STRATEGIC MANAGEMENT

STRATEGIC MANAGEMENT

An Integrated Approach

CHARLES W. L. HILL
University of Washington

GARETH R. JONES
Texas A & M University

HOUGHTON MIFFLIN COMPANY   **Boston**   **Toronto**
Dallas   Geneva, Illinois   Palo Alto   Princeton, New Jersey

For my wife Jennifer
    G.R.J.
For Alexandra, Elizabeth, and Charlotte
    C.W.L.H.

Senior Sponsoring Editor:	*Patrick Boles*
Development Editor:	*Julie Hogenboom*
Project Editor:	*Liza Martina*
Assistant Design Manager:	*Pat Mahtani*
Cover & Interior Designer:	*Sandra González*
Production Coordinator:	*Renée Le Verrier*
Manufacturing Coordinator:	*Sharon Pearson*
Marketing Manager:	*Mary Jo Conrad/Diane McOscar*

Cover Photo: Michael Tcherevkoff/The Image Bank

Printed in the U.S.A.

Library of Congress Catalog Card Number: 91-71987

ISBN: 0-395-59245-3

CDEFGHIJ–D–98765432

Contents

Preface

The favorable reception of the first edition of *Strategic Management: An Integrated Approach* has led us to build and expand upon its principles for the second edition. We utilized feedback from users of the first edition to increase the book's value. We have maintained comprehensive and up-to-date coverage of the burgeoning strategic management literature. We have reexamined the balance between strategy formulation and strategy implementation and added to the flow of material so that a more comprehensive picture of the strategic management process is created. We have also replaced or revised virtually every case in the book. The high quality of cases in this edition should continue to meet the expectations of professors and students in terms of their interest and the importance of the issues they raise.

Comprehensive and Up-To-Date Coverage

In many places we have added to the text to expand and improve our coverage of relevant material. From the most current research, we have created new chapters and improved existing ones. In particular, we have greatly expanded our treatment of business and corporate level strategy by writing two completely new chapters and revising three from the last edition. Some of the additional material discussed includes the following.

- New material on managerial motives, ethics, and social responsibility (Chapter 2).
- Discussion of the role of distinctive competences and barriers to imitation in building and sustaining a company's competitive advantage (Chapter 4).
- A view of the strategic implications of flexible manufacturing systems, design for manufacturing, total quality control, just-in-time inventory systems, and self-managing work teams (Chapter 4).
- Discussion of the way in which competition at the business level often revolves around how a company can pursue a cost leadership and a differentiation strategy simultaneously (Chapter 5).
- A new chapter on the relationship between business-level strategy and industry structure (Chapter 6). This outlines how the characteristics of different industry environments affect the way a firm chooses to compete. For example, we discuss how innovating companies in emerging industries can establish and exploit a first-mover advantage. We discuss how pricing strategy, capacity-expansion strategy, and strategy towards suppliers and distributors becomes a crucial competitive weapon in mature consolidated industries. And we discuss strategies for coping with industry decline.

- Due to the increased interest in global strategy, we have split our corporate-level strategy chapter into two new chapters. Chapter 7 deals with vertical integration and diversification, and Chapter 8 deals with global competition and global strategy. In each of these chapters we offer an account of the latest research and thinking. Included are discussions of long-term contracting and strategic alliances as alternatives to vertical integration and diversification (Chapter 7), and the strategic characteristics of the transnational corporation (Chapter 8).
- New sections on joint ventures and strategic alliances as ways of securing a competitive advantage in new industry environments (Chapter 9).
- A new look at how to design structure so as to simultaneously secure a low cost and a differentiation advantage, and a new look at global strategy and the choice of the appropriate structure and control systems to implement the strategy (Chapter 12).

Balanced and Integrated Progression of Topics

We have incorporated this new material into our existing framework in a way that preserves the balance and flow of the text. As in the first edition, this book is designed so that each chapter builds upon the previous. The new chapters on business and corporate-level strategy provide students with a strong foundation for understanding the process of value creation that underlies strategic management.

In addition, we have maintained our approach of going beyond the uncritical presentation of text material, to debate at length the strengths and weaknesses of various strategic management techniques, and the advantages and disadvantages of different strategies and structures. Our objective continues to be to demonstrate to students that in the real world, strategic issues are inevitably complex, and necessarily involve a consideration of pros and cons, and a willingness to accept tradeoffs. At the same time we have made the text very accessible to students.

To achieve balance we have not allowed any one disciplinary orientation to determine the content of this text. In addition to the strategic management literature, we have drawn on the literature of economics, marketing, organizational theory, operations management, finance, and international business. The perspective of this book is truly strategic in that it integrates the contributions of these diverse disciplines into a comprehensive whole.

Cases

In preparing and selecting cases for the new edition we have been fortunate to draw upon a large number of excellent cases provided to us by case authors, many of whom used the previous edition of this book. For this edition we selected thirty cases that we are certain will appeal to both students and professors in terms of interest and illumination of complex strategic-management issues. As with the first edition, we have chosen cases that illustrate the key subject areas covered in the text. Many of the cases are new, including seven that we have written ourselves. In addition, we have retained and updated two cases from the last edition. We have included several international business cases, as well as new cases on small businesses and entrepreneurship. We feel the selection we offer is second to none, and we are grateful to the case authors who have contributed to this edition. They include

Sexton Adams
North Texas State University

Stephen Barndt
Pacific Lutheran University

Frank C. Barnes
University of North Carolina,
Charlotte

James W. Clinton
University of Northern Colorado

Phil Fisher
University of South Dakota

John A. Grant
Arizona State University

Richard Levin
University of North Carolina

Michael P. Mokwa
Arizona State University

Phillip Phan
University of Washington

Timothy Polymer
Arizona State University

Rhonda K. Reger
Arizona State University

Gordon Shillinglaw
Columbia University

Paul Strebel
International Management
Development Institute

George Toucher
International Management
Development Institute

Sandra Waddock
Boston College

Richard E. White
Arizona State University

Instructor's Resource Manual

We have maintained and refined the format of the Instructor's Resource Manual that users found so beneficial last time. With the case authors' **teaching notes** we have developed in-depth analyses that highlight the important issues in each case and relate them to the text material. Each teaching note offers a **detailed synopsis** of the case and a step by step analysis of the issues contained in it. We also provide a comprehensive list of **true/false** and **multiple choice questions** and **answers** (over 700 questions in all), a series of **discussion questions** and **answers,** a **chapter synopsis,** and a **lecture outline** for each chapter in the book. In addition we offer sample **course outlines** for the material that we have class-tested and found to work.

Teaching Aids

With the second edition of *Strategic Management,* we offer an expansive support package. First, a **videotape** containing information on select cases is available to instructors. This illuminates many issues of interest in the cases.

Second, a package of 75 **color transparencies** accompanies the book. These include all of the art found in the text. In addition, transparency masters of most of the book's figures and tables can be found in the Instructor's Resource Manual.

Finally, *Policy Expert,* a **software package** for case analysis is available with the book. This software package allows students to input financial data from the cases and perform several kinds of strategic and financial analyses. These include the calculation of a wide variety of business formulas, the carrying out of "what if" scenarios, the development of strategic management models in an expert system, and other applied applications useful for case analysis and presentation.

Together, the Instructor's Resource Manual and teaching aids provide an integrated package that supports the approach we have taken throughout the book. Further details for using the support package can be found in the Instructor's Resource Manual.

Acknowledgments

This book is far more than the product of two authors. We wish to thank again the case authors for allowing us to use their material, and the authors of other teaching materials. We also wish to thank the Departments of Management at the University of Washington and Texas A & M University for providing the setting and atmosphere in which the book could be written, and the students of these universities who reacted to and provided input for many of our ideas. In addition, the following reviewers provided valuable suggestions for improving the manuscript from its original form to its current form.

Thomas H. Berliner
The University of Texas at Dallas

Geoffrey Brooks
Western Oregon State College

Gene R. Conaster
Golden State University

Eliezer Geisler
Northeastern Illinois University

Lynn Godkin
Lamar University

W. Grahm Irwin
Miami University

Geoffrey King
California State University—Fullerton

Robert J. Litschert
Virginia Polytechnic Institute and
State University

Lance A. Masters
California State University—
San Bernadino

Joanna Mulholland
West Chester University of
Pennsylvania

Malika Richards
Indiana University

Joseph A. Schenk
University of Dayton

Barbara Spencer
Clemson University

Bobby Vaught   Robert P. Vichas
Southwest Missori State   Florida Atlantic University

Finally, thanks are due to our families for their patience and support during the course of this revision process. We would like to thank our wives, Alexandra Hill and Jennifer George, for their ever increasing support and affection.

C.W.L.H.

G.R.J.

STRATEGIC MANAGEMENT

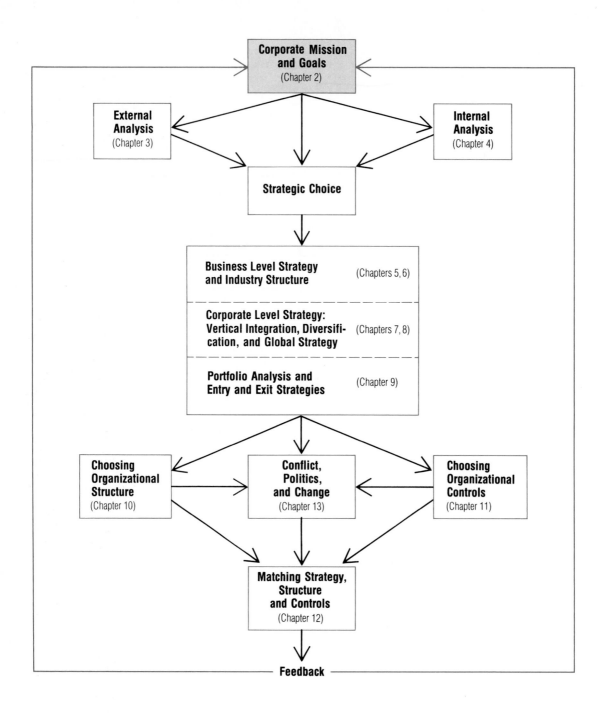

P A R T

I

INTRODUCTION

Chapter 1

THE STRATEGIC MANAGEMENT PROCESS

1.1 OPENING INCIDENT: ROYAL DUTCH/SHELL

Royal Dutch/Shell, the world's largest oil company, is well known for its addiction to strategic planning. Despite the fact that many management gurus and CEOs now consider strategic planning an anachronism, Shell is convinced that long-term strategic planning has served the company well. Part of the reason for this success is that at Shell, planning does not take the form of complex and inflexible ten-year plans generated by a team of corporate strategists far removed from operating realities. Rather, planning involves the generation of a series of "what if" scenarios whose function is to try to get general managers at all levels of the corporation to think strategically about the environment in which they do business.

The strength of Shell's scenario-based planning system was perhaps most evident during the early 1980s. At that time, the price of a barrel of oil was hovering at around $30. With exploration and development costs running at an industry average of around $11 per barrel, most oil companies were making record profits. Moreover, industry analysts were generally bullish; many were predicting that oil prices would increase to around $50 per barrel by 1990. Shell, however, was mulling over a handful of future scenarios, one of which included

the possibility of a breakdown of the OPEC oil cartel's agreement to restrict supply, an oil glut, and a drop in oil prices to $15 per barrel. In 1984 Shell instructed the managers of its operating companies to indicate how they would respond to a $15 per barrel world. This "game" set off some serious work at Shell exploring the question "What will we do if it happens?"

By early 1986 the consequences of the "game" included efforts to cut exploration costs by pioneering advanced exploration technologies, massive investments in cost-efficient refining facilities, and a process of weeding out the least-profitable service stations. All this planning occurred at a time when most oil companies were busy diversifying outside the oil business rather than trying to improve the efficiency of their core operations. As it turned out, the price of oil was still $27 per barrel in early January 1986. But the failure of the OPEC cartel to set new production ceilings in 1985, new production from the North Sea and Alaska, and declining demand due to increased conservation efforts had created a growing oil glut. In late January the dam burst. By February 1 oil was priced at $17 per barrel, and by April the price was $10 per barrel.

Because Shell had already visited the $15 per

barrel world, it had gained a head start over its rivals in its cost-cutting efforts. As a result, by 1989 the company's average oil and gas exploration costs were less than $2 per barrel, compared with an industry average of $4 per barrel. Moreover, in the crucial refining and marketing sector Shell made a net return on assets of 8.4 percent in 1988, more than double the 3.8 percent average of the other oil majors: Exxon, BP, Chevron, Mobil, and Texaco.

As Shell enters the 1990s, its future scenarios depict a world of radical environmentalism, initially among private consumers, and then increasingly among nation-states. In anticipation of this trend, Shell's strategies for the 1990s stress products that are less environmentally harmful. Shell started investing in capacity to produce unleaded gasoline earlier than many of

its competitors and last year sold more unleaded gasoline than any other oil company worldwide. By 1989 nearly 60 percent of the gasoline it sold was unleaded—a quarter as much again as the industry average—compared with 30 percent in 1984. Natural gas, which is less environmentally harmful than oil, is the other main part of Shell's green plan. Shell is currently investing $700 million in a synthesis plant in Malaysia that will convert natural gas into refined oil products. In addition, Shell is well down the road toward developing an economical process for converting natural gas to gasoline. The conversion will not pay unless oil prices stabilize above $20 per barrel, but Shell's future scenarios see that price level as likely by the end of the century.[1]

1.2 OVERVIEW

Why do some organizations succeed and others fail? What makes some profit-seeking organizations, such as IBM, Hewlett-Packard, Royal Dutch/Shell, and the pharmaceutical giant Merck, excellent performers year after year, while others, such as Chrysler, Navistar International Corporation, and USX, go through periods during which they struggle to survive? Why have some not-for-profit organizations, such as the United Way, been able to build up a stable constituency of charitable givers, while others, such as Farm Aid, have been unable to sustain their operations for any length of time? An answer can be found in the subject matter of this book: strategic management. We consider the advantages that accrue to organizations that think strategically. We also examine how organizations that understand both their operating environment and their own internal strengths and weaknesses can identify and exploit strategies successfully.

The techniques that we discuss are relevant to many different kinds of organizations: from large, multibusiness enterprises to small, one-person enterprises; from manufacturing enterprises to service enterprises; and from publicly held profit-seeking corporations to not-for-profit organizations. Although we tend to think of strategic management as primarily concerned with profit-seeking organizations, even a small not-for-profit organization, such as a local theater or church charity, has to make decisions about how best to generate revenues, given the environment in which it is based and the organization's own strengths and weaknesses. Such decisions are, by their very nature, strategic in form and content, involving such factors as an analysis of the "competition." For example, the local church-run charity has to compete with other charities for the limited resources that individuals are prepared to give to charitable causes. Identifying how best to do so is a strategic problem.

The objective of this book is to give you a thorough understanding of the analytical techniques and skills necessary to identify and exploit strategies successfully. The first step toward achieving this objective involves an overview of the main elements of the strategic management process, and an examination of the way in which these elements fit together. That is the function of the present chapter. In subsequent chapters we consider the individual elements of the strategic management process in greater detail.

1.3 DEFINING STRATEGY

The Traditional Approach

Reflecting the military roots of strategy, *Webster's New World Dictionary* defines *strategy* as "the science of planning and directing military operations."[2] The *planning* theme remains an important component of most management definitions of *strategy*. For example, Harvard's Alfred Chandler defined *strategy* as "the determination of the basic long-term goals and objectives of an enterprise, and the adoption of courses of action and the allocation of resources necessary for carrying out these goals."[3] Implicit in Chandler's definition is the idea that strategy involves rational planning. The organization is depicted as choosing its goals, identifying the courses of action (or strategies) that best enable it to fulfill its goals, and allocating resources accordingly. Similarly, James B. Quinn of Dartmouth College has defined *strategy* as "the pattern or plan that integrates an organization's major goals, policies, and action sequences into a cohesive whole."[4] And finally, along the same lines, William F. Glueck defined *strategy* as "a unified, comprehensive, and integrated plan designed to ensure that the basic objectives of the enterprise are achieved."[5]

The case of Royal Dutch/Shell, discussed in the Opening Incident, is a good example of how strategic planning works and how superior planning can result in a competitive advantage. The scenario-based planning used at Shell is designed to educate general managers about the complex and dynamic nature of the company's environment. As a result of that process, the company's general managers understood their business environment better than the competition did. Accordingly, Shell was able to anticipate the crash in oil prices that occurred during 1986. Unlike its competitors, Shell by 1986 had taken steps to ensure that it would remain profitable if this contingency came to pass. In contrast, most of Shell's competitors were operating under the comforting illusion that oil prices would remain strong during the 1980s.

A New Approach

For all their appeal, planning-based definitions of *strategy* have recently evoked criticism. As Henry Mintzberg of McGill University has pointed out, the planning approach incorrectly assumes that an organization's strategy is always the outcome of rational planning.[6] According to Mintzberg, definitions of *strategy* that stress the role of planning ignore the fact that strategies can emerge from within an organization without any formal plan. That is to say, even in the absence of intent, strategies can emerge from the grassroots of an organization. Mintzberg's point is that strategy is more than what a company intends or plans to do; it is also what it actually does. With this in mind, Mintzberg has defined *strategy* as "*a pattern in a stream of decisions or actions,*"[7] the pattern being a product of whatever *intended* (planned) strategies are actually realized and of any *emergent* (unplanned) strategies. The scheme proposed by Mintzberg is illustrated in Figure 1.1.

Mintzberg's argument is that emergent strategies are often successful and may be more appropriate than intended strategies. Richard T. Pascale of Stanford University has described how this was the case for the entry of Honda Motor Co., Ltd., into the U.S. motorcycle market.[8] When a number of Honda executives arrived in Los Angeles from Japan in 1959 to establish an American subsidiary, their original aim (intended strategy) was to focus on selling 250cc and 305cc machines to confirmed motorcycle enthusiasts, rather than 50cc Honda Cubs, which were a big hit in Japan. Their instinct told them that the Honda 50s were not suitable for the U.S. market, where everything was bigger and more luxurious than in Japan.

However, sales of the 250cc and 305cc bikes were sluggish, and the bikes themselves were plagued by mechanical failure. It looked as if Honda's strategy was going to fail. At the same time the Japanese executives were using the Honda 50s to run errands around Los Angeles, attracting a lot of attention. One day they got a call from a Sears, Roebuck buyer who wanted to sell the 50cc bikes to a

FIGURE 1.1   Emergent and deliberate strategies

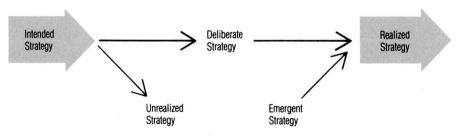

Source: Reprinted from "Strategy Formation in an Adhocracy," by James Mintzberg and Alexandra McHugh, published in *Administrative Science Quarterly*, Vol. 30, No. 2, June 1985, by permission of *Administrative Science Quarterly*. Copyright © 1985 by Administrative Science Quarterly.

broad market of Americans who were not necessarily already motorcycle enthusiasts. The Honda executives were hesitant to sell the small bikes for fear of alienating serious bikers who might then associate Honda with "wimp" machines. In the end they were pushed into doing so by the failure of the 250cc and 305cc models. The rest is history. Honda had stumbled onto a previously untouched market segment that was to prove huge: the average American who had never owned a motorbike. Honda had also found an untried channel of distribution: general retailers rather than specialty motorbike stores. By 1964 nearly one out of every two motorcycles sold in the United States was a Honda.

The conventional explanation of Honda's success is that the company redefined the U.S. motorcycle industry with a brilliantly conceived *intended* strategy.[9] The fact was that Honda's intended strategy was a near disaster. The strategy that *emerged* did so not through planning but through unplanned action taken in response to unforeseen circumstances. Nevertheless, credit should be given to the Japanese management for recognizing the strength of the emergent strategy and for pursuing it with vigor.

The critical point that emerges from the Honda example is that in contrast to the view that strategies are planned, successful strategies can emerge within an organization without prior planning. As Mintzberg has noted, strategies can take root in all kinds of strange places, virtually wherever people have the capacity to learn and the resources to support that capacity.

In sum, Mintzberg's revision of the concept of strategy suggests that strategy involves more than just planning a course of action. It also involves the recognition that successful strategies can emerge from deep within an organization. In practice, the strategies of most organizations are probably a combination of the intended and the emergent. The message for management is that it needs to recognize the process of emergence and to intervene when appropriate, killing off bad emergent strategies but nurturing potentially good ones. To make such decisions, however, managers must be able to judge the worth of emergent strategies. They must be able to think strategically.

1.4 COMPONENTS OF STRATEGIC MANAGEMENT

The strategic management process can be broken down into a number of different components. These components are illustrated in Figure 1.2, and each forms a chapter of this book. Thus you need to understand how the different components fit together. The components include selection of the corporate mission and major corporate goals, analysis of the organization's external competitive environment and internal operating environment, the selection of appropriate business- and corporate-level strategies, and the designing of organizational structures and control systems to implement the organization's chosen strategy. The task of analyzing the organization's external and internal environment and then selecting an appropriate strategy is normally referred to as **strategy formulation.** The task

FIGURE 1.2   Components of strategic management

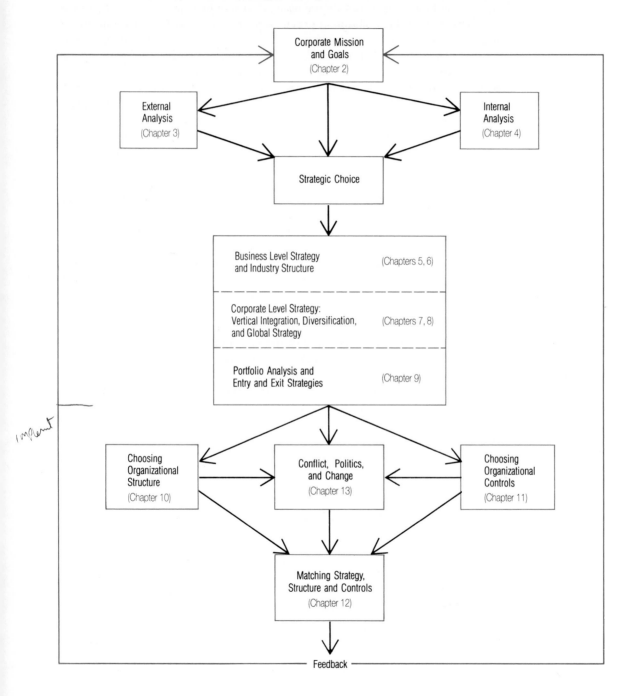

of designing appropriate organizational structures and control systems, given the organization's choice of strategy, is usually called **strategy implementation.**

The traditional approach has been to stress that each of the components illustrated in Figure 1.2 constitutes a *sequential* step in strategic management. In the traditional view, each *cycle* of the process begins with a statement of the corporate mission and major corporate goals. The mission statement is followed by environmental analysis and strategic choice, and the strategy making ends with the design of the organizational structure and control systems necessary to implement the organization's chosen strategy. In practice, however, that sequence is likely to be the case only for the formulation and implementation of *intended* strategies.

As noted earlier, emergent strategies arise from within the organization without prior planning—that is to say, without going through the steps illustrated in Figure 1.2 in a *sequential* fashion. However, top management still has to evaluate emergent strategies. Such evaluation involves comparing each emergent strategy with the organization's goals, external environmental opportunities and threats, and the organization's own internal strengths and weaknesses. The objective is to assess whether the emergent strategy fits the organization's needs and capabilities. In addition, Mintzberg stresses that an organization's capability to produce emergent strategies is a function of the kind of corporate culture fostered by the organization's structure and control systems.

In other words, the different components of the strategic management process are just as important from the perspective of emergent strategies as they are from the perspective of intended strategies. The essential differences between the strategic management process for intended and for emergent strategies are illustrated in Figure 1.3. The formulation of intended strategies is basically a top-down process, whereas the formulation of emergent strategies is a bottom-up process.

Mission and Major Goals

The first component of the strategic management process is defining the **mission** and **major goals** of the organization. This topic is covered in depth in Chapter 2. The mission and major goals of an organization provide the context within which intended strategies are formulated and the criteria against which emergent strategies are evaluated.

The mission sets out why the organization exists and what it should be doing. For example, the mission of national airline might be defined as satisfying the needs of individual and business travelers for high-speed transportation at a reasonable price to all the major population centers of North America.

Major goals specify what the organization hopes to fulfill in the medium to long term. Most profit-seeking organizations operate with a hierarchy of goals in which the maximization of stockholder wealth is placed at the top. Secondary goals are objectives judged necessary by the company if it is to maximize stockholder wealth. For example, General Electric operates with a secondary goal of

FIGURE 1.3   The strategic management process for intended and emergent strategies

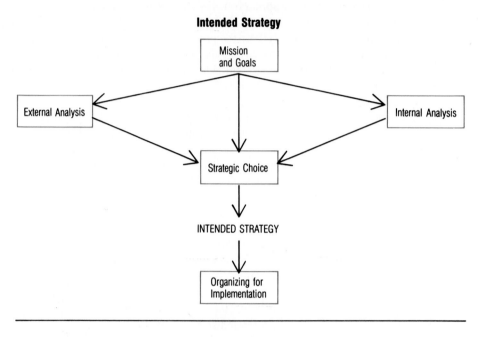

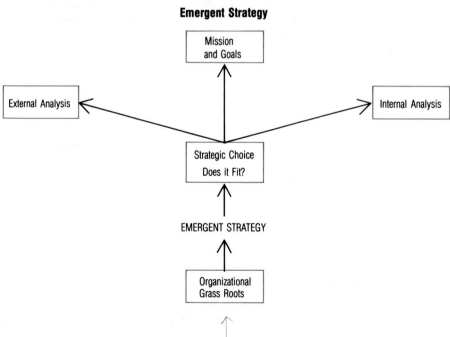

being first or second in every major market in which it competes. This secondary goal reflects the belief at General Electric that building market share is the best way to achieve the primary goal of maximizing stockholder wealth. Not-for-profit organizations typically have a more diverse set of goals. The major goal of Band Aid, for example, was to alleviate starvation in Ethiopia, whereas the goal of a performing arts theater might be to provide high-quality cultural entertainment at a reasonable cost to the general public.

External Analysis ②

The second component of the strategic management process is the analysis of the organization's external operating environment. This topic is covered in detail in Chapter 3. The objective of external analysis is to identify strategic **opportunities** and **threats** in the organization's operating environment. Two interrelated environments should be examined at this stage: the immediate, or industry, environment in which the organization operates and the wider macroenvironment.

Analyzing the industry environment involves an assessment of the competitive structure of the organization's industry, including the competitive position of the focal organization and its major rivals, as well as the stage of industry development. Analyzing the macro-environment consists of examining macroeconomic, social, government, legal, international, and technological factors that may affect the organization. Again consider Royal Dutch/Shell. Its external opportunities included the OPEC oil cartel reaching a sustainable agreement to restrict oil production. The agreement would increase crude oil prices and hence profits for oil majors like Shell. The threats included the possibility of a continued oil glut and radical environmentalism (both of which the company had considered during its scenario planning).

Internal Analysis ③

The next component of the strategic management process, internal analysis, serves to pinpoint the **strengths** and **weaknesses** of the organization. Such analysis involves identifying the quantity and quality of resources available to the organization. These issues are considered in Chapter 4, where we use the concept of the value chain to examine the factors that determine the quantity and quality of an organization's resources in manufacturing, marketing, materials management, research and development, information systems, personnel, and finance. We also discuss the role of distinctive competencies (unique company strengths) in building and sustaining a company's competitive advantage.

In addition to this, for a multibusiness enterprise, identifying strengths and weaknesses also involves assessing whether the balance of different businesses in its portfolio is a strength or a weakness. For example, if a company's businesses are concentrated in highly competitive and unprofitable industries, then the balance is a weakness. Conversely, if its businesses are concentrated in very profitable industries, then the balance is a strength. Assessing the corporate portfolio is an issue that we discuss in Chapter 9.

decision steps~

Strategic Choice 4

The next component involves generating a series of strategic alternatives, given the goals of the firm, its internal strengths and weaknesses, and external opportunities and threats. This issue is covered in Chapter 14. We do not deal with the issue until this stage in the text because we must first lay out the different strategic alternatives open to the firm and describe complexities of organizational structure and control systems. Remember, however, that for strategic decision makers who know the full range of strategic options, strategic choice follows directly from an analysis of the organization's external and internal environments.

The comparison of **s**trengths, **w**eaknesses, **o**pportunities, and **t**hreats is normally referred to as a **SWOT** analysis.[10] A SWOT analysis might generate a series of strategic alternatives. To choose among the alternatives, the organization has to evaluate them against each other with respect to their ability to achieve major goals. The objective is to select the strategies that ensure the best **alignment,** or **fit,** between external environmental opportunities and threats and the internal strengths and weaknesses of the organization. For a single-business organization, the objective is to match the company's strengths to environmental opportunities in order to gain a competitive advantage and thus increase profits. For a multibusiness organization, the goal is to choose for its portfolio of businesses strategies that align the strengths and weaknesses of the portfolio with environmental opportunities and threats.

Again consider Royal Dutch/Shell. The current strategy of investing in processes that convert natural gas to environmentally clean gasoline can be seen as a counter to a potential threat by building on a company strength. The potential threat is radical environmentalism, which may lead to strict limits on auto emissions and auto use, thereby reducing demand for gasoline. The company *strength* is that Shell currently has the largest natural gas reserves and natural gas production of any major oil company. Thus, Shell's strategy is aimed at securing the company's future by aligning a company strength with an environmental threat.

Business-Level Strategy

For the organization operating in a single competitive environment (industry), the outcome of the process of strategic choice is the identification of an appropriate business-level strategy. The different strategic alternatives are discussed in

Chapters 5 and 6. In Chapter 5 we review the pros and cons of three generic business-level strategies: a strategy of cost leadership, a strategy of differentiation, and a strategy of focusing on a particular market niche. The organization's objective when pursuing its chosen strategy should be to establish a sustainable competitive advantage. In addition, Chapter 5 examines the different investment strategies needed to support each of these main strategic alternatives. The argument developed in Chapter 5 is that a company must vary its investment strategy with the stage of development of its industry in order to make its business-level strategy successful.

In Chapter 6 we consider the relationship between business-level strategy and industry structure in greater depth. We are particularly concerned in this chapter with the different strategic options that confront companies in radically different industry settings. Thus, for example, we discuss the advantages and disadvantages of establishing a first-mover advantage in a newly formed or embryonic industry. We discuss the role of market signaling, price leadership, and product differentiation for sustaining a competitive advantage in mature industries. And we discuss the different strategic options that a company can choose from in a declining industry.

Corporate-Level Strategy

An organization's corporate-level strategy must answer this question: What businesses should we be in to maximize the long-run profitability of the organization? For many organizations, the answer involves focusing the organization's full attention on continuing to compete within a single business area. However, competing successfully within a single business area also often involves **vertical integration** and **global expansion.** In some segments of the electronics industry, for example, global markets are necessary to generate the sales volume to achieve full economies of scale. Establishing a low-cost position within a single industry may thus require global expansion. Similar arguments can be made regarding vertical integration. Beyond this, organizations that are successful at establishing a sustainable competitive advantage may find that they are generating resources in excess of their investment requirements within their primary industry. For such organizations, maximizing long-run profitability may entail **diversification** into new business areas.

The strategies of vertical integration, global expansion, and diversification fall under the rubric of corporate-level strategies. We consider the benefits and costs of vertical integration and diversification in Chapter 7. In that chapter we also consider the role of strategic alliances as an alternative to vertical integration and diversification. The benefits and costs of a strategy of global expansion are considered in detail in Chapter 8. In addition, that chapter explores the benefits and costs of global strategic alliances, the different entry modes that can be used to enter a foreign market, and the role of host-government policies in influencing a company's choice of global strategy.

Analyzing the Corporate Portfolio

Substantially diversified companies face the problem of how best to make sense out of their many different activities. General Electric, for example, has more than 100 different business units. How do the different activities fit together? What is the relative contribution of each activity to corporate profitability? What is the outlook for each activity? Portfolio analysis offers a body of techniques designed to help organizations answer such questions. In Chapter 9, we examine these techniques and consider their strengths and weaknesses.

Portfolio analysis may indicate that a company needs to leave some existing business areas or enter new ones. A number of different entry and exit strategies are available. The options for entering new businesses include acquisitions, joint ventures, and internal new venturing. The options for exiting from an existing business include harvest, divestment, and liquidation. We discuss the merits of these entry and exit strategies in Chapter 9.

Designing Organizational Structure

To make a strategy work, regardless of whether it is intended or emergent, the organization needs to adopt the correct structure. The main options here are re-viewed in Chapter 10. Choosing a structure entails allocating task responsibility and decision-making authority within an organization. The issues covered in-clude how best to divide an organization into subunits and how to distribute authority among the different levels of an organization's hierarchy. The options reviewed include whether an organization should function with a tall or a flat structure, how centralized or decentralized decision-making authority should be, and to what extent an organization should be divided up into semi-autonomous subunits (that is, divisions or departments).

Choosing Integration and Control Systems

Strategy implementation involves more than an organization's choice of struc-ture. It also involves the selection of appropriate organizational integration and control systems. The main options here are reviewed in Chapter 11. Strategy implementation often requires collective action or coordination between semi-autonomous subunits (such as product departments) within an organization. Thus we consider integration mechanisms that foster coordination between semi-autonomous subunits. An organization must also decide how best to assess the performance and control the actions of subunits. Its options range from market and output controls to bureaucratic and clan controls, all of which we tackle in Chapter 11.

Matching Strategy, Structure, and Controls

Implementing a strategy requires the adoption of appropriate organizational structures and control systems. After reviewing various structures and control systems in Chapters 10 and 11, in Chapter 12 we consider how to achieve a *fit* among an organization's strategy, structure, and controls. Different strategies and environments place different demands on an organization and therefore require different structural responses and control systems. For example, a strategy of cost leadership demands that an organization be kept simple (so as to reduce costs) and that controls stress productive efficiency. On the other hand, a strategy of differentiating an organization's product by unique technological characteristics generates a need for integrating the activities of the organization around its technological core and for establishing control systems that reward technical creativity. The appropriate structure and control systems are very different in these two cases.

Conflict, Politics, and Change

Although in theory the strategic management process is characterized by *rational* decision making, in practice organizational politics plays a key role. Politics is endemic to organizations: Different subgroups (departments or divisions) within an organization have their own agendas. Typically, the agendas of different subgroups conflict. Thus departments may compete with each other for a bigger share of an organization's finite resources. Such conflicts may be resolved as much by the relative distribution of power between subunits as by a rational evaluation of relative need. Similarly, individual managers often engage in contests with each other over what the correct policy decisions are. Power struggles and coalition building are major consequences of such conflicts and clearly play a part in strategic management. Strategic change tends to bring such power struggles to the fore, since by definition change entails altering the established distribution of power within an organization. In Chapter 13, we analyze the sources of organizational power and conflict and consider how organizational politics influences strategic management and can inhibit strategic change. In addition, we examine how an organization can manage conflicts to fulfill its strategic mission and implement change.

Feedback

Strategic management is an ongoing process. Once a strategy is implemented, its execution must be monitored to determine the extent to which strategic objectives are actually being achieved. This information passes back to the corporate level through feedback loops. At the corporate level it is fed into the next round of strategy formulation and implementation. It serves either to reaffirm existing corporate goals and strategies or to suggest changes. For example, when put into practice, a strategic objective may prove to be too optimistic, and so the next time more conservative objectives are set. Alternatively, feedback may reveal that strategic objectives were attainable but implementation was poor. In that case, the next round in strategic management may concentrate more on implementation. Because feedback is an aspect of organizational control, it is considered in detail in Chapter 11.

1.5 STRATEGIC MANAGERS

To compete in today's complex and ever-changing environment, an organization must have somebody who is responsible for managing strategy development. The task normally falls on the shoulders of **strategic managers.** Strategic managers are individuals who bear responsibility for the overall performance of the organization or for one of its major self-contained divisions. Their overriding concern is for the health of the _total_ organization under their direction. (Many textbooks refer to such individuals as _general managers._) Strategic managers are distinct from **functional managers** within an organization. Functional managers bear responsibility for specific business functions, such as personnel, purchasing, production, sales, customer service, and accounts. Thus their sphere of authority is generally confined to one organizational activity, whereas strategic managers oversee the operation of the whole organization. This responsibility puts strategic managers in the unique position of being able to direct the total organization in a strategic sense.

 Edward Wrapp of the University of Chicago has written extensively about the characteristics of successful strategic managers.[11] In Wrapp's view, five skills are especially significant. They are summarized in Table 1.1.

First, successful strategic managers keep themselves _well informed_ about a wide range of operating decisions being made at different levels in the organization. They develop a network of information sources in many different parts of the organization, which enables them to remain in touch with operating realities. Second, successful strategic managers know how best to _allocate their time and_

TABLE 1.1   Major characteristics of successful strategic managers

---

Successful strategic managers are

1. Well informed
2. Skilled at allocating their time and energy
3. Good politicians (consensus builders)
4. Experts at being imprecise
5. Able to push through programs in a piecemeal fashion

energy among different issues, decisions, or problems. They know when to delegate and when to become involved in a particular decision. Third, successful strategic managers are *good politicians*. They play the power game with skill, preferring to build consensus for their ideas, rather than using their authority to force ideas through. They act as members or leaders of a coalition rather than as dictators.

Fourth, successful strategic managers are able to satisfy the organization that it has a sense of direction without actually committing themselves publicly to precise objectives or strategies. In other words, they are experts at *being imprecise.* At first glance this skill may seem curious, since so much of the received wisdom in the management literature suggests that part of the job of strategic managers is to set precise objectives and formulate detailed strategies. However, in a world where the only constant is change, there is value in being imprecise. Strategic managers would be foolish to commit themselves to a precise objective, given the constant state of environmental flux. *Deliberate imprecision* can often give both the organization and the manager room for maneuver and an enhanced ability to adapt to environmental change. This does not mean that the organization should operate without objectives but rather that the objectives should be open-ended. Thus a strategic manager might commit the organization to becoming number one in its industry without specifying a precise timetable for reaching this goal.

Similarly, successful strategic managers often hesitate to commit themselves publicly to detailed strategic plans, since in all probability the emergence of unexpected contingencies will require adaptation. Thus a successful strategic manager might commit the organization to diversification without stating precisely how or when this will be achieved. It is also important to note that successful strategic managers often have precise private objectives and strategies that they would like to see the organization pursue. However, they recognize the futility of public commitment, given the likelihood of change and the difficulties of implementation.

The fifth skill that Wrapp claims successful strategic managers possess is the *ability to push through programs in a piecemeal fashion.* Successful strategic managers recognize the futility of trying to push total packages or strategic programs through the organization, since significant objections to at least part of such programs are likely to arise. Instead, the successful strategic manager is willing to take less than total acceptance in order to achieve modest progress toward a goal. The successful strategic manager tries to push through his or her ideas in a piecemeal fashion, so that they appear as incidentals to other ideas, though in fact they are part of a larger program or hidden agenda that moves the organization in the direction of the manager's objectives.

Wrapp's picture of the successful strategic manager is thus very different from the picture of the rational decision maker presented in much of the strategic management literature. In Wrapp's view, successful strategic managers are skilled organizational politicians who can build coalitions that get their programs pushed through with a minimum of friction. Furthermore, successful strategic managers recognize the futility of commitment to a precise course of action in a world of constant change. Rather, they keep their options open.

1.6 LEVELS OF STRATEGIC MANAGEMENT

Within a multibusiness company, strategic managers are found not just at the apex of the organization but also at different levels within its hierarchy. Essentially, a typical multibusiness company has three main levels of management: the corporate level, the business level, and the functional level (see Figure 1.4). Strategic managers are found at the first two of these levels but their roles differ, depending on their sphere of responsibility. In addition, functional managers too have a strategic role, though of a different kind. We now look at each of the three levels and the strategic roles assigned to managers within them.

Corporate Level

The corporate level of management consists of the chief executive officer (CEO), other senior executives, the board of directors, and corporate staff. These individuals occupy the apex of decision making within the organization. The CEO is the main strategic manager at this level. His or her strategic role is *to oversee*

FIGURE 1.4   **Levels of strategic management**

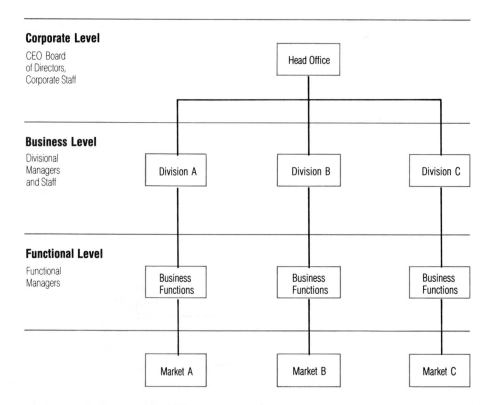

the development of strategies for the total organization. Typically, this role involves defining the mission and goals of the organization, determining what businesses it should be in, allocating resources among the different business areas, and formulating and implementing strategies that span individual businesses.

For example, consider General Electric. The company is involved in a wide range of businesses, including lighting equipment, major appliances, motor and transportation equipment, turbine generators, construction and engineering services, industrial electronics, medical systems, aerospace, and aircraft engines. The main strategic responsibilities of its CEO, Jack Welch, include setting overall strategic objectives, allocating resources among the different business areas, deciding whether the firm should divest itself of any of the businesses, and determining whether it should acquire any new ones. In other words, it is up to Welch to develop strategies that span individual businesses. He is concerned with building and managing the corporate portfolio of businesses. It is not his specific responsibility, however, to develop strategies for competing in the individual business areas, such as aerospace or major appliances. The development of such strategies is the responsibility of business-level strategic managers.

Besides overseeing resource allocation and managing the divestment and acquisition processes, corporate-level strategic managers also provide a link between the people who oversee the strategic development of a firm (strategic managers) and those who own it (stockholders). Corporate-level strategic managers, and particularly the CEO, can be viewed as the guardians of stockholder welfare. It is their responsibility to ensure that corporate strategies pursued by the company are consistent with maximizing stockholder wealth. If they are not, then ultimately the CEO is likely to be called to account by the stockholders.

Business Level

In a multibusiness company, the business level consists of the heads of individual business units within the organization and their support staff. In a single-industry company, the business and corporate levels are the same. A business unit is an organizational entity that operates in a distinct business area. Typically, it is self-contained and has its own functional departments (for example, its own finance, buying, production, and marketing departments). Within most companies, business units are referred to as *divisions*. For example, General Electric has more than 100 divisions, one for each business area that the company is active in.

The main strategic managers at the business level are the heads of the divisions. Their strategic role is to translate general statements of direction and intent from the corporate level into concrete strategies for individual businesses. Thus while corporate-level strategic managers are concerned with strategies that span individual businesses, business-level strategic managers are concerned with strategies that are specific to a particular business. As noted earlier, at General Electric the corporate level has committed itself to the objective of being first or second in every business in which the corporation competes. However, it is up to the

FIGURE 1.5   **The flow of information**

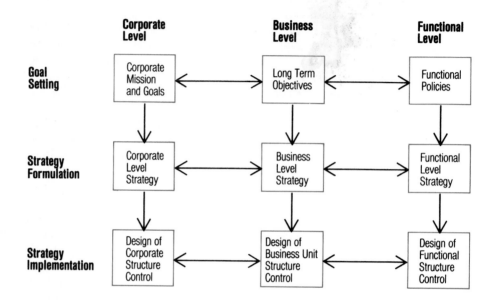

strategic managers who head each division to work out for their business the details of a strategy that is consistent with this objective.

Functional Level

By definition, there are no strategic managers at the functional level. Functional managers bear responsibility for specific business functions, such as personnel, purchasing, production, marketing, customer service, and accounts. They are not in a position to look at the big picture. Nevertheless, they have an important strategic role, for their responsibility is to develop functional strategies in production, marketing, purchasing, and so on, that help fulfill the strategic objectives set by business- and corporate-level general managers. In the case of General Electric's major appliance business, for example, manufacturing managers are responsible for developing manufacturing strategies consistent with the corporate objective of being first or second in that industry. An equally great responsibility for managers at the functional level involves strategy implementation—the execution of corporate- and business-level decisions.

1.7 STRATEGIC INFORMATION SYSTEMS

Goal setting, strategy formulation, and strategy implementation involve personnel at all levels within the organization. Communication among personnel at different levels is necessary to ensure that corporate-, business-, and functional-level strategies are *attainable* and *consistent* with each other and with corporate goals and objectives.

For example, strategic managers at the business level cannot hope to formulate realistic business-level strategies unless they receive input from functional-level managers concerning the strengths and weaknesses of each functional area. Without such input, business-level managers might decide on a strategy that the company does not have the functional resources to pursue. Similarly, corporate-level strategic managers cannot hope to formulate realistic corporate-level strategies unless they receive input from business-level managers about the strengths and weaknesses of each business unit, as well as the market opportunities and threats that each unit faces. Strategic managers also have to make certain that the strategies being pursued by different levels of the organization are consistent with overall corporate goals. The need for such information necessitates further communication among managers at the different levels.

To ensure that the strategies being pursued at each level are consistent and attainable, most organizations go to some length to establish companywide strategic information systems. Often, a committee structure within the firm is designed to facilitate communication between different levels of the hierarchy. For example, at Chrysler five- to seven-member teams are to be found at every level in the corporation from the shop floor on up. The lowest-level teams meet each quarter with their supervisors to set goals, evaluate past performance, and discuss the company's operations. The supervisor of each team is in turn a member of a higher team. The higher teams, too, meet with their supervisors on a quarterly basis. The teams continue to meet up the hierarchy until they reach the top group, which consists of the company's top executives and its CEO. This system facilitates the flow of information within the organization. It helps ensure that higher-level managers do not lose touch with operating realities and consequently pursue strategic objectives that are not attainable.

In addition to committee structures, many companies set up periodic planning conferences that are designed to bring together managers from different levels to discuss strategic problems and strategic directions. In the best-run companies, these conferences provide a forum for higher-level managers to learn about the problems confronting lower-level managers, and for lower-level managers to learn about the strategic objectives of higher-level managers. At such a conference, the merits of different strategies can be debated by all interested parties, and some kind of meaningful synthesis can be worked out.

Figure 1.5 illustrates how these information systems work, at least in theory. On the horizontal axis are the levels of corporate, business, and functional management. On the vertical axis are the three key strategic management tasks: goal setting, strategy formulation, and strategy implementation. In the boxes are the various components of strategic management just discussed. The arrows in the figure represent the way that information flows up and down the organization from level to level and from one component of strategic management to the next. Notice that the setting of corporate goals provides the context for the development of business- and functional-level objectives and vice versa. Notice too that goal setting provides, for each level, the context for strategy formulation and implementation so that a fit can be achieved in this direction as well.

1.8 STRATEGIC PLANNING IN PRACTICE

The last three sections described what might be considered a rational model of the strategic management process. In this model, a company goes through a number of well-defined steps in order to formulate *intended* strategies that align organizational strengths and weakness with environmental opportunities and threats. It is pertinent to ask whether such systems work. Do they help companies establish a sustainable competitive advantage? The answer to this question would seem to be a qualified yes. Strategic planning systems do work, but only if they are correctly designed. Moreover, as with any rational process, their efficiency is subject to the limitations of human decision makers. Even the best-designed planning system will fail to produce the desired results if corporate decision makers fail to use the information at their disposal effectively. In this section we examine common errors in the design of strategic planning systems and consider ways of guarding against the adverse effects of poor strategic decision making.

Does Strategic Planning Work?

Do companies that go through the kind of process outlined above actually generate superior performance relative to those that do not? Clearly, we would expect planning to have some positive effects; empirical evidence does indeed suggest that *on the average* companies that plan outperform those that do not. Of fourteen studies reviewed in a recent survey by Lawrence C. Rhyne, eight found varying degrees of support for the hypothesis that strategic planning improves company performance, five found no support for the hypothesis, and one reported a negative relationship between planning and performance.[12] Moreover, an empirical study by Rhyne, reported in the same article, concluded that "firms with strategic planning systems more closely resembling strategic management theory were found to exhibit superior long-term financial performance both relative to their industry and in absolute terms."[13]

In recent years, however, the use of formal planning systems has been increasingly questioned. Thomas J. Peters and Robert H. Waterman, the best-selling authors of *In Search of Excellence,* are among those who have raised doubts about the usefulness of formal planning systems.[14] Similarly, Henry Mintzberg's revision of the concept of strategy suggests that *emergent* strategies may be just as successful as the *intended* strategies that are the outcome of formal planning. Moreover, it is true that business history is filled with examples of companies that have made poor decisions on the basis of supposedly comprehensive strategic planning.[15] For example, Exxon's decisions to diversify into electrical equipment and office automation and to offset shrinking U.S. oil reserves by investing in shale oil and synthetic fuels were the product of a 1970s planning exercise that was overly pessimistic about the demand for oil-based products. Exxon foresaw ever higher prices for oil and predicted sharp falls in demand as a result. However, oil prices actually tumbled during the 1980s, invalidating one of the basic assumptions of Exxon's plan (see the Opening Incident). In addition, Exxon's diversification failed because of poor acquisitions and management problems in office automation.

Inappropriate Planning Systems

One reason for the poor reputation of strategic planning is that many executives, in their initial enthusiasm for planning techniques during the 1960s and 1970s, adopted inappropriate planning systems. As at Exxon, a common problem was that executives often assumed that it was possible to forecast the future accurately. In practice, the future is unpredictable. In the real world, the only constant is change. Even the best-laid plans can fall apart if unforeseen contingencies occur.

The recognition that in an uncertain world the future cannot be forecasted with sufficient accuracy led Royal Dutch/Shell to pioneer the scenario approach to planning discussed in the Opening Incident. Rather than try to forecast the future, Shell's planners attempt to model the company's environment and then use that model to predict a range of possible scenarios. Executives are then asked to devise strategies to cope with the different scenarios. The objective is to get managers to understand the dynamic and complex nature of their environment and to think through problems in a strategic fashion. This approach seems to work far better than the inflexible forecasting approach to planning that was popular during the 1960s and 1970s.

A further problem is that many companies have made the mistake of treating strategic planning as an exclusively corporate-level function. The result is that strategic plans are often formulated in a vacuum by planning executives who have little understanding or appreciation of operating realities. As a consequence, they formulate strategies that do more harm than good. For example, when demographic data indicated that houses and families were shrinking, planners at General Electric's appliance group concluded that smaller appliances were the wave of the future. Because the planners had little contact with homebuilders and retailers, they did not realize that kitchens and bathrooms were the two rooms that were not shrinking. Nor did they appreciate that working women wanted big refrigerators to cut down on trips to the supermarket. The result was that General Electric wasted a lot of time designing small appliances for which there was only limited demand.

The ivory-tower concept of planning also has the unfortunate effect of creating damaging tensions between corporate- and business-level personnel. The experience of General Electric's appliance group is again illuminating. Many of the planners in this group were recruited from consulting firms or from top-flight business schools. Many of the operating people believed this pattern of recruitment implied that corporate executives thought that operating managers were not smart enough to think through strategic problems for themselves. Out of this impression grew an us-versus-them state of mind that quickly escalated into out-and-out hostility. As a result, even when the planners were right, operating managers would not listen to them. In the 1970s the planners correctly recognized the importance of the globalization of the appliance market and the emerging Japanese threat. However, operating managers, who then saw Sears, Roebuck as the competition, paid them little heed.

Correcting the ivory-tower approach to planning involves recognition that if strategic planning is to be successful, it is an activity that must embrace all levels of the corporation. To some extent, this goal can be achieved by setting up the kind of strategic information systems discussed in the previous section. These systems are designed to ensure that the strategies pursued by different parts of the organization are consistent and attainable. Beyond this, however, it is important to understand that much of the best planning can and should be done by operating managers. They are the ones closest to the facts. The role of corporate-level planners should be that of facilitators who help operating managers do the planning.

Poor Strategic Decision Making

Even the best-designed strategic planning systems will fail to produce the desired results if strategic decision makers fail to use the information at their disposal in an effective manner. Poor strategic decision making most often arises from a failure to question the assumptions underlying a plan, even when readily available information shows the assumptions to be fundamentally flawed.

An interesting example of this phenomenon concerns the 1979 acquisition of Howard Johnson Co. by Britain's Imperial Group.[16] Imperial is the third largest tobacco company in the world, after British American Tobaccos and Philip Morris Companies, Inc. In the 1970s it began a diversification program designed to reduce its dependence on the declining tobacco market. Part of this program included a plan to acquire a major U.S. company. Imperial spent two years scanning the United States for a suitable acquisition opportunity. It was looking for an enterprise in a high-growth industry that had a high market share, a good track record, and good growth prospects and that could be acquired at a reasonable price. Imperial scanned more than 30 industries and 200 different companies before deciding on Howard Johnson.

When Imperial announced its plans to buy Howard Johnson for close to $500 million in 1979, the company's shareholders threatened rebellion. They were quick to point out that at $26 per share Imperial was paying double what Howard Johnson had been worth only six months previously, when share prices stood at $13. The acquisition hardly seemed to be at a reasonable price. Moreover, the motel industry was entering a low- rather than a high-growth phase, and growth prospects were poor. Besides, Howard Johnson did not have a good track record. Imperial ignored shareholder protests and bought the lodging chain. Five years later, after persistent losses, Imperial was trying to divest itself of Howard Johnson. The acquisition had been a complete failure.

What went wrong? Why, after a two-year planning exercise, did Imperial buy a company that so patently did not fit its own criteria? The answer would seem to lie not in the planning but in the quality of strategic decision making. Imperial bought Howard Johnson in spite of its planning, not because of it. What happened at Imperial was that the CEO decided independently that Howard Johnson was a good buy. A rather authoritarian figure, the CEO surrounded himself with subordinates who agreed with him. Once he had made his choice, his advisers concurred with his judgment and shared in developing rationalizations for it. No one questioned the decision itself, even though information was available to show that it was flawed. Instead, strategic planning was used to justify a decision that in practice did not conform with strategic objectives.

The Imperial example is a case of what has been referred to by social psychologist Irving L. Janis as *groupthink*.[17] Groupthink occurs when a group of decision makers embarks on a course of action without questioning underlying assumptions. Typically, a group coalesces around a person or policy. It ignores or filters out information that can be used to question the policy and develops after-the-fact rationalizations for its decision. Thus commitment is based on an emotional, rather than an objective, assessment of what is the correct course of action. The consequences can be poor decisions.

This phenomenon probably explains, at least in part, why, in spite of sophisticated strategic management, companies often make poor strategic decisions. Janis traced many historical fiascoes to defective policy making by government leaders who received social support from their in-group of advisers. In a series of case studies,[18] he suggested that the following three groups of policy advisers, like the group surrounding Imperial's CEO, were dominated by concurrence seeking or groupthink and collectively avoided information that challenged their assumptions:

1. *President Harry Truman's advisory group.* The members of this group supported the decision to escalate the war in North Korea despite firm warnings by the Chinese Communist government that U.S. entry into North Korea would be met with armed resistance from the Chinese.

2. *President John Kennedy's inner circle.* The members of this group supported the decision to launch the Bay of Pigs invasion of Cuba even though available information showed that it would be an unsuccessful venture and would damage U.S. relations with other countries.

3. *President Lyndon Johnson's close advisers.* The members of this group supported the decision to escalate the war in Vietnam despite intelligence reports and other information indicating that this action would not defeat the Vietcong

or the North Vietnamese and would entail unfavorable political consequences within the United States.

Janis observed that these groupthink-dominated groups were characterized by strong pressures toward uniformity, which inclined their members to avoid raising controversial issues, questioning weak arguments, or calling a halt to soft-headed thinking.

The groupthink phenomenon raises the problem of how to bring critical information to bear on the decision mechanism so that strategic decisions made by the company are realistic and based on thorough evaluation. Two techniques known to counteract groupthink are devil's advocacy and dialectic inquiry.

Devil's Advocacy and Dialectic Inquiry

The traditional approach to strategic decision making might be called the *expert approach*.[19] This approach involves a recommended course of action based on a set of assumptions. The generation of a single plan by a knowledgeable planner or by a planning committee whose members share assumptions is an example of the expert approach. The problem with this approach is that it is vulnerable to groupthink. In addition, the assumptions are critical. If they are incorrect, then the approach is likely to generate poor decisions.

Devil's advocacy and dialectic inquiry have been proposed as two means of guarding against the weaknesses of the expert approach.[20] Devil's advocacy involves the generation of both a plan and a critical analysis of the plan. One member of the decision-making group acts as the devil's advocate, bringing out all the reasons that might make the proposal unacceptable. In this way, decision makers can be made aware of the possible perils of recommended courses of action.

Dialectic inquiry is more complex, for it involves the generation of a plan (a thesis) and a counterplan (an antithesis). According to R. O. Mason, one of the early proponents of this method in strategic management, the plan and the counterplan should reflect plausible but conflicting courses of action.[21] Corporate decision makers consider a debate between advocates of the plan and counterplan. The purpose of the debate is to reveal problems with definitions, recommended courses of action, and assumptions. As a result, corporate decision makers and planners are able to form a new and more encompassing conceptualization of the problem, which becomes the final plan (a synthesis).

Each of the three decision-making processes is illustrated in Figure 1.6. Logic suggests that both devil's advocacy and dialectic inquiry are likely to produce better decisions than is the traditional expert approach. If either of those processes had been used in the Imperial case, it is likely that a different (and probably better) decision would have been made. However, there is considerable dispute over which of the two nontraditional methods is better.[22] Researchers have come to conflicting conclusions, and the jury is still out on this issue. From a practical

FIGURE 1.6   **Three decision-making processes**

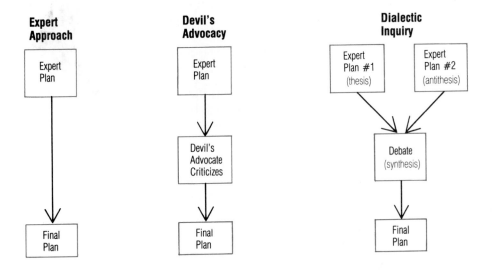

point of view, however, devil's advocacy is probably the easier method to imple-ment because it involves less commitment in terms of time than dialectic inquiry.

1.9 SUMMARY OF CHAPTER

This chapter provides a broad overview of the strategic management process. In discussing the scope and complexity of the strategic management process, we have made the following major points:

1. The techniques of strategic management are applicable to a wide range of organizations, from large, multibusiness organizations to small, one-person businesses, from manufacturing to service organizations, and from profit-seeking to not-for-profit organizations.

2. Traditional definitions of *strategy* stress that an organization's strategy is the outcome of a rational *planning* process.

3. Mintzberg's revision of the concept of strategy suggests that strategy can *emerge* from within an organization in the absence of any prior intentions.

4. The major components of the strategic management process include defin-ing the mission and major goals of the organization; analyzing the external and internal environments of the organization; choosing business and corporate-level strategies that align the organization's strengths and weak-nesses with external environmental opportunities and threats; and adopting

organizational structures and control systems to implement the organization's chosen strategy.

5. Strategic managers are individuals who bear responsibility for the overall performance of the organization or for one of its major self-contained divisions. Their overriding concern is for the health of the *total* organization under their direction.

6. Successful strategic managers are well informed, skilled at allocating their time and energy, good politicians (consensus builders), and experts at being imprecise; they are also able to push through programs in a piecemeal fashion.

7. Strategic management embraces the whole company. Specifically, three levels of strategic management have been identified: the corporate level, the business level, and the functional level.

8. Strategic management involves communication among individuals at different levels of the organization to ensure that the strategies being pursued are attainable and consistent.

9. Strategic planning often fails because executives do not plan for uncertainty and because ivory-tower planners lose touch with operating realities.

10. In spite of systematic planning, companies may adopt poor strategies if their decision making does not question underlying assumptions and guard against the dangers of groupthink.

11. Techniques for enhancing the effectiveness of strategic decision making include devil's advocacy and dialectic inquiry.

Discussion Questions

1. What do we mean by *strategy*?

2. What are the strengths of formal strategic planning? What are its weaknesses?

3. Evaluate the 1987 Iran-Contra affair from a strategic decision-making perspective. Do you think different decisions would have been made if the Reagan administration had used a dialectic inquiry or a devil's advocacy approach when making strategic decisions? Was the sale of arms to Iran the result of an intended or an emergent strategy?

Endnotes

1. "According to Plan," *The Economist*, July 22, 1989, pp. 60–63. Arie P. de Geus, "Planning as Learning," *Harvard* *Business Review* (March–April 1988), 70–74. Pierre Wack, "Scenarios: Uncharted Waters Ahead," *Harvard Business*

Review (September–October 1985), 73–89. Toni Mack, "It's Time to Take Risks," *Forbes,* (October 6, 1986), pp. 125–133.

2. Definition of "strategy" from *Webster's New World Dictionary,* Third College Edition. Copyright © 1988. Used by permission of the publisher, New World Dictionaries/ A division of Simon & Schuster, New York, NY.

3. Alfred Chandler, *Strategy and Structure: Chapters in the History of the American Enterprise* (Cambridge, Mass.: MIT Press, 1962).

4. James B. Quinn, *Strategies for Change: Logical Incrementalism* (Homewood, Ill.: Irwin, 1980).

5. William F. Glueck, *Business Policy and Strategic Management* (New York: McGraw-Hill, 1980).

6. Henry Mintzberg, "Patterns in Strategy Formulation," *Management Science,* 24 (1978), 934–948.

7. Ibid. Italics added.

8. Richard T. Pascale, "Perspectives on Strategy: The Real Story Behind Honda's Success," *California Management Review,* 26 (1984), 47–72.

9. The conventional explanation was championed by the Boston Consulting Group. See BCG, *Strategy Alternatives for the British Motorcycle Industry* (London: Her Majesty's Stationery Office, 1979).

10. K. R. Andrews, *The Concept of Corporate Strategy* (Homewood, Ill.: Dow Jones Irwin, 1971). H. I. Ansoff, *Corporate Strategy* (New York: McGraw-Hill, 1965). C. W. Hofer and D. Schendel, *Strategy Formulation: Analytical Concepts* (St. Paul, Minn.: West, 1978).

11. Edward Wrapp, "Good Managers Don't Make Policy Decisions," *Harvard Business Review* (September–October 1967), 91–99.

12. For a summary of fourteen major studies up to 1985, see Lawrence C. Rhyne, "The Relationship of Strategic Planning to Financial Performance," *Strategic Management Journal,* 7 (1986), 423–436.

13. Lawrence C. Rhyne, "The Relationship of Strategic Planning to Financial Performance," *Strategic Management Journal,* 7 (1986), 432.

14. Thomas J. Peters and Robert H. Waterman, *In Search of Excellence* (New York: Harper & Row, 1982).

15. For some examples, see S. Tilles, "How to Evaluate Corporate Strategy," *Harvard Business Review,* 41 (1963), 111–121. Also see "The New Breed of Strategic Planner," *Business Week,* September 17, 1984, pp. 62–68.

16. The story ran on an almost daily basis in the *Financial Times* of London during the autumn of 1979.

17. Irving L. Janis, *Victims of Groupthink,* 2nd ed. (Boston: Houghton Mifflin, 1982).

18. All these cases are discussed in detail in Janis, *Victims of Groupthink.* Further implications of the phenomenon are examined in I. L. Janis and L. Mann, *Decision Making* (New York: Free Press, 1977).

19. R. O. Mason, "A Dialectic Approach to Strategic Planning," *Management Science,* 13 (1969), 403–414.

20. R. A. Cosier and J. C. Aplin, "A Critical View of Dialectic Inquiry in Strategic Planning," *Strategic Management Journal,* 1 (1980), 343–356. I. I. Mintroff and R. O. Mason, "Structuring III—Structured Policy Issues: Further Explorations in a Methodology for Messy Problems," *Strategic Management Journal,* 1 (1980), 331–342.

21. Mason, "A Dialectic Approach to Strategic Planning," pp. 403–414.

22. D. M. Schweiger and P. A. Finger, "The Comparative Effectiveness of Dialectic Inquiry and Devil's Advocacy," *Strategic Management Journal,* 5 (1984), 335–350.

Chapter 2

CORPORATE MISSION, GOALS, AND STAKEHOLDERS

2.1 OPENING INCIDENT: ALLEGIS CORPORATION

In the early 1980s, Dick Ferris, the CEO of United Airlines, had a vision of the future in which United Airlines was one component of a "worldwide door-to-door travel service." Ferris believed that a company that provided flight, rental car, and hotel services could realize significant synergies. He spoke with zeal about a future in which travel agents around the world would sit in front of their computer screens, coordinating reservations for his airline, his hotels, and his rental cars.

Assembling the assets for this travel empire had begun in 1970 with the purchase of Westin Hotel Company. Under Ferris's leadership, United Airlines bought Hertz Company from RCA in 1985 for $587 million. In March 1987 United bought Hilton International for $980 million. At the same time United Airlines officially changed its name to Allegis Corporation in a symbolic attempt to emphasize the company's rebirth as an integrated travel operation.

The problem with this strategy was that it did not have the support of two major stake- holder groups: the company's airline pilots and stockholders. Ferris's problems with the pilots began in mid 1985 when he demanded wage and productivity concessions from the pilots union, the Air Line Pilots Association of United Airlines (ALPA), in order to compete with low-cost carriers such as People Express and Continental. He succeeded in getting the pilots to accept his demands, but only after a 29-day strike that soured management-labor relations and produced a $92 million quarterly loss. Then, in April 1985, ALPA offered to buy the airline for $4.5 billion. According to F. C. Dubinsky, ALPA chairman at United, the bid was motivated by the pilots' fear that "the airline is no longer the focus of the company. The management is a hotel management team. We want to return to our core business." The bid was refused by corporate leadership.

While these events were unfolding, a number of corporate raiders were beginning to take an interest in the company. In March 1987, Allegis's stock was trading in the $55-to-$60 range.

According to stock analysts and many institutional investors, at that price the stock was grossly undervalued. Several investment experts judged that the company would be worth at least $100 per share if its operations were sold separately. Buoyed by such estimates, real estate mogul Donald Trump was the first raider to surface. He purchased 5 percent of Allegis's stock. After issuing several statements critical of Ferris, Trump sold his stake, but not before he had "talked up" the company's stock price and made a profit of $50 million on the transaction. Then, in May 1987, Coniston Partners, an investment fund, disclosed that it had purchased 13 percent of the company's stock. Coniston's intention was to remove the board of directors and sell off the company's constituent businesses.

Ferris's reaction to the takeover bids from Coniston and ALPA was to initiate two takeover defenses. First, as part of a $15-billion jet order, Allegis provided the Boeing Company with new issue convertible notes valued at $700 million. Should a single investment entity purchase more than 40 percent of Allegis's stock, the interest rates on the notes would increase drastically, thereby severely raising the costs of any hostile takeover attempt. This tactic, however, failed to reassure the majority of Allegis's stockholders, who were becoming increasingly dissatisfied with Ferris. In response, the Allegis board suggested a massive recapitalization plan that would immediately repay stockholders $60 per share in cash and leave them with stock worth an estimated $28 per share. The problem was that this plan would add more than $3 billion to the $2.4 billion in long-term debt already on the company's balance sheet. Such a debt load would have been perilous in the competitive airline industry, and the resulting interest payments might have wiped out profits.

Ultimately the Allegis board could not countenance piling up heavy debt to salvage a master plan that shareholders disliked. Nor could it support a CEO who had so clearly alienated both Wall Street investors and many of the company's employees. Consequently, in June 1987 the board ousted Dick Ferris; repudiated his travel supermarket strategy; announced that Hertz, Westin, and Hilton International would all be sold; decided to consider selling a major stake in United Airlines to its employees; and announced plans to change the company's name back to United Airlines. In effect, after supporting Dick Ferris through two difficult years, the board reversed itself under pressure from employees and stockholders. Coniston and ALPA responded by dropping their takeover bids. In the view of both parties, the board was now proposing to do what they had wanted all along.[1]

2.2 OVERVIEW

Allegis failed to satisfy the interests of two of its major constituencies, or stakeholders: its stockholders and its employees. As a consequence, CEO Dick Ferris, the architect of Allegis's strategy, lost his job. To avoid the problems that Allegis faced, companies can and should identify and incorporate the claims of various stakeholder groups into strategic decision making. This chapter is concerned with identifying how this can be done.

The corporate mission statement is the first key indicator of how an organization views the claims of its stakeholders. The mission statement defines the business of an organization and states basic goals, characteristics, and guiding philosophies. Its purpose is to set the organizational context within which strategic decisions will be made—in other words, to give an organization strategic focus and direction. All strategic decisions flow from the mission statement. In examining how organizations formulate such statements, we concentrate on the three main components that strategy writers have recommended for inclusion in a corporate mission statement:

1. A definition of the organization's business
2. A statement of major corporate goals
3. A statement of corporate philosophy[2]

An example of a mission statement appears in Table 2.1, which shows the mission statement of NCR Corporation. The six points set out major corporate commitments to the following stakeholder groups: customers, stockholders, employees, suppliers, and the community.

After examining how to construct a mission statement, we consider a company's various **stakeholders:** individuals or groups, either within or outside the organization, that have some claim on it (see Figure 2.1). Their interests must be taken into account when a mission statement is formulated. Then we look closely

TABLE 2.1   **NCR's corporate mission statement**

NCR's mission: create value for our stakeholders

NCR is a successful, growing company dedicated to achieving superior results by assuring that its actions are aligned with stakeholder expectations. Stakeholders are all constituencies with a stake in the fortunes of the company. NCR's primary mission is to create value for our stakeholders.

We believe in conducting our business activities with integrity and respect while building mutually beneficial and enduring relationships with all of our stakeholders.

We take customer satisfaction personally: we are committed to providing superior value in our products and services on a continuing basis.

We respect the individuality of each employee and foster an environment in which employees' creativity and productivity are encouraged, recognized, valued, and rewarded.

We think of our suppliers as partners who share our goal of achieving the highest quality standards and the most consistent level of service.

We are committed to being caring and supportive corporate citizens within the worldwide communities in which we operate.

We are dedicated to creating value for our shareholders and financial communities by performing in a manner that will enhance returns on investments.

Source: Courtesy of NCR Corporation.

FIGURE 2.1   The relationship between the mission, stakeholders, and strategies

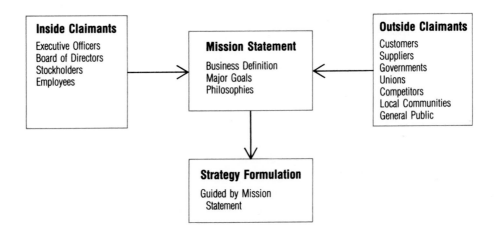

at two particularly important stakeholder groups, **stockholders** and **the general public,** analyzing how stockholders can and do influence the corporate mission, and hence corporate strategies, and considering the issue of **corporate social responsibility.**

2.3 DEFINING THE BUSINESS

The first component of a mission statement is a clear definition of the organization's business. Essentially, defining the business involves answering these questions: "What is our business? What will it be? What should it be?"[3] The answers vary, depending on whether the organization is a single-business or a diversified enterprise. A single-business enterprise is active in just one main business area. For example, U.S. Steel in the 1950s was involved just in the production of steel. By the 1980s, however, U.S. Steel had become USX, a diversified company with interests in steel, oil and gas, chemicals, real estate, transportation, and the production of energy equipment. For USX, the process of defining itself is complicated by the fact that to a large extent the concern of a multibusiness enterprise is *managing businesses.* Thus the business definition of USX involves different issues than did the definition of U.S. Steel. In this section, the problem of how to define the business of a single-business company is considered first. Discussion of the problem of how best to define the business of a diversified enterprise follows.

A Single-Business Company

To answer the question "What is our business?" Derek F. Abell has suggested that a company should define its business in terms of three dimensions: (1) Who is being satisfied (what customer groups)? (2) What is being satisfied (what customer needs)? (3) How are customer needs being satisfied (by skills or by distinctive competencies)?[4] Figure 2.2 illustrates these three dimensions.

Abell's approach stresses the need for a *consumer-oriented* rather than a *product-oriented* business definition. A product-oriented business definition focuses just on the products sold and the markets served. Abell maintains that such an approach obscures the company's function, which is to satisfy consumer needs. A product is only the physical manifestation of applying a particular skill to satisfy a particular need for a particular consumer group. In practice, there often are

FIGURE 2.2   **Abell's framework for defining the business**

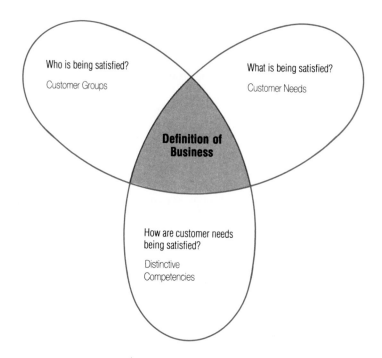

Source: Derek F. Abell, *Defining the Business: The Starting Point of Strategic Planning* (Englewood Cliffs, N.J.: Prentice-Hall, 1980), p. 17.

different ways of serving the particular need of a particular consumer group. Identifying these ways through a broad, consumer-oriented business definition can safeguard companies from being caught unawares by major shifts in demand. Indeed, by helping anticipate demand shifts, Abell's framework can assist companies in capitalizing on the changes in their environment. It can help answer the question "What will our business be?"

Unfortunately, the need to take a customer-oriented view of a company's business has often been ignored. Consequently, history is littered with the wreckage of once-great corporations that failed to define their business or that defined it incorrectly. These firms failed to see what their business would become, and ultimately they declined. Theodore Levitt described the fall of the once-mighty U.S. railroads in terms of their failure to define their business correctly:

> The railroads did not stop growing because the need for passenger and freight transportation declined. That grew. The railroads are in trouble today not because the need was filled by others (cars, trucks, airplanes, even telephones), but because it was not filled by the railroads themselves. They let others take customers away from them because they assumed themselves to be in the railroad business rather than in the transportation business. The reason they defined their industry wrong was because they were railroad oriented instead of transport oriented; they were product oriented instead of customer oriented.[5]

If the railroads had used Abell's framework, they might have anticipated the impact of technological change and decided that their business was transportation. In that case, they might have transferred their early strength in rail into dominance in today's diversified transport industry. Sadly, most railroads stuck to a product-oriented definition of their business and went bankrupt.

In contrast, IBM correctly foresaw what its business would be. Originally, IBM was a leader in the manufacture of typewriters and mechanical tabulating equipment using punch-card technology. However, IBM viewed itself as providing a means for information processing and storage, rather than as a supplier of mechanical tabulating equipment and typewriters. Given this definition, the company's subsequent moves into computers, software systems, office systems, and copiers seem logical.

The question "What should our business be?" can also be answered using Abell's framework. Recall that IBM decided that its business should be computers, word processors, and office systems—all natural extensions of its original business. Other companies do not see as much promise in their original business, perhaps because of negative and irreversible changes in consumer needs and technologies. These companies decide to switch to something different, and they diversify away from their original business. In the 1960s, many companies reduced their dependence on their original business by moving into unrelated areas. Conglomerates such as ITT Corporation, Gulf & Western Industries, and Textron are a result of this diversification movement.[6]

TABLE 2.2   **Examples of business definitions**

Bethlehem Steel Corp.:
Bethlehem is a large, integrated steel producer which makes and sells a wide variety of steel mill and manufactured steel products. Bethlehem is also engaged in the production and sales of coal and other raw materials, . . . in the construction and servicing of mobile offshore drilling rigs and ships, . . . in the manufacture of railroad cars and parts, . . . in the sale of equipment and supplies to the oil and gas industries, . . . and in the manufacture of home building products and custom-molded plastic products. Bethlehem also sells technology domestically and internationally.

Litton Industries, Inc.:
Litton is a technology-based company applying advanced electronics products and services to business opportunities in defense, industrial automation, and geophysical markets. Research and product engineering emphasis is on developing advanced products which the company manufactures and supplies worldwide to commercial, industrial, and government customers.

Polaroid Corp. (late 1970s definition):
Polaroid manufactures and sells photographic products based on inventions of the company in the field of one-step instant photography and light polarizing products, utilizing the company's inventions in the field of polarized light. The company considers itself to be engaged in one line of business.

Polaroid Corp. (mid 1980s definition):
Polaroid designs, manufactures, and markets worldwide a variety of products based on its inventions, primarily in the photographic field. These include instant photographic cameras and films, light polarizing filters and lenses, and diversified chemical, optical, and commercial products. The principal products of the company are used in amateur and professional photography, industry, science, medicine, and education.

Zale Corporation:
Zale's business is specialty retailing. Retailing is a people-oriented business. The corporation's business existence and continued success are dependent upon how well it meets its responsibilities to serve critically important groups of people.

Source: Adapted from company annual reports.

Table 2.2 details how a number of companies define their business. Perhaps the best example of a consumer-oriented business definition in the table is that of Zale Corporation. Given this definition, it is not surprising that Zale is one of the most successful national jewelry retailers. Yet until 1980 Zale was primarily product oriented, and that outlook endangered the company's health. According to Zale's chairman, Donald Zale, the first, foremost, and primary change has been to acquire a consumer orientation. The company makes about half of the jewelry it sells. In the past, manufacturing operations largely decided what products would be made. For a decade manufacturing ground out so-called mother's rings—rings set with children's birthstones. Zale wasn't watching the market. The business died and the company was left with a worthless inventory. This experience forced Zale to rethink its business definition.[7]

Like Zale's early definition, Polaroid's business definition until the 1980s was product oriented, stressing the company's involvement in one-step instant photography. This myopic definition has not served Polaroid well. The development of quick-turnaround photo developing and high-quality, low-cost 35mm cameras—a product that Polaroid's founder, Edwin Land, once rejected—has taken away much of Polaroid's market. At the height of its popularity in 1978, more than 8 million instant cameras were sold in the United States. Four years later the figure was closer to 5 million. Polaroid's net earnings declined from nearly $120 million in 1978 to $23.5 million in 1982. Its problem was defining its business as one-step instant photography rather than as the recording of images and memories. In other words, its business definition was guided by the products it manufactured rather than by the needs it served. Somewhat belatedly, Polaroid realized its mistake, changed its business definition, and attempted to broaden its product base—but with only limited success.[8]

Part of the reason for its difficulty in producing a turnaround is that its current business definition is still primarily product oriented. Polaroid still defines its business in terms of the products it manufactures and sells, rather than the customer needs it is seeking to satisfy.

A Diversified Company

A diversified company faces special problems when trying to define its business because it actually operates several businesses. In essence, the corporate business is often one of managing a collection of businesses. For example, USX, formerly U.S. Steel, is still known primarily for its steel interests. A consumer-oriented definition of USX's steel interests might be something like this: "USX seeks to satisfy customers' needs for a high-strength construction and fabricating material." However, USX is, in fact, a diversified company that in 1986 generated only 33 percent of its revenues from steel. The rest came from oil and gas, chemicals, real estate, transportation, and energy equipment. Clearly, the consumer-oriented definition given above applies only to the company's steel operations; it does not suffice as a definition of its *corporate* businesses.

In a diversified enterprise, the question "What is our business?" must be asked at two levels: the business level and the corporate level. At the business level, such as USX's steel operations, the focus should be on a consumer-oriented definition. But at the corporate level, management cannot simply aggregate the various business definitions, for doing so will lead to an unfocused and confusing statement. Instead, the corporate business definition should be *portfolio oriented*. In this context, **portfolio** refers to a company's collection of businesses. A portfolio-oriented definition should include the following:

1. The purpose of the company's portfolio of businesses
2. The desired scope (diversity) of the portfolio
3. The balance desired between different businesses in the portfolio

The purpose of a portfolio—the gains that a portfolio of businesses can bring a company—is discussed in more detail in Chapters 7 and 9. At this stage, it is

FIGURE 2.3   **Summary of factors important in business definitions**

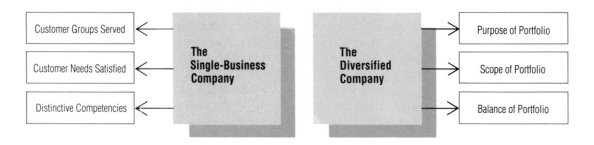

enough to note that a company should define its corporate business so that its strategic objective is clear. For example, in building its portfolio of businesses, USX wanted to become less dependent on its ailing steel operations. Unless it has a clear objective, a company runs the risk of building a portfolio without identifying the underlying industrial or financial logic behind its actions—indeed, without knowing why it is building a portfolio. This criticism has been leveled at the early U.S. conglomerates. A number of commentators claim that these companies built diversified portfolios for no reason other than to be fashionable.[9]

For similar reasons, a portfolio-oriented definition must include the desired scope of the portfolio; otherwise, the company risks pursuing portfolio diversification for its own sake. If no constraint is placed on scope, the company can diversify too widely. Finally, the company must consider the important issue of desired balance among the different businesses in its portfolio. It must decide whether it wants a balanced portfolio of activities, with each business making an equal contribution toward corporate earnings, or an unbalanced portfolio, where the size of the constituent businesses varies considerably. Most companies prefer a balanced portfolio, perhaps because an unbalanced portfolio can result in top management focusing too much attention on large businesses at the expense of the smaller ones.

A summary of factors important in the definitions of both single-business and diversified companies is given in Figure 2.3.

2.4 SETTING CORPORATE GOALS

As we indicated at the start of this chapter, the first major component of a mission statement is a definition of the company's business and the second is a statement of major corporate goals. Corporate goals spell out formally what the organization is trying to achieve; they give direction to the corporate mission statement and help guide the formulation of strategy. For example, a major corporate goal of General Electric is to be first or second in every market in which it competes.

Accordingly, General Electric's businesses typically seek market leadership rather than a secure market niche and therefore center their strategies on how to achieve market leadership. Profit-seeking organizations may operate with a variety of major corporate goals; but in theory at least, all these goals should be directed toward one end: the maximization of stockholder wealth.

Maximizing Stockholder Wealth

Stockholders provide a company with capital and in exchange expect an appropriate return on their investment. A company's stockholders are its legal owners. Consequently, the overriding goal of most corporations is to maximize stockholder wealth, which involves increasing the long-run returns earned by stockholders from owning shares in the corporation. Stockholders receive returns in two ways: (1) from dividend payments and (2) from capital appreciation in the market value of a share (that is, by increases in stock market prices).

The best way for a company to maximize stockholder wealth is to pursue strategies that maximize its own return on investment (ROI), which is a good general indicator of a company's efficiency. In short, the more efficient a company is, the better its future prospects look to stockholders and the greater is its ability to pay dividends. Furthermore, higher ROI leads to greater demand for a company's shares. Demand bids up the share price and leads to capital appreciation.

Secondary Goals

However, as management theorist Peter F. Drucker and many others have pointed out, there is danger in emphasizing only ROI.[10] An overzealous pursuit of ROI can misdirect managerial attention and encourage some of the worst management practices, such as maximizing short-run rather than long-run ROI. A short-run orientation favors such action as cutting expenditures judged to be nonessential in that span of time—for instance, expenditures for research and development, marketing, and new capital investments. Although decreasing current expenditure increases current ROI, the resulting underinvestment, lack of innovation, and poor market awareness jeopardize long-run ROI. Yet despite these negative consequences, managers do make such decisions, because the adverse effects of a short-run orientation may not materialize and become apparent to stockholders for several years. By that time, the management team responsible may have moved on, leaving others to pick up the pieces.

In a major *Harvard Business Review* article, Robert H. Hayes and William J. Abernathy argue that the widespread focus on short-run ROI has been a major factor in the long-run loss of international competitiveness by U.S. companies.[11] MIT economist Lester Thurow likewise faults the short-run orientation of many American businesses for some of their problems. He cites declining R&D expenditures and reduced innovative activity within American enterprises as evidence of this orientation.[12] The household products and drug company American

Home Products Corp., which manufactures Advil, is a case in point.[13] American Home has a history of impressive financial performance, regularly recording a return of more than 30 percent on equity. Since 1983, however, American Home has been showing signs of fatigue. Pretax income, which grew at double-digit rates for a decade, increased only 3 percent annually between 1984 and 1986.

The reason for such a decline in profit growth is the company's difficulty in coming up with new products. Its tight cost controls and focus on current profitability have stunted spending on research and development. In 1983, spending on R&D at American Home was only 3 percent of sales, compared with a drug industry average of 6.1 percent.[14] Moreover, American Home expects a new product to show profit in a year and a half rather than in three years or more, which is the norm for most companies. Thus American Home illustrates the adverse effects of short-run profit maximization.

To guard against short-run behavior, Drucker suggests that companies adopt a number of secondary goals in addition to ROI. These goals should be designed to balance short-run and long-run considerations. Drucker's list includes secondary goals relating to these areas: (1) market share, (2) innovation, (3) productivity, (4) physical and financial resources, (5) manager performance and development, (6) worker performance and attitude, and (7) social responsibility. Although such secondary goals need not be part of a mission statement, sometimes the most important ones are. Recall that General Electric stresses a market-share goal: to be first or second in every business in which it competes. Given the strong positive relationship between market share and profitability, this goal is consistent with long-run profit maximization.[15]

Even if a company does not recognize secondary goals explicitly, it must recognize them implicitly through a commitment to long-run profitability. Take Hewlett-Packard, one of the companies that Thomas J. Peters and Robert H. Waterman cite as being an "excellent" company.[16] The following quotation from Hewlett-Packard's mission statement clearly expresses the importance of an orientation toward maximizing long-run profitability and can serve as a model:

> In our economic system, the profit we generate from our operations is the ultimate source of the funds we need to prosper and grow. It is the one absolutely essential measure of our corporate performance over the long term. Only if we continue to meet our profit objective can we achieve our other corporate objectives.[17]

2.5 CORPORATE PHILOSOPHY

The third component of a mission statement is a statement of corporate philosophy, reflecting the basic beliefs, values, aspirations, and philosophical priorities that the strategic decision makers are committed to and that guide their management of the company. It tells how the company intends to do business and often

TABLE 2.3   Johnson & Johnson's credo

Our Credo

We believe our first responsibility is to the doctors, nurses and patients,
to mothers and fathers and all others who use our products and services.
In meeting their needs everything we do must be of high quality.
We must constantly strive to reduce our costs
in order to maintain reasonable prices.
Customers' orders must be serviced promptly and accurately.
Our suppliers and distributors must have an opportunity
to make a fair profit.

We are responsible to our employees,
the men and women who work with us throughout the world.
Everyone must be considered as an individual.
We must respect their dignity and recognize their merit.
They must have a sense of security in their jobs.
Compensation must be fair and adequate,
and working conditions clean, orderly and safe.
Employees must feel free to make suggestions and complaints.
There must be equal opportunity for employment, development
and advancement for those qualified.
We must provide competent management,
and their actions must be just and ethical.

We are responsible to the communities in which we live and work
and to the world community as well.
We must be good citizens—support good works and charities
and bear our fair share of taxes.
We must encourage civic improvements and better health and education.
We must maintain in good order
the property we are privileged to use,
protecting the environment and natural resources.

Our final responsibility is to our stockholders.
Business must make a sound profit.
We must experiment with new ideas.
Research must be carried on, innovative programs developed
and mistakes paid for.
New equipment must be purchased, new facilities provided
and new products launched.
Reserves must be created to provide for adverse times.
When we operate according to these principles,
the stockholders should realize a fair return.

Johnson & Johnson

Source: Courtesy of Johnson & Johnson.

reflects the company's recognition of its social responsibility (corporate social responsibility is discussed in a later section of this chapter).

Many companies establish a philosophical creed to emphasize their own distinctive outlook on business. Thus a company's creed forms the basis for establishing its corporate culture (an issue considered in Chapter 11). Take the creed of Lincoln Electric Company. It states that productivity increases should be shared primarily by customers and employees through lower prices and higher wages. This belief distinguishes Lincoln Electric from many other enterprises and, by all accounts, is acted on by the company in terms of its specific strategies, objectives, and operating policies.[18]

Another company whose philosophical beliefs are famous is health-care giant Johnson & Johnson. Johnson & Johnson summarizes its philosophy in a credo, which is reproduced in Table 2.3. The credo articulates Johnson & Johnson's belief that the company's first responsibility is to the doctors, nurses, and patients who use J&J products, followed by the employees, the communities in which Johnson & Johnson employees live and work, and finally the company's stockholders. The credo is prominently displayed in every manager's office; and according to the J&J managers, the credo guides all important decisions.

Strong evidence of the credo's influence was apparent in the company's response to the Tylenol crisis. In 1982 seven people in the Chicago area died after taking Tylenol capsules that had been laced with cyanide. Johnson & Johnson immediately withdrew all Tylenol capsules from the U.S. market at an estimated cost to the company of $100 million. At the same time the company embarked on a comprehensive communication effort involving 2,500 Johnson & Johnson employees and targeted at the pharmaceutical and medical communities. By such means, Johnson & Johnson successfully presented itself to the public as a company that was willing to do what was right, regardless of the cost. As a consequence, the Tylenol crisis enhanced rather than tarnished Johnson & Johnson's image. Indeed, because of its actions, the company was able to retain its status as a market leader in painkillers in a matter of months.[19]

2.6 CORPORATE STAKEHOLDERS

Stakeholders and the Mission Statement

Recall that stakeholders are individuals or groups that have some claim on the company. Stakeholders can be divided into internal claimants and external claimants.[20] Internal claimants are stockholders or employees, including executive officers and board members. External claimants are all other individuals and groups affected by the company's actions. Typically, they comprise customers, suppliers, governments, unions, competitors, local communities, and the general public.

All stakeholders can justifiably expect that the company will attempt to satisfy their particular demands. As John A. Pearce, a prominent strategy writer, has noted, stockholders provide the enterprise with capital and expect an appropriate return on their investment in exchange. Employees provide labor and skills and in exchange expect commensurate income and job satisfaction. Customers want value for money. Suppliers seek dependable buyers. Governments insist on adherence to legislative regulations. Unions demand benefits for their members in proportion to their contributions to the company. Rivals seek fair competition. Local communities want companies that are responsible citizens. The general public seeks some assurance that the quality of life will be improved as a result of the company's existence.

A company has to take these claims into account when formulating its strategies, or else stakeholders may withdraw their support. Stockholders may sell their shares, employees leave their jobs, and customers buy elsewhere. Suppliers are likely to seek more dependable buyers, whereas governments can prosecute the company. Unions may engage in disruptive labor disputes, and rivals may respond to unfair competition by anticompetitive moves of their own or by filing antitrust suits. Communities may oppose the company's attempts to locate its facilities in their area, and the general public may form pressure groups, demanding action against companies that impair the quality of life. Any of these reactions can have a disastrous impact on the enterprise.

A mission statement enables a company to incorporate stakeholder claims into its strategic decision making and thereby reduce the risk of losing stakeholder support. The mission statement thus becomes the company's formal commitment to a stakeholder group; it carries the message that its strategies will be formulated with the claims of those stakeholders in mind. We have already discussed how stockholder claims are incorporated into the mission statement when a company decides that its primary goal is maximizing long-run profitability. Any strategies that the company generates should reflect this major corporate goal. Similarly, the mission statement should recognize additional stakeholder claims, in terms of secondary goals or as philosophies.

Stakeholder Impact Analysis

A company cannot always satisfy the claims of all stakeholders. The claims of different groups may conflict, and in practice few organizations have the resources to manage all stakeholders. For example, union claims for higher wages can conflict with consumer demands for reasonable prices and stockholder demands for acceptable returns. Hence often the company must make choices. To do so, it must identify the most important stakeholders and give highest priority to pursuing strategies that satisfy their needs. Stakeholder impact analysis can provide such identification. Typically, stakeholder impact analysis involves the following steps:

1. Identify stakeholders.
2. Identify stakeholders' interests and concerns.

3. As a result, identify what claims stakeholders are likely to make on the organization.
4. Identify the most important stakeholders from the perspective of the organization.
5. Identify the resultant strategic challenges.[21]

   The analysis allows the company to identify the stakeholders most critical to its continued survival and to incorporate their claims into the mission statement explicitly. From the mission statement, stakeholder claims then feed down into the rest of the strategy formulation process. For example, if community involvement is identified as a critical stakeholder claim, it must be incorporated in the mission statement, and any strategies that conflict with it must be rejected.

2.7 CORPORATE GOVERNANCE AND STRATEGY

Satisfying stockholders' demands typically receives a great deal of attention in many corporate mission statements. As providers of capital and owners of the corporation, stockholders play a unique role. Ultimately, an enterprise exists for its stockholders. In the case of most publicly held corporations, however, stockholders delegate the job of controlling the company and determining strategies to corporate managers, who become the agents, or employees, of the stockholders.[22] Accordingly, corporate managers should pursue strategies that are in the best interest of their employers, the stockholders. They should pursue strategies that maximize stockholder wealth. Managers, however, do not always act in this fashion.

Management Goals Versus Stockholder Goals

Why should managers want to pursue strategies other than those consistent with maximizing stockholder wealth? The answer depends on the personal goals of professional managers. Many writers have argued that managers are motivated by desires for status, power, job security, income, and the like.[23] A large company can satisfy such desires better than a small one. A manager gets more status, power, job security, and income as a senior manager at General Motors than as a senior manager in a small local enterprise. Consequently, managers are thought to favor the pursuit of corporate growth goals at the expense of long-run profitability. To quote Carl Icahn, one of the most renowned corporate raiders of the 1980s,

> make no mistake, a strongly knit corporate aristocracy exists in America. The top man, what's more, usually finds expanding his power more important than rewarding owners (stockholders). When Mobil and USX had ex-

cess cash, did they enrich shareholders? Of course not. They bought Mar-cor and Marathon—disastrous investments, but major increases in the size of the manor.[24]

Thus, instead of maximizing stockholder wealth, managers may trade long-run profitability for greater growth. Figure 2.4 graphs profitability against a company's growth rate. A company that does not grow is probably missing out on some profitable opportunities.[25] A growth rate of G_0 in Figure 2.4 is not consistent with maximizing profitability ($P_1 < P_{MAX}$). A moderate growth rate of G_1, on the other hand, does allow a company to maximize profitability, producing profits equal to P_{MAX}. Past G_1, further growth involves lower profitability (that is, past G_1 the investment required to finance further growth does not produce an adequate return). Yet G_2 might be the growth rate favored by managers, for it increases their power and status. At this growth rate, profits are only equal to P_2. Because P_{MAX} is greater than P_2, a company growing at this rate is clearly not maximizing its profitability and hence the wealth of its stockholders. However, a growth rate of G_2 may be consistent with attaining managerial goals of power, status, and income.

The problem facing stockholders, therefore, is how to *govern* the corporation so that managerial desires for excessive growth or "empire building" are held in check. In addition, there is a need for mechanisms that allow stockholders to

FIGURE 2.4   **The tradeoff between profitability and growth rate**

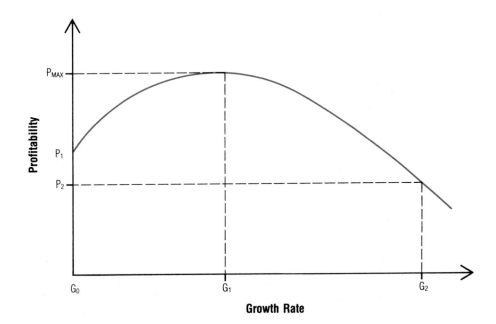

remove incompetent or ineffective managers. A number of *governance mechanisms* perform this function: shareholder meetings, the board of directors, stock-based compensation schemes, and the takeover market.

Stockholder Meetings

The constitution of most publicly held corporations specifies that companies should hold stockholder meetings at least once a year. These meetings provide a forum in which stockholders can voice their approval or discontent with management. In theory, at such meetings stockholders can propose resolutions that, if they receive a majority of stockholder votes, can shape management policy, limit the strategies management can pursue, and remove or appoint key personnel.

In practice, however, until recently stockholder meetings functioned as little more than rubber stamps for management resolutions. Stockholders must finance their own challenges and, in many cases, meet stiff regulations limiting the number of proxy votes they can solicit. Thus proposing resolutions critical of management was normally considered too expensive and difficult to be worthwhile. Rather, it was understood that stockholders could best show dissatisfaction with a company by selling their shares.

However, the recent emergence of powerful institutional investors as major stockholders is beginning to change all that. By 1987, the stock holdings of all institutional investors—pension funds, mutual funds, insurance companies, banks, brokers, and dealers—amounted to more than one-third of all corporate stock. The figure is much higher among the big companies that make up the Standard & Poor 500-stock index. For example, in 1987 the institutions held 63 percent of the stock of the Ford Motor Company, 81 percent of the stock of Digital Equipment, 79 percent of the stock of K Mart, and 72 percent of the stock of Citicorp.[26]

The significance of the growing concentration of stock in institutional hands is that institutions can no longer sell their shares without pushing down the price and taking a loss on the transaction. Jose Arau, principal investment officer for the California Public Employees Retirement System, one of the nation's largest institutional investors, has observed: "In the past you could always vote with your feet, but if you hold a thousand stocks, it's tough to do that."[27]

The lack of room to sell is putting pressure on institutions to show their dissatisfaction with management by voting proxies more aggressively. As a result, there is growing evidence that institutions are beginning to band together and put pressure on management teams that are perceived as being incompetent or pursuing strategies that are inconsistent with maximizing long-run returns.

For example, in early 1987 a group of institutional investors with major holdings in General Motors met with GM chairman Roger Smith. The institutions were angry at the $700 million "hushmail" payment made to dissident director H. Ross Perot when he quit the GM board. In addition, they criticized

Smith for GM's falling profits and market share, its weak stock price, and its poor productivity despite investments of over $40 billion in new equipment since 1979. In view of all these problems, they were also disturbed at the big bonus that GM had recently announced for its senior executives. The institutions then threatened to introduce at the next shareholder meeting a resolution that would be critical of management. In response, within a matter of weeks GM's management announced a series of major policy changes. The company stated that it would buy back stock, cut capital spending, trim production capacity, reduce excessive inventories, and replace cash bonuses for managers with a stock-based compensation plan linked to long-term performance. The institutional shareholders then withdrew their proposal.[28] Direct pressure from institutional investors had succeeded in changing critical aspects of strategy at General Motors.

The Role of the Board

Stockholder interests are looked after within the company by the board of directors. Board members are directly elected by stockholders, and under corporate law the board represents the stockholders' interests in the company. Thus the board can be held legally accountable for the company's actions. Its position at the apex of decision making within the company allows the board to monitor corporate strategy decisions and ensure that they are consistent with stockholder interests. In addition, the board has the legal authority to hire, fire, and compensate corporate employees, including, most importantly, the CEO.[29] Thus, if the board's sense is that corporate strategies are not in the best interest of stockholders, it can apply sanctions. In the case of Allegis Corporation, discussed in the Opening Incident, one factor that led to the dismissal of CEO Dick Ferris was that his strategies lost the support of the Allegis board.

The typical board comprises a mix of insiders and outsiders. Inside directors are required because they have valuable information about the company's activities. Without such information the board cannot adequately perform its monitoring function. However, since insiders are full-time employees of the company, their interests tend to be aligned with those of management. Thus, outside directors are required to bring objectivity to the monitoring and evaluation processes. Outside directors are not full-time employees of the company. Many of them are full-time professional directors who hold positions on the boards of several companies. The need to maintain a reputation as competent outside directors gives them an incentive to perform their tasks as objectively and effectively as possible.

Critics charge that inside directors may be able to dominate the outsiders on the board. Insiders can use their position within the management hierarchy to exercise control over the content of company-specific information that the board receives. Thus, they can present information in a way that puts management in a favorable light. In addition, insiders have the advantage of intimate knowledge of the company's operations. Because superior knowledge and control over information are sources of power (see Chapter 13), insiders may be better positioned to influence board-room decision making than outsiders. Hence, the board may become the captive of insiders and serve merely as a rubber stamp for management decisions, rather than as a guardian of stockholder interests. A board dominated by insiders may pursue strategies consistent with the interests of management rather than of stockholders.

Some critics even contend that most boards are dominated by the company CEO.[30] In support of this view, they point out that both inside and outside directors are often the personal nominees of the CEO. The typical inside director is subordinate to the CEO in the company's hierarchy and therefore is unlikely to criticize his or her immediate boss. In addition, since outside directors too are often the nominee of the CEO, even they can hardly be expected to evaluate the CEO objectively. Thus the loyalty of the board may be biased toward the CEO as opposed to stockholders. This problem has prompted management gurus such as Peter Drucker to comment that the one thing all boards have in common is that they do not function.

Nevertheless, there are signs that many corporate boards are moving away from merely rubber-stamping top-management decisions and are beginning to play a much more active governance role. The catalyst has been an increase in the number of lawsuits filed by stockholders against board members. The trend started in 1985 when a Delaware court ruled that the directors of Trans Union Corporation had been too quick to accept a takeover bid. The court held the directors personally liable for the difference between the offer they accepted and the price the company might have fetched in a sale. The directors then agreed to make up the $23.5 million difference. Since then, a number of major suits have been filed by stockholders against board members. These include suits directed against board members at Holly Farms, Northrop Corporation, Lincoln Savings & Loan, Lotus Development Corp., and RJR Nabisco.[31]

Spurred on by the threat of legal action, increasing numbers of boards have started to assert their independence from company management in general and from corporate CEOs in particular. For example, at ALCOA the board engineered the resignation of CEO Charles W. Parry, who had pursued an unsuccessful diversification strategy. They replaced Parry with a fellow director, Paul O'Neill, and gave him the task of refocusing the company on its core aluminum business.

It must also be said, however, that many boards still have a tendency to act as rubber stamps and seem reluctant to challenge CEOs. For example, Sunstrand CEO Evans Erikson resigned under pressure from institutional investors in 1988 after the company pleaded guilty to defense fraud. But for years, Sunstrand's lavish spending and lax financial controls went unquestioned by directors, prompting the Defense Department to take on oversight responsibility.[32] In summary, it would seem that although many board members are beginning to take their governance responsibilities more seriously, a large number of weak boards still remain.

Stock-based Compensation Schemes

To get around the problem of captive boards, stockholders have urged many companies to introduce stock-based compensation schemes for their senior executives. For example, the introduction of stock-based incentive schemes at General Motors was in response to direct pressure from institutional investors (see above). These schemes are designed to align the interests of managers with those of stockholders. In addition to their regular salary, senior executives are given stock options in the firm, so they receive a major portion of their income from dividend payments and stock price appreciations. Thus, they have a direct interest in adopting strategies consistent with maximizing stockholder wealth for, as significant stockholders themselves, they will gain from such strategies. Lee Iacocca, for example, earned $20 million in 1986 from the sale of Chrysler stock that he was given when he arrived at Chrysler in 1979 to head the company. This gain can be viewed as Iacocca's reward for adopting strategies consistent with the best interests of Chrysler's stockholders.

Recent studies have confirmed that stock-based compensation schemes for senior executives can align management and stockholder interests. For instance, one study found that managers were more likely to consider the effects of their acquisition decisions on stockholder wealth if they themselves were significant shareholders.[33] According to another study, managers who were significant stockholders were less likely to pursue diversification strategies consistent with maximizing the size of the company rather than its profitability.[34] For all their attractions, stock-based compensation schemes have yet to be universally adopted by American companies. Some critics argue that the schemes do not always have the desired effect, since stock compensation plans can harm stockholders by diluting their interests and rewarding management unjustifiably for improvements in stock prices. Critics note that stock prices often increase more because of improvements in the overall economy than because of managerial effort, and they ask why management should be rewarded for such an increase. In addition, when stock prices are falling because of factors outside the company's control, as can occur during a slump in general economic activity, then executives may see the value of their stockholdings decline rapidly. Under such circumstances, stock-based compensation schemes give managers little incentive to align their goals with those of stockholders in general.

The Takeover Constraint and Corporate Raiders

If the board is loyal to management rather than to stockholders or if stock-based compensation schemes have not been adopted by the company, then, as suggested earlier, management may pursue strategies that maximize the company's growth rate rather than its profitability. Stockholders, however, still have some residual power, for they can always sell their shares. If they start doing so in large numbers, the price of the company's shares will decline. If the share price falls far enough, the company might be worth less on the stock market than the book value of its assets, at which point it may become a takeover target.

The risk of being bought out is known as the **takeover constraint.** The takeover constraint effectively limits the extent to which managers can pursue strategies that put their own interests above those of stockholders. If they ignore stockholder interests and the company is bought out, senior managers typically lose their independence and probably their jobs as well. So the threat of takeover can constrain management action. The experience of Allegis Corporation, presented in the Opening Incident, is one example of this process.

Increasingly, the threat of takeover is being enforced by **corporate raiders.** The corporate raider is a phenomenon that emerged in a big way during the late 1970s and early 1980s. Corporate raiders are individuals or institutions who buy up large blocks of shares in companies that they think are pursuing strategies inconsistent with maximizing stockholder wealth. They argue that if these companies pursued different strategies, they could create more wealth for stockholders. Raiders buy stock in a company either (1) to take over the business and run it more efficiently or (2) to precipitate a change in the top management, replacing the existing team with one more likely to maximize stockholder welfare.

Raiders, of course, are motivated not by altruism but by gain. If they succeed in their takeover bid, they can institute strategies that create value for stockholders—including themselves. Icahn's 1985 takeover of TWA for $400 million illustrates the process. TWA was in deep trouble when Icahn bought the company. Its high cost structure was pricing the airline out of lucrative international routes and out of business. Icahn cut costs by persuading pilots and machinists to agree to pay cuts of up to 26 percent. He broke a flight attendants' strike, replacing veterans with younger workers whose pay was up to 50 percent lower. By deciding not to renew leases for three Boeing 747 jumbo jets and selling a fourth, he also pared overhead costs. In all, TWA's cost reductions amounted to $600 million per year.[35]

Even if a takeover bid fails, raiders can still earn millions, for their stockholdings will typically be bought out by the defending company for a hefty premium. Called **greenmail,** this source of gain has stirred much controversy and debate about its benefits. The 1986 bid by international financier Sir James Goldsmith for the Goodyear Tire & Rubber Company, the largest U.S. tire manufacturer, provides a good example of some of the issues raised.[36]

During the slump of the late 1970s and early 1980s, Goodyear, like most auto-related businesses, faced severe financial constraints.[37] The recovery of the auto industry did not help much. Between 1983 and 1985, Goodyear's tire sales rose barely 2 percent and gross profits from tires fell 15 percent. However, between 1983 and 1985, its heavy depreciation policy helped Goodyear generate a strong, positive cash flow amounting to more than $2 billion.

What did Goodyear do with that money? It lacked the confidence to invest heavily in making tires; the competition was too intense. Goodyear could have returned the money to stockholders, who could then have reinvested it in more productive companies. That at least would have been consistent with maximizing stockholder wealth. Instead Goodyear chose to expand by diversifying into the oil industry—an area that it knew nothing about. In 1983 Goodyear bought Celeron Corp., an exploration and production company in the area of oil and gas, and ended up investing $1.2 billion in this business. Stockholders were not happy. Despite a bull market, by October 1986 Goodyear's stock was trading at $32 a share, just about where it had been three years before. Moreover, Goodyear's price-to-earnings ratio was a little more than half of that of the average stock.

Stockholders on their own could do little to change Goodyear's strategy. They could and did sell their shares, but since the company was not dependent on the stock market for new capital, the effect of declining share prices was minimal. Goodyear's stockholders were also too dispersed to get together and effectively pressure management to change its strategy. When Goodyear shares dropped to $32, Goldsmith saw an opportunity to make some money out of the company. He started buying shares, accumulating 12.5 million, and then offered to buy the rest for $4.7 billion. In effect, Goldsmith was saying, "I think that Goodyear is worth at least 50 percent more than the market values it—but only if I run the company myself."

Goldsmith stated his strategy for Goodyear. Specifically, he wanted the company to get back into the business it knew best, tires, and leave the business it did not know at all, oil. He also wanted Goodyear to trim back its tire operations, closing plants and reducing capacity in order to increase efficiency. Goldsmith's bid seemed likely to succeed until the insider-trader scandal concerning Ivan Boesky broke into the news. The uncertainty caused by the scandal persuaded Goldsmith to drop the bid and sell his shares back to Goodyear—for a profit of $93 million. One commentator at the time noted,

> Goodyear in effect bribed Goldsmith to take a walk. Management dipped into the corporate treasury to save its own hide. But the company also, as *The Wall Street Journal* put it, largely agreed—to carry out Sir James's ideas for the company's future. It will focus again on tires, and it will sell off businesses in which it isn't expert—presumably oil and aerospace.[38]

The Goodyear case illustrates both the bad and the good aspects of the corporate raider phenomenon. Some would argue that Goldsmith blackmailed (greenmailed) Goodyear for $93 million. The resultant debt that the company incurred will burden it for years to come. Others, however, might counter that without Goldsmith's intervention, inefficient management teams would have gone on pursuing their own desires for bigger size rather than maximizing stockholder welfare. In that context, the $93 million earned by Goldsmith can be considered a generous consulting fee rather than greenmail. Though these opposing views may never be reconciled, perhaps the most important conclusion is that a

company would probably not have to deal with a takeover bid and its consequences if it were already perceived as providing stockholders with a satisfactory
long-run return on their investment.

Junk Bonds, Poison Pills, and Golden Parachutes

During the 1980s, the threat of hostile takeover increased significantly, in part
because of the easy availability of junk-bond financing. Popularized by the now
bankrupt investment bank Drexel Burnham Lambert, junk bonds carry interest
rates from 3 to 5 percent higher than the yields on government bonds of comparable maturity. The junk-bond concept is similar to that of a home mortgage.
Individuals raise money to purchase their home using the house plus their down
payment as collateral for the mortgage. Similarly, with junk-bond financing a
corporate raider can raise the cash necessary to acquire a takeover target by using
the assets and projected cash flow of the takeover target plus the raider's own
equity contribution as collateral. A junk-bond issue is typically arranged for a
raider by an investment bank and subscribed to by institutional investors (who
are attracted by the high interest rates). Junk bonds have enabled raiders to raise
large sums of money to finance takeovers without having to contribute a great
deal in the way of equity. This possibility has made even the largest companies
vulnerable to takeover by raiders who, in financial terms, are relatively small.

Although the growth of junk-bond financing has undoubtedly strengthened
the takeover constraint, further limiting the extent to which managers can pursue
strategies that put their own interests above those of stockholders, the widespread
use of junk bonds has also raised serious concerns. Critics charge that the level of
debt taken on in junk-bond-financed takeovers significantly increases the risk
of bankruptcy and forces managers to focus on short-term profits at the expense
of long-term investments in R&D and new capital equipment.[39] For example, the
collapse of Campeau's Allied and Federated Department Stores, two large chains
(including Bloomingdale's, Filene's, and others,) has been attributed to Campeau
Corporation's high level of debt. Campeau financed both purchases with junk
bonds.

On the other hand, the bankruptcy of Drexel Burnham Lambert in 1990,
the main investment bank in the junk-bond market, took a lot of the steam out
of junk-bond issues and will, in all probability, lead to a reduction in the number
of junk-bond-financed hostile takeovers over the next few years. In particular,
institutional investors appear to be far more cautious about subscribing to highly
leveraged junk-bond issues than they were prior to Drexel's demise. However,
as many commentators have pointed out, junk bonds themselves are here to stay.
Evidence of this can be found in the rush among well-regarded investment banks,
such as Merrill Lynch, Morgan Stanley, Salomon Brothers, and Goldman Sachs,
to grab a share of Drexel's junk-bond business.[40]

One response by management to the threat posed by junk-bond-financed takeovers has been to create so-called *poison pills*. The purpose of a poison pill is to make it difficult for a raider to acquire a company. The poison pill devised by Household International in 1985 is typical. The Household board of directors unilaterally changed the company's constitution. In response to any takeover bid involving a premium over market value of less than $6 billion, stockholders could not sell their stock without the prior permission of the board. At that time, Household had a market value of less than $2 billion, so the constitution change effectively gave the board the ability to reject any takeover attempt that offered less than $8 billion for Household. Because no raiders in their right mind would offer $8 billion for a company valued at less than $2 billion, the tactic essentially nullified the takeover constraint with regard to Household.

The right of companies to create poison pills has been challenged on several occasions in the law courts by stockholders who object to the unilateral restrictions imposed by management on their right to sell stock to a prospective acquirer. To date the courts have tended to side with management (the right of Household's board to issue restrictions was upheld by a Delaware court). However, there are many examples of stockholders at stockholder meetings introducing resolutions that effectively limit the ability of a company to devise a poison-pill defense, so it remains to be seen just how successful and widespread this tactic is going to be.

Another response to the threat posed by junk-bond-financed takeovers has been the increasing use of *golden parachute contracts*. Golden parachutes are severance contracts that handsomely compensate top-level managers for the loss of their jobs in the event of a takeover. These contracts came into being because of fears that takeover threats were forcing managers to focus on maximizing short-term earnings in an attempt to boost the company's current stock price, thereby reducing the risk of takeover at the expense of long-run investments in R&D and new capital equipment. Managers also complained that the threat of takeover reduced their willingness to fund risky but potentially profitable investments. By reducing managers' concerns about the loss of their jobs, advocates argue, golden parachute contracts encourage managers to focus on long-run investments and to take necessary risks. In addition, because management is less concerned with possible job loss, golden parachute contracts can increase the probability that top management will review takeover proposals objectively, taking stockholder interests into account when deciding how to respond.

For these reasons, golden parachute contracts, when used properly, can be beneficial. On the other hand, some stockholders see golden parachutes as little more than an "insurance against incompetence" or as a "reward for failure," and they argue that managers should not be rewarded for losing their job.[41] One way of ensuring that this does not occur while still preserving the beneficial aspects of golden parachute contracts may be to link the payment of a golden parachute to the premium earned by stockholders in the event of a takeover bid.

The Efficacy of
Corporate Governance

As we have seen, in theory managers are constrained by stockholder meetings, the board of directors, stock compensation schemes, and the threat of takeover to adopt strategies consistent with maximizing stockholder wealth. Notwithstanding recent developments, however, in practice management often dominates stockholder meetings and the board of directors. Thus these institutions have a tendency to rubber-stamp managerial decisions. Also, as noted above, stock compensation schemes are not universally adopted and do not always work as intended. In addition, critics contend that in practice the threat of takeover is an imperfect constraint on managerial action.[42] For example, research evidence suggests that only the most unprofitable companies face a greater than average chance of being acquired. Mediocre companies are apparently no more likely to be acquired than are excellent companies, even though mediocre companies are probably not using their resources to the best effect. Thus there seems to be considerable scope for managers to pursue strategies inconsistent with stockholder wealth before they face a hostile takeover bid. Moreover, the use of poison-pill contracts may nullify the takeover constraint.

For all these reasons, the governance mechanisms discussed here do not always provide complete protection for stockholder interests. In some circumstances it may be difficult for stockholders to remove incompetent managers or managers who pursue empire-building growth strategies at the expense of company profitability. Several writers have observed that although corporate governance mechanisms normally succeed in removing incompetent managers when a company is facing a financial crisis, they are not very effective at placing limits on managerial discretion in noncrisis situations. Thus, for example, the board of Diamond Shamrock Corp. supported the company's CEO, Bill Bricker, over a ten-year period, during which he pursued an aggressive but unprofitable diversification strategy designed to transform what was originally a chemical company into a big-league energy conglomerate. The board continued to support Bricker despite considerable stockholder opposition and the failure of the company to show any profit from its energy operations. Only after a loss of over $600 million, a crash in the company's stock price, and three hostile takeover bids in twelve months did the board finally withdraw its support for Bricker and ask him to resign. If the board had been functioning as theory says it should, in all probability Bricker would have been removed years earlier.[43]

Leveraged Buyouts

The imperfections in corporate governance mechanisms have been used by Harvard Business School professor Michael Jensen to explain the dramatic growth of leveraged buyouts (LBOs) in the United States.[44] The total value of the 76 LBOs undertaken in 1979 was $1.4 billion (in 1988 dollars). In comparison, the total value of the 214 LBOs undertaken in 1988 exceeded $77 billion—nearly one-third of the value of all mergers and acquisitions in the United States.

Whereas in a typical takeover a raider buys enough stock to gain control of a company, in an LBO a company's own executives are often (but not always) among the buyers. Most LBOs are financed by junk bonds. The management group undertaking an LBO typically raises cash by issuing bonds and then uses that cash to buy the company's stock. Thus, LBOs involve a swap of equity for debt. In effect, the company replaces its stockholders with creditors (bondholders), thereby transforming the corporation from a public into a private entity. However, often the same institutions that were major stockholders prior to an LBO are also major bondholders after an LBO. The difference is that as stockholders they were not guaranteed a regular dividend payment, whereas when they become bondholders they are guaranteed regular payment from the company.

Jensen's theory is that LBOs solve many of the problems created by imperfect corporate governance mechanisms. According to Jensen, a major weakness and source of waste in the public corporation is the conflict between stockholders and managers over the payout of *free cash flow*. He defines *free cash flow* as cash flow in excess of that required to fund all investment projects with positive net present values when discounted at the relevant cost of capital. Since free cash flow is by definition cash that cannot be profitably reinvested within the company, Jensen argues that it should be distributed to stockholders.

However, managers generally resist distributing surplus cash resources to stockholders. Rather, for reasons discussed earlier, they have a tendency to invest such cash in growth-maximizing or empire-building strategies. Jensen makes his point with reference to the Ford Motor Company:

> A vivid example is the Ford Motor Company which sits on nearly $15 billion in cash and marketable securities in an industry with excess capacity. Ford's management has been deliberating about acquiring financial service companies, aerospace companies, or making some other multibillion-dollar diversification move—rather than deliberating about efficiently distributing Ford's excess cash to its owners so they can decide how to re-invest it.[45]

Jensen sees a solution to this problem in LBOs. Although management does not have to pay out dividends to stockholders, it does have to make regular debt payments to bondholders or face bankruptcy. Thus, according to Jensen, the debt used to finance an LBO helps limit the waste of free cash flow by compelling managers to pay out excess cash to service debt payments, rather than spending it on empire-building projects with low or negative returns, excessive staff, indulgent perquisites, and other organizational inefficiencies. Further, Jensen sees debt as a way of motivating managers to look for greater efficiencies. The need to service high debt payments is argued to force managers to slash unsound investment programs, reduce overhead, and dispose of assets that are more valuable outside the company. The proceeds generated by these restructurings can then be used to reduce debt to more sustainable levels, creating a leaner, more efficient, and more competitive organization.

However, by no means all commentators are as enthusiastic about the potential of LBOs. Robert Reich, professor of political economy and management at Harvard's John F. Kennedy School of Government, is one of the most vocal critics of LBOs.[46] Reich sees LBOs as being driven by the desires of Wall Street's "paper entrepreneurs" to collect lucrative fees, rather than by desires to improve efficiency. For illustration, he points out that the RJR Nabisco LBO generated almost $1 billion in fees, including $153 million in advisory fees, $294 million in financing fees for investment banks, and $325 million in commercial-bank fees.

Furthermore, Reich sees two main problems with LBOs. First, he argues that the necessity of paying back large loans forces management to focus on the short term and cut back on long-term investments, particularly in R&D and new capital spending. The net effect is likely to be a decline in the competitiveness of LBOs. Second, Reich believes that the debt taken on to finance an LBO significantly increases the risk of bankruptcy. The strong economy of the 1980s may have obscured this fact. Strong demand has allowed companies to service high debt payments. But what might happen if a recession hits? Reich cites a study by the Brookings Institute, which examined the effects of a recession similar in severity to that which rocked the United States in 1974 and 1975. The Brookings computer simulation revealed that, with the levels of corporate debt prevailing in the late 1980s, 1 in 10 U.S. companies would succumb to bankruptcy.

Although it is still too early to say for sure whether Reich or Jensen is closer to the truth, it is interesting to note that the high-visibility bankruptcies of a number of junk-bond-financed LBOs during 1989 and 1990 seemed to reduce dramatically the number of new LBOs during 1990. The bankruptcies, which included Hillsborough Holdings, SCI Television, and Leaseway, were brought about by the inability of these LBOs to meet their debt payments, which is exactly the problem that Reich argues can be expected with junk-bond-financed LBOs.

2.8 CORPORATE SOCIAL RESPONSIBILITY

The Concept of Social Responsibility

Corporate responsibility refers to corporate actions that protect and improve the welfare of society along with the corporation's own interests.[47] Strategic decisions of large corporations inevitably involve social as well as economic consequences; the two cannot be separated.[48] Moreover, the social consequences of economic actions typically affect the company's outside claimants, especially local communities and the general public. For example, if a large company decides for economic reasons to close a plant employing thousands of workers in a small community, the social impact of the closing on that community is both direct and fundamental. Many steel towns in the Midwest have turned into ghost towns after such closings. Similarly, when a manufacturing enterprise builds a major plant in a rural community, it probably changes the social fabric of that community forever. Thus, when selecting a strategy on the basis of economic criteria, a company is also making a choice that will have wider social consequences.

Why Be Socially Responsible?

Should companies be socially responsible? Should they build certain social criteria or goals into their strategic decision making? Many companies do incorporate broad declarations of social intent into their mission statement. Indeed, for a number of good reasons, companies should be socially responsible.

In its purest form, social responsibility can be supported for its own sake simply because it is the noble, or right, way for a company to behave. Less pure but perhaps more practical are arguments that socially responsible behavior is in a company's self-interest. Since economic actions have social consequences affecting a company's outside claimants, if a company wants to retain the support of the claimants, it must take those social consequences into account when formulating strategies. Otherwise it may generate ill will and opposition. For example, if a community perceives a company as having an adverse impact on the local environment, it may block the company's attempts to build new facilities in the area.

Edward H. Bowman of the University of Pennsylvania's Wharton School has taken this point further, arguing that social responsibility is actually a sound investment strategy.[49] He maintains that a company's social behavior affects the price of its stock. In other words, socially responsible policy can also benefit a company's important inside claimants, the stockholders. According to Bowman, many investors view companies that are not socially responsible as riskier investments. Moreover, many institutional investors, such as churches, universities, cities, states, and mutual funds, pay attention to corporate social behavior and thus influence the market for a company's stock.

Evidence can certainly be found in favor of Bowman's arguments. The withdrawal of American assets from South Africa by companies such as IBM and General Motors in 1986, for example, can at least in part be attributed to a desire to create a favorable impression with investors. At that time, for social or political reasons, many investors were selling any stock they held in companies that maintained a substantial presence in South Africa. Similarly, Union Carbide saw its market value plunge more than 37 percent in 1985 in the aftermath of the gas leak at its Bhopal plant in India (which killed 1,757 people and left 17,000 seriously injured) and subsequent revelations concerning poor safety procedures at many Union Carbide plants. For Union Carbide, the consequence was a takeover bid from GAF Corporation (which ultimately failed), extended litigation, and a negative image problem.

Bowman has also shown that companies concerned about social responsibility tend to.be more profitable.[50] To test the effect of social responsibility on profits, Bowman performed a line-by-line content analysis of the 1973 annual reports of food-processing companies in order to ascertain the amount of prose devoted to issues of corporate social responsibility. He then used this figure as a surrogate for actual company concern. He found that companies with some social responsibility prose performed better than those with none (14.7 percent return on equity against 10.2 percent return on equity over the previous five years).

On the other hand, there are those who argue that a company has no business pursuing social goals. Nobel laureate Milton Friedman, for one, insists that concepts of social responsibility should not enter the corporate strategic decision process:

> What does it mean to say that the corporate executive has a social responsibility in his capacity as a businessman? If this statement is not pure rhetoric, it must mean that he is to act in some way that is not in the interests of his employers. For example . . . that he is to make expenditures on reducing pollution beyond the amount that is in the best interests of the corporation or that is required by law in order to contribute to the social objective of improving the environment. . . . Insofar as his actions in accord with his social responsibility reduce returns to stockholders, he is spending their money. Insofar as his actions raise the price to customers, he is spending the customer's money. Insofar as the actions lower the wages of some employees, he is spending their money.[51]

Essentially, Friedman's position is that a business has only one kind of social responsibility: to use its resources for activities that increase its profits, *so long as it stays within the rules of the game,* which is to say, so long as it engages in open and free competition without deception or fraud.

Corporate Social Responsibility and Regulation

Friedman's views cannot be ignored, particularly in a country like the United States, where the rules of the game are well established. American society recognizes that businesses, if left to themselves, will not always behave in a socially responsible manner. The need to generate profit can conflict with society's desire for responsible behavior. For this reason, governments, acting in the interests of society as a whole, have enacted legislation to regulate corporate behavior. Thus there are rules to safeguard consumers from abuse by companies, rules to ensure fair competition, and rules to protect the environment (from pollution, for example).

Unfortunately, companies do not always obey these rules. In a major survey of corporate crimes from 1970 to 1980, *Fortune* magazine found plenty of evidence to this effect.[52] Of 1,043 major corporations in the study, 117, or 11 percent, were involved in at least one major delinquency during the period covered. Some companies were multiple offenders. In all, 188 citations were given by *Fortune,* covering 163 separate offenses: 98 antitrust violations; 28 cases of kickbacks, bribery, or illegal rebates; 21 cases of illegal political contributions; 11 cases of fraud; and 5 cases of tax evasion.

Bethlehem Steel illustrates the kind of cases identified here. The company pleaded guilty to criminal activity over the five-year period 1972–1976. It was operating a kickback scheme for the purpose of bribing representatives of ship-lines to steer repair work to Bethlehem's seven shipyards. Another case involves Archer-Daniels-Midland Company, which was successfully prosecuted in 1976 for defrauding grain buyers by short-weighing. Still another instance of corporate crime is offered by E. I. Du Pont de Nemours's dye group. Wanting to raise prices, in late 1970 the executives of Du Pont's dye business contacted the competition and won an agreement for a follow-the-leader scheme. In January 1971, Du Pont announced a 10 percent price increase; the competition followed suit in February and March. When charged with price fixing, the nine companies involved all pleaded no contest and were fined between $35,000 and $50,000 each.

The very fact that companies do not always behave lawfully is in itself an argument for stressing social responsibility in the mission statement of an enterprise. By expressing its commitment to "free enterprise" or to "maintaining fair relationships with our customers," a company is sending a message both to its own employees and to important stakeholders that it intends to act within the bounds of the law.

The Practice of Social Responsibility

How should a company decide which social issues it will respond to and to what extent it will trade profits for social gain? The spectrum of actual corporate behavior among companies that espouse social responsibility is quite broad. It encompasses mere reaction to the strict requirements of the law, some response to direct pressure from interest groups, and commitment to incorporating wider social concerns within the corporate ethic.

Although the concept of social responsibility implies voluntary response by the company, some degree of external coercion, perhaps from government or from other pressure groups, is likely to occur in a number of situations. Such prodding may be difficult to resist. Where no pressure exists, the incentive to adopt a social policy commitment will be less. There are, however, some criteria that a company may apply to help it choose which social action to undertake. This approach is to judge both the private and the social effects of particular strategies. A company can rank them according to their profitability and their social benefits, as shown in Figure 2.5.[53]

FIGURE 2.5   Comparing profitability and social returns from strategies

Profitability

	Negative	Low	Medium	High
Negative				
Low				
Medium			**Favored Strategies**	
High				

(Social Returns, vertical axis label)

If this framework is used, strategies showing both high profitability and high social benefits would be the most likely to be adopted. Those with high profitability but negative social effects would worry a socially responsible company and probably would not be pursued. On the other hand, even the most socially concerned company would hesitate to adopt strategies with high social gains but negative or low profitability.

2.9 SUMMARY OF CHAPTER

The primary purpose of this chapter is to identify various factors that constitute the organizational context within which strategies are formulated. Normally, these factors are explicitly recognized through the corporate mission statement. The mission statement thus sets the boundaries within which strategies must be contained. Specifically, the following points are made:

1. The mission statement is the starting point of strategic management. It sets the context within which strategies are formulated.

2. The mission statement contains three broad elements: a definition of the company's business, a statement of the major goals of the corporation, and a statement of corporate philosophy.

3.   For a single-business company, defining the business involves focusing on consumer groups to be served, consumer needs to be satisfied, and the technologies by which those needs can be satisfied. This amounts to a consumer-oriented business definition.

4.   For a diversified company, defining the business involves focusing on the purpose behind owning a portfolio of businesses, the desired scope of the enterprise, and the desired balance between the constituent businesses in the portfolio.

5.   A company's major corporate goal should reflect concern for the welfare of the company's owners—its stockholders. Maximizing long-run profits is the major goal consistent with maximizing stockholder wealth.

6.   To avoid adverse short-run consequences of an overzealous focus on profitability, a company needs to adopt a number of secondary goals that balance short-run and long-run considerations.

7.   A company's corporate philosophy makes clear how the company intends to do business. A statement of this philosophy reflects the company's basic values, aspirations, beliefs, and philosophical priorities.

8.   Every company has its stakeholders—individuals who have some claim on the organization. They can be divided into inside and outside claimants. The company needs to recognize their claims in its mission statement, for if it does not, it may lose their support.

9.   The claims of stakeholders can conflict. Frequently, a company does not have the resources to satisfy all claimants. Thus it has to identify the stakeholder groups that are most important to its continued survival and satisfy their claims first. It can uncover this information through a stakeholder impact analysis.

10.   Stockholders are among a company's most important internal claimants. If stockholder wealth is not maximized, then the company runs the risk of becoming a takeover target. Companies sometimes fall into this trap because of managerial obsessions with the size of the business and the power and status that it brings. Corporate raiders have become a major means of disciplining such companies through takeover bids.

11.   Satisfying a company's claimants often involves stressing corporate social responsibility. Social responsibility is important because a company's economic actions inevitably have social consequences that directly affect its claimants. Thus stressing social responsibility is in the company's best interest.

12.   Deciding which social issues to respond to can prove difficult for a company. However, by comparing the social impact of strategies against their economic returns, a company can identify strategies with negative or positive social consequences.

Discussion Questions

1. Why is it important for a company to take a consumer-oriented view of its businesses? What are the possible shortcomings of such a view?

2. What are the strategic implications of a focus on short-run returns? Discuss in terms of the impact on product innovation, marketing expenditure, manufacturing, and purchasing decisions.

3. Are corporate raiders a positive or negative influence on the U.S. economy? How can companies reduce the risk of takeover?

4. Companies should always be socially responsible, whatever the cost. Discuss.

Endnotes

1. Kenneth Labich, "How Dick Ferris Blew It," *Fortune*, July 6, 1987, pp. 42–46. Jodi Klein, "The Lack of Allegiance at Allegis," *Business & Society Review* (Spring 1988), 30–33. James Ellis, "The Unraveling of an Idea," *Business Week*, June 22, 1987, pp. 42–43.

2. Derek F. Abell, *Defining the Business: The Starting Point of Strategic Planning* (Englewood Cliffs, N.J.: Prentice-Hall, 1980). K. Andrews, *The Concept of Corporate Strategy* (Homewood, Ill.: Dow Jones Irwin, 1971). John A. Pearce, "The Company Mission as a Strategic Tool," *Sloan Management Review* (Spring 1982), 15–24.

3. These three questions were first proposed by P. F. Drucker. See Drucker, *Management—Tasks, Responsibilities, Practices* (New York: Harper & Row, 1974), pp. 74–94.

4. Abell, *Defining the Business*, p. 17.

5. Theodore Levitt, "Marketing Myopia," *Harvard Business Review* (July–August 1960), 45–56.

6. F. J. Weston and S. K. Mansinghka, "Tests of the Efficiency Performance of Conglomerate Firms," *Journal of Finance*, 26 (1971), 919–935.

7. T. Mack, "Polishing the Gem," *Forbes*, January 28, 1985, p. 64.

8. For details, see "Polaroid: Turning Away from Land's One Product Strategy," *Business Week*, March 2, 1981, pp. 108–112; "Polaroid Can't Get Its Future in Focus," *Business Week*, April 4, 1983, pp. 31–32; "Polaroid Hopes to Snap Out of Sales Slump," *The Wall Street Journal*, November 11, 1985, p. 6; and "The Marketing Man Who Hopes to Reform Polaroid," *International Management* (June 1986), 35.

9. S. R. Reid, "A Reply to the Weston and Mansinghka Criticisms Dealing with Conglomerate Mergers," *Journal of Finance*, 26 (1971), 937–940.

10. Peter F. Drucker, *The Practice of Management* (New York: Harper, 1954).

11. Robert H. Hayes and William J. Abernathy, "Managing Our Way to Economic Decline," *Harvard Business Review* (July–August 1980), 67–77.

12. Lester C. Thurow, *The Zero Sum Solution* (New York: Simon and Schuster, 1985), 69–89.

13. "Too Much Penny-Pinching at American Home?" *Business Week*, December 22, 1986, pp. 64–65.

14. Figures are taken from Standard & Poor's COMPUSTAT service.

15. The evidence of the Profit Impact of Market Strategy (PIMS) data base provides strong support for this proposition, although the direction of causation has not been proven. See R. D. Buzzell, T. G. Bradley, and R. G. M. Sultan, "Market Share: A Key to Profitability," *Harvard Business Review* (January–February 1975), 97–106.

16. Thomas J. Peters and Robert H. Waterman, *In Search of Excellence* (New York: Harper & Row, 1982).

17. Excerpt from Hewlett-Packard's Mission Statement. Courtesy of Hewlett-Packard Company.

18. M. D. Richards, *Setting Strategic Goals and Objectives* (St. Paul, Minn.: West, 1986).

19. For details, see "Johnson & Johnson (A)," *Harvard Business School Case* #384-053, Harvard Business School.

20. Pearce, "The Company Mission," pp. 15–24.

21. I. C. Macmillan and P. E. Jones, *Strategy Formulation: Power and Politics* (St. Paul, Minn.: West, 1986), 66.

22. M. C. Jensen and W. H. Meckling, "Theory of the Firm: Managerial Behavior, Agency Costs and Ownership Structure," *Journal of Financial Economics*, 3, (1976), 305–360.

23. For example, see R. Marris, *The Economic Theory of Managerial Capitalism* (London: Macmillan, 1964); and J. K. Galbraith, *The New Industrial State* (Boston: Houghton-Mifflin, 1970).

24. Carl Icahn, "What Ails Corporate America—And What Should Be Done?" *Business Week,* October 27, 1986, p. 101.

25. E. T. Penrose, *The Theory of the Growth of the Firm* (London: Macmillan, 1958).

26. Bruce Nussbaum and Judith Dobrzynski, "The Battle, for Corporate Control," *Business Week,* May 18, 1987, pp. 102–109.

27. Quoted in Christopher Power and Vick Cahan, "Shareholders Aren't Just Rolling Over Anymore," *Business Week,* April 27, 1987, pp. 32–33.

28. Nussbaum and Dobrzynski, "The Battle for Corporate Control," pp. 102–109.

29. O. E. Williamson, *The Economic Institutions of Capitalism* (New York: Free Press, 1985).

30. M. L. Mace, *Directors: Myth and Reality* (Cambridge, Mass.: Harvard University Press, 1971). S. C. Vance, *Corporate Leadership: Boards of Directors and Strategy* (New York: McGraw-Hill, 1983).

31. Michele Galen, "A Seat on the Board is Getting Hotter," *Business Week,* July 3, 1989, pp. 72–73.

32. Judith Dobrzynski, Michael Schroeder, Gregory Miles, and Joseph Weber, "Taking Charge: Corporate Directors Flex Their Muscle," *Business Week,* July 3, 1989, pp. 66–71.

33. W. G. Lewellen, C. Eoderer, and A. Rosenfeld, "Merger Decisions and Executive Stock Ownership in Acquiring Firms," *Journal of Accounting and Economics,* 7 (1985), 209–231.

34. C. W. L. Hill and S. A. Snell, "External Control, Corporate Strategy, and Firm Performance," *Strategic Management Journal,* 9, (1988), pp. 577–590.

35. "Carl Icahn: Raider or Manager?" *Business Week,* October 27, 1986, pp. 98–104.

36. J. K. Glassman, "Aprés Ivan," *The New Republic,* December 15, 1986, pp. 11–13.

37. See "The Two Worlds of Jimmy Goldsmith," *Business Week,* December 1, 1986, pp. 98–102; "Goodyear May Be Acquired by Goldsmith," *The Wall Street Journal,* November 19, 1986, p. 2; and Glassman, "Aprés Ivan," p. 12.

38. Glassman, "Aprés Ivan," p. 12.

39. For an interesting discussion of the issues here, see Chapter 1 of J. C. Coffee, L. Lowebstein, and S. Rose-Ackerman, *Knights: Raiders & Targets* (Oxford: Oxford University Press, 1988). See also M. C. Jensen, "The Takeover Controversy: Analysis and Evidence," Chapter 20 in the same volume.

40. J. H. Dobrzynski, "After Drexel," *Business Week,* February 26, 1990, pp. 37–40.

41. H. Singh and F. Harianto, "Management-Board Relationships, Takeover Risk, and the Adoption of Golden Parachutes," *Academy of Management Journal,* 32 (1989), pp. 7–24.

42. A. J. Singh, *Takeovers: Their Relevance to the Stockmarket and the Theory of the Firm* (Cambridge, England: Cambridge University Press, 1971).

43. See "The Downfall of a CEO," *Business Week,* February 16, 1987, pp. 76–84.

44. See Michael C. Jensen, "Agency Costs of Free Cash Flow, Corporate Finance, and Takeovers," *American Economic Review,* (1986), 323–329; and Michael C. Jensen, "The Eclipse of the Public Corporation," *Harvard Business Review* (September–October 1989), 61–74.

45. Jensen, ibid., p. 66.

46. Robert B. Reich, "Leverage Buyouts: America Pays the Price," *The New York Times Magazine,* January 29, 1989, pp. 32–40.

47. K. Davis, W. C. Frederick, and R. L. Blomstrom, *Business and Society; Concepts and Policy Issues* (New York: McGraw-Hill, 1980).

48. Henry Mintzberg, "The Case for Corporate Social Responsibility," *Journal of Business Strategy* (December 1983), 3–15.

49. Edward H. Bowman, "Corporate Social Responsibility and the Investor," *Journal of Contemporary Business* (Winter 1973), 21–43.

50. Edward H. Bowman and M. Haire, "Strategic Posture Towards Corporate Social Responsibility," *California Management Review* (Winter 1975), 49–58.

51. Milton Friedman, "A Friedman Doctrine: The Social Responsibility of Business Is to Increase Its Profits," *The New York Times Magazine,* September 13, 1970, pp. 33.

52. I. Ross, "How Lawless Are Big Companies?" *Fortune,* December 1, 1980, pp. 56–64.

53. J. F. Pickering and T. T. Jones, "The Firm and Its Social Environment," in J. F. Pickering and T. A. J. Cockerill, Eds., *The Economic Management of the Firm* (Oxford: Philip Allan, 1984), pp. 277–323.

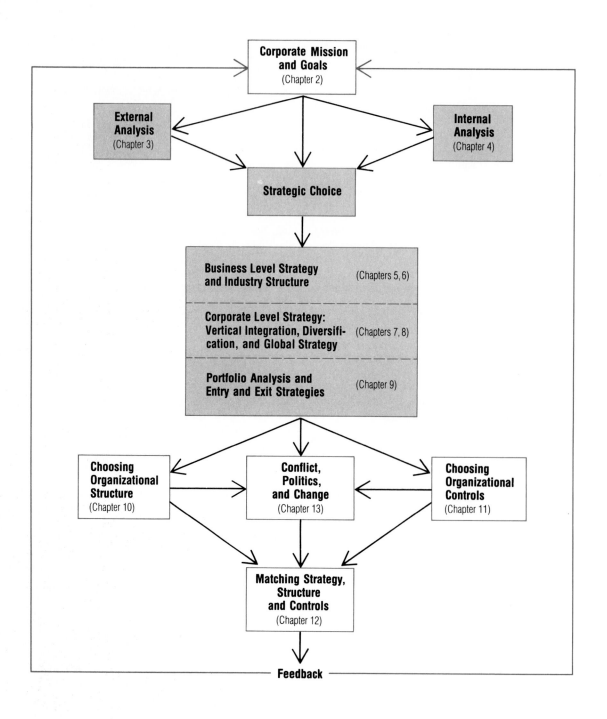

II

STRATEGY FORMULATION

Chapter 3

ANALYZING THE EXTERNAL ENVIRONMENT: THE IDENTIFICATION OF OPPORTUNITIES AND THREATS

3.1 OPENING INCIDENT: USX

U.S. Steel, the forerunner of USX, was formed in the early 1900s by merging ten steel companies. For more than half a century U.S. Steel dominated the American steel industry. Into the 1960s the company accounted for as much as 55 percent of the industry's sales. By 1986, however, the market share of the steel-making arm of USX had fallen to 17 percent, and in that year steel operations posted enormous losses (estimated at $1.4 billion). The once-dominant force in a consolidated domestic industry found itself struggling to hold on to a dwindling market share in a highly competitive global industry.

Most of the decline in the company's market share occurred after the boom years of 1972–

1974, when demand for steel was at an all-time high. Since then the American steel market has been dealt a number of blows. For instance, low-cost foreign producers, utilizing state-of-the-art production facilities, captured a large share of the domestic market. In 1980, foreign steel mills held 16 percent of the domestic market; by 1985, benefiting from a strong dollar, they had captured 22 percent. In addition, new steel-making technologies, based on electric arc furnaces, have allowed domestic minimills to produce steel at a lower cost than the large, integrated operations of the steel majors, which, in some cases, are still based on the technology of the 1930s. As a result, minimills and specialty steel companies increased their share of

NUCOR

69

the market from 21 percent in 1980 to around 40 percent in 1985.

Another blow to the mature industry has been the growing popularity of high-tech synthetic substitutes for steel, which are pushing out steel products in many market segments. For example, auto manufacturers increasingly prefer plastic rather than steel body panels. Moreover, the high costs of severance pay, pensions, and insurance for terminated workers and the low liquidation value of steel plants have made the shutdown of steel-making capacity expensive. In 1983, it cost USX $1.2 billion to shut down 16 percent of its capacity and shed 15,400 jobs. These high costs of exit have made it difficult for established companies to reduce their capacity in line with demand. As a direct result, 40 percent of total domestic capacity was lying idle in 1987.

Hindsight is always 20/20, so it is easy to criticize USX for failing to respond to those market threats until it was too late. Nevertheless, there is little doubt that if USX had responded to the threats as they began to emerge in the 1960s, it would not be facing problems of such magnitude today. The company could have made massive cost-reducing investments while it was making good money; it could have become a major player in the minimills and specialty steel segments; or it could have diversified into the manufacture of synthetics. However, instead of formulating strategic responses to these environmental threats, USX, along with other steel majors, continued to indulge in cozy price-leadership agreements and to lobby Washington for import controls. In short, USX continued to behave like a dominant company in a strong domestic industry, whereas it was fast becoming a high-cost manufacturer in a much larger, and rapidly changing, global industry.[1]

3.2 OVERVIEW

A company's external environment can be broken down into two parts: the industry environment that the company competes in and the macro-environment. Both environments and their relationship to the company are illustrated in Figure 3.1. A company's industry environment consists of elements that directly affect the company, such as competitors, customers, and suppliers. The macro-environment consists of the broader economic, social, demographic, political, legal, and technological setting within which the industry and the company are placed.

For a company to succeed, its strategy must be consistent with the external environment. Superior performance is the product of a good fit between strategy and environment. To achieve a good fit, managers must first understand the forces that shape competition in the external environment. This understanding enables them to identify external environmental trends and to respond by adopting appropriate strategies. In other words, they make the correct strategic choices in relation to the environment, thereby maximizing the company's profitability. In contrast, companies that fail often do so because their managers do not understand the forces that shape competition in the external environment. Consequently, they make poor strategic choices (the company's strategy does not fit the environment), and the company's profitability suffers. USX, discussed in the Opening Incident, is a company whose strategy did not fit its environment. USX

FIGURE 3.1   The external environment

failed to anticipate the threats to its position that arose from changes in the environment of the steel industry. The strategy USX was pursuing in the early 1980s was suited to the environment of the steel industry in the 1960s but not in the 1980s, and USX's market share and profitability declined.

The objective of this chapter is to discuss a number of models that can assist strategic managers in analyzing the external environment. The models provide a framework that can be used to identify environmental *opportunities* and *threats*. Opportunities arise when environmental trends create the potential for a company to increase profits. For example, the baby boom of the 1950s and early 1960s gave Mothercare Stores, Inc., the opportunity to expand its maternity ware and child-care products business into a national operation. Threats arise when environmental trends endanger the integrity and profitability of a company's business: Trends in the steel industry threatened USX's business.

Having identified profitable opportunities, strategic managers need to formulate strategies that enable the company to exploit those opportunities and maximize its return on investment. Because external threats can squeeze profitability out of a company, strategic managers must also formulate strategies that defend a company's profitability against such threats. The different strategic alternatives that a company can adopt to maximize opportunities and counter threats are discussed in Chapters 5, 6, 7 and 8. In this chapter, we focus on the issue of identifying opportunities and threats.

We begin with a discussion of a model for analyzing the industry environment. Next we discuss the competitive implications that arise when groups of companies within an industry pursue similar strategies. We then move on to consider the nature of industry evolution. Finally, we review a number of macroenvironmental issues. By the end of this chapter, you should be familiar with the main factors that strategic managers have to take into consideration when analyzing a company's external environment for opportunities and threats.

3.3 ANALYZING THE INDUSTRY ENVIRONMENT

An *industry* can be defined as a group of companies offering products or services that are close substitutes for each other. Close substitutes are products or services that satisfy the same basic *consumer* needs. For example, the metal and plastic body panels used in automobile construction are close substitutes for each other. Despite different production technologies, auto supply companies manufacturing metal body panels are in the same basic industry as companies manufacturing plastic body panels. They are serving the same consumer need, that of auto assembly companies for body panels.

The task facing strategic managers is to analyze competitive forces in an industry environment in order to identify the opportunities and threats that confront a company. Michael E. Porter of the Harvard School of Business Administration has developed a framework that helps managers do this.[2] Porter's framework is known as the **five forces model.** It focuses on five forces that shape competition within an industry: (1) the risk of new entry by potential competitors, (2) the degree of rivalry among established companies within an industry, (3) the bargaining power of buyers, (4) the bargaining power of suppliers, and (5) the closeness of substitutes to an industry's products (see Figure 3.2).

Porter's argument is that the stronger each of these forces is, the more limited are established companies in their ability to raise prices and earn greater profits. Within Porter's framework, a strong competitive force can be regarded as a threat since it depresses profits. A weak competitive force can be regarded as an opportunity since it allows a company to earn greater profits. Because of factors beyond a company's direct control, such as industry evolution, the strength of the five forces may change through time. In such circumstances, the task facing strategic managers is to recognize opportunities and threats as they arise and to formulate appropriate strategic responses. In addition, it is possible for a company, through its choice of strategy, to alter the strength of one or more of the

FIGURE 3.2   Porter's five forces model

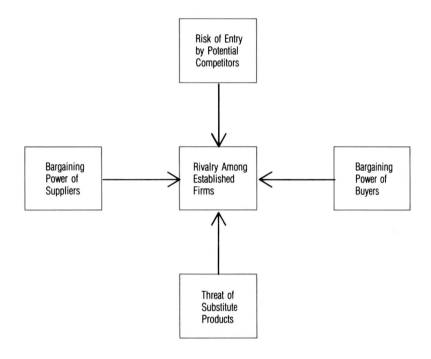

five forces to its advantage. This is part of the subject matter of the following chapters. In this chapter, we focus on understanding the impact that each of the five forces has on a company.

Potential Competitors

Potential competitors are companies that currently are not competing in an industry but have the capability to do so if they choose. The American Telephone & Telegraph Company, for example, was regarded as a potential competitor in the personal computer industry in the early 1980s, for it had the technology, sales force, and capital necessary to manufacture and sell PCs. AT&T, in fact, did enter the industry in 1985. Established companies try to discourage potential competitors from entering, since the more companies enter an industry, the more difficult it becomes for established companies to hold their share of the market and to generate profits. Thus a high risk of entry by potential competitors represents a threat to the profitability of established companies. On the other hand, if the risk of new entry is low, established companies can take advantage of this opportunity to raise prices and earn greater returns.

The strength of the competitive force of potential rivals is largely a function of the height of barriers to entry. The concept of barriers to entry implies that there are significant costs to joining an industry. The greater the costs that potential competitors must bear, the greater are the barriers to entry. High entry barriers keep potential competitors out of an industry even when industry returns are high. The classic work on barriers to entry was done by economist Joe Bain, who identified three main sources of barriers to new entry: brand loyalty, absolute cost advantages, and economies of scale.[3]

Brand loyalty   Brand loyalty is buyers' preference for the products of established companies. A company can create brand loyalty through continuous advertising of brand and company names, patent protection of products, product innovation through company research and development programs, an emphasis on high product quality, and good after-sales service. Significant brand loyalty makes it difficult for new entrants to take market share away from established companies. Thus brand loyalty reduces the threat of entry by potential competitors who may see the task of breaking down well-established consumer preferences as too costly.

Absolute cost advantages   Lower absolute costs give established companies an advantage that is difficult for potential competitors to match. Absolute cost advantages can arise from superior production techniques as a result of past experience, patents, or secret processes; control of particular inputs required for production, be they labor, materials, equipment, or management skills; or access to cheaper funds because existing companies represent lower risks than established companies. If established companies have an absolute cost advantage, then again the threat of entry is significantly reduced.

Economies of scale   Economies of scale are the cost advantages associated with large company size. Sources of scale economies include cost reductions gained through mass-producing a standardized output, discounts on bulk purchases of raw-material inputs and component parts, the spreading of fixed costs over a large volume, and scale economies in advertising.[4] If these cost advantages are significant, then a new entrant faces the dilemma of either entering on a small scale and suffering a significant cost disadvantage or taking a very large risk by entering on a large scale and bearing significant capital costs. A further risk of large-scale entry is that the increased supply of products will depress prices and result in vigorous retaliation by established companies. Thus, when established companies have scale economies, the threat of entry is reduced.

If established companies have built brand loyalty for their products, have an absolute cost advantage with respect to potential competitors, or have significant scale economies, then the risk of entry by potential competitors is significantly reduced. When this risk is low, established companies can charge higher prices and earn greater profits than otherwise would have been possible. Clearly, it is in the interest of companies to pursue strategies consistent with these aims. Indeed, empirical evidence suggests that the height of barriers to entry is *the most important* determinant of profit rates in an industry.[5] Examples of industries where entry barriers are significant include pharmaceuticals, household detergents, and aerospace. In the first two cases, product differentiation achieved through substantial expenditures for research and development and for advertising has built brand loyalty, making it difficult for new companies to enter these industries on a significant scale. So successful have the differentiation strategies of Procter & Gamble and Unilever been in household detergents that these two companies dominate the global industry.

In the aerospace industry, the barriers to entering the commercial airline market are primarily due to scale economies. Development costs alone can be staggering. For example, before McDonnell Douglas Corp. sold a single MD-11, the wide-body jetliner designed to take the company well into the twenty-first century, more than $1.5 billion was spent on development and tooling.[6] Industry analysts estimate that, just to break even on a new model like the MD-11, a company has to sell more than 200 aircraft, a figure representing 13 percent of expected industry sales of wide-body jets between 1990 and 2000. In addition, the cost disadvantages of not achieving an efficient scale of production are substantial in airplane manufacture. Companies that are able to achieve only half of the market share necessary to break even face a 20 percent unit-cost disadvantage.[7] In aerospace, the up-front capital costs, the need to achieve a significant market share to break even, and the cost disadvantages of not achieving an efficient scale of production are likely to deter all but the most determined potential competitors from entry. In spite of this, it should be noted that Airbus Industrie, a European consortium, did manage to enter successfully the commercial aerospace industry in the 1980s, although with the help of significant government backing.

Rivalry Among Established Companies

The second of Porter's five competitive forces is the extent of rivalry among established companies within an industry. If this competitive force is weak, companies have an opportunity to raise prices and earn greater profits. If this competitive force is strong, however, significant price competition, including price wars, may result from the intense rivalry among companies. Price competition limits profitability by reducing the margins that can be earned on sales. Thus intense rivalry among established companies constitutes a strong threat to profitability. The extent of rivalry among established companies within an industry is largely a function of three factors: (1) industry competitive structure, (2) demand conditions, and (3) the height of exit barriers in the industry.

Competitive structure   Competitive structure refers to the number and size distribution of companies in an industry. Different competitive structures have different implications for rivalry. Structures vary from **fragmented** to **consolidated.** A fragmented industry contains a large number of small or medium-size companies, none of which is in a position to dominate the industry. A consolidated industry is dominated by a small number of large companies or, in extreme cases, by just one company (a monopoly). Examples of fragmented industries include agriculture, video rental, health clubs, real estate brokerage, and sun-tanning parlors. Examples of consolidated industries include aerospace, automobiles, and pharmaceuticals. The most common competitive structure in the United States is a consolidated structure—what economists call an *oligopoly*.[8] The range of structures and their different characteristics are illustrated in Figure 3.3.

Many fragmented industries are characterized by low entry barriers and commodity-type products that are hard to differentiate. The combination of these characteristics tends to result in boom-and-bust cycles. Low entry barriers imply that whenever demand is strong and profits are high there will be a flood of new entrants hoping to cash in on the boom. Examples can be found in the explosion in the number of video stores, health clubs, and sun-tanning parlors during the 1980s. Often, the flood of new entrants into a booming fragmented industry creates excess capacity. Once excess capacity develops, companies start to cut prices in order to utilize their spare capacity. The difficulty companies face when trying to differentiate their products from those of competitors can worsen this tendency. The result is a price war, which will depress industry profits, force some companies out of business, and deter any more new entrants. Thus, for example, after a decade of expansion and booming profits, many health clubs are now finding that they have to offer large discounts in order to hold on to their membership. In general, the more commodity-like an industry's product, the more vicious will be the price war. This bust part of the cycle will continue until overall industry capacity is brought in line with demand (through bankruptcies), at which point prices may stabilize again.

In other words, a fragmented industry structure constitutes a threat rather than an opportunity. Most booms will be relatively short-lived because of the

FIGURE 3.3   **The continuum of industry structures**

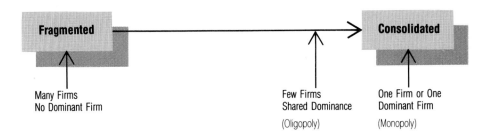

Fragmented   Consolidated

Many Firms
No Dominant Firm

Few Firms
Shared Dominance
(Oligopoly)

One Firm or One
Dominant Firm
(Monopoly)

ease of new entry, and will be followed by price wars and bankruptcies. Since differentiation is often difficult in these industries, the best strategy for a company to pursue in such circumstances may be one of cost minimization. It will allow a company to rack up high returns in a boom and survive any subsequent bust.

The nature and intensity of competition for consolidated industries are much more difficult to predict. The one certainty about consolidated industries is that the companies are *interdependent*. Interdependence means that the competitive actions of one company directly effect the profitability of others in the industry. For example, General Motors' introduction of cut-rate financing to sell autos in 1986 had an immediate negative impact on the sales and profits of Chrysler Corp. and Ford Motor Company, which then had to introduce similar packages in order to protect their market share.

Thus, in a consolidated industry, the competitive action of one company directly affects the market share of its rivals, forcing a response from them. The consequence can be a dangerous competitive spiral, with rival companies trying to undercut each other's prices and pushing industry profits down in the process. The fare wars that racked the airline industry during the seven years after the deregulation of 1979 provide a good illustration of what can happen when companies are highly interdependent. As a result of the fare wars, in 1982 the airline industry as a whole lost over $700 million. Braniff International Corporation and Continental Airlines Corp. were pushed into bankruptcy, and Eastern and People Express sold out to Texas Air to avoid bankruptcy.

Clearly, the interdependence of companies in consolidated industries and the possibility of a price war constitute a major threat. Companies often attempt to reduce this threat by following the price lead set by a dominant company in the industry. However, companies must be careful, for explicit price-fixing agreements are illegal, although tacit agreements are not. (A tacit agreement is one arrived at without direct communication. Instead, companies watch and interpret each other's behavior. Normally, tacit agreements involve following the price lead set by a dominant company.)[9] However, tacit price-leadership agreements are prone to breakdown under adverse economic conditions. This is essentially what is now beginning to occur in the beer industry. For most of the 1980s Anheuser-Busch was the acknowledged price leader in this industry. The resulting absence of price competition helped keep industry profits high. However, slow growth in beer consumption during the late 1980s put pressure on the earnings of all beer majors and persuaded Philip Morris' Miller Brewing division and Adolph Coors Co. to break ranks and institute a policy of deep and continuous discounting for most of their beer brands. In late 1989 market leader Anheuser-Busch announced that it would start offering similar discounts in order to protect its sales volume. Thus, following the breakdown of a tacit price-leadership agreement, the beer industry seems to be sliding toward a price war.

More generally, when price wars are a threat, companies often compete on nonprice factors such as product quality and design features. This type of competition constitutes an attempt to build brand loyalty and minimize the likelihood of a price war. The effectiveness of this strategy, however, depends on how easy it is to differentiate the industry's product. Although some products (such as autos) are relatively easy to differentiate, others (such as airline travel) are essentially commodities that are very difficult to differentiate.

Demand conditions   Industry demand conditions are another determinant of the intensity of rivalry among established companies. Growing demand tends to moderate competition by providing greater room for expansion. Demand grows when the market as a whole is growing through the addition of new consumers or when existing consumers are purchasing more of an industry's product. When demand is growing, companies can increase revenues without taking market share away from other companies. Thus growing demand gives a company a major opportunity to expand operations.

Conversely, declining demand results in more competition as companies fight to maintain revenues and market share. Demand declines when consumers are leaving the marketplace or when each consumer is buying less. When demand is declining, a company can attain growth only by taking market share away from other companies. Thus declining demand constitutes a major threat, for it increases the extent of rivalry between established companies. The issue of what determines demand conditions is discussed in more detail later in the chapter, when we consider industry evolution.

Exit barriers   Exit barriers are a serious competitive threat when industry demand is declining. Exit barriers are economic, strategic, and emotional factors that keep companies competing in an industry even when returns are low. If exit barriers are high, companies can become locked into an unfavorable industry. Excess productive capacity can result. In turn, excess capacity tends to lead to intensified price competition, with companies cutting prices in an attempt to get the orders necessary to utilize their idle capacity.

Common exit barriers include the following: *KH*

1.   Investments in plant and equipment that have no alternative uses and cannot be sold off. If the company wishes to leave the industry, it has to write off the book value of these assets.

2.   High fixed costs of exit, such as severance pay to workers who are being made redundant.

3.   Emotional attachments to an industry, such as when a company is unwilling to exit from its original industry for sentimental reasons.

4.   Strategic relationships between business units. For example, within a multi-industry company, a low-return business unit may provide vital inputs for a high-return business unit based in another industry. Thus the company may be unwilling to exit from the low-return business.

5.   Economic dependence on the industry, such as when a company is not diversified and so relies on the industry for its income.

The steel industry illustrates the adverse competitive effects of high exit barriers. A combination of declining demand and new low-cost sources of supply created overcapacity in the global steel industry during the late 1980s. American companies, with their high-cost structure, were on the sharp end of this decline. Demand for American steel fell from a 1977 peak of 160 million tons to 70 million tons in 1986. The result was excess capacity amounting to an estimated 45 million tons in 1987, or 40 percent of total productive capacity.[10] In order to try to utilize this capacity, many steel companies slashed their prices. As a consequence of the resulting price war, industry profits were low, and several of the majors, including the LTV Corp. and Bethlehem Steel, faced bankruptcy.

Since the steel industry was characterized by excess capacity for most of the 1980s, why did companies not reduce that capacity? The answer is that many tried to, but the costs of exit slowed this process and prolonged the associated price war. For example, in 1983 USX shut down 16 percent of its raw steel-making capacity at a cost of $1.2 billion. USX had to write off the book value of these assets; they could not be sold. In addition, it had to cover pensions and insurance for 15,400 terminated workers.[11] Given such high exit costs, companies such as USX have remained locked into this unprofitable industry. The effect of impeded exit has been more intense price competition than might otherwise have been the case. Thus high exit barriers, by slowing the speed with which companies leave the industry, threatens the profitability of all companies within the steel industry.

Interactions between factors   The extent of rivalry among established companies within an industry is a function of competitive structure, demand conditions, and exit barriers. Particularly within a consolidated industry, the *interaction* of these factors determines the extent of rivalry. For example, the environment

TABLE 3.1   Demand conditions and exit barriers as determinants of opportunities and threats in a consolidated industry

| | | **Demand conditions** | |
		Demand decline	Demand growth
Exit barriers	High	High threat of excess capacity and price wars	Opportunities to raise prices through price leadership and to expand operations
	Low	Moderate threat of excess capacity and price wars	Opportunities to raise prices through price leadership and to expand operations

of a consolidated industry may be favorable when demand growth is high. Under such circumstances, companies might seize the opportunity to adopt price-leadership agreements. However, when demand is declining and exit barriers are high, the probable emergence of excess capacity is likely to give rise to price wars. Thus, depending on the interaction between these various factors, the *extent* of rivalry between established companies in a consolidated industry might constitute an opportunity or a threat. These issues are summarized in Table 3.1.

The Bargaining Power of Buyers

The third of Porter's five competitive forces is the bargaining power of buyers. Buyers can be viewed as a competitive threat when they force down prices or when they demand higher quality and better service (which increase operating costs). Alternatively, weak buyers give a company the opportunity to raise prices and earn greater returns. Whether buyers are able to make demands on a company depends on their *power* relative to that of the company. According to Porter, buyers are most powerful in the following circumstances:

1. When the supply industry is composed of many small companies and the buyers are few in number and large. These circumstances allow the buyers to dominate supply companies.
2. When the buyers purchase in large quantities. In such circumstances, buyers can use their purchasing power as leverage to bargain for price reductions.
3. When the supply industry depends on the buyers for a large percentage of its total orders.
4. When the buyers can switch orders between supply companies at a low cost, thereby playing off companies against each other to force down prices.
5. When it is economically feasible for the buyers to purchase the input from several companies at once.
6. When the buyers can use the threat to supply their own needs through vertical integration as a device for forcing down prices.

An example of an industry whose buyers are powerful is the auto components supply industry. Auto-component suppliers are numerous and typically small in scale. Their customers, the auto manufacturers, are large in size and few in number. Chrysler, for example, does business with close to 2,000 different component suppliers and normally contracts with a number of different companies to supply the same part. The auto majors have used their powerful position to play off suppliers against each other, forcing down the price they have to pay for component parts and demanding better quality. If a component supplier objects, then the auto major uses the threat of switching to another supplier as a bargaining tool. Additionally, both Ford and General Motors have used the threat of manufacturing a component themselves rather than buying it from auto-component suppliers as a device for keeping component prices down.

The opposite circumstances arise when a company has more power than its buyers. For example, by virtue of its patent, Xerox Corporation had a twenty-five-year monopoly in the production of photocopiers. Buyers were dependent on Xerox, which was the only source of supply. This power gave Xerox the opportunity to raise prices above those that would have been set under more competitive conditions, such as the prices currently prevailing in the industry.

The Bargaining Power of Suppliers

The fourth of Porter's competitive forces is the bargaining power of suppliers. Suppliers can be viewed as a threat when they are able to force up the price that a company must pay for input or reduce the quality of goods supplied, thereby depressing the company's profitability. Alternatively, weak suppliers give a company the opportunity to force down prices and demand higher quality. As with buyers, the ability of suppliers to make demands on a company depends on their *power* relative to that of the company. According to Porter, suppliers are most powerful in the following circumstances:

1. When the product that suppliers sell has few substitutes and is important to the company.

2. When the company's industry is *not* an important customer to the suppliers. In such circumstances the health of suppliers does not depend on the company's industry. Thus suppliers have little incentive to reduce prices or improve quality.

3. When suppliers' respective products are differentiated to such an extent that it is costly for a company to switch from one supplier to another. In such circumstances, the company is dependent on its suppliers and *unable* to play them off against each other.

4. When suppliers can use the threat of vertically integrating forward into the industry and competing directly with the company as a device for raising prices.

5. When buying companies are *unable* to use the threat of vertically integrating backward and supplying their own needs as a device for reducing input prices.

For a long time the airlines exemplified an industry whose suppliers were powerful. In particular, the airline pilots and aircraft mechanics unions, as suppliers of labor, were in a very strong position with respect to the airlines. The airlines depended on union labor to fly and service their aircraft. Because of labor agreements and the probability of damaging strikes, nonunion labor was not regarded as a feasible substitute. The unions used this position to raise pilots' and mechanics' wages above the level that would have prevailed in more competitive circumstances, such as those currently found in the industry. This situation persisted until the early 1980s, when the resultant high-cost structure of the airline industry was driving many airlines into bankruptcy. The airlines then used the threat of bankruptcy to break union agreements and drive down labor costs, often by as much as 50 percent.

The Threat of Substitute Products

The final element of Porter's five forces model is the competitive force of substitute products. Substitute products are the products of industries that serve similar consumer needs to those of the industry being analyzed. For example, companies in the coffee industry compete indirectly with those in the tea and soft-drinks industries. (All three industries serve consumer needs for drinks.) The prices that companies in the coffee industry can charge are limited by the existence of substitutes such as tea and soft drinks. If the price of coffee rises too much relative to that of tea or soft drinks, then coffee drinkers will switch from coffee to those substitutes. This phenomenon occurred when unusually cold weather destroyed much of the Brazilian coffee crop in 1975–1976. The price of coffee rose to record highs, reflecting the shortage, and consumers began to switch to tea in large numbers.

The existence of close substitutes constitutes a strong competitive threat, limiting the price a company can charge and thus its profitability. However, if a company's products have few close substitutes (that is, if substitutes are a weak competitive force), then, other things being equal, the company has the opportunity to raise prices and earn additional profits; and its strategies should be designed to take advantage of this fact.

3.4 IDENTIFYING GROUPS WITHIN INDUSTRIES

The Concept of Strategic Groups – MAP

So far we have had little to say about how companies in an industry might differ from each other and what implications the differences might have for the opportunities and threats that they face. In practice, companies in an industry often differ from each other with respect to factors such as distribution channels used, market segments served, product quality, technological leadership, customer service, pricing policy, advertising policy, and promotions. Within most industries, it is possible to observe groups of companies in which each member follows the same basic strategy as other companies in the group but a strategy different from the one followed by companies in other groups. These groups of companies are known as **strategic groups.**[12]

Normally, a limited number of groups captures the essence of strategic differences between companies within an industry. For example, the global auto industry contains a number of different strategic groups. First, there is a group of companies that manufacture a restricted range of cars aimed at serving market segments at the bottom, or basic transportation, end of the market. These companies compete primarily on price. Their strategy is to minimize costs through the attainment of scale economies and competitive pricing to gain market share. Members of this group include Hyundai Motor Company (of South Korea) and Yugo GV (of Yugoslavia).

Second, there is a group of companies that manufacture a restricted range of cars aimed at serving segments at the top, or luxury, end of the market. For these companies, luxury, quality, and outstanding performance, rather than cost, are the critical competitive dimensions. The strategy of these companies is to stress the uniqueness of their product, its outstanding quality and performance, and the status of owning such a car. Examples of such companies include BMW AG, Daimler-Benz AG (Mercedes-Benz), and Jaguar Cars, Inc. They command a high price for their products.

Third, there is a group of companies whose strategy is to manufacture a comprehensive model range of cars aimed at serving the majority of market segments. This strategy focuses on minimizing cost through the realization of scale economies so that the companies can compete on price in the low end of the

FIGURE 3.4   **Strategic groups in the automobile industry**

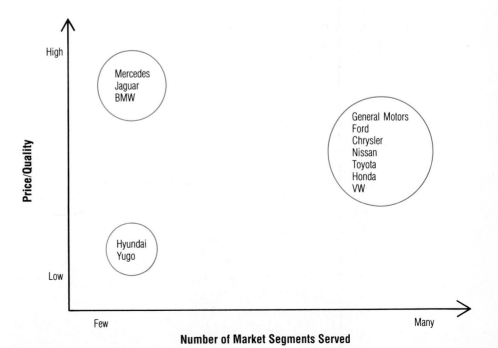

market. At the same time it stresses quality and performance so that the companies can compete at the top end of the market on quality. General Motors, Ford, Chrysler, Nissan Motor Company, Honda, Toyota Motor Corp., and Volkswagen AG are among the companies pursuing such a strategy.

As our discussion suggests, it should be possible to plot these three strategic groups along two main dimensions: price/quality and number of market segments served. This has been done in Figure 3.4. In practice, however, there are more than three strategic groups in the auto industry. We have limited our discussion to three groups for the sake of clarity. Figure 3.4 is also a simplification, since it focuses on only two strategic dimensions.

Implications of Strategic Groups

The concept of strategic groups has a number of implications for industry analysis and the identification of opportunities and threats. First, a company's immediate competitors are those in its strategic group. Since all the companies in a strategic group are pursuing similar strategies, consumers tend to view the products of such enterprises as being direct substitutes for each other. Thus a major threat to a company's profitability can come from within its own strategic group.

Second, different strategic groups can have a different standing with respect to each of Porter's five competitive forces. In other words, the risk of new entry by potential competitors, the degree of rivalry among companies within a group, the bargaining power of buyers, the bargaining power of suppliers, and the competitive force of substitute products can all vary in intensity among different strategic groups within the same industry.

For example, in the auto industry, companies in low-volume strategic groups, such as the now-defunct American Motors Company, traditionally lacked the buying power of those in high-volume strategic groups, such as General Motors. This put companies from low-volume strategic groups in a much weaker position vis-à-vis suppliers than companies in high-volume strategic groups. Thus AMC was unable to bargain down suppliers' prices in the way GM could.

Some strategic groups, then, are more desirable than others, for they have a lower level of threats and greater opportunities. Managers must evaluate whether their company would be better off competing in a different strategic group. If the environment of another strategic group is more benign, then moving into that group can be regarded as an opportunity.

Yet this opportunity is rarely without costs, mainly because of **mobility barriers** between groups. Mobility barriers are factors that inhibit the movement of companies between groups in an industry. They include the barriers to entry into a group and the barriers to exit from a company's existing group. For example, BMW would encounter mobility barriers if it attempted to enter the high-volume strategic group to which General Motors, Chrysler, and Ford belong. These mobility barriers would include the capital costs of building mass-production facilities to manufacture a comprehensive model range of cars (barriers to entry) and the probable loss of BMW's unique, or luxury, status (barriers to exit). Thus a company contemplating entry into another strategic group must evaluate the height of mobility barriers before deciding whether the move is worthwhile.

Mobility barriers also imply that companies within a given group may be protected to a greater or lesser extent from the threat of entry by companies based on other strategic groups. If mobility barriers are low, then the threat of entry from companies in other groups may be high, effectively limiting the prices companies can charge and the profits they can earn without attracting new competition. If mobility barriers are high, then the threat of entry is low, and companies within the protected group have an opportunity to raise prices and earn higher returns without attracting entry.

3.5 COMPETITIVE CHANGES DURING INDUSTRY EVOLUTION

The Industry Life-Cycle Model

Over time most industries pass through a series of well-defined stages, from initial growth, through maturity, and eventually into decline. These stages have different implications for the nature of competition. Specifically, the strength of each of Porter's five competitive forces typically changes as an industry evolves. The changes give rise to different opportunities and threats at each stage of an industry's evolution.[13] The task facing strategic managers is to anticipate how the strength of each force will change with the stage of industry development and to formulate strategies that take advantage of opportunities as they arise and that counter emerging threats.

The industry life-cycle model is a useful tool for analyzing the effects of industry evolution on competitive forces. The model is similar to the product life-cycle model discussed in the marketing literature.[14] Using the industry life-cycle model, we can identify five industry environments, each occurring during a distinct stage of an industry's evolution: (1) an embryonic industry environment, (2) a growth industry environment, (3) a shakeout environment, (4) a mature industry environment, and (5) a declining industry environment. Figure 3.5 illustrates them.

An *embryonic* industry is one that is just beginning to develop (for example, the hand-held calculator industry in the late 1960s). Typically, growth at this stage is slow because of such factors as buyers' unfamiliarity with the industry's product, high prices due to the inability of companies to reap any significant scale economies, and poorly developed distribution channels.

Once demand for the industry's product begins to take off, the industry develops the characteristics of a growth industry. In *growth* industry, first-time demand is expanding rapidly as many new consumers enter the market. Typically, industry growth takes off when consumers become familiar with the product,

FIGURE 3.5   **Stages of the industry life cycle**

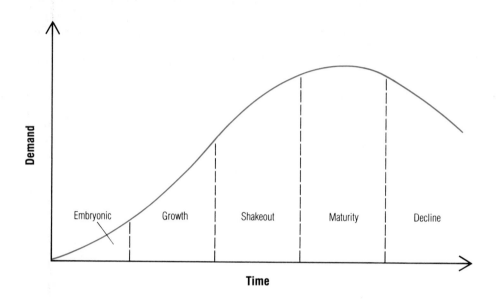

when prices fall because of the attainment of experience and scale economies, and as distribution channels develop. The personal computer industry was at this stage of development between 1981 and 1984. In the United States, 55,000 PCs were sold in 1981. By 1984 the figure had risen to 7.5 million—a 136-fold increase in just three years.[15]

Explosive growth of the type experienced by the PC industry in the early 1980s cannot be maintained indefinitely. Sooner or later the rate of growth slows, and the industry enters the shakeout stage. In the *shakeout* stage, demand approaches saturation levels. In a saturated market, there are few potential first-time buyers left. Most of the demand is limited to replacement demand. A dramatic example of a shakeout occurred in the PC industry during 1984–1986. The average annual growth rate of demand between 1984 and 1986 was 3.3 percent, compared with an average annual growth rate of 3,000 percent between 1981 and 1984.

The shakeout stage ends when the industry enters its *mature* stage. In a mature industry, the market is totally saturated and demand is limited to replacement demand. During this stage, growth is low or zero. What little growth there is comes from population expansion bringing new consumers into the market.

Eventually, most industries enter a decline stage. In the *decline* stage, growth becomes negative for a variety of reasons, including technological substitution (for example, air travel for rail travel), social changes (greater health consciousness hitting tobacco sales), demographics (the declining birthrate hurting the market for baby and child products), and international competition (low-cost foreign competition pushing the American steel industry into decline).

Finally, it is important to remember that the industry life-cycle model is a generalization. In practice, industry life cycles do not always follow the pattern illustrated in Figure 3.5. In some cases, growth is so rapid that the embryonic stage is skipped altogether, as happened in the personal computer industry. In other instances, industries fail to get past the embryonic stage, as occurred with the ill-fated laser disk. Industry growth can be revitalized after long periods of decline, either through innovations or through social changes. For example, the health boom brought the bicycle industry back to life after a long period of decline. The time span of the different stages can also vary significantly from industry to industry. Some industries can stay in maturity almost indefinitely if their products become basic necessities of life, as is the case for the automobile industry. Others skip the mature stage altogether and go straight into decline. That is essentially what occurred in the vacuum-tube industry. Vacuum tubes were replaced by transistors as a major component in electronic products while the industry was still in its growth stage. Still other industries may go through not one but several shakeouts before they enter full maturity.

Implications of Industry Evolution

For strategic managers, the most important aspect of industry evolution concerns its impact on Porter's five competitive forces and, through them, on opportunities and threats. Industry evolution has major implications for two of the five competitive forces—potential competitors and rivalry among established companies—and less substantial implications for the competitive forces of buyers, suppliers, and substitutes. We discuss each in turn.

Potential competitors and industry evolution   The ways in which entry barriers change with industry evolution are summarized in Table 3.2. In an embryonic industry and in the early stages of a growth industry, entry barriers are usually based on the control of technological knowledge.[16] Consequently, at those stages the threat of entry by potential competitors tends to be relatively low. This gives industry incumbents what is commonly known as a *first-mover advantage*. However, the importance of technological knowledge as a barrier to entry is typically short-lived. Sooner or later potential rivals manage to work out the technological requirements for competing in an industry, and technological barriers to entry decline in importance.

The best thing for a company to do when technological entry barriers are high is to take advantage of the relative lack of new competition to build up market share and brand loyalty. For example, in the embryonic stage of the PC industry, Apple Computer had a virtual monopoly of the relevant knowledge (that is, Apple had a first-mover advantage). This technological advantage allowed Apple to become the market leader. Thus, when technological entry

TABLE 3.2   How barriers to entry change with industry evolution

		Embryonic	Growth	Shakeout	Maturity	Decline
		Stage of industry evolution				
	Technology	High to medium	Medium to low	Low	Low	Low
Entry barriers	Scale economies	Low	Low to medium	Medium to high	Medium to high	Medium to high
	Brand loyalty	Low	Low to medium	Medium to high	Medium to high	Medium to high

barriers were eroded by imitators such as IBM, Apple had already established a degree of brand loyalty for its products. This enabled Apple to survive in the industry when competitive pressures increased.

Normally, the importance of control over technological knowledge as a barrier to entry declines significantly by the time an industry enters its growth stage. In addition, because few companies have yet achieved significant scale economies or differentiated their product sufficiently to guarantee brand loyalty, other barriers to entry tend to be low at this stage. Given the low entry barriers, the threat from potential competitors is normally highest at this point. However, paradoxically, high growth usually means that new entrants can be absorbed into an industry without a marked increase in competitive pressure.

As an industry goes through the shakeout stage and enters maturity, barriers to entry increase and the threat of entry from potential competitors decreases. As growth slows during the shakeout, companies can no longer maintain historic growth rates merely by holding on to their market share. Competition for market share develops, driving down prices. Often the result is a price war, as happened in the airline industry during the 1980–1986 shakeout. To survive the shakeout, companies begin to focus both on costs minimization and on building brand loyalty. The airlines, for example, tried to cut operating costs by hiring nonunion labor and to build brand loyalty by introducing frequent-flyer programs. By the time an industry matures, the surviving companies are those that have brand loyalty and low-cost operations. Because both of these factors constitute a significant barrier to entry, the threat of entry by potential competitors is greatly diminished. High entry barriers in mature industries give companies the opportunity to increase prices and profits.

Finally, as an industry enters the decline stage, entry barriers remain high and the threat of entry is low. Economies of scale and brand loyalties are by now well established. In addition, the low profitability characteristic of this stage makes the industry less attractive to potential competitors.

Rivalry among established companies and industry evolution   The extent and character of rivalry among established companies also change as an industry evolves, presenting a company with new opportunities and threats. These are summarized in Table 3.3. In an embryonic industry, rivalry normally focuses on perfecting product design and educating consumers. This rivalry can be intense, as in the race to develop superconductors, and the company that is the first to solve design problems often has the opportunity to develop a significant market position. An embryonic industry may also be the creation of one company's innovative efforts, as happened with personal computers (Apple) or vacuum cleaners (the Hoover Company). In such circumstances, the company has a major opportunity to capitalize on the lack of rivalry and build up a strong hold on the market.

During an industry's growth stage, rivalry tends to be low. Rapid growth in demand enables companies to expand their revenues and profits without taking market share away from competitors. A company has the opportunity to expand its operations. In addition, a strategically aware company takes advantage of the relatively benign environment of the growth stage to prepare itself for the intense competition of the coming industry shakeout.

As an industry enters the shakeout stage, rivalry between companies becomes intense. What typically happens is that companies that have become accustomed to rapid growth during an industry's growth phase continue to add capacity at rates consistent with past growth. Managers use historic growth rates

TABLE 3.3   **How rivalry among established firms changes with industry evolution**

		Stage of industry evolution				
		Embryonic	Growth	Shakeout	Maturity	Decline
Competitive features	Price competition	Low	Low	High	Normally low-medium, can be high	High
	Brand loyalty	Low	Low	Medium to high	High	High
	Overall rivalry	Low	Low	High	Medium, can be high	High

to forecast future growth rates, and they plan expansions in productive capacity accordingly. As an industry approaches maturity, however, demand no longer grows at historic rates. The consequence is the emergence of excess productive capacity. This is illustrated in Figure 3.6, where the solid line indicates the growth in demand over time and the dotted line indicates the growth in productive capacity over time. As can be seen, past point t_1, the growth in demand slows as the industry becomes mature. However, capacity continues to grow until time t_2. The gap between the solid and dotted lines signifies excess capacity. In an attempt to utilize this capacity, companies often cut prices. The result can be an intense price war that drives many of the most inefficient companies into bankruptcy.

A good example of this phenomenon recently occurred in the semiconductor industry. In 1983, there were twenty plants in operation worldwide producing dynamic random-access memories (DRAMs). Propelled by strong market growth and optimistic predictions, by early 1985 the number of plants had more than doubled. By mid 1985, however, there was a significant unanticipated slow-down in the growth rate of the market. As a consequence, by the end of 1985 from 30 to 40 percent of industry DRAM capacity was standing idle. Overca-pacity triggered fierce price cutting and the withdrawal of several incumbent pro-

FIGURE 3.6   Growth in demand and capacity

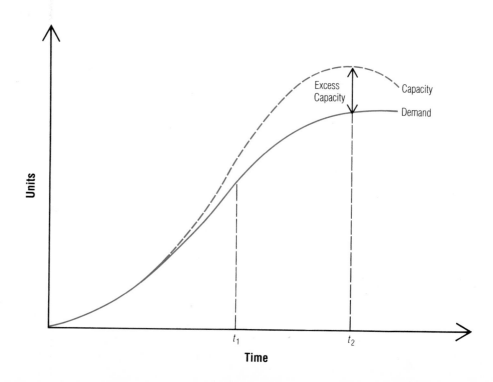

ducers. As a result, by 1987 the number of plants producing DRAMs had fallen 30 percent from the 1985 high.

As a result of the shakeout, most industries by maturity have consolidated and become oligopolies. In the airline industry, for example, as a consequence of the shakeout, the top five companies controlled 85 percent of the industry in 1990, up from only 50 percent of 1984.[17] In mature industries, companies tend to recognize their interdependence and try to avoid price wars. Stable demand gives them the opportunity to enter into price-leadership agreements. The net effect is to reduce the threat of intense rivalry among established companies, thereby allowing greater profitability. However, as noted earlier, the stability of a mature industry is always threatened by further price wars. A general slump in economic activity can depress industry demand. As companies fight to maintain their revenues in the face of declining demand, price-leadership agreements break down, rivalry increases, and prices and profits fall.

The periodic price wars that occur in the gasoline market illustrate this situation. During periods of strong demand for oil, most producers followed the price lead set by OPEC. As demand for oil weakened in the mid 1980s, however, the price lead set by OPEC broke down and severe price competition developed. Mature industries thus are characterized by long periods of price stability, when rivalry is relatively mild, interspersed with periods of intense rivalry and price wars, brought on by a general worsening of macroeconomic conditions. The threat of a price war never disappears. Given this factor, companies should look for opportunities to reduce the sensitivity of their product to price changes.

Finally, within a declining industry, the degree of rivalry among established companies usually increases. Depending on the speed of the decline and the height of exit barriers, competitive pressures can become as fierce as in the shakeout stage.[18] The main problem in a declining industry is that falling demand leads to the emergence of excess capacity. In an attempt to utilize this capacity, companies begin to cut prices, thus sparking a price war. As noted earlier, the American steel industry has experienced these problems because of the attempt of steel companies to utilize their excess capacity (40 percent of the steel industry's total productive capacity was classified as excess in 1986).[19] Exit barriers play a part in adjusting excess capacity. The greater the exit barriers, the harder it is for companies to reduce capacity and the greater is the threat of severe price competition.

Buyers, suppliers, and industry evolution   Industry evolution can change the nature of the relationships between an industry and its buyers and suppliers. As an industry evolves toward maturity, it becomes both larger and more consolidated. These changes enhance the bargaining power of companies in the industry vis-à-vis suppliers and buyers in a number of ways. First, the larger a company is, the more important it is to suppliers as a customer for their products and the greater its bargaining power. Second, the more consolidated an industry is, the less suppliers are able to play off companies against each other in an attempt to increase prices. Third, the more consolidated an industry is, the less buyers are able to play off companies against each other in an attempt to drive down prices.

Hence, as an industry moves toward maturity, the competitive power of buyers and suppliers shrinks.

Substitute products and industry evolution   The competitive force of substitute products depends to some extent on the ability of companies in an industry to build brand loyalty for their own products. Other things being equal, the greater the brand loyalty for an industry's products, the less likely are consumers to switch to the products of substitute industries. Generally, as an industry evolves toward maturity, companies within it begin to expend more effort on differentiating their products to create brand loyalty. This gives a company some protection not only from companies in its own industry, but also from those in substitute industries. Thus, as it moves toward maturity, an industry begins to develop a greater degree of protection against the competitive force of substitute products. However, the emergence of significant new substitutes may push a mature industry into decline, as synthetic materials have done in the steel industry.

Summary: Industry Evolution

The discussion of the effects of industry evolution on competition suggests that the strength of Porter's five competitive forces varies across an industry's life cycle. Rapid expansion makes for weak competitive forces in growth industries. Opportunities for expansion and capturing market share are greatest during this stage. Competitive threats then increase sharply during the shakeout period. The threat of price competition is one of the most important problems that strategic managers have to deal with at this stage. As an industry enters maturity, competitive threats tend to decline and the opportunity exists to limit price competition through price-leadership agreements. Thus, mature industries tend to be characterized by relatively high profitability.[20] Nonprice competition may often play a greater role at this stage, so it is important for a company to capitalize on opportunities to differentiate its product. This situation changes again when an industry enters the decline stage. Competitive intensity increases, particularly when exit barriers are high, profits fall, and the threat of price wars once more becomes substantial.

3.6 ANALYZING THE MACRO-ENVIRONMENT

Macro-environmental factors are factors external to an industry that influence the level of demand within it, directly affecting company profits. Many of these factors are constantly changing, and the change process itself gives rise to new opportunities and threats. Strategic managers must understand the significance of macro-environmental factors and be able to assess the impact of changes in the macro-environment on their company and on the opportunities and threats it faces. Seven elements of the macro-environment are of particular importance here: the macroeconomic environment, the technological environment, the social environment, the demographic environment, the political and legal environment, and the global environment.

The Macro-Economic Environment

The state of the macroeconomic environment determines the general health and well-being of the economy. This, in turn, affects companies' ability to earn an adequate rate of return. The four most important macroeconomic indicators in this context are the growth rate of the economy, the interest rates, currency exchange rates, and inflation rates.

Economic growth   The rate of growth in the economy has a direct impact on the level of opportunities and threats that companies face. Because it leads to an expansion in consumer expenditure, economic growth tends to produce a general easing of competitive pressures within an industry. This gives companies the opportunity to expand their operations. Because economic decline leads to a reduction in consumer expenditure, it increases competitive pressures and constitutes a major threat to profitability. Economic decline frequently causes price wars in mature industries. This happened in the heavy construction equipment industry during the recession of 1979, when many of the major companies, such as International Harvester, came close to bankruptcy.

Although the precise level of economic growth is notoriously difficult to predict, strategic managers need to be aware of the outlook for the economy. For example, it would make little sense to embark on an ambitious expansion strategy if most forecasters are expecting a sharp economic downturn. Conversely, if the economy is currently in poor shape but a general upturn in activity is forecasted, companies might be well advised to take up an expansion strategy.

Interest rates   The level of interest rates can determine the level of demand for a company's products. Interest rates are important whenever consumers routinely borrow money to finance their purchase of these products. The most obvious example is the housing market, where the mortgage rate directly affects demand, but interest rates also have an impact on the sale of autos, appliances, and capital equipment, to give just a few examples. For companies in such industries, rising interest rates are a threat and falling rates an opportunity.

Interest rates also determine the cost of capital for a company. This cost can be a major factor in deciding whether a given strategy is feasible. For instance, a company may finance an ambitious expansion strategy with borrowed money. This course of action may make good sense if interest rates are low and are predicted to stay at that level, but it would be folly if forecasts predict that interest rates will rise to record levels.

Currency exchange rates   Currency exchange rates define the value of the dollar relative to the value of the currencies of other countries. Movement in currency exchange rates has a direct impact on the competitiveness of a company's products in the global marketplace. When the value of the dollar is low compared with the value of other currencies, products made in the United States are relatively inexpensive and products made overseas are relatively expensive. A low or declining dollar reduces the threat from foreign competitors while creating opportunities for increased sales overseas. For example, the 45 percent fall in the value of the dollar against the Japanese yen between 1985 and 1987 sharply increased the price of imported Japanese cars, giving American manufacturers some degree of protection against the Japanese threat. (Actually, the subsequent decline in Japanese auto imports was offset by the increase in U.S.-based production by Japanese companies.) However, when the value of the dollar is high, as it was during the 1984–1985 period, then imports become relatively cheap and the threat from foreign producers increases. A high dollar also limits opportunities for overseas sales because of the relatively high price of goods manufactured in the United States.

Inflation rates   Inflation can destabilize the economy, producing slower economic growth, higher interest rates, and volatile currency movements. If inflation keeps increasing, investment planning becomes a hazardous business. The key characteristic of inflation is that it makes the future less predictable. In an inflationary environment, it may be impossible to predict with any accuracy the real value of returns that can be earned from a project five years hence. Such uncertainty makes companies less willing to invest. Their holding back, in turn, depresses economic activity and ultimately pushes the economy into a slump. Thus high inflation is a threat to companies.

The Technological Environment

Since World War II, the pace of technological change has accelerated, unleashing a process that has been called a "perennial gale of creative destruction."[21] Technological change can make established products obsolete overnight. At the same time it can create a host of new product possibilities. Thus it is both creative and destructive—both an opportunity and a threat. Since accelerating technological change also shortens the average product life cycle, organizations need to anticipate the changes that new technologies bring with them: They need to analyze their environment strategically.[22]

Witness recent changes in the electronics industry. For forty years, until the early 1960s, vacuum tubes were a major component in radios and then in record players and early computers. The advent of transistors destroyed the market for vacuum tubes but at the same time created new opportunities connected with transistors. Transistors took up far less space than vacuum tubes, encouraging a trend toward miniaturization that continues.

The transistor held its position as the major component in the electronics industry for just a decade. In the 1970s microprocessors were developed, and the market for transistors declined rapidly. At the same time, however, the microprocessor created yet another set of new product opportunities—hand-held calculators (which destroyed the market for slide rules), compact disk players, and personal computers, to name just a few. Strategically aware electronics companies, by anticipating the effects of change, benefited from the progression of new technologies. Unaware companies went out of business.

New technologies also give rise to new ways of manufacturing established products. In turn, these new processes give rise to opportunities and threats. Robotics, especially as applied to the automation of vehicle assembly plants, is one example of a new process technology. Another is the steel industry's development of minimills using new electric arc smelting techniques. This particular technology took away from large, integrated steel operations, such as U.S. Steel and Bethlehem Steel, the considerable advantage they once enjoyed because of economies of scale. Thus minimills have emerged as a major threat to established American steel manufacturers. Many minimills can now turn out steel at a lower cost than can large, integrated plants that use thirty-year-old technology. Indeed, by 1985 minimills and specialty steel mills held 40 percent of the U.S. market, and domestic integrated companies had a 38 to 40 percent market share, down from close to 70 percent ten years earlier.[23]

The Social Environment

Like technological change, social change creates opportunities and threats. One of the major social movements of the 1970s and 1980s was the trend toward greater health consciousness. Its impact has been immense, and companies that recognized the opportunities early have often reaped significant gains. Philip Morris, for example, capitalized on the growing health trend when it acquired Miller Brewing Company and then redefined competition in the beer industry with its introduction of low-calorie beer (Miller Lite). Similarly, PepsiCo was able to gain market share from its archrival, Coca-Cola Company, by introducing diet colas and fruit-based soft drinks first. The health trend has also given rise to booming sales of mineral waters, with a market growth of 15 percent per year during the mid 1980s. In an attempt to capitalize on this opportunity, many of the country's largest beverage companies are currently expanding into this fragmented industry. At the same time the health trend has created a threat for many industries. The tobacco industry, for example, is now in decline as a direct result of greater consumer awareness of the health implications of smoking. Similarly, the sugar industry has seen sales decline as consumers have decided to switch to artificial sweeteners.

The Demographic Environment

The changing composition of the population is another factor that can create both opportunities and threats. For example, as the baby-boom generation of the 1960s has moved through the population, it has created a host of opportunities and threats. Currently, baby boomers are getting married and creating an upsurge in demand for the consumer appliances normally bought by couples marrying for the first time. Thus companies such as Whirlpool Corporation and General Electric are looking to capitalize on the predicted upsurge in demand for washing machines, dishwashers, spin dryers, and the like. The other side of the coin is that industries oriented toward the young, such as the toy industry, have seen their consumer base decline in recent years.

The Political and Legal Environment

Political and legal factors also have a major effect on the level of opportunities and threats in the environment. One of the most significant trends in recent years has been the move toward deregulation. By eliminating many legal restrictions, deregulation has opened a number of industries to intense competition. The deregulation of the airline industry in 1979, for example, created the opportunity to establish low-fare carriers—an opportunity that Texas Air, People Express, and others tried to capitalize on. At the same time, the increased intensity of competition created many threats, including, most notably, the threat of prolonged fare wars, which have repeatedly thrown the airline industry into turmoil during the last decade.

Deregulation apart, companies also face serious legal constraints, which limit their potential strategic options. Antitrust laws, for example, can prevent companies from trying to achieve a dominant market position through acquisitions. In 1986, both PepsiCo and Coca-Cola attempted to buy up smaller soft-drink manufacturers, Pepsi bidding for the Seven-Up Company and Coca-Cola for Dr. Pepper Co. Both acquisitions were forbidden by the Federal Trade Commission on the grounds that if they went through, Pepsi and Coca-Cola between them would control more than 80 percent of the soft-drink market. Seven-Up subsequently merged with Dr. Pepper, a move that has created the possible threat (to Pepsi and Coca-Cola) of a third major company emerging in the industry.

For the future, fears about the destruction of the ozone layer, acid rain, and global warming may be near the top of the political agenda in the 1990s. Given these concerns, governments seem increasingly likely to enact tough environmental regulations to limit air pollution. Rather than resisting this trend, companies should try to take advantage of it. For example, back in 1974, when ozone depletion was still a theory, E. I. Du Pont de Nemours & Company decided to start research into substitutes for ozone-damaging chlorofluorocarbons (CFCs), widely used in aerosols, air conditioners, and refrigeration equipment. At the same time, Du Pont made a pledge to phase out production of CFCs if they were shown to be a threat to public health. In March 1988, in response to NASA data, Du Pont honored that commitment and promised to phase out production of CFCs within ten years. Although Du Pont stands to lose $600 million per year from the sales of CFCs, since the mid 1970s the company's research has yielded three viable alternatives to CFCs, each of which is now produced commercially. Thus, by anticipating regulations and undertaking appropriate action, Du Pont is now well positioned to take a large share of the market for CFC substitutes if, as seems increasingly likely, CFCs are banned.

The Global Environment

Changes in the global environment can create both opportunities for market expansion and serious threats to a company's domestic and international market share. As the world enters the 1990s, developments are occurring that may have great significance for the future of American enterprise. The first is the emergence of the European Community as a free-trade block containing a single market that is half again as large as the United States. After the removal of trade barriers between Community members in 1992, the European Community could have the fastest growing and potentially most wealthy economy in the industrialized world. American business would be well advised to take advantage of this growth and to recognize the threat posed by major European companies. European companies may use their strong domestic economy as a springboard from which to invade U.S. markets, much as the Japanese did in the 1970s. American companies need to anticipate these developments rather than ignore them as was all too often the case with the Japanese.

A second development is in Eastern Europe, where the collapse of state communism and the rapid shift toward free-market economies by several Eastern European countries has created potentially enormous growth opportunities. The challenge facing American enterprise is to capitalize on these opportunities before Western European and Asian competitors do. A third development concerns the continuing emergence of "Asian tigers." In particular, Thailand looks set to join a list of major Asian competitors that already includes Japan, South Korea, and Taiwan. As a group, these countries will pose a significant competitive threat for the foreseeable future. At the same time, their markets represent largely untapped growth opportunity.

3.7 SUMMARY OF CHAPTER

This chapter details a framework that strategic managers can use to analyze the external environment of their company, enabling them to identify opportunities and threats. The following major points are made in the chapter:

1. Superior performance is the result of a fit between strategy and the environment. In order to achieve such a fit, strategic managers must be able to identify environmental opportunities and threats.

2. The main technique used to analyze competition in the industry environment is the five forces model. The five forces are (a) the risk of new entry by potential competitors, (b) the extent of rivalry among established firms, (c) the bargaining power of buyers, (d) the bargaining power of suppliers, and (e) the threat of substitute products. The stronger each of these forces is, the more competitive is an industry and the lower is the rate of return that can be earned in that industry.

3. The risk of entry by potential competitors is a function of the height of barriers to entry. The higher the barriers to entry are, the lower is the risk of entry and the greater are the profits that can be earned in the industry.

4. The extent of rivalry among established companies is a function of an industry's competitive structure, demand conditions, and barriers to exit. Strong demand conditions moderate the competition among established companies and create opportunities for expansion. When demand is weak, intensive competition can develop, particularly in consolidated industries with high exit barriers.

5. Buyers are most powerful when a company depends on them for business but they themselves are not dependent on the company. In such circumstances, buyers are a threat.

6. Suppliers are most powerful when a company depends on them for business but they themselves are not dependent on the company. In such circumstances, suppliers are a threat.

7. Substitute products are the products of companies based in industries serving consumer needs similar to the needs served by the industry being analyzed. The more similar the substitute products are to each other, the lower is the price that companies can charge without losing customers to the substitutes.

8. Most industries are composed of strategic groups. Strategic groups are groups of companies pursuing the same or a similar strategy. Companies in different strategic groups pursue different strategies.

9. The members of a company's strategic group constitute its immediate competitors. Since different strategic groups are characterized by different opportunities and threats, it may pay a company to switch strategic groups. The feasibility of doing so is a function of the height of mobility barriers.

10. Industries go through a well-defined life cycle, from an embryonic stage, through growth, shakeout, and maturity, and eventually into decline. Each stage has different implications for the competitive structure of the industry, and each stage gives rise to its own set of opportunities and threats.

11. Important components of the macro-environment include the macroeconomic environment, the technological environment, the social environment, the demographic environment the political and legal environment, and the global environment. Although largely outside of the company's direct control, macro-environmental trends can profoundly affect the magnitude of opportunities and threats facing a company.

Discussion Questions

1. Under what environmental conditions are price wars most likely to occur in an industry? What are the implications of price wars for a company? How should a company try to deal with the threat of a price war?

2. Discuss Porter's five forces model with reference to what you know about the airline industry. What does the model tell you about the level of competition in this industry?

3. Identify a growth industry, a mature industry, and a declining industry. For each industry, identify the following: (a) the number and size distribution of companies, (b) the nature of barriers to entry, (c) the height of barriers to entry, and (d) the extent of product differentiation. What do these factors tell you about the nature of competition in each industry? What are the implications for the company in terms of opportunities and threats?

4. Assess the impact of macro-environmental factors on the likely level of enrollment at your university over the next decade. What are the implications of these factors for the job security and salary level of your professors?

Endnotes

1. Sources include "It's USX vs. Everybody," *Business Week*, October 6, 1986, pp. 26–27; Organization for Economic Cooperation and Development, *Steel in the 80s* (Paris: OECD, 1980); "Better 'X' Than Steel," *Industry Kbek*, July 21, 1986, p 23; and Frank Koelble, "Strategies for Restructuring the U.S. Steel Industry," *33 Metal Producing* (December 1986), 28–33.

2. Michael E. Porter, *Competitive Strategy—Techniques for Analyzing Industries and Competitors* (New York: Free Press, 1980). See also Porter, *Competitive Advantage: Creating and Sustaining Superior Performance* (New York: Free Press, 1985).

3. Joe S. Bain, *Barriers to New Competition* (Cambridge, Mass.: Harvard University Press, 1956).

4. For a more complete discussion of the sources of scale economies, see Chapter 4.

5. Most of this information on barriers to entry can be found in the industrial organization economics literature. See especially the following works: Bain, *Barriers to New Competition;* M. Mann, "Seller Concentration, Barriers to Entry and Rates of Return in 30 Industries," *Review of Economics and Statistics,* 48 (1966), 296–307; and W. S. Comanor and T. A. Wilson, "Advertising, Market Structure and Performance," *Review of Economics and Statistics,* 49 (1967), 423–440.

6. S. Greenhouse, "Dicey Days at McDonnell Douglas," *The New York Times,* February 22, 1987, p. 4.

7. C. F. Pratten, *Economies of Scale in Manufacturing Industry* (London: Cambridge University Press, 1971).

8. F. M. Scherer, *Industrial Market Structure and Economic Performance* (Chicago: Rand McNally, 1981).

9. For a discussion of tacit agreements, see I. C. Schelling, *The Strategy of Conflict* (Cambridge, Mass.: Harvard University Press, 1960).

10. Koelble, "Strategies," pp. 28–33.

11. "It's USX vs. Everybody," pp. 26–27.

12. The development of strategic-group theory has been a strong theme in the strategy literature during recent years. Important contributions include the following: R. E. Caves and Michael E. Porter, "From Entry Barriers to Mobility Barriers," *Quarterly Journal of Economics* (May 1977), 241–262; K. R. Harrigan, "An Application of Clustering for Strategic Group Analysis," *Strategic Management Journal,* 6 (1985), 55–73; K. J. Hatten and D. E. Schendel, "Heterogeneity Within an Industry: Firm Conduct in the U.S. Brewing Industry, 1952–71," *Journal of Industrial Economics,* 26 (1977), 97–113; and Michael E. Porter, "The Structure Within Industries and Companies' Performance," *The Review of Economics and Statistics,* 61 (1979), 214–227.

13. Indeed, Charles W. Hofer has argued that life-cycle considerations may be the most important contingency when formulating business strategy. See Charles W. Hofer, "Towards a Contingency Theory of Business Strategy," *Academy of Management Journal,* 18 (1975), 784–810. There is also empirical evidence to support this view. See C. R. Anderson and C. P. Zeithaml, "Stages of the Product Life Cycle, Business Strategy, and Business Performance," *Academy of Management Journal,* 27 (1984), 5–24; and D. C. Hambrick and D. Lei, "Towards an Empirical Prioritization of Contingency Variables for Business Strategy," *Academy of Management Journal,* 28 (1985), 763–788.

14. The difference is that individual products can have their own life cycle within the broader context of an industry life cycle.

15. "The PC Wars: IBM vs. the Clones," *Business Week,* July 28, 1986, pp. 62–68.

16. Porter, *Competitive Strategy,* pp. 215–236.

17. "Nice Going, Frank, But Will It Fly?" *Business Week,* September 29, 1986, pp. 34–35.

18. The characteristics of declining industries have been summarized by K. R. Harrigan, "Strategy Formulation in Declining Industries," *Academy of Management Review,* 5 (1980), 599–604.

19. J. J. Innace, "Slippery Footing and the Fall of the Axe," *33 Metal Producing* (December 1986), 25–27.

20. The evidence of the effect of industrial organization economics on the relationship between profitability and market structure would seem to support the idea that mature industries are characterized by high profitability. For a review, see D. A. Hay and D. J. Morris, *Industrial Economics: Theory and Evidence* (Oxford: Oxford University Press, 1979).

21. The phrase was originally coined by J. Schumpeter, *Capitalism, Socialism and Democracy* (London: Macmillan, 1950), p. 68.

22. See M. Gort and J. Klepper, "Time Paths in the Diffusion of Product Innovations," *Economic Journal* (September 1982), 630–653. Looking at the history of forty-six different products, Gort and Klepper found that the length of time before other companies entered the markets created by a few inventive companies declined from an average of 14.4 years for products introduced before 1930 to 4.9 years for those introduced after 1949.

23. Innace, "Slippery Footing," pp. 25–27.

Chapter 4

INTERNAL ANALYSIS: STRENGTHS, WEAKNESSES, AND DISTINCTIVE COMPETENCIES

4.1 OPENING INCIDENT: CATERPILLAR TRACTOR CO.

Caterpillar Tractor's first half-century was one of remarkable success. To quote one commentator, "Caterpillar has combined lowest-cost manufacturing with higher cost but truly outstanding distribution and after-market support to differentiate its line of construction equipment. As a result, Caterpillar, ranking as the 24th largest and 39th most profitable company in the United States, is well ahead of its competitors and most of the Fortune 500 glamor companies."[1] In essence, Caterpillar had capitalized on distinctive competencies in two of its major functional areas, manufacturing and marketing, to build a strong competitive position.

In 1982, however, things suddenly went bad for Caterpillar. The company reported its first loss in forty-eight years. A dramatic slump in world demand for heavy earth-moving and construction equipment, a strong dollar that increased the costs of Caterpillar's exports, and intense new low-cost competition from Komatsu of Japan combined to make 1982 the worst year in the company's history. Caterpillar's response to these threats was to re-examine the basis of its former competitive advantage. It found that although it still had by far the best dealer network in the industry, it had lost its cost advantage to Komatsu. Instead of having distinctive competencies in two major areas, Caterpillar now had them in only one—and that was not enough.

To re-establish its former cost advantage, Caterpillar embarked on an aggressive new manufacturing strategy, involving a $1-billion plant modernization program called PWAF

(Plant with a Future). New high-tech machine tools (including robots) were purchased and grouped with existing machines in work areas called *cells*. Each cell is a self-contained work unit that undertakes a major amount of assembly on an individual product. In an operation such as Caterpillar's PWAF, a large number of cells work in parallel. The use of cells improved product quality, lowered inventory requirements, and strengthened employee morale; it also decreased operating costs. In addition, Caterpillar installed sophisticated computer-controlled just-in-time inventory systems in its PWAF, reducing the need to hold expensive inventories of parts and equipment.

The result of Caterpillar's attempts to regain its low-cost position was impressive. Between 1982 and the end of 1986 Caterpillar cut operating costs by 22 percent and aimed to reduce costs by a further 15 to 20 percent by 1990. Although Caterpillar has a long way to go, its manufacturing strategy is having a positive effect on performance. After three years of losses, in 1985 and 1986 Caterpillar netted profits while continuing to hold on to its 35 to 40 percent share of the U.S. market.[2]

4.2 OVERVIEW

In Chapter 3, we reviewed the elements of the external environment that determine the opportunities and threats facing a company. In this chapter, we focus on identifying a company's *strengths* and *weaknesses* and examine functional-level strategies that can build and exploit the strengths and correct the weaknesses. For example, historically, Caterpillar's low-cost manufacturing position was one of its strengths. When Caterpillar lost this advantage to Komatsu of Japan, its manufacturing function turned into a weakness. The company's manufacturing strategy in the 1980s was designed to correct this weakness and to build a new distinctive competence for Caterpillar in manufacturing by the 1990s.

The term **distinctive competence** refers to company strengths that competitors cannot easily match or imitate. Distinctive competencies represent the *unique* strengths of a company. Building a competitive advantage involves the strategic exploitation of distinctive competencies; they form the bedrock of a company's strategy. For example, Caterpillar has always exploited its distinctive competence in distribution and after-sales service to maintain buyer loyalty and protect its market share. This distinctive competence has allowed the company to charge higher prices and earn greater profits than its competitors. Similarly, the 3M Company has been able to exploit its distinctive competence in research and development to produce a wide range of product innovations that have allowed 3M to earn high profits.

We begin this chapter by considering the source of distinctive competencies. Next, we look at the **value chain** concept and consider the way in which distinctive competencies help a company maximize value created through its value chain. The objective is to show how the different functional areas of a firm—such as manufacturing, marketing, materials management, and R&D—are related to each other. Third, we review each functional area in depth. The objective here is to identify both the sources of company-level strengths and weaknesses and the basic **functional strategies** that can be used to build strengths and correct weaknesses. Functional strategies are simply the strategies pursued by the individual functional areas of a company. Thus, we talk about manufacturing strategy, marketing strategy, R&D strategy, human-resources strategy, and the like.

Bear in mind that functional-level strategies are formulated not in a vacuum but in the context set by business-level strategies. Furthermore, strategy formulation is not a top-down process (see Chapter 1). Distinctive competencies help determine the set of feasible business-level strategies. In other words, an examination of a company's strengths and weaknesses at the functional level tells management what the company *can* and *cannot* do at the business level. Thus strategy formulation is an interactive process, and functional-level strategies and considerations are an integral part of it.

4.3 DISTINCTIVE COMPETENCIES

Strategically, the importance of a company's distinctive competencies is that they enable the company to outperform competitors and earn greater profits. Competitors are motivated to try to imitate these distinctive competencies, and if successful, they ultimately eliminate the company's competitive advantage. Many personal computer companies, for example, are trying to imitate the image-oriented graphics that constitute a major distinctive competence of Apple Computer. The more difficult it is for competitors to imitate a company's distinctive competencies, the more *sustainable* is the company's competitive advantage.

Source of Distinctive Competencies

Distinctive competencies arise from two complementary sources: a company's *resources* and its *capabilities*. Resources are the financial, physical, human, technological, and organizational assets of the firm. They can be divided into *tangible resources* (land, buildings, plant, and equipment) and *intangible resources* (brand names, reputation, patents, and technological or marketing know-how). To give rise to a distinctive competence, a company's resources must be both *unique* and *valuable*. A unique resource is one that no other company has. For example, Polaroid's distinctive competence in instant photography was based on a unique intangible resource: the technological know-how involved in instant film processing. This know-how was protected from imitation by a thicket of patents. A resource is valuable if it in some way helps create strong demand for the company's products. Thus, Polaroid's technological know-how was valuable because it created strong demand for Polaroid's photographic products.

Capabilities are a company's skills at coordinating its resources and putting them to productive use. These skills reside in an organization's routines—that is, in the way a company makes decisions and manages its internal processes to achieve organizational objectives. More generally, a company's capabilities are the product of its organizational structure and control systems. These systems specify how and where decisions are made within a company, the kind of behaviors that will be rewarded by the company, and the cultural norms and values of the company. (We discuss how organizational structure and control systems help a company obtain capabilities in Chapters 10 and 11.) It is important to keep in mind that capabilities are, by definition, intangible. They reside not so much in individuals as in the way individuals interact, cooperate, and make decisions within the context of an organization.[3]

The distinction between resources and capabilities is of the utmost importance in understanding the source of a distinctive competence. A company may have unique and valuable resources; but unless it has the capability to use those resources effectively, it may not be able to create or sustain a distinctive competence. For illustration, consider the case of EMI Ltd. and the CAT scanner. The CAT scanner is the greatest advance in radiology since the discovery of X-rays in 1895. CAT scanners generate cross-sectional views of the human body. They were invented by Godfrey Hounsfield, a senior research engineer at EMI, who subsequently won a Nobel Prize for his achievement. As a result of Hounsfield's work, EMI initially had sole possession of a unique and valuable intangible resource: the technological know-how necessary to make CAT scanners. However, EMI lacked the capability to exploit that resource successfully in the marketplace. It lacked the marketing skills required to educate potential consumers about the benefits of the product, and it lacked the after-sales service and support skills necessary to market such a technologically complex product successfully. As a result, eight years after introducing the CAT scanner, EMI was no longer in the CAT scanner business and an imitator, General Electric, had become the market leader. In other words, despite possessing a unique and valuable intangible resource (technological know-how) EMI was unable to establish a distinctive competence and generate high profits because of its lack of capability to exploit that resource.

It is also important to recognize that a company may not need unique and valuable resources to establish a distinctive competence as long as it has capabilities that no competitor possesses. For example, the steel minimill operator Nucor is widely acknowledged to be the most cost-efficient steel maker in the United States. Nucor's distinctive competence in low-cost steel making, however, does not come from any unique and valuable resources. Nucor has the same resources (plant, equipment, skilled employees, know-how) as many other minimill operators. What is different about Nucor is the company's unique capability to manage its resources in a highly productive manner. Nucor's structure, control systems, and culture promote efficiency-seeking at all levels within the company.

In sum, for a company to have a distinctive competence, it (like Polaroid) must at a minimum possess a unique and valuable resource and the capabilities (skills) necessary to exploit that resource, or it (like Nucor) must have some unique capability to manage common resources. A company's distinctive competence is strongest when the company possesses *both* unique and valuable resources *and* unique capabilities to manage those resources.

Barriers to Imitation

Since distinctive competencies allow companies to earn superior profits, competitors want to imitate them. However, the greater the barriers to imitation, the more difficult imitation is and, therefore, the more sustainable a company's competitive advantage is. It is important to note at the outset, however, that ultimately almost any distinctive competence can be imitated by a competitor. The critical issue is the *time* that competitors take to do this. The more time competitors need to imitate a distinctive competence, the greater is the opportunity for the company to build both a strong market position and a *reputation* with consumers that is subsequently difficult for competitors to attack. Moreover, the longer it takes competitors to imitate a company's distinctive competence, the greater is the opportunity for the company to improve on that competence or build other competencies, thereby staying one step ahead of the competition.

Imitating resources   The easiest distinctive competencies for competitors to imitate tend to be based on possession of unique and valuable *tangible* resources such as buildings, plant, and equipment. Such resources are visible to competitors and can often be purchased on the open market. For example, if a company's competitive advantage is based on sole possession of efficient-scale manufacturing facilities, competitors may move fairly quickly to establish similar facilities. Thus, although Ford gained a competitive advantage over General Motors in the 1920s by virtue of being the first to adopt an assembly-line manufacturing technology to produce automobiles, General Motors quickly imitated that innovation and competed away Ford's distinctive competence.

Intangible resources can be more difficult to imitate. This is particularly true of brand names, which are important because they symbolize a company's reputation. In the computer industry, for example, the IBM brand name is synonymous with high quality and superior after-sales service and support. Similarly, the Christian Dior brand name stands for exclusive *haute couture* clothing. Customers often display a preference for the products of such companies, primarily because *the brand name is an important guarantee of high quality*. Although competitors might like to imitate well-established brand names, the law prohibits them from doing so.

Marketing and technological know-how are also important intangible resources. However, unlike brand names, company-specific marketing and technological know-how can be relatively easy to imitate. The movement of skilled marketing personnel between companies may facilitate the general diffusion of know-how. For example, in the 1970s Ford was generally acknowledged to be the best marketer among the big three U.S. auto companies. In 1979 Ford lost a lot of its marketing know-how to Chrysler when Ford's most successful marketer,

Lee Iacocca, joined Chrysler after being fired by Henry Ford III following "personal disagreements." Iacocca subsequently hired many of Ford's top marketing people to work with him at Chrysler. More generally, successful marketing strategies are relatively easy to imitate because they are so visible to competitors. Thus, Coca-Cola quickly imitated PepsiCo's Diet Pepsi brand with the introduction of its own brand, Diet Coke.

In theory, the patent system should make technological know-how relatively immune to imitation. Patents give the inventor of a new product a seventeen-year exclusive production agreement. Thus, for example, pharmaceutical giant Merck recently patented a cholesterol-reducing drug that is marketed under the brand name of Mevacor. Approved by the FDA in August 1987, Mevacor generated sales of $430 million in 1988 and is targeted to generate annual sales of $1 billion by 1992. It is relatively easy to use the patent system to protect a chemical compound from imitation; however, many other inventions are not so easily protected. In electrical and computer engineering, it is often possible to "invent around" patents. Although EMI took out patents on the CAT scanner, General Electric was able to use reverse engineering skills to figure out how the CAT scanner worked. It then developed a product that though not identical to EMI's CAT scanner (and thus not in violation of EMI's patent) was very similar and performed the same basic function. A study found that 60 percent of patented innovations were successfully invented around in four years.[4] The study suggests that, in general, distinctive competencies based on technological know-how can be relatively short-lived.

Imitating capabilities   Imitation of a company's capabilities tends to be more difficult than imitation of its tangible and intangible resources. A principal reason is that a company's capabilities are often *invisible* to outsiders. Remember that capabilities are based on the way in which decisions are made and processes are managed deep within a company. It is difficult for outsiders to discern the nature of a company's internal operations. Thus, for example, it may be difficult for outsiders to identify with precision why 3M is so successful at developing new products or why Nucor is such an efficient steel producer.

On its own, the invisible nature of capabilities would not be sufficient to halt imitation. In theory, competitors could still gain insights into how a company operates by hiring people away from that company. However, a company's capabilities rarely reside in a single individual. Rather, they are the product of how numerous individuals interact within a unique organizational setting. Thus it is possible that no one individual within a company may be familiar with the totality of a company's internal operating routines and procedures. When this is the case, hiring people away from a successful company may not be sufficient to imitate key capabilities.

Consider the way in which a football team works. The success of a team is not the product of any one individual. Rather, it is the product of how individuals work together *as a team;* it is the product of an unwritten or tacit understanding between the players of the team. Thus the transfer of a star player from a winning team to a losing team may not be sufficient to improve the performance of the losing team.

Summary: The Durability of Distinctive Competencies

We have seen how distinctive competencies arise from a company's resources and capabilities. For a company to have a distinctive competence, at a minimum it must possess a unique and valuable resource and the capabilities (skills) necessary to exploit that resource or it must possess unique and valuable capabilities. We have also seen how resources are easier to imitate than capabilities. Thus, a distinctive competence that is based on a company's unique capabilities is probably more durable (less imitable) than one based on its resources.

At this juncture two other factors regarding the durability of a distinctive competence also need to be noted. First, the time that it takes competitors to imitate a company's distinctive competence is a major determinant of durability. The slower competitors are to respond, the greater is the competitive advantage and reputation that a company can build, and the more difficult it will be to attack the company's position later. For example, the failure of U.S. auto manufacturers to react quickly to the distinctive competence of Japanese auto companies in the manufacture of compact, low-cost, high-quality motor cars gave the Japanese companies time to build a strong market position and reputation that is now proving difficult to attack.

Second, durability is also dependent on the stability of the environment. Resources and capabilities that are suited to one environmental state may not be suited to another. Thus, although the resources and capabilities of U.S. Steel gave the company a distinctive competence in the steel industry of the 1950s and 1960s, this was no longer true by the 1970s and 1980s (see the Opening Incident of Chapter 3). What had changed in the intervening period was not so much U.S. Steel as the environment of the global steel industry. As a result, U.S. Steel's resources and capabilities no longer constituted a distinctive competence.

As a general point, it should be noted that the increasing pace of technological change in recent years has reduced the life span of many resources—particularly those related to plant, equipment, and technological know-how. Proprietary technology, for example, is increasingly subject to a high risk of obsolescence due to competitors' discoveries. *diffusion, imitation?*

4.4 THE VALUE CHAIN

The value a company creates is measured by the amount that buyers are willing to pay for a product or service.[5] A company is profitable if the value it creates exceeds the cost of performing value-creation functions, such as procurement, manufacturing, and marketing. To gain a competitive advantage, a company must either perform value-creation functions at a lower cost than its rivals or perform them in a way that leads to differentiation and a premium price. To do either, it must have a distinctive competence in one or more of its value-creation functions. If it has significant weaknesses in any of these functions, it will be at a competitive disadvantage.

Value creation can be illustrated with reference to a concept called the value chain, which has been popularized by Professor Michael E. Porter of the Harvard School of Business Administration.[6] The form of the value chain is given in Figure 4.1. The value chain is divided between *primary* activities and *support* activities. Each activity adds value to a product.

Primary activities have to do with the physical creation of a product, its marketing and delivery to buyers, and its support and after-sales service. In this chapter, we consider the activities involved in the physical creation of a product to be *manufacturing* and those involved in marketing, delivery, and after-sales service to be *marketing*. Thus establishing distinctive competencies in primary value-creation activities means establishing them in manufacturing and marketing.

Support activities provide the inputs that allow the primary activities of manufacturing and marketing to take place. The *materials-management function* controls the transmission of physical materials through the value chain, from procurement through operations and into distribution. The efficiency with which

FIGURE 4.1   The value chain

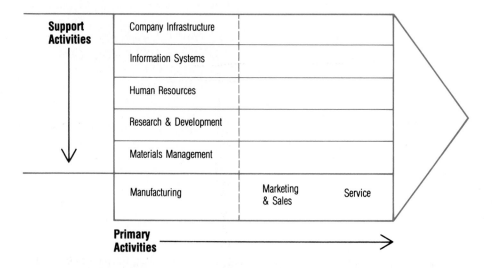

this movement is carried out can significantly lower the cost of value creation. In addition, effective materials management can monitor the quality of inputs to manufacturing, thereby increasing the quality of a company's outputs and facilitating premium pricing. The *R&D function* develops new product and process technologies. Technological developments can lower manufacturing costs and result in the creation of more attractive products that demand a premium price. Thus R&D can affect primary manufacturing and marketing activities and, through them, value creation. The *human-resources function* ensures that the company has the right mix of people to perform its primary manufacturing and marketing activities and that it meets the staffing requirements of other support activities. The *information-systems function* makes certain that management has the information to maximize the efficiency of its value chain and to exploit information-based competitive advantages in the marketplace. Finally, *company infrastructure* consists of a number of activities, including general management, planning, finance, and legal and government affairs. The infrastructure embraces all other activities of the company and can be viewed as setting the context within which they take place. As with primary activities, establishing a distinctive competence in support activities can give the company a competitive advantage.

If a company can gain a distinctive competence in a primary or a support value-creation function, its profit margin will increase. On the other hand, when those functions are weak, the company's value creation will lead to higher cost or to an output that is valued less by consumers. In either case, its profit margin will be squeezed.

4.5 MANUFACTURING

With the rise of low-cost overseas competition, American companies have come to recognize the importance of manufacturing strategy. The objective of a company's manufacturing strategy should be to produce cost-competitive goods that are sufficiently high in quality. If a company can achieve this objective, its manufacturing function can be classified as a strength. If not, manufacturing must be regarded as a weakness. Three factors warrant particular attention in a consideration of manufacturing strategy and manufacturing strengths and weaknesses: the experience curve, the product-process life cycle, and the recent emergence of flexible manufacturing technologies.

The Experience Curve

The concept of the experience curve was popularized by management consultants at the Boston Consulting Group (BCG) in the 1970s, although the basic idea had been around for at least thirty years before that.[7] The experience curve refers to systematic manufacturing-cost reductions that occur over the life of a product.

FIGURE 4.2   **A typical experience curve**

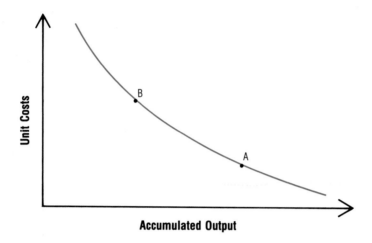

The BCG has noted that manufacturing costs for a product typically decline by some characteristic amount each time *accumulated* output is doubled. The relationship was first observed in the aircraft industry, where it was found that each time accumulated output of airframes was doubled, unit costs typically declined to 80 percent of their previous level.[8] Thus, the fourth airframe typically cost only 80 percent of the second airframe to produce, the eighth airframe only 80 percent of the fourth, the sixteenth only 80 percent of the eighth, and so on. The outcome of this process is a relationship between unit manufacturing costs and accumulated output similar to that illustrated in Figure 4.2.

The strategic significance of the experience curve is clear. It suggests that increasing a company's product volume and market share will also bring cost advantages over the competition. Thus because company A in Figure 4.2 is farther down the experience curve than company B, it has a clear cost advantage over company B. Manufacturing is a strength for company A but a weakness for company B. Two reasons explain the cost reductions that underlie the experience curve: learning effects and plant-level economies of scale.

Learning effects   Learning effects refer to cost savings that come from learning by doing. Labor learns by repetition how best to carry out a task such as assembling airframes. In other words, labor productivity increases over time as individuals learn the most efficient way to perform a particular task. Equally important, it has been observed that in new manufacturing facilities, management typically learns how best to run the new operation. Hence production costs eventually decline because of increasing labor productivity and management efficiency.

Learning effects tend to be most significant in situations where a technologically complex task is repeated, since there is more to learn. Thus learning effects are more significant in an assembly process involving 1,000 complex steps than in an assembly process involving 100 simple steps. No matter how complex a task, however, learning effects typically die out after a limited period of time. Indeed, it has been suggested that they are really important only during the start-up period of a new process and cease after two or three years.[9] Any decline in the experience curve after such a point, therefore, is due to economies of scale.

Economies of scale   Economies of scale at the plant level refer to unit-cost reductions achieved through mass-production techniques. The classic example of such economies is Ford's Model T automobile. The world's first mass-produced car, the Model T Ford was introduced in 1923. Until then it had cost Ford approximately $3,000 (in 1958 dollars) to build and assemble an automobile. By introducing mass-production techniques, the company achieved greater division of labor (that is, splitting assembly into small, repeatable tasks) and specialization and reduced the cost of manufacturing cars to less than $900 per unit (in 1958 dollars) at large output volumes.[10]

As in the Model T case, so in many other situations plant-level scale economies lower costs. Du Pont, for example, was able to reduce the cost of rayon fiber from 53 cents per pound to 17 cents per pound in less than two decades, mainly through plant-level scale economies. But these economies do not continue indefinitely. Indeed, most experts agree that after a certain **minimum efficient scale (MES)** is reached, there are few, if any, plant-level scale economies to be had from expanding volume.[11] Minimum efficient scale refers to the minimum plant size necessary to gain significant economies of scale. In other words, as shown in Figure 4.3, the long-run unit-cost curve of a company is L-shaped. At outputs beyond MES in Figure 4.3, additional cost reductions are hard to achieve.

FIGURE 4.3   A typical long-run unit-cost curve

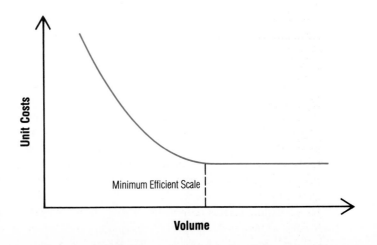

Strategic implications   The experience-curve concept is clearly important. If a company wishes to attain a low-cost position, it must try to ride down the experience curve as quickly as possible. This involves constructing efficient-scale manufacturing facilities, even before the company has the demand, and aggressively pursuing cost reductions from learning effects. The company probably also needs to pursue an aggressive marketing strategy, cutting prices to the bone and stressing heavy sales promotions in order to build up cumulative volume as quickly as possible. Once down the experience curve, the company is likely to have a significant cost advantage vis-à-vis its competitors, for it will have gained a distinctive competence in low-cost manufacturing.

However, the company farthest down the experience curve must not become complacent about its cost advantage—for three reasons. First, since neither learning effects nor economies of scale go on forever, the experience curve is likely to bottom out at some point, and further cost reductions will be hard to achieve. Thus in time other companies can catch up with the cost leader. Once this happens, a number of low-cost companies can have cost parity with each other. In such circumstances, establishing a sustainable competitive advantage must involve strategic factors in addition to the minimization of production costs.

Second, cost advantages gained from experience effects can be made obsolete by the development of new technologies. For example, the price of television picture tubes followed the experience-curve pattern from the introduction of television in the late 1940s until 1963. The average unit price dropped from $34 to $8 (in 1958 dollars) in that time. The advent of color television interrupted the experience curve. Manufacturing picture tubes for color TVs required a new manufacturing technology, and the price for color TV tubes shot up to $51 by 1966. Then the experience curve reasserted itself. The price dropped to $48 in 1968, $37 in 1970, and $36 in 1972.[12] In short, technological change can alter the rules of the game, requiring former low-cost companies to take steps to reestablish their competitive edge.

A final reason for avoiding complacency is that high volume does not necessarily give a company a cost advantage. Some technologies have different cost functions. For example, the steel industry has two alternative manufacturing technologies: an integrated technology based on the basic oxygen furnace and a minimill technology based on the electric arc furnace. As illustrated in Figure 4.4, the electric arc furnace is cost efficient at relatively low volumes, whereas the basic oxygen furnace is most efficient at high volumes. Even when both operations are producing at their most efficient output levels, steel companies with basic oxygen furnaces do not have a cost advantage over minimills. Consequently, the pursuit of experience economies by an integrated company using basic oxygen technology may not bring the kind of cost advantages that a naive reading of the experience-curve phenomenon would lead the company to expect. Indeed, in recent years integrated companies have not been able to get enough orders to run at optimum capacity. Hence their production costs have been considerably higher than those of minimills.[13] More generally, as we shall discuss shortly, in

FIGURE 4.4   Unit production costs in an integrated steel mill and a minimill

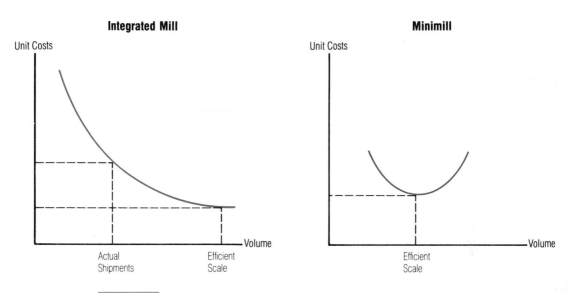

Source: Adapted from D. F. Barnett and R. W. Crandall, *Up From the Ashes: The Rise of the Steel Minimills in the United States* (Washington, D.C.: Brookings Institute, 1986), p. 40. Reprinted by permission.

many industries new flexible manufacturing technologies hold out the promise of allowing small manufacturers to produce at unit costs comparable to those of large assembly-line operations.

The Product-Process Life Cycle

A second concept that has played a role in the development of manufacturing strategy and the identification of manufacturing strengths and weaknesses is the product-process life cycle, originally developed by former Harvard Business School professors Robert H. Hayes and Steven G. Wheelwright.[14] The process-product life cycle suggests that manufacturing efficiency is optimized when a company matches its manufacturing process with its product structure.

Product-process framework   A version of Hayes and Wheelwright's framework appears in Figure 4.5. The horizontal axis summarizes a company's product structure; the vertical axis summarizes different process technologies (process structure). Hayes and Wheelwright suggest that in the first instance manufacturing efficiency is optimized for companies on the diagonal of this matrix.

For example, typical of a company positioned in the upper left-hand corner of the matrix is a commercial printer. In such a company, each job is unique, and

FIGURE 4.5   Product and process structure

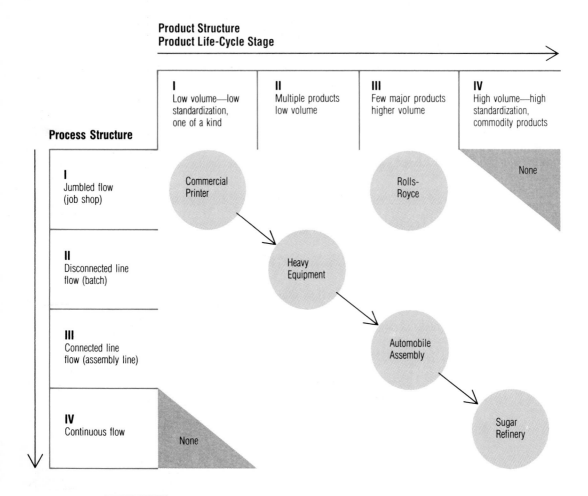

a jumbled flow (or job-shop processing) is usually selected as most effective in meeting product requirements. The characteristics of the product require a flexible, job-shop type of technology. Farther down the diagonal, we find a manufacturer of heavy equipment, such as Caterpillar or Navistar. These companies produce a range of different products, some of which may be customized. The fact that each item is <u>not unique</u> allows the company to attain some economies of scale by moving from a job-shop technology to a disconnected line flow (or batch processing), where batches of a given model proceed irregularly through a series of work stations.

Still farther down the diagonal are mass-production operations such as high-volume auto assembly. The company's product structure is characterized by a limited range of high-volume products. By adopting a connected line flow (or full assembly-line technology), the company can realize significant economies of scale (as in the classic example of the Model T Ford). Finally, in the right-hand corner of the matrix are refinery operations, such as sugar refining and petroleum refining. These operations use continuous-flow technology to manufacture high volumes of a standardized, commodity-type product.

In Figure 4.5, the two shaded corners of the matrix are void of individual companies. The upper right-hand corner characterizes a commodity product produced by a job-shop process. Such an arrangement would be uneconomical, if not impractical. The lower left-hand corner represents a one-of-a-kind product that is made by a continuous-flow process. Again, such an arrangement would not be practical; continuous-flow processes do not have the flexibility to manufacture one-of-a-kind products.

Strategic implications   Hayes and Wheelwright's framework has both static and dynamic implications. From a static perspective, it suggests that matching product structure with process structure is the best way to minimize manufacturing costs. Companies off the diagonal are unlikely to be able to minimize unit costs. For example, the framework suggests that it is not cost efficient for a company to attempt to produce a few high-volume products utilizing a disconnected line flow. Thus, from the perspective of manufacturing costs, a match of product and process structure might be considered a company strength, and a mismatch might be considered a weakness.

However, Hayes and Wheelwright also recognize that under certain conditions it may be profitable for a company to seek a position off the diagonal. For example, Rolls-Royce Motors, Ltd., makes a limited product line of automobiles using a process that is more like a job shop than an assembly line (see Figure 4.5). As a result, Rolls-Royce's manufacturing costs are considerably above those of an automobile company on the diagonal, such as Ford or Chrysler. Nevertheless, because of its reputation for high quality and luxury stemming from its job-shop process, Rolls-Royce can charge a price high enough to cover its high manufacturing costs. In other words, Rolls-Royce carries out its value-creation activities in a way that leads to differentiation and a premium price. It pays Rolls-Royce to be off the diagonal because the company competes primarily on the basis of quality and image rather than cost. A company like Ford, however, has to remain on the diagonal if it is to compete effectively, because Ford competes on the basis of cost (price).

From a dynamic perspective, the main implications of the product-process framework stem from the fact that for some industries at least, industry evolution takes place down the diagonal of the matrix. The first three stages of the product-structure dimension, for example, roughly correspond to the kind of product structures found within companies in the embryonic, growth, and maturity phases of an industry's evolution. The implication is that *companies competing on cost* need to match their process structure with the requirements of industry evolution. Thus in embryonic industries a jumbled flow may be most appropriate, whereas in mature industries a connected line flow may work best. However, these relationships are not inevitable. The heavy-equipment industry, for example, has reached maturity, and yet most companies still produce a low volume of multiple products—because that is what the market demands. Nevertheless, from a dynamic perspective, the framework is of some use in predicting how a company should change its process structure to match the stage of industry evolution.

Flexible Manufacturing Technology   Toyota

Implicit in the product-process life-cycle approach to manufacturing strategy is the idea that a tradeoff exists between cost and quality. In order to achieve greater quality, the product-process life cycle suggests that a penalty has to be accepted in the form of greater costs. Recent advances in manufacturing technology are beginning to make this view outdated. In particular, the rise of flexible manufacturing technologies may allow companies to achieve both low costs and high quality simultaneously. The term *flexible manufacturing technology* refers to a collection of computer-based technologies that are designed to (1) increase the utilization of individual machines through better scheduling, (2) reduce set-up times, and (3) improve quality control at all stages of the manufacturing process.

Because of those features, Patricia Nemetz of Eastern Washington University, and Louis Fry, have argued that flexible manufacturing technologies allow companies to be highly responsive to unique customer demands, yet also able to compete on the basis of cost, while maintaining superior quality and dependability.[15] A company using flexible manufacturing technology may be able to produce many small batches of products for different groups of consumers at a cost that at one time could be achieved only through mass production of a highly standardized output. As a result, the age-old tradeoff between cost and quality may be disappearing.[16]

Flexible manufacturing technologies vary in their sophistication and complexity. The two most common technologies are **flexible machine cells** and **flexible manufacturing systems.**[17]

A flexible machine cell is a grouping of various types of machinery, a common materials handler, and a centralized cell controller (computer). Each cell normally contains from four to six machines capable of performing a variety of operations. The typical cell is dedicated to the production of a family of parts or products. The settings on machines are controlled by computer. This type of control allows each cell to switch quickly between the production of different parts or products.

Improved capacity utilization and reductions in work-in-progress and in waste are major benefits of flexible machine cells. Improved capacity utilization results from the reduction in set-up times and from the computer-controlled co-ordination of production flow between machines (which eliminates bottlenecks). The tight coordination between machines also reduces work-in-progress (for example, stockpiles of partly finished products). Reductions in waste result from the ability of computer-controlled machinery to identify how to transform inputs into outputs while producing a minimum of unusable waste material. As a consequence of all these factors, a free-standing machine might be in use 50 percent of the time, but the same machines when grouped into a cell can be used more than 80 percent of the time and produce the same end product with half the waste. Increases in productivity and lower costs are the results.

Flexible manufacturing systems are more complex than cells. A flexible manufacturing system achieves centralized coordination between a number of independent cells by utilizing a sophisticated centralized computer—that is, a computer responsible for coordinating the activities of all the cells in a work place. Flexible manufacturing systems are designed to be efficient for the production of small batches of products or parts. The enhanced coordination of production flow between cells allows for improved logistics in materials handling over that which can be achieved by each cell individually. In addition, by using several cells operating in parallel to perform the same function, the production process does not come to a halt if a single cell breaks down. The results include further reductions in work-in-progress and increases in capacity utilization and productivity. The net effect is to reduce costs. At the same time, the centrally controlled materials-handling system allows for the introduction of superior statistical quality-control procedures.

The benefits of installing flexible manufacturing systems can be dramatic. For example, after the introduction of a flexible manufacturing system, General Electric's locomotive operations reduced the time needed to produce locomotive motor frames from sixteen days to sixteen hours. IBM's flexible manufacturing plant in Austin, Texas, can turn out a lap-top computer in less than six minutes, with 75 percent greater efficiency than a conventional plant. Caterpillar Tractor cut its unit costs by 22 percent between 1982 and 1986 after the introduction of cell-based flexible manufacturing technologies. Similarly, after introducing a flexible manufacturing system, Fireplace Manufacturers Inc., one of the country's largest fireplace businesses, reduced scrap left over from the manufacturing process by 60 percent, increased inventory turnover threefold, and increased labor productivity by more than 30 percent.[18]

Nevertheless, reported implementation difficulties have resulted in a failure to realize the potential benefits inherent in flexible manufacturing systems. The difficulties seem to arise from a failure to understand the full benefits of flexible manufacturing technologies and a lack of integration of the manufacturing function with other functions of the firm.[19] If flexible manufacturing technologies are to realize their promise, they need to be closely integrated with other functions. For example, integration with R&D allows engineers to design products for efficient manufacturing. In addition, integration with materials management allows for the efficient implementation of just-in-time inventory systems, which are necessary for improved logistics. Both of these issues are discussed in subsequent sections of this chapter.

4.6 MARKETING

In recent years there has been an increasing tendency to view marketing (as well as manufacturing) from a strategic perspective.[20] Three key decision areas are central to strategic marketing management and the development of marketing competencies: (1) the selection of target market segments that determine *where* the company will compete; (2) the design of the marketing mix (price, promotion, product, place) that determines *how* the company will compete in these target markets; and (3) positioning strategy. A company that performs each of these tasks well can create a differential advantage for itself in the marketplace. The marketing function is a strength for such a company. If a company fails to create a differential advantage, its marketing function must be regarded as a weakness.

Selection of Target Market Segments

Markets are rarely homogeneous (except in the cases of certain commodities). The typical market is made up of different types of buyers with diverse wants regarding such critical factors as product characteristics, price, distribution channels, and service. A market segment is a group of buyers with similar purchasing characteristics. For example, the auto market might be divided into a compact segment, a status segment, a sports vehicle segment, and so on.

The critical strategic choice that a company faces is how to position itself vis-à-vis different market segments. It has three basic alternatives (see Figure 4.6). In **undifferentiated marketing,** a single marketing mix is offered to the entire market. This strategy rarely succeeds, given the different demands of different segments. In **differentiated marketing,** a different marketing mix is offered to each segment served. In **focused marketing,** the company competes in just one segment and develops the most effective marketing mix to serve that segment.

The classic example showing why undifferentiated marketing is normally a major weakness is the strategy that Ford adopted for the Model T in the 1920s. To minimize production costs, Henry Ford proclaimed that consumers could have any car "as long as it is black." This strategy worked fine until Alfred Sloan of General Motors realized the potential for adopting a differentiated marketing strategy, offering different cars to different segments. Even though differentiation meant that GM spent more than Ford to produce a car, the strategy worked because it recognized the diversity of consumer needs and wants.

FIGURE 4.6   Market segmentation and marketing strategy

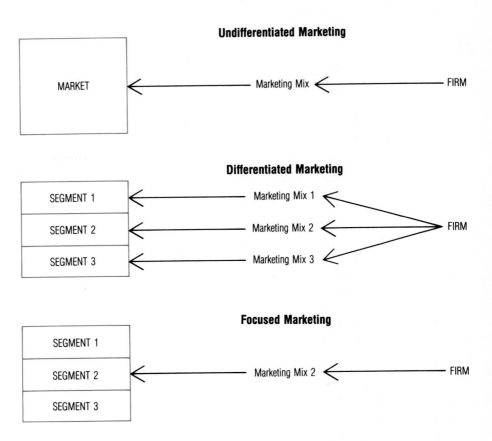

An example of a focused strategy is that pursued by Rolls-Royce. By focusing on the needs of status-conscious high-income consumers, Rolls-Royce has established a profitable niche for itself in the auto industry (and has eliminated the need for the company to adopt a low-cost manufacturing position).

One of the most difficult choices faced by many companies is the choice between a focused and a differentiated marketing strategy. A differentiated marketing strategy lets a company capture customers from many different market segments, thus permitting greater growth. Its drawback is that a broadened customer base may cause the company to lose the unique appeal generated by focusing on just one segment. Rolls-Royce, for example, would probably lose much of its prestige appeal if it began to manufacture compact cars. Making such a choice involves business-level strategy considerations, and we take up this dilemma in the next chapter.

Designing the Marketing Mix

The marketing mix is the set of choices that determine a company's offer to its target market(s). The marketing mix is normally defined in terms of the four P's of marketing: product, price, promotion, and place. Table 4.1 summarizes these main components. A company alters its marketing mix to discriminate among different segments. For example, the market for personal computers consists of a number of segments, including a segment of scientific users, an office segment, an educational segment, and a home-user segment. Each segment is likely to desire different product characteristics (the scientific segment, for example, might require specialist features that other segments do not need). The distribution channels utilized will also vary, as will advertising, promotional, and pricing strategies. Zenith Data Systems Corp., for example, has done well in the educational segment by offering 40 percent price discounts to colleges that buy its PC-compatible machines and by giving away free software to academic and student users as a promotional tool. IBM has excelled in the business segment by capitalizing on its reputation and using its substantial sales force to sell PCs directly to businesses. Hewlett-Packard has done well in the scientific segment by designing its machines to suit the specific requirements of engineers and research scientists.

A company's objective when designing a marketing mix is to try to create a **differential advantage** or to exploit any differential advantage it already has. A differential advantage enables a company to distinguish its offer from that of its competitors in the segments in which it competes. In other words, a differential advantage helps the company establish a distinctive competence, or strength, in marketing. It may be obtained through any element of the marketing mix: creation of a superior product or a more attractive design, better after-sales service, better advertising, more persuasive point-of-sales promotions, and so on. For example, much of IBM's differential advantage stems from name recognition. Caterpillar's comes from its dealer network, spare-parts availability, and reputation for turning out a high-quality product. Anheuser-Busch derives its differential advantage from name recognition of its Budweiser brand beer, as well as

TABLE 4.1   Components of the marketing mix

Product	Price	Promotion	Place
Quality	List price	Advertising	Distributors
Features	Discounts	Sales promotions	Direct selling
Name/reputation	Allowances	Packaging	Retailers
	Credit		Locations
			Inventory
			Transport

from its competitive pricing and promotional skills. In most industries, only by creating a differential advantage can a company ordinarily obtain high profits. Thus companies lacking any differential advantage must view their marketing function as a major weakness.

Positioning

As the final element of marketing strategy, positioning draws on the two earlier principles of marketing strategy: (1) the choice of target market segments that a company decides to focus on and (2) the design of the marketing mix to create a differential advantage that defines how the company will compete with rivals in each segment. For example, Porsche is positioned in the prestige segment of the auto market with a differential advantage based on technical performance. Similarly, Rolls-Royce is positioned in the prestige segment of the auto market with a differential advantage based on status, quality, and luxury. In contrast, Chrysler has positioned itself in a number of different segments of the auto market, including the compact segment, midsize-family-car segment, and high-performance-car segment. A company's success in positioning its products generally determines whether the company has a distinctive competence in marketing or not.

4.7 MATERIALS MANAGEMENT

The role of materials management is to oversee purchasing, production planning and control, and distribution.[21] Sometimes referred to as *logistics management,* materials management is becoming an increasingly important function in many companies because it can help a company both to lower its costs and to boost product quality.

Cost Reductions

For the average U.S. manufacturing enterprise, materials and transport costs account for nearly 60 percent of sales revenues. Minimizing these costs leads to more value. In addition, according to the *Census of Manufactures,* U.S. manufacturing companies annually reinvest four or five times more capital in inventories than in new plant and equipment.[22] Efficient materials management can reduce the amount of cash a company has tied up in inventories, freeing money for investment in plant and equipment.

One technique specifically designed to reduce materials-management costs is the just-in-time (JIT) inventory system. Under a JIT system, inputs are shipped from suppliers to manufacturers at the last possible moment. JIT requires that a company enter into a close relationship with its suppliers. This relationship includes the establishment of computer links between suppliers and the company to facilitate coordination and scheduling. The major cost saving comes from increasing inventory turnover, which reduces inventory-holding costs, such as warehousing and storage costs. For example, Ford's switch to JIT systems in the early 1980s reportedly brought the company a huge one-time saving of $3 billion. At Ford, minimal inventory now turns over nine times a year instead of the former, six, and carrying costs have been reduced by a third.

JIT systems have also helped improve the competitive position of many service companies. For example, Kroger, a nationwide grocery, drug, and convenience store, grades its suppliers on the timing of delivery. Goods that are sent too soon increase the space needed to store inventory, slow the turnover, and create the probability that goods will have to be paid for before they are resold. Kroger's grading system allows the company to track suppliers and know which are the most reliable and the fastest.

The drawback of JIT systems is that they leave a company without a buffer stock of inventory. Although inventory stockpiles are inefficient and expensive, they can help tide a company over shortages of inputs brought on by labor disputes among suppliers or other unforeseen disruptions. However, in general, the advantages far outweigh the risks.

In addition to setting up JIT systems with suppliers, effective materials management can assist with internal logistics—that is, with optimizing the flow of materials through the company's manufacturing process and out to buyers. To a large degree, flexible manufacturing systems attempt to replicate JIT principles *within* a company's manufacturing process. Thus, each work cell in a flexible manufacturing cell system is served by a common materials handler that delivers the right parts to the right machines "just in time," thereby further reducing work-in-progress. The function of materials management is to oversee these internal logistics and to coordinate them with external logistics (such as relationships with suppliers) so that the whole system runs smoothly.

Quality Control

Materials management also has an important responsibility for quality control. Utilizing sophisticated statistical quality-control procedures in conjunction with JIT systems, the materials-management function can monitor the quality of inputs from suppliers. By rejecting substandard parts before they enter the manufacturing process, materials management can significantly reduce the number of defects in finished products. In addition, along with manufacturing, materials management should be responsible for monitoring the quality of component parts as they go through the manufacturing process. This monitoring can be done by applying stringent quality-testing procedures to products as they pass from work station to work station. The ultimate objective is to eradicate all defects from finished products.

The long-run results of increased quality control are illustrated in Figure 4.7a. Increased quality control improves the performance reliability of a compa-

FIGURE 4.7a   **The effect of quality on market share**

FIGURE 4.7b   **The effect of quality on costs**

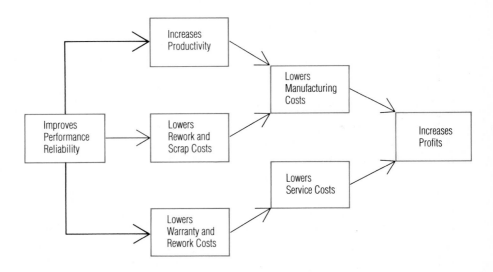

Source: Adapted from "What Does Product Quality Really Mean?" by David A. Garvin, *Sloan Management Review,* 26, Fall 1984, Fig. 1, pp. 37, by permission of the publisher. Copyright © 1984 by the Sloan Management Review Association. All rights reserved.

ny's end product (there are fewer defects). In turn, this increases a company's reputation for quality and may enable a company to charge a premium price for its product. In addition, a reputation for quality may result in an increase in market share, which can help the company realize experience-based scale economies. The overall effect is to increase company profitability.

There is an important relationship between quality control and cost savings.[23] It is illustrated in Figure 4.7b, which shows that increased performance reliability of a company's end products reduces costs from three sources. First, productivity increases because labor time is not wasted assembling poor-quality products that cannot be sold. This saving leads to a direct reduction in unit costs. Second, increased reliability means lower rework and scrap costs. Third, greater product reliability means lower warranty and rework costs. The net effect is to increase value-added by reducing both manufacturing and service costs.

Materials-Management Organization

According to materials-management specialists Jeffrey G. Miller and Peter Gilmour of Harvard Business School, the concept of a materials-management function reflects the fact that purchasing, production, and distribution are not separate activities but three aspects of one basic task: controlling the flow of materials and products from sources of supply through manufacturing and channels of distribution and into the hands of customers—in other words, through the value chain.[24] Tight coordination and control of the flow of materials allow a company to take advantage of cost savings, inventory reductions, and performance improvement opportunities unavailable without a materials-management function.

Despite the cost and quality-control advantages of a materials-management function, according to Miller and Gilmour, only about half of U.S. companies actually operate with such a function. Those that do not include many companies in which purchasing costs, inventories, and customer service levels are important and interdependent aspects of establishing a competitive advantage. Such companies typically operate with a traditional organization structured along the lines illustrated in Figure 4.8a. In such an organization, purchasing, planning and control, and distribution are not integrated. Indeed, planning and control are part of the manufacturing function, and distribution is seen as part of the marketing function. Such companies are unable to establish materials management as a major strength and consequently may face higher production costs. Figure 4.8b shows what a typical materials-management organization looks like. Its purchasing, planning and control, and distribution are all integrated within a single materials-management function. This arrangement allows the company to transform materials management into an important strength, or distinctive competence.

4.8 RESEARCH AND DEVELOPMENT

Investment in research and development often produces spectacular results. Examples include Xerox's twenty-five-year domination of the photocopier market

FIGURE 4.8a   **Traditional reporting relationships**

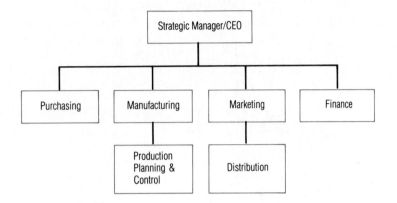

FIGURE 4.8b   **Materials-management organization**

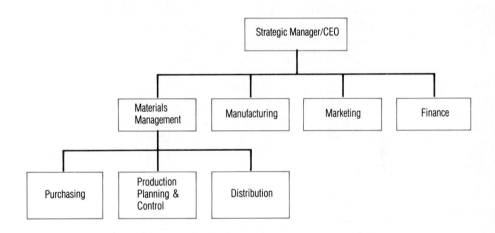

after the company's initial development of the invention; Du Pont's steady stream of inventions such as Cellophane, nylon, Freon (used in all air conditioners), and Teflon (nonstick pans); Sony's development of the Walkman; and Bausch & Lomb's development of contact lenses. However, research and development also involves great risks of failure: Only about 12 to 20 percent of R&D-based projects actually generate profit when they get to the marketplace.[25] The remaining 80 to 88 percent fail. Two well-publicized recent failures were AT&T's losses on its venture into the computer industry (which amounted to a staggering $1.25 billion in 1986) and Sony's development of Betamax video players, which have lost out to VHS systems (in 1986 Betamax had only a 5 percent share of the video player market).[26]

The High Failure Rate of New Products

Four main reasons have been advanced to explain why 80 to 88 percent of new products fail to generate an economic return. The first reason is uncertainty. Developing new products is a risky business. No one can really predict what the demand for a new product will be. Although good market research can reduce the risks of failure, it cannot eradicate them altogether.

Poor commercialization is often cited as a second reason for failure. This occurs when there is an intrinsic demand for a new technology but the technology is not well adapted to consumer needs. One reason many of the early personal computers failed to sell, for example, is that you needed to be a computer programmer to be able to use them. It took Steve Jobs at Apple Computer to understand that if the technology could be made "user friendly" there would be an enormous market for it. Thus, the original personal computers marketed by Apple incorporated little in the way of radical new technology, but they did succeed in making existing technology accessible to the average person.

A third reason for failure is that companies often make the mistake of marketing a technology for which there is not enough demand. One of the best examples is the Anglo-French supersonic jetliner, Concorde. A miracle of high technology, Concorde can carry 140 passengers at twice the speed of sound, reducing the trans-Atlantic flight time by 60 or 70 percent. However, only eight Concordes were ever sold. The reason was simple: At the price that it cost to produce the aircraft, there was never any demand for it. Thus the whole venture was a costly mistake.

A fourth reason for failure is that many companies are slow to get their products to market. The longer the time between initial development and final marketing, the more likely it is that someone else will beat you to market and gain a first-mover advantage.

Nevertheless, despite the high failure rate of new products, a number of companies have managed to establish an undisputed distinctive competence in R&D. These include 3M, Du Pont, Merck, and (despite Betamax) Sony. Such competence can be achieved by formulating an R&D strategy that stresses a close relationship with R&D skills—that is, the risk of failure can be reduced by matching R&D strategy to R&D skills.

R&D Strategy and R&D Skills

A company's R&D strategy can be broken down into three types: (1) strategies of product innovation, aimed at developing entirely new products ahead of competitors; (2) strategies of product development, aimed at improving the quality or features of existing products; and (3) strategies of process innovation, aimed at improving manufacturing to reduce costs and increase quality.[27] The basic R&D skills necessary to support each strategy vary along the lines illustrated in Figure 4.9. They include skills (1) in basic scientific and technological research, (2) in exploiting new scientific and technological knowledge, (3) in project management, (4) in prototype design and development, (5) in integrating R&D with manufacturing, and (6) in integrating R&D with marketing. Possession of these skills constitutes a strength in R&D.

The first two skills require the employment of research scientists and engineers and the establishment of a work environment that fosters creativity. A number of top companies try to achieve this by setting up university-style research facilities where scientists and engineers are given time to work on their own research projects in addition to projects that are linked directly to ongoing company research. At Hewlett-Packard, for example, the company labs are open to engineers around the clock. In addition, Hewlett-Packard encourages its corporate researchers to devote 10 percent of company time to exploring their own ideas—and does not penalize them if they fail. Similarly, at 3M there is the "15 percent

FIGURE 4.9   **Strategy and R&D skills**

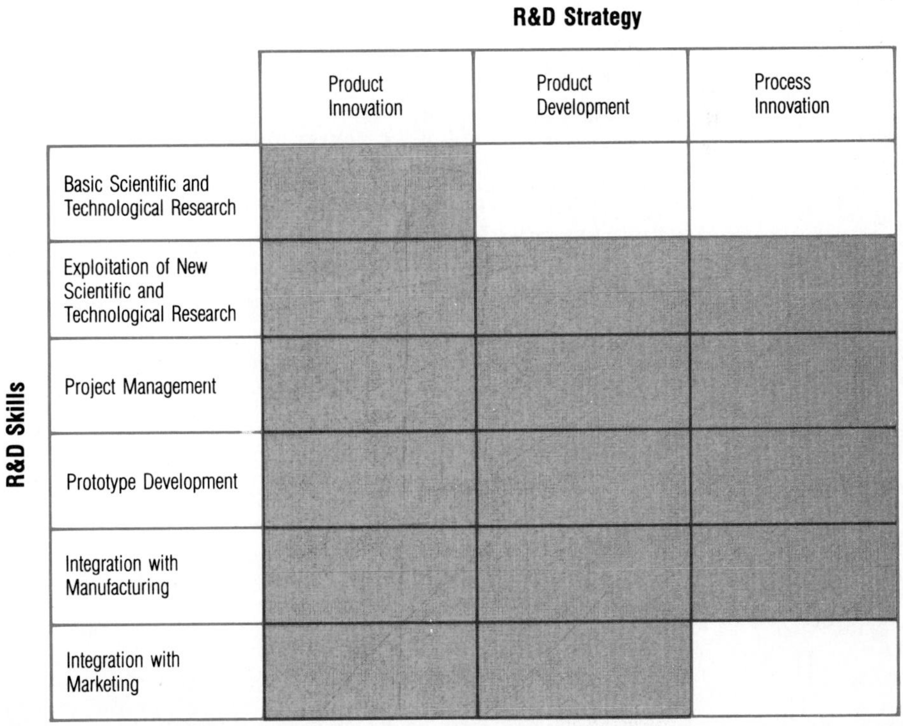

R&D Strategy

R&D Skills	Product Innovation	Product Development	Process Innovation
Basic Scientific and Technological Research	▓		
Exploitation of New Scientific and Technological Research	▓	▓	▓
Project Management	▓	▓	▓
Prototype Development	▓	▓	▓
Integration with Manufacturing	▓	▓	▓
Integration with Marketing	▓	▓	

rule," which allows researchers to spend 15 percent of the workweek researching any topic that they want to investigate, as long as there is the potential of a payoff for the company. The most famous outcome of this policy is the ubiquitous yellow Post-it Notes. The idea for them evolved from a researcher's desire to find a way to keep the bookmark from falling out of his hymn book. Post-its are now a major 3M consumer business, with 1988 revenues of around $300 million.

Project management requires two important skills. The first is the ability to select among competing projects at an early stage of development so that the most promising receive funding and potential costly failures are killed off. The second, which is often overlooked, is the ability to take a new product from its inception to the marketplace in as short a time as possible. This skill is absolutely essential when several companies are racing to get competing products to the market so that they can gain a first-mover advantage. For example, after Intel Corporation's introduction of its powerful 386 microprocessor in 1986, a number of companies, including IBM and Compaq, were racing to be the first to introduce a 386-based personal computer. Compaq beat IBM by six months and gained a major share of the high-power market as a result.

A major reason for Compaq's success is that it utilizes a team approach to project management. The project-management team includes engineers and marketing, manufacturing, and finance people. Each function works in parallel rather than sequentially. While engineers are designing the product, manufacturing people are setting up the manufacturing facilities, marketing people are working on distribution and are planning marketing campaigns, and finance people are working on project funding. The net effect of this approach can be to reduce the time it takes to get a product from the drawing board to the marketplace by over 50 percent when compared with sequential development.

Skills in prototype design and development are particularly important for technologically complex products or processes where major bugs may have to be worked out before the product or process is ready for the market. Prototypes of commercial jetliners, for example, must undergo extensive testing and refinement before mass production can begin.

Skills in integrating R&D with manufacturing are perhaps the most overlooked and yet among the most critical skills of all. The essence of these skills is the ability to design products that are easy to manufacture. The easier products are to manufacture, the lower manufacturing costs are and the less room there is for making mistakes. Designing for manufacturing can lower costs and increase product quality. For example, after Texas Instruments redesigned an infrared sighting mechanism that it supplies to the Pentagon, the company found that it had reduced the number of parts from 47 to 12, reduced the number of assembly steps from 56 to 13, reduced the time spent fabricating metal from 757 minutes per unit to 219 minutes per unit, and reduced unit assembly time from 129 minutes to 20 minutes. The result was a dramatic decline in manufacturing costs and product defects.

Finally, skills in integrating R&D and marketing are crucial if a new product is to be properly commercialized. Without integration with marketing, a company runs the risk of developing products for which there is little or no demand, such as the Concorde.

Product innovation   As Figure 4.9 shows, product innovation requires the most skills. The company must be able to carry out basic research, exploit the results of that research to develop new products, screen new products to select only those that have the greatest probability of success, ensure that it has the ability to manufacture these products, and make certain that there is a market for them and that they meet market requirements.

Given the cost of establishing all these skills, only the largest companies in an industry tend to pursue a new product innovation strategy *on a continual basis* (although it is not unusual for small companies to generate important one-time innovations). Only companies such as AT&T, Du Pont, 3M, Hewlett-Packard, and IBM have the requisite funds to support basic research laboratories, and only they can afford to bear the risks. AT&T and IBM, for example, have spent millions of dollars during the last few years in an attempt to develop superconducting materials. Yet despite spectacular advances, both companies predict that another twenty years may pass before they develop marketable products.[28] Clearly, most small and medium-size companies cannot support research efforts on that scale.

Product development   As Figure 4.9 shows, a product development strategy typically involves lower risks than does product innovation. The company is not introducing a totally new product but rather is refining an existing one with a known demand. It does not have to undertake basic research, nor need it develop skills to exploit *new* scientific knowledge and technologies. Instead, the company takes on existing technology and refines or extends the products associated with it. Such companies are often classified as imitators. In the Japanese electronics industry, for example, Sony has been the traditional innovator, and Matsushita Electric Industrial Co., Ltd., with its Panasonic brand, and Sharp Electronics Corporation have been major followers or imitators.

Product development, however, need not mean imitation. One of the most notable developers of products has been Apple Computer. The original founders of Apple took computer technology that had originally been worked out by Intel, Texas Instruments, and NASA and used that technology to develop a dramatic extension of existing computer products—the first personal computer.

Many companies undertake product development on a regular basis to upgrade their own product line continually. Nowhere is this more evident than in the automobile industry: Its annual model changes involve incremental product developments. Leadership in product design, rather than the creation of new markets or the imitation of market innovators, is the distinctive competence being sought. Thus auto companies tend to stress prototype development and integration of R&D with marketing to ensure that new models appeal to consumers. The failure of General Motors to do this in recent years reduced the company's sales and market share at the end of the 1980s.

Process innovation   The motive for process innovation differs from the motive for product innovation and development strategies. In the latter cases, market expansion is normally the primary goal. In the former, the strategic aim is cost reduction and an increase in product quality. Although process innovation does not usually require basic technological and scientific research, it does demand skills to exploit new scientific and technological know-how. Because the goal is related to manufacturing efficiency, close integration between manufacturing and R&D is also called for. Caterpillar's PWAF project, cited in the Opening Incident, is one example of a cost-motivated process innovation. IBM's development of a low-cost assembly line to turn out its PS/2 personal computers is another.

Industry Life-Cycle Factors

Industry life-cycle factors affect the propensity of companies to pursue different R&D strategies.[29] Figure 4.10 illustrates the implications of life-cycle factors for R&D strategies. The rate of new product innovation is greatest in the embryonic

FIGURE 4.10   **R&D strategy over the industry life cycle**

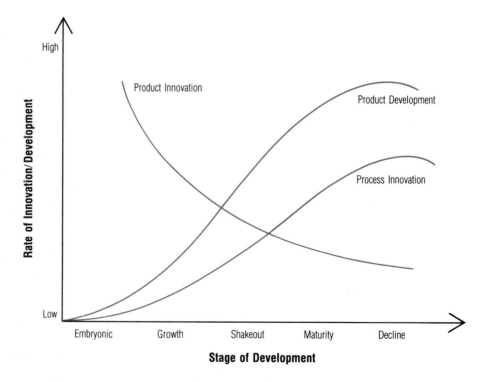

and early growth stages of an industry, falling off thereafter. At those stages, an innovating company has the chance to set the technological context for industry development. That was Sony's thrust when it introduced the Betamax video player. Its innovation lost out to the rival VHS system; however, had Sony succeeded in establishing Betamax as the industry standard, the company would have reaped substantial rewards.

As an industry matures, basic product characteristics become more standardized, and the significance of innovations declines. Complementing this trend, product development strategies become more important. Detroit's obsession with annual model changes is an example of how the phenomenon manifests itself in the auto industry. At maturity, company R&D tends to be oriented less toward basic research and more toward product development and design. A similar trend can be observed with respect to process innovations. Early in an industry's development, rapid growth permits companies with efficient and inefficient manufacturing processes to coexist, but as growth slows and competitive intensity increases, manufacturing efficiency becomes an important precondition for survival. At this stage, companies devote more attention to cost-reducing process innovations. Caterpillar's Plant with a Future and IBM's high-tech personal computer assembly line can be seen as natural responses to the increase in competitive pressure as an industry enters a shakeout.

4.9 HUMAN RESOURCES

"Our people are our greatest resource" is one of the statements most commonly found in corporate annual reports; it is also one of the most important. Without the right people in the right positions, no strategy, however well formulated in other respects, is likely to succeed. This recognition has led to the recent development of strategic human-resource management.[30] Strategic human-resource management has two important objectives: (1) to manage the human resources of a company so as to achieve the highest possible employee commitment and productivity; (2) to match people with a company's short-run and long-run strategic requirements. To achieve the first objective, companies are increasing employee participation in the work process. To achieve the second, companies are adopting work-force planning.

Employee Participation

Poor productivity is the scourge of American industry. Low labor productivity increases the costs of value creation. Low productivity growth relative to our major competitors has contributed to the relative decline in U.S. competitiveness. For example, between 1977 and 1982 U.S. manufacturing productivity grew at a sluggish 0.6 percent per year compared with 2.1 percent in West Germany, 2.7 percent in the United Kingdom, and 3.4 percent in Japan.[31] In response to this problem, many U.S. companies are turning to employee participation to boost productivity and product quality. Quality circles and self-managing teams are perhaps the most significant approaches to participation.

Quality circles   Quality circles were introduced in the United States as long ago as the 1920s. However, they fell into disuse until they were picked up by the Japanese after World War II. Since the late 1970s they have been adopted by an increasingly large number of U.S. businesses. The typical quality circle consists of from five to twelve volunteers drawn from different areas of a function. They meet one or two hours a week to discuss ways of improving quality, efficiency, and the work environment. Quality circles can generate ideas that reduce costs and improve product quality; however, they do not organize work more efficiently or force managers to adopt a participatory style. As a result, they tend to fade away after a few years.

Self-managing teams   Self-managing teams are a relatively recent phenomenon in American industry. Few companies used them until the mid 1980s, but since then they have spread rapidly. The growth of flexible manufacturing cells, which group workers into teams, has undoubtedly facilitated the spread of self-managing teams. The typical team consists of from five to fifteen employees who produce an entire product instead of subunits. Team members learn all tasks and rotate from job to job. A more flexible work force is one result. Team members can fill in for absent coworkers and respond quickly to changes in models and production runs. Teams also take over managerial duties such as work and vacation scheduling, ordering materials, and hiring new members. The greater responsibility that is thrust on team members is seen as a motivator. People generally respond well to being given greater autonomy and responsibility. In addition, performance bonuses linked to team production and quality targets work as a further motivator.

The net effect of these changes is reportedly an increase in productivity of 30 percent or more and a substantial increase in product quality. Further cost savings arise from eliminating supervisors and creating a flatter organizational hierarchy. Perhaps the most potent combination is that of self-managing teams and flexible manufacturing cells. The two seem to be designed for each other. For example, following the introduction of flexible manufacturing technology and work practices based on self-managing teams in 1988, a General Electric plant in Salisbury, North Carolina, increased productivity by a remarkable 250 percent compared with GE plants that produced that same products in 1985.[32] By the same token, however, it must be remembered that teams are no panacea. Unless they are integrated with flexible manufacturing technology, self-managing teams in all probability will fail to live up to their potential.

Work-Force Planning

The aim of a work-force plan is to match people with a company's strategic requirements, both in the short run and in the long run. The critical elements of a work-force plan are (1) forecasts that estimate the company's labor needs, (2) an inventory that establishes whether there is a match between the company's current human resources and future needs, (3) an analysis of the supply and demand for human resources, and (4) the formulation of alternative approaches to head off human-resource imbalances.[33]

4.10 INFORMATION SYSTEMS

We live in an information age. The sharp reduction in the cost of information-systems (IS) technology has allowed computer systems to move from back-office support applications to applications offering a significant competitive advantage.[34] The applications of IS technology are many and embrace all the primary and support activities of the value chain. Table 4.2 offers examples of applications and shows that IS technology enhances a company's control over its costs and helps create a differential advantage.

TABLE 4.2   Examples of information systems applications

Activities	Applications	Implications
Manufacturing	Computer-controlled manufacturing systems	Lower costs/better quality control
Marketing	Telemarketing	Increased orders/differential advantage
	Remote terminals for salespersons	Increased orders/differential advantage
	Electronic market research	Increased orders/differential advantage
Materials management	Automated warehousing/just-in-time inventory systems	Lower costs
	Automated order processing	Lower costs
	Computer-scheduled distribution	Lower costs
Research and development	Computer-aided design	Lower costs/differential advantage
Human resources	Automated personnel scheduling	Lower costs

Specific examples of the strengths of IS technology come from a range of companies: Caterpillar applied IS technology in its PWAF project to manage just-in-time inventory systems and manufacturing cells. Major airlines depend on computer-controlled reservation systems to create a differential advantage and capture customers. Auto manufacturers rely on computer-aided design systems to make fuel-efficient automobiles and speed up product development (thereby lowering costs). Salespeople count on remote computer terminals to help them increase the scope and speed of price quotes. In addition, IS technology has fostered the growth of new products, such as credit cards. It has also enabled companies to change their competitive scope. For example, Dow Jones & Co., Inc., publisher of *The Wall Street Journal,* pioneered a page transmission technology that links seventeen U.S. printing plants to produce a truly national newspaper. Using the same technology, Dow Jones has also started *The Asian Wall Street Journal* and *The Wall Street Journal Europe;* it can maintain control over much of the editorial content while printing the paper in plants all over the world.

According to Michael E. Porter and V. E. Millar, creating a distinctive competence in information systems and exploiting information-based competitive advantages require the following steps[35]:

1. *Assess information intensity.* The first task is to evaluate the existing and potential information intensity of the company's processes and products. An information-intensive manufacturing process is one that involves many complex assembly steps. Assembling an automobile, for instance, requires the bringing together of as many as 7,500 different parts. Clearly, the scope for IS technology to reduce costs through better manufacturing coordination and control is much greater in such a case than in an assembly process involving 20 parts. An information-intensive product is one that has a high information content, such as Dun & Bradstreet's service for corporate analysts.

2. *Identify how IS technology might create a competitive advantage.* Managers need to evaluate in a systematic way how IS technology can create a competitive advantage. This evaluation requires assessing the impact of IS technology on the value chain and on industry competition (that is, on the five competitive forces discussed in Chapter 3), for the stronger the impact of IS technology on the value chain, the greater is the potential change in industry competition. Through investments in IS technology, many companies have succeeded in altering the basis of competition in their favor and have created an IS-based distinctive competence. Citibank N.A. did so in the early 1970s with its introduction of automated teller machines, and American Airlines did so in the 1960s with the introduction of the first computerized reservation system.

3. *Develop a plan for taking advantage of IS technology.* To create or exploit a distinctive competence in IS technology, a systematic IS plan must be worked out. This plan should rank the strategic investments needed in hardware and software, as well as in new product development activities that are necessary

to establish a distinctive competence. Organizational changes reflecting the role that IS technology can play both within functional activities and in linking functional activities need to be recognized. In essence, the IS function needs to be closely integrated with other functions to exploit information-based competitive advantages to their full extent.

If those steps are followed, a company may place itself in a position where it has a distinctive competence in information systems. This support function helps it establish distinctive competencies in other areas, thus contributing toward overall value creation in a number of different ways. By the same token, however, a company that does not develop a distinctive competence in information systems will find its ability to establish distinctive competencies in other areas limited. Low-cost manufacturing and materials management, for example, are difficult to achieve without mastery of IS technologies. Thus strengths in information systems are becoming increasingly important. A company whose information system skills are weak will almost certainly find itself at a competitive disadvantage.

4.11 COMPANY INFRASTRUCTURE

Company infrastructure is the last support function in the value chain. It consists of the activities that set the organizational context within which other support and primary functions take place. Strategic management, planning, finance, accounting, legal affairs, and government relations are all part of the infrastructure. These activities are often viewed as overhead—a somewhat unjust view, since they can be an important source of competitive advantage.[36] By helping a company identify its strengths, weaknesses, opportunities, and threats, planning skills are often a major strength. Many strategic mangers, such as Chrysler's Lee Iacocca, can be considered a company strength. Financial and accounting skills are perhaps among the most important company strengths. The ability of Texas Air to keep on growing by acquisitions in the airline industry, despite depressed profits, can largely be attributed to the company's skills in raising finance and keeping lines of credit open. In addition, legal skills and skills in government relations can also be an important source of competitive advantage, particularly for companies that depend on government contracts for business (such as defense contractors) or for companies that must negotiate with regulatory bodies on a regular basis (such as telephone companies).

More generally, and perhaps more importantly, a company's culture, organizational structure, and internal control systems can all be viewed as part of the infrastructure within which other value-creation activities take place. Organizational structure, control systems, and culture all help define where decisions are made and how processes are managed. They help define the organizational routines or *capabilities* of a company. In turn, as noted early in this chapter, a company's capabilities are major determinants of whether the company has a distinctive competence in one or more of its value-creation activities. Thus, in a very real sense, a company's ability to create value depends on the nature of its infrastructure.

A company's organizational structure and control systems (its capabilities) also help achieve coordination between the different activities of the value chain. Establishing a competitive advantage often requires close coordination between different value-creation activities. We have already observed how coordination between (1) R&D and marketing, (2) R&D and manufacturing, and (3) manufacturing and materials management are all-important preconditions for establishing distinctive competencies. More generally, meeting consumer needs almost always involves coordination among the different activities of the value chain. The role of a company's capabilities in achieving coordination is of the utmost importance.

Given the importance of the company infrastructure—and in particular organization structure, controls, and culture—in establishing capabilities and achieving coordination within the value chain, we shall return to discuss these issues in greater depth in the implementation chapters in Part III.

4.12 FINANCIAL RESOURCES   (436-9)

As already noted, a company's financial position can constitute either a strength or a weakness. Indeed, it can seriously affect the company's ability to build distinctive competencies in other areas, given that doing so often requires substantial investments. The critical considerations here are cash flow, credit position, and liquidity.

Cash Flow

Cash flow—perhaps the most important financial consideration for a company—refers to the surplus of internally generated funds over expenditures. A positive cash flow enables a company to fund new investments without borrowing money from bankers or investors. This ability is obviously a strength, since the company avoids paying interest or dividends. If current operations cannot generate a positive cash flow, the company is in a relatively weak financial position.

A company's cash-flow position often depends on the industry life cycle. In the embryonic and early growth stages of an industry, most companies reinvest all their cash in operations. Companies in such industries are cash hungry. They have to construct manufacturing capacity to meet demand, undertake research to perfect basic product design, and bear marketing expenditures to expand demand for the product. Later in an industry's development, the necessary production facilities will have been built and basic product design features perfected. Consequently, demands for cash tend to be less substantial as an industry matures, enabling companies to generate a strong positive cash flow. Thus cash flow may move from being a weakness to a strength as the company's industry matures.

Credit Position

Even if cash flow is a weakness, a company can still establish a reasonably secure overall financial standing if it has a good credit position. A good credit position can enable a company to expand by using borrowed money. To establish good credit, a company must (1) have a low level of current debt or (2) be viewed by bankers and investors as having good prospects. Many bio-technological companies, for example, have a negative cash flow but a strong overall financial position—because investors are willing to underwrite short-term losses in anticipation of big profit gains from innovations in genetic engineering.

To a large extent, a company's ability to establish a good credit position depends on how the company projects itself to bankers and investors. Companies based in embryonic or high-growth industries have an advantage, since the outlook for their business is generally more positive than for companies based in mature or declining industries. However, even a troubled company based in a highly competitive mature industry can establish good lines of credit if it is able to build up the confidence of investors. This is exactly what Lee Iacocca did in 1979 when he persuaded the U.S. government to underwrite a $1.5-billion loan for Chrysler.

Liquidity   (pp. 436 439)

A company is said to be *liquid* when its current assets exceed its current liabilities. Liquidity takes the form of idle working capital, such as marketable securities, or funding in reserve, such as unused lines of credit. A company's liquidity is a measure of its ability to meet unexpected contingencies—for instance, a sudden dip in demand or a price war. Companies that lack liquidity are in a weak financial position because they may be unable to meet these contingencies. Companies with major investments in fixed assets, such as steel mills or auto plants, tend to be less liquid than companies with a lower level of fixed assets. The reason is that fixed assets cannot be easily translated into cash and often require major fixed costs, which place heavy demands on the company's cash reserves in times of trouble.

4.13 SUMMARY OF CHAPTER

This chapter shows how distinctive competencies arise out of the unique strengths found within a company's individual functions, or value-creation activities. These competencies enable a company to establish a sustainable competitive advantage, whereas their lack places a company at a considerable competitive disadvantage. The pursuit of functional strategies can help a company (1) exploit existing distinctive competencies and (2) establish new distinctive competencies. The main points made in this chapter can be summarized as follows:

1. Distinctive competencies derive from unique company-level strengths. They are the bedrock of a company's strategic advantage. They are based on a company's resources and capabilities. The life span of a competence depends on its durability and imitability.

2. To gain a competitive advantage, a company must either perform value-creation activities at a lower cost than its rivals or perform them in a way that leads to differentiation and a premium price. To do either, a company must have a distinctive competence in one or more of its value-creation functions.

3. Strengths in manufacturing enable a company to minimize manufacturing costs for a given level of product quality. Establishing a distinctive competence in manufacturing involves exploiting experience-curve economies and matching process structure with product structure. A company that attains both of these objectives will find that its manufacturing costs are at least as low as, if not lower than, those of its nearest rivals. In addition, flexible manufacturing systems can give companies a manufacturing-based competitive advantage.

4. Strengths in marketing enable a company to differentiate its product. Establishing a distinctive competence in marketing involves appropriate market segmentation and the design of a marketing mix that enables the company to establish a differential advantage. A company that achieves this will be able to increase volume sold or charge a higher price than a company that does not.

5. Strengths in materials management enable a company to minimize the costs of logistics functions and improve product quality. Establishing a distinctive competence in materials management involves creating a materials-management function that oversees purchasing, production planning, and distribution activities. A company that achieves this will be able to minimize costs in each of these areas and enhance product quality.

6. Strengths in R&D enable a company to create new market opportunities through product innovation, differentiate its product through product development, or minimize product costs for a given quality through process innovation. Establishing a distinctive competence in R&D involves matching R&D skills to the requirement of an R&D strategy. Companies that lack appropriate skills will not be able to build an R&D-based competitive advantage.

7. Strengths in human-resource management enable a company to motivate its work force and to match people to strategic labor requirements. Motivating the work force requires the introduction of team-based approaches to production. Establishing a distinctive competence in human resources also involves planning to acquire individuals with the requisite mix of skills and experience.

8. Strengths in information systems enable a company to exploit information-based competitive advantages in other business functions, from manufacturing to human-resource management. Establishing a distinctive competence in information systems involves assessing the information intensity of company products and processes, identifying ways in which information systems can lead to a competitive advantage, and developing a company-wide plan for taking advantage of information systems.

9. A company's infrastructure consists of activities that set the organizational context within which other support and primary functions take place. These activities include general management, planning, finance, accounting, legal affairs, and government relations. A distinctive competence in any of these areas can assist a company in obtaining a sustainable competitive advantage.

10. The most critical components of a company's financial resources are its cash flow, credit, and liquidity positions. A positive cash flow, good credit, and high liquidity constitute strengths, whereas a negative cash flow, poor credit (high debt), and low liquidity are weaknesses.

Discussion Questions

1. What is the purpose of the value chain? How can it assist strategic managers in identifying a company's strengths and weaknesses with respect to (a) operating costs and (b) differentiation?

2. What functional strategies might a company pursue for each of the value-creation activities to minimize its overall operating costs?

3. What functional strategies might a company pursue for each of the value-creation activities to maximize the uniqueness of its product?

4. To what extent are the strategies you listed in response to Question 2 incompatible with the strategies you listed in response to Question 3?

Endnotes

1. W. K. Hall, "Survival Strategies in a Hostile Environment," *Harvard Business Review* (September–October 1980), 75–85.

2. "Caterpillar Is Betting on Pint-sized Machines," *Business Week,* November 25, 1985, p. 41. "For Caterpillar the Metamorphosis Isn't Over," *Business Week,* August 31, 1987,

pp. 72–74. "Where to Find the Top 100s," *Forbes,* July 13, 1987, p. 164.

3. Among others, the source of organizational capabilities has been discussed by the following: Jay Barney, "Organizational Culture: Can It Be a Source of Competitive Advantage?" *Academy of Management Review,* 11 (1986), 656–665; S. A. Lipperman and R. P. Rumelt, "Uncertain Imitability: An Analysis of Inter-Firm Differences Under Competition," *Bell Journal of Economics,* 23 (1982), 418–438; and Richard R. Nelson and Sidney G. Winter, *An Evolutionary Theory of Economic Change* (Cambridge, Mass.: Belknap, 1982).

4. See Edwin Mansfield, "How Economists See R&D," *Harvard Business Review* (November–December 1981), 98–106.

5. Michael E. Porter, *Competitive Advantage: Creating and Sustaining Superior Performance* (New York: Free Press, 1985).

6. Ibid.

7. See W. J. Abernathy and K. Wayne, "Limits of the Learning Curve," *Harvard Business Review* (September–October 1974), 109–119; Boston Consulting Group, *Perspectives on Experience* (Boston: Boston Consulting Group, 1972); G. Hall and S. Howell, "The Experience Curve from an Economist's Perspective," *Strategic Management Journal,* 6 (1985), 197–212; and W. B. Hirschmann, "Profit from the Learning Curve," *Harvard Business Review* (January–February 1964), 125–139.

8. A. A. Alchian, "Reliability of Progress Curves in Airframe Production," *Econometrica,* 31 (1963), 679–693.

9. Hall and Howell, "The Experience Curve," pp. 197–212.

10. Abernathy and Wayne, "Limits of the Learning Curve," pp. 109–119.

11. For example, see F. M. Scherer, A. Beckenstein, E. Kaufer, and R. D. Murphy, *The Economies of Multiplant Operations* (Cambridge, Mass.: Harvard University Press, 1975).

12. Abernathy and Wayne, "Limits of the Learning Curve," pp. 109–119.

13. D. F. Barnett and R. W. Crandall, *Up from the Ashes: The Rise of the Steel Minimill in the United States* (Washington, D.C.: Brookings Institute, 1986).

14. For example, see these three articles by Robert H. Hayes and Steven G. Wheelwright: "Link Manufacturing Process and Product Life Cycles," *Harvard Business Review* (January–February 1979), 133–153; "The Dynamics of Process-Product Life Cycles," *Harvard Business Review* (March–April 1979), 127–136; and "Competing Through Manufacturing," *Harvard Business Review* (January–February 1985), 99–109.

15. Patricia Nemetz and Louis Fry, "Flexible Manufacturing Organizations: Implications for Strategy Formulation and Organization," *Academy of Management Review,* 13(4) (1988), 627–638.

16. For further details see Nigel Greenwood, *Implementing Flexible Manufacturing Systems* (New York: Halstead Press, 1986); and Richard Schonberger, *Japanese Manufacturing: Nine Hidden Lessons in Simplicity* (London: Free Press, 1986).

17. This description is based on Patricia Nemetz, "Flexible Manufacturing Strategies, Technologies, and Structures: A Contingency Based Empirical Analysis" (Ph.D. diss. University of Washington, 1990).

18. "Factories That Turn Nuts into Bolts," *U.S. News and World Report,* July 14, 1986, pp. 44–45. Joel Kotkin, "The Great American Revival," *Inc.* (February 1988), 52–63.

19. This was a finding of Nemetz, "Flexible Manufacturing Strategies."

20. For example, see J. M. Hulbert and N. E. Toy, "A Strategic Framework for Marketing Control," *Journal of Marketing,* 41 (1977), 12–20; R. M. Johnson, "Market Segmentation: A Strategic Management Tool," *Journal of Marketing Research,* 8 (1971), 15–23.

21. D. Ammer, "Materials Management as a Profit Center," *Harvard Business Review* (January–February 1969), 49–60. Jeffrey G. Miller and Peter Gilmour, "Materials Managers: Who Needs Them?" *Harvard Business Review* (July–August 1979), 57.

22. Miller and Gilmour, "Materials Managers," p. 57.

23. David Garvin, "What Does Product Quality Really Mean?" *Sloan Management Review,* 26 (1984), 25–44.

24. Miller and Gilmour, "Materials Managers," p. 57.

25. These figures are averages taken from research by Edwin Mansfield and his associates. For example, see Edwin Mansfield, "How Economists see R&D," *Harvard Business Review* (November–December 1981), 98–106; and Edwin Mansfield, J. Rapoport, J. Schnee, S. Wagner, and M. Ham-

burger, *Research and Innovation in the Modern Corporation* (New York: Norton, 1971).

26. For details, see P. Petre, "AT&T's Epic Push into Computers," *Fortune,* May 25, 1987, pp. 42–50.

27. V. Scarpello, W. R. Boulton, and C. W. Hofer, "Reintegrating R&D into Business Strategy," *Journal of Business Strategy,* 6 (Spring 1986), 49–56.

28. See "Our Life Has Changed," *Business Week,* April 6, 1987, pp. 94–100.

29. W. J. Abernathy and J. M. Utterback, "Patterns of Industrial Innovation," *Technology Review,* 80 (1978), 1–9.

30. C. Fomrun, N. Tichy, and M. A. Devanna, *Strategic Human Resource Management* (New York: Wiley, 1983).

31. See Charles W. L. Hill, Michael Hitt, and Robert Hoskisson,

"Declining U.S. Competitiveness: Reflections on a Crisis," *Academy of Management Executive,* 2 (1988), 51–60.

32. John Hoerr, "The Payoff from Teamwork," *Business Week,* July 10, 1989, pp. 56–62.

33. J. Sweet, "How Manpower Development Can Support Your Strategic Plan," *Journal of Business Strategy,* 2 (Summer 1981), 78–81.

34. See F. W. McFarland, "Information Technology Changes the Way You Compete," *Harvard Business Review* (May–June 1984), 98 103; and Michael E. Porter and V. E. Millar, "How Information Gives You a Competitive Advantage," *Harvard Business Review* (July–August 1985), 149–160.

35. Porter and Millar, ibid.

36. Porter, *Competitive Advantage,* p. 43.

Chapter 5

BUSINESS-LEVEL
STRATEGY

5.1 OPENING INCIDENT: HOLIDAY INNS INC.

The history of the Holiday Inns Inc. motel chain is one of the great success stories in American business. Its founder, Kemmons Wilson, vacationing in the early 1950s, found existing motels to be small, expensive, and of unpredictable quality. This discovery, along with the prospect of unprecedented highway travel that would come with the new interstate highway program, triggered a realization: There was an unmet customer need, a gap in the market for quality accommodations. Holiday Inns was to meet that need.

From the beginning, Holiday Inns set the standard for motel features like air conditioning and ice makers, while keeping room rates reasonable.[1] These amenities enhanced the motels' popularity, and a Wilson invention, motel franchising, made rapid expansion possible. By 1960 Holiday Inns motels dotted America's landscape; they could be found in virtually every city and on every major highway. Before the 1960s ended, more than 1,000 of them were in full operation, and occupancy rates averaged 80 percent. The concept of mass accommodation had arrived.

By the 1970s, however, the motel chain was in trouble. The service offered by Holiday Inns appealed to the average traveler, who wanted a standardized product (a room) at an average price. In essence, Holiday Inns had been target-

ing the middle of the hotel-room market. But travelers were beginning to make different demands on hotels and motels. Some wanted luxury and were willing to pay higher prices for better accommodations and service. Others sought low prices and accepted rock-bottom quality and service in exchange. Although the market had fragmented into different groups of customers with different needs, Holiday Inns was still offering an undifferentiated, average-cost, average-quality product.[2]

Holiday Inns missed the change in the market and thus failed to respond appropriately to it, but the competition did not. Companies like Hyatt Corp. siphoned off the top end of the market, where quality and service sold rooms. Chains like Motel 6 and Days Inn captured the basic-quality, low-price end of the market. In between were many specialty chains that appealed to business travelers, families, or self-caterers—people who want to be able to cook in their hotel rooms. Holiday Inns' position was attacked from all sides. The company's earnings declined as occupancy rates dropped drastically, and marginal Holiday Inns motels began to close as competition increased.

Wounded but not dead, Holiday Inns is counterattacking. The original chain has been upgraded to suit quality-oriented travelers. At the same time, to meet the needs of different kinds of travelers, the company has created new hotel and motel chains, including the luxury Holiday Inn Crowne Plazas; the Hampton Inns, which serve the low-price end of the market; and the all-suite Embassy Suites. Holiday Inns has attempted to meet the demands of the many niches, or segments, in today's hotel market. However, although it is still the biggest motel operator, it has lost its leading role in the industry. Now it is simply one company in a mature and overcrowded market.[3]

5.2 OVERVIEW

As the Holiday Inns example suggests, this chapter examines *how a company can compete effectively in a business or industry* and scrutinizes the various strategies that a company can adopt to maximize its competitive advantage and profitability. Chapter 3, on the industry environment, provided concepts for analyzing industry opportunities and threats. Chapter 4 discussed how a company can develop distinctive competencies at the functional level in order to gain a competitive edge. The purpose of Chapter 5 is to consider the business-level strategies that a company can use to compete effectively in the marketplace.

We begin by examining the basis of all business-level strategy: the process of deciding what products to offer, what markets to compete in, and what distinctive competencies to pursue. Second, we discuss three **generic competitive business-level strategies:** cost leadership, differentiation, and focus. The discussion centers on how to organize and combine decisions about product, market, and distinctive competencies so that a company can follow one of the generic strategies. We then look at how the industry lifecycle affects the choice of a generic strategy. Third, we examine the various **investment strategies** that a company may adopt at the business level to match its generic competitive strategies. Two factors are important in the choice of investment strategy: (1) a company's relative competitive strength in the industry and (2) a company's stage in the industry life cycle. By the end of the chapter, you will understand how the successful choice of business-level strategy is a product of matching environmental opportunities and threats (discussed in Chapter 3) to a company's strengths and weaknesses (discussed in Chapter 4). Then in Chapter 6 we extend this analysis and discuss how a company should tailor its business-level strategy to the industry structure in which it competes.

5.3 FOUNDATIONS OF BUSINESS-LEVEL STRATEGY

In Chapter 2, on defining the business, we discussed how Derek F. Abell saw the process of business definition as one involving decisions about (1) customer needs, or what is to be satisfied, (2) customer groups, or who is to be satisfied, and (3) distinctive competencies, or how customer needs are to be satisfied.[4]

These three decisions are at the heart of business-level strategy choice because they provide the sources of a company's competitive advantage over its rivals and determine how the company will compete in a business or industry. Consequently, we need to look at the ways in which companies can gain a competitive advantage at the business level.

Customer Needs and Product Differentiation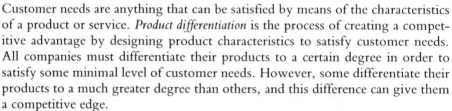

Customer needs are anything that can be satisfied by means of the characteristics of a product or service. *Product differentiation* is the process of creating a competitive advantage by designing product characteristics to satisfy customer needs. All companies must differentiate their products to a certain degree in order to satisfy some minimal level of customer needs. However, some differentiate their products to a much greater degree than others, and this difference can give them a competitive edge.

Some companies offer the customer a low-price product without engaging in much product differentiation.[5] Others seek to create something unique about their products so that they satisfy customer needs in ways that other products cannot. The uniqueness may relate to the physical characteristics of the product, such as quality or reliability, or it may lie in the product's appeal to customers' psychological needs, such as need for prestige or status.[6] Thus a Japanese auto may be differentiated by its reputation for reliability, and a Corvette or a Porsche may be differentiated by its ability to satisfy customers' status needs. Alternatively, product differentiation may be achieved by the number or diversity of models offered by the company. For example, in a recent catalogue, Sony offered twenty-four different 19-inch color television sets aimed at the top end of the market. Similarly, Baskin-Robbins provides at least thirty-one flavors of ice cream aimed at ice-cream lovers, and Foot Locker stocks the largest selection of athletic shoes available to appeal to the greatest number of buyers. Another way to differentiate a product is through a company's distinctive competence, as we discuss below. In practice, the kind of product differentiation that a company pursues is closely linked to the customer groups it serves.

Customer Groups and Market Segmentation

Market segmentation may be defined as the way a company decides to group customers, based on important differences in their needs or preferences, in order to gain a competitive advantage.[7] In general, a company can adopt three alternative strategies toward market segmentation.[8] First, it may choose not to recognize that different groups of customers have different needs and may adopt the approach of serving the average customer. Holiday Inns did this for much of its history. Second, a company may choose to segment its market into different constituencies and develop a product to suit the needs of each group. This approach matches that of Holiday Inns after it lost market share. Third, a company can choose to recognize that the market is segmented but concentrate on servicing only one market segment, or niche.

Why would a company want to make complex product/market choices and create a different product tailored to each market segment rather than create a single product for the whole market? The answer is that the decision to provide many products for many market niches allows a company to satisfy customer needs better. As a result, customer demand for the company's products rises and generates more revenue than would be the case if the company offered just one product for the whole market.[9] The contest between Ford and General Motors back in the 1920s illustrates this point.

Ford produced more motor cars in the 1920s than any other company. It was also the lowest-cost producer, for Henry Ford believed that one product would satisfy the entire market. The strategy worked well until GM's Alfred Sloan recognized the potential of segmenting the market and offering differentiated products.[10] Sloan developed five car divisions—Chevrolet, Pontiac, Oldsmobile, Cadillac, and Buick—each producing a wide range of different kinds of cars. Although this approach cost more, GM could recoup the costs with a differentiated pricing policy: Different car models were directed at different socioeconomic market segments. Because the product policy satisfied different customer needs, it was wildly successful. GM passed Ford in market share and profit and stayed ahead until 1986. Essentially, *Ford and GM made different decisions about which customer groups and customer needs to satisfy, and as a result they obtained different competitive advantages*. Holiday Inns made the same mistake that Ford made in the 1920s. It failed to realize that a company has to respond to customer groups and needs if it is to maximize profitability.

Sometimes, however, the nature of the product or the nature of the industry does not allow much differentiation—for example, bulk chemicals or cement.[11] In these cases, there is little opportunity for obtaining a competitive advantage through product differentiation and market segmentation because there is little opportunity for serving customer needs and customer groups in different ways. Instead, price is the main criterion used by customers to evaluate the product, and the competitive advantage lies with the company providing the lowest-priced product.

Deciding on Distinctive Competencies

The third issue in business-level strategy is to decide what distinctive competence to pursue in order to satisfy customer needs and groups.[12] Here we define *distinctive competence* as the means by which a company attempts to satisfy customer needs and groups in order to obtain a competitive advantage. Thus, for example, some companies use their production technology to develop a distinctive competence in manufacturing as a way of satisfying customer needs. The company tries to ride down the experience curve to provide customers with lower-cost products. Other companies may choose to concentrate on research and development to build a distinctive competence in technology and satisfy customer needs through the design and performance characteristics of their products. Still others may decide to satisfy customer needs by the quality of their service and the responsiveness of service personnel—that is, they may focus on developing competence in sales and marketing. The point is that, in making business strategy choices, a company must decide how to *organize and combine* its distinctive competencies in order to gain a competitive advantage. The source of these distinctive competencies is discussed at length in Chapter 4.

In sum, a product/market/distinctive-competence perspective provides a framework for understanding the foundations of competitive business-level strategy. Each of the generic competitive strategies discussed below is the result of different product/market/distinctive-competence decisions made to obtain a competitive advantage over industry rivals.

5.4 CHOOSING A GENERIC COMPETITIVE STRATEGY AT THE BUSINESS LEVEL

In this section, we examine the strategies that enable companies to compete effectively in a business or industry. Companies pursue a business-level strategy to gain a competitive advantage that allows them to outperform rivals and achieve above-average returns. They can choose from three generic competitive ap-

TABLE 5.1   **Product/market/distinctive-competence choices and generic competitive strategies**

	Cost leadership	Differentiation	Focus
Product differentiation	Low (principally by price)	High (principally by uniqueness)	Low to high (price or uniqueness)
Market segmentation	Low (mass market)	High (many market segments)	Low (one or a few segments)
Distinctive competence	Manufacturing and materials management	Research and development, sales and marketing	Any kind of distinctive competence

proaches: **cost leadership, differentiation,** and **focus.**[13] These strategies are called *generic* because all businesses or industries can pursue them regardless of whether they are manufacturing, service, or not-for-profit enterprises. Each of the generic strategies results from a company's making consistent choices on product, market, and distinctive competencies—choices that reinforce each other. Table 5.1 summarizes the choices appropriate for each generic strategy.

Cost-Leadership Strategy

A company's goal in pursuing a cost-leadership or low-cost strategy is to outperform competitors by producing goods or services at a cost lower than theirs. Two advantages accrue from this strategy. First, because of its lower costs, the cost leader is able to charge a lower price than its competitors yet make the same level of profit as they do. If companies in the industry charge similar prices for their products, the cost leader makes a higher profit than its competitors because of its lower costs. Second, if price wars develop and companies start to compete on price as the industry matures, the cost leader will be able to withstand competition better than the other companies because of its lower costs. For both these reasons, cost leaders are likely to earn above-average returns. But how does a company become the cost leader? It achieves this position by means of the product/market/distinctive-competence choices that it makes to gain a low-cost competitive advantage. Table 5.1 outlines these strategic choices.

Strategic choices   The cost leader chooses a low level of product differentiation. Differentiation is expensive, and if the company produces a wide range of products or expends resources to make its products unique, then its costs rise.[14] The cost leader aims for a level of differentiation not markedly inferior to that of the differentiator (a company that competes by spending resources on product development) but a level obtainable at low cost.[15] The cost leader does not try to be the industry leader in differentiation; it waits until customers want a feature or service before providing it. For example, a cost leader does not introduce stereo sound in television sets. It adds stereo sound only when it is obvious that consumers want it.

The cost leader also normally ignores the different market segments and aims for the average customer, again for the sake of lowest cost. Thus, in product/market terms, the company seeks a level of product differentiation that appeals to the average customer. Even though no customer may be totally happy with the product, the fact that *the company normally charges a lower price than its competitors* puts the product within a customer's range of choices.

The development of a distinctive competence in manufacturing is most important to a low-cost company, which attempts to ride down the experience curve so that it can lower its manufacturing costs. Since the company charges less for its products, it can attract the extra sales volume that allows it to obtain these experience-curve effects (that is, costs go down as production output increases). Besides, cost minimization means matching product and process structures and adopting efficient materials–management techniques. Consequently, the manufacturing and materials-management functions are the center of attention in the cost-leadership company, and the other functions shape their distinctive competencies to meet the needs of manufacturing.[16] For example, the sales function develops the competence of capturing large, stable sets of customer orders that allow manufacturing to make longer production runs and so reduce costs. The research and development function specializes in process improvements to lower the costs of manufacture, as well as product improvements to make production easier. Chrysler, for example, reduced the number of parts involved in manufacturing a car from 75,000 to 40,000 in order to decrease costs.

In short, the cost leader gears all its strategic product/market/distinctive-competence choices to the single goal of squeezing out every cent of production costs to provide a competitive advantage. A company like Heinz is an excellent example of a cost leader. Beans and canned vegetables do not permit much of a markup. The profit comes from the large volume of cans sold (each can having only a small markup). Therefore the H. J. Heinz Company goes to extraordinary lengths to try to reduce costs—by even 1/20th of a cent per can—because this will lead to large cost savings and thus bigger profits over the long run. As you will see in the chapters in Part III on strategy implementation, the other source of cost savings in pursuing cost leadership is the design of the organization structure to match this strategy, since structure is a major source of a company's costs. As we discuss in Chapter 12, a low-cost strategy implies tight production controls and rigorous use of budgets to control the production process.

Advantages and disadvantages   The advantages of each generic strategy are best discussed in terms of Porter's five forces model introduced in Chapter 3.[17] The five forces involve threats from competitors, from powerful suppliers, from powerful buyers, from substitute products, and from new entrants. The cost leader is protected from *prospective competitors* by its cost advantage. Its lower costs also mean that it will be less affected than its competitors by increases in the price of inputs if there are *powerful suppliers* and less affected by a fall in the price it can charge for its products if there are *powerful buyers*. Moreover, since cost leadership usually requires a big market share, the cost leader purchases in relatively large quantities, increasing bargaining power vis-à-vis suppliers. If *substitute products* start to come into the market, the cost leader can reduce its price to compete with them and retain its market share. Finally, the leader's cost advantage constitutes a *barrier to entry,* since other companies are unable to enter the industry and match the leader's costs or prices. The cost leader is therefore relatively safe as long as it can maintain its cost advantage.

The principal dangers of the cost-leadership approach lurk in competitors' ability to find ways of producing at lower cost and beat the cost leader at its own game. For instance, if technological change makes experience-curve economies obsolete, new companies may apply lower-cost technologies that give them a cost advantage over the cost leader. The specialty steel mills discussed in Chapter

3 gained this advantage. Competitors may also draw a cost advantage from labor-cost savings. Foreign competitors in Third World countries have very low labor costs; for example, wage costs in the United States are on the order of 600 or so percent more than in South Korea or Mexico. Many American companies now assemble their products abroad as part of their low-cost strategy; many are forced to do so simply to compete.

Competitors' ability to easily *imitate* the cost leader's methods is another threat to the cost-leadership strategy. For example, the ability of IBM-clone manufacturers to produce IBM-compatible products at costs similar to IBM's (but, of course, sell them at a much lower price) is a major worry for IBM. Finally, the cost-leadership strategy carries a risk that the cost leader, in the single-minded desire to reduce costs, may lose sight of changes in customer tastes. Thus a company may make decisions that reduce costs but drastically affect demand for the product. Holiday Inns experienced that problem. Similarly, the Joseph Schlitz Brewing Co. reduced the quality of its beer's ingredients, substituting inferior grains to reduce costs. Consumers immediately caught on; demand for the product dropped dramatically; and the company was eventually absorbed into the Stroh Brewing Co. As mentioned earlier, the cost leader cannot abandon product differentiation, and even low-priced products, such as Timex watches, cannot be too inferior to the more expensive Seikos if the low-cost/low-price policy is to succeed.

Although all companies try to contain their costs, the cost leader takes an extreme position in this regard and makes all its product/market/distinctive-competence choices with cost minimization in mind. Its ability to charge a lower price is the competitive advantage that allows it to be the industry price setter. However, given the huge growth in low-cost competition from abroad, it appears that cost leadership may become increasingly difficult to pursue in many industries. Even Japanese countries are now experiencing this problem. Their cost edge has been eroded by companies in Taiwan and Korea, such as Gold Star and Samsung, which are now the cost leaders. Japanese companies are increasingly looking to differentiation as a competitive strategy. Honda, for example, began building Acura to compete in the luxury car market, and Toyota and Nissan quickly responded with Lexus and Infiniti, respectively.

Differentiation Strategy

The objective of the generic strategy of differentiation is to achieve a competitive advantage by creating a product or service that is *perceived* by customers to be unique in some important way. The differentiated company's ability to satisfy a customer need in a way that its competitors cannot means that it can charge a **premium price.** The ability to increase revenues by charging premium prices (rather than by reducing costs like the cost leader) allows the differentiator to outperform its competitors and make above-average returns. The premium price is usually substantially above the price charged by the cost leader, and customers pay it because they believe the product's differentiated qualities to be worth the difference. Consequently, the product is priced on the basis of what the market will bear.[18] Thus Mercedes-Benz autos are much more expensive in the United States than in Europe because they confer more status here. Similarly, a basic BMW is not a lot more expensive to produce than an Oldsmobile, but its price is determined by customers who perceive that the prestige of owning a BMW is something worth paying for. Similarly, Rolex watches do not cost much to produce; their design has not changed very much for years; and their gold content is only a fraction of the watch price. Customers, however, buy the Rolex because of the unique quality they perceive in it: its ability to confer status on its wearer. In stereos, the name Bang & Olufsen of Denmark stands out, in jewelry Tiffany & Company, in airplanes Lear jets. All these products command premium prices because of their differentiated qualities.

Strategic choices   As Table 5.1 shows, a differentiator chooses a high level of product differentiation. As noted earlier, product differentiation can be achieved in a wide variety of ways. Procter & Gamble claims that its product quality is high and that Ivory soap is 99.44 percent pure. The Maytag Co. stresses reliability and the best repair record of any washer on the market. Sony emphasizes the quality of its television sets. In technologically complex products, technological features are the source of differentiation, and many people pay a premium price for the items. Differentiation can also be based on *service,* the ability of the company to offer comprehensive after-sales service and product repair—an especially important consideration when one buys complex products such as autos and domestic appliances, which are likely to break down periodically. Companies like IBM and Federal Express have excelled in service and reliability. In service organizations, quality of service attributes are also very important. Why can Neiman-Marcus and Nordstrom charge premium prices? They offer an exceptionally high level of service. Similarly, firms of lawyers or accountants stress the service aspects of their operations to clients: their knowledge, professionalism, and reputation.

Finally, a product's appeal to customers' psychological desires can become a source of differentiation. The appeal can be to prestige or status, as it is with BMWs and Rolex watches; to patriotism, as with buying a Chevrolet; to safety of home and family, as with Prudential Insurance; or to value for money, as with Sears, Roebuck and J. C. Penney. Differentiation can also be tailored to age groups as well as to socioeconomic groups. Indeed, the bases of differentiation are endless.

A company that pursues a differentiation strategy attempts to differentiate itself along as many dimensions as possible. The less it resembles its rivals, the more it is protected from competition and the wider its market appeal. Thus BMWs are not just prestige cars; they also offer technological sophistication, luxury, and reliability, as well as good, although very expensive, repair service. All these bases of differentiation help increase sales.

Generally, a differentiator chooses to segment its market into many niches. Now and then a company offers a product designed for each market niche and chooses to be a **broad differentiator,** but a company might choose to serve just those niches where it has a specific differentiation advantage. For example, Sony produces twenty-four models of television, filling all the niches from midpriced to high-priced sets. However, its lowest-priced model is always priced about $100 above that of its competitors, bringing into play the premium price factor. You have to pay extra for a Sony. Similarly, although Mercedes-Benz has recently filled niches below its old high-priced models with its 190 and 290 series, nobody would claim that Mercedes is going for every market segment. As we mentioned earlier, GM was the first company that tried to fill most of the niches, from the cheapest Chevrolet to the highest-priced Cadillac and Corvette.

Finally, in choosing which distinctive competence to pursue, a differentiated company concentrates on the organization function that provides the sources of its differentiation advantage. Differentiation on the basis of technological competence depends on the research and development function. Attempts to increase market segments are aided by the marketing function. A focus on a specific function does not mean, however, that manufacturing and the control of production costs are unimportant. A differentiator does not want to increase costs unnecessarily and tries to keep them somewhere near those of the cost leader. However, since developing the distinctive competencies needed to provide a differentiation advantage is expensive, a differentiator usually has higher costs than the cost leader. Still, it must control those costs so that the price of the product does not exceed what customers are willing to pay. The cost of producing some differentiated products, such as Rolex watches, is relatively low and the markup is relatively high; in such cases, companies can manipulate the price to match the market segments they serve. Nevertheless, since bigger profits are earned by controlling costs, as well as by maximizing revenues, it pays to control production costs, though not to minimize them to the point of losing the source of differentiation.[19]

Advantages and disadvantages   The advantages of the differentiation strategy can now be discussed in the context of the five forces model. Differentiation safeguards a company against *competitors* to the degree that customers develop **brand loyalty** for its products. Brand loyalty is a very valuable asset because it protects the company on all fronts. For example, *powerful suppliers* are rarely a problem because the differentiated company's strategy is geared more toward the price it can charge than toward the costs of production. Thus a differentiator can tolerate moderate increases in the prices of its inputs better than the cost leader can. Differentiators are unlikely to experience problems with *powerful buyers* because buyers are at their mercy. Only they can supply the product, and they command brand loyalty. Differentiators can pass on price increases to customers because customers are willing to pay the premium price. Differentiation and brand loyalty also create an *entry barrier* for other companies seeking to enter the industry. New companies are forced to develop their own distinctive competence to be able to compete, and doing so is very expensive. Finally, the threat of *substitute products* depends on the ability of competitors' products to meet the same customer needs as the differentiator's products and to break customers' brand loyalty. This can happen, as when IBM-clone manufacturers captured a large share of the home-computer market, but many people are still willing to pay the price for an IBM even though there are many IBM clones about. The issue is how much of a premium price a company can charge for uniqueness before customers switch products.

The main problems with the differentiation strategy center on the company's long-term ability to maintain its perceived uniqueness in customers' eyes. We have seen in the last ten years how quickly competitors move to *imitate and copy* successful differentiators. This has happened in many industries, such as computers, autos, and home electronics. Patents and first-mover advantages—the advantages of being the first to market a product or service—last only so long, and as the overall quality of products goes up, brand loyalty declines. Furthermore, the increasing use of consumer magazines that objectively compare the quality of competing products has helped consumers to become more knowledgeable in the marketplace. The result is that differentiators always have to be one step ahead of their imitators; otherwise, they will get left behind. No longer are consumers afraid of taking a risk. If the price is right and the features are minimally suitable, consumers will switch products, giving the cost leader an advantage over the differentiator.

One final threat to the differentiator is that the source of a company's uniqueness may be overridden by changes in consumer tastes and demands. The Opening Incident describes how Holiday Inns lost its competitive advantage because the market had segmented into complex niches while the company was still serving the needs of the average customer. A company must be constantly on the lookout for ways to match its unique strengths to changing product/market opportunities and threats. Otherwise it will be outperformed by its competitors. Clothing manufacturers know this well, and they change their clothes' styles every year to keep up with consumers' changing tastes.

Thus the disadvantages of this strategy are the ease with which competitors can imitate a differentiator's product and the difficulty of maintaining a premium price.[20] When differentiation stems from the design or physical features of the product, differentiators are at great risk because imitation is easy. The risk is that over time products like VCRs or stereos become *commodity-like* products for which the importance of differentiation diminishes as the price starts to fall. When differentiation stems from service quality or reliability or from any *intangible source,* like the Federal Express guarantee or the prestige of a Rolex, a company is much more secure. It is difficult to imitate intangibles, and the differentiator can reap the benefits of this strategy for the long run.

In summary, strategy of differentiation requires the firm to develop a competitive advantage by making product/market/distinctive-competence choices that reinforce one another and together increase the value of a product or service in the eyes of consumers. When a product has uniqueness in customers' eyes, differentiators can charge a premium price. However, they must watch out for imitators and be careful that they do not charge a price higher than the market will bear. Assessing the price they can charge for the uniqueness of a product is a crucial part of this strategy because the accuracy of the assessment is what determines the long-run profitability of differentiation.

Both Cost Leadership and Differentiation

Recently, changes in production technique—in particular, the development of flexible manufacturing technologies (discussed in Chapter 4)—have made the choice between cost-leadership and differentiation strategies less clear-cut. Because of technological developments it has become increasingly possible for a company to take advantage of the benefits of both. The reason is that the new flexible technologies allow firms to pursue a differentiation strategy at a low cost.

Traditionally, differentiation was obtainable only at high cost because the necessity of producing different models for different market segments meant that firms had to have short production runs, which raise manufacturing costs. In addition, the differentiated firm had to bear higher marketing costs than the cost leader because it was servicing many market segments. As a result, differentiators had higher costs than cost leaders that could produce large batches of standardized products. However, flexible manufacturing may enable a firm pursuing differentiation to manufacture a range of products at a cost comparable to those of the cost leader. The use of robots and flexible manufacturing cells reduces the costs of retooling the production line and the costs associated with small production runs. Indeed, a factor promoting the current trend toward market fragmentation and niche marketing in many consumer goods industries is the substantial reduction of the costs of differentiation by flexible manufacturing.

Another way that a differentiated producer may be able to realize significant scale economies is by standardizing many of the component parts used in its end products. For example, in the mid 1980s Chrysler began to offer twelve different models of cars to different segments of the auto market. However, despite different appearances, all twelve models were based on a common platform, known as the K-car platform. Very different models of K-cars used many of the same components, including axles, drive units, suspensions, and gear boxes. As a result, Chrysler was able to realize significant scale economies in the manufacture and bulk purchase of standardized component parts.

Another way that a firm can reduce both production and marketing costs is by limiting the number of models in the product line by offering packages of options rather than letting consumers decide exactly what options they require. It is increasingly common for auto manufacturers, for example, to offer an economy auto package, a luxury package, and a sports package to appeal to the principal market segments. Package offerings substantially reduce manufacturing costs because long production runs of the various packages are possible. At the same time, the firm is able to focus its advertising and marketing efforts on particular segments so that these costs are also reduced. Once again the firm is getting gains from differentiation and from low cost at the same time.

Just-in-time inventory systems can also help reduce costs and improve the quality and reliability of a company's products. This is important to differentiated firms where quality and reliability are essential ingredients of the product's appeal. Rolls-Royces, for example, are never supposed to break down. Improved quality control enhances a company's reputation and thus allows it to charge a premium price.

Taking advantage of the new production and marketing developments, some firms are managing to reap the gains from cost-leadership and differentiation strategies simultaneously. Since they can charge a premium price for their products compared with the price charged by the pure cost leader, and since they have lower costs than the pure differentiator, they are obtaining at least an equal, and probably a higher, level of profit than firms pursuing only one of the generic strategies. Hence the combined strategy is the most profitable to pursue, and companies are quickly moving to take advantage of the new production, materials-management, and marketing techniques. Indeed, American companies must take advantage of them if they are to regain a competitive advantage, for the Japanese pioneered many of these new developments. This explains why firms like Toyota and Sony are currently much more profitable than their U.S. counterparts, General Motors and Zenith. However, American firms like McDonald's, Apple Computer, and Intel are currently pursuing both strategies simultaneously.

Focus Strategy

The third pure generic competitive strategy, the focus strategy, differs from the other two chiefly because it is directed toward serving the needs of a *limited customer group or segment*. A focused company concentrates on serving a particular market niche, which may be defined geographically, by type of customer, or by segment of the product line.[21] For example, a geographical niche may be defined by region or even by locality. Selecting a niche by type of customer might mean serving only the very rich or the very young or the very adventurous. Concentrating only on a segment of the product line means focusing only on vegetarian foods or on very fast motor cars or on designer clothes. In following a focus strategy, a company is *specializing in* some way.

Having chosen its market segment, a company may pursue a focus strategy through either a differentiation or a low-cost approach. In essence, a focused company is a specialized differentiator or cost leader. Few focus firms are able to pursue both cost leadership and differentiation together because of their small size. If a focus firm uses a low-cost approach, it competes against the cost leader in the market segments where it has no cost disadvantage. For example, in local lumber or cement markets, the focuser has lower transportation costs than the low-cost national company. The focuser may also have a cost advantage because it is producing complex or custom-built products that do not lend themselves easily to economies of scale in production and therefore offer few experience-curve advantages. With a focus strategy, a company concentrates on small-volume custom products, where it has a cost advantage, and leaves the large-volume standardized market to the cost leader.

If a focuser pursues a differentiation approach, then all the means of differentiation that are open to the differentiator are available to the focused company. The point is that the focused company competes with the differentiator in only one or in just a few segments. For example, Porsche, a focused company, competes against General Motors in the sports car segment of the car market but not in other market segments. Focused companies are likely to develop differentiated product qualities successfully because of their knowledge of a small customer set (such as sports car buyers) or knowledge of a region. Furthermore, concentration on a small range of products sometimes allows a focuser to develop innovations faster than a large differentiator. However, the focuser does not attempt to serve all market segments because doing so would bring it into direct competition with the differentiator. Instead, a focused company concentrates on building market share in one market segment and, if successful, may begin to serve more and more market segments and chip away at the differentiator's competitive advantage.

Strategic choices   Table 5.1 shows the specific product/market/distinctive-competence choices made by a focused company. Differentiation can be high or low because the company can pursue a low-cost or a differentiation approach. As for customer groups, a focused company chooses specific niches in which to compete, rather than going for whole market, like the cost leader, or filling a large number of niches, like a broad differentiator. A focuser may pursue any distinctive competence because it can pursue any kind of differentiation or low-cost advantage. Thus it might seek a cost advantage and develop a low-cost manufacturing competence within a region. Or it could develop a service competence based on its ability to serve the needs of regional customers in ways that a national differentiator would find very expensive.

The many avenues that a focused company can take to develop a competitive advantage explain why there are so many small companies in relation to large ones. A company has enormous opportunity to develop its own niche and compete against low-cost and differentiated enterprises, which tend to be larger. A focus strategy provides an opportunity for an entrepreneur to find and then exploit a gap in the market by developing a product that customers cannot do without.[22] The small specialty mills discussed in the preceding chapter are a good example of how focused companies that specialize in one market can grow so efficient that they become the cost leaders. Many large companies started with a focus strategy, and, of course, one means by which companies can expand is to take over other focused companies. For example, Saatchi & Saatchi DFS Compton Inc., a specialist marketing company, grew by taking over several companies that were also specialists in their own market, such as Hay Associates, Inc., the management consultants.

Advantages and disadvantages   A focused company's competitive advantages stem from its distinctive competence. It is protected from *rivals* to the extent that it can provide a product or service that they cannot provide. This ability also gives the focuser power over its *buyers,* because they cannot get the same thing from anyone else. With regard to *powerful suppliers,* however, a focused company is at a disadvantage, because it buys in small volumes and thus is in the suppliers' power. But as long as it can pass on price increases to loyal customers, this disadvantage may not be a significant problem. *Potential entrants* have to overcome the customer loyalty that the focuser has generated; and, in turn, the development of customer loyalty reduces the threat from *substitute products.* This protection from the five forces allows the focuser to earn above-average returns on its investment. Another advantage of the focus strategy is that it permits a company to stay close to its customers and to respond to their changing needs. The problem that a large differentiator sometimes experiences in managing a large number of market segments is not an issue for a focuser.

Since a focuser produces at a small volume, its production costs often exceed those of a low-cost company. Higher costs can also reduce profitability if a focuser is forced to invest heavily in developing a distinctive competence—such as expensive product innovation—in order to compete with a differentiated firm. However, once again flexible manufacturing systems are opening up new opportunities for focused firms: Small production runs become possible at a lower cost. Increasingly, small specialized firms are competing with large companies in specific market segments where their cost disadvantage is much reduced.

A second problem is that the focuser's niche can suddenly disappear because of technological change or changes in consumer tastes. Unlike the more generalist differentiator, a focuser cannot move easily to new niches, given its concentration of resources and competence in one or a few niches. For example, a clothing manufacturer focusing on heavy-metal enthusiasts will find it difficult to shift to other segments if heavy-metal loses its appeal. The disappearance of niches is one reason that so many small companies fail.

Finally, there is the prospect that differentiators will compete for a focuser's niche by offering a product that can satisfy the demands of the focuser's customers; for example, GM's new top-of-the-line models are aimed at BMW and Mercedes-Benz. The cost leader may compete by providing a product whose low price may lure customers into switching; for example, IBM reduced its price to gain market share from the clone manufacturers. A focuser is vulnerable to attack and therefore has to constantly defend its niche.

Being Stuck in the Middle ??

Each generic strategy requires a company to make consistent product/market/ distinctive-competence choices to establish a competitive advantage. In other words, a company must achieve a fit among the three components of business-level strategy. Thus, for example, a low-cost company cannot go for a high level of market segmentation like a differentiator or provide a wide range of products because doing so would raise production costs too much and the company would lose its low-cost advantage. Similarly, a differentiator with a technological competence that tries to reduce its expenditures on research and development, or one that specializes in comprehensive after-sales service and tries to economize on its sales force to reduce costs is asking for trouble because it will lose its competitive advantage as its distinctive competence disappears.

Successful business-level strategy choice involves serious attention to all elements of the competitive plan. There are many examples of companies that, through ignorance or through mistakes, did not do the planning necessary for success in their chosen strategy. Such companies are said to be **stuck in the middle** because they have made product/market choices in such a way that they have been unable to obtain or sustain a competitive advantage.[23] As a result, they have below-average performance and suffer when industry competition intensifies.

Some stuck-in-the-middle companies started out pursuing one of the three generic strategies but made wrong decisions or were subject to environmental changes. Losing control of a generic strategy is very easy unless management keeps close track of the business and its environment, constantly adjusting product/market choices to suit changing industry conditions. We saw in the Opening Incident how this can happen. There are many paths to being stuck in the middle. Sometimes a low-cost company may decide to use some of its profits to diversify into product markets where it has little expertise or to invest in research and development that management thinks may bolster the prestige of the organization. Such actions are expensive and have no guarantee of success. Bad strategic decisions can quickly erode the cost leader's above-average profitability.

Quite commonly, a focuser can get stuck in the middle when it becomes overconfident and starts to act like a broad differentiator. People Express is a good example of a company in this situation. It started out as a specialized carrier serving a narrow market niche: low-priced travel on the Eastern Seaboard. In pursuing this focus strategy based on cost leadership, it was very successful; but when it tried to expand to other geographical regions and began taking over other airlines to increase its number of planes, it lost its niche. People Express became one more carrier in an increasingly competitive market, where it had no special competitive advantage against the other national carriers. The result was financial troubles. People Express was swallowed up by Texas Air and incorporated into Continental Airlines.

Differentiators, too, can fail in the market and end up stuck in the middle if competitors attack their markets with more specialized or low-cost products that blunt their competitive edge. This happened to IBM in the large-frame computer market. The increasing movement toward flexible manufacturing systems will increase the problems faced by cost leaders and differentiators. Many large firms will become stuck in the middle unless they make the investment needed to pursue both strategies simultaneously. No company is safe in the jungle of competition, and each must be constantly on the lookout to exploit competitive advantages as they arise and to defend the advantages it already has.

In sum, successful management of a generic competitive strategy requires strategic managers to attend to two main things. First, they need to ensure that the product/market/distinctive-competence decisions they make are oriented toward one specific competitive strategy. Second, they need to monitor the environment so that they can keep the firm's strengths and weaknesses in tune with changing opportunities and threats.

Generic Strategies and the Industry Life Cycle

In Chapter 3, on analyzing the industry environment, Table 3.3 summarizes how the basis of rivalry among companies changes as their industry ages during the life cycle. The table shows that competition by price and by product differentiation becomes increasingly pronounced at later stages of the industry life cycle. We discuss the effect of these changes on business-level strategy in detail in the next chapter; however, the industry life cycle has several implications for companies pursuing a specific generic strategy. First, it implies that pursuing a cost-leadership strategy is least important at early stages in the life cycle because companies can sell all they can produce. Thus, although low costs help increase profit margins, at the embryonic stage most companies are trying to differentiate their products in order to develop customers' tastes for them.

By the growth stage, however, companies must choose which competitive strategy to follow, because the growth stage is succeeded by the shakeout, where only the strongest survive. Some companies attempt to become the *cost leaders;* others strive to become *differentiators;* still others *focus* their efforts on their chosen niche. Some will be better in making their product/market choices than others, so that by the shakeout stage the companies *stuck in the middle* will be the ones to exit the industry first.

By the maturity stage, an industry is composed of a *collection of companies pursuing each of the generic strategies.* This is where the strategic group concept, discussed in Chapter 3, becomes important. Essentially, all the companies pursuing a low–cost strategy can be viewed as composing one strategic group, and all those pursuing differentiation constitute another; the focusers form a third group.[24] The *mobility barrier* surrounding each group is based on the generic business-level strategy pursued by companies in the group. That is, once a company has made an investment in one generic strategy, changing to another is very expensive, and the expense restricts intra-industry competition. For example, if a company invests resources to develop a distinctive competence in cost leader-ship, it will find entering the differentiator group very difficult because it lacks the extensive sales force or advanced technological competence necessary to com-pete with the differentiator. Similarly, differentiators cannot enter the low-cost group unless they have the capacity to reduce their costs to the level of companies in that group because they *have* made an investment in the necessary sales force or technology. Thus, when strategic groups are based on different generic com-petitive strategies, there is likely to be a stable pattern of industry competition over time.

This is why the development of a cohesive set of product/market/distinctive-competence choices to pursue a generic strategy is so important early on. The strategy sets the scene for profitability in later stages of the industry life cycle because the emergence of strategic groups defined by strategy type simultane-ously protects companies from potential industry entrants and limits the degree to which companies pursuing different strategies can compete against each other.

The advent of companies pursuing both a cost-leadership and a differentia-tion strategy further complicates this picture. As this trend continues, the impli-cation is that these companies will have little trouble attacking the strategic groups presently made up of pure differentiators or pure cost leaders because they possess the competencies of companies already in these groups. Companies pur-suing both strategies simultaneously will become the dominant competitors in an industry—that is, the ones who set industry pricing and output decisions. Increasingly, it appears that firms will be confronting other firms in head-on com-petition, and the battle for competitive advantage will become more acute in the industry setting. We discuss the relationship between business-level strategy and the industry structure environment in considerable detail in the next chapter. There we examine how the gains from a generic competitive strategy also depend on the structure of industry competition and competitive relations between com-panies in the industry.

Summary: Three Generic Strategies

The three generic strategies represent the principal ways in which organizations can compete in an industry. They protect companies from the five forces of com-petition and ultimately, for the companies that survive the shakeout stage, pro-vide protection by means of mobility barriers. However, many companies do fail along the way. Sometimes companies do not continue to develop the functional competencies necessary to sustain their dominance. Sometimes they lose their product differentiation advantage to a competitor. Sometimes the market changes, and the niches or segments they were filling disappear. It is therefore not enough just to choose a generic competitive strategy. If above-average returns are to be consistently obtained, as many resources must be devoted to maintain-ing a competitive strategy as to establishing it. Consequently, if a company is to pursue a generic competitive strategy or develop two strategies simultaneously, it must evaluate the potential returns from the strategy against the cost of the resources that have to be invested in order to develop it. This is the issue to which we now turn.

5.5 CHOOSING AN INVESTMENT STRATEGY AT THE BUSINESS LEVEL

We have been discussing business-level strategy in terms of making product/ market/distinctive-competence choices to gain a competitive advantage. However, there is a second major choice to be made at the business level: the choice of which type of investment strategy to pursue in support of the competitive strategy.[25] An *investment strategy* refers to the amount and type of resources—both human and financial—that must be invested to gain a competitive advantage. Generic competitive strategies provide competitive advantages, but they are expensive to develop and maintain. Differentiation is the most expensive of the three because it requires that a company invest resources in many functions, such as research and development and sales and marketing, to develop distinctive competencies. Cost leadership is less expensive to maintain once the initial investment in a manufacturing plant and equipment has been made. It does not require such sophisticated research and development or marketing efforts. The focus strategy is cheapest because fewer resources are needed to serve one market segment than to serve the whole market.

In deciding on an investment strategy, a company must evaluate the potential returns from investing in a generic competitive strategy against the cost of developing the strategy. In this way, it can determine whether a strategy is likely to be profitable to pursue and how profitability will change as industry competition changes. Two factors are crucial in choosing an investment strategy: the strength of a company's position in an industry relative to its competitors and the stage of the industry life cycle in which the company is competing.[26]

Competitive Position

Two attributes can be used to determine the strength of a company's relative competitive position. First, the larger a company's *market share,* the stronger is its competitive position and the greater are the potential returns from future investment. This is because a large market share provides experience-curve economies and suggests that the company has developed brand loyalty. The strength and uniqueness of a company's *distinctive competencies* are the second measure of competitive position. If it is difficult to imitate a company's research and development expertise, its manufacturing or marketing skills, its knowledge of particular customer segments, or its reputation or brand-name capital, the company's relative competitive position is strong and its returns from the generic strategy increase.

In general, the companies with the largest market share and strongest distinctive competence are in the best position.

These two attributes obviously reinforce one another and explain why some companies get stronger and stronger over time. A unique competence leads to increased demand for the company's products, and then, as a result of larger market share, the company has more resources to invest in developing its distinctive competence. Companies with a smaller market share and little potential for developing a distinctive competence are in a weaker competitive position.[27] Thus they are less attractive sources for investment.

Life-Cycle Effects

The second main factor influencing the investment attractiveness of a generic strategy is the *stage of the industry life cycle*. Each life cycle stage is accompanied by a particular industry environment, presenting different opportunities and threats. Each stage, therefore, has different implications for the investment of resources needed to obtain a competitive advantage. For example, competition is strongest in the shakeout stage of the life cycle and least important in the embryonic stage, so the risks of pursuing a strategy change over time. The difference in risk explains why the potential returns from investing in a competitive strategy depend on the life-cycle stage. Table 5.2 summarizes the relationship among the stage of the life cycle, competitive position, and investment strategy at the business level.

TABLE 5.2   **Choosing an investment strategy at the business level**

		Strong competitive position	Weak competitive position
Stage of industry life cycle	Embryonic	Share building	Share building
	Growth	Growth	Market concentration
	Shakeout	Share increasing	Market concentration or harvest/liquidation
	Maturity	Hold-and-maintain or profit	Harvest or liquidation/divestiture
	Decline	Market concentration, harvest, or asset reduction	Turnaround, liquidation, or divestiture

Choosing an Investment Strategy w/ finance

Embryonic strategy   In the embryonic stage, all companies, weak and strong, emphasize the development of a distinctive competence and a product/market policy. During this stage, investment needs are great because a company has to establish a competitive advantage. Many fledgling companies in the industry are seeking resources to develop a distinctive competence. Thus the appropriate business-level investment strategy is a **share-building strategy.** The aim is to build market share by developing a stable and unique competitive advantage to attract customers who have no knowledge of the company's products.

Companies require large amounts of capital to build research and development competencies or sales and service competencies. They cannot generate much of this capital internally. Thus a company's success depends on its ability to demonstrate a unique competence to attract outside investors, or venture capitalists. If a company gains the resources to develop a distinctive competence, it will be in a relatively stronger competitive position. If it fails, its only option may be to exit the industry. In fact, companies in weak competitive positions at all stages in the life cycle may choose to exit the industry to cut their losses.

Growth strategies   At the growth stage, the task facing a company is to consolidate its position and provide the base it needs to survive the coming shakeout. Thus the appropriate investment strategy is the **growth strategy.** The goal is to maintain a company's relative competitive position in a rapidly expanding market and, if possible, to increase it—in other words, to grow with the expanding market. However, other companies are entering the market and catching up with the industry innovators. As a result, companies require successive waves of capital infusion to maintain the momentum generated by their success in the embryonic stage. For example, differentiators are engaging in massive research and development, and cost leaders are investing in plant to obtain experience-curve economies. All this investment is very expensive.

The growth stage is also the time when companies attempt to consolidate existing market niches and enter new ones so that they can increase their market share. Increasing the level of market segmentation is also expensive. A company has to invest resources to develop a new sales and marketing competence. Consequently, at the growth stage companies fine-tune their competitive strategy and make business-level investment decisions about the relative advantages of a differentiation, low-cost, or focus strategy, given financial needs and relative competitive position. For example, if one company has emerged as the cost leader, the other companies in the industry may decide not to compete head-on with it. Instead, they pursue a growth strategy using a differentiation or focus approach and invest resources in developing unique competencies. Because companies spend a lot of money just to keep up with growth in the market, finding additional resources to develop new skills and competencies is a difficult task for strategic managers.

Companies in a weak competitive position at this stage engage in a **market concentration strategy** to consolidate their position. They move to specialize in some way and adopt a focus strategy in order to reduce their investment needs. If very weak, they may also choose to exit the industry.

Shakeout strategies   By the shakeout stage, demand is increasing slowly and competition by price or product characteristics has become intense. Thus companies in strong competitive positions need resources to invest in a **share-increasing strategy** to attract customers from weak companies that are exiting the market. In other words, companies attempt to maintain and increase market share despite fierce competition. The way companies invest their resources depends on their generic strategy.

For cost leaders, because of the price wars that can occur, investment in cost control is crucial if they are to survive the shakeout stage. Differentiators in a strong competitive position choose to forge ahead and become broad differentiators. Their investment is likely to be oriented toward marketing, and they are likely to develop a sophisticated after-sales service network. They also widen the product range to match the range of customer needs. Differentiators in a weak position reduce their investment burden by withdrawing to a focused strategy—the market concentration strategy—in order to specialize in a particular niche or product. Weak companies exiting the industry engage in a harvest or liquidation strategy, both of which are discussed below.

Maturity strategies   By the maturity stage, a strategic group structure has emerged in the industry, and companies have learned how their competitors will react to their competitive moves. At this point companies want to reap the rewards of their previous investments in developing a generic strategy. Until now profits have been reinvested in the business, and dividends have been small. Investors in strong companies have obtained their rewards through capital appreciation because the company has reinvested most of its capital to maintain and increase market share. As market growth slows in the maturity stage, a company's investment strategy depends on the level of competition in the industry and the source of the company's competitive advantage.

In environments where competition is high because technological change is occurring or where barriers to entry are low, companies need to defend their competitive position. Strategic managers need to continue to invest heavily in maintaining the company's competitive advantage. Both low-cost companies and differentiators adopt a **hold-and-maintain** strategy to support their generic strategies. They expend resources to develop their distinctive competencies so as to remain the market leaders. For example, differentiated companies may invest in improved after-sales service, and low-cost companies may invest in the latest production technologies, such as robotics. Doing so is expensive but is warranted by the revenues that will accrue from maintaining a strong competitive position.

Additionally, companies move to develop both a low-cost and a differentiation strategy simultaneously. Differentiators take advantage of their strong position to develop flexible manufacturing systems in order to reduce their production costs. Cost leaders move to start differentiating their products to expand their market share by serving more market segments. For example, Gallo moved into the premium wine and wine cooler market segments to take advantage of low production costs.

However, when a company is protected from industry competition, it may decide to exploit its competitive advantage to the full by engaging in a **profit strategy.** A company pursuing this strategy attempts to maximize the present returns from its previous investments. Typically, it reinvests proportionally less in its business and increases returns to shareholders. The strategy works well as long as competitive forces remain relatively *constant,* so that the company can maintain the profit margins developed by its competitive strategy. However, the company must constantly remain alert for threats from the environment and must take care not to become complacent and unresponsive to changes in the competitive environment.

All too often market leaders fail to exercise such vigilance, imagining that they are impregnable to competition. For example, General Motors felt secure against foreign car manufacturers until changes in oil prices precipitated a crisis. Kodak, which had profited for so long from its strengths in film processing, was slow to respond to the threat of electronic imaging techniques. Paradoxically, the most successful companies often fail to sense changes in the market. For example, Holiday Inns' failure to perceive changes in customer needs was to some extent the result of its single-minded efforts to develop its existing motel chain. Developing two chains side by side would have required more resources, but that was what the market demanded. A company's ability to raise capital becomes very important in such situations; otherwise, its distinctive competence may disappear.

Companies in a weak competitive position at the maturity stage use the decline strategies discussed below.

Decline strategies   The decline stage of the industry life cycle begins when demand for the industry's product starts to fall. There are many possible reasons for decline, including foreign competition and product substitution. A company may lose its distinctive competence as its rivals enter with new or more efficient technologies. Thus it must decide what investment strategy to adopt in order to deal with new industry circumstances. Table 5.2 lists the strategies that companies can resort to when their competitive position is declining.[28]

The initial strategies that companies can adopt are market concentration and asset reduction.[29] With a **market concentration strategy,** a company attempts to consolidate its product and market choices. It narrows its product range and exits marginal niches in an attempt to redeploy its investments more efficiently and improve its competitive position. Reducing customer needs and the customer groups served may allow the company to pursue a focus strategy in order to survive the decline stage. (As noted earlier, weak companies in the growth stage tend to adopt this strategy.) That is what International Harvester did as the demand for farm machinery fell. It now produces only medium-size trucks under the name Navistar.

An **asset reduction strategy** requires a company to limit or reduce its investment in a business and to extract, or milk, the investment as much as it can. This approach is sometimes called a **harvest strategy** because the company reduces to a minimum the assets it employs in the business and foregoes investment for the sake of immediate profits.[30] A market concentration strategy generally indicates that a company is trying to turn around its business so that it can survive in the long run. A harvest strategy implies that a company will exit the industry once it has harvested all the returns it can. Low-cost companies are more likely to pursue a harvest strategy simply because a smaller market share means higher costs and they are unable to move to a focus strategy. Differentiators, in contrast, have a competitive advantage in this stage if they can move to a focus strategy.

At any stage of the life cycle, companies that are in weak competitive positions may apply **turnaround strategies.**[31] The question that a company has to answer is whether there is a viable way to compete in the industry and how much will such competition cost. If a company is stuck in the middle, then it must assess the investment costs of developing a generic competitive strategy. Perhaps a company pursuing a low-cost strategy has not made the right product or market choices, or a differentiator has been missing niche opportunities. In such cases, the company can redeploy resources and change its competitive strategy.

Sometimes a company's loss of competitiveness may be due to poor strategy implementation. If so, the company must move to change its structure and control systems rather than its strategy. For example, Dan Schendel, a prominent management researcher, found that 74 percent of the turnaround situations he and his colleagues studied were due to inefficient strategy implementation. The strategy-structure fit at the business level is thus very important in determining competitive strength.[32] We discuss it in detail in Chapter 12.

If a company decides that turnaround is not possible, either for competitive or for life-cycle reasons, then the two remaining investment alternatives are **liquidation** and **divestiture.** As the terms imply, the company moves to exit the industry either by liquidating its assets or by selling the whole business. Both can be regarded as radical forms of harvesting strategy because the company is seeking to get back as much as it can from its investment in the business. Often, however, it can only exit at a loss and take a tax write-off. Timing is important, because the earlier a company senses that divestiture is necessary, the more it can get for its assets. There are many stories about companies that buy weak or declining companies, thinking that they can turn them around, and then realize their mistake as the new acquisitions become a drain on their resources. Often the acquired companies have lost their competitive advantage, and the cost of regaining it is too great. However, there have also been spectacular successes, like that achieved by Lee Iacocca, who engaged in a low-cost strategy involving the firing of more than 45 percent of Chrysler's work force.

5.6 SUMMARY OF CHAPTER

The purpose of this chapter is to discuss the factors that must be considered if a company is to develop a business-level strategy that allows it to compete effectively in the marketplace. The formulation of business-level strategy involves matching the opportunities and threats in the environment to the company's strengths and weaknesses by making choices about products, markets, technologies, and the investments necessary to pursue the choices. All companies, from one-person operations to the strategic business units of large corporations, must develop a business strategy if they are to compete effectively and maximize their long-term profitability. The chapter makes the following main points:

1. Selecting a business-level strategy involves two main decisions: (a) choosing a generic competitive strategy and (b) choosing an investment strategy.

2. At the heart of generic competitive strategy are choices concerning product differentiation, market segmentation, and distinctive competence.

3. The combination of those three choices results in the specific form of generic competitive strategy employed by a company.

4. The three generic competitive strategies are cost leadership, differentiation, and focus. Each has advantages and disadvantages. A company must constantly manage its strategy; otherwise, it risks being stuck in the middle.

5. Increasingly, developments in manufacturing technology are allowing firms to pursue both a cost-leadership and a differentiation strategy and thus obtain the economic benefits of both strategies simultaneously. Technical developments also allow small firms to compete with large firms on equal footing in particular market segments and hence increase the number of firms pursuing a focus strategy.

6. The choice of generic competitive strategy is affected by the stage of the industry life cycle.

7. The second choice facing a company is an investment strategy for supporting the competitive strategy. The choice of investment strategy depends on two main factors: (a) the strength of a company's competitive position in the industry and (b) the stage of the industry life cycle.

8. The main types of investment strategy are share building, growth, share increasing, hold-and-maintain, profit, market concentration, asset reduction, harvest, turnaround, liquidation, and divestiture.

Discussion Questions

1. Why does each generic competitive strategy require a different set of product/market/dis-tinctive-competence choices? Give examples of pairs of companies in the (a) computer industry

and (b) auto industry that pursue different competitive strategies.

2. How can companies pursuing a cost-leadership, differentiation, or focus strategy become stuck in the middle? In what ways can they regain their competitive advantage?

3. Over the industry life cycle, what investment strategy choices should be made by (a) differentiators in a strong competitive position and (b) differentiators in a weak competitive position?

4. How do technical developments affect the generic strategies pursued by firms in an industry? How might they do so in the future?

Endnotes

1. "The Holiday Inns Trip: A Breeze for Decades, Bumpy Ride in the '80s," *The Wall Street Journal,* February 11, 1987, p. 1.

2. Holiday Inns, *Annual Report,* 1985.

3. Bureau of Labor Statistics, *U.S. Industrial Outlook* (Washington, D.C., 1986).

4. Derek F. Abell, *Defining the Business: The Starting Point of Strategic Planning* (Englewood Cliffs, N.J.: Prentice-Hall, 1980), p. 169.

5. Michael E. Porter, *Competitive Strategy: Techniques for Analyzing Industries and Competitors* (New York: Free Press, 1980).

6. R. Kotler, *Marketing Management,* 5th ed. (Englewood Cliffs, N.J.: Prentice-Hall, 1984). M. R. Darby and E. Karni, "Free Competition and the Optimal Amount of Fraud," *Journal of Law and Economics,* 16 (1973), 67–86.

7. Abell, *Defining the Business,* p. 8.

8. Michael E. Porter, *Competitive Advantage: Creating and Sustaining Superior Performance* (New York: Free Press, 1985).

9. R. D. Buzzell and F. D. Wiersema, "Successful Share Building Strategies," *Harvard Business Review,* 59 (1981), 135–144. L. W. Phillips, D. R. Chang, and R. D. Buzzell, "Product Quality, Cost Position, and Business Performance: A Test of Some Key Hypotheses," *Journal of Marketing,* 47 (1983), 26–43.

10. Alfred R. Sloan, *My Years at General Motors* (New York: Doubleday, 1972).

11. Porter, *Competitive Strategy,* p. 45.

12. Abell, *Defining the Business,* p. 15.

13. Although many other authors have discussed cost leadership and differentiation as basic competitive approaches (e.g., F. Scherer, *Industrial Market Structure and Economic Performance,* 2nd ed. [Boston: Houghton Mifflin, 1980]), Porter's model (Porter, *Competitive Strategy*) has become the dominant approach. Consequently, this model is the one developed below, and the discussion draws heavily on his definitions. The basic cost-leadership/differentiation dimension has received substantial empirical support (e.g., D. C. Hambrick, "High Profit Strategies in Mature Capital Goods Industries: A Contingency Approach," *Academy of Management Journal,* 26 [1983], 687–707).

14. Porter, *Competitive Advantage,* p. 37.

15. Porter, *Competitive Advantage,* pp. 13–14.

16. D. Miller, "Configurations of Strategy and Structure: Towards a Synthesis," *Strategic Management Journal,* 7 (1986), 217–231.

17. Porter, *Competitive Advantage,* pp. 44–46.

18. Charles W. Hofer and D. Schendel, *Strategy Formulation: Analytical Concepts* (St. Paul, Minn.: West, 1978).

19. W. K. Hall, "Survival Strategies in a Hostile Environment," *Harvard Business Review,* 58(5) (1980), 75–85. Hambrick, "High Profit Strategies in Mature Capital Goods Industries," pp. 687–707.

20. Porter, *Competitive Strategy,* p. 46.

21. Ibid., p. 38.

22. Peter F. Drucker, *The Practice of Management* (New York: Harper, 1954).

23. Porter, *Competitive Strategy*, p. 43.

24. G. Dess and R. Davies, "Porter's (1980) Generic Strategies as Determinants of Strategic Group Membership and Organizational Performance," *Academy of Management Journal*, 27 (1984), 467–488.

25. Hofer and Schendel, *Strategy Formulation*, pp. 102–104.

26. Our discussion of the investment, or posturing, component of business-level strategy draws heavily on Hofer and Schendel's discussion in *Strategy Formulation*, especially Chapter 6.

27. Hofer and Schendel, *Strategy Formulation*, pp. 75–77.

28. K. R. Harrigan, "Strategy Formulation in Declining Industries," *Academy of Management Review*, 5 (1980), 599–604.

29. Hofer and Schendel, *Strategy Formulation*, pp. 169–172.

30. L. R. Feldman and A. L. Page, "Harvesting: The Misunderstood Market Exit Strategy," *Journal of Business Strategy*, 4 (1985), 79–85.

31. C. W. Hofer, "Turnaround Strategies," *Journal of Business Strategy*, 1 (1980), 19–31.

32. Hofer and Schendel, *Strategy Formulation*, p. 172.

Chapter 6

BUSINESS-LEVEL STRATEGY AND INDUSTRY STRUCTURE

6.1 OPENING INCIDENT: THE AIRLINE INDUSTRY

Before deregulation in 1978, competition over fares and ticket prices was not permitted in the airline industry, and the airlines had to find other ways to compete for customers. Their response was to attract customers by offering more frequent flights and better service. However, since they all imitated one another, no airline was able to get a competitive advantage over its rivals, and each airline's costs rose dramatically because of the cost of extra flights, improved meals, and so on. To cover their higher costs, the airlines continuously applied for fare increases. As a result, customers paid higher and higher fares to compensate for the airlines' inefficiency. In an attempt to cure this problem, Congress decided to deregulate the industry and allow competition over ticket prices and free entry into the industry. Although the airlines did not want deregulation (Why should they? They were receiving a nice profit as a protected industry.), deregulation took place in 1979. The result was chaos.

Deregulation destroyed the old competitive rules of the game. Before deregulation, the major airlines knew how they could compete and were able to signal their intentions to one another so they understood each other's competitive moves. In the new world of price competition, entry into the industry was easy, and a host of small airlines entered to compete with the majors. During regulation each airline had not had to develop a generic strategy. There had been no incentive to keep costs low because cost increases could be passed on to consumers; and all firms had used the same means to differentiate themselves, so no airline had a competitive advantage in being unique. With no rules to tell them how to compete and no experience of free competition, the result was a price war as new, low-cost entrants like People Express and Southwest Air sought to gain market share from the majors.

For several years, price competition remained the principal competitive behavior in the airline industry, and the result was a low level of industry profitability. Most airlines lost money. However, by 1988, the airline industry had gone through a shakeout. Many of the new entrants that had precipitated the crisis had either gone bankrupt because of the price wars or had been swallowed up by the majors. Also, the majors had developed sophisticated business-level strategies based on the development of hub-and-spoke networks, which allowed them to build national route structures at low cost. These networks also made it difficult for new firms to enter the industry because the majors held all the available gates at large airports. Through all these means the majors had created new barriers to entry and therefore reduced the threat of new entrants. They were thus in a position to develop new competitive rules of the game to stabilize industry competition and prevent price competition.

Inside the industry, the majors also adopted competitive techniques to reduce the level of competitive rivalry. Very quickly, the airlines imitated one another's pricing policies. On most route segments the prices charged by the airlines diverged by less than 5 percent, and the airlines used market signaling to communicate their intention of making changes such as raising prices. By 1990 they exercised their new market power to start a policy of issuing nonrefundable tickets to reduce their costs and transfer risk to the consumer. Airline profits rocketed. By stabilizing industry competition by means of new competitive rules, they restored industry profitability and set the scene for competition in the 1990s. However, by 1991 the Gulf War had totally altered the industry environment in which the airlines operated, and a new competitive situation arose where not only the profitability but the very survival of many airlines was at stake.

6.2 OVERVIEW

As the Opening Incident suggests, even when companies have developed successful generic competitive strategies and have supported these strategies with appropriate investment strategies, they still face a crucial problem: how to respond to the actions of industry competitors, each of which is seeking to maximize its own competitive advantage and profitability. The purpose of this chapter is to discuss this crucial element of business-level strategy: the management of competitive relations in dynamic industry environments where companies are interdependent—that is, where the outcome of one company's actions depends on the responses of its rivals. Our intention is to show how the success of a company's business-level strategy also depends on the way the company manages the competitive industry environment.

In Chapter 5, we examined how the stages of the industry life cycle affect the choice of generic competitive strategy and investment strategy. The industry life cycle also determines the level and type of competition present in the industry environment, that is, its **industry structure.** Using the concepts developed in Chapter 3 on the industry environment, we start by analyzing the factors that create competition or rivalry in industry relations. Then we turn to the competitive problems that companies encounter in different industry structures and discuss how companies should manage their interactions with other companies in these contexts to maximize their competitive advantage. Different industry structures require different responses by companies if companies individually and the industry as a whole are to be highly profitable. First, we focus on how companies in *fragmented industries* try to develop competitive strategies that support their generic strategies to manage industry relations. Second, we look at the problems of developing and sustaining a first-mover advantage to exploit the potential of a generic competitive strategy in *embryonic and growth industries*. Third, we consider the nature of competitive relations in *mature industries*. Here, we focus on how a set of companies that have been pursuing successful generic competitive strategies can use a variety of competitive techniques to manage the high level of competitive interdependency found in such industries. Finally, we look at the problems of managing a company's generic competitive strategy in *stagnant* or *declining industries* where industry rivalry is high because market demand is slowing or falling. By the end of the chapter, you will understand how the successful pursuit of a generic strategy depends on the selection of the right competitive moves to deal with the actions of industry competitors.

6.3 FACTORS AFFECTING THE LEVEL OF INDUSTRY COMPETITION

Industry competition refers to the manner in which companies in an industry act to obtain a competitive advantage over their rivals. As discussed in Chapter 3, a principal factor affecting the level of industry competition is the nature of an industry's structure. Some industries are fragmented, or have many small companies. Others are consolidated, or have a few large companies. In general, industry competition is highest when there are a few large companies in the market, because the companies are highly interdependent and thus the actions of one company impinge directly on the actions of another. In consolidated industries, companies' cost, pricing, and output decisions—decisions that are the consequence of generic competitive strategy—are *interdependent,* so the potential profitability of any one company can be calculated only if the actions of other companies are taken into account. By contrast, in fragmented industries, companies are small and can be treated as if they are acting in isolation. Thus each company can make its own cost, pricing, and output decisions independent of its competitors. Emerging industries are fragmented because firms are small and are just developing generic strategies.

A second determinant of industry competition is market demand. We have already seen how market demand changes over the industry life cycle and how growing or declining demand affects the level of industry competition. Since market demand is the source of company revenue and industry profits, companies compete for their share of market demand, or market share, at all stages of the life cycle. The different ways in which companies compete when demand is growing, stable, or declining lead to different forms of competitive relations in different industry structures. Once again, companies' pricing and output decisions are crucially affected by the nature of market demand.

Finally, since the profitability of a generic strategy is, in part, a function of the value-added that a company puts into the strategy as a result of investing in its value-creation functions, the cost of developing functional competencies is very important for a company. Consequently, a third factor affecting industry competition is competition for the scarce resources—inputs of all kinds, technological, human, financial—that affect the costs at which value creation takes place and that all companies in an industry are in competition to obtain at the lowest price. Here, we are interested in company strategies toward buyers and suppliers to reduce costs or obtain a differentiation advantage. Some of these strategies are covered in this chapter and some in the next chapter, where we consider vertical integration.

To understand business-level strategy in different industry structures, we have to understand how companies seek to realize the benefits from their generic strategies by formulating these strategies to deal with interdependencies with their rivals, customers, and buyers and suppliers. This is the issue to which we now turn.

6.4 STRATEGY IN FRAGMENTED INDUSTRIES

A fragmented industry is one composed of a large number of small and medium-size companies among whom competitive interdependence is at a minimum. No company by itself is in a strong enough position to influence industry pricing and output decisions, so each company seeks its own best competitive strategy. An industry may consist of many small companies rather than a few large ones for several reasons.[1] If there are few economics of scale to be achieved, entry barriers may be low. Furthermore, customer needs may differ from region to region so that each particular market segment is small. These factors make it hard to obtain a cost advantage, and they make differentiation very difficult. In addition, customer needs may be so specialized that only small job lots of products are required, and thus there is no room for a large mass-production operation to satisfy the market. Finally, if transportation costs are high, regional production may be the only efficient way to satisfy customer needs.

For some fragmented industries, these factors dictate the competitive strategy to pursue, and the focus strategy stands out as a principal choice. Companies may specialize by customer group, customer need, or geographical region, so that a proliferation of small specialty companies operates in local or regional market segments. All kinds of custom-made products—furniture, clothing, rifles, and so on—fall into this category, as do all small service operations that cater to particular customer needs, such as laundries, restaurants, health clubs, and rental stores. Indeed, service companies make up a large proportion of the enterprises in fragmented industries because they provide personalized service to clients and therefore need to be close to clients.

However, if a company can overcome the limitations of a fragmented market, it can often reap the benefits of a cost-leadership or differentiation strategy. Entrepreneurs are eager to gain the cost advantages of pursuing a low-cost strategy or the sales-revenue-enhancing advantages of differentiation by circumventing the problems of a fragmented industry. The returns from consolidating a fragmented industry are often huge. And, of course, during the last twenty-five years many companies have overcome industry structure problems and consolidated many fragmented industries. These companies are large retailers like Wal-Mart Stores, Inc., Sears, and J. C. Penney, fast-food chains like McDonald's and Burger King, as well as chains of health clubs, repair shops, and even lawyers and consultants. What business strategies are these companies using to grow and become the industry leaders?

Chaining

Companies like Wal-Mart Stores and Midas International Corporation are pursuing a *chaining* strategy in order to obtain the advantages of a cost-leadership strategy. They establish networks of linked merchandising outlets that are so interconnected that they function as one large business entity. The amazing buying power that these companies possess through their nationwide store chains allows them to negotiate large price reductions with their suppliers and promotes their competitive advantage. These companies overcome the barrier of high transportation costs by establishing sophisticated regional distribution centers that can economize on inventory costs and maximize responsiveness to the needs of stores and customers (this is Wal-Mart's specialty). Last but not least, they realize economies of scale from the sharing of managerial skills across the chain and from nationwide rather than local advertising.

Franchising

For differentiated companies in fragmented industries, such as McDonald's or Century 21 Real Estate Corporation, the competitive advantage comes from the business strategy of *franchising*. With franchising, a local store operation is both owned and managed by the same person. When the owner is also the manager, he or she is strongly motivated to control the business closely and make sure quality and standards are consistently high so that customer needs are always satisfied. Such motivation is particularly critical in a strategy of differentiation, where it is important for a company to maintain its uniqueness. One reason that industries fragment is the difficulty of maintaining control over, and the uniqueness of, the many small outlets that must be operated. Franchising avoids this problem. In addition, franchising lessens the financial burden of swift expansion, allowing rapid growth of the company. Finally, a differentiator can also reap the advantages of large-scale advertising as well as the purchasing, managerial, and distribution economies of a large company, as McDonald's does very efficiently. Indeed, McDonald's is able to pursue cost leadership and differentiation simultaneously only because franchising allows costs to be controlled locally and differentiation can be achieved by marketing on a national level.

Horizontal Merger

Companies like Dillard's and Texas Air have been choosing a business-level strategy of *horizontal merger* to consolidate their respective industries. Such companies have essentially arranged for the merger of small companies in an industry to create a few large companies. For example, Dillard's arranged for the merger of regional store chains to create a national company; Texas Air bought Eastern and People Express to add to Continental to reduce the number of companies in the airline industry. By pursuing horizontal merger, companies are able to obtain economies of scale or secure a national market for their product. As a result they are able to pursue a cost-leadership or a differentiation strategy.

In fragmented industries, companies can pursue all three business-level strategies: focus, cost leadership, and differentiation. The challenge is to choose the most appropriate means—franchising, chaining, or horizontal merger—of overcoming a fragmented market and thus allowing the advantages of the generic strategy to be realized. The huge increase in franchising and the emergence of chain stores and restaurants in manufacturing and service industries have had a great impact on consumers in the last twenty-five years. Their effect on America has been startling. Identical fast-food chains and stores in every shopping mall are now part of the American scene. It is difficult to think of any major service activities—from consulting and accounting firms to businesses satisfying the smallest consumer need, such as beauty parlors and car-repair shops—that have not been merged and consolidated into chains.

6.5 STRATEGY IN EMBRYONIC AND GROWTH INDUSTRIES

Because economic forces prevent entrepreneurs from consolidating an industry, fragmented industries usually contain a large number of small companies. Embryonic industries often consist of large numbers of small companies because companies are newly formed or created and competitive pressures are still low. Rivalry with competitors, for example, is low for two reasons. First, the rules of the competitive game have yet to be worked out. Second, companies are not yet competing for one another's customers; they are preoccupied with developing their technical competencies. Each company can make competitive moves in relative isolation because there are two main sources of uncertainty: (1) *technological uncertainty* about what product is likely to emerge as the industry norm or leader, about what unique characteristics the product ultimately will possess, and about how it will be manufactured; (2) *strategic uncertainty* about the distinctive competencies and generic competitive strategies that will be the most profitable to pursue in order to satisfy customer needs or groups. In essence, in an embryonic industry several newly formed companies are simultaneously formulating new product/market strategies and are seeking to develop the distinctive competencies that lead to a successful generic competitive strategy.

In this competitive situation, all companies are trying to develop technological innovations that allow them to earn profits higher than their competitors'. The profits may come from product innovations that allow companies to charge a premium price for their products or from process innovations that lower the costs of value creation and increase the quality of output so companies can charge a premium price. However, over time, as the paths to technological success in the new industry environment become established—for example, as dominant product designs emerge from competing technologies—the best ways to compete in the industry become apparent. Furthermore, the high profits earned by the industry innovators act as market signals to potential competitors that want to enter the industry to try to imitate the innovation. As a result, as more and more companies compete to be first with the next round of technical improvements, companies are brought into direct competition and begin to compete for the customers of their rivals.

In this new competitive environment, the innovators who pioneered the development of new products and processes often lose their competitive advantage to the new imitators. Examples are such companies as Royal Crown, which pioneered diet cola only to lose its advantage to Coca-Cola and PepsiCo; EMI, which developed the CAT scanner but lost out to General Electric in the development race; and Bowman, which invented the pocket calculator only to see Texas Instruments reap the long-run rewards of the innovation. Embryonic industry environments present difficult competitive challenges for companies seeking to maintain their competitive advantage into the growth stage of the industry and avoid being also-rans. Why do innovators lose out to the new competitors, and how can they maximize their chances of remaining industry leaders into the growth stage and beyond? These are the issues we now discuss.

Managing First-Mover Advantages to Profit from Innovation

The key to profiting from innovation in embryonic and growth environments is to create, exploit, and sustain a first-mover advantage over industry rivals. A first-mover advantage is the competitive advantage that accrues when a company is first into the market with a new product. This advantage confers on a company a *cost-leadership or a differentiation advantage,* which allows the company to develop a successful generic competitive strategy.

Identifying first-mover advantages   There are four principal first-mover advantages. First, being first into the market may confer a *reputation effect,* which leads to a differentiation advantage. A first mover may be able to build brand loyalty simply by being the pioneer. For example, in England, Hoover was the first company to bring vacuum cleaners to the market, and even today vacuum cleaners are known there as "Hoovers." Similarly, ball-point pens are known as "Bics" after the company that developed them. In computers, Apple Computer obtained a massive reputation effect by being the first to bring a personal computer to market; Microsoft obtained a similar effect from its innovative software.

Second, being the pioneer can confer on a company an experience-curve effect that leads to a low-cost advantage. The first mover may be able to move down the experience curve rapidly, thereby achieving a cost advantage and creating a barrier to entry. For example, Du Pont's development of titanium oxide gave Du Pont a cost advantage that imitators have been unable to match. Third, being first allows a company to pre-empt and take control of scarce assets, thus raising the costs of potential imitators. For example, Alcoa's control of the lowest-cost deposits of bauxite gave it long-term control over aluminum smelting, and Wal-Mart's policy of locating stores in small southern towns that competitors had ignored pre-empted the ability of rivals to target this market segment.

Finally, by being first to the market, a company can tie up customers by making it either very difficult or very expensive for them to switch to the products of competitors—that is, customers incur *switching costs* if they move to a competitor's product. For example, in changing from one particular software package to another, a consumer incurs the costs of learning a new operating system. Similarly, someone who replaces an Apple computer with an IBM model incurs the costs of learning how to operate the IBM hardware.

Exploiting first-mover advantages   To exploit first-mover advantages, a company must try to improve product design and quality in order to build and strengthen reputation effects. It also must invest resources to support the aggressive pricing and marketing efforts required to build brand loyalty and exploit experience-curve effects in the growth stage—that is, it has to invest in developing its generic competitive strategy. If it fails to do either of these things, it is opening the way for existing or potential competitors to overtake it. Kodak, for example, put an early emphasis on product quality and in the 1920s developed sophisticated distribution and after-sales service to protect product quality and build brand loyalty. In contrast, DeHavilland, the early leader in airline manufacturing, experienced increasing technical problems with its jet aircraft that allowed Boeing to capture market share. Similarly, Texas Instruments was able to enter the pocket-calculator industry because Bowman lacked the resources to exploit production and marketing first-mover advantages. The inability to exploit first-mover advantages is the primary reason that innovators fail in the race for industry dominance.

Creating barriers to imitation   The creation of barriers to imitation also prevents competitors from imitating an innovation and protects the first-mover advantage. Barriers slow competitors' responses, allowing the first mover to remain one step ahead in the development process. Even though competitors may copy the first innovation, a company will always be one step ahead of its competition if it can create barriers that allow it to consolidate a first-mover advantage.

Barriers to imitation include patents and secret processes. In some industries, patents are a powerful device for controlling entry into the market. In the chemical and drug industries, patents provide a company with control of the market for many years. In industries such as electronics and aerospace, however, patents often provide only weak protection because they are easy to invent around. Edwin Mansfield of the Wharton Business School found that 60 percent of patented innovations were invented around within four years.[2] Thus secret processes are often better than patents. If a key process can be kept secret, imitation may be difficult and companies should not patent their techniques and hence reveal their methods. For example, Coca-Cola has never patented the formula for Coke.

First-Mover Disadvantages

There are strong advantages to be obtained from being a first mover, and the first-mover advantage is the source of many companies' industry dominance—for example, Xerox, Apple, and McDonald's. Nevertheless, several factors can turn a first-mover advantage into a weakness and make it better to be late, rather than early, into the market.

Resolution of technological uncertainty   Sometimes late movers benefit from the resolution of uncertainty about the technological processes or standards that will become the industry norm. The first mover can become locked into a technology that is rapidly replaced; rapid technological changes can make early investments obsolete. For example, Philco, an early industry leader in semiconductors, invested in a state-of-the-art manufacturing process that was quickly superseded by one developed by Texas Instruments, which became the industry leader. Similarly, Sony, the early leader in video with its Betamax system, failed to convince competitors to make Betamax the industry standard. When VHS became the dominant system, Sony's competitive advantage was eroded.

Resolution of strategic uncertainty   Sometimes late movers can benefit from the resolution of uncertainty about the basis of future competition in an industry. The basis of competition may change as a market develops, and the distinctive competencies that give a company a competitive advantage in the embryonic stage may not be the competencies that will work in the growth stage and beyond. Consequently, a first mover might invest all its resources in developing the wrong strategic capabilities; such a mistake can cause the company to lose its competitive advantage. For example, Apple initially lost out to IBM in personal computers because Apple's strategy emphasized retail distribution and educational use while IBM's emphasized a direct sales force and business use—and business users were the most rapidly growing market segment.

Free-rider effect   Late movers may be able to take advantage of a free ride on a first mover's investments in research and development, buyer education, and the development of the industry's infrastructure, including its purchasing and distribution channels. The first mover bears the costs of educating new customers and creating the market for companies that enter later. IBM is a classic example of a company that waited until the potential for the personal computer was proven before entering the market and rapidly developing a machine to take advantage of its brand name. Apple bore all the up-front costs of proving that the market existed.

Complementary assets   A number of factors can work to a first mover's disadvantage and give late movers a competitive edge. These disadvantages, however, can be overcome by a company that recognizes the need to change with the market and does not rest on its early innovations. The competitive advantage of the brand name achieved from being the first mover can be set against these disadvantages. As long as a company is open to the need to respond to technological and strategic changes, it will be able to handle the challenge by late movers successfully, as Apple has done with IBM. However, the success of a first mover's strategy in the industry growth stage is affected by its ability to develop *complementary assets,* and the existence of barriers to imitation.

Complementary assets are the assets required to exploit core technological know-how and maintain a first-mover advantage. They include (1) competitive manufacturing facilities capable of handling rapid market growth; (2) marketing know-how, a trained sales force, and access to industry distribution systems; (3) after-sales service and support networks; and (4) complementary technology—for example, software to support computer hardware. In essence, a first mover has to develop its value-creation functions and not rely purely on its technological expertise; otherwise, competitors will find it easy to attack the first mover's position as the industry develops.

Developing these competencies is expensive, and companies pursing growth and share-increasing strategies need large infusions of capital. It is for this reason that first movers often lose out to late movers that are large successful companies, established in other industries, that have the resources to develop quickly a presence in the new industry. Moving into an industry that is related to a company's principal industry by technological similarities is an example of pursuing the strategy of related diversification (discussed in the next chapter). A company like 3M is a good example of a company that moves quickly to capitalize on the opportunities presented by the opening of new product markets like those in compact disks and floppy disks. 3M is a late mover to be feared.

Choosing the Right Strategy

Given the advantages and disadvantages of being a first mover in the growth stages of an industry, a company must decide what is the best way to exploit the potential profits from an innovation. In general, the three strategic choices facing a company are (1) to develop and market the technology itself; (2) to develop and market jointly with other companies through a strategic alliance or joint venture; (3) to license the technology to others and let them develop the market. These three strategies and the two factors, complementary assets and barriers to imitation, that affect a company's choice of strategy are summarized in Table 6.1.

In general in a solo venture a first mover prefers to develop and market the technology itself when the company has or can obtain the needed complementary assets quickly *and* can erect high barriers to imitation. Usually, a company must be large to pull this off—that is, the firm must be an established company; however, there are exceptions, such as Apple Computer.

Developing and marketing the technology jointly is the preferred option when a company controls the technology but lacks the resources to build one or more of the complementary assets needed to gain a competitive advantage—that is, the company cannot fund a share-building or a growth strategy. In that situation, a small company will join a large company to capitalize on the potential profits. However, it may be possible to attract venture capitalists to fund the company, although they will demand a large share of the profits. By joining forces with venture capitalists, the company reduces the risk that a large company in a joint alliance will steal the technology and expropriate know-how.

Finally, if barriers to imitation are likely to be hard to develop and maintain because they can be invented around, *and* a company lacks the resources to develop the necessary complementary assets, the best strategy may be to sell or license the technology. The company will collect royalty payments from would-be imitators but faces the risk that they will quickly invent around the technology

TABLE 6.1   **Choosing a competitive strategy in embryonic and growth industries**

Means of developing and marketing technology	Does innovator have complementary assets?	Likely barriers to imitation
Firm in solo venture	Yes	High
Jointly by strategic alliance	No	High
Licensing established firms	No	Low

so that the royalties will soon dry up. RCA had this experience after licensing its color television technology to the Japanese. They quickly superseded RCA's technology and became the market leaders.

Summary: Embryonic and Growth Strategies

In embryonic and growth industries, there are complex industry dynamics to be dealt with if companies are to survive and prosper into the shakeout stage. During the embryonic and growth stages companies must exploit a technological advantage successfully in order to exploit a product market and develop a sustainable generic competitive strategy. Product and process innovation allows companies to charge a premium price for their product or lowers the costs of value creation. The way a company makes its choices in the growth stage determines its future profitability and its ability to cope with the dynamics of industry competition in the mature, consolidated industry setting.

6.6 STRATEGY IN MATURE INDUSTRIES

As a result of fierce competition in the shakeout stage, an industry often becomes consolidated, and so a mature industry is often one composed of a small number of large companies. This is not to suggest that a mature industry does not contain either medium-size companies or a host of small specialized ones. The large companies, however, determine the structure of industry competition because they can influence the five competitive forces. Indeed, these are the companies that developed the most successful generic competitive strategies to deal with the industry environment.

By the end of the shakeout stage, strategic groups composed of companies pursuing similar generic competitive strategies have emerged in the industry. Companies have learned to analyze each other's strategies, and they know that their competitive actions will stimulate a competitive response from rivals in their strategic group and from companies in other groups that may be threatened by their actions. For example, a differentiator that starts to lower prices because it has adopted a more efficient technology not only threatens other differentiators in its group but also threatens low-cost companies that see their competitive edge being eroded away. Hence, by the mature stage of the industry life cycle, *companies have learned the meaning of competitive interdependence*.

In mature industries, companies choose competitive moves and techniques to maximize their competitive advantage *within the structure of industry competition*. Indeed, to understand business-level strategy in mature industries, one must understand how large companies try to collectively, although indirectly (since explicit collusion among companies violates antitrust law), help stabilize industry competition to prevent entry, industry overcapacity, or cutthroat price competition that would hurt all companies. In Chapter 5 we assumed that companies in an industry can pursue a generic strategy successfully, regardless of what other companies are doing. In practice, the issue is more complicated than this because the strategy pursued by one company directly affects other companies. Because each company is trying to make maximum profits, it is bound to come into conflict with its competitors. How, therefore, can companies manage industry competition so as to *simultaneously* protect their individual competitive advantage and maintain industry rules that preserve industry profitability? (Remember that no generic strategy will generate above-average profits if competitive forces are so strong that companies are at the mercy of each other, powerful suppliers, and powerful customers.) The answer is by using competitive moves and techniques to reduce the threat of each competitive force.

In the discussion that follows, we consider the various price and nonprice methods that companies can use to simultaneously build barriers to entry and reduce industry rivalry. We then discuss methods by which firms can manage relationships with suppliers and buyers and ways to counter the threat of substitute products. In general, competitive moves involve product/market decisions concerning *differentiation, pricing, and output.* Differentiation decisions are important because differentiation is expensive and raises a company's costs. Building barriers to entry or managing rivalry through differentiation therefore raises a company's costs. Similarly, pricing decisions are important because lower product prices mean less company and industry profit. If firms are forced to lower prices to deter entry or to compete in the market, profits will be reduced. Finally, output decisions are important because the higher the level of output produced by the industry as a whole, the lower is the price that can be obtained for each unit of output and the lower are revenues. Collectively, companies want to have rules about product/market decisions to deter entry and protect industry profitability. However, at the same time companies individually want to be able to exploit their distinctive competencies by making pricing and output decisions to maximize their competitive advantage. A number of competitive techniques can help accomplish both of these goals.

Market Signaling

All industries start out fragmented, with small companies battling for market share. Then, over time, the leading players emerge, and companies start to interpret each other's competitive moves. *Market signaling* is the first means by which companies attempt to structure industry competition in order to deter entry and control rivalry.[3] Market signaling is the process by which companies convey their intentions to potential entrants and to existing competitors about product/market strategy and how they will compete in the future or how they will react to the competitive moves of their rivals. Market signaling can benefit product/market strategy in several ways.

First, companies may use market signaling to announce that they will respond vigorously to hostile competitive moves that threaten them. For example, companies may signal that if one company starts to cut prices aggressively, they will respond in kind. Or companies may signal that if one company makes a differentiation move—for instance, extends car warranties, as GM did—then all other companies will follow, to maintain the status quo and prevent any company from gaining a competitive advantage. Similarly, companies may signal to potential entrants that if the latter do enter the market, they will fight back by reducing prices or by other aggressive competitive moves. Market signaling *protects* the existing structure of competitive advantages by deterring potential imitators who wish to copy other companies' generic strategies.

Second, market signaling can be used to pre-empt competitors. One company may inform the others that it is proceeding with new product innovations or with investment in new industry production capacity that will provide a competitive advantage that the others will be unable to imitate effectively because their entry into the market will be too late. For example, software companies like Microsoft often announce new operating systems years in advance. The purposes of such an announcement are to deter prospective competitors from making the huge investments necessary to compete with the industry leaders and to let customers know that a company still has the competitive edge so important to retaining consumer loyalty. However, pre-emptive signaling can backfire, as IBM found out when it announced that its new PS/2 operating system would not be compatible with the operating systems presently standard in the industry. Other companies in the industry collectively signaled to IBM and to IBM's customers that they would band together to protect the existing operating systems, thus preserving industry standards and preventing IBM from obtaining a competitive advantage from its new technology. IBM subsequently backed down. A pre-emptive move, therefore, has to be *credible:* Competitors must believe that a company will respond as it signals and stick to its position. If a threat is not credible, the signaling company weakens its position because it cried "wolf."

A third purpose of market signaling is to allow companies to coordinate their actions indirectly and avoid costly competitive moves that lead to a breakdown in industry product policy. One company may signal that it intends to lower prices because it wishes to attract customers who are switching to the products of another industry, not because it wishes to stimulate a price war. On the other hand, signaling can be used to improve industry profitability. The airline industry is a good example of the power of market signaling. In the 1980s signals of lower prices set off price wars. In the 1990s the airlines have used market signaling to obtain uniform price increases. Similarly, the introduction of non-refundable tickets was a market signal by one company that was quickly copied by all other companies in the industry. In sum, market signaling allows companies to give to one another information that enables them to understand each other's competitive product/market strategy and make coordinated competitive moves.

Price Leadership

Price leadership, where one company takes the responsibility for setting industry prices, is a second way of enhancing the profitability of product/market policy among companies in a mature industry.[4] By setting prices, the industry leader implicitly creates the price standards that other companies will follow. The price leader is generally the strongest company in the industry, the one with the best ability to threaten other companies that might cut prices or increase their output to seize more market share. For example, vast oil reserves made Saudi Arabia the price leader in the oil industry and allowed the Saudis to threaten that if other countries raised their output, so would Saudi Arabia, even though the price of oil would decline. Similarly, De Beers controls the price of diamonds because it controls the worldwide distribution of diamonds.

Formal price leadership, or price setting by companies jointly, is illegal under antitrust laws, so the process of price leadership is often very subtle. In the auto industry, for example, auto prices are set by imitation. The price set by the weakest company—that is, the company with the highest costs—is often used as the basis for competitors' pricing. Thus U.S. automakers set their prices, and Japanese automakers then set theirs with reference to the U.S. prices. The Japanese are happy to do this because they have lower costs than U.S. companies and are making many times the profit of the U.S. automakers without competing with them by price. Pricing is often done by market segment. The prices of different auto models in the model range indicate the customer segments that the companies are aiming for and the price range they believe the market segment can tolerate. Each manufacturer prices a model in the segment with reference to the prices charged by its competitors, not by reference to competitors' costs. Price leadership thus helps differentiators charge a premium price, and it helps low-cost companies by increasing their margins. Obviously, it makes a combined cost-leadership/differentiation strategy very profitable.

Price leadership can stabilize industry relations by preventing head-to-head competition, and it raises the level of industry profitability to allow companies funds for future investments and profitable returns to shareholders. However, the dangers of price leadership are worth noting. Price leadership helps companies with high costs; it allows them to survive without becoming more productive or more efficient. This means that they may become complacent and hide behind their own pricing policy, extracting profits that they do not reinvest to improve their productivity. In other words, they follow a profit strategy, as discussed in the Chapter 5. This practice has the long-term effect of making them vulnerable to new entrants who have lower costs because they have developed new productive techniques. This of course is what happened to U.S. automakers and in the electronics industry when the Japanese entered the market. After years of tacit price fixing with General Motors as the leader, the automakers were subject to growing low-cost Japanese competition to which they were unable to respond. Only because the Japanese automakers were foreign companies are many U.S.

auto companies surviving today in the new competitive environment. If they had been new U.S. entrants, there would be no Chrysler, and both Ford and General Motors would be much smaller and wiser companies. }

Competitive Product Differentiation

An important element of product/market strategy in consolidated industries is the use of product differentiation not as a means of creating uniqueness and protecting a company's generic competitive strategy but as a way of preventing competitors from obtaining access to a company's customers and attacking its market share. Product differentiation can be used to deter potential entrants and manage industry rivalry. Product differentiation also allows companies to compete for market share by using *nonprice competitive* methods, such as offering products with different or superior features or applying different marketing techniques. Those methods minimize the risk that companies will use price competition, which hurts everyone because it reduces industry profitability.

To understand how product differentiation can be used competitively, it is useful to analyze the ways in which companies can use differentiation in a consolidated industry to achieve different goals. Table 6.2 uses two dimensions—products and market segments—to identify four product/market strategies that capitalize on the use of competitive product differentiation (notice that in this model we are considering new market segments, not new markets).

Market penetration   When a company concentrates on expanding market share in its existing product markets, it is engaging in a strategy of *market penetration*.[5] Market penetration involves using advertising to promote and build product differentiation. In a consolidated industry, advertising is used to influence consumers' brand choice and create a *brand-name reputation* for the company and

TABLE 6.2   **Four product differentiation strategies**

		Products	
		Existing	New
Market Segments	Existing	Market penetration	Product development
	New	Market development	Product proliferation

its products. In this way, a company can increase its market share by attracting the customers of its rivals. Because brand-name products often command premium prices, building market share in this situation is a very profitable business.

In some mature industries—for example, the soap and detergent, disposable diapers, and brewing industries—a market penetration strategy often becomes a way of life.[6] In these industries all companies engage in intensive advertising and battle for market share, and each company is afraid not to advertise for fear it will lose market share to rivals. As a result, in the soap and detergent industry, for example, over 10 percent of sales revenues is used for advertising to maintain and perhaps build market share. These huge advertising outlays constitute a barrier to entry for prospective entrants. Furthermore, since advertising is a form of nonprice competition, companies are competing primarily through the perceived quality of their products and not by price and are thus reducing harmful competition.

Product development   Product development is the creation of new or improved products to replace existing ones.[7] The wet shaving industry exemplifies an industry based on product replacement to create successive waves of consumer demand that, in turn, create new sources of revenue for industry companies. In 1989, Gillette came out with its new Sensor shaving system, which gave a massive boost to its market share. In turn, Wilkinson Sword responded with its version of the product.

Product development is important for maintaining product differentiation and building market share. For example, the laundry detergent Tide has gone through over fifty different changes in formulation over the past forty years to improve its performance. Tide is what is advertised, but Tide is a different product each year. The battle over diet colas is another example of the use of competitive product differentiation by product development. Royal Crown developed Diet Rite, the first diet cola. However, Coca-Cola and Pepsi-Co responded quickly with their versions of the soft drink and by massive advertising soon took over the market. Refining and improving products is an important element of defending a company's generic competitive strategy in a consolidated industry. This kind of competition can be as vicious as a price war.

Market development   Market development involves finding new market segments in which to exploit a company's products. A company pursuing this strategy wishes to capitalize on the brand name it has developed in one market segment by finding new market segments in which to compete. In this way, it is able to exploit the product differentiation advantages of its brand name. The Japanese auto manufacturers offer an interesting example of the use of market development. With their initial entry, each Japanese manufacturer offered cars aimed at the economy segments of the auto market. Thus, for example, the Toyota Corolla was aimed at the small economy car segment of the market as was the Honda Accord. However, over time, the Japanese upgraded each car, and now each is directed at more expensive market segments. The Accord is now a leading contender in the mid-size luxury sedan segment, and the Corolla fills the small-car segment that used to be occupied by the Celica, which is now aimed at a sportier market segment. By redefining their product offerings, Japanese manufacturers have profitably developed their market segments and successfully attacked their industry rivals, wresting market share from these companies. Although the Japanese used to compete as low-cost producers, market development has allowed them to become differentiators as well.

Product proliferation   Companies seldom produce just one product. Most commonly, companies produce a range of products aimed at different market segments so that they have broad product lines. Sometimes, to reduce the threat of entry, companies tailor their range of products to fill a wide array of niches because doing so increases the difficulty of entry by potential competitors.[8] The strategy of pursuing a broad product line to deter entry is known as *product proliferation*.

Because the large U.S. automakers were slow to fill the small-car market niches, they were vulnerable to the entry of the Japanese into these market segments in the United States. They really had no excuse for this situation, for in their European operations they had a long history of small-car manufacturing. They should have seen the opening and filled it ten years earlier, but in their view small cars meant small profits. Similarly, in the breakfast cereal industry, competition is based on the production of new kinds of cereal to satisfy or create new consumer desires; thus the number of breakfast cereals proliferates. This proliferation makes it very difficult for prospective entrants to attack a new market segment.

As an example of the use of product proliferation to deter entry consider Figure 6.1. It depicts product space in the restaurant industry along two dimensions: (1) atmosphere, which ranges from "fast food" to "candlelight dining," and (2) quality of food, which ranges from average to gourmet. The circles represent product spaces filled by restaurants located along the two dimensions. Thus McDonald's is situated in the average-quality/fast-food area. A gap in the product space gives a potential entrant or an existing rival an opportunity to enter the market and make inroads. The shaded unoccupied product space represents areas where new restaurants can enter the market. However, filling all the product spaces makes it very difficult for an entrant to gain a foothold in the market and differentiate itself.

The strategy of product proliferation usually means that all large companies in an industry have a product in each market segment or niche and compete head-to-head for customers. If a new niche develops, like convertibles or oat bran cereals, then the leader gets a first-mover advantage; but soon all the other companies catch up, and once again competition is stabilized and industry rivalry is reduced. Product proliferation not only deters entry, it also allows stable industry competition based on product differentiation not price—that is, it allows nonprice competition based on the development of new products. The battle is over a product's perceived quality and uniqueness, not its price.

FIGURE 6.1   **Product proliferation in the restaurant industry**

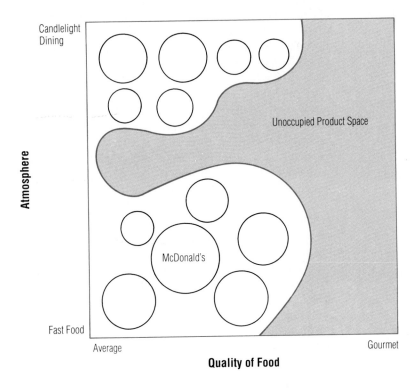

Competitive Pricing

So far, we have been discussing forms of nonprice competition in consolidated industries and techniques used by companies to avoid cutthroat competition, which reduces both company and industry levels of profitability. However, in some industries, price competition periodically breaks out, most commonly when there is industry overcapacity—that is, when companies collectively produce so much output that reducing price is the only way to dispose of it. If one company starts to cut prices, the others quickly follow because they fear the price cutter will be able to sell all its inventory and they will be left with unwanted goods. Since price wars drastically hurt each company's profits, price reductions are never the preferred form of competitive move except, perhaps, in the short run by companies that have a cost advantage.

However, in some situations strategies involving price cutting can be used to deter entry by other companies, thus protecting the profit margins of companies already in an industry. These strategies are called *limit pricing strategies*.[9] Suppose an industry has emerged where profitability is high and existing companies are earning high profit margins. Normally, new companies are attracted to this market because of the prospect of high returns. Companies enter the industry, establish productive capacity, and increase the industry's output. The result is that profit margins fall. Existing companies, however, know that high short-term prices will attract new entrants and lead to low profits. Thus one possible strategy for existing companies is to cut or hold down prices to a level where they earn an above-normal level of profit—but profit that is not high enough to signal to competitors the real potential profitability of the market. The purpose of this strategy, which is called *limit pricing,* is to encourage potential competitors to believe that prices (and hence profits) are relatively low now and will be low in the future, so it is not worthwhile for competitors to make the investments necessary to establish a generic strategy and enter the industry. Essentially, existing companies are trying to bluff potential competitors by keeping prices below the level the market will bear.

Whether limit pricing can be pursued in many industry contexts is debatable. Imitation occurs more and more quickly in today's competitive environment, and the norm these days is for cheap imitations to flood the market, rapidly bringing down prices until some kind of shakeout has occurred and stability is reestablished. It may be extremely risky for companies to depart from the normal competitive pricing practice, which is to charge a high short-term price to exploit an innovation and then to successively reduce prices as new companies enter the market in order to maintain and build market share. Sacrificing short-term high profits for the prospect of uncertain long-run returns from limit pricing is a risky strategy.

Given these problems, a second competitive pricing strategy becomes a possibility: to initially charge a high price for a product and seize short-term profits but then to aggressively cut prices in order to simultaneously build market share *and* deter potential entrants.[10] The incumbent companies signal to potential entrants that if they do enter the industry, the incumbents will use their competitive advantage to drive price down to a level where new companies will be unable to cover their costs.[11] Thus incumbents are able to pursue a market penetration strategy and build an industry reputation while deterring entry. This strategy of pricing for market penetration also allows a company to *ride down the experience curve and obtain substantial economies of scale.* Hence, even though prices are falling, so are costs so profit margins may still be maintained.

Although this strategy may work with a weak competitor and deter entry, it is unlikely to work with an established company that is trying to find profitable investment opportunities in other industries. For example, it is difficult to imagine a 3M being afraid to enter an industry because companies already there are threatening to drive down prices. 3M has the resources to withstand any short-term losses. Thus it may be in the interests of incumbent companies to accept new entry gracefully and give up market share gradually to new entrants to prevent price wars from developing.

At each stage of the industry life cycle, a company is maximizing the price it can obtain for its product given current competitive conditions. Which pricing strategy incumbent companies choose depends on their forecasts about the likely returns from their generic competitive strategies given their cost and differentiation advantages. *Companies should always be concerned to make pricing decisions that maximize the stream of profits in the long run.* Short-term profit maximization may lead to this goal, or the goal may be achieved with long-term price restraint or successive waves of price cutting to reduce costs and build market share. In general, it will depend on the industry context.

Most evidence suggests that companies first skim the market and charge high prices during the growth stage, maximizing short-run profits.[12] Then they move to a market penetration strategy and charge a lower price to rapidly expand the market and develop a reputation and obtain economies of scale, driving down costs and preventing entry. As competitors enter, they reduce prices to retard entry and give up market share to create a stable industry context where they can use nonprice competitive methods to maximize long-run profits. At that point, competitive product differentiation becomes the main basis of industry competition and prices are quite likely to rise as competition stabilizes. Competitive price and non-price decisions are therefore linked and determined by the way a company manages its generic strategy to maximize profits when companies are highly interdependent.

Capacity Control Strategies

A final competitive technique that allows companies to simultaneously deter entry and manage industry rivalry is capacity control strategies. As noted above, excess industry capacity can be a major factor influencing the level of competition in an industry because it leads to price cutting and reduced industry profitability. Excess capacity may result from a shortfall in demand, as when a recession lowers the demand for automobiles and causes companies to give customers price incentives. In this case companies can do nothing except wait for better times. However, in many cases excess capacity results because industry companies *simultaneously* respond to favorable conditions by investing in new plant in order to be able to take advantage of a predicted upsurge in demand. Paradoxically, each individual company's attempt to outperform the others results in companies' collectively producing an industry capacity problem that hurts them all. This situation is illustrated in Figure 6.2. Although demand is increasing, the result of each company's decision to increase capacity is a surge in industry capacity, which will drive down prices.

To prevent the emergence of costly excess capacity, companies in consolidated industries must devise strategies that allow them to control or at least benefit from capacity expansion programs. Before we look at these strategies, however, we need to explore in more detail the factors that cause excess capacity.[13]

Factors causing excess capacity   Capacity problems are often the result of technological factors. The introduction of new, low-cost technology sometimes causes a problem because, to prevent being left behind, all companies introduce it simultaneously. A capacity problem occurs because the old technology is still

FIGURE 6.2   **Changes in industry capacity and demand**

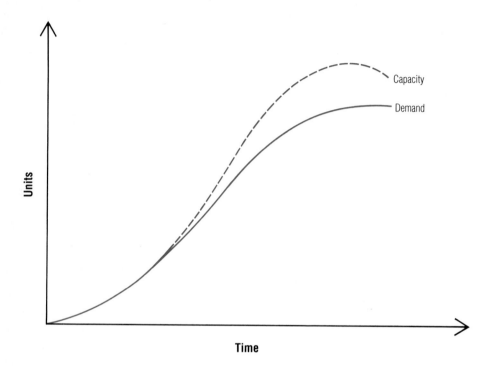

being used to produce output. In addition, new technology is often introduced in large increments that generate overcapacity. For example, an airline that needs more seats on a route must add another plane, thereby adding hundreds of seats even though only fifty may be needed. Similarly, a new chemical process may operate efficiently only at the rate of a 1,000 gallons a day, whereas the previous process was efficient at 500 gallons a day. If all industry companies change technologies, industry capacity doubles and enormous problems result.

Industry competitive factors also cause overcapacity. Obviously, entry into an industry is a major factor causing excess capacity. Japan's entry into the semiconductor industry caused massive overcapacity and price declines in microchips. Similarly, the collapse of OPEC was due to the entry of new countries able to produce oil at competitive prices. Sometimes the age of a company's plant can cause a problem. For example, in the hotel industry, given the rapidity with which the quality of hotel furnishings declines, customers are always attracted to new hotels. The building of new hotel chains next to old chains, however, can cause excess capacity. Often, companies are simply making simultaneous competitive moves based on industry trends, but those moves eventually lead to head-to-head competition. Most fast-food chains, for example, establish new outlets whenever demographic data show population increases. However, they seem to forget that all chains use such data. Thus a locality that has no fast-food outlets may suddenly see several being built simultaneously. Whether all can survive depends on the growth rate of demand relative to the growth rate of the fast-food chains.   "bunching" entries

Choosing a capacity control strategy   Given the variety of ways in which capacity can expand, it is obvious that companies need to find some means of controlling it. Companies will be unable to recoup the investments in their generic strategies if they are always plagued by price cutting and price wars, and low industry profitability produced by overcapacity causes the exit not just of the weakest companies but sometimes of major industry players as well. In general, the strategic choices are for each company individually to try to *pre-empt its rivals* and seize the initiative or for companies collectively to find indirect means of *coordinating with other companies* so that companies become aware of the mutual effects of their actions.

Pre-emptive strategy   To pre-empt rivals, a company must forecast a large increase in demand in the product market and then move rapidly to establish large-scale operations that will be able to satisfy the forecasted demand. Achieving a first-mover advantage may deter other companies from entering the market because the implication is that the pre-empter will be able to move down the experience curve, reduce its costs, and hence reduce prices and threaten a price war if necessary.

This strategy, however, is extremely risky because it involves the investment of resources in a generic strategy before the extent and profitability of the future market are clear. Wal-Mart, with its strategy of locating in small rural towns to tap an underexploited market for discount goods, has pre-empted Sears and K Mart. Wal-Mart has been able to engage in market penetration and market expansion with the secure base established in its rural strongholds.

A pre-emptive strategy is also risky if competitors are not deterred from entry but decide to enter the market. If they have a stronger generic strategy or more resources, like an AT&T or IBM, they can make the pre-empter suffer greatly. Thus, for the strategy to be successful, the pre-empter generally must be a credible company with enough resources to withstand a possible price war.

Coordination strategy   Although collusion over the timing of new investments is illegal under antitrust law, tacit coordination is found in many industries as companies attempt to understand and forecast the competitive moves of their rivals. Generally, companies use market signaling to secure coordination. They make announcements about their future investment decisions in trade journals and newspapers. In addition, they share information about their production levels and their forecasts of industry demand so as to bring industry supply and demand into equilibrium. Thus a coordination strategy reduces the risks associated with investment in the industry. The principal danger to companies comes from potential entrants that may disrupt the stability of the industry. In the U.S. car market, for example, the relative market shares and outputs of General Motors, Chrysler, and Ford were stable for many years until Japanese automakers showed them the meaning of overcapacity. Thus the avoidance of socially wasteful losses from simultaneous investments in industry capacity should not come at the expense of inefficiency or from lack of attention to maintaining a viable generic competitive strategy.

Supply and Distribution Strategy

As we saw in Chapter 3, as an industry becomes consolidated and composed of a few large companies, it becomes stronger vis-à-vis its suppliers and customers. Suppliers become dependent on the industry for buying their inputs, customers for obtaining industry outputs. By the mature stage, in order to protect market share and improve product quality, many companies are interested in taking over more of the distribution of their products and in controlling the source of inputs crucial to the production process. When they seek to own supply or distribution operations, they are pursuing a strategy of *vertical integration,* which is considered in detail in the next chapter. Here, we discuss how the choice of a means of controlling the relationships between a company and its suppliers and distributors is an important determinant of the way in which a company supports its generic strategy and develops a competitive advantage.

One important reason to control supplier/distributor relationships is that a company that can ensure its ability to dispose of its outputs or acquire inputs in a timely, reliable manner is able to reduce costs and improve product quality. A good way to analyze the issues involved in choosing a distribution/supplier strategy is to contrast the situation that exists between a company and its suppliers and distributors in Japan with the situations that exist in the United States. In this country, it is normal for a company and its suppliers to have an antagonistic relationship. Each tries to drive the best bargain to make the most profit. Moreover, the relationship between a company's buyers and suppliers tends to be superficial and anonymous because purchasing and distribution personnel are routinely rotated to prevent kickbacks. In contrast, in Japan, the relationship between a company and its suppliers and distributors is based on long-term personal relationships and trust. Suppliers in Japan are responsive to the needs of the company, respond quickly to changes in the specification of inputs, and adjust supply to meet the needs of a company's just-in-time inventory system. The results of this close relationship are lower costs and the ability to respond to unexpected changes in customers' demand. The close supplier/distributor relationship supports Japanese companies' generic strategy. Clearly, it pays a company to develop a long-term strategy toward its suppliers and distributors.

A company has many options to choose from in deciding on the appropriate way to distribute its products to gain a competitive advantage. A company may distribute its products to an independent distributor, who in turn distributes to retailers. Or a company might distribute directly to retailers or even to customers. In general, the complexity of a product and the amount of information needed about its operation and maintenance determine the distribution strategy chosen. For example, automakers typically use franchisees to control the distribution of their autos rather than a general car dealership. The reason is the high level of after-sales service and support necessary to satisfy customers. Automakers are able to penalize franchisees by withholding cars from a dealership if customer complaints rise; thus they have effective control over franchisee behavior. Also by controlling the franchisees, they can tailor price and nonprice competition to industry conditions, and this allows the large automakers to coordinate their actions by controlling the thousands of separate dealerships across the country effectively.

On the other hand, the large electronics manufacturers and the producers of consumer durables like appliances generally prefer to use a network of distributors to control distribution. To enhance market share and control the way products are sold and serviced, manufacturers choose five or six large distributors per state to control distribution. The distributors are required to carry the full line of a company's products and invest in after-sales service facilities. The result is that the manufacturer receives good feedback on how its products are selling, and the distributor becomes knowledgeable about a company's products and thus helps the company maintain and increase its control over the market. The company is able to discipline its distributors if they start to discount prices or otherwise threaten the company's reputation or generic strategy.

Large manufacturers like Johnson & Johnson, Procter and Gamble, and General Foods typically sell directly to a retailer and avoid giving profits to a distributor or wholesaler. In part, they do this because they have lower profit margins than do the makers of electronic equipment and consumer durables. However, this strategy also allows them to influence a retailer's behavior directly. For example, they can refuse to supply a particular product that a retailer wants unless the retailer stocks the entire range of the company's products. Also, the companies can ensure shelf space for new products. Coca-Cola and PepsiCo are two companies that are able to influence retailers to exclude or reduce the shelf space given to competing products. They can do so because soft drinks have the highest profit margins of any product sold in supermarkets. Gallo is one of the few wine makers that control the distribution and retailing of their own products. This is one reason Gallo is so consistently profitable.

In sum, devising the appropriate strategy for acquiring inputs and disposing of outputs is a crucial part of competitive strategy in mature industry environments. Companies can gain a competitive advantage through the way they choose to control their relationships with distributors and suppliers. By choosing the right strategy, they are able to control their costs, their price and nonprice strategies, and their reputation and product quality. These are crucial issues in mature industries.

Summary: Mature Strategies

Business-level strategy in mature industries involves the development of the means by which companies can pursue the hold-and-maintain or profit strategies discussed in Chapter 5. To maximize profitability, companies rationalize their product/market choices to reduce costs and increase revenues, and they develop means to stabilize industry competition to increase the industry's level of profitability. Controlling the five forces of industry competition—in particular, developing competitive techniques to deter entry and manage industry rivalry—is the crucial part of this process. The principal means of achieving these goals are market signaling; price leadership; the development of competitive price, differentiation, and capacity control strategies; and the selection of a strategy for dealing with suppliers and distributors. Business-level strategy involves developing rules of the game to manage relationships with competitors and with suppliers and customers. Conditions in the macro-environment, such as changes in technology or in foreign competition or in consumer tastes, sometimes change the basis of industry interdependence, alter the sources of competitive success, and reduce the ability of companies collectively to coordinate their actions. That is why periods of stability in an industry are followed by unrest and intense competition as companies jockey for position in the changed industry environment. Managing such change is the goal of business-level strategy in mature industry environments.

6.7 STRATEGY IN DECLINING INDUSTRIES

In a mature industry, demand slows and is often limited to replacement demand. Thus there is increased competition between companies for market share. Once demand starts to fall, an industry is said to be in decline, and competitive pressures become even more intense. Since declining industries are often consolidated, we need to consider how a reduction or fall in market growth affects industry competition and how it presents a new set of problems for companies to deal with.

In general, companies in declining industries still have to manage all the various aspects of competitive strategy identified in the last section—for example, price and nonprice competition. However, new options become important.

Falling market demand means that companies individually need to fine-tune their generic competitive strategies to face the new competitive situation, and collectively they need to coordinate their behavior to head off vicious price wars. Falling demand means lower industry revenues, so it becomes especially important for companies to streamline their cost structures and find the best way to invest their resources in value creation in order to maximize value-added. Since price competition reduces total industry revenues, it puts all companies at risk.

Manipulating Product/ Market Strategies

Companies manipulate their competitive product/market strategies in several ways to match a new situation.[14] Since increased competition often emerges over product quality, cost, and price, companies need to take a hard look at their product offerings to make sure they are offering the appropriate range of products and the right mix of product attributes to attract the most buyers at the least cost. Product proliferation, for example, may have gone too far, and now the sheer number of products sold is starting to raise costs with no compensating increase in demand. If this is the case, the company should concentrate more on product and market development to find new uses for its products or new products that better fit customer needs. Since all companies will be increasing their attempts at market penetration, it is important for the company to keep its advertising in line with them or risk losing market share. In terms of price policy, companies should pay particular attention to price changes by competitors; and if prices start to fall, they should keep in line with competitors.

In this situation, the benefits of pursuing a combined cost-leadership and differentiation strategy become clear. If a company can maintain its differentiation advantage, then it may be able to maintain its premium price even as prices come down. Even if some price discounts are forced by the situation, pursuing a dual strategy keeps the company the most profitable company. Thus, even if industry profitability falls, the low-cost differentiator is unlikely to suffer. Moreover, this company will be at the forefront of process innovation, so it will be the first to take advantage of new technical developments. Such a company is able to reap first-mover advantages at all stages of the industry.

Weaker companies experience competitive problems most forcefully. Thus they attempt to initiate coordinated moves and signal their willingness to follow a price leader as price cuts occur. Whether such attempts at coordination work depends on the severity of competition. As we saw in the Opening Incident, in very uncertain and competitive environments preventing price wars can be particularly difficult because all companies are acting purely in their own interests. However, if companies have forecasted slowing demand early enough, they may be able to signal their willingness to find ways of avoiding a price war. For example, they may signal their willingness to reduce industry capacity, thereby removing the dangers of excess capacity. Reducing capacity may also allow them to reduce their costs because their oldest and most inefficient plants can be liquidated first. Additionally, they may signal their intention to retreat from some market segments and consolidate in others, so they increasingly specialize only in the segments of the product line where they have a competitive advantage. In this way they can also reduce competition.

Finally, companies can move to increase industry consolidation by purchasing smaller and weaker competitors. Such purchases increase their market share and make it more difficult for potential competitors to enter the industry. The beer industry is a good example of a mature industry where in the last twenty years the big players have absorbed most of the small players (that is, the regional brewers) to create a stable industry situation in which nonprice brand-name competition and the development of new products have been the main forms of competition. The large brewers have used business-level strategy to create a highly profitable industry.

In sum, in a situation of declining demand, companies must manipulate their generic competitive strategy to reap the most returns from the changed industry environment. They must decide how to compete based on their distinctive competencies, and they should invest resources where they will have maximum effect—for example, in value-chain activities that result in lower costs or in a differentiation advantage, or in purchasing smaller competitors to reduce excess industry capacity and to increase market share. Companies must be careful not to make decisions that result in their being *stuck in the middle*. If a company fails to recognize the implications of the changed environment, or if it fails to make the right competitive moves, it may be the one purchased by its competitors and liquidated.

Market Concentration and Asset Reduction

The competitive moves discussed above are most applicable in industries where demand is falling slowly and competitive pressures are least intense. When demand is falling rapidly, more radical competitive moves become necessary. To some extent we have already discussed this issue in Chapter 5, where we noted how companies can pursue market concentration and asset reduction investment strategies in their attempt to maximize the profits associated with a declining market.

With market concentration, companies are increasing their investments in certain industry segments so as to be able to dominate the industry and obtain a competitive advantage over their rivals. In essence, they are seeking to pre-empt their rivals by seeking a *leadership position,* which will give them a first-mover advantage in the competitive battle to come.[15] This position will also allow them to become the price leader and determine the competitive rules of the declining situation. To the extent that they are focusing their investments in only one or in a few segments, they may be said to be following a *niche strategy*. Here, they are content to defend one market segment as, for example, International Harvester did when it became Navistar and only produced trucks.

On the other hand, if a company does not perceive that the returns from investing in the industry are warranted, it may choose an asset reduction strategy. Here, it may try to divest the business quickly, try to milk its investments and harvest the business to maximize cash flow, or move to liquidate the investment and exit the industry quickly. In Chapter 9, we present a model showing how a company chooses among these three strategies.

6.8 SUMMARY OF CHAPTER

The purpose of this chapter is to discuss how the structure of the industry in which companies compete affects the level of company and industry profitability. Developing a generic competitive strategy and an investment strategy is only the first part, albeit a crucial part, of business-level strategy. Tailoring that generic strategy to the industry structure by choosing industry-appropriate competitive moves and product/market strategies is the second part of successful strategy formulation at the business level. The chapter makes the following main points:

1. The main factors affecting the level of industry competition are the number and relative size of the companies in an industry, the level of market demand and whether it is growing or declining, and the availability of the resources necessary for reducing the costs of value creation.

2. In fragmented industries composed of a large number of small companies, the principal forms of competitive strategy are chaining, franchising, and horizontal merger.

3. In embryonic and growth industries, managing first-mover advantages to profit from technical innovations is a crucial aspect of competitive strategy. Companies must learn how to exploit these advantages while avoiding the disadvantages of being first in the market.

4. They can do so by choosing the right strategy to exploit the innovation. The three choices are for the company to develop and market the technology itself, to do so jointly with another company, or to license the technology to existing companies.

5. Mature industries are composed of a few large companies whose actions are so highly interdependent that the success of one company's strategy depends on the responses of its rivals.

6. The principal competitive moves and strategies used by companies in mature industries are market signaling, price leadership, competitive product differentiation, competitive pricing, capacity control, and supply and distribution strategy.

7. These strategies are interdependent and must be matched to a company's generic competitive strategy.

8. In declining industries where market demand has leveled off, companies must tailor their price and nonprice strategies to the new competitive environment. They also need to manage industry capacity to prevent the emergence of capacity expansion problems. When demand is falling, companies can adopt leadership or niche strategies to exploit the potential of a declining market; or, if prospects are poor, they can employ divestment and liquidation strategies to exit the market quickly.

Discussion Questions

1. Why are industries fragmented? What are the main ways in which companies can turn a fragmented industry into a consolidated one?

2. What are the key problems involved in maintaining a competitive advantage in a growth industry environment? What are the dangers associated with being the leader?

3. Discuss how companies can use (a) product differentiation and (b) capacity control strategies to manage rivalry and increase industry profitability.

Endnotes

1. This discussion draws heavily on Michael E. Porter, *Competitive Strategy: Techniques for Analyzing Industries and Competitors* (New York: Free Press, 1980), pp. 191–200.

2. Edwin Mansfield, "How Economists see R&D," *Harvard Business Review* (November–December 1981), 98–106.

3. Porter, *Competitive Strategy*, pp. 76–86.

4. F. M. Scherer, *Industrial Market Structure and Economic Performance*, 2nd ed. (Boston: Houghton Mifflin, 1980), Ch. 6.

5. H. Igor Ansoff, *Corporate Strategy* (London: Penguin Books, 1984), pp. 97–100.

6. Robert D. Buzzell, Bradley T. Gale, and Ralph G. M. Sultan, "Market Share—A Key to Profitability," *Harvard Business Review* (January–February 1975), 97–103. Robert Jacobson and David A. Aaker, "Is Market Share All That It's Cracked Up to Be?" *Journal of Marketing*, 49 (Fall 1985), 11–22.

7. Ansoff, *Corporate Strategy*, pp. 98–99.

8. J. Brander and J. Eaton, "Product Line Rivalry," *American Economic Review*, (June 1984), (74), 323–334.

9. Scherer, *Industrial Market Structure and Economic Performance*, Ch. 8.

10. P. Milgrom and J. Roberts, "Predation, Reputation, and Entry Deterrence," *Journal of Economic Theory*, 27 (1982), 280–312.

11. Sharon M. Oster, *Modern Competitive Analysis* (New York: Oxford University Press, 1990), pp. 262–264.

12. Donald A. Hay and Derek J. Morris, *Industrial Economics: Theory and Evidence* (New York: Oxford University Press, 1979), pp. 192–193.

13. The next section draws heavily on Marvin B. Lieberman, "Strategies for Capacity Expansion," *Sloan Management Review*, (8) (Summer 1987), 19–27; and Porter, *Competitive Strategy*, pp. 324–338.

14. Michael E. Porter, *Competitive Advantage: Creating and Sustaining Superior Performance* (New York: Free Press, 1985), pp. 254–274.

15. Kathryn Rudie Harrigan and Michael E. Porter, "End-Game Strategies for Declining Industries," *Harvard Business Review* (July–August 1983), 111–120.

Chapter 7

CORPORATE-LEVEL STRATEGY: VERTICAL INTEGRATION AND DIVERSIFICATION

7.1 OPENING INCIDENT: HANSON INDUSTRIES

In 1973 Gordon White, cofounder of British conglomerate Hanson Trust PLC, arrived in the United States to start the North American arm of Hanson Trust. Thirteen years later the company he set up, Hanson Industries, was ranked ninety-seventh among the Fortune 500 Industrials. Hanson Industries' achievement in joining the elite of U.S. companies capped a twenty-two-year period during which Hanson Trust's pretax profits had grown at an average rate of 45 percent a year. This phenomenal growth was based on a carefully thought-out corporate strategy of diversification by acquisition into many unrelated industries. Between 1984 and 1986 alone Hanson Industries bought three major U.S. companies: U.S. Industries, a building and industrial products company; SCM Corporation, a typewriter and chemicals conglomerate; and Kaiser Cement Corporation.

The basis of the company's diversification strategy has been to acquire businesses cheaply, often against the existing management's will, liquidate surplus assets, and manage what is left in such a way as to increase earnings and generate cash for the next acquisition. When seeking companies to acquire, Hanson looks for cyclical businesses that earn good returns over the long run but may be suffering from a short-term setback. It also looks for companies in which a weak division or two have depressed overall performance, as well as for once-weak companies whose stock prices do not yet reflect recent turnarounds. All these factors keep down the price of the acquisition. In addition, Hanson seeks businesses in mature industries, where demand is predictable and new capital requirements are likely to be minimal. The company deliberately steers clear of high-tech industries, where capital requirements are large and technological change makes the future uncertain.

Once Hanson acquires a company, it economizes further by selling headquarters buildings and eliminating staff jobs or pushing them down into operations. Underperforming divisions are either turned around quickly or sold. The divisions that remain are given substantial operating autonomy but are held accountable for their performance through a system of tight financial controls. Strong profit incentives are introduced to encourage divisional executives to focus on the bottom line. Hanson's objective is to markedly improve the profitability of the companies it acquires.

The working out of all these factors can produce remarkable results. For example, Hanson Industries paid $930 million for SCM in January 1986, after a bitterly contested takeover battle. By September 1986 it had sold off a number of SCM subsidiaries for more than $1 billion. Hanson held on to the typewriter and chemicals businesses, which in effect cost nothing and

which earned record pretax profits of $165 million in 1987. Since 1987, the chemicals and typewriter businesses acquired with SCM have shown a further significant improvement in performance.

Consider Smith-Corona, SCM's typewriter business. Under Hanson, Smith-Corona reduced the number of parts in its leading products from 1,400 to 400 and the required time for assembly from 8 hours to 1.5 hours. In addition, employment was cut from 5,200 workers in 1985 to 3,100 by 1988. By such moves, Smith-Corona has been able to establish a cost advantage over its major Japanese competitors. As a consequence, by 1989 Smith-Corona had regained its hold on more than 50 percent of the American typewriter market, after seeing its share sink as low as 32 percent in 1986.[1]

7.2 OVERVIEW

Corporate-level strategy is concerned with answering this question: How should we manage the growth and development of the company to maximize long-run profitability? Answering it involves choosing (1) the *businesses* and (2) the *markets* that a company is going to compete in. With regard to different businesses, the company may decide to (a) concentrate on a single business, (b) vertically integrate into adjacent businesses, or (c) diversify into new business areas. With regard to markets, the company may decide to (a) compete just within its domestic marketplace or (b) expand globally and compete in the international arena. Table 7.1 illustrates this range of choices.

In this chapter, we review in depth the decisions to concentrate on a single business, vertically integrate, and diversify into new businesses. In the next chapter we look at the issue of global expansion and discuss the different ways in which multinational companies can create value. Throughout both chapters we emphasize that to succeed, corporate strategies should *add value* to the corporation. To understand what this means, we have to go back to the concept of the value chain, introduced in Chapter 4. *To add value, a corporate strategy should enable a company, or one or more of its business units, to perform one or more of the value-creation functions at a lower cost, or perform one or more of the value-creation functions in a way that allows for differentiation and a premium price.* Thus a company's *corporate* strategy should help in the process of establishing a distinctive competence *at the business level.*

TABLE 7.1   **Corporate-level strategy options**

		Businesses		
		Single business	Vertical integration	Diversification
Markets	Domestic	e.g., Domino's Pizza, Inc.	e.g., Nucor Corporation	e.g., Southland Corporation
	Global	e.g., Holiday Inns Inc.	e.g., Exxon Corporation	e.g., Hanson Trust

For example, Hanson Trust's restructuring of SCM, discussed in the Opening Incident, reduced the operating costs of SCM's typewriter and chemicals businesses, thereby increasing the *value added* by each of these businesses. Because Hanson eliminated excess staff, reduced corporate overhead, and encouraged divisional heads to focus on the bottom line, the value-creation functions of the businesses acquired from SCM could be performed at a lower cost.

We must emphasize at the outset that companies frequently make mistakes when pursuing corporate-level strategies and may end up reducing rather than adding value. Consequently, at the end of this chapter, we discuss strategic retrenchment and turnaround as a response to failed corporate strategies.

7.3 CORPORATE GROWTH AND DEVELOPMENT

Stages of Corporate Development

Most companies begin as single-business enterprises competing within the confines of their domestic market. For such companies, maximizing long-run profitability means identifying how best to compete within their market. As you saw in Chapter 5, this process requires management to consider differentiation, cost leadership, and focus. However, it may also involve vertical integration, either backward, to gain a strategic advantage from owning supply sources, or forward, to gain a strategic advantage from owning distribution outlets. In addition, as we see in the next chapter, in today's marketplace, a company often needs a global presence in order to compete successfully. For example, global electronics manufacturers, such as Sony, have a cost advantage over domestic companies, such as Zenith and RCA Consumer Electronics Division, that comes from their huge global volume and the resulting scale economies.

Beyond these considerations, a company that manages to establish a sustainable competitive advantage in its original industry may find itself generating financial resources _in excess_ of those required to maintain its position. It must then decide how to invest the excess resources in order to maximize its long-run profitability. One option may be to return the excess to stockholders in the form of higher dividends or stock buybacks. Another option is to diversify into new business areas. Diversification can take several forms but, to be viable, must _add value_ to the corporation. In the case of Hanson Trust, value is added by restructuring acquired companies to reduce costs and generate extra profits. Diversification can also create value through resource sharing between businesses, by transferring skills from one business to another, and by operating an internal capital market.

Thus the growth and development of a typical modern enterprise can be divided into three main stages. At stage 1, a company operates as a single business within the confines of a single national market. At stage 2, vertical integration and global expansion strengthen the competitive position of the company's core activity; vertical integration and global expansion _support_ a company's business-level strategy. Stage 3 begins when a company is generating resources _in excess_ of those necessary to maintain a competitive advantage in its core activity. Typically, at this stage a company looks for diversification opportunities outside its core business to generate value from the investment of excess resources. Figure 7.1 summarizes these stages.

The model proposed in Figure 7.1 differs from that offered by Alfred Chandler of Harvard University.[2] On the basis of historical research, Chandler suggested that most U.S. companies first grew as single businesses, then vertically integrated, then diversified into related businesses, and only at that point expanded globally. Historical analogies, however, are a poor guide to

FIGURE 7.1   **Stages of corporate growth and development**

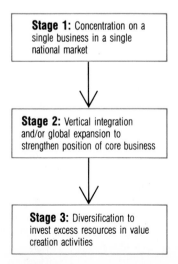

Stage 1: Concentration on a single business in a single national market

Stage 2: Vertical integration and/or global expansion to strengthen position of core business

Stage 3: Diversification to invest excess resources in value creation activities

modern conditions because the emergence of truly global markets and global competition is a phenomenon of the late twentieth century. Today the imperatives of global competition often force companies to become global before they diversify.

Limits to Growth

Vertical integration, diversification, and global expansion can all create value for a company.[3] However, past some point, the value created by these strategies is also subject to the basic economic "law" of *diminishing returns*. All that this means is that in general the value added by each successive expansion move is likely to be less than the value added by the previous move. For example, a company might pursue its most promising diversification opportunity first, its next most promising diversification move second, and its next most promising move third. Although each successive diversification move may add value, each adds less value than the previous move.

Of course, in practice things do not happen quite like this. For example, a company may not know which is its most promising diversification opportunity, so it pursues its least promising opportunity first. Similarly, at least initially, successive expansions overseas tend to generate *increasing returns* as the company realizes experience-based scale economies from global volume. Nevertheless, the basic point holds: *Past some point,* extensive diversification, vertical integration, or international expansion tends to be associated with a decline in value added at the margin. The decline occurs because the most profitable opportunities have already been exploited by the company and only less profitable opportunities exist. The notion of diminishing returns to vertical integration, diversification, or global expansion implies that the *marginal value-added* associated with each successive expansion move tends to decline. (The term *marginal value-added* simply refers to the value created by each additional expansion move.)

The decline is illustrated for diversification in Figure 7.2 The extent of diversification is measured on the horizontal axis, and dollars are measured on the vertical axis (the horizontal axis could just as well measure the extent of vertical integration or global expansion). The marginal-value-added curve, *MVA,* is shown to decline, signifying that each successive diversification move adds less value than the previous move.

In addition, the bureaucratic costs of managing successive expansion moves tend to increase. This means that as a company becomes ever more vertically integrated, diversified, or global in its scope, the task of managing ever greater complexity gives rise to increasingly difficult problems of coordination and control. For example, consider the problems associated with managing an organization that has the size and complexity of General Motors. General Motors is vertically integrated (it manufactures 70 percent of all component parts used in its auto assembly operation); it is diversified with operations in autos, aerospace, data systems, and finance; and it is global in scope with assembly operations on four continents. Managing such a complex organization composed of so many

FIGURE 7.2   Marginal value-added and costs of expansion

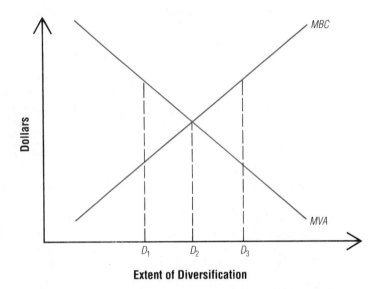

interdependent parts can be a bureaucratic nightmare. We consider the source of these problems in more detail later in this chapter and the next. In addition, we consider bureaucratic costs more closely in the section on strategy implementation when we look at how companies should design their structures and control systems to match their strategy. For now it is enough to note that ultimately, this phenomenon can result in control loss and declining economic performance.

The implication is that the *marginal bureaucratic costs* associated with each successive expansion move will tend to increase (the term *marginal bureaucratic costs* simply refers to the costs of managing each additional expansion move). This is illustrated in Figure 7.2 by the upward-sloping marginal-bureaucratic-cost curve (*MBC*).

If we now consider both the marginal value-added and the marginal bureaucratic costs associated with expansion, the implication of this discussion is that *there is a definite limit to the profitable expansion of any company*. In Figure 7.2 this limit is at the point where the two curves intersect—that is, where $MVA = MBC$. The logic is as follows: For a company that has diversified up to D_1 on the horizontal axis, the marginal value-added of diversification, although declining, still exceeds the marginal bureaucratic costs of managing that additional diversification ($MVA > MBC$). Thus it pays to pursue further diversification because the company can still create additional value by doing so. For a company that has pursued diversification up to D_3 on the horizontal axis, however, the marginal value-added exceeds the marginal bureaucratic costs ($MVA < MBC$). In this case, it pays to reduce diversification because the last (or marginal) diversification move gave rise to more bureaucratic costs than to value-added. Thus, the optimal level of diversification for this company is at D_2, where $MVA = MBC$.

In practice, of course, it is difficult to identify the optimal level of diversification, vertical integration, or global expansion. However, this does not invalidate the analysis given above. We can surmise from observation that companies often continue to pursue a strategy beyond the point at which it is profitable to do so. For example, many of the go-go conglomerates of the 1960s and 1970s, such as Esmark Corporation, General Electric, ITT, Textron, Tenneco, and United Technologies, clearly diversified beyond the point at which it was profitable to do so. As a result, all of these companies suffered a decline in profitability and subsequently spent most of the 1980s restructuring themselves, selling off many of their diversified activities, and refocusing on their strategic core.[4]

A final point is that the MVA and MBC curves depicted in Figure 7.2 are not fixed for all time; they can shift. For example, administrative innovations can reduce the bureaucratic costs of managing organizational complexity. Thus Alfred Chandler has observed how the development of the multidivisional structure at General Motors and Du Pont during the 1920s and 1930s enabled those companies to solve the problem of how to manage a moderate degree of diversification.[5] Similarly, current advances in information technology, by enabling top managers to call up detailed data about an operation at the push of a button, may have reduced the bureaucratic costs of managing large complex organizations and made greater size possible.

The effect of such administrative innovations is illustrated in Figure 7.3. Following an administrative innovation that lowers the bureaucratic costs of managing a complex organization, the marginal-bureaucratic-cost curve declines from MBC_1 to MBC_2. As a result, the optimum level of diversification for the company increases from D_1 to D_2. Put another way, because of administrative

FIGURE 7.3   **The effect of an administrative innovation**

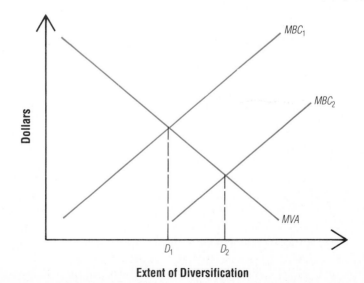

innovation the company can now profitably manage a greater degree of diversification than was previously the case.

Now that we have considered in a general sense the factors that determine the limits to profitable growth, we move on to look at each of the various corporate-level strategies in turn. We start by considering the advantages and disadvantages of concentrating on a single business before moving on to consider vertical integration and diversification.

7.4 CONCENTRATION ON A SINGLE BUSINESS

All companies begin by concentrating on a single business within the confines of their domestic market. For such companies, corporate- and business-level strategy are synonymous. To maximize profitability, they must pursue cost-leadership, differentiation, or focus strategies. Even when a company has established a sustainable competitive advantage, however, it can still benefit from continuing to serve a single business.

Advantages

By concentrating on one operation, a single-business company can focus the total human, physical, and financial resources of the organization toward competing successfully within its market. This can be important in growth industries, where demands on the company's resources are likely to be substantial but the long-term profits from establishing a competitive advantage are also substantial.

Besides, the top managers of a single business in a single national market are likely to have an intimate knowledge of the business the company is involved in, whereas in multibusiness and multinational enterprises, top managers may have to struggle just to keep abreast of the different operations of the individual subsidiary companies. Such knowledge is a major asset when a company's business is based in an intensely competitive and technologically dynamic industry that requires quick and informed top-management decision making.

Disadvantages

Concentrating on just one business has significant disadvantages as well. A company may be able to increase value-added by vertically integrating or diversifying. Vertical integration may be necessary to establish a sustainable competitive advantage within an industry. For example, even in a young, technologically dynamic, high-growth industry such as the personal computer industry, IBM's strategy for establishing a competitive advantage involves backward integration into the manufacture of proprietary components that are difficult for competitors to copy.

Beyond this, companies that concentrate on just one line of business face two other major constraints in trying to maximize profitability, and both of these constraints push profit-seeking companies toward corporate diversification. First, single-business enterprises that are based in mature industries may find opportunities for profitable growth limited by a lack of investment opportunities within their core industry. At this stage, concentrating on a single business may not represent the best use of the company's resources—especially if the company has established a competitive advantage and is now generating financial resources *in excess* of those needed to maintain that advantage. To make better use of such excess resources, companies often begin to diversify into new business areas. For example, Philip Morris, finding its growth limited by a mature tobacco industry but nevertheless generating strong cash flows from its dominant position in tobacco, diversified into the brewing industry with the acquisition of Miller Brewing Company and into the food industry with the acquisition of General Foods and Kraft.

Companies that concentrate on a single business also risk missing out on profitable opportunities stemming from the application of a company's distinctive competencies to other industries. Thus, had Philip Morris not acquired Miller Brewing, it would have missed out on the opportunity to apply its distinctive competence in marketing one consumer product (cigarettes) to marketing another (beer).

7.5 VERTICAL INTEGRATION

Vertical integration means that a company is producing its own inputs (backward integration) or is disposing of its own outputs (forward integration). A steel company that supplies its iron ore needs from company-owned iron ore mines exemplifies backward integration. An auto manufacturer that sells its cars through company-owned distribution outlets illustrates forward integration. Figure 7.4 illustrates five main stages in a typical raw-material-to-consumer production chain. For a company based in the assembly stage, backward integration involves moving into intermediate manufacturing and raw-material production. Forward integration involves movement into distribution and retail.

In addition to forward and backward integration, it is also possible to distinguish between **full integration** and **taper integration** (see Figure 7.5).[6] A

FIGURE 7.4   **Different stages in the raw-material-to-consumer production chain**

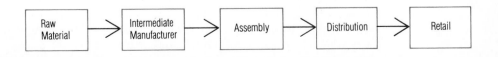

FIGURE 7.5   **Full and taper integration**

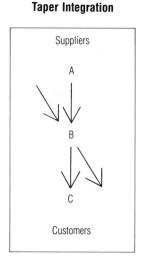

company achieves full integration when it produces all of a particular input needed for its processes or when it disposes of *all* of its output through its own operations. Taper integration occurs when a company buys from independent suppliers in addition to company-owned suppliers or when it disposes of its output through independent outlets in addition to company-owned outlets. The advantages of taper integration over full integration are discussed later in this chapter.

Creating Value Through Vertical Integration

A company pursuing vertical integration is normally motivated by a desire to strengthen the competitive position of its original, or core, business.[7] Through this strategy, the company can add value from the following sources: (1) production cost savings, (2) avoidance of market costs, (3) improved quality control, and (4) protection of proprietary technology. At the very least, these sources of additional value allow the company either to reduce its overall cost position in its core business or to charge a premium price for its product. Vertical integration, then, is consistent with a company's attempt to establish itself as the cost leader or as a differentiated player in its core business.

Reducing production costs   When vertical integration permits technologically complementary processes to be carried out in quick succession, a company can save on production costs. For example, the ability to roll steel when hot from refining offers an advantage to steel refineries with their own rolling mills. The newly refined steel does not have to be reheated to make it malleable. Similarly, the ability to turn wood pulp into newsprint without drying and reconstituting it—as would have to be done if the pulp were to be delivered to a different organization for further processing—gives an advantage to integrated pulp and paper mills.

Further production cost savings arise from the easier planning, coordination, and scheduling of adjacent processes made possible in vertically integrated organizations. For example, in the 1920s Ford profited from the tight coordination and scheduling that are possible with backward vertical integration. Ford integrated backward into steel foundries, iron ore shipping, and iron ore mining. Deliveries at Ford were coordinated to such an extent that iron ore landed at Ford's steel foundries on the Great Lakes was turned into engine blocks within twenty-four hours. Thus Ford substantially reduced its production costs by eliminating the need to hold excessive inventories.

Avoiding market costs If a company buys its inputs or sells its outputs on the open market, it often has to bear buying and selling costs. Many of these costs, such as advertising, maintaining a sales force, and running a procurement department, can be reduced or even eliminated through vertical integration. Moreover, vertical integration can also dispose of the need to pay profits to market middlemen (commodity brokers, warehouse operators, transport companies, and the like). Since it avoids market costs, a company may find it easier to become the cost leader in its core business.

Further costs of using the market arise when a company depends on a limited number of powerful suppliers for important inputs. The suppliers may take advantage of such a situation to raise prices above those that would be found in more competitive circumstances. The company ends up having to pay exorbitantly high prices for its inputs. These prices are the costs of using the market. If the company would integrate backward and supply its own inputs, it could avoid these costs. The same arguments apply when a company sells to a limited number of powerful buyers. Recognizing the company's dependence on them for orders, the buyers can squeeze down prices, costing the company potential profit. By integrating forward, the company can circumvent powerful buyers and earn greater returns on its final sales.[8]

Protection of product quality By protecting product quality, vertical integration enables a company to become a differentiated player in its core business. The banana industry illustrates this situation. Historically, a problem with the banana industry has been the variable quality of delivered bananas, which often arrived on the shelves of American stores either too ripe or not ripe enough. To correct this problem, major American food companies, such as General Foods, have integrated backward to gain control over supply sources. Consequently, they have been able to distribute bananas of a standard quality at the optimal time for consumption to American consumers. Knowing that they can rely on the quality of these brands, consumers are willing to pay more for them. Thus by integrating backward into plantation ownership, the banana companies have built consumer confidence, which enables them in turn to charge a premium price for their product. Similarly, when McDonald's decided to open up its first restaurant in Moscow, it found, much to its initial dismay, that in order to serve food and drink indistinguishable from that served in McDonald's restaurants elsewhere, it had to vertically integrate backward and supply its own needs. The quality of Russian-grown potatoes and meat was simply too poor. Thus, to protect the quality of its product, McDonald's set up its own dairy farms, cattle ranches, vegetable plots, and food-processing plant within the Soviet Union.

The same kind of considerations can result in forward integration. Ownership of distribution outlets may be necessary if the required standards of after-sales service with complex products are to be provided. For example, in the 1920s Kodak owned retail outlets for distributing photographic equipment. The company felt that few established retail outlets had the skills necessary to sell and service its photographic equipment. By the 1930s, however, Kodak decided that it no longer needed to own its retail outlets because other retailers had begun to provide satisfactory distribution and service for Kodak products. The company then withdrew from retailing.

Protection of proprietary technology   Proprietary technology is technology that is unique to a company and can give it an advantage over competitors. Proprietary technology can allow a company to establish more efficient production processes, thus reducing manufacturing costs, or it can be embodied in the design of a company's product, permitting the company to charge a premium price. Vertical integration makes good sense when a company needs to prevent its competitors from knowing too much about its technology. When proprietary technology involves an innovative process, vertical integration helps a company to protect its know-how and to establish itself as a cost leader in its core operation. When proprietary technology relates to a product innovation, vertical integration assists the company in establishing itself as a differentiated player in its core operation.

Recently, IBM integrated backward into the manufacture of microcircuits to protect the innovations incorporated in its new PS/2 personal computer system from being duplicated by competitors. The information pathways and graphics of the PS/2 machines are created by proprietary chips, manufactured by IBM itself, that will be difficult for competitors to decipher. By taking this step, IBM hopes to avoid the widespread copying of its machines that occurred in the case of the company's original PC system—that is, it hopes to differentiate itself.[9]

Disadvantages of Vertical Integration

Vertical integration has its disadvantages, however. Most important among them are (1) cost disadvantages, (2) disadvantages that arise when technology is changing fast, and (3) disadvantages that arise when demand is unpredictable. These disadvantages can give rise to bureaucratic costs, making the benefits of vertical integration not always as substantial as they might seem initially. When deciding whether to integrate, strategic managers need to weigh the value created by vertical integration against the bureaucratic costs of implementing the strategy. In many cases, the bureaucratic costs are such that vertical integration may reduce rather than increase value.

Cost disadvantages   Although often undertaken to gain a cost advantage, vertical integration can bring higher costs if a company becomes committed to purchasing inputs from company-owned suppliers when low-cost external sources of supply exist. For example, currently General Motors is at a cost disadvantage in relation to Chrysler because it makes 70 percent of its own components, whereas Chrysler makes only 30 percent. GM has to pay United Auto Workers wages to workers in its own component supply operations, and these wages are generally $2 more per hour than the wages paid by independent component suppliers. Thus, as General Motors exemplifies, vertical integration can be a disadvantage when a company's own sources of supply have higher operating costs than those of independent suppliers.

Company-owned suppliers might have high operating costs, relative to independent suppliers, because company-owned suppliers know that they can always sell their output to other parts of the company. The fact that they do not have to compete for orders with other suppliers reduces their incentive to minimize operating costs. Indeed, the managers of the supply operation may be tempted to pass on any cost increases to other parts of the company in the form of higher transfer prices, rather than looking for ways to reduce those costs. In essence, this lack of incentive to reduce costs can give rise to substantial *bureaucratic costs*. The problem may be less serious, however, when the company pursues taper, rather than full, integration, since the need to compete with independent suppliers can produce a downward pressure on the cost structure of company-owned suppliers.

Technological change   When technology is changing fast, vertical integration poses the hazard of tying a company to an obsolescent technology.[10] Consider a radio manufacturer who in the 1950s integrated backward and acquired a manufacturer of vacuum tubes. When in the 1960s transistors replaced vacuum tubes as a major component in radios, this company found itself tied to a technologically obsolescent business. Switching to transistors would have meant writing off its investment in vacuum tubes. Thus the company was reluctant to change and instead continued to use vacuum tubes in its radios while its nonintegrated competitors were rapidly switching to the new technology. Since it kept making an outdated product, the company rapidly lost market share. Thus vertical integration can inhibit a company's ability to change its suppliers or its distribution systems to match the requirements of changing technology.

Demand uncertainty   Vertical integration can also be risky in unstable or unpredictable demand conditions. When demand is stable, higher degrees of vertical integration might be managed with relative ease. Stable demand allows better scheduling and coordination of production flows among different activities. When demand conditions are unstable or unpredictable, achieving close coordination among vertically integrated activities may be difficult. The resulting inefficiencies can give rise to significant bureaucratic costs.

The problem involves balancing capacity among different stages of a process. For example, an auto manufacturer might vertically integrate backward to acquire a supplier of carburetors that has a capacity exactly matching the auto manufacturer's needs. However, if demand for autos subsequently falls, the automaker will find itself locked into a business that is running below capacity. Clearly, this would be uneconomical. The auto manufacturers could avoid this situation by continuing to buy carburetors on the open market rather than making them itself.

If demand conditions are unpredictable, taper integration might be somewhat less risky than full integration. When a company provides only part of its total input requirements from company-owned suppliers, in times of low demand it can keep its in-house suppliers running at full capacity by ordering exclusively from them.

Summary: Vertical Integration

Although vertical integration can create value, it may also result in substantial costs. These costs arise from the lack of incentive that company-owned suppliers have to reduce their operating costs and from a possible lack of strategic flexibility in the face of changing technology or uncertain demand conditions. Together, these costs form a major component of the bureaucratic costs of vertical integration. Their existence places a limit on the amount of vertical integration that can be profitably pursued.

However, the pursuit of taper integration rather than full integration may reduce the bureaucratic costs of vertical integration. In terms of the framework introduced earlier, taper integration can be viewed as lowering the marginal-bureaucratic-cost curve. In turn, this allows a company to profitably pursue more extensive vertical integration. This is illustrated in Figure 7.6, where MBC_F is the marginal-bureaucratic-cost curve for a company pursuing full integration and MBC_T is the marginal-bureaucratic-cost curve for a company pursuing taper integration. With full integration it pays a company to pursue vertical integration up to V_1 on the horizontal axis. Taper integration, however, creates an incentive for in-house suppliers to reduce their operating costs and increases the company's ability to respond to changing demand conditions. Thus a switch from full to taper integration reduces the marginal-bureaucratic-cost curve from MBC_F to MBC_T and allows the company to vertically integrate up to V_2 on the horizontal axis. In other words, a company that pursues taper integration can profitably

FIGURE 7.6   **Comparing the marginal bureaucratic costs of taper and full integration**

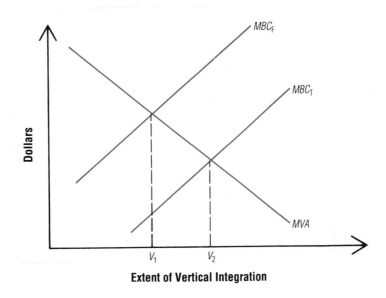

manage greater levels of vertical integration than can a company that pursues full integration. Ultimately, however, although the pursuit of taper integration may reduce bureaucratic costs, it cannot eliminate them altogether. Thus there is a very real limit to extent of vertical integration that a company can profitably manage.

7.6 ALTERNATIVE TO VERTICAL INTEGRATION: LONG-TERM CONTRACTING

The Benefits of Long-Term Contracting

One strategy that companies can adopt in order to capture some if not all of the benefits of vertical integration, without having to deal with many of the bureaucratic costs that accompany vertical integration (whether taper or full integration), is to enter into long-term contracts with suppliers or buyers. Long-term contracts are long-term cooperative relationships between two companies. One agrees to supply the other; the other agrees to continue purchasing from that supplier; and both commit themselves to working together to look for ways of lowering the costs or raising the quality of inputs into the downstream company's value-creation process. If attainable, such a stable long-term relationship allows the participating companies to share the value that might be created by vertical integration while avoiding many of the bureaucratic costs associated with ownership of an adjacent stage in the raw-material-to-consumer production chain. Thus long-term contracts can be a substitute for vertical integration.

For example, as noted in Chapter 6, many of the Japanese auto companies have cooperative relationships with their component-parts suppliers that go back decades. These relationships involve the auto companies and their suppliers in getting together and working out ways to increase value-added through, for example, the implementation of just-in-time inventory systems, or by cooperating on component-part designs for improving quality and lowering assembly costs. Thus the Japanese auto majors have been able to capture many of the benefits from vertical integration, particularly those arising from production cost savings and the protection of product quality, without having to bear the bureaucratic costs associated with formal vertical integration. The component-parts suppliers also benefit from these relationships, since they grow with the company they supply and share in its success.

In stark contrast, U.S. auto companies have tended to pursue formal vertical integration to a much greater degree than their Japanese counterparts. General Motors manufactures 70 percent of its own component parts, Ford 50 percent, and Chrysler 30 percent, compared with less than 20 percent among most Japanese auto companies.[11] The increased bureaucratic costs of managing extensive vertical integration have lowered the profits of the U.S. companies relative to their Japanese counterparts.

Moreover, when the U.S. auto companies decide not to vertically integrate, instead of entering into cooperative long-term relationships with independent component suppliers, they have tended to use their powerful position to play their component suppliers off against each other, frequently dictating terms to them. For example, in 1986 Chrysler instructed its part suppliers to cut their prices by 5 percent, regardless of prior pricing agreements. Chrysler used the threat to weed out suppliers that did not obey as a means of forcing through the policy. Such action may yield short-term benefits for an auto major, but there is a long-term cost to be born in the form of lack of trust and hostility between the company and its suppliers. This may inhibit the introduction of just-in-time inventory systems, make it difficult for suppliers and manufacturers to work together on component-part designs for lowering costs and improving quality, and generally make component suppliers hesitant to commit themselves to cost-reducing investments that make them too dependent on the business of any one auto major.

As a consequence of their inability to establish cooperative long-term relationships with their suppliers, the U.S. auto majors tend to have higher-cost and lower-quality inputs. For example, according to industry estimates, in 1985 for comparable $6,000 small cars U.S. manufacturers spent an average of $3,350 on parts, materials, and services, whereas the average Japanese company spent $2,750—a cost saving of $600 achieved largely through more efficient handling of relationships with suppliers. Long-term contracting as practiced by the Japanese was apparently associated with the lowest cost of material inputs, while *both* vertical integration *and* the lack of long-term cooperative relationships between auto majors and independent suppliers, as is typical in the United States, appear to have raised the costs and lowered the quality of inputs.[12] All this suggests that in many ways, a cooperative long-term relationship between supplier and buyer is better than formal vertical integration.

Impediments to Long-Term Contracting

Given the obvious benefits of long-term contracting, why is it not more widely practiced? The main problem seems to be a lack of trust, which makes companies hesitant to enter into long-term relationships. Lack of trust is particularly likely when one of the companies has to make substantial capital investments in *specialized assets* in order to enter into the relationship. A specialized asset is one that has few if any alternative uses. For example, an aluminum smelter is a specialized asset because it can be used to smelt only aluminum and not any other metal. An investment in specialized assets can be viewed as a sunk cost. Once made, it cannot be recovered.

Lack of trust between companies might arise from a fear that once a company has incurred sunk costs, its partner might use the expenditure as a lever to seek more favorable terms. For example, consider the case of an aluminum company trying to decide where to locate a $500-million aluminum smelter. Smelting aluminum is an energy-intensive process, so energy costs are likely to be a prime determinant of the location decision. Imagine that the aluminum company decides to site its smelter next door to a power station, after having agreed to buy power at a previously agreed-to price. The danger is that once the aluminum company incurs the $500-million investment associated with establishing its operations (that is, once the company incurs sunk costs), the power company might break its prior agreement and raise energy prices. It can do this secure in the knowledge that having committed $500 million to the new smelter, the aluminum company is in no position to close its operations and set up elsewhere.

However, there are ways of designing long-term cooperative relationships to build trust and reduce the hazards associated with making investments in specialized assets. We consider these in the next section.

Establishing Long-Term Agreements

One way of designing long-term cooperative relationships to build trust and reduce the possibility of a company reneging on an agreement is for the company making investments in specialized assets to demand a *hostage* from its partner. Another is by establishing a *credible commitment* on the part of both parties to build a trusting long-term relationship.[13]

Hostage taking   The idea behind hostage taking is that when a company makes investments in specialized assets in order to enter into a long-term relationship with a partner, it seeks a hostage from its partner that can be used as a guarantee that its partner will not subsequently renege on any agreement between the two. Thus the aluminum-smelting company discussed above, before investing any money, might demand that the power company invest in a bond that is held in trust by a third party and transferred to the aluminum company if the power company raises prices above previously agreed-to levels. The bond is the hostage used to ensure that the power company does not renege on pricing agreements.

For an example of a hostage-taking situation, consider the cooperative relationship between Boeing and Northrop. Northrop is a major subcontractor for Boeing's commercial airline division, providing many component parts for the 747 and 767 aircraft. In order to serve the special needs of Boeing, Northrop has had to make substantial investments in specialized assets. In theory, because of the sunk costs associated with such investments, Northrop is dependent on Boeing and Boeing is thus in a position to renege on previous agreements and use the threat to switch orders to other suppliers as a way of driving down prices. However, in practice Boeing is unlikely to do this since the company is also a major supplier to Northrop's defense division, providing many parts for the Stealth bomber. Boeing has had to make substantial investments in specialized assets in order to serve the needs of Northrop. Thus both companies are *mutually dependent* on each other. Boeing, therefore, is unlikely to renege on any pricing agreements with Northrop, since it knows that Northrop could respond in kind. In other words, each company holds a hostage that can be used as insurance against the other company's unilaterally reneging on prior pricing agreements.

Credible commitments   A credible commitment is a believable commitment to support the development of a long-term relationship between companies. To understand the concept of credibility in this context, consider the relationship between General Electric and IBM. GE is one of the major suppliers of advanced semiconductor chips to IBM, and many of the chips are customized to IBM's own requirements. In order to meet IBM's specific needs, GE has had to make substantial investments in specialized assets that have little other value. As a consequence, GE is dependent on IBM and faces a risk that IBM will take advantage of this dependence to demand lower prices. In theory IBM could back up its demand with the threat to switch to another supplier. However, GE reduced the risk of this occurring by getting IBM to enter into a contractual agreement that committed IBM to purchase chips from GE until the end of the 1990s. In addition, IBM agreed to share in the costs of developing the customized chips, thereby reducing GE's investments in specialized assets. Thus, by publicly committing itself to a long-term contract, and by putting some money into the development of the customized chips, IBM has essentially made a *credible commitment* to continue purchasing those chips from GE.

Summary   By establishing credible commitments or by taking hostages, companies may be able to use long-term contracts to realize much of the value associated with vertical integration, without having to bear the bureaucratic costs of formal vertical integration. As a general point, it should be noted that the growing importance of just-in-time inventory systems as a way of reducing costs and enhancing quality is increasing the pressure for companies to enter into long-term agreements in a wide range of industries. Thus we might reasonably expect to see a growth in the popularity of such agreements in the future. However, it is not always possible to reach such agreements, in which case formal vertical integration may be called for.

7.7 DIVERSIFICATION

There are two major types of diversification: *related diversification* and *unrelated diversification*. Related diversification is diversification into a new activity that is linked to a company's existing activity by commonality between one or more components of each activity's value chain. Normally, these linkages are based on manufacturing, marketing, materials management, and technological commonalities. The diversification of Philip Morris into the brewing industry with the acquisition of Miller Brewing is an example of related diversification because there are marketing commonalities between the brewing and tobacco business (both are consumer product businesses in which competitive success depends on brand-positioning skills). Unrelated diversification is diversification into a new activity that has no obvious commonalities with any of the company's existing activities. The acquisitions made by Hanson Trust, considered in the Opening Incident, are an example of unrelated diversification.

In this section, we begin by looking at how diversification can create value for a company and then we examine some reasons why so much diversification apparently dissipates rather than creates value. We include a consideration of the bureaucratic costs of diversification. Finally, we consider some of the factors that determine the choice between the strategies of related and unrelated diversification.

Creating Value Through Diversification

Most companies first consider diversification when they are generating financial resources *in excess of* those necessary to maintain a competitive advantage in their original, or core. business.[14] The question they must tackle is how to invest the excess resources in order to create value. Diversification can create value in four main ways: (1) through an internal capital market, (2) by restructuring, (3) by transferring skills among businesses, and (4) by sharing functions or resources.

Establishing an internal capital market   A diversified company can create value by establishing within the company an internal capital market that takes over some of the functions of the stock market. In an internal capital market, the head office has three major roles: (1) to perform strategic planning functions concerning the composition of the corporate portfolio (decisions about acquisitions and divestments); (2) to set financial targets and monitor the subsequent performance of business units, intervening selectively in underperforming units to correct any problems; and (3) to allocate corporate capital among the competing claims of different business units. The business units themselves are set up as autonomous profit centers, subject only to financial controls from the head office.

Advocates of this strategy contend that the head office can monitor business-unit performance and allocate financial resources among units more efficiently than the stock market could do if each business unit were an independent company.[15] The reason is that the head office, as an internal investor, has access to better information about the performance of business units and is better able to use that information than could stock market investors if each business unit were independent.

For example, the head office can use its authority to demand detailed information on the efficiency of a business unit's operations, whereas stock market investors have to make judgments on the basis of whatever information a company chooses to release to them. The head office can also intervene selectively in underperforming business units and fine-tune their operations (for instance, by making relatively minor management changes), whereas the stock market can make only drastic adjustments (such as a takeover). Consequently, the stock market may fail to discipline underperforming management teams adequately and may allocate too few capital resources to some companies and too many to others. The head office of a diversified company can both discipline underperforming management teams and allocate resources much more effectively.

Since a company is more efficient than the stock market in monitoring performance and allocating capital, it should acquire potentially strong but poorly managed enterprises that are undervalued by the stock market. By exposing acquired companies to the discipline of tight financial controls and efficient capital allocation, an internal capital market encourages and rewards aggressive profit-seeking behavior by the acquired company's management. The result can be an increase in the efficiency of the value-creation process within the acquired company. Specifically, the managers of the acquired company might be motivated to look for ways to reduce the costs of value creation and to perform individual value-creation functions in a way that leads to differentiation and a premium price. Such improvements in the efficiency of value creation within the acquired company also add value to the acquiring corporation.

However, the strategy has its critics. Some contend that today's computer-drive stock market efficiently allocates resources and penalizes poorly managed companies by forcing proxy votes on key elements of corporate strategy.[16] If this is true, and it is a debatable point, the whole basis for the strategy has been destroyed. Others argue that overly tight financial controls can lead to short-run profit maximization within the business units of companies trying to create value through an internal capital market.[17] In turn, the arms-length relationship between the head office and the business units allows such behavior to go undetected until a good deal of damage has been done. The poor performance of portfolio diversifiers, such as Gulf & Western Industries, Consolidated Foods Corporation, and ITT, has lent weight to these criticisms. However, there are also some spectacular examples of how successful the strategy can be—for instance, the Anglo-American conglomerate BTR Inc.[18] More than anything else, these conflicting examples suggest that the strategy is difficult to implement.

Restructuring A restructuring strategy has a lot in common with an internal capital market strategy. The essential differences have to do with the degree to which the head office becomes involved in business-unit operations. Companies that pursue a restructuring strategy seek out poorly managed, underperforming, or undeveloped companies. The objective is to acquire such companies and then intervene in a *proactive* fashion, frequently changing the acquired company's management team, developing new business-level strategies, and infusing the company with new financial or technological resources. If all goes well, the upshot is a dramatic improvement in the competitive position and financial health of the acquired company, creating value for the acquiring enterprise.

The diversification strategy of Hanson Trust, described in the Opening Incident, is based on restructuring. Hanson seeks out companies that are not maximizing stockholder wealth. Such companies are normally characterized by excess organizational slack. This means that they use more resources than necessary to run their business. For example, managers may be given expensive company cars as perks; corporate headquarters may be lavishly decorated and overstaffed; and the company may own a ranch to entertain its visiting executives or run a fleet of jets to fly its managers around the country.

Because of their inefficiency, companies with a high degree of organizational slack are often undervalued by the stock market. Companies such as Hanson Trust can acquire them at a reasonable price and then reorganize them to increase their efficiency. Excess staff are likely to be laid off and the executive jets, company cars, and expensive headquarters sold. Typically, unwanted subsidiary companies are also sold at this stage. Whatever remains is then subjected to central financial controls designed to instill profit discipline and efficiency awareness. The result, as in the case of the Hanson/SCM acquisition, is improved performance through lower operating costs or increased differentiation. Thus the acquiring company creates value for its stockholders by improving the efficiency of value creation in acquired companies.

Transferring skills   Companies that base their diversification strategy on transferring skills seek out new businesses related to their existing business by one or more value-creation functions (for example, manufacturing, marketing, materials management, and R&D—see Chapter 4). They may want to create value by drawing on the distinctive skills in one or more of their existing value-creation functions in order to improve the competitive position of the new business. Alternatively, they may acquire a company in a different business area in the belief that some of the skills of the acquired company might improve the efficiency of their existing value-creation activities. If successful, such skill transfers can lower the costs of value creation in one or more of a company's diversified businesses or enable one or more of a company's diversified businesses to undertake their value-creation functions in a way that leads to differentiation and a premium price.

An example is Germany's Daimler Benz, the maker of Mercedes-Benz cars. In recent years Daimler has diversified into household goods, defense electronics, automation systems, and aerospace. The strategy is based on a belief that the transfer of state-of-the-art technological know-how between the different businesses of the company will enhance the competitive position of each, enabling all of Daimler Benz's businesses to better differentiate themselves with regard to technology.

For such a strategy to work, the skills being transferred must involve activities that are important for establishing a competitive advantage. All too often, companies assume that any commonality is sufficient for creating value. General Motors' acquisition of Hughes Aircraft, made simply because autos and auto manufacturing were going electronic and Hughes was an electronics concern, demonstrates the folly of overestimating the commonalities among businesses. To date, the acquisition has failed to realize any of the anticipated gains for GM, whose competitive position has only worsened. (One may similarly raise questions about the value that Daimler Benz might create from transferring technological know-how between autos and aerospace.)

Philip Morris's transfer of marketing skills to Miller Brewing, discussed earlier, is perhaps one of the classic examples of how value *can* be created by skill transfers. Drawing on its marketing and brand-positioning skills, Philip Morris pioneered the introduction of Miller Lite, the product that redefined the brewing industry and moved Miller from number six to number two in the market. Rockwell International's diversification into factory automation with the company's 1985 acquisition of Allen-Bradley Canada Ltd. is another example of skill transfers. In this case, skill transfers were based on technological linkages between different activities. Rockwell has given Allen-Bradley strong research and development support and Rockwell's own electronics technology, and Allen-Bradley's factory automation expertise is boosting efficiency in Rockwell's commercial and defense factories.[19]

Sharing resources   Like skill transfers, diversification to share resources is possible only when there are significant commonalities between one or more of the value-creation functions of a company's existing and new activities. By *resources* we mean manufacturing, marketing, R&D, human resources, and the like. The objective of sharing resources is to create value from the realization of **economies of scope**.[20] Economies of scope arise when two or more business units share manufacturing facilities, distribution channels, advertising campaigns, R&D costs, and so on. Each business unit that shares resources has to invest less in the shared functions. For example, the costs of General Electric's advertising, sales, and service activities in major appliances are low because they are spread over a wide range of products. In addition, such a strategy can utilize the capacity of certain functions better. For example, by producing the components for the assembly operations of two distinct businesses, a component-manufacturing plant may be able to operate at a greater capacity, thereby realizing *economies of scale* in addition to economies of scope.

Thus a diversification strategy based on resource sharing can help a company attain a low-cost position in each of the businesses in which it operates. As such, diversification to share resources can be a valid way of *supporting* the generic business-level strategy of cost leadership. However, strategic managers need to be aware that the bureaucratic costs of coordination necessary to achieve resource sharing within a company often outweigh the value that can be created by such a strategy.[21] Consequently, the strategy should be pursued only when sharing is likely to generate a *significant* competitive advantage in one or more of a company's business units.

Procter & Gamble's disposable diaper and paper towel businesses offer one of the best examples of successful resource sharing. These businesses share the costs of procuring certain raw materials (such as paper) and developing the technology for new products and processes. In addition, a joint sales force sells both products to supermarket buyers, and both products are shipped by means of the same distribution system. This resource sharing has given both business units a cost advantage that has enabled them to undercut their less diversified competitors.[22]

Summary   There are four ways in which a diversified company can create value. However, as discussed early in this chapter, the *marginal value* added by each additional diversification move tends to decline as a company exploits its most profitable diversification opportunities. This suggests that there are limits to the amount of value that can be created through diversification. In addition, as also discussed early in this chapter, when considering how much diversification a company can profitably pursue, it is necessary to consider the bureaucratic costs of diversification.

The Bureaucratic Costs of Diversification

In a study that looked at the diversification of thirty-three major U.S. corporations between 1950 and 1986, Michael Porter observed that the track record of corporate diversification has been dismal.[23] Porter found that most of the companies had divested many more diversified acquisitions than they had kept. He concluded that the corporate diversification strategies of most companies have dissipated value instead of creating it. More generally, a large number of academic studies have come to the general conclusion that *extensive* diversification tends to depress rather than improve company profitability.[24] This research begs the question of why diversification so often fails.

One reason so much diversification fails is that all too often the bureaucratic costs of diversification exceed the value created by the strategy. Companies often diversify past the point at which it is profitable to do so (in terms of Figure 7.2, they diversify to the point where *MVA* is less than *MBC*). The bureaucratic costs of diversification arise from two sources: (1) the number of businesses in a company's portfolio and (2) the extent of coordination required between the different businesses of the company in order to realize value from a diversification strategy. We consider each of these sources in turn.

Number of businesses   The greater the number of businesses in a company's portfolio, the more difficult it is for corporate management to remain informed about the complexities of each business. Management simply does not have the time to process all of the information that is required to assess the strategic plan of each business unit objectively. This problem began to occur at General Electric in the 1970s. As then-CEO Reg Jones commented:

> I tried to review each plan in great detail. This effort took untold hours and placed a tremendous burden on the corporate executive office. After awhile I began to realize that no matter how hard we would work, we could not achieve the necessary in-depth understanding of the 40-odd business unit plans.[25]

One consequence of information overload in extensively diversified companies is that corporate-level management ends up making important resource allocation decisions on the basis of only the most superficial analysis of the competitive position of each business unit. Thus, for example, a promising business unit may be starved of investment funds while other business units receive far more cash than they can profitably reinvest in their operations. Another consequence is that the lack of familiarity with operating affairs on the part of corporate-level management increases the probability that business-level managers will be able to deceive corporate-level managers. For example, business-unit managers may be able to justify poor performance on the grounds that it is a consequence of difficult competitive conditions, when in reality it is the consequence of poor management.

Thus information overload can result in substantial inefficiencies within extensively diversified companies. These inefficiencies include the suboptimal allocation of cash resources within the company and a failure by corporate management to successfully encourage and reward aggressive profit-seeking behavior by business-unit managers. In other words, information overload can make it extremely difficult to create value by establishing an internal capital market within a diversified company or by pursuing a restructuring strategy.

The inefficiencies that arise from information overload can be regarded as one component of the bureaucratic costs of extensive diversification. Of course, these costs can be reduced to manageable proportions if a company limits the scope of its diversification. Indeed, a desire to reduce these costs lay behind the 1980s divestments and strategic concentration strategies of conglomerates of the 1960s and 1970s such as Esmark Corporation, General Electric, ITT, Textron, Tenneco, and United Technologies. Under the leadership of Jack Welch, for example, GE switched its emphasis from forty main business units to sixteen main business units contained within three clearly defined sectors. In terms of Figure 7.2, discussed earlier, the inefficiencies from information overload arise when a company diversifies beyond the point at which *MVA* equals *MBC*.

Coordination between businesses   A second source of bureaucratic costs arises from the coordination required to realize value from a diversification strategy based on skill transfers or resource sharing. Both transferring skills and sharing resources require close coordination between business units. The bureaucratic mechanisms necessary to achieve that coordination give rise to bureaucratic costs. (We discuss the mechanisms for achieving coordination in Chapter 11.)

More seriously, however, substantial bureaucratic costs can arise from an inability to identify the unique profit contribution of a business unit that is sharing resources with another unit. Consider a company that has two business units—one producing household products (such as liquid soap and laundry detergent) and another producing packaged food products. The products of both units are sold through supermarkets. In order to lower the costs of value creation, the parent company decides to pool the marketing and sales functions of each business unit. Pooling allows the business units to share the costs of a sales force (one sales force can sell the products of both divisions) and gain cost economies from using the same physical distribution system. The organizational structure required to achieve this might be similar to that illustrated in Figure 7.7. The company is organized into three main divisions: a household products division, a food products division, and a marketing division.

Although such an arrangement may create value, it can also give rise to substantial control problems and hence bureaucratic costs. For example, if the performance of the household products business begins to slip, identifying who is to be held accountable—the management of the household products division or the management of the marketing division—may prove difficult. Indeed, each may blame the other for poor performance: The management of the household products division might blame the marketing policies of the marketing division, and the management of the marketing division might blame the poor quality and high costs of products produced by the household products division. Although this kind of problem can be resolved if corporate management directly audits the affairs of both divisions, doing so is costly in both the time and the effort that corporate management must expend.

FIGURE 7.7   **The structure of a company sharing marketing between two business units**

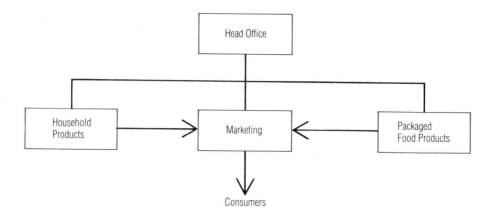

FIGURE 7.8   **Marginal-bureaucratic-cost curves and the need for coordination**

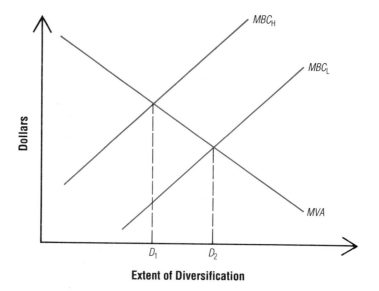

Now imagine the situation within a company that is trying to create value by sharing marketing, manufacturing, and R&D resources across ten businesses rather than just two. Clearly, the accountability problem could become far more serious in such a company. Indeed, the problem might become so serious that the effort involved in trying to tie down accountability might create a serious information overload for corporate management. When this occurs, corporate management effectively loses control of the company. The consequences of not being able to tie down accountability may include an inability by corporate management to encourage and reward aggressive profit-seeking behavior by business-unit managers, poor resource allocation decisions, and a generally high level of organizational slack. All of these inefficiencies can be considered part of the bureaucratic costs of diversification to share resources.

Summary   Although diversification can create value for a company in a number of ways, it inevitably involves bureaucratic costs. The costs tend to be greater (1) the greater the number of business units within a company and (2) the greater the need for coordination between those business units. Thus bureaucratic costs are much greater in a company that has twenty businesses, all of which are trying to share resources, than in a company that has ten businesses, none of which are trying to share resources.

The implications are illustrated in Figure 7.8. The marginal bureaucratic costs of a diversified company with a high need for coordination between business units (MBC_H) are compared with the marginal bureaucratic costs of a diversified company with a low need for coordination between business units (MBC_L). A company with a high need for coordination is one that is trying to create value through resource sharing. A company with a low need for coordination is one that is trying to create value through the operation of an internal capital market or by restructuring. As can be seen, at every level of diversification, MBC_H is greater than MBC_L. If we assume that both companies have the same marginal-value-added curve, the implication is that the company with a low need for coordination can profitably manage a greater extent of diversification than can the company with a high need for coordination. (The company with a low need for coordination can manage $0-D_2$ diversification profitably, and the company with a high need for coordination can manage only $0-D_1$ diversification profitably.) This analysis has implications for a company's choice between a strategy of related and unrelated diversification, which is discussed in a later section.

Diversification That Dissipates Value

Another reason so much diversification apparently fails to create value is that many companies diversify for the wrong reasons. As a consequence, they end up dissipating value rather than creating it. This is particularly true of diversification to "pool risks" or to "achieve greater growth," both of which are often given by company managers as reasons for diversification.

Consider *diversification to pool risks*. The benefits of risk pooling are said to come from merging imperfectly correlated income streams to create a more stable income stream. An example of risk pooling might be USX's diversification into the oil and gas industry in an attempt to offset the adverse effects of cyclical downturns in the steel industry. According to the advocates of risk pooling, the more stable income stream reduces the risk of bankruptcy and is in the best interests of the company's stockholders.

However, this argument ignores two facts. First, stockholders can easily eliminate the risks inherent in holding an individual stock by diversifying their own portfolios, and they can do so at a much lower cost than the company can. Thus, far from being in the best interests of stockholders, attempts to pool risks through diversification represent an unproductive use of resources. Second, the vast majority of research on this topic suggests that corporate diversification is not a very effective way to pool risks.[26] The business cycles of different industries are not easy to predict and in any case tend to be less important than a general economic downturn that hits all industries simultaneously. International Harvester illustrates the point. By 1979 International Harvester had diversified into three major businesses: agricultural equipment, construction equipment, and trucks. These businesses were supposed to follow different business cycles, cushioning the company against severe fluctuations. In the early 1980s, however, all these businesses suffered a downturn at the same time, cumulating a $2.9-billion loss for Harvester.

Now consider *diversification to achieve greater growth*. Such diversification is not a coherent strategy because growth on its own does not create value. Growth should be the *by-product,* not the objective, of a diversification strategy. However, companies sometimes diversify for reasons of growth alone, rather than to gain any well-thought-out strategic advantage. ITT under the leadership of Harold Geneen took this path. Geneen turned ITT from an international telecommunications company into a broadly based conglomerate consisting of more than 100 separate businesses with interests in such diverse areas as baking, car rental, defense electronics, fire hydrants, insurance, hotels, paper products, and telecommunications. The strategy seemed to have more to do with Geneen's desire to build an empire than with maximizing the company's value.[27] Since Geneen's departure in 1979, ITT's management has been trying to divest many of the businesses acquired under his leadership and to concentrate on insurance and financial services.

Related or Unrelated Diversification?

One issue that a company must resolve is whether to diversify into businesses related to its existing business by value-chain commonalities or into totally new businesses. The distinction here is between related diversification and unrelated diversification. By definition, a related company can create value by resource sharing and by transferring skills between businesses. It can also carry out some restructuring and create value by applying internal capital market concepts to the management of its diverse activities. By way of contrast, since there are no commonalities between the value chains of unrelated businesses, an unrelated company cannot create value by sharing resources or transferring skills between businesses. Unrelated diversifiers can create value only by restructuring and creating an internal capital market.

Since related diversification can create value in more ways than unrelated diversification can, one might think that related diversification should be the preferred strategy. In addition, related diversification is normally perceived as involving fewer risks because the company is moving into business areas about which top management has some knowledge. Probably because of those considerations, most diversified companies display a preference for related diversification.[28] However, research suggests that the average related company is no more profitable than the average unrelated company.[29] How can this be, if related diversification is associated with more benefits than is unrelated diversification?

The answer to this question is actually quite simple. Bureaucratic costs arise from (1) the number of businesses in a company's portfolio and (2) the extent of coordination required between the different businesses in order to realize value from a diversification strategy. An unrelated company does not have to achieve coordination between business units. Thus it has to cope only with the bureaucratic costs that arise from the number of businesses in its portfolio. In contrast, a related diversified company has to achieve coordination between business units if it is to realize the value that comes from skill transfers and resource sharing. As a consequence, it has to cope with the bureaucratic costs that arise *both* from the number of business units in its portfolio *and* from coordination between business units. Thus, although it is true that related diversified companies can create value in more ways than unrelated companies can, they have to bear higher bureaucratic costs in order to do so. These higher costs may cancel out the higher benefits, making the strategy no more profitable than one of unrelated diversification. This is summarized in Table 7.2.

How then is a company to choose between these strategies? The choice depends on a comparison of the relative value-added and bureaucratic costs associated with each strategy. In making this comparison, it is important to note that the opportunities for creating value from related diversification are a function of the extent of commonalities between the skills required to compete in the company's core business and the skills required to compete in other industrial and commercial areas. Some companies' skills are so specialized that they have few applications outside the core businesses. For example, since the commonalities

TABLE 7.2   **Comparing related and unrelated diversification**

Strategy	Ways of creating value	Source of bureaucratic costs
Related	Internal capital market	Number of businesses
	Restructuring Transferring skills Sharing resources	Coordination between businesses
Unrelated	Internal capital market Restructuring	Number of businesses

between steel making and other industrial or commercial operations are few, most steel companies have diversified into unrelated industries (LTV into defense contracting, USX into oil and gas). When companies have less specialized skills, they can find many more related diversification opportunities outside the core business. Examples include chemical companies (such as Dow Chemical and Du Pont) and electrical engineering companies (such as General Electric). Consequently, the opportunities available to them to create value from related diversification are much greater.

Thus it pays a firm to concentrate on related diversification when (1) the company's core skills are applicable to a wide variety of industrial and commercial situations and (2) the bureaucratic costs of implementation do not exceed the value that can be created through resource sharing or skill transfers. The second condition is likely to hold only for companies that are moderately diversified. At high levels of related diversification, the bureaucratic costs of additional diversification are likely to outweigh the value created by that diversification, and the strategy may become unprofitable.

By the same logic, it may pay a company to concentrate on unrelated diversification when (1) the company's core skills are highly specialized and have few applications outside the company's core business and (2) the bureaucratic costs of implementation do not exceed the value that can be created by establishing an internal capital market or pursuing a restructuring strategy. Once again, however, the second condition is unlikely to hold for companies that are highly diversified. Thus, no matter whether a company pursues a related or an unrelated diversification strategy, the existence of bureaucratic costs suggests that there are very real limits to the profitable growth of the company.

7.8 ALTERNATIVE TO DIVERSIFICATION: STRATEGIC ALLIANCES

Diversification can be unprofitable because of the bureaucratic costs associated with implementing the strategy. One way of trying to realize the value associated with diversification, without having to bear the same level of bureaucratic costs, is to enter into a strategic alliance with another company to start a new business venture.

In this context, strategic alliances are essentially agreements between two or more companies to share the costs, risks, and benefits associated with developing new business opportunities. Many strategic alliances are constituted as formal joint ventures in which each party has an equity stake. Other alliances take the form of a long-term contract between companies in which they agree to undertake some joint activity that benefits both. Agreements to work together on joint R&D projects often take this form.

Strategic alliances seem to be a particularly viable option when a company wishes to create value from transferring skills or sharing resources between diversified businesses. Alliances offer companies a framework within which to share the resources required to establish a new business. Alternatively, alliances enable companies to swap complementary skills to produce a new range of products. For example, consider the recent alliance between United Technologies and Dow Chemical to build plastic-based composite parts for the aerospace industry. United Technologies is already involved in the aerospace industry (it builds Sikorsky helicopters), and Dow Chemical has skills in the development and manufacture of plastic-based composites. The alliance calls for United Technologies to contribute its advanced aerospace skills and Dow its skills in developing and manufacturing plastic-based composites to a joint venture in which each company will have a 50 percent equity stake. The joint venture will then undertake the task of developing, manufacturing, and marketing a new line of plastic-based composite parts for the aerospace industry. Through the alliance, both companies will become involved in new activities. They will, in short, be able to realize some of the benefits associated with related diversification without having to merge activities formally or bear the costs and risks of developing the new products on their own.

Bureaucratic costs are reduced because neither Dow nor United Technologies is actually expanding its own organization, nor does either company have to coordinate internal skill transfers. Rather, after incorporation the joint venture will operate as an independent company, and both Dow and United Technologies will receive payment in the form of dividends.

Of course, there is a down side to such alliances. For one thing, profits must be split with an alliance partner, whereas with full diversification a company gets to keep all of the profits. Another problem is that when a company enters into an alliance, it always runs the risk that it might give away critical know-how to its alliance partner, who might then use that know-how to compete directly with the company in the future. Thus, for example, having gained access to Dow's expertise in plastic-based composites, United Technologies might dissolve the alliance and produce these materials on its own. However, as in the case of vertical integration, the risk can be minimized if Dow gets a *credible commitment* from United Technologies. By entering into a formal joint venture, rather than a more loosely structured alliance, United Technologies has given such a commitment because it has had to invest substantial amounts of capital. Thus, if United Technologies tried to produce plastic-based composites on its own, it would essentially be competing against itself.

7.9 RETRENCHMENT AND TURNAROUND

Vertical integration and diversification are strategies for profitable expansion. However, for many of the reasons discussed above, corporate strategies sometimes fail and corporate decline ensues. Retrenchment is not so much a corporate strategy as a strategic response to corporate decline. The objective of retrenchment is to restructure the operations of a troubled company in order to halt corporate decline and return the company to profitability. In this section, we review the causes of corporate decline and then examine the steps toward successful retrenchment and turnaround.

The Causes of Corporate Decline

Six main causes stand out in most cases of corporate decline: poor management, overexpansion, inadequate financial controls, high costs, the emergence of powerful new competition, and unforeseen shifts in demand.[30] Normally, several, if not all, of these factors are present in a decline situation. For example, Chrysler's decline toward near-bankruptcy in the 1970s was brought on by poor top management, which had failed to put adequate financial controls in place. As a result, Chrysler's cost structure got out of line, inhibiting Chrysler's ability to respond to powerful, new, low-cost Japanese competition. In addition, the unforeseen shift in demand toward compact and subcompact cars after the oil price hikes of 1974 and 1979 left Chrysler, as a manufacturer of intermediate- and full-size models, ill prepared to serve the market.

Poor management   "Poor management" covers a multitude of sins, ranging from sheer incompetence to neglect of core businesses and an insufficient number of good managers. Although not necessarily a bad thing, one-person rule often seems to be at the root of poor management. One study found that the presence of a dominant and autocratic chief executive with a passion for empire-building strategies often characterizes many failing companies.[31] Another study of eighty-one turnaround situations found that in thirty-six cases troubled companies suffered from an autocratic manager who tried to do it all and, in the face of complexity and change, could not.[32] Examples of autocratic CEOs include Bill Bricker, the former CEO of Diamond Shamrock; Harold Geneen, the former CEO of ITT; and Roy Mason, the former CEO of the one-time Fortune 500 and later bankrupt Charter Company.

In a review of the empirical studies of turnaround situations, Richard Hoffman identified a number of other management defects commonly found in declining companies.[33] These included a lack of balanced expertise at the top (for example, too many engineers), a lack of strong middle management, a failure to provide for orderly management succession by a departing CEO (which may result in an internal succession battle), and a failure by the board of directors to monitor management's strategic decisions adequately.

Overexpansion   The empire-building strategies of autocratic CEOs such as Bricker, Geneen, and Mason often involve rapid expansion and extensive diversification. Much of this diversification tends to be poorly conceived and adds little value to a company. As observed above, the consequences of too much diversification include loss of control and an inability to cope with recessionary conditions. Moreover, companies that expand rapidly tend to do so by taking on large amounts of debt financing. Adverse economic conditions can limit a company's ability to meet its debt requirements and can thus precipitate a financial crisis.

Inadequate financial controls   The most common aspect of inadequate financial controls is a failure to assign profit responsibility to key decision makers within the organization. A lack of accountability for the financial consequences of their actions can encourage middle-level managers to employ excess staff and spend resources beyond what is necessary for maximum efficiency. In such cases, bureaucracy may balloon and costs spiral out of control. This is precisely what happened at Chrysler during the 1970s. As Lee Iacocca later noted, Jerry Greenwald, whom Iacocca brought in to head the finance function in 1980, "had a hell of a time finding anybody who could be identified as having specific responsibility for anything. They would tell him, 'Well, everyone is responsible for controlling costs.' Jerry knew very well what that meant—in the final analysis nobody was."[34]

High costs   Inadequate financial controls can lead to high costs. Beyond this, the most common cause of a high-cost structure is low labor productivity. It may stem from union-imposed restrictive working practices (as in the case of the auto and steel industries), management's failure to invest in new labor-saving technologies, or, more often, a combination of both. Other common causes include high wage rates (a particularly important factor for companies competing on costs in the global marketplace) and a failure to realize economies of scale due to low market share.

New competition   For U.S. companies, powerful new competition typically comes from overseas, and many companies have been caught unprepared for its emergence. The auto majors initially ignored the Japanese threat; by the time they responded, they had already given up substantial market share. Similarly, U.S. manufacturers of microprocessors made the mistake of discounting Asian competition, only to see their market share plummet during the mid 1980s in the face of new low-cost competition.

Unforeseen demand shifts   Unforeseen, and often unforeseeable, shifts in demand can be brought about by major changes in technology, economic or political conditions, and social and cultural norms. Although such changes can open up market opportunities for new products, they also threaten the existence of many established enterprises, necessitating restructuring. The classic example is clearly the 1974 OPEC oil price increase, which, among other things, hit the demand for autos, oil-fired central heating units, and many oil-based products, such as vinyl phonographic records. Similarly, the oil price collapse of 1983–1986 devastated many oil field drilling companies and forced them into undertaking drastic restructuring.

The Main Steps of Retrenchment and Turnaround

There is no standard model of how a company should respond to a decline. Indeed, there can be no such model because every situation is unique. However, in most successful turnaround situations, a number of common features are present. They include changing the leadership, redefining the company's strategic focus, divesting or closing unwanted assets, taking steps to improve the profitability of remaining operations, and, occasionally, making acquisitions to rebuild core operations.

Changing the leadership   Since the old leadership bears the stigma of failure, new leadership is an essential element of most retrenchment and turnaround situations. At Chrysler Lee Iacocca replaced John Riccardo; at U.S. Steel David Roderick replaced the autocratic Edgar Speer; and at Apple Computer John Sculley replaced the erratic, emotional, but sometimes brilliant Steve Jobs. To resolve a crisis, the new leader should be someone who is able to make difficult decisions, motivate lower-level managers, listen to the views of others, and delegate power when appropriate.

Redefining strategic focus   For a single-business enterprise, redefining strategic focus involves a re-evaluation of the company's business-level strategy. A failed cost leader, for example, may reorient toward a more focused or differentiated strategy. For a diversified company, redefining strategic focus means identifying the businesses in the portfolio that have the best long-term profit and growth prospects and concentrating investment there. For example, in response to the profit debacle of the early 1980s, International Harvester sold its construction and agricultural equipment businesses and concentrated on heavy and medium trucks and spare parts, in which it was number one in the United States.

Asset sales and closures   Having redefined its strategic focus, a company should divest as many unwanted assets as it can find buyers for and liquidate whatever remains. It is important not to confuse unwanted assets with unprofitable assets. Assets that no longer fit in with the redefined strategic focus of the company may be very profitable. Their sale can bring the company much-needed cash, which it can invest in improving the operations that remain.

Improving profitability   Improving the profitability of the operations that remain after asset sales and closures involves a number of steps. They may include the following: (1) layoffs of white- and blue-collar employees; (2) investments in labor-saving equipment; (3) assignment of profit responsibility to individuals and subunits within the company, by a change of organizational structure if necessary; (4) tightening financial controls; and (5) cutting back on marginal products.

Kodak recently took several of these steps in an attempt to regain the market share it had lost to foreign competition. Between 1983 and 1987 Kodak cut its total work force by 20 percent; most of the job losses affected white-collar employees. The company scrapped an archaic organization based on centralized functions (manufacturing, R&D, marketing, and the like) and reorganized into twenty-four business units, each with its own profit-and-loss responsibility. In addition, a 1985 study showed that 80 or 90 percent of Kodak's products generated only 10 or 20 percent of its profits. In response, by 1987 the company had discontinued 10,000 products, reducing its total to 55,000.

Acquisitions   A somewhat surprising but quite common turnaround strategy involves making acquisitions, primarily to strengthen the competitive position of a company's remaining core operations. For example, Champion International Corporation used to be a very diversified company manufacturing a wide range of paper and wood products. After years of declining performance, in the mid 1980s Champion decided to focus on its profitable newsprint and magazine paper business. The company divested many of its other paper and wood products businesses, but at the same time it paid $1.8 billion for St. Regis Corp., one of the country's largest manufacturers of newsprint and magazine paper.   WSJ, '94

7.10 SUMMARY OF CHAPTER

The purpose of this chapter is to examine the different corporate-level strategies that companies pursue in order to maximize their value.

1. Corporate-level strategy is concerned with answering the question of how to manage a company's growth and development in order to maximize long-run profitability. The answer involves choices of both the *businesses* and the *markets* that the company is going to compete in.

2. Corporate strategies should *add value* to a corporation. To add value, a corporate strategy should enable the company, or one or more of its business units, to perform one or more of the value-creation functions at a lower cost or in a way that allows for differentiation and a premium price.

3. The advantages of concentrating on a single business include focusing the company's resources on establishing a distinctive competence within one business area and keeping top management in touch with operating realities. These benefits are particularly significant in growth industries.

4. The disadvantages of concentrating on a single business are that the company may need to integrate vertically or expand globally in order to establish a low-cost or differentiated position in its core operation. A single-business company may also miss out on opportunities to expand its market to other nations or apply its distinctive competencies to profit opportunities that arise in other industries.

5.   Vertical integration allows a company to create value through production cost savings and by avoiding the costs of using the market, protecting product quality, and protecting proprietary technology.

6.   The disadvantages of vertical integration include cost disadvantages if a company's internal source of supply is a high-cost one and a lack of flexibility when technology is changing fast or when demand is uncertain.

7.   Taper integration is normally preferable to full integration because taper integration exposes in-house suppliers and distributors to some degree of competitive pressure, thereby keeping costs low. Taper integration also enables a company to adopt a more flexible posture toward uncertainties in demand.

8.   Entering into a long-term contract can enable a company to realize many of the benefits associated with vertical integration without having to bear the same level of bureaucratic costs. However, to avoid the risks associated with becoming too dependent on its partner, when entering into a long-term contract a company needs to seek a credible commitment from its partner or establish a mutual hostage-taking situation.

9.   Diversification can create value through the pursuit of a portfolio strategy, restructuring, skill transfers, and resource sharing. Diversification for other reasons is unlikely to add value.

10. The bureaucratic costs of diversification are a function of (a) the number of independent business units within the company and (b) the extent of coordination between those business units.

11. Diversification motivated by a desire to pool risks or achieve greater growth is often associated with the dissipation of value.

12. Related diversification is preferred to unrelated diversification because it enables a company to engage in more value-creation activities and is less risky. If a company's skills are not transferrable, the company may have no choice but to pursue unrelated diversification.

13. Strategic alliances can enable companies to realize many of the benefits of related diversification without having to bear the same level of bureaucratic costs. However, when entering into an alliance, a company does run the risk of giving away key technology to its partner. The risk of this occurring can be minimized if a company gets a credible commitment from its partner.

14. The causes of corporate decline include poor management, overexpansion, inadequate financial controls, high costs, the emergence of powerful new competition, and unforeseen shifts in demand.

15. Responses to corporate decline include changing the leadership, redefining the company's strategic focus, divestment or closure of unwanted assets,

taking steps to improve the profitability of the operations that remain, and occasionally, acquisitions to rebuild core operations.

Discussion Questions

1. When will a company choose related diversification and when unrelated diversification? Discuss with reference to an electronics manufacturer and an ocean shipping company.

2. Why was it profitable for General Motors and Ford to integrate backward into component-parts manufacturing in the past, and why are both companies now trying to buy more of their parts from outside?

3. Under what conditions might concentration on a single business be inconsistent with the goal of maximizing stockholder wealth? Why?

4. General Motors integrated vertically in the 1920s, diversified in the 1930s, and expanded overseas in the 1950s. Explain these developments with reference to the profitability of pursuing each strategy. Why do you think vertical integration is normally the first strategy to be pursued after concentration on a single business?

Endnotes

1. Hope Lampert, "Britons on the Prowl," *The New York Times Magazine,* November 29, 1987, pp. 22–24, 36, 38, 42. Thomas Moore, "Old Line Industry Shapes Up," *Fortune,* April 27, 1987, pp. 23–32, and "Goodbye Corporate Staff," *Fortune,* December 21, 1987, pp. 65–76. Barnaby Feder, "Hanson's Meteoric Rise," *The Wall Street Journal,* July 1989, pp. 1, 38.

2. Alfred D. Chandler, *Strategy and Structure: Chapters in the History of the Industrial Enterprise* (Cambridge, Mass.: MIT Press, 1962).

3. The argument outlined in this section is based on that of G. R. Jones and Charles W. L. Hill, "A Transaction Cost Analysis of Strategy-Structure Choice," *Strategic Management Journal,* 9 (1988), 159–172.

4. For details see Jeffrey R. Williams, Betty Lynn Paez, and Leonard Sanders, "Conglomerates Revisited," *Strategic Management Journal,* 9 (1988), 403–414.

5. Chandler, *Strategy and Structure.*

6. K. R. Harrigan, "Formulating Vertical Integration Strategies," *Academy of Management Review,* 9 (1984), 638–652.

7. This is the essence of Chandler's argument. See his *Strategy and Structure.* The same argument is also made by Jeffrey Pfeffer and Gerald R. Salancik, *The External Control of Organizations* (New York: Harper & Row, 1978). See also K. R. Harrigan, *Strategic Flexibility* (Lexington, Mass.: Lexington Books, 1985); K. R. Harrigan, "Vertical Integration and Corporate Strategy," *Academy of Management Journal,* 28 (1985), 397–425; and F. M. Scherer, *Industrial Market Structure and Economic Performance* (Chicago: Rand McNally, 1981).

8. One interpretation of the dynamics involved in this type of situation can be found in resource dependence models of organizations. See Pfeffer and Salancik, *The External Control of Organizations,* pp. 113–142. Another can be found in transaction cost analysis. See Oliver E. Williamson, *Markets and Hierarchies: Analysis and Antitrust Implications* (New York: Free Press, 1975), pp. 82–131.

9. See "IBM, Clonebuster," *Fortune,* April 27, 1987, p. 225; and "How IBM Hopes to Skin the Copycats," *Business Week,* April 6, 1987, p. 40.

10. Harrigan, *Strategic Flexibility,* pp. 67–87.

11. Standard & Poor's Industry Survey, *Autos–Auto Parts,* April 23, 1987.

12. Ibid.

13. O. E. Williamson, *The Economic Institutions of Capitalism* (New York: Free Press, 1985).

14. This resource-based view of diversification can be traced back to Edith Penrose's seminal book, *The Theory of the Growth of the Firm* (Oxford: Oxford University Press, 1959).

15. See, for example, Jones and Hill, "A Transaction Cost Analysis of Strategy-Structure Choice," pp. 159–172; and Williamson, *Markets and Hierarchies,* pp. 132–175.

16. See Michael E. Porter, "From Competitive Advantage to Corporate Strategy," *Harvard Business Review* (May–June 1987), 43–59.

17. See C. W. L. Hill, M. A. Hitt, and R. E. Hoskisson, "Declining U.S. Competitiveness: Reflections on a Crisis," *Academy of Management Executive,* 2 (February 1988), 51–59.

18. See C. W. L. Hill, "Profile of a Conglomerate Takeover: BTR and Thomas Tilling," *Journal of General Management,* 10 (1984), 34–50.

19. "Rockwell: Using Its Cash Hoard to Edge Away from Defense," *Business Week,* February 4, 1985, pp. 82–84.

20. D. J. Teece, "Economies of Scope and the Scope of the Enterprise," *Journal of Economic Behavior and Organization,* 3 (1980), 223–247.

21. For a detailed discussion, see C. W. L. Hill and R. E. Hoskisson, "Strategy and Structure in the Multiproduct Firm," *Academy of Management Review,* 12 (1987), 331–341.

22. Michael E. Porter, *Competitive Advantage: Creating and Sustaining Superior Performance* (New York: Free Press, 1985), p. 326.

23. Porter, "From Competitive Advantage to Corporate Strategy," pp. 43–59.

24. For a survey of the evidence see V. Ramanujam and P. Varadarajan, "Research on Corporate Diversification: A Synthesis," *Strategic Management Journal,* 10 (1989), 523–551.

25. C. R. Christensen et al., *Business Policy Text and Cases* (Homewood, Ill.: Irwin, 1987), p. 778.

26. For a survey of the evidence, see C. W. L. Hill, "Conglomerate Performance over the Economic Cycle," *Journal of Industrial Economics,* 32 (1983), 197–212; and D. T. C. Mueller, "The Effects of Conglomerate Mergers," *Journal of Banking and Finance,* 1 (1977), 315–347.

27. Michael Brody, "Caught in the Cash Crunch at ITT," *Fortune,* February 18, 1985, pp. 63–72.

28. For example, see C. W. L. Hill, "Diversified Growth and Competition," *Applied Economics,* 17 (1985), 827–847; and R. P. Rumelt, *Strategy, Structure and Economic Performance* (Boston: Harvard Business School Press, 1974).

29. See H. K. Christensen and C. A. Montgomery, "Corporate Economic Performance: Diversification Strategy Versus Market Structure," *Strategic Management Journal,* 2 (1981), 327–343; and Jones and Hill, "A Transaction Cost Analysis of Strategy-Structure Choice," pp. 159–172.

30. See J. Argenti, *Corporate Collapse: Causes and Symptoms* (New York: McGraw-Hill, 1976); R. C. Hoffman, "Strategies for Corporate Turnarounds: What Do We Know About Them?" *Journal of General Management,* 14 (1984), pp. 46–66; D. Schendel, G. R. Patton, and J. Riggs, "Corporate Turnaround Strategies: A Study of Profit Decline and Recovery," *Journal of General Management,* 2 (1976); and S. Siafter, *Corporate Recovery: Successful Turnaround Strategies and Their Implementation* (Harmondsworth, England: Penguin Books, 1984), pp. 25–60.

31. See Siafter, *Corporate Recovery,* pp. 25–60.

32. D. B. Bibeault, *Corporate Turnaround* (New York: McGraw-Hill, 1982).

33. Hoffman, "Strategies for Corporate Turnarounds," pp. 46–66.

34. Lee Iacocca, *Iacocca: An Autobiography* (New York: Bantam Books, 1984), p. 254.

Chapter 8

CORPORATE-LEVEL STRATEGY: THE GLOBAL DIMENSION

8.1 OPENING INCIDENT: THE MEDIA AND ENTERTAINMENT INDUSTRY

One of the biggest mergers of 1989 was between Time Inc., the largest publisher in the United States, and Warner Communications Inc., an entertainment conglomerate. The resulting company, Time Warner Inc., will generate more than $10 billion in annual revenues from a wide range of products and services, including movies, television shows, records, magazines, books, and cable television. The merger promises to make Time Warner the world's biggest media and entertainment company.

The merger was conceived by Time and Warner executives as a response to the rapid globalization of the media and entertainment industry. Many in the industry argue that we are witnessing the development of an integrated global media and entertainment network. In this vision of the future, global citizens will get their news from CNN and their music from MTV and will see worldwide best-selling novels serialized on global television networks. Enterprises that are global in scope will be able to realize significant economies in the costs of developing and running television, film, video, book, and music productions by distributing

them to global audience. Global entertainment organizations will be able to gain a competitive advantage from using the profits generated in one national market to finance expansion in other markets. And they will be better able to take products developed in one nation and sell them in another. At the forefront of globalization in the industry have been a number of foreign media conglomerates, including Germany's Bertelsmann, Britain's Maxwell Communications Corp., and Rupert Murdoch's News Corp. All of these companies have been investing heavily in the United States.

Murdoch, for example, started by building a global empire of low-priced tabloid newspapers that specialized in scandal, gossip, and contests. Then, in 1985, he turned his attention to U.S. motion pictures and television. He began his television empire in 1985, when he bought seven television stations from Metromedia Inc. for $2 billion. In 1986 he added Twentieth Century-Fox Film Corp. for $1.6 billion. As a result, Murdoch can now produce movies and television shows that he can sell or air on Sky Television, his European satellite venture, and on his Fox networks. Moreover, he can publicize his productions in *TV Guide* and *Premiere* magazines, which he also owns. During the same time period, Germany's Bertelsmann made a number of major acquisitions in the United States, including Doubleday and Co. Inc. (a book publisher), and RCA Records. Maxwell Communications Corp. purchased Macmillan Publishing Company. And Sony shocked the U.S. entertainment and media establishment with its acquisition of CBS Records and Columbia Pictures Inc.

Because of these developments, by the late 1980s both Time Inc. and Warner Communications were beginning to look like second-string competitors in their own country, and both feared being squeezed by integrated global competitors. The merger of the two was seen as a way of putting an American company back in the top league of the media industry. Time Warner Inc. promises to deliver significant synergies and have a global reach. In theory, Time Warner can now publish a book, serialize it in a magazine, turn it into a movie, sell the video rights, show the film on Home Box Office, feature the film on Time Warner's cable system, and then put the score on a compact disk. Also, Warner Communications can help Time crack the vast and fast growing overseas market—something that Time has had trouble doing. In 1988, Time generated only 6 percent of its revenues outside the United States. Strong foreign distribution systems helped Warner Communications generate 40 percent of its revenues overseas in 1988.

Whether the merger will live up to its advance billing will not be apparent for a number of years. One thing is clear, however. The merger was forced on Time and Warner Communications by the rapid globalization of the media and entertainment industry.[1]

8.2 OVERVIEW

The United States emerged from the Second World War as the most powerful industrial nation. For the next thirty-five years, U.S. enterprises had things largely their own way. U.S. companies were among the biggest in the world, and U.S. multinationals dominated a wide range of industries in countries around the globe (*multinational companies* are companies that do business in two or more countries). In 1973, for example, 126 of the world's 260 largest multinationals were U.S. enterprises, including 15 of the largest 25 multinationals.[2]

During the 1980s, things began to change rapidly. West German, French, British, Dutch, Italian, South Korean, and Japanese companies began to take an ever greater share of their own domestic markets away from U.S. multinationals. At the same time, they began to challenge U.S. companies in the North American market. Lulled into a false sense of security by years of dominance, U.S. companies all too often proved ill equipped to take on this challenge. As a result, the trade balance, one index of America's competitiveness in the global economy, steadily deteriorated. Until the late 1960s the U.S. generally ran a trade surplus with the rest of the world. Beginning in 1973, however, the trade balance began to dip into the red, and by the 1980s the problem was becoming serious, cumulating in a record $175-billion trade defect in 1986.[3]

As a result of these changes, there has been a growing awareness that a new reality is confronting American business: global competition and global competitors. The Opening Incident describes how this new reality is transforming the structure of the U.S. media and entertainment industry. Similar trends can be observed in a wide range of other industries, from autos and banking to semiconductor chips and tire manufacturing. Consider semiconductors. In 1975 both of the key global players were U.S. companies: Motorola and Texas Instruments. Now the list of key global players also includes NEC, Fujitsu, Hitachi, and Toshiba. A similar trend has occurred in consumer electronics. In 1975, the key global players were General Electric and RCA, both U.S. enterprises. Now the list of key global players also includes Matsushita, Philips, and Sony.

This chapter describes the strategic choices that confront companies doing business in a global environment. We begin by discussing how global expansion creates value for a company. Next, we look at the different strategies that companies can pursue in the global arena and consider the factors that influence a company's choice of strategies. We consider the various options that a company has for entering a foreign market. We then discuss the motives, benefits, and costs of building global strategic alliances with competitors. The chapter closes with a look at how foreign governments' policies influence global strategy.

8.3 VALUE CREATION

Global expansion involves establishing significant operations and market interests outside a company's home country. Global expansion enables a company to add value in a number of ways not available to domestic enterprises. These arise from the ability of global enterprises to (1) transfer core skills overseas, (2) use global volume to cover product development costs, (3) realize economies of scale from global volume, and (4) configure the company's value chain so that individual value-creation functions are performed in locations where value-added is maximized.

Transferring Core Skills Overseas

The competitive advantage that many multinational companies enjoy over local competitors is based on core technological, marketing, or management skills and know-how that local competitors lack. These skills typically allow a multinational to perform one or more value-creation functions in a way that leads to differentiation and a premium price. For these multinationals, global expansion is a way of earning greater returns from their existing skills and know-how by expanding the size of their potential market. It is a way of exploiting the profit potential that their skills represent.

IBM, Xerox, and Kodak, for example, all profited from the transfer overseas of their core skills in technology and R&D. Those skills have enabled these companies to charge a premium price. Marketing skills have formed the basis of global competitive advantage for other multinationals. The overseas success of U.S. multinationals like Kellogg, Coca-Cola, H. J. Heinz, and Procter & Gamble is based more on marketing know-how than on technological know-how. Still other multinationals have based their competitive advantage over local competitors on general management skills. Such an advantage may arise from better trained or educated managers, a superior organizational structure, and more sophisticated management techniques in areas such as finance. Such factors explain the growth of international hotel chains such as Hilton International, Interconti-nental, and Sheraton.

Using Global Volume to Cover Product Development Costs

Were it not for global markets, some companies would have great difficulty re-couping their investment in new product development. For example, it costs pharmaceutical companies anywhere from $50 million to $150 million to put a new drug on the market. To recoup this expenditure, pharmaceutical companies need global markets; the U.S. market alone is too small. Similarly, without global markets, aircraft manufacturers like Boeing would probably be unable to cover the billions of dollars of development costs necessary to produce a new aircraft. Thus global markets may be necessary to reap the full value of invest-ment in product development. Put another way, selling a new product to the global market allows a multinational company to spread the fixed costs of new product development over greater sales volume, thereby lowering the relative cost of investments in R&D—that is, thereby lowering the relative cost of the R&D function of the value chain.

Realizing Economies of Scale from Global Volume

By offering a standardized product to the global marketplace and by manufac-turing that product in a single location or in a few choice locations, a global company can reap from its global volume scale economies that are not available to smaller domestic enterprises. By lowering the costs of value creation, these scale economies can assist a company in becoming a low-cost player in the global industry. Thus global expansion may be consistent with the generic business-level strategy of cost leadership.

For example, by using centralized manufacturing facilities and global mar-keting strategies, Sony was able to become the low-cost player in the global television market. Thus Sony was able to take market share in the global televi-sion market away from competitors such as Philips N.V., RCA, and Zenith, all of whom traditionally based manufacturing operations in each of their major markets and therefore lacked scale economies similar to Sony's. Similarly, Japanese manufacturers of electronic components, such as NEC Corporation, are beginning to dominate the global market, primarily because their huge global volume for a standardized product has enabled them to ride down the experience curve and gain significant cost economies over their rivals.

Configuring the Global Value Chain

Porter

The costs of factors of production, such as labor, energy, and raw material inputs, vary from country to country. The availability of certain skills, particularly skilled labor, can also vary from country to country. One way to increase value-added is to perform different value-creation functions in the locations where the mix of factor costs and skills is most favorable. By doing so, a company may be able to lower the costs of value creation and perform key value-creation functions in a way that results in greater differentiation and a premium price.

For example, consider manufacturing operations. The main factors determining the most favorable locations for global manufacturing are (1) labor costs, (2) energy costs, (3) access to a work force with appropriate skills, (4) access to the necessary infrastructure (such as roads, rail networks, and favorable political climate), and (5) proximity to important global markets (particularly when transport costs are high). After considering such issues, in the late 1980s European subsidiaries of Ford and General Motors began shifting much of their European auto production from West Germany to Great Britain because labor costs in Britain were 45 percent less than those in West Germany and productivity gains among British auto workers had been averaging 10 to 12 percent annually, against 8 percent in West Germany.[4] In short, GM and Ford were moving their operations from a high-cost, high-skill location to a low-cost, high-skill location in order to lower the costs of value creation. Similarly, Volkswagen has recently shifted production of its low-priced Polos from Wolfsburg, Germany, to Spain, where labor costs are lower. This move has enabled Volkswagen to lower the costs of manufacturing Polos. At the same time, the strategy has freed high-wage, high-skilled German labor to concentrate on the production of higher-priced Golf cars. By using high-skilled labor to produce Golf cars, Volkswagen has maintained the high quality of the Golf, which in turn allows the company to achieve greater differentiation and charge a higher price.[5]

8.4 COMPARING GLOBAL AND MULTIDOMESTIC STRATEGIES

One of the major strategic choices faced by multinational companies is whether to pursue a *global strategy* or a *multidomestic strategy*.[6] The differences between the pure versions of these two strategies are summarized in Table 8.1. A multidomestic strategy—the time-honored way in which global companies compete—is based on the assumption that national markets differ widely in consumer tastes

TABLE 8.1   **Dimensions of global and multidomestic strategies**

Dimensions	Pure multidomestic strategy	Pure global strategy
Product offering	Fully customized to each country	Fully standardized worldwide
Manufacturing	Manufacturing in each country	Manufacturing based where the factor-cost/skill mix is most favorable
Marketing	Locally determined	Centrally determined
Competitive strategy	Responsibility of national subsidiaries	Integrated across countries and centrally directed

and preferences, competitive conditions, operating conditions, and political, legal, and social structures. To deal with these differences, multidomestic companies decentralize manufacturing, marketing, and strategic decisions to national subsidiaries. Thus each national subsidiary has its own marketing function and its own manufacturing facilities. The attributes of the product vary among nations according to the tastes and preferences of local consumers, and the managers in each country decide on business-level strategy without regard for what happens in other countries.

In contrast, a pure global strategy is based on the assumption that between countries there are no tangible differences in consumer tastes and preferences. This working assumption enables a multinational company to market a standardized product to the global marketplace and to manufacture that product in a limited number of locations where the mix of factor costs and skills is most favorable so that the company can realize significant scale economies from its global volume. For example, Levi 501 blue jeans are sold as a standardized product the world over and are manufactured in a few choice locations where the mix of factor costs and skills is most advantageous. Thus Levi Strauss & Co. manufactures in Scotland most of its blue jeans sold in Western Europe, primarily because Scotland offers a relatively low-cost skilled labor force, generous government subsidies, and access to the major markets of the European Community.

In addition, companies pursuing a pure global strategy can integrate competitive moves across countries, using the profits generated in one country to support competitive attacks in another. Frequently a competitor is attacked in one country in order to drain its resources from another. For example, when Fuji Photo Film Co. began cutting deep inroads into Kodak's home market, Kodak launched powerful counterattacks in Fuji's home market, cutting the prices at which its Japanese subsidiary sold film. The result was that Kodak checked Fuji's invasion of the U.S. market by keeping Fuji busy defending its home market.

Both strategies have advantages and disadvantages, which are discussed below. The factors that determine which strategy a company should pursue are discussed in Section 8.5.

The Advantages and Disadvantages of a Pure Global Strategy

Pure global companies are able to create value in all of the ways discussed earlier. They can transfer core skills between nations to enhance value-added. They can spread the fixed costs of new product development over their global volume. They can realize scale economies by serving the global marketplace from centralized manufacturing facilities. They can site their manufacturing facilities in locations where the mix of factor costs and skills is most favorable. Above all else, the ability to realize cost economies from integrated global manufacturing suggests that a pure global strategy is most consistent with the generic business-level strategy of cost leadership. In addition, as noted above, companies pursuing a pure global strategy have the advantage of being able to coordinate competitive moves across countries. Thus they can use the profits generated in one country to support competitive attacks in another.

On the other hand, because they manufacture a standardized global product, companies pursuing a pure global strategy have to give up a certain degree of responsiveness to different national conditions. This surrender can give rise to significant disadvantages and can be very damaging. In particular, the result of attempts to lower costs through global product standardization can be a product that does not entirely satisfy anyone. For example, Procter & Gamble stumbled when it tried to introduce its Cheer laundry detergent into Japan without changing the U.S. product or marketing message (which was that the detergent was effective in water of all temperatures). In Japan, Cheer was a failure for a couple of reasons. Because the Japanese use a great deal of fabric softener, it did not make enough suds. Because the Japanese usually wash clothes in cold water, the claim that Cheer works in all temperatures was irrelevant.

Often overlooked by those who enthusiastically advocate global strategies are the organizational problems that arise from the effort to achieve coordination between national subsidiaries. A pure global strategy can give rise to significant bureaucratic costs because of the increased coordination, reporting requirements, and even the added staff that such a strategy requires. Moreover, companies pursuing a global strategy have to wrestle with the difficult issue of how to price transfers of goods and services between components of the company's value chain based in different countries. Transfer pricing problems are difficult enough to resolve within just one country. In the context of a global company, identifying the appropriate transfer price can be further complicated by volatile exchange rates.

The Advantages and Disadvantages
of a Pure Multidomestic Strategy

A pure multidomestic strategy explicitly recognizes differences among nations. That is its principal advantage. The strategy can assist a company in tailoring its products and business-level strategy to the unique conditions in each country. The central idea is to customize a product to different national requirements. Thus the extent of product differentiation may vary from country to country, depending on the tastes and preferences of consumers in each country.

Another advantage is that a pure multidomestic strategy raises far fewer difficult organizational issues than does a pure global strategy. Within multidomestic companies, the need for coordination is lower than it is within global companies. Most national subsidiaries can be managed on an arm's-length basis with relatively little input from world corporate headquarters. Also, since each national subsidiary is essentially a self-contained unit, there are few transfers of goods and services between subsidiaries. Thus the transfer pricing problem is far less complicated in multidomestic companies than in global companies. In sum, the bureaucratic costs of implementing a pure multidomestic strategy are far lower than the bureaucratic costs of implementing a pure global strategy.

A major disadvantage of a pure multidomestic strategy is that a multidomestic company has fewer ways than a global company to create value. A multidomestic company can transfer core skills between its international operations. In addition, a multidomestic company may be able to spread the fixed costs of new product development over its global volume (although the scope for doing this is limited by the need to customize a product to the unique conditions of each national market). However, by definition, a company pursuing a pure multidomestic strategy lacks the ability to realize scale economies from centralizing manufacturing facilities and offering a standardized product to the global marketplace. Moreover, because manufacturing and marketing functions are based in each country, pure multidomestic companies are unable to configure the global value chain so that different value-creation functions are performed in locations where the mix of factor costs and skills is most favorable. For these reasons, the manufacturing costs of companies pursuing a pure multidomestic strategy are likely to be significantly higher than those of a company pursuing global strategy.

In addition, because a company pursuing a pure multidomestic strategy decentralizes business-level strategy decisions to each national subsidiary, it lacks the ability to launch coordinated global attacks against subsidiaries' competitors. This can constitute a significant disadvantage for a company facing multinational competitors that have this ability.

Tradeoffs

The foregoing discussion suggests that a number of important tradeoffs are involved in the choice between a pure global and a pure multidomestic strategy.

TABLE 8.2   **Advantages and disadvantages of multidomestic and global strategies**

	Manufacturing costs	Bureaucratic costs	Strategic coordination	Consumer responsiveness
Multidomestic strategy	High	Low	Low	High
Global strategy	Low	High	High	Low

The issues are summarized in Table 8.2. As the table shows, although companies pursuing a pure global strategy have the advantage of low manufacturing costs and a high level of strategic coordination between countries, they have the disadvantages of high bureaucratic costs and a lack of responsiveness to the needs of consumers in different countries. Alternatively, although companies pursuing a pure multidomestic strategy have the advantage of low bureaucratic costs and a high level of responsiveness to the needs of consumers in different countries, they have the disadvantage of high manufacturing costs and a low level of strategic coordination between countries.

8.5 CHOOSING BETWEEN GLOBAL AND MULTIDOMESTIC STRATEGIES

Given the tradeoffs, which strategy should a multinational company choose? According to C. K. Prahalad and Yves L. Doz, the answer can be gleaned from a comparison of *pressures for global integration* and *pressures for local responsiveness.*[8] When the pressures for global integration are high and the pressures for local responsiveness are low, a company should choose a pure global strategy. When the pressures for global integration are low and the pressures for local responsiveness are high, a company should choose a pure multidomestic strategy. Of course, in practice companies often face high pressures for both global integration and local responsiveness. In such circumstances the appropriate strategic response may require a hybrid strategy that mixes elements of global and multidomestic strategies. This response is discussed later in the chapter. First, however, we discuss the factors that create pressures for global integration and local responsiveness.

Pressures for Global Integration

Pressures for global integration arise from (1) the need for cost reduction, (2) the existence of universal needs, and (3) global strategic coordination by competitors.

Need for cost reduction   The global integration of manufacturing is often a response to competitive pressures for cost reduction. Cost reduction can be of particular importance in industries producing commodity-type products where differentiation is difficult, price is the main competitive weapon, and competition is intense. Examples include hand-held calculators and semiconductor chips. Cost reduction is also important in industries where key international competitors are based in countries that have low factor costs—for example, low labor and energy costs. The need to configure the value chain in order to supply the product from low-factor-cost locations or to exploit economies of scale from global volume can drive a company toward a global strategy. This is what happened to the Dutch multinational Philips N.V. Long a multidomestic company, Philips switched to a global strategy after seeing much of its global market share in televisions being taken by Sony during the 1970s. Similarly, Britain's Imperial Chemical Industries, one of the world's largest chemical companies, switched from a multidomestic strategy to a global strategy in 1983 in direct response to cost pressures arising from a severe recession in the global chemical business. The continuing emergence of low-cost competitors based in newly industrialized countries such as South Korea is likely to make cost considerations even more important in the future.

Universal needs   The existence of universal needs creates strong pressures for a global strategy. Universal needs exist when the tastes and preferences of consumers in different countries are very similar if not identical. Products that serve universal needs require little adaptation across national markets. In such circumstances, global integration is obviously facilitated. This is clearly the case in many industrial markets. Electronic products such as capacitors, resistors, and semiconductor chips are good examples of products that meet universal needs.

Harvard Business School professor Theodore Levitt has taken this point farther than most. Levitt argues that many consumer goods markets are becoming characterized by universal needs.[9] According to Levitt, modern communications and transport technologies have created the conditions for a convergence of the tastes and preferences of consumers from different nations. The result is the emergence of enormous global markets for standardized consumer products. Levitt cites worldwide acceptance of McDonald's hamburgers, Coca-Cola, Levi Strauss blue jeans, and Sony television sets, all of which are sold as standardized products, as evidence of the increasing homogeneity of the global marketplace.

Levitt's argument, however, has been characterized as extreme by many commentators.[10] For example, Christopher Bartlett of Harvard Business School and Sumantra Ghoshal of INSEAD, a French business school, have observed that in the consumer electronics industry consumers reacted to an overdose of standardized global products by showing a renewed preference for differentiated products. They note that Amstrad, the fast-growing British computer and electronics company, got its start by recognizing and responding to local consumer need. Amstrad captured a major share of the British audio market by moving away from the standardized inexpensive music centers marketed by global companies such as Sony and Matsushita. Amstrad's product was encased in teak rather than in metal cabinets and had a control panel tailor-made to appeal to British consumers. In response, Matsushita had to reverse its bias toward standardized global design and place more emphasis on product differentiation. From fifteen models in its portable audio product range in 1980, the company increased the line to thirty in 1985.

Global strategic coordination by competitors   The presence of competitors engaged in global strategic coordination creates pressures for global integration. As noted earlier, to gain market share, global companies can use profits generated in one market to subsidize prices in other markets. This strategy enables them to move down the experience curve, realize greater cost economies, and thus increase long-run profits. This is what Canon, Hitachi, and Seiko did in order to build global market share. Reacting to such threats calls for global strategic coordination and thus creates pressures to centralize at corporate headquarters decisions about the competitive strategy of different national subsidiaries. Thus, when one multinational company in an industry adopts global strategic coordination, its competitors may be forced to respond in kind, lest they lose out.[11]

An example of this phenomenon occurred in the tire industry during the 1970s. At that time the world tire market was dominated by three multinationals: Michelin Tire Corporation, Goodyear, and Firestone Tire & Rubber. Each of these companies pursued a multidomestic strategy, thus decentralizing manufacturing, marketing, and competitive strategy to various national subsidiaries around the globe. In the early 1970s, Michelin used its strong European profits to attack Goodyear's North American home market. Goodyear could have retaliated by cutting its North American prices. However, Michelin was exposing only a small amount of its worldwide business in North America and had little to lose from a North American price war. Goodyear, in contrast, saw a major threat to profits in its largest market and struck back by cutting prices and expanding its operations in Europe. The action forced Michelin to slow its attack on Goodyear's North American market and to think again about the costs of taking market share away from Goodyear. Michelin's decision to engage in global strategic coordination forced Goodyear to respond in kind. The result was an increase in pressures for global integration in the tire industry.[12]

Pressures for Local Responsiveness

Pressures for local responsiveness arise from (1) differences in consumer tastes and preferences, (2) differences in infrastructure and in traditional practices, (3) differences in distribution channels, and (4) host-government demands.

Differences in consumer tastes and preferences   Strong pressures for local responsiveness emerge when consumer tastes and preferences differ significantly between countries. In such cases, product and marketing messages have to be customized to appeal to local consumers. Customizing typically creates pressures for the delegation of manufacturing and marketing functions to national subsidiaries. In the automobile industry, for example, there is a strong demand among individual North American consumers for pickup trucks, especially in the South and West, where many families have a pickup truck as a second or third car. In contrast, in European countries pickup trucks are seen purely as utility vehicles and are purchased primarily by companies rather than by individuals. Thus marketing messages must take into account the different nature of demand in North America and Europe.

Also in the automobile industry, Nissan has found that it has had to develop "lead country" models—products carefully tailored to the dominant and distinctive needs of individual national markets. In the United States, Nissan decided that it needed a sporty "Z" model as well as a four-wheel-drive family vehicle to serve strong consumer preferences. Neither model is in great demand in Japan and Europe. Thus Nissan sells about 5,000 "Z" cars a month in the United States but only 500 a month in Japan.[13]

Differences in infrastructure and in traditional practices   Pressures for local responsiveness emerge when there are differences in infrastructure and in traditional practices between countries. In such circumstances, a product may need to be customized to the distinctive infrastructures and practices of different nations. This customizing may necessitate the delegation of manufacturing and marketing functions to foreign subsidiaries. For example, in North America consumer electrical systems are based on 110 volts, but in some European countries 240-volt systems are standard. Thus domestic electrical appliances have to be customized to take this difference in infrastructure into account. Traditional practices often vary across nations. For example, in Britain people drive on the left-hand side of the road, thus creating a demand for right-hand-drive cars, whereas in France people drive on the right-hand side of the road, thus creating a demand for left-hand-drive cars. Automobiles have to be customized to take this difference in traditional practices into account.

Differences in distribution channels   A company's marketing strategies may have to be responsive to international differences in distribution channels. Such differences may necessitate the delegation of marketing functions to national subsidiaries. In laundry detergents, for example, five retail chains control 65 percent of the market in Germany, but no chain controls more than 2 percent of the market in neighboring Italy. Thus retail chains have considerable buying power in Germany but relatively little in Italy. Dealing with these differences requires detergent companies to use different marketing approaches. Similarly, in the pharmaceutical industry the Japanese distribution system is radically different from the U.S. system. Japanese doctors do not accept or else respond unfavorably to an American-style high-pressure sales force. Thus pharmaceutical companies have to adopt different marketing practices in Japan and the United States (soft sell versus hard sell).

Host-government demands   The term *host country* is used to signify a foreign country in which a multinational is doing business. Economic and political demands imposed by host-country governments may necessitate a degree of local responsiveness. For example, the politics of health care around the world requires that pharmaceutical companies manufacture in multiple locations. Pharmaceutical companies are subject to local clinical testing, registration procedures, and pricing restrictions, all of which require the manufacturing and marketing of a drug to meet local requirements. Moreover, since governments and government agencies control a significant proportion of the health-care budget in most countries, they are in a powerful position and can demand a high level of local responsiveness. More generally, threats of protectionism, economic nationalism, and local content rules (which require a certain percentage of a product to be manufactured locally) all dictate that multinational companies manufacture locally. Part of the motivation for Japanese auto companies setting up U.S. pro-

FIGURE 8.1   **Pressures for global integration and local responsiveness: the integration-responsiveness grid**

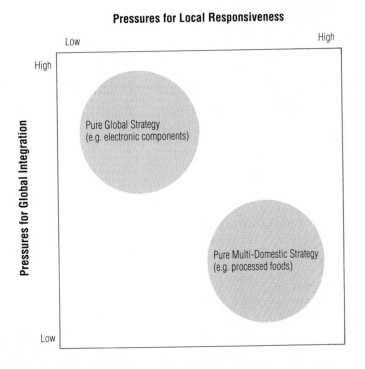

duction operations, for example, is to counter the threat of protectionism that is being increasingly voiced by Congress.

Choosing a Strategy

What is the best strategy for a company to pursue? The answer depends on a consideration and balancing of the various factors discussed above. One way to identify which strategy is best is to plot a company's position on an integration-responsiveness grid similar to the one shown in Figure 8.1.[14] The vertical dimension of this grid measures pressures for global integration; the horizontal dimension measures pressures for local responsiveness. A pure global strategy is appropriate when the pressures for global integration are high and the pressures for local responsiveness are low. This is the case in the electronic components industry. Obviously, in such cases a company should pursue a global strategy. A pure multidomestic strategy is appropriate when the pressures for global integration are low and the pressures for local responsiveness are high. This is the case in the processed-foods and cookware industries. Obviously, in such cases a company should pursue a pure multidomestic strategy.

FIGURE 8.2a   **Pressures for global integration and local responsiveness in the television industry**

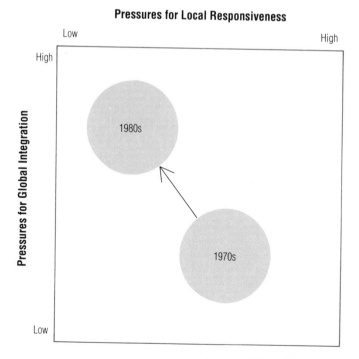

For many companies, however, the issue is not so clear-cut. Two factors complicate the picture. First, the relative importance of pressures for global integration and local responsiveness may change through time, necessitating a change in strategy. In the television industry, for example, the advent of low-cost global manufacturers such as Sony in the 1970s increased the importance of global integration for other companies in the industry (see Figure 8.2a). Thus, in order to compete on a cost basis with Sony, companies like Philips were forced to switch from a multidomestic strategy to a global strategy.

Nevertheless, despite all the talk of increasing globalization, it would be wrong to view this as the only kind of change. In some industries the need for local responsiveness has increased in recent years. As discussed earlier, in the audio market Amstrad's success in focusing on local needs increased pressures for local responsiveness in the industry (see Figure 8.2b). In particular, in an attempt to recover market share from Amstrad, competitors such as Matsushita moved away from a pure global strategy and incorporated more multidomestic elements in their strategic posture. Similarly, some researchers have reported a marked shift toward greater local responsiveness in the prepared-food industry between 1973 and 1983 (see Figure 8.2c).

FIGURE 8.2b   **Pressures for global integration and local responsiveness in the audio products industry**

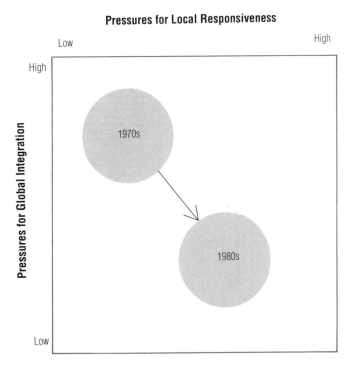

FIGURE 8.2c   **Pressures for global integration and local responsiveness in the prepared foods industry**

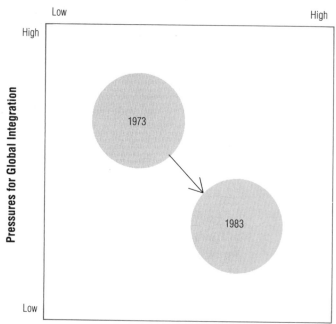

The second complicating factor is that most companies do not fall into the upper-right or lower-left corner of the integration-responsiveness grid. Indeed, it is possible for companies to be positioned anywhere on the grid. Thus some companies may have to balance conflicting demands for global integration and for local responsiveness.

8.6 THE TRANSNATIONAL COMPANY

Christopher Bartlett and Sumantra Ghoshal coined the term *transnational company* to describe companies that face pressures for both global integration and local responsiveness.[15] The strategy often adopted by such companies is neither a pure multidomestic strategy nor a pure global strategy. Rather, they combine elements of both strategies in a hybrid known as a *transnational strategy*. According to Bartlett and Ghoshal, in practice many multinational companies must simultaneously deal with demands for global integration and for local responsiveness and thus must pursue transnational strategies.

Caterpillar Tractor is a good example of a transnational company.[16] The need to compete with low-cost competitors such as Komatsu forced Caterpillar to look for greater cost economies by centralizing global production at locations where the factor-cost/skill mix was most favorable. At the same time, variations in construction practices and government regulations across countries mean that Caterpillar has to be responsive to local needs. On the integration-responsiveness grid, therefore, Caterpillar is situated toward the top right corner (see Figure 8.3).

To deal with these simultaneous demands, Caterpillar has designed its products to use many identical components and invested in a few large-scale component-manufacturing facilities to fill global demand and realize scale economies. At the same time the company augments the centralized manufacturing of components with assembly plants in each of its major global markets. At these plants, Caterpillar adds local product features, tailoring the finished product to local needs. Thus Caterpillar is able to realize many of the benefits of global manufacturing while at the same time responding to pressures for local responsiveness by differentiating its product among national markets.

Achieving a balance between the demands of global integration and local responsiveness raises difficult and complex implementation issues. Organizational

FIGURE 8.3   Caterpillar's position on the integration-responsiveness grid

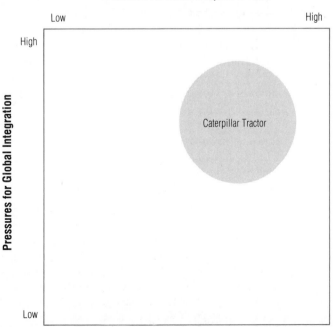

structures that are supportive of (1) collaborative information sharing and problem solving, (2) cooperative support and resource sharing, and (3) collective action among product, geographical, and functional management must be developed. To achieve this without developing a stultifying bureaucracy, companies need managers who understand the need for multiple strategic capabilities, who are able to view problems simultaneously from both local and global perspectives.

8.7 THE CHOICE OF ENTRY MODE

What is the best means of achieving global expansion? There are basically five different ways of entering an overseas market: (1) exporting, (2) licensing, (3) franchising, (4) entering into a joint venture with a host country company, and (5) setting up a wholly owned subsidiary in the host country. Each entry mode has advantages and disadvantages that strategic managers need to consider carefully.[17]

Exporting

Most manufacturing companies begin their global expansion as exporters and only later switch to one of the other modes for serving a foreign market. Exporting does have two distinct advantages. First, exporting avoids the costs of having to establish manufacturing operations in the host country. Since these costs are often substantial, this is not a trivial advantage. Second, exporting is consistent with a pure global strategy. By manufacturing the product in a centralized location and then exporting it to other national markets, a company may be able to realize substantial scale economies from its global sales volume. This is how Sony came to dominate the global television market and how many of the Japanese auto companies originally made inroads into the U.S. auto market.

On the other hand, there are a number of drawbacks to exporting. First, exporting from the company's *home* base may not be appropriate if there are lower-cost locations for manufacturing the product abroad. Thus, particularly for a company pursuing a pure global strategy, it may pay to manufacture in a location where the mix of factor costs and skills is most favorable and then export from that location to the rest of the globe in order to achieve scale economies. This, of course, is not so much an argument against exporting as an argument against exporting from a company's *home* country. Many U.S. electronics companies have moved some of their manufacturing to the Far East because of the availability of low-cost, high-skilled labor. They then export from that location to the rest of the globe, including the United States.

A second drawback to exporting is that high transport costs can make exporting uneconomical, particularly in the case of bulk products. One way of getting around this problem is to manufacture bulk products on a regional basis. This strategy enables a company to realize some economies from large-scale production while at the same time limiting the transport costs that it has to bear. Many multinational chemical companies manufacture their products on a regional basis, serving several countries in a region from one facility.

A third drawback to exporting is that tariff barriers can make the strategy uneconomical. Similarly, the threat to impose tariff barriers by the government of a host country can make the strategy very risky. Indeed, the implicit threat from Congress to impose tariff barriers on Japanese autos imported into the United States led directly to the decision by many Japanese auto companies to set up manufacturing plants in the United States. As a consequence of this trend, by 1990 almost 50 percent of all Japanese cars sold in the United States were manufactured locally, up from 0 percent in 1985.

A fourth drawback to exporting arises when a company delegates marketing activities to a local agent in each country in which it does business. This practice is common among companies that are just beginning to export. Unfortunately, there is no guarantee that a foreign agent will act in a company's best interest. Foreign agents often carry the products of competing companies and as a result have divided loyalties. Thus a foreign agent may not do as good a job as the company would do if it managed marketing itself. There are ways around this problem, however. One solution is to set up a wholly owned subsidiary in the host country to handle local marketing. By doing this, a company can reap the cost advantages that arise from manufacturing the product in a single location and simultaneously exercise tight control over marketing strategy in the host country.

Licensing

International licensing is an arrangement whereby a foreign licensee buys the rights to manufacture a company's product in the licensee's country for a negotiated fee (normally, royalty payments on the number of units sold). The licensee then puts up most of the capital necessary to get the overseas operation going. The advantage of licensing is that a company does not have to bear the development costs and risks associated with opening up a foreign market. This can make licensing a very attractive option for companies that lack the capital to develop operations overseas. In addition, licensing may be an attractive option for companies that are unwilling to commit substantial financial resources to an unfamiliar or politically volatile foreign market.

On the other hand, there are two serious drawbacks to licensing. First, licensing does not give the tight control over manufacturing, marketing, and strategic functions in foreign countries that is required if a company is going to pursue a global strategy. Typically, each licensee sets up its own manufacturing operations. This severely limits the ability of the company to realize economies of scale by manufacturing its product in a centralized location. Thus, when economies of scale are likely to be important, licensing may not be the best way of expanding overseas. In addition, pursuing a global strategy may require a company to coordinate strategic moves across countries so that the profits earned in one country can be used to respond to competitive attacks in another. Licensing, by its very nature, severely limits the ability of a company to do this. A licensee will not let a multinational company take its profits (beyond those due in the form of royalty payments) and use them to support an entirely different licensee operating in another country.

A second problem with licensing arises when a company licenses its technological know-how to foreign companies. Technological know-how constitutes the basis of the competitive advantage of many multinational companies. Most companies wish to maintain control over the use to which their technology is put. By licensing its technology, a company can quickly lose control over it. Many companies have made the mistake of thinking that they could maintain control over their know-how within the framework of a licensing agreement. Unfortunately, this has often proved not to be the case. For example, RCA once licensed its color television technology to a number of Japanese companies. The Japanese companies quickly assimilated RCA's technology and then used it to enter the U.S. market. Now the Japanese have a bigger share of the U.S. market than the RCA brand does. Similar concerns are now surfacing over the 1989 decision by Congress to allow Japanese companies to produce the advanced FSX fighter under license from McDonnell Douglas. Critics of this decision fear that the Japanese will use the FSX technology to support the development of a commercial airline industry that will compete with Boeing and McDonnell Douglas in the global marketplace.

Franchising

In many respects franchising is similar to licensing. However, whereas licensing is a strategy pursued primarily by manufacturing companies, franchising is a strategy employed primarily by service companies. Both McDonald's and Hilton International, for example, have expanded overseas by franchising. In the case of franchising, a company (the franchiser) sells limited rights to use its brand name to franchisees in return for a lump-sum payment and a share of the franchisee's profits. However, unlike the parties to most licensing agreements, the franchisee agrees to abide by strict rules defining how it does business. Thus, when McDonald's enters into a franchising agreement with a foreign company, it expects that company to run its restaurants in the same way that McDonald's restaurants elsewhere in the world are run.

The advantages of franchising as an entry mode are similar to those of licensing. Specifically, a franchiser does not have to bear the development costs and risks associated with opening up a foreign market on its own. The franchisee typically assumes those costs and risks. Thus, using a franchising strategy, a service company can build up a global presence quickly and at a low cost.

The disadvantages are less pronounced than in the case of licensing. Since franchising is a strategy used by service companies, a franchiser does not have to consider the need to coordinate manufacturing in order to achieve economies of scale. Nevertheless, franchising may inhibit the ability of a company to achieve global strategic coordination.

A more significant disadvantage of franchising concerns quality control. The foundation of franchising arrangements is the notion that a company's brand name conveys a message to consumers about the quality of the company's product. Thus a business traveler booking into a Hilton International hotel in Hong Kong can reasonably expect the same quality of room, food, and service as she or he would receive in New York. The Hilton brand name is a guarantee of the consistency of product quality. Foreign franchisees, however, may not be as concerned about quality as they should be, and the result of poor quality can go beyond lost sales in the foreign market to include a decline in a company's worldwide reputation. For example, a business traveler who has a bad experience at the Hilton in Hong Kong may never go to another Hilton hotel and urge colleagues to do likewise. The geographical distance of a franchiser from its foreign franchisees, however, makes poor quality control difficult to detect. In addition, the sheer number of individual franchisees, which in the case of McDonald's runs into the tens of thousands, can make the detection of poor quality difficult. Because of these factors, quality problems may persist.

One way around this disadvantage is to set up a subsidiary in each country or region in which a company expands. The subsidiary might be wholly owned by the company, or it might be a joint venture with a foreign company. The subsidiary assumes the rights and obligations to establish franchisees throughout that particular country or region. The combination of close proximity and the limited number of independent franchisees that have to be monitored reduces the quality-control problem. In addition, because the subsidiary is at least partly owned by the company, the company can place its own managers in the subsidiary to ensure that it does a good job of monitoring the quality of franchisees within the country or region for which it is responsible. This organizational arrangement has proved very popular in practice and is being used by McDonald's, Kentucky Fried Chicken, Hilton International, and other companies to expand international operations.

Joint Ventures vs. "Strategic Alliances"

Establishing a joint venture with a foreign company has long been a popular way to enter a new market. Joint ventures have a number of advantages. First, a multinational may feel that it can benefit from a local partner's knowledge of a host country's competitive conditions, culture, language, political systems, and business systems. Thus for many U.S. companies, joint ventures have involved the American company providing technological know-how and products and the local partner providing the marketing expertise and local knowledge necessary to compete within the country. Second, when the development costs and risks of opening up a foreign market are high, a company might gain by sharing these costs and risks with a local partner. Third, in many countries political considerations make joint ventures the only feasible entry mode. For example, historically many U.S. companies found it much easier to get permission to set up operations in Japan if they went in with a Japanese partner than if they tried to enter on their own (Texas Instruments and IBM have been notable exceptions to this rule.) Furthermore, research suggests that joint ventures with local partners experience a low risk of nationalization, apparently because local equity partners, who may have some influence on host-government policy, have a vested interest in speaking out against nationalization.[18]

There are two major disadvantages to joint ventures. First, as in the case of licensing, a company that enters into a joint venture runs the risk of losing control over its technology to its venture partner. For example, the joint venture between Boeing and a consortium of Japanese companies to build the 767 commercial jetliner raised fears that Boeing was unwittingly giving away its commercial airline technology to the Japanese. (Ways of constructing joint-venture agreements to minimize this risk are discussed in Section 8.8 on global strategic alliances.)

A second disadvantage is that a joint venture does not give a company the tight control over different subsidiaries that it might need if it wishes to pursue a global strategy. Consider the entry of Texas Instruments (TI) into the Japanese semiconductor market. When TI established semiconductor facilities in Japan, it did so for the sole purpose of checking the market share of Japanese manufacturers and limiting the amount of cash available to them to invade TI's global market. In other words, TI was engaging in global strategic coordination. To implement this strategy, TI's Japanese subsidiary had to be prepared to take instructions from TI's corporate headquarters regarding competitive strategy. The strategy also required the Japanese subsidiary to be run at a loss if necessary. Clearly, a Japanese joint-venture partner would have been unlikely to accept such conditions because they would have meant a negative return on investment. Thus, in order to implement this strategy, TI set up a wholly owned subsidiary in Japan rather than entering by means of a joint venture.

Wholly Owned Subsidiaries

Establishing a wholly owned subsidiary is generally the most costly method of serving a foreign market. Companies doing this have to bear the full costs and risks associated with setting up overseas operations (in contrast with joint ventures, where the costs and risks are shared, or licensing, where the licensee bears most of the costs and risks). Despite this considerable disadvantage, however, two clear advantages are associated with setting up a wholly owned subsidiary.

First, when a company's competitive advantage is based on control over a technological competence, a wholly owned subsidiary is normally the preferred entry mode because it reduces the risk of losing control over that competence.

For this reason, many high-tech companies prefer to set up wholly owned subsidiaries overseas rather than enter into joint ventures or licensing arrangements. Thus wholly owned subsidiaries tend to be the favored entry mode in the semiconductor, electronics, and pharmaceutical industries.

Second, a wholly owned subsidiary gives a company the kind of tight control over operations in different countries that is necessary if a company is going to pursue a global strategy. When the pressures for global integration are high, it may pay a company to configure its value chain in such a way that value-added at each stage is maximized. Thus a national subsidiary may specialize in manufacturing only part of the product line or certain components of the end product, exchanging parts and products with other subsidiaries in the company's global system. Establishing such a global manufacturing system necessarily requires a high degree of *control* over the operations of national affiliates. Different national operations have to be prepared to accept centrally determined decisions about how they should produce, how much they should produce, and how their output should be priced for transfer between operations. Licensees or joint-venture partners are unlikely to accept such a subservient role.

Choosing Between Entry Modes

As the preceding discussion demonstrates, both advantages and disadvantages are associated with the different entry modes. They are summarized in Table 8.3. Inevitably, because of these advantages and disadvantages, tradeoffs affect the choice of an entry mode. For example, when considering entry into an unfamiliar country with a track record for nationalizing foreign-owned enterprises, a company might favor a joint venture with a local enterprise. Its rationale might be that the local partner will help it to establish operations in an unfamiliar environment and will speak out against nationalization if the possibility arises. However, if the company's distinctive competence is based on proprietary technology, entering into a joint venture would mean running a risk of losing control over that technology.

Given such tradeoffs, making hard and fast recommendations about what a company should do is difficult. However, a number of rough generalizations can be made. First, if a company's competitive advantage is based on control over proprietary technology, licensing and joint-venture arrangements should be avoided if possible (in order to minimize the risk of losing control over that technology). Thus, if a high-tech company is considering setting up manufacturing operations in a foreign country, it should do so through a wholly owned subsidiary.

Second, for service companies the combination of franchising and subsidiaries to control franchisees within a particular country or region seems to work well. The subsidiary may be wholly owned or a joint venture. In most cases, however, service companies have found that entering into a joint venture with a local partner in order to set up a controlling subsidiary in a country or region

TABLE 8.3   Advantages and disadvantages of different entry modes

Entry mode	Advantage	Disadvantage
Exporting	Ability to realize global scale economies	High transport costs
		Tariff barriers
		Problems with local marketing agents
Licensing	Low development costs and risks	Difficulties achieving global strategic coordination
		Lack of control over technology
Franchising	Low development costs and risks	Difficulties achieving global strategic coordination
		Problems of quality control
Joint ventures	Access to local partner's knowledge	Difficulties achieving global strategic coordination
	Sharing of development costs and risks	Lack of control over technology
	Political acceptability	
Wholly owned subsidiaries	Protection of technology	Assumption by company of all development costs and risk
	Establishment of tight control necessary for achieving global strategic coordination	

works best. A joint venture is often politically more acceptable to the host government and brings a degree of local knowledge to the subsidiary.

Third, the greater the pressures for global integration, the more likely it is that a company will want to pursue some combination of exporting and wholly owned subsidiaries. By manufacturing in locations where the mix of factor costs and skills is most favorable, a company may be able to realize substantial cost economies. The company might then want to export the finished product to marketing subsidiaries based in various countries. These subsidiaries are typically wholly owned and have the responsibility for overseeing distribution in a particular country. Setting up wholly owned marketing subsidiaries is preferable to a joint-venture arrangement or to using a foreign marketing agent because it gives a company the tight control over strategic decisions in the host country that might be necessary to pursue global strategic coordination.

8.8 GLOBAL STRATEGIC ALLIANCES

The term *global strategic alliances* refers to cooperative agreements between potential or actual multinational competitors. Alliances range from formal joint ventures, in which two or more multinational companies have an equity stake, to short-term contractual agreements in which two companies may agree to cooperate on a particular problem (such as developing a new product). There is no doubt that collaboration between competitors is in fashion. The 1980s saw a virtual explosion in the number of strategic alliances. For example, in the global auto industry the number of alliances between the 23 largest competitors increased from less than 10 pairwise linkages in 1978 to 52 pairwise linkages in 1988.[19] Examples in other industries include the following:

1. A cooperative arrangement between Boeing and a consortium of Japanese companies to produce the 767 wide-body commercial jet
2. An alliance between General Electric and Snecma of France to build a family of low-thrust commercial aircraft engines
3. An agreement between Siemens and Philips to develop new semiconductor technology
4. An agreement between ICL, the British computer company, and Fujitsu of Japan to develop a new generation of mainframe computers capable of competing with IBM's products
5. An alliance between Eastman Kodak and Canon of Japan under which Canon manufactures a line of medium-volume copiers for sale under Kodak's name
6. An agreement between Texas Instruments and Kobe Steel Inc. of Japan to make logic semiconductors in Japan.

The Pros and Cons of Global Strategic Alliances

Critics warn that global strategic alliances, like formal joint ventures, give competitors a low-cost route to gain new technology and market access. For example, Harvard Business School professors Robert Reich and Eric Mankin have argued that strategic alliances between U.S. and Japanese companies are part of an implicit Japanese strategy to keep higher-paying, higher-value-added jobs in Japan and to gain the project engineering and production process skills that underlie the competitive success of many U.S. companies.[20]

On the other hand, a number of commentators have argued that strategic alliances can be to the advantage of both parties.[21] Alliances can be seen as a way of sharing the high fixed costs and high risks associated with new product development or with the opening up of new markets. The alliance between Boeing and the Japanese consortium to build the 767, for example, arose because Boeing was looking for assistance to share in the increasingly heavy burden of aircraft development (development costs for a new commercial aircraft can run into billions of dollars). Similarly, strategic alliances are becoming increasingly common in the global pharmaceutical industry, where the cost of developing a new drug can amount to $150 million.

Alternatively, an alliance can be seen as a way of bringing together complementary skills and assets that neither company could easily develop on its own.

Consider the strategic alliance between France's Thompson and Japan's JVC to manufacture videocassette recorders. JVC and Thompson are trading skills; Thompson needs product technology and manufacturing skills, and JVC needs to learn how to succeed in the fragmented European market. Both sides believe that there is an equitable chance for gain. Similarly, in 1990 AT&T struck a deal with NEC Corporation of Japan to trade technological skills. AT&T will give NEC some of its computer-aided-design technology. In return, NEC will give AT&T access to the technology underlying NEC advanced logic computer chips. Such equitable skill swaps seem to underlie many of the most successful strategic alliances.

Thus, contrary to Reich and Mankin's argument, alliances need not be high-tech giveaways, and they can evolve into mutually beneficial relationships. However, in order for this to occur, alliances must be structured so that (1) a company does not unintentionally give away proprietary technology to its alliance partner and (2) a company learns important skills from its alliance partner.

Protecting Technology in Alliances

Thomas Roehl of the University of Michigan and Frederick Truitt of the University of Washington have argued that a company in an alliance can take several approaches to protecting its technology.[22] First, alliances can be designed to make it difficult or impossible to transfer technology that is not meant to be transferred. Specifically, the design, development, manufacture, and service of the alliance product are structured to *wall off* the most sensitive technologies and prevent their leakage to the other participant. In the alliance between General Electric and Snecma to build commercial aircraft engines, General Electric tried to reduce the risk of "excess transfer" by walling off certain sections of the production process. The modularization effectively cut off the transfer of what GE felt was key competitive technology while permitting Snecma access to final assembly. Similarly, in the alliance between Boeing and the Japanese to build the 767, Boeing walled off research, design, and marketing functions considered central to Boeing's competitive position but allowed the Japanese to share in production technology. Boeing also walled off new technologies not required for 767 production.

Second, the sharing of technology and information can be linked to long-term commitments that require such complex intertwining of facilities and personnel and such large expenditures on capital equipment usable only in the context of the partnership that the risk of separation and head-to-head competition is substantially reduced. The most obvious way of doing this is for both companies to enter into a formal joint venture to which they commit substantial equity. In this case, the commitment of equity by each party to the alliance is the source of protection—a kind of mutual hostage taking (as discussed in Chapter 7). However, companies often prefer not to get involved in a formal joint venture with competitors because that involvement can limit their ability to exit from the alliance when they feel it has served its purpose.

A third possibility involves linking the release of technology to an alliance partner to specific performance requirements. Motorola, for example, has taken an incremental, incentive-based approach to technology transfer in its venture with Toshiba. The agreement calls for Motorola to release its microprocessor technology incrementally as Toshiba delivers on its promise to increase Motorola's penetration of the Japanese semiconductor market. The greater Motorola's market share becomes, the greater will Toshiba's access to Motorola's technology be. This arrangement guarantees that Motorola does not give away control over its technology without first getting something in exchange.

Learning from Alliance Partners

After a five-year study of fifteen strategic alliances between major multinationals, Gary Hamel, Yves Doz, and C. K. Prahalad came to the conclusion that one of the major forces determining how much a company gains from an alliance is its ability to learn from alliance partners.[23] They focused on a number of alliances between Japanese companies and Western (European or American) partners. In every case in which a Japanese company emerged from an alliance stronger than its Western partner, the Japanese company had made a greater effort to learn. Indeed, few Western companies seemed to want to learn from their Japanese partners. They tended to regard the alliance purely as a cost-sharing or risk-sharing device rather than as an opportunity to learn about how a potential competitor does business.

Consider the alliance between General Motors and Toyota to build the Chevrolet Nova. The alliance is structured as a formal joint venture called New United Motor Manufacturing Inc. Both parties have a 50 percent equity stake. The venture owns an auto plant in Fremont, California. According to one of the Japanese managers, Toyota achieved most of its objectives from the alliance: "We learned about U.S. supply and transportation. And we got the confidence to manage U.S. workers."[24] All that knowledge was then quickly transferred to Georgetown, Kentucky, where Toyota opened a plant of its own in 1988. On the other hand, although General Motors got a new product, the Chevrolet Nova, some GM managers complain that their knowledge was never put to good use inside General Motors. They say that they should have been kept together as a team to educate GM's engineers and workers about the Japanese system. Instead they were dispersed to different GM subsidiaries.[25]

A company entering an alliance must try to learn from its alliance partner and then put that knowledge to good use within its own organization. To do this, it has been suggested, all operating employees must be well briefed on the partner's strengths and weaknesses and understand how acquiring particular skills will bolster their company's competitive position. Hamel, Doz, and Prahalad observed that this is already standard practice among Japanese companies. They made the following observation:

> We accompanied a Japanese development engineer on a tour through a partner's factory. This engineering dutifully took notes on plant layout, the

number of production stages, the rate at which the line was running, and the number of employees. He recorded all this despite the fact that he had no manufacturing responsibility in his own company, and that the alliance did not encompass joint manufacturing. Such dedication greatly enhances learning.[26]

For such learning to be of value, the knowledge acquired from an alliance must be diffused through the organization (this was not done in GM after the GM-Toyota joint venture). The managers involved in an alliance should be used specifically to educate their colleagues within the company about the skills of the alliance partner.

8.9 THE ROLE OF HOST-GOVERNMENT POLICIES

One of the major differences between a purely domestic company and a multinational company is that the multinational has to deal with host-government policies. These policies can add another dimension of difficulty to the problem of strategy formulation and implementation. The governments of independent nation-states have their own set of priorities and objectives that may conflict with the strategic objectives of a multinational. Host governments can enact all kinds of measures that limit the freedom of a multinational to pursue the strategies of its choice and alter the attractiveness of various choices. These measures include trade policies, local content requirements, tax policies, exchange controls, and price policies. In addition, host governments may require a multinational wishing to do business in their country to enter into a joint venture with a domestic enterprise.

In terms of the framework introduced earlier in this chapter, the effect of host-government policies may be to limit the ability of a multinational to pursue global integration and to increase pressures for local responsiveness. For example, as illustrated in Figure 8.4, although economic and competitive conditions may suggest a high need for integration and a low need for local responsiveness (that is, the company should pursue a pure global strategy), host-government demands may require a company to be responsive to local needs. This situation is occurring in the auto industry.

Economic and competitive conditions in the auto industry have been pushing auto companies toward global strategies. However, host-government demands for local production, coupled with the threat to raise import tariffs on autos, have forced companies to be more locally responsive than they would probably choose to be. Thus, faced with the threat of significant tariff barriers, Japanese companies have recently been setting up production plants in the United States and Western Europe—despite their previous preference for the global strategy of centralizing production in Japan and exporting.

Alternatively, a multinational may be able to establish with a host govern-

FIGURE 8.4   **The impact of host-government demands on the integration-responsiveness grid**

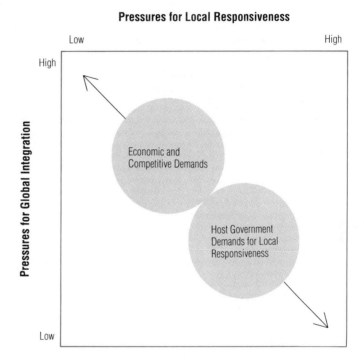

ment a cooperative relationship that is to the benefit of both parties. Host governments often try to attract multinationals by offering generous subsidies and privileged access to their local markets. For example, economic problems and high unemployment prompted Ireland to provide large subsidies in an effort to attract multinationals that can create jobs. In spite of a relatively small domestic market, Ireland is becoming an attractive site for multinational production because it offers free access to the markets of the European Community, of which it is a member.

The Concerns of Host Governments

If a multinational company is to develop effective strategies for dealing with host governments, it must first understand their concerns about their balance of payments, transfer pricing, competitiveness, and national sovereignty.[27]

Balance of payments   The balance of payments is an important policy issue for host governments, for a balance-of-payments deficit may act as a constraint on economic growth and lead to a decline in the value of the host country's currency. When a multinational exports its production to a host country, as the Japanese auto companies used to do with regard to the United States, exporting has a negative effect on the balance of payments of the host country. Threats of protectionism and the imposition of tariffs are always possibilities in this situation, even from countries nominally committed to the preservation of "free trade." Such threats may be sufficient to force a multinational to establish production in a host country even though it would prefer to export to that country. Thus, in response to growing protectionist pressures from Congress, the Japanese auto companies rapidly increased their direct investment in the United States between 1985 and 1990. By 1990 around 20 percent of U.S.-based auto-making capacity was Japanese owned, up from 0 percent in 1985.

Even when a multinational establishes a subsidiary in a host country, however, host-government concerns about the balance of payments may not be allayed. If the subsidiary is seen as an assembly plant—that is, if most of the components are manufactured overseas and imported into the host country for final assembly—a negative balance-of-payments effect may still exist. To correct it, many host governments have enacted local content requirements specifying that a certain percentage of a multinational's output in the host country be manufactured in the host country. For example, permission from the British government for Japanese electronics companies to invest in the United Kingdom was made conditional on the use of a high proportion of British-made components.

Another issue concerns the payment of dividends, interest, royalties, or administrative charges to the parent company. The capital outflows that such payments represent can push the balance of payments into deficit and precipitate a decline in the exchange value of the host country's currency. Such concerns have prompted host governments to enact tight exchange-control regulations. These make it difficult for a multinational to send its earnings back to its home country. For example, U.S. multinationals have long considered Brazil a profitable location for direct investment. However, Brazilian exchange controls have often forbidden multinationals from taking their profits out of the country. Such policies limit a multinational's ability to use the profits generated in one country to fight competitive battles in other countries. They limit a multinational's ability to achieve global strategic coordination.

Transfer pricing   Another important issue relating to the balance of payments is transfer pricing. The *transfer price* is the price at which goods are sold between the subsidiaries of a multinational company. Multinationals can and do use transfer prices both as a means of circumventing exchange controls and as a way of consolidating profits in the most favorable locations for tax purposes (for example, tax havens such as the Bahamas). Thus a multinational may circumvent tight exchange controls by charging an artificially high price for material inputs supplied to a host-country subsidiary from one of its home-country operations. In addition to the negative impact on a host country's balance of payments, artificially high transfer prices may also result in local shareholders' losing part of their legitimate profits. The host government may also lose tax revenue because of the decline in the earnings of the multinational's host-country subsidiary implied by high transfer prices.

An investigation by the British Monopolies and Mergers Commission brought to light the excessive prices charged for drugs in the United Kingdom by Hoffmann–La Roche, a Swiss pharmaceutical company.[28] According to the company, transfer prices were determined by "what is reasonable for tax purposes." The drugs in question were purchased by the U.K. subsidiary of Hoffman–La Roche at 46 times the price at which the same goods were available on the open market. In another example, a study of transfer pricing by the Colombian government for the period 1967–1970 estimated that transfer prices within multinationals were significantly inflated. With regard to the Colombian subsidiaries of foreign multinationals, transfer prices for pharmaceuticals were 87 percent greater than the world price, 44 percent greater for rubber, 25 percent greater for chemicals, and 54 percent greater for electrical components.[29] The expansion of intracompany trade that has accompanied the growth of globally integrated manufacturing strategies has only increased host-government concerns about such transfer pricing policies.

By its nature, transfer pricing is difficult to detect, but as concern has grown in host countries, greater efforts are being made to do so. Some countries now scrutinize transfer prices and fix them directly. For example, members of the Andean Pact (Colombia, Ecuador, Peru, Bolivia, Chile, and Venezuela) have adopted a common system for attempting to control transfer prices. This involves regular screening of the transfer prices paid for technology and products within multinationals and comparing them against world prices.

Competitiveness   Host governments often fear that the subsidiaries of foreign multinationals possess greater economic power than do indigenous competitors. In particular, they worry that a multinational may be able to use its aggregate financial strength to outspend domestic competitors and drive them out of business. This fear is particularly prevalent among the governments of less-developed countries, which may be concerned that the lack of indigenous competitors creates a potential monopoly problem. To forestall this situation, host governments may require foreign multinationals to share ownership of local subsidiaries with local enterprises or with the government itself. Clearly this requirement is not always in the best interest of the multinational, for shared ownership limits its ultimate control over the operations of the subsidiary.

National sovereignty   Another fear of host governments is that if their economy becomes too dependent on foreign multinationals, their ability to pursue desired policies may be limited. For example, a multinational enterprise is less responsive than an indigenous company to monetary policy measures because it can draw on funds elsewhere. Host-government fiscal policies may be circumvented by transfer pricing. Trade policy may be determined by marketing considerations of the parent company or by political considerations imposed on the multinational by the home-country government, and so on.

Host governments in less-developed countries may also be particularly concerned that multinationals may use their dominant position in the host economy to demand tax concessions, subsidies, and expensive infrastructure investments that the host country cannot easily afford. These demands may be reinforced by threats to relocate operations elsewhere in the world, taking away jobs, unless the host government complies. Finally, host governments may be concerned about foreign domination of strategic industries—such as aircraft manufacture, shipbuilding, and steelmaking—that may be important for the country in times of war. Because of this concern, Britain, France, and many other developed countries have restricted foreign direct investment in certain industries.

All of these concerns are particularly worrying for the governments of countries whose economy is dominated by foreign multinationals—countries like Mexico, where half of the largest 300 manufacturing firms in the mid 1970s were the subsidiaries of foreign multinationals, or Brazil, where 147 of the 300 largest manufacturing enterprises and 59 of the 100 largest were foreign owned.[30] Host governments try to protect their national sovereignty vis-à-vis multinationals by pursuing policies designed to reduce the power of multinationals: nationalization of foreign-owned assets, requiring joint ventures from foreign-owned enterprises, and setting up a screening procedure that gives access only to multinationals whose investments will clearly benefit the host. For example, Kenya has an elaborate screening system to ensure that only multinationals that will be of benefit to Kenya are let in.

Strategies for Dealing with Host Governments

In some cases a multinational can do little to alleviate host-government concerns, other than accept the solutions imposed by the host government. If those solutions are not acceptable, the best thing for the multinational to do is not invest in that host country. For example, when the government of India began to demand that local investors have a majority ownership stake in the subsidiaries of all foreign-owned multinationals, a number of U.S. companies responded by shutting down their Indian operations. One such company was Coca-Cola, which felt that it might no longer be able to protect its secret formula if majority control of its Indian operation was given to local investors. Another was IBM, which feared losing control over its technology.

Generally, however, many multinationals are in a relatively strong bargaining position with host governments. In many cases, by setting up production facilities in the host country, they may be able to attenuate the demands of the host government even if they cannot fully alleviate its concerns. The fact is that many host governments need the capital investment, jobs, and technology that a multinational can provide. A multinational can use this need as a lever to gain access to a country's market on reasonably favorable terms. Thus, although a multinational may still have to agree to a degree of local ownership, it might be limited to a relatively small minority stake that offers little real local control.

The bargaining position of a multinational is further increased if it intends to use the host country as an export base to serve a regional market. Host governments can be expected to solicit such investments actively. For example, the British government offered substantial subsidies in an ultimately successful effort to persuade Nissan to base its European manufacturing operation in Britain rather than Spain.

Alternatively, it may pay a multinational to enter into a strategic alliance with an indigenous company, partly as a means of guaranteeing access to an otherwise protected market. On this point, there is little doubt that part of the motivation underlying the recent flurry of joint ventures between Japanese and U.S. auto companies (for example, General Motors and Toyota, Ford and Mazda, and Chrysler and Mitsubishi), at least from the Japanese perspective, is a belief that such alliances will moderate growing protectionist tendencies in Congress.

Perhaps most importantly, however, multinationals can further their case with host governments if they are able to stress the benefit to both parties of a long-term cooperative relationship. In particular, a tacit or explicit commitment to sharing value with the host government may alleviate concerns. IBM, for example, is willing to incur what it calls "citizenship costs" in various countries in order to be allowed to continue to operate worldwide as it sees fit. Thus IBM goes to some lengths to ensure that host-country governments are satisfied with its presence. These range from progressive labor policies, to grants for education, to efforts to manage its globally integrated manufacturing network in a way that does not have a major adverse impact on any one host country's trade balance.

8.10 SUMMARY OF CHAPTER

In this chapter we describe the strategic choices that confront companies doing business in the global environment. We see how global expansion can create value for a company, and we examine the pros and cons of the different strategies that companies can pursue in the global arena. The following points are made during the course of this discussion:

1. A new reality is confronting American business: global competition and global competitors.

2. Global expansion enables a company to add value from (a) transferring core skills overseas, (b) using global volume to cover product development costs, (c) realizing economies of scale from global volume, and (d) configuring the company's value chain so that individual value-creation functions are performed in locations where value-added is maximized.

3. One of the major strategic choices made by multinationals is whether to compete on a multidomestic or a global basis. A multidomestic strategy is based on the assumption that national markets differ. A global market is based on the assumption that a product can be standardized across national markets.

4. A tradeoff is necessary when a company chooses between a multidomestic and a global strategy. Companies pursuing a global strategy gain cost economies from the integration of manufacturing, marketing, and competitive strategy across national boundaries, but they must give up a certain degree of responsiveness to national conditions. The opposite is true of companies pursuing a multidomestic strategy.

5. Pressures for global integration arise from (a) the need for cost reduction, (b) the existence of universal needs, and (c) global strategic coordination by competitors.

6. Pressures for local responsiveness arise from (a) differences in consumer tastes and preferences, (b) differences in infrastructure and in traditional practices, (c) differences in distribution channels, and (d) host-government demands.

7. Although some companies are clearly pure global enterprises and others are pure multidomestic enterprises, most companies have to deal with competing pressures for global integration and local responsiveness.

8. Companies that attempt to deal simultaneously with pressures for global integration and local responsiveness are called *transnational companies.*

9. There are five different ways to enter an overseas market: (a) exporting, (b) licensing, (c) franchising, (d) entering into a joint venture, and (e) setting up a wholly owned subsidiary. Each mode has its advantages and disadvantages.

10. Strategic alliances are cooperative agreements between potential or actual competitors. Critics warn that strategic alliances are little more than high-tech giveaways. Proponents suggest that they are a valuable way of (a) sharing risks and costs and (b) bringing together complementary skills.

11. An alliance need not be a high-tech giveaway so long as (a) the alliance is structured to prevent the unintentional transfer of technology and (b) companies learn to learn from their alliance partners.

12. A major difference between a purely domestic enterprise and a multinational is that the multinational has to deal with host-government policies.

13. If a multinational is to develop effective strategies for dealing with host governments, it must first understand their concerns about their balance of payments, transfer pricing, competitiveness, and local sovereignty.

14. Multinationals can often further their cause with host governments if they are able to stress the benefit to both parties of a long-term cooperative relationship.

Discussion Questions

1. Pick a major diversified multinational company and attempt to plot the position of its various businesses on the integration-responsiveness grid (see Figure 8.1). Justify your choice of positioning.

2. Licensing proprietary technology to overseas competitors is the best way to give up a company's competitive advantage. Discuss.

3. What kind of companies stand to gain most from entering into a strategic alliance with potential competitors? Why?

Endnotes

1. David Lieberman, "Keeping Up with the Murdochs," *Business Week,* March 20, 1989, pp. 32–34. David Lieberman, "Will It Happen? Will It Work?" *Business Week,* March 20, 1989, p. 34. Judith H. Dobrzynski, "Giant Steps Toward the Global Village: Or an Ego Trip?" *Business Week,* March 20, 1989, p. 36.

2. Neil Hood and Stephen Young, *The Economics of the Multinational Enterprise* (London: Longman, 1979).

3. Charles W. L. Hill, Michael Hitt, and Robert Hoskisson, "Declining U.S. Competitiveness: Reflections on a Crisis," *Academy of Management Executive,* 2 (1988), 51–60.

4. "West German and British Cars: A Tale of Two Motor Industries," *The Economist,* February 13, 1988, p. 65.

5. George S. Yip, "Global Strategy in a World of Nations?" *Sloan Management Review* (Fall 1989), 29–41.

6. For example, see T. Hout, Michael E. Porter, and E. Rudden, "How Global Companies Win Out," *Harvard Business Review* (September–October 1982), 98–108; Theodore Levitt, "The Globalization of Markets," *Harvard Business Review* (May–June 1983), 92–102; and S. Ghoshal, "Global Strategy: An Organizing Framework," *Strategic Management Journal,* 8 (September–October 1987), 425–440.

7. Yip, "Global Strategy in a World of Nations?" pp. 29–41.

8. C. K. Prahalad and Yves L. Doz, *The Multinational Mission: Balancing Local Demands and Global Vision* (New York: Free Press, 1987).

9. Theodore Levitt, "The Globalization of Markets," *Harvard Business Review* (May–June 1983), 92–102.

10. Levitt's critics include Kenichi Ohmae, "Managing in a Borderless World," *Harvard Business Review* (May–June 1989), 152–161; and Christopher A. Bartlett and Sumantra Ghoshal, "Managing Across Borders: New Strategic Requirement," *Sloan Management Review* (Summer 1987), 7–17.

11. Prahalad and Doz, *The Multinational Mission.*

12. Gary Hamel and C. K. Prahalad, "Do You Really Have a Global Strategy," *Harvard Business Review* (July–August 1985), 139–148.

13. Ohmae, "Managing in a Borderless World," 152–161.

14. See Prahalad and Doz, *The Multinational Mission.*

15. Christopher A. Bartlett and Sumantra Ghoshal, *Managing Across Borders: The Transnational Solution* (Boston: Harvard Business School Press, 1989).

16. Hout, Porter, and Rudden, "How Global Companies Win Out," 98–108.

17. This section draws on the following two studies: Charles W. L. Hill, Peter Hwang, and W. Chan Kim, "An Eclectic Theory of the Choice of International Entry Mode," *Strategic Management Journal,* 11 (February 1990), 117–128; and Charles W. L. Hill and W. Chan Kim, "Searching for a Dynamic Theory of the Multinational Enterprise: A Transaction Cost Model," *Strategic Management Journal,* 9, Special Issue (1988), 93–104.

18. David G. Bradley, "Managing Against Expropriation," *Harvard Business Review* (July–August, 1977), 75–83.

19. Charles W. L. Hill and W. Chan Kim, "Cooperative Alliances in the Global Auto Industry" (Working paper, University of Washington, 1990).

20. Robert B. Reich and Eric D. Mankin, "Joint Ventures with Japan Give Away Our Future," *Harvard Business Review* (March–April 1986), 78–90.

21. See Gary Hamel, Yves L. Doz, and C. K. Prahalad, "Collaborate with Your Competitors: And Win," *Harvard Business Review* (January–February 1989), 133–139; Kenichi Ohmae, "The Global Logic of Strategic Alliances," *Harvard Business Review* (March–April 1989), 143–154; and Thomas W. Roehl and J. Frederick Truitt, "Stormy Open Marriages Are Better," *Columbia Journal of World Business* (Summer 1987), 87–95.

22. Roehl and Truitt, "Stormy Open Marriages Are Better," pp. 87–95.

23. Hamel, Doz, and Prahalad, "Collaborate with Your Competitors," pp. 133–139.

24. Bernard Wysocki, "Cross-Border Alliances Become Favorite Way to Crack New Markets," *The Wall Street Journal,* March 4, 1990, p. A1.

25. Ibid., pp. A1, A6.

26. Hamel, Doz, and Prahalad, "Collaborate with Your Competitors," pp. 138–139.

27. Hood and Young, *The Economics of the Multinational Enterprise.*

28. Monopolies Commission, *Chlordiazepoxide and Diazepan* (London: Her Majesty's Stationery Office, 1973).

29. S. Lall, "Transfer Pricing by Multinational Manufacturing Firms," *Oxford Bulletin of Economics and Statistics,* 35 (1973), 173–195.

30. Hood and Young, *The Economics of the Multinational Enterprise.*

Chapter 9

ANALYZING AND CHANGING THE CORPORATE PORTFOLIO

9.1 OPENING INCIDENT: ROCKWELL INTERNATIONAL

In 1974 Robert Anderson succeeded Willard Rockwell as chairman of the board of Rockwell International Corp., a broadly diversified group with activities in aerospace, automotive equipment, electronics, and consumer appliances. Anderson's task was to make some sense out of this portfolio of businesses. He focused resources on the businesses that had the best long-term growth and profit prospects and divested businesses that had poor prospects. The winner in this process was the defense-oriented aerospace business.

The focus on defense began to pay big dividends in 1981, when Congress ordered 100 B-1B bombers from Rockwell. The contract was worth $15 billion. As a consequence, in 1984 aerospace activities accounted for nearly 45 percent of Rockwell's revenues, up from around 30 percent five years earlier. However, this growth brought problems. The B-1B contract was due to end in 1988; and with few signs of congressional eagerness to order more B-1Bs, Rockwell faced the problem of how to maintain

eleven years of continuous growth. Management was also worried that Rockwell now depended too much on defense contracts. After five years of expansion, the federal defense budget would not grow indefinitely, particularly given growing political unrest over the size of the federal deficit. To make matters worse, Rockwell's nondefense activities were concentrated in the mature industrial and automotive sectors, where growth prospects were low.

In short, by the mid 1980s Rockwell International's corporate portfolio was no longer balanced. Too great a percentage of earnings came from defense contracts and mature nondefense activities. If the company was to continue growing, it had to change the mix of businesses in its portfolio. In January 1985 Rockwell took a major step toward this goal with the $1.65-billion acquisition of Allen-Bradley, a leader in computerized factory automation. Allen-Bradley gave Rockwell a fifth area that complemented its four core areas—aerospace, electronics, automotive components, and industrial products. The acquisition put Rockwell at the forefront of an expanding industry in which sales were predicted to grow from \$5 billion to \$20 billion between 1985 and 1990. In essence, Rockwell took the cash harvest from the B-1B bomber and invested it for the 1990s in a business with star potential.[1]

9.2 OVERVIEW

Chapter 7 reviewed the corporate-level strategies that companies pursue in order to become multibusiness enterprises. This chapter examines various techniques used by multibusiness enterprises like Rockwell to analyze their portfolio of businesses. These techniques are referred to as **portfolio techniques.** They give strategic managers an overview of the long-term prospects and competitive strengths and weaknesses of a company's various businesses, enabling them to evaluate whether a portfolio is adequate from the perspective of long-term corporate growth and profitability. For example, in the mid 1980s management's assessment was that Rockwell's portfolio provided the company with too few prospects for long-term growth and profit.

When most companies analyze their portfolios, the objective is to identify what needs to be done to construct a balanced portfolio of businesses. A **balanced portfolio** can be defined as an assortment of businesses that enables a company to achieve the growth and profit objectives associated with its corporate strategy without exposing the company to undue risks. If a company does not have the right balance of businesses in its portfolio, it needs to pursue strategies designed to correct the imbalance. Thus Rockwell acquired Allen-Bradley in an attempt to shift the balance of activities in its portfolio toward businesses with greater long-term growth and profit prospects.

In this chapter, we discuss the advantages and limitations of three different portfolio techniques: (1) a portfolio matrix developed by management consultants at the Boston Consulting Group, (2) a portfolio matrix developed originally by management consultants McKinsey & Company for use at General Electric, and (3) an industry evolution matrix developed by Charles Hofer, of the University of Georgia. We also look at the pitfalls of portfolio planning in general.[2]

After examining the different portfolio techniques, we consider the means that companies employ to change the composition of their portfolios. These means include *entry strategies* (acquisition, internal new venturing, and joint ventures) and *exit strategies* (divestment, harvest, and liquidation). Acquisition and internal new venturing and joint ventures are alternative ways of entering new business areas, and we look at the factors that influence the choice between them. Divestment, harvest, and liquidation are alternative ways of exiting from existing business areas, and we examine the factors that affect a company's choice among them.

9.3 THE BOSTON CONSULTING GROUP BUSINESS MATRIX

The main objective of the Boston Consulting Group (BCG) technique is to help strategic managers identify the cash-flow requirements of the different businesses in their portfolio. The BCG approach involves three main steps: (1) dividing a company into strategic business units (SBUs) and assessing the long-term prospects of each, (2) comparing SBUs against each other by means of a matrix that indicates the relative prospects of each, and (3) developing strategic objectives with respect to each SBU.

Defining and Evaluating Strategic Business Units

A company must create an SBU for each economically distinct business area that it competes in. When strategic managers identify **SBUs,** their objective is to divide a company into strategic entities that are relevant for planning purposes. Normally, a company defines its SBUs in terms of the product markets they are competing in. For example, Rockwell International divides itself into five SBUs—aerospace, automotive components, electronics, factory automation, and industrial products—each reflecting a particular product market. Alternatively, companies that have significant vertically integrated operations might define all the businesses involved in a single vertically integrated chain of operations as one SBU. For example, the company shown in Figure 9.1 has divided itself into three SBUs. The first contains three closely related operations in the chemical industry; the second, a business operating in the automotive components industry; and the third, three vertically integrated businesses in the industries of iron ore mining, steel refining, and steel fabricating.

Having defined SBUs, strategic managers then assess each according to two criteria: (1) the SBU's relative market share and (2) the growth rate of the SBU's industry.

Relative market share The objective when identifying an SBU's relative market share is to establish whether that SBU's market position can be classified as a strength or a weakness. *Relative market share* is defined as the ratio of an SBU's market share to the market share held by the largest rival company in its industry. If SBU X has a market share of 10 percent and its largest rival has a market share of 30 percent, then SBU X's relative market share is 10/30, or 0.3. Only if an SBU is a market leader in its industry will it have a relative market share greater than 1.0. For example, if SBU Y has a market share of 40 percent and its largest rival has a market share of 10 percent, then SBU Y's relative market share is 40/10 = 4.0.

According to the Boston Consulting Group, market share gives a company cost advantages from economies of scale and learning effects (we discussed the

FIGURE 9.1   **The division of activities into SBUs**

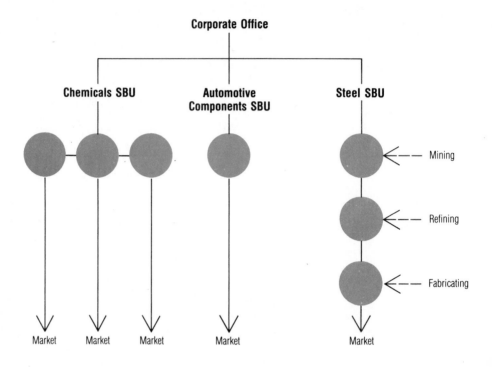

details in Chapter 4). An SBU with a relative market share greater than 1.0 is assumed to be farthest down the experience curve and therefore to have a significant cost advantage over its rivals. By similar logic, an SBU with a relative market share smaller than 1.0 is assumed to be at a competitive disadvantage because it lacks the scale economies and low-cost position of the market leader. Thus a relative market share greater than 1.0 can be characterized as a *strength*, and a relative market share smaller than 1.0 is a *weakness*. BCG characterizes SBUs with a relative market share greater than 1.0 as having a *high* relative market share and SBUs with a relative market share smaller than 1.0 as having a *low* relative market share.

Industry growth rate   The objective when assessing industry growth rates is to determine whether industry conditions offer opportunities for expansion or whether they threaten the SBU (as in a declining industry). The growth rate of an SBU's industry is assessed according to whether it is faster or slower than the growth rate of the economy as a whole. Industries with growth rates faster than the average are characterized as having *high* growth. Industries with growth rates slower than the average are characterized as having *low* growth. BCG's position is that high-growth industries offer a more favorable competitive environment and better long-term prospects than slow-growth industries. In other words, high-growth industries present an *opportunity,* low growth industries a *threat.*

Comparing Strategic Business Units

The next step of the BCG approach is comparing SBUs against each other by means of a matrix based on two dimensions: relative market share and high growth. Figure 9.2 provides an example of such a matrix. The horizontal dimension measures relative market share; the vertical dimension measures industry growth rate. Each circle represents an SBU. The center of each circle corresponds to the position of that SBU on the two dimensions of the matrix. The size of each circle is proportional to the sales revenue generated by each business in the company's portfolio. The bigger the circle, the larger is the size of an SBU relative to total corporate revenues.

The matrix is divided into four cells. SBUs in cell 1 are defined as **stars,** in cell 2 as **question marks,** in cell 3 as **cash cows,** and in cell 4 as **dogs.** BCG argues that these different types of SBUs have different long-term prospects and different implications for corporate cash flows.

Stars   The leading SBUs in a company's portfolio are the *stars.* They have a high relative market share and are based in high-growth industries. In the language of

FIGURE 9.2   **The Boston Consulting Group matrix**

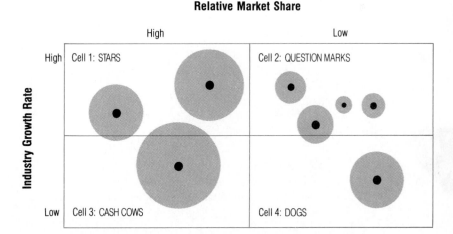

Source: Boston Consulting Group Matrix. Reprinted by permission of the Boston Consulting Group, Inc. Adapted from p. 12 in "Strategy and the Business Portfolio" by F. Hedley in *Long Range Planning,* (February 1977).

SWOT analysis, they have both competitive strengths and opportunities for expansion. Thus they offer excellent long-term profit and growth opportunities. Generally, BCG predicts that *established stars* are likely to be highly profitable and therefore can generate sufficient cash for their own investment needs. *Emerging stars,* in contrast, may require substantial cash injections to enable them to consolidate their market lead.

Question marks   SBUs that are relatively weak in competitive terms, that have low relative market shares, are *question marks.* However, they are based in high-growth industries and thus may offer opportunities for long-term profit and growth. A *question mark* can become a *star* if nurtured properly. To become a market leader, a *question mark* requires substantial net injections of cash; it is cash hungry. The corporate head office has to decide whether a particular *question mark* has the potential to become a *star* and is therefore worth the capital investment necessary to achieve stardom.

Cash cows   SBUs that have a high market share in low-growth industries and a strong competitive position in mature industries are *cash cows.* Their competitive strength comes from being farthest down the experience curve. They are the cost leaders in their industries. BCG argues that this position enables such SBUs to remain very profitable. However, low growth implies a lack of opportunities for future expansion. As a consequence, BCG argues that the capital investment requirements of *cash cows* are not substantial, and thus they are depicted as generating a strong positive cash flow.

Dogs   SBUs that are in low-growth industries but have a low market share are *dogs.* They have a weak competitive position in unattractive industries and thus are viewed as offering few benefits to a company. BCG suggests that such SBUs are unlikely to generate much in the way of a positive cash flow and indeed may become cash hogs. Though offering few prospects for future growth in returns, dogs may require substantial capital investments just to maintain their low market share.

Strategic Implications

The objective of the BCG portfolio matrix is to identify how corporate cash resources can best be used to maximize a company's future growth and profitability. BCG recommendations include the following:

1.   The cash surplus from any *cash cows* should be used to support the development of selected *question marks* and to nurture *emerging stars.* The long-term objective is to consolidate the position of *stars* and to turn favored *question marks* into *stars,* thus making the company's portfolio more attractive.

2. *Question marks* with the weakest or most uncertain long-term prospects should be divested so that demands on a company's cash resources are reduced.

3. The company should exit from any industry where the SBU is a *dog*—by divestment, harvesting market share, or liquidation (exit strategies are discussed later in this chapter).

4. If a company lacks sufficient *cash cows, stars,* or *question marks,* it should consider acquisitions and divestments to build a more balanced portfolio. A portfolio should contain enough *stars* and *question marks* to ensure a healthy growth and profit outlook for the company and enough *cash cows* to support the investment requirements of the *stars* and *question marks*

Strengths and Weaknesses of the BCG Matrix

The major strength of the BCG matrix is that it focuses attention on the cash-flow requirements of different types of businesses and points out ways of using cash flows to optimize the value of the corporate portfolio. The BCG matrix also indicates when a company needs to add another SBU to its portfolio and when it needs to remove an SBU.

However, the BCG matrix has a number of significant shortcomings. The model is simplistic. An assessment of an SBU in terms of just two dimensions, market share and industry growth, is bound to be misleading, for a host of other relevant factors should be taken into account. Although market share is undoubtedly an important determinant of an SBU's competitive position, companies can also establish a strong competitive position by differentiating their product to serve the needs of a particular segment of the market (see Chapter 5). Thus a business having a low market share can be very profitable and have a strong competitive position in certain segments of a market. The auto manufacturer Rolls-Royce is in this position, yet the BCG matrix would classify Rolls-Royce as a *dog* because it is a low-market-share business in a low-growth industry. Similarly, industry growth is not the only factor determining industry attractiveness. Many factors besides growth determine competitive intensity in an industry and thus its attractiveness (see Chapter 3).

The connection between relative market share and cost savings is not as straightforward as BCG suggests. Chapter 4 made clear that a high market share does not always give a company a cost advantage. In some industries—for example, the U.S. steel industry—low-market-share companies using a low-share technology (minimills) can have lower production costs than high-market-share companies using high-share technologies (integrated mills). The BCG matrix would classify minimill operations as the *dogs* of the American steel industry, whereas in fact their performance over the last decade has characterized them as *star* businesses.[3]

Furthermore, a high market share in a low-growth industry does not necessarily result in the large positive cash flow characteristic of *cash-cow* businesses. The BCG matrix would classify General Motors' auto operations as a *cash cow*. However, the capital investments needed to remain competitive are so substantial in the auto industry that the reverse is more likely to be true: Low-growth industries can be very competitive, and staying ahead in such an environment can require substantial cash investments.

The BCG approach, then, carries the risk of misclassifying businesses. The McKinsey matrix was developed to counter some of its weaknesses.

9.4 THE McKINSEY MATRIX

The technique developed by management consultants McKinsey & Company also divides a company into SBUs. As in the BCG matrix, each SBU is assessed along two dimensions, but the dimensions are based on many more factors. The dimensions are (1) the attractiveness of the industry in which an SBU is based and (2) an SBU's competitive position within that industry.

Assessing Industry Attractiveness

The assessment of industry attractiveness is a four-step process. Each step can be illustrated with reference to Table 9.1. The table shows how Rockwell International might assess the attractiveness of the factory automation industry, in which it now operates (see the Opening Incident). The steps are as follows:

1. Strategic managers identify a set of criteria that determine the attractiveness of an industry. The set typically includes factors acknowledged to be important determinants of industry attractiveness—factors such as growth, size, capital intensity, and competitive intensity. The competitive forces discussed in Chapter 3 are normally found in this kind of list, either individually or summarized by some aggregate criterion such as competitive intensity.

2. Strategic managers then assign a weight to each criterion in the set to indicate the relative importance of each *to the company*. To ensure consistency, the sum of the weights should add up to 1. For example, Rockwell International is shown in Table 9.1 to rank "industry growth" as the most important attractiveness criterion, assigning it a weight of 0.30. The rationale for this ranking is that Rockwell is involved in too many mature industries and needs to move into high-growth ones.

3. Next, strategic managers rate the attractiveness of each industry in the corporate portfolio according to the various attractiveness criteria. Normally, a scale of 1 to 5 is used, where 1 is unattractive and 5 is very attractive. Deci-

TABLE 9.1   **Assessing industry attractiveness: factory automation industry**

Industry attractiveness criteria	Weight	Industry rating	Weighted score
Industry size	0.10	3	0.30
Industry growth	0.30	5	1.50
Industry profitability	0.20	4	0.80
Capital intensity	0.05	5	0.25
Technological stability	0.10	5	0.50
Competitive intensity	0.20	3	0.60
Cyclicality	0.05	2	0.10
Totals	1.00		4.05

sions about the attractiveness of the criteria will reflect the company's objectives. Thus "industry growth" in Table 9.1 is rated 5 by Rockwell because factory automation is a high-growth industry and Rockwell is looking for high growth. Notice that an attractive criterion can be viewed as providing the company with an *opportunity* to realize its corporate objectives, but an unattractive criterion must be viewed as a *threat*.

4. Finally, strategic managers compute a total weighted score for each industry in the corporate portfolio. To arrive at this score, *weight* is multiplied by the *rating* for each of the attractiveness criteria, to get a *weighted score;* then the weighted scores are added. Thus in Table 9.1 Rockwell assigns to "competitive intensity" a weight of 0.20, and the factor automation industry is given a rating of 3 against this criterion. Thus the weighted score is $0.20 \times 3 = 0.60$. Adding the weighted scores together gives a *total weighted score* for each industry in the company's portfolio. The total weighted score is an index of how attractive each industry is to the company. The maximum value that this index can have is 5 and the minimum is 1; the average score is around 3. The total score of 4.05 for the factory automation industry indicates to Rockwell that the attraction of the industry is above average.

Assessing Competitive Position Within an Industry

Assessing an SBU's competitive position within its industry involves four steps similar to those followed in assessing industry attractiveness. Each step can be illustrated with reference to Table 9.2, which shows how Rockwell might assess the competitive position of its factory automation business (Allen-Bradley) within the factory automation industry.

TABLE 9.2   **Assessing competitive position: factory automation SBU**

Key success factors	Weight	Industry rating	Weighted score
Market share	0.15	5	0.75
Technological know-how	0.25	5	1.25
Product quality	0.15	4	0.60
After-sales service/maintenance	0.20	5	1.00
Price competitiveness	0.05	2	0.10
Low operating costs	0.10	3	0.30
Productivity	0.10	3	0.30
Totals	1.00		4.30

1. Strategic managers identify the *key success factors* in each of the industries in which the company competes. In the case of Rockwell's factory automation business, the factors are market share, technological know-how, product quality, after-sales service/maintenance, price competitiveness, low operating costs, and productivity.

2. Next, strategic managers assign a weight to each success factor, indicating its relative importance for establishing a strong competitive position within the industry being considered. As before, to ensure consistency, the weights must add up to 1. Table 9.2 shows that Rockwell views "technological know-how" as the most important success factor in the factory automation industry, followed by "after-sales service/maintenance."

3. Then strategic managers rate the competitive strengths of each SBU against relevant success factors in the various industries. As before, a scale of 1 to 5 is normally used, where 1 is very weak and 5 is very strong. Table 9.2 shows that Rockwell's factory automation SBU is in a very strong position with respect to market share, technological know-how, and after-sales service/ maintenance—all-important success factors in the factory automation industry. In other words, the *strengths* (distinctive competencies) of Rockwell's factory automation business include market share, technological know-how, and service/maintenance. Its *weaknesses* include price competitiveness, operating costs, and productivity.

4. Finally, strategic managers compute a total weighted score, which can then be used as an index of an SBU's competitive position. This score is derived by multiplying *weight* by *industry rating* to get a *weighted score* for each success factor and then adding the weighted scores to obtain the *total weighted score*. The value of the total weighted score will be between 5 (very strong com-

petitive position) and 1 (very weak competitive position), with 3 being the average. Table 9.2 shows that Rockwell's factory automation SBU is in a strong competitive position, with a total weighted score of 4.30.

Comparing Strategic Business Units

Once the foregoing analysis has been completed, the actual position of each SBU can be plotted on a matrix similar to the one shown in Figure 9.3. Industry attractiveness is plotted on the vertical dimension, competitive position on the horizontal dimension. Each circle represents an SBU. The position of the center of

FIGURE 9.3   The McKinsey matrix

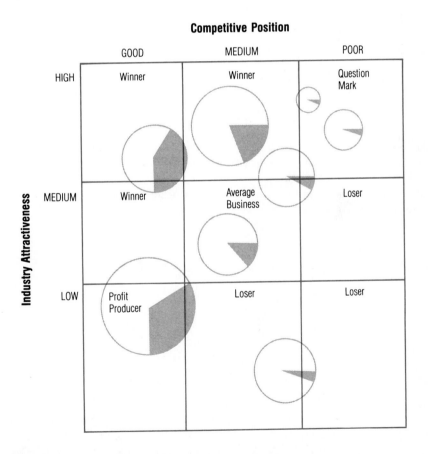

each circle is determined by the score that the SBU received on the two dimensions. The size of each circle is proportional to the size of the industry in which the SBU is based (measured total industry sales). The shaded wedge indicates an SBU's market share in that industry.

The McKinsey matrix is divided into nine cells. SBU's falling into three of the cells are characterized as **winners,** or the most desirable businesses. They are based in industries of medium to high attractiveness and have medium to strong competitive positions. Rockwell's factory automation business might be characterized as a *winner.* Three other cells are characterized as containing **losers.** These are the least desirable businesses. They have relatively weak competitive positions in unattractive industries.

One cell contains a *question mark.* As in the BCG matrix, **question marks** have an uncertain but potentially promising future. They have a weak competitive position in an attractive industry. With proper nurturing, they could become *winners;* however, they also run the risk of developing into *losers.* One cell contains **profit producers.** Analogous to the BCG matrix *cash cows,* these businesses have a strong competitive position in an unattractive industry. Finally, one cell contains **average businesses.** These businesses have no great strengths, but neither are they particularly weak.

Strategic Implications

The strategic implications of the McKinsey analysis are straightforward. *Losers* should be divested, liquidated, or told to harvest market share (a process described in detail later in the chapter). The position of *winners* and *developing winners* should be consolidated, if necessary by net injections of cash. The company should also nurture selected *question marks* in an attempt to turn them into *winners.* Since *profit producers* are based in industries whose long-term prospects are poor, these businesses should use their strong competitive position to generate profits, which can then be invested to support *winners* and selected *question marks.* The company should either try to turn *average businesses* into *winners* or consider divesting them because they are unlikely to offer the best long-term returns.

One objective of the McKinsey analysis is to identify how far out of balance a company's portfolio actually is. In this context, a **balanced portfolio** can be defined as one that contains mostly *winners* and *developing winners,* plus a few *profit producers,* to generate the cash flow necessary to support the *developing winners,* and a few small *question-mark* businesses with the potential to become *winners.*[4] Such a portfolio is balanced because it offers the company good profit and growth prospects without straining its cash-flow position.

More typically, however, a company has an unbalanced portfolio—a portfolio that places too many demands on the company's cash-flow position and offers inadequate prospects for profit and growth. Table 9.3 shows several different kinds of unbalanced portfolios, along with appropriate corrective strategies. To correct an unbalanced portfolio, strategic managers must change the compo-

TABLE 9.3   **Four basic types of unbalanced portfolios**

Problem action	Typical symptoms	Typical corrective
Too many *losers*	Inadequate cash flow Inadequate profits Inadequate growth	Divest/liquidate/harvest *losers* Acquire *profit producers* Acquire *winners*
Too many *question marks*	Inadequate cash flow Inadequate profits	Divest/harvest/liquidate selected *question marks*
Too many *profit producers*	Inadequate growth Excessive cash flow	Acquire *winners* Nurture/develop selected *question marks*
Too many *developing winners*	Excessive cash demands Excessive demands on management Unstable growth and profits	Divest selected developing winners if necessary Acquire *profit producers*

Source: Adapted from p. 52 in *Successful Strategic Management* by C. W. Hofer and M. J. Davoust. Copyright © 1977 by A. T. Kearney. Reprinted by permission.

sition of the corporate portfolio, adding or removing SBUs. For example, Rockwell International's portfolio in the early 1980s suffered from having too many *profit producers;* it was unbalanced. To correct this situation, Rockwell acquired a *developing winner,* Allen–Bradley.

Strengths and Weaknesses of the McKinsey Matrix

The McKinsey matrix is a great improvement on the BCG matrix because it is more comprehensive and avoids the simplifications and unwarranted assumptions of the BCG approach. One of its greatest strengths is its flexibility. The McKinsey matrix recognizes that different industries are characterized by different success factors, and it incorporates this fact into the analysis. Moreover, the McKinsey analysis can cover a much greater range of strategically relevant variables.

Nevertheless, the McKinsey approach is not perfect. One of the main difficulties is that it produces numbers to give strategic decisions legitimacy but does not explicitly recognize that the numbers are all subjectively derived. Strategic managers must be careful, therefore, not to let their own subjective biases enter into the analysis. Another problem is that the analysis is basically a static one. It looks at the *current* position of SBUs but does not take into account how their *future* position might change as a result of industry evolution. It does not depict the position of businesses across different stages of the industry life cycle. For example, it does not depict what might happen to a *question mark* as its industry enters the growth stage or to a *winner* as its industry enters the shakeout stage. This is where the industry evolution matrix becomes relevant.

9.5 THE INDUSTRY EVOLUTION MATRIX

To offset the shortcomings of the McKinsey matrix, Charles Hofer has suggested that companies use a portfolio matrix based on industry evolution.[5]

Evaluating and Comparing Strategic Business Units

Using the industry evolution matrix, strategic managers start by dividing business areas into SBUs. Next, using techniques similar to those of the McKinsey approach, they assess the competitive position of each SBU. The position of each SBU is plotted on a fifteen-cell matrix similar to the one shown in Figure 9.4. The horizontal dimension indicates an SBU's competitive position. The vertical dimension shows the different stages of industry evolution. Each circle represents an SBU. The size of the circle is proportional to the size of the industry in which the SBU is based (measured by total industry revenues), and the shaded wedge indicates the market share of the SBU.

The power of the industry evolution matrix lies in the story that it can tell about the distribution of a company's businesses across different stages of the industry life cycle. Using descriptive terminology similar to that of the McKinsey approach, we might characterize business A in Figure 9.4 as a *high-potential question mark*. It has a strong competitive position in the early stage of an industry's development. Thus it is well placed to capitalize on opportunities for expansion when its industry enters the growth stage. Similarly, business B is a *developing winner*. It has a strong position in a growth industry. It, too, can capitalize on opportunities for expansion. Business C, however, although also based in a growth industry, looks like a *developing loser*. Such a business is unlikely to survive the threat of the shakeout stage. The industry in which business D is based is currently undergoing a shakeout. Although this makes the industry environment a threat, business D has a strong competitive position and will probably survive and enter into maturity as a market leader or *profit producer*. Businesses E and F look to be *profit producers*, whereas business G is a definite *loser*.

Strategic Implications

The strategic implications of this analysis center on the different stages of the life cycle at which the various businesses are found. *High-potential question marks* and *developing winners*, such as businesses A and B, should be nurtured, for they may

FIGURE 9.4   **The industry evolution matrix**

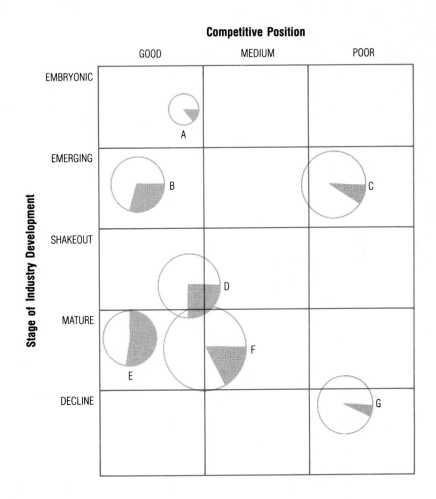

Source: Adapted from Charles W. Hofer, "Conceptual Constructs for Formulating Corporate and Business Strategies." (Dover, MA: Lord Publishing, #BP 0041, p. 3.) Copyright © 1977 by Charles W. Hofer. Reprinted by permission.

become the *established winners* and *profit producers* of the future. Potential *losers*, such as business C, should be divested as quickly as possible. Similarly, businesses such as G have few long-term prospects. The company needs to adopt an exit strategy for such operations. Business D is unlikely to be earning good returns currently, but its prospects are good. Businesses in this kind of position need to be supported. Businesses E and F should be managed in a way that consolidates and maintains their competitive strengths. Any surplus cash flows from these businesses should be used to support *developing winners* and companies going through a shakeout.

Like the McKinsey approach, the industry evolution matrix enables strategic managers to assess whether a corporate portfolio is balanced or unbalanced. A balanced portfolio should consist mainly of *established winners* and *profit producers,* such as businesses E and F; a few *developing winners,* such as business B; and a few *high-potential question marks,* such as business A. Most companies, however, find that they have unbalanced portfolios similar to those described in Table 9.3.

Unlike the McKinsey approach, the industry evolution matrix enables a company to assess how its portfolio of current operations is likely to develop over the next few years. A company with a number of *potential losers* based in currently profitable high-growth emerging industries might foresee that several years down the line it could be faced with an unbalanced portfolio containing too many *losers.* By taking corrective action now, it can avoid this situation.

Strengths and Weaknesses of the Industry Evolution Matrix

The strength of the industry evolution matrix is that it shows the distribution of a company's activities across different stages of the life cycle. As a result, a company can predict how its current portfolio might develop, and it can take immediate action to ensure that its portfolio is balanced. The industry evolution matrix has the additional advantage of focusing the attention of corporate-level personnel on potential business-level strategies. As you recall from Chapters 3 and 4, the industry life cycle is one of the most important determinants of strategic choice at the business level. For example, developing *winners,* such as business B in Figure 9.4, are at the development stage where the realization of cost economies from experience-curve effects is most important. Thus by using the industry evolution matrix, corporate-level personnel can perceive strategic requirements at the business level. No other approach has this advantage.

The drawback of the industry evolution matrix is that it does not focus on all the relevant factors of industry attractiveness. As the McKinsey matrix illustrates, the stage of industry evolution is an important but not the sole determinant of industry attractiveness. Other factors are also significant and have an impact that is independent of the stage of industry evolution.

9.6 BENEFITS AND PITFALLS OF PORTFOLIO ANALYSIS

Benefits

As a planning tool, portfolio techniques have a number of benefits. First, they enable strategic managers to analyze the diverse activities of a multibusiness company in a systematic fashion and so help make sense out of enterprise diversity. Second, they highlight the different cash-flow implications and requirements of different business activities. Such highlighting can assist the corporate head office in carrying out its resource allocation function.

Third, the concept of a balanced portfolio prods strategic managers to identify the kinds of adjustments that need to be made in the composition of the company's portfolio so that long-term growth and profitability can be optimized. Essentially, a balanced portfolio constitutes a company *strength,* an unbalanced portfolio a company *weakness.* Portfolio analysis can be used to identify gaps in the corporate portfolio that need to be filled in order to strike a balance. Thus in the early 1980s Rockwell International saw the lack of any *developing winners* as a gap in its portfolio and filled the gap with the purchase of Allen-Bradley. By the same token, portfolio analysis can indicate when there are too many businesses of a certain type in a company's portfolio. Exiting from these businesses will correct the portfolio's imbalance.

Of the three techniques discussed in this chapter, the BCG business matrix is perhaps the least useful, for it oversimplifies and makes unwarranted assumptions about the relationship between market share and performance. Both the McKinsey technique and the industry evolution matrix are more comprehensive and realistic. A strong case can be made for using them together and giving strategic managers two different but complementary perspectives of a company's portfolio. The McKinsey technique provides the company with an overview of the attractiveness of its *current* portfolio, whereas the industry evolution matrix can be used to project how the attractiveness of that portfolio might alter in the *future.*

Pitfalls

The merits of the different techniques apart, it must be recognized that the whole process of portfolio planning has its own pitfalls. Although these pitfalls do not invalidate the concept of portfolio planning, they suggest that companies should be cautious about relying too heavily on portfolio-planning techniques. Three major areas of concern can be identified.[6]

First, portfolio techniques explicitly assume that a company can be divided into a reasonable number of SBUs for the purpose of analysis. In practice, many companies are very diverse and have a large number of different business units. General Electric, for example, now has close to 300 businesses. Grouping such a large number of businesses into SBUs still results in a large number of SBUs to be managed by the head office. Large numbers of SBUs can create problems of **information overload** at the corporate office. It has been suggested that information overload starts becoming a serious problem when a company contains forty to fifty SBUs.[7] When information overload develops, the corporate office's analysis of each SBU becomes increasingly superficial. Strategic managers at the corporate office simply do not have the time to undertake the kind of thorough analysis needed to make portfolio techniques work. Thus the head office may commit large sums of money to different SBUs on the basis of insufficient knowledge of the activities involved and of the different industries that the company is active in. Poor decisions and poor performance are the inevitable results.

Second, when an SBU contains a number of different but related product divisions, as is often the case, conflicts of interest can develop between the internal cash-flow priorities of the SBU and the cash-flow priorities of the company as a whole. For example, an SBU may be defined as a *dog,* told to harvest its market share, and denied any significant capital investments. However, this SBU may contain a product division that strategic managers at the SBU level see as a *rising star.* To realize its full potential, the *rising star* needs significant capital investments, but the corporate analysis does not uncover this fact. The result can be damaging political conflict between strategic managers at the SBU level and at the corporate level over the lack of fund allocations to the *rising star.*

Third, a naive application of portfolio-planning techniques can create problems for vertically integrated companies and for companies that have pursued a strategy of related diversification. In a vertically integrated company, one SBU might be supplying inputs to another. Portfolio planning might suggest that the supplying SBU should be divested. However, divesting might be absurd if benefits in the form of lower production costs are being derived from the internal source of supply. Similarly, in a related-diversification company, two SBUs might be coordinating their activities to realize benefits from the exploitation of marketing and production synergies. Portfolio planning might suggest that one of these SBUs be divested. However, divestiture would mean the loss of the benefits derived from exploiting those synergies.

In short, a naive application of portfolio techniques can obscure important strategic relationships between SBUs. This potential limitation, however, can be overcome if strategic managers take the time to weigh the conflicting considerations of achieving a balanced portfolio against the loss of valuable strategic relationships among the SBUs.

9.7 ENTRY STRATEGIES

As noted above, correcting an imbalance in a company's corporate portfolio frequently requires entry into new business areas, adding *question marks, winners,* or *profit producers* to the portfolio. This means adding new business areas to the company through related diversification, unrelated diversification, or international expansion. In Chapter 7, we reviewed factors that influence a company's choice among these different generic corporate-level strategies. In this section, we examine the *means* of entry into a new business area (as distinct from the *type* of generic corporate-level strategy being pursued). The basic choices that strategic managers face are entry through **acquisition** and entry through **internal new venturing.** Sometimes neither is the optimal choice; in such cases, entry through a **joint venture** may prove to be the best option.

Acquisition Versus Internal New Venturing

Entry into a new business area through acquisition involves purchasing an established company, complete with all its facilities, equipment, and personnel. Entry into a new business area through internal new venturing involves starting a business from scratch: building facilities, purchasing equipment, recruiting personnel, opening up distribution outlets, and so on. Such projects are often called *greenfield projects* because the company starts with nothing but a green field.

The choice between acquisition and internal new venturing as the preferred entry strategy is influenced by a number of factors: (1) barriers to entry, (2) the relatedness of the new business to existing operations, (3) the comparative speed and development costs of the two entry modes, (4) the risks involved in the different entry modes, and (5) industry life-cycle factors.[8]

Barriers to entry   Recall from Chapter 3 that barriers to entry arise from factors associated with product differentiation (brand loyalty), absolute cost advantages, and economies of scale. When barriers are substantial, a company finds entering an industry through internal new venturing difficult. To do so, a company may have to construct an efficient-scale manufacturing plant, undertake massive advertising to break down established brand loyalties, and quickly build up distribution outlets—all hard-to-achieve goals that are likely to involve substantial expenditures. In contrast, by acquiring an established enterprise, a company can circumvent most entry barriers. It can purchase a market leader that already benefits from substantial scale economies and brand loyalty. Thus the greater the barriers to entry, the more is acquisition the favored entry mode.

Relatedness   The more related a new business is to a company's established operations, the lower are the barriers to entry and the more likely it is that the company has accumulated experience with this type of business. These factors heighten the attractiveness of new venturing. For example, IBM entered the personal computer market in 1981 by new venturing. The entry was very successful, enabling IBM to capture 35 percent of the market within two years. IBM was able to enter by this mode because of the high degree of relatedness between the personal computer market and IBM's established computer mainframe operations. IBM already had a well-established sales force and brand loyalty, and it had considerable expertise in the computer industry. Similarly, companies such as Du Pont and Dow Chemical Co. have successfully entered closely related chemical businesses through internal new venturing.

In contrast, the more unrelated a new business is, the more likely is entry to be through acquisition. By definition, unrelated diversifiers lack the specific expertise necessary to enter a new business area through greenfield development. An unrelated diversifier choosing internal new venturing has to develop its own expertise for competing in an unfamiliar industry. The learning process can be lengthy and involve costly mistakes before the company fully understands its new industry. In the case of an acquisition, however, the acquired business already has a management team with accumulated experience in competing in that particular industry. When making an acquisition, a company is also buying knowledge and experience. Thus widely diversified conglomerates such as ITT, Textron, Gulf & Western, and Hanson Trust have all expanded through acquisition.

Speed and development costs   As a rule, internal new venturing takes years to generate substantial profits. Establishing a significant market presence can be both costly and time consuming. In a study of corporate new venturing, Ralph Biggadike of the University of Virginia found that on the average it takes eight years for a new venture to reach profitability and ten to twelve years before the profitability of the average venture equals that of a mature business.[9] He also found that cash flow typically remains negative for at least the first eight years of a new venture. In contrast, acquisition is a much quicker way to establish a significant market presence and generate profitability. A company can purchase a market leader in a strong cash position overnight, rather than spend years building up a market-leadership position through internal development. Thus, when speed is important, acquisition is the favored entry mode.

Risks of entry   New venturing tends to be an uncertain process with a low probability of success. Studies by Edwin Mansfield of the University of Pennsylvania concluded that only between 12 percent and 20 percent of R&D-based new ventures actually succeed in earning an economic profit.[10] Indeed, business history is strewn with examples of large companies that lost money through internal new venturing. For example, in 1984 AT&T entered the computer market through an internal new venture. Company officials predicted that by 1990 AT&T would rank second in data processing, behind IBM. So far there are few signs of that happening. In 1985 AT&T's computer division lost $500 million, and in 1986 it lost $1.2 billion.[11]

When a company makes an acquisition, it is acquiring known profitability, known revenues, and known market share; thus it avoids uncertainty. Essentially, internal new venturing involves the establishment of a *question-mark* business, whereas acquisition allows a company to buy a *winner*. Thus many companies favor acquisition.

Industry life-cycle factors   We considered the general importance of the industry life cycle in Chapter 3. The industry life cycle has a major impact on many of the factors that influence the choice between acquisitions and internal new venturing. In embryonic and growth industries, barriers to entry are typically lower than in mature industries because established companies in the former are still going through a learning process. They do not have the same experience advantages as the established companies in a mature industry environment. Given these factors, entry by an internal new venture during the early stage of the industry life cycle means lower risks and development costs, as well as fewer pen-

alties in terms of expansion speed, than entry into a mature industry environment. Thus internal new venturing tends to be the favored entry mode in
embryonic and growth industries, whereas acquisition tends to be the favored
mode in mature industries. Indeed, many of the most successful internal new
ventures have been associated with entry into emerging industries—for instance,
IBM's entry into the personal computer arena and John Deere Co.'s entry into
the snowmobile business.

Summary   In sum, internal new venturing seems to make most sense when the
following conditions exist: when the industry to be entered is in its embryonic
or growth stage; when barriers to entry are low; when the industry is closely
related to the company's existing operations (the company's strategy is one of
related diversification); and when the company is willing to accept the attendant
time frame, development costs, and risks.

In portfolio terms, internal new venturing makes most sense when a company needs more *question marks* in its portfolio or when it sees a strong possibility
of establishing an *emerging winner* in an embryonic or growth industry. On the
other hand, acquisition makes the most sense when a company needs more *established winners* or *profit producers* in its portfolio. Table 9.4 summarizes these
situations.

In contrast, acquisition makes most sense when the following conditions
exist: when the industry to be entered is mature; when the barriers to entry are
high; when the industry is not closely related to the company's existing operations (the company's strategy is one of unrelated diversification); and when the
company is unwilling to accept the time frame, development costs, and risks of
internal new venturing.

Pitfalls of Acquisition

Despite the popularity of acquisition, it often does not bring the gains predicted.[12]
For example, management consultants McKinsey & Company put fifty-eight
major acquisitions undertaken between 1972 and 1983 to two tests: (1) Did the
return on the total amount invested in the acquisitions exceed the cost of capital,
and (2) did the acquisitions help their parent companies outperform the compe-

TABLE 9.4   **Portfolio gaps and entry strategies**

Portfolio gap	Entry strategy
Insufficient *cash cows*	Acquire companies in mature industries
Insufficient *winners*	Acquire companies in mature industries
Insufficient *question marks* or *developing winners*	Internal venture in growth or embryonic industry

tition in the stock market? Twenty-eight out of the fifty-eight clearly failed both tests, and six others failed one.[13] In terms of the generic corporate strategies discussed in Chapter 7, these test results indicate that many acquisitions fail to establish the *strategic advantages* that company's managers originally planned for. Consequently, far from acquiring an *established winner* or a *profit producer,* a company may find that it has added a *dog* to its portfolio.

Why does this happen? Why do so many acquisitions fail? There appear to be four major reasons: (1) Companies often experience difficulties when trying to integrate divergent corporate cultures. (2) Companies overestimate the potential gains from synergy. (3) Acquisitions tend to be very expensive. (4) Companies often do not adequately screen their acquisition targets.

Integration   Having made an acquisition, the acquiring company has to integrate the acquired one into its own organizational structure. Integration can entail the adoption of common management and financial control systems, the joining together of operations from the acquired and the acquiring company, or the establishment of linkages to share information and personnel. When integration is attempted, many unexpected problems can occur. Often they stem from differences in corporate cultures. After an acquisition, many acquired companies experience high management turnover because their employees do not like the acquiring company's way of doing things. The loss of management talent and expertise, to say nothing of the damage from constant tension between the businesses, can set back the realization of gains from an acquisition by several years.

For example, four years after Fluor bought St. Joe Minerals Corporation in one of the largest acquisitions of 1981, only seven of the twenty-two senior managers who had run St. Joe before the acquisition remained. Instead of reaping gains from an established *winner,* Fluor found itself struggling to transform a business that was fast becoming a *loser.* The crux of the problem was a clash in corporate cultures between Fluor, a centralized and autocratic organization, and St. Joe, a decentralized company. St. Joe's senior management resented the centralized management style at Fluor, and many managers left in protest.[14]

Overestimated synergies   Even when companies achieve integration, they often overestimate the extent of synergy between the different businesses. They overestimate the strategic advantages that can be derived from the acquisition and thus pay more for the target company than it is probably worth. For example, Coca-Cola once thought that it could use its marketing skills to dominate the U.S. wine industry. It reasoned that a beverage is a beverage. But after buying three wine companies and enduring seven years of marginal profits, Coca-Cola finally conceded that wine and soft drinks are very different products, with different kinds of appeal, pricing systems, and distribution networks. In 1983 the wine operations were sold to Joseph E. Seagram & Sons, Inc., for $210 million— the price Coca-Cola had paid for the purchases and a substantial loss when adjusted for inflation.[15]

The expense of acquisition Acquisitions of companies whose stock is publicly traded tend to be very expensive. When a company bids to acquire the stock of another enterprise, the stock price frequently gets bid up by speculators hoping to gain from the acquisition. Thus the acquiring company often must pay a premium over the current market value of the target. In the early 1980s acquiring companies paid an average premium of 40 to 50 percent over current stock prices for an acquisition. The debt taken on to finance the acquisition can later become a noose around the acquiring company's neck, particularly if interest rates rise.

Inadequate preacquisition screening Many companies make acquisition decisions without thoroughly analyzing the potential benefits and costs. Thus they often find that they have bought a *dog* instead of a *winner* or a *profit producer*. Philip Morris, for example, thought it could apply the same brand-management skills that it had used so successfully with cigarettes and beer to turn 7Up into another Coca-Cola. After investing eight years and hundreds of millions of dollars, Philip Morris finally faced up to something that Seven-Up Company researchers had known all along: Lemon-lime soft drinks have limited appeal. The Seven-Up Company was sold. If Philip Morris had screened Seven-Up thoroughly before acquiring the company, it could have saved itself a lot of money.

Guidelines for Successful Acquisition

To avoid pitfalls and make successful acquisitions, companies need to take a structured approach that involves three main components: (1) target identification and preacquisition screening, (2) bidding strategy, and (3) integration.[16]

Screening Thorough preacquisition screening increases a company's knowledge about potential takeover targets, leads to a more realistic assessment of the problems involved in executing an acquisition and integrating the new business into the company's organizational structure, and lessens the risk of purchasing a *dog*. The screening should begin with a detailed assessment of the strategic rationale for making the acquisition and an identification of the kind of company that would make an ideal acquisition candidate. Hanson Trust exemplifies a company that has a very clear idea of its ideal acquisition candidate (see the Opening Incident in Chapter 7).

Next, the company should scan a target population of potential acquisition candidates, evaluating each according to a detailed set of criteria that focus on (1) financial position, (2) product market position, (3) management capabilities, and (4) corporate culture. Such an evaluation should enable the company to identify the strengths and weaknesses of each candidate, the extent of potential synergies between the acquiring and the acquired companies, potential integration problems, and the compatibility of the corporate cultures of the acquiring and the acquired companies.

The company should then reduce the list of candidates to the most-favored ones and evaluate them further. At this stage, it should sound out third parties, such as investment bankers, whose opinions may be important and who may be able to give valuable insights about the efficiency of target companies. The company that leads the list after this process should be the acquisition target.

Bidding strategy   The objective of bidding strategy is to reduce the price that a company must pay for an acquisition candidate. The essential element of a good bidding strategy is timing. Hanson Trust, for example, always looks for essentially sound businesses that are suffering from short-term problems due to cyclical industry factors or from problems localized in one division. Such companies are typically undervalued by the stock market and thus can be picked up without payment of the standard 40 or 50 percent premium over current stock prices. With good timing, a company can make a bargain purchase.

Integration   Despite good screening and bidding, an acquisition will fail unless positive steps are taken to integrate the acquired company into the organizational structure of the acquiring one. Integration should center on the source of the potential strategic advantages of the acquisition—for instance, marketing, manufacturing, procurement, R&D, financial, or management synergies. Integration should also be accompanied by steps to eliminate any duplication of facilities or functions. In addition, any unwanted activities of the acquired company should be sold. Finally, if the different business activities are closely related, they will require a high degree of integration. In the case of a company like Hanson Trust, the level of integration can be minimal, for the company's strategy is one of unrelated diversification. But a company such as Rockwell International requires greater integration because its strategy is one of related diversification.

Pitfalls of Internal New Venturing

Science-based companies that use their technology to create market opportunities in related areas tend to favor internal new venturing as an entry strategy. Du Pont, for example, has created whole new markets for the chemical industry with products such as cellophane, nylon, Freon, and Teflon—all internally generated innovations. Another company, 3M, has a near-legendary knack for shaping new markets from internally generated ideas. Internal new venturing, however, need not be based on radical innovations. Although IBM was an imitator rather than an innovator, it successfully entered the personal computer market in 1981 through a venture-based strategy rather than by acquisition. Similarly, the Gillette Company successfully diversified into the manufacture of felt-tip pens, and John Deere diversified into snowmobiles—both through internal new venturing.

As noted earlier, internal new ventures often fail, and even when they succeed, it may take years before they become profitable. In terms of portfolio techniques, new ventures are by definition *question marks*. However, management can reduce the probability of failure by avoiding three common pitfalls: (1) entering on too small a scale, (2) poor commercialization of the new venture, and (3) poor corporate management of the venture process.

Scale of entry   Research suggests that large-scale entry into a new business is the best way for an internal venture to succeed. Although in the short run large-scale entry means significant development costs and substantial losses, in the long run (that is, after eight to twelve years) it brings greater returns than small-scale entry.[17] Figure 9.5 plots the relationships among scale of entry, profitability, and cash flow over time for successful small-scale and large-scale ventures. The figure shows that successful small-scale entry involves lower losses, but in the long run large-scale entry generates greater returns. However, perhaps because of the costs of large-scale entry, many companies prefer a small-scale entry strategy. Acting on this preference can be a major mistake, for the company fails to build up the market share necessary for long-term success.

FIGURE 9.5   **The impact of large-scale versus small-scale entry on profitability and cash flow**

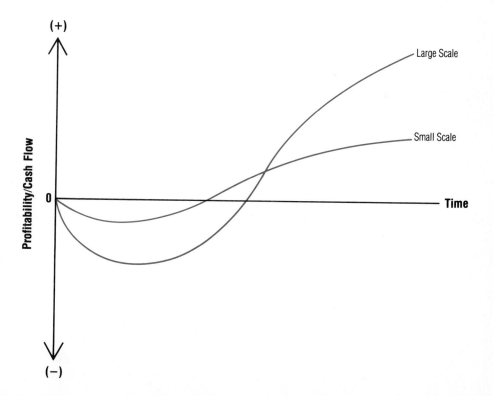

Commercialization   To be commercially successful, science-based innovations must be developed with market requirements in mind. Many internal new ventures fail when a company ignores the basic needs of the market. A company can become blinded by the technological possibilities of a new product and fail to analyze market opportunities properly. Thus a new venture may fail because of lack of commercialization, as happened when the British and French governments underwrote the development of the Concorde supersonic jet airplane.

Poor implementation   Managing the new venture process raises difficult organizational issues.[18] Although we deal with the specifics of implementation in later chapters, we must note some of the most common mistakes here. The shotgun approach of supporting many different internal new venture projects can be a major error, for it places great demands on a company's cash flow and can result in the best ventures being starved of the cash they need for success.

Another mistake involves a failure by corporate management to set the strategic context within which new venture projects should be developed. Simply taking a team of research scientists and allowing them to do research in their favorite field may produce novel results, but the results may have little strategic or commercial value.

Failure to anticipate the time and costs involved in the venture process constitutes a further mistake. Many companies have unrealistic expectations of the time frame involved. Reportedly, some companies operate with a philosophy of killing new businesses if they do not turn a profit by the end of the third year—clearly an unrealistic view, given Biggadike's evidence that it can take eight to twelve years before a venture generates substantial profits.

Guidelines for Successful Internal New Venturing

To avoid the pitfalls just discussed, a company should adopt a structured approach to managing internal new venturing. New venturing typically begins with R&D. To make effective use of its R&D capacity, a company must first spell out its strategic objectives and then communicate them to its scientists and engineers. Research, after all, makes sense only when it is undertaken in areas relevant to strategic goals.[19]

To increase the probability of commercial success, a company should foster close links between R&D and marketing personnel, for this is the best way to ensure that research projects address the needs of the market. The company should also foster close links between R&D and manufacturing personnel, to ensure that the company has the capability to manufacture any proposed new products.

Many companies achieve close integration between different functions by setting up project teams. Such teams comprise representatives of the various functional areas. The task of these teams is to oversee the development of new products. For example, Compaq's success in introducing new products in the personal computer industry has been linked to its use of project teams that oversee the development of a new product from its inception to its market introduction.

Another advantage of such teams is that they can significantly reduce the time it takes to develop a new product. Thus, while R&D personnel are working on the design, manufacturing personnel can be setting up facilities, and marketing personnel can be developing their plans. Because of such integration, Compaq needed only six months to take the first portable personal computer from an idea on a drawing board to a marketable product.

To use resources to the best effect, a company must also devise a selection process for choosing only the ventures that demonstrate the greatest probability of commercial success. Picking *future winners,* however, is a tricky business, since by definition new ventures are *question marks* with an uncertain future. A study by Edwin Mansfield and G. Beardsley found that the uncertainty surrounding new ventures was so great that a company typically took four to five years after launching the venture before it could reasonably estimate its future profitability.[20] Nevertheless, some kind of selection process is necessary if a company is to avoid spreading its resources too thinly over too many projects.

Once a project is selected, management needs to monitor the progress of the venture closely. Evidence suggests that the most important criterion for evaluating a venture during its first four to five years is market-share growth rather than cash flow or profitability. In the long run, the most successful ventures are those that increase their market share. A company should have clearly defined market-share objectives for an internal new venture and decide to retain or kill it in its early years on the basis of its ability to achieve market-share goals. Only in the medium term should profitability and cash flow begin to take on greater importance.

Finally, the association of large-scale entry with greater long-term profitability suggests that a company can increase the probability of success for an internal new venture by thinking big. Thinking big means construction of efficient-scale manufacturing facilities ahead of demand, large marketing expenditures, and a commitment by corporate management to accept initial large losses as long as market share is expanding.

Joint Ventures

In some situations a company prefers internal new venturing over acquisition as an entry strategy but is nevertheless hesitant to commit itself to an internal new venture because of the risks and costs involved in building a new operation up from the ground floor. Such a situation is most likely to occur when a company sees the possibility of establishing an *emerging winner* in an embryonic or growth industry but the risks and costs associated with the project are more than it is willing to assume on its own. In such circumstances, the company may prefer to enter into a joint venture with another company and use the joint venture as a vehicle for entering the new business area. Such an arrangement enables the company to share the substantial risks and costs involved in a new project.[21]

For example, in 1990 IBM and Motorola set up a joint venture whose purpose is to provide a service that will allow computer users to communicate over radio waves. Customers buying the service will use hand-held computers, made by Motorola, to communicate by means of a private network of radio towers that IBM had built across the United States. The venture is aimed at the potentially enormous market of people who could benefit from using computers in the field, such as people who repair equipment in offices and insurance claims adjusters. Analysts estimate that the market for such a service is currently in the tens of millions of dollars but could reach the billions over the next decade.

Because of the embryonic nature of the industry, the venture faces substantial risks. A number of competing technologies are on the horizon. For example, laptop computers are being fitted with modems that can communicate with host computers through cellular telephone networks. Although cellular networks are more crowded and less reliable than radio networks, that state of affairs could change. Thus there is no guarantee that communication between computers over radio waves is the technology of the future. Given this uncertainty, it makes sense for IBM and Motorola to combine in a joint venture and share the risks associated with building up this business.

In addition, a joint venture makes sense when a company can increase the probability of successfully establishing a new business by joining forces with another company. For a company that has some of the skills and assets necessary to establish a successful new venture, teaming up with another company that has complementary skills and assets may increase the probability of success.

Again, the joint venture between IBM and Motorola provides an example. Motorola dominates the market for mobile radios and already manufactures hand-held computers, but it lacks a nationwide radio network that users of hand-held computers might use to communicate with each other. IBM lacks radio technology, but it does have a private network of radio towers (originally built for communicating with 20,000-plus IBM service people in the field) that covers more than 90 percent of the country. Combining Motorola's skills in radio technology with IBM's radio network in a single joint venture increases significantly the probability of establishing a successful new business.

However, there are three main drawbacks with such an arrangement. First, a joint venture allows a company to share the risks and costs of developing a new business, but it also requires the profits to be shared if the new business is successful. Second, a company that enters into a joint venture always runs the risk of giving critical know-how away to its joint-venture partner, who might use that know-how to compete directly with the company in the future. As we pointed out in Section 8.8 on global strategic alliances, however, joint ventures may be structured to minimize this risk. Third, the venture partners must share control. If the partners have different business philosophies, time horizons, or investment preferences, substantial problems can arise. Conflicts over how to run the joint venture can tear it apart and result in business failure.

In sum, although joint ventures often have a distinct advantage over internal new venturing as a means of establishing a new business operation, they also have certain drawbacks. Thus when deciding whether to go it alone or to cooperate with another company in a joint venture, strategic managers need to assess carefully the pros and cons of the alternatives.

9.8 EXIT STRATEGIES

Just as building a balanced portfolio requires entry into new business areas, so it also requires exit from existing business areas. As Table 9.3 suggested, exit is normally required when a company has too many *losers* or *question marks* and sometimes when it has too many *developing winners*. (It is not unusual for a company to sell a *developing winner* if the business does not fit the basic strategic thrust of the corporation.) Exit strategies are also normally a critical component of corporate retrenchment strategies. How should a company deal with the exit problem? In essence, it has three choices: divest, harvest, or liquidate. Which strategy is best in a given situation depends on two factors: the characteristics of the relevant industry and the characteristics of the business to be divested.

Divestment, Harvest, and Liquidation

Divestment Divestment involves selling a business to another company or to the management of the business itself. As an exit option, divestment is becoming an increasingly popular strategy. In 1986 the number of divestments in the United States reached an all-time high of 1,317.[22] Divestment makes sense if the prospects for the business to be sold seem good—that is, if the business, to be divested is a *developing winner* or a particularly promising *question mark*. In these circumstances, the unit to be divested can command a high price. Divestment can be difficult to implement if the prospects for the business are poor, as in the case of a *loser*. For example, when the Bendix Corporation decided to exit from the troubled machine tool industry in 1984, it could get only $74 million for its operation. Yet five years earlier, when the machine tool industry was booming, Bendix had paid $300 million to acquire just part of the business it sold in 1984.[23]

Harvest A harvest strategy involves controlled disinvestment in a business unit to optimize cash flow as the company exits from an industry. To increase cash flow, management eliminates or severely curtails new investment, cuts maintenance of facilities, and reduces advertising and research while reaping the benefits of past good will.[24] The effects are illustrated in Figure 9.6. The business unit loses market share, but in the short run cash flow out of the business increases markedly. The cash generated by the harvest strategy can be invested elsewhere in the corporation. Once the cash flow begins to decline, liquidation is normally considered. Divestment is difficult because by this time the business is run-down and its long-term prospects are poor.

The trouble with a harvest strategy is that it can be difficult to implement. It creates motivational problems in the business being harvested and can lead to a lack of confidence on the part of customers and suppliers once they perceive what is occurring. Thus the strategy may be administratively more difficult to manage than it is worth.

Liquidation   Liquidation involves closing an operation. Liquidation is normally the exit option of last resort. It is selected only when all other options have

FIGURE 9.6   **The impact of a harvest strategy on cash flow**

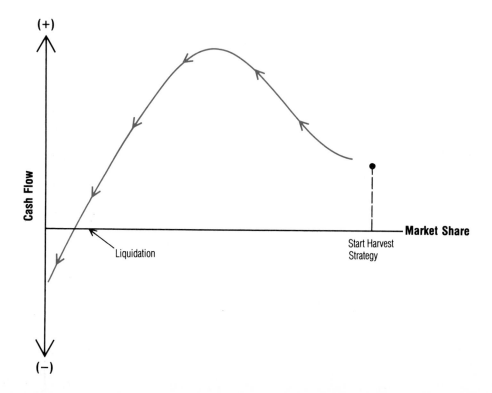

failed, because a company must take substantial write-offs on the closure of an operation and bear the fixed costs of exit, such as severance pay to employees.

Choice of Exit Strategy

The choice of exit strategy is governed by the characteristics of the business unit to be sold and the competitive intensity of the industry in which it is based. The characteristics of the business unit to be sold can be summarized by its portfolio category: *developing winner, question mark,* or *loser.* Relevant industry characteristics include factors that determine competitive intensity: barriers to entry, life-cycle factors, exit barriers, product characteristics, and so on (see Chapter 3). An industry's characteristics can be summarized by its overall competitive prospects, which are either *favorable* or *unfavorable.*

Other things being equal, a company chooses the exit strategy that maximizes the payoffs of exit. Given that liquidation normally has a negative payoff, the preferred choice is between divestment and harvest. Within this framework, the range of preferred exit strategies is illustrated in Table 9.5. By definition, *developing winners* are most likely to be found in industries with favorable prospects. Divestment makes most sense in these circumstances, since an abundance of buyers will bid up the purchase price.

Losers can be found in industries with both favorable and unfavorable prospects. The poor competitive position of *losers* makes it unlikely that they can be divested at a reasonable price. When an industry's prospects are favorable, a harvest strategy may be preferred. Even in such circumstances, however, difficulties associated with implementing a harvest strategy may prompt a company to divest *losers* at a bargain price rather than try to manage decline.

When industry prospects are unfavorable, divestment may be out of the question for *losers,* since there will be no buyers. The preferred strategy will be harvest. However, if the industry is facing rapid decline in sales, even a harvest strategy may not generate much in the way of positive cash flow. Liquidation is the only option in such circumstances.

TABLE 9.5   **Exit strategies**

Business characteristic	Favorable industry	Unfavorable industry
Developing winner	Divest	
Loser	Harvest/divest	Harvest/liquidate
Question mark	Divest	Liquidate

For *question marks* operating in a favorable industry environment, divestment is the favored option. In such cases, a company can often sell the business to its managers through a leveraged buyout. When the industry environment is unfavorable, however, few buyers are likely to be found. A harvest strategy does not work because the market share of most *question marks* is typically too low to make the strategy viable. Thus liquidation may be the only option.

9.9 SUMMARY OF CHAPTER

This chapter reviews three main techniques for analyzing the portfolio of a multibusiness company. The rationale for undertaking such an analysis is to identify what needs to be done to build a balanced portfolio. Building a balanced portfolio typically involves entry and exit strategies. The choice between different entry and exit strategies, and the pitfalls involved, are reviewed. The following points are made:

1. There are three main portfolio techniques that companies can use: the Boston Consulting Group matrix, the McKinsey matrix, and the industry evolution matrix devised by Hofer.

2. The strength of the BCG matrix is its focus on cash-flow requirements. Weaknesses include the simplistic categorization of businesses and untenable assumptions about relationships among market share, growth, and profitability.

3. The strength of the McKinsey matrix is its ability to incorporate a wide range of strategically relevant variables into the analysis. The main weakness is that the analysis is essentially static and tells little about how industry evolution might change business attractiveness.

4. The strength of the industry evolution matrix lies in what it tells about the distribution of a company's businesses across different stages of the industry life cycle. The weakness of the technique is that it ignores many strategically relevant industry factors.

5. In general, portfolio analysis helps companies conceptualize their diversity, assists in the allocation of corporate cash, and identifies the adjustments necessary to achieve a balanced portfolio. However, it has the following weaknesses: the assumption that a company can be divided into a reasonable number of strategic business units, a tendency to ignore potential conflicts of interest that might emerge between corporate cash-flow priorities and

cash-flow priorities within an SBU, and a tendency to ignore interrelationships among business units.

6. Correcting an imbalance in a corporate portfolio typically requires entry strategies (acquisition, internal new venturing, and joint ventures) and exit strategies (divestment, harvest, and liquidation).

7. The choice of an appropriate entry strategy is influenced by barriers to entry, relatedness, speed and development costs of entry, risks of entry, and industry life-cycle considerations. In general, internal new venturing makes the most sense when the strategic goal is to establish *question marks* or perhaps *developing winners*. Acquisition makes the most sense when the strategic goal involves establishing *profit producers* or *winners*.

8. Many acquisitions fail because of poor postacquisition integration, overestimation of the potential gains from synergy, the high cost of acquisition, and poor preacquisition screening. Guarding against failure involves structured screening, good bidding strategies, and positive attempts to integrate the acquired company into the organization of the acquiring one.

9. Many internal new ventures fail because of entry on too small a scale, poor commercialization, and poor corporate management of the internal venture process. Guarding against failure involves a structured approach toward project selection and management, integration of R&D and marketing to improve commercialization of a venture idea, and entry on a significant scale.

10. Exit strategies include divestment, harvest, and liquidation. The choice of exit strategy is governed by the characteristics of the relevant business unit and the competitive intensity of the relevant industry.

Discussion Questions

1. Why might diversified companies that use portfolio analysis techniques have an advantage over diversified companies that do not? How do you think cash flows are allocated in companies that do not use portfolio analysis techniques?

2. Under what circumstances might it be best to enter a new business area by acquisition, and under what circumstances might internal new venturing be the preferred entry mode?

3. In the face of the obvious difficulties of succeeding with acquisitions, why do so many companies continue to make them?

4. What are the main pitfalls of portfolio planning? How might these pitfalls be avoided?

Endnotes

1. For details, see "Rockwell: Using Its Cash Hoard to Edge Away from Defense," *Business Week,* February 4, 1985, pp. 82–84; "Bob Anderson Has New Miracles to Work at Rockwell," *Business Week,* March 31, 1986, pp. 64–65; and "Rockwell's Hard Place," *Business Week,* February 29, 1988, pp. 46–47.

2. For further details of portfolio techniques, see R. A. Bettis and W. K. Hall, "Strategic Portfolio Management in the Multibusiness Firm," *California Management Review,* 24 (1981), 23–38; P. Haspeslagh, "Portfolio Planning: Uses and Limits," *Harvard Business Review* (January–February 1983), 58–73; B. Hedley, "Strategy and the Business Portfolio," *Long Range Planning,* 10 (1977), 9–15; and Charles W. Hofer and Dan Schendel, *Strategy Formulation: Analytical Concepts* (St. Paul, Minn.: West, 1978).

3. For evidence, see D. F. Barnett and R. W. Crandall, *Up from the Ashes: The Rise of the Steel Miner* (Washington, D.C.: The Brookings Institute, 1986), pp. 1–17.

4. As defined by Hoter and Schendel, *Strategy Formulation,* p. 82.

5. Charles W. Hofer, *Conceptual Constructs for Formulating Corporate and Business Strategies* (Boston: Intercollegiate Case Clearing House, #9-378-754, 1977).

6. For details, see R. A. Bettis and W. K. Hall, "The Business Portfolio Approach: Where It Falls Down in Practice," *Long Range Planning,* 12 (1983), 95–105; and Haspeslagh, "Portfolio Planning," pp. 58–73.

7. Bettis and Hall, "The Business Portfolio Approach," pp. 95–105.

8. For further details, see H. L. Ansoff, *Corporate Strategy* (New York: McGraw-Hill, 1965); E. R. Biggadike, *Corporate Diversification: Entry, Strategy and Performance* (Cambridge, Mass.: Division of Research, Harvard Business School, 1979); M. S. Salter and W. A. Weinhold, *Diversification Through Acquisition: Strategies for Creating Economic Value* (New York: Free Press, 1979); and G. S. Yip, "Diversification Entry: Internal Development Versus Acquisition," *Strategic Management Journal,* 3 (1982), 331–345.

9. E. R. Biggadike, "The Risky Business of Diversification," *Harvard Business Review* (May–June 1979), 103–111.

10. Edwin Mansfield, "How Economists See R&D," *Harvard Business Review* (November–December 1981), 98–106.

11. Peter Petre, "AT&T's Epic Push into Computers," *Fortune,* May 25, 1987, pp. 42–50.

12. See D. C. Mueller, "The Effects of Conglomerate Mergers: A Survey of the Empirical Evidence," *Journal of Banking and Finance,* 1 (1977), 315–342, and *The Determinant and Effects of Mergers* (Cambridge, Mass.: Oelgeschlager, Gunn & Hain, 1980). See also M. H. Lubatkin, "Merger and the Performance of the Acquiring Firm," *Academy of Management Review,* 8 (1983), 218–225.

13. "Do Mergers Really Work?" *Business Week,* June 3, 1985, pp. 88–100.

14. "Fluor: Compounding Fractures from Leaping Before Looking," *Business Week,* June 3, 1985, pp. 92–93.

15. "Coca-Cola: A Sobering Lesson from Its Journey into Wine," *Business Week,* June 3, 1985, pp. 96–98.

16. For views on this issue, see L. L. Fray, D. H. Gaylin, and J. W. Down, "Successful Acquisition Planning," *Journal of Business Strategy,* 5 (1984), 46–55; C. W. L. Hill, "Profile of a Conglomerate Takeover: BTR and Thomas Tilling," *Journal of General Management,* 10 (1984), 34–50; and D. R. Willensky, "Making It Happen: How to Execute an Acquisition," *Business Horizons* (March–April 1985), 38–45.

17. Biggadike, "The Risky Business of Diversification," pp. 103–111.

18. R. A. Burgelman, "A Process Model of Internal Corporate Venturing in the Diversified Major Firm," *Administrative Science Quarterly,* 28 (1983), 223–244.

19. I. C. MacMillan and R. George, "Corporate Venturing: Challenges for Senior Managers," *Journal of Business Strategy,* 5 (1985), 34–43.

20. G. Beardsley and Edwin Mansfield, "A Note on the Accuracy of Industrial Forecasts of the Profitability of New Products and Processes," *Journal of Business,* (1978), 127–130.

21. Paul B. Carroll, "IBM, Motorola Plan Radio Link for Computers," *The Wall Street Journal,* January 29, 1990, pp. B1, B5.

22. "1986 Profile," *Mergers and Acquisitions,* 21 (1986), 57–61.

23. "Bendix: A Buy That Really Was Too Good to Be True," *Business Week,* June 3, 1985, pp. 93–94.

24. K. R. Harrigan and Michael E. Porter, "End-Game Strategies for Declining Industries," *Harvard Business Review* (July–August 1983), 111–120.

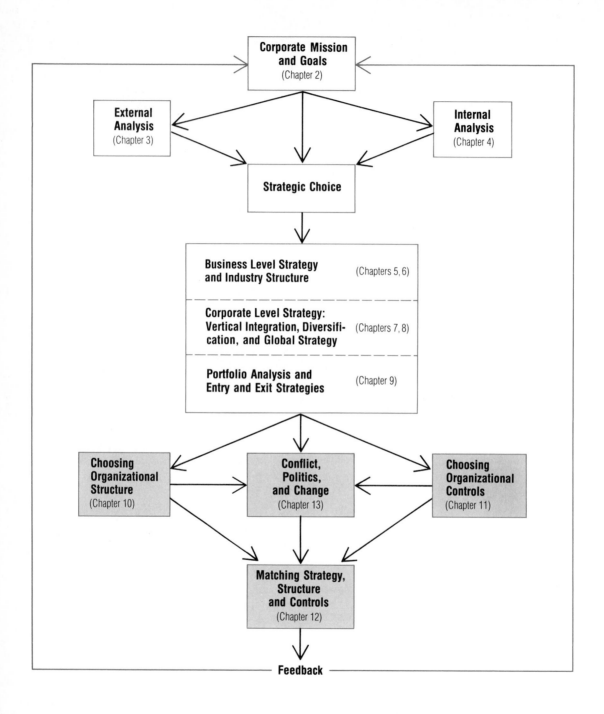

STRATEGY IMPLEMENTATION

Chapter 10

DESIGNING

ORGANIZATIONAL

STRUCTURE

10.1 OPENING INCIDENT: APPLE COMPUTER

Incorporated in 1977, Apple Computer, Inc., designs, manufactures, and markets personal computers for use in business, education, and the home.[1] Apple Computer was created in 1976, when two engineers, Steven Jobs and Steven Wozniak, collaborated to produce a computing board for personal use. As early orders for their system increased, Jobs and Wozniak realized that they needed to create an organization with a structure that could handle capital acquisitions, marketing, management and strategic planning, engineering, and production. In essence, they needed to formalize the functions necessary in any complex business. In true entrepreneurial fashion, they created a flat, decentralized structure designed to allow people to be creative, flexible, and responsive to the uncertainty in the new home computer industry. With few rules and only a vague hierarchy, the organization operated on the basis of personal contact between people in different functions through teams and task forces, many of which were chaired by Jobs and Wozniak.

By 1982 Apple's structure was taller, with more levels of management. A new chief executive, Hugh Sculley, had been hired to take control of the management side of the business. Fast growth and the introduction of a wider range of products—the Lisa and Macintosh computers—led to greater organizational differentiation. As a result, Apple moved to a divisional structure, in which each product was manufactured in a self-contained division and each division had its own set of specialist functions such as marketing, research and development, and product engineering. Problems arose with this structure, however.[2] Jobs championed the Macintosh computer against the Lisa computer for development and triggered hostile competition for resources among the divisions. Overhead costs rose dramatically because specialist functions were duplicated in each division. Furthermore, Sculley's role and the role of top managers in running the business became unclear in the organization because all direction seemed to come from the divisions and especially from Jobs. The unsettling outcome of these conditions was that IBM overtook Apple as leader in the personal computer industry.

By 1985 the recession in the computer industry had exacerbated these problems and made reorganization imperative. Sculley took total control of the company and once again changed its structure.[3] He created a structure in which one set of specialist functions served the needs of all the various product lines—a product structure. The production system was also changed so that products were manufactured in one central production department, in which one management team had overall control, rather than in separate divisions by different managers. This change reduced costs massively, and centralized management control allowed the company to respond more quickly to market developments. In addition, Apple adopt-

ed company-based, rather than division-based, plans for achieving corporate objectives.

Apple Computer started out with a flat, decentralized functional structure and had moved to a second form, the divisional structure, which inhibited its development and growth. Today Apple uses a more centralized product structure and is in good financial shape. Its streamlined management team is able to address the strategic and operational needs of the business as Apple seeks to expand its market share.

10.2 OVERVIEW

As the discussion of Apple suggests, this chapter examines the creation of the right organizational structure for managing a company's strategy. In the first chapter of this book, we define strategy implementation as the way in which a company created the organizational arrangements that allow it to put its strategic plan into operation most efficiently and to achieve its objectives. Strategy is implemented through organizational design. Organizational design involves selecting the combination of organizational structure and control systems that lets a company pursue its strategy most efficiently. Different kinds of structure and control systems provide strategic planners with alternative means of pursuing different strategies because they offer the company and the people within it a variety of different ways to act.

In this chapter, the organizational structures available to strategic managers are examined. In Chapter 11, we consider the integration mechanisms that companies use to coordinate the structure, as well as the control systems through which they monitor and evaluate corporate, divisional, and functional performance. Chapter 12 traces the ways in which different strategy choices lead to the use of different kinds of structure and control systems. After reading this section of the book, you will be able to choose the right organizational design for implementing a company's strategy. You will understand why Apple Computer chose to change organizational structures as it grew and developed.

10.3 DESIGNING ORGANIZATIONAL STRUCTURES

After formulating a company's strategy, management must make designing the structure its next priority, for strategy can only be implemented through organizational structure. The activities of organizational personnel are meaningless unless some type of structure is used to assign people to tasks and connect the activities of different people or functions.[4] The terms used to describe the characteristics of organizational structure are differentiation and integration. **Differentiation** is the way in which a company allocates people and resources to organizational tasks.[5] First, management chooses how to distribute *decision-making authority* in the organization; these are **vertical differentiation** choices.[6] Second, it chooses how to divide labor in the organization and group organizational tasks; these are **horizontal differentiation** choices. **Integration** is the means by which a company seeks to coordinate people and functions to accomplish organizational tasks.[7] These means include the use of integrating mechanisms and the whole apparatus of organizational control. In short, differentiation refers to the way in which a company divides itself up into parts, and integration refers to the way in which the parts are then combined. Together the two processes determine how an organizational structure will operate and how successfully managers will be able to implement their chosen strategies.

As a comparison, consider the structure of a chemical compound such as water. It consists of different types of atoms: two of hydrogen and one of oxygen. It also comprises bonds between the atoms. The properties of the chemical—the way it functions—are a consequence both of its individual atoms (differentiation) and the way these are bonded or connected (integration). The same is true of organizational structure: The way it functions depends on what it is made up of and how it is put together—its differentiation and integration. Strategic managers must design the organization correctly if it is to be effective for a particular strategy.

10.4 VERTICAL DIFFERENTIATION

The aim of vertical differentiation is to specify the reporting relationships that link people, tasks, and functions at all levels of a company. Fundamentally, this means that management chooses the appropriate number of hierarchical levels and the correct span of control for implementing a company's strategy most effectively. The organizational hierarchy establishes the authority structure from the top to the bottom of the organization. The **span of control** is defined as the number of subordinates a manager directly manages.[8] The basic choice is whether to aim for a **flat structure,** with few hierarchical levels and thus a relatively wide span of control, or a **tall structure,** with many levels and thus a relatively narrow span of control (Figure 10.1). Tall structures have many hierarchical levels relative to size; flat structures have few levels relative to size.[9] For example, research suggests that the average number of hierarchical levels for a company employing 3,000 persons is seven. Thus an organization having nine levels would be called tall, whereas one having four would be called flat. With its 4,000 employees and four hierarchical levels, Liz Claiborne, for instance, has a relatively flat structure.

FIGURE 10.1   **Tall and flat structures**

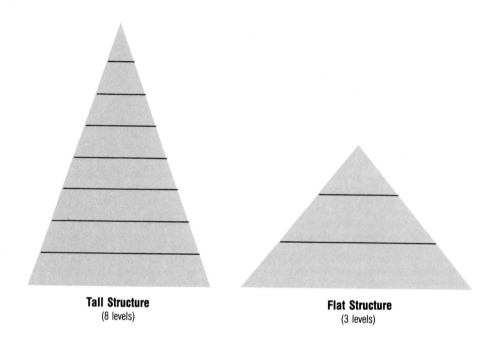

Tall Structure
(8 levels)

Flat Structure
(3 levels)

On the other hand, before reorganization, Westinghouse, with its ten hierarchical levels, had a relatively tall structure. Now it has seven levels—the average for a large organization.

Companies choose the number of levels they need on the basis of their strategy and the functional tasks necessary to achieve their strategy. For example, manufacturing companies often pursue a low-cost strategy to minimize production costs and increase operating efficiency. As a result, these companies are usually tall, with many levels in the hierarchy and prescribed areas of authority, so that managers can exert tight control over personnel and resources.[10] On the other hand, high-tech companies often pursue a strategy of differentiation based on service and quality. Consequently, these companies are usually flat, giving employees wide discretion to meet customers' demands without having to refer constantly to supervisors.[11] (We discuss this subject further in Chapter 12.) The crux of the matter is that the allocation of authority and responsibility in the organization must match the needs of corporate-, business-, and functional-level strategy.

Disadvantages of Tall Hierarchies

As a company grows and diversifies, choosing the right number of levels for managing its business becomes important because research shows that the num-

FIGURE 10.2   **Relationship between company size and number of hierarchical levels**

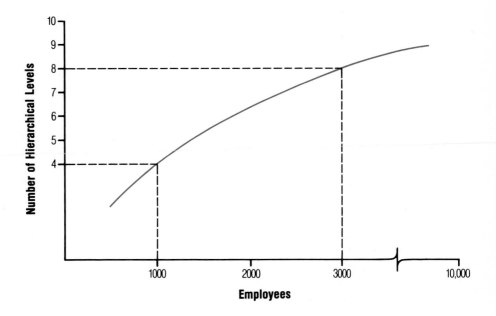

ber of hierarchical levels relative to company size is predictable as the size increases.[12] This finding demonstrates an interesting lesson in organization design concerning the correct choice of the number of hierarchical levels. The relationship between size and number of levels is presented in Figure 10.2. Companies with approximately 1,000 employees usually have four levels in the hierarchy: chief executive officer, departmental vice presidents, first-line supervisors, and shop-floor employees. By 3,000 employees, they have increased their level of vertical differentiation by raising the number of levels to eight. Beyond 3,000 employees, however, something interesting happens: Even when companies grow to 10,000 employees or more, the number of hierarchical levels rarely increases beyond nine or ten. As organizations grow, managers apparently try to limit the number of hierarchical levels. When companies become too tall, problems occur, making strategy more difficult to implement and the company less efficient in pursuing its mission.[13]

Communication problems   Too many hierarchical levels impede communication. Communication between the top and the bottom of the hierarchy takes much longer as the chain of command lengthens. This leads to inflexibility, and valuable time is lost in bringing a new product to market or in keeping up with technological developments.[14] For Federal Express, communication is vital in its business; the company therefore allows a maximum of only five layers of management between the employee and the chief executive officer to avoid communication problems.[15] On the other hand, because of its tall hierarchy, Procter & Gamble needed twice as much time as its competitors to introduce new products until it recently moved to streamline its structure.[16]

More subtle, but just as important, are the problems of information distortion that accompany the transmission of information up and down the hierarchy. Going down the hierarchy, managers at different levels (for example, divisional or corporate managers) may misinterpret information, either through accidental garbling of messages or on purpose, to suit their own interests. In either case, information from the top may not reach its destination intact. For instance, a request to share divisional knowledge among divisions to achieve gains from synergy may be overlooked or ignored by divisional managers who perceive it as a threat to their autonomy and power. This attitude among managers was one of the problems that led Iacocca to reorganize Chrysler to coordinate cost-cutting measures across divisions.

Information transmitted upward in the hierarchy may also be distorted. Subordinates may transmit to their superiors only information that improves their own standing in the organization. The greater the number of hierarchical levels, the more scope subordinates have to distort facts, so that top managers may lose control over the hierarchy. Similarly, managers may compete with each other, and, when they are free from close corporate supervision, they may hoard information to promote their own interests at the expense of the organization's.

Motivational problems   A proliferation of levels reduces the scope of managerial authority. As the number of levels in the hierarchy increases, the amount of authority possessed by managers at each hierarchical level falls. For example, consider the situation of two identically sized organizations, one of which has three levels in the hierarchy and the other seven. Managers in the flat structure have much more authority, and greater authority increases their motivation to perform effectively and take responsibility for the organization's performance. Moreover, when there are fewer managers, their performance is more visible, and therefore they can expect greater rewards when the business does well. By contrast, in the tall organization, managers' ability to exercise authority is limited, and their decisions are being constantly scrutinized by their superiors. As a result, the tendency is for managers to pass the buck and refuse to take the risks that are often necessary when pursuing new strategies. The shape of the organization's structure strongly affects the behavior of people within it and thus the way in which strategy is implemented.[17]

High costs of operation   Another problem facing tall structures is simply that many hierarchical levels imply many managers, and employing managers is expensive. Managerial salaries, benefits, offices, and secretaries are a huge expense for an organization. If the average middle manager costs a company a total of $200,000 a year, then employing 100 surplus managers will cost $20 million a year. U.S. oil companies recognized this fact when oil prices fell in 1986. When these companies made billions of dollars in profits, they had no incentive to control the number of levels in the hierarchy and the number of managers. Once they grew aware of the cost of these managers, however, companies such as ARCO and Exxon Corporation ruthlessly purged the hierarchy, reducing the number of levels, and thus of managers, to reduce costs and restore profitability.

To offer another example, when companies grow and are successful, they often hire personnel and create new positions without much regard for the effect of these actions on the organizational hierarchy. Later, when managers review that structure, it is quite common to see the number of levels reduced because of the disadvantages just discussed. Deregulation also quite often prompts a reduction in levels and personnel. In a deregulated environment, companies must respond to increased competition. After deregulation, AT&T, as well as a number of airline companies, reduced costs and streamlined their structures so that they could respond more rapidly to opportunities and threats brought about by increased competition. An examination of the nature of vertical differentiation in an organization is one means by which strategic planners are able to assess organizational strengths and weaknesses.

In sum, many problems arise when companies become too tall and the chain of command becomes too long. Strategic managers tend to lose control over the hierarchy, which means that they lose control over their strategies. Disaster often follows. One way that such problems can be partially overcome, however, is by the decentralization of authority. That is, authority is vested in lower levels in the hierarchy as well as at the top. Because this is one of the most important implementation decisions a company can make, we discuss it next in more detail.

Centralization or Decentralization?

Centralization of authority exists when managers at the upper levels of the organizational hierarchy retain the authority to make the most important decisions. When authority is decentralized, it is delegated to divisions, functional departments, and managers at lower levels in the organization. If top management delegates authority to lower levels in the hierarchy, the communication problems described earlier are avoided because information does not have to be constantly sent to the top of the organization for decisions to be made. Decentralization or delegation of authority has several other advantages. First, if strategic managers delegate *operational decision making* to lower levels, they can spend more time on *strategic decision making*. As a result, they make more effective decisions and are better at long-term planning. Second, decentralization also promotes flexibility and responsiveness because lower-level managers can make on-the-spot decisions. Thus the bottom layers in the organization can more easily adapt to local situations. As IBM has demonstrated, this can be an enormous advantage for business strategy. For example, IBM has a tall structure, but it is well-known for the amount of authority it delegates to lower levels. Operational personnel can respond quickly to customer needs and so ensure superior service, which is a major source of IBM's competitive advantage. Similarly, to revitalize its product strategy, Westinghouse has massively decentralized its operations to give divisions more autonomy and encourage risk taking and quick response to customer needs.[18]

If decentralization is so effective, why do not all companies decentralize decision making and avoid the problems of tall hierarchies? The answer is that centralization has its advantages, too. Centralized decision making allows easier coordination of the organizational activities needed to pursue a company's strategy. If managers at all levels can make their own decisions, planning becomes extremely difficult, and the company may lose control of its decision making. Centralization also means that decisions fit broad organization objectives. For example, when its branch operations were getting out of hand, Merrill Lynch & Co. increased centralization by installing more information systems to give corporate managers greater control over branch activities. Similarly, Hewlett-Packard centralized research and development responsibility at the corporate level to provide a more directed corporate strategy. Furthermore, in times of crisis, centralization of authority permits strong leadership because authority is focused on one person or group. This focus allows for speedy decision making and a concerted response by the whole organization. Perhaps Iacocca personifies the meaning of centralization in times of crisis. He provided the vision and energy for Chrysler managers to respond creatively to Chrysler's problems and designed a cohesive plan for restoring its profitability.

Summary: Vertical Differentiation

Managing the strategy-structure relationship when the number of hierarchical levels becomes too great is difficult and expensive. Depending on a firm's situation, the problems of tall hierarchies can be avoided by decentralization. As firm size increases, however, decentralization becomes less effective. How, therefore, as firms grow and diversify can they maintain control over their structures and strategies without becoming taller or more decentralized? That is, how can a firm like Exxon control 300,000 employees without becoming too tall and inflexible? There must be alternative ways to create organizational arrangements to achieve corporate objectives. The first of these ways is through the choice of form of horizontal differentiation: by deciding on the correct way to group organizational activities and tasks.

10.5 HORIZONTAL DIFFERENTIATION

Whereas vertical differentiation concerns the division of authority, horizontal differentiation focuses on the division and grouping of tasks to meet the objectives of the business.[19] Because, to a large degree, an organization's tasks are a function of its strategy, the dominant view is that companies choose a form of horizontal differentiation or structure to match their organizational strategy. Perhaps the first person to address this issue formally was the Harvard business historian Alfred D. Chandler.[20] After studying the organizational problems experienced in large U.S. corporations such as Du Pont and General Motors as they grew and diversified in the early decades of this century, Chandler reached two conclusions: (1) that in principle organizational structure follows the growth strategy of a company, or, in other words, the range and variety of tasks it chooses to pursue; and (2) that American enterprises go through stages of strategy and structure changes as they grow and diversify. In other words, a company's structure changes as its strategy changes in a predictable way.[21] The kinds of structure that companies adopt are discussed in this section.

Simple Structure

The simple structure is normally used by the small, entrepreneurial company involved in producing one or a few related products for a specific market segment. Often in this situation, one person, the entrepreneur, takes on most of the managerial tasks. No formal organization arrangements exist, and horizontal differentiation is low because employees perform multiple duties. A classic example of this structure is Apple Computer in its earliest stage. As a venture between two persons, Steven Jobs and Steven Wozniak, worked together in a garage to perform all the necessary tasks to market their personal computer. The success of their product, however, made this simple structure outdated almost as soon as it was adopted. To grow and perform all the tasks required by a rapidly expanding company, Apple needed a more complex form of horizontal differentiation.

Functional Structure

As companies grow, two things happen. First, the range of tasks that must be performed expands. For example, it suddenly becomes apparent that the services of a professional accountant or production manager are needed to take control of specialized tasks. Second, no one person can successfully perform more than one organizational task without becoming overloaded: For example, the entrepreneur can no longer simultaneously produce and sell the product. The issue arises, then, as to what grouping of activities, or what form of horizontal differentiation, can most efficiently handle the needs of the growing company. The answer for most companies is the **functional structure.** In functional structures, people are grouped on the basis of their common expertise and experience or because they use the same resources.[22] For example, engineers are grouped in a function because they perform the same tasks and use the same skills or equipment. Figure 10.3 shows a typical functional structure. Here, each of the triangles represents a different functional specialization—sales and marketing, manufacturing, research

FIGURE 10.3   **Functional structure**

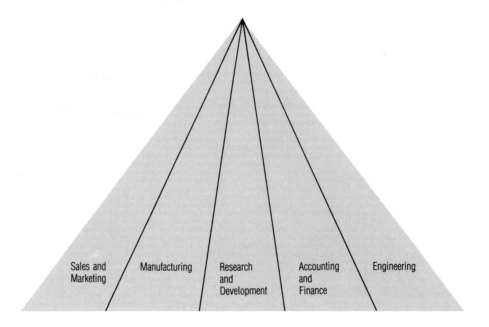

and development, and so on—and each function concentrates on its own specialized task.

Advantages of a functional structure   The functional structure has several advantages. First, if people who perform similar tasks are grouped, they can learn from one another and become better—more specialized and productive—at what they do. Second, they can monitor one another and make sure that others are doing their tasks effectively and not shirking their responsibilities. As a result, the work process becomes more efficient, reducing costs and increasing operational flexibility.

A second important advantage of the functional structure derives from its ability to give managers more control of organizational activities. As already noted, many difficulties arise when the number of levels in the hierarchy increases. If you group people into different functions, however, each with its own managers, then several different hierarchies are created, and the company can avoid becoming too tall. For example, there will be one hierarchy in manufacturing and another in accounting and finance. Managing the business is much easier when different groups specialize in different organizational tasks and are managed separately.

Problems with a functional structure   In adopting a functional structure, a company increases its level of horizontal differentiation to handle more complex task requirements. The structure allows it to keep control of its activities as it grows. This structure serves the company well until it begins to grow and diversify. If the company becomes geographically diverse and begins operating in many locations or if it starts producing a wide range of products, control problems arise. Specifically, **control loss** problems develop in the functional structure, and the company is no longer able to coordinate its activities.[23]

Communications problems   As functional hierarchies evolve, functions grow more remote from one another. As a result, it becomes increasingly difficult to communicate across functions to implement strategy. This communication problem stems from **functional orientations**.[24] With increasing differentiation, the various functions develop different orientations to the problems and issues facing the organization. Different functions have different time or goal orientations. Some functions, such as manufacturing, see things in a short time framework and are concerned with achieving short-run goals, such as reducing manufacturing costs. Others, like research and development, see things from a long-term point of view, and their goals (that is, product development) may have a time horizon of several years. Moreover, different functions may have different interpersonal orientations—a further impediment to good communication. As a result of all these factors, each function may develop a different view of the strategic issues facing the company. For example, manufacturing may see a problem as the need to reduce costs, sales may see it as the need to increase responsiveness to customer needs, and research and development may see it as the need to introduce new products. In such cases, the functions find it difficult to communicate and coordinate with one another, and implementation suffers.

Measurement problems   As the number of its products proliferates, a company may find it difficult to measure the contributions of one or a group of products to its overall profitability. Consequently, the company may be turning out some unprofitable products without realizing it and may also be making poor decisions on resource allocation. In essence, the company's measurement systems are not complex enough to serve its needs.

Location problems   Location factors may also hamper coordination and control. If a company is producing or selling in many different regional areas, then the centralized system of control provided by the functional structure no longer suits it because managers in the various regions must be flexible enough to respond to the needs of these regions. Thus the functional structure is not complex enough to handle regional diversity.

Strategic problems   Sometimes the combined effect of all these factors is that long-term strategic considerations are ignored because management is preoccupied with solving communication and coordination problems. As a result, a company may lose direction and fail to take advantage of new opportunities.

Experiencing these problems is a sign that the company does not have an appropriate level of differentiation to achieve its objectives. It must change its mix of vertical and horizontal differentiation to accommodate more complex organizational tasks. To this end, many companies reorganize to a product or geographical structure.

Product or Geographical Structure

In the product or geographical structure, activities are grouped by either product lines or geographical location. In the product structure, the production function is broken down into different product lines based on the similarities and differences among the products. Figure 10.4 presents a product structure typical of a drug or pharmaceutical company. In this company, products are grouped in terms of their being wet drugs, dry drugs, or powders. Inside each product group, there may be many similar products manufactured.

FIGURE 10.4   **Product or geographical structure**

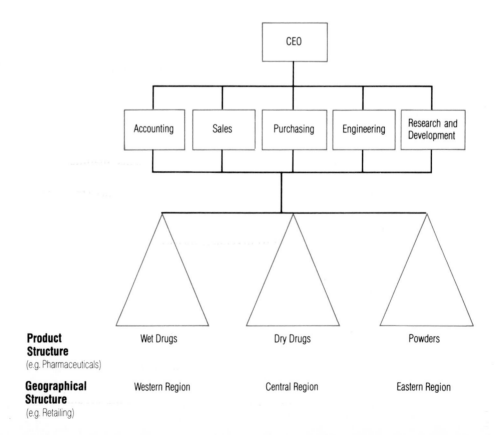

| Product Structure (e.g. Pharmaceuticals) | Wet Drugs | Dry Drugs | Powders |
| Geographical Structure (e.g. Retailing) | Western Region | Central Region | Eastern Region |

Because three different product groupings now exist, the degree of horizontal differentiation in this structure is higher than in the functional structure. The specialized support functions, such as accounting or sales, are centralized at the top of the organization, but each support function is divided in such a way that personnel tend to specialize in one of the different product categories to avoid communication problems. Thus there may be three groups of accountants, one for each of the three product categories. In sales, separate sales forces dealing with the different product lines may emerge, but because a single sales function brings economies of scale to selling and distribution, these groups will coordinate their activities. Unisys Corporation, for example, recently moved to a product structure based on serving the product needs of different customer groups: the commercial and the public sectors are two such groups. Unisys's salespeople specialize in one customer group, but all groups coordinate their sales and software activities to ensure good communication and the transfer of knowledge among product lines.

The use of a product structure, then, reduces the problems of control and communication associated with the functional structure. It pushes aside barriers among functions because the product line, rather than each individual function, becomes the focus of attention. In addition, the profit contribution of each product line can be clearly identified, and resources can be allocated more efficiently. Note also that this structure has one more level in the hierarchy than the functional structure—that of the product line manager. This increase in vertical differentiation allows managers at the level of the production line to concentrate on day-to-day operations and gives top managers more time to take a longer-term look at business opportunities.

Another example of a company that adopted a product structure to manage its product lines is Maytag. Initially, when it manufactured only washers and dryers, Maytag used a functional structure. In trying to increase its market share, however, Maytag bought two other appliance manufacturers: Jenn-Air, known for its electric ranges, and Hardwick, which produces gas ranges. To handle the new product lines, Maytag moved to the product structure presented in Figure 10.5. Each company was operated as a product line, and the major specialized support services were centralized as in the drug company shown in Figure 10.4. Maytag continued to diversify, however, and, as we discuss in the next section, it was forced to move to a multidivisional structure.

When a company operates as a geographical structure, geographical regions become the basis for the grouping of organizational activities. Thus the three parts in Figure 10.4 might be named Western Region, Central Region, and Eastern Region. The same range of products are manufactured in each region. Like a product structure, a geographical structure provides more control than a functional structure because there are several regional hierarchies carrying out the work previously performed by a single centralized hierarchy. A company like Federal Express clearly needs to operate a geographical structure to fulfill its corporate goal: next-day mail. Large merchandising organizations, such as Neiman-Marcus, also moved to a geographic structure soon after they started building

FIGURE 10.5   **Maytag's product structure**

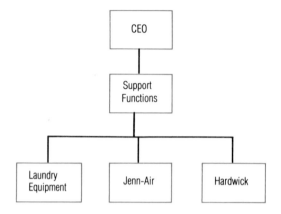

stores across the country. With a geographical structure, different regional cloth-ing needs—sun wear in the West, down coats in the East—can be handled as required. At the same time, because the purchasing function remains centralized, one central organization can buy for all regions. Thus a company both achieves economies of scale in buying and distribution and reduces coordination and com-munication problems.

Once again, however, the usefulness of the product or geographical structure depends on the size of the company and its range of products and regions. If a company starts to diversity into unrelated products or to integrate vertically into new industries, the product structure would not be capable of handling the in-creased diversity. The reason is that it does not provide managers with enough control over organizational activities to allow them to manage the company effectively; it is not complex enough to deal with the needs of the large, multi-business company. At this point in its development, a company would normally adopt the multidivisional structure.

Multidivisional Structure

The multidivisional structure possesses two main innovations that let a company grow and diversify while overcoming control loss problems. First, each distinct product line or business unit is placed in its own self contained unit or division with all support functions. For example, Pepsi-Cola has three major divisions, soft drinks, snack foods, and restaurants, and each division has its own functions such as marketing and research and development. The result is a higher level of horizontal differentiation. Second, the office of corporate headquarters staff is created to monitor interdivisional activities and exercise financial control over each of the divisions.[25] This staff contains corporate managers who oversee all divisional and functional activities, and it constitutes an additional level in the

FIGURE 10.6   Multidivisional structure

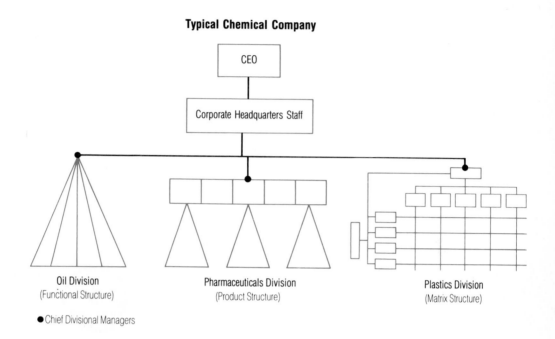

Typical Chemical Company

CEO

Corporate Headquarters Staff

Oil Division
(Functional Structure)

Pharmaceuticals Division
(Product Structure)

Plastics Division
(Matrix Structure)

● Chief Divisional Managers

organizational hierarchy. Hence there is a higher level of vertical differentiation in a multidivisional structure than in a product structure. Figure 10.6 presents a typical divisional structure found in a large chemical company such as Du Pont. Although this company might easily have seventy operating divisions, only three—the oil, drugs, and plastics divisions—are represented here.

As a self contained business unit, each division possesses a full array of support services. That is, each has self-contained accounting, sales, and personnel departments, for example. Each division functions as a profit center, making it much easier for corporate headquarters staff to monitor and evaluate the activities of each.[26]

Each division is also able to adopt the structure that best suits its needs. Figure 10.6 shows that the oil division has a functional structure because its activities are standardized, the drug division has a product structure for reasons discussed earlier, and the plastics division has a matrix structure, which is discussed in detail later in this chapter. Similarly, General Motors operates the whole corporation through a multidivisional structure, but each auto division operates a product structure, in which product lines are based on the type of auto made.

In the Maytag example noted earlier, we mention that Maytag continued to diversify its operations. It purchased two more appliance manufacturers, Magic Chef Company, which produces a wide variety of air conditioners and refrigerators, and Admiral, a maker of small appliances. Management originally intended

FIGURE 10.7   **Maytag's multidivisional structure**

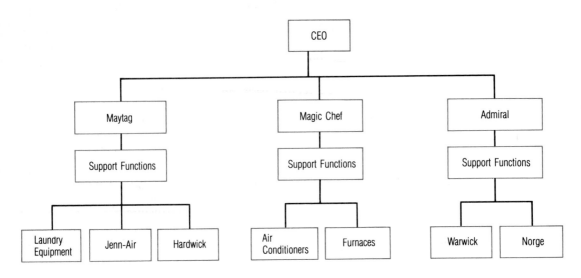

to operate the businesses as product lines through a product structure but soon realized that it would not be feasible to market several different brands in every category of the appliance industry with centralized support services.[27] The company, therefore, reorganized to a multidivisional structure with three autonomous divisions, each of which was given its own support functions. Then, within each division, a product structure was used. This change in structure proved to be very efficient and is shown in Figure 10.7.

In the multidivisional structure, day-to-day operations of a division are the responsibility of divisional management; that is, divisional management has **operating responsibility**. Corporate headquarters staff, however, which includes members of the board of directors as well as top executives, is responsible for overseeing long-term plans and providing the guidance for interdivisional projects. This staff has **strategic responsibility**. Such a combination of self-contained divisions with a centralized corporate management represents a higher level of both vertical and horizontal differentiation, as we note earlier. These two innovations provide extra control necessary to manage growth and diversification. Because this structure is now adopted by 60 percent of all large U. S. corporations, we need to consider its advantages and disadvantages in more detail.

Advantages of the Multidivisional Structure

There are several advantages that a multidivisional structure possesses when it is managed effectively by both corporate and divisional managers. Together, these advantages can raise corporate profitability to a new peak because they allow the organization to operate more complex kinds of corporate level strategy.

Enhanced corporate financial control   The profitability of different business divisions is clearly visible in the multidivisional structure.[28] Because each division is its own profit center, financial controls can be applied to each business on the basis of profit criteria. Typically, these controls involve establishing targets, monitoring performance on a regular basis, and selectively intervening when problems arise. Corporate headquarters is also in a better position to allocate corporate financial resources among competing divisions. The visibility of divisional performance also means that corporate headquarters can identify the divisions in which investment of funds would yield the greatest long-term returns. In a sense, the corporate office is in a position to act as the investor or banker in an internal capital market, channeling funds to high-yield uses.

Enhanced strategic control   The multidivisional structure frees corporate staff from operating responsibilities. The staff thus gains time for contemplating wider strategic issues and for developing responses to environmental changes. The multidivisional structure also enables headquarters to obtain the proper information to perform strategic planning functions. For example, separating individual businesses is a necessary prerequisite for the application of portfolio planning techniques.

Growth   The multidivisional structure enables the company to overcome an organizational limit to its growth. By reducing information overload at the center, headquarters personnel can handle a greater number of businesses. They can consider opportunities for further growth and diversification. Communication problems are reduced by applying accounting and financial control techniques as well as by implementing policies of "management by exception," meaning that corporate headquarters intervenes only when problems arise.

Stronger pursuit of internal efficiency   Within a functional structure, the interdependence of functional departments means that performance of functions within the company cannot be measured by objective criteria. For example, the profitability of the finance function, marketing function, or manufacturing function cannot be assessed in isolation, as they are only part of the whole. This often means that within the functional structure considerable degrees of organizational slack can go undetected. Resources might be absorbed in unproductive uses. For example, the head of the finance function might employ a larger staff than required for efficiency to reduce work pressures inside the department. Generally, a larger staff also brings a manager higher status. But because a divisional structure prescribes divisional operating autonomy, the divisions' efficiency can be directly observed and measured in terms of profit. Autonomy makes divisional managers accountable for their own performance; they can have no alibis. The general office is thus in a better position to identify inefficiencies.

A multidivisional structure then has a number of powerful advantages. No doubt that is why this structure appears to be the preferred choice of most large diversified enterprises today. Indeed, research suggests that large business companies that adopt this structure outperform those that retain the functional structure.[29]

Disadvantages of the Multidivisional Structure

A multidivisional structure has its disadvantages as well. Good management can eliminate some of them, but others are inherent in the way the structure operates and require constant attention. They are discussed next.

Establishing the divisional–corporate authority relationship   The authority relationship between corporate headquarters and the divisions must be correctly established. The multidivisional structure introduces a new level in the hierarchy—the corporate level. The problem is to decide how much authority and control to assign to the operating divisions and how much authority to retain at corporate headquarters. This problem was first noted by Alfred Sloan, the founder of General Motors. He introduced the multidivisional structure into General Motors, which became the first company to adopt it.[30] He created General Motors' familiar five-automobile divisions—Oldsmobile, Buick, Pontiac, Chevrolet, and Cadillac. The problem he noted was that when headquarters retained too much power and authority, the operating divisions lacked sufficient autonomy to develop the business strategy that might best meet the needs of the division. When too much power was delegated to the divisions, however, they pursued divisional objectives with little heed to the needs of the whole corporation. For example, all the potential gains from synergy discussed earlier would not be achieved. Thus the central issue in managing the multidivisional structure is how much authority should be centralized at corporate headquarters and how much should be decentralized to the divisions. This issue must be decided by each company in reference to the nature of its business and its corporate-level strategies. There are no easy answers, and over time, as the environment changes or the company alters its strategies, the balance between corporate and divisional control will also change.

Distortion of information   If corporate headquarters puts too much emphasis on divisional return on investment, for instance, by setting very high and stringent return on investment targets, divisional managers may choose to distort the information they supply top management and paint a rosy picture of the present situation at the expense of future profits. That is, divisions may maximize short-run profits—perhaps by cutting product development or new investments or marketing expenditures. This may cost the company dearly in the future. The problem stems from too tight financial control. General Motors has suffered from this problem in recent years, as declining performance has made managers attempt to make their divisions look good to corporate headquarters. On the other hand, if the divisional level exerts too much control, powerful divisional managers may resist attempts to use their profits to strengthen other divisions and therefore disguise their performance. Thus managing the corporate-divisional interface involves coping with subtle power issues.

Competition for resources   The third problem of managing the divisional structure is that the divisions themselves may compete for resources, and this rivalry will prevent gains from synergy from emerging. For example, the amount of money that corporate personnel has to distribute to the divisions is fixed. Generally, the divisions that can demonstrate the highest return on investment will get the lion's share of the money. But that large share strengthens them in the next time period, and so the strong divisions grow stronger. Consequently, divisions may actively compete for resources, and by doing so, reduce interdivisional coordination. For example, at Procter & Gamble, the struggle among divisions for resources has actually led to a loss in market share because resources had been inefficiently distributed as a result of competition.

see Rohm
~ Haas
case

Transfer pricing   Divisional competition may also lead to battles over **transfer pricing.** As we discuss in Chapter 8, one of the problems with vertical integration or related diversification is setting transfer prices between divisions. Rivalry among divisions increases the problem of setting fair prices. Each supplying division tries to set the highest price for its outputs to maximize its own return on investment. Such competition can completely undermine the corporate culture and make the corporation a battleground. Many companies have a history of competition among divisions. Some, of course, may encourage competition, if managers believe that it leads to maximum performance.

Short-term research and development focus   If extremely high return on investment targets are set by corporate headquarters, there is a danger that the divisions will cut back on research and development expenditures to improve the financial performance of the division. Although this will inflate divisional performance in the short term, however, it will reduce the ability of a division to innovate new products and lead to a fall in the stream of long-term profits. Once again, corporate headquarters personnel must carefully control their interactions with the divisions to ensure that both the short- and long-term goals of the business are being achieved.

Operations costs   Because each division possesses its own specialized functions, such as finance or research and development, these multidivisional structures are expensive to run and manage. Research and development is especially costly, and so some companies centralize such functions at the corporate level to serve all divisions, as is done in the product structure. The duplication of specialist services, however, is not a problem if the gains from having separate specialist functions outweigh the costs. Again, management must decide if duplication is financially justified. Activities are often centralized in times of downturn or recession—particularly advisory services and planning functions. Divisions, however, are retained as profit centers.

The advantages of divisional structures must be balanced against their disadvantages, but, as already noted, the disadvantages can be managed by an observant, professional management team that is aware of the issues involved. The multidivisional structure is the dominant one today, which clearly suggests its usefulness as the means of managing the multibusiness corporation.

Strategic Business Unit (SBU) Structure

As corporations have grown and developed, new variants of the multidivisional structure have emerged. The increased size of many companies has resulted in a structure with an even higher level of horizontal differentiation: the **strategic business unit (SBU)**. When a company has 200 to 300 different divisions, as does Beatrice Foods Company or General Electric, corporate management finds it almost impossible to retain control over the organization. As we note earlier, problems of information overload at the center can emerge, and with 300 divisions to control, corporate staff may not have the time to examine the operations of each division thoroughly.

To simplify this control problem, the organization may introduce yet another level in the hierarchy and split the company into groups of divisions operating in similar areas. The idea is to group divisions to realize synergies among them. Typically, these groups are referred to as strategic business units, and each SBU is controlled by an SBU headquarters staff. Each SBU, as well as each division inside each SBU, becomes a profit center, and it is the SBU headquarters staff's job to maximize the profitability of its SBU. For example, in Beatrice Foods, one SBU comprises all the divisions that produce in the food industry, and another comprises all those in the consumer products industry. Each SBU is operated independently and evaluated separately. An example of an SBU structure is shown in Figure 10.8. Each triangle represents a self-contained division, and each circle represents a collection of related divisions managed by an SBU headquarters staff. Thus one more level in the hierarchy is created.

As originally conceived, the role of the **SBU office** is to control the divisions inside the SBU and allocate resources among them. The role of corporate headquarters thus becomes to control the SBUs and allocate resources among them. As a result, the corporation becomes more manageable. Nevertheless, SBUs are not ideal solutions, and the arguments for and against their creation are similar to those for the multidivisional structure.

On the positive side, SBUs reduce the work of corporate personnel by decreasing the span of control to a manageable level and permitting the decentralization of authority. Moreover, the SBU structure can provide an effective integrating device for coordinating the needs of companies inside a group. SBU personnel are more in touch with the needs and interests of those companies than a corporate office is likely to be. They are able to promote gains from synergy between companies in their group.

On the negative side, because the corporate office is now more remote, it

FIGURE 10.8   **Strategic business unit structure**

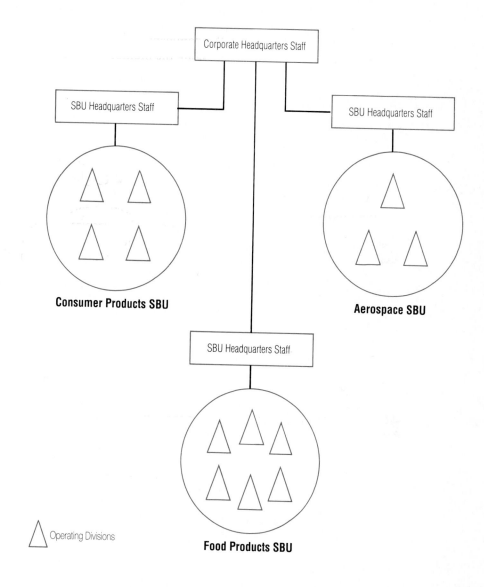

Corporate Headquarters Staff

SBU Headquarters Staff

SBU Headquarters Staff

Consumer Products SBU

Aerospace SBU

SBU Headquarters Staff

Operating Divisions

Food Products SBU

can lose touch with individual operating divisions inside an SBU because the SBU structure intervenes between it and the operating divisions. Corporate staff may not realize the seriousness of divisional problems until it is too late for counteractive measures. Besides, conflicts of interest may arise between the SBU and the corporate staff over funds for development. For example, using the Boston Consulting Group (BCG) matrix, the corporate office may define the SBU as a *dog* and limit its access to corporate capital. The SBU may also contain a *star* business, however, which would now be starved for cash. The SBU staff's challenging the authority of corporate staff would further weaken integration and accountability. Finally, the introduction of the SBU level in the organizational hierarchy may slow information transfers and communication and reduce the flexibility of the company as a whole.

On balance, then, it appears that the usefulness of this structure depends on the strategy with which the company is operating. The SBU structure is only appropriate for the companies that can group their divisions into separate, distinct categories, so that the benefits of this form of structure can be exploited. Such companies are likely to be related diversifiers.

Conglomerate Structure

The conglomerate structure is another main variant of the multidivisional form.[31] Whereas the SBU structure works best when commonalities link the various divisions or businesses in the company's portfolio, the conglomerate structure is used when there are no commonalities among divisions. The conglomerate form functions as a holding company, and each division is evaluated as a totally autonomous profit center. Textron and BAT Industries are good examples of companies that pursue unrelated diversification using a conglomerate structure.

The role of the corporate staff in a conglomerate structure is purely to perform portfolio analyses of the company's businesses. Decisions to acquire or divest businesses are linked to the goal of maximizing the profitability of the *corporate portfolio*. In contrast to the ordinary multidivisional or SBU structure, in the conglomerate structure problems of control and communication are at a minimum because the corporate staff makes no attempt to intervene in divisional strategy. This structure is therefore economical to manage because, even if the corporate staff controls as many as 300 businesses, the same portfolio matrix techniques can be applied to each business. For example, American Express Company operates its divisions loosely and treats its businesses as autonomous and self-financing fund generators. American Express believes that to attract able managers, its divisions must be given independence, and management views the divisions as "players" and the parent company as "referee." Corporate headquarters is active, however, in setting objectives, reviewing performance, and allocating capital to divisions.

Matrix Structure

A matrix structure differs from the structures discussed so far in that the matrix is based on two forms of horizontal differentiation rather than on one, as in the functional or product structure.[32] In the usual matrix design, activities on the vertical axis are grouped by *function,* so that we get a familiar differentiation of tasks into functions such as production, research and development, and engi-

ABB

FIGURE 10.9   **Matrix structure**

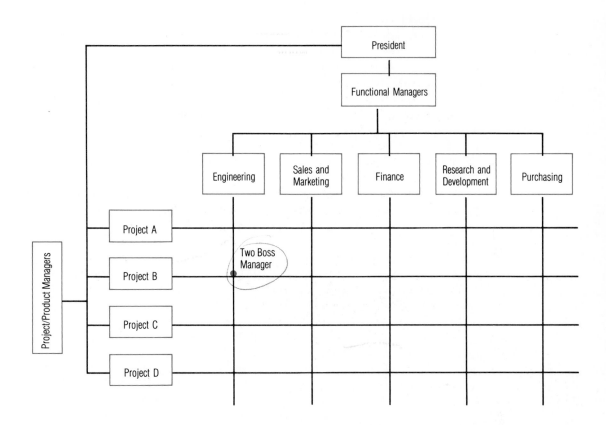

neering. In addition, superimposed on this vertical pattern is a horizontal pattern based on differentiation by *product or project*. The result is a complex network of reporting relationships among projects and functions, as depicted in Figure 10.9.

This structure also employs an unusual kind of vertical differentiation. Although matrix structures are flat, with few hierarchical levels, employees inside the matrix have two bosses: a **functional boss**, who is the head of a function, and a **project boss**, who is responsible for managing the individual projects. Employees work on a project team with specialists from other functions and report to the project boss on project matters and the functional boss on matters relating to functional issues. These employees are called **subproject managers** and are responsible for managing coordination and communication among the functions and projects.

Matrix structures were first developed by companies in high-technology industries such as aerospace and electronics—by companies such as TRW Inc. and Apple Computer. These companies are developing radically new products in uncertain, competitive environments, and speed of product development was the crucial consideration. They needed a structure that could respond to this strategy, but existing functional and product structures were too inflexible to allow the complex role and task interactions necessary to meet new product development requirements. Moreover, employees in these companies tend to be highly qualified and professional, and perform best in autonomous, flexible working conditions: The matrix structure provides such conditions. For example, this structure requires a minimum of direct hierarchical control by supervisors. Employees control their own behavior, and participation in project teams allows them to monitor other team members and learn from each other. Further, as the project goes through its different phases, different specialists from various functions are required. Thus, for example, at the first stage the services of research and development specialists may be needed, and then at the next stage engineers and marketing specialists are needed to make cost and marketing projections. As the demand for the type of specialist changes, employees can be moved to other projects that need their services. As a result, the matrix structure can make maximum use of employee skills as existing projects are completed and new ones come into existence. Finally, the freedom given by the matrix not only provides the autonomy to motivate employees, it also leaves top management free to concentrate on strategic issues because they do not have to become involved in operating matters. On all these counts, the matrix is an excellent tool for creating the flexibility necessary for quick reactions to competitive conditions.

There are disadvantages to the matrix structure, however.[33] First, it is expensive to operate compared with a functional structure. Employees tend to be highly skilled, and therefore both salaries and overheads are high. Second, the constant movement of employees around the matrix means that time and money are spent in establishing new team relationships and getting the project off the ground. Third, the subproject manager's role, balancing as it does the interests of the project with the function, is difficult to manage, and care must be taken to avoid conflict between functions and projects over resources. Over time, it is possible that project managers will take the leading role in planning and goal setting, in which case the structure works more like a product or divisional structure. If function and project relationships are left uncontrolled, they can lead to power struggles among managers, and the result is not increased flexibility, but stagnation and decline. Finally, the larger the organization, the more difficult it is to operate a matrix structure, because task and role relationships become complex. In such situations, the only option may be to change to a product or divisional structure.

Given these advantages and disadvantages, the matrix is generally used only when a company's strategy warrants it. There is no point in using a more complex structure than necessary because it will only cost more to manage. In dynamic product/market environments, the benefits of the matrix in terms of flexibility and innovation are likely to exceed the extra cost of using it, and so it becomes an appropriate choice of structure. Companies in the mature stage of the industry life cycle or those pursuing a low-cost strategy, however, would rarely choose this structure. We discuss it further in Chapter 12.

10.6 SUMMARY OF CHAPTER

This chapter introduces the issues involved in designing a structure to meet the needs of a company's strategy. The reasons that Apple Computer changed its structure over time and the problems that can arise when companies make such changes should now be clear. As the discussion in this chapter suggests, companies can adopt a large number of structures to match changes in their size and strategy over time. The structure that a company selects will be the one whose logic of grouping activities (that is, its form of horizontal differentiation) best meets the needs of its business or businesses. The company must match its form of horizontal differentiation to vertical differentiation. That is, it must choose a structure and then make choices about levels in the hierarchy and degree of centralization or decentralization. It is the combination of both kinds of differentiation that produce its internal organizational arrangements. As previously noted, however, once the company has divided itself into parts it must then integrate itself. This is discussed in the next chapter. We stress the following points:

1. Implementing a strategy successfully depends on selecting the right structure and control system to match a company's strategy.

2. The basic tool of strategy implementation is organizational design.

3. Differentiation and integration are the two design concepts that decide how a structure will work.

4. Differentiation has two aspects: (a) vertical differentiation, which refers to how a company chooses to allocate its decision-making authority; and (b) horizontal differentiation, which refers to the way that a company groups organizational activities into functions or departments or divisions.

5. The basic choice in vertical differentiation is whether to have a flat or a tall structure. Tall hierarchies have a number of disadvantages, such as problems with communication and information transfer, motivation, and cost. Decentralization or delegation of authority, however, can solve some of these problems.

6. The structures that a company can adopt as it grows and diversifies include the functional, product, and multidivisional forms. Each structure has advantages and disadvantages associated with it.

7. Other specialized kinds of structures include the matrix, conglomerate, and strategic business unit (SBU) forms. Each has a specialized use, and to be chosen, must match the needs of the organization.

Discussion Questions

1. What is the difference between vertical and horizontal differentiation? Rank the various structures discussed in this chapter along these two dimensions.

2. What kind of structure best describes the way your (a) business school and (b) university operates? Why is the structure appropriate? Would another structure fit better?

3. When would a company decide to change from a functional to a product structure? From a product to a multidivisional structure?

4. When would a company choose a matrix structure? What are the problems associated with managing this structure?

Endnotes

1. "Apple Computer, Inc.—Background History," Apple Computer, Inc., 1986.

2. "Apple Takes On Its Biggest Test Yet," *Business Week,* January 31, 1983, p. 79.

3. Bro Uttal, "Behind the Fall of Steve Jobs," *Fortune,* August 5, 1985, pp. 20–24.

4. J. R. Galbraith, *Designing Complex Organizations* (Reading, Mass.: Addison-Wesley, 1973).

5. J. Child, *Organization: A Guide for Managers and Administrators* (New York: Harper & Row, 1977), pp. 50–72.

6. R. H. Miles, *Macro Organizational Behavior* (Santa Monica, Calif.: Goodyear, 1980), pp. 19–20.

7. Galbraith, *Designing Complex Organizations.*

8. V. A. Graicunas, "Relationship in Organization," in L. Gulick and L. Urwick (eds.), *Papers on the Science of Administration* (New York: Institute of Public Administration, 1937), pp. 181—185. J. C. Worthy, "Organizational Structure and Company Morale," *American Sociological Review,* 15 (1950), 169–179.

9. Child, *Organization,* pp. 50—52.

10. G. R. Jones, "Organization-Client Transactions and Organizational Governance Structures," *Academy of Management Journal,* 30 (1987), 197–218.

11. H. Mintzberg, *The Structuring of Organizations* (Englewood Cliffs, N. J.: Prentice-Hall, 1979), p. 435.

12. Child, *Organization,* p. 51.

13. R. Carzo, Jr., and J. N. Yanousas, "Effects of Flat and Tall Organization Structure," *Administrative Science Quarterly,* 14 (1969), 178–191.

14. A. Gupta and V. Govindardan, "Business Unit Strategy, Managerial Characteristics, and Business Unit Effectiveness at Strategy Implementation," *Academy of Management Journal,* 27 (1984), 25–41. R. T. Lenz, "Determinants of Organizational Performance: An Interdisciplinary Review," *Strategic Management Journal, 2 (1981), 131–154.*

15. W. H. Wagel, "Keeping the Organization Lean at Federal Express," *Personnel* (March 1984), 4.

16. J. Koter, "For P&G Rivals, the New Game Is to Beat the Leader, Not Copy It," *Wall Street Journal,* May 6, 1985, p. 35.

17. G. R. Jones, "Task Visibility, Free Riding and Shirking; Explaining the Effect of Organization Structure on Employee Behavior," *Academy of Management Review,* 4 (1984), 684–695.

18. "Operation Turnaround—How Westinghouse's New Chairman Plans to Fire Up An Old Line Company," *Business Week,* December 14, 1983, pp. 124–133.

19. R. L. Deft, *Organizational Theory and Design,* 2nd ed. (St. Paul, Minn.: West, 1986), p. 215.

20. Alfred D. Chandler, *Strategy and Structure* (Cambridge, Mass.: MIT Press, 1962).

21. The discussion draws heavily on Chandler, *Strategy and Structure,* and B. R. Scott, "Stages of Corporate Development" (Cambridge, Mass.: Intercollegiate Clearing House, Harvard Business School, 1971).

22. J. R. Galbraith and R. K. Kazanjian, *Strategy Implementation: Structure System and Process,* 2nd ed. (St. Paul, Minn.: West, 1986). Child, *Organization.* R. Duncan, "What Is the Right Organization Structure?" *Organizational Dynamics* (Winter 1979), 59–80.

23. O. E. Williamson, *Markets and Hierarchies: Analysis and Antitrust Implications* (New York: Free Press, 1975).

24. P. R. Lawrence and J. Lorsch, *Organization and Environment* (Boston: Division of Research, Harvard Business School, 1967).

25. Chandler, *Strategy and Structure.* Williamson, *Markets and Hierarchies.* L. Wrigley, "Divisional Autonomy and Diversification" (Ph.D. diss., Harvard Business School, 1970).

26. R. P. Rumelt, *Strategy, Structure, and Economic Performance* (Boston: Division of Research, Harvard Business School, 1974); Scott, "Stages of Corporate Development." Williamson, *Markets and Hierarchies.*

27. K. Deveny, "Maytag's New Girth Will Test Its Marketing Muscle," *Business Week,* February 16, 1987, p. 68.

28. The discussion draws on each of the sources cited in endnotes 20–27, and also on G. R. Jones and C. W. L. Hill,

"Transaction Cost Analysis of Strategy-Structure Choice," *Strategic Management Journal,* 9 (1988), 159–172.

29. H. O. Armour and D. J. Teece, "Organizational Structure and Economic Performance: A Test of the Multidivisional Hypothesis," *Bell Journal of Economics,* 9 (1978), 106–122.

30. Alfred Sloan, *My Years at General Motors* (New York: Doubleday, 1983), Ch. 3.

31. N. A. Berg, "Strategic Planning in Conglomerate Companies," *Harvard Business Review,* 43 (1965), 79–92. K. N. M. Dundas and R. R. Richardson, "Implementing the Unrelated Product Strategy," *Strategic Management Journal,* 3 (1982), 287–301.

32. S. M. Davis and R. R. Lawrence, *Matrix* (Reading, Mass.: Addison-Wesley, 1977). J. R. Galbraith, "Matrix Organization Designs: How to Combine Functional and Project Forms," *Business Horizons,* 14 (1971), 29–40.

33. Duncan, "What Is the Right Organizational Structure?" Davis and Lawrence, *Matrix.*

Chapter 11

CHOOSING

INTEGRATION AND

CONTROL SYSTEMS

11.1 OPENING INCIDENT: TRW

TRW Information Services, one of America's most successful high-tech companies, was heavily involved in the intercontinental ballistic missile (ICBM) research program and has continued to be a leader in electronics, defense, and space program development. It was one of the first companies to introduce the matrix structure as a means of coordinating and integrating its complex and constantly changing product lines. To make the matrix structure work, TRW also adopted a variety of integration and control systems to encourage high performance and increase the level of coordination between functions. First, it relied heavily on the recruitment and selection of highly skilled, professional employees with strong internal motivation to perform.[1] Second, it established project teams in which employees were able to work and integrate with employees in other functions. In addition, TRW reinforced employee commitment to high performance by avoiding employee layoffs and by developing a decentralized, freewheeling organization culture that rewarded risk taking, innovation, and creativity. Its innovative strategic organization design brought TRW huge success. It grew from a

company valued at $500,000 in 1965 to one valued at more than $6 billion in 1990.[2]

With rapid growth, however, came major problems. Each project group inside its matrix structure developed into a full-fledged division within a multidivisional structure. As a result, integration among divisions dissipated, and the kind of controls that the company could use when it was small and decentralized no longer suited a high-tech giant. In fact, the company was running into the very integration problems that it had sought to avoid by developing a matrix structure. The various divisions in TRW—defense, electronics, and automotive products—were not cooperating with one another and were sharing their research and development know-how less and less. Actually, they were competing,[3] which was an enormous problem for a company that depended on technological advances for its future growth and success.

The reason for the lack of integration was that divisional managers were saying, "Why should I spend billions of dollars investing in research for my own product lines and then this other division can just come along and get the knowledge free and apply it to its own products, especially when I am evaluated on bottom-line performance?" In other words, divisions were competing rather than cooperating because the old kind of controls used by TRW were no longer appropriate, and the company had not yet developed a new set of controls to coordinate its new organizational structure. Rube Mettler, TRW's chairman, faced the problem of finding new ways to integrate divisions and new control systems that would encourage cooperation among them and prepare the corporation for future growth.

TRW attempted to improve integration by introducing new types of incentive schemes to stimulate cooperation rather than competition. For example, divisional managers' bonuses, promotions, and pay raises were linked to the results of cooperation among divisions. The company also developed a transfer pricing scheme that allowed divisions to charge a fair price for technology transferred to other divisions. In addition, to improve performance, it tried to develop a corporate culture based on cooperative corporate values rather than competitive divisional values. These efforts were just one part of TRW's overall control system, which also monitored costs, productivity, quality, and all the other indicators of organizational performance.

11.2 OVERVIEW

In Chapter 10, we discuss the various kinds of structures available to companies when they implement their strategies. As the example of TRW suggests, in this chapter we consider the various kinds of integrating mechanisms and control systems that companies use to make these structures operate efficiently. **Integrating mechanisms** coordinate the various functions and divisions of the business. More complex structures require the use of more complex kinds of integrating mechanisms. Through **control systems**, organizations can monitor, evaluate, and change their performance. These systems provide information on how well a company's strategy is working and how well the structure used to implement the strategy is working. **Strategic control** is the process of selecting the types of controls at the corporate, business, and functional levels in a company that allow strategic managers to evaluate whether the company's strategy and structure are achieving organizational objectives.

We first take up the kinds of integrating mechanisms that companies can activate. Then we outline the process of strategic control and examine in detail the types of control that companies can use. These include market control, output control, bureaucratic control, and clan control and culture. Finally, we discuss how the design of reward systems is an important element of the strategic control process. In the next chapter, we consider in detail how to match organizational structure and control to corporate-, business-, and functional-level strategy.

11.3 INTEGRATION AND INTEGRATING MECHANISMS

Matching Differentiation with Integration

As we discuss in Chapter 10, an organization must choose the appropriate form of differentiation to match its strategy. Greater diversification, for example, requires that a company move from a product structure to a divisional structure. Differentiation, however, is only one design decision to be made. Another decision concerns the level of integration necessary to make the structure work effectively. **Integration** is defined as the extent to which the organization seeks to coordinate the various activities of the organization and make them interdependent. The design issue can be summed up simply: The higher a company's level of differentiation (that is, the more complex its structure), the higher is the level of integration needed to make the structure perform effectively.[4] Thus if a company adopts a more complex form of differentiation, it requires a more complex form of integration to accomplish its goals. For example, Federal Express needs an enormous amount of integration and coordination to allow it to fulfill its promise of next-day package delivery. It is renowned for its innovative use of integrating mechanisms, such as customer-liaison personnel, to manage its transactions quickly and efficiently. Similarly, if managers adopt a multidivisional structure to manage a strategy of related diversification, they must establish means to integrate across divisions to achieve the gains from synergy. Take the problem facing Texas Air, the nation's biggest airline company. Its acquisition of Eastern Airlines, People Express, and New York Air doubled its size, and integrating these airlines with Continental caused enormous problems for the company. It was its inability to coordinate the airlines that led to its current misfortunes.

Forms of Integrating Mechanisms

Jay R. Galbraith, a prominent management theorist, has identified a series of integrating mechanisms that a company can use to increase its level of integration as its level of differentiation increases.[5] These mechanisms—on a continuum from simplest to most complex—are listed in Table 11.1 together with the examples of the individuals or groups that might perform these integrating roles.

Direct contact   The aim behind establishing direct contact among managers is to set up a context within which managers from different divisions or functional departments can work together to solve mutual problems. As TRW's experience suggests, however, several problems are associated with establishing contact among managers in different functional departments or divisions. Managers from different functional departments have different subunit orientations but equal authority and so may tend to compete rather than cooperate when conflicts arise.

TABLE 11.1   **Types and examples of integrating mechanisms**

Direct contact	Sales and production managers
Liaison roles	Assistant sales and plant managers
Task forces	Representatives from sales, production, and research and development
Teams	Organizational executive committee
Integrating roles	Assistant vice president for strategic planning or vice president without portfolio
Integrating departments	Corporate headquarters staff
Matrix	All roles are integrating roles

For example, in a typical functional structure, the heads of each of the functions have equal authority; the nearest common point of authority is the CEO. Consequently, if disputes arise, no mechanism exists to resolve the conflicts apart from the authority of the boss. In fact, one sign of conflict in organizations is the number of problems sent up the hierarchy for upper-level managers to solve. This wastes management time and effort, slows down strategic decision making, and makes it difficult to create a cooperative culture in the company. For this reason, companies choose more complex integrating mechanisms to coordinate interfunctional and divisional activities.

Interdepartmental liaison roles   A company can improve its interfunctional coordination through the interdepartmental liaison role. When the volume of contacts between two departments or functions increases, one of the ways of improving coordination is to give one person in *each* division or function the responsibility for coordinating with the other. These people may meet daily, weekly, monthly, or as needed. Figure 11.1a depicts the nature of the liaison role, the small circle representing the individual inside the functional department who has responsibility for coordinating with the other function. The responsibility for coordination is part of an individual's full-time job, but through these roles, a permanent relationship forms between the people involved, greatly easing strains between departments. Furthermore, it offers a way of transferring information across the organization, which is important in large, anonymous organizations whose employees may know no one outside their immediate department.

Temporary task forces   When more than two functions or divisions share common problems, then direct contact and liaison roles are of limited value because they do not provide enough coordination. The solution is to adopt a more complex form of integrating mechanism called a task force. The nature of the task force is represented diagrammatically in Figure 11.1b. One member of each function or division is assigned to a task force created to solve a specific problem. Essentially, task forces are *ad hoc committees,* and members are responsible for reporting back to their departments on the issues addressed and solutions recommended. Task forces are temporary because, once the problem is solved,

FIGURE 11.1   **Forms of integrating mechanisms**

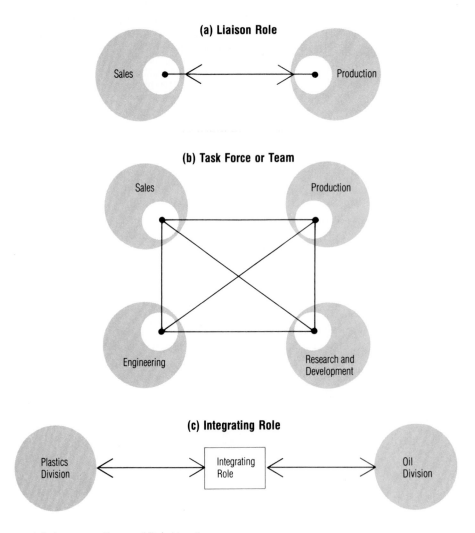

(a) Liaison Role

Sales   Production

(b) Task Force or Team

Sales   Production

Engineering   Research and Development

(c) Integrating Role

Plastics Division   Integrating Role   Oil Division

● Indicates manager with responsibility for integration

members return to their normal roles in their departments. Task force members also perform many of their normal duties while serving on the task force.

Permanent teams   In many cases, the issues addressed by a task force are recurring problems. To solve these problems effectively, an organization must establish a permanent integrating mechanism such as a permanent team. An example of a permanent team is a new product development committee, which is responsible for the choice, design, and marketing of new products. Such an activity obviously requires a great deal of integration among functions if new products are to be successfully introduced, and establishing a permanent integrating mechanism accomplishes this. Intel, for instance, emphasizes teamwork. It formed a council system based on approximately ninety cross-organizational groups, which meet regularly to set functional strategy in areas such as engineering and marketing and develop business-level strategy.

The importance of teams in the management of the organizational structure cannot be overemphasized. Essentially, permanent teams are the organization's *standing committees,* and much of the strategic direction of the organization is formulated in these meetings. Henry Mintzberg, in a study of how the managers of corporations spend their time, discovered that they spend almost 60 percent of their time in these committees.[6] The reason is not bureaucracy but rather that integration is possible only in intensive, face-to-face sessions, in which managers can understand others' viewpoints and develop a cohesive organizational strategy. The more complex the company, the more important these teams become. Westinghouse, for example, has established a whole new task force and team system to promote integration among divisions and improve corporate performance.

Integrating roles   The integrating role is a new role whose only function is to prompt integration among divisions or departments; it is a full-time job (see Figure 11.1c.). As you see, it is independent of the subunits or divisions being integrated. The role is staffed by an independent expert, who is normally a senior manager with a great deal of experience in the joint needs of the two departments. The job is to coordinate the decision process among departments or divisions to allow the synergetic gains from cooperation to be obtained. One study found that Du Pont had created 160 integrating roles to provide coordination among the different divisions of the company and improve corporate performance.[7] Once again, the more differentiated the company, the more common are these roles. Often people in these roles take the responsibility for chairing task forces and teams, and this provides additional integration.

Integrating departments   Sometimes the number of integrating roles becomes so high that a permanent integrating department is established at corporate headquarters. Normally, this occurs only in large, diversified corporations, which see the need for integration among divisions. This department consists mainly of strategic planners and may indeed be called the strategic planning department. Corporate headquarters staff in a divisional structure can also be viewed as an integrating department from the divisional perspective.

Matrix structure   Finally, when differentiation is very high and the company must be able to respond quickly to the environment, a matrix structure becomes the appropriate integrating device. The matrix contains many of the integrating mechanisms already discussed: The subproject managers integrate among functions and projects, and the matrix is built on the basis of temporary task forces.

Summary: Integration and Integrating Mechanisms

It is clear that firms have a large number of options open to them when they increase their level of differentiation as a result of increased growth or diversification. The implementation issue is for managers to match differentiation with the level of integration to meet organizational objectives. Note that while too much differentiation and not enough integration will lead to failure of implementation, the converse is also true. That is, the combination of low differentiation and high integration will lead to an overcontrolled bureaucratized organization where flexibility and speed of response is reduced and not enhanced by the level of integration. Also, integration is expensive for the company because it raises management costs. For these reasons the goal is to decide on the optimum amount of integration necessary for meeting organizational goals and objectives. It is in this connection that strategic control becomes important because it allows managers to assess whether their integration mechanisms are coordinating their structures.

11.4 STRATEGY IMPLEMENTATION AND CONTROL

In Chapter 10, we mention that implementation involves selecting the right combination of structure and control for achieving a company's strategy. Structure assigns people to tasks and roles (differentiation) and specifies how these are to be coordinated (integration). Nevertheless, it does not of itself provide the mechanism through which people can be *motivated* to make the structure work. Hence the need for control. Put another way, management can develop *on paper* an elegant organization structure with the right integrating mechanisms, but only appropriate control systems will make this structure work. For example, at TRW, top management established a complex system of teams and integrating roles to link the various divisions in the company and solve the problem of cooperation. Although this solution seemed good on paper, in practice, management found that different divisional teams were not cooperating because the company offered no rewards for cooperation. Top management had to establish a monitoring system to evaluate the divisions' attempts at cooperating with each other and also had to introduce rewards for cooperation. For a company like TRW, the right control system was vital for achieving the gains from synergy on which the company's dominance in the high-tech field depends.

TRW demonstrates that a structure will not work without the complex web of controls that allow a company to monitor, evaluate, and reward its parts—divisions, functions, and individual personnel. In the rest of this chapter, we discuss the various options open to companies in designing such a control system. First, however, we examine in more detail what a control system is.

11.5 STRATEGIC CONTROL SYSTEMS

Strategic control systems are the formal target-setting, monitoring, evaluation, and feedback systems that provide management with information about whether the organization's strategy and structure are meeting strategic performance objectives. An effective control system should have three characteristics: It should be *flexible* enough to allow managers to respond as necessary to unexpected events; it should provide *accurate information,* giving a true picture of organizational performance; and it should provide managers with the information in a *timely manner* because making decisions on the basis of outdated information is a recipe for failure.[8] As Figure 11.2 shows, designing an effective strategic control system requires four steps.[9]

1. *Establish the standards or targets against which performance is to be evaluated.* The standards or targets that managers select are the ways in which a company chooses to evaluate its performance. Generally, these targets are derived from the strategy pursued by the company. For example, if a company is pursuing a low-cost strategy, then "reducing costs by 7 percent a year" might be a target. If the company is a service organization like McDonald's, its standards might include time targets for serving customers or guidelines for food quality.

2. *Create the measuring or monitoring systems that indicate whether the targets are being achieved.* The company establishes procedures for assessing whether work goals at all levels in the organization are being achieved. In many cases, measuring performance is a difficult task because the organization is engaged in many complex activities. For example, managers can measure quite easily

FIGURE 11.2   **Steps in designing an effective control system**

Establish Standards and Targets

↓

Create Measuring and Monitoring Systems

↓

Compare Actual Performance Against
the Established Targets

↓

Evaluate Result and Take Action if Necessary

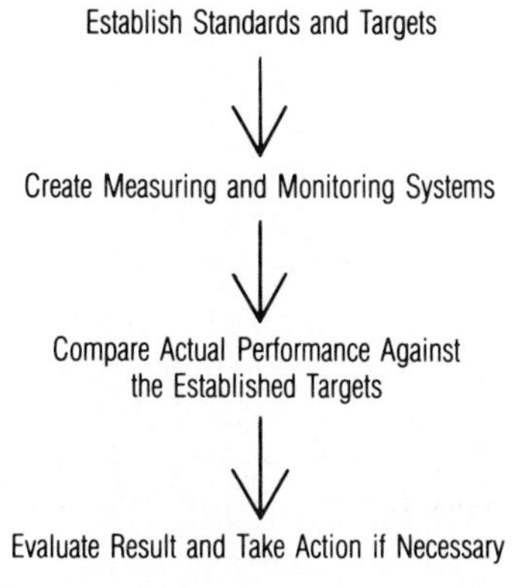

how many customers their employees serve: they can count the number of receipts from the cash register. Yet how can they judge how well their research and development department is doing when it may take five years for products to be developed? Or how can they measure the company's performance when the company is entering new markets and serving new customers? Or how can they evaluate how well divisions are integrating? The answer is that they need to use various types of control, which we discuss later in this chapter.

3. *Compare actual performance against the established targets.* Managers evaluate whether—and to what extent—performance deviates from the targets developed in step 1. If performance is higher, management may decide that it had set the standards too low and may raise them from the next time period. The Japanese are renowned for the way they use targets on the production line to control costs. They are constantly trying to raise performance, and they constantly raise the standards to provide a goal for managers to work toward. On the other hand, if performance is too low, managers must decide whether to take remedial action. This decision is easy when the reasons for poor performance can be identified—for instance, high labor costs. More often, however, the reasons for poor performance are hard to uncover. They may involve external factors, such as a recession. Or the cause may be internal. For instance, the research and development laboratory may have underestimated the problems it would encounter or the extra costs of doing unforeseen research. For any form of action, however, step 4 is necessary.

4. *Evaluate the result and initiate corrective action when it is decided that the target is not being achieved.* If managers decide to begin corrective action, they have two choices. They can *alter the control systems* being used to measure and monitor the performance of divisions, departments, or individuals—they may change budgets or replace rules for example. In adopting this response, managers are acting on the work system itself to correct the deviation, and they may push for more creative decision making or try to increase productivity by offering better bonuses. The other option available to managers is to *act on the target itself.* Perhaps a target was incorrectly set—for example, a sales target was too optimistic or too high. In this situation, the objective would be to change the target rather than the type of control being used to achieve it. Essentially, then, managers can act on the *means,* that is, the actual types of controls used, or the *ends,* that is, the standards or targets.

The simplest example of a control system is the thermostat in a home. By setting the thermostat, you establish the standard with which actual temperature is to be compared. The thermostat contains a sensing or monitoring device, which measures the actual temperature against the desired temperature. Whenever there is a difference between them, the furnace or air-conditioning unit is activated, to bring the temperature back to the standard: in other words, corrective action is initiated. Note that this is a simple control system for it is entirely self-contained and the target (temperature) is easy to measure.

Obviously, establishing targets and designing measurement systems is much more difficult in the strategic arena because there are many different targets or standards to choose from. We turn to this issue next.

11.6 SELECTING PERFORMANCE STANDARDS

In selecting performance standards, managers are deciding what criteria they will use to evaluate the organization's performance. Standards or measures of a company's performance fall into four basic categories.[10] These are summarized in Table 11.2, along with the individual kinds of measures within each category.

Performance Standards

The first category contains standards that measure a company's ability *to meet efficiency goals.* Thus standards relating to productivity, cost, or quality of production are set up and used as the base line measures for evaluating performance. The second category consists of standards that measure *human resources* in an organization. A company creates targets concerning the level of absenteeism, turnover, or job satisfaction that is acceptable in the organization. Much more difficult to formulate are standards pertaining to the *internal functioning and responsiveness* of the organization, which make up the third category. Here managers are concerned with factors such as creativity, flexibility, decision making, and organizational communication. In the fourth, and last, category standards relate to an organization's ability to *exploit the environment and obtain scarce resources.* Hence such measures as ability to respond to changes in the environment or to manage external constituencies, such as stockholders, customers, or the government, are important. These standards are also difficult to devise.

Generally, performance is measured at four levels in the organization: the corporate, divisional, functional, and individual levels. Managers at the corporate level are most concerned with overall and abstract measures of organizational

TABLE 11.2   Types and examples of performance targets

Efficiency targets	Productivity, profit, quality, output, costs
Human resource targets	Absenteeism, turnover, job satisfaction, morale, commitment, cooperation
Internal functioning targets	Flexibility, planning, goal-setting, communication, conflict management
Environmental targets	External constituency building, political legitimacy, control of scarce inputs and outputs

FIGURE 11.3   Levels of organizational control

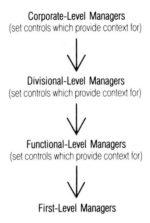

Corporate-Level Managers
(set controls which provide context for)

Divisional-Level Managers
(set controls which provide context for)

Functional-Level Managers
(set controls which provide context for)

First-Level Managers

performance such as profit, return on investment, or total labor force turnover. The aim is to choose performance standards that measure overall corporate performance. Similarly, managers at the other levels are most concerned with developing a set of standards to evaluate business- or functional-level performance. These measures should be tied as closely as possible to the work activities needed to meet strategic objectives at each level. Care must be taken, however, to ensure that the standards used at each level do not cause problems at the other levels—for example, that divisions' attempts to improve their performance do not conflict with corporate performance. Furthermore, controls at each level should provide the basis on which managers at the levels below can select their control systems. Figure 11.3 illustrates these links.

Problems with Selecting Standards

Selecting the appropriate standards for evaluating performance is one of the most important decisions that strategic managers can make because these standards determine what the company should be doing—that is, its strategic mission. But managers must watch out for some problems.

First, because so many different kinds of standards are available, assessments of a company's performance can vary according to the measure selected. If managers choose measures that emphasize productivity but ignore those concerning the environment, they may end up with conflicting impressions of a company's performance. A classic case is that of the large American car makers at the time of high oil prices. Although car makers were very efficient—they could produce large cars at low cost—they were hardly effective because nobody wanted to buy large cars. Thus they were not satisfying their outside constituencies—customers or shareholders. Thus through the measures they select and try to control, managers can create a misleading impression of a company's performance. It is vital, therefore, that they measure the right things.

Second, the four categories of standards are not always consistent and may be incompatible—that is, pursuing one type of standard may stop a company from achieving another. For example, a company's attempts to minimize cost and maximize productivity often lead to higher employee absenteeism and turnover because employees must work under more intense pressure. As another example, companies often like to maintain large inventories of spare parts or components to ride out shortages in stocks of finished goods and respond properly to customer needs. Nevertheless, maintaining buffer stocks and inventory is expensive and therefore raises costs. In such a situation, a company is trading off efficiency against its internal flexibility.

An important tradeoff at the heart of this second problem is that between short-run efficiency and long-term effectiveness. For example, the competitive advantage that the Japanese have over U.S. manufacturers is often attributed to their long-term planning, large investments of funds in research and development, and expectation of a slower payoff (or return on investment). U.S. corporations, on the other hand, are so concerned with maximizing short-run returns that they limit investment in research and development and, in general, try to reduce costs in the short run. As a result, they suffer in the long run because they have not made the investment for the future. The kind of measures management adopts to evaluate its performance can strongly influence whether this will occur, and large companies such as General Motors are now building long-term quality standards into their control system. For example, in its attempt to catch up with the Japanese, General Motors has increased its research and development budgets. In the last five years, it has spent so much on improving its product quality that it could have easily bought Toyota on the stock exchange and still have had money to spare. A company must design a control system that can evaluate whether it is meeting all the objectives necessary to accomplish its strategic mission.

The third problem is that the measures chosen to evaluate performance may depend on whose interests are at stake. You see in Chapter 2 that a company's primary function is to maximize stockholder wealth, but what path should be pursued to achieve this? Suppose some stockholders prefer short-term dividends whereas others prefer long-term capital appreciation. Which measure of performance should management adopt? Furthermore, if it adopts the standard of maximizing long-term wealth, how should it move toward this goal? Should it reduce costs, maximize its ability to deal with the environment, maximize employee welfare to encourage productivity, or maximize research and development spending? Although these are all possible targets, no easy rules determine which of them are best. Some companies are more successful than others simply because they adopt the right kind of measures.

Management needs to use all four categories of standards to create the mix of standards necessary to pursue a successful long-term strategy. Specifically, management must minimally satisfy all the constituencies that have an interest in the company.[11] As we identify in Chapter 1, these constituencies include shareholders, customers, and the company's employees. In satisfying their interests, management will be balancing the needs of short-run operating efficiency against long-run strategic effectiveness.

11.7 TYPES OF CONTROL SYSTEMS

The control systems that managers can use range from those measuring **organizational outputs** to those measuring and controlling **organizational behaviors**.[12] In general, outputs are much easier to measure than behaviors because outputs are relatively tangible or objective. Hence output controls tend to be the first type that a company employs. In many situations, however, organizational outputs cannot be easily measured or evaluated. For example, measuring organizational creativity or flexibility objectively is difficult. In addition, the more complex the organizational tasks, the harder it is to use output control because evaluating the work of people such as research and development personnel or strategic planners is both difficult and expensive. Similarly, the higher the interdependence among functions or divisions—for instance, when a company is seeking to achieve gains from synergy—the tougher it is for a company to pinpoint divisional contributions to performance.

In these situations, a company usually adopts control systems that shape the behaviors necessary to reach its targets.[13] Although such behavior control systems are generally more expensive to employ, they are often the only means a company has to monitor and evaluate performance when organizational activities are complex. Table 11.3 shows the various types of control systems along this output-to-behavior control continuum. We discuss each of these types in turn and also consider the use of different kinds of control mechanisms at the various organizational levels—corporate, divisional, functional, and individual.

TABLE 11.3   Types of control systems

Market control	Output control	Bureaucratic control	Clan control
Stock price	Divisional goals	Rules and procedures	Norms
ROI	Functional goals	Budgets	Values
Transfer pricing	Individual goals	Standardization	Socialization

Market Control

Market control is the most objective kind of output control and is achieved by setting a *system of prices* to monitor and evaluate performance. Market control can therefore be used only when an organization is able to establish objective financial measures of performance. In practice, this means that there must be competition of some kind, because only through a competitive market mechanism can a fair price be established.

Types of market control systems   There are three common forms of market control: stock market price, return on investment, and transfer pricing.

Stock market price   Stock price is a useful measure of a company's performance primarily because the price of the stock is determined competitively by the number of buyers and sellers in the market. Movements in the price of a stock provide top management with feedback on its performance. They act as a powerful means of control because managers tend to be sensitive to falls in the stock market prices, since their compensation is often related to stock price. Falls in stock price may also stimulate takeover attempts, and this factor also serves to control managerial action. Finally, because stock price reflects the long-term future return from the stock, it can be regarded as an indicator of the company's long-run potential.

Return on investment   Return on investment (ROI), determined by dividing net income by invested capital, is another form of market control. At the corporate level, the performance of the whole company can be evaluated *against* other companies, and it is in this sense that ROI acts as a market control. ROI can also be used *inside* the company, however, at the divisional level, to evaluate the relative performance of one operating division either against similar free-standing businesses or against other internal divisions. For example, one reason for selecting the multidivisional structure is that each division can be evaluated as a self-contained profit center. Consequently, management can directly measure the performance of one division against another. The ability to use this standard was one of the reasons for General Motors' original move to a divisional structure. ROI is a powerful form of market control at the divisional level when managers are concerned with the performance of the whole corporation.

Transfer pricing   Transfer pricing involves establishing the price at which one division will transfer outputs (goods or services) to another—for example, the price at which the oil division will transfer petroleum products to the chemical division, as in Conoco Inc., or the price at which the aerospace division at TRW will transfer research and development knowledge to the vehicle division. There are two basic methods of setting transfer prices. The **market-based method** is the more objective one because the price charged in the external market is the gauge. Competitors' prices are commonly used to set the internal price. In the

cost-based method, on the other hand, prices are set relative to some standard-cost or full-cost method, but the problem lies in determining the markup to be charged to the buying division.

Both methods are used equally, and each has its drawbacks.[14] With the cost-based method, the issue is determining how much profit the supplying division should earn. Internal transfer prices between divisions can be difficult to set, and sometimes divisions fight over prices to be charged, creating additional problems for corporate managers. When the market-based method is used, the price may be set too high because the supplying division may have a cost advantage over its competitors. This doubly penalizes the buying divisions: Not only are they paying more to the selling division than is really necessary, but, as a result, they may have to charge a price in the market for their product that would rob them of sales. The conflicts stemming from transfer price decisions are among the hardest problems that a vertically integrated and related company must face. Unrelated companies, obviously, are spared these difficulties because there are no transactions between divisions.[15]

Problems with market controls   The use of market controls such as ROI and transfer pricing are two prime ways in which strategic managers can evaluate corporate and divisional performance. As this section suggests, however, market control is appropriate only under one condition: when some form of comparison system exists. In comparisons with other companies, market controls such as ROI or stock market price function well. But whether market control can work at the divisional level depends on the skills of managers and their willingness to reach equitable solutions over transfer prices for products. Finally, failure to meet stock price or ROI targets also indicates that corrective action is necessary. It signals the need for corporate reorganization to meet corporate objectives, and such reorganization could involve a change in structure or liquidation and divestiture of businesses.

Output Control

The next most objective method of organizational control is **output control**. When no market system can be devised to allocate and price organizational resources because no system of comparison (between companies or divisions) exists, companies must turn to alternative methods of control. The easiest and cheapest kind of control available it output control. To apply output control, a company must be able to estimate or forecast appropriate targets for its various divisions, departments, or personnel.

Common forms of output controls   We next discuss the most common forms of output controls.

Divisional goals   In creating divisional goals, corporate management is setting the standards against which divisional performance will be judged. Such standards include sales, productivity, growth, and market share goals. Divisional managers use the standards as the basis for designing the organizational structure to meet the objectives. Generally, corporate managers try to raise these standards over time to force divisions to adopt more efficient forms of structure. Goal setting is also used to evaluate divisions' attempts to cooperate for the sake of achieving synergies or to measure the efficiency of scheduling resources among divisions. Thus divisional goals are a way of assessing the alignment of structure with strategy.

Functional goals   Output control at the functional level is achieved by setting goals for each function. For example, sales goals are the typical means through which managers control the sales function. Sales targets are established for the whole function, and then individual personnel are given specific goals, which they in turn are required to achieve. Functions and individuals are then evaluated on the basis of achieving or not achieving their goals, and, of course, compensation is pegged to achievement. As at the divisional level, functional goals are established to encourage development of functional competencies that provide the company with a competitive advantage at the business level. The achievement of these goals is a sign that the company's strategy is working and meeting organizational objectives.

Individual goals   Output control at the individual level is also common. You have already seen how sales compensation is normally based on individual performance. In general, whenever employee performance can be easily monitored and evaluated, output controls are usually appropriate. Thus, for example, piece-rate systems, in which individuals are paid according to exactly how much they produce, are characteristic output control systems. For many jobs, output control is impossible because individuals' performance cannot be evaluated. For example, if individuals work in teams, it is impossible or very expensive to measure their individual outputs. Similarly, if their work is extremely complex, such as research and development, it makes little sense to control people on the basis of how much they produce. In general, to prevent problems, individual goals must be set with the functional strategy in mind.

Problems with output control   The inappropriate use of output control at all levels of the organization can lead to unintended and unfortunate consequences. For instance, the wrong goals may be used to evaluate divisions, functions, or individuals. If short-term measures of performance, such as quantity produced, are used, they can conflict with quality goals. In a classic example of the unintended consequence of output control, an employment placement agency rewarded its workers on the basis of how many people they placed weekly in new jobs. The result was that they directed prospective applicants to job positions for which they were totally unsuited—for instance, they sent accountants to production line jobs. Realizing its mistake, the agency changed the reward system to emphasize how long new employees stayed in their positions after placement.

The moral of the story is clear: Monitoring, evaluating, and rewarding employee behavior requires the right set of controls.

The same is true at the functional and divisional levels. The use of the wrong reward system can have the unintended effect of producing conflict among departments, which start to compete for resources, as happened at TRW. To give another example, F. W. Whyte, a famous researcher, was studying the effect of reward systems on the relation between the production function and packaging and distribution in a manufacturing organization. Management introduced a new output control system for production personnel. Performance rose sharply, and employee salaries increased proportionately. These unskilled workers were now making more than semiskilled workers in packaging and distribution, however. Chaos ensued when the other workers insisted that their salaries be raised above the production people's salaries. Because such raises would have led to high salary levels, management responded by removing the output control system, and all the gains from productivity were forfeited as production workers reverted to their previous performance levels.

We note earlier that clashes over transfer prices may occur at the divisional level. In general, setting across-the-board output targets, such as ROI targets, for divisions can lead to destructive results if divisions single-mindedly try to maximize divisional profits at the expense of the corporate objectives. Moreover, to reach output targets, divisions may start to distort the numbers and engage in strategic manipulation of the figures to make their divisions look good.[16] Thus strategic managers need to design output controls that stimulate divisions to pursue long-run profitability goals at the divisional and corporate levels. In practice, output or market controls must be used in conjunction with bureaucratic (and clan) controls if the right strategic behaviors are to be achieved.

Bureaucratic Control

Market and output controls require that relatively objective, measurable standards exist for monitoring and evaluating performance. When measurable standards are difficult or expensive to develop, and when they are not sufficient to fulfill corporate objectives, managers must turn to bureaucratic control. **Bureaucratic control** is control through the establishment of a comprehensive system of rules and procedures to direct the actions or behavior of divisions, functions, and individuals.[17] In using bureaucratic control, the intention is not to specify the goals, but the best *means* to reach the goals.

Types of bureaucratic control   Types of bureaucratic control include not only impersonal rules and procedures, but also budgets and the standardization of activities. The specific types of bureaucratic controls chosen by an organization to direct employee behavior will be the ones best matched to its particular strategy. Each of the various types of bureaucratic control available to strategic planners is discussed next.

Rules and procedures   Rules and procedures are important sources of control in most organizations. The power of the rule is that it standardizes behavior. If employees follow the rules, then actions or decisions are performed the same way time and time again. The result is predictability and accuracy, which are the goals of all control systems. Rules are essentially guides to action that can be followed in all routine situations. The more unusual the situation, however, the less useful are the rules, for if frequent exceptions have to be made, the rules cease to serve the purpose of a simple guide to action. Nevertheless, much routine business is done through written rules, which specify how different functions are to coordinate their behavior and how people are to perform their tasks and roles. As strategy changes over time, the kinds of rules and procedures a company uses also change. The point is to devise a system of rules and procedures that will accomplish the activities necessary to pursue a particular strategy.

Budgets   Budgets are a second source of bureaucratic control. **Budgets** are essentially collections of rules for allocating resources, principally financial resources.[18] Organizations establish budgets for divisions, functions, and individuals. Then they organize their behavior around the rules the budget establishes.[19] For example, the research and development department normally has a budget for new product development. Managers know that if they spend too much on one project, they will have less to spend on other projects. Hence they modify their behavior to suit the budget. Similarly, sales personnel have budgets that indicate how much money they can spend on advertising or distributing their products. These rules control the behavior of salespeople and lead to decisions about the best way to use scarce resources to meet the company's strategy. The main types of budgets are (1) operating budgets, which specify what the company intends to produce and the resources needed to produce it; (2) sales budgets, which focus on the revenue the company expects to earn from sales per time period; and (3) expense budgets, which specify the resources that managers in various functions have to conduct activities and meet their goals.[20] Merck, the chemical company, is well known for its innovative design and use of budgets in manufacturing to squeeze out costs; by these means it has gained a major cost advantage over competitors.

As with the other means of control, care must be taken to design the budget so that it does not lead to conflict or competition among functions. Such feuding frequently occurs in sales/production relationships. For example, production is often evaluated on its ability to reduce production costs and come in under budget. Therefore production managers try to reduce costs by lengthening production runs, which lowers costs, because less time is spent on changing the production line specifications to turn out other products. Although such action allows production managers to beat their budgets (and get appropriately rewarded), it often hurts the sales function because sales can reduce its costs only by selling more and can sell more only by being able to respond quickly to customer demands. Production personnel will not respond to sales' needs, however, because rescheduling production to satisfy sales customers will increase production costs. The result is that the two functions frequently clash because each follows the needs of its own budget, and the company as a whole suffers.

The budget thus becomes the *goal* to be strived for rather than remains a set of rules that simply guide decision making. Managers are driven into short-term behavior paths to meet the budget, and the performance of the whole organization suffers. Changes in the environment can worsen this problem if management cannot respond creatively to changing circumstances because an inflexible budget has put it in a straightjacket. An advantage of budgets, however, is that they provide the guidelines that let managers monitor their own behavior effectively and enable superiors to measure functional activities accurately. They also provide a natural means through which the company can link functional and divisional activities to the corporate mission. The goals of the organization—for instance, high-quality products or customer service—can be built into the size of the budgets allocated to each function, and such action aligns employee behavior with the company's strategy.

Standardization   Standardization is a potent weapon that organizations can use to influence behaviors.[21] Indeed, to a large degree, bureaucratic control is based on standardization. Rules are a part of the standardization process, but only one part of it. In practice, there are three things that an organization can standardize: its *inputs,* its *throughput activities,* and its *outputs.*

1. *Standardization of inputs.* One way in which an organization can control the behavior of both people and resources is by standardizing the inputs into the organization. This means that the organization screens inputs and allows only those that meet its standards to enter. For example, if employees are the input in question, then one way of standardizing them is to recruit and select only those people who possess the qualities or skills needed by the organization. Arthur Andersen & Company, the accounting firm, is very selective in the way it recruits people into the organization, and so are most prestigious organizations. If the inputs in question are raw materials or component parts, then the same considerations apply. The Japanese are renowned for high quality and precise tolerances they demand from component parts to minimize problems with the product at manufacturing stage.

2. *Standardization of throughput activities.* The aim of standardization of throughputs is to program work activities so that they are done the same way time and time again. The goal is predictability. As already noted, the use of bureaucratic controls such as rules and procedures in one main way in which organizations can standardize throughputs. Another way is to organize production tasks to facilitate the movement of semifinished goods from one stage to the next and to reduce the time and resources needed to produce outputs. The goal is to improve the efficiency with which goods are produced and to find improved ways to control and standardize production. Output controls are important because they provide the means by which management monitors and evaluates the success of its efforts.

3. *Standardization of outputs.* The goal of standardizing outputs is to specify what the performance characteristics of the final product or service should be—what the dimensions or tolerances of the product should conform to, for example. To ensure that their products are standardized companies apply quality control and use various criteria to measure this standardization. One criterion might be the number of goods returned from customers or the number of customer complaints. On production lines, periodic sampling of products can indicate whether they are meeting performance characteristics. Given the intensity of foreign competition, companies are devoting extra resources to standardizing outputs, not just to reduce costs but to retain customers, because companies will retain their customers' business if the product's performance satisfies the customers. For example, if you buy a Japanese car and have no problems with its performance, which car are you most likely to buy next time? That is why companies such as U.S. car makers have been emphasizing the quality dimension of their products. They know how important standardizing outputs is in a competitive market.

McDonald's is an excellent example of a company that uses all three types of standardization. First, the quality of its inputs is standardized through controlling food supplies and franchise holders. Then, at the throughput phase, its food operations are totally standardized, and so, at the output phase, we get uniform burgers and strict output control over employee behavior. In general, fast-food restaurants, convenience stores, and all types of service-oriented chain stores use standardization as a main means of control.

Problems with bureaucratic control   As with other kinds of controls, the use of bureaucratic control is accompanied by problems, and they must be managed if the organization is to avoid unforeseen difficulties. Because bureaucratic control is central to the operation of all large organization structures, these problems are considered in more detail.

First, management must be careful to monitor and evaluate the usefulness of bureaucratic controls over time. Rules lead to standardized, predictable behavior and constrain people's behaviors. Rules are always easier to establish than to get rid of, however, and over time the number of rules an organization uses tends to increase. As new developments lead to additional rules, often the old rules are not discarded, and the company becomes overly bureaucratized. Consequently, the organization and the people in it become inflexible and therefore unable to deal effectively with changing or unusual circumstances. Such inflexibility hampers strategy implementation and makes the company slow to react. Managers must therefore continually be on the alert for reducing the number of rules and procedures necessary to manage the business and should always prefer to discard a rule rather than use a new one.

The second major problem is the cost of using bureaucratic controls. Just as structure is expensive, so is bureaucratic control. To give a dramatic example, according to a recent estimate, 20 percent of the cost of health care is spent on managing the paperwork necessary to satisfy organizational and government health care rules and procedures. This amount runs to billions of dollars a year. Hence reducing the number of rules and procedures to the essential minimum is important. Management frequently neglects this task, however, and often only a change in strategic leadership brings the company back on course.

Because outputs are relatively easy to evaluate but behaviors are not, bureaucratic control costs much more than market or output control. For this reason, output controls are selected first and bureaucratic controls second. They are most useful when combined: For example, in a divisional structure, market controls may be used to monitor divisional performance, and inside the division, bureaucratic controls such as budgets or standardization become appropriate. To prevent short-term profit-seeking behaviors from emerging because of the sole emphasis on output control, it is necessary to apply bureaucratic controls to evaluate other aspects of a division's or function's performance.

When rules are used, authority is delegated to lower levels in the hierarchy. If subordinates are not monitored closely, however, functions or divisions may develop their own goals at the expense of organizational goals. This is the control loss phenomenon, which we discuss in Chapter 10. Care must be taken that the rules corporate headquarters devises minimize control loss problems; otherwise the structure will not work, as managers may start to distort information or even compete with other divisions for resources.

Managers must realize that much of the decision making and work that gets done in the organization gets done not formally through prescribed bureaucratic controls, but through managers themselves meeting and communicating informally. Indeed, in many cases a fourth form of control is being used in the organization—a very subtle form, often taken for granted by people who fail to realize the important effect it has on their behavior. This is control through the development of common norms and values.

Clan Control and Culture

Clan control is control through the establishment of an internal system of organizational norms and values.[22] The goal of clan control is self-control: Individuals feel responsible for working to the best of their ability in the interests of the organization. With clan control, employees are not controlled by some external system of constraint, such as direct supervision, outputs, or rules and procedures. Rather, employees are said to internalize the norms and values of the organization and make them part of their own value system.[23] Just as we internalize the values of society—for instance, "thou shalt not steal"—so in organizations employees internalize the expectations of the organization and act in terms of them. The value of clan control for an organization is its ability to specify the beliefs, norms, and values that govern employee behavior.[24] Wal-Mart is a good example of a company that actively promotes organizational norms and values. Its employees are called "associates" and are encouraged to take initiative as partners in the organization.

Clan control is initially expensive to use because it requires a great amount of time and resources to generate norms and values strong enough to control employee behavior. Consequently, clan control is used particularly in small companies or in departments staffed by professional employees, who, through their training, have already developed a professional orientation toward their job. In fact, clan control is used more often in conjunction with standardization of inputs. In other words, the first company recruits experts or professionals, and then it allows them to develop their own codes of behavior to guide their work activities. That is why in professional contexts, such as research and development teams, you find a common code of dress or language in the group. For example, clan control is most likely to thrive in a matrix structure or in an organization such as Apple Computer, in which employees were guided by the common vision of creating a desk-top computer, or in IBM, where a commitment to service is a major value.

Much of the most recent research, however, does not talk about clan control, but rather about the development of an organizational culture for managing a company's strategy. The terms *clan control* and *culture* are similar and are used interchangeably in the following discussion.

Culture refers to that specific collection of norms, standards, and values that are shared by members of an organization and affect the way an organization does business.[25] The principal difference between the way this concept controls behavior and, say, the organization's mission statement, is that culture is implicit in the way people act in the organization; it does not need to be written to be understood. Socialization is the term used to describe how people learn organizational culture. Through socialization, people internalize the norms and values of the culture and learn to act like existing personnel.[26] Control through culture is so powerful because, once these values are internalized, they become a part of the individual, and the individual follows organizational values without thinking about them. As shown in Figure 11.4, culture may be transmitted in the organization by several means.

FIGURE 11.4   **Ways of transmitting culture**

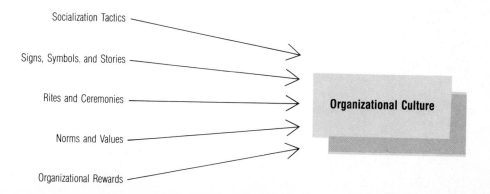

Socialization Tactics

Signs, Symbols, and Stories

Rites and Ceremonies

Norms and Values

Organizational Rewards

Organizational Culture

Traits of strong corporate cultures   Several scholars in the field have tried to uncover the common traits that strong corporate cultures share and to find out whether there is a particular set of values that dominates strong cultures but is missing from the weak. Perhaps the best-known attempt is T. J. Peters and R. H. Waterman's account of the norms and values characteristic of successful organizations and their cultures.[27] They argue that successful organizations show three common value sets. First, successful companies have values promoting a *bias for action*. The emphasis is on autonomy and entrepreneurship, and employees are encouraged to take risks—for example, to create new products, even though there is no assurance that these products will be winners. Managers are closely involved in the day-to-day operations of the company and do not simply make strategic decisions isolated in some "ivory tower," and employees have a "hands-on, value-driven approach."

The second set of values stems from the *nature of the organization's mission*. The company must stick with what it does best and maintain control over its core activities. A company can easily get side-tracked into pursuing activities outside its area of expertise just because they seem to promise a quick return. Management should cultivate values so that a company "sticks to the knitting," which means staying with the businesses it knows best. A company must also establish close relations with the customer as a way of improving its competitive position. After all, who knows better about a company's performance than those who use its products or services? By emphasizing customer-oriented values, organizations are able to learn customer needs and improve their ability to develop products and services customers desire. All these management values are strongly represented in companies such as IBM, Hewlett-Packard, and Toyota that are sure of their mission and take constant steps to maintain it.

The third set of values bear on *how to operate the organization*. A company should try to establish an organizational design that will motivate employees to do their best. Inherent in this is the belief that productivity is obtained through people and that respect for the individual is the primary means by which a company can create the right atmosphere for productive behavior. As William Ouchi has noted, a similar philosophy pervades the culture of Japanese companies.[28] Many U.S. companies pay this kind of attention to their employees—for instance, Kodak, Procter & Gamble, and Levi Strauss. An emphasis on entrepreneurship and respect for the employee leads to establishing a structure that gives employees the latitude to make decisions and motivates them to succeed. Because a simple structure and a lean staff best fit this situation, the organization should be designed with only the number of managers and hierarchical levels that are necessary to get the job done. The organization should also be sufficiently decentralized to permit employee participation but centralized enough for management to make sure that the company pursues its strategic mission and that cultural values are followed.

These three main sets of values are at the heart of an organization's culture, and management transmits and maintains them through stories, myths, symbols, and socialization. Pursuing these values is not enough to ensure organizational success, however, and over time cultural values should change to suit the environment in which the company is operating. A company needs to establish the values that are good for it and base its organizational structure and control system on them. When that is accomplished, only those people who fit the values are recruited into the organization, and, through training, they become a part of the organization's culture. Thus the types of control systems chosen should reinforce and build on one another in a cohesive way. Although, as we note earlier, culture is difficult and expensive to develop, it is a powerful form of control. Nevertheless, it is not free of problems, and we now consider its debit side.

Problems with clan control The development of unique systems of norms and values at the divisional and functional levels can lead to communications problems across divisions and functions. Thus when clan control is used, care must be taken that integration does not suffer because of such failures in communication. Moreover, clan control is not suitable where rapid growth or changes in the environment do not provide a context within which stable norms and values can develop. A classic case of the failure of clan control under these conditions is People Express, which started off with a system based on a team structure, where clan control was used as the main means of getting the work done. As the company grew quickly through its takeover of other airlines and rapid increase in flights, it could not maintain control of its operations, and its costs rose dramatically.

Clan control is also not appropriate when employee turnover is high because there is no time to develop a stable system of values and the costs rise dramatically with increased turnover. Consequently, it is of little use in most production line systems. The Japanese, however, can use clan control in their factories because turnover there is typically low, and if lifetime employment exists, turnover is negligible.

Finally, organizational culture cannot by itself control organizational performance and make structure work. It must be backed by output and bureaucratic controls and matched to a reward system so that employees will in fact cultivate organizational norms and values and modify their behavior to organizational objectives. Because of the expense involved, many companies abandon culture in favor of tight objective control and close supervision of behavior.

Summary: Types of Control Systems

Choosing a control system to match the firm's strategy and structure offers management a number of important challenges. Management must select controls that provide a framework to accurately monitor, measure, and evaluate the standards or targets organizations choose to achieve their strategic objectives at step 1 in the control process. Market and output controls are the cheapest and easiest to use, but they must be backed up with bureaucratic and clan control to ensure that the firm is achieving its goals in the most efficient way possible. In general, these controls should reinforce one another, and care must be taken to ensure that they do not result in unforeseen consequences such as competition between functions, divisions, and individuals.

11.8 STRATEGIC REWARD SYSTEMS

A final way in which organizations attempt to control employee behavior is by linking reward systems to their control systems.[29] An organization must decide which behaviors it wishes to reward, adopt a control system to measure these behaviors, and then link the reward structure to them. How to relate rewards to performance is a crucial strategic decision because it affects the way managers and employees at all levels in the organization behave. For example, in designing a pay system for salespeople, the choice would be whether to employ salespeople on the basis of straight salary or salary plus a bonus based on how much is sold. Neiman-Marcus, the luxury retailer, pays employees a straight salary because it wants to encourage high-quality service but discourage hard sell. Thus there are no incentives based on quantity sold. On the other hand, the pay system for rewarding car salespeople typically contains a high bonus for the number of cars sold.

What behaviors to reward is therefore an important decision, tied closely to a company's business-level strategy, as we discuss in Chapter 12. Next we consider the types of reward systems available to strategic managers.[30] Generally, reward systems are found at the individual and group or total organizational levels. Often these systems are used in combination; for example, merit raises at the individual level may be accompanied by a bonus based on divisional or plant performance. Within each type, several forms of reward systems are available.

Individual Reward Systems

Piecework plans   Piecework plans are used when outputs can be objectively measured. Essentially, employees are paid on the basis of some set amount for each unit of output produced. Piecework plans are most commonly used for employees working on production lines, where individuals work alone and their performance can be directly measured. Because this system encourages quantity rather than quality, the company normally applies stringent quality controls to ensure that the quality is acceptable.

Commission systems   Commission systems resemble piecework systems, except that they are normally tied not to what is produced but to how much is sold. Thus they are most commonly found in sales situations. Often the salaries of salespeople are based principally on commission to encourage superior performance. Thus first-rate salespeople can earn more than $1 million per year.

Bonus plans   Bonus plans at the individual level generally reward the performance of a company's key individuals, such as the CEO or senior vice presidents. The performance of these people is visible to the organization as a whole and to stakeholders such as shareholders. Consequently, there is a strong rationale for paying these individuals according to some measure of functional or divisional performance. A company must proceed carefully, however, if it is to avoid problems such as emphasis on short-run rather than long-term objectives. For example, paying bonuses based on quarterly or yearly ROI rather than on five-year growth can have a markedly different effect on the way strategic managers behave.

Group and Organizational   TRW
Reward Systems

Group and organizational reward systems provide additional ways in which companies can relate pay to performance. In general, the problem with these systems is that the relationship is less direct and more difficult to measure than in the case of individually based systems. Consequently, they are viewed as less motivating. The most common reward systems at these levels involve group bonuses, profit sharing, employee stock options, and organization bonuses.

Group-based bonus systems   Sometimes a company can establish project teams, or work groups, that perform all the operations needed to turn out a product or provide a service. This arrangement makes it possible to measure group performance and offer rewards on the basis of group productivity. The system can be highly motivating because employees are allowed to develop the best work procedures for doing the job and are responsible for improving their own productivity. For example, Wal-Mart supports a group bonus plan based on controlling shrinkage (i.e., employee theft).

Profit-sharing systems   Profit-sharing plans are designed to reward employees on the basis of the profit a company earns in any one time period. Such plans encourage employees to take a broad view of their activities and feel connected with the company as a whole. Wal-Mart uses this method as well to develop its organizational culture.

Employee stock option systems   Rather than reward employees on the basis of short-term profits, a company sometimes allows them to buy its shares at below-market prices, heightening employee motivation. As shareholders, the employees will focus not only on short-term profits, but also on long-term capital appreciation, for they are now the company's owners. Over time, if enough employees participate, they can control a substantial stock holding, as did the employees of Eastern Airlines, and thus become vitally interested in the company's performance.

Organization bonus systems   Profit is not the only basis on which a company can reward organization-wide performance. Rewards are also commonly based on cost savings, quality increases, or production increases obtained in the last time period. Because these systems usually require that outputs be measured accurately, they are most common in production line organizations or in service companies, where it is possible to cost out the price of the services of personnel. The systems are mainly a back-up to other forms of pay systems. In rare situations, however, such as at The Lincoln Electric Company, a company renowned for the success of its cost-savings group plan, they become the principal means of control.

Control through organizational reward systems complements all the other forms of control we discuss in this chapter. The reward systems help determine how output or clan control, for example, will work. Rewards act as the oil for making a control system function effectively. To ensure that the right strategic behaviors are being rewarded, rewards should be closely linked to an organization's strategy. Moreover, they should be so designed that they do not lead to conflicts among divisions, functions, or individuals.

11.9 SUMMARY OF CHAPTER

The purpose of this chapter is to discuss the types of integrating mechanisms and control systems available to strategic planners to influence organizational performance. Companies must use more complex integrating mechanisms when they adopt more complex structures. They must also select the combination of controls that will make the structure work and meet the company's strategic objectives. Companies may use a variety of controls because different types of controls may suit different divisions or functions or different types of employees.

The essential task for companies is to select controls that are consistent with one another and also match the organizational structure. Companies with a high level of differentiation and integration require a more complex set of controls than those with a low degree of differentiation and integration. For example, as we discuss in the opening incident about TRW, controls should spur divisions to cooperate rather than compete. The control system has to provide rewards for both cooperation based on establishing a fair price for each division's technological know-how and sharing knowledge (such as group bonus plans). In the case of simple functional structures, on the other hand, output controls can monitor each function's performance separately from the others, making control much easier to achieve. In the next chapter, we consider in detail how structure and control should be jointly matched to the company's corporate- and business-level strategies.

This chapter makes the following main points:

1.   The more complex the company and the higher its level of differentiation, the higher is the level of integration needed to manage its structure.

2. The kinds of integrating mechanisms available to a company range from direct contact to matrix structure. The more complex the mechanism, the greater are the costs of using it. A company should take care to match these mechanisms to its strategic needs.

3. Strategic control is the process of setting targets, monitoring, evaluating, and rewarding organizational performance.

4. Control takes place at all levels in the organization: corporate, divisional, functional, and individual.

5. Effective control systems are flexible, accurate, and able to provide quick feedback to strategic planners.

6. There are four steps to designing an effective control system: establishing performance standards, creating measuring systems, comparing performance against targets, and evaluating the result taking corrective action.

7. Many kinds of performance standards are available for strategy implementation. The kinds of measures managers choose affect the way a company operates.

8. Control systems range from those directed at measuring outputs or productivity to those measuring behaviors or actions.

9. The three main forms of market control are stock market price, return on investment, and transfer pricing.

10. Output control establishes goals for divisions, functions, and individuals. It can be used only when outputs can be objectively measured.

11. Bureaucratic control is used to control behaviors when it is impossible to measure outputs. The main forms of bureaucratic control are rules and procedures, budgets, and standardization.

12. When neither outputs nor behaviors can be monitored and evaluated, organizations turn to clan control. Clan control is control through a system of norms and values that individuals internalize as they are socialized into the organization. Organizational culture is a collection of the norms and values that govern the way in which people act and behave inside the organization.

13. An organization's reward systems constitute the final form of control. A company links its reward systems to organizational goals and objectives to provide an incentive for employees to perform well.

14. Organizations use all these forms of controls simultaneously. Management must select and combine those that are consistent with each other and with the strategy and structure of the organization.

Discussion Questions

1. What are the relationships among differentiation, integration, and strategic control systems? Why are these relationships important?

2. For each of the structures we discuss in Chapter 10, outline the integrating mechanisms and control systems most suitable for matching them.

3. What kinds of integration and control systems does your (a) business school and (b) university use to operate its structure and control personnel?

4. List the kinds of integration and control systems you would be likely to find in (a) a small manufacturing company, (b) a chain store, (c) a gourmet restaurant, and (d) a big five accounting firm.

Endnotes

1. Robert Sheehan, "Thompson Ramo Wooldridge: Two Wings in Space," *Fortune,* February 1963, p. 95.

2. TRW Inc. Annual Report, 1990.

3. "TRW Leads a Revolution in Managing Technology," *Business Week,* November 15, 1982, p. 124.

4. P. R. Lawrence and J. Lorsch, *Organization and Environment* (Homewood, Ill.: Irwin, 1967), pp. 50–55.

5. J. R. Galbraith, *Designing Complex Organizations* (Reading, Mass.: Addison-Wesley, 1977), Ch. 1. J. R. Galbraith and R. K. Kazanjian, *Strategy Implementation: Structure, System, and Process* (St. Paul, Minn.: West, 1986), Ch. 7.

6. Henry Mintzberg, *The Nature of Managerial Work* (Englewood Cliffs, N.J.: Prentice-Hall, 1973), Ch. 10.

7. Lawrence and Lorsch, *Organization and Environment,* p. 55.

8. W. G. Ouchi, "The Transmission of Control Through Organizational Hierarchy," *Academy of Management Journal,* 21 (1978), 173–192. W. H. Newman, *Constructive Control* (Englewood Cliffs, N.J.: Prentice-Hall, 1975.

9. K. A. Merchant, *Control in Business Organizations* (Marshfield, Mass.: Pitman, 1985). E. E. Lawler III and J. G. Rhodes, *Information and Control in Organizations* (Pacific Palisades, Calif.: Goodyear, 1976).

10. J. P. Campbell, "On the Nature of Organizational Effectiveness," in R. S. Goodman and J. M. Pennings (eds.) *New Perspectives on Organizational Effectiveness* (San Francisco: Jossey-Bass, 1977), pp. 13–55.

11. T. Connolly, E. J. Conlon, and S. J. Deutsch, "Organizational Effectiveness: A Multiple-Constituency Approach," *Academy of Management Review,* 5 (1980), 211–217: R. E. Quinn and J. Rohrbaugh, "A Spatial Model of Effectiveness Criteria: Towards a Competing Values Approach to Organizational Analysis," *Management Science,* 29 (1983), 33–51.

12. W. G. Ouchi, "The Relationship Between Organizational Structure and Organizational Control," *Administrative Science Quarterly,* 22 (1977), 95–113.

13. J. D. Thompson, *Organizations in Action* (New York: McGraw-Hill, 1967), Ch. 10. W. G. Ouchi, "A Conceptual Framework for the Design of Organizational Control Systems," *Management Science,* 25 (1979), 833–848.

14. R. F. Vancil, *Decentralization: Managerial Ambiguity by Design* (Homewood, Ill.: Dow-Jones Irwin, 1978).

15. R. G. Eccles, *The Transfer Pacing Problem* (Lexington, Mass.: Lexington Books, 1985), Ch. 2.

16. E. Flamholtz, "Organizational Control Systems as a Managerial Tool," *California Management Review* (Winter 1979), 50–58.

17. O. E. Williamson, *Markets and Hierarchies* (New York: Free Press, 1975). W. G. Ouchi, "Markets, Bureaucracies, and Clans," *Administrative Science Quarterly,* 25 (1980), 129–141.

18. P. Lorange, *Corporate Planning* (Englewood Cliffs, N. J.: Prentice-Hall, 1980). G. A. Welsch, *Budgeting: Profit Planning and Control,* 4th ed. (Englewood Cliffs, N.J.: Prentice-Hall, 1976).

19. C. S. Trapani, "Six Critical Areas in the Budgeting Process," *Management Accounting,* 64 (1982), 52–58.

20. Trapani, "Six Critical Areas," p. 54.

21. H. Mintzberg, *The Structuring of Organizations* (Englewood Cliffs, N.J.: Prentice-Hall, 1979), pp. 5–9.

22. Ouchi, "Markets, Bureaucracies, and Clans," p. 130.

23. G. R. Jones, "Socialization Tactics, Self-Efficacy, and Newcomers' Adjustments to Organizations," *Academy of Management Journal,* 29 (1986), 262–279.

24. M. R. Louis, "Surprise and Sensemaking: What Newcomers Experience in Entering Unfamiliar Settings," *Administrative Science Quarterly,* 25 (1980), 226–251.

25. L. Smircich, "Concepts of Culture and Organizational Analysis," *Administrative Science Quarterly,* 28 (1983), 339–358.

26. J. Van Maanen and E. H. Schein, "Towards a Theory of Organizational Socialization," in B. M. Staw (ed.), *Research in Organizational Behavior* (Greenwich, Conn.: JAI Press, 1979), pp. 1, 209–264.

27. T. J. Peters and R. H. Waterman, *In Search of Excellence: Lessons from America's Best-Run Companies* (New York: Harper & Row, 1982).

28. W. G. Ouchi, *Theory Z. How American Business Can Meet the Japanese Challenge* (Reading, Mass.: Addison-Wesley, 1981).

29. E. E. Lawler III, *Motivation in Work Organizations* (Monterey, Calif.: Brooks/Cole, 1973). Galbraith and Kazanjian, *Strategy Implementation,* Ch. 6.

30. E. E. Lawler III, "The Design of Effective Reward Systems," in J. W. Lorsch (ed.), *Handbook of Organizational Behavior* (Englewood Cliffs, N.J.: Prentice-Hall, 1987), pp. 386–422. R. Mathis and J. Jackson, *Personnel,* 2nd ed. (St. Paul, Minn.: West, 1979), p. 456.

Chapter 12

MATCHING
STRUCTURE AND
CONTROL TO
STRATEGY

12.1 OPENING INCIDENT: TEXAS INSTRUMENTS

Texas Instruments (TI) was started by two entrepreneurs, Clarence Karcher and Eugene McDermott, who invented the technique of using sound waves to map underground strata. This technique became the dominant way for oil companies to prospect for oil, and its applications for sonar and radar in the military became evident. The real breakthrough for TI, however, came in the 1950s, when it pioneered transistors small enough for use in radios and developed silicon transistors for use in military operations. Miniaturization of electronic circuits became TI's chief competitive advantage and allowed the company to grow rapidly, even when companies such as General Electric and RCA entered the market. It solidified its competitive advantage by emphasizing efficiency, and it emerged as the lowest-cost producer of these circuits.[1]

To maintain its technological edge, TI adopted a decentralized matrix structure, so that product and technological knowledge could be shared across its many divisions. Divisional sharing gave TI a leading edge in two fast-growing and highly profitable businesses: computers and consumer electronics. In controlling the matrix, the president of TI at this time, Patrick E. Haggerty, decentralized decision making to the divisional level. He made little attempt to interfere in the various divisions' business-level strategies. He saw the role of the corporate center as one of managing a portfolio of investments and instituted a strict set of financial controls to evaluate divisional performance. Under his leadership, and then under J. Fred Bucy's, the company prospered and grew.[2] By 1983, however, the company was experiencing problems.

TI faced substantial competition from Japanese companies that had imitated many of TI's products and technical innovations, while usurping its cost-leadership position. In addition, the company received a major blow to its morale when its consumer products business reported record losses and plunged TI into its first quarterly loss ever. Bucy, in a statement to stockholders, explained the company's downturn: "TI is suffering from the problems of the company's success. As it passes through phases of corporate life, it must accommodate its organization and structures to these phases as it grows. This failure to adjust affected operating and strategic structures."[3]

TI realized that it had to alter its structure and control system as its competitive position changed over time. To restore profitability, TI abandoned its matrix structure because it had begun to fragment both people and resources, making it almost impossible for management to exert effective control over divisional operations. TI moved to a more centralized, divisional structure, where control could be exercised more easily. In the new structure, divisional managers were evaluated on their division's performance as a profit center. In addition, corporate-level personnel designed new control systems to promote the sharing of information and knowledge across divisions more efficiently and to promote synergies. In essence, TI went to a strategic business unit (SBU) structure, which, when coupled with the right mix of integrating mechanisms and divisional controls, put the company back on track.

TI realized that its structure had to match its business- and corporate-level strategy. It recognized, too, that as changes in the competitive environment caused changes in its strategy, management would have to keep moving quickly to implement the structure and control system best suited to its objectives.

12.2 OVERVIEW

At Texas Instruments, strategic managers moved to implement the right mix of structure and control systems to allow the company to deal with changes in its strategy and the competitive environment. In this chapter, we discuss how strategic choice at the corporate, business, and functional levels affects the choice of structure and control systems—in other words, how to match different forms of structure and control to strategy. As we emphasize in Chapter 1, the issue facing strategic managers is to match strategy formulation with strategy implementation. All the tools of strategy formulation and implementation are discussed in previous chapters. Now we put the two sides of the equation together and examine the issues involved in greater detail.

First, we consider how functional-level strategy affects structure and control and then how a company's choice of generic business-level strategy affects the choice of structure and control for implementing the strategy. Next, we take up the special problems that different kinds of corporate-level strategy pose for strategic managers in designing a structure and note how changes in corporate-level strategy over time affect the form of structure and control systems adopted by a company, paying particular attention to ways of implementing international strategy. Finally, we examine the problems relating to the two entry strategies we discussed in Chapter 9: managing mergers and acquisitions and providing the setting that encourages internal venturing. By the end of this chapter, you will understand why Texas Instruments and all companies go through a series of transitions in structure and control as they attempt to deal with the changing nature of their strategy and environment.

12.3 STRUCTURE AND CONTROL AT THE FUNCTIONAL LEVEL

In Chapter 4, in our discussion of strategy formulation at the functional level, we emphasize that a company must develop distinctive competencies to give it a competitive advantage. We discuss how different competencies could be developed in each function and then, in Chapter 5, we note that at the business level different generic competitive strategies require the development of different types of distinctive competencies. In this section, we consider how a company can create a structure and control system that permit the development of various distinctive functional competencies or skills.

Decisions at the functional level fall into two categories: choices about the level of vertical differentiation and choices about monitoring and evaluation systems. (Choices about horizontal differentiation are not relevant here because we are considering each function individually.) The choices made depend on the distinctive competence that a company is pursuing.

Manufacturing

In manufacturing, functional strategy usually centers on reducing production costs. A company must create an organizational setting in which managers can learn from experience curve effects how to economize on costs. To move down the experience curve quickly, the company must exercise tight control over work activities and employees, so that it can squeeze out costs wherever possible. This is why manufacturing generally has the tallest structure of all the functions.

Besides supervision from the hierarchy, however, manufacturing also relies on bureaucratic and output controls to reduce costs. Standardization is frequently used to squeeze out costs. For example, human inputs are standardized through the recruitment and training of personnel, the work process is standardized or programmed to reduce costs, and quality control is used to make sure that outputs are being produced correctly. In addition, managers are closely monitored and controlled through output control and production budgets.

Finally, in some manufacturing settings, especially those run on Japanese-style principles, companies attempt to develop a production culture. Employees are given benefits that normally only management receives, quality control circles are created to exchange information and suggestions about problems and work procedures, and workers share in the increases in output through some form of bonus system. The aim is to match structure and control so that they jointly create a low-cost competence and the function achieves its strategy.

Research and Development

In contrast, the functional strategy for a research and development department is to develop a technological distinctive competence. Consequently, the structure should produce a setting in which personnel can develop innovative products or processes. In practice, research and development departments have flatter structures than any other function in an organization (that is, they usually have the fewest number of hierarchical levels relative to their size). Flatter structures give research and development personnel the freedom and autonomy to be innovative. Furthermore, because evaluating research and development personnel is difficult, adding layers of hierarchy would waste resources.[4]

Controlling the research and development function is somewhat problematical because it is difficult to monitor employee behavior. Using output controls for the purpose is difficult and expensive. The solution, therefore, is to use input control and recruit only highly trained employees. Research and development departments also rely heavily on small teams and clan control to reinforce innovation, and a professional culture emerges to control employee behavior.

Sales

Like research and development, the sales function usually has a flat structure. Most commonly, three hierarchical levels—sales director, regional or product sales managers, and individual salespeople—can accommodate even large sales forces. Flat structures are possible because the organization does not depend on direct supervision for control. Salespeople's activities are often complex; moreover, because they are dispersed in the field, these employees are difficult to monitor. Rather than depend on the hierarchy, the sales function usually implements output and behavioral controls. These controls take the form of specific sales goals as well as detailed reports that salespeople must file describing their interactions with customers.[5] Supervisors can then review salespeoples's performance easily.

Similar considerations apply to the other functions, such as accounting, finance, engineering, or personnel. Managers must select the right combination of structure and control mechanisms to achieve functional objectives. Table 12.1 lists the appropriate choices of structure and control for all the principal organizational functions.

TABLE 12.1   **Structure and control at the functional level**

Function	Type of structure	Main type of control
Production	Tall/centralized	Output control (e.g., cost targets)
Materials management	Flat/centralized	Output control (e.g., inventory and purchasing targets)
Research and development	Flat/decentralized	Clan control (e.g., norms, values, and culture)
Sales	Flat/decentralized	Output control (e.g., sales targets)
Accounting/finance	Tall/decentralized	Bureaucratic control (e.g., budgets)
Human resources	Flat/centralized	Bureaucratic control (e.g., standardization)

12.4 STRUCTURE AND CONTROL AT THE BUSINESS LEVEL

Generic Business-Level Strategies

Designing the right mix of structure and control at the business level is a continuation of designing a company's functional departments. Having implemented the right structure and control system for each individual function, the company must then implement the organizational arrangements so that all the functions can be managed together to achieve business-level strategy objectives. Because the focus is on managing interfunctional relationships, the choice of *horizontal differentiation* (division of organizational activities) and *integration* for achieving business-level strategies becomes very important.[6] Control systems must also be selected with the monitoring and evaluating of interfunctional activities in mind. Table 12.2 summarizes the appropriate organizational structure and control systems that companies can use when following a low-cost, differentiation, or focused strategy.

Cost-leadership strategy and structure   The aim of the cost-leadership strategy is to make the company pursuing it the lowest-cost producer in the market.[7] At the business level, this means reducing costs not just in production, but across all functions in the organization—including research and development and sales and marketing.

If a company is following a cost-leadership strategy, its research and development efforts probably focus on process engineering rather than on the more expensive product research, which carries no guarantee of success. In other words, the company stresses research that lowers the cost of making existing

TABLE 12.2   Generic strategy, structure, and control

	Strategy		
	Cost leadership	Differentiation	Focus
Appropriate structure	Functional or product	Product or matrix	Functional
Integrating mechanisms	Center on manufacturing	Center on R&D or marketing	Center on product or customer
Output control	Great use (e.g., cost control)	Some use (e.g., quality goals)	Some use (e.g., cost and quality)
Bureaucratic control	Some use (e.g., budgets, standardization)	Great use (e.g., rules, budgets)	Some use (e.g., budgets)
Clan control	Little use (e.g., quality control circles)	Great use (e.g., norms and culture)	Great use (e.g., norms and culture)

products. Similarly, the company tries to decrease the cost of sales and marketing by offering a standard product to a mass market rather than by offering different products aimed at different market segments.[8]

To implement such a strategy, the cost leader chooses the simplest structure—the one with the lowest level of differentiation that can meet the needs of the strategy. Simple structures are the least expensive to operate and thus match the needs of the low-cost strategy. In practice, the structure chosen is normally a functional or perhaps a product structure. Each of these structures allows manufacturing activities to be programmed or standardized, a major source of cost saving.[9] The two structures are also relatively easy to manage because they require a low degree of integration. The company does not need to coordinate as many new products or innovations and so avoids the expense of creating task forces or teams. Seagate Technology, producer of hard disks, is an example of a cost leader that continually streamlines its structure to maintain a competitive advantage. It periodically reduces levels in the hierarchy and institutes strict production controls to minimize costs. This process puts it substantially ahead of its Japanese competitors.

To reduce costs, cost-leadership companies want to use the cheapest and easiest forms of control available—output controls. For each function, a company adopts output controls that allow it to monitor and evaluate functional performance closely, so that waste is curtailed and cost savings maximized. In the production function, for example, the company imposes tight controls and stresses meeting budgets based on production or cost targets.[10] In research and development, too, the emphasis falls on the bottom line. Research and development personnel concerned with demonstrating their contribution to saving costs may focus their efforts on improving process technology, where actual savings are calculable. Heinz Foods clearly illustrates such efforts. In following a cost-leadership strategy, it places enormous emphasis on production improvements that can reduce the cost of a can of beans. Like manufacturing and research and development, the sales function is closely monitored, and sales targets are usually challenging. Cost-leadership companies, however, are likely to reward employees by generous incentive and bonus schemes to encourage high performance. Often their culture is based on values that emphasize the bottom line, such as in Heinz, Lincoln Electric, and PepsiCo.

In short, pursuing a successful cost-leadership strategy requires close attention to the design of structure and control to economize on costs. Managers, rules, and organizational control mechanisms cost money, and low-cost companies must try to economize when implementing their structures. When a company's competitive advantage depends on achieving and maintaining a low-cost advantage, adopting the right organizational arrangements is vital.

Differentiation strategy and structure   To pursue a differentiation strategy, a company must develop a distinctive competence in a function such as research and development or marketing and sales. To make its product unique in the eyes of the customer, the differentiated company must design its structure and control systems around the *particular source* of its competitive advantage.[11] As a result, the differentiated company usually employs a more complex structure—that is, a structure with a higher level of differentiation and integration than the cost leader.

For example, suppose the differentiator's strength lies in technological competence; the company has the cutting-edge technology. In this case, the company's structure and control systems should be designed around the research and development function. Implementing a *matrix structure,* as Texas Instruments and TRW have done, helps develop technological innovations, for it allows for the cross-fertilization of ideas among functions. Integrating mechanisms, such as tasks forces and teams, help transfer knowledge among functions and are designed around the research and development function. For example, sales, marketing, and production targets are geared to research and development goals, marketing devises advertising programs that focus on technological possibilities, and salespeople are evaluated on their understanding of new product characteristics and their ability to inform potential customers about them. Stringent sales targets are unlikely to be set in this situation because the goal is quality of service.

When the source of the differentiator's advantage is in the breadth of its product range or the number of different market segments it serves, a different structure is required. In such cases, companies design a structure around their products, and thus a *product* or *geographical* structure fits best. Consequently, if a company manufactures a distinctive range of products, research and development or sales are organized by product, and task forces and teams have a product, not a research orientation. If designed around types of customers, the company may have a structure based on regional needs or even on different types of customers such as businesses, individual consumers, or the government. For example, both Compaq and Rockwell have recently reorganized their structures to concentrate on the needs of specific customers or regions to gain a competitive advantage.

The control systems used to match the structure can also be geared to the company's distinctive competence. For the differentiator, it is important that the various functions do not pull in different directions; indeed, cooperation among the various functions is vital. But when functions work together, output controls become much harder to use. In general, it is much more difficult to measure the performance of people in different functions when they are engaged in cooperative efforts. As a result, a company must rely more on behavior controls and clan control when pursuing a strategy of differentiation. That is why companies pursuing a differentiation strategy often have a markedly different kind of culture than those pursuing a low-cost strategy. Because the quality of human resources is often the source of differentiation—good scientists, designers, or marketing people—these organizations have a culture based on professionalism or collegiality, a culture that emphasizes the distinctiveness of the human resource rather than the high pressure of the bottom line.[12] Hewlett-Packard, IBM, and Frito-Lay, Inc., all of which emphasize some kind of distinctive competence, exemplify firms with professional cultures.

The structure and control system of the differentiator are more expensive than the cost leader's, but the benefits are also greater if companies reap the rewards of a premium price.

Focus strategy and structure   In Chapter 5, we define a focus strategy as one that was directed at a particular customer segment. A company focuses on a product or range of products directed at one sort of customer or region. This strategy tends to have higher production costs than the other two strategies because output levels are lower, making it harder to obtain substantial economies of scale. As a result, a focused company must exercise cost control. On the other hand, because some attribute of its product usually gives the focused company its unique advantage—possibly its ability to provide customers with high-quality, personalized service—a focused company has to develop a unique competence. For both these reasons, the structure and control system adopted by the focused company have to be inexpensive to operate but flexible enough to allow a distinctive competence to emerge.

The focused company normally adopts a functional structure to meet these needs. This structure is appropriate because it is complex enough to manage the activities necessary to service the needs of the market segment or produce a narrow range of products. At the same time, a functional structure is also relatively easy to control, and there is less need for complex, expensive integrating mechanisms. This structure permits more personal control and flexibility than the other two, and so reduces the costs of control while fostering the development of a distinctive competence.[13] Given its small size, a focused company can rely less on bureaucratic control and more on clan control and culture, which is vital to the development of a service competence. Although output controls need to be used in production and sales, this form of control, as with clan control, is inexpensive in a small organization.

The combination of functional structure and low cost of control help offset the higher costs of production while still allowing the firm to develop unique strengths. It is little wonder, then, that there are so many focused companies. Additionally, because a focused company's competitive advantage is often based on personalized service, the flexibility of this kind of structure allows it to respond quickly to customer needs and change its products in response to customer requests. The structure, then, backs up the strategy and helps the firm develop and maintain its distinctive competence.

Au Bon Pain Company, Inc., a fast-food chain specializing in fancy coffees and baked goods such as croissants, is a good example of a company that recognized the need to design a structure and control system to match a focused strategy aimed at an upscale customer group. To encourage franchises to perform highly and satisfy customer needs, it decentralized control to each franchise, making each a self-contained functional unit. Then, through a profit-sharing plan that rewarded cost cutting and quality, it gave each franchise manager the incentive to create a set of control arrangements that minimized costs but maximized quality of service. The result was a strategy-structure fit that led to a massive increase in franchise profits.

Although research corroborates that these are appropriate forms of structure and control associated with different kinds of strategies, these forms are ideals. Many companies do not use the right forms. Quite likely, they are not as successful or may not survive as long as those that do match their strategy, structure, and control systems.[14] In Chapter 13, we discuss some of the problems that companies may encounter when they attempt to change their structures or strategies, and we also examine the reasons that their structures do not match their strategies.

Business Strategies and the Industry Life Cycle

Although the choice of generic strategy is at the heart of a company's business-level strategy, the stage of the industry life cycle that the company is in also influences its business strategy. Table 12.3 shows the relationship between industry life cycle strategy and form of organizational structure and control.

TABLE 12.3   **Life cycle strategy and structure and control**

Life cycle strategy	Appropriate structure	Integrating mechanisms	Type of control		
			Output	Bureaucratic	Clan
Embryonic	Simple	Personal and group meetings	Little use	Little use (e.g., sales targets)	Great use (e.g., entrepreneurial culture)
Growth	Functional, product, or matrix	Liaison roles task forces and teams (e.g., product innovation committee)	Little use	Little use	Little use
Shakeout	Product or matrix (depends on generic strategy)	Fully developed teams and task forces (e.g., product development committee)	Some to great use	Some to great use (depends on generic strategy)	Some to great use
Maturity	Product/functional	Teams and task forces (e.g., process development committee)	Some to great use	Some to great use (depends on generic strategy)	Some to great use
Decline	Move to simplify structure (e.g., product to functional)	Streamline integrating mechanisms	Great use	Great use	Some use

Embryonic stage strategy and structure   In the embryonic industry stage, the principal problem facing companies at the business level is to perfect the product and educate the customer about the product. The computer industry in the early 1970s is a good example of an industry in the embryonic stage. At this stage, a *share-building strategy* is the appropriate choice because the company's objective is to establish a reputation and market share. Generally, because the company is small at this stage, it has a flat structure, and its founder probably exercises a great deal of centralized control.

In terms of horizontal differentiation, a functional structure is likely to emerge as a firm establishes its goals and objectives and begins to group activities by function. Developing market share depends primarily on product development; hence the research and development and the marketing functions take precedence in the new structure. Integration, in turn, will be organized around that function providing the distinctive competence that the company is trying to develop.

Companies in embryonic industries are likely to be entrepreneurial, with a fast-moving culture that stems mainly from a technological or marketing orientation. Clan control, like that used by Apple Computer in its early years, is the main type of control because the company is essentially discovering how to do things right. These companies settle for loose control because output controls or stringent rules and procedures do not suit a company that does not know as yet what targets it can achieve. In fact, establishing targets can hurt the company by lowering aspirations and stifling creativity. Thus structure and control are best kept simple and fluid.

Growth-stage strategy and structure   By the time it reaches the growth stage of the life cycle, an organization has learned how to do the right things in the right way. It therefore adopts a *growth strategy* to retain its share of the rapidly expanding market.[15] By now, it has established a relatively stable grouping of functional activities, and functional managers have emerged to take control of the functions, lessening the burden on the founding entrepreneur. Consequently, the company is also taller, with a higher level of vertical differentiation. More managerial control results as well. These changes mean that the company is operating with a fully developed functional structure that gives it a firm foundation on which to build. The boundaries among functions are still likely to be fluid, however, and cross-functional communication that integrates the organization persists. As the company grows and becomes more complex, it increasingly uses teams and task forces. At this stage, the company's goal should be to perfect its manufacturing operations to ride down the experience curve, and to design its structure to suit its distinctive competence.

Nevertheless, problems can occur at this stage when companies do not change their structure and controls to suit future contingencies. Because of the large increase in market growth, many companies neglect their costs because they can still sell all they can produce. As there is no pressure to cut costs, a company has a lot of slack, and it has little incentive to exert tight control over itself. Often companies develop complex structures with little concern for their costs. You saw earlier in the Opening Incidents to this chapter and Chapter 10 how lax control was at Texas Instruments and Apple Computer during their period of unprecedented growth. Apple thought it had the luxury to develop the expensive divisional structure that duplicated design, research and development, and marketing activities for each product line. When the next stage of the life cycle, the shakeout stage, arrived, Apple scrambled to restructure itself more efficiently. Similarly, at Texas Instruments, managers recognized the consequences of using an expensive matrix structure in a maturing market. Organizational design during growth almost inevitably determines a company's success in future stages.

Shakeout strategy and structure   In the shakeout stage, a *share-maintaining* or *share-increasing* strategy is the appropriate choice. In a shakeout, the market is increasing, but at a decreasing rate: excess capacity develops throughout the industry as demand growth slows. To survive, a company must hold onto its share of the market. The companies that have perfected their manufacturing systems and streamlined their structures are in the best position because they have accumulated more experience and lowered costs faster than the others. Companies that paid close attention to adopting the right organizational structure and controls in the growth stage now find themselves in the best position to develop their generic business-level strategy and to sustain their competitive advantage in the shakeout. Such companies control their structures and can choose the right organizational arrangements to capitalize on generic strategy. As discussed earlier, companies at this stage are forced to decide what kind of structure they need because cost leadership and differentiation have different kinds of structure and control requirements.

To increase market share and reduce costs, both low-cost and differentiated companies usually adopt a product structure based on product lines or market segments. This structure allows a low-cost company to control its production system efficiently. For a differentiator, such a structure helps increase market share because the company can group its activities to mirror its market segments and different kinds of customers. The company's integration mechanisms can be closely tied to its product lines, which also makes coordination easier. Apple's reorganization to a product structure as it went after the school market, home market, and so on, illustrates this point. Similarly, Hewlett-Packard, faced with increasing competition from the Japanese, reorganized its structure around six product/market segments to achieve a fit between its strategy and structure.

A company's controls also change. Managers quite likely are more attentive to the bottom line and develop tough performance standards for the various functions. Standardization of inputs, throughputs, and outputs is the chief concern. Bonuses for key employees in the management team and for salespeople are usually linked to increases in market share. The culture of the organization probably changes as well, to reflect the more competitive and uncertain industry environment. Management must become less freewheeling and more efficiency oriented, and rewards are tied to cost effectiveness. Marketing, not just selling, is emphasized. If the company is a differentiator, customers have to be convinced of its dedication to product quality, reliability, or after-sales service.[16] Thus a marked shift in the kind of controls companies use occurs at this stage in the industry life cycle. Dealing with the new reality of the competitive environment is hard on strategic managers, and consequently many organizations go into decline and fail. Companies undergo major changes in competitive position and advantage as they are forced to readjust their structure and control system to the new competitive conditions.

Maturity strategies and structure   In the maturity stage, _hold-and-maintain_ market share and _profit strategies_ are most likely. Companies try to exploit the benefits of having made the right strategy-structure choices at the previous stages and enjoy their competitive advantage. At this stage, the goals of the research and development and production functions are to keep up with incremental product and process innovations. Products have been standardized, and a company's principal concern is to increase the product range to suit different kinds of customers and iron out any distribution difficulties to maximize sales. Its competitive strategy determines how the company strives to hold and maintain its position at this stage and to reap profits.

With a strategy of differentiation, a hold-and-maintain position means concentrating resources on developing the customer base. Companies use resources to improve marketing, distribution, and after-sales service. Decentralization occurs, and autonomy is granted to lower-level employees so that they can respond creatively and flexibly to customer needs. A high level of interfunctional communication is emphasized. The sales force feeds information to research and product development personnel so that they can refine products to enhance customer satisfaction, and research and development coordinates with manufacturing to bring new products on line. Because it needs as much integration as possible, the company frequently relies on task forces to trade and share information. Structure is buttressed by a culture that stresses service and customer satisfaction. IBM is renowned for its cultural values that allow it to respond effectively to customer needs.

Although a company may be following a differentiation strategy, costs are still a concern, especially if a profit strategy is being pursued. In production, strict cost control is likely to be stringently enforced, and in fact, production may be contracted out to Third World countries with lower labor costs.

If the company is following a low-cost strategy, both the hold-and-maintain and profit positions require continuing attention to materials management and the regulation of procurement, production, and distribution to control costs. Thus control is likely to become increasingly stringent. These companies also develop tall structures, with rigid rules and procedures that standardize organizational activities. Output controls increase and include strict accounting procedures and quantitative and qualitative measures of performance.[17] The culture of a company pursuing a profit strategy will combine a rigid cost-cutting mentality with a heavy managerial emphasis on the bottom line. Bonus systems linked directly to cost reduction or sales targets tied to increases in the customer base dominate the reward system and reinforce the production culture.[18] The combined result of all these measures is an organization that is a far cry from the decentralized and flexible differentiating company. It reaps profits from its meticulous attention to cost cutting. Crown Cork & Seal Company, Inc., is the epitome of a company in the mature stage and has remained the cost leader in the bottling and capping market for many years because of its innovative cost-cutting methods.

Decline strategies and structure   As all the decline strategies we discuss in Chapter 5—harvest, asset reduction, divestiture, and others—suggest, companies choosing to remain in the industry must shift to a structure and control system that reduces their total costs of production. Otherwise they cannot respond to the inevitable fall in demand in a declining industry. Because the industry has excess capacity, companies must change their structure and move rapidly to remove excess capacity by closing down plants. If they operate with a product structure, product lines should be trimmed and consolidated. General Motors did so, though very belatedly, when the demand for its vehicles declined. It shut down plants across the country, streamlined its structure, and cut costs by reducing its numbers of white-collar employees. Similarly, Kodak responded to increasing competition and a stagnating market by reducing capacity and combining many of its operating facilities both at home and abroad.

The move to streamline structure is often accompanied by a centralization of authority at the top levels in the organization.[19] That is, management moves to reassert tight personal control over lower levels in the hierarchy. Increased control is often attended by a reduction in the number of hierarchical levels as the company streamlines its structure. After deregulation, AT&T eliminated two levels in the hierarchy and recentralized control.

Obviously, decline is difficult for companies to manage. Employees, accustomed to prosperity, find that promotion opportunities and bonuses have dried up and that layoffs may ensue. Layoffs threaten morale and exacerbate the problems that the company is trying to deal with. Corporate culture deteriorates. Large oil companies suffered these consequences when they terminated thousands of employees during the oil price slump. During decline, top management continually tightens control, autonomy at lower levels is reduced, and any function or activity that cannot demonstrate bottom-line results is in danger. Output controls work in a punitive fashion and are reinforced by strict accounting procedures and bureaucratic control.

The resulting structure is far less costly to operate, and the company is in a better position to survive. If the company is pursuing a low-cost strategy, its only option is to move quickly to reduce costs even further. The cost leader may be able to survive comfortably for many years as other, less efficient, companies are driven out of the market. For the differentiator in a declining situation, cost cutting will mean reducing distribution costs. Although it must protect its distinctive competence, the differentiator may have room to reduce its product range or trim marginal customer segments to reduce costs without hurting revenues too much. In essence, it pursues a strategy of market concentration, which lowers costs but permits the company to retain its differentiated appeal. Many companies may also decide to specialize in one niche and essentially move to a focused strategy, serving one customer segment. These companies can streamline and simplify their structure because they have simplified their strategies. They can reduce the costs of coordination and control by selecting a simplified structure that has a lower level of differentiation and integration.

Summary: Structure and Control at the Business Level

Companies must match their structures and control systems to their business level strategies if they are to survive and prosper in competitive environments. Not only does the basic choice between a low cost and a differentiation strategy require the company to make a different set of choices, but choices of structure and control must be continually changed and modified to suit the nature of the industry life cycle. This is a complex job for strategic managers and one that many companies do not do well. The evidence suggests that strategy, structure, and performance are strongly linked at the business level: Companies that do not alter their structures do not perform as well as those that do.

12.5 STRUCTURE AND CONTROL AT THE CORPORATE LEVEL

At the corporate level, a company needs to choose the organizational structure that will enable it to operate efficiently in a number of different businesses. Although product structures are sometimes used to manage the multibusiness company, the structure normally chosen at the corporate level is the multidivisional structure or one of its variants (discussed in Chapter 10). The larger and more diverse the businesses in the corporate portfolio, the more likely is the company to have a multidivisional structure. The reason is that each division requires the services of full-scale specialist support functions and that a headquarters corporate staff is needed to oversee and evaluate divisional operations. Once it selects a divisional structure, a company must make two more choices: the right mix of integrating mechanisms to match the particular divisional structure and the right control systems to make the divisional structure work.

In Chapters 7 and 8, we discuss the various types of corporate strategy that a company can pursue. For the first of these types—concentration on a single business—the corporate- and business-level strategies are identical. Thus the previous discussion of structure and business-level strategy covers the issue of choice of structure and control for the single-business firm. We next discuss how the corporate-level strategies of vertical integration, related diversification, and unrelated diversification affect the choice of structure and control systems. Then we consider how to implement international strategy.

As we discuss in Chapter 7, the main reason a company pursues vertical integration is to achieve *economies of integration* among divisions.[20] For example, the company can coordinate resource scheduling decisions among divisions to reduce costs. For instance, locating a rolling mill next to a steel furnace saves the costs of reheating steel ingots. Similarly, the chief gains from related diversification come from obtaining *synergies* among divisions: Divisions benefit by sharing distribution and sales networks or research and development knowledge. With both of these strategies, the benefits to the company come from some transfer of resources among divisions. To secure these benefits, the company must coordinate activities between divisions. Consequently, structure and control must be designed to handle the transfer of resources among divisions.

In the case of unrelated diversification, however, the benefits to the company come from the possibility of achieving an *internal capital market,* which allows corporate personnel to make better allocations of capital than the external capital market. With this strategy, there are no transactions or exchanges among divisions; each operates separately. Structure and control must therefore be designed to allow each division to operate independently.

A company's choice of structure and control mechanisms thus depends on the degree to which the company must control the interactions among divisions. The more interdependent the division—that is, the more they depend on each other for resources—the more complex are the structure and control mechanisms required to make the strategy work.[21]

Table 12.4 indicates what forms of structure and control companies should

TABLE 12.4   Corporate strategy and structure and control

Corporate strategy	Appropriate structure	Need for Integration	Type of control — Market	Type of control — Bureaucratic	Type of control — Clan
Unrelated diversification	Conglomerate	Low (no exchanges between divisions)	Great use (e.g., ROI)	Some use (e.g., budgets)	Little use
Vertical integration	Multidivisional	Medium (scheduling resource transfers)	Great use (e.g., ROI, transfer pricing)	Great use (e.g., standardization, budgets)	Some use (e.g., shared norms and values)
Related diversification	Multidivisional SBU	High (achieve synergies between divisions by integrating roles)	Little use	Great use (e.g., rules, budgets)	Great use (e.g., develop corporate culture)

adopt to manage the three corporate strategies. We examine them in detail in the next sections.

Unrelated Diversification

Because there are *no linkages* among divisions, unrelated diversification is the easiest and cheapest strategy to manage. The main requirement of the structure and control system is that it lets corporate personnel easily and accurately evaluate divisional performance. Thus the *conglomerate structure,* discussed earlier, is the appropriate choice, and market and bureaucratic controls are used with it. Each division is evaluated by strict return on investment criteria, and each division is given a budget in relation to its return on investment. The company also applies sophisticated accounting controls to obtain information quickly from the divisions so that corporate managers can readily compare divisions on several dimensions. Textron is a good example of a company that operates a conglomerate structure through the use of sophisticated computer networks and accounting controls, which allow it almost daily access to divisional performance.

Divisions in the conglomerate structure usually have considerable autonomy unless they fail to reach their return on investment objectives. Generally, corporate headquarters is not interested in the types of business-level strategy pursued by each division unless there are problems. If problems arise, corporate headquarters may step in to take corrective action, perhaps replacing managers or providing additional financial resources, depending on the reason for the problem. If they see no possibility of a turnaround, however, corporate personnel may just as easily decide to divest the division. This structure therefore allows the unrelated company to operate its businesses as a portfolio of investments, which can be bought and sold as business conditions change. Usually, managers in the various divisions do not know one another, and they may not know what companies are in the corporate portfolio.

The use of market controls to manage a company means that no integration among divisions is necessary. Thus the costs of managing an unrelated company are low. The biggest problem facing corporate personnel is to decide on capital allocations to the various divisions to maximize the overall profitability of the portfolio. They also have to oversee divisional management and make sure that divisions are achieving return on investment targets.

Vertical Integration

Vertical integration is an expensive strategy to manage because *sequential resource flows* from one division to the next must be coordinated. The multidivisional structure effects such coordination. This structure provides the centralized control necessary for the vertically integrated company to achieve benefits from the control of resource transfers. Corporate personnel assume the responsibility for devising market and bureaucratic controls to promote the efficient transfer of resources among divisions. Complex rules and procedures are instituted to manage interdivisional relationships and specify how exchanges are to be made. In addition, an internal transfer pricing system is created to allow one division to sell its products to the next. As we previously note, these complex links can lead to ill will among divisions, and so corporate personnel must try to minimize divisional conflicts.

Centralizing authority at corporate headquarters must be done with care in vertically related companies. It carries the risk of involving corporate personnel in operating issues at the business level to the point where the divisions lose their autonomy and motivation. As we note in Chapter 10, the company must strike the right balance of centralized control at corporate headquarters and decentralized control at the divisional level if it is to implement this strategy successfully.

Because their interests are at stake, divisions need to have input into scheduling and resource transfer decisions. For example, the plastics division in a chemical company has a vital interest in the activities of the oil division, for the quality of the products it gets from the oil division determines the quality of its own products. Divisional integrating mechanisms can bring about direct coordination and information transfers among divisions.[22] To handle communication among divisions, the company can set up task forces or teams for the purpose. At the very least, it should establish liaison roles; in high-tech and chemical companies, integrating roles among divisions are common. Thus a strategy of vertical integration is managed through a combination of corporate and divisional controls. Although the organizational arrangements for managing this strategy cost more than those for operating unrelated diversification, the benefits derived from vertical integration often outweigh its costs.

Related Diversification

In the case of related diversification, divisions share research and development knowledge, information, customer bases, and goodwill to obtain gains from synergy. The process is difficult to manage, and so a multidivisional structure is used to facilitate the transfer of resources to obtain synergies. Even with this structure, however, high levels of resource sharing and joint production by divisions make it hard for corporate managers to measure the performance of each individual division. Besides, as you read in the Opening Incident in Chapter 11 about TRW, the divisions themselves may not want to exchange products or knowledge because transfer prices—inherently difficult to set—are perceived as unfair. If a related company is to obtain gains from synergy, it has to adopt complicated forms of integration and control at the divisional level to make the structure work efficiently.

First, market control is impossible because resources are shared, so the company needs to develop a corporate culture that stresses cooperation among divisions and to set corporate, rather than divisional, goals. Second, corporate managers must establish sophisticated integrating devices to ensure coordination among divisions. Integrating roles and teams are crucial because they provide the context in which managers from different divisions can meet and develop a common vision of corporate goals. Hewlett-Packard, for example, created three new high-level integrating teams to make certain that the new products developed by its technology group made their way quickly to its product divisions.

An organization with a multidivisional structure must have the right mix of incentives and rewards for cooperation if it is to achieve gains from synergy. With unrelated diversification, divisions operate autonomously, and the company can quite easily reward managers on their division's individual performance. With related diversification, however, rewarding divisions is more difficult because they are engaged in joint production, and strategic managers must be sensitive and alert to achieve equity in rewards among divisions.

In this situation, the strategic business unit (SBU) structure, discussed in earlier chapters, can prove useful. If the company designs its structure around the basic commonalities among divisions, it can evaluate divisional performance more easily. Thus, for example, one SBU could be operated around a customer group, such as chain stores, whereas another SBU could be operated around technological similarities. SBUs make it easier to integrate and control the performance of the company and allow management to sense opportunities and threats as well as develop the company's distinctive competencies. The aim always is to design the structure so that it can maximize the benefits from the strategy at the lowest management cost.

Managing a strategy of related diversification also raises the issue of how much authority to centralize and how much to decentralize. Corporate managers need to take a close look at how their controls affect divisional performance and autonomy. If corporate managers get too involved in the day-to-day operations of the divisions, they can endanger divisional autonomy and undercut divisional managers' decision making. Corporate managers, after all, see everything from a corporate, rather than a divisional, perspective. For example, in the Heinz case previously mentioned, management attempted to develop one form of competitive advantage, low-cost advantage, in every division.[23] Although this approach may work well for Heinz, it may be markedly inappropriate for a company that is operating a totally diverse set of businesses, each of which needs to develop its own unique competence. Too much corporate control can put divisional managers in a straightjacket, and performance suffers.

Global Expansion

In Chapter 8, we note how most large companies have an international, or global, dimension to their strategy because they produce and sell their products in international markets. For example, Procter & Gamble and food companies such as Heinz, Kellogg Co., and Nestlé Enterprises, Inc. have production operations throughout the world, as do the large auto companies and computer makers. In this section, we examine how the need to manage foreign operations affects a company's choice of structure and control and how a company changes its structure as it expands internationally.

In general, the choice of structure and control systems for managing an international business is a function of three factors. The first is the need to choose a level of vertical differentiation that provides effective supervision of foreign operations. Companies operating in international markets must create a hierarchy of authority that clarifies the responsibilities of domestic managers for handling the sale of products abroad and also allocates responsibility for foreign operations between domestic and foreign managers. Second, such companies must choose a level of horizontal differentiation that groups foreign operation tasks with domestic operations in a way that allows the company to market its products abroad and serve the needs of foreign customers in the most effective way. In practice, a company's choice of structure is a function of the complexity and the extent of its foreign operations. Third, the company must choose the right kinds of market, bureaucratic, and clan controls to make the structure function effectively.

When a company sells only domestically made products in foreign markets, problems of coordinating foreign and domestic operations are minimal. Companies like Mercedes-Benz or Jaguar, for example, make no attempt to produce in the foreign market; rather they sell or distribute their domestic products internationally. Such companies usually just add a **foreign operations department** to their existing structure and continue to use the same control system. If a company is using a functional structure, this department has the responsibility for coordinating manufacturing, sales, and research and development activities according to the needs of the foreign market. In the foreign country, the company usually establishes a subsidiary to handle sales and distribution. For example, Mercedes-Benz's foreign subsidiaries have the responsibility for allocating dealerships, organizing supplies of spare parts, and, of course, selling cars. A system of bureaucratic controls is then established to keep the home office informed of changes in sales, spare parts requirements, and so on, in the foreign countries.

A company with many different products or businesses operating from a multidivisional structure has a more serious coordination problem: to coordinate the flow of different products across different countries. To manage these transfers, many companies create an **international division**, which they add to their existing divisional structure.[24] International operations are managed as a separate divisional business whose managers are given the authority and responsibility for coordinating domestic product divisions and foreign markets. The international division also controls the foreign subsidiaries that market the products and decides how much authority to delegate to foreign management. This arrangement permits the company to engage in more complex foreign operations.

The next level of complexity arises when companies establish **foreign subsidiaries** to produce goods and services abroad. In terms of vertical differentiation, the problem for the company is how to allocate responsibility for foreign operations between management in the United States and management in the foreign country. Clearly, the lines of communication and chain of command lengthen in managing foreign production operations making control more difficult. The company has to maintain control of the strategy of the foreign subsidiary while giving the management of the foreign branch the flexibility it needs to deal with its own unique situation. Because strategic managers are much farther away from the scene of operations, it makes sense to decentralize control and grant decision-making authority to managers in the foreign operations while using market and bureaucratic controls to keep abreast of foreign developments. Many companies adopt the policy of creating autonomous foreign operating divisions, which, like home divisions, are evaluated on the basis of their rate of return, growth in market share, or operations costs. Chrysler and General Motors both did just that when they moved into Europe and began developing, producing, and marketing cars to suit Europeans' particular needs. In this situation, developing the right mix of controls that give foreign managers sufficient autonomy but keep home management informed of the current situation is critical.

When synergies can be obtained from cooperation between a company's home divisions and its autonomous foreign subsidiaries, an organization must choose a structure and control system to exploit these synergies. One solution lies in grouping foreign subsidiaries into world regions; the domestic divisions then coordinate with world regions rather than with individual subsidiaries. For example, when a company makes and sells the same products in many different markets, it often groups its foreign subsidiaries into world regions to simplify the coordination of products across countries; Europe might be one region, the Pacific Basin another, and the Middle East a third. This sort of grouping across world markets results in an **international SBU structure** in which subsidiaries inside each SBU are grouped on the basis of geographical region and the same set of market and bureaucratic controls can be applied to all subsidiaries. This allows companies to obtain synergies from dealing with broadly similar cultures because information can be transmitted more easily. For example, consumer preferences regarding product design and marketing are likely to be more similar among countries in one world region than among countries in different world regions.

Sometimes the potential gains from sharing product, marketing, or research and development knowledge between home and foreign operations are so great that companies adopt **an international matrix structure** for organizing their international activities. Such a structure appears in Figure 12.1. The figure represents the structure adopted by a large chemical company such as Du Pont. On the vertical axis, instead of functions, are the company's *product divisions,* which provide product and marketing information to the foreign subsidiaries. For example, these might be the petroleum, plastics, drug, or fertilizer divisions. On the horizontal axis are the company's foreign subsidiaries in the various *countries or world regions* in which it operates. Managers in the foreign subsidiary control foreign operations and through a system of bureaucratic controls report to divisional personnel back in the United States. They are also responsible, together with U.S. divisional personnel, for developing control and reward systems that permit marketing or research and development information to be shared to

FIGURE 12.1   An international matrix structure

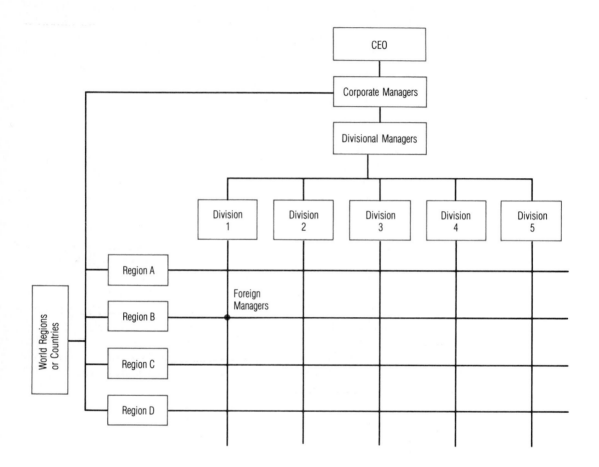

achieve gains from synergies. This structure therefore both provides a great deal of local flexibility and gives divisional personnel in the United States considerable access to information about local affairs. Additionally, the matrix form allows knowledge and experience to be transferred among geographical regions and among divisions and regions. The matrix structure, providing as it does a great deal of opportunity for face-to-face contact between domestic and foreign managers, makes the transmission of company norms and values easier so that it facilitates the development of clan control. This is especially important for an international company in which lines of communication are longer and information is subject to distortion. Club Med Inc. fully exploits these synergies in the way it manages its holiday resorts. The matrix also allows each home division to rationalize (that is, balance) production so that, for example, a lack of demand in one world region can be compensated by increased demand in another. Philip

Morris does this with cigarettes. Slumping demand in the United States is countered by supplying regions where cigarette sales are expanding. Similarly, Japanese car manufacturers plan their international strategy to compensate for import restrictions or currency changes in the world market.

Most large companies have an international component in their organizational structures. The issue with multinational companies, as with all others, is to adopt the structure and control system that best meets the needs of their strategy. The need to implement international strategy successfully has put an increasing burden on corporate managers to design the company's structure and controls to respond to the challenges of the world market.

12.6 CHANGES IN CONTROLS AND STRUCTURE

As we discuss in Chapter 10, the main growth path for U.S. corporations is from vertical integration to related diversification. Given the previous discussion, this means that, to succeed, a company has to alter its structure and control systems as it changes from one strategy to another. It must change the controls that were appropriate when it was pursuing a strategy of vertical integration to those that suit a strategy of related diversification. In practice, this means moving from transfer prices and output controls to bureaucratic and clan control.

But often corporate and divisional managers do not understand that the benefits from related diversification cannot be achieved using the old market controls. Managers do not foresee the new pattern of relationships successfully and do not choose controls matched to the new strategy.[25] As a result, companies fail to realize the benefits from their new strategy. The Greyhound Corporation is an example of a company that is experiencing problems in managing its new acquisition strategy because it seems to be unable to decide if it is pursuing related or unrelated diversification.

Mixing two strategies leads to similar problems. For example, companies pursuing a strategy of related diversification often buy unrelated businesses and pursue both related and unrelated diversification simultaneously. What often happens is that managers tend to apply the same types of controls across all divisions. Thus if they control their unrelated companies using controls appropriate for related ones their new unrelated businesses perform badly. That is the situation at Greyhound. Strategic managers have not put the right controls in place to achieve internal capital market gains.

Switching strategies in midstream thus creates some serious implementation problems. Managers must be sensitive to the need to readjust their controls and form of divisional structure to achieve their objectives. Mixed structural forms such as the strategic business unit (SBU) structure are useful for this purpose because this structure can be designed to allow companies to pursue different strategies together. For example, an SBU structure permits companies to manage the strategies of vertical integration, related diversification, and unrelated diversification simultaneously because divisions can be grouped into business units based on the similarities or differences among their businesses. When companies are grouped according to the types of benefit expected from the strategy, the costs of managing them are reduced and many of the problems just outlined are avoided. In the next sections, we look in more detail at the strategy implementation problems that emerge when companies acquire new businesses, develop new businesses through internal corporate venturing, or both.

12.7 MERGERS, ACQUISITIONS, AND STRUCTURE

In Chapter 9, we note that mergers and acquisitions are principal vehicles by which companies enter new product markets and expand the size of their operations.[26] We discuss earlier the strategic advantages and disadvantages of mergers. We now consider how to design structure and control systems to manage the new acquisitions. This issue is important because, as we note elsewhere, many acquisitions are unsuccessful, and one of the main reasons is that many companies do a very poor job of integrating the new divisions into their corporate structure.[27]

The first factor that makes managing new acquisitions difficult is the nature of the businesses that a company acquires. If a company acquires businesses related to its existing businesses, it should find it fairly easy to integrate these businesses into its corporate structure. The controls already being used in the related company can be adapted to the new divisions. To achieve gains from synergies, the company can expand its task forces or increase the number of integrating roles, so that the new divisions are drawn into the existing divisional structure.

If managers do not understand how to develop connections among divisions to permit gains from synergy, the new businesses will perform poorly. Some authors have recently argued that that is why the quality of management is so important. A company must employ managers who have the ability to recognize synergies among apparently different businesses and so derive benefits from acquisitions and mergers.[28] For instance, Porter cites the example of Philip Morris, the tobacco maker, which took over Miller Brewing Company.[29] On the surface these seem to be very different businesses. When their products are viewed as consumer products that are often bought and consumed together, however, the possibility of sales, distribution, and marketing synergies becomes clearer. Because both businesses require the same kind of managerial skills, even management synergies are feasible. Because it is usually easier to see the potential synergies between very similar businesses, companies should take over only related businesses, where they have the knowledge and expertise to manage the new acquisitions and make them profitable.

If companies acquire businesses for the sake of capital market gains alone, however, strategy implementation is easier. If companies acquire unrelated businesses and seek to operate them only as a portfolio of investments, they should have no trouble managing the acquisitions. Implementation problems are likely to arise only when corporate managers try to interfere in businesses that they know little about or when they use inappropriate structure and controls to manage the new business and attempt to achieve the wrong kind of benefits from the acquisition. For example, if managers try to integrate unrelated companies with related ones, apply the wrong kinds of controls at the divisional level, or interfere in business-level strategy, corporate performance suffers. These mistakes explain why related acquisitions are sometimes more successful than unrelated ones.[30]

Strategic managers therefore need to be very sensitive to the problems involved in taking over new businesses through mergers and acquisitions. Like other managers, they rarely appreciate the real issues inherent in managing the new business until they have to deal with these issues personally. Even in the case of acquiring closely related businesses, new managers must realize that each business has a unique culture or way of doing things. Such idiosyncrasies must be understood to manage the new organization. Over time new management can change the culture and alter the internal workings of the company, but this is a difficult implementation task, as we discuss in the next chapter, when politics and strategic change are considered.

12.8 INTERNAL NEW VENTURES AND STRUCTURE

The main alternative to growth through acquisition and merger is for a company to develop new businesses internally. In Chapter 9, we call this strategy the *new venturing process,* and we discuss its advantages for growth and diversification. Now we consider the design of the appropriate internal arrangements for encouraging the development of new ventures. At the heart of this design process must be the realization by corporate managers that internal new venturing is a form of entrepreneurship. The design should encourage creativity and give new venture managers the opportunity and resources to develop new products or markets. Hewlett-Packard, for example, gives managers a great deal of latitude in this respect. To encourage innovation, it allows them to work on informal projects while they carry out their assigned tasks.[31] More generally, management must choose the appropriate structure and controls for operating new ventures.[32]

One of the main design choices is the creation of **new venture divisions**. To provide new venture managers with the autonomy to experiment and take risks, the company sets up a new venture division separate from other divisions and makes it a center for new product or project development. Away from the day-to-day scrutiny of top management, divisional personnel pursue the creation of new business as though they were external entrepreneurs. The division is operated by controls that reinforce the entrepreneurial spirit. Thus market and output controls are inappropriate because they can inhibit risk taking. Instead, the company uses clan control and develops a culture for entrepreneurship in this division to provide a climate for innovation. Care must be taken, however, to institute bureaucratic controls that put some limits on freedom of action. Otherwise costly mistakes may be made and resources wasted on frivolous ideas.

In managing the new venture division, it is important to use integrating mechanisms such as task forces and teams to screen new ideas. Managers from research and development, sales and marketing, and product development are heavily involved in this screening process. Generally, the champions of new products must defend their projects before a formal evaluation committee, consisting of proven entrepreneurs and experienced managers from the other divisions, to secure the resources for developing them. Companies such as 3M, IBM, and Texas Instruments are examples of successful companies that use this method for creating opportunities internally.

Care must be taken to preserve the autonomy of the new venture division. As mentioned earlier, the costs of research and development are high and the rewards uncertain. After spending millions of dollars, corporate managers often become concerned about the division's performance and introduce tight output controls or strong budgets to increase accountability. These measures hurt the entrepreneurial culture.

Sometimes, however, after creating a new invention, the new venture division wants to reap the benefits by producing and marketing it. If this happens, then the division becomes an ordinary operating division and entrepreneurship declines.[33] Strategic managers must take steps to provide a structure that can sustain the entrepreneurial spirit.[34] Hewlett-Packard has a novel way of dealing with new venturing. In the operating divisions, as soon as a new, self-supporting product is developed, a new division is formed to produce and market the product. By spinning off the product in this fashion, the company keeps all its divisions small and entrepreneurial. The arrangement also provides a good climate for innovation. In the last few years, however, Hewlett-Packard found that having many new venture divisions was too expensive and so has merged some of them. The company appears to be moving toward the creation of a single new venture division.

Internal new venturing is an important means by which large, established companies can maintain their momentum and grow from within.[35] The alternative is to acquire small businesses that have already developed some technological competence and to pump resources into them. This approach can also succeed, and it obviously lessens management's burden if the company operates the new business as an independent entity. In recent years Kodak has taken this path to diversification, buying a share in many small companies. In practice, companies are likely to operate in both ways, acquiring some new businesses and developing others internally. Recently, many companies have made acquisitions when increasing competition from abroad has threatened their dominance in existing businesses and has forced them to evaluate opportunities for maximizing long-term growth in new businesses.

12.9 SUMMARY OF CHAPTER

This chapter brings together strategy formulation and strategy implementation and examines how a company's choice of strategy affects the form of its structure and control systems. The cause of Texas Instrument's problems with its structure should now be clear: Its structure no longer fit the strategy that the company had to pursue to regain its competitive advantage. The following are the main points of the chapter:

1. At the functional level, each function requires a different kind of structure and control system to achieve its functional objectives.

2. At the business level, the structure and control system must be designed to achieve business-level objectives, which involves managing the relationships among all the functions to permit the company to develop a distinctive competence.

3. Cost-leadership and differentiation strategies each require different structures and control systems if the company is to develop a competitive advantage.

4. The form of the company's structure and control systems varies at different stages of the industry life cycle.

5. At the corporate level, the company must choose the structure and control system that will allow it to operate a collection of businesses.

6. Unrelated diversification, vertical integration, and related diversification require different forms of structure and control if the benefits of pursuing the strategy are to be realized.

7. As companies grow and enter foreign markets, international considerations affect their choice of structure and control. Consequently, companies develop foreign divisions to operate in these markets. When there are gains to be derived from synergy, companies often adopt an international matrix form to trade knowledge and expertise.

8. As companies change their corporate strategies over time, they must change their structures because different strategies are managed in different ways.

9. The profitability of mergers and acquisitions depends on the structure and control systems that companies adopt to manage them and the way a company integrates them into its existing businesses.

10. To encourage internal new venturing, companies must design a structure that gives the new venture division the autonomy it needs in order to develop new products and protect it from excessive interference by corporate managers.

Discussion Questions

1. How should (a) a high-tech company, (b) a fast-food franchise, and (c) a small manufacturing company design their functional structures and control systems to implement a generic strategy?

2. How should (a) a differentiated company and (b) a low-cost company alter their structures and control systems over the industry life cycle?

3. If a related company begins to buy unrelated businesses, in what ways should it change its structure or control mechanisms to manage the acquisitions?

4. How would you design a structure and control system to encourage entrepreneurship in a large, established corporation?

Endnotes

1. "Texas Instruments Inc.," *Moody's Industrial Manual,* 2 (1986), 6120.

2. "TI: Shot Full of Holes and Trying to Recover," *Business Week,* March 6, 1984, pp. 82–84.

3. "Texas Instruments Cleans Up Its Act," *Business Week,* September 19, 1983, p. 56.

4. W. G. Ouchi, "The Relationship Between Organizational Structure and Organizational Control," *Administrative Science Quarterly,* 22 (1977), 95–113.

5. K. M. Eisenhardt, "Control: Organizational and Economic Approaches," *Management Science,* 16 (1985), 134–148.

6. J. R. Galbraith, *Designing Complex Organizations* (Reading, Mass.: Addison-Wesley, 1973). P. R. Lawrence and J. W. Lorsch, *Organization and Environment* (Cambridge, Mass.: Harvard University Press, 1967). D. Miller, "Strategy Making and Structure: Analysis and Implications for Performance," *Academy of Management Journal,* 30 (1987), 7–32.

7. Michael E. Porter, *Competitive Strategy: Techniques for Analyzing Industries and Competitors* (New York: Free Press, 1980). D. Miller, "Configurations of Strategy and Structure," *Strategic Management Journal,* 7 (1986), 233–249.

8. D. Miller and P. H. Freisen, *Organizations: A Quantum View* (Englewood Cliffs, N.J.: Prentice-Hall, 1984).

9. J. Woodward, *Industrial Organization: Theory and Practice* (London: Oxford University Press, 1965). Lawrence and Lorsch, *Organization and Environment.*

10. R. E. White, "Generic Business Strategies, Organizational Context and Performance: An Empirical Investigation," *Strategic Management Journal,* 7 (1986), 217–231.

11. Porter, *Competitive Strategy.* Miller, "Configurations of Strategy and Structure."

12. E. Deal and A. A. Kennedy, *Corporate Cultures* (Reading, Mass.: Addison-Wesley, 1985). "Corporate Culture," *Business Week,* October 27, 1980, pp. 148–160.

13. Miller, "Configurations of Strategy and Structure." R. E. Miles and C. C. Snow, *Organizational Strategy, Structure, and Process* (New York: McGraw-Hill, 1978).

14. Lawrence and Lorsch, *Organization and Environment.*

15. C. W. Hofer and D. Schendel, *Strategy Formulation: Analytical Concepts* (St. Paul, Minn.: West, 1978).

16. Porter, *Competitive Strategy.*

17. T. Burns and G. M. Stalker, *The Management of Innovation* (London: The Tavistock Institute, 1961). Lawrence and Lorsch, *Organization and Environment.*

18. G. R. Jones, "Transaction Costs, Property Rights, and Organizational Culture: An Exchange Perspective," *Administrative Science Quarterly,* 28 (1983), 454–467.

19. D. A. Whetten, "Sources, Responses, and Effects of Organizational Design," in J. R. Kimberly and R. H. Miles (eds.), *The Organizational Life Cycle* (San Francisco: Jossey Bass, 1980).

20. G. R. Jones and C. W. L. Hill, "Transaction Cost Analysis of Strategy-Structure Choice," *Strategic Management Journal,* 9 (1988), 159–172.

21. Jones and Hill, "Transaction Cost Analysis of Strategy-Structure Choice."

22. Lawrence and Lorsch, *Organization and Environment.* Galbraith, *Designing Complex Organizations.* Porter, *Competitive Advantage: Creating and Sustaining Superior Performance.*

23. Porter, *Competitive Strategy.*

24. J. Stopford and L. Wells, *Managing the Multinational Enterprise* (London: Longman, 1972).

25. C. K. Prahalad and R. A. Bettis, "The Dominant Logic: A New Linkage Between Diversity and Performance," *Strategic Management Journal,* 7 (1986), 485–501.

26. M. S. Salter and W. A. Weinhold, *Diversification Through Acquisition* (New York: Free Press, 1979).

27. F. T. Paine and D. J. Power, "Merger Strategy: An Examination of Drucker's Five Rules for Successful Acquisitions," *Strategic Management Journal,* 5 (1984), 99–110.

28. Prahalad and Bettis, "The Dominant Logic." Porter, *Competitive Strategy.*

29. Ibid.

30. H. Singh and C. A. Montgomery, "Corporate Acquisitions and Economic Performance," unpublished manuscript, 1984.

31. T. J. Peters and R. H. Waterman Jr., *In Search of Excellence* (New York: Harper & Row, 1982).

32. R. A. Burgelman, "Managing the New Venture Division: Research Findings and the Implications for Strategic Management," *Strategic Management Journal,* 6 (1985), 39–54.

33. N. D. Fast, "The Future of Industrial New Venture Departments," *Industrial Marketing Management,* 8 (1979), 264–279.

34. Burgelman, "Managing the New Venture Division."

35. R. A. Burgelman, "Corporate Entrepreneurship and Strategic Management: Insights from a Process Study," *Management Science,* 29 (1983), 1349–1364.

Chapter 13

CONFLICT, POLITICS AND CHANGE IN STRATEGY-STRUCTURE CHOICE

13.1 OPENING INCIDENT: CBS INC.

CBS Inc. is a diversified entertainment and information company engaged in the principal businesses of broadcasting, recorded music, and publishing. One of America's most prestigious organizations, CBS experienced much turmoil in recent years. Its troubles began when outside investors, deciding that the company's profitability and return on assets were under par, led several takeover attempts against it. In successive attacks, Jesse Helms, a senator from North Carolina, Ivan Boesky, an arbitrager, and finally Ted Turner, the founder of Turner Broadcasting System, Inc., announced takeover attempts.[1] CBS realized that it had to take these takeover attempts seriously if it wanted to remain independent.

First, Thomas Wyman, the chairman of CBS at the time, authorized a repurchase of CBS stock for $150 a share (Turner's offer was only $130). This increased CBS's debt from $510 million to $1.4 billion. Next, CBS searched for a white knight who would buy a major portion of CBS stock in the event that a hostile bid seemed likely to succeed. Laurence Tisch of Loew's Companies, Inc. agreed to play this role. By 1986, however, Tisch had purchased 25 percent of CBS stock, making him the largest stockholder, and board members, including Wyman, began to fear that he would take over CBS. Tisch did nothing to stop these rumors.[2]

Tisch began to take a more active role in CBS to question or disagree with Wyman's policies. Wyman himself was now suffering on two fronts. Although he had been brought in by the legendary founder of CBS, William Paley, Paley had become increasingly disturbed that Wyman was not consulting him on CBS policy, particularly because CBS was going through bad times. Tensions increased, and at a board meeting at the end of 1986 Wyman revealed that he had been secretly negotiating with Coca-Cola for the sale of CBS to the soft drink company. Board members were shocked and withdrew their support. Wyman resigned, Paley became acting chairman, and Tisch became acting CEO.

After this power struggle, the pressing issue facing the company became to change CBS's

N. turri – morie

strategy and structure to increase its ratings. The CBS news division posed a problem. It had been CBS's most prestigious operation since the golden days of Edward Murrow and Walter Cronkite, but the recruitment of a new president for the division, Van Gordon Sauter, had led to conflict between management and staff. Sauter believed that to earn the highest ratings, the news should be entertaining, whereas the news staff believed that the news should remain free of entertainment value, as in the past. In the ensuing conflict, Dan Rather, Bill Moyers, and Don Hewitt, executive producer of "60 Minutes," all offered to buy the news division and take it out of CBS. The offer was refused, but Tisch decided to remove Sauter to restore stability to the division.[3]

The next problem was reorganizing CBS's structure and control systems. The trend in the three main networks was to increase efficiency by downsizing and reducing staff and costs. Tisch, as the chief executive officer of CBS, began this change process by laying off staff. He eliminated more than 1,500 employees, about 9 percent of the CBS work force; this number included 150 people from the news division. He also severely cut expense accounts and reduced the slack that CBS personnel had previously enjoyed. Tisch's goal was to change CBS so that it functioned like a company in the maturity stage of the industry life cycle and to attain a 12 percent return on investment goal.[4] This change process caused more conflict and further hurt morale at CBS, however, particularly in the news division.

13.2 OVERVIEW

As the example of CBS suggests, this chapter is about organizational politics, conflict, and the problems that occur when companies attempt to change their strategy and structure. Until now in our study of strategic management, we have treated strategy formulation and implementation from an impersonal, rational perspective, where decisions are made coldly and logically. In reality, this picture of how companies make decisions is incomplete because politics and conflict influence the decision-making process and the selection of organizational objectives. CBS most likely would not have made the tough choices it did if Tisch, an outsider with concern for the bottom line, had not approached the problems facing CBS's broadcasting division with a fresh perspective—one that was not colored by years spent in a CBS culture, where this division's dominance was taken for granted and the bottom line got scant attention.

The power struggle at CBS for control of the corporation indicates the importance of politics at the company. Wyman's failure to share power with Tisch and Paley and their subsequent removal of him is an example of the use of power in organizations to change organizational objectives. The problems in the news division underscore not only the issue of power, but also that of conflict between different interests—between a manager who wanted high ratings by being entertaining and a news staff that wanted ratings based on the quality of the news broadcasts. The time it took to recognize the need for organizational change and the difficulties CBS had in pushing changes through exemplify the problems of implementing strategic change.

In this chapter, we look at each of these issues. We probe the sources of organizational politics and discuss how individuals, departments, and divisions seek to increase their power so that they can influence organizational decision making. Then we examine the nature of organizational conflict and note how managers must deal with conflict to make better strategy-structure choices. Finally, we consider why it is difficult to change organizations, and we outline ways in which managers can direct organizational change so that their company's strategy and structure matches new competitive environments.

13.3 ORGANIZATIONAL POLITICS AND POWER

So far, we have assumed that in formulating the corporate mission and setting policies and goals strategic managers strive to maximize corporate wealth. This picture of strategic decision making is known as the **rational view**. It suggests that managers achieve corporate goals by following a calculated, rational plan, in which only shareholders' interests are considered. In reality, strategic decision making is quite different. Often, strategic managers' decisions further their personal, functional, or divisional interests. In this **political view** of decision making, goals and objectives are set through compromise, bargaining, and negotiation.[5] Top-level managers constantly clash over what the correct policy decisions should be, and, as at CBS, power struggles and coalition building are a major part of strategic management. As in the public sphere, politics is the name given to the process in which different individuals or groups in the organization try to influence the strategic management process to further their own interests.

In this section, we examine the nature of organizational politics and the process of political decision making. **Organizational politics** is defined as the process by which self-interested but interdependent individuals and groups seek to obtain and use power to influence the goals and objectives of the organization to further their own interests.[6] First, we consider the sources of politics and why politics is a necessary part of the strategic management process. Second, we look at how managers or divisions can increase their power so that they can influence the company's strategic direction. Third, we explore the ways in which the organization can manage politics to help it fulfill its strategic mission.

Sources of Organizational Politics

According to the political view of organizational decision making, several factors foster politics in corporate life. Figure 13.1 contrasts these factors with those underlying the rational view of organizational decision making.

The rational view assumes that complete information is available and no uncertainty exists about outcomes, but the political view suggests that strategic managers can never be sure that they are making the best decisions.[7] From a

FIGURE 13.1   **Rational and political views of decision making**

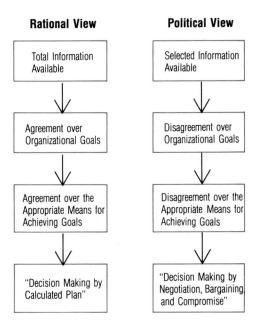

Rational View

Total Information Available

↓

Agreement over Organizational Goals

↓

Agreement over the Appropriate Means for Achieving Goals

↓

"Decision Making by Calculated Plan"

Political View

Selected Information Available

↓

Disagreement over Organizational Goals

↓

Disagreement over the Appropriate Means for Achieving Goals

↓

"Decision Making by Negotiation, Bargaining, and Compromise"

political perspective, decision making always takes place in uncertainty, where the outcomes of actions are difficult to predict. According to the rational view, moreover, managers lack consensus about appropriate organizational *goals* and the appropriate *means,* or strategies, for achieving these goals. According to the political view, on the other hand, the choice of goals and means is linked to each individual's, function's, or division's pursuit of self-interest. Disagreement over the best course of action is inevitable in the political view because the strategic decisions made by the organization necessarily help some individuals or divisions more than others. For example, if managers decide to invest in resources to promote and develop one product, other products will not be created. Some managers win, and others lose.

Given this point of view, strategy choices are never right or wrong; they are simply better or worse. As a result, managers have to promote their ideas and try to lobby support from other managers so that they can build up backing for a course of action. Thus coalition building is vital in strategic decision making.[8] Managers join coalitions to lobby for their interests, because in doing so they increase their political muscle in relation to their organizational opponents.

Managers also engage in politics for personal reasons. Because organizations are shaped like pyramids, individual managers realize that the higher they rise the more difficult it is to climb the next position.[9] If their views prevail and the organization follows their lead, however, *and* if their decisions bear results, they reap rewards and promotions. Thus by being successful at politics, they increase their visibility in the organization and make themselves contenders for high organizational office.

The assumption that personal, rather than shareholder or organizational, interest governs corporate actions is what gives the word *politics* bad connotations in many people's minds. But because no one knows for certain what decision is truly best, letting people pursue their own interest may in the long run mean that the organization's interests are being followed. Competition among managers stemming from self-interest may improve strategic decision making, with successful managers moving to the top of the organization over time. If a company can maintain checks and balances in its top management circles, politics can be a healthy influence, for it can prevent managers from becoming complacent about the status quo and thus avert organizational decline.

If politics grows rampant and if powerful managers gain such dominance that they can suppress the views of managers who oppose their interests, however, major problems may arise. Checks and balances fade, debate is restricted, and performance suffers. For example, at Gulf & Western, as soon as its founder died, the company sold off fifty businesses that the new top management considered pet projects (and therefore his political preferences) and not suited to the company's portfolio. Ultimately, companies that let politics get so out of hand that shareholder interests suffer are taken over by aggressive new management teams, as happened at Diamond Shamrock.

If kept in check, politics can be a useful management tool in making strategic decisions. The best chief executive officers recognize this fact and create a strategic context in which managers can fight for their ideas and reap the rewards from their lobbying efforts. For example, 3M is well known for its top management committee structure, in which divisional managers who request new funds and new venture managers who champion new products must present their projects to the entire top management team and lobby for support for their ideas. All top managers in 3M experienced this learning process, and presumably the ones in the top management team are those who succeeded best at mobilizing support and commitment for their concepts.

To play politics, managers must have power. **Power** can be defined as the ability of one individual, function, or division to cause another individual, function, or division to do something that it would not otherwise have done.[10] Power differs from authority, which stems from holding a formal position in the hierarchy. Power comes from the ability to informally influence the way other parties behave. Perhaps the simplest way to understand power is to look at its sources.

Sources of Power

To a large degree, the relative power of organizational functions and divisions derives from a company's corporate- and business-level strategies. Different strat-

FIGURE 13.2   **Sources of power**

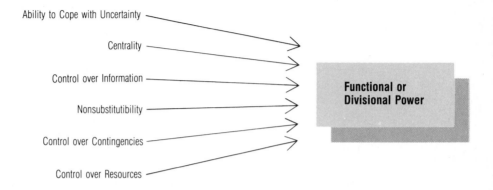

egies make some functions or divisions more important than others in achieving the corporate mission. We consider sources of power at the *functional or divisional level,* rather than at the individual level, because we are primarily interested in the links between politics and power and business- and corporate-level strategy. Figure 13.2 lists the sources of power that we discuss next.

Ability to cope with uncertainty   A function or division gains power if it can reduce uncertainty on behalf of another function or division.[11] Let us suppose that a company is pursuing a strategy of vertical integration. A division that controls the supply and quality of inputs to another division has power over it because it controls the uncertainty facing the second division. At the business level, in a company pursing a low-cost strategy, sales has power over production because sales provide information about customer needs necessary to minimize production costs. In a company pursuing a differentiation strategy, research and development have power over marketing at the early stages in the product life cycle because it controls product innovations. But once innovation problems are solved, marketing is likely to be the most powerful function because it supplies research and development with information on customer needs. Thus a function's power depends on the degree to which other functions rely on it.

Centrality   Power also derives from the **centrality** of a division or function.[12] Centrality refers to the extent to which a division or function is at the center of resource transfers among divisions. For example, in a chemical company, the division supplying specialized chemicals is likely to be central because its activities are critical to both the petroleum division, which supplies its inputs, and the end-using divisions such as plastics or pharmaceuticals, which depend on its outputs. Its activities are central to the production process of all the company's businesses.

Therefore it can exert pressure on corporate headquarters to pursue policies in its own interest.

At the functional level, the function that has the most centrality and therefore power is the one that provides the distinctive competence on which a company's business-level strategy is based. For example, at Apple Computer the function with the greatest centrality is research and development because the company's competitive advantage rests on a technical competence. On the other hand, at Wal-Mart the purchasing and distribution function is the most central because Wal-Mart's competitive advantage depends on its ability to provide a low-cost product.

Control over information   Functions and divisions are also central if they are at the heart of the information flow—that is, if they can control the flow of information to other functions or divisions (or both).[13] Information is a power resource, because by giving or withholding information, one function or division can cause others to behave in certain ways. For example, sales can control the way production operates. If sales manipulates information to satisfy its own goals—for instance, responsiveness to customers—production costs will rise, but production may be unaware that costs could be lowered with a different sales strategy. Similarly, research and development can shape managers' attitudes to the competitive prospects of different kinds of products by supplying favorable information on the attributes of the products it prefers and by downplaying others.

In a very real sense, managers in organizations are playing a subtle information game when they form policies and set objectives. We discuss in Chapter 10 how divisions can disguise their performance by providing only positive information to corporate managers. The more powerful a division, the easier it can do this. In both strategy formulation and implementation, by using information to develop a power base, divisions and functions can strongly influence policy in their own interests.

Nonsubstitutability   A function or division can accrue power proportionately to the degree to which its activities are **nonsubstitutable**—that is, cannot be duplicated.[14] For example, if a company is vertically integrated, supplying divisions are nonsubstitutable to the extent that the company cannot buy what they produce in the marketplace. Thus the petroleum products division is not very powerful if a large supply of oil is available from other suppliers. In an oil crisis, the opposite would be true. On the other hand, the activities of a new venture division—a division in which new products are developed—are nonsubstitutable to the extent that a company cannot buy another company that possesses similar knowledge or expertise. If knowledge or information can be bought, the division is substitutable.

The same holds true at the functional level. A function and the managers inside that function are powerful to the extent that no other function can perform their task. As in the case of centrality, which function is nonsubstitutable depends on the nature of a company's business-level strategy. If the company is pursuing a low-cost strategy, then production is likely to be the key function, and research and development or marketing has less power. But if the company is pursuing a strategy of differentiation then the opposite is likely to be the case.

Thus the power that a function or division gains by virtue of its centrality or nonsubstitutability derives from the company's strategy. Eventually, as a company's strategy changes, the relative power of the functions and divisions also changes. This is the next source of power that we discuss.

Control over contingencies   Over time, the nature of the contingencies—that is, the opportunities and threats—facing a company from the competitive environment will change as the environment changes.[15] The functions or divisions that can deal with the problems confronting the company and allow it to achieve its objectives gain power. Conversely, the functions that can no longer manage the contingency lose power. To give an example, if you look at which functional executives rose to top management positions during the last fifty years, you find that generally the executives who reached the highest posts did so from functions or divisions that were able to deal with the opportunities and threats facing the company.[16]

In the 1950s, for example, the main contingency problem a company confronted was to produce goods and services. Pent-up demand from the years of World War II led to a huge increase in consumer spending for automobiles, homes, and durable goods. Goods needed to be produced quickly and cheaply to meet demand, and during this period the managers who rose to the top were from the *manufacturing* function or consumer products divisions. In the 1960s, the problem changed: Most companies had increased their productive capacity, and the market was saturated. Producing goods was not as difficult as selling them. Hence, *marketing and sales* functions rose to prominence. The rise of executives in companies reflected this critical contingency, for greater numbers of them emerged from the sales function and from marketing-oriented divisions than from any other groups. In the 1970s companies began to realize that competitive conditions were permanent. They had to streamline their strategies and structures to survive in an increasingly hostile environment. As a result, *accounting and finance* became the function that supplied most of the additions to the top management team. Today a company's business- and corporate-level strategy determines which group gains preeminence.

Control over resources   The final source of power that we examine is the ability to control and allocate scarce resources.[17] This source gives corporate-level managers their clout. Obviously, the power of corporate managers depends to a large extent on their ability to allocate capital to the operating divisions and to allot cash to or take it from a division on the basis of their expectations of its future success.

But power from this source is not just a function of the ability to allocate resources immediately; it also comes from the ability to *generate resources in the future*. Thus individual divisions that can generate resources will have power in the corporation. For example, if the Boston Consulting Group matrix is used to categorize divisions, rising stars have power because of the future resources they are expected to generate, whereas cash cows have power because of their ability to generate resources right away. This balance of power between the stars and cash cows explains why corporate management must intervene to allocate resources. Left to themselves, the divisions would never agree on the correct price to charge for capital or on the most efficient way to allocate capital among divisions. Obviously, from a resource perspective, dogs have no power at all, and question marks are in a very weak position, unless they have a strong corporate champion. At the functional level, the same kinds of considerations apply. The ability of sales and marketing to increase customer demand and generate revenues explains their power in the organization. In general, the function that can generate the most resources has the most power.

The most powerful division or function in the organization, then, is the one that can reduce uncertainty for others, is most central and nonsubstitutable, has control over resources and can generate them, and is able to deal with the critical external strategic contingency facing the company. In practice, each division in the corporation has power from one or more of these sources, and so there is a distribution of power among divisions. This condition gives rise to organizational politics, for managers form coalitions to try to get other power holders on their side and thus gain control over the balance of power in the organization.

Effects of Power and Politics on Strategy-Structure Choice

Power and politics strongly influence a company's choice of strategy and structure because the company has to maintain an organizational context that is responsive both to the aspirations of the various divisions, functions, and managers and to changes in the external environment. The problem companies face is that the internal structure of power always lags behind changes in the environment because, in general, the environment changes faster than companies can respond. Those in power never voluntarily give it up, but excessive politicking and power struggles reduce a company's flexibility and may erode its competitive advantage.

For example, if power struggles proceed unchecked, divisions start to compete and to hoard information or knowledge to maximize their own returns. As we note in the Opening Incident to Chapter 11, this condition prevailed at TRW. It also occurred at Digital Equipment Corp. when its product groups became self-contained units that cared more about protecting their interests than about achieving organizational goals. In such situations, exchanging resources among divisions becomes expensive, and gains from synergy are difficult to obtain. These factors in turn lower a company's profitability and reduce organizational growth. Similar problems arise at the functional level: If one function starts to exercise its political muscle, the other functions are likely to retaliate by decreasing their cooperation with the function in question and not responding to its demands. For example, in a company pursuing a low-cost strategy, if the manufacturing function starts to exploit its position and ignores the need of sales to be responsive to customers, over the long run sales can hurt manufacturing by accepting bigger orders but at lower prices or even by seeking many small customer accounts to deliberately elevate production costs and so squeeze profits for the manufacturing function.

Managing Organizational Politics

To manage its politics, a company must devise organizational arrangements that create a **power balance** among the various divisions or functions so that no single one dominates the whole enterprise. In the divisional structure, the corporate headquarters staff plays the balancing role because they can exert power even over strong divisions and force them to share resources for the good of the whole corporation. In a single-business company, a strong chief executive officer is important because he or she must replace the corporate center and balance the power of the strong functions against the weak. The forceful CEO takes the responsibility for giving the weak functions an opportunity to air their concerns and interests and tries to avoid being railroaded into decisions by the strong function pursuing its own interests.

The CEO of a large divisional corporation also has great potential for exerting power. Here the CEO plays another important role, however, that of arbiter of acceptable political decision making. Politics pervade all companies, but the chief executive officer and top-level managers can shape its character. In some organizations, power plays are the norm because chief executive officers themselves garnered power in that way. However, other companies—especially those founded by entrepreneurs who believed in democracy or in decentralized decision making—may not tolerate power struggles, and a different kind of political behavior becomes acceptable. It is based on a function or division manager's competence or expertise rather than on her or his ability to form powerful coalitions. At PepsiCo, politics is of the cutthroat power-play variety, and there is a rapid turnover of managers who fail to meet organizational aspirations. At Coca-Cola, however, ideas and expertise are much more important in politics than power plays directed at maximizing functional or divisional self-interest. Similarly, Intel Corporation does not tolerate politicking or lobbying for personal gain; instead, it rewards risk taking and makes promotion contingent on performance, not seniority.

To design an organizational structure that creates a power balance, strategic managers can use the tools of implementation that we discuss in Chapters 10 and 11. First, they must create the right mix of integrating mechanisms to allow functions or divisions to share information and ideas. A multidivisional structure offers one means of balancing power among divisions, and the matrix structure among functions. A company can then develop norms, values, and a common culture that emphasize corporate, rather than divisional, interests and that stress the company's mission. In companies such as IBM or 3M, for instance, culture serves to harmonize divisional interests with the achievement of corporate goals. Finally, as we note earlier, strong hierarchical control by a gifted chief executive officer can also create the organizational context in which politics can be put to good use and its destructive consequences avoided. When chief executive officers use their expert knowledge as their power, they provide the strong leadership that allows a company to achieve its corporate mission. Indeed, it should be part of the strategic manager's job to learn how to manage politics and power to further corporate interests because politics is an essential part of efficiently allocating scarce organizational resources.

13.4 ORGANIZATIONAL CONFLICT

Politics implies an attempt by one party to influence the goals and decision making of the organization to further its own interests. Sometimes, however, the attempt of one group to further its interests thwarts another group's ability to attain its goals. The result is conflict within the organization. **Conflict** can be defined as a situation that arises when the goal-directed behavior of one organizational group blocks the goal-directed behavior of another.[18] In the discussion that follows, we examine (1) the effect of conflict on organizational performance, (2) the sources of conflict, (3) the ways in which the conflict process operates in the organization, and (4) the ways in which strategic managers can regulate the conflict process using effective conflict resolution practices so that—just as in the case of politics—it yields benefits rather than costs.

Conflict: Good or Bad?

The effect of conflict on organizational performance is continually debated. In the past, conflict was viewed as always bad, or dysfunctional, because it leads to lower organizational performance.[19] According to that view, conflict occurs because managers have not implemented strategy correctly and have not designed the appropriate structure that would make functions or divisions cooperate to achieve corporate objectives. Without doubt, bad implementation can cause conflict and good design can prevent it. If carefully managed, however, conflict can increase organizational performance.[20] The graph in Figure 13.3 indicates the effect of organizational conflict on performance.

The graph shows that to a point conflict increases organizational performance. The reason is that conflict leads to needed organizational change because it exposes weaknesses in organizational design. Managers can respond by changing structure and control systems, thus realigning the power structure of the organ-

FIGURE 13.3   **Effect of conflict on performance**

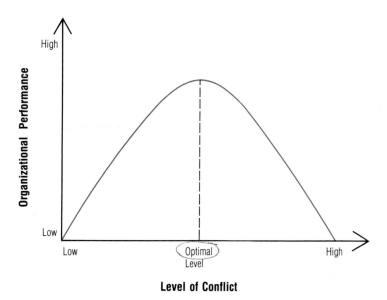

Level of Conflict

ization and shifting the balance of power in favor of the group that can best meet the organization's needs. Conflict signals the need for change. After the optimum point, however, a rise in conflict leads to a decline in performance, for conflict gets out of control and the organization fragments into competing interest groups. Astute managers prevent conflict from passing the optimum point and therefore can use it to increase organizational performance. Managing conflict, then, like managing politics, is a means of improving organizational decision making and of allocating resources and responsibilities. Politics, however, does not necessarily cause conflict, and effective management of the political process is a way of avoiding destructive clashes among groups. Conflict in organizations has many sources, and strategic managers need to be aware of them, so that when conflict does occur it can be quickly controlled or resolved.

Sources of Conflict

As we note elsewhere, conflict arises when the goals of one organizational group thwart those of another. Many factors inherent in the way organizations operate can produce conflict among functions, divisions, and individuals.[21] We focus on three main sources of organizational conflict, and they are summarized in Figure 13.4 on the following page.

FIGURE 13.4   **Sources of organizational conflict**

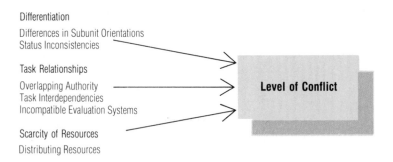

Differentiation
Differences in Subunit Orientations
Status Inconsistencies

Task Relationships
Overlapping Authority
Task Interdependencies
Incompatible Evaluation Systems

Scarcity of Resources
Distributing Resources

Level of Conflict

Differentiation   In Chapter 10, we define differentiation as the way in which a company divides authority and task responsibilities. The process of splitting the organization into hierarchical levels and functions or divisions may produce conflict because it brings to the surface the differences in the goals and interests of groups inside the organization. This kind of conflict has two main causes.

Differences in subunit orientations   As differentiation leads to the emergence of different functions or subunits in a company, each group develops a unique orientation toward the organization's major priorities, as well as its own view of what needs to be done to increase organizational performance. Goals of the various functions naturally differ. For example, production generally has a short-term, cost-directed efficiency orientation. Research and development is oriented toward long-term, technical goals, and sales is oriented toward satisfying customer needs. Thus production may see the solution to a problem as one of reducing costs, sales as one of increasing demand, and research and development as product innovation. Differences in subunit orientation make strategy hard to formulate and implement because they slow a company's response to changes in the competitive environment and reduce its level of integration.

Differences in orientation are also a major problem at the divisional level. For example, cash cow divisions emphasize marketing goals, whereas stars promote technological possibilities. Consequently, it is extremely difficult for divisions such as these to find a common way of viewing the problem. In large corporations, such disagreements can do considerable harm because they reduce the level of cohesion and integration among divisions, hamper cooperation and synergy, and thus lower corporate performance. Many large companies, such as DEC International, Inc., Westinghouse, and Procter & Gamble, have had to cope with this handicap; they responded by reorganizing their structure and improving integration.

Status inconsistencies   In a differentiated company, over time some functions or divisions come to see themselves as more vital to its operations than others.

As a result, they make little attempt to adapt their behaviors to the needs of other functions, thus blocking the goals of the latter. For example, at the functional level, production usually sees itself as the linchpin in the organization and the other functions as mere support services. This leads to line and staff conflict, where production, or line, personnel thwart the goals of staff, or support, personnel.[22] The kind of business-level strategy that a company adopts may intensify line and staff conflict because it increases the status of some functions relative to others. In low-cost companies, production is particularly important, and in differentiators, marketing or research and development is most important.

At the divisional level, the divisions that are more central to the company's operations—for example, those that supply resources to the end-using divisions—may come to see themselves as the system's linchpins. They also may pay little attention to the needs of the end users (for example, developing new products). The end users may retaliate by buying in the marketplace or, more typically, by fighting over transfer prices, which, as we discuss earlier, is a major sign of conflict among divisions. Thus the relationships among divisions must be handled carefully by corporate headquarters to prevent conflicts from flaring up and damaging interdivisional relationships.

Task relationships   As we discuss in Chapter 10, several features of task relationships may generate conflict among functions and divisions.[23]

Overlapping authority   If two different functions or divisions claim authority and responsibility for the same task, then conflict may develop in the organization. This often happens when the organization is growing, and thus functional or divisional relationships are not yet fully worked out. Likewise, when changes occur in task relationships, for instance, as when divisions start to share sales and distribution facilities to reduce costs, disputes over who controls what emerge. As a result, divisions may fight for control of the resource and thus spawn conflict.

Task interdependencies   To develop or produce goods and services, the work of one function flows horizontally to the next so that each function can build on the contributions of the others.[24] If one function does not do its job well, then the function next in line is seriously hampered in its work, and this too, generates conflict. For example, the ability of manufacturing to reduce costs on the production line depends on how well research and development has designed the product for cheap manufacture and how well sales has attracted large, stable customer accounts. At the divisional level, when divisions are trading resources, the quality of the products supplied by one division to the next affects the quality of the next division's products.

The potential for conflict is great when functions or divisions are markedly interdependent. In fact, the higher the level of interdependence, the higher is the potential for conflict among functions or divisions.[25] Interdependence among functions, along with the consequent need to prevent conflict from arising, is the reason that managing a matrix structure is so expensive. Similarly, managing a strategy of related diversification is expensive because conflicts over resource transfers arise and have to be continually dealt with. Conversely, with unrelated diversification, the potential for interdivisional conflict is minimal because divisions do not trade resources.

The merger between Burroughs Corporation and Sperry Corporation to create Unisys Corporation created the types of problems that must be managed to prevent conflict from task interdependence. The CEO of Burroughs, W. M. Blumenthal, has taken enormous pains to manage new task interdependences to avoid major conflicts among divisions and has used a variety of integrating mechanisms to bring the two companies together. The problem is so severe because each company has the same set of functions, which, in the long run, must be merged.

Incompatible evaluation systems   We mention in Chapter 11 that a company has to design its evaluation and reward systems so that they do not interfere with task relationships among functions and divisions. Inequitable performance evaluation systems stir up conflict.[26] Typical problems include finding a way of jointly rewarding sales and production to avoid scheduling conflicts and setting budgets and transfer prices so that they do not lead to competition among divisions. Again, the more complex the task relationships, the harder it is to evaluate each function's or division's contribution to revenue, and the more likely is conflict to arise.

Scarcity of resources   Competition over scarce resources also produces conflict.[27] This kind of conflict most often occurs among divisions and between divisions and corporate management over the allocation of capital, although budget fights among functions can also be fierce when resources are scarce. As we discuss in other chapters, divisions resist attempts to transfer their profits to other divisions and may distort information to retain their resources. Other organizational stakeholders also have an interest in the way a company allocates scarce resources. For example, shareholders care about the size of the dividends, and unions and employees want to maximize their salaries and benefits.

Given so many potential sources of conflict in organizations, conflict of one kind or another is always present in strategic decision making. We need to consider how a typical conflict process works itself out in the organization and whether there are any guidelines that corporate managers can use to try to direct conflict and turn its destructive potential to good strategic use. A model developed by Lou R. Pondy, a famous management theorist, helps show how the conflict process operates in organizations.[28] We discuss this in the next section.

The Organizational Conflict Process

Conflict is so hard to manage strategically because it is usually unexpected. The sources of conflict that we have just discussed are often inherent in a company's

FIGURE 13.5   **Stages in the conflict process**

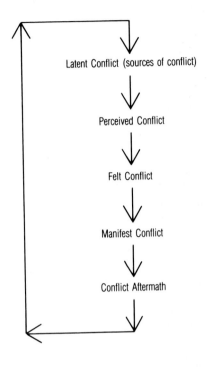

mode of operation. The first stage in the conflict process, then, is *latent conflict—* potential conflict that can flare up when the right conditions arise. (The stages in the conflict process appear in Figure 13.5.) Latent conflicts are frequently activated by changes in an organization's strategy or structure that affect the relationship among functions or divisions. For example, if a company has been pursuing a dominant product strategy using a functional structure to implement the strategy, it might decide to widen its product range. To overcome problems of coordinating a range of specialist services over many products, the company may adopt a product structure. The new structure changes task relationships among product managers, and this in turn changes the relative status and areas of authority of the different functional and product managers. Conflict between functional and product managers or among product managers is likely to ensue.

Because every change in a company's strategy and structure alters the organizational context, conflict can easily arise unless the situation is carefully managed to avoid it. But avoidance is not always possible, and consequently the latent stage of the conflict process quickly leads to the next stage: *perceived conflict.*

Perceived conflict means that managers become aware of the clashes. After a change in strategy and structure, managers discover that the actions of another function or group are obstructing the operations of their group. Managers start to react to the situation, and from the perceived stage, they go quickly to the *felt conflict* stage. Here managers start to personalize the conflict. Opinions polarize, as one function or division starts to blame the others for causing the conflict. Production might blame the inefficiency of sales for a fall in orders, while sales might blame production for a fall in product quality. Typically, there is a marked lack of cooperation at this stage, and integration among functions or divisions breaks down as the groups start to polarize and develop an "us versus them" mentality. If not managed, this stage in the conflict process leads quickly to the next stage, *manifest conflict*.

At this point, the conflict among functions or divisions comes into the open, and each group strives to thwart the goals of the other. Groups compete to protect their own interests and block the interests of other groups. Manifest conflict can take many forms. The most obvious is open aggression among top managers as they start to blame other functions or divisions for causing the problem. Other forms of manifest conflict are transfer pricing battles and knowledge hoarding. Defamatory information about other divisions is also likely to be circulated at this stage in the conflict process. These actions are much worse than political maneuvering because divisions are trying not simply to promote their interests but also to damage the performance of the other divisions. As a result, the company cannot achieve any gains from scheduling resource transfers or from developing synergy between divisions.

At the functional level, the effects of conflict can be equally devastating. A company cannot pursue a low-cost strategy if the functions are competing. If sales makes no attempt to keep manufacturing informed about customer demands, manufacturing cannot maximize the length of production runs. Similarly, a company cannot successfully differentiate if marketing does not inform research and development about changes in consumer preferences or if product engineering and research and development are competing over product specifications. Companies have experienced each of these conflicts at one time or another and suffered a loss in performance and competitive advantage because of them.

The long-term effects of manifest conflict emerge in the last stage of the conflict process, the *conflict aftermath*. Suppose that in one company a change in strategy leads to conflict over transfer prices. Then divisional managers, with the help of corporate personnel, resolve the problem to everyone's satisfaction and re-establish good working relationships. In another company, however, the conflict between divisions over transfer prices is resolved only by the intervention of corporate managers, who *impose* a solution on divisional managers. A year later, a change in the environment occurs that makes the transfer pricing system in both companies no longer equitable, and prices must be renegotiated. How will the two companies react to this situation? The managers in the company in which the conflict was settled amicably will approach this new round of negotiations with a cooperative, and not an adversarial, attitude. In the company in which divisions never really established an agreement, however, a new round of intense clashes is likely, with a resulting fall in organizational performance.

The conflict aftermath in each company was different because in one company conflict was resolved successfully but in the other it was not. The conflict aftermath sets the scene for the next round of conflict that will certainly occur because conflict is inherent in the ways companies operate and the environment is constantly changing. The reason that some companies have a long history of bad relations among functions or divisions is that their conflict has never been managed successfully. In companies in which strategic managers have resolved the conflict, a cohesive organizational culture obtains. In those companies, managers adopt a cooperative, not a competitive, attitude when conflict occurs. The question we need to tackle, however, is how best to manage the conflict process strategically to avoid its bad effects and make transitions in strategy-structure choice as smooth as possible.

Managing Conflict Strategically

Given the way the conflict process operates, the goal of strategic managers should be to intervene as early as possible so that conflict does not reach the felt, and particularly the manifest, stage. At the manifest stage, conflict is difficult to resolve successfully and is much more likely to lead to a bad conflict aftermath. At what point, then, should managers intervene?

Ideally, managers should intervene at the latent stage and act on the sources of conflict.[29] Good strategic planning early can prevent many of the problems that occur later. For example, when managers are changing a company's strategy, they should be consciously thinking about the effects of these changes on future group relationships. Similarly, when changing organizational structure, strategic managers should anticipate the effects the changes will have on functional and divisional relationships. Many large organizations do act in this way and require that the potential effect of strategy-structure changes on the organization be included in the strategic planning process to prevent conflict from arising later on.

Nevertheless, often it is impossible to foresee the ramifications of changes in strategy. Organizations are complex, and many unexpected things can happen as managers implement organizational change. Consequently, managers cannot always intervene at the latent stage to prevent conflict from arising. Thus changes in strategy or structure may lead to failure, as when Apple Computer went to a divisional structure or when Kodak's instant camera proved a financial disaster.

Frequently, intervention is only possible between the felt and the manifest stage. It is here that managers may have the best chance to find a solution to the problem. Managers can adopt a number of different solutions, or conflict resolution strategies, and we consider them next.

Conflict Resolution Strategies

Using authority   As we discuss in Chapter 11, integration among functions and divisions is a major problem because they have equal authority and thus cannot control each other. When functions cannot solve their problems, these problems are often passed on to corporate managers or to the chief executive officer, who has the authority to impose a solution on parties. In general, there are two ways of using authority to manage conflict. First, the chief executive officer or corporate managers can play the role of arbiters and impose a solution on the parties in conflict. Second, they can act as mediators and try to open up the situation so that the parties in conflict can find their own solution. Research shows that the latter approach works better because it leads to a good conflict aftermath.

Change task relationships   In this approach, the aim is to change the interdependence among functions or divisions so that the source of the conflict is removed. Task relationships can be altered in two ways: First, strategic managers can *reduce* the degree of dependence among the parties. For example, they can develop a structure in which integration among groups is easier to accomplish. Thus a shift from a functional to a divisional structure can reduce the potential for conflict. Similarly, establishing a strategic business unit structure can lessen the chances of conflict among divisions.

Alternatively, conflict may arise because the correct integrating mechanisms for managing task interdependence have not been adopted. In this case, managing the conflict means *increasing* integration among divisions and functions. Thus in high-tech companies, in which functions are very highly task interdependent, managers can use a matrix structure to provide the integration necessary to resolve conflict. In a divisional structure, managers can use integrating roles and establish integrating departments to allow divisions to price and transfer resources. At Hewlett-Packard, corporate staff created three integrating committees to allow divisions to share resources and minimize conflict over product development. Increased integration prevents conflicts from emerging. Managers also use structure through the process of strategy implementation to solve conflicts.

Changing controls   Conflict can also be managed by altering the organization's control and evaluation systems. For example, in some organizations it may be possible to develop joint goals among functions and divisions and to create a reward system based on the achievement of these joint goals, as when sales and production are jointly rewarded on the basis of how much revenue they generate. Similarly, corporate evaluation systems can be created to measure the degree to which divisions cooperate with one another. We discuss in an earlier chapter how TRW attempted to develop such evaluation systems so that divisions could share information and knowledge while being appropriately rewarded for it. Finally, to some degree, conflict is the result of managers in one function not appreciating the position of those in another. To give managers a broader perspective and to overcome differences in subunit orientations, managers can be rotated among divisions and given assignments at the corporate level to show them the problems faced by managers elsewhere in the company.

Summary: Organizational Conflict

Conflict is an ever present organizational phenomenon that must be managed if the firm is to achieve its objectives. The whole process of strategy-structure choice creates the potential for conflict, and in a rapidly changing environment conflict is increasingly likely. It is a part of the strategic manager's job to develop the personal skills and abilities needed to solve conflict problems. These skills involve the ability to analyze the organizational context to pinpoint the source of the problem and handling managers who are in conflict. It is possible now to consider the process of managing organizational change.

13.5 MANAGING CHANGES IN STRATEGY-STRUCTURE CHOICE: STEPS IN THE CHANGE PROCESS

In the modern corporation, change rather than stability is the order of the day. Rapid changes in technology, the competitive environment, and customer demands have increased the rate at which companies have to alter their strategies to survive in the marketplace.[30] Consequently, companies have to go through rapid structural reorganizations as they outgrow their structures. E. F. Hutton, for example, estimates that more than half of the top 800 major corporations have undergone major restructuring in recent years.[31] In this section, we discuss the problems associated with managing such changes in strategy and structure.

The management of strategic change involves a series of distinct steps that managers must follow if the change process is to succeed. These steps are listed in Figure 13.6.

FIGURE 13.6   Stages in the change process

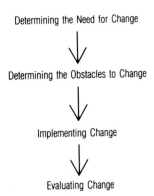

Determining the Need for Change

The first step in the change process involves strategic managers' determining the need for change. Sometimes this change is obvious, as when divisions are fighting or competitors introduce a product that is clearly superior to anything that the company has in production. More often, however, managers have trouble determining that something is going wrong in the organization. Problems may develop gradually, and organizational performance may be slipping for a number of years before it becomes obvious. At CBS, for example, profitability fell, but because it was a reputable stock, the fall caused little stir. After a lapse of time, however, investors realized that the stock had been undervalued and that CBS could be made to perform better. In other words, outside investors realized sooner than inside management did that there was a need for change.

Thus the first step in the change process occurs when the company's strategic managers or others in a position to take action recognize that there is a gap between desired company performance and actual performance.[32] Using measures such as falls in stock price or market share as indicators that change is needed, managers can start looking for the source of the problem. To discover it, they conduct a SWOT analysis. First, they examine the company's strengths and weaknesses. For example, management conducts a strategic audit of the functions and divisions and looks at their contribution to profitability over time. Perhaps some divisions have become dogs without management's realizing it or the company has too many rising stars. Management also analyzes the company's level of differentiation and integration to make sure that it is appropriate for its strategy. Perhaps a company does not have the integrating mechanisms in place to achieve gains from synergy. Management then examines environmental opportunities and threats that might explain the problem. For instance, the company may have had intense competition from substitute products without being aware of it, or a shift in consumer tastes or technology may have caught it unawares.

Once the source of the problem has been identified, management must determine the ideal future state of the company—that is, how it should change its strategy and structure. A company may decide, like CBS, to lower its costs by streamlining its operation. Or, like General Motors, it may increase its research and development budget or diversify into new products to increase its future profitability. Essentially, strategic managers apply the conceptual tools that this book has described to work out the best choice of strategy and structure to maximize profitability. The choice they make is specific to each individual company, and, as noted earlier, there is no way that managers can determine its correctness in advance. This is the adventure of strategic management.

Thus the first step in the change process involves determining the need for change, analyzing the organization's current position, and determining the ideal future state that strategic managers would like it to attain. This process is diagrammed in Figure 13.7.

FIGURE 13.7   **A model of change**

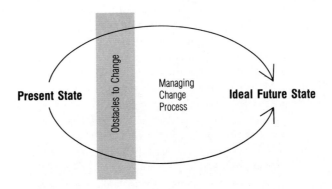

Determining the Obstacles to Change

The second step in the change process involves determining the obstacles to change.[33] Strategic managers must analyze the factors that may prevent the company from reaching its ideal future state. Obstacles to change are found at four levels in the organization: corporate, divisional, functional, and individual levels.

At the corporate level, there are several potential obstacles to consider. First, changing strategy or structure even in seemingly trivial ways may significantly affect a company's behavior. For example, suppose that to reduce costs the company decides to centralize all divisional purchasing and sales activities at the corporate level. Such consolidation could severely damage each division's ability to develop a unique strategy for its own individual markets. Or suppose that in response to low-cost foreign competition the company decides to pursue a policy of differentiation. This action would change the balance of power among functions and lead to politicking and even conflict as functions start fighting to retain their status in the organization. A *company's present structure and strategy* are powerful obstacles to change. They produce a massive amount of inertia that has to be overcome before change can take place. This is why change is usually such a slow process.

The *type of structure* a company uses can also impede change. For example, it is much easier to change strategy if a company is using a matrix, rather than a functional, structure, or if it is decentralized rather than centralized, or if it has a high, rather than a low, level of integration. Decentralized, matrix structures are more flexible than highly controlled functional structures. It is easier to change subunit orientations, and thus there is a lower potential for conflict.

Some *corporate cultures* are easier to change than others. For example, change is notoriously difficult in the military because everything is sacred to obedience and the following of orders. Some cultures, however, such as Hewlett-Packard's, are based on values that emphasize flexibility or change itself. Consequently, they are much easier to change when change becomes necessary.

Similar factors operate at the divisional level. Change is difficult at the divisional level if divisions are *highly interrelated and trade resources,* because a shift in one division's operations will affect other divisions. Consequently, it is more difficult to manage change if a company is pursuing a strategy of related, rather than unrelated, diversification. Furthermore, changes in strategy affect divisions in different ways because change generally favors the interests of some divisions over those of others. Divisions may thus have different attitudes to change, and some will not support the changes in strategy that the company makes. Existing divisions may resist establishing new product divisions because they will lose resources and their status inside the organization may fall.

The same obstacles to change exist at the functional level as well. Like divisions, different functions have different strategic orientations and react differently to the changes management proposes. For example, in a decline situation, sales will resist attempts to cut back on sales expenditures to reduce costs if it believes the problem stems from inefficiency in manufacturing. At the individual level, too, people are notoriously resistant to change because change implies uncertainty, which breeds insecurity and the fear of the unknown.[34] Because managers are people, this individual resistance reinforces the tendency of each function and division to oppose changes that may have uncertain effects on them.

All these obstacles make it difficult to change organizational strategy or structure quickly. That is why American car manufacturers took so long to respond to the Japanese challenge. They were accustomed to a situation of complete dominance and had developed inflexible, centralized structures that inhibited risk taking and quick reaction. Paradoxically, companies that experience the greatest uncertainty may become best able to respond to it. When they have been forced to change often, they develop the ability to handle change easily.[35] Strategic managers must understand all these potential obstacles to change as they design a company's new strategy and structure. All these factors are potential sources of conflict and politics that can dramatically affect a company's ability to move quickly to exploit new strategic opportunities. Obstacles to change must be recognized and incorporated into the strategic plan. The larger and more complex the organization, the harder it is to implement change.

Implementing Change

Implementing—that is, introducing and managing—change raises several questions. For instance, who should actually carry out the change: internal managers or external consultants? Although internal managers may have the most experience or knowledge about a company's operations, they may lack perspective because they are too much a part of the organization's culture. They also run the risk of appearing to be politically motivated and of having a personal stake in the changes they recommend. Companies therefore often turn to external consultants who can view the situation more objectively. Outside consultants, however, must spend a lot of time learning about the company and its problems before they can propose a plan of action. Thus the issue of who should manage the change is complex, and most companies create a task force consisting of both internal managers and external consultants. In this way, companies can get the benefits of inside information and the external perspective.

Generally, a company can take two main approaches to change: top-down change or bottom-up change.[36] With **top-down change**, the change task force analyzes how to alter strategy and structure, recommends a course of action, and then moves quickly to implement change in the organization. The emphasis is on speed of response and management of problems as they occur. **Bottom-up change** is much more gradual. The change task force consults with managers at all levels in the organization. Then, over time, it develops a detailed plan for change, with a timetable of events and stages that the company will go through. The emphasis in bottom-up change is on participation and keeping people informed about the situation, so that uncertainty is minimized.

The advantage of bottom-up change is that it removes some of the obstacles to change by incorporating them into the strategic plan. In addition, the aim of consulting with managers at all levels is to reveal potential problems. The disadvantage of bottom-up change is its slowness. On the other hand, in the case of the much speedier top-down change, the problems may emerge later and may be difficult to resolve. In general, the type of change that companies adopt depends on the nature of their situation. Flexible companies that are used to change risk fewer problems with top-down change. For corporate lumbering giants, bottom-up change may be the only way of getting anything done because managers are so unaccustomed to and threatened by change.

Evaluating Change

The last step in the change process is to evaluate the effects of the changes in strategy and structure on organizational performance. A company must compare the way it operates after implementing change with the way it operated before. Managers use indices such as changes in stock market price or market share to assess the effects of change in strategy. It is much more difficult, however, to assess the effects of changes in structure on company performance because they are so much more difficult to measure. Whereas companies can easily measure the increased revenue from increased product differentiation, they do not have any sure means of evaluating the effects that moving from a product to a divisional structure has had on performance. Managers can be surveyed, however, and over time it may become obvious that organizational flexibility and the company's ability to manage its strategy have increased. Managers can also assess whether the change has decreased the level of politicking and conflict and strengthened cooperation among the divisions and functions.

Organizational change is a complex and difficult process for companies to manage successfully. The problem starts from the beginning in getting managers to realize that change is necessary and to admit that there is a problem. Once the need for change is recognized managers can go about the process of recommending a course of action and analyze potential obstacles to change. Depending on the organization and the nature of the problem the company is dealing with, either bottom-up or top-down change is appropriate. However, in both cases it is best to use a mix of internal managers and external consultants to implement the change. After implementing change, managers assess its effects on organizational performance and then the whole process is repeated as companies strive to increase their level of performance. This is why companies in which change is a regular occurrence find it much easier to manage than do companies in which complacent managers only start a change effort when the company is already in trouble.

13.6 SUMMARY OF CHAPTER

This chapter has examined the political side of strategy formulation and implementation and discussed the problems that can arise in managing changes in strategy and structure. It should now be apparent that organizations are not just rational decision-making systems in which managers coldly calculate the potential returns from their investments. Organizations are arenas of power, in which individuals and groups fight for prestige and possession of scarce resources. In the pursuit of their interests, managers compete and engage in conflict. The very nature of the organization makes this inevitable. Managers have to deal with politics and conflict creatively to achieve organizational benefits from them. They also have to manage the process of organizational change so that the company can maximize its ability to exploit the environment. The most successful companies are those in which change is regarded as the norm and managers are constantly seeking to improve organizational strengths and eliminate weaknesses so that they can maximize future profitability. This chapter makes the following main points:

1. Organizational decision making is a combination of both rational and political processes. Formation of coalitions, compromise, and bargaining are integral parts of the strategic management process.

2. Organizational politics occurs because different groups have different interests and different perceptions of the appropriate means to further their interests.

3. To play politics, managers must have power. Power is the ability of one party to cause another party to act in the first party's interest.

4. The sources of power available to strategic managers include coping with uncertainty, centrality, control over information, nonsubstitutability, and control over contingencies and resources.

5. Politics must be managed if the company is to obtain benefits from the process, and one of the best ways of doing so is to create a power balance in the organization. A strong chief executive officer or a well-designed structure can create a power balance.

6. Organizational conflict exists when divisions, functions, or individuals go beyond competition and strive to thwart each other's goals. Conflict can be defined as a situation that occurs when the goal-directed behavior of one group blocks the goal-directed behavior of another.

7. Whether conflict is good or bad for the organization depends on the way it is managed. In general, conflict is useful in exposing organizational weaknesses, but it must be managed quickly, before it gets out of hand.

8. Conflict is inherent in the nature of an organization's design. The sources of conflict include differentiation, task relationships, and scarcity of resources.

9. Conflict can be regarded as a process with a series of stages. These stages are latent conflict, perceived conflict, felt conflict, manifest conflict, and conflict aftermath.

10. Organizational change is the process by which companies alter their strategy and structure to improve performance.

11. Organizational change is managed through a series of stages. First, the need for change must be recognized, and the company must decide on its ideal future state. Then the obstacles to change must be analyzed and incorporated into the change plan, and change must be implemented. Finally, the change process must be evaluated to assess its effects on organizational performance.

12. Well-run organizations are constantly aware of the need to monitor their performance, and they institutionalize change so that they can realign their structures to suit the competitive environment.

Discussion Questions

1. How can managing (a) politics and (b) conflict in organizations lead to improved organizational decision making? How might a company create a system of checks and balances in the organization through the design of its structure and control systems?

2. How might conflict and politics affect the formulation and implementation of (a) generic competitive strategies and (b) corporate-level strategies?

3. What are some of the political problems a company might encounter if it takes over a related business and tries to integrate it into its organizational structure? (Hint: Use the sources of power to frame your answer.)

4. Discuss how you would set up a plan for change for an unrelated company that is starting to pursue a strategy of related diversification. What problems will the company encounter? How should it deal with them?

Endnotes

1. "Corporate Shoot-Out at Black Rock," *Time,* September 22, 1986, pp. 68–72.

2. "Civil War at CBS," *Newsweek,* September 15, 1986, pp. 46–54.

3. P. W. Barnes, "Tisch Wins Praise for Fast Action at CBS," *The Wall Street Journal,* October 28, 1986, p. 5.

4. P. J. Boyers, "Three New Bosses are Slashing Operations and Putting Nearly Everyone's Job on the Line," *The New York Times,* November 2, 1986, p. 26.

5. A. M. Pettigrew, *The Politics of Organizational Decision Making* (London: Tavistock, 1973).

6. R. H. Miles, *Macro Organizational Behavior* (Santa Monica, Calif.: Goodyear, 1980).

7. J. G. March and H. A. Simon, *Organizations* (New York: Wiley, 1958).

8. J. G. March, "The Business Firm as a Coalition," *The Journal of Politics,* 24 (1962), 662–678. D. J. Vredenburgh and J. G. Maurer, "A Process Framework of Organizational Politics," *Human Relations,* 37 (1984), 47–66.

9. T. Burns, "Micropolitics: Mechanism of Institutional Change," *Administrative Science Quarterly,* 6 (1961), 257–281.

10. R. A. Dahl, "The Concept of Power," *Behavioral Science,* 2 (1957), 201–215. G. A. Astley and P. S. Sachdeva, "Structural Sources of Intraorganizational Power," *Academy of Management Review,* 9 (1984), 104–113.

11. This section draws heavily on D. J. Hickson, C. R. Hinings, C. A. Lee, R. E. Schneck, and D. J. Pennings, "A Strategic Contingencies Theory of Intraorganizational Power," *Administrative Science Quarterly,* 16 (1971), 216–227; and C. R. Hinings, D. J. Hickson, J. M. Pennings, and R. E. Schneck, "Structural Conditions of Interorganizational Power," *Administrative Science Quarterly,* 19 (1974), 22–44.

12. Hickson et al., "A Strategic Contingencies Theory."

13. Pettigrew, *The Politics of Organizational Decision Making.*

14. Hickson et al., "A Strategic Contingencies Theory." Pettigrew, *The Politics of Organizational Decision Making.*

15. Hickson et al., "A Strategic Contingencies Theory."

16. H. A. Landsberger, "The Horizontal Dimension in Bureaucracy," *Administrative Science Quarterly,* 6 (1961), 299–232.

17. G. R. Salancik and J. Pfeffer, "The Bases and Use of Power in Organizational Decision Making: The Case of a University," *Administrative Science Quarterly,* 19 (1974), 453–473.

18. J. A. Litterer, "Conflict in Organizations: A Reexamination," *Academy of Management Journal,* 9 (1966), 178–186. S. M. Schmidt and T. A. Kochan, "Conflict: Towards Conceptual Clarity," *Administrative Science Quarterly,* 13 (1972), 359–370. Miles, *Macro Organizational Behavior.*

19. Miles, *Macro Organizational Behavior.*

20. S. P. Robbins, *Managing Organizational Conflict: A Nontraditional Approach* (Englewood Cliffs, N.J.: Prentice-Hall, 1974). L. Coser, *The Functions of Social Conflict* (New York: Free Press, 1956).

21. This discussion owes much to the seminal work of the following authors: Lou R. Pondy, "Organizational Conflict:

Concepts and Models," *Administrative Science Quarterly, 2* (1967), 296–320; and R. E. Walton and J. M. Dutton, "The Management of Interdepartmental Conflict: A Model and Review," *Administrative Science Quarterly,* 14 (1969), 62–73.

22. M. Dalton, *Men Who Manage* (New York: Wiley, 1959). Walton and Dutton, "The Management of Interdepartmental Conflict."

23. Walton and Dutton, "The Management of Interdepartmental Conflict." J. McCann and J. R. Galbraith, "Interdepartmental Relationships," in P. C. Nystrom and W. H. Starbuck (eds.), *Handbook of Organizational Design* (New York: Oxford University Press, 1981).

24. J. D. Thompson, *Organizations in Action* (New York: McGraw-Hill, 1967).

25. Walton and Dutton, "The Management of Interdepartmental Conflict," p. 65.

26. Ibid., p. 68.

27. Pondy, "Organizational Conflict," p. 300.

28. Ibid., p. 310.

29. Ibid., p. 316.

30. T. J. Peters and R. H. Waterman Jr., *In Search of Excellence* (New York: Harper & Row, 1982).

31. J. Thackray, "Restructuring Is the Name of the Hurricane," *Euromoney* (February 1987), 106–108.

32. R. Beckhard, *Organizational Development* (Reading, Mass.: Addison-Wesley, 1969). W. L. French and C. H. Bell Jr., *Organization Development,* 2nd ed. (Englewood Cliffs, N.J.: Prentice-Hall, 1978).

33. L. C. Coch and R. P. French Jr., "Overcoming Resistance to Change," *Human Relations* (August 1948), 512–532. P. R. Lawrence, "How to Deal with Resistance to Change," *Harvard Business Review* (January–February 1969), 4–12.

34. P. Kotter and L. A. Schlesinger, "Choosing Strategies for Change," *Harvard Business Review* (March–April 1979), 106–114.

35. J. R. Galbraith, "Designing the Innovative Organization," *Organization Dynamics* (Winter 1982), 5–25.

36. M. Beer, *Organizational Change and Development* (Santa Monica, Calif.: Goodyear, 1980). L. E. Greiner, "Patterns of Organizational Change," *Harvard Business Review* (May–June 1967), 3–5.

P A R T IV

CASE STUDY ANALYSIS

Chapter 14

ANALYZING AND WRITING A CASE STUDY

14.1 WHAT IS CASE STUDY ANALYSIS?

Case study analysis is an integral part of a course in strategic management. The purpose of a case study is to provide students with experience of the strategic management problems faced by actual organizations. A case study presents an account of what happened to a business or industry over a number of years. It chronicles the events that managers had to deal with, such as changes in the competitive environment, and charts the managers' response, which usually involved changing the business- or corporate-level strategy. The cases in Part IV of this book cover a wide range of issues and problems that managers have had to confront. Some cases are about finding the right business-level strategy to compete in changing industry conditions. Some are about companies that grew by acquisition, with little concern for the rationale behind their growth, and how this affected their future profitability. Each case is different because each organization is different. The underlying thread in all the cases, however, is the use of strategic management techniques to solve business problems.

Cases prove valuable in a strategic management course for several reasons. First, cases provide you, the student, with experience of organizational problems that you probably have not had the opportunity to experience firsthand. In a relatively short period of time, a semester, you will have the chance to appreciate and analyze the problems faced by many different companies and to understand how managers tried to deal with them.

Second, cases illustrate the theory and content of strategic management—that is, all the information that we have presented to you in the previous thirteen chapters of this book. This information has been collected, discovered, and distilled from the observations, research, and experience of managers and academics. The meaning and implication of this information are made clearer when they are applied to case studies. The theory and concepts help reveal what is going on in the companies studied and allow you to evaluate the solutions that specific companies adopted to deal with their problems. Consequently, when you analyze cases, you will be like a detective who, with a set of conceptual tools, probes what happened and what or who was responsible, and then marshals the evidence that provides the solution. Top managers enjoy the thrill of testing their problem-solving abilities in the real world. After all, it is important to remember that no one knows what the right answer is. All that managers can do is to make the best guess. In fact, managers say repeatedly that they are happy if they are right only half the time in solving strategic problems. Strategic management is an uncertain game, and using cases to see how theory can be put to practice is one way of improving your skills in diagnostic investigation.

The third advantage of case studies is that they provide you with the opportunity to participate in class and gain experience in presenting your ideas. Sometimes the instructor will call on students as a group to identify what was going on in a case, and through classroom discussion the issue and solutions to the problem in the case will reveal themselves. In this situation, you will have to organize your views and conclusions so that you can present them to the class. Be prepared for a discussion of your ideas. Because your classmates may have analyzed the issues differently from you, they will want you to argue your points before you can convince them, and so be prepared for debate. This mode of discussion is an example of the dialectical approach to decision making that you may recall from Chapter 1. This is how decisions are made in the actual business world. Sometimes instructors will assign an individual, or more commonly a group, to analyze the case before the whole class. The individual or group will probably be responsible for a thirty- to forty-minute presentation of the case to the class, and in that presentation must cover the issues involved, the problems facing the company, and a series of recommendations for resolving those problems. Then the discussion will be thrown open to the class, and you will have to defend your ideas. Through such discussions and presentations, you will experience how to convey your ideas effectively to others. Remember that a great deal of managers' time is spent in these kinds of situations, presenting their ideas and engaging in discussion with other managers, who have their own views about what is going on. Thus you will experience in the classroom the actual process of strategic management, and this will serve you well in your future career.

If you work in groups to analyze case studies, you will also learn about the group process involved in joint work. When people work in groups, it is often difficult to schedule time and allocate responsibility for the case analysis. There will always be group members who shirk or who are so sure of their own ideas that they try to dominate the group's analysis. Most of strategic management takes place in groups, however, and it is best if you learn about these problems now.

14.2 ANALYZING A CASE STUDY

As just mentioned, the purpose of the case study is to let you apply the concepts of strategic management when you analyze the issues facing a specific company. Thus to analyze a case study, it is necessary to closely examine the issues with which the company is involved. This will often take several readings of the case: a first reading, to grasp the overall picture of what is happening to a company, and then subsequent readings, to discover and grasp the specific problems.

Generally, detailed analysis of a case study should include eight areas:

1. The history, development and growth of the company over time
2. The identification of the company's internal strengths and weaknesses
3. The nature of the external environment surrounding the company
4. A SWOT analysis
5. The kind of corporate-level strategy pursued by a company
6. The nature of the company's business-level strategy
7. The company's structure and control systems and how they match its strategy
8. Recommendations

To analyze a case, you need to apply the course concepts to each of these areas. Which concepts to use is obvious from the chapter titles. For example, to analyze the company's environment, you would use Chapter 3, on environmental analysis. To help you further, we next offer a brief guide to some of the main strategic management concepts that can be used to analyze the case material for each of the points we have just noted.

1. *Analyzing the company's history, development and growth.* A convenient way to investigate how a company's past strategy and structure affect it in the present is to chart the critical incidents in its history—that is, the events that were the most unusual or the most essential for its development into the company it is today. Some of the events have to do with its founding, its initial products, how it made new product market decisions, and how it developed and chose functional competencies to pursue. Its entry into new businesses and shifts in its main lines of business are also important milestones to consider.

2. *Identification of the company's internal strengths and weaknesses.* Once the historical profile is completed, you can begin the SWOT analysis. Take all the incidents you have charted and use them to develop an account of the company's strengths and weaknesses as they have emerged historically. Examine each of the value creation functions of the company, and identify the functions in which the company is currently strong and currently weak. Some companies might be weak in marketing, and some strong in research and development. Make lists of these strengths and weaknesses. Table 14.1 gives examples of what might go in these lists.

3. *Environmental analysis.* The next step is to identify environmental opportunities and threats. Here you should apply all the concepts from Chapter 3, on industry and macroenvironments, to analyze the environment the company is confronting. Of particular importance at the industry level is Porter's five forces model and the stage of the life cycle model. Which factors in the macroenvironment will appear salient depends on the specific company being analyzed. However, use each concept in turn—for instance, demographic factors—to see if it is relevant for the company in question.

TABLE 14.1   **A SWOT checklist**

Potential internal strengths	Potential internal weaknesses
Many product lines?	Obsolete, narrow product lines?
Broad market coverage?	Rising manufacturing costs?
Manufacturing competence?	Decline in R&D innovations?
Good marketing skills?	Poor marketing plan?
Good materials management systems?	Poor materials management systems?
R&D skills and leadership?	Loss of customer good will?
Information system competencies?	Indequate information systems?
Human resource competencies?	Inadequate human resources?
Brand name reputation?	Loss of brand name capital?
Portfolio management skills?	Growth without direction?
Cost or differentiation advantage?	Bad portfolio management?
New-venture management expertise?	Loss of corporate direction?
Appropriate management style?	Infighting among divisions?
Appropriate organizational structure?	Loss of corporate control?
Appropriate control systems?	Inappropriate organizational structure and control systems?
Ability to manage strategic change?	High conflict and politics?
Well-developed corporate strategy?	Poor financial management?
Good financial management?	Others?
Others?	
Potential environmental opportunities	**Potential environmental threats**
Expand core business(es)?	Attacks on core business(es)?
Exploit new market segments?	Increases in domestic competition?
Widen product range?	Increase in foreign competition?
Extend cost or differentiation advantage?	Change in consumer tastes?
Diversify into new growth businesses?	Fall in barriers to entry?
Expand into foreign markets?	Rise in new or substitute products?
Apply R&D skills in new areas?	Increase in industry rivalry?
Enter new related businesses?	New forms of industry competition?
Vertically integrate forward?	Potential for takeover?
Vertically integrate backward?	Existence of corporate raiders?
Enlarge corporate portfolio?	Increase in regional competition?
Overcome barriers to entry?	Changes in demographic factors?
Reduce rivalry among competitors?	Changes in economic factors?
Make profitable new acquisitions?	Downturn in economy?
Apply brand name capital in new areas?	Rising labor costs?
Seek fast market growth?	Slower market growth?
Others?	Others?

Having done this analysis, you will have generated both an analysis of the company's environment and a list of opportunities and threats. Table 14.1 also lists some common environmental opportunities and threats that you might look for, but the list you generate will be specific to your company.

4. *The SWOT analysis.* Having identified the company's external opportunities and threats, as well as its internal strengths and weaknesses, you need to

consider what your findings mean. In other words, you need to balance strengths and weaknesses against opportunities and threats. Is the company in an overall strong competitive position? Can it continue to pursue its current business- or corporate-level strategy profitably? What can the company do to turn weaknesses into strengths and threats into opportunities? Can it develop new functional, business, or corporate strategies to accomplish this change? *Never merely generate the SWOT analysis and then put it aside.* Because it provides a succinct summary of the company's condition, a good SWOT analysis is the key to all the analyses that follow.

5. *Analyzing corporate-level strategy.* To analyze a company's corporate-level strategy, you first need to define the company's mission and goals. Sometimes the mission and goals will be stated explicitly in the case; at other times you will have to infer them from available information. The information you need to collect to find out the company's corporate strategy includes such factors as its line(s) of business and the nature of its subsidiaries and acquisitions. It is important to analyze the relationship among the company's businesses. Do they trade or exchange resources? Are there gains to be achieved from synergy? Or is the company just running a portfolio of investments? This analysis should enable you to define the corporate strategy that the company is pursuing (for example, related or unrelated diversification, or a combination of both) and also to conclude whether the company operates in just one core business. Then take your SWOT analysis and debate the merits of this strategy. Is it appropriate, given the environment the company is in? Could a change in corporate strategy provide the company with new opportunities or transform a weakness into a strength? For example, should the company diversify from its core business into new businesses?

There are other issues to be considered as well. How has the company's strategy changed over time? Why? What is the claimed rationale for the change? Often it is a good idea to apply a *portfolio matrix technique* to the company's businesses or products to analyze its situation and identify which divisions are stars or dogs. It is also useful to explore how the company has built its portfolio over time. Did it acquire new businesses or did it internally venture its own? All these factors provide clues about the company and indicate ways of improving its future performance.

6. *Analyzing business-level strategy.* Once you know the company's corporate-level strategy and have done the SWOT analysis, the next step is to identify the company's business-level strategy. If the company is a single-business company, then its business-level strategy is identical to its corporate-level strategy. If the company is in many businesses, then each business will have its own business-level strategy. You will need to identify the company's generic competitive strategy—differentiation, low cost, or focus—and its investment strategy, given the company's relative competitive position and the stage of the life cycle. The company may also market different products using different business-level strategies: For example, it may offer a low-cost prod-

uct range and a line of differentiated products. You should be sure to give a full account of a company's business-level strategy to show how it competes.

Identifying the functional strategies that a company pursues to achieve its business-level strategy is very important. The SWOT analysis will have provided you with information on the company's functional competencies. You should further investigate production, marketing, or research and development strategy to gain a picture of where the company is going. For example, pursuing a low-cost or a differentiation strategy successfully requires a very different set of competencies. Has the company developed the right ones? If it has, how can it exploit them further?

The SWOT analysis is especially important at this point if the industry analysis, particularly Porter's model, has revealed the threats to the company from the environment. Can the company deal with these threats? How should it change its business-level strategy to counter them? To evaluate the potential of a company's business-level strategy, you must first perform a thorough SWOT analysis that captures the essence of its problems.

Once you complete this analysis, you will have a full picture of the way the company is operating and be in a position to evaluate the potential of its strategy. Thus you will be able to make recommendations concerning the pattern of its future actions. But first you need to consider strategy implementation, or the way the company tries to achieve its strategy.

7. *Analyzing structure and control systems.* The aim of the analysis here is to identify what structure and control systems the company is using to implement its strategy and to evaluate whether that structure is the appropriate one for the company. As we discuss in Chapter 12, different corporate and business strategies require different structures. The chapter, and particularly Tables 12.2, 12.3, and 12.4, provide you with the conceptual tools to determine *the degree of fit between the company's strategy and structure.* For example, you need to assess whether the company has the right level of vertical differentiation (for instance, does it have the appropriate number of levels in the hierarchy or decentralized control?), or horizontal differentiation (does it use a functional structure when it should be using a product structure?). Similarly, is the company using the right integration or control systems to manage its operations? Are managers being appropriately rewarded? Are the right rewards in place for encouraging cooperation among divisions? These are all issues that should be considered.

In some cases, there will be little information on these issues, whereas in others there will be a lot. Obviously, in writing each case, you should gear the analysis toward its most salient issues.

In some cases, organizational conflict, power, and politics will be important issues. Try and analyze why these problems are occurring. Is it because of bad strategy formulation or bad strategy implementation? Organizational change is an issue in most of the cases because companies in the cases are attempting to alter their strategies or structures to solve strategic problems. Thus as a part of the analysis, you might suggest an action plan that the company in question could use to achieve its goals. For example, you might list the steps it would need to go through to alter its business-level strategy from differentiation to focus in a logical sequence.

8.   *Making recommendations.* The last part of the case analysis process involves making recommendations based on your analysis of the case. Obviously, the quality of your recommendations is a direct result of the thoroughness with which you prepared the case analysis. The work you put into the case analysis is obvious to the professor from the nature of your recommendations. Recommendations are directed at solving whatever strategic problem the company is facing and at increasing its future profitability. Your recommendations should be in line with your analysis, that is, should follow logically from the previous discussion. For example, your recommendations will generally center on the specific ways of changing functional, business, and corporate strategy and organizational structure and control to improve business performance. The set of recommendations will be specific to each case, and so it is difficult to discuss these recommendations here. Such recommendations might include an increase in spending on specific research and development projects, the divesting of certain businesses, a change from a strategy of unrelated to related diversification, an increase in the level of integration among divisions by using task forces and teams, or a move to a different kind of structure to implement a new business-level strategy. Again, make sure your recommendations are mutually consistent and are written in the form of an action plan. The plan might contain a timetable that sequences the actions for changing the company's strategy and a description of how changes at the corporate level will necessitate changes at the business level and subsequently at the functional level.

After following all these stages, you will have performed a thorough analysis of the case and will be in a position to join in class discussion or present your ideas to the class, depending on the format used by your professor. Remember that you must tailor your analysis to suit the specific issue discussed in your case. In some cases, you might omit completely one of the stages of the analysis because it is not relevant to the situation you are considering. You must be sensitive to the needs of the case and not apply the framework we have discussed in this section blindly. The framework is meant only as a guide, and not as an outline that you must use to do a successful analysis.

14.3 WRITING A CASE STUDY

Often, as part of your course requirements, you will need to write up one or more of the cases and present your instructor with a written case analysis. This may be an individual or a group report. Whatever the situation, there are certain guidelines to follow in writing a case that will improve the evaluation that your analysis will receive from your teacher. Before we discuss these guidelines, and before you use them, make sure that they do not conflict with any instructions your teacher has given you.

The main point is how to structure the writing of a case study. Generally, if you follow the stages of analysis just discussed, *you will already have a good structure for your written discussion.* All reports begin with an *introduction* to the case. In it, you outline briefly what the company does, how it developed historically, what problems it is experiencing, and how you are going to approach the issues in the case write-up. Do this sequentially, saying, "First, we discuss the environment of Company X . . . third, we discuss Company X's business-level strategy . . . Last, we provide recommendations for turning around Company X's business."

In the second part of the case, the strategic analysis section, do the SWOT analysis, analyze and discuss the nature and problems of the company's business-level and corporate strategy, and then analyze its structure and control systems. Make sure you use plenty of headings and subheadings to structure your analysis. For example, have separate sections on any important conceptual tool you use. Thus you might have a section on Porter's five forces model as part of your analysis of the environment. Or you might offer a separate section on portfolio techniques when analyzing a company's corporate strategy. Tailor the sections and subsections to the specific issue of importance in the case.

In the third part of the case write-up, present your solutions and recommendations. Be comprehensive, do this in line with the previous analysis so that the recommendations fit together, and move logically from one to the next. The recommendations section is very revealing because, as we mentioned earlier, your teacher will have a good idea of how much work you put into the case from the quality of your recommendations.

Following this framework will provide a good structure for most written reports, though obviously it must be shaped to fit the individual case being considered. Some cases are about excellent companies experiencing no problems. In such instances, it is hard to write recommendations. Instead, you can focus on analyzing why the company is doing so well and using that analysis to structure the discussion. There are some minor points to note that can also affect the evaluation you receive.

1. Do not repeat in summary form large pieces of factual information from the case and feed them back to the instructor in the report. The instructor has also read the case and knows what is going on. Rather, use the information in the case to illustrate your statements, to defend your arguments, or to make salient points. Beyond the brief introduction to the company, you must avoid being *descriptive;* instead, you must be *analytical.*

2. Make sure the sections and subsections of your discussion flow logically and smoothly from one to the next. That is, try to build on what has gone before so that the case study builds to a climax. This is particularly important for

group cases. With group cases there is a tendency for people to split up the work and say, "I'll do the beginning, you take the middle, and I'll do the end." The result is bad because the parts of the analysis do not flow from one to the next, and it is obvious to the instructor that no real group work has been done.

3. Avoid grammatical and spelling errors. They make the paper seem sloppy.

4. Some cases dealing with well known companies end in 1986 or 1987 because no later information was available when the case was written. If possible, do a library search for more information on what has happened to the company since then. Following are sources of information for performing this search:

   Datext is a service on compact disk that gives an amazing amount of good information.
   F&S Predicasts provide a listing on a yearly basis of all the articles written about a particular company. Simply reading the titles gives an indication of what has been happening in the company.
   10K annual reports often provide an organizational chart.
   Write to the company for information.
   Fortune and *Business Week* have many articles on companies featured in the cases in this book.
   Standard & Poor's industry reports provide detailed information about the competitive conditions facing the company's industry.

5. Sometimes the instructor will hand out questions for each case to help you in your analysis. Use these as a guide for analyzing and writing the case because they often illuminate the important issues that have to be covered in the discussion.

   If you follow the guidelines in this section, you should be able to write a thorough and effective evaluation.

14.4 THE ROLE OF FINANCIAL ANALYSIS IN CASE STUDY ANALYSIS

Another important aspect of analyzing and writing a case study is the role and use of financial information. A careful analysis of the company's financial condition immensely improves a case write-up. After all, these figures represent the concrete results of the company's strategy and structure. Many useful financial performance ratios can be derived from a company's balance sheet and profit and loss accounts. These can be broken down into four different subgroups: profit ratios, liquidity ratios, leverage ratios, and shareholder-return ratios. In addition to these performance ratios, a company's *cash flow* position is of critical importance and should be assessed.

Profit Ratios

Profit ratios measure the efficiency with which the company uses its resources. The more efficient the company, the greater is its profitability. It is useful to compare a company's profitability against that of its major competitors in its industry. Such a comparison will tell you whether the company is operating more or less efficiently than its rivals. In addition, the change in a company's profit ratios over time will tell you whether its performance is improving or declining.

A number of different profit ratios can be used, and each of them measure a different aspect of a company's performance. The most commonly used profit ratios are as follows:

1. *Gross profit margin.* The gross profit margin gives an indication of the total margin available to cover operating expenses and yield a profit. It is a measure of the value a company creates net of the cost of performing value creation activities. It is defined as follows:

$$\text{Gross Profit Margin} = \frac{\text{Sales Revenue} - \text{Cost of Goods Sold}}{\text{Sales Revenue}}$$

2. *Return on total assets.* This measures the return earned on the total investment in a company. It is defined as follows:

$$\text{Return on Total Assets} = \frac{\text{Profits After Tax} + \text{Interest}}{\text{Total Assets}}$$

Total assets refer to fixed assets, plus current assets. Interest payments are added back to after-tax profits to account for the financing of current assets by creditors.

3. *Return on stockholders' equity.* Often referred to as return on net worth, this measures the rate of return on stockholders' investment in the company. In theory, a company attempting to maximize the wealth of its stockholders should be trying to maximize this ratio. It is defined as follows:

$$\text{Return on Stockholders' Equity} = \frac{\text{Profit After Tax and Interest}}{\text{Total Stockholders' Equity}}$$

Liquidity Ratios

A company's liquidity is a measure of its ability to meet unexpected contingencies such as a prolonged strike or price war. An asset is termed "liquid" if it can be quickly converted into cash. A company's current assets are liquid assets. Liquidity can be in the form of idle working capital, marketable securities, or funding in reserve, such as unused lines of credit. A company that lacks liquidity is in a weak financial position. For example, if a company whose sales revenues are hurt by a strike lacks liquidity, it might not be able to generate the cash necessary to meet the claims of short-term creditors, such as banks. Bankruptcy could ultimately result from such a scenario. Companies with major investment in fixed assets, such as steel mills or auto plants, tend to be less liquid than companies with a lower level of fixed assets. This is because fixed assets cannot be easily translated into cash and because they often necessitate major fixed costs, which place heavy demands on a company's cash reserves in times of trouble.

Two commonly used liquidity ratios are as follows:

1. *Current ratio.* The current ratio measures the extent to which the claims of short-term creditors are covered by assets that can be quickly converted into cash. If a company's current ratio declines to less than 1, the company could be in serious trouble should an unexpected contingency arise. The ratio is defined as follows:

$$\text{Current Ratio} = \frac{\text{Current Assets}}{\text{Current Liabilities}}$$

2. *Quick ratio.* The quick ratio measures a company's ability to pay off the claims of short-term creditors without relying on the sale of its inventories. This is a valuable measure since in practice the sale of inventories is often difficult. It is defined as follows:

$$\text{Quick Ratio} = \frac{\text{Current Assets} - \text{Inventories}}{\text{Current Liabilities}}$$

Leverage Ratios

A company is said to be highly leveraged when it relies on external sources of funds rather than internally generated funds to finance its investments. In some situations, it may make good sense for a company to be highly leveraged. For example, many successful high-tech start-ups have relied almost entirely on external sources of funds to finance their initial investments. On the other hand, high leverage can become a terminal weakness, particularly when rising interest rates increase the cost of debt beyond a company's ability to service that debt. Generally, a highly leveraged company is more vulnerable to changes in the cost of finance than a company that funds its investments from internally generated cash.

Three commonly used leverage ratios are as follows:

1. *Debt-to-assets ratio.* The debt-to-assets ratio is the most direct measure of the extent to which borrowed funds have been used to finance a company's investments. It is defined as follows:

$$\text{Debt-to-Assets} = \frac{\text{Total Debt}}{\text{Total Assets}}$$

Total debt is the sum of a company's current liabilities and its long-term debt, and total assets are the sum of fixed assets and current assets.

2. *Long-term debt-to-equity ratio.* The long-term debt-to-equity measure indicates the balance between debt and equity in a company's long-term capital structure. This is perhaps the most widely used measure of a company's leverage. It is defined as follows:

$$\text{Debt-to-Equity} = \frac{\text{Long-term Debt}}{\text{Total Stockholders' Equity}}$$

3. *Times-covered ratio.* The times-covered ratio measures the extent to which a company's gross profit covers its annual interest payments. If the times-covered ratio declines to less than 1, then the company is unable to meet its interest costs and is technically insolvent. The ratio is defined as follows:

$$\text{Times-covered Ratio} = \frac{\text{Profits Before Interest and Tax}}{\text{Total Interest Charges}}$$

Shareholder–Return Ratios

Shareholder-return ratios measure the return earned by shareholders from holding stock in the company. Given the goal of maximizing stockholder wealth, providing their shareholders with an adequate rate of return is a primary objective of most companies. As with profit ratios, it can be helpful to compare a company's shareholder returns against those of similar companies. This will give you a yardstick for determining how well the company is satisfying the demands of this particularly important group of organizational constituents. Two commonly used ratios are given below.

1. *Total shareholder returns.* Total shareholder returns measure the returns earned by time $t + 1$ on an investment in a company's stock made at time t. (*Time* t is the time at which the initial investment is made.) Total shareholder

returns include both dividend payments and appreciation in the value of the stock (adjusted for stock splits) and are defined as follows:

$$\text{Total Shareholder Returns} = \text{Stock Price}(t + 1) - \text{Stock Price}(t)$$

$$\frac{+ \text{ Sum of Annual Dividends per Share}}{\text{Stock Price}(t)}$$

Thus if a shareholder invests $2 at time t, and at time $t + 1$ the share is worth $3, while the sum of annual dividends for the period t to $t + 1$ has amounted to $0.2, total shareholder returns are equal to $(3 - 2 + 0.2)/2 = 0.6$, that is a 60-percent return on an initial investment of $2 made at time t.

2. *Dividend yield.* The dividend yield measures the return to shareholders received in the form of dividends. It is defined as follows:

$$\text{Dividend Yield} = \frac{\text{Dividends per Share}}{\text{Market Price per Share}}$$

Market price per share can be calculated for the first of the year, in which case the dividend yield refers to the return on an investment made at the beginning of the year. Alternatively, the average share price over the year may be used. A word of caution: a company that pays out high annual dividends may leave itself with too few cash reserves to meet its investment needs and may have to borrow more than it would choose to do from external sources of finance. In turn, the subsequent high level of debt may depress the market value of a company's stock. Thus a high dividend yield is not always a good thing.

Cash Flow

A company's cash flow position is an important indicator of its financial status. Cash flow refers to the surplus of internally generated funds over expenditure. Some businesses are cash hungry, whereas others are net generators of cash. Cash flow is important for what it tells us about a company's financing needs. A strong positive cash flow enables a company to fund future investments without having to borrow money from bankers or investors. This is desirable because the company avoids the need to pay out interest or dividends. A weak or negative cash flow means that a company has to turn to external sources to fund future investments. Generally, companies in high-growth industries often find themselves in a poor cash flow position (because their investment needs are substantial), whereas successful companies based in mature industries find themselves in a strong cash flow position.

A company's internally generated cash flow is calculated by adding back its depreciation provision to profits after interest, taxes, and dividend payments. If this figure is insufficient to cover proposed new investment expenditures, the company has little choice but to borrow funds to make up the shortfall—or curtail investments. If this figure exceeds proposed new investments, the company can use the excess to build up its liquidity (that is, through investments in financial assets) or to repay existing loans ahead of schedule.

14.5 CONCLUSION

When evaluating a case, it is important to be *systematic*. Analyze the case in a logical fashion, beginning with the identification of operating and financial strengths and weaknesses and environmental opportunities and threats. Move on to assess the value of a company's current strategies only when you are fully conversant with the SWOT of the company. Ask yourself whether the company's current strategies make sense, given its SWOT. If they do not, what changes need to be made? What are your recommendations? Above all, link any strategic recommendations you may make to the SWOT analysis. State explicitly how the strategies you identify take advantage of company strengths to exploit environmental opportunities, how they rectify company weaknesses, and how they counter environmental threats. And do not forget to outline what needs to be done to implement your recommendations.

CASES

S E C T I O N

A

SMALL BUSINESS CASES

Case 1

PARENTS
IN A PINCH, INC.

During the spring of 1989 the owners of Parents In A Pinch, Barbara Marcus and Davida Manon, began to assess their current position within the childcare industry and their alternatives for expansion. By 1989 Parents In A Pinch had become Boston's best-known provider of short-term, emergency, and long-term childcare in the child's home (see Exhibit 1). The two owners believed that Parents In A Pinch was positioned perfectly to tap into a trend of increasing in- and out-of-home childcare, but were concerned because their current level of profitability was below expectations. They also thought their service filled a specific market niche that few others were currently serving, but that there was room for expansion within the market. Further, Marcus and Manon had been approached by several parties interested in franchising their operation. Marcus and Manon thought this would increase profits with minimal investment on their part; however, neither fully understood what the implications of such a change were for themselves or for Parents In A Pinch.

The owners knew little about franchising or whether a more appropriate means might not be found to ensure continued growth and enhance profitability. They were considering several other possible ways of expanding including development of new programs serving the corporate market and expansion of their current efforts to new regions. Faced with the franchising requests, Marcus and Manon had to evaluate Parents In A Pinch's future, determine what business they wanted to be in in the long term as well as how to develop a strategy for success within that business.

BACKGROUND: PARENTS IN A PINCH, INC.

Parents In A Pinch, Inc. began on a shoestring budget in 1983 with a goal of providing short-term and emergency childcare in the child's home. The firm

This case was prepared by Sandra A. Waddock, The Wallace E. Carroll School of Management, Boston College, Chestnut Hill, MA 02167, with Carol Ann Barber, MBA, and Laura Rhodes, MBA, Boston College, class of 1989.

EXHIBIT 1   Parents In A Pinch profile

Company:	Parents In A Pinch, Inc. 45 Bartlett Crescent Brookline, MA 02146 (617) 739-KIDS
Owners:	Davida Manon Barbara Marcus
Company description:	Parents In A Pinch is a professional childcare placement service in the Boston metropolitan area. It provides quality childcare in parents' home for children of all ages.
Short-term services:	Available for a day, evening, weekend, or overnight when regular childcare cannot be used, when a child is sick, and when parents are ill or need extra help.
Long-term services	Arranged for both full and part time schedules including regular after school care, full or partial days several times a week, and full time childcare for working parents.
Corporate services:	Available to employees of participating corporations for short-term emergency childcare through their benefits packages.
Placement statistics:	(August 1987 through August 1988):
Short term:	Total jobs filled = 3756 (approximately 22,000 hours) Successful match rate = 97%
Long term:	Total placements = 154 (111 placed for up to 4 months; 43 placed for 4+ months) Successful match rate = 94%
Sitters:	Acceptable sitters available = 1,341
Clients:	Total clients = 2,484

served as a temporary placement agency matching babysitters with parent needs. By the end of its fifth year of operation, Parents In A Pinch had serviced over 4,000 clients, provided over 20,000 hours of short-term babysitting hours per year, and since 1985 offered long-term placement as well, placing 150 long-term sitters annually (see Exhibit 1 for a summary). In 1988, Parents In A Pinch was comprised of a small core of staff with 150 babysitters on call at any one time and an additional 150 babysitters in long-term placement. In addition, the firm had a network of clients, some of whom used Parents In A Pinch regularly and others only sporadically. Parents In A Pinch had only five permanent employees supporting this babysitter and client network, including the two owners who still participated actively in the day-to-day operation of the firm.

In 1988, short-term and long-term sitting each accounted for fifty percent of revenues (see Exhibit 2). During fall of 1988 a corporate benefit service, which provided emergency childcare services to employees of companies who paid Parents In A Pinch a retainer, had been test marketed. Based on the initial success of

EXHIBIT 2   1988 revenues and expenses

Revenues	1988
Short term	60,778
Registration	19,525
Long term	63,602
Miscellaneous	6,711
Corporate benefit	0
Total	150,616

Expenses	
Payroll	
Staff	40,400
Directors	35,000
Contract lab	2,500
Advertising	18,137
Postage	1,960
Prof. fees	8,000
Telephone	6,040
Rent	7,980
Printing	3,000
Insurance	675
Office expense	3,000
Health benefits	4,600
Miscellaneous	17,770
Total	148,062
Net profit	2,554

the corporate benefit service, Marcus and Manon planned to begin marketing it to their entire service area of greater Boston in 1989. The owners expected the corporate benefit program to increase significantly as a proportion of revenues over the next five years.

When the agency opened in 1983, the owners hoped to provide emergency childcare service to parents at all income levels. As working parents themselves, they recognized the growing market need for high quality, reliable childcare, both on an emergency basis and for longer periods of time. To implement their business, they developed extensive babysitter screening processes that ensured that all sitters met high quality standards. This screening process continued to be an integral part of Parents In A Pinch's success, since the business relied on a solid reputation that reassured anxious parents that their children would be well cared for, even when the provider was brought in at the last minute and did not already know the child. As Parents In A Pinch's business grew, the owners recognized that to cover the costs of providing short-term, specialized childcare services, they had to price Parents In A Pinch out of the middle income market for childcare and focus on a more upscale target population that could afford the price they needed to charge to remain viable.

Like many new ventures, Parents In A Pinch's first three years of operation were financially unstable, in part because their services were new to the market. Parents In A Pinch had to educate the market about when and how to use services, as well as establish its sitters' reliability, skills, and trustworthiness. Early marketing efforts generated positive publicity as well as numerous word-of-mouth referrals among clients. By the fourth year of operation, the financial picture had stabilized as a result of streamlining and improving operations. In 1988, Parents In A Pinch made its first profit of approximately $2,000 on nearly $150,000 of revenues, in addition to paying modest salaries to the directors (see Exhibits 2 and 3). Parents In A Pinch also began to expand its service area by moving into an "office" in Framingham, a western suburb of Boston. The Framingham "office" was managed by an outside, part-time employee working on a beeper system to interview and funnel sitters in the western suburbs to the main Parents In A Pinch location for placement. As of 1989, there was no formal office or separate system for the branch, with the exception of a local telephone number, trunked into the Brookline office.

Goals and Objectives

Over time, Marcus and Manon had developed a specific mission and goal statement for the business, along with short- and long-term objectives for the early 1990s. Long-term goals involved responding with high quality babysitters to the childcare needs of families, while continuing to be a leader in innovative childcare options. In the short term they focused on the recruitment of sitters, corporate relations, and improving their training package, while evaluating alternative

EXHIBIT 3   **Monthly cash receipts 1987 and 1988**

	1987	1988
January	13,808	10,581
February	8,723	12,329
March	13,063	14,779
April	11,184	10,795
May	14,194	15,475
June	11,843	15,301
July	14,897	15,301
August	10,976	9,456
September	13,119	15,959
October	10,619	12,683
November	9,439	10,994
December	9,138	11,749

revenue-raising programs. Long-term objectives focused on profitability, management development, and diversification. Specific goals and objectives as developed by the owners are detailed in Exhibit 4.

Description of Current Services

Parents In A Pinch's operations consisted of the two primary services of short-term emergency childcare and long-term placement. In addition, the owners hoped to grow the new corporate service into a third major offering.

EXHIBIT 4   **Parents In A Pinch mission and goal statement**

Mission and goals

Parents In A Pinch, Inc. is a childcare placement service which responds to the in-home needs of families in Eastern Massachusetts.

Goals

To respond to temporary and permanent childcare needs of families

To insure that qualified childcare personnel are referred to parents

To respond to working parents in collaboration with their workplace

To insure timely response to parent requests

To maintain open communication with parents

To assist others who wish to establish an in-home temporary or long-term childcare placement agency

To offer different models of temporary childcare, in-home and out-of-home

Short-term objectives

Recruit a qualified pool of 150 short-term sitters who will be able to respond to a minimum of 10 job requests per day.

Recruit a pool of 100 sitters three times/year who will be able to respond to a minimum of 75 requests in September, January, and May, and a continuing pool of providers for months in between.

Develop a relationship with 5 corporations, businesses, or service firms to provide emergency childcare as an employee benefit.

Revise the written training package, with clear definitions and emphasis on childhood illness and clear indicators about when to call a physician.

Plan and develop a franchise package and marketing plan.

Develop a marketing plan for consultation.

Long-term objectives

Increase profits to the agency at a rate of 25% each year.

Redistribute the time/energy of the owners from daily operations to developing franchises, consulting and planning. Hire office manager(s).

Develop feasibility study regarding drop-in center/indoor playground.

Short-term emergency childcare   Both owners considered short-term babysitting the core business, since it was a unique service offered by Parents In A Pinch in the Boston market. This service provided emergency care, quickly and efficiently, to parents who were unable to use their regular childcare provider (for instance, when the sitter or child is ill) or who required temporary services for some reason.

Parents needing emergency care initiated Parents In A Pinch's response by phoning in a request for a babysitter. When a request was received, employees at Parents In A Pinch went through their files to determine which babysitters in the labor pool best matched the parents' needs. Records detailing each sitter's preferences for infants, toddlers, or school-age children were maintained on a computerized data base system at Parents In A Pinch, although much of the matching was still being done by hand in 1989. The partners were planning to purchase a computer that could hasten the matching process within the next several months. Records on the sitters' location, mobility, references, and prior babysitting experiences were maintained so that within a couple of hours of the initial call, the sitter arrived at the child's home. To ensure that babysitters were available when needed, Parents In A Pinch maintained a computerized list of at least 100 babysitters, who were actively seeking babysitting jobs.

All job requests were fully documented when received. Files were also kept up to date and elaborated by follow-up telephone calls to both clients and sitters after the babysitting experience. This thorough documentation enabled Parents In A Pinch to provide high quality service because they knew the individual characteristics of both sitters and clients. Though the complete documentation improved service, it also complicated the administration of the matching process, as it necessitated extensive attention to detail and constant updating of the records.

The emergency childcare service had two types of users: registered clients who paid an annual fee of $35, then paid an hourly rate of $9.50, and unregistered clients who were charged an hourly rate of $12.00. At the completion of a job parents wrote two checks: one directly to the babysitter at a rate of $6.00 per hour, and one to Parents In A Pinch for $3.50 per hour (or $6.00 if the parent is unregistered). The babysitter mailed Parents In A Pinch's check in to the agency and the process was complete. Parents In A Pinch was able to place babysitters with 97% of the parents who called in 1988.

Because the short-term services were completely dependent on demand, on any given day requests ranged from as few as three to as many as 30. This fluctuation made providing emergency short-term care both labor intensive and administratively complex. Despite high administrative costs, however, Parents In A Pinch's greatest challenge was securing the stable labor pool to enable it to meet demand.

Long-term childcare   In addition to short-term childcare, Parents In A Pinch acted as a placement agency for long-term childcare providers. Parents In A Pinch screened potential caretakers in an attempt to ensure an appropriate match be-

EXHIBIT 5   Parents In A Pinch long-term placement fees

Hours of childcare	Length of contract	
Per week	1–4 months	More than 4 months
10–25	$400.00	$ 750.00
26–35	$550.00	$1000.00
36 +	$700.00	$1200.00

tween the parents' needs and the experience and skills of the potential babysitter. For its efforts, Parents In A Pinch received a one time placement fee based on the hours of childcare per week and the length of the babysitting contract (see Exhibit 5).

Long-term placements were an easier and less costly service for the agency to provide. Although the matching process was far more extensive for long-term placements, the revenues from a successful match were proportionately much greater than those for a short-term job. The greatest challenge the owners faced in this aspect of the business was actually recruiting long-term babysitters. The success rate of placement requests was about 50%, while the success rate of actual long-term placements was 94%, due in part to their ability to adequately find and screen potential babysitters.

Corporate benefit service   The corporate benefit service provided emergency childcare for a company's employees. Corporations were charged an annual registration fee based on projected use of Parents In A Pinch's services during the year. This retainer entitled all company employees to use Parents In A Pinch's services, paying the rate as registered clients. In addition, the corporation subsidized the registration fee for the employee because it also covered the agency's portion of the babysitting fee. Therefore, the employee paid only for the babysitting.

COMPETITIVE ENVIRONMENT

The childcare industry was characterized by a wide variety of different types of providers, most of them small. Providers ranged from in-home childcare by relatives and friends, to family day care in the provider's home, to single site centers, rapidly growing day-care chains, and live-in nannies, the highest growth segment in childcare. Numerous innovations were occurring in childcare.

Recently, a few Boston-area hospitals had begun offering short-term sick child services, and some local colleges provided temporary services similar to those provided by Parents In A Pinch. There had also been a proliferation of day-care centers, some independent and some associated with employers. Day-care chains were rapidly growing, while numerous independent day-care facilities were springing up, along with family day care provided in the home by individuals. Still, the competition for the services Parents In A Pinch provided was low, in part because the market was not saturated and in part because of the high degree of fragmentation and lack of organized structure among potential competitors. Most of the attention of the larger competitors was focused on providing day care on a regular not emergency basis.

Because of dramatic demographic changes, childcare had become one of the major public issues facing corporations. Companies were increasingly being forced to deal with childcare issues proactively, as more women with young children entered the workforce. To remain competitive, some companies provided in-company day care that helped employees with dual or single income households. Many companies were reluctant to enter the childcare business directly, preferring instead to provide information to employees, or to offer other forms of childcare support, such as those provided by Parents In A Pinch. Marcus and Manon thought that by being among the first providers to explicitly deal with this emerging need, they could place Parents In A Pinch on the forefront of corporate childcare.

Market Characteristics

Parents In A Pinch faced both a seasonal and cyclical childcare industry. Demand for childcare fluctuated depending on the school year, holidays and vacations. Large cash inflows occurred in September and May, when many childcare decisions were made regarding day care, extended day care, and summer camping (Exhibit 3). Short-term fees increased during holidays because of the increase in demand for short-term childcare when children were on vacation. Additionally, Parents In A Pinch's income tended to fluctate on a cyclical basis from year to year as household income responded to economic conditions, falling under poorer economic conditions.

Nature of demand   Demand for childcare was influenced by two key factors. First, the demand for childcare was extremely price sensitive; affordability was critical. Second, childcare decisions were based as much on emotion as on reason; as far as anxious parents were concerned, the quality of care provided to their children was an overriding concern.

Extent of demand   During the 1970s and 1980s, there had been a dramatic change in the nation's labor force. By the late 1980s, women comprised more than 50% of the nation's workforce; this proportion was expected to continue to increase in the foreseeable future. In addition, over 60% of American families consisted of two working parents. The rapid growth of single-parent families also meant a greater demand for childcare services. The Executive Office of Economic Affairs of the Commonwealth of Massachusetts estimated that in 1955

EXHIBIT 6   Massachusetts family income and estimated total number of children
in different age groups

	Low	Moderate	High	Total
0 to 1 year old	41,076	58,813	63,481	163,370
2 to 3 years old	39,029	61,614	56,946	157,589
4 to 5 years old	50,411	74,683	41,076	166,170
6 to 8 years old	64,414	82,152	71,883	218,449
9 to 12 years old	61,614	83,085	76,550	221,249
All children under 13	256,544	360,347	309,936	926,827

Low: Those with family income below 71% of the adjusted median ($20,592 for a family of four).

Moderate: Those with family income between 71% and 135% of the adjusted median ($39,684 for a family of four).

Source: *The Economics of Child Care in Massachusetts.* The Commonwealth of Massachusetts, June 24, 1988.

EXHIBIT 7   Households with married couples earning $50,000+ as a joint income

Children ages	Massachusetts	Boston
Under 18	21,404	13,979
Under 6	3,379	2,316

two-thirds of people entering the workforce would be women, an increase from
54 percent in 1986.

The number of children was also increasing because the "baby boomers"
were finally having their own children. These trends in the labor force and family
life suggested that there would be approximately 250,000 children under 6 years
of age and 161,000 children between 6 and 12 years of age who would require
childcare in Massachusetts alone. This growth represented an increase of 23% in
ten years. Parents In A Pinch was particularly interested in targeting households
with two working parents in high income brackets, since these parents have specialized childcare needs and the resources to afford them. Exhibits 6 and 7 provide
further detail on the characteristics of the market.

Competition

Childcare providers fell into four categories:

- In-home childcare
- Family day care

- Single site centers
- Childcare chains

These providers served the ongoing childcare needs of parents, full- and part-time. They were supplemented by programs located within schools and by after-school programs. In general, however, they presented little competitive threat to Parents In A Pinch's core business, since they met a different set of needs.

Recently, a new group of competitors had emerged that competed directly with Parents In A Pinch. In Boston, the competition for short-term care centered around two types of services offered by different types of childcare providers:

- Agencies providing in-home, short-term childcare
- Hospitals providing temporary and sick childcare

Parents In A Pinch was in the first category. Two other firms in the Boston area provided similar short-term care: Cambridge Care and Personal Touch. Cambridge Care developed from an elderly care agency and represented a group of potential competitors that posed a significant threat because of the existing base of qualified babysitters. Personal Touch began as and was still predominantly a cleaning service; it currently focused its babysitting on the hotel market. Another competitor, Boston Babysitters, had recently gone out of business. Parents In A Pinch had achieved the strongest reputation for quality emergency babysitting services in the market area.

Specialized childcare alternatives such as those offered through corporations or emergency/sick care were very new. Specialized services had begun to be introduced because of increasing awareness of the problems faced by working parents with sick children, changing norms concerning childcare, and increasing competition for labor as more women entered the workforce and became unavailable as providers. Some hospitals, facing serious economic problems, viewed these trends as an opportunity to stabilize their own revenues and workforce and established in-house programs that provided temporary care to mildly ill children. These services were used primarily by hospital staff.

A few large companies in the greater Boston area had developed on-site day-care programs for employees. Most corporations, however, preferred to provide supportive services to parents rather than becoming directly involved in either emergency or longer-term childcare. Thus, they often developed referral networks that aided parents in their search for childcare. Few corporations, as yet, had become actively aware of the need for short-term emergency care of the sort that Parents In A Pinch provided. None actually provided such services.

Family day-care providers, the large group of individuals who took children into their homes, posed little threat to Parents In A Pinch, as they had to be known to parents and were frequently unavailable on a short-term basis. In addition, they almost never took mildly ill children and had limited slots for infants. Their cost, however, was likely to be significantly less than that of agencies such as Parents In A Pinch.

A few new competitors were emerging, though they could not yet be classified as serious competition. Models on the cutting edge of short-term childcare included drop-in day-care centers such as an area in a shopping mall where parents can leave children to play while shopping. In recent months, at least two drop-in centers had opened within Parents In A Pinch's service area.

Neither owner considered direct competition to Parents In A Pinch's emergency services likely to experience the rapid growth occurring in other areas of the childcare industry. One reason for this belief was the labor intensive nature of emergency service. To be successful in emergency childcare, a firm needed to maintain a large labor pool capable of providing service on short notice. Developing the labor pool required an up-to-date network of potential babysitters, administrative talent, excellent record keeping systems, and an immediate outreach capacity. All of these capacities took time and initiative to develop. Parents In A Pinch's owners believed that they had developed a first-mover advantage in this regard.

Labor Pool

The labor pool for the childcare industry consisted of many different types of people. In-home childcare providers are a mixed group: foreigners, people with minimal formal skills, people in transition and, for part-time jobs, college students. Family day care typically drew its labor pool from young mothers who wanted to stay at home with their own children and needed the extra income to support themselves. Single site centers and chain day-care centers obtained personnel from various sources including education and early childhood teachers. These people were usually devoted to the childcare profession and were willing to suffer the relatively low wages offered. Employment tended to be relatively temporary and turnover was quite high.

Parents In A Pinch's ability to find and maintain its large babysitter network was a key factor in its success. In part, this ability was a product of location: maintaining an extensive babysitter network meant that the organization needed to be located in an area in which the supply of potential babysitters was plentiful. Potential babysitters were individuals with schedules that were flexible enough to permit them to work on an as-needed basis. Boston provided an ideal location for this type of worker, with its numerous universities and colleges providing an abundant source of students with the need for part-time, flexible work and the desire to earn spending money.

Regulation

With the growth of the childcare industry, the regulatory environment had become more restrictive. Recent adverse publicity had raised concerns about the quality of childcare and, in particular, the potential for child abuse in day-care environments. Numerous well-publicized incidents of abuse or poor quality care had made parents and industry observers aware of the need for more stringent regulation.

Most existing regulation of childcare settings took place at the state rather than the federal level, with each state having different licensing and regulation requirements. In general, however, regulation had been difficult to enforce because of limited state resources for monitoring the numerous childcare settings, specifically family day care. In Massachusetts alone, there were over 12,000 licensed childcare providers.

The federal government had some legislative involvement in childcare. Recent tax legislation, for example, provided a tax subsidy for families using childcare. In addition, the Bush administration had targeted the issue as a major priority during the 1988 campaign. Exactly what changes could be expected at the federal regulatory level were not clear.

As a referral agency, Parents In A Pinch was not subject to this regulatory scrutiny. Despite their current relative freedom from regulatory constraints, Marcus and Manon were aware of the continued need to stay on top of industry growth and regulation to maintain their competitive advantage and avoid potential regulatory problems. This was especially important as many states had already begun addressing the regulation and licensing of childcare for sick children.

One major problem that all childcare providers faced was liability. In a society increasingly involved in lawsuits, adequate insurance was essential, but obtaining insurance for childcare agencies had been extremely difficult because of malpractice liabilities. Although some easing of an earlier crisis atmosphere around insuring childcare had occurred, having adequate insurance continued to be a major problem as well as a major expense for childcare agencies. Companies like Parents In A Pinch had even greater difficulty than day-care centers in obtaining insurance because the care they provided was in the home and not directly supervised by the agency. Parents In A Pinch had recently overcome this problem, however, by obtaining liability coverage after a four year search. This put, as the owners stated, "the stamp of approval" on the business. Several competitors, however, were bonded, which Parents In A Pinch was not, a factor important to hotel babysitting.

Owners' Perspective on Parents In A Pinch's Market Position

By 1989, Parents In A Pinch had stable annual earnings and solid financial record keeping, which included in-depth knowledge of the expenses associated with the emergency childcare service. The owners continually monitored prices and expenses in comparison to market conditions to ensure that they remained competitive in the high-end childcare market. Although the owners kept good records and had a good understanding of financial information, they knew they could improve financial accounting controls by computerizing the financial information, which was kept manually. Computerization, they believed, would save time in comparing past with present performance.

Marcus and Manon believed that the stage was set for Parents In A Pinch to be the leader in providing emergency childcare benefits. There was little competition and demand was growing. Of course, they recognized that success depends on their own ability to maintain a comprehensive network of screened and trained babysitters and a constantly growing and satisfied client base. Long-term care provision was another growth market, in which Parents In A Pinch already had an established position. Competition was much more intense in this market than in emergency care, with numerous agencies springing up to provide both foreign and domestic live-in nannies for long-term placement. The corporate service, if developed properly, did provide an opportunity for long-term growth in revenues that would not be as cyclical as were short-term emergency care revenues from individual parents. Both owners recognized, however, that marketing to corporations required a different set of skills than they had tapped in the past, as well as some significant organizational changes.

Neither owner had marketing expertise or any formal education in management. They compensated for this gap in part by seeking outside help when appropriate. Nonetheless, it had become clear that if the organization were to grow to any great extent, additional management expertise might be needed.

Although Parents In A Pinch's reputation in the childcare market was excellent, it was also perceived as a high cost way of obtaining emergency childcare. Much of Parents In A Pinch's past success could be attributed to the energy and drive that the two owners had brought to the business. Their imagination and commitment had pulled the organization through its rough first years. Other factors needed to be considered as Marcus and Manon attempted to plan for Parents In A Pinch's growth. Childcare had historically been a low margin industry and Parents In A Pinch's operations to date were no exception. Although Parents In A Pinch's babysitters were paid by the clients, the costs of administering the service were fixed, including rent, insurance, administrative salaries, and advertising. In the long term these costs were expected to increase incrementally with the growth of the business. Depending on the growth options chosen, the fixed costs would shift.

POSSIBLE GROWTH STRATEGIES

The Franchising Option

Parents In A Pinch had been approached on a number of occasions by individuals interested in franchising. Because they knew little about the pros and cons of franchising, Marcus and Manon contacted a team of MBA students to help them analyze this option. In exploring the franchise option with the help of the team, Marcus and Manon found some guidance on what makes a franchise successful.

First, they realized that the current operation must be successful both operationally and financially if it is to be amenable to franchising. The prospective franchisor must be able to show the prospective franchisee that s/he is capable of providing a proven idea or there will be little buyer interest. The franchisee must see a benefit, such as potential profit, in the relationship before he or she will be willing to invest.

Second, successful franchises must be based on a concept that is capable of being duplicated but that cannot be easily copied by outsiders. In order to be transferable or sold to a franchisee, operating systems must be standardized to the point that an individual other than the founder can take on the concept and implement it. This requires development of operating manuals that are standardized, an idea that cannot be easily replicated by competitors, name recognition or brand identity associated with the franchisor, and/or systems in place that provide a competitive advantage to the franchisee not available to the sole entrepreneur.

Third, standardized operating procedures that allow the business to be taught to franchisees need to be in place. To the extent that a business depends on the initiatives of any individual entrepreneur or group of entrepreneurs, it becomes less easy to franchise. As McDonald's has learned, the thoroughness and quality of operating systems makes it difficult for competitors to duplicate the company's success but provide an adequate basis for a franchisee to replicate the concept consistently throughout the franchised system.

Fourth, successful franchisors provide continuing support, allowing the entire franchise system to capitalize, for instance, on economies of scale in marketing, advertising, and operations, on new marketing techniques, or new product/service developments. This ongoing support helps franchisors avoid the potential problems that can arise when a franchisee has learned the system and feels independent enough to operate without the franchisor's advice and help.

Marcus and Manon believed these criteria were reasonable and were concerned about the extent to which Parents In A Pinch's concept and operations met them. The revenues from franchising the operation might help stabilize cash flow, but franchising would create costs, for instance increased legal fees, more marketing, and training and support for franchisees.

Estimated capital requirements for franchising   A franchise operation requires capital for legal fees, inventory, and start-up costs unless the primary business generates enough cash by itself to support the new system. The capital requirements to initiate a franchising strategy appeared to be significant for Parents In A Pinch in light of its cash flow. Marcus and Manon believed that franchising Parents In A Pinch could require anywhere from $60,000 to $250,000 in start-up capital. Because Parents In A Pinch was a service organization that did not require inventory, the bulk of the capital would be needed for legal fees for the franchise agreement. The owners had one estimate of $100,000 for legal fees for the first two years of getting the project started. Other expenses of franchising included:

- Increased advertising expenditures to solicit franchisees
- Travel costs to monitor franchise start-up and performance

- Developing and printing operating and training manuals
- Developing and printing administrative forms

These expenses would be partially offset by a franchising fee estimated at $10,000 and franchising royalties at 3% of the franchisees' gross revenues, figures in line with other franchise fees and royalties in similar businesses.

Operational and managerial requirements   In addition to the capital requirements, Marcus and Manon needed to explore the operational and managerial requirements of running Parents In A Pinch. The two entrepreneurs wondered whether they had the managerial capacities within their small organization to develop a successful franchise operation, particularly since franchising would require a great deal of their own attention. Further, they wondered whether there might not be other ways to grow that were less risky and therefore concurrently explored several alternative growth strategies.

Alternative Growth Options

One possible growth option was to grow via expansion, such as had already occurred through the Framingham branch or through licensing of the concept. Another was to pursue diversification through the corporate benefit program, through obtaining corporate endorsements of Parents In A Pinch's services, or to more broadly diversify, for example, into elderly care or consulting.

Branch offices   Branch offices might provide a way for Parents In A Pinch to expand its primary market, while maintaining close control over operations. The "office" in Framingham had had limited success because it was not managed as an independent unit, but rather as an extension of Parents In A Pinch's main unit. Successful branch offices appeared to be "clones" of the primary organization, perhaps on a smaller scale. It appeared that the branch offices had to be organized and managed as independent units with their own management, labor pool, client base, and staff, rather than as outgrowths of the main office. In addition, good branch managers were essential.

On the pro side, branch offices did not need a large capital investment. Office space and equipment could be obtained inexpensively in outlying areas, or the branch could even operate out of the manager's home during start-up. This method of growth would allow Parents In A Pinch to retain control of the operation while minimizing its capital and managerial investments.

The Framingham area, where the trial branch was located, was similar in some respects to Boston. For example, it had an adequate local supply of college students who could serve as babysitters, as well as market demand from professionals working in the Route 128 "high technology belt" to the west of Boston. Despite the apparent advantages of control, Manon and Marcus were still concerned about the amount of managerial time, training, and support that would have to be devoted to branch managers. They knew that they would need to undertake some market research and develop a business plan, and that branches would require nearly as much support as would franchises.

Licensing   Licensing involved developing a legal contract with the licensee to purchase Parents In A Pinch's name, computer software, and operations manuals and forms. The license relationship ends at the sale of the package. Under this arrangement, Parents In A Pinch would basically provide a start-up kit in return for a one-time fee. On the plus side, licensing offered the potential for smoothing out or at least increasing cash flows, while bringing a much greater market recognition to the organization. The problem with this relationship, however, was lack of control over future operations of businesses carrying the Parents In A Pinch name. Unlike most successful license ventures, Parents In A Pinch was a service organization; this meant Parents In A Pinch could not control its licensees through inventory management and product quality, techniques available to product-oriented licensors, and instead had to depend on the quality of management running licensed operations.

Corporate benefit program   Both owners believed that one way to diversify that could help smooth cash flows as well as increase revenues would be to expand the corporate benefit program they had initiated in 1988. This program tapped their expertise in providing emergency childcare while greatly expanding their potential market. It did require, however, knowledge of the local corporate market, sales directly to corporate purchasers, and probably a rather extensive educational campaign directed at corporations to make them aware of the benefits of participating in such a program.

Corporate benefits services were priced according to the number of employees in a company joining the service. Rates ranged from $1500 for 200 service hours to $3500 for 600 service hours. When hours contracted for are used up, employers could renew the contract. The extent of market demand for this service was not known.

Corporate endorsements   For those corporations that would not commit fully to the corporate benefit plan, Parents In A Pinch's owners believed that they could increase their marketing efforts to obtain a corporate endorsement for their services, which would simply mean marketing their services differently rather than developing a new strategy. This recommendation would indicate to employees who needed short-term childcare that Parents In A Pinch was a feasible solution to their problems that had been fully checked out by their employers. Marcus and Manon thought it had the potential to increase the demand for their services by increasing both corporate and parent awareness of what Parents In A Pinch could offer, which would increase revenues and profits. Additionally, this networking could provide inroads to major employers for Parents In A Pinch to pursue as future clients of the corporate benefit plan.

Elderly care   Another possibility was a more complete diversification of the sort that similar agencies had already taken. For instance, Parents In A Pinch might expand its services to include elderly care, which was similar to childcare in requiring an extensive, highly flexible and trained labor pool providing high quality service. Since Parents In A Pinch had already proven itself capable of providing emergency care services, it might be easy to use the systems already in place to service a new market. Growth in elderly care was also expected to be significant as baby boomers in dual career families approached middle age and their own parents required care, and as the general population aged, and as the availability of facilities caring for the elderly became scarcer. By getting into elderly care early, Parents In A Pinch might be able to refine its systems and adjust for problems specific to the elderly care market.

Consulting   One opportunity that occurred to the owners was consulting to individuals interested in the childcare industry. Both had a working knowledge of the childcare industry as well as firm-specific experience that could prove beneficial to new entrants. This option could provide additional revenues, but also might give direct competition insight into some of the ways Parents In A Pinch had developed to maintain its success. Although the most likely format consisted of one- or two-day seminars, Marcus and Manon knew that consulting would be a drain on their time and energy and might direct attention away from internal problems that developed at Parents In A Pinch.

FUTURE DIRECTIONS

With all of these alternatives facing them, Barbara Marcus and Davida Manon knew that they had to make some choices and begin planning Parents In A Pinch's future. With financial and managerial resources a primary concern in this decision, the puzzle was which direction to choose and how to best plot a path toward a successful future.

Case 2

ACME LEASING COMPANY (FRESNO TRUCK SALES CORPORATION)

> Our goal is to add value to the franchise regardless of the size. The leasing company often becomes the number one or two customer for the dealership in parts, service and new truck sales. We seem to forget that sometimes and it is important.
>
> Frank Fuller
> President, Truck Leasing Corporation

Fresno Truck Sales Corporation,[1] in business for 20 years, is a highly successful retailer of class 7 and 8 commercial trucks. The firm is located in a company owned office building along Highway 99 in the San Joaquin Valley.

Currently, it operates a 16-bay service shop with 23 full time mechanics, and a 200,000 square foot sales, parts, and service facility. Fresno Truck Sales had grown from a small independent dealer of trucks to a $15 million a year operation specializing in the sale of U.S. manufactured commercial trucks, parts, and service. Ten years ago, David Krose, its current owner, took over active management from his father, who had started the firm.

OPPORTUNITIES FOR DIVERSIFICATION

In 1985, Dave Krose was approached by John Russo, Area Manager for Truck Leasing Corporation, and asked to consider entering the LeaseCorp full service

Doctoral Candidate Phillip H. Phan and Assistant Professor John E. Butler, of the University of Washington, prepared this case as a basis for class discussion rather than to illustrate either effective or ineffective handling of an administrative situation.
[1]Acme Leasing Company is a fictitious franchise built up from interviews with actual truck lease/rental franchises. Financial data has been disguised, and names have been changed.

460

truck rental and leasing network as a franchise. At the time, full service rental/leasing was a relatively new concept in the Fresno area. It entailed the rental/leasing and maintenance of medium, and heavy-duty trucks for commercial use. In addition to maintenance and other transportation services, the LeaseCorp franchise also provided truck financing, fuel and mileage tax reporting services, state license applications, substitute rental vehicles, insurance, and driver safety programs for its customers.

After considering the pros and cons of the offer, Dave decided it was a logical extension to his current business. Always one to take the lead in his marketplace, he saw full service leasing as the most viable transportation alternative to owning for private carriers. It relieved these carriers of having to deal with the administrative and maintenance headaches associated with owning a fleet of trucks. He also felt that some companies currently using common carriers could be converted to full service maintenance leasing. These customers would have to be shown that the services offered with leasing were comprehensive enough to relieve them of the administrative burdens and costs incurred through dealing with a second party common carrier.

Coincidentally, at the time he spoke with John, Dave was already looking for opportunities to diversify. In 1985 the economy was recovering from a slight recession, competition was becoming more intense, and profit margins in the dealership were shrinking. Dave saw starting the leasing company as a way to build and preserve the customer base of the dealership. This could create a steady stream of income that would help reduce extreme revenue fluctuations that are common in this business.

Dave had also spoken with Frank Fuller, president of Truck Leasing Corporation before considering a franchise arrangement. Frank told him,

> Current trends indicate that 40% of all new Class 8 trucks sold in the next few years will end up in truck leasing/rental companies. Sixty-four percent (64%) of the projected growth in the truck leasing industry will come from existing customers. Ninety-four percent (94%) of customers who lease become attached to the leasing concept and will continue to remain full service lease customers. This means that, one, your leasing company will become your dealership's biggest and most loyal customer in the years to come. Two, if you treat your leasing customers right, you are almost guaranteed of a strong repeat business base, and three, you can participate in 100% of your market. If you follow the LeaseCorp system, and adhere to our guidelines, you'll make a good profit—competitive to what you are earning in your dealership now.

Further assurances were given by John,

> LeaseCorp will provide all the necessary administrative and operational support through our various programs. You must keep in mind that this is a management intensive business—you cannot forget that.

After consulting with his lawyer, Dave agreed to join the LeaseCorp network.

ACME LEASING COMPANY ORGANIZATION

David Krose selected Thomas Kelley, his son-in-law, as general manager in charge of the new operation, now known as Acme Leasing. Acme Leasing was structured as an autonomous subsidiary of Fresno Truck Sales (see the organization chart depicted in Exhibit 1). Associated with the leasing company was a dedicated service department, originally staffed by a mechanic transferred from the dealership. Eager to get the new venture off to a running start, Dave selected his best mechanic for the job. As the fleet size increased, more mechanics were added and by 1989, Acme Leasing had a total of 4 mechanics assigned to it. Major engine repair, and warranty jobs were subcontracted to the dealership's service department because they possessed the equipment necessary to do the work. The dealership service manager, Ted Ketch, was in overall charge of both service departments, and reported directly to Dave.

The leasing service department started with a service bay and added another after the fleet size exceeded 40 units. The facilities, including capital equipment, were rented from the dealership. Thus, as part of its housing overheads, Acme paid a monthly rental fee to the dealership.

Tom, a recent Master's degree graduate in history from the University of California at Irvine, had a short work history with the firm and no experience in the leasing business. After graduating in 1983, Dave hired him as a salesman for the dealership. Tom, a personable young man, demonstrated a natural flair for selling. He rose to be top performer in the company after only 18 months. He was extremely enthusiastic, a good conversationalist, and was good at motivating the other salesmen. Tom seemed a logical choice for the position when the LeaseCorp franchise was started. Dave saw an opportunity to groom Tom for a future senior management position, and decided this was a good place to start. He also knew that Tom felt himself to be over-qualified for the sales job. Dave, inclined toward keeping the business a family affair, welcomed the chance to nurture a future leader for the business.

Tom Kelley, eager to establish himself in the company, was glad for the opportunity to be his own boss. In this capacity, Tom was responsible for the day to day running of the leasing operation, soliciting new business and, with the help of the dealership's credit manager, making decisions on credit matters. In addition, he was provided administrative and operational support from Truck Leasing Corporation, such as licensing and reporting services, training programs, operating manuals, and frequent on-site visitations by experienced field personnel. Working for Tom was a secretary to handle the daily paperwork, and a rental salesman.

EXHIBIT 1   **Acme Leasing Company**
(A subsidiary of Fresno Truck Sales Corporation)

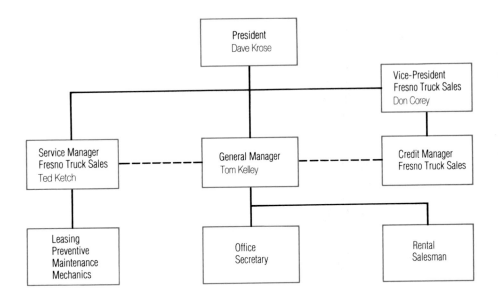

COMPENSATION SCHEMES

As a manager, Tom was paid a base salary. In addition, because he was also responsible for lease sales, he was given a commission for each truck lease he sold. The rental manager was compensated on a base salary plus bonus basis. The bonus was tied directly into the amount of rental business he generated. Tom's secretary was paid a salary. All personnel in the leasing company were given medical and dental insurance benefits, paid annual leave, and participated in incentive travel programs related to their job performances.

OPERATING HISTORY

The first two years of the new venture passed uneventfully. Revenue increased steadily during the second year (see Exhibit 2) as more agricultural produce packing companies in the area became aware of LeaseCorp. In the third and fourth years, however, revenues increased dramatically, reaching $1.6 million in 1989. The economy moved toward another recessionary trend in early 1989, and more agricultural companies turned to the leasing alternative in order to ease their capital commitments, and improve their cash flows

EXHIBIT 2   Acme Leasing Company income statement*

Revenues	1985	1986	1987	1988	1989
Fixed					
Full service lease—fixed	166,400	287,200	645,000	840,800	998,800
Rental—fixed	68,279	128,720	152,899	197,485	279,985
Total fixed	234,679	415,920	797,899	1,038,285	1,278,785
Variable					
Full service lease—variable	36,600	78,150	196,150	207,500	222,700
Rental—variable	38,943	44,550	55,048	80,659	99,789
Total variable revenue	75,543	122,700	251,198	288,159	322,489
Total Revenues	310,222	538,620	1,049,097	1,326,444	1,601,273
Expenses					
Fixed					
License, permits, PPT, FHUT	23,805	40,390	80,960	105,510	128,455
Outside vehicle costs—subs.		9,917	16,840	28,222	36,218
Insurance	6,000	11,040	22,560	29,520	36,240
Interest expense	3,968	8,080	14,760	17,280	22,280
Deprec.—vehicles in service	21,450	38,350	42,200	45,860	47,970
Vehicles—sub-lease	121,800	208,400	442,580	577,530	714,000
Total Fixed Costs	177,023	316,167	619,900	803,922	985,163
Variable					
Fuel use taxes	0	389	0	841	888
State mileage taxes	0	432	0	423	536
Oil, antifreeze, and lubricants	3,591	6,910	15,379	21,905	28,493
Repair labor	14,590	30,835	70,990	90,898	104,898
Repair parts	10,780	23,632	57,954	81,579	85,388
Outside repairs	817	14,991	32,549	45,820	88,778
Damage repairs	0	735	0	449	525
Tires	14,012	25,062	49,118	64,906	80,838
Warranty (credit)		−1,389	−1,955	−1,203	−1,383
Total Variable Costs	43,790	101,599	224,036	305,617	388,961
Total Fixed & Variable Exp.	220,813	417,766	843,936	1,109,540	1,374,124
Gross Profit	89,409	120,854	205,161	216,904	227,149
Overheads					
Maintenance overhead					
Mechanics labor and fringe	24,876	24,928	53,785	72,789	95,782
Shop supplies	966	1,432	1,696	2,325	3,643
Service vehicle exp	986	1,358	2,664	2,890	2,523
Shop equip exp	1,638	2,699	3,103	3,991	4,175
Total maintenance overhead	28,466	30,417	61,249	81,995	106,123
Personnel overhead	57,410	67,389	78,800	79,745	77,700
Housing cost overhead	16,000	22,000	37,728	37,846	38,174
Administrative overhead	9,674	10,573	12,902	13,515	17,130
Total Overhead Expenses	111,551	130,379	190,679	213,101	239,127
Total Expenses	332,364	548,145	1,034,615	1,322,641	1,613,251
Total Operating Profit	−22,142	−9,525	14,482	3,803	−11,978

EXHIBIT 2   **Acme Leasing Company income statement* (*cont.*)**

Revenues	1985	1986	1987	1988	1989
Adjustments					
Gain/loss on sale of vehicles			− 1,057	− 4,120	− 6,067
Misc. other income/(expense)**	1,303	1,281	985	1,604	1,435
Income Before Taxes	− 20,839	− 8,244	14,410	1,287	− 16,610
Provision for income tax	0	0	0	0	0
Net Income	− 20,839	− 8,244	14,410	1,287	− 16,610

*Abbreviated and Disguised Statement
**Includes transfers to dealership

An additional side effect, which seemed fortuitous at the time, was the increase in business with common carriers during the seasonal highs. In order to reduce the cash commitment required for owning sufficient specialized trucks to meet the seasonal demands, the trucking companies in the area turned to signing 3-year leases and to renting heavily from LeaseCorp. In addition, because Acme Leasing also offered a contract maintenance package and rental of additional trucks to leasing customers, these companies were able to save substantially on operational costs and, at the same time, reduce revenue lost due to truck downtime. It seemed the perfect marriage because the common carriers needed additional vehicles during seasonal peaks, and Acme Leasing found a substantial additional source of revenue. During the seasonal peak periods, rental utilization typically ran 90% to 100%. This was reduced to 40% during the lows; but with a steady base of lease business, overall utilization did not fall below 70% throughout the year.

THE ISSUE OF FUTURE GROWTH

Currently, in 1990, Acme Leasing is facing the prospect of another surge of growth. Two weeks ago, Tom approached Dave for capital to expand their service facilities, and to acquire 10 trucks. He said he needed 5 trucks to replace those Acme was planning to retire during the current year. In addition, he needed 5 more because the rental business was taking off and he could not keep up with demand given the current size of their rental fleet. This was the third time in 5 years that Acme would be expanding its operation. Growth, Dave admitted to himself, had been spectacular. From a 4 truck operation at startup, the fleet now consisted of 84 units. In addition to an increasing number of regular renters, they were currently servicing 15 leasing customers. As further proof, Tom submitted a 5 year income statement and balance sheet, showing the growth in lease and rental revenues, and total assets (see Exhibits 2 and 3).

> The pace of growth in the leasing business continues to be unrelenting. This is particularly pronounced in the Valley because transportation happens to be a very important component of production in the agriculture industry,

he said. To drive his point home, he cited a recent special report in *Successful Dealer* (July/August 1990) which indicated that,

> lease/rental is becoming increasingly popular. As dealership customers try to concentrate on their main business, they are looking to turn their transportation needs over to a professional.

Tom said,

> You don't see many trucks parked out in the yard do you? It has been like this for the last year and a half. Already, Ryder is moving in on the Fresno market, and if we don't do something about increasing our capacity, our potential customers will be lost to competitors who will have the capacity to handle them. We are sitting on a gold mine, but if we wait, we'll lose it for sure.

Dave was inclined to agree with Tom's general assessment. However, because Tom was requesting so many additional trucks Dave wanted to be sure. Besides, there was the question of where the money was going to come from. The dealership side of the business had not been doing well recently. Last year, the dealership took several large credit losses after two fleet customers filed for Chapter 11 bankruptcy. Furthermore, owner-operators have been scaling back on new truck purchases in order to weather the continuing economic downturn. Realistically, there was no way for expansion funds to be generated from the dealership at this time.

However, Dave could not ignore the need for growth. He reasoned that in this business, stagnation was fatal. Then, he turned his attention to the financial statements Tom submitted. In doing so, he realized that this was the first time since startup he had seriously looked at Acme Leasing's financial structure. In general, he received informal feedback from Tom and his service manager, Ted, during the weekly operations meetings. In addition, he usually received a consolidated profit and loss statement at the end of each quarter, and as long as he did not see a negative bottom line, Dave did not question Tom's management.

> If you can't trust your managers, then you shouldn't hire them,

was his operating philosophy.

EXHIBIT 3   Acme Leasing Company balance sheet*

Assets	1985	1986	1987	1988	1989
Cash	1,603	2,074	3,125	1,118	1,437
Receivables					
Lease receivables	38,462	80,101	202,214	318,689	452,966
Other receivables	3,127	5,156	8,137	14,127	16,127
Total Receivables	41,589	85,257	210,351	332,816	469,093
Total Inventory	10,305	11,615	14,725	15,239	12,256
Other assets					
Prepaid expenses	19,917	10,795	13,633	15,647	15,001
Misc. other assets	4,955	9,611	10,529	15,327	17,278
Total Other Assets	24,872	20,406	24,162	30,974	32,279
Fixed assets					
Units for leasing	165,000	295,000	240,000	345,000	345,000
(Accumulated deprec.)	− 21,450	− 59,800	− 91,000	− 135,850	− 180,700
Other fixed assets	35,596	31,945	32,895	35,493	37,710
(Accumulated deprec.)	− 8,862	− 5,974	− 13,478	− 15,896	− 16,726
Total Fixed Assets	170,284	261,171	168,417	228,747	185,284
TOTAL ASSETS	248,653	380,521	420,780	608,894	700,349
Liabilities & Capital					
Acct payable & accrued exp					
Accounts payable—trade	167,427	291,189	293,286	419,031	494,460
Accounts payable—misc	55,485	59,931	45,634	72,264	95,346
Intercompany payable	7,820	7,600	8,112	8,934	10,685
Other accrued expenses	8,920	6,964	22,421	29,889	30,652
Total Accts Pay & Accrued Exp	239,651	365,684	369,453	530,119	631,143
Long term debt					
Notes payable lease equip	4,840	8,920	21,000	27,160	34,200
Total Long Term Debt	4,840	8,920	21,000	27,160	34,200
TOTAL LIABILITIES	244,491	374,604	390,453	557,279	665,343
Capital					
Capital Stock Par Value	25,000	35,000	45,000	65,000	65,000
Retained earnings					
Beginning balance		− 20,839	− 29,083	− 14,672	− 13,385
YTD earnings	− 20,839	− 8,244	14,410	1,287	− 16,610
Net Retained Earnings	− 20,839	− 29,083	− 14,672	− 13,385	− 29,995
TOTAL CAPITAL	4,161	5,917	30,328	51,615	35,005
TOTAL LIABILITY & CAPITAL	248,653	380,521	420,780	608,894	700,349

*Abbreviated and Disguised Statement

HISTORICAL FINANCIAL PERFORMANCE

As Dave examined the financial and sales data for the past 5 years, he began to realize that things were not going as well as his general manager had been projecting in his verbal reports (see the statement of income and balance sheet in Exhibits 2 and 3). In particular, operating profits in the current year had declined (see Exhibit 4). Further, even though total revenue had been growing in previous years, it became evident that its rate of growth had started to slow three years ago. Dave was concerned because the signs of slowing growth had not been detected and brought to his attention at the time. Although the recessionary trend had weakened by late 1989, promising a stronger economy for the future, Dave Krose did not see this improved economy reflected in Acme's income statement. This was especially disturbing because general economic forecasts, provided by various trade journals and industry experts, indicated an accelerating increase in the use of the leasing alternative over the next five years. As more agricultural and transportation companies, concerned with maintaining a healthy cash flow, began to realize the benefits of leasing, this upward trend was also expected to continue in the Fresno area.

EXHIBIT 4   **Acme Leasing Company income statement**

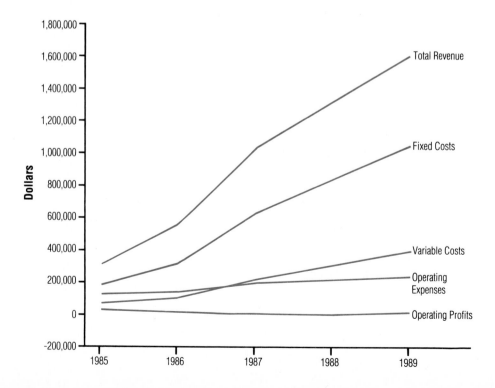

A possible explanation for the reduced rate of growth in revenues could be the recently established Ryder truck leasing outlet, which heated up competition in the Fresno area. However, Fresno was a growing market for leasing, so it stood to reason that a loss of market share did not provide all the answers. Other possible causes of decreasing growth in revenues could be the increase in rentals in the rental/lease mix. Subject to seasonal demand, increases in rental units may have sometimes resulted in more trucks parked for longer periods of time.

Comparing the *LeaseCorp Standard Operations Handbook* key ratios summary (see the LeaseCorp standard ratios in Exhibit 5) with Acme's operating ratios, Dave found that certain components of his cost structure had also increased dramatically (see the summary of operating ratios in Exhibit 6). Both of these factors, declining rate of growth in sales, and increasing growth in costs, contributed to an overall decline in profits.

Dave Krose wanted to reverse these trends and insure a strong position for his business in the future. The leasing company has been making positive profits, and there still exists a lot of upside potential. Thus, no thought was being given to abandoning the business.

In order to identify the issues he must address, and then to correctly deal with them, Dave assigned Donald Corey, his vice-president, to determine the causes for the decline in profit growth. Dave had never taken an accounting course, and found financial statements to be of little assistance as a decision making aid. However, he needed to know why the rate of growth in revenues has declined, despite the upward industry trend for leasing, and secondly, why certain cost components have risen so rapidly.

Don was also recently promoted from his general manager's position with

EXHIBIT 5   **LeaseCorp standard ratios summary**

Fixed expenses:

Sub-lease expense/revenue	<46%
(License + permits + FHUT)/total revenue	<8%
Outside subs/total revenue	<1.5%
Total fixed expense/total revenue	<58%

Variable expenses:

(Oil, lube + labor + parts + outside)/total revenue	<17%
Tires/total revenue	<4%
Warranty/total revenue	>2%
Total maintenance/total revenue	<21%

Gross profit: 20–28% of Total Revenue

Overhead: Total Overhead < Gross Profit

Net profit: 5–10%

EXHIBIT 6   Acme Leasing Company selected ratios & statistics*

	1985	1986	1987	1988	1989
Fixed Cost Percentage of Total Revenue					
License, permits, PPT, FHUT	7.67	7.50	7.72	7.95	8.02
Outside vehicle costs—subs.	0.00	1.84	1.61	2.13	2.26
Vehicles—sub-lease	39.26	38.69	42.19	43.54	44.59
Total Fixed Costs	57.06	58.70	59.09	60.61	61.52
Variable Cost Percentage of Total Revenue					
Oil, lube, labor, parts, outside repairs	9.60	14.18	16.86	18.11	19.21
Tires	4.52	4.65	4.68	4.89	5.05
Warranty	0.00	−0.26	−0.19	−0.09	−0.09
Total variable costs	14.12	18.86	21.36	23.04	24.29
Gross profit on revenue	0.29	0.22	0.20	0.16	0.14
Overheads Percentage of Total Revenue					
Total maintenance overheads	9.18	5.65	5.84	6.18	6.63
Personnel overhead	18.51	12.51	7.51	6.01	4.85
Housing cost overhead	5.16	4.08	3.60	2.85	2.38
Administrative overhead	3.12	1.96	1.23	1.02	1.07
Total overhead expenses	35.96	24.21	18.18	16.07	14.93
Net income on revenue	−6.72%	−1.53%	1.37%	0.10%	−1.04%
Liquidity Ratios					
Current ratio	0.22	0.27	0.62	0.66	0.76
Quick ratio	0.18	0.24	0.58	0.63	0.75
Days receivables	48.93	57.77	73.18	91.58	106.93
Days expenses in cash	2.65	1.81	1.35	0.37	0.38
Working capital to sales	−0.60	−0.50	−0.13	−0.14	−0.09
Leverage Ratios					
Total balance sheet debt to equity	58.76	63.31	12.87	10.80	19.01
Total debt to equity (incld LRL)	176.28	204.71	71.47	55.72	100.90
Total debt to total assets	0.98	0.98	0.93	0.92	0.95
Accounts receivable to payables	0.17	0.23	0.57	0.63	0.74
Sustainable Growth Rate	−1088.35%	−772.38%	−81.23%	−105.47%	−237.52%

*Sustainable growth rate is the max. future annual rate of growth that is achievable without new equity, a change in the debt/equity ratio, and with all net profits retained to fund growth. In general, use a 5-year running average for a more accurate indicator of this ratio.

| **Net Working Capital** | −186,155 | −266,739 | −141,252 | −180,946 | −148,357 |

the dealership. Eager to prove his worth, he attacked the project with enthusiasm. In order to make sure he covered all aspects of the business, he requested additional help from Frank Fuller. Frank assigned John Russo as the LeaseCorp representative, and operations troubleshooter. Together, Don and John went over the entire operation with a fine-tooth comb. In two weeks, Don submitted a memo that summarized his findings, with general comments and personal observations about the various issues (see Exhibit 7).

EXHIBIT 7   ## Fresno Truck Sales Corporation memorandum

To: David Krose, President, Fresno Truck Sales

From: Donald Corey, Vice-President, Fresno Truck Sales

Re: *Report on Acme Leasing Company's 5 year financial performance.*

Following your request dated August 6th, 1990, I have tried to discover, with the help of John Russo, the origins of the problems you highlighted in Acme's 5 year income statement. During the course of my analyses I have also come across other additional problems. As I originally suggested, much of the fluctuation in revenues has come from rentals to private carriers who currently own part of their fleets. About 31% of our fleet is currently designated rental. Operating margins tend to be higher in the short run for this segment due to customers' price insensitivity to short-term rentals, but the market is highly seasonal. In particular, our periods of high demand tend to start in July and run through to September during the fresh produce peak seasons. There is less demand between March and June, and almost no demand at all between October and February.

As I see it, the first issue to address is the optimal rental/lease mix for our fleet. A related issue is our dependence on a single industry for the major portion of our business. The private carriers we are dealing with are mostly in the agricultural produce industry. The trucking companies that we deal with are divisions of companies servicing the agricultural sector in this area.

Another feature I noticed in our operation is that, of the 15 lease customers we are currently servicing, 4 are trucking companies. In analyzing the individual truck profit and loss statements, it seemed apparent that the vehicles belonging to the trucking companies consistently produced lower returns than those of the other companies. Conversations with Ted Ketch revealed that trucking companies run on very tight schedules in order to maximize their revenues per truck. Thus, they are not as conscientious in keeping to their P.M. schedules. On the revenue side, other problems with this customer segment were also evident. It is undeniable that trucking companies constitute a large portion of the market, but we need to reassess our leasing policy for them.

I noticed that our lease and rental rates are extremely competitive with Ryder's. While staying competitive is important to maintaining our presence in the marketplace, it is possible that in the bid to remain ahead, we may have under-priced some of our contracts.

The operative word, I believe, has been 'volume' rather than 'margin'. I have been told, "*If we are able to get volume, then sacrificing margin is justified.*" In addition, because many of our contracts with trucking companies are for only 3 years, the cost accelerator clauses in several of them, especially with our high volume customers, have been waived. We really need to define some parameters with respect to the kinds of contracts we are willing to pursue.

In connection with the contract writing issue, I have discovered a large number of high mileage trucks with high residual values. High mileage used trucks with high residual values cause two things to happen. High mileage lowers their resale values, while high residuals require their resale prices to be high. This incongruity has forced Acme to absorb some losses resulting from the sales of such vehicles. In addition, most of our vehicles are specialized to service the agricultural transport industry.

EXHIBIT 7   Fresno Truck Sales Corporation memorandum (*cont.*)

A tour of our leasing company's service shop impressed on me the short amount of time it took to turn a truck around during a preventive maintenance service. This did not seem to be the case with lease trucks in the dealership's shop. John pointed out the difference is in the nature of the work done during preventive maintenance versus repair maintenance. John also suggested that the dealership mechanics have been trained to sell labor to the customer, whereas the leasing company's mechanics are supposed to repair at minimum cost. Coupled with this problem, you will notice that most of our fleet is at the point where lease variable revenue rates will not cover our actual variable maintenance costs (see Attachment 1).

Excluding the trucking companies, a quick telephone survey of our remaining customers indicated that 40% do not plan to renew their leases. Some preferred to rent during the short, peak seasons. One indicated that Ryder offered them better terms, and the rest cited poor maintenance and maintenance scheduling as major reasons. To verify the last reason, I found that our use of substitute trucks was unusually high. Six of our vehicles have to be put on standby rental just to deal with the need for substitutes when they are required. We need to look into this problem because it will affect our repeat customer base in the long run.

In the area of operational support from Truck Leasing Corporation, I found that while much information was provided by LeaseCorp's regular company visitation reports, they did not seem to translate into positive action by Acme Leasing. The most common complaint I received from various personnel in the company

ATTACHMENT 1   Acme Leasing Company analysis of truck variable cost per mile

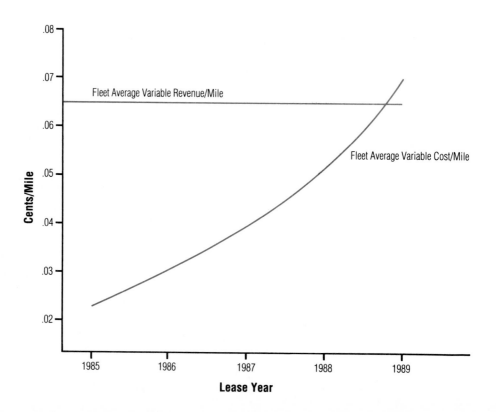

EXHIBIT 7   **Fresno Truck Sales Corporation memorandum (*cont.*)**

hinted at the lack of time available to implement many of the suggestions. I feel we need to address these issues because they affect how the company sees its relationship with Truck Leasing Corporation.

Finally, an analysis of the receivables revealed that they are growing at a faster rate than sales. Credit gaining, while important for garnering business, is a sensitive issue. On the other hand, collecting is just as important for maintaining current receivable accounts. We should review our policies with respect to this matter as soon as possible. I have investigated the possibility of using our credit department at the dealership to do the collections. We have the capacity to take on the extra work and can simply charge the leasing company for services rendered.

Please contact me if you have any questions, or wish to discuss this report further.

Attachment.

STRATEGIC CONCERNS

Dave had not anticipated that Tom's simple request for more funds would snowball into an operations audit of this nature. However, he reasoned, it was better that the problems got caught now, rather than later. In general, some of the problems the memo highlights seemed to indicate a fundamental conflict between the needs of a retail dealership, and those of a leasing franchise. It appears that certain strategies adopted by the company, although appropriate at the time of startup, might now need some modifications. Finally, it is apparent that Dave Krose has to rethink the philosophy of the leasing operation. Specifically, while initially seen as an adjunct to the main business of selling trucks, it has grown too large to be treated as such. Using the leasing company simply as a customer for the dealership was a good idea, but for the operation to grow and prosper, a basic realignment of its strategic goals and objectives appeared necessary. Tom Kelley's, and Dave's own roles in the business also have to be resolved. Time, attention, and resources have to be committed in order to ensure that the leasing company succeeds, and adds value to the entire business. Otherwise, continuing on this course will end up hurting the entire corporation instead.

David Krose believed that timely decision making is critical to the long-term growth of the firm. On one count, at least, Tom was right. They were sitting on a gold mine, and if they did not act quickly, opportunities would be lost. Given the competitiveness of the dealership business, it is foreseeable that leasing will become as competitive in the future. Opportunities lost will not be easily regained. If they want to get in on the ground floor of what will prove to be a growing market, they need to make plans now. Dave feels he cannot afford to wait another year and adopt a "wait and see" attitude. In addition to all this, Dave has to think about where the funds for the expansion are going to come from should he decide to pursue growth.

Due to the rising costs of doing business, Dave is already cash strapped in his dealership—no money can come from there. The cash situation in the leasing company is just as poor. Thus, he would have to look elsewhere in order to obtain funds.

As a matter of policy, LeaseCorp will overfinance the purchase price of a new vehicle.[2] However, Dave has always felt that in the interest of minimizing the costs of keeping liquid assets, the excess cash had to be used rather than kept idle as reserves. Thus, he was in the habit of redirecting these funds into his dealership to meet his cash flow needs or for capitalization purposes. Currently, these cash reserves are unavailable, because they are locked up in capital equipment and inventory.

Dave forwarded a copy of Don's memo to Tom Kelley, John Russo, and Ted Ketch. He called a meeting with Tom, Don, John, and Ted for Friday of the following week to discuss the issues raised. He also requested that all of them attend with suggestions for the next step.

THOMAS KELLEY

Tom was uncertain what the memo meant, but he had once said to Dave,

> You can't really tell if you've made any money until the contract runs its full course. What with constantly changing costs, and with competition from Ryder, you may get to the end of the lease period and find you haven't made any money at all.

Tom believed that was what they were now witnessing. Several contracts had expired and, on reflection, they probably came out just breaking even. It was a real problem because he was trying to predict events over a 5 year time horizon with rates that cover all contingencies, yet having to remain competitive.

The way he got around that problem was to do more rental business. During the seasonal highs, he could rent tractors at $575 a week and 14 cents a mile with no loss in business. The extra 5 tractors targeted for rental will bring in even more revenue. He was uncertain as to the reasons why Don felt rental business was overemphasized. He was confident there was nothing wrong with his marketing.

Tom decided that cost was the cause of the problems. The leasing company was made to pay full retail prices for the services and parts used during repair maintenance work by the dealership's service department. He reasoned to himself,

> It's close to impossible to compete with Ryder, who gets the best fleet rates from their suppliers, when I have to bear full retail cost for parts and service from my own dealer's service shop.

[2]Actually, the overfinancing is intended to be used to help the lease franchises offset vehicle startup costs, i.e., licensing, sales commissions, pre-delivery and inspection, etc.

Tom couldn't understsand why Dave allowed this practice to continue. He had previously said to Dave,

> After all, LeaseCorp is your best customer. We are 100% loyal, come to you for everything, even though we can sometimes get better prices outside. With an 84 unit fleet, we are now your largest single customer! Good treatment is not too much to ask for is it?

This has been the focus of a running battle he conducts with Ted Ketch, the service manager. Ted's reluctance to give him any price breaks is why Tom felt the most important thing was to get the customer signed to a contract, whether lease or rental. Often, this meant that he had to cut rates in order to be competitive, but as a salesman, he knew that high volumes *did* justify lower margins.

TED KETCH

Ted had his own thoughts on the matter. If Tom had built the right cost per mile allowances into the contracts he sold, he wouldn't be in this bind. There's no way that he will service a truck for the kind of rates Tom wants,

> Why should I sacrifice my bottom line for the leasing company so that they can give away the house? I can't see myself wasting resources to work on a lease truck for $35 an hour when I can be increasing my margins with customer work at $45 an hour. It just doesn't make sense.

FRANK FULLER

Frank was thinking about the phone conversation he had with Dave in which Dave had asked for more funds to acquire the 10 trucks. In looking at the income statement, Frank was in agreement that revenues were good. But Dave's balance sheet did not seem to reflect the same story. He was overleveraged, cash poor, and had major loan commitments that were coming due in the near future. Technically, Dave should have had additional equity in his leasing company if he had not been transferring the excesses from the 6% overfinancing to the dealership. With the additional equity, Truck Leasing would be more willing to finance his trucks. As it stood, expansion seemed a poor idea at this stage.

From what Frank gathered through their conversation, Acme Leasing had a lot of "shop cleaning" to do before taking the next step. Frank was always willing to lend a hand, but was hestitant to commit any funds at this point. On hearing Dave's complaints about his cash position, Frank had informed him over the phone,

Do you realize the excesses from the overfinancing is really a low interest loan for you to take care of your future expansion needs? Dave, you know that Truck has always backed you. Almost all your trucks are now being financed by us. We have never turned you down before, but you have to realize that the first thing any finance officer looks for is equity in a company before considering a loan. Truck Leasing Corp. has to see some equity in Acme.

Frank felt it wasn't up to him to dictate how the franchises ran their businesses, but it was in Truck Leasing's interest that the franchises all did well for themselves, and he was glad Dave called on him at the time he did.

Before sending John out, Frank expressed his concern over Acme's poor record of used truck sales,

Find out why Acme's used truck sales have been so poor. This is an area where they can easily pick up extra cash. I want us to help them sort this out because the impact on their bottom line will be immediate. Find out what they have been doing and see what can be done to change things.

Despite his concerns, Frank was confident that with John's expertise, and Dave's willingness to improve his operations, Acme Leasing would get through this slump in good shape.

JOHN RUSSO

John, on receiving the memo, was pleased that some action was being taken. To his mind, there were two major issues with which Dave had to deal. One was the question of growth. Sure, timing was important, but, if asked, he would advise strongly against growing now. The simple reason was that Acme Leasing did not have the managerial capabilities to handle growth at this point in time. Yet, he agreed that Dave must move quickly if he wanted to capitalize on the current growth in the area. This led to the second issue. The relationship between Dave and Tom. This was a sensitive issue, and though it was not like him to express unsolicited opinions, he felt that using the leasing company as a training ground for Tom was proving to be too expensive. John felt a sense of urgency in the kind of danger signs he was witnessing. Lack of cash flow, receivable buildups, increasing costs, decreasing revenue growth, and the lack of cooperation between the leasing company and dealership service department on basic policy issues. Issues such as the disagreement over intercompany charges make for an inflated cost burden that can potentially lead to collapse. Yet, he feels, these are merely the superficial symptoms of a deeper, more subtle problem.

There appears to be a lack of appreciation for the finer aspects of managing a leasing business. The business is different, radically different, from that of a dealership. In fact, about the only thing they have in common are the trucks,

he once said to Don Corey during the operations analysis they conducted.

URGENT NEED FOR ACTION

Dave was anxious to get something going. The agriculture peak season was 2 months away. With that, business from the trucking companies was expected to increase. He knew that Ryder in Fresno had already put in an order for more trucks to handle the extremely profitable peak season rentals. Acme could use the additional revenue, and he had no wish to be shortchanged on any business he could get out of the harvest season. But at this point, it seemed that everything hinged on the outcome of the next meeting.

GLOSSARY OF TERMS

Common carrier	Generally a generic term that refers to companies engaged in the business of selling commercial transportation. In this case, we are dealing with trucking companies.
FHUT	Federal Highway Utilization Tax—imposed on class 8 heavy trucks
Fixed and variable revenues	Fixed revenues are the base lease rate charged for the truck. Variable revenues refer to the additional cents per mile, and other mileage or time related charges. Akin to the base rate plus mileage charges imposed by car rental companies.
Fleet customers	Leasing customers with leases on more than two trucks
Full service leasing	A truck leasing contract that includes regular preventive maintenance, normal wear spare parts (such as tires, hoses, oil, lubrication, etc.), and other administrative services (such as fuel tax reporting, substitute truck rentals, 24 hour emergency service, etc.) as part of the package. The price of the contract should take into account all these expenses to arrive at the profit margin. Thus, once the contract is signed, the leasing company must try to protect that predetermined margin.
Intercompany pricing	Most leasing companies are set up as units autonomous from the dealership or holding company. Thus, work done by the dealership service department is usually charged back to the leasing company as expense items. This may take two forms: full retail rates, or special intra-company preferred rates.
Sub-lease	A financing program offered by the franchisor in which the franchisee leases the trucks it needs from the parent in order to sub-lease them to customers. The lease arrangements are usually on a case by case basis. In general, leases run anywhere from 5 to 6 years with a certain residual value built into the truck at the end of the contract. The residual is determined by considering the type of vehicle, the number of miles per year, and the expected wear on the truck. By using this type of arrangement, the franchisee does not have

to put up vast amounts of capital up front. In a sense, it is a "pay as you earn" scheme, devised to allow franchisees to expand quickly as demand grows. At the end of the lease period, the trucks are usually bought over from the parent at the residual price and then resold in the used trucks market, ideally at the residual or a higher price.

National account

In which a leasing customer is serviced by more than one LeaseCorp franchise over a wide geographical area.

P.M.

Preventive maintenance

LeaseCorp

The name of the Truck Leasing Corporation franchising system. The franchise system consists of privately owned truck sales dealerships that add truck leasing/rental to their service options by becoming a LeaseCorp franchise, stand alone truck leasing/rental companies that join the system, and Truck Leasing Corporation owned leasing outlets. The franchising provides various administration and operational reporting services including truck financing, training, operations analysis, etc.

PPT

Personal Property Taxes—imposed by county governments for the ownership of trucks

Private carrier

A goods manufacturing company that transports its own products. Transportation is an essential but not primary component of its business.

Rebillable line items

Some expenses incurred by the leasing company are chargeable to the customer as extraordinary items. Such as taxes, outside repairs for damages that are caused by abuse of the equipment, etc.

Specialized trucks

Generally trucks that have been custom designed to meet the specific needs of certain industries. Thus, the most common specialized trucks used in the agriculture transport industry are the refer straight trucks (refrigerated trucks), and stake body (box) straight truck.

Case 3

SIGNS R US

It was February 1989 and the 1988 financial statements for the Signs R Us sign shop of Columbia, South Carolina, had just been delivered. Looking them over, 55-year-old owner Wilma Simmons realized that some changes were needed. The shop had suffered a net loss on its third straight year of declining sales. Over the last forty years, Signs R Us has survived some pretty lean times and would probably survive the current slowdown. But for the first time, Wilma faced the possibility of going out of business.

HISTORY

After several years as a traveling jazz musician, Wilma's father, Walter, opened Signs R Us in 1948. Over the years, he took on several partners, but none stayed more than a couple of years. They apparently did not agree with Walter's business approach—putting most of his time into creating signs and very little of it into running the shop. But for thirty-five years his approach worked and the shop was modestly successful.

The key to Signs' longevity (besides Walter's skill) had been an evolving core of steady customers, albeit demanding different products. During the late 1940's and early 1950's they produced elaborate neon signs for drive-in theaters. Business was so good during this period that Walter had as many as ten men working for him, blowing and bending the glass tubing and installing the signs. This period was followed by a long relationship with a telephone equipment manufacturer who contracted for screen-printed electronic circuits.[1]

Oil companies, opening stations in the expanding suburbs, carried the shop from the sixties until the 1973 oil crisis. From the mid-seventies through the mid-eighties, grocery store chains gave the Simmons all the business they could handle with signs that touted things like weekly specials and two-for-one coupons.

[1]The desired circuitry is miniaturized, then transferred onto a screen, through which a molten conductive metal is applied directly onto a ceramic base.

EXHIBIT 1   Signs R Us Sign Shop income statement, 1987 and 1988

	1988	1987
Total Sales	$95,123	$103,553
Expenses		
Salary	20,000	24,000
Employee wages	36,605	35,629
[1]Employee benefits & taxes	4,811	5,068
Material	12,856	13,997
Supplies/postage	230	242
Rent	9,600	9,240
Utilities	3,821	3,728
Insurance	2,474	2,414
[2]Depreciation—equipment	0	2,674
[3]Truck maintenance	985	857
Telephone	1,566	1,812
Yellow pages ad	5,250	4,300
Accounting & legal	450	410
Interest & debt repayment	5,635	3,327
Miscellaneous	124	347
Total Expenses	104,407	108,045
Net Income (Loss)	($9,285)	($4,492)

Notes: 1. Based on 8.5% of salary plus employee wages.
2. Pick-up truck with 3-year depreciable life.
3. Includes gasoline, registration fees, and repairs.

EXHIBIT 2   Signs R Us Sign Shop balance sheet, 1987 and 1988

Assets	12/31/88	12/31/87
Cash	$ 944	$ 1,941
Notes & accounts receivable	4,099	8,010
Current assets	5,043	9,951
Equipment	13,315	10,641
Less accum dep'n	(13,315)	(10,641)
Non-current assets	0	0
Total assets	$ 5,043	$ 9,951

Liabilities & stockholder's equity		
Accounts payable in less than 1 year	$ 332	$ 117
Current liabilities	332	117
Loans from stockholders	21,400	21,400
Notes payable in 1 year or more	5,038	10,673
Capital stock—common	3,200	3,200
Retained earnings	(24,927)	(25,439)
Total liabilities & stockholder's equity	$ 5,043	$ 9,951

However, since the grocers' 1985 switch to "everyday low prices" Signs R Us had been unable to establish a new corps of repeat clients and sales had fallen by 25% (Exhibits 1 and 2).

PRODUCTS AND SERVICES

Signs R Us offers a variety of products and services including banners, silk-screened postcards, painted plywood, and vinyl-letter signs. They will letter vehicles, provide design assistance, custom-design signs, and create one-of-a-kind items such as books or commemorative plaques. They also provide delivery and installation on large jobs.

Vinyl-letter signs and postercards are the most popular items (Exhibit 3).

EXHIBIT 3   **Signs R Us Sign Shop list of jobs for part of July 1988**

Date ordered	Customer	Type of job*	Description**	Quantity	Price	Deposit	By
Week 1							
7/2	People's Insurance	PC	25 × 28 cards	10	400.00		Hank
7/3	SC Dept of Ag.	PC	7 × 11 cards	750	325.00		Jim
Week 2							
7/6	Perry & Plummer	V	Letters on van	1	400.00		Saundra/Hank
7/6	Insite Developers	S	18 × 40 sign	40	452.00		Hank
7/9	Hardees	B	4 ft × 10 ft banner	2	425.00		Jim
7/9	Hardees	PC	22 × 28 cards	6	210.00	35.00	Saundra
7/9	Best Company	V	Letters—no sign	12	22.50		Saundra
7/9	Century Data	PC	22 × 28 card	1	52.50		Saundra
7/10	Capital Center	PC	28 × 44 cards	2	90.00		Saundra
Week 3							
7/13	Ready-Lite	V	Letters on 2 ft × 3 ft plywood	1	370.20		Saundra/Jim
7/14	Lawyers Title	PC	24 × 28 cards	6	300.00	50.00	Saundra
7/15	SC Trial Lawyers	PC	24 × 28 cards	10	565.50		Saundra/Hank
7/15	Columbia Herald	B	4 ft × 6 ft, 4 ft × 12 ft banner	1 ea.	250.00		Jim
7/16	Nationwide Ins.	PC	22 × 28 cards	16	440.00	40.00	Saundra
7/17	P & P Builders	V	Letters on truck	1	350.00		Hank
7/17	Ready-Lite	V	Letters on 5 × 15 plywood	5	80.70		Saundra/Jim

Notes: *PC = Postcards   S = Painted plywood sign   P = Plastic sign
       V = Vinyl letters   B = Banner
       **In inches unless otherwise noted

Custom-designed items and banners are the most profitable. According to Wilma, they used to do a lot more design work for people, but over the last ten years much of that business had been lost to local advertising agencies. As a result, they often end up working with a design that they could have created. Most customers are surprised when they are told that design assistance is available.

Vinyl-letter signs prepared on a computer are fast becoming the dominant market item. The computers, which cost about $10,000 (the model Signs has cost $9,200, in 1987), are as easy to use as a typewriter. The operator installs a roll of adhesive-backed vinyl, types in the message, and selects the desired print-type (i.e., Gothic, block letters, all capitals, etc.). The letters are then mounted on a painted plywood, canvas, or plastic background. "There's not much real sign painting going on anymore," laments Wilma. "With these computers, anybody can get into the business. Shoot, the guy up the street (All American Sign Shop) has three computers and five high school kids running them. They can't actually paint anything over there, but he's doing a great business."

CUSTOMERS

Signs R Us serves a variety of customers. Government agencies, a large nearby university, construction companies, equipment rental shops, builders and realtors, assorted small businesses, and shopping malls have all ordered some type of sign or banner at one time or another. Some, such as the builders, are very cost-conscious whereas others (small businesses) are more interested in the quality and durability of the work. However, none of the above groups could be considered "regular" customers.

COMPETITION

Wilma considers budget sign shops to be her greatest competition. These shops do most of their business in the computer generated vinyl-letter signs and stress low price and fast turn-around. All are relatively new. All American Sign Shop, a franchise, has been open just three years. According to Wilma, since it opened, eight or ten similar shops have opened in town or out in the suburbs (Exhibit 4). "But I think half of them have already gone out of business," she adds.

"Used to be, all the signers in town knew each other and there was plenty of work for everybody, but not anymore. There's only a couple of shops left from more than ten years ago. It's almost all computer stuff now. As far as I know, Wilson Sign Company is the only other shop in town that still does hand-painting. He's a young guy who took over for his father. I don't know much more about him, but I did hear that he's not doing too well."

EXHIBIT 4   **Signs R Us Sign Shop list of competitors in Columbia**

Name	Location*	Advertising emphasis**
All Star Signs	South	Professional custom signs at lowest competitive prices 1-day service on most orders
All American Sign Shop	Downtown	Speedy signs at budget prices Small signs are our specialty Computer generated pre-spaced vinyl lettering
BC Graphics	North	Specializing in handlettered banners, postercards, windows & doors, truck graphics, real estate signs
Dave's Signs	North	Great signs, no waiting! Custom graphics Sandblasted wood signs, banners, vehicles
Econosign	West	Specializing in custom designed small signs at affordable prices 1-Hour signs and banners When you need it now!
Express Sign Company	North	High quality—fast service Visit our convenient location
R&T Sign Services	East	Specializing in real estate signs Fast, economical, high quality Construction signs, tree signs, sandblasted signs, sign frames
Signs & Screen Prints	South	Custom magnetic signs Computer cut vinyl letters Engraved signs
Today's Signs, Etc.	Downtown	Over 20 years experience Vinyl lettering Banners and postercards
Wilson Sign Company	Downtown	Constant quality since 1927 Design, production, installation Handpainted signs, graphics & logos

Notes: *Downtown vs. suburbs
         **Taken from yellow pages ad

FINANCES

Wilma does not like to owe anyone money. The company's only debt is a non-collateralized personal line of credit which she secured from a nearby bank. Also, despite long-standing relationships with most of her suppliers, Wilma pays for all purchases C.O.D. All equipment in the shop (darkroom equipment, the computer, easels) plus furniture and fixtures, and a 1985 pick-up truck are owned outright.

With the exception of one share of stock held by her father, Wilma owns all 3,200 shares of the incorporated company. Her personal assets include a 2-bedroom house and furnishings (she lives alone) and a six-year-old car, both of which are fully paid off. Despite the company's recent problems, Wilma has not been forced to draw upon her personal assets to keep it going.

PERSONNEL

only 4

Including Wilma, there are four employees at Signs R Us. She handles the finances, project scheduling, purchasing, writing up of (most) bids, and general shop management. She also makes calls on prospective customers and does some sign painting and design if time allows.

Wilma practically grew up at the shop, working off and on helping her father. However, it was not until the early 1970's that she began working there full-time. She studied history in college, and has recently taken two evening courses in classical art. Her work experience includes designing sets for a television station and some graphic design. She gradually took over running the day-to-day operations in the late 1970's, although Walter continued to work until just recently. According to Wilma: "He liked not having to make all the decisions, but he never let me forget that it was his company."

Jim Davis has been with Signs for just over four years and was at one time Wilma's right-hand man. He does a lot of the commercial work and most of the banners. Wilma says that he has ". . . a mill mentality—he works rather slowly, as if when he's done with that particular job, he'll be laid off. So he stretches it out. Well, he knows I won't lay him off but he works slow anyway. But he does good work, so I don't complain."

Hank Richards handles most of the vehicle lettering and custom design jobs, both of which require a great deal of skill. He also checks out potential jobs and writes up bids for the work. Hank is Wilma's number one guy: "He has a real good feel for what works and what doesn't. He has taken on a lot of the responsibility that I had originally thought Jim was going to handle. I would like to give him a raise, but I don't know where the money is going to come from." Like Wilma, Hank's background is in graphic design.

Saundra Cox, a senior at the university, works part-time. The bulk of her time (80%–90%) is spent running the computer. Most of the jobs that she works on take 2 to 3 hours and are in the customer's hands by the next day. When she is not at the computer, Saundra does odd jobs around the shop (i.e., mixing paints, cleaning up, running errands, etc.). According to Wilma, she is a good worker but at times is preoccupied with other things, and as a result may need to be told something several times. Saundra has hinted that she will be leaving after she graduates in May.

Wilma is generally happy with her employees. Having been together for over three years, Jim and Hank have developed a good working relationship and seem to complement each other's strengths. Saundra, although new, has managed to fit in fairly well. However, Wilma does not feel comfortable leaving the shop for more than a couple of hours. She trusts them and has faith in their abilities, but she says that she gets anxious whenever she has been away from the shop for very long. "I would like to make more sales calls than I do now. I guess I'm over-protective because it's my business," she reasons.

OPERATIONS

Although each employee has his or her strengths in one area or another, they often work on projects in pairs. This is partly due to the mix of activity on projects, and to the fact that it helps to smooth the workload. This arrangement is different from other sign shops where each project is handled by one person who is paid a commission for his work. At Signs the employees are all paid by the hour.

The shop is rented on a no-lease, verbal contract basis for $800 per month. When the original three-year lease expired, the landlord never bothered to draw up a new one. Wilma is not worried about him disappearing; he operates a Chinese restaurant right next door. Signs has been in the same location, within walking distance of both the university and the state house, for six years.

The shop includes (front to back) a reception area, Wilma's office, the computer room, the darkroom, the banner room, and "the back" (Exhibit 5). The darkroom is used for reproducing and enlarging images that customers have brought in, requesting that they be included on a sign. Most signs are produced in "the back." In addition to the painting, drying, and assembly of signs, "the back" also serves as a storage area for paint, wood, and canvas.

EXHIBIT 5   **Signs R Us Sign Shop shop floor diagram**

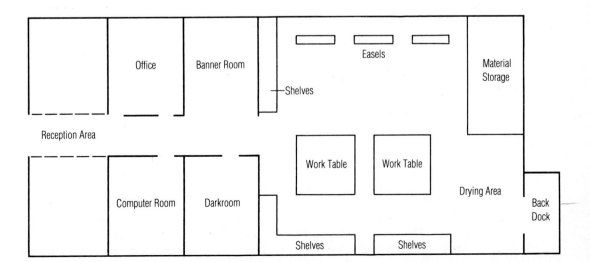

MARKETING

Signs R Us' marketing efforts could best be described as a mixed bag. In 1987, a full-color brochure was put together and sent to fifty recent customers. Not a single order or response was ever received. When Wilma had a chance to ask some of the recipients about the brochure, most did not even recall having seen it. Signs' most effective means of attracting customers is their ad in the Columbia area Yellow Pages. "We doubled the size of the ad from last year, and it really seems to have helped," said Wilma. "A good number of our orders start out from telephone calls. Of course lots of people are just calling to get prices, but it also lets them know we're here."

Personal sales are considered the key to the larger, less frequent, contracted jobs. Both Wilma and Hank make personal calls on customers or go to meetings where contracts are put out for bids. Wilma feels that, although somewhat shy, Hank has potential in personal selling: "Customers really like him once they have worked with him. In fact, a few of them have been back in and asked for him specifically. He's developed sort of a following."

In an attempt to secure additional business, Wilma has joined the city Chamber of Commerce four of the last five years. She would also like to make some connections within the Columbia business community. However, she has not received a referral in months and is very disappointed: "I go to the meetings and all the officers do is argue. They never make any effort to get ideas from the members, or to help us out. It's all really political. I have decided this is the last year that I'm going to join."

When asked whether their downtown location helps or hurts business, Wilma is not sure. As the suburbs grow and more services become available there, fewer people need to come into the city. Nevertheless, proximity to government agencies and the university does generate some business. "I think in some instances a convenient location helps, but price and quick turn-around are the real drivers right now."

Wilma put away the financial statements and thought about the company's situation. If business did not pick up soon, things would really get tight. She had already cut back her own salary once. What alternatives did she have? A new computer would allow them to double their vinyl-letter business; she could do more personal selling, going after the large government jobs; to cut expenses, she could forgo replacing Saundra whenever she leaves; or she could target and aggressively pursue the high-end, custom-design market. To Wilma, none of the choices sounded all that great. Maybe there was something that she was missing?

Case 4

SOLARCARE, INC.

In the summer of 1988, Battle Brown and Bill Hinchey, two recent MBA graduates, faced a decision that would have a significant and lasting impact on their business careers. They were attempting to decide whether to continue to pursue an entrepreneurial venture into the sun care industry or return to the secure jobs they previously held with large corporations.

GRADUATE BUSINESS SCHOOL

In 1986, Brown and Hinchey received their degrees from the Graduate School of Industrial Administration at Carnegie-Mellon University in Pittsburgh. During the course of their studies, they developed an idea for an innovative sunscreen product called SunSense. The formulation of SunSense was nothing radical by industry standards; most sunscreens were created from a standard list of ingredients that had been pre-approved by the Food and Drug Administration. The innovative feature of SunSense would be its means of delivery: a disposable towelette moistened with a high protection sunscreen that users could simply wipe on and throw away.

The concept began in a first-year product development class. Brown and Hinchey, along with several classmates, were placed in hypothetical positions as product managers at a major consumer products company that had a heavy presence in the sun care market.

They were challenged with developing a new extension for one of the company's existing lines. At the time, the group noticed three major factors influencing the sun care market. The demographic changes associated with the aging baby boom population, the perceived deterioration of the earth's protective ozone layer that was receiving considerable public attention, and President Ronald Reagan's skin cancer surgery all helped focus attention on the potential hazards of over-exposure to the sun (following his surgery, Reagan even told reporters that the bandage on his nose was a sign warning people to stay out of the sun).

This case was prepared by Temple D. Brown under the direction of Professor Dick Levin at the University of North Carolina with the assistance of SolarCare, Inc., for the purposes of classroom discussion. © 1990 Graduate School of Business Administration, The University of North Carolina at Chapel Hill.

Thus, Brown and Hinchey saw what they characterized as a "groundswell" of awareness of the need for products that offered protection from the sun. In a subsequent buyer behavior class, their research indicated that the primary attributes of a potential entrant into this market should be convenience and a greaseless formulation that would allow use outside the conventional beach and pool setting.

Combining their findings, the two determined that their product should be designed for active outdoor users who want protection from the sun without having to use lotion from a messy, leaky bottle. Their solution was a high sun protection factor ("SPF") sunscreen packaged as a single towelette along the lines of Handi-Wipes cleansing towelettes.

AFTER CARNEGIE-MELLON

After graduating from CMU, Brown accepted an offer to work in direct marketing for Harte-Hanks Communications Inc., and Hinchey accepted an offer in brand management at Procter & Gamble Co. During this time, they recruited Mike Gausling, a financial analyst and MBA who also worked at P&G, and Dr. Sam Niedbala, a research chemist from Hoffman-LaRoche in New Jersey.

Together, the four worked at nights and on weekends to refine their idea and attempt to develop a business plan. Eventually they developed a plan for their company, to be called SolarCare, that addressed in greater detail the marketing, production, and finance issues that would be crucial for launching SunSense in the market place.

THE SUN CARE MARKET

The sun care market had a wide variety of products and was characterized by low brand loyalty among consumers. Several large companies dominated the market with brands such as Coppertone and Shade (Schering-Plough), Sundown (Johnson & Johnson), and Bain de Soleil (Procter & Gamble). The market was highly fragmented and very competitive: approximately 60 firms sold sun care products, and the top 25 products together controlled only 55% of the market. Furthermore, the market was very seasonal, with 65% of revenues coming from sales during the summer months.

Additionally, the market was segmented into sunscreens, products that had an SPF greater than six, and tanning lotions and accelerators, products that had an SPF of six or below. SunSense would have an SPF of 15, a level that blocked out over 90% of the sun's harmful rays and provided a level of protection 15 times greater than if no protection were used.

Most sun care products were delivered in 4-oz. bottles that were available in discount drug stores at prices ranging from $5.50 to $6 for "normal" range SPF's (i.e., SPF's below 15). Lotions with SPF's as high as 40 were available in the $6 to $7 range. At non-discount stores, prices for identical products were generally 15–36% higher.

While the broader market grew at an annual rate of 6% in the mid-1980s, sunscreen sales grew at 15% per year and comprised 44% of the $265 million in overall retail sun care product sales in 1987.

Typically, retail displays were dominated by products of the large companies who had well-established distribution networks and armies of field representatives on hand to replenish constantly the store inventories as they were depleted. Smaller companies had to contract with store representatives for these reshelving and restocking services. These representatives generally were employed by a regional or national service firm and were assigned to work in one store, providing stocking services for the firm's clients only.

Hinchey, from his marketing experience at P&G, believed that sales to major retailers were best negotiated directly by the manufacturer, although many manufacturers sold only to distributors. Major retailers sometimes requested guaranteed sales provisions, whereby unopened product cases could be returned to the manufacturer at the end of the season for a refund. In addition, major accounts usually demanded extended credit, paying 25–50% on receipt of the product, and the balance after September 1, the date traditionally considered to mark the end of the sun care season. These major players generally demanded cooperative advertising support as well, which could mean another 2–3% expense for the manufacturer.

Sales to specialty retail markets, which included golf and tennis pro shops, ski resort shops, sporting goods stores, public sporting events, and amusement parks, were generally carried out through distributors that had the resources to establish direct contact with the retailers. Terms to distributors were typically net 30 days, and thus had a more favorable impact on the manufacturer's cash flow.

MANUFACTURING

The team felt that it was unreasonable to believe that SolarCare could acquire enough capital to control its own manufacturing facility. Accordingly, they contacted several large suppliers of cleansing towelettes and discovered that they could contract to have the SunSense formula mixed to their own specifications and packaged in finished form, ready to ship. The cost of this procedure to SolarCare would be approximately 16 cents per towelette for 15,000 cases (a total of 1,080,000 individual towelettes).

The SunSense package would be similar to a Handi-Wipes towelette package, only larger. The outer wrapping would be of a polyester design to prevent leakage when stored in athletic bags or other locations where the pack might encounter stress. The folded towelette inside would be roughly a 6 × 9 inch paper-based cloth saturated with SolarCare's specially formulated sunscreen.

The manufacturer would mix the sunscreen to SolarCare's specifications, saturate the towelettes, package them individually, box them in cases of 72 towelettes each, and deliver them on skids to SolarCare. SolarCare would then ship as needed to individual retailers.

SolarCare planned to have three types of cases available: 12 six-count boxes, three 24-count counter display boxes, or 72 loose towelettes. Additionally, SolarCare planned to offer a "clip-strip" package, which was a display featuring two hanging strips that held 36 towelettes attached to a heavy cardboard sign with the SunSense logo. Shoppers could simply pull off the number of towelettes they wanted. SolarCare felt that this display concept would encourage trial usage among consumers who were unwilling to purchase 6 pieces of an unknown product. The cases of loose towelettes could be used to replenish the clip-strips as they were depleted.

FINANCING

The group determined that internal financing would be sufficient to carry the company through a small test marketing effort. Together, the four could make equity contributions of $200,000 to get the company started. Looking beyond a test market, however, they realized quickly that any national or region-by-region

EXHIBIT 1   **Projected sales and earnings, Years 1–5**

	Year 1	Year 2	Year 3	Year 4	Year 5
Shipments	200,000	900,000	1,600,000	1,800,000	2,000,000
Gross sales	820,000	3,690,000	6,560,000	7,380,000	8,420,000
Allowances (22%)	(180,400)	(811,800)	(1,443,200)	(1,623,600)	(1,852,400)
Net Sales	639,600	2,878,200	5,116,800	5,756,400	6,567,600
Cost of goods	200,000	855,000	1,440,000	1,620,00	1,800,000
Operating expense	328,350	468,000	504,000	584,500	667,000
Selling expense	76,650	92,000	105,000	115,500	123,000
Packaging	30,000	40,000	40,000	40,000	40,000
Advertising	1,500,000	1,750,000	1,250,000	1,250,000	1,250,000
Total Cost	2,135,000	3,205,000	3,339,000	3,610,000	3,880,000
Operating Income	(1,495,400)	(326,800)	1,777,800	2,146,400	2,687,600

Source: Company records

rollout of SunSense would require significant outside funding of some form. In their business plan, they estimated that major cash inflows would be needed by the end of 1988. At that time, they estimated that the company would need $2.7 million in capital. Allowing a 10% "working pad," they rounded this number to an even $3 million. Exhibit 1 details what SolarCare felt were reasonable sales and income projections provided it could achieve this level of financing.

Messrs. Brown, Hinchey, Gausling, and Dr. Niedbala felt that successful test marketing results would virtually guarantee the future availability of financing and thus would ensure the long-term success of SolarCare.

THE TEST MARKET OF 1988

In late 1987, SolarCare contracted with a manufacturer to produce a small quantity of SunSense towelettes to be used in a test market. Testing of SunSense in 1988 consisted of both mass- and specialty-market efforts, as well as a direct mail campaign to put samples of the product directly in the hands of consumers.

SolarCare's sales in 1988 were slightly more than $50,000, and these sales were primarily made of sales to two accounts, K Mart (Florida and California stores only) and Phar-Mor, a discount drug chain with stores in Chicago and along the east coast from Pennsylvania to Florida. Other accounts included small regional drug and convenience stores and some specialty retail markets (Exhibit 2).

In June of 1988, after all product had been shipped and had presumably been on shelves for 3–4 weeks, SolarCare hired a marketing specialist to evaluate the movement of SunSense in Florida and California. The consultant found that from early May through June, each Phar-Mor store on average had sold 28.5% of its initial supply of SunSense, while each K Mart on average sold 7.3%. The average price per towelette was 52 cents, though K Mart stores offered the product only in six-count boxes (Phar-Mor offered roughly 60% of its supply as individual towelettes).

Neither chain ordered additional supplies of SunSense. However, neither chain returned unsold product and both seemed interested in continuing to carry the product.

Kings Island amusement park in Cincinnati ordered two cases of SunSense, which it placed on sale in its gift shops for $1.00 per towelette. The supply sold out in less than two weeks, and Kings Island subsequently ordered 42 additional cases, which also sold out. Other retail outlets offered SunSense for an average price of 89 cents per towelette and sold nearly all the product received.[1]

---

[1] These outlets were located in and around the Allentown-Bethlehem area where SolarCare was headquartered and where substantial local media coverage increased consumer awareness of SunSense. SolarCare also received national television news coverage on cable superstation WWOR of New York and was featured in a prominently placed article in *The Wall Street Journal* in May 1988.

EXHIBIT 2   **1988 sales summary**

	K Mart	Phar-Mor	Other retail	Total: major retail	Specialty
Number of cases**					
6-count	656	202	16	874	0
Single	0	212	239	451	440
Total	656	414	255	1,325	440
Average retail ($)					
6-count	3.57	2.85	4.50	3.52	0.00
Single	0.00	0.50	0.89	0.69	1.00
Wholesale $					
6-count	2.52	2.28	2.52	2.45	0.00
Single	0.00	0.39	0.42	0.40	0.50
Number of stores	200	82	130	412	300
Sales	$19,837	$11,480	$7,711	$38,684	$15,840
				Total Sales:	**$54,524**

**6-count and individual cases each contain 72 towelettes.

Source: Company records

In all, SolarCare was pleased with the results of 1988. Perhaps most importantly, Hinchey felt, the company had succeeded in establishing a "bigger than life perception" among consumers that helped build consumer confidence in the product. In reality, they were merely a small team with very limited resources attempting to revolutionize a segment of a highly competitive industry. As Hinchey quipped, "We're just four guys and a dog on a hill."

THE DECISION

The young entrepreneurs were assessing their situation. They were trying to determine if they should go ahead with the venture, and if so, how they could finance the growth of SolarCare beyond the test market. In addition, they were attempting to identify any potential risks that they might have overlooked in formulating their business plan, such as market reaction and competitive response risks.

Case 5

WALL DRUG STORE:
FACING THE '90S

SIZZLING STEAK: WALL DRUG
WESTERN ART: WALL DRUG
BEAUTIFUL WESTERN ART: WALL DRUG
FREE COFFEE AND DO-NUTS FOR VIETNAM VETERANS: WALL DRUG
FREE COFFEE AND DO-NUTS FOR HONEYMOONERS: WALL DRUG
MAKE YOUR DAY: WALL DRUG
W'ALL MAKE YOU HAPPY: WALL DRUG
FREE ICE WATER: WALL DRUG

Travelers driving across the rolling prairie of western South Dakota on Interstate Highway 90 are amused, irritated, and beguiled by scores of roadside signs and billboards advertising the attractions of something called Wall Drug. There are signs promising 5 cent coffee, homemade rolls, and roast beef dinners; signs intended to amuse (HAVE YOU DUG WALL DRUG?; W-A-A-L I'LL BE DRUGGED); signs publicizing publicity (FEATURED ON TODAY SHOW: WALL DRUG; WALL DRUG FEATURED IN PEOPLE; WALL DRUG AS TOLD BY WALL ST. JOURNAL; WALL DRUG AS TOLD BY TIME) and signs advertising Black Hills gold jewelry, cowboy boots, and camping supplies. By the time travelers reach the little (pop. 770) town of Wall, more than half of them are curious enough to exit under the friendly stare of an 80 foot, bright green, concrete brontosaurus which towers over the Wall Auto Livery, a Sinclair station. Two blocks to the left they find Main Street and a block-long business district with a hardware store, a grocery store, a dozen gift shops, restaurants, museums, and Wall Drug, the self-proclaimed "Worlds Largest Drug Store."

The Wall Drug Store occupies half of the east side of this block. Behind the iron hitching posts lining the curb and the pine board store front are a restaurant and twenty odd small shops selling souvenirs, western clothing, moccasins and

This case was prepared by Professor Phil Fisher and Professors Emeritus Robert Johnson and James Taylor of the University of South Dakota. It was presented at the North American Case Research Meeting, 1990. All rights reserved to the authors and the North American Case Research Association.

boots, Indian pottery, western jewelry, western books, stuffed jackalopes,[1] fudge, posters, oil paintings and, of course, prescription drugs. Life-sized concrete or fiberglass Old West characters lounge on benches in an enclosed mall giving tourists opportunities for photos of themselves sitting on a cowboy's lap or with an arm around a dance hall girl. Two animated, life-sized, mannequin cowboy orchestras play and sing for the crowds, and nearby a more menacing mannequin shouts out challenges to passers to try and match his quick draw in a gun fight for only fifty cents.

In back of the store is an open yard ringed with buildings featuring more animated displays, including a piano playing gorilla, and a singing family on a Sunday drive in a restored 1908 Hupmobile. This area, termed the "backyard," includes a six foot stuffed rabbit, a stuffed buffalo, a stuffed bucking horse, and a large, saddled fiberglass jackalope all providing more photo opportunities for visiting tourists. An old-fashioned covered well dispenses free ice water for coolers and Thermos bottles from a modern faucet.

A private collection of over 300 original paintings portraying the American West is displayed on the walls of the restaurant dining rooms. Throughout the store, those walls not covered with shelves of merchandise are covered with photographs. There are old photographs of Sioux chiefs, and western characters such as Calamity Jane, General Custer, and Wild Bill Hickock. There are hundreds of photographs of less famous cowboys and homesteaders. There are photographs showing people standing in front of signs giving the mileage to Wall Drug from such places as Paris, Amsterdam, Cairo, London, New Delhi, and Tokyo. And there are pictures of the generations of the Hustead family who created, own, and manage this unique drug store which is visited each year by approximately 2 million people.

As the tourist season opened in the Spring of 1990, Bill Hustead, the CEO of Wall Drug, his parents, Ted and Dorothy, his wife, Marjorie, and his sons, Rick and Ted, made last-minute preparations for the flood of expected customers. At the same time they continued to consider the pros and cons of plans for the most ambitious expansion in the company's history.

WALL DRUG HISTORY

Ted Hustead graduated from the University of Nebraska with a degree in pharmacy in 1929. In December of 1931, in the depths of the depression, Ted and his wife, Dorothy, bought the drugstore in Wall, South Dakota, for $2,500. Dorothy, Ted and their four-year-old son, Bill, moved into living quarters in the back twenty feet of the store. Business was not good (the first month's receipts were $350) and prospects in Wall did not seem bright. Wall, South Dakota, in 1931 is described in the following selection from a book about the Wall Drug Store.

[1]Jackalopes are stuffed jackrabbits with antelope or deer antlers. Flying jackalopes have pheasant wings. These creations of taxidermy were priced from $99 to $129.

Wall, then, a huddle of poor wooden buildings, many unpainted, housing some 300 desperate souls; a 19th century depot and wooden water tank; dirt (or mud) streets; few trees; a stop on the railroad, it wasn't even on the highway. U.S. 16 and 14 went right on by, as did the tourists speeding between the Badlands and the Black Hills. There was nothing in Wall to stop for.[2]

Neither the drugstore nor the town of Wall prospered until Dorothy Hustead conceived the idea of placing a sign promising free ice water to anyone who would stop at their store. The first sign was a series of small signs along the highway that read "GET A SODA/GET A BEER/TURN NEXT CORNER/ JUST AS NEAR/TO HIGHWAY 16 AND 14/FREE ICE WATER/WALL DRUG." On a blazing hot Sunday afternoon in the summer of 1936, Ted put the signs up and travelers were turning off the highway to stop at the drugstore before he got back. Located at the western edge of the Badlands National Monument, and near the major highway between the Monument and the Black Hills 50 miles farther to the west, they began to draw a stream of weary, thirsty tourists into the store.

Ted began putting signs up all along the highways leading to Wall. One series read "SLOW DOWN THE OLD HACK/WALL DRUG CORNER/ JUST ACROSS THE RAILROAD TRACK." The attention-catching signs were a boon to Wall Drug Store and the town of Wall prospered too. In an article in *Good Housekeeping* in 1951, the Husteads' signs were called "the most ingenious and irresistible system of signs ever devised."

Just after World War II, a friend of the Husteads, traveling across Europe for the Red Cross, got the idea of putting up Wall Drug signs overseas. The idea caught on and soon South Dakota servicemen who were familiar with the signs back home began to carry small Wall Drug signs all over the world. Many wrote the store requesting signs. For example, a sign was placed in Paris, "WALL DRUG STORE, 4278 MILES." Wall Drug signs were placed all over the world including areas near the North and South Poles, the 38th parallel in Korea and on jungle trails in Vietnam. The Husteads sent more than 200 signs to servicemen requesting them from Vietnam. These signs led to news stories and publicity which further increased the reputation of the store.

Articles about Ted Hustead and the Wall Drug Store began appearing in newspapers and magazines. In August, 1950, *Redbook Magazine* carried a story which was later condensed in *Reader's Digest*. The number of newspapers and magazines carrying feature stories or referring to Wall Drug increased over the years. As of May, 1990, Wall Drug Store files contained over 700 clippings of stories about the store. The store had also been featured on several network and cable television shows.

The store and its sales grew steadily. From 1931 to 1941, the store was in a

[2]Jennings, Dana Close; *Free Ice Water: The Story of Wall Drug;* North Plains Press; Aberdeen, South Dakota, 1969, p. 26.

rented building on the west side of Wall's Main Street. In 1941, the Husteads bought an old lodge hall in Wasta, S.D. (15 miles west of Wall), and moved it to a lot on the east side of the street. This building became the core around which the current store was built.

Tourist travel greatly increased after World War II, and the signs brought increasing numbers of people to the store. Bill Hustead recalls that he was embarrassed because the facilities were not large enough to service the crowds of customers. The store did not even have modern rest rooms, but sales during this period grew to $200,000 annually by 1950.

In 1951, Bill Hustead, now a pharmacy graduate of South Dakota State University, joined his parents in the store. In 1953, they expanded the store into a former store room to the south. This became the Western Clothing Room. In 1954, they built an outside store on the south of the Western Clothing Room. This resulted in a 30% increase in sales. In 1956, a self-service cafe was added on the north side of the store. The cafe expansion was built around a large cottonwood tree which remained, its trunk rising out of the center of the dining area up through the roof.

By 1958, the Wall Drug Store had two men in a truck working full time to maintain 600 signs displayed along highways throughout the Midwest. The store also gave away thousands of small signs each year to people who requested them.

In the early 1960's, Highway 16, the main east-west route across South Dakota to the Black Hills, was replaced by Interstate Highway 90. The new highway was routed near the south edge of Wall. The Husteads, who had been considering building an all new Wall Drug Store along with a gasoline service station near the old highway, did build the station, the Wall Auto Livery, at the new highway interchange.

In 1963, they added a new fireproof construction coffee shop. A new kitchen, also of fireproof construction, was added to the back of the coffee shop the following year. Also in 1964 and 1965, new administrative offices and a new pharmacy were opened on a second floor over the kitchen. Another dining room and the backyard area were added in 1968. This was followed in 1971 with the Art Gallery Dining Room. By the early 70's annual sales volume had reached $1,000,000.

In 1971, the Husteads bought a theater that bordered their store on the south. The next year they demolished it and constructed a new addition, called the Wall Drug Mall. All previous expansions had been financed from profits of the business or short-term loans. Ted and Bill broke with this by borrowing $250,000 for 10 years to finance the Mall.

The Mall was designed as a miniature western town within a large enclosure. The strolling mall was designed as a street between shops fashioned like two-story frontier stores. The store fronts and interiors were made of various kinds of American wood—pine, black walnut, gumwood, cedar, hackberry, maple, and oak. The store fronts were recreated from photographs of Western towns in the 1880's. These shops stocked products which were more expensive than the souvenir merchandise of the older shops. In 1983, the Mall was extended to in-

EXHIBIT 1   Wall Drug Store sales and net income

Year	Sales (000)	Net income (000)
1975	2,679	118
1976	3,464	165
1977	3,777	155
1978	4,125	206
1979	3,552	33
1980	3,970	185
1981	4,821	224
1982	4,733	203
1983	4,851	257
1984	5,055	285
1985	5,273	161
1986	5,611	233
1987	6,142	249
1988	6,504	204
1989	7,419	242

Source: Company records

clude a half dozen more shops, a travelers' chapel modeled after one built by Trappist Monks in Dubuque, Iowa, in 1850, and a replica of the original 1931 drugstore called Hustead's Apothecary, which serves as a museum of Hustead family and Wall Drug artifacts.

The store was also expanded on the north end in 1975 and 1976 and on the south of the original Mall in 1978. Wall Drug continued to have increased sales every year until 1979. That year, a revolution in Iran started a chain of events which resulted in a doubling of the price of crude oil and temporary shortages of gasoline in the United States. This caused many service stations to experience periods of time that summer when they were out of gasoline. Travel by automobile decreased, and the Wall Drug Store was one of many businesses hit by a decrease in sales. By 1981, however, sales had recovered. Exhibit 1 gives sales and net income after taxes for 1975 through 1989. In 1990, the store and its backyard covered 48,000 square feet and sales were $7.4 million.

THE HIGHWAY BEAUTIFICATION ACT AND WALL DRUG STORES

In 1965, Congress passed the Highway Beautification Act, which was designed to reduce the number of roadside signs. Anticipating the removal of many Wall Drug signs, the Husteads invested in new signs that were allowed under the initial legislation. Since these signs could be no closer than 660 feet from the highway, they had to be very large and cost around $9,000 each. By the time they were installed, the laws had been amended to exclude them.

In the late 1960's, concerned about the effects of losing their roadside signs, the Husteads began advertising in unusual and unlikely places. They began taking small advertisements in the European *International Herald Tribune* and Greenwich Village's *Village Voice*. They advertised 5 cent coffee, 49 cent breakfasts and veterinary supplies. They put advertisements on double-decker buses in London, on the walls in the Paris Metro (subway), along the canals in Amsterdam and in rail stations in Kenya. These ads brought letters and telephone calls and then news articles. First, *The Village Voice* carried an article, and in 1971, the Sunday *New York Times*. Bill Hustead appeared on the network television show "To Tell the Truth." In all, 260 articles about the store were printed in the 1970's and approximately the same number during the 1980's.

Passage of the Highway Beautification Act did not mean an end to roadside signs. Compliance with this legislation was slow in many states. Disputes over whether sign owners should be compensated for removed signs, and a lack of local support for the law meant that some signs remained.

Bill Hustead served in the South Dakota state legislature during the 1960's and was Chairman of the state joint senate-house Committee on Transportation when the Highway Beautification Act was passed. He and his committee wrote South Dakota's compliance law, which resulted in the removal of 22,000 of the 28,000 roadside signs in the state. The federal government then fined the state for noncompliance, objecting to the establishment of commercial zones in which signs were permitted. The owners of roadside businesses challenged this federal enforcement and were successful. The federal government finally accepted a plan which allowed county governments to establish zones where signs were permitted. In South Dakota, this zoning resulted in an additional 1,000 signs being erected bringing the total to 7,000. Bill also testified at federal and state legislative hearings on laws to comply with the federal law. In 1981, Bill Hustead was appointed to the South Dakota Highway Commission, a position he still held in 1990.

By 1990, most remaining Wall Drug roadside signs were located in South Dakota, and there were fewer than 300. Existing signs were being permitted, but no new signs could be erected. Existing signs could be maintained and repainted, but could not be moved or enlarged. Federal legislation proposed in 1989 would have removed these signs without compensation, but the proposed bill was not passed; and the Husteads were more optimistic about the future of roadside advertising than they had been in many years.

Wall Drug sign coverage was still fairly intensive along Interstate 90. In 1990, a count of signs over a 250 mile stretch of I-90 east of Wall identified 86 Wall Drug signs. No two signs were alike, although about half had a characteristic design. These contained a short message, HAND MADE JEWELRY, for example, in dark green letters on a white background, and the logo, WALL DRUG, below in yellow letters on a dark green background. Other signs had a variety of colors and formats. A crew still serviced the signs twice a year, and all signs observed in 1990 were in excellent condition.

BUSINESS ENVIRONMENT

Wall is located at the northwest edge of the Badlands National Park (see Exhibit 2). The Badlands Park is an area of over 244,000 acres of barren ridges and peaks formed by centuries of erosion which exposed colorful layers of different minerals and fossil remains of prehistoric animals. Approximately one million people visit the Monument each year.

Rapid City, South Dakota (population 44,000), is 50 miles to the west of Wall. Rapid City is on the eastern rim of the Black Hills, a forested mountain region and the source of most of the gold mined in the United States. The Black Hills is also the site of the Mount Rushmore Memorial, which attracts about 2 million visitors each year. Forest Service visitation figures for the Badlands and Mount Rushmore are given in Exhibit 3.

Interstate Highway 90 is the only east-west interstate highway in South Dakota. It passes near the Badlands National Park and through the Black Hills,

EXHIBIT 2   South Dakota: location of Wall Drug Store

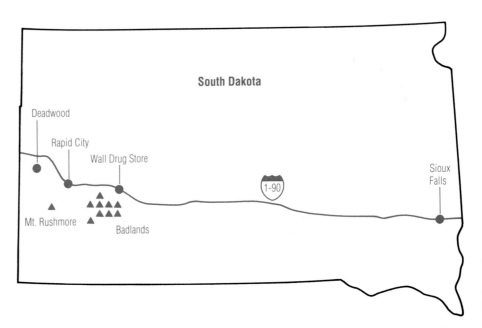

EXHIBIT 3   **Annual visitors**

	Badlands National Park	Mount Rushmore Memorial
1971	1,293,011	2,314,522
1973	1,400,000	NA
1975	1,165,161	1,994,314
1977	1,303,471	2,271,838
1979	870,000	1,642,757
1981	1,187,970	2,054,567
1983	1,038,981	1,983,710
1985	962,242	2,112,281
1987	1,186,398	1,949,902
1988	1,122,040	2,013,749
1989	1,249,956	2,075,190

Source: U.S. Forest Service

carrying most of the tourists which visit these areas. Exhibit 4 gives the traffic count on I-90 by month for 1988 and 1989. According to Ted Hustead, counts of traffic in the area of Wall showed that 78% of all cars which left Interstate 90 to drive a parallel road through the Badlands also entered Wall. For westbound I-90 traffic, 55% exited at Wall, and 45% of eastbound traffic turned off at the Wall exit. These counts were made during the summer months.

There were seven other gift shops in Wall, and an Old West wax museum, a wildlife museum, a taffy shop, and a Cactus Saloon and a Badlands Bar on Wall's Main Street. All depended primarily upon tourist business during the summer months. In the spring of 1990, the Hustead family was preparing two new gift shops for June 1 openings. These shops were across the street from the main store. They were called Dakota Mercantile and The Tumbleweed.

Voters in South Dakota approved a referendum in 1988 to permit limited betting ($5) casino gambling to be licensed in the city of Deadwood, South Dakota (pop. 2409). Situated in the Black Hills 90 miles west of Wall and 11 miles off Interstate Highway 90, Deadwood was founded by gold miners and is near to several still active gold mines. During the 1880's it was home to well-known western characters such as Calamity Jane and Will Bill Hickock. Hickock, in fact, was shot in the back and killed while playing poker in Deadwood. Legal gambling began again in November of 1989. While the full impact of the Deadwood gambling casinos on tourism in South Dakota could not yet be measured in early 1990, it was expected to result in an increase in traffic on Interstate 90, the most direct highway from the East. Exhibit 5 shows sales for all eating establishments and hotels and motels in Wall and Deadwood by two-month periods from January 1988 through February 1990.

EXHIBIT 4   **Automatic traffic recorder data**

Average daily traffic on I-90 near Wall, S.D.

	1988	**1989**
January	1674	1975
February	1867	1954
March	2184	2353
April	2567	2606
May	3361	3420
June	4919	5160
July	5615	5847
August	5629	6086
September	3875	4233
October	3401	3609
November	2675	3141
December	2372	2374
Annual daily average	3345	3563

Source: South Dakota Department of Transportation

MANAGEMENT

Bill Hustead, 63, was the President and Chief Executive Officer of the Wall Drug Store. Bill and his wife, Marjorie, owned 60 percent of the stock in the company. Marjorie was the corporation Secretary and was active in the business and in charge of merchandise buying. Ted and Dorothy Hustead owned the remaining 40 percent of the stock. Both were in their late 80's and still participated in the store management. Ted was Chairman of the Board and was involved primarily in public and employee relations. Dorothy was also an officer of the corporation and managed the store's cash receipts, accounting and banking.

Two of Bill and Marjorie's sons, Rick, 40, and Teddy, 39, were also active in store management. Rick had a Master's degree in guidance and counseling and had worked as a high school guidance counselor before joining the store in 1980. His primary responsibility was managing restaurant operations. Teddy had a degree in business and had worked for several years in the Alaskan oil fields before Rick persuaded him to join the store in 1988. He was responsible for day to day management of the shops. Both brothers participated in strategic planning and policy making for the overall business.

While neither Rick or Teddy were pharmacists, Rick's wife, Kathy, was a registered pharmacist and worked three days a week managing the store's prescription drug business. In 1990, Teddy married and his wife, Karen, was to

EXHIBIT 5   Sales receipts (000's)

Eating and lodging establishments

	Wall, S.D.		Deadwood, S.D.	
	Eating	Lodging	Eating	Lodging
1988				
Jan.–Feb.	$106	$ 16	$275	$172
Mar.–Apr.	118	37	285	145
May–Jun.	358	366	502	318
Jul.–Aug.	550	740	823	613
Sep.–Oct.	270	204	372	434
Nov.–Dec.	115	32	296	158
1989				
Jan.–Feb.	83	13	277	201
Mar.–Apr.	124	45	295	141
May–Jun.	385	414	538	344
Jul.–Aug.	641	911	883	724
Sep.–Oct.	328	300	434	243
Nov.–Dec.	134	54	495	265
1990				
Jan.–Feb.	103	28	715	363

Source: South Dakota Department of Revenue

become the newest member of the Hustead family management team. Karen was the Executive Vice President of the Badlands and Black Hills Association. This was an organization of the tourism-related businesses in the region. It was expected that she would start as a floating troubleshooter involved in day to day store operations to learn the business, and that she would also have a role in public and governmental relations for the store.

Bill spoke about the significant roles of his mother and wife in the success of the Wall Drug Store.

It's known as Ted and Bill Hustead's Wall Drug, but for years Dorothy was the backbone of the store. A few years ago, Dad and I were honored at a banquet and as I sat there and listened to the speeches a voice deep within me cried, Dorothy, Dorothy. She was the one with the idea to put up the signs. She was the one who worked behind the counter and in the restaurant.

My wife, Marjorie, is the most valuable asset we have. After she took over the buying, we raised our net from the jewelry store by $50,000. She has a wide sphere of influence and is a stabilizing force.

If the Wall Drug Store was a family institution, it was also seen as an institution of great importance to the town of Wall and the store's full-time employees. Bill Hustead's conversations about the Wall Drug Store frequently emphasized the importance of the business to the economy of the town of Wall, its importance as the only source of income in Wall for most of its full-time employees, and of the need to secure its continued success for the sake of the town and the store's employees. He also spoke of the business in terms of personal and family pride.

> The priest here in Wall thought I might have a calling for the priesthood, so my folks sent me to Trinity High School in Sioux City, Iowa. . . . One time I had a date with a girl who took me to her home. Some relatives, a married sister, I think, and her husband were there, and they made some slighting remarks about that "little store with all the signs." I was embarrassed. Gosh, Mom had the idea about the signs but then did Dad have to put them up all the way from Wisconsin to Montana?
>
> Then, when I worked in the store during the summer, I was embarrassed sometimes at some of the things customers would say about the store. Our facilities were so poor. We didn't even have indoor rest rooms.

There were two key managers who were not family members. Mike Huether worked with Rick in managing restaurant operations. The two were about the same age and had the same level of responsibility, but Bill noted that, "Mike isn't as likely to go to the mat with me." Huether was a long-time employee who had worked at the Wall Drug Store since he was 18. Karen Poppe with 16 years' experience was the personnel manager. As the store grew and the competition for seasonal employees increased, this function had become critical to the store's ability to grow or even function at the current level of operations.

The Wall Drug Store had no organization chart or written job descriptions, but all the managers believed that they had clear understandings as to their responsibilities and authority. Rick explained, "There is overlap. Ted (Teddy) and I have specific and joint responsibility. Ted's focus is more in retail. My focus is more in the restaurant. There is no organizational chart, but we spend enough time talking to each other so that our roles are defined."

Rick thought the store needed a more complete management staff but that they had made progress toward that in his ten years there. "Bill is a builder and a brilliant businessman. What I wanted to do is run the business more efficiently. It's paid off with more profits."

MANAGEMENT SUCCESSION

Asked about the difficulties of having three generations of the family active in the store management, Bill spoke of his own plans. "I went to a religious retreat earlier this month, then attended my cousin's funeral in the East and a funeral of a high school friend and I'm ten days behind in my work. Sometimes I think this darn job is killing me. I can't work ten or twelve hour days anymore."

The aspirations of his sons were a factor also. "My forty-year-old sons will have to have independence. The boys in the store (a brother and three sisters were not involved with the store) will get as much of the store as I can give them, but it's not that good a business. There's too much pressure." Asked about the fact that his father at 87 was still active in the business, he said, "I love my father. He's the best P.R. man anybody ever had."

He elaborated more on his past contributions to the business. "My plan was to work for a while and then buy a drugstore in Jackson Hole, Wyoming, but Dad and Mom encouraged me to come here. They needed me desperately. Dad was never a floor man and they really needed someone on the floor."

Rick discussed the issue of management succession from his perspective. "We have a clear understanding with some documentation but no timetable. Teddy came in with the understanding that we'd be partners. I'd like to see my Dad stay on as long as he wants. He is politically influential. He's a tremendous businessman. He's an asset to the business and to us. I hope he'll keep involved to the point he enjoys it. Control is not a major issue. If anyone is concerned about succession, it's Bill." Rick also pointed out that the family had life insurance protection to assure that the business would not be crippled by inheritance taxes should anyone in the family die.

Ted Sr. made it clear that he no longer expected to take an active role in making policy decisions. The 1989 South Dakota legislature had approved the licensing of video poker and keno machines which would accept bets up to two dollars. The Husteads had installed a few in the Western Art Gallery Dining Room, where they had a liquor license and bar. Their intent was to evaluate the results and either remove them or install more depending on their profitability and their perceived contribution or detraction from the atmosphere. Asked about his attitude toward the decision to install video lottery machines, Ted said, "They don't need to ask me, and I don't want them to ask me, but if they had, I'd have said I didn't think much of them" (the video lottery machines).

Speaking of Bill's contribution to the store, Ted Sr. commented, "My son Bill is an idea man. The Mall was his. He called in an architect and gave him the plans. Bill has built the art collection. He has a great appreciation for art. I bought the first few paintings; Bill bought the rest."

STORE OPERATIONS

The Wall Drug Store had approximately 30 permanent employees. Peak summer employment would reach 225. About 100 people from the local area were employed to do seasonal work and 120 college students were recruited to complete the work force. Ninety-five percent of the local seasonal employees would be people who had worked at Wall Drug in previous years. Many were housewives and senior citizens who could begin work in May and work during September and October when the college students were not available. About forty percent of the college students each year were repeat employees from previous years, but Wall Drug had to recruit about 70 new employees each year.

Student recruiting was handled by Karen Poppe. Each year 200 colleges and universities were sent recruitment information just prior to the Christmas break. She also made recruiting trips to about six colleges and attended several "job fairs." Recruitment of seasonal employees was becoming increasingly difficult and was seen by the Wall Drug management as a potential limit to their growth.

Mrs. Poppe and the Husteads thought that Wall's remoteness was a major obstacle to recruitment of summer employees from college campuses. The nationwide increase in the tourism industry meant that there were more companies recruiting from the same source. At the job fairs, Mrs. Poppe found herself competing with such major attractions as Disney World and other theme parks, and better known vacation areas such as Yellowstone Park. This made persuading students to choose the little town of Wall on the treeless plains of South Dakota more difficult each year.

Summer employees were housed in small dormitories and houses owned by the store. The store owned a swimming pool for employees and would have social gatherings such as picnics or volleyball games. Summer employees were paid $4.00 an hour and worked 40 hours plus 8 hours of overtime for which they were paid time-and-a-half. They paid $25 per week for their rooms. Students who stayed through the Labor Day weekend also got a 5 percent bonus and a rent reduction of $17 per week for the entire summer.

While the gambling casinos in Deadwood, South Dakota, 90 miles to the West were expected to result in increased traffic on I-90, they also competed for seasonal employees. In 1990, unskilled casino employees in Deadwood were being paid $7.00 an hour.

Wall Drug had formerly hired 1 of every 5 applicants for summer jobs. By 1990, they were having difficulty filling their positions. The labor scarcity had also had an effect on their personnel policies. As Bill explained, "We would exercise discipline. We expected to send a few people home just to let everyone know that we were serious. Now we get them out here and try to make it work. If they can't make change, we try to find a place for them. And it works better. We have a better atmosphere now."

New employees were trained to be courteous and informed about the Badlands, Black Hills, and other sites of interest in the area. Karen Poppe coordinated new employee orientation, but most of the members of the Hustead family participated. Ted Sr. studied the applications and pictures of all summer employees so that he could greet them by name when they arrived and whenever he saw them working in the store.

The Wall Drug Store and restaurant had a total area of 48,000 square feet. By comparison, the average Wal-Mart store covered a little more than 56,000 square feet. In 1989, Wall Drug merchandise sales were $5.6 million. The restaurant was a self-service restaurant with seating for 500; it had sales of $1.8 million.

In 1989, the average McDonald's had $1.6 million in sales. The opening of the two new stores, Dakota Mercantile and The Tumbleweed, would add another 6,000 square feet.

Wall Drug visitors frequently asked about purchasing items by mail. For several years the store had about $50,000 in mail order sales without catalogs or order forms. In 1989, Teddy designed a simple order form with the title, "Order By Mail Year Around From WALL DRUG." It listed a few items under the categories of jewelry, western art, boots and moccasins, western wear, western books and "Etc., Etc., Etc." Items listed under this last category were "jackalopes, flying jackalopes, steer skulls, rattlesnake ashtrays, horse twitches, and souvenirs galore." This one-page sheet also included a map of the store but listed no prices. It was available at cash registers for customers to take with them. Mail order sales increased to over $87,000 in 1989 and sales for the first three months of 1990 were up 47 percent over 1989. Most mail order sales were for bigger ticket items such as jewelry. The store also sold over 60 jackalopes by mail in 1989.

Commenting on Teddy's success with increasing mail order sales, Rick said, "A catalog would be the next step. We talk about building a model for this business, but we need to hire the talent to run it."

The Husteads were also trying to expand their tour bus business. Bus tours were an increasingly important factor in tourism. They were especially popular with senior citizens and foreign visitors. The Husteads believed that the ability to provide fast food service from their 500-seat, self-service restaurant would be a reason for bus tours to include them as a stop. They were also interested in persuading tour operators now running buses from Denver to the Black Hills to include the 100-mile round trip from Rapid City to the Badlands as part of the tour. This would also include a stop at Wall Drug. Attracting more of this business was assigned to Teddy, who had increased the store's promotional efforts at bus tour operator conventions and trade shows. This had resulted in some increase in business, and about 90 buses were expected to include Wall Drug as a stop in 1990.

FINANCE

Exhibits 6 and 7 present income statements and balance sheets from 1983 through 1989. Historically, the store's growth and expansion projects had been financed through retained earnings and loans of up to ten years' duration. The long-term debt of $151,000 outstanding in 1989 consisted of approximately $82,000 owed on a stock repurchase agreement and a $69,000 interest bearing note. These debts were held by Hustead family members not active in the business and were being paid in monthly installments.

Wall Drug had a profit sharing plan for all employees who worked more than 1000 hours during any year. At the discretion of the four senior Husteads

EXHIBIT 6   **Wall Drug Store income statement (000's)**

	1983	1984	1985	1986	1987	1988	1989
Net sales	$4,851	$5,055	$5,273	$5,611	$6,142	$6,504	$7,419
Cost of goods sold	2,586	2,553	2,793	2,854	3,338	3,579	4,164
Gross profit	$2,265	$2,502	$2,480	$2,757	$2,804	$2,925	$3,255
General and administrative							
Wages and salaries	$1,006	$1,129	$1,233	$1,274	$1,305	$1,443	$1,541
Officers' salaries	143	154	135	151	164	155	178
Depreciation	123	136	148	149	170	168	200
Profit sharing contribution	100	113	119	135	126	146	157
Advertising	93	82	99	122	107	123	44
Utilities	84	111	106	124	120	129	141
Conventions and conferences	1	1	3	3	16	14	21
Other	356	424	465	501	505	534	655
Total G & A expenses	$1,906	$2,150	$2,308	$2,459	$2,513	$2,712	$2,937
Income from operations	$359	$352	$172	$298	$291	$213	$318
Dividend and interest income	48	57	52	68	71	69	63
Other income and (expenses)	13	18	6	15	2	−4	−7
Pre tax income	$420	$427	$230	$381	$364	$276	$374
Income tax	162	143	69	148	115	72	132
Net income	$258	$284	$161	$233	$249	$204	$242
Preferred stock dividend	1	1	0	2	1	1	1
Add to retained earnings	$257	$283	$161	$231	$248	$203	$241

Source: Company records

who were the corporate officers, the plan paid up to 15% of employees' salary into a retirement trust fund managed by an independent financial institution. Profits had always been sufficient to pay the full 15 percent. The store terminated a smaller noncontributory defined benefit plan in 1988. All participating employees were fully vested in their earned benefits under the old plan.

Inventory levels are shown as of December 31. Orders for the coming season began arriving in December, but most would arrive from January through April. Peak inventory levels would reach $2.5 million. Many suppliers would postdate invoices for July and August, which eased the cash flow burden of financing this seasonal inventory.

The art collection was used primarily to attract customers and repeat customers. Prices for the paintings were not established. When paintings were sold the prices were negotiated. The collection was carried in the accounts as merchandise inventory and valued at cost.

A small part of the inventory consisted of gold bullion which would be sold

EXHIBIT 7   Wall Drug Store balance sheets (000's)

| | Assets Years Ended December 31 | | | | | | |
	1983	1984	1985	1986	1987	1988	1989
Assets							
Current assets							
Cash	$ 40	$ 12	$ 18	$ 29	$ 70	$ 59	$267
Current marketable securities	205	0	0	1	1	2	0
Accounts receivable	13	25	24	25	36	48	41
Merchandise inventory	405	616	718	968	1,322	1,429	1,330
Prepaid taxes and other	33	32	114	57	68	112	52
Total current assets	$ 696	$ 685	$ 874	$1,080	$1,497	$1,650	$1,690
Investments and other assets							
Noncurrent marketable securities	402	489	600	785	739	646	487
Life insurance and other	7	7	7	8	14	13	79
Total other assets	$ 409	$ 496	$ 607	$ 793	$ 753	$ 659	$ 566
Property and equipment							
Land	$ 174	$ 177	$ 187	$ 186	$ 171	$ 181	$ 181
Building and improvements	1,935	2,057	2,112	2,160	2,434	2,495	2,567
Equipment, furniture and fixture	1,065	1,232	1,278	1,372	1,492	1,628	1,795
Construction in progress	0	0	0	55	0	0	148
Total property and equipment	$3,174	$3,466	$3,577	$3,774*	$4,097	$4,304	$4,691
Less accumulated depreciation	1,475	1,609	1,732	1,869	2,032	2,182	2,385
Net property and equipment	$1,699	$1,857	$1,845	$1,905*	$2,065	$2,122	$2,306
Goodwill at cost less accumulated amortization	16	14	12	10	9	7	5
TOTAL ASSETS	$2,820	$3,052	$3,338	$3,788	$4,324	$4,438	$4,567

periodically to the store's main jewelry supplier in Rapid City. This practice provided a hedge against rising gold prices. In 1990, because of the need to finance the new stores, the stocks of bullion were low.

The $300,000 reserve for self insurance was established in 1982. The store was a self insurer for collision and comprehensive coverage of its motor vehicles, of the deductible portion of its employees' medical coverage and a portion of the casualty coverage of some buildings and their contents. A portion of the store's marketable securities funded this reserve.

EXPANSION PLANS FOR THE 1990'S

As he prepared for the 1990 tourist season, Bill Hustead, CEO of Wall Drug, was making plans for the store's most ambitious expansion. This expansion

EXHIBIT 7   Wall Drug Store balance sheets (000's) *(cont.)*

| | Liabilities and equity | | | | | | |
	1983	1984	1985	1986	1987	1988	1989
Liabilities							
Current liabilities							
Current maturities of long-term debt	$ 40	$ 10	$ 2	$ 2	$ 2	$ 2	$ 2
Notes payable	50	85	175	310	598	500	275
Accounts payable	61	40	41	54	60	44	77
Taxes payable	93	67	75	95	81	75	128
Accrued profit sharing contribution	100	113	119	135	127	146	157
Accrued pension plan payable	0	0	29	25	31	15	0
Accrued payroll and bonuses	65	50	34	48	56	56	73
Accrued interest payable	4	2	4	1	7	5	2
Total current liabilities	$ 413	$ 367	$ 479	$ 670	$ 962	$ 843	$ 714
Long-term debt	182	173	173	172	156	154	152
Deferred income taxes	10	25	27	56	68	101	121
Stockholders' equity							
Preferred stock	$ 30	$ 30	$ 30	$ 30	$ 30	$ 30	$ 30
Class A common stock	48	48	48	48	48	48	48
Class B common stock (nonvoting)	53	53	53	53	53	53	53
Capital in excess of par	52	52	52	52	52	52	52
Reserve for self insurance	300	300	300	300	300	300	300
Retained earnings	1,732	2,004	2,176	2,407	2,654	2,857	3,097
Total stockholders' equity	$2,215	$2,487	$2,659	$2,890	$3,137	$3,340	$3,580
Total liabilities and equity	$2,820	$3,052	$3,338	$3,788	$4,322	$4,438	$4,567

*These numbers may be slightly off due to rounding.

Source: Company records

would include a large open mall ringed with shops to be built to the rear of the existing backyard area. Houses along the street to the rear of the store, already owned by the Husteads, would be moved or razed to make room for this expansion.

New shops with a combined floor space of nearly 15,000 square feet would include a shop selling Indian handicraft items, a poster store, a yogurt shop, a fast food hamburger shop, and a store for motorcyclists. (Sturgis, South Dakota, in the Black Hills is the site of an annual summer motorcycle rally which attracts thousands of motorcyclists from all over North America.) A major feature of the new addition would be a free gallery displaying a recently acquired collection of over 700 old photographs of cattle drives, rodeos, Indians, cowboys, and other early settlers of South Dakota and Montana. The Husteads estimated that approximately twelve to fourteen additional employees would be required to staff this expansion during the peak season.

Bill planned to build this expansion over a period of three to five years. As with previous expansions, he planned to act as his own general contractor and direct the actual construction. When the project was finished, the existing backyard would be removed. This was constructed of metal buildings and had about 3,000 square feet of floor space.

The last project being planned was to build the Wall Drug Western Art Gallery and guest house. This would be a three story mansion, a replica of an old Southern plantation house, to display the best of the Wall Drug Store's western art collection. It would also display beautiful furnishings, elegant table settings, crystal, and other accoutrements of graceful living. The Hustead art collection included 30 paintings portraying Christmas in the West. Bill planned to have a Christmas room in the mansion to display these paintings and a permanent Christmas tree with antique ornaments. The third floor was planned as a theater which would show films or videotapes about some of the artists and a film or a videotape about the Wall Drug Store. Some rooms in the mansion were to be set aside as guest quarters.

Bill planned to charge a small admission fee to the mansion. This income would be used to purchase new paintings for the art collection. Bill explained,

> There is more to business than just profit. We are aiming at sophisticated people who will get a kick out of this. Forty percent of our business is from repeat customers so we've got to keep moving in such a way as to impress people. We've got to keep forward momentum.

Bill believed that the very survival of the business and the jobs and aspirations of his full time employees depended on the Wall Drug Store's continued development.

> We are not Wal-Mart. We are in the entertainment business. We can't just sit here with what we've got and expect people to keep coming.

Bill Hustead was aware that his two sons had serious reservations about his expansion plans. Commenting on the proposed expansion, Rick said,

> Dad is more oriented to seeing the business as a real attraction—a "must stop" attraction. I'm more concerned with the nuts and bolts. I want to be profitable. I want a better handle on our inventory and labor. My concern is always that we are profitable and don't overextend or build things that won't be profitable. What he plans to do is interesting, but I have real questions about the mansion. Are we going to realize a profit? This could cost one and a half or two million dollars. Fortunately it is the farthest down the road. We should expand the food service first.
>
> I'm conservative. I resisted the new shops (Dakota Mercantile and The Tumbleweed) at first. The building estimates were $210,000. They cost

$300,000. They are nice shops but getting personnel to run them is an issue.

The Husteads did not use a formal system of evaluating return on investment in making decisions about expansion. Rick noted, however, that these decisions were subjected to analysis. "Dad knows his expenses and his volumes. We know that we have to gross $200,000 or better in the new shops to be successful."

Bill estimated that the new stores would have a payback of approximately five years. He reported that their cost had actually been about $240,000. As to the expense of the proposed expansion plans, he said, "There is no way we are going to spend one and a half to two million dollars. The total cost of the backyard expansion and the art gallery will be between eight to nine hundred thousand and one and a half million dollars."

Teddy felt that he was somewhere in the middle on the expansion plans:

> We have got to replace the backyard and make the store more interesting, but the mansion never has made too much sense to me. I have a lot of respect for my father, but he got this idea from homes in the South. I don't know if it applies to the West. On the other hand, we are getting to have a world class collection of western art. I don't ever want to underestimate him.

Teddy also pointed out that the existing building needed extensive repairs. "The roof around the tree needs to be replaced. A few years ago the tree was trimmed back, and it died so now it has to go." Teddy estimated that these repairs would cost $200,000. He noted further that the store's administrative offices had been built in 1964 for a much smaller staff and were inadequate for current operations.

Bill commented on the objection his sons had raised to the mansion style art gallery. "People from the South settled in South Dakota and some houses of this type were built here, but it wouldn't have to be a southern style mansion. It could be another type of building."

In May, the 1990 season began on a promising note. The first two weeks of sales in the Dakota Mercantile and Tumbleweed stores were very good. "It's now or never," Bill commented, reflecting on the seasonal character of their business. Sales in the main store were also running ahead of 1989's, and bus loads of travelers bound for Deadwood were stopping to eat and shop.

S E C T I O N

B

BUSINESS-LEVEL CASES

Case 6

THE EVOLUTION OF THE AIR EXPRESS INDUSTRY, 1973–1991

INTRODUCTION

This case describes the evolution of the air express industry from 1973 to 1991. The air express industry is the segment of the air cargo industry that specializes in rapid (normally overnight) delivery of small packages. It is generally agreed that the air express industry began with Fred Smith's vision for Federal Express Company, which started operations in 1973. Federal Express essentially transformed the structure of the existing air cargo industry and paved the way for rapid growth in the overnight package segment of that industry. A further impetus to industry development was the 1977 deregulation of the air cargo industry. Deregulation allowed Federal Express (and its emerging competitors) to buy large jets for the first time. The story of the industry during the 1980s was one of rapid growth and increasing competition for Federal Express from new entrants such as United Parcel Service (UPS) and Airborne Express. The result was severe price cutting, which drove some of the weakest competitors out of the market and touched off a wave of consolidation. As the industry enters the 1990s, industry structure within the United States seems to be stabilizing and price competition is abating somewhat. However, the industry now faces significant new challenges in the global marketplace.

THE INDUSTRY IN 1973

In 1973 roughly 1.5 billion tons of freight were shipped annually in the United States. Most of this tonnage was carried by surface transport, with air freight

This case was prepared by Charles W. L. Hill, University of Washington.

513

accounting for less than 2 percent of the total.[1] Although shipment by air freight was often quicker than shipment by surface freight, the high cost of air freight had kept down demand. The typical users of air freight at this time were suppliers of time-sensitive, high-priced goods, such as computer parts and medical instruments, which were needed at dispersed locations but were too expensive for customers to hold as inventory.

The main cargo carriers in 1973 were major passenger airlines, which operated a number of all-cargo planes and carried additional cargo in the bellies of their passenger planes, along with a handful of all-cargo airlines such as Flying Tiger. From 1973 onward the passenger airlines moved steadily away from all-cargo planes and began to concentrate cargo freight in the bellies of passenger planes. This change was a response to increases in fuel costs, which made the operation of many old cargo jets uneconomical.

With regard to distribution of cargo to and from airports, in 1973 about 20 percent of all air freight was delivered to airports by the shipper and picked up by the consignee. The bulk of the remaining 80 percent was accounted for by three major intermediaries: (1) Air Cargo Incorporated, (2) freight forwarders, and (3) the U.S. Postal Service. Air Cargo Incorporated was a trucking service, wholly owned by twenty-six airlines, which performed pickup and delivery service for the airlines' direct customers. Freight forwarders were trucking carriers who consolidated cargo going to the airlines. They purchased cargo space from the airlines and retailed it in small amounts. They dealt primarily with small customers, providing pickup and delivery services in most cities, either in their own trucks or through contract agents. The U.S. Postal Service used air service for transportation of long-distance letter mail and air parcel post.[2]

THE FEDERAL EXPRESS CONCEPT

Federal Express, founded by Fred Smith Jr., was incorporated in 1971 and began operations in 1973. At that time a significant proportion of small-package air freight flew on commercial passenger flights. Smith believed that there were major differences between packages and passengers, and he believed that the two had to be treated differently. Most passengers moved between major cities and wanted the convenience of daytime flights. Cargo shippers preferred nighttime service to coincide with late-afternoon pickups and next-day delivery. Because small-package air freight was subservient to the requirements of passengers' flight schedules, it was often difficult for the major airlines to achieve next-day delivery of air freight.

Smith's aim was to build a system that could achieve next-day delivery of

---

[1]Christopher H. Lovelock, "Federal Express (B)," *Harvard Business School Case #579-040,* 1978.
[2]Standard & Poor's Industry Surveys, *Aerospace & Air Transport,* January 1981.

small-package (under 70 pounds) air freight. He set up Federal Express with his $8-million family inheritance and $90 million in venture capital. Federal Express established what was at that time a unique "hub and spoke" route system. The hub of the system was Memphis, chosen for its good weather, central location, and the fact that it was Smith's hometown. The spokes were regular routes between Memphis and shipping facilities at public airports in the cities serviced by Federal Express. Every weeknight, aircraft would leave their home cities with a load of packages and fly down the "spokes" to Memphis (often with one or two stops on the way). At Memphis all packages were unloaded, sorted by destination, and reloaded. The aircraft then returned to their home cities in the early hours of the morning. Packages were ferried to and from airports by Federal Express couriers driving company vans and working to a tight schedule. Thus, from door-to-door the package was in Federal Express's hands. This system guaranteed that a package picked up from a customer in New York at 5 P.M. would reach its final destination in Los Angeles (or any other major city) by noon the following day. It enabled Federal Express to realize economies in sorting and to utilize its air cargo capacity efficiently. Federal Express also pioneered the use of standard packaging with an upper weight limit of 70 pounds and a maximum length plus girth of 108 inches. This limitation helped Federal Express to gain further efficiencies from mechanized sorting at its Memphis hub. Later entrants into the industry copied Federal Express's package standards and "hub and spoke" operating system.

To accomplish overnight delivery, Federal Express had to operate its own planes. However, restrictive regulations enforced by the Civil Aeronautics Board (CAB) prohibited the company from buying large jet aircraft. To get around this restriction, Federal Express bought a fleet of twin-engine executive jets, which it converted to mini-freighters. These planes had a cargo capacity of 6,200 pounds, which enabled Federal Express to get a license as an "air taxi" operator.

After 1973 Federal Express quickly built up volume. By 1976 it had an average daily volume of 19,000 packages, a fleet of 32 aircraft, 500 delivery vans, and 2,000 employees, and it had initiated service in 75 cities. Moreover, after three loss-making years, the company turned in a profit of $3.7 million on revenues of $75 million.[3] However, volume had grown to the point where Federal Express desperately needed to use larger planes to maintain operating efficiencies. As a result, Smith's voice was added to those calling for Congress to deregulate the airline industry and allow greater competition.

DEREGULATION AND ITS AFTERMATH

In November 1977, one year before passenger services were deregulated, Congress loosened regulations controlling competition in the air cargo industry. The

---

[3]Lovelock, "Federal Express (B)."

result was a drastic loosening of standards of entry into the industry. The old CAB authority to name the carriers that could operate on the various routes was changed to the relatively simple authority to decide who among candidate carriers was fit, willing, and able to operate an all-cargo route. In addition, CAB controls over pricing were significantly reduced. The immediate effect was an increase in rates for certain types of shipments, particularly minimum- and high-weight categories, suggesting that prices had been held artificially low by regulation. As a result, the average yield (revenue per ton-mile) on domestic air freight increased 10.6 percent in 1978 and 11.3 percent in 1979.[4]

Freed by deregulation, Federal Express immediately began to purchase larger jets and quickly established itself as a major carrier of small-package air freight. However, despite the increase in yields, at first new entry into the air cargo industry was limited, mainly because of the high capital requirements involved in establishing an all-cargo carrier. Indeed, by the end of 1978 there were only four *major* all-cargo carriers serving the domestic market: Airlift International, Federal Express, Flying Tiger, and Seaboard World Airlines. All of these had increased their route structure following deregulation, but only Federal Express specialized in next-day delivery for small packages. Yet demand for a next-day delivery continued to boom. Industry estimates suggest that the small-package priority market had grown to about 82 million pieces in 1979, up from 43 million in 1974.[5]

At the same time, in response to increasing competition from the all-cargo carriers, the passenger airlines continued their retreat from the all-cargo business (originally begun in 1973 as a response to high fuel prices). Between 1973 and 1978 there was a 45 percent decline in the mileage of all-cargo flights by the airlines. This was followed by a 14 percent decline between 1978 and 1979. Instead of all-cargo flights, the airlines concentrated their attention on carrying cargo in the bellies of passenger flights. This practice hurt the freight forwarders badly. The freight forwarders had long relied on the all-cargo flights of major airlines to achieve next-day delivery. Now the freight forwarders were being squeezed out of this segment by a lack of available lift at the time needed to ensure next-day delivery.

This problem led to one of the major postderegulation developments in the industry: the acquisition and operation by freight forwarders of their own fleets of aircraft. Between 1979 and 1981 five of the six largest freight forwarders became involved in this activity. The two largest of these were Emery Air Freight and Airborne Express. Emery operated a fleet of 66 aircraft at the end of 1979, the majority of which were leased from other carriers. In mid 1980 this fleet was providing service to approximately 129 cities, carrying both large-volume shipments and small-package express.

Airborne Express acquired its own fleet of aircraft in April 1980 with the

[4]Standard & Poor's Industry Surveys, *Aerospace and Air Transport,* January 1981.
[5]Ibid.

purchase of Midwest Charter Express, an Ohio-based all-cargo airline. Then, in 1981, Airborne opened a new hub in Wilmington, Ohio, which became the center of its small-package express operation. This enabled Airborne to provide next-day delivery for small packages to 125 cities in the United States.[6] Other freight forwarders that moved into the overnight-mail market included Purolator Courier and Gelco Courier, both of which offered overnight delivery by air on a limited geographical scale.

INDUSTRY EVOLUTION, 1980–1986

New Products and Industry Growth

In 1981 Federal Express expanded its role in the overnight market with the introduction of an Overnight Letter service, with a limit of 2 ounces. This guaranteed overnight delivery service was set up in direct competition with the U.S. Postal Service's Priority Mail. The demand for such a service was illustrated by its expansion to about 17,000 letters per day within its first three months of operation.

More generally, the air express industry was changing from being predominantly a conduit for goods to being a distributor of information—particularly company documents, letters, contracts, drawings, and the like. As a result of the growth in demand for information distribution, new product offerings such as the Overnight Letter, and Federal Express's own marketing efforts, the air express industry enjoyed high growth during the early 1980s, averaging 20 percent per year.[7] Indeed, many observers attribute most of the growth in the overnight delivery business at this time to Federal Express's marketing efforts. According to one industry participant, "Federal Express pulled off one of the greatest marketing scams in the industry by making people believe they absolutely, positively, had to have something right away."[8]

Increasing Price Competition

Despite rapid growth in demand, competitive intensity in the industry increased sharply in 1982 following the entry of UPS into the overnight-delivery market. UPS was already by far the largest private package transporter in the United States. UPS had an enormous ground-oriented distribution network and reve-

[6]Ibid.
[7]Standard & Poor's Industry Surveys, *Aerospace and Air Transport*, January 1984.
[8]Carol Hall, "High Fliers," *Marketing and Media Decisions*, (August 1986), 138.

nues in excess of $4 billion per year. In addition, UPS had for a long time offered second-day air service for priority packages, primarily by using the planes of all-cargo and passenger airlines. In 1982 UPS acquired a fleet of twenty-four used Boeing 727-100s and added four DC-8 freighters from Flying Tiger, enabling it to introduce next-day air service in September of that year—at roughly half the price Federal Express was charging at the time![9]

Federal Express countered almost immediately by announcing that it would institute 10:30 A.M. delivery (at a cost to the company of $18 million). However, none of the other carriers followed suit, reasoning that most of their customers are usually busy or in meetings in the morning hours, so delivery before noon is not really that important. Instead, by March 1983 most of the major carriers in the market (including Federal Express) were offering their high-volume customers contract rates that matched the UPS price structure. Then three new services introduced by Purolator, Emery, and Gelco Courier pushed prices even lower.

What followed was something of a competitive free-for-all: Constant price changes and volume discounts were offered by all industry participants. Not surprisingly, these developments began to hit the profit margins of the express carriers. Between 1983 and 1984 Federal Express saw its average revenue per package fall nearly 14 percent, and Emery saw a 15 percent decline in its yield on small shipments.[10]

Another factor driving price down at this time was the growing tendency for customers to group together and negotiate for lower prices. For example, Xerox set up accounts with Purolator and Emery that covered not only Xerox's express packages but also those of fifty other companies including Mayflower Corp., the moving company, and the Chicago Board of Trade. By negotiating as a group, these companies were able to achieve prices as much as 60 percent lower than those they could get on their own.[11]

The main beneficiary of the price war was UPS, which by 1985 had gained the number-two spot in the industry with 15 percent of the market. Federal Express, meanwhile, had seen its market share slip back to 37 percent from around 45 percent two years earlier. The other four major players in the industry at this time were Emery Air Freight (14 percent market share), Purolator (10 percent), Airborne Express (8 percent), and the U.S. Postal Service (8 percent).[12] The survival of all four of these carriers in the air express business was in question by 1986. Emery, Purolator, and the U.S. Postal Service were all reporting losses on their air express business, and Airborne had seen its profits slump 66 percent in the first quarter of 1986 and now had razor-thin margins.

[9]Standard & Poor's Industry Surveys, *Aerospace and Air Transport,* January 1984.
[10]Standard & Poor's Industry Surveys, *Aerospace and Air Transport,* December 1984.
[11]Brian Dumaine, "Turbulence Hits the Air Couriers," *Fortune,* July 21, 1986, pp. 101–106.
[12]Ibid.

$SWO\ \textcircled{T}$

The Specter of Fax

To make matters worse, by the mid 1980s there were increasing concerns that electronic mail would take much of the information distribution business away from the air express operators. In particular, as the speed and quality of facsimile machines improved and the price of the equipment fell, fax emerged as a very real threat to the volume of document traffic handled by the air express carriers.

Federal Express responded to this perceived threat by its 1984 entry into the electronic mail business with its ZAPMAIL product. The company established fax equipment in Federal Express retail outlets, as well as in some Federal trucks. Federal's existing courier service picked up documents and then transmitted them by fax to a Federal Express receiver. The document was then delivered to its destination by the courier service. The aim was to provide door-to-door service within two hours. Unfortunately for Federal Express, fax technology developed so rapidly that it became cost effective for corporate clients to buy their own equipment rather than use Federal's. In 1986, after two years of large losses, Federal Express admitted its mistake and abandoned ZAPMAIL.

The growth of facsimile continued to be a threat, however, and undoubtedly squeezed the growth rate in document traffic. Federal Express's experience is illuminating. During 1986 its year-to-year gains in monthly overnight document traffic were in the 50–60 percent range. By late 1988 the gains were down in the 9–10 percent range.[13] However, a 1988 study by Airborne Express of the impact of fax machines puts this threat in some perspective. Eighty-one percent of executives contacted for a study by Airborne said that their use of fax had increased over the past year. However, those same executives said that fax was having a limited impact on air express: Approximately 77 percent said use of air express had either remained constant or increased during the same period.[14]

INDUSTRY EVOLUTION, 1987–1990

Industry Consolidation

A slowdown in the growth rate of the air express business due to increasing geographical saturation, along with the inroads made by electronic transmission, stimulated further price discounting in 1987 and early 1988. Predictably, this cre- ✔ ated problems for the weakest companies in the industry. The first to go was Purolator Courier, which had lost $65 million during 1985 and 1986. Purolator's problems stemmed from a failure to install an adequate computer system. The

---

[13]Standard & Poor's Industry Surveys, *Aerospace and Air Transport,* May 1989.
[14]"Are Faxes Putting the Whammy on Air Express? This Study Says No," *Distribution,* (January 1989), 22.

company was unable to track shipments, a crucial ability in this industry, and its best corporate customers were billed 120 days late.[15] In 1987 Purolator agreed to be acquired by Emery. The latter, however, was unable to effect a satisfactory integration of Purolator and sustained large losses in 1988 and early 1989.

In April 1989, Consolidated Freightways, a major trucking company and parent of CF AirFreight, the third largest heavy shipment specialist in the United States, acquired Emery for $478 million. However, CF AirFreight soon found itself struggling to cope with Emery's problems. In its first eleven months with CF, Emery lost $100 million. One of the main problems was Emery's billing and tracking system, described as a "rats nest" of conflicting tariff schedules, which caused customer overbillings and made tracking packages en route a major chore. In addition, CF enraged corporate customers by trying to add a "fuel surcharge" ranging from 4 to 7 percent to prices in early 1989. Competitors held the line on prices and picked up business from CF/Emery.[16]

As a result of the decline of the CF/Emery/Purolator combination, the other firms in the industry were able to pick up market share. As of mid 1990, estimates suggest that Federal Express had about 50 percent of the air express market, UPS had 20 to 22 percent, and Airborne Express had 14 to 15 percent.[17]

The other major acquisition in the industry during this time was the purchase of Flying Tiger by Federal Express for $880 million in December 1988. Although Flying Tiger had some air express operations in the United States, its primary strength was as a heavy-cargo carrier with a global route structure. The acquisition was a step toward Federal Express's goal of becoming a major player in the international air express market (more about this later). However, the acquisition was not without its problems. For one thing, many of Flying Tiger's biggest customers, including UPS and Airborne Express, are Federal's competitors in the domestic market. These companies have long paid Tiger to carry packages to countries where they have no landing rights. It seems unlikely that these companies will continue to push international business toward their biggest domestic competitor. Further problems have arisen in the process of trying to integrate the two operations. These include the scheduling of aircraft and pilots, the servicing of Tiger's fleet, and the merging of Federal's non-union pilots with Tiger's union pilots.[18]

During this period there were also hints of further consolidations. TNT Ltd., a large Australia-based air cargo operation with a global network, made an unsuccessful attempt to acquire Airborne Express in 1986. TNT's bid was frustrated by opposition from Airborne and by the difficulties inherent in getting

[15]Chuck Hawkins, "Purolator: Still No Overnight Success," *Business Week,* June 16, 1986, pp. 76–78.

[16]Joan O'C. Hamilton, "Emery Is One Heavy Load for Consolidated Freightways," *Business Week,* March 26, 1990, pp. 62–64.

[17]Interview with Roy Liljebeck, Executive Vice President and Chief Financial Officer, Airborne Express.

[18]"Hold That Tiger: FedEx Is Now A World Heavyweight," *Purchasing,* September 14, 1989, pp. 41–42.

around U.S. law, which currently limits foreign firms from having more than a 25 percent stake in U.S. airlines. Nevertheless, the law may change and TNT still holds a minority stake in Airborne. In addition, DHL Airways, the U.S. subsidiary of DHL International, a large Brussels-based air courier with global reach, has been reportedly attempting to enlarge its presence in the United States and may be on the lookout for an acquisition.[19]

Pricing Trends

In October 1988, UPS offered new discounts to high-volume customers in domestic markets. For the first time since 1983, competitors declined to match the cuts. Then in January 1989 UPS announced a price increase of 5 percent for next-day air service—its first price increase in nearly six years. Federal Express, Airborne, and Consolidate Freightways all followed suit with moderate increases. Further rate increases of 5.9 percent on next-day air letters were announced by UPS in February 1990. Federal Express was expected to follow suit in April. Airborne also implemented selective price hikes on noncontract business of 5 percent, or 50 cents a package on packages up to 20 pounds.[20]

Product Trends

Having seen a slowdown in the growth rate of the next-day document delivery business due to fax machines and market saturation, the major operators in the air express business have begun to look for new product opportunities to sustain their growth and margins. The major U.S. players are rapidly introducing services designed to assist business customers in their warehousing, distribution, and assembly operations. The emphasis of this business is on helping customers reduce the time involved in their production cycles and gain distribution efficiencies.

To capture some of this business, Federal Express has set up the Business Logistics Services (BLS) division. The new division evolved from Federal Express's Parts Bank. The Parts Bank stores critical inventory for clients, most of whom are based in the high-tech electronics and medical industries. On request, Federal Express will ship this inventory to a client's customers. The service saves clients from having to invest in their own distribution systems. It also allows them to achieve scale economies by making large production runs and then storing the inventory at the Parts Bank.

The BLS division has expanded this service to include some assembly operations, customs brokerage, and assistance in achieving just-in-time manufacturing. Thus, for example, one U.S. computer company relies on BLS to deliver

[19]Standard & Poor's Industry Surveys, *Aerospace and Air Transport*, April 1988.
[20]Robin Goldwyn Blumenthal, "UPS Move to Lift Rates Could Spur Increases by Rivals," *The Wall Street Journal*, February 13, 1990, pp. B1, B4.

electronic subassemblies from the Far East as a key part of its just-in-time system. Federal Express brings the products in on its aircraft, clears them through customs with the help of a broker, and manages truck transportation to the customer's dock.[21]

Airborne Express has also made a significant push into this end of the business. A number of Airborne's corporate accounts utilize a warehousing service called Stock Exchange. As with Federal Express's Parts Bank, clients warehouse critical inventory at Airborne's hub in Wilmington, Ohio, and Airborne ships those items on request to clients' customers. In addition, Airborne has begun operating a "commerce park" on 1,000 acres around its Wilmington hub. The park is aimed at companies that want to contract out logistics to Airborne and can gain special advantages by locating at the company's hub. Not the least of these advantages is the ability to make shipping decisions as late as 2 A.M. Eastern time.

Globalization

Perhaps the most important development for the long run was the increasing globalization of the air freight industry during the late 1980s. A healthy U.S. economy, a strong and expanding Pacific Rim, and the move toward economic integration in 1992 among the twelve Economic Community countries of Western Europe—all offer strong opportunities for growth in the international air cargo business. Moreover, the increasing globalization of companies in a range of industries from electronics to autos, and from fast food to clothing, is beginning to dictate that the air express operators follow suit.

Global manufacturers want to keep inventories at a minimum and deliver just-in-time as a way of keeping down costs and fine-tuning production. Thus some electronics companies manufacture key components in one location, ship them by air to another for final assembly, and then deliver them by air to a third location for sale. This is particularly true among industries producing small high-value items (such as electronics, medical equipment, and computer software), which can be economically transported by air, and where just-in-time inventory systems are crucial for keeping down costs. It is also true in the fashion industry, where timing is all-important. For example, the clothing chain The Limited manufactures clothes in Hong Kong and then ships them by air to the United States to keep from missing out on fashion trends.[22] In addition, more and more wholesalers are beginning to turn to international air express as a way of meeting delivery deadlines. In the autumn of 1988, for example, one wholesaler used in-

[21]Peter Bradley, "Good Things Come in Small Packages," *Purchasing,* November 9, 1989, pp. 58–64.
[22]Joan M. Feldman, "The Coming of Age of International Air Freight," *Air Transport World,* (June 1989), 31–33.

ternational express air service to meet the video distribution deadline for the movie *ET*.[23]

The emergence of integrated global corporations is also increasing the demand for global shipment of contracts, confidential papers, computer printouts, and other documents that are far too bulky for fax machines to handle. Major U.S. corporations are increasingly demanding for their far-flung global operations the same kind of service that they receive from air express operators within the United States.

As a consequence of these trends, rapid growth is predicted in the global arena. Worth around $6.5 billion in annual sales in 1989, the market for international air express is expected to increase between 20 percent and 30 percent every year through the 1990s.[24] In response, the race is on among the major air cargo operators to build global air and ground transportation networks that will enable them to deliver goods and documents between any two points on the globe within forty-eight hours.

Currently the company with the most extensive international operations is DHL. Started in 1969 and based in Brussels, DHL is smaller than many of its rivals but has managed to capture as much as an 80 percent share in some markets, such as documents leaving Japan, by concentrating solely on international air express. The potential strength of DHL was enhanced in June 1990 when Lufthansa, Japan Air Lines, and the Japanese trading company Nisho Iwai announced that they intended to invest as much as $500 million for a 57.5 percent stake in DHL. Although Lufthansa and Japan Air Lines are primarily known for their passenger flights, they also are among the top five air freight haulers in the world, both because they carry cargo in the holds of their passenger flights and because each has a fleet of all-cargo aircraft.[25]

TNT Ltd., a $4.4-billion Australian conglomerate, is another big player in the international air express market. TNT has courier services from 184 countries as well as package express and mail services. It owns 15 percent of Airborne Express and may acquire more (although U.S. law on the foreign ownership of airlines currently limits its potential stake to 25 percent). TNT has a rapidly growing fleet of aircraft, and in 1989 it announced that it would buy XP, a Dutch surface carrier, as the foundation for expanding its express service in Western Europe in anticipation of the 1992 economic integration of the Economic Community.

Among U.S. carriers, Federal Express was first off the blocks in the race to build up a global air express network. Between 1984 and 1989 Federal Express purchased seventeen other companies worldwide in an attempt to build up its global distribution capabilities, cumulating in the $880-million purchase of Flying

---

[23]Ibid.

[24]Clemens P. Work, "The Flying Package Trade Takes Off," *U.S. News & World Report,* October 2, 1989, pp. 47–50.

[25]Byron Acohido, "Expansion Express," *The Seattle Times,* June 30, 1990, pp. E1, E6.

Tiger. The main asset of Flying Tiger was not so much its aircraft as its landing rights overseas. The Flying Tiger acquisition gave Federal Express service to 103 countries, a combined fleet of 328 aircraft, and revenues of $5.2 billion in fiscal 1989.[26]

However, Federal Express has yet to show a profit on its international operations. Start-up costs have been heavy, in part because of the enormous capital investments required to build an integrated air and ground network worldwide. In addition, faced with heavy competition, Federal Express has yet to generate the international volume required to fly its planes at above breakeven capacity on many international routes. Trade barriers have also proved very damaging to the bottom line. Customs regulations require a great deal of expensive and time-consuming labor, such as checking paperwork and rating package contents for duties. This obviously inhibits the ability of international air cargo carriers to effect express delivery. Federal Express has been particularly irritated by Japanese requirements that each inbound envelope be opened and searched for pornography, a practice that seems to be designed to slow the company's growth in the Japanese market.

UPS has also moved quickly to build up an international presence. Privately held UPS is already the largest package delivery company in the world, having 230,000 employees worldwide and 1988 revenues in excess of $11 billion. But about 85 percent of its business comes from the slow-growing ground network, and most is concentrated in North America. Since entering the air express business in 1982, UPS has built up a fleet of 115 large jets and leases an additional 240 smaller aircraft. In 1988 UPS bought eight smaller European air freight companies and Hong Kong's Asian Courier Service and announced air service and ground delivery in 175 countries and territories.

However, all has not been smooth sailing for UPS either. UPS had been using Flying Tiger for its Pacific shipments. The acquisition of Flying Tiger by Federal Express leaves UPS in the difficult situation of shipping its parcels on a competitor's plane. UPS is concerned that its shipments could get pushed to the back of the aircraft. Since there are few alternative carriers, UPS is pushing for authority to run an all-cargo route to Tokyo, but approval could take some time. Moreover, "beyond rights" to carry cargo from Tokyo to more distant destinations (such as Singapore and Hong Kong) must also be negotiated in laborious discussions. Of course, Federal Express finessed that problem by buying Flying Tiger, which already had a route structure in place and international landing rights. Because of these problems, along with other start-up costs, UPS does not anticipate breakeven on its international routes until 1993 at the earliest. On the other hand, UPS has deep pockets, and with $7 billion in debt-free assets the company can afford to invest for the long haul.

The other U.S. carrier that is making a determined push overseas is Airborne Express. However, Airborne's strategy differs from that of Federal Express and UPS in that it is not investing in its own international air fleet and ground operations. Airborne's strategy has two aspects. First, it will continue to fly its own planes in the United States while booking space on other air carriers for shipments going overseas. Second, it has been looking for strategic alliances with foreign companies that would give it market access and ground operations overseas. In 1989 the company announced an alliance with Mitsui & Co., a $125-billion-a-year Japanese trading and finance firm, and Tonami Transportation Co., operators of a ground-based express delivery service in Japan called Panther Express. The deal calls for Mitsui to purchase $40-million worth of Airborne stock and to provide $100 million in aircraft financing over the next five years and for the partners to collaborate in building volume in the lucrative Japan-U.S. air express market. Non-Japanese firms currently only handle 15 percent of the air shipments going in and out of Japan. But now that Mitsui owns part of Airborne, the Seattle-based company is counting on getting the inside track on the other 85 percent of the market.[27]

[27]Acohido, "Expansion Express," pp. E1, E6.

AIRBORNE EXPRESS

INTRODUCTION

Airborne Express is an air express transportation company, providing next-morning delivery of small packages (under 70 pounds) and documents throughout the United States. The company owns and operates an airline and a fleet of ground transportation vehicles to provide a complete door-to-door service. It is also an air freight forwarder, moving shipments of any size on a worldwide basis. As of 1990, Airborne Express held third place in the U.S. air express industry with 14 or 15 percent of the overnight market. Its main domestic competitors are Federal Express, which has about 50 percent of the market; United Parcel Service (UPS), which has from 20 to 22 percent of the market; and Consolidate Freightways (CF), which holds less than 10 percent of the market. Airborne Express survived a prolonged period of severe price competition that followed the 1982 entry of UPS into the industry. The company now appears poised to take advantage of consolidation in the industry and moderating price competition. Operating margins increased to 5.2 percent in 1989, up from 2.9 percent in 1988.

The evolution of the air express industry and the current structure of competition in the industry are discussed in Case 6, "The Evolution of the Air Express Industry, 1973–1991." The current case focuses on the operating structure, competitive strategy, organizational structure, and culture of Airborne Express.

HISTORY OF AIRBORNE EXPRESS

Airborne Express was originally known as Pacific Air Freight when it was founded in Seattle at the close of World War II by Holt W. Webster, a former Army Air Corps officer. The company was merged with Airborne Freight Corporation of California in 1967, taking the name of the California company but retaining management direction by the former officers of Pacific Air Freight.

This case was prepared by Charles W. L. Hill, University of Washington, with the assistance of Daniel Bodnar, Laurie Martinelli, Brian McMullen, Lisa Mutty, and Stephen Schmidt. The case was made possible by the generous assistance of Airborne Express. The information was provided by Airborne Express. The case is intended as a basis for classroom discussion, rather than to illustrate either effective or ineffective handling of an administrative situation.

Airborne was initially an exclusive air freight forwarder. Freight forwarders like Airborne arranged for the transportation of air cargo between any two destinations. They purchased cargo space from the airlines and retailed the space in small amounts. They dealt primarily with small customers, providing pickup and delivery services in most cities, either in their own trucks or through contract agents.

After the 1977 deregulation of the airline industry, Airborne entered the air express industry by leasing the airplanes and pilots of Midwest Charter Express, a small airline operating out of its own airport in Wilmington, Ohio. However, Airborne quickly became dissatisfied because the limited control it was able to exercise over Midwest made the tight coordination and control of logistics that were necessary to become a successful air express operator very difficult to achieve. Instead of continuing to lease Midwest's planes and facility, in 1980 Airborne decided to buy "the entire bucket of slop; company, planes, pilots, airport and all."

Among other things, the Midwest acquisition put Airborne in the position of being the only industry participant to own an airport. Airborne immediately began the job of developing a "hub and spoke" route system capable of supporting a nationwide distribution. An efficient sorting facility was established at the Wilmington hub. Airborne upgraded Midwest's fleet of prop and prop-jet aircraft, building a modern fleet of DC-8s, DC-9s, and YS-11s. These planes left major cities every evening, flying down the spokes carrying letters and packages to the central sort facility in Wilmington. There the letters and packages were unloaded, sorted according to their final destination, and then reloaded and flown to their final destination for delivery before noon next day.

During the late 1970s and early 1980s dramatic growth in the industry attracted many competitors (see Exhibit 1 for data on Airborne's domestic shipment growth). As a consequence, despite a high growth rate, price competition became intense, forcing a number of companies to the sidelines by the late 1980s (see Case 6). Airborne was able to survive this period by pursuing a number of strategies that increased productivity and drove costs down to the lowest levels in the industry (see Exhibit 2 and Exhibit 3 for data on productivity growth and revenues). As a consequence, by the late 1980s Airborne had pulled away from a pack of struggling competitors to become one of the top three companies in the industry.

AIR EXPRESS OPERATIONS

The Domestic Delivery Network

Airborne Express has divided the country into 13 regions. Each region has between 9 and 18 stations, which are essentially the ends of the spokes in Airborne's "hub and spoke" system (the hub being Wilmington, Ohio; see Exhibit 4). In

EXHIBIT 1   Domestic shipment growth, 1984–1989

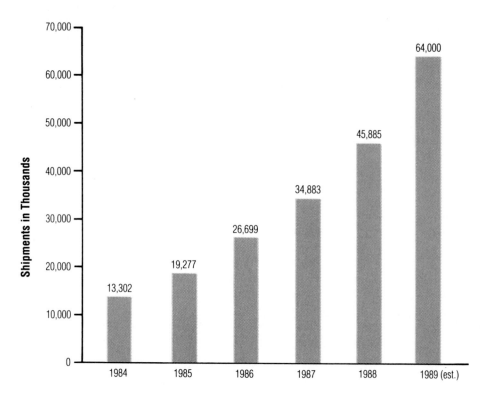

EXHIBIT 2   Productivity growth, 1984–1989

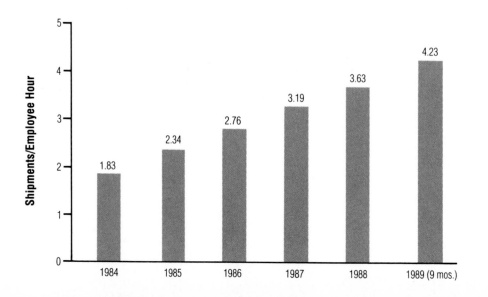

EXHIBIT 3   Unit revenues and costs, 1984–1989

	Revenue per shipment	Operating cost per shipment
1984	$30.17	$28.52
1985	23.25	22.36
1986	19.51	18.49
1987	17.49	16.95
1988	16.20	15.73
1989 (9 mos.)	14.42	13.72

EXHIBIT 4   The "hub and spoke" system

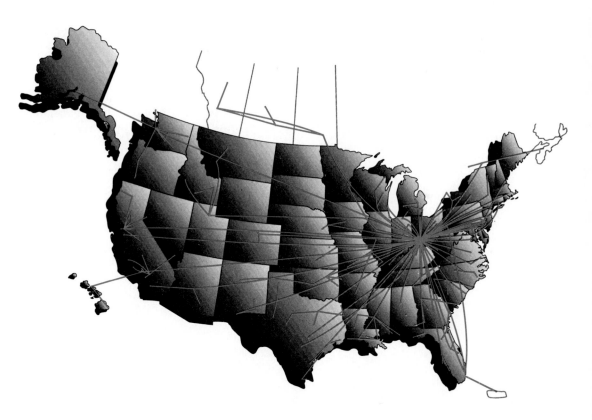

each station there are from 50 to 55 or so drivers plus staff. About 80 percent of Airborne's 12,000-plus employees are found at this level (see Exhibit 5 for data on operating characteristics). The stations are the basic units in Airborne's delivery organization. Their primary task is to ferry packages between clients and the local air terminal.

Airborne's drivers make their last round of major clients at 5 P.M. The drivers collect packages either directly from clients or from one of the company's 4,900-plus drop boxes, strategically located in the lobbies of major commercial buildings. To give clients a little more time, in most major cities a few central drop boxes are not emptied until 6 P.M. If a client who needs still more time gets a package to the airport by 7 P.M., the package will make the evening flight.

When a driver picks up a package, she or he uses a hand–held scanner to read a bar code on the package. This information is fed directly into Airborne's FO-CUS (Freight, On-line Control and Update System) computer system, which has global coverage. The FOCUS system records shipment status at key points in the life cycle of a shipment. Thus a customer can call Airborne on a 24–hour basis and find out where in Airborne's system a package is.

When a driver has completed the pickup route, she or he takes the load to Airborne's loading docks at the local airport. There the packages are loaded into "C-containers" (the specifications of a C-container are given below). Several C-containers are then towed by hand or by tractor to a waiting aircraft. They are loaded onto a conveyor belt, and one by one they pass through the passenger door of the plane. Before long the plane is loaded and takes off. It either flies directly to the company's hub at Wilmington or makes one or two stops along

EXHIBIT 5   **Operating characteristics as of December 31, 1989**

Company aircraft in service	
DC-8s	14
DC-9s	23
YS-11s	12
Chartered aircraft	58
Regional hubs	5
Employees	
U.S. full time	5,111
U.S. part time	3,863
Overseas	374
Total	9,348
Offices	
United States	162
Overseas	20
Total	182
Delivery vehicles	4,537
Drop boxes	3,850

the way to pick up more packages. Sometime between midnight and 2 A.M. most of the aircraft land at Wilmington. An old Strategic Air Command base, Wilmington's location places it within a 600-mile radius (overnight drive or one-hour flying time) of 60 percent of the U.S. population. Wilmington also has the advantage of good weather. In the ten years that Airborne has operated at Wilmington, air operations have been "fogged out" on only four days.

After arrival at Wilmington the plane taxis down the runway and parks alongside planes that are already disgorging their load of C-containers. Within minutes the C-containers are removed from the plane by conveyor belt and towed to the sort facility by a tractor. The sort facility contains 284,000 square feet, has a 10-mile-long conveyor belt, and is capable of handling 763,000 packages per night. Here the bar codes on the packages are read again; then the packages are directed through a labyrinth of conveyor belts and are sorted according to final destination. Part of the sorting is done by hand; part is automated. At the end of this process, packages are grouped by final destination and loaded into a C-container. An aircraft bound for the final destination is then loaded with C-containers, and by 5 A.M. most aircraft have taken off.

On arrival at the final destination, the plane is unloaded and the packages are sorted according to their delivery points in the surrounding area. Airborne couriers then take the packages on the final leg of their journey. Packages have a 75 percent probability of being delivered to clients by 10:30 A.M. and a 98 percent probability of being delivered by noon.

Regional Hubs

Although the majority of packages are transported by air and pass through Wilmington, Airborne has also established five regional hubs. The first was opened in Allentown, Pennsylvania, which is centrally located in the Northeast. This hub handles packages that are being transported to points between Washington, D.C., and Boston. Instead of being shipped by air, packages to be transported within this area are sorted by the drivers at pickup and delivered from the driver's home station by scheduled truck runs to the Allentown hub. There they are sorted according to destination and taken to the appropriate station on another scheduled truck run for final delivery.

In addition to the Allentown hub, Airborne has established regional hubs at Atlanta; Orlando; South Bend, Indiana; Columbia, Missouri; and Richmond, Virginia. One advantage of ground-based transportation through regional hubs is operating costs that are much lower than corresponding costs for air transportation. However, because customers assume that all packages are flown, Airborne can charge the same price for ground-transported packages as for air-transported packages and makes a much higher return on the former. The trucking hubs also ease the load at the Wilmington hub, which is currently operating at about 90 percent capacity.

International Operations

In addition to its domestic express operations, Airborne is also an international company providing service to over 180 countries worldwide. International operations currently account for about 25 percent of total revenues. This share is expected to increase with the forecasted growth in the international air express industry (see Case 6).

Airborne offers two international products: freight products and express products. Freight products are commercial size, large-unit shipments. This is a door-to-airport service. Goods are picked up domestically from the customer and then shipped to the destination airport. A consignee or an agent of the consignee gets the paperwork and must clear the shipment through customs. Express products are small packages, documents, and letters. This is a door-to-door service, and all shipments are cleared through customs by Airborne.

Airborne does not fly any of its own aircraft overseas. It contracts for space on all-cargo airlines such as FDX/Tigers (purchased by Federal Express in 1989) or in the cargo holds of passenger airlines. Airborne owns facilities overseas in Japan, Taiwan, Hong Kong, Singapore, Australia, New Zealand, and London. These facilities function in a manner similar to Airborne's domestic stations—that is, they have their own trucks and drivers and are hooked into the FOCUS tracking system. The majority of foreign distribution, however, is carried out by foreign service partners. Foreign service partners are large, local, well-established surface delivery companies. Recently Airborne entered into a number of exclusive strategic alliances with large foreign agents, including Purolator (Canada) and Mitsui (Japan). The rationale for entering strategic alliances, along with Airborne's approach to global expansion, is discussed in greater detail later in this case.

Another aspect of Airborne's international operations is the creation at its Wilmington hub of the only privately certified Foreign Trade Zone (FTZ) in the United States. While in an FTZ, merchandise is tax free; no customs duty is paid on it until it leaves the zone. Thus a foreign-based company may store critical inventory in the FTZ and have Airborne deliver the merchandise just-in-time to U.S. customers. The foreign company is therefore able to hold inventory in the United States without paying customs duty on it until it is actually needed.

Aircraft Purchase and Maintenance

As of early 1990 Airborne Express owned fourteen DC-8s, twenty-three DC-9s, and twelve YS-11s (see Exhibit 5). In addition, the company charters fifty-eight aircraft on a regular basis, and there are plans to add six DC-9s to the fleet in 1990. To keep down capital expenditures, Airborne buys used planes, converting them to its specifications at a maintenance facility based at its Wilmington hub. Once it gets a plane, Airborne typically guts the interior and installs state-of-the-art electronics and avionics equipment. The company's philosophy is to put as many upgrades as possible into an aircraft. Although implementing this policy can cost a lot up front, the payback is an increase in aircraft reliability and a reduction in service downtime. Airborne also standardizes cockpits as much as possible, making it easy for crews to switch from one aircraft to another if the need arises. According to the company, the total purchase and modification of a secondhand DC-9 costs about $10 million; an equivalent new plane would cost $40 million. An additional factor reduces operating costs: Airborne's DC-9 and YS-11 aircraft require two-person cockpit crews, not the three-person crews required in most Federal Express and UPS aircraft.

After conversion, Airborne strives to keep aircraft maintenance costs down by carrying out virtually all of its own fleet repairs (it is the only all-cargo carrier to do so). The Wilmington maintenance facility can handle everything except major engine repairs and has the capability to machine critical aircraft parts. The company sees this in-house facility as a major source of cost saving. It estimates that maintenance labor costs are around $16 per hour, versus the industry standard of $65 per hour for subcontract labor.

C-Containers

C-containers are uniquely shaped 60-cubic-foot containers developed by Airborne Express in 1985 at a cost of $3.5 million. They are designed to fit through the passenger doors of DC-8 and DC-9 aircraft. They replaced the much larger A-containers widely used in the air cargo business. At six times the size of a C-container, A-containers can be loaded only through specially built cargo doors and require specialized loading equipment. The loading equipment required for C-containers is a modified belt loader, similar to that used for loading baggage onto a plane and about 80 percent less expensive than the equipment needed to load A-containers. The use of C-containers also means that Airborne does not have to bear the $1-million per plane cost required to install cargo doors that take A-containers. The C-containers are shaped to allow maximum utilization of a plane's interior loading space. Fifty containers fit into a converted DC-9, and about 83 fit into a DC-8-62. Moreover, a C-container filled with packages can be moved by a single person, making it easy to load and unload. Airborne Express has taken out a patent on the design of the C-containers.

Information Systems

Airborne utilizes three information systems—LIBRA, FOCUS, and FIRST—to help it boost productivity and improve customer service. LIBRA computer equipment installed in the mail room of major corporate clients allows clients to input all of the necessary shipment information directly onto a computer disk. Airborne's driver takes the disk back to her or his station. There, all of the information is uploaded directly to Airborne's mainframe computer by means of disk-to-disk transfer, which eliminates the need to rekey the data and is a significant source of accuracy and cost savings. Prior to the introduction of LIBRA, the average data entry rate was 69 airbills per hour. Now over 30 percent of all airbills are entered into Airborne's computer system via LIBRA, and the average data entry rate has increased to 117 airbills per hour.

The FOCUS system is essentially a worldwide tracking system. The bar codes on each package are read at various points (for example, pickup, sorting at Wilmington, arrival) with hand-held scanners, and this information is fed into Airborne's computer system. Using FOCUS, Airborne can track the progress of a shipment through its national and international logistics system. The major benefit is in customer service. Airborne can inform customers on a 24-hour basis where in the system their shipment is.

FIRST (Freight Inventory, Release and Shipment Tracking) is a recent extension of FOCUS. The FIRST system integrates Airborne's computer system with the computer systems of its biggest customers. The objective of FIRST is to eliminate much of the paperwork that flows between Airborne and its customers as cargo is moved between nations and to replace that paperwork with computer-to-computer transmission. The FIRST system automatically accomplishes many tasks that are done by clerks. Airborne is marketing the system to international shippers of heavy freight (300 to 400 pounds) who depend on just-in-time inventory programs to keep their costs down. The system goes into effect after customers place orders with suppliers. It transfers responsibility for all of the documentation to Airborne, which moves the cargo, generates paperwork such as bills of lading, commercial invoices, and customer documents, and automatically transfers necessary information into customers' computer systems. As a subset of FOCUS, the FIRST system also provides the customer with continuous information about a cargo's movement. Such information is vital for customers attempting to coordinate global just-in-time inventory systems.

Logistics Services

Although small-package express delivery remains Airborne's main business, the company is beginning to experiment with a range of services designed to embrace the logistics functions of corporate clients, including assistance in establishing and managing just-in-time inventory systems. Data Products Corp., for example, a producer of computer printers, takes advantage of low labor costs to carry out significant assembly operations in Hong Kong. Microprocessors and many of the other primary component parts for its printers, however, are manufactured in the United States and have to be shipped to Hong Kong. The finished product is then shipped back to the United States for sale.

In setting up a global manufacturing system, Data Products had a decision to make: whether to consolidate the parts from its hundreds of suppliers in-house and then arrange for shipment to Hong Kong or instead contract out to someone who could handle the whole logistics process. Data Products decided to contract out and picked Airborne Express to consolidate the component parts and arrange for shipments.

Airborne controls the consolidation and movement of component parts from the component-parts suppliers through to the Hong Kong assembly operation in such a way as to minimize inventory-holding costs. The key feature of Airborne's service is the collection of all of Data Products' materials at Airborne's facility at Los Angeles International Airport. Data Products' Hong Kong assembly plants can then tell Airborne what parts to ship by air as and when they are needed. Airborne is thus able to provide inventory control for Data Products. In addition, by scheduling deliveries so that year-round traffic between Los Angeles and Hong Kong can be guaranteed, Airborne has been able to negotiate a favorable air rate from Japan Air Lines for the transportation of component parts.

In addition to such services, an increasing number of Airborne's corporate clients are beginning to utilize a warehousing service called Stock Exchange. The basic idea is that clients warehouse critical inventory at Airborne's Wilmington hub. Often these items are not required all at once. A manufacturer, however, can realize substantial scale economies by manufacturing them in large production runs. Under the Stock Exchange system neither manufacturer nor user need commit to warehousing space. Rather, the manufacturer contracts out the warehousing and logistics function to Airborne Express. Airborne stores the inventory at Wilmington and delivers parts to users as and when they are needed—that is, just-in-time. Regional warehousing brings products closer to the end-user, shortening delivery time. Hub warehousing is available for customers who want to maintain their own inventories.

STRATEGY

Positioning Strategy

In the early 1980s Airborne Express tried hard to compete head to head with Federal Express. Airborne attempted to establish broad market coverage, including both frequent and infrequent users.

To build broad market coverage, Airborne followed Federal Express's lead, funding a television advertising campaign designed to build consumer awareness. However, by the mid 1980s Airborne decided that this was an expensive way to build market share. The advertising campaign bought recognition but little penetration. One of the principal problems was that serving infrequent users was expensive. Infrequent users demanded the same level of service as frequent users but typically had only one shipment per pickup, compared with ten or more shipments per pickup from frequent users. Far more pickups from infrequent users were required to generate the volume of business produced by frequent users. Given the extremely competitive nature of the industry at this time, such an inefficient utilization of capacity was of great concern to Airborne.

Consequently, in the mid 1980s Airborne decided to become a niche player in the industry and focused on serving the needs of high-volume corporate accounts. The company slashed its advertising expenditure, pulled the plug on its television ad campaign, and invested more resources in building a 250-strong direct sales force. By focusing on high-volume corporate accounts, Airborne was able to establish scheduled pickup routes and use its ground capacity more efficiently. As a result the company achieved significant reductions in its unit costs. Partly because of this factor, Airborne executives reckon that their costs are as much as $3 per shipment less than the costs of their primary competitor, Federal Express.

Of course there was a downside to this strategy. High-volume corporate customers have a great deal more bargaining power than infrequent users, so they can and do demand substantial discounts. In March 1987 Airborne achieved a major coup when it won an executive three-year contract to handle all of IBM's express packages weighing less than 150 pounds. However, to win the IBM account, Airborne had to offer rates up to 84 percent below Federal Express's list prices! Nevertheless, so far the strategy seems to have worked. As of 1990 Airborne had established numerous high-volume corporate accounts, most of them secured through competitive bidding. The concentrated volume that this business represents has helped Airborne to drive down costs and widen margins.

Delivery Time, Reliability, and Flexibility

Another feature of Airborne's strategy was the decision *not* to try to compete with Federal Express on delivery time. Federal Express and UPS are the only companies to guarantee delivery by 10:30 A.M. Airborne guarantees delivery by midday. Guaranteeing delivery by 10:30 A.M. would stretch Airborne's already tight scheduling system to the limit. To meet its 10:30 A.M. deadline, Federal Express has to operate with a 5-P.M. deadline for the previous day's pickups. Airborne can afford to be a little more flexible and can arrange pickups at 6 P.M. or later if that suits a corporate client's particular needs. Later pickups clearly benefit the shipper, who is after all the paying party.

In addition, Airborne executives feel that a guaranteed 10:30 A.M. delivery is unnecessary. The extra hour and a half does not make a great deal of difference to most clients, and they are willing to accept the extra time in exchange for lower prices. In addition, Airborne stresses the reliability of its delivery schedules. As one executive put it, "A package delivered consistently at 11:15 A.M. is as good as delivery at 10:30 A.M." This reliability is enhanced by Airborne's ability to provide shipment tracking through its FOCUS system.

Second-Day Delivery

Because of a slowdown in the growth of the overnight delivery market toward the end of the 1980s, Airborne has set up second-day air service (Federal Express and UPS also offer second-day service). The problem is that the lower pricing on second-day delivery does not support the purchase of additional aircraft to provide the service.

One way around this problem is to utilize space in the cargo holds of commercial passenger flights to establish the service. As a rule, passenger carriers do have spare capacity in their cargo holds (estimated at 15 to 18 million pounds daily—more capacity than Federal Express, UPS, and Airborne combined). An alliance between Airborne Express and a passenger airline could be a mutually beneficial way of setting up a second-day service. The airline would provide the lift, and Airborne could provide the logistics and ground support operation (that is, delivery trucks). The airline would get a piece of business that it would not otherwise get without expensive capital investments in ground support operations, and Airborne should benefit from the diversification of its product offering. Problems to be solved, however, include working out whether the baggage-handling systems of commercial aircraft are suitable for handling small packages, whether the scheduling of a passenger airline will support a second-day service, and which airline (if any) to form an alliance with.

International Strategy

Perhaps the major strategic challenge currently facing Airborne (and the other air express carriers) is how best to establish international service levels that are comparable to its domestic service. Many of Airborne's major corporate clients are becoming ever more global in their strategic orientation, and they are increasingly demanding a compatible air express service. In addition, the rise of companies with globally dispersed manufacturing operations that rely on just-in-time delivery systems to keep inventory-holding costs down has created a demand for a global air express services that can transport critical inventory between operations located in different areas of the globe.

The response of Federal Express and UPS to this challenge has been to undertake massive capital investments to establish international airlift capability and international ground operations based on the U.S. model (for details see Case 6). Their rationale seems to be that a wholly owned global delivery network is necessary to establish the tight control, coordination, and scheduling required for a successful air express operation.

Airborne has decided on a different strategy, in part born of financial necessity because Airborne lacks the capital necessary to imitate Federal Express and UPS. Airborne has decided to pursue a *variable-cost strategy*. It involves two main elements: (1) the utilization of international airlift space on existing air cargo planes and passenger aircraft to get packages overseas and (2) entry into strategic alliances with foreign companies that already have established ground delivery networks. Airborne hopes to be able to establish global coverage without having to undertake the kind of capital investments that Federal Express and UPS are currently bearing.

Airborne executives defend their decision to continue to purchase space on international flights, rather than fly their own aircraft overseas, by making a number of points. First, they point out that Airborne's international business is currently 70 percent outbound and 30 percent inbound. If Airborne were to fly its own aircraft overseas, the inbound planes would be half empty. Second, on many routes Airborne simply does not yet have the volume necessary to justify flying its own planes. Third, currently national air carriers are giving Airborne good prices. If Airborne began to fly directly overseas, the company would be seen as a competitor and might no longer be given price breaks. Fourth, getting international airlift space is currently not a problem. Although space can be limited in the third and fourth quarters of the year, Airborne is such a big customer that it usually has few problems getting lift.

Nevertheless, the long-term viability of this strategy is questionable given the rapid evolution in the international air express business. Flying Tiger was once one of Airborne's major providers of international lift. However, after the purchase of Flying Tiger by Federal Express, Airborne reduced its business with Flying Tiger (the business Airborne gave to Flying Tiger dropped from $27 million in 1988 to $14 million in 1989). Apart from concerns about giving business to a competitor, Airborne fears that its packages will be "pushed to the back of the plane" whenever Flying Tiger has capacity overload problems. Another, potentially adverse, development occurred in June 1990. The trio of Japan Air Lines, Lufthansa, and the Japanese trading company Nissho Iwai purchased a nearly 57 percent stake in DHL, a major international delivery operator with an extensive ground network in many industrialized nations, and announced intentions to invest $500 million in DHL. Since Japan Air Lines has been a major carrier of Airborne's packages around the Pacific Rim, this partnership could have negative implications for Airborne.

Airborne has many alliances, or service partnerships, using indigenous companies that know the norms and culture of their own country or region. Airborne currently has major alliances with Purolator (Canada) and Mitsui & Co. (Japan). The Purolator alliance dates back to October 1987. Purolator is primarily a ground service with 2,200 delivery vehicles, 5,600 employees, and delivery to 8,000 points within Canada. Airborne flies direct to a number of Canadian destinations, and Purolator handles the ground deliveries.

The alliance with Mitsui was announced in December 1989. Mitsui is one of the world's leading trading companies. Together with Tonami Transportation Co., Mitsui owns Panther Express, one of the top five express carriers in Japan and a company with a substantial ground network. The deal established a joint venture between Airborne, Mitsui, and Tonami. Known as Airborne Express Japan, the joint venture combined Airborne's existing Japanese operations with

Panther Express. Airborne handles all of the shipments to and from Japan. The joint venture is owned 40 percent by Airborne, 40 percent by Mitsui, and 20 percent by Tonami. The agreement specifies that board decisions must be made by consensus among the three partners. A majority of two cannot outvote the third. In addition, the deal calls for Mitsui to invest $40 million in Airborne Express through the purchase of a new issue of nonvoting 6.9 percent cumulative convertible preferred stock and for a commitment to Airborne from Mitsui of up to $100 million for aircraft financing. Airborne executives see the Mitsui deal as a major coup, both financially and in terms of market penetration into the huge Japanese market.

The primary advantage claimed by Airborne executives for expanding by means of strategic alliances is that the company gets an established ground-based delivery network overseas without having to make enormous capital investments. There are reports that Airborne is currently looking for a major European partner to complement its deal with Mitsui. This approach has been criticized by the likes of Fred Smith, the CEO of Federal Express. Smith's view is that to succeed internationally a company has to fly its own planes and build its own ground-based delivery system. Otherwise it is not possible to get the tight control over logistics necessary to make an international air express operation work. Federal Express, however, is currently losing money on its international operations (as is UPS). Airborne is not.

ORGANIZATION

The Top-Management Team

Airborne Express Corporation is the trade name used by Airborne Freight Corporation. The organizational structure is flat (to keep lines of communication short) and is arranged on a functional basis. The top level is shared by Robert Cline, the CEO, and Robert Brazier, the president and COO. Brazier has been with the company since 1964, Cline since 1965. Brazier and Cline are the only members of the management team to sit on the board of directors (Cline is chairman).

Reporting directly to these two men are six senior managers. The following three senior managers report directly to Cline: Graham Dorland, chairman of ABX Air, Inc. (airline subsidiary); Roy Liljebeck, executive vice president and chief financial officer; and Dick Goodwin, vice president for human resources.

Dorland bears primary responsibility for the ABX Air, Inc. subsidiary. He specializes in airline operations, which includes managing the Wilmington hub, the package-sorting facility, and all aircraft and flight maintenance operations. Working under him are more than 3,000 employees: 300 pilots and 2,500 airport, aircraft maintenance, and sorting workers.

Liljebeck's responsibilities center on the finance and administrative functions. His departments include treasurer, controller, accounting, purchasing, information systems, data processing, and archiving. Of the approximately 1,200 people working at headquarters, between 700 and 800 fall within these areas.

Goodwin handles all human-resource functions. Since there are no field personnel officers (except at Wilmington), everything related to employment is handled through the Seattle head office—recruiting, hiring, compensation and benefits, training, and employee communications.

The following three senior managers report directly to Braizer: Kent Freudenberger, executive VP marketing and sales; Ray Van Bruwaene, executive VP field services; and Jack Cella, executive VP international.

Freudenberger's concern is marketing the express product (not freight), both nationally and internationally, and making direct pricing decisions. The 250-person direct sales force is responsible to Freudenberger.

Van Bruwaene deals with operations—the "service" that Airborne sells: picking up the package, getting it to the stations, and delivering it to the final destination. He is responsible for managing the delivery network and for the associated functions such as customer service and data entry in the field. The stations, along with the drivers and station staff, are under Van Bruwaene's control.

Cella deals with international issues such as joint-venture agreements, marketing agreements, agent and broker relations, and pricing decisions.

A striking feature of this top-management team is its longevity of service. The most recent arrival has been with Airborne for fifteen years, and many of the top officers have spent their entire careers with the company. Despite their long service, most of the senior managers still have from 10 to 15 years to go before retirement. The advantage of a long-serving top-management team is that the members know each other well, having established a solid working relationship over a long number of years. Among other things, this consistency means that many of the interpersonal and communications difficulties that can plague top-management teams were worked out long ago. The potential disadvantage is that the team could become somewhat inbred and myopic, although there is no evidence that this has occurred at Airborne.

Decision Making, Control, and Culture

The philosophy at Airborne is to keep the organizational structure as flat as possible—to shorten lines of communication and allow for a free flow of ideas within the managerial hierarchy. The top managers generally feel that they are open to ideas suggested by lower-level managers. At the same time, decision making is fairly centralized. The view is that interdependence between functions makes centralized decision making necessary. To quote one executive, "Coordination is the essence of this business. We need centralized decision making in order to achieve this."

Control at Airborne Express is geared toward boosting productivity, lowering costs, and maintaining a reliable high-quality service. These goals are achieved through a combination of budgetary controls, pay-for-performance incentive systems, and a corporate culture that stresses key values.

Consider the procedure used to control stations, which contain about 80 percent of all employees. Station operations are reviewed on a quarterly basis by means of a budgetary process. Control and evaluation of station effectiveness stress four categories. The first is *service*, measured by the time between pickup and delivery. The goal is to achieve between 95 and 97 percent of all deliveries before noon. The second category is *productivity*, measured by total shipments per employee-hour. The third category is *controllable cost*. The fourth is *station profitability*. Goals for each category are determined each quarter in a bottom-up process that involves station managers in the goal setting. The goals are then linked to an incentive pay system whereby station managers can earn up to 10 percent of their quarterly salary just by meeting their goals, and there is no maximum on the up side if they exceed the goals.

The direct sales force also has an incentive pay system. The target pay structure for the sales organization is 70 percent base pay and a 30 percent commission. There is, however, no cap on commissions for salespeople. So in theory there is no limit to what a salesperson can earn. There are also contests that are designed to boost performance. For example, there is a "Top Gun" competition for the sales force, where the top salesperson for each quarter wins a $10,000 prize.

Incentive pay systems apart, however, Airborne is not known as a high payer. The company's approach is not to be the compensation leader. Rather, the company tries to set its salary structure to position itself in the middle of the labor market. Thus, according to Dick Goodwin, VP for human resources, "We target our pay philosophy (total package: compensation plus benefits) to be right at the fiftieth percentile plus or minus 5 percent."

A degree of self-control is also achieved by trying to establish a corporate culture that focuses employees' attention on the key values required to maintain a competitive edge in the air express industry. The values continually stressed by top managers at Airborne, and communicated throughout the organization by the company newsletter and a quarterly video, are serving customers' needs, maintaining quality, "doing it right" the first time around, and excellent service. There is also a companywide emphasis on productivity and cost control. One executive, when describing the company's attitude to expenditures, said, "We challenge everything. . . . We're the toughest sons of bitches on the block." Another noted: "Among managers I feel that there is a universal agreement on the need to control costs. This is a very tough business, and our people are aware of that. Airborne has an underdog mentality—a desire to be a survivor."

FINANCIAL STRATEGY

A summary of Airborne's financial situation is given in Exhibit 6. Airborne's principal source of liquidity for capital expenditures has been internally generated cash flows. Credit agreements with a group of banks provide for a total commitment of $165 million. Management has set a self-imposed limit of senior debt to total capital of 40 percent and a limit of total long-term debt to capital of 50 percent. As debt levels reach these limits, Airborne issues new equity shares. The last equity issue was in July 1990.

Other sources of financing for Airborne are sales/leasebacks of aircraft and the joint venture with Mitsui (which provided $40 million and a commitment of $100 million in aircraft financing). During 1989 Airborne sold and leased back nine planes. This action reduced the company's debt and generated $83 million in cash. Airborne wants to continue to lease back from 20 to 30 percent of its aircraft.

AN INTERVIEW WITH ROBERT CLINE

Robert Cline is the CEO of Airborne Freight, Corp. the parent company of Airborne Express. Here are selections from an interview with Cline conducted by Charles Hill in February 1990.

HILL: The margins in this business are often described as "razor thin." Airborne is already an efficient operation. Do you see any hope of margins' widening in the future?

CLINE: I do see hope. The industry is consolidating, which is resulting in much greater price stability. Instead of ten viable players, in our portion of the industry there are now really just three. Last year we saw the most stable pricing environment in a decade, and I think it's going to continue. The reason I say that is that we are seeing UPS raise rates, and there is a very good chance from all we hear that Federal Express will follow. So that with price stability and our continued ability to bring down costs, it should lead to continued margin improvement.

HILL: Do you ever fear being squeezed out in a price war between Federal Express and UPS? Although Airborne has the lowest-cost structure, the company still lacks the financial resources to compete head to head with Federal Express and UPS in a price war.

CLINE: That's always been a concern that we have had . . . that the two elephants will wrestle around in the grass and accidentally roll over us. Our best guess is that won't happen. One, because at this point in time UPS has not decided to discount. They are not really bidding for

EXHIBIT 6   **Financial statements**

	1986	1987	1988	1989 (9 mos.)
Revenues	100%	100%	100%	100%
Operating expenses				
Transportation purch.	36%	37%	38%	35.6%
Ground costs	28	28	28	28.1
Flight ops and maintenance	12	12	12	11.8
S, G + A	14	13	12	12.8
Operating expenses before depreciation	90	90	90	88.3
Depreciation	5	7	7	6.8
Total operating expenses	95	97	97	95.1
Earnings from operations	5	3	3	4.9

	12/31/87	12/31/88	9/30/89
Senior long-term debt	$86,284	$120,553	$141,431
Subordinated long-term debt	50,000	50,000	46,395
Deferred taxes	28,906	31,315	33,108
Net worth	124,445	127,418	137,889
	$289,635	$329,286	$358,823
% Senior debt to total	30%	37%	39%
% All debt to total	47%	52%	52%

corporate accounts. Now will they eventually get into it? It's a difficult one to say. We take the position that we don't think they will, but we'd better be prepared for it. But you know, if UPS does get into discounting in the air, they'd better be prepared to do it on the ground as well.

As for Fed Ex, you never know, they might. I would feel more comfortable against Fed Ex, quite honestly, than I would against UPS because of their size, and they have this surface element to subsidize air. Our costs are definitely lower than Fed Ex's. Sure, if they went to an all-out price war, it would be difficult to match them, but their balance sheet is not that strong.

HILL: Why do you think Fed Ex is losing money internationally?

CLINE: I think it's a tough nut to crack. They are flying their planes over there, and they don't have enough volume to justify it. The volume just isn't there, especially the backhaul. I'm sure it's killing them. They have built this enormous overhead and now the volume has to catch up with it. Because of their international problems, it wouldn't make much sense for them to get into a domestic price war and erode the only good margins they have.

HILL: How do you see the global market for express mail developing over the next decade?

CLINE: It's in its infancy. It's where the U.S. market was eight to ten years ago. There will be very rapid growth, I think, especially in the ller-package business. Who the players will be has yet to be decided. UPS and Federal have got the resources and have leaped in with direct service, flying their aircraft, and operating stations. Then you have the guys who aren't flying planes. Ourselves, DHL, who probably has the biggest franchise going right now. TNT, the Australian firm that own[ed] 15 percent of us, is also a very big player, especially in Europe.

We will remain an indirect carrier. We are not flying. We don't intend to fly—we don't really need to fly—there are all kinds of capacity available. Take Europe. UPS goes into Cologne and Federal goes into Brussels. We use scheduled airlines, so we have a choice. If it's to Paris, we go direct. If it's to London, we go direct. Whereas they have to go into a hub and redistribute. So actually, in many cases we have a service advantage over them. The only advantage they are going to have over us is if they can fill their aircraft with high-yielding freight; then their cost structure will be lower.

HILL: Fred Smith (CEO of Federal Express) says that to succeed internationally, you have to fly your own planes and build your own ground network to get tight control over distribution.

CLINE: That was his whole theory in the United States, and he was right because we didn't have the service. But I don't know if that's necessary internationally. I mean, there are so many flights, a lot of capacity. Now once we develop enough volume both ways on a consistent basis, we might fly. The only problem with flying the scheduled airlines is that you are subject to their pricing schedules, and their prices do go up and down.

HILL: Where would you like Airborne to be in the global market by the year 2000?

CLINE: Our global program is to develop strategic alliances. Our deal with Mitsui is a major step in that direction. The advantage is what they can bring to the table in the way of business, their knowledge of the area (Japan), their ability to get into markets that we as an American company cannot. Federal Express is kidding themselves if they think they are ever really going to make a dent in the Japanese market.

HILL: It's often said that the prime motive that Japanese companies have for entering into joint ventures is that they want to learn from their U.S.

partners—and once they have learned what they want to learn, they often quit. Do you think there is any danger of this occurring?

CLINE: I doubt it. I don't think Mitsui could ever develop its own U.S. airline system because of the foreign ownership problem (foreign ownership of U.S. airlines is limited to 25 percent). We have a unique franchise, and there is really nobody else they can go to. So I don't worry about that too much. Besides, we did get a commitment from them for $140 million. If they walk away from this thing, they also walk away from a pretty big investment.

HILL: What is the current state of your relationship with TNT? Are they likely to try another takeover bid?

CLINE: It's an uneasy relationship. We actually do work together in certain areas of the world . . . but those are arm's-length transactions. I think that TNT has backed away from any future takeover bid, primarily because of the foreign ownership rule.

HILL: What is the impact on your margins of rising fuel costs?

CLINE: Fuel costs amount to 4 percent of our total costs, so it's not a major impact. On the other hand, if fuel costs go up by 50 percent, it will knock down our margins by 2.5 percent. And since our margins are only 5 percent, it would have an effect.

CONCLUSION

As Airborne Express enters the 1990s, a number of key strategic opportunities and emerging threats confront the company:

1. The rapid globalization of the air express industry
2. The development of logistics services based on rapid air transportation
3. The growth potential for second-day air service
4. Capacity constraints (Airborne is currently utilizing from 80 to 85 percent of its airlift capacity and thus has little margin for error should aircraft need repairs.)
5. The growing specter of economic recession in the United States
6. The increase in fuel costs that followed the 1990 invasion of Kuwait by Iraq (In the first five weeks after the invasion, the price of jet fuel rose by nearly 50 percent.)

The company must decide how to position itself vis-à-vis each of these opportunities and threats.

Case 8

THE DRUGSTORE
INDUSTRY

INTRODUCTION

The label "drugstore industry" does not accurately describe those stores that to-day call themselves drugstores. For the first half of this century, small neighbor-hood drugstores provided customers with prescription medicines, nonprescription over the counter (OTC) remedies, and health-related merchandise. Many of these corner drugstores also featured soda fountains.

Today's "drugstore" consists of a wide variety of retail combinations. A few, amazingly, are images of the past, continuing to focus on prescriptions and nonprescription medicines. They can properly be described as pharmacies. Even the soda fountain is making a comeback—although on a very small scale. For the most part, however, drugstores now carry a broad line of merchandise, including items commonly available at supermarkets, discount stores, camera shops, jew-elry and department stores, gift shops, sporting goods stores, etc.

In 1986, there were 50,900 drug/proprietary stores in the United States, a decline of 1,100 drugstores since 1982. Drug/proprietary sales totaled $56 billion in 1987, an increase of $19.6 billion over 1982 sales of $36.4 billion. Sales by multi-unit drugstores (11 or more) in 1987, $32.9 billion, accounted for 58.7% of total sales of $56 billion (*U.S. Statistical Abstract,* 1989).

At the same time that drugstores have expanded lines of merchandise, the number and types of retail outlets at which pharmacy services are available have multiplied, blurring the distinction between pharmacy, drugstore, supermarket, etc. Supermarkets and discount stores prominently promote their pharmacy services.

Prescription medicines now are available directly from physicians, hospitals, clinics, and mail-order organizations that compete for the consumers' medical

This case was prepared by James W. Clinton of the University of Northern Colorado and is intended to be used as a basis for class discussion rather than to illustrate either effective or inef-fective handling of the situation. Presented and accepted by the Midwest Society for Case Re-search. All rights reserved to the author and MSCR. Copyright © 1989 by James W. Clinton.

dollar. Just as large shopping centers attempt to provide the mobile shopper with one-stop shopping service, more and more health care providers offer one-stop medical service that includes prescription medicines.

THE COMPETITIVE ENVIRONMENT

The chief players in the drugstore industry consist of (a) independent single-store druggists, (b) small independent drugstore chains, (c) large independent drugstore chains, (d) drugstore chains controlled by parent companies, (e) supermarkets with pharmacies (called combination stores)—including single units, independent chains, and subsidiary chains, (f) discount retailers with pharmacies, (g) department stores and retail specialty shops carrying merchandise or selling services that overlap drugstores' line of products and services, (h) hospital and clinic pharmacies, including Health Maintenance Organizations (HMOs), (i) physicians who sell prescription medicines to patients, (j) independent mail-order services of either health and beauty aids or prescription medicines, (k) mail-order pharmacy services provided as part of an overall health insurance program, and (l) independent health and beauty consultants who visit the consumer at home.

Independent Pharmacists

Thousands of independent drugstores continue to operate in today's complex environment, competing on the basis of personal service to customers and neighborhood convenience. According to Martha Glaser (*Drug Topics,* November 21, 1988), "independents constitute about two-thirds of all community pharmacies; they fill about 80% of all Medicaid Rxs (prescriptions)."

Independents, like their larger competitors, are serviced by about 80 national drug wholesalers whose sales have grown from $8.6 billion in 1981 to $19.5 billion in 1987, according to Val Cardinale (*Drug Topics,* November 21, 1988). One of these wholesalers is the product of a merger of Affiliated Drug Stores and Associated Chain Drug Stores, representing "more than 100 chains with more than 10,000 stores . . . ," according to Iris Rosendahl (*Drug Topics,* September 19, 1988). The wholesaler, because of volume buying, offers members lower prices, particularly for generic drugs.

An alternative for the independent pharmacist is the franchise. Medicine Shoppe, with 750 units, is the largest pharmacy franchise in the country. Prescriptions account for 90% of sales for both Medicine Shoppe and Medicap (another franchisor), according to Marianne Wilson (*American Druggist,* October 1988). In addition to conventional pharmacy franchises, deep-discount drugstore franchise outlets, such as Drug Emporium and Drug Castle, emphasize low prices for a broad line of products.

Independent Chain Drugstores

Fidelity Prescriptions   Fidelity Prescriptions, a small independent drug chain located in the midwest United States, operates specialty pharmacies. A ten-store chain of 1,500-square-foot drugstores, Fidelity drugstores sell prescription medications and offer limited home health care and services. Fidelity's prime customers are the over-45-year-olds, "pre-teen, teen, and college students looking for dermatological items and young mothers who have pre-schoolers" (*Chain Store Age Executive,* May 1988).

Walgreen   The largest drugstore chain in the country—independent or otherwise—in terms of total sales and profits is the Walgreen Company. Walgreen operates over 1,400 drugstores in 30 states. Walgreen opened more than 400 new drugstores between 1984 and 1988. During the fiscal year ending August 31, 1988, Walgreen opened 88 new stores, remodeled 60 stores, and expanded pharmacies in 50 stores. Walgreen plans to remodel an additional 165 stores during fiscal 1989. Pharmacy sales represent 27% of Walgreen's sales. Walgreen also owns and operates four photo-processing facilities.

Rite-Aid   Rite-Aid, another independent drugstore chain, is a fast-growing drug chain whose growth has been fueled by acquisition of other drugstore chains. The typical Rite-Aid drug store has 6,700 square feet of selling space and averages $1.1 million in sales. Rite-Aid, formed in 1962, operated 2,128 drugstores in 22 Northeastern, Mid- and South Atlantic, and Midwestern states, and the District of Columbia.

Rite-Aid purchased 533 stores from Kroger (SupeRx), Gray Drug, and Drug Fair in 1987 (*1988 Annual Report*). "Rite-Aid's strength lies in its ability to buy stores cheap that lost money for others and quickly turn them around" (*Forbes,* July 13, 1987). During 1987, Rite-Aid added 99 stores on its own, enlarged or relocated 47 others, and closed 33 stores. During fiscal 1989, Rite-Aid plans to add 90 new stores and renovate 225 stores acquired in 1987.

In the spring of 1989, Rite-Aid purchased the Lane Drug Company from Peoples Drug Stores, adding 114 drugstores located primarily in Ohio. Rite-Aid carries more than 1,000 private label products which account for over 14% of sales. Pharmacies account for over 39% of sales, and third-party transactions (purchases reimbursed either to the consumer or the drugstore through a medical insurance program—the third party) represent about 40% of prescription sales. Rite-Aid emphasizes discount prices instead of frequent sale prices.

Rite-Aid drugstores typically locate in low-rent strip malls and low-income areas. Rite-Aid targets Medicaid patients, ". . . health clinics, group health plans, and any other state, federal or company-funded insurance programs" (*Forbes,* July 13, 1987).

Longs Drug   Longs Drug Stores is an independent drugstore chain of 236 outlets, concentrated in California (200) and Hawaii (21). Longs began as a single pharmacy in 1939 and, unlike Rite-Aid and Walgreen, emphasizes decision-making at the store manager level. Almost 87% of store merchandise is shipped directly by vendors to the drugstores, enabling managers to tailor store inventories to local customer tastes. Less than 14% of merchandise sold by Longs in 1988 was processed through the company's three redistribution centers (warehouse operations).

Longs drugstores vary in size from 15,000 to 40,000 square feet. During the last five years, newly opened Longs drugstores averaged 23,000 square feet (*Annual Report, 1989*). Longs earned a record $55.9 million on record sales of $1.9 billion in fiscal 1989 vs. $49.2 million on $1.7 billion in sales the previous year.

Hook-SuperX   Hook-SuperX, Inc. (HSI), of Cincinnati, Ohio, was incorporated in October, 1986, to acquire on a leveraged basis, portions of the retail drugstore business owned by the Kroger Company of Cincinnati, Ohio. In November, 1987, HSI acquired 19 drugstores from Jack Eckerd Corporation. In June, 1988, HSI acquired all of the stock of Brooks Drug, Inc., a drugstore chain of 348 retail stores, for $80 million, from the Andrews Group—which previously acquired Brooks from Revlon in September, 1986, for $95 million. Brooks drugstores operated under the names of Brooks, Brooks Drugs, Brooks Pharmacy, Brooks Discount Center, Mall Drug, Sav-A-Lot, Nescott, Eckerd Drug, and Whelan Drug Company. The Andrews Group lost $3.7 million on revenues of $385.3 million in 1987 vs. a loss of $3.2 million on revenues of $155.7 million in 1986.

HSI operates 357 Hook drugstores, 323 SupeRx drugstores, 348 Brooks drugstores, 30 Hook convalescent aid centers, and 13 SupeRx deep discount drugstores—a total of 1,071 outlets. Hooks' Indianapolis, Indiana, warehouse processed 87% of all merchandise sold by Hook drugstores in fiscal 1988. Similarly, 80% of all Brooks Drugs' sales moved through Brooks' Pawtucket, Rhode Island, warehouse. For fiscal 1988, HSI lost $402,000 on sales of $1.3 billion.

Dart Drug   Dart Drug was incorporated in 1928 as the United Drug Company. The company's name changed to United Rexall in 1945, to Rexall Drug Company in 1946, Rexall Drug and Chemical in 1959, and in 1969, to Dart Industries. In 1984, the Drug Store Division of Dart Group Corporation was taken private in a leveraged buyout. The company operated 58 drugstores and five deep discount drugstores in the Washington, D.C., and Richmond, Virginia, markets. Most stores were located in suburban shopping centers. All store locations were leased. The merchandising department at company headquarters in Landover, Maryland, makes most product selections for the company's stores. Eight district managers oversee store operations.

In 1987, Dart Drug went public. Dart lost $23.6 million on sales of $218.2 million in 1988 vs. a loss of $1.8 million on revenues of $265.6 million in 1987. In 1988, the company had a negative net worth of $11.1 million. The company's name recently was changed to Fantle Drug Stores under CEO Sheldon Fantle. As of August, 1989, Fantle Drug was unable to pay interest payments on its debt

(Exhibit 1 summarizes selected data for major independent drugstore chains discussed above).

Drugstore Subsidiaries

Osco/Sav-On   Osco/Sav-On Drug Stores, formerly an independent drug chain, is now a subsidiary of American Stores. (American Stores moved its headquarters from Salt Lake City, UT, to Irvine, CA, in 1988, but then returned to Salt Lake in 1989 (*Value Line,* March 15, 1989). At present, Osco's California stores are converting to the Sav-On name to improve economies of scale possible in advertising and distribution; when the conversion is complete, Sav-On will operate 160 drug stores in California.

American Stores' *1987 Annual Report* noted that "Osco Drug, Inc. . . . did not reach . . . Objectives. . . . Operating profits decreased 24.4% to $97 million on a sales increase of 4.2% to $3 billion." American Stores, as 1988 began, operated 1,460 retail food and drug stores in 39 states concentrated primarily in the Western United States: Acme Markets, Alpha Beta Stores (supermarkets), American Superstores, Jewel Food Stores, Osco Drug, Skaggs Alpha Beta (combination supermarket/drug), and Star Market, Inc. During 1987, Osco Drug remodeled 25 drugstores, opened six stand-alone stores, and closed ten stores. Ten large drug/food combination stores also were opened. American Stores earned $154.3 million in 1987 on sales of $14.3 billion vs. $144.5 million in 1986 on sales of $14 billion.

Thrifty Drug   Thrifty Corporation of Los Angeles, California, a chain of drugstores and sporting good outlets, recently was acquired by Pacific Enterprises, a conglomerate engaged also in natural gas transmission, energy, and financial services. Thrifty operates full-sized Thrifty Drug Discount Stores and Thrifty Jr. convenience stores. Thrifty operated a total of 801 stores at the close of 1987, an increase of 89 stores from the previous year—20 of which were Thrifty Drug Discount Stores and 27 Thrifty Jr. stores.

EXHIBIT 1   **Independent drugstore chains' sales ($ billions), net income ($ millions), and numbers of stores, 1988**

Chain	Sales	Net income	Number of stores
Walgreen	$4.9	$129.1	1,421
Rite-Aid	2.9	95.2	2,312
Longs Drug	1.9	55.9	236
Hook-SuperX	1.3	(0.4)	1,041
Drug Emporium	.4	7.2	74
Dart Drug	.2	(23.6)	63

Thrifty's operating income was $66 million in 1988 on sales of $2.4 billion vs. net income of $39.5 million in 1987 on $1.84 billion in sales (*1988 Annual Report*). Parent Pacific Enterprises earned $251.2 million net income on $5.4 billion sales in 1987. In June, 1988, Thrifty acquired 110 Pay N' Save drugstores in the Pacific Northwest (*Value Line,* September 15, 1988). Thrifty plans annual growth of 4–7% in number of drugstores "over the near term" (*1987 Annual Report*).

Thrift Drug   J. C. Penney, this country's fourth largest retailer (*Standard and Poor's,* Corporation Records), owns and operates as a subsidiary operation 434 Thrift Drug Stores (not to be confused with Thrifty Drug, described above). Penney's operates department stores, catalog stores, supermarkets, and drugstores, and is involved in banking, insurance, real estate, telemarketing, and travel services. Penney's earned $608 million in 1988 on $15.3 billion revenues vs. $530 million net income on $14.7 billion 1987 revenues.

Pay Less Drug   Retailer K Mart acquired Pay Less Drug Stores Northwest in 1986 and planned to upgrade and modernize the 254 newly acquired stores. Pay Less operates drugstores in Oregon, Washington, Idaho, and Nevada. K Mart's net income in 1988 was $802.9 million on sales of $27.3 billion; 1987 income was $692.2 million on sales of $25.6 billion.

Note: Comprehensive financial data (including number of stores) pertaining specifically to subsidiary drugstore chains owned by American Stores, Pacific Enterprises and K Mart, i.e., Osco/Sav-On, Thrifty, and Pay Less, respectively, are not readily available since most operating data for these companies are consolidated and comingled under their larger parent companies.

Peoples Drug   Imasco, Ltd., of Montreal, Quebec, a diversified Canadian company, acquired Peoples Drug Stores in 1985. Peoples, at that time, consisted of a chain of 831 company-owned drugstores, the sixth largest chain in the United States. Peoples drugstores operated under trade names of Peoples, Lane, Reed, Lee, Health Mart, Rea and Derick, and Bud's. Peoples drugstores were located in 150 markets in 14 states and the District of Columbia.   + C V S

Imasco's Imperial Tobacco subsidiary controls over one-half of the Canadian cigarette market; Imasco owns the Hardees fast food chain of over 3,000 outlets, and operates Canada's largest drugstore chain, Shoppers Drug Mart—614 outlets (*Value Line,* June 30, 1989). About 40% of Imasco's common stock is owned by BAT Industries. Imasco netted $314.3 million in 1988 on $6.0 billion in sales.

As noted above, Rite-Aid purchased 114 drugstores from Imasco's Peoples in the spring of 1989. Peoples planned, in 1989, to sell a total of 300 outlets that fell below management's profit expectations.

Imasco's 1987 annual report noted that Peoples drugstores suffered an operating loss of $32 million on revenues of $1.9 billion and an additional extraordinary charge of $39 million before taxes because of "costs associated with restructuring and disposing of certain assets and unproductive store locations." The previous year Peoples' operating earnings were $46.4 million on $1.8 billion in sales.

Peoples is leader or second best in market share in most of its markets (*1987 Annual Report*). Because of problems in distribution, operating margins, and excessive inventory, Peoples inaugurated a program called CSP that is expected to improve store performance. Basic elements of CSP are: (a) convenient store locations, (b) pharmacists whom customers perceive as community health professionals, and (c) a wide range of products and services.

Deep Discount Drug Chains

Deep discount drugstores are expected to total 650 (including Canada) by 1990, over twice their number of 1985—313. Major retailers operating deep discount drug chains are: (a) Wal-Mart's "dot" drugstores, (b) F. W. Woolworth's "Rx Place," and (c) Safeway's "Drugs for Less."

F&M Distributors operate 52 deep discount drugstores in the Midwest and Middle Atlantic states, averaging sales of $700 per square foot in its 25,000-square-foot stores. F&M "has merchandise . . . shipped directly from manufacturers to stores unless . . . warehousing (is more) . . . profitable" (*Chain Store Age Executive*, March, 1988).

Contract Pharmacies

True Quality Pharmacies (McKinney, TX) operates 31 contract pharmacy units in Wal-Mart stores. True Quality provides customers with health care information, including delivery of brochures to local nursing homes (*Chain Store Age Executive*, December, 1987).

Discount Retailers

Discounters, such as Wal-Mart, K Mart, and Target, normally feature cut-rate generic prescription drugs and house brands of nonprescription drugs. Their lines of merchandise overlap and duplicate drugstore product lines.

Supermarkets

Supermarkets' merchandise includes food items, sundries, and pharmaceuticals, etc. These combination stores generally occupy over 30,000 square feet in size with $12 million in annual sales. Over 3,500 supermarket combination stores operate in the United States, many of them owned by major food chains such as Safeway, Kroger, Albertson's, Giant Foods (Washington, D.C.), and King Soopers. Average sales volume of health and beauty aid (HBA) sections in combina-

tion stores ($1.1 million) typically is twice that of the average chain drugstore.
HBA combination store sales in 1987 were $3.9 billion.

> Total pharmacy dollars generated in supermarkets in 1987 are estimated at
> $2.75 billion . . . nearly one-third as much as the $8.47 billion generated by
> the nation's 19,412 chain drugstores in 1986. (*Progressive Grocer,* Febru-
> ary, 1988)

Hyper-markets

Hyper-markets are another dimension beyond supermarkets in size, product line,
and product variety. Wal-Mart opened "hypermarts" in Topeka, KS, and Gar-
land, TX, during 1988. Wal-Mart's Hypermart USA Topeka store is 200,000
square feet and features a pharmacy accessible from an adjoining mall for the
convenience of older shoppers. Wal-Mart's Hypermart is over 100 times the size
of the average independent Fidelity Prescriptions drugstore, cited earlier (see Exhibit 2).

Specialty Stores

Specialty stores, such as camera shops, gift shops, and beauty shops, carry merchandise lines offered by most drugstores.

Mail-Order Services

Mail-order operations, such as the American Association of Retired People
(AARP), offer discounted prices on prescription drugs to members. AARP's
membership is in the millions because of the rapid growth in the "senior citizen"
population. AARP offers prescription, travel, and financial services, and health,

EXHIBIT 2   **Average store size in <u>square feet</u>, selected drugstore chains, supermarkets, and
hyper-markets**

Retail outlet	Store size
Fidelity Prescriptions	1,500
Rite-Aid	6,700
Longs Drugs	23,000
F&M Distributors	25,000
Supermarkets	30,000 +
Hyper-markets	200,000 +

life, and automobile insurance. AARP's support for the 1988 Catastrophic Health
Care Bill was considered by many instrumental in passage of the bill.

Medco, a mail-order firm, recently obtained a contract to provide prescription services for 190,000 retired California employees and their dependents. Medco plans to serve customers through the company's mail-order service pharmacies and through the Public Employees Retirement System network of 50,000 member pharmacies (*Drug Topics,* July 17, 1988).

Third Party Providers

Third party providers are organizations, such as Blue Cross, that receive policyholder health insurance premium payments, and in turn, reimburse the health professional or agency (doctor, nurse, or hospital) that provided products or services to the insured. They are called third party providers because they serve as intermediaries between the two parties—patient and health care provider—and provide funds to the health care professionals for their services. Some third party providers contract with either mail-order pharmacies or other pharmacies for prescription medicines at discounted prices. The third party provider may even, as part of the health insurance policy, require members to have their prescriptions filled at the contract pharmacy.

Health Maintenance
Organizations (HMOs)

HMOs receive member insurance payments directly from members and provide services that include discounted prescription medicines. Kaiser operates HMOs, among other locations, at San Francisco, CA, Portland, OR, and Denver, CO.

Hospitals

More than 13% of this country's hospitals include pharmacies that furnish prescription medicines to patients and others. An additional 13% of all hospitals are considering adding pharmacies to hospital facilities (*Drug Topics,* August, 1988).

TECHNOLOGY

Some of the related activity in technology within the industry includes:

Walgreen is installing checkout scanners and expects to have them in all stores by 1991 (*Value Line,* March 30, 1989). Scanners are part of Walgreen's Information Network (WIN), intended to: (a) speed customer checkout, (b) reduce labor costs, (c) improve pricing accuracy, (d) simplify promotional pricing, and (e) keep stock in better condition because of higher inventory turnover. WIN is part of Walgreen's Strategic Inventory Management System (SIMS) expected to improve inventory control and reduce merchandise delivery costs (*Value Line,* March 30, 1989). Walgreen newspaper ads note that all Walgreen stores are linked to one another through in-store computers.

Rite-Aid's 265,000 square foot distribution center in Winnsboro, South Carolina, serves 426 stores in six states and has the capacity, according to management, to serve 650 units. Rite-Aid's *1988 Annual Report* notes that:

> Store managers place orders through a computerized inventory system with the Harrisburg (PA) warehouse but are allowed no other buying or pricing decisions. Their order arrives prepriced and accompanied by a detailed diagram of how to display it in the store . . . all the stores look exactly alike.

Thrifty Corporation completed computerization of its pharmacy operations during 1987; computerized point-of-sale cash registers in 385 drugstores in 1988; and plans to introduce unit pricing code (UPC) technology in all stores over the next four years (*1988 Annual Report*).

The Catastrophic Health Act calls for the federal Health Care Financing Administration to provide a free computer terminal and related software to pharmacists who request such equipment—to facilitate delivery of prescription medicines to Medicare patients. (Under this Act, consumers pay for prescriptions until a deductible cap is reached. Beyond this deductible cap, Medicare pays for the prescriptions.) Doctors who wish to dispense prescription medicine directly to Medicare customers also are eligible to receive both hardware and software free of charge (*Drug Topics,* October 3, 1988).

INDUSTRY ASSESSMENT

Vice-President William Combs of Longs Drugs, Walnut Creek, California, noted at an April 14, 1989, presentation to the Hawaii Security Analysts:

> The 45 to 64 age group will increase by 33% in the next ten years. This group requires more medication. In addition, hospital stays are shorter (as patients attempt to avoid high hospital in-patient charges by leaving the hospital early), more people self-medicate (to keep medical care costs down), and there is a greater awareness of health.
>
> . . . In 1991, conservative estimates indicate the Catastrophic Health Bill will add between a billion and a half to two billion dollars in prescription drug sales, represented by a projected 700 million prescription claims in the mid-90s. Longs expects to be part of the pharmacy provider network which will be used by Medicare (for the over-65 population).

Walgreen Drug identified the following factors as <u>favorable</u> to the drugstore industry: (a) aging of the population, (b) increasing number of births, (c) shorter hospital stays, and (d) more working women (*Value Line,* March, 1989).
Value Line believes:

> . . . Drug stores are, as a group, less vulnerable to the vagaries of the business cycle than most other industries. That's because of the inelasticity of much of their product line—especially pharmacy items. [See Exhibit 3 for recent drugstore chain financial data.]

Value Line's assessment is confirmed by the steady upward movement of health care costs. Medical care, which includes pharmaceuticals, accounted for $360.3 billion of consumers' personal consumption expenditures in 1987, $404.1 billion in 1988, and increased to an annual rate of $439.9 billion for the first quarter of calendar 1989 (*Survey of Current Business,* June, 1989).
During the past year drug manufacturers increased prices charged wholesalers 10%, according to Richard Koenig (*Wall Street Journal,* April 6, 1989),

(see pp 436-439)

EXHIBIT 3   **Selected financial ratios, drug chains, 1986–1988**

	Industry	Longs	Walgreen	Rite-Aid
Current ratio				
1988	1.9 to 1	1.39	1.99	1.62
1987	2.1	1.51	1.77	1.9
1986	1.9	1.56	1.85	1.7
Quick ratio				
1988	.5 to 1	.296	.65	.375
1987	.6	.271	.28	.424
1986	.5	.232	.43	.369
Inventory turnover				
1988	6.1 turns	9.0	7.5	4.8
1987	5.8	9.2	6.2	4.8
1986	5.8	9.0	6.6	4.1
Net profit margin				
1988	2.6%	2.9	2.6	3.32
1987	2.5	2.8	2.4	3.77
1986	2.7	2.4	2.8	4.44
Return on net worth				
1988	15.5%	16.5	18.1	15.0
1987	14.9	16.4	16.6	16.4
1986	15.6	13.3	18.6	17.2

Source: *Value Line Investment Survey* and *RMA: Annual Statement Studies, 1988.*

pass thru?

while pharmacists raised prices to consumers only 7.6%. Since third parties, such as insurance companies or governmental health programs, pay for over one-third of prescription sales, druggists can expect continued pressure on margins.

POSSIBLE CHANGES FACING THE INDUSTRY   *SWOT?*

Analysis of the drugstore industry has become increasingly complex and difficult as drugstore chains are acquired by larger companies and as store labels, such as drugstore, supermarket, and discount store, no longer accurately represent either the nature or scope of merchandise offered to customers. These acquisitions, along with increased overlap in merchandise lines, indicate that further changes in the industry are likely.

Possible changes include: (a) fewer independent chains due to additional acquisitions by larger corporations; (b) cooperative arrangements between physicians, hospitals, and third party providers for filling prescriptions that reduce those filled by drugstores and combination stores; (c) development of computerized lifetime prescription drug histories as a marketing tool; (d) computer networks tied to vendors that enable individual chain drugstores (and perhaps even independent drugstores) to reorder merchandise as economically as if centrally ordered; (e) federal health care programs that assure that no one is denied needed medication due to a lack of funds; (f) cooperative arrangements between colleges and universities and drugstore chains that arrange for contract pharmacies on campuses; (g) development of major retirement communities that contract for both pharmacy and nonprescription drug items for residents; and (h) widespread formation of associations of consumers that contract as a group for prescriptions and other "drugstore merchandise" at discounted prices. *MIS*

Independent pharmacists, operators of drugstore chains, supermarket operators, health care providers, health insurance companies, government agencies, and consumers can expect continued change in the structure of the drugstore *stage?* industry and how goods and services are made available to consumers. Each industry stakeholder must develop his or her own vision of what the future drugstore environment is going to be and how best to adjust to, and perhaps even profit from, that environment.

Case 9

LONGS DRUG STORES

PREFACE

Longs Drug Stores, as of January 1989, operated 236 retail drug stores in six western states: California (200 stores), Hawaii (21), Nevada (6), Colorado (5), Alaska (2), and Arizona (2). Total sales were $1.9 billion for the fiscal year ending January 26, 1989; net profit was $55.9 million; both totals were records for the company.

Note: Case data were obtained from interviews, company Annual Reports and Quarterly Reports, company publications, and business publications. Opinions expressed in the case may not necessarily reflect the opinions of the company.

COMPANY HISTORY

In the mid-1920s, a few years before the Great Depression, brothers Thomas and Joseph Long lived with their parents in Covelo, a very small town in northern California. Their father ran a general merchandise store in a rural, agricultural community, extending credit to customers, most of whom were farmers. In 1928, the arrival of an agricultural depression made it impossible for most farmers to pay their bills—and their father's country store, with no income coming in to pay off creditors, closed its doors.

From this personal experience with a credit operation, the Long brothers, who worked their way through the University of California at Berkeley, believed

This case was prepared by James W. Clinton of the University of Northern Colorado and is intended to be used as a basis for class discussion rather than to illustrate either effective or ineffective handling of the situation. Presented and accepted by the Midwest Society for Case Research. All rights reserved to the author and MSCR. Copyright © 1989 by James W. Clinton.

they could succeed in retailing by operating a self-service drug store on a cash and carry basis. Consequently, on May 12, 1938, Thomas and Joseph Long opened a 7,000 square foot retail drug store, Long's Self Service Drugs, in Oakland, California. The store was a success and the Long brothers opened another store in Alameda, California. Joe Long managed the Alameda store and Tom Long managed the Oakland store. According to the late vice-president and former board member, Norm Adams, lobby department manager of the Alameda store in 1939, the hours were long, but working together as a team (Adams and founder Joseph Long) was satisfying.

A third store was opened in San Jose in 1941 and a fourth store in Fresno, California. For several months, until an ad writer was found, Joe Long commuted to Fresno once a week from a newly opened general office in Alameda to write the store's newspaper ads. World War II slowed the Longs' expansion program. In 1950, five years after the war's end, Longs Drugs consisted of seven stores.

In 1949, while vacationing in Hawaii, Joseph Long became upset with the high prices he paid for items at a local drug store, and decided to open a drug store in Honolulu. It was not until 1953, however, that Long obtained the Hotel and Bishop Street location in downtown Honolulu he wanted. Longs' first Hawaii drug store opened in 1954; a second was added in 1959 at the Ala Moana shopping center (at that time one of the world's largest shopping malls) near Waikiki. In 1967, Longs created a district office and the company's first distribution center—in Honolulu—to break down shipping containers received from the United States mainland into smaller lot sizes for efficient delivery of merchandise to the two Hawaii stores. By 1960, Longs Drugs consisted of 16 drug stores in California and Hawaii. In 1961, Longs Drugs stock went public. By 1971, Longs operated 54 drug stores.

Longs' headquarters initially was located in Alameda, but later was relocated to Oakland. To allow for future expansion not available at the Oakland location, and to provide employees with a work location closer to their homes, Longs later moved the General Office to its present site—Walnut Creek, California.

When Robert Long, son of co-founder and present board chairman Joseph Long, was appointed President in 1975, Longs Drugs operated approximately 92 drug stores.

Longs entered the Phoenix, Arizona, market in 1978, and by 1987 operated 15 stores in metropolitan Phoenix. In 1987, however, Longs sold its Phoenix drug stores to the Osco/Sav-On Drug Store division of American Stores in exchange for 12 Osco drug stores—eleven in northern California and one in Colorado. At the time of the sale, Longs' major Phoenix competitors consisted of the Walgreen, Thrifty, Revco, Osco, and SupeRx drug chains. Industry analysts evaluated the exchange favorably because Longs withdrew from a market of firmly entrenched competitors in which Longs was relatively weak (in terms of: [a] number of stores, [b] market penetration, [c] market share, and [d] profitability—when compared with Longs' more successful and well-established California stores) in return for stores that added to Longs' already strong position in the San Francisco Bay area.

MANAGEMENT'S PHILOSOPHY

In September, 1988, CEO Robert M. Long, concerned that the size of Longs Drugs made it less likely that all employees would personally meet the company's founders, Thomas and Joseph Long, and benefit directly from their expressed values, put the company's beliefs into writing. According to Long, the company's first principle is the "Golden Rule," that is, "treating others, as we ourselves would like to be treated." Long also believed that:

> Our first responsibility is to our customers. . . . Everything we do and sell must be of high quality. . . . We are responsible to our employees, who must be treated as individuals. . . . We care about their growth and success. . . . We must develop competent management, and their actions must be just and ethical. . . . We are responsible to the communities in which we reside. . . . We are responsible to our shareholders. Our business must make a sound profit, and reserves created for adverse times. . . . We believe that when we honor these responsibilities, and operate by these principles and beliefs, all of us will realize a fair return.

Founders Joseph and Thomas Long encouraged informality and open communications among managers, a tradition continued today. "Longs Drugs, 1938–1988, 50th Anniversary Commemorative Album" described the Long brothers' approach to management:

> The first organized management meeting . . . took place in the late 1940s at Joe Long's cabin at Lake Tahoe . . . (and) involved approximately eight to ten managers (drug managers and lobby managers). Everyone stayed in the cabin. . . . You'd wake up in the morning to the smell of breakfast cooking in the kitchen. . . . Joe (Long) would be cooking bacon and eggs and sausage. . . . After breakfast . . . everyone would sit around that same table for the meetings. There was no agenda . . . in those days. . . . Joe and Tom would talk about everything—about running a store, about merchandising, about one-on-one with our employees. . . . We came back inspired. . . . In later meetings, other speakers were added . . . on operating topics. . . . Many managers refer to the camaraderie that has been a special part of their careers with Longs. . . . No one can really understand what we shared.

Longs' underlying values are reflected in company policies and store practices, some of which are unique to the industry. Each store, for example, is autonomous. The store manager operates his store as if an independent entrepreneur, selecting, buying, and pricing as he chooses. Longs also attempts to provide a merchandise mix desired by customers at prices competitive or lower. Key employees, through stock options, participate in the company's growth and profitability. The Long brothers believed managers who shared in profits would recognize that they literally worked for themselves and work that much harder. Store managers and assistant managers receive a percentage of the profits from their own stores, based on the principle that the more they earn for the company, the more they earn for themselves.

MANAGEMENT AND ORGANIZATION

In a presentation to security analysts in Hawaii given on April 14, 1989, President R. M. Long stated that:

> The conventional organizational chart places the president and CEO on top with subordinate layers underneath. Our organization is just the reverse; cashiers and clerks are on the top, because they're closest to the customer, And I'm at the bottom. . . . Compared to other drug chains our corporate headquarters is very small. Our general office's primary function is to serve the stores. We perform those tasks which could take store management away from the customer, such as accounting, legal work, and site selection. At Longs, attention is focused on the stores and their ability to serve customers.

BOARD OF DIRECTORS

Joseph M. Long (co-founder), Chairman of the Board, age 76.
Robert M. Long, President and Chief Executive Officer, director since 1968, 50.
Thomas J. Long (co-founder), Retired Chairman of the Board, 78.
Richard M. Brooks, President and CEO, SF Adams Management Corporation; formerly V-P Finance and Treasurer, Lucky Stores (appointed August, 1988), 61.
William G. Combs, Vice-President, Administration and Treasurer (joined Longs in 1943; Treasurer since 1961; director since 1980), 58.
E. E. Johnston, Insurance Consultant (Member, Audit Committee); director since 1972, 71.

D. E. McHenry, Chancellor Emeritus, University of California–Santa Cruz (Member, Audit Committee); director since 1974, 78.

Ronald A. Plomgren, Senior Vice-President, Development (joined Longs in 1950; Senior V-P since 1983; director since 1972), 54.

Steven D. Roath, Executive Vice-President (hired as a staff pharmacist in 1964; Senior V-P since 1983; director since 1979; currently responsible for store operations and Management Information Systems), 48.

I. W. Rowland, Pharmacy Consultant, Dean Emeritus, School of Pharmacy, Univ. of the Pacific (Member, Audit Committee); director since 1971, 79.

S. B. Stewart, Attorney-at-Law (Member, Audit Committee), 80.

T. R. Sweeney, Vice-President, district manager; director since 1978; 50.

CORPORATE OFFICERS

In addition to officers identified above, viz., J. M. Long, R. M. Long, W. G. Combs, R. A. Plomgren, S. D. Roath, and T. R. Sweeney, Longs has four Senior Vice-Presidents:

William Brandon, regional senior vice-president (of Southern California stores; began as a clerk in 1959, promoted to district manager in 1974).

George A. Duey, regional senior vice-president (of Northern California, Colorado, Alaska and Arizona stores; joined Longs in 1958; promoted to district manager in 1972).

Orlo D. Jones, Properties and Secretary (joined Longs as an attorney in 1971; V-P since 1979).

Daniel R. Wilson, Marketing (joined Longs as a pharmacist in 1964; appointed district manager in 1981; V-P since 1983).

Other officers are:

Al A. Arrigoni, Construction (joined Longs in 1972 as a project coordinator; appointed V-P in 1988).

Lester C. Anderson, Personnel (joined Longs as a manager in 1972; V-P since 1979).

David J. Fong, Pharmacy (joined Longs as a pharmacist in 1975; appointed V-P in 1988).

Michael K. Raphel, Real Estate (V-P since 1988; joined 1978).

Kyle J. Westover, Training (joined in 1968; V-P since 1988).

The remaining vice-presidents are:

District Managers Jack Daleth, Sal Petrucelli, and Victor H. Howe; D. D. England, R. W. Vienop, R. W. Wilson; and Grover L. White, Controller.

At the close of fiscal 1989, Longs had approximately 12,400 employees, of whom approximately 400 were located at corporate headquarters.

Longs' area of operations is divided into two regions and eleven districts: (1) Northern, (2) Sacramento, (3) Delta, (4) Coast, (5) East Bay, (6) Santa Clara, (7) Central, (8) East Los Angeles, (9) Los Angeles West, (10) San Diego, and (11) Hawaii.

MERCHANDISING AND OPERATIONS

Store Siting and Store Size

Of Longs' 236 drugstores, Longs owns both the land and buildings of 42% of the stores and the buildings on leased land of 16% of the stores. The remaining store buildings and store land sites are leased. (See Exhibit 1.)

Before choosing a store site, Longs Drug conducts demographic studies to evaluate: population of the surrounding area, access to the shopping area, the nature of the competition (with regard to pharmacy, cosmetics, photo, liquor, and general sundry products as well as competitive pricing), average family income in the area to be served, etc. Longs also plays a role in selecting co-tenants in a new shopping center. According to former board member Norm Adams:

> We attempt to (choose) our competition in the small shopping center (typically consisting of two anchors: a grocery and a drug store) for the mere

EXHIBIT 1   Longs Drugs, store data: total, openings, closings, and sq. ft., by fiscal year, 1980–1989

Fiscal year	Year end totals	Opened	Sold/closed (net)	Total sq. ft. (000)
1989	236	11	4*	6,046
1988	229	10	3**	5,877
1987	222	15	1	5,614
1986	208	17	0	5,272
1985	191	13	0	4,845
1984	178	5	0	4,507
1983	173	12	1	4,360
1982	162	14	1	4,089
1981	149	19	0	3,728
1980	130	11	1	3,212

Note: *two stores sold; two stores closed.
**15 stores sold; 11 stores acquired.

fact that a grocery store will be in the shopping center is enough competition. Grocery stores now carry large quantities of over-the-counter drugs as
well as many sundries. . . . We, in turn, carry many grocery items, but . . .
only buy them when they are good buys and pass them on to the public.
. . . By featuring spectacular grocery prices we generate traffic in the shopping center at no cost to (the grocery store) . . . and frequently the grocery
stores ask us to let them know when we are coming out with a "hot" ad so
they can put on additional help to take care of the increased business—
business on which they can make a profit.

Longs seeks centers with adequate parking. Longs attempts to locate its
stores in a center away from fast food restaurants or theaters because of the latter's
high utilization of parking spaces. Longs also prefers aggressive shopping center
tenants who generate foot traffic for several of the center's stores. A center that
contains a variety of stores, representing a truly one-stop shopping center, is also
high on Longs' site priorities.

Local zoning sometimes denies Longs a prime store location. In other cases,
leasing costs are so high Longs cannot justify joining the site as a tenant. District
managers recommend new store sites to a real estate committee composed of key
executives in the General Office—who make the final decision. Longs prefers to
buy or lease the land and build their own store but will accept a turnkey (site and
space ready for fixtures) lease if the terms are attractive.

Longs' 1989 Annual Report notes:

Most stores range in size from 15,000 to 40,000 square feet. Stores which
opened in the last five years averaged approximately 23,000 square feet,
with 66% selling space. . . . Sales of merchandise averaged $8.3 million per
store for the year ended January 26, 1989.

Longs is becoming increasingly flexible in store siting decisions. CEO Robert Long told a group of Hawaii security analysts on April 14, 1989:

We are looking at more than just sites which can accommodate Longs' typical 25,000 square foot store with a supermarket as a co-tenant. Today's varied marketplace calls for a diversity of retail applications. . . . Later this year
(for example) we will open a 17,000-square-foot store in Davis, California
(home to the U. of California–Davis agricultural college), which will feature
what the architect calls "a contemporary agricultural, college decor." Another store will experiment with new colors and large backlit transparencies,
while another will be built in a downtown location. . . . Many have asked why
we're only opening 12 to 14 stores this year compared to others. The reason is, we are more selective in choosing our locations. We don't build
cookie-cutter stores; we stylize our stores to conform to the particular requirements of a given location.

Store closings, as Exhibit 1 shows, are rare and usually the result of an unusual combination of circumstances. The Bakersfield, California, store, for example, was closed down after two earthquakes and low volume. The National City, California, store, located between San Diego and the Mexican border, was closed after Mexico devalued the peso. Many customers were Mexican nationals from whom Longs accepted pesos for store purchases. As the value of the peso dropped, however, Longs experienced significant currency exchange losses, and business generated by local residents was insufficient to operate the store profitably.

Store Inventories

CEO Long views Longs' market niche to be "a drug and convenience store." Store pharmacies are considered to be community health centers, and represent the prime focus of the store. All stores include cosmetics and photo departments and carry health-oriented merchandise. Longs, in addition to carrying brand name merchandise, also features house brand merchandise, including over-the-counter medications and liquors. (Longs' product mix, as tabulated in *Chain Drug Review,* November 7, 1988, appears in Exhibit 2.)

Longs' market research, according to Vice-President Combs, shows that most customers want to shop quickly (in and out) and conveniently (close to home). Superstores carry most of the items frequently purchased by consumers—groceries, personal care needs, and prescription items. Strip center stores (a small group of stores not including a superstore) also carry most of these convenience

EXHIBIT 2   **Longs Drugs' product mix, 1988**

Prescription drugs	18%
Cosmetics	10%
Housewares and appliances	9%
Candy	7%
Liquor, wine, and beer	7%
Over the counter drugs	6%
Food	6%
Household supplies	6%
Photofinishing/camera supplies	6%
Stationery and greeting cards	5%
Related drug items	4%
Sporting goods and toys	3%
Toiletries	2%
Tobacco and magazines	2%
Miscellaneous	9%
Total	100%

items. Longs, to appeal to customers' diverse needs, therefore, carries groceries and other items customers might wish to purchase at a single shopping stop.

Longs' store managers select and price merchandise in line with the co-founders' belief that decision-making should be pushed down to the operating level where employees meet the customer. Store managers purchase most merchandise, therefore, directly from manufacturers and wholesalers.

Forbes, in an October 31, 1988, article titled "Managers as Entrepreneurs," noted the freedom exercised by Longs' store managers:

> One store, (close to) . . . a large retirement community, stocks plenty of aspirin, laxatives, and other products used primarily by senior citizens. . . .
> The Longs store across town, however, serves a neighborhood dominated by upper-income professionals with young families. Store manager Danny Van Allen does especially well selling videocassette recorders, stereos and cameras.
> "I like to think of myself as the chairman of an $8 million company," said one Longs manager.

Store managers have an incentive to choose inventories carefully and move them quickly. The store manager and assistant store manager receive quarterly bonuses based on a percentage of net profit for their store. Hence, they strive to keep their costs of doing business down. The department managers' bonus, on the other hand, is based on gross profit. Thus, they work hard to keep volume up.

Redistribution Centers

In January of 1989, Longs was utilizing four redistribution centers. The three located in California—Ontario, San Diego, and Vacaville—were not owned by Longs. According to Vice-President Combs, "Longs is not in the warehouse business." By not being tied to a particular mode of distribution, Longs is able to select (in California's very competitive environment) the most effective and economical distribution channel. Longs does, however, own and operate the company's fourth redistribution center, located in Honolulu, Hawaii. The centers range in size from approximately 10,000 square feet (San Diego) to 250,000 square feet (Vacaville). Store managers staff committees that decide which merchandise the centers purchase. In fiscal 1989, over 13% of Longs' merchandise, consisting primarily of promotional and seasonal goods, flowed through these four centers to Longs' retail drug stores.

Longs also opened a pharmacy distribution center in Southern California at the close of 1988 which, by the end of 1989, was expected to supply pharmacy items to 90% of Longs' drug stores. The center does not stock every pharmacy item, only those high-volume items that offer the advantage of ordering in bulk.

The centers, through economies of scale, enable Longs to reduce distribution costs. According to Executive Vice-President Roath, as quoted in the November 7, 1988, issue of *Chain Drug Review,* the distribution center concept:

> has made the ordering of ad merchandise easier for managers . . . without diluting at all the manager's role in ad or seasonal item selection. . . . We will not use distribution centers (however) where using them adversely impacts or reduces the authority of our store managers to select merchandise.

Longs presently is studying whether or not additional merchandise, specifically health and beauty aids items, should be shipped through distribution centers.

Promotion

Longs' General Office receives a steady stream of salesmen offering promotional "buys." The General Office disseminates merchandise information to the stores pertaining to merchandise sources—such as jobbers and manufacturers—and prices available.

Store managers have joined to form what are termed "ad groups," logical store groupings with a common major advertising medium. For example, approximately twenty Longs Drug Stores have combined to form an ad group in Contra Costa County, California, because each of the twenty stores draws customers from readers of the *Contra Costa Times,* a local newspaper. Store managers meet once a week to develop a single ad for the twenty stores. Store managers are assigned merchandise categories and asked to recommend promotional items and selling prices for inclusion in a common ad. The managers review merchandise data provided by the General Office and submit their recommendations to the ad group. The store managers review and then vote on whether to accept or reject these merchandise suggestions. Store managers individually determine quantities ordered for their stores. Their orders, however, are then combined with those of other ad group members to achieve economies of scale.

In addition to the major ad group, store managers may use another, smaller newspaper, either exclusively or with one or several other store managers, to form another ad group. Composition of this secondary ad group is determined by the extent to which the medium's circulation matches the selling area of the store or stores. Merchandise selection and pricing is determined by the same process outlined above for the larger ad group. Essentially, store managers determine which merchandise will be promoted, at what price merchandise will be sold, and in which medium the merchandise will be advertised.

In 1988, Longs, to differentiate itself from competitors and increase consumer awareness of the company, circulated a newspaper advertising supplement, "Health News," containing health information on such topics as cholesterol and generic drugs. A companion insert, "Longs Beauty News," discussed questions frequently asked by customers. Still a third supplement, "Today's Lifestyles," promotes products directed at a variety of customer segments. Consumer surveys conducted after distribution of these supplements, accompanied by increased employee contact with customers and a broader line of merchandise, indicated customers had a clearer perception of Longs. The difference that set Longs apart from competitors was Longs' employees' closer attention to customer needs. The promotion was considered a success and additional supplements are planned. Longs' stores also conduct senior citizen health fairs and provide free cholesterol and blood pressure screenings.

Longs first used corporate-level advertising in 1982. Prior to 1982, all Longs' advertising was placed at the store or multi-store level. Currently, most of Longs' advertising continues to be prepared at the store level or by ad groups. Only a small proportion of Longs' advertising is prepared at the corporate level.

Employee Training

Store managers hire, train, and promote store employees. A library of video tapes is supplied to store managers by the corporate headquarters, covering such subjects as: operating the cash register, cosmetics, photography, special occasions, the difficult customer, shoplifting, inventory, etc. The corporate telecommunications studio facility at Walnut Creek distributes a video, entitled "Merchandising Muscle," to each store every six to eight weeks. According to Executive Vice-President Roath:

> "Merchandising Muscle" shares ideas from throughout the chain. . . . (It) is also used to relate hero stories about Longs people who exemplify Longs service ethic. . . . (Longs also conducts) specialty education programs, such as our pharmacy and cosmetic schools and photo seminars. . . . Recently in our East Los Angeles District we have begun testing a training center prototype where we can provide computer training in groups to our stores . . . (through) our pharmacy computer system. . . . A second, more advanced prototype of a Longs training center is currently under construction . . . in Hawaii.

Longs believes their trained employees enable the company to provide superior customer service of a specialized and personalized nature.

Technology

Each store pharmacy has a computer tied into Longs' Pharmacy Information System, maintained at corporate headquarters, that not only provides pharmacy item price and sales data specific to the store, but also enables each store manager to access merchandise purchase information on non-pharmacy items pertaining to his store. The System also allows store managers to communicate almost instantaneously with all other stores and the Walnut Creek headquarters. Satellite links join Hawaii stores to this management information network. Longs designed its own retail management software.

Longs' stores do not presently use optical scanning devices at checkout stands. Costs of installing such devices in all Longs' stores are estimated to exceed $25 million. Currently, however, Longs is testing scanners in two of its stores. Two additional stores are scheduled to test and evaluate the equipment of other scanner manufacturers. If the tests are successful, other stores will adopt the scanners. Longs is trying to determine if scanner technology is compatible with (and economically justified in) Longs' decentralized management structure in which pricing and merchandise decisions are made at the store level.

During 1988, Longs modernized prescription departments at 22 locations, introducing conveyors and specially designed fixtures. These pharmacies, called "Super Pharmacies," reduce time required to fill prescriptions and reduce customer waiting time.

Longs recently built a new facility to process prescriptions by mail. The facility significantly expanded Longs' mail-order processing capability, and currently represents less than 5% of total prescriptions filled.

Longs produces its own video programs, as noted above, in a Longs owned and operated studio. Longs' video network, to which all stores are connected, can distribute videos to all stores in one day.

PERSONNEL

Longs, as a general rule, promotes only from within. Fifteen of Longs' twenty corporate officers previously served as store managers. If a particular skill, however, is needed that is not available within the firm, Longs will go outside the company to obtain that needed expertise. Recently, for example, Longs hired a corporate executive skilled in applications of computer technology to very large operations.

Department managers and above are eligible to purchase low-cost group life insurance up to $200,000—based upon salary. Employees are eligible, after one year's service, or 1,000 hours, to participate in a profit-sharing plan, financed by company contributions, but administered by a committee of employees. Employees are vested gradually into the plan until fully vested after 7 years. Company contributions to the plan have averaged about 15% of the payroll since the plan was adopted in 1956. Longs' 1989 Annual Report noted that:

> At the end of our fiscal year 1989, the (ESOP) Plan held 11.3% of the Company's stock. In March of 1989, the Company guaranteed a loan to the Plan from an outside source of approximately $25 million to purchase 696,864 shares of Longs common stock from the Company, increasing the Plan holdings to 14.3%. The loan will be repaid from future Company contributions and dividends on stock held by the Plan.

LONGS' COMPETITIVE PERFORMANCE

Longs' competitors include other independent drug chains; drug chains that are subsidiaries of conglomerates; supermarkets that feature pharmacies (combination stores); independent drug stores; deep discount drug stores (that feature low-priced prescription medicines); discount retailers such as K Mart and Wal-Mart that include pharmacies; health maintenance organizations (HMOs), such as Kaiser Permanente, hospitals, and physicians who dispense prescription medicines directly to patients; department and retail stores that carry health and beauty aids, camera supplies, etc., also carried by Longs; independent mail order prescription drug services; mail order prescription drugs available through consumers' health insurance contracts; etc.

Longs Drug ranks fourteenth in total number of stores in the chain drug store industry but eighth in sales and third in net income. Longs is industry leader in sales per square foot ($455 vs. $326 for Walgreen Drugs, and $275 for Osco—according to *Forbes*, October 31, 1988) and number of inventory turns (7.1 versus an industry average of 4). (See Exhibit 3.)

EXHIBIT 3   Selected financial ratios, drug chains, 1986–1988

	Industry	Longs	Walgreen	Rite-Aid
Current ratio				
1988	1.9 to 1	1.39	1.99	1.62
1987	2.1	1.51	1.77	1.9
1986	1.9	1.56	1.85	1.7
Quick ratio				
1988	.5 to 1	.296	.65	.375
1987	.6	.271	.28	.424
1986	.5	.232	.43	.369
Inventory turnover				
1988	6.1 turns	9.0	7.5	4.8
1987	5.8	9.2	6.2	4.8
1986	5.8	9.0	6.6	4.1
Net profit margin				
1988	2.6%	2.9	2.6	3.32
1987	2.5	2.8	2.4	3.77
1986	2.7	2.4	2.8	4.44
Return on net worth				
1988	15.5%	16.5	18.1	15.0
1987	14.9	16.4	16.6	16.4
1986	15.6	13.3	18.6	17.2

Source: *Value Line Investment Survey* and *RMA: Annual Statement Studies, 1988.*

Longs' definition of earning power, that is, margin multiplied by inventory turnover, leads the industry. Longs' average store sales, over $8 million, also is the industry leader. *Drug Store News* reported drug store industry prescriptions increased 1% in 1988; drug chains' prescriptions increased by 7%; and Longs Drugs' prescriptions increased by 19%. Longs, according to *Forbes,* has a 20% share of the California market.

FINANCE

The Board of Directors amended an earlier 1986 Shareholders Rights Plan on November 15, 1988, according to a Longs' press release: "to provide (stockholders) additional protection against abusive takeover tactics." (During the past few years Longs has been the subject of takeover rumors.) If someone acquires 20% or more of Longs' common stock, existing Longs' shareholders will have the right to acquire additional common stock at one-half the stock's market value. Longs believes such rights "will not prevent a takeover, but should encourage anyone seeking to acquire the company to negotiate with the Board of Directors before making a takeover attempt." (Longs' insiders, i.e., founders, officers, and employees [through the ESOP], own over 40% of the company's outstanding stock.)

In fiscal years 1987–1989, Longs repurchased approximately three million shares of the company's common stock. Dividends paid by the firm have increased for 25 consecutive years. (Pertinent financial data appear in Exhibits 4–7.)

EXHIBIT 4   **Longs Drugs, selected financial data, 1980–1989**

Fiscal year	Cash flow per share	Earnings per share	Book value per share	Net profit margin	Return on net worth
1989*	$3.60	$2.75	$16.25	2.9%	16.5%
1988	3.09	2.33	14.59	2.8	16.4
1987	2.42	1.78	13.74	2.4	13.3
1986	2.29	1.74	13.33	2.6	13.0
1985	2.31	1.88	12.23	2.9	15.4
1984	2.10	1.72	10.57	3.0	16.2
1983	1.79	1.46	9.38	2.8	15.5
1982	1.72	1.43	8.42	3.0	17.0
1981	1.45	1.23	7.44	2.9	16.5
1980	1.46	1.27	6.62	3.5	19.1

*Adapted from *Value Line,* January 20, 1989, p. 789.

EXHIBIT 5   Longs Drugs, consolidated balance sheet, 1988–1989 ($ millions)

| | Fiscal year ending | |
	1989	1988
Assets		
Current assets		
Cash and equivalents	$ 21.8	$ 20.3
Pharmacy/other receivables	23.0	15.7
Merchandise inventories	196.7	192.3
Other	8.3	6.2
Total current assets	$249.8	$234.5
Property		
Land	$ 54.4	$ 49.1
Building/leasehold		
improvements	177.5	165.7
Less depreciation	(94.5)	(81.9)
Equipment/fixtures	114.2	100.4
Beverage licenses	6.5	6.2
Property, net	$257.8	$239.5
Total Assets	$507.6	$474.0
Liabilities and Stockholders' Equity		
Current liabilities		
Accounts payable	$105.7	$ 96.7
Compensation	29.0	23.3
Income taxes	5.0	4.3
Other taxes	21.9	18.5
Other	18.0	13.0
Total current liabilities	$179.6	$155.8
Deferred income taxes	18.9	18.4
Stockholders' equity		
Common stock	$ 10.0	$ 10.3
Additional capital	31.5	21.4
Common stock contributions to		
benefit plans	.7	4.5
Retained earnings	266.9	263.6
Total stockholders' equity	$309.1	$299.8
Total Liabilities and Stockholders' Equity	$507.6	$474.0

Note: Shares outstanding for fiscal years 1986–1989 were 21.7, 21.1, 20.5, and 19.9 million, respectively. The Board, in February, 1988, authorized repurchase of up to 2.0 million shares.

EXHIBIT 6   **Longs Drugs, income and retained earnings, fiscal years 1987–1989 ($ millions)**

		Fiscal years	
	1989	**1988**	**1987**
Sales	$1,925.5	$1,772.5	$1,635.4
Cost of goods sold	1,445.9	1,333.2	1,241.3
Gross margin	479.6	439.3	394.1
Other expenses:			
Operating/administration	315.4	284.1	258.3
Occupancy	71.5	66.8	60.9
Total	$386.9	$350.9	$319.2
Income before taxes	92.7	88.4	74.9
Taxes	36.8	39.1	36.3
Net income	55.9	49.3	38.6
Retained earnings, start of year	263.6	260.9	266.9
Repurchase of common stock	(35.1)	(29.7)	(28.3)
Dividends	(17.5)	(16.8)	(16.3)
Add net income	55.9	49.3	38.6
Retained earnings, end of year	266.9	263.7	260.9
Earnings per share of common stock	$2.75	$2.33	$1.78
Dividends paid per share common	.86	.79	.75
Stock price range	$31–38	$25–41	$27–35

EXHIBIT 7   **Longs Drugs, consolidated cash flows, 1987–1989 ($ millions)**

		Fiscal year ending	
	1989	**1988**	**1987**
Cash receipts			
Customer sales	$1,918.1	$1,770.1	$1,632.5
Sale of property	3.1	17.4	3.0
Stock options exercised	6.5	3.5	2.3
Total cash receipts	$1,927.7	$1,791.0	$1,637.8
Cash disbursements			
Inventory purchases	$1,441.3	$1,332.0	$1,235.0
Operating, administrative, occupancy expenses	357.1	323.5	294.8
Income tax payments	35.6	38.8	30.7
Investment in property	37.6	41.5	41.9
Repurchase common stock	37.0	31.2	29.3
Dividend payments	17.5	16.8	16.3
Total cash disbursed	$1,926.1	$1,783.8	$1,648.0
Net additions to cash	1.6	7.2	(10.2)

Note: totals may differ due to rounding.

FUTURE PROSPECTS

According to *Value Line* analyst Claire Mencke (January 20, 1989, p. 789):

> With its high sales per store, booming market area, and debt-free balance sheet, Longs has the resources to be a more aggressive market force. Our projections, however, assume it will continue on a cautious path of expansion over the (next) 3- to 5-year period.

Several years ago, former board member Norm Adams echoed the philosophy of the company's founders:

> ... we *have* to be bullish (about the future). We owe it to our employees and to our stockholders. Without opening new stores we would lessen the chances for advancement for our employees. We would not have an orderly expansion in sales and profits. We could not increase our dividends to our stockholders in an orderly fashion. ...

MICROSOFT CORPORATION

Microsoft Corporation has changed the way U.S. business works by creating some of the most widely used personal computer software. In 1986, Bill Gates, the cofounder of Microsoft, took his company public in a stock offering that subsequently made him a billionaire. Founded in 1974 with virtually no capital or resources but Gates's and a few colleagues' raw computing talent, Microsoft became the largest computer software company in the United States by 1988 and has grown steadily every since (see Exhibit 1). The company has always been more profitable than its competitors; and now, with sales of over $1 billion annually, it is seeking to increase its dominance in the fiercely competitive software industry. However, competitors are responding to the threat of Microsoft's dominance with an increased wave of merger and joint-venture activity, and Microsoft has a number of thorny problems to handle if it is to protect its industry position as it grows. In order to understand Microsoft's current situation, it is useful to go back to its early beginnings.

HISTORY

William (Bill) H. Gates III, cofounder, chief executive officer, and chairman of the board of Microsoft, is the son of a prominent Seattle family. His father is a partner at a leading Seattle law firm, now Microsoft's law firm; his mother is a regent of the University of Washington and a director of Pacific Northwest Bell. Gates started writing programs for computers at age 14, when with three high school computing friends he started the Lakeside Programming Group. He and his friends started to write programs for such things as his school's payroll accounts, and the applications of computers soon became his overriding obsession. In 1973, he enrolled in Harvard University, but his practical interest in computers led him to leave. Joined by his high school friend Paul Allen, who had left the

This case was prepared by Gareth R. Jones, Texas A&M University. Copyright, Gareth R. Jones, 1991.

EXHIBIT 1   Microsoft Corporation financial highlights (in thousands, except net income per share)

	1989	1988	Year ended June 30 1987	1986	1985
For the year					
Net revenues	$803,530	$590,827	$345,890	$197,514	$140,417
Net income	170,538	123,908	71,878	39,254	24,101
Net income per share	3.03	2.22	1.30	0.78	0.52
At year-end					
Working capital	$310,131	$227,827	$164,353	$118,452	$41,442
Total assets	720,598	493,019	287,754	170,739	65,064
Stockholders' equity	561,780	375,498	239,105	139,332	54,440
Key ratios					
Current ratio	3.0	2.9	4.4	5.0	4.9
Return on net revenues	21.2%	21.0%	20.8%	19.9%	17.2%

Source: Microsoft Corporation, *Annual Report,* 1990.

University of Washington, he founded, with Allen, Microsoft in 1974 in Albuquerque, New Mexico.

In the early 1970s, the personal computer industry was in its infancy. Steven Jobs and Steve Wozniak had just created the Apple computer. There were no established personal computer programs or even a standard computer language, and anyone with the capacity to develop and write programs was uniquely placed to seize a large part of the growing market. In January 1975, an opportunity for Gates and Allen to enter the market presented itself in a *Popular Electronics* story about a company called MITS, which sold computer kits that used a new microprocessor from Intel. MITS needed somebody to write a programming language that would allow users to write programs on their MITS machines. The race was on to develop the program, and Gates and Allen beat their competitors to the post, writing a condensed version of the BASIC computer language that fit the MITS personal computer's limited memory. They founded Microsoft to produce the program for MITS, but MITS folded when its machine never took off. However, Gates realized the market potential of developing a widely accepted operating-system program. In order to prepare for the future, Gates and Allen moved their company back to their hometown, Seattle, and set about developing an improved operating system.

Gates and Allen's chance to capitalize on their skills arrived in the unexpected form of IBM, the computer giant. IBM had held back from the home computer market, waiting to see how companies like Apple fared before committing resources to enter the marketplace. When the potential of the market became clear, IBM realized that it had missed the boat, and in order to recover, it was forced to develop its own personal computer rapidly. On the hardware side, to develop a machine quickly, IBM was forced to buy a lot of computer components from other companies (as a result, the IBM machines were easy to clone later). On the software side, IBM was looking for a software operating system. An operating system is the language that links the keyboard, screen, printer, microprocessor, and computer and allows the parts to communicate. It also provides a basic programming language for the development of applications programs, such as word-processing programs, that can run on the computer. IBM approached Microsoft for an operating system.

Gates and Allen's computer language would not work on the new system; and they could not develop a new language quickly enough for IBM's needs, so they declined IBM's offer, recommending another firm with a language that would work. That firm, unwilling to customize its language for IBM and sign IBM's nondisclosure agreement, also refused IBM's offer. In the meantime, Gates had realized the potential of being in control of IBM's operating system.

With its vast resources and reputation, IBM was very likely to sell millions of machines. Anybody who could provide an operating system would have a ready-made market for the system because it would accompany each machine sold by IBM. Realizing the financial potential of the offer, Gates bought the rights to an operating system from a firm called Seattle Computer Products for $50,000 and then approached IBM to sign an agreement to develop it for IBM's machine. The rest is history. MS-DOS, the name of the new operating system that was developed for the IBM machine, became the industry standard once IBM chose it. Gates's inspired move in buying into the new language made Microsoft a principal player in the software industry. Ironically, the start of Microsoft was an acquisition that IBM surely wishes it had made.

PRODUCTS AND MARKETS

In the Microsoft 1990 annual report, the company's principal business activities are described as "the development, production, marketing, and support of a wide range of software for professional use including operating systems, languages, and application programs, as well as the books and hardware for the microcomputer marketplace."[1] Since the introduction of MS-DOS with IBM's personal computer in 1981, the history of Microsoft has been synonymous with the introduction of new products and entry into new markets.

The first step in product development was customizing the MS-DOS operating system to work on all Original Equipment Manufacturers' (OEMs) machines. Microsoft receives a royalty for every copy of MS-DOS sold with an IBM machine. When clone-makers like Tandy and Compaq developed their own IBM-compatible machines, Microsoft developed an IBM-compatible MS-DOS

[1]Microsoft Corporation, *Annual Report*, 1990.

system to work on the other computer manufacturers' machines; thus Microsoft receives a royalty payment from them too. Ironically, IBM cannot claim a royalty from clone-manufacturers for its hardware, but Microsoft can claim a royalty for its software. Moreover, all the programming applications using IBM-compatible systems have to be MS-DOS compatible to run on IBM machines, so Microsoft has an advantage over other software developers, who have to have knowledge of new developments in operating languages to be able to write software applications programs. Microsoft has risen on IBM's coattails. MS-DOS still accounts for about half of Microsoft's revenues.

With the growth in demand for Microsoft's operating system, the company quickly grew. Gates, often described as a workaholic, puts in long hours and demands the same of his employees. He immediately saw that the operating-language side of the business was only one potential moneymaker. The applications side is another. Gates quickly had the company at work developing a wide range of computer software applications to suit the needs of personal computer users. One of the first products was Microsoft Word, a word-processing package, which entered the highly competitive word-processing market. Microsoft Word quickly became a big seller, exploiting the Microsoft brand name, and ranks behind only WordPerfect in popularity among personal computer users.

In 1982, Microsoft recognized the growing importance of business customers in the microcomputer market. Building on its established expertise in system/language products, the company introduced its first business productivity program—the Microsoft Multiplan spreadsheet. Since then, more than a million copies of Multiplan have been distributed around the world. It is available for more than seventy brands of microcomputers and in more than a dozen foreign languages.

The next logical step was to customize software applications for non-IBM-compatible operating systems. In January 1984, Microsoft introduced Multiplan for Apple's Macintosh computer, and in 1985 Macintosh Word was introduced. Although Apple had its own software programs, Gates saw the need to develop applications that could take advantage of Apple's user-friendly graphics capabilities. Microsoft has been so successful at developing these software applications that it has become the number-one seller of applications programs for the Macintosh, outselling even Apple's own programs.

The experience that Microsoft gained in graphics from work on the Macintosh had an important effect on Microsoft's future product strategy. Gates realized that programs based on user-friendly graphics-based software, rather than on numerical or character-based software, would become the dominant standard; moreover, graphics-based applications would be important in the development of the next generation of operating systems for IBM-compatible computers so that IBM could compete with Apple on this basis. Consequently, Gates put his programmers to work on developing a graphics-based operating system. The result was seen in November 1984, when Microsoft Windows was announced. Windows runs on the MS-DOS system but allows users to run several applica-

tions programs at the same time. It works with the standard applications programs that users already possess and provides a foundation for graphics-based
applications that use drop-down menus and icons and mix text and graphics to give
the user a natural, intuitive way to interact with the computer. These graphics-
based applications represent a major step forward in software technology,
making computers easier to use while allowing developers to bring sophisticated
new capabilities to their programs.

To support the improved MS-DOS Windows operating system, Microsoft
actively encourages the development of Windows-based software applications by
other companies. Already, more than 500 developers—including several industry
leaders—have developed products that will run under Microsoft Windows. Many
organizations, like the U.S. Air Force in a major computer purchase from Zenith
Corporation, specify that Microsoft Windows be supplied with each MS-DOS
system. As a result, Windows is becoming increasingly popular.

The original Windows system, however, had several defects, most noticeably graphics capabilities inferior to those of the Macintosh system. The defects
slowed sales. Microsoft hoped that sales of Windows will flourish in 1990 and
1991 with the introduction of Windows Version 3.0 and of applications programs
like Microsoft® Word for Windows, document creation and management program that has attracted rave reviews. The coupling of Windows with MS-DOS
has led to improved sales of Microsoft's operating systems and applications programs and is likely to have a significant impact on Microsoft's revenues into the
future. Microsoft expected to sell $500-million worth of Windows 3.0 by mid
1991.

Microsoft's foray into graphics has not been totally smooth. Apple Computer filed suit against Microsoft and Hewlett-Packard in March 1988, alleging
that the visual displays in Microsoft Windows infringe on certain Apple copy-
rights. However, the court ruled in 1989 that 179, or almost 95 percent, of the
189 visual displays that Apple alleged to be infringing on its copyright were licensed under a 1985 agreement between Microsoft and Apple. The remaining
area of dispute is not yet resolved but has become a relatively minor issue as a
result of the 1989 judgment. Clearly, Apple did not like the way Microsoft was
able to pick up the idea of user-friendly graphics and run with it.

A new generation of Microsoft applications software came into being in 1985
when Microsoft introduced its graphically oriented spreadsheet program—
Microsoft® Excel. From the beginning the spreadsheet market has been dominated by Lotus Corporation's 1-2-3 system. This spreadsheet system and
Microsoft's prior system, Multiplan, are numerically based—that is, information
is displayed conventionally in columns and rows. Graphically oriented Excel is
capable of displaying numerical information in a wide variety of ways depending
on users' needs. Although Lotus still holds the lion's share of the spreadsheet
market, Excel has been making rapid inroads and is in the number-two position.

Microsoft seems happy to be in the number-one or number-two position in
all important computer applications markets. On the operating-system side, it is

the acknowledged industry leader with MS-DOS and Windows. On the software side, it is market leader in several Macintosh applications and in several specifically DOS applications categories; it is second to WordPerfect Corporation in word processing and second to Lotus in spreadsheets.

MORE OPERATING LANGUAGE DEVELOPMENTS

The successes of MS-DOS and Windows operating systems did not lead Gates to become complacent. He quickly saw that operating systems must adapt to new computer hardware technologies and that the most important of these was ever faster microprocessors. Intel Corporation's introduction of the 80286 system was followed with its new generation of 80386 chips, and the full potential of these chips could be exploited only if new, more powerful operating languages capable of exploiting the power of the new microprocessors were developed. Moreover, competition between OEMs such as Compaq and IBM was based increasingly on machine speed and memory capacity. IBM in particular was smarting over the fact that IBM-clone OEMs had seized the lion's share of the computer market by offering machines that were much cheaper and often quicker than its own. IBM desperately needed a new product that would re-establish its dominance in the personal computer market. IBM believed that the way to proceed was to develop new hardware and software that was compatible neither with the last generation of its machines nor with MS-DOS, so that the advantage of IBM-compatible OEMs would be wiped out. In April 1987, only a short time after Microsoft had introduced its new Windows application software (which was MS-DOS compatible), Microsoft and IBM announced the joint development of the OS/2 operating system to run IBM's next generation of personal computers, the new PS/2. In December 1987, OS/2 1.0 was shipped with the new IBM PS/2 machine, and a new round of uncertainty and competition in the software industry began as existing OEMs strongly resisted IBM's attempts to establish the PS/2–OS/2 combination as the new industry standard.

The OS/2 system was designed, via a Presentation Manager system, to be compatible with the MS-DOS system; thus the new system can access and process all MS-DOS files. This capability was intended to lessen MS-DOS users' resistance to changing to the new system. Nevertheless, users have been slow to move to the OS/2 system. The cost of the hardware required to run it—including a required 4 megabytes of memory, larger disk space, and color monitors—has deterred users from buying the new machines and moving to the new software. An operating system's success depends on the number of applications available to use with it. Applications companies, however, have been slow to develop applications programs for OS/2 because of limited demand for such programs. Also, users have not been clear about the advantages of an OS/2 system over improved MS-DOS with Windows. Buyers' familiarity with their present system and the time needed to learn a new system are other obstacles to change in the industry. Because the costs of switching to a new system are high, upgrading to the OS/2 has been slow. All this has hurt both Microsoft and, in particular, IBM, which saw the PS/2–OS/2 combination as a way of winning back the market.

As a result, a two-tier operating-system environment may emerge: In this environment, MS-DOS with Windows would remain the standard for the ordinary microcomputer user and OS/2 would become the standard for high-end microcomputers, especially for systems requiring networking and multiuser capabilities. However, Compaq and other OEMs continue strongly to resist such a move since their machines are not PS/2 compatible. There is thus ongoing uncertainty in the industry.

Uncertainty has also increased because of the concurrent development of another advanced operating system called UNIX. UNIX is explicitly designed for advanced computer networking where computers can be linked so that users can share information and files and share programs and resources such as data bases and printers. A networking system also supplies the hardware and software that link mainframe computers with microcomputers, as well as interlinking microcomputers. Some claim that UNIX will become the standard operating system for the office of the future. UNIX was developed by AT&T's Bell Laboratories to have multiuser, multitasking, and networking capabilities. Its introduction suffered because, like IBM with its proprietary PS/2 system, AT&T entered an exclusive agreement with Sun Microcomputer to produce the machines to meet UNIX requirements. However, other OEMs and software companies, not willing to let AT&T and Sun acquire a dominant position in the huge networking market, refused to cooperate by writing applications for UNIX. In essence, they prevented UNIX from becoming the industry standard.

Nevertheless, the power and capabilities of UNIX are becoming increasingly apparent, and Microsoft was forced to develop a UNIX operating system. It developed Xenix, a version of UNIX to run on IBM microcomputers. So now Microsoft has yet another operating system for which software applications are required. Moreover, as networking becomes popular in the advanced end of the market, users are demanding connectivity and compatibility with other hardware and software systems. Companies are asking OEMs to make sure their machines are compatible and software makers to make sure their software systems can operate across different OEMs' machines.

The battle over industry standards is fierce. The company that succeeds in setting industry standards will have an enormous competitive advantage in developing applications and determining the development of the industry. Microsoft, by virtue of its investments in all operating systems, is uniquely placed to influence the course of industry development. In fact Gates has said that although UNIX remains dominant on high-end workstations, it will not become the standard of the desktop of the future. He prefers to bet on Windows. Moreover, at present OS/2 cannot be upscaled to run efficiently on larger, networked systems.

Windows is becoming increasingly popular among consumers who are demanding industry standards to help them get the most for their computing dollars. Recently, most applications companies have become interested in Windows. Both Lotus and Word-Perfect, the other two major software firms, have announced their intention of bringing out Windows products. The evolution of the computing environment will be interesting, as will Microsoft's part in shaping it.

MORE SOFTWARE DEVELOPMENTS

Microsoft's applications business grew rapidly, and by 1989 applications systems were generating more revenue than the operating-system side of the business. Microsoft constantly improves the quality of its word-processing and spreadsheet programs and its operating systems and is constantly trying to improve the quality and user friendliness of its products. This ongoing effort is especially important in the applications business because users have cited (1) product quality and after-sales service and (2) the user friendliness and the start-up costs of a new product as the two biggest factors affecting the choice of applications systems.

Microsoft has experienced some trouble in bringing out new versions of its applications programs. In early 1989, Microsoft was late in bringing out its new version of Microsoft® Word software, and the early versions of both Windows and OS/2 were introduced before analysts felt they should have been. There have also been complaints about poor documentation to support the systems, resulting in high learning costs for users. Such problems slow sales of Microsoft products as users put off buying updates of programs until they feel the investment warrants the purchase. Recently, Microsoft has dramatically increased the number of programming personnel and has put more resources into Microsoft Press, a division that publishes how-to guides for Microsoft products.

Microsoft has been quick to enter the CD-ROM applications business, which uses compact discs as the information storage vehicle. CD-ROM (Compact Disc Read Only Memory) is a new technology that has already had a major impact in the recording industry. Microsoft believes that the computer applications of this technology will be very affordable because a single CD-ROM disc can contain a thousand times more information than a floppy disk. It can also allow multimedia presentation combining text, video, and audio. Microsoft has set up an advanced research and development group dedicated to CD-ROM, and the company sponsored a major conference on CD-ROM technology, attended by nearly 1,000 people from the publishing and computer industries. Microsoft foresees that CD-ROM can be used in a large number of ways—for data-base storage, as a software distribution medium, for electronic publishing of books and documentation, and for mass storage of fonts or images. Future CD-ROM applications might include everything from electronic encyclopedias to medical data bases to home entertainment products. Microsoft believes that these new technologies offer exciting possibilities that will continue to move the company forward in its mission: to make the microcomputer a valuable tool on every desk and in every home. Microsoft has seized a large share of this market.

On the other hand, Microsoft's networking program, LAN (Local Area Network) Manager, is increasing steadily with existing versions for OS/2 and UNIX as well as significantly better connectivity to Windows. The big seller is Novell Inc.'s Netware program, which can link hundreds of programs and has 66 percent of the market. Microsoft is desperately trying to catch up in this market.[2]

MICROSOFT'S COMPETITORS

For the last five years, there has been a movement toward consolidation in the microcomputer industry. The movement has been caused by consumer demands for computer systems applications that are broad based enough to integrate and connect the hardware and software systems of different firms in the computer industry. Given the high costs of investing in computer systems, consumers fear buying into systems that might become obsolete because of technological developments. Also, the time and effort involved in making one manufacturer's software applications compatible with another's on the same computer system have led software companies to realize that firms need to offer a comprehensive package of applications that meets the needs of end users. Applications must include a word-processing program, a spreadsheet program, and a data-base management program that are all compatible with a networking system and all capable of working on a wide variety of machines utilizing different chip sizes.

Another pressure toward integration results from the fact that although small firms often are the most innovative and staffed with the ablest computer programmers, they lack the capital for expansion and for investment in research and development and marketing and are likely to be swallowed up by larger companies with established distribution networks and the resources to develop software applications. Mergers and acquisitions valued at $8.4 billion took place in 1988, and this trend has been accelerating. The same is true in the personal computer market, which is splitting into two camps: high quality, high performance for the top end of the market; high volume, low cost for the clone end of the market. In the first category, IBM, Apple, and Compaq dominate, with IBM losing market share to the others. In the second, Japanese, Taiwanese, and Korean manufacturers dominate. The way the personal computer market develops obviously has important implications for the way software firms invest their resources.

---

[2]Richard Brandt, "Who'll Plug into Microsoft's No. 2 Slot?" *Business Week,* January 15, 1990, p. 28.

Today, although hundreds of companies make software products, the industry is dominated by three companies. Microsoft, Lotus, and Ashton-Tate are the respective industry leaders in operating systems, spreadsheet software, and database management systems. These companies have over a 50 percent share of the software market for personal computers. They all have very large, loyal customer bases, established and protected distribution channels for their products, and large amounts of internally generated cash to fund new product developments. As these companies start to widen their product offerings, industry competition is likely to increase.

In introducing new products, Microsoft has been one of the main developers of the computer software industry. In a very real sense, Microsoft has created the structure of the industry because of its control over MS-DOS, the world's dominant operating language. Since all applications software depends on the structure of the operating language, other computer applications firms depend on Microsoft for information about future product developments. Some industry observers claim that the overlap between Microsoft's operating-language and applications businesses gives Microsoft an unfair advantage over its industry rivals.[3] Its applications group receives information faster than competitors about ongoing or future changes or advances in programming. As a result, critics claim, Microsoft has too much industry dominance. They point to Apple, which spun off its applications business into a separate company called Claris to prevent the conflict of interest. Microsoft claims that its two main groups do not share proprietary information before competitors receive it and that its own applications group receives updates at the same time as competitors. Nevertheless, it seems obvious that Gates can suggest new lines of research to the applications group because of his knowledge of the operating-language group's activities even if no detailed information is passed between groups. There *is* considerable potential for Microsoft to benefit from the overlap between the groups' activities.

Lotus has customized its spreadsheet program to run on Windows, and WordPerfect has customized its word-processing program to run on Windows. Microsoft is dependent on these and other software companies' customizing their programs to run on its new operating systems. However, if software applications companies believe that Microsoft is taking unfair advantage of its position as the setter of industry operating-language standards to gain a first-mover advantage in applications, they can refuse to write new applications programs for Xenix, Windows, and OS/2. Companies in the industry are therefore in a kind of mutual hostage situation: If one tries to take advantage of the others, they can retaliate through their product plans. In fact, the slow sales of the OS/2 system have been attributed to the fact that few software companies are writing programs for it.

Nevertheless, there is considerable scope for competition. The features of

---

[3]Richard Brandt, "Microsoft Is Like an Elephant Rolling Around, Squashing Ants," *Business Week*, October 30, 1989, pp. 148–152.

the new product applications are changing yearly as firms try to redefine the markets for their products, as Microsoft did when it introduced graphics-based Excel. Also, the ability of software producers to upgrade existing software quickly and match upgrades to new operating languages and new hardware is crucial. In this respect, the brand-name reputation of existing producers is very important. For example, Lotus still controls the spreadsheet industry, and Microsoft had to make its Excel compatible with Lotus to seize a share of the market. One of the reasons for brand-name power is the reluctance of consumers to switch products because of the high costs of learning a new operating or applications system. Since the only technical requirement for entering the industry is programming ability, brand loyalty and name recognition are important organizational resources.

Another important element of Microsoft's environment was its close relationship with IBM. Some industry observers believe that the principal reason that Microsoft brought out OS/2 so quickly was IBM's demand for a new product standard that would be incompatible with the old industry standard. The development of a new standard would force users to switch to new machines and would protect IBM from competition with clone-manufacturers. Microsoft had to bear the cost of developing a new operating language or risk losing its special relationship with IBM. However, Gates got IBM to support the Windows operating system in return, so Microsoft is now able to develop Windows side by side with OS/2, albeit at high cost.

Because OS/2 and Windows are not compatible, customer uncertainty has been considerable. Buyers are waiting to see which system will emerge as the dominant one. Moreover, Compaq, Tandy, and other OEMs have banded together to prevent OS/2 from becoming the new industry standard because the PS/2 personal computer possesses proprietary technology that cannot be duplicated by other OEMs. They have jointly announced that they will continue to develop the MS-DOS Windows applications and resist IBM's attempts to change industry standards. The problem over hardware standards has lessened the sales of the PS/2 and OS/2, and the future is uncertain.

However, no matter which operating system eventually dominates, Microsoft will be the winner because it has developed all three—MS-DOS, Windows, and OS/2. Although sales may be slow now, they are certain to pick up as the dominant operating system emerges, and Microsoft may be able to recoup its high development costs. Even now, profits from MS-DOS are paying for the new research and for much more. No matter which OEM eventually dominates, or if the OEMs share the market, Microsoft will be the leading maker of operating systems.

On the applications side too, Microsoft is taking full advantage of its industry position. The profits from MS-DOS fund its research in software applications, so that unlike other applications-only software firms, it has the enormous advantage of being able to generate funds internally. Microsoft is also able to reap advantages from exploiting its brand name across different applications segments of the market. For example, it can spread its advertising costs across the word-processing, spreadsheet, file management, graphics, communications, and project management segments and hence reap economies of scope and scale in advertising. Also, it can apply its technical and research and development knowledge across many market segments, unlike competitors such as Lotus and WordPerfect, which are one-product companies. As a result, Microsoft can reap cost advantages here as well. Similarly, its vast output of programs gives it an advantage on the distribution end. Being so large and powerful, it can ensure that its products are picked up by the three or four main wholesale distributors that decide which software reaches the market. Moreover, because its operating systems accompany each computer sold, it has access to customers that are denied to applications-only software firms.

NEW INDUSTRY DEVELOPMENTS

Increasing competition is on the horizon for Microsoft. As the hardware side of the computer business becomes less profitable, OEMs themselves are expanding their efforts to develop new software. In 1987, IBM established its own Application Systems Division to beef up its output of software applications. In 1987, IBM derived 11 percent of its revenues from software products; it wanted that figure to be over 33 percent by 1991. IBM is clearly a powerful competitor and could eventually become a head-to-head competitor with Microsoft if new-generation operating languages come to dominate the market.

Moreover, in April 1990 Lotus announced that it was acquiring Novell Inc. in a $1.5-billion deal that would result in a corporation at least as big as Microsoft with estimated 1990 revenues of $1.25 billion compared with Microsoft's $1,050 billion. This takeover provides Lotus with the technical and financial leverage to compete head to head with Microsoft in the important new software applications areas discussed earlier. Novell is the leader in networking software with its Netware product. At the same time, Lotus arranged deals with WordPerfect and with DSybase, which makes data-base management software, to make the different application systems compatible and thereby allow Lotus to provide a range of software offerings equal to Microsoft's. Since the $5-billion network market is increasing at an annual rate of 30 percent, Lotus's action is a strong threat to Microsoft. Microsoft recently responded with a strong commitment of resources to the networking area.

Despite these developments, Microsoft is still in an enviable industry position. As a producer of applications software, it is a strong competitor with other applications firms, and as a producer of operating systems, it is essentially a supplier to the other applications companies. This dual role gives Microsoft dominance and has led to the charge that Microsoft is in too powerful an industry position. Several critics have compared Microsoft's position with IBM's position in the mainframe market of the 1970s. Antitrust legislation forced IBM to separate its applications group from its hardware group and to reveal its hardware specifications to other firms. Critics suggest that Microsoft's dominance may stifle industry innovation and bankrupt competitors. Microsoft, however, has been careful to prevent this perception from becoming widespread and has taken steps to enter joint-venture and long-term agreements with other companies.

JOINT VENTURES

Joint ventures are becoming an increasingly important part of Microsoft's strategy as it continues to expand into new operating-language and applications markets. Several motivations are behind these joint ventures. Microsoft seems to be using long-term contracts and joint ventures with competitors as a means of reducing competitors' fears about Microsoft's future competitive intentions. In specific applications categories Microsoft is willing to share information with a rival so that both can share the market. For example, it entered into an agreement with Apple (with which it is involved in a lawsuit) whereby Microsoft's Presentation Manager and Macintosh's system software will share the same font scaling and printer/page description technology. This venture will effectively give Apple a large share of the market for font software.

Microsoft also entered into agreements to obtain the specialized knowledge that other firms possess in special new software areas, so that Microsoft can enter these areas quickly. For example, to enter the CD-ROM applications market, Microsoft entered into a joint venture with IBM to create a new industry standard for multimedia computer systems. It also worked closely with Ashton-Tate and Sybase Inc. to develop the Ashton-Tate/Microsoft SQL (Structure Query Language) Server, an applications program for a multiuser data-base system. Originally, Microsoft and Ashton-Tate were expected to compete head to head for this market; however, they have combined forces to position the new product as the accepted industry standard to beat the competition, which includes IBM and Lotus, which also have products in the area. Microsoft has also joined with Digital Communications Associates to produce DCA/Microsoft Communications Server, designed to manage network connectivity across 3,270 environments. LAN systems allow computers to communicate and share resources. Clearly, Microsoft is not averse to sharing some markets with companies that share similar vision. One advantage of this strategy is short product development time, which is important in an environment of global competition.

Moreover, being at the center of a complex series of linkages between all major software and hardware producers allows Bill Gates to push hard for the industry standards he wants and take advantage of his enhanced industry knowledge to position Microsoft's products for the next generation. The ability to control standards—for example, to push for Windows rather than for Xenix—is of vital importance, for the system that becomes dominant will be the one for which a new generation of software applications will be written.

Microsoft's long-term growth strategy also involves acquiring firms to gain access to new computer programming skills quickly. For example, it acquired Dynamical Systems Research to obtain its Modrian product, which is compatible with the applications written for IBM's TopView operating system but runs 30 times faster and requires 50 percent less RAM. The acquisition is intended to help Microsoft move from the icon-based DOS Windows, which is controlled by a mouse, to a character-based DOS windowing environment. It was also intended to help Microsoft lure away IBM's small but lucrative base of Fortune 1,000 firms currently using TopView. Microsoft also acquired Cytation, a small research and development firm that had been working on computer products using laser and compact-disc technology. T. M. Lopez, president of Cytation, was hired to act as head of Microsoft's CD-ROM division.

THE DANGERS OF BEING FIRST

Microsoft's industry dominance is not without its hazards. First, supporting the development of so many industry operating-system platforms puts a severe strain on Microsoft's resources. Gates has committed his company to over ten operating system platforms, together with the obligation to develop software applications for each operating system. Obviously, working toward this goal dilutes the effort that can be applied to each platform.[4] But the advantage of this strategy is that Microsoft is sure to be a winner for the platforms that survive and become industry standards. The strategy, however, has resulted in delays for some of Microsoft's major products. For example, Microsoft was late to market with its updates of Microsoft Word in 1989, and the delay sent its stock plummeting. Microsoft has more than doubled its work force in the last five years to handle its development needs, and this increase has resulted in a large increase in its operating expenses. Clearly, the desire to be the leader is expensive.

Another problem for Microsoft is its relationship with IBM. Microsoft has to maintain a delicate balance with IBM in many areas of software development. On several occasions IBM and Microsoft have supported different standards— for example, for font specifications—and Microsoft has had great difficulty in getting IBM's support for Windows because of IBM's commitment to making its new PS/2 system the industry standard in hardware. As other OEMs develop new technologies with new operating-system requirements, Gates may have difficulty managing his special relationship with IBM.

Similarly, the sensitive relationship with software applications competitors is likely to be a continuing problem if uncertainty over industry operating systems continues. Microsoft's dominance in operating systems will always give it a potentially unfair advantage over competitors, and Microsoft will have to be careful to avoid charges of monopoly. Gates will need all his political skills to manage these relationships. Luckily for him, as one commentator has put it, he is "part evangelist, part arm-twisting horse trader."[5] If anyone can set industry standards, it will be Gates.

[4]Sandra Reed, *Personal Computing*, 13 (July 1989), 75.
[5]Ibid.

A STRONG INTERNATIONAL PRESENCE

In the same way that Microsoft has expanded and enhanced its product line over the past ten years, the company has expanded its reach internationally. Activities outside the United States have increased at a rapid pace, generating more than 40 percent of Microsoft's business revenues in 1990. Microsoft has built its international business on some important principles. Microsoft has realized that it has to adapt its products to the needs of the countries in which it operates. This "product localization" means adapting products to a country's language and standards. More than 150 local-language versions of Microsoft products are currently on the market. User messages in each program and all documentation are in the native language. Special characters are supported on the screen, and local conventions—such as dates and monetary references—are handled correctly. Both the Microsoft Windows and the Macintosh programming environments have a technical design made specifically with international localization in mind.

At the same time, Microsoft insists on maintaining the same quality in its foreign products as in its domestic products, so that a customer buying a Microsoft product abroad gets the same commitment to quality as an American customer. Finally, the company insists on a strong marketing effort to keep customers informed about its products and devotes considerable resources to backing up the sales and after-sales service offered by its foreign distributors. All these policies have contributed to Microsoft's differentiated image and led to strong foreign sales. These principles have paid off, and Microsoft expects a continued increase in international revenues as foreign markets evolve. Any new computer sold anywhere in the world represents a chance of revenue generation for Microsoft.

To foster continued growth in overseas markets, Microsoft has taken several steps to strengthen its international organization. For example, sales offices have been opened in Italy, Sweden, and the Netherlands; and Japanese operations have been transferred from ASCII, an exclusive sales representative, to Microsoft KK, a wholly owned subsidiary. In other parts of the world, Microsoft is represented by independent sales representatives. The leading source of revenues in Europe, Canada, and Australia is Microsoft's retail operations. OEM distribution has been responsible for a greater percentage of revenues in the Far East and other regions.

In December 1985, Microsoft started operations in a new manufacturing facility in Dublin, Ireland, primarily to serve the European retail market. The Dublin facility has proved that it is able to meet the same stringent quality-control requirements that Microsoft insists on in the United States. Recently, Microsoft obtained international distribution rights for products produced by Microrim, Micrografx and other U.S. companies. Internationally, these products carry the Microsoft name and Microsoft provides worldwide marketing and support for them.

International strength is important to Microsoft's marketing efforts, especially because Microsoft believes that this strength is of increasing importance to corporate customers—both domestic and international—as they equip their facilities around the world with office information systems. By establishing an international presence today, Microsoft will be able to provide a high level of support to meet the future computing needs of these corporations. In addition, OEMs such as IBM and, increasingly, Compaq and Tandy are also internationalizing rapidly, so that Microsoft needs to support the efforts of these customers too. Clearly, Microsoft is at the center of a web of relationships involving hardware manufacturers, software manufacturers, and end users.

MICROSOFT'S STRUCTURE

Microsoft tailors its structure and control systems to suit its products and markets. In order to manage the rapid development of new products, it introduced forty-three new and enhanced products in 1988, fifty-three in 1989. It organizes itself functionally by dividing its software specialists into three principal operating groups: the systems and languages group, responsible for developing operating systems and languages; the applications group, responsible for developing Microsoft's applications business; and the hardware and books group, which handles hardware developments like the Microsoft mouse and the writing of books and information to keep customers informed about the capabilities of Microsoft's products. The last group is very necessary because a key part of Microsoft's strategy is to inform customers about the superior quality of its products.

These groups contain the computer specialists responsible for product development and are small research and development units responsible for developing new technologies to exploit new software opportunities. The division between operating systems and applications is also a response to the need to keep the activities of the two groups separate. Recall that competitors have claimed that Microsoft's applications group receives information before they do and thus has an unfair advantage.

In 1989, because of the expected growth in applications activities over the next five years, Microsoft subdivided the applications group into separate business groups. The new grouping gives Gates more control over activities inside each business group and allows the profit contributions of each business unit to be compared closely. In addition, it allows close monitoring of the business group's performance and an opportunity to align performance with rewards. Also, given that Microsoft's core competence is the skills of its employees, the division of activities into smaller groups allows each group to become more specialized and knowledgeable in the area of its specialty. This gives Microsoft an advantage over its competitors.

In fact, Microsoft is constantly altering its structure to suit the growth in its product lines. For example, to develop and enhance its networking applications programs, in 1990 it folded the Workgroup Services Group, which was responsible for developing the SQL Communication Server, into the Network Business Unit. The rationale for this change was to connect these groups with Microsoft's networking group, which develops Microsoft LAN Manager, Microsoft's main networking program, in order to exploit synergies between the groups' activities.

Inside each operating group hundreds of programmers work in small teams of 10 to 15 employees.[6] The team is the basis of how Microsoft functions, and as the company grows, its team structure becomes more and more sophisticated. In 1980, Microsoft had 80 employees. By 1989, the company had 4,000 employees worldwide. Employment grew to 5,200 by the middle of 1990 and is expected to increase to 8,000.[7]

Gates learned much about the importance of teams from IBM, which used teams to handle product development. Using teams allows Microsoft to keep product development projects on schedule, something most start-up companies find hard to do. Microsoft holds regular meetings of new product teams and sets strict deadlines for software development. In this way it is able to control its flat, decentralized group operations. Gates describes Microsoft's current development process as about "one-third IBM's and two-thirds Microsoft's."

When Gates starts work on a new project, he selects a team of about ten people from engineering and marketing. The team sets goals, divides up the work, then meets every couple of weeks to solve problems. At team meetings, Gates can be most intimidating. One executive in charge of developing applications software for Microsoft said, "Bill has toughened us up. He used to just beat us up, and we went away feeling bad. You have to be able to take this abuse and fight back. If you back down, he loses respect. It's part of the game."[8] This team spirit permeates Microsoft and provides the company with unifying values and goals.

Finally, the grouping of activities gives Microsoft close control over technical development. The programming staff is working with a substantial collection of proprietary development tools that make possible the transfer of technology from one product to another. This means lower-cost development and faster time to market.

The other main division that Microsoft makes is by the markets or channels it serves. Microsoft is not just a research and development company. From the beginning it realized that being close to customers and informing them about company products was as important to revenue generation as was designing new products. A problem facing all small companies is in the commercialization of their products. Microsoft has never had this problem because it has distribution groups organized by the markets that Microsoft serves. The five distribution groups are Domestic Original Equipment Manufacturers (OEMs), Domestic Retail, International OEMs, International Retail, and Microsoft Press. This division parallels the way Microsoft looks at its revenues. It does so from two perspectives: the products that revenues are derived from and the markets that products

[6]Douglas Gantnbein, "Microsoft Magic," *Business Week Careers,* (February 1988), Vol. 10, p. 100.
[7]Microsoft Corporation, *Annual Report,* 1990.
[8]Richard Brandt, "The Waiting Game That Microsoft Can't Lose," *Business Week,* April 13, 1987, p. 72.

are sold in. Exhibit 2 shows how revenues are broken down by product group and by channel. Microsoft is proud of the fact that its products are pretty evenly sold across markets and across products because this lessens risk in any one market.

Each marketing/distribution group can liaise with each software operating group to ensure that respective markets are being served with the right products. In addition, each marketing/distribution group can feed back to the operating groups information gathered on customer attitudes to Microsoft's products and new market opportunities to exploit.

In 1989, when revenue from foreign operations contributed over 40 percent of Microsoft's total revenues (a percentage that is increasing each year), the company changed this structure somewhat to meet the increasing international needs of the corporation. The company realized that most of its OEM customers have an increasingly international focus because they too sell their products around the world. As a result, the domestic and international OEM groups were combined so that they could better share information and tailor their activities to meet the needs of OEMs. However, as noted earlier, Microsoft has an ever increasing need to customize its software to the country in which it sells its products. In fact, much of the growth in employment in the company comprises staff additions attributable to the need for product localization. Retail distribution groups are still separate to serve the needs of their different markets. All this strongly suggests the attention that Microsoft pays to organizing its human resources to meet the needs of its products and markets at home and abroad.

CONTROL IN MICROSOFT

Given its team structure, Microsoft has some particularly difficult control problems. As a team finishes an assignment, the team dissolves and members are sent to new teams or even to business units to address new product needs. (Competitors claim that this movement of employees is how Microsoft informally transfers knowledge between the operating-system division and the applications division.) This movement causes problems of integration between the groups.

Moreover, Microsoft is a very decentralized company. At Microsoft, Gates willingly delegates authority, but he is fussy about how it is used. Vern Raburn, for example, resigned in 1982 as president of Microsoft's Consumer Products Group after Gates decided that "he wasn't doing his best work." Microsoft therefore has a problem coordinating its activities. To solve this problem, team supervisors and managers spend a lot of time in scheduled meetings coordinating operating strategy and sharing information and knowledge. Although employees can set their own work hours, times for meetings are rigidly adhered to.

As Microsoft grows, it may run into coordination problems unless steps are taken to coordinate the activities of its rapidly growing work force. At the same time, it will need to avoid the problem experienced by IBM: centralization in

EXHIBIT 2   Revenue by product group and by channel

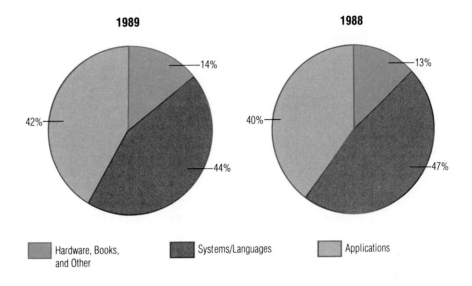

1989

14%
44%
42%

1988

13%
47%
40%

Hardware, Books, and Other   Systems/Languages   Applications

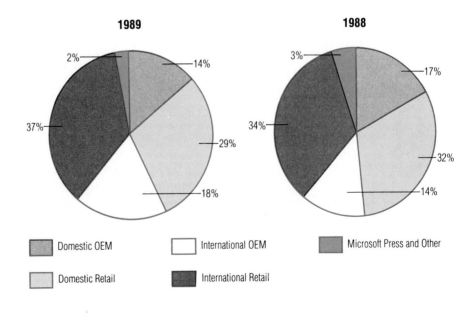

1989

2%
14%
29%
18%
37%

1988

3%
17%
32%
14%
34%

Domestic OEM   International OEM   Microsoft Press and Other

Domestic Retail   International Retail

Source: Microsoft Corporation, *Annual Report*, 1990.

decision making with organizational growth. IBM moved to decentralize itself, to return to a more flexible team structure. Microsoft must take steps to ensure that it does not encounter the same problem. Already its facilities are spreading out as it expands its physical campus in Redmond, Washington, just outside Seattle. Similarly it will have growing difficulty coordinating its international activities as time goes on. One step it already has taken is having foreign employees spend six months at its headquarters in Redmond, Washington, learning the intricacies of Microsoft operations.

Gates and Microsoft spend a lot of time developing a relaxed, informal atmosphere at corporate headquarters, but Gates's personality dominates the company. Microsoft employees work long hours, and Gates sets the standard. As chief strategist, he oversees extensive product development efforts and meets regularly with his top executives, often on weekends. On weekdays he is at work from about 9:30 A.M. to midnight. The environment at Microsoft has been described as "equal parts family and West Coast informality."[9] There are frequent picnics and parties, and every employee gets a free membership at a nearby health club. Dress is casual—even for executives. For example, executives usually wear ties when visiting a customer but not when they are hosts. Gates believes that informality works.

Many Microsoft programmers earn less salary than they could in other organizations, yet Microsoft's annual turnover is less than 10 percent. However, Microsoft has a stock option plan, and its rewards systems are closely tied to employee performance. This is of course vital, for Microsoft's distinctive competence is in the creativity of its employees. In order to attract and keep the most talented employees, Microsoft gives them room to be creative and rewards them well for working hard.

Microsoft's compensation and promotion plan to increase employee loyalty is similar to the one employed by law firms and accounting firms. Essentially, employees work to become partners. Microsoft has rating levels for programmers, and rewards increase as they reach senior status. Unless employees feel that they are equitably compensated, they will have no incentive to put forward the effort that Microsoft requires to stay ahead of its competitors. After all, the best programmers can always leave to found their own firms. The rapid pace of the computer software industry makes it essential to get products to market in a timely manner and to respond quickly to technological change. Motivated employees and an operating structure that allows them to be productive are vital to a high-tech company.

THE FUTURE

Microsoft is investing in all new technologies to keep the company at the forefront of its industry. It is investing heavily in research and development and mar-

---

[9]Ibid.

keting expenditures to support product development. In the short run this investment has increased the proportion of operating expenses as a percent of revenue, hurting financial results. What will be the long-run effects of this investment? Some industry analysts argue that Microsoft's present strong position can only weaken over the long run. Given the rapid pace of industry change, the uncertainty over industry standards, and the ability of small new companies to create new programs in an increasingly short amount of time, Microsoft may lose its dominance in the industry. Moreover, as Microsoft grows larger and its already expanding work force grows rapidly, internal innovation might falter. Commenting on the Lotus merger with Novell, Gates observed that big companies are hard to run and that Microsoft is having problems now. What will happen to Microsoft as it grows? Will it be able to maintain the volume of new products at the current rate? Will it be able to establish OS/2 as the industry standard, particularly if IBM continues to lose its dominance? Will the development of UNIX result in a free-for-all? How should Microsoft deal with Lotus, which may become the largest software company? Clearly, Gates has problems ahead to manage. Exhibit 3 shows key selected financial data for Microsoft.

EXHIBIT 3   **Microsoft Corporation selected five-year financial data (in thousands, except employee and per share data)**

			Year ended June 30		
	1989	1988	1987	1986	1985
For the year					
Net revenues	$803,530	$590,827	$345,890	$197,514	$140,417
Cost of revenues	204,185	148,000	73,854	40,862	30,447
Research and development	110,220	69,776	38,076	20,523	17,108
Sales and marketing	218,997	161,614	85,070	57,668	42,512
General and administrative	27,898	23,990	22,003	17,555	9,443
Operating income	242,230	187,447	126,887	60,906	40,907
Non-operating income	16,566	10,750	8,638	5,078	1,936
Stock option program (expense)	(8,000)	(14,459)	(14,187)	—	—
Income before income taxes	250,796	183,738	121,338	65,984	42,843
Provision for income taxes	80,258	59,830	49,460	26,730	18,742
Net income	170,538	123,908	71,878	39,254	24,101
At year-end					
Current assets	468,949	345,348	213,002	147,980	52,066
Property, plant, and equipment—net	198,825	130,108	70,010	19,544	11,190
Other assets	52,824	17,563	4,742	3,215	1,808
Total assets	720,598	493,019	287,754	170,739	65,064
Liabilities	158,818	117,521	48,649	31,407	10,624
Stockholders' equity	561,780	375,498	239,105	139,332	54,440
Total liabilities and stockholders' equity	720,598	493,019	287,754	170,739	65,064
Working capital	310,131	227,827	164,353	118,452	41,442
Number of employees	4,037	2,793	1,816	1,153	910

EXHIBIT 3   **Microsoft Corporation selected five-year financial data (in thousands, except employee and per share data) (*cont.*)**

| | Year ended June 30 | | | | |
	1989	1988	1987	1986	1985
Common stock data					
Net income per share	3.03	2.22	1.30	0.78	0.52
Book value per share	10.29	7.00	4.54	2.73	1.26
Cash and short-term investments per share	5.51	3.41	2.51	2.01	0.44
Average common and common equivalent shares outstanding	56,245	55,818	55,270	50,400	46,520
Shares outstanding at year-end	54,586	53,663	52,713	51,040	43,066
Key ratios					
Current ratio	3.0	2.9	4.4	5.0	4.9
Return on net revenues	21.2%	21.0%	20.8%	19.9%	17.2%
Return on average total assets	28.1%	31.7%	31.4%	33.3%	42.8%
Return on average stockholders' equity	36.4%	40.3%	38.0%	40.5%	56.6%
Growth percentages—increases					
Net revenues	36.0%	70.8%	75.1%	40.7%	44.0%
Net income	37.6%	72.4%	83.1%	62.9%	51.8%
Net income per share	36.5%	70.8%	66.7%	50.0%	48.6%
Book value per share	47.0%	54.2%	66.3%	116.7%	75.0%

Source: Microsoft Corporation, *Annual Report*, 1990.

ASHTON-TATE CORPORATION

Mike Philips poured himself another cup of coffee and sat down to ponder his future. He had just come from his final interview with Ashton-Tate Corporation, and had been offered a job on its management team. However, he had job offers from two other companies, and was being pressed to make a decision. Mike had just completed an MBA in Administrative Management, and was delighted to find his skills and talents in such high demand. But now he was faced with a difficult decision, and the solution to his dilemma was unclear.

Ashton-Tate had offered him the highest salary and the most attractive position for the utilization of his skills and for advancement. However, he was concerned with rumors that the company was faced with an assortment of problems. Mike had worked long and hard to complete the MBA program; he didn't want to take a position with a company whose future appeared questionable.

After much thought, Mike came to the conclusion that the only way he could make an informed and intelligent decision about his future was to thoroughly investigate and analyze the past and current performance of Ashton-Tate. Perhaps new information would give him the enlightenment he needed.

INDUSTRY OVERVIEW

The foundation for the microcomputer industry was laid in 1969 when Dr. Ted Hoff of the Intel Corporation designed the first silicon chip, called a microprocessor. Initially, microcomputers were regarded to be for hobbyists; however, the development of the first spreadsheet program in 1979 made these computers an asset for businesses and individuals. The entry of IBM into the market in 1981

This case was prepared by Lori Bachman, Shirong Chen, Sherry Christe, Sally Danforth, and Susanne Wegner under the supervision of Professor Sexton Adams, University of North Texas, and Professor Adelaide Griffin, Texas Woman's University. © Sexton-Adams and Adelaide Griffin.

and the rapid growth rate of the industry attracted many new companies, and by 1984, there were 350 companies producing microcomputers.[1] IBM became the standard for this market, and microprocessors were categorized according to their compatibility with IBM's machines.

Computers were directed to perform various operations by a series of instructions called computer programs, or computer software. Software not only told the computer what to do, but what order in which to do it. Although some people wrote their own programs, most packages were written by trained programmers employed by software corporations.

The computer software market fell into three major categories: operating systems, languages, and applications software. Application software encompassed those programs which performed an application-related function on a computer. Some common uses of application software were managing home finances, word processing and creating databases.[2]

By 1986, the microcomputer software market had blossomed into a $5 billion industry, consisting of 14,000 companies and 27,000 different products.[3] The question facing the industry became: How many of these companies, some very tiny, would survive in this highly competitive market? In 1985, 23 small software companies were bought out; in 1986, this number increased to 57.[4]

The customer had undergone changes as well. Prior to 1986, typical software consumers were individuals who used PCs at home and occasionally at work. The new customers were corporate clients interested in tying their computers into information networks, and they were a tough sell. As G. M. K. Hughes, vice president of systems and communications at Pfizer Pharmaceuticals, said, "The package has got to be from someone reputable, it's got to be bug-free, the manual's got to be good, and it's got to be teachable."[5] By mid-1989, the PC software market had grown to a $9 billion industry with 65% of all software being purchased by corporate clients.[6]

By early 1989, it was obvious that the software industry was experiencing difficulties. First, market analysts and consumers were wearying with the industry's tendency to promote "vaporware"—programs promised but not delivered. This problem was twofold: (1) companies frequently promised product features that they were eventually unable to develop, and (2) several of the large companies had encountered as many as three lengthy delays before a product was finally released.[7] These delays were doubly costly, because they gave smaller competitors a chance to gobble up precious market share. Second, investors had been burned on software stocks, which tended to be highly volatile. A missed deadline could send a software company's stock into a tailspin, as Microsoft's founder William Gates discovered when he lost $174 million on paper in a single day.[8] Finally, as software companies fought to come up with bigger and more sophisticated products, development and testing became exceedingly expensive and time-consuming. Richard Shaffer, editor of *The Computer Letter,* compared the testing problem to, "writing *War and Peace* and having the entire book worthless if you have a comma out of place."[9] As a result of these factors, the software industry was forced to move away from its earlier trend of developing new and innovative programs toward an emphasis on reliability in product and delivery.

The software market began showing signs of a substantial slowdown in 1989. A trade group released figures showing PC software sales were up just 9% in the second quarter of 1989, down 41 points from the same period in 1988.[10] This slowdown was attributed to several factors. First, PC sales were slowing; predictions for the year ended July, 1990, showed only 10% growth, as compared to the 25% annual growth experienced in recent years. In addition, software companies had been slow to adapt their software to OS/2, a new operating system developed jointly by IBM and Microsoft. Finally, because of the premature announcements being made by companies concerning updates of existing products, many users were waiting for these new versions instead of purchasing those already on the shelves.[11]

The industry presented some bright spots, too. The European computer market, which lagged behind the U.S. in maturity, was an area of potential growth. Software that tied PCs to network systems was also showing tremendous growth. These markets combined would keep software sales growing; however, many analysts felt that the days of huge, double-digit growth in the PC software market were over.[12]

COMPANY HISTORY

Although Ashton-Tate (also referred to as A-T) is a relatively young company, its achievements in its eight-year history have been extraordinary. The company was founded in 1980 when George Tate and Hal Lashlee formed a partnership in order to market mail-order software; they called the company Software Plus.[13]

In the summer of 1980, the partnership acquired the exclusive rights to W. Wayne Ratliff's database program called Vulcan. Ratliff had been marketing the software himself through mail-order catalogs, but had been unable to respond to the resulting onslaught of orders. After purchasing Vulcan, Lashlee and Tate set out to market their product. They hired Hal Pawluk of Abert, Newhoff and Burr, a prestigious Los Angeles advertising company. Because of the immaturity of Lashlee and Tate's operation, Pawluk initially hesitated in taking the pair as clients, but was convinced, after trying the program, that they had a winner.

Pawluk's first act was to change the name of the program from Vulcan to dBASE II. "It was Britishy, and with the small 'd' and capital letters, it looked good in type," said Pawluk.[14] Although there was never a dBASE I, the use of the II implied an improved product. Pawluk also gave the company a new name: Ashton-Tate. dBASE II proved to be a huge success, and subsequent versions of this immensely popular program eventually drew over 3 million customers.[15]

But by 1985, A-T's management was able to see the dangers of remaining a one-product company, and embarked on a plan for long-term growth through product development and horizontal acquisition. A-T purchased Forefront Corporation and Multimate International Corporation in 1985, Decision Resources Inc. in 1986, and Ann Arbor Softworks in 1988. These acquisitions enabled A-T to enter new markets, and experience earnings growth. During the second quarter of 1986, A-T's earnings rose 87% over the same quarter of the year before, from $3.5 to $6.5 million. "Ashton-Tate has become more diversified and less dependent on revenue from any one product," said Michael Goulde of a Boston-based market research firm. "They have made some very smart acquisitions."[16] The company was the darling of Wall Street as its stock price soared.

In 1989, however, A-T's growth slowed as the company struggled to develop and release its latest database version, dBASE IV. The long-awaited update was released in January, 1989, and was, without question, flawed.[18] It was estimated that as many as 450,000 lines of dBASE IV's code contained as many as 100 "bugs"—a term used by programmers to define flaws—that caused problems with functions such as filesorting.[19] Denis Bellemare, a Montreal lawyer and dBASE user, said, "This program is nothing but a stick-up. It's so bug-ridden I can't use it."[20]

In addition, competition began to eat into A-T's database market share with faster and less expensive dBASE clones. Although the U.S. PC database market grew almost 200% between 1985 and 1988, A-T saw its share of that market cut by a third. In 1988, Ashton-Tate held 45% of the U.S. PC database market, down from 68% in 1985.[21] Although no one company gained the share lost by A-T, all competitors benefitted from the company's stalled sales.

As the company's reputation as a developer slipped, so did the price of its stock. It appeared that the stock was driven down by the market's perception as much as by slowing sales growth. By October, 1989, A-T's stock price had dropped to less than $10 per share, down from $27 per share just a year and a half earlier.

THE ORGANIZATION

Management

Ashton-Tate differentiated itself immediately upon its entrance into the software market. Its management philosophy was based on high quality, and customer service activities including discounts, timely deliveries, and toll-free assistance numbers.

Management experts outline three key management phases in a high-tech company. Initially, the company is run by the scientist-engineer who develops the product, then by the entrepreneur who markets the product, and finally, by a professional manager who takes over as the highflier matures.[22] A-T's management progression clearly parallels these three phases. Phase 1 ended when W. Wayne Ratliff, the developer of the program that would later become dBASE II, sold the program to George Tate and Hal Lashlee. As entrepreneurs already established in the software mail-order business, Tate and Lashlee entered Phase 2.

Hal Pawluk, an executive at the first advertising company employed by A-T, stated that George Tate's marketing savvy was the real secret to the company's success.[23] Tate himself elaborated on his competitors' weaknesses, "they lose touch with what they're doing and selling, and they forget all about the customer."[24]

While the early years were characterized by what Tate described as a "seat-of-the-pants" management approach, Tate recognized that a professional manager would be required to direct the rapidly growing company.[25] With the appointment of David Cole as Chief Executive Officer in 1982, the company entered Phase 3 in the management evolution. Cole's background in the study of corporations and management, as well as his practical expertise at CBS, Prentice-Hall, and management consulting, gave him the credentials Tate wanted in a successor.[26] By the time George Tate died in August, 1984, at the age of 40, he had little involvement in the day-to-day operations of Ashton-Tate.[27]

David Cole was described as charismatic and entrepreneurial, but lacking the ability to create a stable, well-organized operation.[28] Cole left abruptly in 1984 to pursue other interests, and was replaced by Edward M. Esber, Jr. "The Harvard MBA replaced Cole's flamboyant, one-man rule with a lower-key, participatory approach."[29] Esber also implemented formalized planning, budgeting, product development, and frequently scheduled meetings.

At the time of Esber's installment in 1984, observers had written A-T off as just another one-product company that couldn't come up with an encore. And Esber, virtually unknown in the industry, did not seem the likely candidate to turn the company around. But Esber proved both supporters and skeptics wrong. He installed a new management system, and made plans for lessening the company's reliance on its database management program, dBASE II, which accounted for over half of the firm's revenues in 1984.[30]

On November 1, 1986, Luther Nussbaum joined A-T as president. Nussbaum had over 15 years of management experience, including four years as a senior executive as Businessland, and was expected to bring added stability to the upper echelons of the company.[31] His appointment was critical to the rapidly growing company because it would allow Chairman and CEO Esber to spend more time on strategic planning. Esber was quoted as saying, "I wish he could start tomorrow . . . It frees me to deal with the demands and the job of building investor relationships, to work on mergers and acquisitions."[32] But many critics felt that Nussbaum's short stint at Businessland did not provide him with an in-depth knowledge of the industry, and that he had few marketing skills. One former A-T employee was quoted as saying, Nussbaum "is more of a listener than a strategy guy."[33]

Many employees hoped that Nussbaum would be able to make a difference; one executive who stayed on said, "He's saying the right things. He's making the action-oriented people smile again, and they haven't been smiling for a long time."[34] Some wondered if Chairman Esber and Roy E. Folk, executive vice president and general manager of A-T's Software Products Division, would allow the new president to be effective.[36]

With his new management in place, Esber embarked on the first long-term strategic planning the company had ever attempted. His plan was to make A-T a one-stop shopping center for applications software through diversification.[37] It was under his leadership that A-T made a series of acquisitions. Esber also increased the company's R&D budget, and A-T released new, improved versions of its database program. His greatest asset was that he always had one eye on the competition; he was once quoted as saying, "Just about the time you begin to believe you're Superman, the world's supply of kryptonite increases."[38]

But, changes in the upper echelons trickled down through the organization, and were less than positively perceived by A-T's employees. While the early days of A-T were described by former employees as entrepreneurial and exciting, by 1986, the adjectives "cautious" and "conservative" were more commonly used to describe the company.[39] According to Wayne Ratliff, the developer of dBase, who resigned in 1986, "Ashton-Tate is moving away from being a software business to becoming a business business. The company has been in a slow decline in its ability to create software because of its sheer mass. The people running the company don't seem to be creators or builders. They are managers and buyers."[40]

Esber shrugged off staff defections as a fact of life in the high-technology industry. When critics called him overly conservative, he denounced their label. "My MBA is a convenient label. If they want to call being held accountable for the responsibilities they have, the decisions they make, and the expectation to be good managers and do good jobs MBAness, then I'll be glad to have that label."[43]

Many observers believe that A-T's success could be directly attributed to Esber. "Esber almost single-handedly turned Ashton-Tate around since he became president and CEO. Ashton-Tate was a one-product company. Its dealers were mad because of its arrogance, its research and development was confused, and it didn't know who its users were," said Osman Eralp, a New York–based analyst with Hambrecht & Quist, Inc.[46] Esber has admitted to some personal pride in "transforming Ashton-Tate from a second-tier player into a well-respected first-tier player"; however, he preferred to dwell on the future.[47] "Five years from now, I want us to be the leading computer software, services, and information supplier in the business," says Esber. "As an industry, we need to be more innovative, to find new markets and new customer bases."[48]

Luther Nussbaum resigned as president and Chief Operating Officer on July 25, 1989. His resignation occurred simultaneously with Ashton-Tate's press release addressing the firm's $19.8 million net loss for the second quarter of 1989.

According to Esber, Nussbaum resigned over "differences in management philosophy."[49] Insiders said that Nussbaum was blamed for loading dBASE IV inventory, the company's latest database version, into retail channels.[50] Esber personally assumed the additional title and responsibilities of president with all staff reporting to him.

Organizational Structure

The company was incorporated in California in 1980. The firm's name was changed to "Ashton-Tate" in 1983, and changed again to the "Ashton-Tate Corporation" in October, 1986, at the time of its re-incorporation in Delaware.

By 1984, A-T had grown from a store-front operation to a company that was large enough to require a reorganization to improve the effectiveness of its operations. The company was split into three divisions: the Software Group, the International Division, and New Business Development. The Software Group accounted for 80% of the company's total revenues in 1984. The charter of the New Business group was to identify new products and markets. Anticipating a tremendous potential market overseas, the company chose to direct its efforts primarily on Western Europe and Asia.[52]

Due to the surge in acquisitions, the company saw the need to restructure again in 1988 with corporate operations grouped into product, function, and geographically based divisions. According to Esber, the "new organizational structure provides us with the flexibility and focus to manage today's business while preparing us for tomorrow's challenges."[53]

In July, 1989, A-T restructured again, forming an Applications group. This group was responsible for products other than dBASE, mainly A-T's Macintosh programs and PC applications, such as word processing and graphics. The new group was based in San Jose, California, and was headed by A-T vice president and general manager Bill Lyons, a former IBM executive.[54] As of March, 1989, A-T had a work force of approximately 1,460 employees worldwide.[55] Exhibit 1 displays an organizational chart.

FOREIGN OPERATIONS

Anticipating a tremendous potential in the world market, A-T entered the international market in 1982. Its international revenues increased 500% between 1984 and 1989.[56] The company had two territories, Europe and International. European operations included the European continent, North Africa, and the Middle East. International included the Pacific Rim—including Asia, Australia, and New Zealand—and Latin America.

EXHIBIT 1   Ashton-Tate organization chart

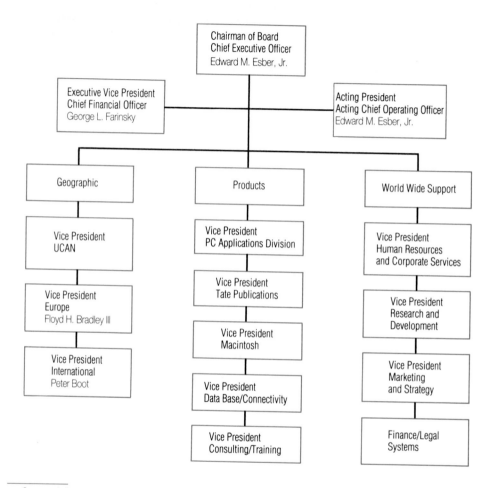

Source: A-T 1989 Annual Report

The European market was especially favorable to A-T because the company had strong marketing links with companies such as the U.K. Javelin Software Company and a French distributor, La Commande Electronique. A-T had five operating subsidiaries and two major distributors in Europe. The opening of the European Manufacturing Facility in Dublin, Ireland, in 1988 was an important step in the company's efforts to maximize production control and efficiency in Europe.[57] During 1988, active marketing and distribution campaigns for dBASE, Framework, and MultiMate were launched in France, U.K., Spain, Germany, and Amsterdam.

In the international arena, A-T operated six subsidiaries and 16 master distributors, and offered a full range of software products. The company began building a manufacturing plant in Singapore, which it hoped to complete in 1990. Peter Boot, vice president of International, called the Pacific Rim, "a hotbed of activity in 1989."[58] Operations also commenced in Japan, New Zealand, Taiwan, Korea, and China. According to Boot, "Long before the turn of the century, A-T's international revenues will contribute significantly to its success."[59] Exhibit 2 displays a breakdown of A-T's U.S. and foreign revenue percentages.

EXHIBIT 2   A-T U.S./foreign breakdown of revenue percentages

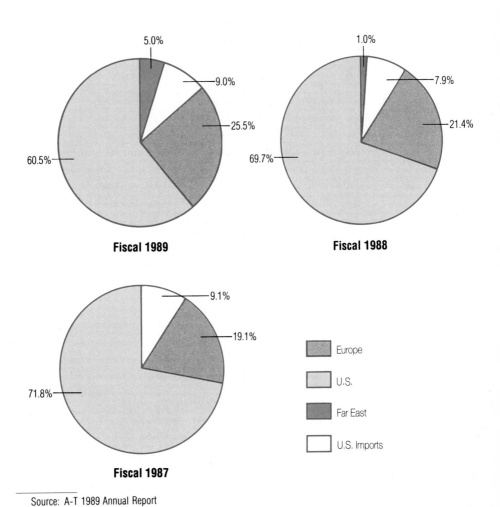

Fiscal 1989

Fiscal 1988

Fiscal 1987

Europe
U.S.
Far East
U.S. Imports

Source: A-T 1989 Annual Report

A-T experienced tremendous success in marketing its product in Japan by drawing on its successes in the United States. When it introduced dBASE in Japan, it positioned it to compete with a single product called Condor. By undercutting Condor in price, and promoting dBASE as a reliable and popular program, A-T was able to snatch a substantial portion of the Japanese database market. A 1984 distribution agreement with the IBM 5550 series of computers gave the product additional legitimacy.[60]

Although the foreign market was very appealing, a menace threatened to destroy U.S. software foreign marketing attempts: piracy—the illegal copying of software. As early as 1986, Ronald S. Posner, Executive Vice President, Sales and International, stated, "The rampant international piracy of software could become one of the most serious trade problems faced by the U.S."[61] Actions have been taken to thwart this problem such as trade legislation, U.S./foreign governmental cooperation and policy-making, and educational seminars. Whether this dilemma will be resolved remains to be seen.

ACQUISITIONS AND MERGERS

Ashton-Tate accumulated many of its products through the acquisition of the firms that developed and introduced them. Building a unified product line through acquisition enables a company to shorten development time, and bring in a fresh crop of technical resources, according to Roy Folk, former executive vice president and general manager of A-T's Software Products Division.[62]

In July, 1985, Ashton-Tate acquired Forefront Corporation, a microcomputer software development company in Sunnyvale, California, that was primarily responsible for designing Framework and Framework II. Framework is A-T's integrated database, word-processing, spreadsheet, and telecommunications package.

When Ashton-Tate purchased Connecticut-based Multimate International Corporation in December, 1985, it marked the beginning of a new age for the firm.[63] The purchase represented the largest deal ever in the microcomputer software industry, and the merging of two financially sound companies. Multimate, which was a privately held company, had become a $21 million business within the two years since its founding. In addition, Multimate was extremely profitable; it had profits of $2 million during the second quarter of 1985—just under A-T's $2.35 million—on sales that were one-third as great.[64]

This acquisition extended A-T's reach beyond the database market into the area of word processing with the Multimate Professional Word Processor package. Not only did it boost A-T's revenues by $21 million, but it gave the California-based Ashton-Tate added national presence in the market. According to InfoCorp, the acquisition was expected to bring Ashton-Tate products' total dollar market share to 13% from its previous 10%.[65] In 1985, Lotus still topped the list with a 22% dollar share of the U.S. software market.[66]

Continuing its aggressive expansion of its product line through acquisition, Ashton-Tate announced in October, 1986, that it had purchased Decision Resources Inc. (DRI) for $13 million in cash. At A-T's annual shareholders meeting, company president Esber described the Connecticut graphics software firm as the "obvious choice . . . an overall good fit" with A-T.[67] Esber was further quoted as saying that DRI was twice the size of its nearest competitor, and was a leading brand-name product choice of many Fortune 500 companies. In addition, Esber felt the personalities and cultures of the two companies matched well.[68]

In reaction to Esber's announcement, market analysts said they did not expect A-T's stock to be affected, nor were they anticipating unusually rapid growth in the business graphics market during 1987 and 1988. According to California market researcher Info-Corp, the business graphics market was valued at approximately $57.8 million in 1986, and was expected to grow to about $78.6 million by 1988. DRI's 1986 sales were $13 million, or about a 22.5% share of the market.[69] A-T's immediate interest was to concentrate on DRI's international sales, which represented about 5% of the company's 1986 business.[70]

DRI's business graphic line included Chart-Master, Diagram-Master, Sign-Master, and Map-Master; A-T intended to retain these names, but package the products with the A-T logo. Esber also stated that he intended to maintain DRI's Connecticut facilities and its 109 employees.[71]

In January, 1988, Ashton-Tate acquired Ann Arbor Softworks, a small, privately owned Macintosh software developer. A-T said it would release several new products to compete directly with Mac products offered by Microsoft, the leading developer of Macintosh applications. A-T and Microsoft were expected to compete in two main areas: word processing and spreadsheets. Ann Arbor, of Newbury Park, Ca., posted 1986 revenues of $2.1 million on sales of FullPaint, its Mac graphics program.[72] A complete listing of A-T's acquisitions appears in Exhibit 3.

EXHIBIT 3   **Ashton-Tate acquisitions**

July 1985	Forefront Corporation Products: Framework, Framework II, integrated business software
December 1985	Multimate International Products: Multimate word processing package
October 1986	Decision Resources Products: Chart-master, Diagram-Master, Sign-Master, Map-Master
January 1988	Ann Arbor Softworks Products: Macintosh applications—graphics, word processing

Source: A-T 1989 10-K

MARKETING

Product Development

Critics had long said that Ashton-Tate lacked the technical vision to maintain its No. 3 ranking in the PC software industry.[73] A-T put a great deal of money and manpower into acquiring its products and selling them through elaborate packaging and advertising; the result was that its reputation as a strong marketing company grew. But at the same time, A-Y cultivated a reputation for being weak in research and development. This image was reinforced by the company's lack of investment in R&D, and the fact that its dBASE product was updated only three times in eight years.[74]

Another growing concern was that A-T's dBASE updates did not meet the needs of its users. Both dBASE III and dBASE III PLUS contained flaws that frustrated developers and alienated corporate users, who did not have the time or the inclination to debug an off-the-shelf product. It became apparent that the company had stopped listening to, or perhaps stopped hearing, its customers.[75]

In September, 1986, A-T held its first Developers Conference. A vocal and frustrated audience of MIS managers and corporate programmers complained about A-T's support programs, long product development cycle, the company's failure to understand how its products were being used, and its unwillingness to listen to its customers' needs.[76] For some time, A-T's response to complaints and requests from customers had frequently been similar to an early quote by dBASE's developer, Wayne Ratliff, "dBASE wasn't meant to be used that way."[77]

Sometime during the two years before the next conference, Ashton-Tate's management understood that it needed a shift in its collective attitude. Chairman and CEO Esber kicked off the October, 1988, conference, dubbed the Meeting of the Minds II, by promising that the company's previous "see-no-evil, hear-no-evil, speak-no-evil" philosophy was a thing of the past.[78] He admitted that A-T had not listened well enough to the dBASE user, and confessed to turning away from users' requests for features and improvements. Esber was openly apologetic, "We're sorry. We made a mistake."[79] The audience ate it up. It was clear that A-T's intent was to reclaim the loyalty of the dBASE community, and that it aimed to become a major player in the database market for computers of all sizes: minicomputers, PCs, and mainframes.[80] A-T also organized an advisory panel of business users on new developments for the dBASE language, and its members felt the company was taking their suggestions seriously.[81]

The disaster that resulted from the release of dBASE IV in 1989 forced Esber to reexamine the company's product development process. Until 1989, A-T's engineers only hunted for bugs after an entire program was written. With dBASE IV, the process was further complicated by an unwieldy development crew of 75.[82] Because of the pressure to get the product to market, serious bugs were allowed to slip through. In July, 1989, then-President Nussbaum announced that, in the future, code would be checked throughout the entire development process, as individual sections of the program were written. The belief was that this would prevent the crash debugging that was performed on dBASE IV. Esber added that the company would not compound its past mistakes by shipping future products until after they had been properly tested.[83]

Products

As the nation's third largest independent software producer, A-T was the leading publisher of microcomputer database management systems.[84] After its various acquisitions, the company began to offer a full range of competitive products in the areas of word processing, desktop publishing, graphics, and other multifunctional software for personal computers. Exhibit 4 shows the product lines offered by Ashton-Tate.

Ashton-Tate began operations with a database product. A database allows the user to create files in which information can be stored, and subsequently retrieved. Although criticized for its difficulty in operating, dBASE II's flexible language programming capabilities attracted a large following of loyal users. Many liked dBase II because it was more powerful and flexible than Basic and Cobol, and allowed database applications to be built more quickly.[85] To insure dBASE II's position in this growing market, and to satisfy the strong demand for versatility and flexibility, A-T introduced several revised versions of the original dBASE II, including dBASE III and dBASE III PLUS.

Framework, a powerful integrated program, was introduced in July of 1984. But when Ashton-Tate postponed shipment of Framework in order to make additional enhancements, they lost multitudinous sales to Symphony, a similar program that Lotus introduced at the same time. Industry analysts estimated that Symphony was outselling Framework 16 to 1 in late 1984.[86] A-T responded to poor sales by announcing enhancements to the Framework program. These changes included allowing the program to run on the PC AT, and permitting it to run off a hard disk, without the use of floppies.

In 1988, Ashton-Tate developed Draw Applause, a presentation graphics software program specifically designed for IBM's PS/2. This product was devised for the more sophisticated user, and was compatible with its dBASE III PLUS. Draw Applause was developed by A-T's Graphics Development Center, formerly Decision Resources.[87] The package offered special effects such as modem transmission, a file-management library, and the easy importation of Lotus 1-2-3 files. The product was targeted at salespeople because of its ability to create business presentation visuals and art.

In early 1988, A-T introduced three major software packages for the Apple Macintosh. FullWrite Professional, a complete Macintosh word-processing program was first shipped in April, 1988. It combined the functionality of a full-featured word processor with the features of desktop publishing and graphics products.[88] Full Impact, a powerful spreadsheet package, was introduced in July,

EXHIBIT 4   Ashton-Tate products/prices

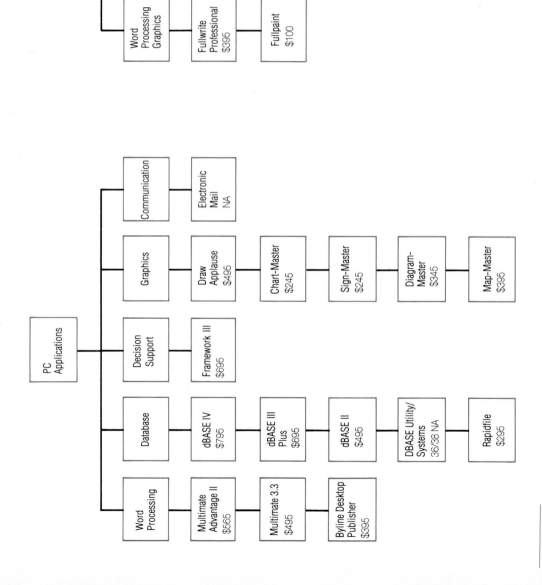

Source: A–T Product Catalog, Fall 1988

1988, and was a presentation spreadsheet for the Macintosh. It combined full spreadsheet capabilities with high-level graphics, presentation capabilities, and word processing.[89] dBASE Mac and dBASE Mac Run Time were database management systems designed to suit the special functions of the Macintosh.[90]

In 1988, A–T released Multimate Advantage II, a full-function word-processing software firmly rooted in the typewriter world.[91] It is designed as a sophisticated, but easy-to-use word processor made for dBASE users. Multimate Advantage II proved to be a major upgrade of the best-selling, but aging word-processing package, Multimate Professional Writer.

In 1988, A–T and Microsoft Corporation formed a joint venture to develop a software program called SQL (Structure Query Language). SQL provides an off-the-shelf solution to Local Area Network (LAN) relational database management. The strengths of SQL are its fast response time, exhaustive data security functions, and advanced networking support with OS/2 and LAN managers.[92] It can offer the user a cost effective alternative to minicomputers and mainframes for departmental applications.

In January, 1989, following two lengthy delays, A–T released dBASE IV version 1.0. The product came on 14 disks with 1,570 pages of documentation contained in 10 manuals.[93] The program was larger than its predecessors in that it required 640k bytes and a hard disk drive. The number of fields per record were increased from 128 to 255, the field and command line length were increased, and the number of memory variables was raised.[94]

In mid-1989, A–T announced a new product strategy for its dBASE IV version, 1.1; the new version was to be offered in two separate forms. Version 1.1 (Plain) would work on small machines (640k memory), and Version 1.1 (Server) would work only on larger machines with 1MB (Megabyte) memory or more. The purpose of this multiple release strategy was to better meet A–T's customers' needs, and to ensure that the low-end product would not be held up by bugs on the more complicated SQL Server Connection program.[95]

In mid-1989, Esber also announced plans to develop an easy-to-use version of dBASE for those PC users who were intimidated by the complexity of dBASE IV. By 1990, he also hoped to introduce "Ashton-Tate Office," a software package that would use dBASE to trade information with other A–T products such as word processors and graphics programs. Industry analysts were not overly impressed. "It's an elegant strategy, but Ashton-Tate's competitors are pursuing it, too," said Richard G. Sherlund of Goldman, Sachs & Co.[96]

Product Support

During the summer of 1986, A–T split its resources into two areas: a software products division, and a systems, service, and information division, which was created to handle customer support and training services. The first phase of the support and service program was launched during the fall of that year. It offered a variety of support plans for individual users, priced from $50 to $150 annually, and for large corporations, priced at $4,000 annually. In addition, the company sought to, "create an ongoing revenue stream through maintenance contracts," according to Ray Posner, the executive vice president and general manager in charge of the new division.[97] Users were given until December, 1986, to decide whether or not they planned to participate; at that time, free support expired. Customer response was mixed. Bob Merkel, a product engineer at Professional Control Corp., said, "We will never pick it up. The frustration for most users of waiting on the phone puts a bad taste in your mouth. When they come up with a pay plan, it is kind of a slap in the face."[98] CEO Esber dismissed talk of user displeasure, "We're trying to take people from nothing—paying no money for unlimited lifetime support—and if it was a penny a call, it would upset some people." By December, 1986, the new program had only 30 subscribers.[99]

Ashton-Tate's program was different from those of other software companies in that it charged one price for all support functions instead of letting users select the options that best addressed their individual needs.[100] Due to the lukewarm reception the new pay-for-support plan received, President Nussbaum announced that the company was considering offering the various options as separate units.

Instead, in November, 1987, the company modified its plan by offering a multiuser electronic bulletin board service that provided free technical support to any microcomputer user. The service, called Ashton-Tate Support BBS, promised to answer all queries within 24 hours. The bulletin board was not expected to replace the pay-for-support plan, but it was hoped that it would relieve users' concerns. Richard Goepel, manager of A-T's support product center said, "From a customer goodwill point of view, it's a good move."[101]

In December, 1988, the company announced plans to air the first batch of user-reported quirks in dBASE IV, along with suggested solutions on major electronic bulletin boards.[102]

Promotions

In the mid-1980s, changes took place in the software industry. As Jim Manzi of Lotus Corporation put it, "The days of writing a hit program, dumping it into distribution, and making an instant killing are over."[103] Many larger software companies began luring executives from consumer goods companies by offering them generous stock options. In 1984, Ashton-Tate brought in David Hull, from Carnation, to market their database programs. The hope was that these marketers would teach high-tech companies to sell their software as a consumer product instead of as a technological wonder.[104]

Part of A-T's strength lay with its success in developing good relations with its retailers; the company protected its distribution channels by not competing with them. While other large companies, such as Lotus, zeroed in early on direct sales, A-T worked to achieve dealer loyalty. With tens of thousands of software packages on the market, the ability to encourage retailers to push a product made a tremendous difference.[105] Ashton-Tate provided its dealers and distributors with technical assistance and merchandising aids that included brochures, point-of-purchase displays, and other promotional items. In addition, the firm furnished product and sales training manuals, conducted seminars and promotions, and engaged in various forms of advertising with its dealers and distributors.[106]

To encourage distributor goodwill, Ashton-Tate allowed its dealers, within limits, to return old products in exchange for new ones. The terms of these exchanges varied according to the type of exchange. Consumers were allowed to return products within three days of purchase, or within 90 days for warranty claims.[107] In addition, consumers were often permitted to "trade-up"; that is, to exchange old software for newer versions for a very minimal fee. In 1988, many distributors offered free upgrades to dBASE IV for customers who bought dBASE III PLUS.[108]

In 1989, the software war became more intense, as the top three companies, Ashton-Tate, Lotus, and Microsoft, all tried to buy their way into the hearts of retailers. Each kicked off new marketing programs to provide incentives to both retailers and their own salespeople with the hopes of building software brand loyalty. A-T initiated a $3 million sales promotion to increase dBASE IV sales.[109] Called the Technical Knockout Campaign, it was made available through A-T's 5,000 dealers. The campaign included financial incentives of up to $50 to salespeople in the form of bonuses for each software package sold.[110] Customers were also included in this campaign; one sweepstakes offered a trip to Las Vegas for the Leonard-Hearns fight. "We wanted a hard-hitting campaign that got rid of the fear, uncertainty and doubt that some people have about dBase IV 1.0," said Joseph Brilando, A-T's vice president of corporate marketing and strategy.[111] Jeffrey Tarter, editor of an industry newsletter called *Soft-Letter,* said that these financial incentives only increased market share temporarily. He added that marketing dollars could be more effectively spent by breaking open new niche markets. "Companies overrate the effectiveness of market-development funds," he said. "They're not addressing the real issues, like lack of interest by customers in the channel itself, or problems like channel-stuffing."[112]

One market that began to attract the attention of the big software companies in mid-1989 was the small business user. These customers had historically been ignored because of the difficulty encountered in creating and marketing software for them. But as other markets became saturated, it became more apparent that these customers might represent software's last big frontier. In September, 1989, it was estimated that only 50% of America's five million small companies were computerized.[113] However, selling to these consumers presented an enormous challenge. Microsoft's Mike Slade said that in small business, "people are impatient. They don't have much time, they're price-sensitive, and they're fairly new to computing."[114] In order to overcome these obstacles and attract these customers, A-T took to direct-mail pitches, better distribution methods, and the education of its sales force and distributors.[115]

A-T's first magazine ad was a bold and daring concept. The headline stated "dBASE II vs. The Bilge Pump." The ad continued,

> We all know that bilge pumps suck, and by now, we have found out—the hard way—that a lot of software seems to work the same way.[116]

Ashton-Tate welcomed the resounding response. As Pawluk stated, "The noise in the computer business was pretty high; you had to grab their attention."[117] In 1982, Tate came up with the idea of floating a helium-filled blimp labeled "dBASE II" through a Las Vegas computer convention. Everyone agreed that this crazy campaign was attracting attention to the tiny company.

A-T continued to use print advertising. Historically, software marketers used only computer periodicals for print ads, but in the late 1980s, the emphasis turned away from these advertisement-laden magazines toward business periodicals and newspapers. The purpose was to target those who may be making the purchasing decision for the office. However, computer periodicals continued to provide a source of inexpensive advertising, and advertisers still believed that most consumers consulted these magazines just before making a purchase.[118]

In 1984, A-T raised the eyebrows of many by running the first television advertisements used in the micro software industry to promote its Framework package. The company purchased nearly $4 million of local and cable television time during the July, 1984, Democratic Convention and the 1984 Olympics in Los Angeles. The first ad was high-tech, featuring a threesome walking through the mist. Upon reaching their destination, they paused, while an ominous voice boomed, "Framework—for thinkers."[119] The ad campaign was designed by Dancer, FitzGerald, and Sample, creators of the "Where's the beef" campaign for Wendy's.[120] Because explaining the product in a 30-minute spot was impossible, the ads went for a dramatic effect. The reviews of Ashton-Tate's TV advertising were mixed; many shareholders argued that it was a waste of their money, and marketers of other software products agreed. But Marty Mazner, director of the Framework marketing efforts for A-T, said, "TV today—because there are very few software ads—is a very quick and valuable way to build image and confidence."[121]

In 1988 and 1989, much effort was put forth by software companies to increase their name recognition among consumers. The intention was to make their products the ones consumers asked for when they wanted a word-processing program or a graphics package. Massachusetts-based International Data Corp., a market research firm, estimated that the typical buyer considers a software purchase for months, and visits a computer store as many as five times during that period.[122] This name recognition didn't come cheaply; the result for many software companies was that marketing costs—advertising, promotion, sales support, and distribution—became their single largest expense.

Distribution

In early 1984, A-T underwent a tremendous reorganization, realigning itself as a market-driven company. It created one of the largest sales forces in the software industry. More than one-fourth of its 410 employees were in sales.[123]

In 1989, Ashton-Tate had 570 marketing, sales, and support personnel worldwide. This included a regional network in Canada and the U.S. of 107 field sales representatives and support personnel, located in eight metropolitan areas of the U.S., and offices in Toronto and Vancouver, Canada. The field sales group provided both distributors and dealers with training, technical assistance, and sales support.[124]

In the U.S. and Canada, there were two major distributors and approximately 15 major dealers of Ashton-Tate's products. A-T's two major distributors in the U.S. were Softsel Computer Products and Ingram Software Distribution Services. These distributors marketed A-T's products to its authorized dealers, and provided product support, merchandising aids and other support services. For the fiscal year ended January, 1989, Softsel accounted for 14%, and Ingram accounted for 8% of A-T's net revenues. All U.S. and Canada distributors accounted for a total of 22% of A-T's net revenues in 1989.[125]

A-T's 15 dealers were predominantly PC hardware and software retail stores. The majority of these 5,000 locations were national and regional chains and franchises such as Businessland, ComputerLand, Corporate Software, and Egghead Discount Software. Sales by authorized dealers accounted for approximately 28% of Ashton-Tate's net revenues for fiscal year 1989.[126]

In addition, A-T sold some of its products, primarily software upgrades and publications, directly to educational and other users. These direct sales accounted for approximately 8% of Ashton-Tate's net revenues during 1989.[127]

Original Equipment Manufacturers (OEMs) accounted for 3% of Ashton-Tate's net revenues during fiscal 1989. OEMs were primarily microcomputer manufacturers who offered A-T's products through the same distribution channels through which their own products were marketed. Ashton-Tate had such royalty agreements with a number of OEMs, including Tandy, Wang, Zenith, Hewlett-Packard, and AT&T.[128]

Other distribution points included Value-Added Remarketers (VARs); VARs contributed to sales by generating their own applications software by adding software enhancements to A-T's dBASE and Framework products. These VARs accounted for less than 1% of A-T's net revenues for fiscal 1989.[129]

In 1989, A-T had operations in ten foreign countries, including the U.K., West Germany and Japan. Each of these locations had field service and technical

personnel to support dealer and distributor sales in those and neighboring countries. These dealers and distributors serviced the principal worldwide markets for
A–T's products. In addition, A–T had OEM agreements with several international
companies, including IBM in Europe and the Far East. In 1989, foreign operations accounted for 30% of net revenues, and exports accounted for 9% of net
revenues.[130] Exhibit 5 shows the changes that occurred between 1988 and 1989 in
points of sale.

Pricing

Software is worth only what people are willing to pay for it. Over the years,
consumers were led to believe that full-function business packages should cost in
the range of $300 to $700, but the fact that sophisticated programs have been

EXHIBIT 5   **Ashton-Tate's points of sale, in millions**

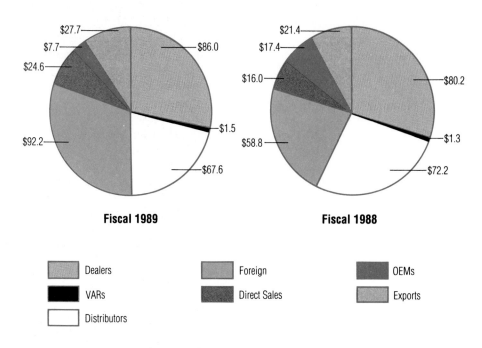

Source: A-T 1989 10K

successfully marketed at prices from $29.95 to $2,995 indicates that prices may often be irrelevant to actual development costs.[131]

In early 1986, A–T announced an increase in the wholesale prices of its entire line in an effort to raise the level of customer service and support provided by its distribution channels.[132] It was predicted that distributors would not accept a decrease in their profit margins, and that the cost to the end-user would eventually rise. Many felt that this "unbundling of support" merely represented a disguised price increase.[133]

To date, price competition has not been a major factor in the microcomputer software market. However, it may become a more significant factor in the future. Ashton-Tate's pricing policies have been fairly competitive in all the areas it serves.

EXHIBIT 6   **Ashton-Tate selected financial data (Ashton-Tate's fiscal year ending January 31st)**

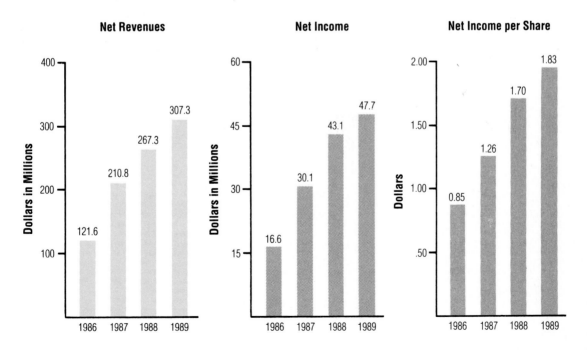

Source: A-T 1989 Annual Report

FINANCE

Until early 1989, Ashton–Tate was an extraordinary software company that grew by leaps and bounds, earning greater revenues each year. The company was taken public in November, 1983, with a $1.7 million stock offering and an average stock price of $14.[134] An additional stock offering was made in 1984. From 1984 to 1988, the company continued to experience revenue growth. Exhibit 6 shows net revenues, net income, and earnings per share for 1986 through 1989.

EXHIBIT 7   **Ashton-Tate sales by product line**

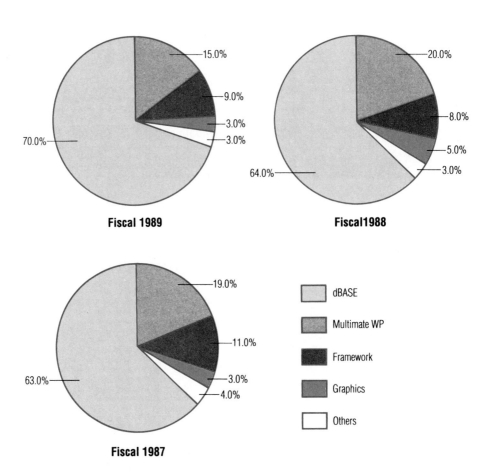

Fiscal 1989

Fiscal1988

Fiscal 1987

dBASE

Multimate WP

Framework

Graphics

Others

Source: Adapted from A-T Value Line, June 16, 1989

Source: Adapted from A-T Value Line, June 17, 1988

Source: Adapted from A-T Value Line, June 19, 1987

By 1989, the financial picture at A-T began to sour. The company incurred its first net loss ever in the second quarter of 1989 in the amount of $8.3 million.[135] The reasons cited by A-T's management included "reduced revenues, lagging dBASE IV sales, and increased competition."[136] The general consensus on Wall Street was that A-T's stock was only for patient investors with strong stomachs because "the depth of internal problems are [sic] great, inventories are excessively high in dealer channels, the dBASE IV release is a terrible product, and there are excessively high expense levels."[137] Exhibit 7 shows Ashton-Tate's revenues broken down by product line for 1988 and 1989.

As early as 1988, A-T began to exhibit a weakness in earnings in comparison to other software vendors. Ashton-Tate showed growth of only 9% during that year, compared to the 62.5% growth rate averaged by other PC software vendors during the same period.[138]

In spite of A-T's aggressive diversification attempts, dBASE continued to be the flagship that kept the company afloat. According to industry analysts, sales from dBASE rose from approximately 50% of sales in 1986 to a whopping 70–75% of total sales in 1988.[139]

A-T experienced an increase in revenues from exports and foreign sales from 28% of total revenues in 1987, to 39.5% of total revenues in 1989.[140] Foreign operating income rose from 26% of total operating income in 1988 to 38.5% of total operating income in fiscal 1989.

A-T invested heavily in research and development during 1988, with R&D costs rising from 13% to 17% of total revenues between fiscal 1988 and fiscal 1989.[141] According to Edward Esber in his 1989 annual shareholders' letter, "Last year was a year of research and development, planning and rationalization of our worldwide manufacturing activities, while calendar 1989 will be a year of sales and marketing."[142]

Like many growth companies, A-T never paid a dividend to its shareholders, but instead reinvested all net income in the firm. A-T was able to finance working capital and capital expenditures from internally generated funds, facilities, and equipment leases, and public stock offerings. As of January 31, 1989, A-T had a $35 million unused line of credit, and $109.4 million in cash and short-term investments.[143]

In early 1989, at least two industry veteran CEOs on the West Coast were contacted be entrepreneurs interested in brokering an acquisition of A-T.[144] Based on its stock price, A-T was a bargain; its stock was hovering at around $23, a level at which analysts speculated that a takeover would be feasible. Estimates of its future cash flows put the value of the company at between $42 and $44 per share.[145]

In February, 1989, A-T announced the adoption of a shareholder rights program. A shareholder received one right for each common share held; that right would allow him to buy one share of common stock for $105 in the case that an outside group acquired a 15% stake in A-T. According to industry observers, this action might fend off the acquisition predators temporarily.[146] Financial statements are displayed in Exhibits 8 and 9.

EXHIBIT 8   Ashton-Tate consolidated balance sheets (in thousands, except share data)

	6 mos. ended June 30, 1989	Jan. 1, 1989	Jan. 1, 1988
Assets			
Current assets:			
Cash and short-term investments (Note 2)	$ 89,035	$109,381	$117,640
Trade accounts receivable,			
less allowance for doubtful accounts of			
$3,032 and $4,002	40,790	70,695	58,417
Inventories (Note 3)	26,712	25,092	8,171
Prepaid expenses and other (Note 9)	9,670	9,327	4,957
Total current assets	$166,207	214,495	189,185
Property and equipment (Note 4)	50,690	44,570	18,053
Product rights (Note 1)	32,831	41,916	39,899
Other	7,242	4,510	2,606
Total assets	$256,970	$305,491	$249,743
Liabilities and stockholders' equity			
Current liabilities:			
Accounts payable:	$ 20,697		
Trade	—	$ 22,362	$ 16,996
Other (Note 12)	—	—	5,750
Accrued payroll and related taxes	6,689	8,987	8,606
Current portion of capital lease obligations	2,161	2,080	2,418
Income taxes payable (Note 9)	2,282	20,308	17,287
Cooperative advertising	—	4,644	5,344
Other	10,826	5,477	6,642
Total current liabilities	$ 42,655	63,858	63,043
Capital lease obligations	3,479	3,569	5,502
Other long-term liabilities	4,474	4,606	2,113
Total liabilities	$ 50,608	72,033	70,658
Commitments and contingencies			
Stockholders' equity			
Common stock: par value, $0.01 per share,			
issued and outstanding 25,706,000 and			
24,768,000 shares, respectively	258	257	248
Additional paid-in capital	87,160	84,427	72,219
Retained earnings	122,200	151,167	103,412
Cumulative foreign currency translation	(296)	1,102	3,740
adjustment			
Employee notes receivable	(2,960)	(3,495)	(534)
Total stockholders' equity	206,362	233,458	179,085
Total liabilities and stockholders' equity	$256,970	$305,491	$249,743

Source: A-T 1989 Annual Report and A-T Form 10-Q for quarterly period ended June 30, 1989.

EXHIBIT 9   **Ashton-Tate consolidated statements of income (in thousands, except per share data)**

	6 mos. ended June 30, 1989	Jan. 31, 1989	Jan. 31, 1988	Jan. 31, 1987
Net revenues	$149,292	$307,283	$267,328	$210,799
Operating costs and expenses:				
Cost of revenues	31,424	47,839	39,684	33,362
Research and development	32,569	52,863	35,463	25,670
Sales and marketing	48,984	79,889	64,697	49,491
Administrative and general	35,505	58,762	54,547	45,848
Total operating costs and expenses	148,482	239,353	194,391	154,371
Operating income	810	67,930	72,937	56,428
Interest income	4,008	6,364	5,162	2,577
Interest expense	(460)	(839)	(1,123)	(844)
Special charges (note 4)*	(11,136)			
Income before provision for income taxes (Loss)	(6,778)	73,455	76,976	58,161
Provision for income taxes	1,500	25,700	33,900	28,061
Net income (Loss)	$ (8,278)	$ 47,755	$ 43,076	$ 30,100
Net income per share (Loss)	$ (.31)	$1.83	$1.70	$1.26
Weighted average outstanding shares	26,381	26,158	25,338	23,902

*Note 4. Special Charges: During the quarter ended June 30, 1989, the Company wrote-off certain product rights and inventories valued at $11.1 million, principally related to the Decision Resources product line which it acquired in 1986.

Source: A-T 1989 Annual Report and A-T Form 10-Q for quarterly period ended June 30, 1989.

COMPETITIVE ENVIRONMENT

Domestic Competition

Since 1987, Ashton-Tate has faced increasing competition in the area of PC-based database management systems (DBMS). Oracle System's Oracle, R-Base by Microrim, Foxbase by Fox Software, Borland International's Paradox, and

Nantucket's Clipper are just a few of the resourceful DBMS packages with which A-T's databases competed. Most recently, Cullinet Software, Inc., Lotus Corporation, and Microsoft Inc. have joined the race to produce DBMS systems. Even IBM, the supreme computer heavyweight, has introduced a less sophisticated PC DBMS product. To add further competitive pressures, small, upstart software companies may develop and introduce breakthrough DBMS products that could completely change the nature of the current DBMS market.

Larry Foster, a senior vice president at Egghead Discount Software, said that once, "people would automatically ask for dBASE. Now, customers are open to other products."[147] Borland, in the No. 2 spot with 7.3% of the database market, expects unit sales of its Paradox program to more than double in 1989 to 150,000 units.

In addition, technological innovations are giving competitors a boost. FoxPro, Fox's newest database, performs up to eight times faster than dBASE, in some benchmark tests. Nantucket's Clipper is easier to customize than dBASE for handling specialized filing and sorting jobs. Nantucket claims to have 175,000 regular customers, and expects its sales to increase 20% in fiscal 1990, to $24 million. Even less sophisticated products such as Symantec's Q&A and Software Publishing Company's Professional File sold nearly 160,000 units combined in 1988.[148]

The competitive environment for DBMS systems turned decidedly nasty in 1988, and A-T began playing competitive hardball. Heated criticisms were exchanged by A-T and Oracle Systems Corporation's management as dBASE IV and Oracle fought for market dominance.[149] Ashton-Tate became more outspoken in attacking its competitors' products and in claiming its exclusive rights to the dBASE technology. Roy Folk, executive VP at Ashton-Tate, was quoted as calling Oracle's database product, "not fully compatible, and old and tired."[150]

In July, 1989, Techtel Corp., a California-based marketing research firm conducted a survey of between 700 and 900 corporate and institutional buyers. According to the survey, only 54.1% of those with any opinion about dBASE IV had a positive opinion about the product. This represented a substantial drop from dBASE's 68.4% positive rating in April, 1989, and an even larger drop from its July, 1988, positive rating of 76.2%.[151] In contrast, Borland's Paradox's ratings remained consistently high, as did ratings for Microrim's R-Base.[152]

In 1984, A-T introduced Framework, its multifunction package, to compete directly with Lotus Corporation's Symphony.[153] Other contenders in this market included IBM, Software AG, and Management Sciences American, Inc. A-T did not enjoy the success in this market that it did in the DBMS market. Although Framework II and Framework III accounted for nearly 19% of all PC integrated software sales in 1988, Lotus continued to dominate the multifunction business software market.[154]

The graphics market was an equally difficult one for Ashton-Tate to penetrate. Shortly after its introduction, Draw Applause received a "Best Buy" rating from *PC Week* in October, 1988.[155] But by October, 1989, *PC Week* readers rated A-T's Draw Applause 1.1 in last place in a poll of eight popular graphics packages. Harvard Graphics and Lotus' Freelance Plus were the clear favorites among graphics package users.[156]

In the word-processing market, A-T faced a multitude of competitors. Although Multimate Advantage held a 10% market share of the word-processing market in 1988, this market was dominated by Microsoft's Word and WordPerfect Corporation's WordPerfect.[157] WordPerfect Corporation posed an additional threat; industry observers predicted that by the end of 1989, it would replace A-T as the third largest independent software manufacturer.[158] WordPerfect's share of the word-processing market grew from 35% to nearly 60% between January, 1988, and September, 1989, and its 1989 second quarter revenues of $67 million topped those of A-T.[159]

Competition seemed more favorable in A-T's foreign markets. A-T had marketing and business links with European resellers and distributors for specific A-T products.[160] The European business communities clamored for state-of-the-art business software applications.

Japanese Competition

Lotus Development Corporation Chairman Jim Manzi told this joke at a recent industry conference, "While Americans, Canadians, and Europeans are busy trying to replicate the recent cold fusion experiment, the Japanese have announced that the fusion Hondas went out yesterday, the fusion Toyotas go out today, and the fusion VCRs will be ready for export tomorrow."[161] The threat of the Japanese in the area of software was quickly becoming a reality, especially to U.S. manufacturers who, in 1989, held a 70% share of the worldwide software market.[162] The Japanese were pouring billions of yen into basic software research, and were racing to produce packaged software to replace the custom software they have traditionally manufactured.

Despite these changing trends, however, many U.S. software executives were not overly concerned. A-T's Esber was quoted as saying, "So far I don't see the Japanese in my part of the software business."[164]

LEGAL ENVIRONMENT

In January, 1987, A-T filed a suit against Queue Associates, Inc., and Gary Balleisen, Queue's principal, contending that they, "intended to release products which would capitalize on the company's proprietary information improperly obtained by them."[165] Queue, in turn, countersued, "alleging breach of contract and seeking specific performance and damages."[166] Esber was not concerned and said, "We can only say heretofore, every one of the actions that have been resolved by the court have been resolved in Ashton-Tate's favor. It is clear that the courts have found significant merit to the charges we have brought in those cases."[167]

In late 1988, A-T shocked the PC software industry by suing dBASE cloner Fox Software, Inc., and its licensee, the Santa Cruz Operation, Inc., for copyright infringement. Ashton-Tate claimed that it legally owned the dBASE language, and that Fox had encroached on this ownership by manufacturing a software program almost identical to dBASE. This represented the first attempt in the personal computer software industry to copyright a language. In his 1989 letter to the shareholders, Esber said, "While we encourage the development of third party add-on software that complements dBASE products, we will exert every effort to prevent the copying of a product that we have developed through the reinvestment of vast amounts of funds which our stockholders have entrusted to our management. We will not allow other companies to capitalize on our development efforts to the detriment of our stockholders."[168]

Although no court had ever ruled that computer languages are protectable, there also existed no legal precedent to indicate that languages could not be safeguarded. In an interview in January, 1989, CEO Esber stated, "The language is ours. We created it. A minute part of it does include other public-domain software that, under law, we can incorporate."[169] To further complicate matters, dBASE author Wayne Ratliff claimed that dBASE was derived from a DBMS that is in the public domain and not proprietary to Ashton-Tate.[170] Esber's response to Ratliff's claim was that Ratliff had been paid handsomely for dBASE, between $15 and $20 million, and "I would be happy to take a refund if he is basically saying he took it."[171]

Fox Software President David Fulton believed the real motivation was to protect dBASE against FoxPro, which he claimed was technically superior to Ashton-Tate's product. Representatives of Fox also stated that A-T's long delay in actively protecting dBASE implied a license for use by such companies as theirs. Fox filed a countersuit denying A-T's claim and charging A-T with attempting to monopolize a market in which they already had a majority of the sales.[172]

The software industry as a whole faced an increasingly hostile legal climate in 1988 and 1989. By July, 1989, most of the large software companies faced lawsuits by shareholders, and in each case, the scenario was similar. A company announced lower than expected earnings and in response, its stock price dropped. Then shareholders sued, claiming that management should have informed them sooner that there was trouble on the horizon. High-tech companies were especially vulnerable to lawsuits because their earnings and stock prices tended to be volatile.[173]

Between June 15 and July 28, 1989, A–T and certain of its directors and managers were named as defendants in three separate lawsuits filed by shareholders. Each of the suits alleged material misstatements and omissions by company officers and directors concerning the firm's condition. Several of the officials named, including CEO Esber, sold shares of stock during the period that the suits alleged improper disclosures were made.[174] A–T maintained its innocence and stated that the claims were without merit. The case has since been settled for an undisclosed amount, with no admission of any wrongdoing.

A FINAL NOTE

As addressed earlier, sluggish sales of A–T's dBASE IV 1.0, released in late 1988, caused a tremendous reduction in cash flows, resulting in a $19.8 million loss for the second quarter of 1989. In October, 1989, the company reported a loss for the third quarter of $19.4 million, on revenues of $53.9 million.[175] In an effort to stem this financial slide, the company announced a significant reduction in its work force in September, 1989. Two hundred and fifty of the company's 1,700 employees worldwide were laid off, with sales, marketing, and administration being the key areas affected. Although these cutbacks were expected to cost the firm $6 million in severance, management anticipated annual savings of twice that amount on a long-term basis.[176]

In addition, Ashton-Tate announced plans to curtail a number of development projects in order to focus company resources after the employee cutbacks. "We have rethought our priorities," said CEO Esber. "Any nonstrategic products have been curtailed or eliminated."[177]

Finally, all signs indicated that the new dBASE IV Version 1.1 would not be ready for a 1989 fall release as had previously been announced. Industry observers felt that the new product would have to be shipped by the beginning of 1990 in order for A–T to remain competitive with such rivals as Borland International's Paradox. Esber, however, said, "We are out of the date business." The product will ship when it is ready."[178]

EPILOGUE

A loud voice over the PA system announced the library would be closing in 15 minutes. Mike closed the last of a large pile of periodicals piled on the table in front of him. After spending an entire afternoon reading, he was more confused than ever. How could a company that had started out so dynamically, with such a bright future ahead of it, have ended up in the predicament in which Ashton-Tate found itself?

Mike decided to go home with the information he had obtained about Ashton-Tate, and try outlining an internal and external analysis. He needed to organize his thoughts by determining the strengths and weaknesses, as well as the threats and opportunities that the company faced. Only then, he was convinced, would he be able to make a decision about his future with the company.

Bibliography

1. Pearce, John A., and Zahra, Shaker A., "The Microcomputer Industry," *An Industry Approach to Cases in Strategic Management,* 1989, p. 27.

2. Shelly, Gary, and Cashman, Thomas J., *Computer Fundamentals with Application Software,* 1986, p. 12.1.

3. Field, Anne R., and Harris, Catherine L., "Software: The Growing Gets Rough," *Business Week,* March 24, 1986, p. 128.

4. Ibid., p. 128.

5. Ibid., p. 128.

6. Cole, Patrick E., and Depke, Deidre A., "The Software Market Is Downright Mushy," *Business Week,* October 2, 1989, p. 98.

7. Schwartz, John, "Hard Times for Software," *Newsweek,* April 3, 1989, p. 42.

8. Ibid.

9. Ibid., p. 43.

10. Cole, Patrick E., and Depke, Deidre A., "The Software Market . . . ," p. 98.

11. Ibid.

12. Ibid.

13. Lynch, Mitchell, "The Wizardry of Ashton-Tate," *PC Magazine,* February 7, 1984, p. 179.

14. Ibid.

15. Cole, Patrick E., "dBASE IV Is a Godsend—to the Competition," *Business Week,* November 13, 1989, p. 102.

16. Maginnis, Minamary, "Diversification, dBASE III PLUS Boost Ashton-Tate Quarterly Revenue 87%," *Computerworld,* August 25, 1986, p. 110.

17. Cole, Patrick E., "dBugs in dBASE IV Spread to the Bottom Line," *Business Week,* July 17, 1989, p. 135.

18. Ibid.

19. Ibid.

20. Ibid.

21. Cole, Patrick E., "dBASE IV Is a Godsend . . . ," p. 102.

22. Lynch, "The Wizardry of Ashton-Tate," p. 180.

23. Ibid.

24. Ibid., p. 180.

25. Ibid.

26. Ibid.

27. "George Tate, Ashton-Tate Chairman, Co-Founder, PC Pioneer Dies at 40," *PC Week,* August 21, 1984, p. 62.

28. Ticer, Scott, "The Dark Horse Who Has Ashton-Tate Galloping Again," *Business Week,* February 10, 1986, p. 88.

29. Ibid.

30. Ibid.

31. Churbuck, David, "Ashton-Tate Announces New President; Chairman Esber to Focus on Planning," *PC Week,* October 14, 1986, p. 140.

32. Ibid.

33. Ibid.

34. Spector, Gregory, "Nussbaum Faces a Long List of Chores as A-T President," *PC Week,* January 27, 1987, p. 39.

36. Ibid.

37. Ticer, Scott, "The Dark Horse . . . ," p. 89.

38. Ibid.

39. From "Ashton-Tate Software Writers Exodus as Company Culture Changes," by David Churbuck, *PC Week,* October 28, 1986, p. 194. Published by Ziff-Davis Publishers.

40. Ibid.

43. Ibid.

46. Wood, Lamont, "Ashton-Tate Mines for Software Gems," *Computer Decisions,* June 30, 1986, p. 48.

47. Ibid.

48. Ibid.

49. Press release from Ashton-Tate dated July 25, 1989, p. 2.

50. Newsclip, "No Search for Nussbaum Successor," *ComputerWorld,* August 7, 1989, p. 8.

52. Horton, Cleveland, "Ashton-Tate Goal: Out-IBM IBM in Software," *Advertising Age,* November 26, 1984, p. 71.

53. Ashton-Tate's Annual Report, April 3, 1989, p. 5.

54. Newsclip, "Ashton-Tate Restructures, Forms Applications Group," *PC Week,* July 10, 1989, p. 11.

55. Form 10-K, Fiscal Year Ended January 31, 1989.

56. Ashton-Tate's Annual Report, April 3, 1989, p. 20.

57. Ibid.

58. Ibid., p. 24.

59. Ibid.

60. Stoll, Marilyn, "U.S. Computer Companies Must Meet Japanese on Their Terms, Study Says," *PC Week,* August 22, 1988, p. 96.

61. DeBakey, George T., and Posner, Ronald S., "Software Piracy Limits U.S. Export Growth," *Business America,* June 9, 1986.

62. Freedman, Beth, "The Search for Encores," *PC Week,* October 14, 1986, p. 47.

63. McEnaney, Maura, "Multimate Acquisition Leaves Some Execs' Futures Uncertain," *Computerworld,* February 10, 1986, p. 132.

64. Gillin, Paul, "Purchase of Multimate Boosts A-T's Market Position," *PC Week,* August 6, 1985, p. 111.

65. Ibid.

66. Ibid.

67. Spector, Gregory, "Ashton-Tate Buys Graphics Software Company for $13M," *PC Week,* August 12, 1986, p. 127.

68. Ibid.

69. Ibid.

70. Ibid., p. 131.

71. Ibid.

72. Lyons, Daniel J., "Database Allies, Now Mac Rivals," *PC Week,* February 16, 1988, p. 133.

73. Cole, Patrick E., "dBugs in dBASE IV . . . ," p. 135.

74. Strehlo, Christine, "Is Ashton-Tate Born Again?" *Personal Computing,* March, 1989, p. 71.

75. Ibid.

76. Liskim, Miriam, "A 'Meeting of the Minds,'" *Personal Computing,* December, 1988, p. 83.

77. Ibid.

78. Ibid.

79. Strehlo, Christine, "Is Ashton-Tate . . . ," p. 73.

80. Liskim, Miriam, "A 'Meeting' . . . ," p. 83.

81. Strehlo, Christine, "Is Ashton-Tate . . . ," p. 71.

82. Cole, Patrick E., "dBugs in dBASE IV . . . ," p. 135.

83. Ibid.

84. *Valueline,* September 1, 1989.

85. Ibid.

86. Horton, Cleveland, "Ashton-Tate Goal . . . ," p. 4.

87. Flynn, Mary Kathleen, "Ashton-Tate Debuts Graphics Package for PS/2," *Datamation,* February 15, 1988, p. 89.

88. Form 10-K, Fiscal Year Ended January 31, 1989, p. 2.

89. Ibid., p. 3.

90. Ibid.

91. Wood, Lamont, "Multimate Advantage II 1.0," *Byte,* May, 1988, p. 108.

92. Deagon, Brian, "A-T Shops New SQL Server to Resellers," *Electronic News,* May, 1989, p. 28.

93. Coffee, Peter C., "Ease, Speed or Power: dBASE IV Developers Must Choose One," *PC Week,* January 23, 1989, p. 5.

94. Lent, Anne Fischer, and Rubel, Malcolm, "dBASE IV: Setting the New Standards?" *Byte,* p. 102.

95. Kidder, Peabody, *Equity Research,* August 16, 1989, p. 2.

96. Cole, Patrick E., "dBugs in dBASE IV . . . ," p. 136.

97. Smith, Gina, "Ashton-Tate Service and Support: Too Soon to Measure Up," *PC Week,* January 27, 1987, p. 46.

98. Barney, Doug, and Watt, Peggy, "Support Program Debated," *Computerworld,* January 26, 1987, p. 37.

99. Smith, Gina, "Ashton-Tate Service . . . ," p. 46.

100. Bridges, Linda, and Freedman, Beth, "Ashton-Tate Acts to Revamp Stalled Corporate Service Plan," *PC Week,* January 27, 1987, p. 1.

101. Jones, Stephen, "Ashton-Tate Opens BBS for Users," *Computerworld,* November 23, 1987, p. 31.

102. Freedman, Beth, "Ashton-Tate to Address dBASE Quirks," *PC Week,* December 5, 1988, p. 5.

103. McComas, Maggie, "The Hard Sell Comes to Software," *Fortune,* September 17, 1984, p. 59.

104. Ibid.

105. Horton, "Ashton-Tate Goal . . . ," p. 71.

106. Form 10-K, Fiscal Year Ended January 31, 1989.

107. Ibid.

108. Lyons, Daniel J., "Ashton-Tate and Lotus Striving to Maintain Sales of Current Versions," *PC Week,* June 14, 1988, p. 119.

109. Doler, Kathleen, " 'Megabuck' Software-Marketing War Begins," *PC Week,* April 3, 1989, p. 70.

110. Ibid.

111. Ibid.

112. Ibid.

113. Depke, Deidre A., "Software's Big Guns Take Aim at Small Business," *Business Week,* September 25, 1989, p. 217.

114. Ibid.

115. Ibid., p. 218.

116. Lynch, "The Wizardry . . . ," p. 179.

117. McComas, "The Hard Sell . . . ," p. 60.

118. Ibid.

119. Duffy, Richard, "Ashton-Tate, Lotus Prepare for TV Ads Showdown," *PC Week,* May 15, 1984, p. 51.

120. Ibid.

121. McComas, "The Hard Sell . . . ," p. 60.

122. Horton, "Ashton-Tate Goal . . . ," p. 4.

123. Form 10-K, Fiscal Year Ended January 31, 1989, p. 5.

124. Ibid.

125. Ibid.

126. Ibid., p. 6.

127. Ibid.

128. Ibid.

129. Ibid.

130. Ibid.

131. Editorial, "Software Industry Price Rumblings," *PC Week,* December 23, 1986, p. 24.

132. Garretson, Rob, "A-T Raises Wholesale Prices on Entire Product Line," *PC Week,* April 1, 1986, p. 1.

133. Editorial, "Software Industry . . . ," p. 24.

134. Mitchell, "The Wizardry . . . ," p. 181.

135. Stevens, Brad, Ashton-Tate Press Release, July 25, 1989.

136. Ibid.

137. McCollum, Timothy R., "Ashton-Tate Research Note #1397," *Equity Research,* August 31, 1989, p. 3.

138. Barrey, Douglas, "Swollen Inventories Come Back to Haunt Ashton-Tate," *Computerworld,* June 19, 1989, p. 4.

139. Cole, Patrick E., "dBugs in dBase IV . . . ," p. 136.

140. Ashton-Tate's Annual Report, April 3, 1989, p. 44.

141. Ibid., p. 32.

142. Ibid., p. 6.

143. Ibid., p. 33.

144. Freedman, Beth, and Lyons, Daniel J., "Ashton-Tate Ripe for Sale?" *PC Week,* February 13, 1989, p. 1.

145. Newsclip, "A-T Adopts Shareholder Plan," *PC Week,* February 20, 1989, p. 69.

146. Freedman, "A-T Ripe . . . ," p. 8.

147. Cole, Patrick E., "dBASE IV Is a Godsend . . . ," p. 102.

148. Ibid.

149. Barrey, Douglas, "Fussin' and Feudin'," *Computerworld,* June 27, 1988, p. 35.

150. Ibid., p. 36.

151. Day-Copeland, Lisa, "dBASE IV's Popularity Diminishes as Buyers' Negative Opinions Mount," *PC Week,* October 16, 1989, p. 150.

152. Ibid.

153. Duffy, "Ashton-Tate, Lotus . . . ," p. 51.

154. Ashton-Tate's Annual Report, April 3, 1989, p. 13.

155. Ibid.

156. "The PC Week Poll of Corporate Satisfaction," *PC Week,* October 30, 1989, p. 117.

157. Ashton-Tate's Annual Report, April 3, 1989, p. 13.

158. Cole, Patrick E., "WordPerfect Looks, Leaps," *Business Week,* October 2, 1989, p. 99.

159. Ibid.

160. Cole, "dBugs in dBase . . . ," p. 136.

161. Lyons, Daniel J., "Japan Eyes U.S. Software Market," *PC Week,* July 10, 1989, p. 115.

162. Ibid.

164. Ibid.

165. Form 10-K, Fiscal Year Ended January 31, 1989.

166. Ibid.

167. *PC Week,* September 29, 1987, p. 149.

168. Ashton-Tate's Annual Report, April 3, 1989, p. 5.

169. Barney, Douglas, "Esber Stands Firm Behind dBASE Lawsuit," *Computer World,* January 23, 1989, p. 45.

170. Ibid.

171. Ibid.

172. Strehlo, Christine, "Litigating a Standard," *Personal Computing,* March, 1989, p. 73.

173. Lyons, Daniel J., "Shareholder Suits Proving Profitable for Legal Eagles," *PC Week,* July 10, 1989, p. 11.

174. Zellner, Wendy, "Ashton-Tate Hits dBasement," *Business Week,* August 28, 1989, p. 36.

175. Press release from Ashton-Tate dated October 15, 1989, p. 2.

176. Von Simson, Charles, "Esber Eyes . . . ," p. 8.

177. Ibid.

178. Ibid.

CAMPBELL SOUP
COMPANY

It was April 1989 and so far, rainfall appeared to be at a normal level. This was good news for food manufacturers, as North America had suffered a severe drought in 1988, causing commodity prices to skyrocket. In addition world supplies of many grains, oilseeds, and other agricultural products were tightened.

However, Campbell Soup Company, a leading food manufacturer, was not out of the woods yet. John "Jack" Dorrance, Jr., the founder's son and family patriarch, had just passed away. His death prompted rumors that the company would be sold. Speculation was further flamed by rumors that the family had named a sale price for the company, that an investment bank had been hired, and that there was a rift in the Dorrance family.[1] Of course these rumors were downplayed by the founder's grandchildren, who were now heading up the family's 58% ownership in Campbell's. At the same time they prompted a major restructuring and were pushing for more say in the company's policies.

On November 1, 1989, Gordon McGovern, the company's chief executive officer and president, took an early retirement. However, people familiar with the Board of Directors and their feelings believe that McGovern was fired.[2] Wall Street analysts feel that the abrupt departure of McGovern gives great evidence that the remaining family members did not wish to give up their control over the company.[3] Market reaction was favorable, as the stock price rose and heavy trading continued. Analysts believed that McGovern's resignation would prove favorable for the company.

However, the rumor mills continued to work. . . .

HISTORY

In 1869, Abram Anderson, an ice box maker, and Joseph Campbell, a fruit merchant, established a canning and preserving business. They were best known for

This case was prepared by Sheila Brock, Jennifer Kemp, and Debye Orr under the supervision of Professor Sexton Adams, University of North Texas, and Adelaide Griffin, Texas Woman's University. © Sexton Adams and Adelaide Griffin.

their jams and jellies, and their reputation for quality food products was established instantly. In 1891, it was incorporated as the Joseph Campbell Company in Camden, New Jersey.[4]

In 1897, John T. Dorrance developed a process for canning soup in condensed form, and Campbell has been best known for this process ever since. However, Campbell has also been manufacturing many other popular products. For example, Swanson, Hungry Man, Prego, Pepperidge Farm, and many more.[5]

The company was owned entirely by the Dorrance family from 1900 to 1954. In 1922, it was incorporated as the Campbell Soup Company, and in 1954 it went public but the Dorrance family retained control. In 1989, they held approximately 60% of the stock.[6]

John T. Dorrance ran the Campbell Soup Company from 1914 until his death in 1930. When he died, Campbell was devoted to engineering, committed to supplying value, and a very secret company. In 1930, his son John T. Dorrance, Jr., began to run the company. Observers noted that management was very centralized under his command. He had final approval on all major decisions made at Campbell. The company was described by employees as a conservative and paternalistic company as a result of the Dorrance family dominance.[7]

Although Campbell diversified into many food-related businesses, the majority of its revenues still came from the sale of their canned soup. Campbell had four major divisions, which included Campbell U.S.A., Campbell Enterprises, Campbell International, and Pepperidge Farm.[8]

THE COMPANY TODAY

After incorporating, the Campbell Soup Company soon became the largest manufacturer of condensed canned soups and ready-to-serve soups. Other manufactured food products were vegetable and tomato juices, pickles, frozen prepared seafood and chicken, frozen meat pies, canned beans, canned pasta products, spaghetti sauces, and bakery products.

In addition to their domestic operations in 24 states and Puerto Rico, Campbell's foreign sales accounted for 21% of total net sales and 13% of operating earnings in 1988. The company had operations in continental Europe, the United Kingdom, Canada, South America, Mexico, and the Far East.[9]

In fiscal 1988 and 1989, Campbell contributed $4.0 million and $4.3 million, respectively, to a wide range of social, educational, and cultural organizations. In addition they donated 6,000 tons of food products and ingredients to organized feeding programs.[10]

INDUSTRY

In the food processing industry one year is relatively undiscernible from the next, from a macroeconomic point of view. Basically, consumption can only grow as the population grows, which for the last two decades, had been stagnant. This had caused the overall U.S. market to become quite mature. Yet, despite such a static environment, major changes were taking place within the processed foods industry.[11]

To begin with, the baby boomers were growing older and presumably wiser. With this maturation came the demand for "more nutritious, lower calorie, lower salt, and lower cholesterol foods that are also easy to prepare."[12] In addition, the structure of the family was changing. There had been an increase in the number of working mothers and a decline of two-parent families within the last decade. This demographic development led to an increased demand for "foods that are easy to prepare, serve and clean up after."[13] According to the Commerce Department's March 1988 *Current Population Survey,* there were 65.1 million families in the United States, the majority of which did not have children under the age of eighteen living at home.[14] Statistics such as these led food processors to change such elements as package size and marketing strategy to help move their products from the stores' shelves to the consumers' tables.

Consumers had also been demanding more fresh and refrigerated foods instead of canned or frozen products. These refrigerated prepared foods were perceived as "more wholesome . . . and closer to the taste and quality of home-cooked food. . . ."[15] These products, which included such items as soups, salads, entrées, pastas, sauces, and desserts, offered food manufacturers opportunities for increased market share (through product expansion) and higher profit margins. There had also been a noticeable preference for richer foods, and sweet and salty snacks. In fact, in 1987, these items replaced juice drinks as the nation's latest fashion in food. Industry analysts attributed these trends to consumers' increased disposable income. Another fashion in food was the increased preference for Hispanic foods. Food companies had been aggressively pursuing this trend in recent years, and Campbell was no exception. In 1986, it acquired Casera Corp., "a comparatively small (257 million in annual sales) producer of a broad range of canned and frozen Spanish foods."[16]

According to Jane Collin, a food, beverage, and tobacco analyst, such acquisitions had not been uncommon. She stated that "a high level of merger and acquisition activity always has been a prominent feature of the foods industry."[17] There were several reasons for this. First, few growth opportunities exist in mature markets. This was evidenced by the fact that in the last decade, per capita consumption of food had remained relatively constant, only averaging about a 1% to 2% annual growth. (Exhibit 1). Secondly, relatively low fixed costs and significantly large excess cash flows had resulted in readily available investment funds.[18] Lastly, food manufacturers had been striving to boost revenues and profits and intensify their pricing power.[19]

EXHIBIT 1   Per capita food consumption by food group

(Index: 1982 = 100)

	1979	1984	1985	1986	1987
Meats	104.6	103.2	104.1	101.3	97.8
Fish	105.7	111.4	117.1	119.5	125.2
Poultry and eggs	98.2	102.5	105.1	106.9	112.8
Dairy products	104.9	100.8	102.0	102.0	101.6
Fruits and vegetables	100.5	107.1	105.1	108.0	109.9
Wheat flour	100.4	101.2	105.7	105.9	109.7
Rice, pasta, and cereals	93.4	97.4	104.6	117.2	131.3
Sugar and sweeteners	121.3	91.4	85.6	81.8	84.5
Other	101.7	100.7	103.7	102.1	96.1
Total foods	103.2	102.2	103.3	104.2	105.1

Source: U.S. Department of Agriculture.

However, acquisitions were not the only way to achieve growth. Some food manufacturers, including Campbell, chose "to grow through new products aimed at increasingly specific market segments."[20] In 1987, food processors introduced 10,182, a record number of new products.[21] These new products helped add some spark to otherwise stale food markets. On the downside, they intensified competition for grocery store shelf space, which had already grown scarce due to the merger activity and the consolidations among the retail chains.[22]

Industry observers noted that the consolidations among retail chains increased the grocers' buying power over the food processors. As Jane Collin noted, "In the 1980's, the retail chains . . . gained more and more pricing power over the manufacturers."[23] She did not believe the balance would shift back to the food processors any time soon.[24] For one thing, grocers were striving to maintain their profits so as to reduce the heavy debt load they assumed during their acquisition phase.[25] Secondly, the manufacturers had already lost considerable bargaining power in that the supermarket chains accounted for an increased proportion of their sales.[26]

Another event impacted the food industry in the late 80's, as noted by one analyst: "One of the newest developments in the food industry is the appearance of upscale, private-label specialty foods designed to take advantage of the wide price differential between national brands and the more expensive gourmet brands."[27] These self-manufactured items gave the retailers a cost advantage (of as much as 35% of the product's total cost) since the items only had to change hands one to two times, as compared to the approximately seven times it traditionally took for the national brand items to reach store shelves. The development of these upscale labels was "in sharp contrast to the inflation-driven generic era of the early 1970's, when food inflation was high and retailers' focus was on maintaining price levels even if it meant sacrificing quality."[28] Without the presence of inflation, the volume of these generic brands only accounted for about 5–10% of all food sold at supermarkets. Yet, analysts believed consumers would still be willing to switch from well-known national brands to the private-label store brands provided quality was not compromised.[29]

Despite this new development, the most valuable asset of any leading food manufacturer was its portfolio of brand-name franchises. *Valueline* stated that "consumers reach first for the names they have come to know and trust, such as Campbell Soup, Kellogg, Heinz, and so forth."[30] These familiar brands were another key to increased asset turnover and profitability in the mature food industry. They helped manufacturers fill distribution pipelines and use production capacity more fully through product-line extensions, category expansions, and product reformulations.[31] This brand strength was the core reason that the food industry continued to outperform the market (Exhibit 2).

ECONOMY

According to industry analysts, "the packaged food industry traditionally has been the beneficiary of inelastic price demand—consumer demand is relatively stable regardless of product prices."[32] However, this relation may be tested in the years beginning after 1988. During the five-year period 1983 through 1988, increases in food prices were less than general inflation. This was mainly due to the fact that manufacturers resisted passing on the burden of incrementally higher costs to the wholesalers and retailers, and ultimately the consumers.[33] But, a severe drought occurred in the spring of 1988, causing commodity prices to skyrocket, thus giving manufacturers plenty of occasion to raise prices.

In addition, general inflation caused other production costs to increase. Packaging costs, the third largest component in food production costs, advanced again in 1988, after a 6.5% increase in 1987. Marketing and advertising costs also escalated. This was in response to the intense competition, both home and abroad, that was so prevalent in the food industry. Additionally, all the merger activity added considerable debt service costs to the industry's list of concerns.[34]

These costs all contributed to the higher food inflation rates (Exhibit 3). For the January to April 1989 period, "prices for all food items . . . advanced 6.2% from a year ago, well ahead of the 4.9% four-month average increase for the Consumer Price Index (CPI)."[35] Most of this rise was felt in the prices for food eaten at home—consumers in this area paid 7.2% more during this period than in the same period for 1988, while only 4.6% more was paid for food eaten away from home. Industry observers expected this inflation to limit the pricing flexibility of the food industry.[36]

An added frustration to this limited pricing flexibility was the fact that growth in consumers' disposable income was slowing, and food and beverage

EXHIBIT 2   Packaged food industry dynamics

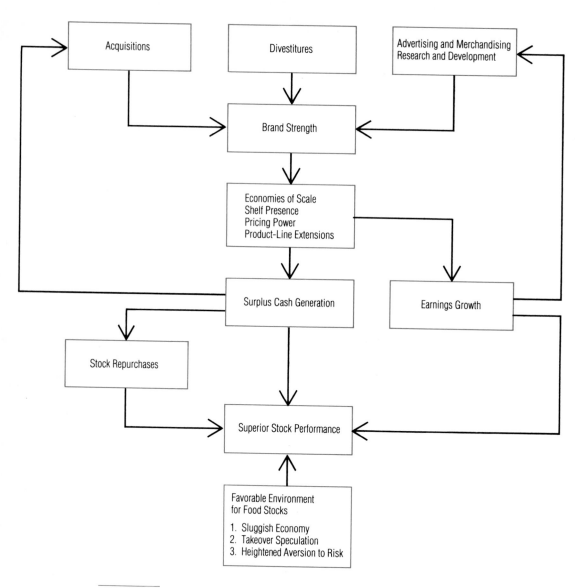

Source: *Valueline*, August 25, 1989, p. 1451.

EXHIBIT 3   **Food price indexes**

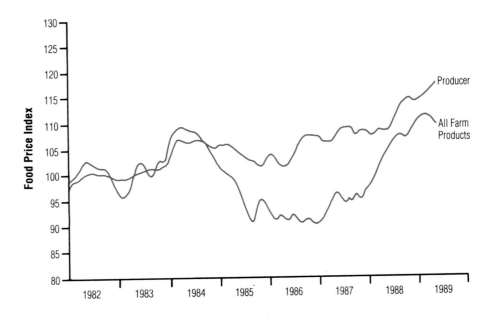

Source: U.S. Department of Agriculture; U.S. Department of Labor.

spending (as a proportion of consumers' total outlays) had been declining (Exhibit 4). However, analysts forecasted "less room in the consumer's budget for luxury items yet enough of a cushion for more spending on groceries."[37]

MANAGEMENT

Prior to Gordon McGovern as CEO and president of Campbell, the company's management was very centralized. In 1980, Gordon McGovern came in and transformed management, by emphasizing a decentralized nature and encouraging managers to take risks and attempt to develop new products. He backed up his new management style with a compensation program as an incentive for those who were taking part in the development of the company through new products. Some of the company's employees were skeptical of the new style and believed that it was an attempt to get the support of the employees and improve his reputation within the company. McGovern believed that the new management style and the restructuring of the divisions would encourage managers to be more aggressive in the development of new products.[38]

McGovern's focus was on being the top introducer of new products in future years. However, as he pushed the development of new products, he gave little

EXHIBIT 4   **Food expenditures as a percentage of disposable income**

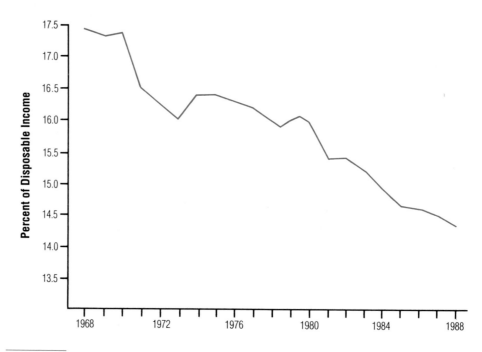

Source: U.S. Department of Commerce.

attention to updating and increasing the efficiency of the production of the soup products. McGovern admitted, "We make it in big kettles like they did in 1910."[39] Janet Novack, an industry observer, stated, "Nostalgic, yes. Efficient, no," but admitted that "What is not out of date is the affection and loyalty that consumers display toward the name. Campbell, according to one recent survey, remains the second most powerful brand name in America, ranked only behind Coca-Cola in consumer recognition and esteem."[40]

With such a strong market share and brand recognition, why was it taking McGovern so long to modernize the company? When he took over as CEO in 1980, he got off to a good start with management decentralization, the introduction of a large number of new products, and increased spending on marketing. However, all of these changes had little influence on the company's net income, and stock performance had not fared well either, as Campbell stock had one of the lowest price-to-earnings ratios within the food processing industry. Boasting a mediocre stock price, low debt and a very powerful brand name would seem to send out a signal to the public that Campbell was a possible target for takeover. Analysts believed, "On the contrary, it's a classic example of a public company run to suit the conservative style and long-term agenda of a controlling family."[41] McGovern plainly stated that "we're not running the company for the stock price."[42] The Dorrances, which consisted of nine families, were 58% owners of the company's stock, and were receiving about a 3% return on their stock, or approximately $65 million a year in dividends, and did not seem to be complaining. The family had always been very secretive about reporting and preferred that McGovern not reveal the goals of the company. An industry observer stated, "McGovern insists the pace of progress has been fine, considering how much is needed to be done."[43] However, the company had had its share of failures, including losses of millions due to introduction of new products that were not properly test-marketed first, and the occasional neglect of their main business of condensed soups. There did not seem to be rifts between the Dorrance family and management, although rumor had it that the Board of Directors were discontent with McGovern's performance. An industry observer stated, "Attractive, rich and single. That the company is, and it is likely to remain that way given the Dorrances' tight control."[44] However, the Board of Directors had to be more concerned with the 40-plus percent of stock that the public held, as their interests in the company could not continue to be ignored. Therefore they were looking ahead and searching for a replacement for McGovern as he had planned to retire in a few years.

On April 9, 1989, John T. Dorrance, Jr., controller of about 32% of the stock, passed away, leaving his shares equally to each of his three children. An industry analyst reported that "Mr. Dorrance has long been perceived by Wall Street as the main stumbling block between Campbell and a lucrative takeover," and, "many analysts said that R. Gordon McGovern, Campbell's chief executive, catered far more to Mr. Dorrance's interests than to those of shareholders."[45] The family members expressed their desire to keep the company independent; however, analysts "say they simply do not have the kind of commitment to the company that the late Mr. Dorrance had."[46] A wait-and-see attitude was then adopted as no one knew whether the family would continue to run the company or whether a takeover bid would be accepted.

On November 2, 1989, the big news broke. McGovern had been forced out as CEO and president. Industry observers noted that this was "the strongest evidence yet of the power that Dorrance family members intend to wield in reshaping the troubled food company."[47] In August of 1989 McGovern had announced a plan for major restructuring, which the family planned to continue to implement as they acquired new businesses and disposed of the unprofitable ones. A new CEO had not been named, and for the time being, Baum, president of Campbell USA, and Harper, the chief financial officer, were running the company as a team, with duties almost evenly split between the two. An industry analyst noted that "Mr. Baum said the two have orders to 'focus on bottom-line profits' and to 'take a hard look at our businesses—what is good and what is not so good,'" something that McGovern was not known for doing.[48] So, it seemed that the remaining family members were looking out not only for their interests, but for the public's interest in the company as well. Management experts and analysts agreed that the board should decide very quickly on a new CEO. Jay Conger, an organizational behavior professor, said, "Human beings need to feel that there is one individual running the show," and a committee approach to leadership "tends to blunt a sense of focus and a sense of vision for the organization."[49] Both men felt that they could do the job together well. Additionally, both men were up for the job individually, so there was the risk of competition between the two as they continued to work together until a new CEO was named. Conger stated that "Inherently, it's an unstable situation. Traditionally, there will be more dividing into camps."[50] The Board of Directors had a big decision to make, one that would have to please both the family as well as the public stockholders.

STRATEGY

The Campbell Soup Company's overall strategy was to focus on the consumer. Management's statement of their strategy was, "All of Campbell's activities begin with our focus on consumers. Our goals are to maximize profitability and shareholder value by marketing consumer food products that lead in quality and value; and to build and defend the first or second position in every category in which we compete."[51] In addition to this overall strategy, management also set goals for the company to achieve each year.

In fiscal year 1988, management's goals were to enhance the core businesses, acquire other companies in strategic markets, and restructure their operations.[52] In management's opinion, these goals were achieved. In fiscal year 1989, management's goals were changed somewhat. The goals were to enhance the core businesses, grow in international markets, and increase their cash return on investments. Management believed that they gained headway on these goals during the year.[53]

Management used various methods to achieve these goals. They acquired three domestic companies in fiscal 1988 to strengthen their core businesses. Marie's salad dressing was acquired and gave Campbell leadership in the refrigerated salad dressing market and strengthened their Fresh Produce Group. The acquisition of Early California ripe olives and Durkee Spanish olives gave the Vlasic Group market leadership in the olive category. And the acquisition of Mrs. Kinser's Home Style Foods, Inc., strengthened the chilled line of products.[54]

Campbell also acquired many foreign companies. In 1988, they made their largest acquisition ever by acquiring Freshbake Foods PLC for $201 million. Freshbake was located in the United Kingdom, and the acquisition price represented 24 times earnings.[55]

In an effort to improve shareholder value, management streamlined the company's infrastructure by eliminating obsolete and inefficient facilities, including the plant closures in Pennsylvania, Illinois, Maryland, and Tennessee. Campbell also reduced their inventories and divested themselves of marginal businesses, such as Pietro's restaurants. Surplus assets were disposed of, and they added new capacity in long-term growth markets such as the salad dressing market with the acquisition of Marie's.[56]

As a result of this effort, several programs were introduced to reduce overhead, especially at corporate headquarters. A hiring freeze was enacted, along with an early retirement program and a review of all headquarters functions. Management believed that these programs would reduce overhead by approximately ten million dollars annually.[57]

Another result of the streamlining strategy was a realignment of the manufacturing organization, with the creation of five manufacturing regions, which was expected to enable Campbell to relate more closely with their wholesale customers. The closer relationship was a major step in improving their information flow and speeding up their deliveries.[58]

Regarding the upcoming fiscal year 1990, Campbell's management stated that they were entering it with a continued commitment to lower costs and to aggressively addressing the weak spots, such as the overseas companies, in their manufacturing and distribution systems. They were also dedicated to aggressively marketing products that were the first or second best sellers in their categories, for example, Marie's salad dressing.[59]

THE RESTRUCTURE

In August of 1989, Campbell announced its plan for a major restructuring that was aimed at modernizing and streamlining operations. The plan called for closing approximately nine plants worldwide and eliminated about 2,800 jobs in the United States and 830 overseas. Goodwill was also written off in Argentina, and top managers were replaced in Britain and Italy.[60]

In 1988 the Mrs. Paul's Kitchens plant in Doylestown, Pennsylvania, was closed and the canned food plant in Chicago, Illinois, was converted to a regional distribution center.[61] Plants closed in 1989 were food processing plants in Pocomoke City and Crisfield, Maryland; Camden, New Jersey; and one in Smyrna, Tennessee. Campbell plants in Ohio, Texas, California, and North Carolina picked up the slack and began operating 24 hours. Campbell's domestic plants had been functioning at about 60% capacity, and were ranked 5% to 6% below the food industry average regarding performance, by one industry analyst. Campbell would not provide any details regarding the overseas closures because the various government authorities had not been notified.[62]

The restructuring resulted in a charge of approximately $343 million, and was expected to be a nonrecurring charge. This resulted in an approximate $261 million charge against fiscal 1989 earnings after taxes. Fiscal 1990 was expected to incur after-tax savings of almost $15 million, and $150 million in savings was expected over the next four years. Management viewed the 1989 earnings of only $13 million (after restructuring charges) as a necessary sacrifice in order to improve long-term profitability.[63] Industry analysts reported that early results from the restructuring had been disappointing, especially in Europe.[64]

Campbell's management believed that the restructuring would give them sufficient capacity for 3 to 6 years. They also believed that it was a necessary plan to become more competitive across the world.[65] Some industry analysts saw the plan as an attempt to slow Campbell's expansion, and to improve the margins and productivity of existing operations.[66] Others believed that it was an attempt to reduce the speculation of a takeover. However, it was also believed by most analysts that much more than the restructuring was needed to be done in order to make Campbell more competitive.[67]

DIVISIONS

Fiscal 1989 saw a change in Campbell's operating divisions. Pepperidge Farm, which was a part of the Campbell U.S.A. division, became a division in itself. The four operating divisions were Campbell U.S.A., Pepperidge Farm, Campbell Enterprises, and Campbell International (Exhibit 5). The percentage of sales and operating earnings that each division contributed in 1988 and 1989 is shown in Exhibit 6.

Campbell U.S.A. was the largest division; their sales were $3,358 million in fiscal 1989, which accounted for 58.3% of total sales, and 63.5%, or $3,087 million, in fiscal 1988. This division consisted of six groups: Soup, Grocery, Convenience Meals, Fresh Produce, Refrigerated Foods, and New Ventures. The year 1989 was strong for this division; operating earnings were up 15%, excluding

EXHIBIT 5   **Campbell soup company organization chart**

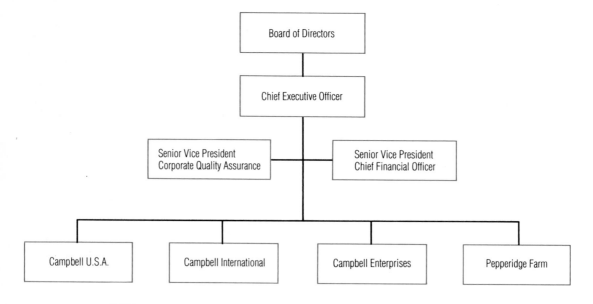

Source: Campbell Soup Company, *Annual Report*, 1989.

EXHIBIT 6   **1988 and 1989 Operating earnings by division (in millions of dollars)**

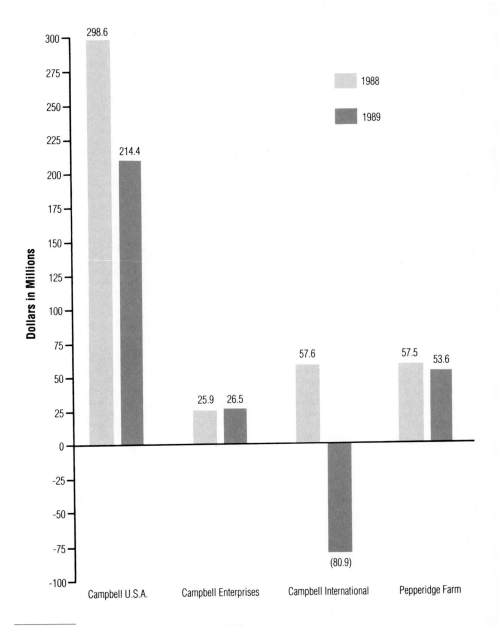

Source: Campbell Soup Company, *Annual Report,* 1989.

restructuring charges; and sales were up 9% over 1988 sales. The performance was attributed to aggressive marketing programs and strong core-brand performance. Campbell U.S.A. also had a 6% volume gain in fiscal 1989. There was exceptionally strong growth in V-8 vegetable juice, Swanson frozen entrées and fried chicken, Prego spaghetti sauces, Franco-American pasta products, Great Starts breakfasts, and Le Menu Lightstyle frozen dinners.[68]

In the Soup Group, the condensed soups showed market declines. These were the products that Campbell was most famous for. However, Special Request, a reduced-sodium soup, showed market increases, and Prego, Franco-American, and V-8 juice of the Grocery Group each had record annual sales volume. This came about by a combination of aggressive consumer marketing efforts, more effective trade promotion support, and more effective advertising. The products in the Convenience Meals Group all showed strength, including the Swanson Homestyle Entrée introduced in 1988, due to successful price positioning and promotion programs. The strong sales gains of the Fresh Produce Group resulted from volume gains in branded mushrooms, and other vegetable lines. The Refrigerated Foods Group improved its sales for the first time in two years. In the New Ventures Group, national sales were scheduled for the Souper Combo early in the fiscal year 1990.[69]

Management believed that much of the strength was due to strong national and local marketing programs, coupled with aggressive regional merchandising and trade programs. Additionally during 1989, a special program was launched called "Quality Proud," which focused on quality achievement at all levels. For the 1990 fiscal year, this division planned to continue its drive to become the low-cost producer in its major product categories.[70]

The Pepperidge Farm division also had a strong operating year in 1989 with sales increases of 11% and operating earnings increases of 6%. Its sales were $548 million in 1989, which accounted for 9.5% of Campbell's total sales, and 10%, or $495 million, in 1988. Its success was mainly attributed to the continued success of American Collection single-serving frozen desserts. Campbell received the American Marketing Association's Best New Product award for this product. Other products in this division also did well, including the Croissant Toaster Tarts and their line of salad croutons. However, there was a slowdown in operating earnings as a result of heavy marketing expenditures spent on American Collection.[71]

In 1988, new products were introduced that management believed would fit with the Pepperidge Farm image and meet consumer demands for imaginative new products of high quality and value. The new products included American Collection single-serving desserts and the Pepperidge Farm frozen danish. Management believed that both products received excellent consumer acceptance.[72]

Also included was a mail order business unit. During 1989 this unit acquired Wooden Spoon, Inc., a specialty cookware mail order company which had softened the impact of seasonality from the other mail order businesses owned by Campbell.[73]

In 1989, plans were announced to construct a $180 million state-of-the-art bakery and cookie plant near Adamstown, Pennsylvania, which would strengthen Campbell's regional ability to deliver increased freshness and value to its consumers.[74]

Campbell Enterprises, the smallest division, was nongrocery. Its sales were $327 million in 1989, which accounted for 5.7% of total sales, and 5.5%, or $321 million, in 1988. In 1988, its earnings accounted for 6% of total operating earnings, or $26 million. It was created in fiscal 1987, to operate businesses outside the traditional grocery channels. The division sold frozen food to restaurants and supermarket delicatessens and Godiva chocolates to department stores. The division reported a strong year for 1989. It reported an 11% increase in sales, and operating earnings rose 5%, excluding the restaurant operations, start-up costs, and restructuring costs. The strong performance was mainly due to the good performance of its two major groups, Campbell Food Service Company and Godiva Chocolatiers.[75]

In fiscal 1989, several new products were introduced. These included cheese sauces for "fast food" outlets, pizza and other red sauces, hot and refrigerated entrées and side dishes, and new varieties of frozen restaurant soups. This division also acquired the Campbell World Trading Company, Inc., in 1989, which marketed foreign-made specialty food products, including six lines of Campbell products.[76]

Campbell International had operations in Argentina, Australia, Belgium, Canada, France, Ireland, Italy, Mexico, Spain, the Netherlands, the United Kingdom, and West Germany. Its purpose was to achieve global competitiveness in prepared convenience foods. Foreign-based manufacturers and retailers forced domestic companies like Campbell to recognize that they must compete on a worldwide basis in order to survive.[77] Management at Campbell believed that the marketplace of the future was outside the U.S., and they began acquiring foreign companies. In 1989, foreign sales were $1,527 million, which accounted for 26.5% of total sales, up from 21% in 1988. Management stated that by 1990 it hoped to have increased this percentage to 40%. In 1988 its earnings accounted for 13% of operating earnings. The increase in international sales over the years is shown in Exhibit 7.[78]

Management's strategy for the European operations was to expand, and they stated "the plan is to leverage our strong domestic frozen food and brand strengths into the fast-growing European market through Freshbake."[79] Freshbake Foods PLC was acquired by Campbell in 1988 and was Britain's largest frozen foods producer. This acquisition was a source of some of the trouble Campbell was having overseas. The acquisition price was $201 million, or 24 times earnings, and investors felt that it was too much to pay for a company with little brand recognition.[80] The acquisition resulted in the U.K. operations having severe overcapacity. Freshbake ranked third in the Britain frozen-food market and faced intense competition. Major competitors were Unilever with 22% of the market share, and United Biscuits with 19%. Analysts felt that Campbell should get rid of Freshbake as they only had 12% of the market and gaining market share was not an easy task.[81]

EXHIBIT 7   Campbell's international sales (in billions of dollars)

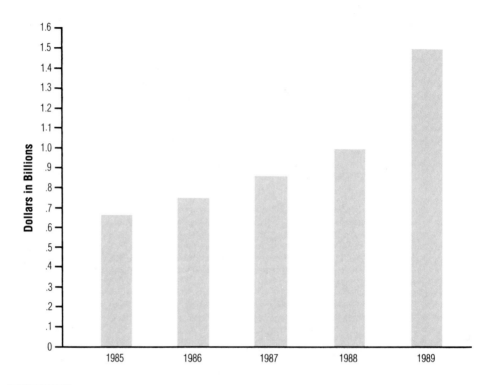

Source: *The Wall Street Journal,* September 26, 1989, p. A6.

Another troubled overseas company was D. Lazzaroni & Co. This company produced Italian cookies, and had been hurt by overproduction and distribution problems, which occurred primarily in its cake business. In 1988, they overestimated Italy's market for Christmas cakes. As a result of the overproduction, they had to reduce the price of the cakes in order to sell them. A company official said that "you could buy cake cheaper than bread."[82] Campbell replaced Lazzaroni's top management and began studying ways to improve distribution.[83]

Not everyone was so optimistic about Campbell's acquisitions; however, industry analysts believed that Campbell's problems had resulted from expanding too fast, especially in Europe. John McMillin, an analyst with Prudential-Bache Securities, Inc., said, "They haven't got a handle on their European businesses."[84]

Much of the concern of the industry analysts regarding Campbell's presence in the international markets stemmed from the intense competition. Analysts were worried about the high cost of competing in the U.K. food market and the errors made by Campbell, such as overproduction and severe overcapacity.[85]

PRODUCTION

McGovern's production philosophy was to focus on quality products. Rather than making products the way that the machines were already designed to make them, McGovern concentrated on what the consumers wanted. In the past, Campbell had emphasized new products that were compatible with existing production facilities.

Consumers became concerned with lowering their blood cholesterol by reducing their intake of fat. Fruits and vegetables were low in fat and consequently Americans began to eat more of them. Campbell saw this as an opportunity to market branded produce. Management felt that consumers liked produce with a brand on it, and would pay for it. So Campbell added value to fresh produce and put the Campbell name on it. Analysts stated that adding value to a product whose best-selling feature was naturalness would take imagination and money; however, technology did make it possible. The technology was hydroponic cultivation, in which plants were grown in a liquid nutrient instead of soil. However, this technique lost its biggest sponsor when General Mills pulled out as they felt that hydroponics would take too long to pay off. An example of the branded produce is Campbell's Farm Fresh Mushrooms introduced in 1979. In 1984 they contributed only $65 million of revenues to Campbell's $3.7 billion; however, management believed that the branded produce would ripen into a $1 billion business by the early 1990s.[86]

Consumers also became very convenience oriented. In response, Campbell began to use "grab-and-eat" packages, which were aimed heavily at convenience stores. They allowed the consumer to buy a carton of soup, pop it into the store microwave, and sip it as he drove away. Analysts said that some 70% of what was bought at convenience stores was eaten within 15 minutes from the time it left the store. To sum up the changes that were occurring and the effects on Campbell, an industry observer said, "The Campbell Kids had better stay healthy and energetic . . . to keep up with the hurried pace of modern life."[87]

Campbell became concerned with their packaging costs. Sometimes it would cost more to produce the container than it would to produce the product contained within the package. In 1984, Campbell decided that the time had come to "can the can" as too expensive, too messy, and too inconvenient for today's world of fast-acting microwave ovens. Consequently, management began a multi-million-dollar search for a new container. A sealed plastic soup bowl that could be popped into a microwave and heated up in a few minutes had been tested, along with several other containers. Management believed that soup bowls conveyed an "image of warmth," but they had not found a bowl design with a color and shape that they liked. Campbell had been consulting their consumers as to their opinion. The sales pitch for the new container would be convenience. Analysts believed that the new packaging would help increase soup consumption overall. In 1984, management stated that a change to plastics would reduce their packaging costs by as much as 15%. However, they stated that it would take a lot of time and money, approximately $100 million, to restructure the production facilities. They also estimated that it would be about five years before the soup can took its final bow. In 1989 Campbell researchers were still working on this project.[88]

In *Garbage,* a new magazine, Campbell was criticized for the packaging of its new microwave product Souper Combo. The editors of this magazine ran a giant diagram of the Souper Combo product and had arrows pointing to the packaging's polystyrene foam, polypropylene, and polyester film. These were all plastic items which were said to be nonbiodegradable and to have created the "landfill monster." However, modifications had been made to the Souper Combo product to make it less of an offender than portrayed, but it still was not one of Campbell's better products regarding recyclability.[89]

The safety stocks and inventories held by Campbell were unbelievably high in years prior to 1986, so Campbell began to drastically reduce their inventory. From 1986 to 1989, they averaged about $35 million a year in inventory reductions. In 1989 they reached the point where a question was raised as to whether further cuts could be made without affecting the promptness of delivery. In the Fayetteville, Arkansas, plant, the just-in-time inventory system was implemented and the additional warehouse space created was turned into productive, value-added running space.[90]

Campbell employed over 44,000 employees to operate their more than 90 manufacturing plants in the United States and 12 plants overseas. One of the main heat processing plants was located in Paris, Texas. The plant produced over 4 million cans of Campbell soups, Campbell beans, V-8 juice, tomato juice, Bounty products, Franco-American pastas, and Swanson products daily, and employed over 1,500 people and operated three different shifts.[91]

MARKETING

Along with McGovern's new management style came a new marketing style. McGovern felt that they would have to make their presence known in the world of advertising and promotion if they were going to try to introduce all the newly developed products. Management believed that in order to ensure long-term growth, new product introduction was vital.[92] Campbell had been at the top for new products introduced. The company's latest focuses had been on microwave foods that came in a microwaveable container, as research in 1987 revealed that 50% of those responding desired a special section at the grocery store for microwaveable foods.[93] The company's introduction of frozen Le Menu's in 1982 proved to be a successful one, until Kraft's Budget Gourmet was introduced at a much lower price and consumers became price-conscious. Campbell then lowered the price and moved marketing expenditures away from the media and toward couponing.[94]

McGovern came on aggressively with increases in expenditures for marketing at greater than 50%. From 1980 to 1989, marketing and sales expense went from $213 million to $818 million (Exhibit 8). In 1983, McGovern felt that consumers had changed from a taste-oriented position (thus the "Mm! Mm! Good" slogan) to a more health-oriented position. Therefore the company's long-time ad agency was replaced and the "Soup is good food" campaign was launched. With this campaign came trouble from the Federal Trade Commission. The company dropped the controversial campaign and returned to the "Mm! Mm! Good" campaign, in 1988.[95]

Campbell continued to increase its marketing and advertising budget and developed new marketing and advertising strategies. The back-to-basics plan called for the majority of the new spending to focus on the core soup business. In addition the plan called for a cutback in new products introduced, in order to keep the attention on product lines that were already well established. However, all new products and strategies were not discouraged. Among new marketing strategies being tested was the use of ATM machines for distribution of coupons, which proved to be a successful strategy in the test markets, with larger test markets being considered.

In continuing with the back-to-basics strategy, Campbell realized that a mass

EXHIBIT 8   **Marketing and sales expenses (in millions of dollars)**

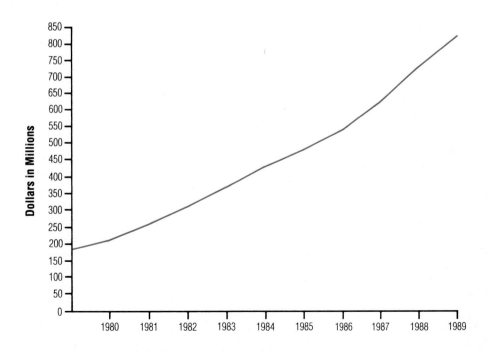

Source: Campbell Soup Company, *Annual Reports,* 1988 and 1989.

market no longer existed for consumers, but instead a number of regional markets existed. Therefore they shifted the focus from production to marketing. The company created over twenty regions for marketing activities, and each was responsible for the planning and spending of their respective regions, rather than the national center giving a budget number and plan to each of the regions.[96] The strategy was engineered by McGovern and put into place by Campbell USA's president, Herbert Baum. According to Baum, there was some resistance in the beginning from the district managers, who had a hard time handling their marketing responsibilities, and from national managers, who felt as if they were losing their control to the district managers.[97]

Once the operations ran smoothly in marketing, Baum organized production into five regions, so that the two could work more closely together. What was the result of the changes? "Revenues . . . posted a 12 percent increase in operating earnings; sales were up by 7 percent."[98] Beginning in fiscal year 1989, Baum planned to regionalize further by evaluating managers' performance on a regional basis as far as profit and loss were concerned. "If he had it his way, the regional units would eventually operate as entirely autonomous units."[99]

Campbell had a strong marketing program and virtually unlimited cash resources, keeping them in a competitive position with other top companies in the industry.

LEGAL

With the launch of Campbell's "Soup is good food" campaign came attacks from the Federal Trade Commission (FTC). The FTC's complaint said that "food marketers using health claims in advertising had better be prepared to disclose any ingredient that dilutes those claims."[100] The FTC complained that the ad was misleading as it did not disclose the fact that the soup was high in sodium, which could increase the risk of heart disease. Campbell planned to contest the case as the company did not believe the ads were misleading. However, if the FTC charges held up, they would require Campbell to disclose the sodium content for soups that contained greater than 500 milligrams, when the company advertised that a soup was "heart-healthy."[101] In February of 1988, Campbell stopped using the ads and returned to the old campaign. In May of 1989, Campbell agreed to pay $315,000 to nine states to settle claims against their advertising.[102]

Another possible legal problem for Campbell came from supermarket chains asking for uniform prices on new and established promotional items across the country. The use of slotting allowances, which were used mainly in regional markets in order to gain shelf space for new products by allowing discounts on other products or payment to the grocer for putting the new items on the shelf, could be threatened by the FTC. The FTC could ban the use of slotting allowances as they may be in violation of the Robinson-Patman Act, prohibiting preferential pricing for any one customer. Should this happen, it would likely have "a major negative implication for companies that focus on specific regional markets such as Campbell's Soup. . . ."[103]

COMPETITION

The food processing industry was an intensively competitive industry. According to Herbert Baum, president of Campbell U.S.A., "prepared foods is a one percent business at best," as far as "unit growth from year to year. So everybody is fighting for market share."[104]

Campbell's competition came from different levels, including international, national, regional, and local food processors. In addition, many retailers had begun to use their own brand-name products.[105]

With approximately 8,000 new food products introduced annually, some products had to be discontinued in order to make room for the new ones on the grocery store shelves. Campbell's canned soup swallowed up 70% of the nation's market, giving the company some advantage when it came to occupying shelf space (Exhibit 9). Competition was fierce in the supermarkets, as each manufacturer wanted to have as many "facings" (products that face outward on the shelf) as possible. Manufacturers whose products had more facings got more attention from the shoppers. As a result of the competition for "facings," some retailers

EXHIBIT 9   **Campbell share of the soup market**

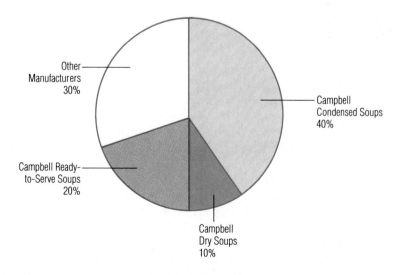

Other Manufacturers 30%

Campbell Condensed Soups 40%

Campbell Ready-to-Serve Soups 20%

Campbell Dry Soups 10%

Source: Campbell Soup Company, *Annual Report*, 1989.

were able to charge the manufacturers a slot fee for occupation of prime shelf space.[106]

FINANCE

As mentioned previously, Campbell's undertook a major restructuring program. This caused current earnings to decline. However, company officials were optimistic—they believed the program would improve operating margins and long-term profitability. A company spokesman said, "We don't intend for earnings to remain flat."[107] John M. McMillin of Prudential-Bache Securities once commented on Campbell, "They have so much on their table that they have a case of indigestion."[108] But he predicted the restructuring would produce a sharper focus for the company. "They finally realized they don't need to be this big," he said.[109]

The costs for this restructuring in 1988 and 1989 were $49.3 million, pretax, and $343.0 million, pretax, respectively. The 1988 charges involved $27.2 million for plant closings and conversions; $13.4 million in expenses for the company's early retirement program; and $8.7 million for the company's ongoing program of asset redeployment, which was included in cost of products sold.[110] According to the annual report, the 1989 charges involved "plant consolidations, work force reductions, and goodwill write-offs."[111] However, it failed to break the charges down into these segments. Excluding these restructuring costs, Campbell posted increases in its operating earnings for both 1988 and 1989. However, net earnings were essentially flat for fiscal 1989. Gross margins continued their four-year upward trend even though cost of products sold continued to escalate (Exhibit 10). Each of Campbell's four major divisions recorded sales increases (Exhibit 11). In fact, overall sales increased 16% in 1989 to $5.67 billion, up from $4.87 billion in 1988. Unit volume increased 14%, with most of this increase attributed to acquisitions. The annual report stated that only 4% of the volume increase came from base businesses (Exhibit 12).[112]

Operating expenses also continued their upward trend, with a 17.1% increase in 1989, and a 16% increase in 1988. Marketing and sales expenses and interest expense, net, had the greatest increases. Campbell sustained its long-standing commitment to improving production facilities. In 1988, it had capital expenditures of $262 million; in 1989, it had spent $302 million for plant assets. Approximately $400 million was needed to complete projects in progress at July 30, 1989.[113]

Campbell Soup Company was a major player in the "merger mania" that began in the late 1980s. In 1988 the company spent over $600 million, including assumption of debt, on acquisitions. Fiscal year 1989's acquisitions totaled $140 million, including assumption of debt. These acquisitions caused major shifts in its liquidity position. As a result of increased borrowing to fund these acquisitions, Campbell's ratio of total debt to total capitalization (including minority

EXHIBIT 10   Campbell soup company, five year review—consolidated

(Millions except per share amounts)	1989	1988	1987	1986	1985
Earnings					
Net sales	5,672.1	4,868.9	4,490.4	4,286.8	3,916.6
Cost of products sold	4,001.6	3,392.8	3,180.5	3,082.7	2,879.7
Marketing and sales expenses	818.8	733.3	626.2	544.4	478.4
Administrative expenses	252.1	232.6	213.9	195.9	151.2
Research and development expenses	47.7	46.9	44.8	42.2	34.5
Interest, net	55.8	20.7	22.2	28.6	32.1
Foreign exchange losses, net	19.3	16.6	4.8	0.7	0.9
Other (income) expense	32.4	(3.2)	(9.5)	5.5	5.4
Restructuring and unusual charges	343.0	40.6			
Equity in earnings of affiliates	10.4	6.3	15.1	4.3	2.1
Minority interests	(5.3)	(6.3)	(4.7)	(3.9)	(2.8)
Earnings before taxes	106.5	388.6	417.9	387.2	333.7
Taxes on earnings	93.4	147.0	170.6	164.0	135.9
Earnings before cumulative effect of accounting change	13.1	241.6	247.3	223.2	197.8
Cumulative effect of change in accounting for income taxes		32.5			
Net earnings	13.1	274.1	247.3	223.2	197.8
Percent of sales	0.2	5.6	5.5	5.2	5.1
Percent of stockholders' equity	0.7	15.1	15.1	15.3	15.0
Per share					
Earnings before cumulative effect of accounting change	0.10	1.87	1.90	1.72	1.53
Cumulative effect of change in accounting for income taxes		0.25			
Net earnings	0.10	2.12	1.90	1.72	1.53
Dividends	116.4	104.6	91.7	84.4	79.1
Retained in business	(103.3)	169.5	155.6	138.8	118.7
Dividends declared per share	0.90	0.81	0.705	0.65	0.61
Depreciation	175.9	162.0	139.0	120.8	119.0
Salaries, wages, pensions, etc.	133.9	1,222.9	1,137.3	1,061.0	950.1
Number of stockholders (in thousands)	43.7	43.0	41.0	50.9	49.5
Average shares outstanding	129.3	129.4	129.9	129.5	129.1
Year-end financial position					
Current assets	1,601.5	1,362.9	1,437.9	1,334.8	1,152.7
Working capital	369.4	499.6	744.1	708.7	579.4
Plant assets—gross	2,543.0	2,539.7	2,355.1	2,089.1	1,856.1
Accumulated depreciation	1,002.4	1,030.8	1,006.1	921.0	828.6
Plant assets purchased	284.1	245.3	303.7	235.3	198.3
Total assets	3,932.1	3,609.6	3,097.4	2,762.8	2,437.5
Long-term debt	629.2	525.8	380.2	362.3	297.1
Stockholders' equity	1,778.3	1,895.0	1,736.1	1,538.9	1,382.5
Per share	13.76	14.69	13.35	11.86	10.69

Source: Campbell Soup Company, *Annual Report,* 1989.

EXHIBIT 11   Campbell soup company, supplemental schedule of sales and earnings

(Million dollars)	1989 Sales	1989 Earnings	1988 Sales	1988 Earnings	1987 Sales	1987 Earnings
Contributions by division:						
Campbell U.S.A.						
Campbell U.S. group	2,776.5	175.1	2,583.8	272.2	2,445.3	284.0
Vlasic Foods	441.4	38.9	352.7	29.9	283.4	21.9
Mrs. Paul's Kitchens	139.8	0.4	150.0	(3.5)	152.7	9.6
	3,357.7	214.4	3,086.5	298.6	2,881.4	315.5
Pepperidge Farm	548.4	53.6	495.0	57.5	458.5	54.0
Campbell Enterprises	327.3	26.5	320.7	25.9	312.8	26.8
Campbell International	1,526.6	(80.9)	1,036.5	57.6	897.8	69.2
Interdivision	(87.9)	—	(69.8)	—	(60.1)	—
Total sales	5,672.1		4,868.9		4,490.4	
Total operating earnings		213.6		439.6		465.5
Unallocated corporate expenses		(31.3)		(12.8)		(18.7)
Interest, net		(55.8)		(20.7)		(22.2)
Foreign currency translation adjustments		(20.0)		(17.5)		(6.7)
Taxes on earnings		(93.4)		(147.0)		(170.6)
Earnings before cumulative effect of accounting change		13.1		241.6		247.3
Cumulative effect of change in accounting for income taxes		—		32.5		—
Net earnings		13.1		274.1		247.3
Per share						
Earnings before cumulative effect of accounting change		0.10		1.87		1.90
Cumulative effect of change in accounting for income taxes		—		0.25		—
Net earnings		0.10		2.12		1.90

Source: Campbell Soup Company, *Annual Report*, 1989.

EXHIBIT 12   **Sales volume increase**

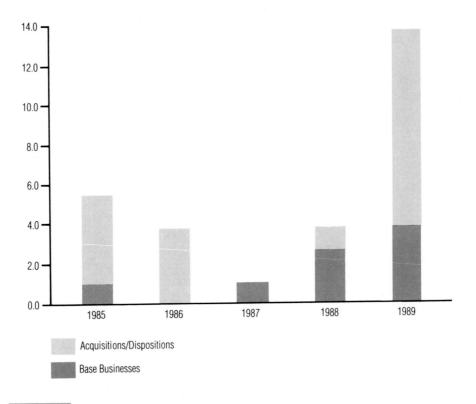

Acquisitions/Dispositions

Base Businesses

Source: Campbell Soup Company, *Annual Report,* 1989.

interests) was 30.5% in 1989, up from 23.1% and 19.1% in 1988 and 1987 respectively.[114]

Management did not appear excessively concerned. According to the 1989 annual report, the company had access to ample source of funds. They had filed a registration statement with the Securities Exchange Commission for the occasional issuance of up to $200 million of debt securities. As of July 30, 1989, none of these securities had been issued. Additionally, Campbell had unused lines of unconditional credit of approximately $630 million.[115]

Despite all of this, in November 1989 Campbell ranked "near the bottom of the food-industry group in terms of return on equity, with 15% compared with about 25% for industry leaders."[116] Yet, according to *Valueline,* stock action had been wild since the death of John Dorrance, Jr. in April. The price of the stock initially rose from the low $30s to the mid $40s, then quickly jumped to more than $60 amid heated takeover speculation before profit-taking set in.[117] The price jumped again in early November 1989 as the resignation of McGovern "sparked a revival of rumors that the company could become a takeover target."[118] Prudential-Bache, in response to the departure, boosted the stock's short-term investment rating. Analyst John McMillin believed the company would turn to new management that was more financially oriented.[119]

FINAL THOUGHTS

In 1989, the future of the food industry looked bright. A relatively stable economy had been forecasted, and ample opportunities remained for the 1990s.[120]

By 1992, the European Common Market would be established and "market boundaries will be all but eliminated as community-wide tariff and quota regulations are relaxed in an effort to build a larger, more cohesive European market."[121] According to *Standard and Poor's,* manufacturers would be reaching abroad through acquisitions and other means for both growth opportunities and access to the common market, while such opportunities still existed.[122]

Industry analysts predicted that "a product that serves consumers' growing appetite for convenient, healthy and satisfying eating experiences could exceed expectations for its category."[123] Jane Collin commented, "products that seem to fill the bill include anything microwaveable, and cereals, seafood and snacks. For food processors, the only risk in these markets seems to be how much consumers will be willing to pay."[124]

Market adviser Robert H. Stovall made the comment that the food industry looked attractive for investments, given the forecasted stable economy. He said, "strong unit volume growth, inelastic price demand and merger and acquisition activity have all stimulated investor interest," and he recommended that "some of the most attractive packaged food stocks are Borden, Campbell Soup, and CPC International."[125]

However, despite this overall sunny forecast, Campbell still had clouds on their horizon.

Endnotes

1. Grant, Stephen E., "Food Processing Industry," *Valueline* (August 25, 1989), p. 1458.

2. Goel, Vindu P., "Campbell Soup's McGovern Forced Out," *The Wall Street Journal,* November 2, 1989, P. A3.

3. Goel, Vindu P., "McGovern Forced Out," p. A3.

4. The Chronology of Campbell Soup Company.

5. Ibid.

6. Ibid.

7. "Campbell Soup: A Company Growing with the Future."

8. Campbell Soup Company, *Annual Report 1989,* p. 14.

9. Ibid., p. 15.

10. Ibid., p. 3.

11. Collin, Jane, "Food, Beverages & Tobacco," *Standard & Poor's Industry Surveys* (February 2, 1989), p. F16.

12. Ibid., p. F16.

13. Ibid., p. F16.

14. Ibid., p. F16.

15. Ibid., p. F16.

16. Ibid., p. F16.

17. Ibid., p. F17.

18. Ibid., p. F17.

19. Ibid., p. F19.

20. Ibid., p. F17.

21. Collin, Jane, "Food, Beverages & Tobacco," *Standard & Poor's Industry Surveys* (June 23, 1988), p. F7.

22. Collin, *Industry Surveys* (February 2, 1989), p. F17.

23. Ibid., p. F17.

24. Ibid., p. F17.

25. Collin, *Industry Surveys* (June 23, 1988), p. F7.

26. Collin, *Industry Surveys* (February 2, 1989), p. F17.

27. Collin, Jane, "Food, Beverages & Tobacco," *Standard & Poor's Industry Surveys* (June 22, 1989), p. F2.

28. Ibid., p. F2.

29. Ibid., p. F2.

30. Grant, *Valueline,* p. 1451.

31. Collin, *Industry Surveys* (June 23, 1988), p. F7.

32. Collin, *Industry Surveys* (June 22, 1989), p. F1.

33. Collin, *Industry Surveys* (February 2, 1989), p. F15.

34. Ibid., p. F15.

35. Collin, *Industry Surveys* (June 22, 1989), p. F1.

36. Ibid., p. F1.

37. Collin, *Industry Surveys* (February 2, 1989), p. F15.

38. *The Wall Street Journal,* September 17, 1984, p. 10.

39. Novack, Janet, "We're Not Running the Company for the Stock Price," *Forbes,* September 19, 1988, p. 41.

40. Ibid., p. 41.

41. Ibid., p. 44.

42. Ibid., p. 44.

43. Ibid., p. 44.

44. Ibid., p. 52.

45. Duetsch, Claudia, "A Sudden Change at Campbell Soup," *The Wall Street Journal,* April 11, 1989.

46. Ibid.

47. Goel, Vindu P., "McGovern Forced Out," p. A3.

48. Ibid., p. A3.

49. Goel, Vindu P., "Campbell Chief Resigns at a Tough Time," *The Wall Street Journal,* November 3, 1989, p. B7.

50. Ibid., p. B7.

51. *Annual Report 1989,* p. 1.

52. Campbell Soup Company, *Annual Report 1988,* p. 2.

53. *Annual Report 1989,* p. 2.

54. *Annual Report 1988,* pp. 2–3.

55. Goel, Vindu P., "Campbell Soup Seeks to Broaden International Presence," *The Wall Street Journal,* September 26, 1989, p. A6.

56. *Annual Report 1988,* p. 3.

57. Ibid., p. 3.

58. Ibid., p. 3.

59. *Annual Report 1989,* p. 4.

60. Goel, Vindu P., "Campbell Soup Posts Big Loss for 4th Period," *The Wall Street Journal,* September 7, 1989, p. A4.

61. *Annual Report 1988,* p. 23.

62. Goel, Vindu P., "Campbell Soup Discloses Plan to Re-structure," *The Wall Street Journal,* August 25, 1989.

63. *Annual Report 1989,* p. 2.

64. Goel, Vindu P., "Campbell Discloses Plan."

65. Goel, Vindu P., "Campbell Discloses Plan."

66. Goel, Vindu P., "Campbell Posts Big Loss," p. A4.

67. Goel, Vindu P., "Campbell Chief Resigns," p. B7.

68. *Annual Report 1989,* p. 15.

69. Ibid., p. 5.

70. Ibid., p. 8.

71. Ibid., p. 9.

72. *Annual Report 1988,* p. 8.

73. *Annual Report 1989,* p. 10.

74. Ibid., p. 10.

75. *Annual Report 1989,* p. 15.

76. Ibid., p. 12.

77. Goel, Vindu P., "Campbell Seeks to Broaden Presence," p. A6.

78. *Annual Report 1988,* p. 14.

79. Goel, Vindu P., "Campbell Seeks to Broaden Presence," p. A6.

80. Ibid., p. A6.

81. Goel, Vindu P., "Campbell Chief Resigns," p. B7.

82. Goel, Vindu P., "Campbell Seeks to Broaden Presence," p. A6.

83. Ibid., p. A6.

84. Ibid., p. A6.

85. Ibid., p. A6.

86. Tracey, Eleanor Johnson, "Here Comes Brand-Name Fruit and Veggies," *Fortune,* February 18, 1985, p. 105.

87. Melloan, George, "The Campbell Kids Fight for the Middle of the Store," *The Wall Street Journal,* March 28, 1989, p. A19.

88. "Canning Campbell's Can," *Newsweek,* April 9, 1984, p. 84.

89. King, Thomas R., "Potential Advertisers May Toss Garbage Magazine in Dumpster," *The Wall Street Journal,* November 2, 1989, p. B6.

90. Melloan, George, "The Campbell Kids Fight," p. A19.

91. "Campbell Soup: A Company Growing."

92. *Annual Report 1989,* p. 3.

93. Fitch, Ed, "Scouts Agree: It's Hot If Its Microwaveable," *Advertising Age.*

94. Erickson, Julie, "Upscale Meals Face a Big Chill," *Advertising Age,* p. 2.

95. Colford, Steven, "FTC Attacks Campbell Ad Health Claim," *Advertising Age,* January 30, 1989, p. 2.

96. Hetzer, Barbara, "Pushing Decisions down the Line at Campbell Soup," *Business Month,* July 1989, p. 63.

97. Ibid., p. 62.

98. Ibid., p. 63.

99. Ibid., p. 63.

100. Colford, Steven, "FTC Attacks Health Claim," p. 2.

101. Ibid., p. 89.

102. "Campbell Soup in Settlement," *The New York Times,* May 19, 1989.

103. Collin, *Industry Surveys* (February 2, 1989), p. F17.

104. Melloan, George, "The Campbell Kids Fight," p. A19.

105. Form 10-K, Campbell Soup Company, 1988.

106. Melloan, George, "The Campbell Kids Fight," p. A19.

107. Goel, "Campbell Posts Big Loss," p. A4.

108. Ibid., p. A4.

109. Ibid., p. A4.

110. *Annual Report 1988,* p. 23.

111. *Annual Report 1989,* p. 23.

112. Ibid., p. 15.

113. Ibid., p. 17.

114. Ibid., p. 17.

115. Ibid., pp. 17, 23.

116. Goel, "Campbell Chief Resigns," p. B7.

117. Grant, *Valueline,* p. 1458.

118. Wilson, David, "Stocks Inch Up in Quiet Trading as Profit-Taking Slows Advance," *The Wall Street Journal,* November 2, 1989, p. B8.

119. Ibid., p. B8.

120. Robert H. Stovall, "Food for Thought," *Financial World* (May 30, 1989), p. 51.

121. Collin, *Industry Surveys* (February 2, 1989), p. F19.

122. Ibid., p. F19.

123. Collin, *Industry Surveys* (June 23, 1988), p. F7.

124. Ibid., p. F7.

125. Stovall, "Food for Thought," p. 51.

NORDSTROM, INC. (A)

Nordstrom, a Seattle-based fashion specialty retail chain, operates 42 apparel, accessory, and shoe department stores, 10 discount clothing stores, and 6 youth-oriented clothing stores in Alaska, California, New Jersey, Oregon, Utah, Virginia, and Washington.

The company has attained a position of leadership and an outstanding reputation for service. Salesperson attention to the customer, selection of goods, product return policy, and amenities to make shopping an enjoyable experience are acknowledged to be extraordinary in the industry. Capitalizing on this trend-setting customer service to differentiate itself from competition, Nordstrom has grown aggressively while major competing chains have not.

After many years as a regional retail chain serving the Northwest states, in the late 1970s Nordstrom started a major expansion into California and Utah. Growth in the Northern and Southern California areas was steady through the 1980s, and in 1988 the company started a move from Western regional focus to that of a national retailer with the opening of a store in Virginia. As a result of growth in number of stores and sales per store, net sales grew nearly 700 percent from 1979 to 1988. Sales in fiscal year 1988 approximated $2.3 billion.

COMPANY HISTORY[1]

John W. Nordstrom immigrated to the United States from Sweden in 1887 at the age of 16 and worked for a number of years as a logger, miner, and laborer. After earning $13,000 gold mining in the Klondike, he settled in Seattle where, in 1901, he opened a shoe store in partnership with shoemaker Carl Wallin. In 1923 Wallin and Nordstrom opened a second store in Seattle. John Nordstrom's three sons bought his interest in the store in 1928 and Carl Wallin's in 1929,

This case was prepared by Stephen E. Barndt, Professor of Management, School of Business Administration, Pacific Lutheran University.

[1]This brief history of Nordstrom, Inc., draws heavily on the Nordstrom 1987 Annual Report, pp. 5–12.

establishing the "family" ownership and management that has continued to the present.

In the early years under John Nordstrom, two basic philosophies were developed that have guided business practice since. The first is a customer orientation in which the company emphasizes offering outstanding service, selection, quality, and value. The second is a policy of selection of managers from among employees who have experience on the sales floor. All of the Nordstrom family members who attained management positions started their careers as salesmen.

Rapid growth did not begin until after World War II. Starting an expansion in 1950 with the opening of two new stores, growth continued so that by 1961 there were eight shoe stores and thirteen leased shoe departments in Washington, Oregon, and California.

In 1963, Nordstrom diversified into women's fashion apparel with the acquisition of Best's Apparel and its stores in Seattle and Portland. Before the 1960s ended, five new Nordstrom Best stores offering clothes, shoes, and accessories had been opened.

The 1970s saw additional changes and rapid, steady growth. Management was passed to the third generation of Nordstroms in 1970, and the company went public in 1971, accompanied by a change in name to Nordstrom, Inc. Continued growth in the Northwest provided the company with 24 stores by 1978. Geographical expansion to California began in 1978 and continued through the 1980s. By 1987, Nordstrom's Southern California presence was reflected in its position of first or second in market share for women's suits, women's blazers, men's tailored pants, women's dresses, women's coats, women's shoes, and men's shoes in the Los Angeles market.[2] In early 1989 Nordstrom operated 26 stores in California including 5 Nordstrom Rack discount stores. The Rack line of stores was started in 1983 and had grown to 10 in the Western states by 1988. Exhibit 1 shows the growth in Nordstrom and Nordstrom Rack stores during the 12 years ended January 31, 1989.

THE FASHION SPECIALTY RETAIL INDUSTRY

Fashion specialty goods include apparel, shoes, and accessories. The market for such goods is relatively mature, with annual and 10-year growth rates approximating 7 percent. In 1988, total U.S. sales of apparel and other fashion goods was $83.4 billion. Approximately 50 percent of this represented women's wear and another 25 percent, men's wear.[3]

The fashion goods market is segmented into several imprecise levels of perceived quality and price. The custom-made goods market is at the high end and

[2]"Nordstrom's Expansion Blitz," *Chain Store Age Executive*, December 1988, pp. 49–50, 53.
[3]Standard & Poor's Industry Surveys, October 1989.

EXHIBIT 1   Nordstrom growth, 1977–1989

Year ended Jan. 31	Company operated stores	Total square footage
1977	20	1,206,000
1978	24	1,446,000
1979	26	1,625,000
1980	29	1,964,000
1981	31	2,166,000
1982	34	2,640,000
1983	36	2,977,000
1984	39	3,213,000
1985	44	3,924,000
1986	52	4,727,000
1987	53	5,098,000
1988	56	5,527,000
1989	58	6,374,000

Source: 1985, 1986, 1987, and 1989 Annual Reports.

followed by designer/style-setting goods; then popular, mid-priced goods; and finally the low-priced utility goods market.

The aging of the population into higher income categories, economic prosperity in general, and increased representation of women in the work force and in higher salaried positions have resulted in greater appeal of the higher quality, style-setting fashions. Retailers that have catered to market segments, such as fashion conscious women that desire upscale goods, have done well. In fact, specialty store sales have grown almost 11 percent per year over the past five years, while department stores have essentially stood still at 5.5 percent growth. Analysts expect specialty niche merchants to continue flourishing if they are able to adapt their lines to changing tastes such as those appropriate to a maturing population of shoppers.

COMPETITION

Fashion retailing has traditionally been a very competitive field with stores relying heavily on product differentiation through an emphasis on quality, service, or other means of adding value. Competitors include traditional department stores, e.g., Ames; general merchandise chain stores, e.g., Sears, K Mart; specialty retailers, e.g., The Limited, Brooks Brothers, I. Magnin, Nordstrom; and independent boutiques.

Most retailers position themselves to serve a single segment of the market. Many department stores are exceptions, offering stylish fashions "upstairs" and

EXHIBIT 2   Competitor specialization by segment

Market segment	Types of stores serving the segment	Emphasis in marketing
Custom	Independent specialty shops	One of a kind quality
Style-setting/fashion conscious	Upscale department stores, fashion specialty chains, boutiques	Name, quality, service
Popular, mid-priced	Department stores, independent and chain specialty stores	Availability, variety, price, service
Low-priced	Discount department stores, general merchandisers	Price, accessibility/convenience

discounted standard or clearance goods in their bargain basement departments. Exhibit 2 provides a general view of the kinds of retailers that tend to serve the various market segments and what they offer.

Competition is often intense with rivals in close proximity to one another. This is especially true for companies locating in shopping malls. Nordstrom, which caters to the upscale, fashion conscious market, locates in malls and downtown shopping districts. As a consequence, Nordstrom is typically in face-to-face competition with a number of strong, major competitors. For example, in its California markets a Nordstrom store is likely to face several of the following competitors: Macy's, Broadway, Robinson's, Buffum's, Neiman-Marcus, Bonwit Teller, I. Magnin, and Saks Fifth Avenue. The Tysons Corner, Virginia, store competes directly with Macy's, Bloomingdale's, and Saks Fifth Avenue, and the Seattle, Washington, store competes with I. Magnin, the Bon Marché, and Frederick and Nelson. All of these competitors are major chain department stores or chain specialty stores. Of course, Nordstrom also faces competing independent boutiques and specialty stores in all of its locations.

COMMON INDUSTRY PRACTICES

Although fashion retailers do not all follow the same strategies, there are several popular strategic moves that have been widely followed to varying degrees. These include market segmentation, selective location, growth through acquisition, cost containment, and price discounting.

Most fashion retailers focus on a single market segment. In recent years the higher priced, higher quality stylish market has been particularly attractive because of the greater growth in this segment and the higher margins available on such goods. This attractiveness has lead some companies to establish new lines of focused stores and others to refocus current stores. Each of these alternatives has presented disadvantages. Developing new retail lines can require considerable capital for new business start-up or acquisition of existing businesses. Refocusing has been difficult for many because an identity, once established, is difficult to change. For example, Sears, long a retailer of low priced and popular fashions, clouded its image and confused potential customers when it tried to upgrade its product offerings.

In contrast to focusing on single market segments, many department stores have sought further market diversification in order to serve higher income customers without losing others. This diversification involves creating stores within a store with departments divided into mini boutiques each aimed at a specific fashion niche.

A shift in shopping from neighborhood and downtown locations to suburban and urban shopping malls has made locating stores in malls or close proximity thereto essential. Picking the malls that are attractive with respect to customer demographics and then gaining access to needed square footage are key factors for success. Companies that gain the new prime locations in growing areas tend to have significant advantages over competitors with older stores in declining shopping areas.

In the mature fashion market with low (7 percent) rate of growth, companies that desire growth must capture the business of competitors. This can involve enticing competitors' customers through superior marketing. Alternatively, it can involve acquiring going-concern competitors to gain market share or broader segment coverage. The latter, a growth through acquisition strategy, has been widely followed in the industry. The Allied Stores Corp., Federated Department Stores, Inc., Macy's, The Limited, the May Department Stores Company, and Carter Hawley Hale Stores, Inc., among others, have engaged in significant use of acquisition for growth.

Rapid expansion through acquisition has left many chains in debt and strapped for cash. For example, Campeau Corp., which owns Allied Stores and Federated Department Stores, faced bankruptcy in late 1989 and planned to sell three of its Federated chains, including Bullock's and I. Magnin, to Macy's and Filene's to the May Department Stores Company. Aside from such drastic measures as divestiture, debt laden companies are commonly in a perpetual search for ways to reduce operating costs. They also tend to be conservative, not investing in innovation or taking major risks. Many such companies are followers, only attempting to duplicate the moves of a competitor after those moves have been proven successful.

Price competition is common, especially among department stores. This includes constant rounds of sale prices in place of stocking top-of-the-line goods to lure customers. Such heavy reliance on price discounting to increase sales rather than on enhanced merchandising and marketing is reflected in advertising that is typically price oriented.

Lower prices (with lower margins), in general, and heavy debt burdens, in particular, have driven many of the larger corporations toward cost reduction. Because labor and inventory are major cost categories, they have been the target of cutbacks. Among many stores, inventories are maintained at low to moderate levels and emphasize a limited breadth of fast turnover styles. Labor cost reduction has affected direct selling and support. Sales cost reductions have been achieved by replacing commission pay with straight hourly wages, increased use of relatively inexperienced lower-pay people for sales, and a reduction of work hours and, therefore, the size of the on-duty sales force. At the same time, centralization of the buying and warehousing functions have reduced support manpower and labor costs.

NORDSTROM STRATEGIC POSTURE

The Nordstrom strategy emphasizes merchandise and service tailored to appeal to the affluent and fashion-conscious shopper without losing its middle class customers. The large Nordstrom specialty department stores cater to their target market with an unparalleled attention to the customers, guaranteed service, and a wide and deep line of merchandise. The success of this strategy has made the company one that competitors fear and attempt to follow. Its competitive strength is implied in the statement ". . . Nordstrom is sometimes known as the 'Black Hole,' into which shoppers disappear, never to enter nearby stores."[4]

In addition to its mainline stores, Nordstrom also operates 6 smaller Place Two specialty stores specializing in youth fashions and 10 Nordstrom Rack stores. The Racks serve as discount outlets offering clearance merchandise from the main stores plus some merchandise purchased directly from manufacturers. They cater to bargain shoppers who value Nordstrom quality.

Store architecture and merchandise differ from store to store. Each is designed to fit lifestyles prevailing in the local geographic and economic environment. For example, the downtown San Francisco and Seattle stores provide their mainstay clientele, the upscale professionals, with large men's clothing and accessories selections. In every location, merchandise selection, local tastes, and customer preferences help shape the store looks on the inside. Approximately 70 percent of the merchandise featured is available at all Nordstrom stores, while the other 30 percent is unique to each store or region.[5]

Product Lines

Nordstrom's specialty department stores carry focused lines of classically styled, relatively conservative merchandise. A *New York Times* writer described the merchandise as ". . . primarily classic and not trendy, the selection limited to styles with broad appeal . . ."[6]

Women's fashions account for the largest share of the Nordstrom product

[4]Jan Shaw, "Executives Catch Nordstrom Fever in Opening Week," *San Francisco Business Times*, October 10, 1988, p. 10.
[5]Nordstrom 1987 Annual Report, p. 12.
[6]Richard W. Stevenson, "Watch Out Macy's, Here Comes Nordstrom," *New York Times Magazine*, August 27, 1989, p. 35.

EXHIBIT 3   Merchandise sales by category

Merchandise category	Share of 1988 sales
Women's apparel	39 percent
Women's accessories	20 percent
Shoes	18 percent
Men's apparel and furnishings	17 percent
Children's apparel and accessories	4 percent
Other	2 percent

line. However, men's wear appears to be gaining in emphasis. Already men's wear comprises 18 percent of the inventory and 21–22 percent of total sales in the new downtown San Francisco store.[7] Exhibit 3 shows the company-wide sales breakdown by merchandise category.

Nordstrom carries both designer and private label merchandise. Private labels are carried on 15 percent of the merchandise. Men's apparel and men's and women's shoes are the largest private label lines where approximately 50 percent of men's clothes and 25 percent of shoes carry the Nordstrom name. Designer lines make up the bulk of the merchandise. Nordstrom features apparel lines by Claude Montana, Gianfranco Ferre, Christian Lacroix, Carolina Herrera, Carolyne Roehm, Calvin Klein, Ann Klein, Donna Karan, Gianni Versace, among others, in its various stores. The Facconnable line of men's wear has recently been added throughout the chain. Selection of lines and styles is largely based on wants indicated in direct customer feedback.

The volume of its orders has allowed Nordstrom to develop a broad supplier base. No one supplier has significant bargaining power.

Merchandising

Nordstrom's merchandising is noted for its extensive inventories and dedicated, helpful sales force. However, Nordstrom also differs from its rivals in several other ways.

The typical store has 50 percent more salespeople on the floor than similar sized competitors. The sales force uses its product knowledge to show appropriate merchandise to customers, assist them in their selections, and suggest accessories. Salespeople keep track of their regular customers' fashion tastes and sizes and then call them or send notes about new merchandise in which they may have an interest.

The company carries a very large inventory, providing an unusually wide selection of colors and sizes. With an inventory almost twice as large per square

[7]Robert Sharoff, "Chicago Seen as Good Move for Nordstrom," *Daily News Record,* January 6, 1989, pp. 2,11.

foot as its department store competitors, Nordstrom has a depth of inventory almost comparable to smaller specialty stores while offering a more complete line. As an indication of the inventory intensity, the San Francisco Center (downtown) store had $100 million invested in opening day inventory, including 100,000 pairs of shoes, 10,000 men's suits, and 20,000 neckties.

Nordstrom is one of the industry leaders in dividing its stores into small boutiques featuring merchandise mixes. Departments are added or changed to serve evolving customer needs. For instance, in response to growth in the number of women in higher level management positions, women's tailored clothing departments have been added. While designer fashions are generally not given special treatment in display, recently the company has started setting up special areas to display some of its higher priced designer apparel. As discussed earlier, Nordstrom has established Facconnable men's wear shops throughout the chain.

Luxurious settings that use polished wood and marble are used in place of the chrome and bright colors common in competing stores. Merchandise is arranged in departments according to lifestyles. Stores feature clusters of antiques and open displays of merchandise, usually arranged at right angles to each other. Mannequins are used sparingly. A piece of antique furniture would be a more commonly used display prop. Merchandise is displayed without bulky anti-theft tags. In addition, there is no closed-circuit television, presenting a less intimidating atmosphere to customers. Instead, Nordstrom relies on the presence of its large sales force to discourage theft.

Nordstrom spends only about 2 percent of sales on advertising, half as much as is commonly spent. The company relies heavily on word-of-mouth to attract customers. What advertising the stores do, emphasizes the styles and breadth of merchandise selection rather than price.

Pricing

Prices are competitive with comparable merchandise. Nordstrom follows the same mark-up practices common to retail fashion stores but prices tend to be high, reflecting the company's selectivity in providing high quality merchandise. However, they are committed to providing value and will not be undersold on their merchandise. If a customer finds an item carried by Nordstrom for sale cheaper at another store, Nordstrom will match that lower price.

Customer Service

High inflation in the 1970s and significant increases in the cost of goods and labor caused most department stores and specialty retailers to cut services to prevent prices from skyrocketing and to remain competitive with the discount retailers that had become popular. This period of rising costs forced consumers to accept the decrease in service in exchange for affordable prices.

Under recent conditions of economic improvement with lower inflation and higher incomes, the public is raising its expectations of service. Many Americans have become tired of self-service or inattentive sales help. Two-income households and busy professionals have become hooked on convenience and are willing to pay for it. At the same time, retailers who shifted to lower levels of customer service are having difficulty in upgrading service. Understaffing in sales positions and overwork coupled with low pay and lack of a career path do not provide the conditions necessary to motivate employees to improve service.

Nordstrom has never cut service and therefore does not have to overcome structural, motivational, or cultural barriers to provide satisfying service. The company is already there—it is the undisputed leader in customer service. Nordstrom's excellent service is anchored on the sales force and supported by company policy and investment in facilities and personnel.

At Nordstrom's a customer can expect to be in a department no longer than two minutes before a salesperson is in attendance to answer questions, explain merchandise, and make suggestions. This salesperson might lead the customer to merchandise in other departments to help find what he or she wants. As an example of this kind of service, a sales representative showed up at a Nordstrom store as it opened at 9:30 A.M. The sales representative, who was dressed in jeans and complimentary causal attire, explained that she needed to be completely outfitted so that she could make a sales presentation at a college over an hour away in two hours. She had arrived in town with only her briefcase. An airline had misdirected her luggage. A sales clerk helped her select a suit and then brought merchandise to fill out the outfit from other departments including such items as shoes, hose, a slip, blouse, and scarf. The sales clerk also facilitated opening a charge account to make the purchase possible. The sales representative left Nordstrom 45 minutes later attired for her presentation.

Sales clerks routinely attend customers in dressing rooms, bringing them alternative items of apparel or sizes to try on. They also routinely send thank-you notes and announcements of sales and arrival of merchandise that should be of interest to the customer. Other examples of the extraordinary out-of-the-way types of service that have been noted of Nordstrom sales personnel include warming up customers' cars on cold days, paying parking tickets for customers who couldn't find legal parking, personal delivery of items to the customer's home, and ironing a newly bought item of apparel so the customer could wear it back to work.

Extraordinary service stems from several mutually supportive factors. First, the number of salespeople on the floor is high—50 percent higher than is common. This means the sales clerks are not so rushed and have the time to wait on customers. Second, the sales force is carefully recruited and then trained. Third, pay is higher than in comparable positions elsewhere and, in addition, is partly based on performance (volume of sales). This means that the sales clerk who satisfies customers earns more. In addition, there is a kind of peer pressure to sell more (satisfy more customers) because those who earn more are seen as role models. Last, Nordstrom has a powerful corporate culture that stresses attentiveness to the customer. This culture is well established, having been instituted under John W. Nordstrom and reinforced ever since. The company has been successful transferring this culture to its new stores at their start-up. A key practice in establishing the Nordstrom culture in new stores is to open them under the leadership of a cadre of experienced Nordstrom managers and salespeople who provide guidance and training to the locally hired personnel.

In keeping with the feeling that the customer is "king" and is always right, Nordstrom has a no-questions-asked merchandise return policy. The company willingly replaces or refunds the price of any item of merchandise whether new or used, with or without a sales receipt. Probably the best known of many refund folklore tales is the case where an individual returned a pair of tires for a refund. The purchase price of the pair of tires was refunded even though Nordstrom does not sell and never has sold tires.

Luxurious settings and furnishings make the shopper feel special. Standard extras in many of the stores include a musician playing enjoyable music on a baby grand piano, free coat and package checking, extra large dressing rooms, free gift wrap at the cash register, and tea for weary customers as they try on apparel in the dressing rooms. Newer, larger stores feature even more extras. For example, the San Francisco Center store has a beauty treatment spa, four restaurants, a pub in the men's department, and valet parking to help it differentiate itself from competition.

Location

Nordstrom targets growing affluent communities for its stores. Although the majority of its stores are located in suburban shopping centers, others are located in large and small city central business districts. In either type of location, Nordstrom chooses to locate close to other retailers because of the drawing power of a concentration of shopping facilities. Exhibit 4 shows the locations and size of Nordstrom and Nordstrom Rack stores in mid 1989.

As a late entrant in many regions, e.g., the East, Southern and Northern California, Nordstrom has had an advantage in its selection of store sites in growing high income areas. Early entrant chains often find themselves doing business in outdated stores in older, less economically attractive areas. However, the industry is mature with most attractive shopping districts saturated with retailers. Finding locations attractive for growth with adequate available square footage requires buying out competitors or a geographically extended search. Following its coverage of virtually all major Pacific Northwest markets in the 1970s and very early 1980s, Nordstrom channeled its growth to California. By the late 1980s, Nordstrom had covered most of the attractive California markets, limiting its further growth there. This forced the company to search for expansion opportunities in several other, slower growing geographical regions. Nordstrom currently plans to open stores in a number of selected locations spread across the East, Northeast, and Midwest, and is considering opening stores in the Southeast

EXHIBIT 4   Nordstrom stores

Store location	State	Sq ft	Year started	Remarks
Portland Lloyd Center (shoes)	OR	14,000	1960	to be replaced 1990
Portland Lloyd Center (apprl)	OR	58,000	1963	to be replaced 1990
Seattle downtown	WA	245,000	1963	
Seattle Northgate	WA	12,000	1965	
Portland downtown	OR	150,000	1966	
Tacoma Mall	WA	132,000	1966	
Bellevue Square	WA	184,000	1967	
Seattle Southcenter	WA	170,000	1968	
Yakima	WA	44,000	1972	
Seattle Aurora Village	WA	71,000	1974	
Spokane	WA	121,000	1974	
Portland Washington Square	OR	108,000	1974	
Anchorage	AK	97,000	1975	
Fairbanks	AK	52,000	1975	
Vancouver	WA	71,000	1977	
South Coast Plaza	CA	235,000	1978	
Alderwood Mall	WA	125,000	1979	
Salem	OR	71,000	1980	
Crossroads Plaza	UT	131,000	1980	
Clackamas Town Center	OR	121,000	1981	
Los Cerritos Shopping Center	CA	122,000	1981	
Fashion Valley	CA	156,000	1981	
Fashion Place Mall	UT	110,000	1981	
Ogden City Mall	UT	76,000	1982	
Hillsdale Mall	CA	149,000	1982	
Clackamas Rack	OR	28,000	1983	
Glendale Galleria	CA	147,000	1983	

and Intermountain West. Such growth is opportunistic, involving new shopping mall space in growth areas and occupancy of vacated space in older shopping centers. An example of the latter is Nordstrom's entry into the Paramus, New Jersey, market in a store vacated when May Department Stores closed its Hahne's chain.

Distribution centers are located in regions to serve stores. Recently a distribution center was opened in Maryland to serve the growing number of stores in surrounding states, making a total of six distribution centers.

MANAGEMENT

Nordstrom practices selective centralized and decentralized decision making. Strategic and significant financial decisions are made at the top level in the organization while operational decisions are made at the region and store level. The

EXHIBIT 4   **Nordstrom stores (*cont.*)**

Store location	State	Sq ft	Year started	Remarks
Santa Anna Rack	CA	32,000	1983	
Topanga Plaza	CA	154,000	1984	
University Towne Center	CA	130,000	1984	
Topanga Rack	CA	48,000	1984	
Broadway Plaza	CA	193,000	1984	
Stanford Shopping Center	CA	187,000	1984	
Pavilion Rack	WA	37,000	1985	
Alderwood Rack	WA	25,000	1985	
Galleria at South Bay	CA	161,000	1985	
Westside Pavilion	CA	150,000	1985	
Horton Plaza	CA	151,000	1985	
San Diego Rack	CA	27,000	1985	
The Village at Corte Madera	CA	115,000	1985	
Oakridge Mall	CA	150,000	1985	
Portland Rack	OR	19,000	1986	
Montclair Plaza	CA	133,000	1986	
North Country Fair Center	CA	156,000	1986	
Seattle Rack	WA	42,000	1987	
Santa Anna Fashion Square	CA	169,000	1987	
Valley Fair Shopping Center	CA	165,000	1987	
Colma Rack	CA	31,000	1987	
Chino Rack	CA	30,000	1987	
Tysons Corner Center	VA	208,000	1988	
Stonestown Galleria	CA	174,000	1988	
San Francisco Center	CA	350,000	1988	
Brea Mall	CA	195,000	1989	replaced 1979 store

Source: Nordstrom Annual Report 1988.

managers in each region, store, and department have responsibility and accountability for profit. They are given the autonomy and authority to make decisions regarding their area. This decentralized management allows managers to be entrepreneurially creative in tailoring each store's merchandise and layout to its customers. Free of decision making for regional and store operations, top management has been able to concentrate on further expansion.

The company structure can be described in terms of three levels of management responsibility—top or executive level, mid level, and store level. The top level consists of three co-chairmen of the board—brothers James F. Nordstrom, 49, and John N. Nordstrom, 52, and cousin Bruce A. Nordstrom, 55—often referred to as the "family"; plus president John A McMillan, 57, who is married to a Nordstrom; and executive vice president Robert E. Bender, 52. The "family" are deeply involved in providing the overall guidance to the company and exercise effective control with about 40 percent ownership. When a new store opens, one or more Nordstroms will be there, on the floor. During a downturn in 1987, family members returned to the floor for stints of selling and visible leadership to help motivate meeting goals. They are visible leaders and approachable to employees and customers but are close-lipped about themselves and the company.

The mid-management level is comprised of the corporate treasurer; geographical group general managers for the Northern California, Southern California, Oregon, Washington, Utah, Alaska, and capital groups of stores; region managers responsible for smaller groups of stores in several of the geographical store groups; and various managers in charge of staff support areas such as public relations, legal affairs, and advertising. Groups or regions have their own buyer organizations to ensure responsiveness to satisfying wants appropriate to the lifestyles in their area.

Operational management of the stores is the responsibility of store managers with the assistance of their staff and department managers. Exhibit 5 shows the general chain of command at Nordstrom.

Throughout the company, idea generation and operational decision making are encouraged, expected, and supported at the lowest levels where the individual has the appropriate information. Managers in the sales departments routinely make decisions on what inventory to carry and whether to accept checks, lower prices to stay competitive, and accept returned merchandise, without consulting higher-level managers or staff specialists.

Units and the individuals in them are goal-driven. As stated by Richard Stevenson in a *New York Times Magazine* article, "the life of a Nordstrom salesperson is defined by goals. Departmental, storewide, and company goals. Qualitative and quantitative goals."[8] Store goals are set for the year and both reflect and influence departmental goals. Department goals influence salesperson goals. Yearly goals are translated into monthly goals. Daily goals are more changeable and reflect pro rata accomplishment of monthly goals as well as historical performance. On a daily basis, departments aim to surpass sales of the same day last year by a set level, and individual goals are adjusted accordingly. If the department is behind in reaching its monthly goal, daily goals of the department and each sales clerk are likely to be pegged higher to get back on track.

Salespeople and departments are kept aware of the level of their goal accomplishment and are provided rewards for goal achievement. Salespeople are reminded of the day's goal and may be asked during the day how they are doing. Those reaching goals are praised; and when longer-term goals, e.g., annual personal goals, are achieved, recognition is public, often in the form of an announcement or letter from a Nordstrom. Top-performing salespeople are admitted to the Pacesetters' Club. Pacesetters receive a certificate, a new "Pacesetter" business card, a 33 percent discount on Nordstrom merchandise (rather than the standard 20 percent), and a night on the town.

The company also promotes performance and conformity to its standards of

---

[8]Stevenson, op. cit., p. 39.

EXHIBIT 5   **Nordstrom management structure**

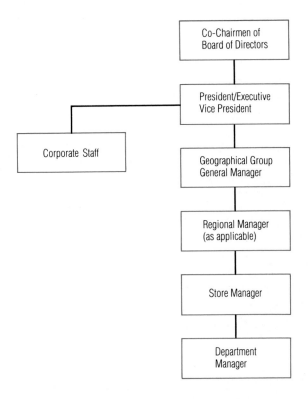

customer service through the widespread use of heroics. The exploits of employees who make unusual or extraordinary efforts to please customers or who have specially noteworthy levels of sales are communicated through the organization, formally and informally, so that they may serve as role models. This technique, along with the use of goals, serves as a powerful indicator of the kinds of behavior the company wants and rewards.

HUMAN RESOURCES

Nordstrom has about 25,000 employees. The company likes to hire young people who have not learned behaviors inconsistent with the Nordstrom customer service values and then start them in sales positions. The actual decision of whom to hire is left to the sales department managers rather than to a staff personnel department. The company's hiring practices, in conjunction with its major expansion in recent years, have left the company with a work force that is relatively young and often college educated. Even its mid- and top-level manager are young. Top managers are in their late 40s to early 50s. Mid-level vice presidents range in age from mid 30s to upper 50s with most less than 45 years of age.

The company follows a promote-from-within policy. Because the company is growing fast, this serves as a motivator to those who aspire to rapid advancement. Promotions to line management positions are made from among employees with sales and customer contact experience. Those who are promoted to higher level positions are encouraged and expected to keep in contact with customers. For example, the company's buyers, who all started in sales positions, spend a large amount of their time on the sales floor to learn what the customers want.

Initial training is brief, taking about one and a half days, and stresses product knowledge and how to work cash registers and attend the customer. Formal indoctrination takes the form of reading a handbook and either viewing a videotape or listening to a lecture on the company's history.

Acceptable behavior is not narrowly specified. For the most part, the culture takes care of that. Employees are given basic guidance in a short, one page 5″ × 8″ employee handbook on card stock that says:

> Our number one goal is to provide
> **outstanding customer service.**
> Set both your personal and
> professional goals high.
> We have great confidence in your
> Ability to achieve them.
> Nordstrom Rules:
> Rule #1: **Use your good
> judgment in all situations.**
> There will be no additional rules.[9]

Other expectations are transmitted in various ways and will bring on corrective actions if violated. One of these is dress. Employees are expected to wear neat business attire. Further, it is understood that the attire *should* be acquired from Nordstrom. Personal business, including telephone calls, is not to be conducted in a customer area. Abuse of employee discount privileges, violation of criminal law, rudeness to a customer, and unacceptable personal conduct are grounds for immediate dismissal. Underperforming employees usually leave on their own as do those who are uncomfortable with constant pressure to meet goals and be nice to the customer no matter what the customer does or how he/ she behaves. Those who remain are loyal to the company and accepting of its cultural values.

To motivate its sales force, Nordstrom uses goals, heroics, recognition, and promotion from within as already discussed. Additional major motivational

---

[9]Nordstrom Employee Handbook, undated.

forces are monetary compensation and morale boosting and attitude shaping programs.

High pay is a very important factor in attracting, retaining, and motivating employees. Pay ranges from about $6 to $9 per hour plus commissions of 6.5 percent to 10 percent. Under combined hourly and commission pay, first year salespeople average $20,000 to $22,000 and after three years about $50,000 per year.[10] Top salespeople can earn $80,000 to $100,000. With these kind of earnings, Nordstrom's sales employees' compensation is high relative to the rest of the industry.

Commission pay ties rewards directly to sales and customer service performance. The higher the sales to satisfied customers, the greater the reward. Since returned merchandise is subtracted from the sales clerk's sales and therefore decreases commission income, selling for the sake of a sale alone is discouraged.

Monetary rewards and public recognition are supplemented with motivational speeches and skits along with pep-talk meetings. The objectives of these techniques are to build employees' confidence in their ability to perform to higher limits, in general, and to get them worked up to capitalize on the selling opportunities associated with one of the four major annual sales, in particular.

FINANCIAL POSITION

Over the ten year period 1979 through 1988, Nordstrom has shown continuous growth in sales and net earnings from year to year (see Exhibits 6 and 7). Although fiscal year 1988, ending January 31, 1989, appears to be the best year of the ten in terms of return on sales, assets, and equity, the entire period reflects consistent, positive performance.

The company is a leader in sales per square foot, a key measure of efficiency in the industry. The department store industry averages $150 in sales per square foot. Although Nordstrom is not directly comparable to general department stores because it sells only apparel, shoes, and accessories that can be densely stocked, it can be compared to specialty department stores. A specialty department store can be considered to be doing very well if it sells between $200 and $250 a square foot.[11] In 1988, Nordstrom stores averaged $380 in sales per square foot. The new Tysons Corner store was expected to reach $450 in its first year and the company's leading store, the South Coast Plaza store, sold $600 per square foot in 1987. As shown in Exhibit 8, per foot sales have risen steadily on both real and constant dollar bases over the last ten years. Nordstrom stores also get off to a quicker start in sales than is common. "On the average, it takes a

[10]Melinda Wilson, "Upscale Nordstrom's May Land in Detroit," *Crain's Detroit Business,* May 23, 1989.
[11]Susan J. Stocker, "Nordstrom's Store Nearing Records," *Washington Business Journal,* August 22, 1988, pp. 1, 16.

EXHIBIT 6   Nordstrom statement of profit and earnings, FY 1979–1988

(Dollars in thousands except per share amounts)

| | Year Ended January 31 | | | | |
	1989	1988	1987	1986	1985
Net sales ($)	2,327,946	1,920,231	1,629,918	1,301,857	958,678
Costs and expenses					
Cost of sales & related					
buying & occupancy	1,564,056	1,300,883	1,095,584	893,874	648,270
Selling, general &					
administrative	582,973	477,488	408,664	326,758	243,845
Net interest	39,977	32,952	34,910	30,482	20,682
Service charge income	(57,492)	(53,825)	(49,479)	(36,636)	(26,630)
Total costs and expenses	2,129,514	1,757,498	1,489,679	1,214,478	886,167
Earnings before taxes	198,432	162,733	140,239	87,379	72,511
Income taxes	75,100	70,000	67,300	37,300	31,800
Net earnings ($)	123,332	92,733	72,939	50,079	40,711
Earnings per share ($)	$1.51	1.13	.91	.65	.54
Dividends per share ($)	$ .22	.18	.13	.11	.10
After-tax return on sales	.053	.048	.045	.038	.042
Asset turnover	1.54	1.56	1.52	1.37	1.34
Return on assets	.082	.075	.068	.053	.057
Return on equity	.21	.19	.19	.17	.16

EXHIBIT 7   Selected indicators of Nordstrom's financial position, FY 1979–1988

(Dollars in thousands)

| | Year ended January 31 | | | | |
	1989	1988	1987	1986	1985
Custom accounts receivable, net	465,929	391,387	344,045	296,030	214,831
Merchandise inventories	403,795	312,696	257,334	226,019	162,361
Total current assets	914,946	730,182	645,326	546,756	402,898
Property, plant equipment, net	594,038	502,661	424,228	397,380	313,818
Total assets	1,511,703	1,234,267	1,071,124	945,880	717,557
Current liabilities	448,165	394,699	324,697	339,503	239,331
Long-term debt & capitalized leases	389,216	260,343	271,054	276,419	199,387
Shareholder's equity	639,941	533,209	451,196	314,119	271,709

EXHIBIT 6   Nordstrom statement of profit and earnings, FY 1979–1988 (*cont.*)

(Dollars in thousands except per share amounts)

	Year Ended January 31				
	1984	**1983**	**1982**	**1981**	**1980**
Net sales ($)	768,677	598,666	512,188	400,614	339,896
Costs and expenses					
Cost of sales & related buying & occupancy	509,133	402,590	393,158	267,646	229,005
Selling, general & administrative	192,813	150,628	126,872	98,228	84,214
Net interest	12,109	11,413	8,345	5,384	3,981
Service charge income	(19,217)	(14,278)	(9,862)	(7,199)	(6,273)
Total costs and expenses	694,838	550,353	468,513	364,059	310,927
Earnings before taxes	73,839	48,313	43,675	36,555	29,069
Income taxes	33,600	21,300	18,900	16,900	12,650
Net earnings ($)	40,239	27,013	24,775	19,655	16,419
Earnings per share ($)	.54	.38	.35	.29	.25
Dividends per share ($)	.07	.0625	.055	.045	.04
After-tax return on sales	.052	.045	.048	.049	.048
Asset turnover	1.49	1.48	1.47	1.35	1.48
Return on assets	.078	.067	.071	.066	.071
Return on equity	.18	.15	.18	.16	.16

Source: Nordstrom Annual Report 1988.

EXHIBIT 7   Selected indicators of Nordstrom's financial position, FY 1979–1988 (*cont.*)

(Dollars in thousands)

	Year ended January 31				
	1984	**1983**	**1982**	**1981**	**1980**
Custom accounts receivable, net	162,610	120,145	95,223	71,924	64.662
Merchandise inventories	129,588	103,674	84,796	65,921	59,240
Total current assets	309,039	241,169	202,292	174,429	132,117
Property, plant equipment, net	205,597	163,957	144,530	121,709	98,060
Total assets	514,679	405,126	347,447	296,792	230,177
Current liabilities	164,628	91,335	92,987	64,606	52,448
Long-term debt & capitalized leases	109,534	110,850	105,302	106,725	68,752
Shareholder's equity	237,734	201,673	149,071	127,783	111,059

Source: Nordstrom Annual Report 1988.

EXHIBIT 8   Nordstrom sales per square foot

Year ended January 31	Sales per square foot	Index of retail apparel price (1979 = 100)	Sales per square foot corrected for price rises
1980	$185	100.0	$185
1981	184	106.2	173
1982	200	110.3	181
1983	205	112.3	183
1984	243	114.5	212
1985	267	116.0	230
1986	293	118.9	246
1987	322	119.1	270
1988	349	124.5	280
1989	380	129.9	293

Note: Retail apparel price index is a composite including men's and boys' apparel, women's and girls' apparel, infants' and toddlers' apparel, footwear, and other apparel.

Sources: Nordstrom Annual Report 1988; U.S. Department of Commerce, *Statistical Abstract of the United States 1989*; and U.S. Bureau of Labor Statistics, *Monthly Labor Review*, January and March 1989.

Nordstrom store between one and two years before it reaches chainwide sales per square foot performance. This compares to an industry average of about three years."[12]

Nordstrom spends considerably less on advertising than is common among competitors. As compared to an industry average of 4 percent of sales, Nordstrom spends less than 2 percent on advertising. Total company advertising expenditures amounted to only $41,566,000, 33,468,000, 29,119,000, 23,299,000, and 17,481,000 in FY 1988, 1987, 1986, 1985, 1984 respectively. The low level of advertising expenditures allows the company to pay more in salesperson compensation without eroding profit margins. In addition, Nordstrom is able to capitalize on the mystique created by the many feature articles that continue to be written about the company and its services.

The company has used internally generated operating earnings, debt, and proceeds from the sale of common stock to finance its growth. Currently, debt is preferred over equity as a source of capital. However, Nordstrom has avoided the high level of debt that plagues many of its competitors. Incremental, store by store growth has been managed so that only relatively modest increases in debt have been needed to supplement operating earnings in financing growth. Most recently, $75,000,000 in long-term debt was added in 1986 and another $150,000,000 in 1988. The company's debt to assets ratio has averaged .58 over

[12]"Nordstrom's Expansion Blitz," op. cit., p. 50.

EXHIBIT 9   Nordstrom liquidity and debt ratios, FY 1986–1988

| | | Year ended January 31 | |
	1989	1988	1987
Current ratio	2.04	1.85	1.99
Quick ratio	1.14	1.06	1.19
Long-term debt/equity	.61	.49	.60
Long-term debt/total assets	.26	.21	.25
Total debt/total assets	.58	.57	.58

Notes: Long-term debt includes long-term obligations under capitalized leases and currently maturing long-term debt. Total debt is calculated as total liabilities and equity less equity.

the last three years with only minor variations from year to year (see Exhibit 9) for leverage and liquidity ratios.

Opening new stores and enlarging present stores is expected to require the expenditure of approximately $500,000,000 through 1991. Of this, the company estimates that $300,000,000 or more will be secured through additional long- and short-term debt without significantly harming its leverage position. Current long-term debt carries with it restrictive covenants that limit the amount of additional long-term debt and lease obligations, require that working capital be the greater of $50,000,000 or 25 percent of consolidated current liabilities, and limit short-term borrowing.

Nordstrom's current ratio was approximately 2.04 at the end of FY 1988 and hovered near 2.0 the preceding two years. Over the last 10 years the current ratio ranged from a low of 1.61 to a high of 2.7. The quick ratio is in excess of one. In addition to its reasonably healthy liquidity position, Nordstrom has available a $150,000,000 line of credit to use as liquidity support for short-term debt.

At the end of FY 1988, 100,000,000 shares of common stock were authorized and 81,465,028 shares issued. Book value per share increased steadily over the 10 years from $1.69 in 1979 to $7.68 in 1988. Exhibit 10 shows total stockholders' equity and other elements of the company's financial structure at the end of fiscal years 1986, 1987, and 1988.

CURRENT INDUSTRY TRENDS

The general trend followed by chain specialty and department stores is to become more like Nordstrom. Nordstrom's success has awakened many of its competitors. They now see customers' satisfaction with sales-force efficiency, competence, and attitudes as a key success factor in market segments other than the low price end. This realization has prompted competing chains to start switching from an emphasis on rock-bottom costs to one of serving the customers.

EXHIBIT 10   Nordstrom balance sheet, FY 1986–1988

(Dollars in thousands)

	Year ended January 31		
	1989	1988	1987
Current assets			
Cash	3,922	4,049	13,608
Short-term investments	12,136	900	14,679
Accounts receivable, net	481,580	404,615	352,662
Merchandise inventories	403,795	312,696	257,334
Prepaid expenses	13,513	7,922	7,043
Total current assets	914,946	730,182	645,326
Property, buildings, equipment, net	594,038	502,661	424,338
Other assets	2,719	1,424	1,570
Total assets	1,511,703	1,234,267	1,071,124
Current liabilities			
Notes payable	95,903	88,795	50,000
Accounts payable	190,755	166,524	177,259
Accrued salaries, wages, taxes	94,369	78,937	63,887
Accrued expenses	26,452	22,267	21,984
Accrued income taxes	20,990	17,085	15,372
Current long-term liabilities	19,696	21,091	5,000
Total current liabilities	448,165	394,699	324,697
Long-term debt	346,471	215,300	241,249
Obligations under leases	23,049	23,952	24,805
Deferred income taxes	54,077	67,107	29,177
Shareholders' equity			
Common stock	147,629	146,317	142,432
Retained earnings	429,312	386,892	308,764
Total shareholders' equity	639,941	533,209	451,196
Total liabilities and equity	1,511,703	1,234,267	1,071,124

Source: Nordstrom Annual Reports 1988 and 1987.

Actually improving services is easier said than done. Years of understaffing and lack of attention to the customer have resulted in sales forces that are not accustomed to providing excellent service. Efforts to upgrade customer service can clash with the corporate culture that has developed in chain stores under these conditions. Changing customer service values is slow and requires consistent communication and reinforcement of desired attitudes and behaviors.

The first and most pronounced change being introduced in major chains to boost sales and upgrade customer service is the conversion of salespeople's compensation from hourly pay to commissions. The general intent of this change to commission compensation is to foster greater concern for satisfying the customer and therefore making the immediate and future sales. The following examples illustrate the scale of the trend toward commission pay. Macy's converted stores located in competition with Nordstrom's to commission sales compensation. Similarly, Frederick and Nelson, a Seattle-area chain of department stores, had 90 percent of its salespeople on commission by 1987. Carter Hawley Hale has its chains and their 113 stores' sales force on 100 percent commission. Campeau Corp. planned to have 90 percent of the salespeople in its Jordan Marsh, Maas Brothers–Jordan Marsh, Stern's, Bon Marché, Abraham & Straus, Bloomingdale's, Burdines, Lazarus, and Rich-Goldsmith's chains on commission by the end of 1990. Bloomingdale's already had 13 of its 17 stores' sales forces on 100 percent commission by mid 1989.

Conversion to commission pay is costly initially and payoffs come slowly. However, the payoffs can be significant. For example, the Frederick and Nelson chain reduced its selling costs as a percent of sales by one percentage point, while at the same time, increasingly sales staff hours by 10 percent.[13]

Several other trends are less pronounced than the movement to commission pay but have a potential impact on service competitiveness. One is the addition of sales staff. Frederick and Nelson was previously cited as having increased its sales force by a modest 10 percent. Macy's has increased both its sales force and their training. Macy's has also eliminated departments such as home furnishings, linens, housewares, and electronics and replaced them with expanded apparel, shoes, and accessories departments. This is indicative of the movement toward focusing on higher margin, higher priced merchandise, including designer labels. In addition, the consolidation of operations and centralization of selected functions has continued and building medium-sized stores is favored.

COMPANY PLANS

Growth can be expected to continue at a minimum rate of three to four new large specialty department stores per year. These large stores will range in size from about 150,000 to 250,000 square feet. In addition, the Nordstrom Racks will continue their steady expansion. Distribution centers will be established to serve the stores that are in geographical areas new to Nordstrom.

Nordstrom has no plans to expand its operations to foreign nations. At least initially, national expansion will be targeted at the Southwest, Washington to Boston corridor, the Southeast, and the Midwest regions.

When the company enters a new area it will open several stores within a very few years to make more efficient use of the required supporting distribution center and the regional staff, including buyers. The company will open its new stores

[13]"Now Salespeople Really Must Sell for their Supper," *Business Week,* July 31, 1989, pp. 50, 52.

under the leadership of experienced employees relocated or promoted from other Nordstrom stores. As in the past, this cadre will be relied on to anchor and communicate the Nordstrom culture.

Company plans call for opening 14 new large specialty stores and expanding 2 present stores between mid 1989 and into 1993 (see Exhibit 11). The schedule reflects an emphasis on gaining a critical mass of stores between Washington and New York City and in the upper Midwest. In addition to the large stores, a Rack is planned for the Los Angeles area in 1989.

The company is actively considering or seeking store sites in the Atlanta, Boston, Phoenix, and Denver areas and a distribution center in the Chicago area. Other current plans call for 8 to 10 specialty stores in North New Jersey and at least 20 in the New York metropolitan area, including Connecticut, Westchester County, and Long Island.[14]

Within stores, service is expected to remain as a major basis of differentiation. Likewise merchandising will remain the same except that the company is moving in the direction of more emphasis on designer apparel with the use of special display areas and shops.

EXHIBIT 11

Planned additions to large specialty store chain

Location		Year	Remarks
Pentagon City (Washington DC)	VA	1989	
Portland (downtown)	OR	1989	expand existing store
Arden Fair (Sacramento)	CA	1989	
Pleasanton	CA	1990	
Lloyd Center (Portland)	OR	1990	replace old, smaller store
Riverside	CA	1990	
Santa Barbara	CA	1990	
Garden State Plaza (Paramus)	NJ	1990	
Menlo Park Mall (Edison)	NJ	1991	
Oakbrook Center Mall (Chicago)	IL	1991	
Towson (Baltimore)	MD	1991	
Montgomery Mall (Bethesda)	MD	1991	
Freehold Raceway Mall (Freehold)	NJ	1992	
Bloomington	MN	1992	
Culver City	CA	1992	
Indianapolis	IN	1993	

[14]Robin Kamen, "Nordstrom Plans 8 N.J. Stores." *The Record,* March 2, 1989, p. C1.

NORDSTROM (B)

For Nordstrom, 1990 was shaping up as a year of few ups and many downs. Labor union charges of unfair labor practices and weak consumer demand offset strategic gains made through new store openings.

LABOR PROBLEMS

From mid 1989, Nordstrom has been engaged in open dispute with locals 1001 and 367 of the United Food and Commercial Workers Union. The union, through these locals, represents approximately 2,000 Nordstrom employees in Western Washington. From 1989 through 1990 the union made a number of unfair labor practice charges against the company.

In late 1989 the union charged that Nordstrom encouraged its salespeople to work off-the-clock, not charging the time they spend attending meetings, taking inventory, writing thank-you notes, making home deliveries, or tracking down hard-to-find garments over the phone. Thus the union was claiming that salespeople spent time working for the company for which they were not compensated. The Washington Department of Labor and Industries subsequently found Nordstrom in violation of state wage laws and directed the company to reimburse workers for work performed without pay. The union followed up with a class-action lawsuit on behalf of 50,000 past and present Nordstrom employees in Washington, Oregon, California, Utah, Alaska, and Virginia, seeking compensatory damages and penalties. Pending determination of the company's liability and a means of settlement of claims, Nordstrom established a $15 million contingency liability reserve for retroactive wage claims.[1]

Members of both locals 1001 and 367, unhappy with the union and its actions, filed petitions with the National Labor Relations Board (NLRB) to decertify United Food and Commercial Workers as their bargaining representative.

This case was prepared by Stephen E. Barndt, Professor of Management, School of Business Administration, Pacific Lutheran University.

[1]Nordstrom Annual Report 1989.

The union countered with complaints to the NLRB that Nordstrom helped organized pro-company rallies, made promises of improved benefits and commission systems if the union were decertified, and otherwise aided in the decertification effort. The NLRB found that Nordstrom did violate labor laws by aiding in the decertification effort. The decertification petitions were thrown out by the NLRB because of the union charges.

In August 1990, Nordstrom reached a settlement with the NLRB in which it promised to refrain from certain activities such as threatening, making promises, providing assistance in decertification, and dealing directly with employees on contract issues. However, another decertification cannot be acted on while there are any union appeals or unfair labor practice charges pending against the company. The union planned to file new allegations, blocking any new decertification election efforts.

The union also engaged in an attempt to discredit Nordstrom's image with consumers. The union alleged the company requires its employees to wear garments it is promoting during work hours, then put them back on the rack, sometimes without cleaning. Nordstrom denied this claim, pointing out that employees are encouraged but not required to wear Nordstrom clothing. The Nordstrom clothing they wear must be purchased and employees can buy at a discount.[2]

In a unrelated incident, a salesclerk in a California Nordstrom store filed a lawsuit alleging that Nordstrom invaded her privacy through use of a hidden video camera placed in a small room used by some employees to change clothes and relieve themselves. Nordstrom contended that the room was not an employee lounge and the camera was there to monitor a safe containing high value merchandise.[3]

FINANCIAL PERFORMANCE

A weakened market from mid 1989 contributed to a downturn in profits at the end of 1989 and a poor showing in the first half of 1990. The weakening market and inattentive management left the company with excess inventory at first. Then, after an overcorrection by management, Nordstrom found it had too little inventory to serve demand. In addition, the generally soft industry-wide demand resulted in competitive price cutting in the attempt to capture sales. This was especially true of the department store chains in financial trouble, e.g., Federated Stores, which was in chapter 11 bankruptcy. However, Nordstrom, because of its overstock position, also resorted to markdowns.

As a result of reduced demand, price cutting, and a $15,000,000 charge for the contingency liability fund to cover off-the-clock pay claims, Nordstrom

2The Morning News Tribune, March 23, 1990, p. A1.
3Seattle Times, July 8, 1990, p. A4.

EXHIBIT 1   Nordstrom consolidated balance sheet

Year ended January 31, 1990

Current assets	
Cash and each equivalent	$ 33,051,000
Accounts receivable, net	536,274,000
Merchandise inventories	419,976,000
Prepaid expenses	21,847,000
Total current assets	1,011,148,000
Property, buildings, & equipment, net	691,937,000
Other assets	4,335,000
Total assets	1,707,420,000
Current liabilities	489,999,000
Long-term debt	418,533,000
Obligations under capitalized leases	22,080,000
Deferred income taxes	43,669,000
Total shareholders' equity	733,250,000
Total liabilities and equity	1,707,420,000

Source: Nordstrom Annual Report 1989.

ended fiscal year 1989 with net earnings of only $114,909,000 on net sales of $2,671,114,000. Net earnings had decreased 6.8 percent from FY 88. At the same time, net sales had increased by 14.7 percent and sales per square foot had gone up to $398 from $380 in the previous year. Total costs and expenses were up to 93.3 percent of sales compared to 91.5 percent in each of the two previous years.[4] The company ended FY 89 with the balance sheet shown in Exhibit 1.

In the first half of 1990 earnings continued depressed. The company's first quarter 1990 earnings were 43 percent and second quarter earnings were 7 percent below the same quarters in 1989.[5] In the first half of 1990, the company experienced earnings of $49,000,000 on sales of $1,360,000,000 compared with $62,000,000 in earnings on $1,241,000,000 in sales in first half 1989.[6]

In response to the drop in sales and profits, in September 1990 Nordstrom announced that it would direct all stores to cut expenses by 3 to 12 percent, depending on the store performance. Store managers will decide how to make these cuts, which could include personnel, inventory, or advertising reductions.

While Nordstrom attributed its reduced profitability to a soft retail market and inadequate inventories, the union problems are an acknowledged distraction, taking attention away from the customers.[7]

[4]Nordstrom Annual Report 1989.
[5]*The Morning News Tribune,* September 8, 1990, p. A.
[6]"Will 'The Nordstrom Way' Travel Well?" *Business Week* September 3, 1990, pp. 82–83.
[7]*The Morning News Tribune,* May 11, 1990, pp. B6, B9.

CONTINUED EXPANSION

In spite of its slackening financial performance, Nordstrom remained committed to expansion. In the latter half of 1989, two new stores were opened, one in the Arden Fair Shopping Center in Northern California and the other at Pentagon City Mall in the Washington, D.C., area. In 1990 new stores were opened in Pleasanton, Northern California; Santa Barbara, Southern California; and in the Garden State Plaza, Paramus, New Jersey. In addition two older stores were enlarged or replaced. The 245,000 square foot Paramus store, the company's most recent, with its personal shoppers to help customers select items, concierge to point customers in the right direction, three restaurants, and a spa, experienced the best initial sales volume of any East Coast store.

Plans continue to call for expansion. In the next five years, Nordstrom wants to open 20 new stores in 13 states.[8] In the immediate future Nordstrom has committed to opening two stores in New Jersey and Maryland plus one in the Chicago area within the next two years.

[8]"Will 'The Nordstrom Way' Travel Well?" *Business Week* September 3, 1990, pp. 82–83.

MERABANK (A)

MeraBank is one of the oldest and largest financial institutions in the Southwest. Formerly First Federal Savings and Loan, MeraBank changed its name creating a new corporate identity to support and enhance its strong commitment to customer service and to facilitate new strategic thrusts. Now, MeraBank must consider the impact of its name and identity change, its expansion and repositioning strategies, and its basic services marketing challenges.

BACKGROUND

On January 1, 1986, First Federal Savings and Loan of Arizona gave banking a great new name, MeraBank (see Exhibit 1). The rich history of First Federal was a foundation and catalyst for the emergence of MeraBank.

Brief History of MeraBank

Arizona was a frontier state in 1925 when State Building and Loan opened its doors for business. State Building and Loan was a forward-thinking company, an enthusiastic group of business people determined to grow with the needs of the nation's newest state. In 1938, the company became First Federal Savings and Loan, and continued to grow becoming the state's oldest and largest thrift.

First Federal was an appropriate name for this innovative company that achieved a long list of "firsts." For example, First Federal was the first Arizona savings and loan to open a branch office. This was achieved in 1948 when a branch office was opened in Yuma. First Federal was the first savings and loan in Arizona to exceed a billion dollars in assets. It was the first savings and loan to acquire other savings and loans with the acquisitions in 1981 of American Savings in Tucson, Mohave Savings in north and northwestern parts of Arizona, and the acquisition in 1982 of Mutual Savings in El Paso, Texas. After becoming

This case was prepared by Michael P. Mokwa, John A. Grant, and Richard E. White of Arizona State University, in cooperation with MeraBank and the First Interstate Center for Services Marketing at Arizona State University. The case was developed as a basis for discussion rather than to illustrate either effective or ineffective management practice. The help of Robba Benjamin, Margaret B. McGuckin, and Barry Iselin of MeraBank is gratefully acknowledged.

EXHIBIT 1   The MeraBank logo

a public company in 1983, First Federal was the first Arizona savings and loan to be listed on the New York and Pacific Stock Exchanges.

In 1984 and 1985, First Federal's growth accelerated, primarily due to the injection of capital from the stock conversion. The company progressed with its mission clearly defined—to be a leading real estate–based financial institution in the Southwest. To achieve its mission, activity centered on diversification with a real estate focus. Three companies were acquired—Realty World, a realty franchising business; First Service Title, a title and escrow service; and F.I.A. Associates, an investment consulting and advisory company. Consumer loan operations were expanded throughout eight western states. In 1985, the company changed its charter from a savings and loan association to a federal savings bank. First Federal officially became MeraBank on January 1, 1986.

In December 1986, MeraBank was acquired by Pinnacle West, formerly AZP, Incorporated. Pinnacle West is Arizona's largest corporation. Pinnacle West is a diversified group of subsidiaries that include: Arizona Public Service Company, a public utility; Suncor Development Company, a real estate development company; El Dorado Investment Company, which invests through limited partnerships in private companies with significant growth potential; and Malapai Resources Company, which locates and develops fuel and uranium reserves. MeraBank with its $6.3 billion in assets and banking presence could be expected to improve short-term earnings and growth potential for the diversified Pinnacle West.

MeraBank's Business Lines

Throughout all of its changes, MeraBank has positioned itself as a family-oriented financial institution, capitalizing on real estate expertise. For over 15 years, MeraBank has set the pace in residential mortgage lending in Arizona with a market share nearly double that of its closest competitor. The company also has been a significant originator and syndicator of commercial real estate development and construction loans on a national basis. As illustrated in Exhibit 2, MeraBank's operations span eight western states. It is the 25th largest thrift in the United States, the largest thrift in Arizona, and the second largest financial institution in Arizona.

EXHIBIT 2   MeraBank's areas of operation

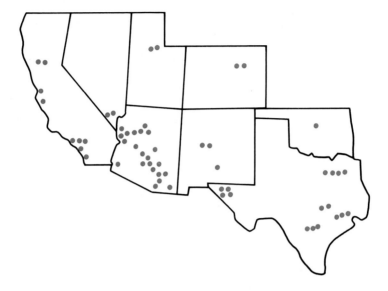

MeraBank has five major business lines: (1) retail banking; (2) consumer lending; (3) real estate lending and mortgage banking; (4) corporate banking; and (5) real estate development.

MeraBank has a well–established retail banking presence. The company offers the convenience of 78 branches including 9 in Texas. Aside from MeraBank's commitment to the Texas region, expansion is being planned for other geographic areas in the Southwest. MeraBank's core products relate to checking and savings, but utilization of electronics and the potential for cross selling are providing new opportunities in retail banking. Currently, MeraBank is a part of the largest ATM (automatic teller machine) system in the state of Arizona.

Phoenix is the largest and strongest area of operation for MeraBank's retail banking. As illustrated in Exhibit 3, MeraBank's market penetration is nearly 18% in Phoenix, which is significantly greater than in the smaller metropolitan areas of Tucson and El Paso. The Phoenix area accounts for over 45% of the bank's business while Tucson is about 10.4% and El Paso is 8.8%. Other parts of Arizona account for 12.8% of the business, other areas of Texas are 4.1%, and other states are 18.2%. By reaching 15% of the Arizona market, MeraBank has a 7.1% share of the total deposit market. Exhibit 4 illustrates MeraBank's position in the total deposit market in comparison with other Arizona financial institutions. The exhibit shows each major competitor's share of the total deposit market. Valley National Bank (VNB) is the leader, followed by First Interstate Bank (FIB), The Arizona Bank (TAB), Western Savings (WS), MeraBank (MB), United Bank (UB), Pima Savings (PS), Great American Savings (GAS), and Southwestern Savings (SWS).

EXHIBIT 3   **Retail household penetration**

Total	3Q85: 231,949	
	3Q86: 251,195	
	3Q87: 280,663	
Total accounts	677,240	
Total deposit dollars	$2.4 billion	
Market penetration	Arizona	15.0%
	Phoenix	17.8%
	Tucson	10.7%
	El Paso	12.2%

EXHIBIT 4   **Major competitors**

Arizona financial market (1986)

Competitor	AZ branches	Assets	Loans	Deposits
			($ In billions)	
Banks				
Valley National	272	$10.7	$7.3	$9.2
First Interstate	183	6.5	4.3	5.7
Arizona Bank	119	4.5	3.2	3.8
United Bank	47	2.7	1.8	2.2
MeraBank	68	6.3	5.1	4.0
Savings and loans				
Western Savings	82	5.5	3.0	3.8
Great American*	32	3.2	2.5	1.4
Southwest Savings	50	2.1	1.7	1.5
Pima Savings	28	2.6	1.8	1.3

*Estimated: AZ operations combined with parent company.

In consumer lending, MeraBank offers customers a variety of secured and unsecured loans, including home equity lines of credit, car loans, RV loans, and boat loans. Credit cards and lines of credit are also important dimensions of the consumer lending package. MeraBank views consumer lending as an expansion area and has opened new consumer lending offices called MeraFinancial Services Corporation in key areas of Colorado, California, and Texas. The bank's goal in this area is to create as large a consumer loan portfolio as possible, commensurate with sound underwriting. The consumer lending group has instituted a detailed program of monthly loan reviews that will keep management well-informed on the status of the portfolio and how it is meeting underwriting standards.

A strong core of MeraBank's expertise lies in real estate financing. The mortgage lending operations originate and service more loans in Arizona than any other finance company. Additionally, Meracor Mortgage Corporation offices operate in Arizona, California, Colorado, Nevada, New Mexico, Texas, and Utah. They handle residential, commercial, and construction loans. A further presence of MeraBank in the real estate lending market is the marketing of its realty brokerage office franchises. Meracor Realty Corporation holds the license for a large segment of the West and Southwest, having franchised more than 135 Realty World offices. Realty World brokers can offer MeraBank mortgages and services to clients, enabling the bank to reach new customers without adding its own branch office. Through ReaLoan, a computerized mortgage application system, a home buyer and broker can use a computer terminal to analyze the dozens of mortgages available through MeraBank.

In 1985, MeraBank expanded into title insurance. This service was designed to provide customers with title insurance and escrow services from national title insurance companies. Further expansion of the mortgage banking business is sought as MeraBank continues to pursue a program of nationwide lending to strengthen its position as a major force nationally in commercial and construction lending. F.I.A. Associates, the bank's real estate advisory and management company, manages over $1.5 billion in real estate properties and is viewed as a way of diversifying in the real estate business through institutional investors.

Corporate banking provides both deposit and lending services to companies throughout the Southwest. MeraBank offers corporate clients a wide variety of deposit, checking, and lending services as well as financing, secured by accounts receivable and inventory. The bank finances equipment acquisition and plant expansions as well. Cash management accounts and high-yield bonds are products that were designed to meet the needs of the corporate banking customers. Corporate banking is a new area for savings institutions, and the bank is branching into this new and challenging business prudently.

MeraBank is also a significant competitor in real estate joint ventures, which include the marketing and property management of joint venture projects. This fifth business line, real estate development, is achieved through Meracor Development Corporation, the bank's joint venture and development company. Meracor activities focus on the management of profitable, high-quality projects in Arizona, and to a lesser extent in Texas, California, Colorado, and New Mexico. Management has made a strategic decision to reduce dependence on this area and to limit the size of joint venture development in the future to assure that MeraBank retains a conservative level of leverage.

The Competitive Market Environment

Competition in financial markets is expanding and intensifying as many new institutions are entering and as traditional market and service boundaries are eroding. The basic financial market in Arizona, MeraBank's largest area of operations, can be segmented fundamentally into (1) banks, and (2) savings and loans.

Information about MeraBank's major competitors in each of the segments can be found in Exhibit 4. In 1985, savings and loans totaled about a 24% share of the Arizona deposit market, while banks maintained the largest overall market share with 70% of the deposits.

With product deregulation, savings and loan institutions have been given freedom to expand much more into consumer banking services. This has allowed savings and loan institutions to compete directly with the banks, which has resulted in a blurring of the distinction between banks and savings and loan institutions. Through mergers and acquisitions that have taken place as a result of geographical deregulation, larger national and international bank holding companies have moved into the Arizona competitive environment and made their presence known. Of the six largest banks in Arizona, four changed hands in 1986. The two largest banks that have not changed hands during this period are Valley National Bank and First Interstate Bank.

Despite increased competition and activity, total deposits in the Arizona market have begun to decline. As illustrated in Exhibit 5, Arizona's deposit base increased by $11.2 billion from 1983 through 1986, reaching a peak of $33.4 billion. However, in 1987, total deposits declined from 1986. Exhibit 6 shows that the leading financial institutions saw a stable or declining market share trend. First Interstate's market share dropped from 19% to 15.4%, while Valley National and MeraBank's market shares declined 2.5 and 1.4 points, respectively. Exhibit 7

EXHIBIT 5   Trend of Arizona's total consumer banking deposits, 1983–1987/Q3

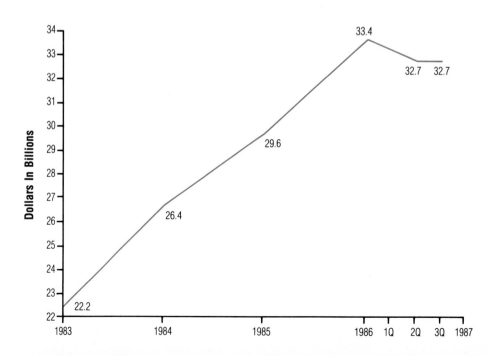

EXHIBIT 6   Market share trend—total consumer banking deposits, 1983–1987/3Q

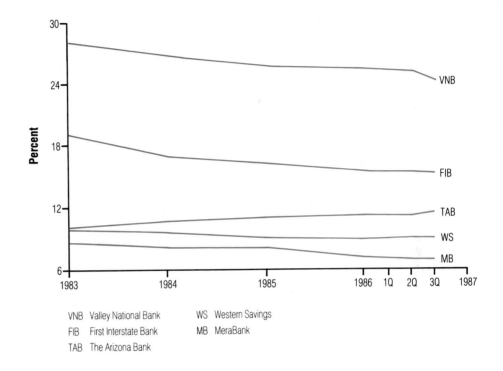

VNB   Valley National Bank   WS   Western Savings
FIB   First Interstate Bank   MB   MeraBank
TAB   The Arizona Bank

shows that all competitors experienced a positive annual growth rate between 1983 and 1986. But in 1987, all but two competitors had a drop in the average deposit per branch from the first quarter of 1987 through the third quarter of 1987. This is illustrated in Exhibit 8.

The decline in bank deposits appears to stem from consumers' desire for higher return investments. As the stock market enjoyed a record bull market period in the first three quarters of 1987, conservative banking products had a continuing decline, as seen in Exhibit 9. Certificates of deposit (CDs), which offer a guaranteed rate of return for a specified period of deposit time, declined while Money Market Accounts (MMA), which offer a varying rate of interest with no time commitment on the deposit, exhibited a dramatic increase in sales. Passbook savings (PB) and interest-bearing checking accounts (NOW) steadily declined in 1987.

The Major Competitors

In the Arizona market, the most formidable competitor has been Valley National Bank with nearly 10 billion dollars in assets. Valley National remains as the only bank that is headquartered in Phoenix. Valley has 277 branches in Arizona. Valley National's 24.1% share of the total deposit market is maintained with 25% of the

EXHIBIT 7   Growth in total deposits by major competitors

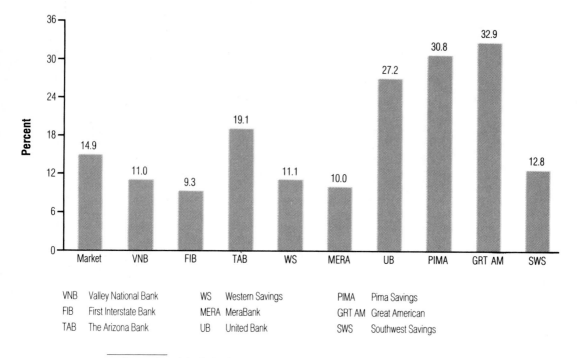

VNB	Valley National Bank	WS	Western Savings	PIMA	Pima Savings
FIB	First Interstate Bank	MERA	MeraBank	GRT AM	Great American
TAB	The Arizona Bank	UB	United Bank	SWS	Southwest Savings

Source: *Deposit Institution Performance Directory.*

branches. Valley National's strategy seems centered on intense penetration and physical presence, supported by regional expansion.

Valley National is also the leader in the Arizona market for electronic banking and is planning further expansion. At present, the Valley National debit card is the most widely accepted in the Arizona market and can be used to make purchases at grocery stores, service stations, convenience stores, even department stores. This electronic funds transfer card has become known as a POS (point of sale). It allows a debit of the customer's bank account as payment for a purchase. The POS is expected to be expanded into more retail outlets by Valley National.

In the lending end of the business, Valley National has instituted a Loan by Phone program. The bank promises answers to loans in 30 minutes. These are some of the services that Valley focuses on in its advertising to create its image as "The Leader in Your Banking Needs."

First Interstate Bank has been very close in asset size to MeraBank, but has over twice as many branch locations in Arizona. First Interstate has 15.2% of the deposit market share and 16.4% of the branches. The bank is also involved in POS capability with their debit card being accepted at all but grocery store locations. First Interstate is an affiliate of First Interstate Bancorp, which is the

EXHIBIT 8   Average consumer banking deposits/branch, third quarter 1987

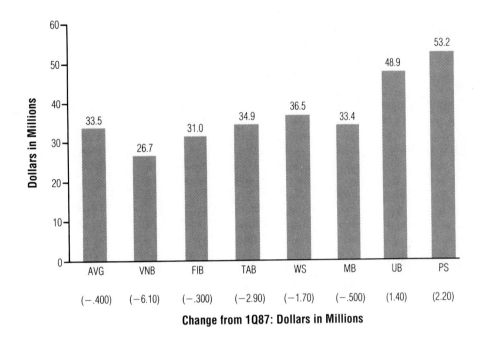

Change from 1Q87: Dollars in Millions

	AVG	VNB	FIB	TAB	WS	MB	UB	PS
Dollars in Millions	33.5	26.7	31.0	34.9	36.5	33.4	48.9	53.2
Change	(−.400)	(−6.10)	(−.300)	(−2.90)	(−1.70)	(−.500)	(1.40)	(2.20)

EXHIBIT 9   Deposit product mix, 1983–1987/3Q

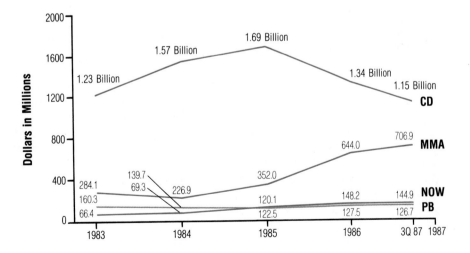

eighth-largest retail banking organization in the nation. First Interstate is a relatively new name for a long-standing competitor. Their advertising theme is "Serving Arizona for 110 years." First Interstate customers are the highest users of the automatic teller machines (ATMs) in Arizona, and First Interstate plans to continue to expand its ATMs, POS, and branches to stay on the leading edge in convenience banking.

The Arizona Bank is another competitor close to MeraBank in asset size, with just under 5 billion dollars. The Arizona Bank with 126 branches in Arizona was acquired in October of 1986 by Security Pacific Corporation, the sixth-largest bank holding company in the United States. The bank's image is tied closely with the state it serves. To convey an Arizona image, a native American Indian is used in the bank's logo with the slogan "The Bank Arizona Turns To" and "Count on Us." The bank's plans include expansion of more branches in the Phoenix metropolitan area and some outlying communities.

The United Bank of Arizona has been a smaller competitor with only 47 branch operations. It has maintained over 2 billion dollars in assets. United Bank has a 5.7 percent share of the total deposits with only 3.9% share of the branches. United Bank was acquired by Union Bancorp in January of 1987. Union Bancorp is a holding bank in Los Angeles, a subsidiary of Standard Chartered PLC, an International Banking Network. United Bank has had the fastest percentage growth in assets, deposits, and loans of all major Arizona banks in the last 5 years. The bank's focus has been on responsiveness to the needs of the middle market, growing businesses. This is reflected in the advertising theme, "Arizona's Business Bank for Over 25 Years." Citicorp has been very interested in United Bank and would like to acquire it to enhance their presence in Arizona.

In the savings and loan segment, the largest competitor has been Western Savings, with approximately 5.8 billion dollars in assets. Headquartered in Phoenix, Western Savings has begun expansion into Tucson and Flagstaff. In their major markets, Western Savings has located branch offices in popular grocery stores. To develop their image as "The Foresight People," Western Savings plans to continue to expand products and services. The company experienced about a 2% drop in CDs but has seen an increasing volume of retail deposits. Western Savings is the only thrift currently involved in POS. It has only been able to have its POS card accepted by about 200 Mobil service stations.

Great American, though substantially smaller, has been aggressively expanding in the Phoenix area following a similar location strategy to that of Western Savings. Headquartered in San Diego, the company plans continued expansion in the Phoenix area, targeting high-income growth markets. Great American has experienced the largest increases in the MMAs and has seen a strong increase in the volume of retail deposits in the last year. They present themselves in the image of a bank, trying to stress the name Great American, "Your Advantage Bank."

Southwest Savings is a smaller institution with 53 branch operations. It has been an independent and closely held organization. Southwest has committed themselves to serving the growing senior citizen population in Arizona. Southwest Savings has experienced the industry trend in product performance with about a 2% drop in CDs, while MMAs were up sharply. However, overall total deposits have been down.

Pima Savings has operated out of Tucson, where they have a 40 percent share of the total savings and loan deposits in Pima County. Pima Savings has a 5.9 percent market share of the total deposits in Arizona with only 3.7 percent of the total branches. Pima Savings has seen continued growth in total deposits and in CDs. The company is viewed in the industry as the investment rate leader. Pima is rapidly expanding branches in the Phoenix area, frequently using Safeway grocery stores as their outlets. Pima is owned by Pima Financial Corporation, which is a subsidiary of Heron Financial Corporation, a U.S. holding company for one of Europe's largest privately owned companies.

To gain insight into the competitive environment, 10 additional exhibits have been included. Exhibit 10 illustrates the net worth of the Arizona financials as a percent of their assets. The composition of loan services is expressed in terms of real estate and consumer loans for the banks in Exhibit 11, and for the savings and loan associations in Exhibit 12.

Other major competitors in the Arizona financial market began to arrive with reinstatement of interstate banking in 1986. Among the newest financial institutions are: Citibank, which took over Great Western Bank & Trust of Arizona and is a subsidiary of Citicorp, the largest bank holding company in the United States; and Chase Bank of Arizona, a division of Chase, the second largest

EXHIBIT 10   GAAP net worth as a percent of unconsolidated assets

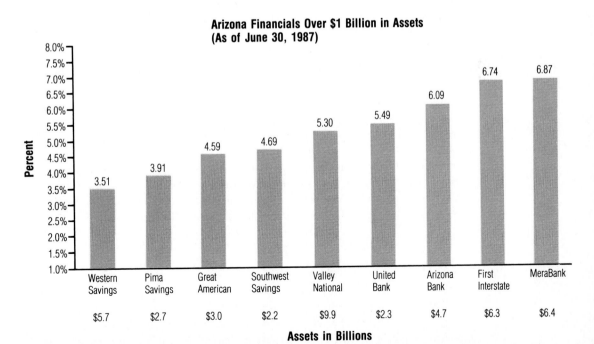

EXHIBIT 11   Major competitors for loan services, banks, September 30, 1986

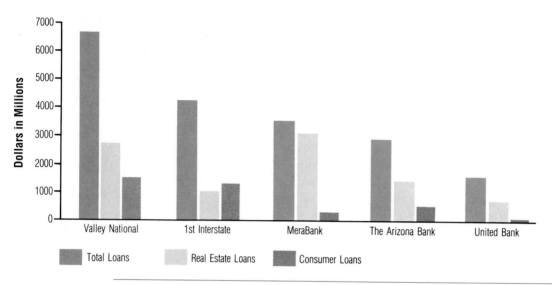

	Dollars (millions)		
	Total loans	Real estate loans	Consumer loans
Valley National	6718	2740	1538
1st Interstate	4307	1078	1345
MeraBank	3595	3138	352
The Arizona Bank	2942	1466	569
United Bank	1632	754	118

Source: *Deposit Institution Performance Directory.*

holding company in the country. Chase took over the former Continental Bank. These acquisitions should have an impact on the Arizona financial market in the near future. Interstate banking has provided the opportunity for the acquisition of Arizona's financial institutions by out-of-state companies and could continue to be a factor in the competitive environment. Also considered as competitors in some segments of MeraBank's lines of business are insurance companies, finance companies, investment companies, money market funds, credit unions, and pension funds. Overall, many organizations are entering financial service markets.

THE NAME AND IDENTITY CHANGE

In 1985, the total population of Arizona was 3.2 million. The state had experienced a five-year increase in its total population, an increase of nearly 25%. Growth had been projected to continue. MeraBank's other dominant market,

EXHIBIT 12   Major competitors for loan services, savings associations, September 30, 1986

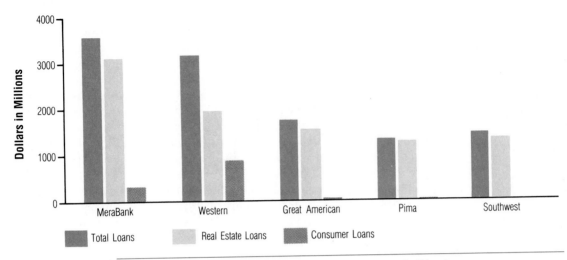

	Dollars (millions)		
	Total loans	Real estate loans	Consumer loans
MeraBank	3595	3138	352
Western	3180	1978	919
Great American	1773	1571	90
Pima	1345	1286	58
Southwest	1477	1343	34

Source: *Deposit Institution Performance Directory.*

Texas, also had been growing. In 1985, it had a much larger population than Arizona, over 15 million people. At that time, First Federal operated 12 offices located throughout Texas, in El Paso, Dallas, Austin, Houston, and Fort Worth.

Even though First Federal was well positioned in its highly competitive markets, banking deregulation and legislative changes were opening doors to interstate banking and to charter changes for thrift institutions. New products and services would soon be available and a significant challenge confronted First Federal. Although First Federal offered a full range of products and services, most consumers perceived banks to be better—more full-service and service-oriented—than savings and loans.

First Federal perceived a name change as a necessity, but the corporate priorities in 1985 were complex. The company hoped to demonstrate superior financial performance, while making customer service its most effective marketing tool. Moreover, the company hoped to protect its current market share from the threat of new competition, while increasing retail banking coverage in Texas and expanding beyond Arizona and Texas.

The board of directors had been considering a name change since the company went public in 1983. The name First Federal was a very common name in financial institutions. There were over 89 First Federals in Texas alone. If expansion was to be considered, the company needed a name it could grow with. Aside from expanding under one name and distinguishing itself to stockholders, the board wanted to include the word "bank" in its name and position itself as a bank in the market.

A market research company from New York was retained to help determine what the new name and bank image should be. However, the board felt the process would be easy, simply changing some signs and forms. The board decided that the First Federal logo could be maintained by simply changing the name to FedBank. The board dismissed the market research team, and by 1984, they were ready to make the change. In August, a new senior Vice President was given the task of implementing the name change. The initial step was to check out regulations regarding the use of the word "bank" in the name of a chartered savings and loan association. However, it was discovered in the legal search that the proposed use of FED in the new name would violate law. There is a regulation banning private organizations from using a name that sounds like a federal agency. In this case, the proposed FedBank name was very similar to the federal bank known as the "FED."

The task of changing the name would have to start over. The first market research company had left with some ill feelings. So in 1985, a new consulting firm, S & O Consultants from San Francisco, was contracted for the project. S & O specialized in corporate identity. They had recently done the name change for First Interstate Bank in Arizona and were familiar with the financial institution market in the area.

The Project Objectives

Objectives were established at the beginning of the project. These objectives are outlined in Exhibit 13. The primary objective was to select a name that conveyed

EXHIBIT 13   Name objectives

The new name for First Federal of Arizona's retail bank should accomplish the following (percentages indicate weights given to each objective when evaluating names):

1. Convey an honest, hard-working, service-oriented bank. (30%)
2. Imply stature and strength. (30%)
3. Appeal to the mass-market retail banking audience. (20%)
4. Be distinctive, memorable, and easy to pronounce. (20%)
5. Be compatible with a range of financial services including retail banking, real estate development, construction lending, mortgage banking, corporate lending, etc.
6. Make no specific reference to Arizona, but may incorporate southwestern flavor.
7. Be available and legally protectable.

a positive image and new identity. The name needed to be legally available in all 50 states. It needed to fit all the business lines—everything from the title company to retail banking to real estate joint ventures. A distinctive identity was to be developed as well. The First Federal logo was very similar to other existing corporate identities and offered little value to the company as an identity. The new name needed to create excitement and set the tone for continued innovation and leadership. It needed to increase the employees' morale and help generate new business. However, the company did not have unlimited resources. So, a very important objective was to accomplish everything within a strict, tight budget and a short time frame.

The Process

Distinct phases were identified in the change process. First, the name itself had to be generated and selected. Second, the logo and identity surrounding the name had to be developed. Third, the identity needed to be communicated in a clear and concise way, and finally, evaluation must be undertaken.

Selecting the name was the first step. Criteria for the new name were established. These included implying stature and strength, and being distinctive, memorable, and easy to pronounce. All the criteria were ranked and weighted in terms of perceived importance. The criteria of conveying a service-oriented bank and of implying stature and strength were ranked as the two most important criteria for the new name.

After a positioning statement was developed for the name itself, the process of generating the name began. Over 800 names were evaluated and critiqued. The top 20 names were further evaluated using a mathematical scoring system, and all the top 20 names were legally searched in all 50 states. The final five that were considered were: First Mark Savings Bank, Interprize Savings Bank, Landmark Savings Bank, Merit Savings Bank, and Pace Savings Bank.

An early favorite was Merit Savings Bank. However, this name was being used elsewhere, particularly in California. And it was associated with a brand of cigarettes. However, the name had some interesting roots. After an arduous series of executive interviews, brainstorming sessions, and stormy meetings, a consensus was reached. The name MeraBank was selected.

In phase two, the logo and identity were developed. The company desired a design that would uniquely identify them and reach across all their business lines. The logo had to be instantly recognizable, even before the name was seen. The company wanted something that would emphasize a commitment to comprehensive financial services. The logo would have to be modern, make a strong retail statement, and incorporate a taste of southwestern imagery, but not limit the bank to Arizona.

Choices were narrowed, and focus group testing began. In Exhibit 14, the leading choices are represented. Focus group reaction favored C, a multicolored logo. Group participants described the identity as "progressive," "modern," and

EXHIBIT 14   Proposed MeraBank logos

A)

B)

C)

"large." Obviously, this met the company's objectives. The colors were described as being "attractive" and "southwestern." The vibrant yellow-gold and orange-red of the sunrise with the royal purple of the mountains were well-understood southwestern images.

Several modifications were made to the logo based on focus group work. For example, the company has had a substantial senior citizen customer base. They expressed some very strong dissatisfaction with the proposed typeface. They perceived the logo as very contemporary, but the typeface was perceived as very different and too modern. What resulted was a new and much more conservative typeface with the same multicolored contemporary logo. Perceptions were much more favorable.

Effective communication of the name and imagery were vital to establishing the identity and accomplishing performance-oriented objectives. A strategic decision was made to communicate the change from the inside out. To accomplish this, a large task force was assembled internally to cover literally every aspect of the identity change. The name change task force began working in July of 1985. It included a project manager, 7 project leaders, and 30 employees. The task force was responsible for the signage, forms, merchant notification, employee notification and promotion, media notification and promotion, and customer notification and promotion.

To direct and guide the task force, several objectives and strategic thrusts were outlined. The first objective was to gain employee awareness and enthusiasm for the name change. Employee support was essential to communicate the name from the inside out. A second objective of the task force was to develop a graphic plan and standards manual that clearly spelled out the proper representation and usage of the new logo. A high priority was given to the delicate task of communicating the change to primary stakeholders, including board members and the stockholders. A major undertaking involved identification and revision of all forms. The effort uncovered the opportunity to reduce by 30% the number of forms used.

The task force also needed to develop an advertising campaign and related promotions for customer notification. A TV spot would provide only 30 seconds to communicate the new identity; a billboard would provide less time. A very complex message had to be refined to its strongest, simplest components. Also, the task force needed to develop branch employee training and information sessions including the revision of the branch operations manuals. Finally, the task force had to be prepared to handle any of the legal questions that could arise concerning the name change. Thus, one of the task force members was a staff attorney.

The plans to generate employee awareness and enthusiasm were initiated within tight time and resource constraints. The task force knew that employee support was essential to market acceptance. The name, but not the logo, was first announced to all employees at the company's big 60th birthday celebration in September 1985. Further internal communication was initiated through a new publication called "The MeraBanker." The employee campaign even included a "mystery shopper" who went into the field asking employees questions about the name change.

A customer awareness program began in November with a teaser advertising campaign. By December, more than 1200 stationery forms and collateral pieces had been redesigned and printed. On January 1, 1986, the new signs and the major campaign theme, "First Federal Gives Banking a Great New Name," were unveiled. Throughout the customer awareness program, the "MeraBanker" term was consistently used for name and identity–related internal communication.

Extensive work was done with the press. Hundreds of press releases were sent out. Early releases included a question and answer piece that did not include the full identity. Later in the program, the logo, the name, and the advertising campaign were released to the press.

MeraBank wanted its identity to be comprehensive and wanted to maintain the integrity and power of the identity. So for the first time in the company's history, a graphic standards manual was developed to state how and for what purposes the logo could be used. This was necessary to determine proper use for advertising, promotions, and brochures, as well as use on checks, credit cards, debit cards, ATM cards, all banking forms, and annual reports. MeraBank even changed their hot-air balloon.

Results of the Name Change

The impact of the name change was very positive. Employees were enthusiastic about the change and scored extremely well on the mystery shopper quizzes. Over 96% of all employees answered questions about the new name correctly. The extensive amount of employee involvement in the name change stimulated a renewed sense of pride in the company. Moreover, the name change was the catalyst generating a new orientation: employees and management perceived themselves as a bank.

Market studies were undertaken to determine consumer response. Consumers were positive about the new name. Over two-thirds recalled the new name, their primary source being television advertising. Fifty-five percent of consumers could identify the new name as MeraBank, and very few people perceived the name change as negative. Overall, post–name change advertising was perceived as more meaningful than previous advertising. In fact, advertising recall doubled and achieved a significant breakthrough in terms of consumer scoring.

The new advertising was very successful in promoting the new MeraBank image. When surveys were conducted after the name change, people began to list MeraBank in the bank category and not with the savings and loan institutions. The ad campaign also helped to promote the trial of MeraBank. Of those surveyed who were likely to try MeraBank, most were impressed with the name change advertising and rated it as being very meaningful to them. Those who were willing to try MeraBank described the company as "progressive" and having a "high level of customer service."

In Exhibit 15, there is a comparison of performance figures. A year after the

EXHIBIT 15   Year-end performance comparison

	December 1985	December 1986	3Q 1987
Assets	$5.2 Billion	$6.3 Billion	6.4 Billion
Retail banking market share	9.1%	8.5%	8.1%
Mortgage lending market share	6.6%*	6.4%*	5.4%*
Advertising awareness	18.0%*	33.0%*	20.1%*

*Phoenix and Tucson metro combined.

name change, MeraBank's assets were up 20%, and its advertising recall was up almost 100%. MeraBank's retail banking and mortgage lending market share had dropped slightly. This was planned through new pricing strategies that were undertaken to reduce the overall cost of funds. MeraBank, now positioned as a bank, lowered interest rates, getting these more in line with bank competitors versus savings and loan competitors.

THE NEW MERABANK

MeraBank began thinking of itself as a bank after the name change. Customers, employees, and the financial market began to refer to MeraBank as a bank, not as a thrift. However, changing the charter and creating new advertising campaigns were just the beginning. A complete repositioning in the market would be necessary to educate, attract, and serve "bank" customers. Changes in products, advertising, service, and facilities would be needed to complete the identity metamorphosis.

Several strategic changes occurred in conjunction with the name change. Advertising positioned MeraBank directly against the banks. Management dropped interest rates on savings deposits to bring them in line with bank rates. In the six months following the name change, the six-month CD rate dropped 1.1%. Through December 1987, the overall interest expense had been reduced by over $20 million as a result of this strategy. Interest rates and fees on credit cards were increased to be aligned with the pricing policies of banks. Customer service did not appear to suffer as a result of these changes. As seen in Exhibit 3, the number of total retail households served by MeraBank increased by 9% the first six months after the name change. By December 1987, the number of households served was up 22%.

The Marketing Group

Overall, changes were initiated to build a new corporate culture emphasizing service and measuring performance against both banks and thrifts. Strategy implementation became the major responsibility of the marketing group. As a result of the successful name change, the Senior Vice President of Marketing was promoted to Executive Vice President and Chief Administrative Officer in charge of marketing, human resources, and long-range planning. She recruited a new senior vice president for the marketing group.

The basic structure of the marketing organization is presented in Exhibit 16. Headed by a senior vice president, the department is organized into four major divisions. The first division, Market Planning, Research and Development, works on analyzing and segmenting the market and on keeping an accurate

EXHIBIT 16   **Organization structure of the marketing group**

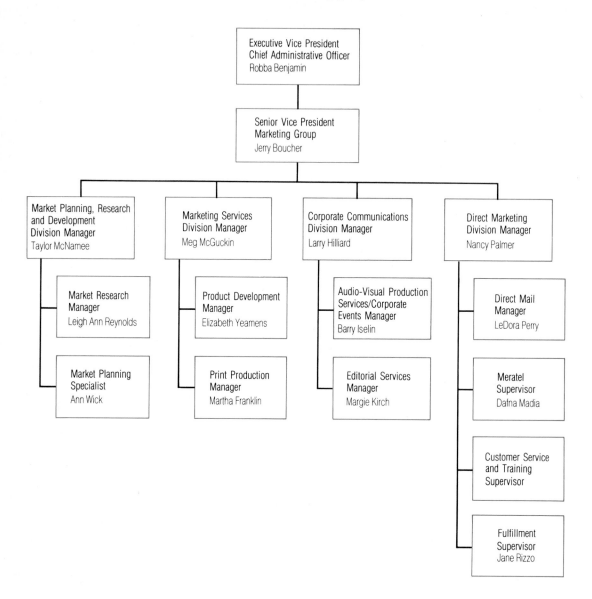

account of MeraBank's position in the financial market. Marketing Services develops and manages products, promotions, advertising, and print production for the company. Corporate Communications is responsible for public relations activities, audio/visual productions, and employee communications. The fourth division, Direct Marketing, oversees direct mail campaigns, telemarketing, customer service, and training. Though the reporting structure is set clearly, the functions interface frequently, and informal relationships appear to be very cooperative.

Consumer Market Segments

The primary demographic factors related to financial product usage appear to be age and income. Financial consumers for the banking industry often are segmented using these two criteria. Segments with the strongest potential for heavy financial product usage are: mid-age middle income; mid-age affluent; pre-retired middle-income; pre-retired affluent; and retired higher income groups. These segments represent 57% of the Phoenix metropolitan population and 47% of the Tucson area, as seen in Exhibit 17.

Using segmentation profiles as a base, MeraBank has begun to target its distribution system as well as its products and communication efforts toward specific market segments, in particular more affluent population segments. A profile of MeraBank's customer segments appears in Exhibit 18. A major indicator of MeraBank's commitment to reach new segments and serve new needs can be seen in their direct marketing budget, which increased 200% from 1985 to 1986. As a result of the repositioning effort and the move to targeting, the total households that were served increased 15%, to well over a quarter of a million households.

Service and Product Development

MeraBank launched two new retail banking services since the name change: the Passport Certificate Account and the Working Capital Account. These new accounts have brought in new deposits at a time when total deposits have been declining. Many existing product lines, such as CDs, have seen a decline in sales. MeraBank has suffered a loss of about 2% of its CD deposits. Passbook savings accounts have also been on a decline. However, MeraBank has increased its share of interest-bearing checking accounts—a conventional "bank" product—despite

EXHIBIT 17   **MeraBank segment penetration**

Phoenix	Population	Tucson	Population
Young, low income	9%	Young, low income	16%
Young, middle income	21	Young, middle income	21
Mid-age, middle income	17	Mid-age, middle income	15
Mid-age, affluent	16	Mid-age, affluent	11
Older, low income	6	Older, low income	9
Pre-retired, middle income	9	Pre-retired, middle income	8
Pre-retired, affluent	5	Pre-retired, affluent	4
Retired, higher income	10	Retired, higher income	9
Retired, lower income	7	Retired, lower income	8

EXHIBIT 18   **Market segmentation profiles**

Mid-age, middle income—These households will be hard to target as an entire segment, because they are widely distributed across all financial styles and thus vary greatly in their attitudes toward financial matters. Households in this segment are family oriented. Much of their financial behavior is focused on protecting their families and planning for their children's future.

Mid-age, affluent—A large portion of this segment are "Achievers" and have the most-in-command financial style. They are likely to be receptive to marketing approaches that appeal to their self-image as successful, knowledgeable, and decisive people.

Households in this segment are value sensitive. They are receptive to distinctive product features, and are able to make price/feature trade-offs. While households in this segment are price sensitive, they are willing to pay for services that they don't have time for, especially the dual earner households. They have positive attitudes toward using electronics and are likely to own computers and other electronic/high technology products.

Pre-retired, middle income—Half of the households in this segment are "Belongers." Their financial style is predominantly more-safe-and-simple. Many of these households will be receptive to marketing approaches that stress traditional, conservative values and emphasize the safety of the institution. In their efforts to minimize taxes and accumulate funds for retirement, these households will require conservative, lower risk products.

Many of these households are shifting their focus away from their children to their own future retirement. Though the family is still important, these households' goals are changing as they enter a new life stage. They place a high value on the reputation of the financial institutions they use and on having trust in them.

Pre-retired, affluent—The financial styles of the pre-retired affluent households are predominantly most-in-command and most-comfortable. They are oriented toward the present and are concerned about retaining their present lifestyles during their retirement. They are sophisticated in their approach to financial matters. These households like having access to people that they perceive as competent, but are receptive to using the telephone for financial dealings.

Retired, higher income—Households in this segment are the most-safe-and-simple and prefer to keep financial affairs uncomplicated and are generally unexperimental. Other households, called most-comfortable, are sophisticated in their approach to their financial affairs. They view themselves as prosperous and financially secure. They highly value security and involvement in financial affairs. These retired households are likely to be receptive to social seminar-type events, because they have the time to attend and the interest in learning.

---

increases in the minimum balance of the NOW account from $100 to $500. Similarly, an increase in credit card fees has had only a minimal effect on the number of credit card accounts and card usage.

The Passport Certificate is targeted to the 55+ age group. The advertising campaign has used primarily newspaper. The core product is very traditional, a certificate of deposit. But the CD is augmented with free checking as well as free and discounted travel services such as car rentals, insurance, and even a 24-hour travel center. The account is made more tangible by giving each customer a wallet-size passport card with the account number and the package benefits included.

The Working Capital Account is targeted to the affluent, middle-aged market segment. It is patterned after a money market account. It is a liquid investment with a very high yield tied to the one-year treasury bill. The account requires a high minimum balance of $10,000, but permits unlimited access to the money. The investor can gain a high-yield CD rate, but maintain checking privileges and access to the money. Once again, newspaper was the primary advertising medium for the product. The Working Capital Account provides its subscribers with monthly statements of the investment and the checking accounts. The account is the only product of its type in the Arizona market. In the first nine months after introduction, it generated a half billion dollars.

MeraBank has a strong commitment to customer service and convenience that goes beyond the traditional branch structure. The direct marketing division supervises the operations of Meratel, which is a customer service hotline and "telephone bank." Customers can open an account, obtain information, or transact business by calling 1-800-MERATEL. This convenience to customers has been well received. Call volume increased 300% during the year following the name change. The effectiveness of the Meratel operation can be evaluated using Exhibit 19. To further improve the level of service performance, MeraBank has initiated direct marketing campaigns to retail customers, contacting them by mail and telephone. The intention is to expand this operation and begin a regular program of calling retail customers to enhance convenience.

MeraBank's management believes that its success is dependent on the capabilities and performance of employees. The company is recruiting and developing employees who are more sales-oriented. Employees are expected to produce superior levels of performance, be customer-oriented, have high standards of integrity, and work in unison with a team spirit. To ensure these service standards, a comprehensive training program has been instituted for the sales staff with an incentive compensation system for frontline personnel. The commission program has resulted in doubling the cross-sales ratio at the front line. The training process has also been revised to reflect more product training and to amend a thrift vocabulary by incorporating banking terms. Periodically, the company will sponsor a contest to encourage high-quality service and improve morale. Internal newsletters provide employees with communication and inspiration to maintain quality service.

Community service also is an important orientation at MeraBank. In 1987, MeraBank contributed over $1.2 million to charity, and many of its employees

EXHIBIT 19   **Meratel**

	Deposit acquisition	Number of calls
1984	$37,600,000	7,831
1985	$58,014,800	22,319
1986	$51,435,700	75,222
1987	$80,234,630	266,000

work in behalf of civic and charitable endeavors. Contributions are divided among worthy cultural, civic, educational, health, and social welfare programs. In one project, MeraBank teamed with Realty World brokers to create a "Dream House." This project benefits victims of cerebral palsy. Strong community spirit is perceived to be a direct expression of MeraBank's service philosophy and culture.

Advertising and Promotion

Advertising and promotional strategy play a key role in positioning MeraBank. Following the name change, advertising objectives emphasized creating awareness and educating the public to the new identity. These objectives have evolved to emphasize increasing both deposits and branch traffic. The initial name change campaign required an increase in promotional expenditures. However, the current advertising budget is only slightly more than it was for First Federal Savings. The primary media used are television and newspaper, while radio is used to a lesser extent. TV advertising is targeted at the 35 + age customer, while newspaper ads are aimed at an older 55 + customer. Direct mail and billboard campaigns are used less often, but have been effective for some products.

MeraBank television advertising has incorporated the new identity of the institution, while maintaining the First Federal campaign theme of "We'll Be There." This theme has been used since 1985, and there are no plans to change the theme for general TV ads. However, MeraBank has tried to develop more sophisticated messages and imagery in their ads. Also, they run special promotional campaigns using television as the primary medium. For example, MeraBank became involved in an advertising campaign promoting CDs and a contest linked with ABC television stations and the 1988 Winter Olympics.

This campaign capitalized on patriotic interest in the Olympics and offered a free trip to the games in Canada as the grand prize. The winner of the contest was announced at the half time of the 1988 Super Bowl. Additional prizes were large interest rates on CDs with MeraBank. TV, newspaper, and direct mail were utilized in this campaign. The campaign also included a contest for employees. Employee Olympics were held to spur interest in the promotion and to encourage outstanding service. Employees were able to nominate peers for sportsmanship, team spirit, and customer service. Given the perceived success of the winter campaign, MeraBank planned to extend this strategy to include the summer games.

Merchandising and
Facility Management

Extending the emphasis placed on promotion, MeraBank has given more attention to branch merchandising. The entire point-of-sale "look" has been revised to reflect the new corporate identity. Signage, brochures, and point-of-purchase material incorporate the company logo and identity color scheme. Though thought has been given to a standardized interior appearance, there is not a uniform branch configuration. However, the newer and remodeled facilities reflect an interior design that is more open and modular in construction. Partitions are utilized to provide a flexible lobby setup. Interior decor and career apparel that would embody MeraBank's corporate identity through style and color schemes both have been under serious consideration. The basic design and exterior of branch locations also is under review.

MeraBank has essentially three prototypes for branch facilities: (1) a large regional center; (2) an intermediate-size complex; or (3) a small shopping center style. However, a pilot project is being undertaken with the Circle K convenience stores. A MeraBank branch and Circle K convenience store are sharing the same building. Though no direct internal connection was made between bank and store, the two facilities share a parking lot and the same foundation. This approach is viewed as a way of saving on construction costs for new branches as well as providing added security to the customers who use the ATM machine outside of the branch, as the convenience store is always open. It is not, however, regarded as an expansion strategy into retail grocery outlets—a strategy that has been popular with competitors.

MeraBank is planning a new corporate headquarters. The new office building is being designed based on a careful study of the company's history and image. The building is to personify the new positioning thrust and corporate culture of MeraBank.

Emerging Technology

MeraBank belongs to an automatic teller machine network that provides its customers with the most extensive coverage of any financial institution in Arizona. Expansion of the ATM machines and a nationwide hookup are being planned. This could lead toward a future where most banking transactions could be done electronically at home using a computer terminal. Home banking appears to be a long-term technological goal of the banking industry.

The current trend in convenience bank merchandising is electronic fund transfers. Electronic fund transfers are used by many banks in the Phoenix area in the form of a debit card, POS. Though it looks like a credit card, it is used to facilitate payment at retail locations. Using the POS, a transaction is automatically debited to an account. While POS has been limited to market tests in most states, penetration in Arizona has been substantial.

A recent survey found the overall rate of POS acceptance to be 26% among financial service consumers. The response varied by age groups. Younger age brackets had higher usage ratings. While the ratings may not seem impressive, they are when compared with the early ratings of ATM acceptance. Investment in POS technology is very high. However, market penetration might generate transaction volumes that reduce transaction costs considerably. Though many of the larger financial institutions have been involved in POS, MeraBank is taking a conservative stance toward electronic technology and is waiting to see how others fare before they follow.

Profitability Perspectives

Examining the profit picture of MeraBank, it is easiest to consider loans as the assets of the bank and deposits as the liabilities. A key to profitability is the diversity of the bank's assets and liabilities. MeraBank attempts to spread its investment risks and not invest too heavily in any one particular business line. Currently, the retail banking, consumer lending, real estate lending, and mortgage banking lines of business contribute most significantly. Corporate banking contributes to a lesser extent. On a limited basis, the real estate development line is profitable.

MeraBank is very competitive in consumer loans such as auto loans, student loans, and RV and boat loans. Home and mortgage loans are a particular strength. The home equity loan is the fastest growing loan in the Arizona market. Commercial loans are a smaller segment of MeraBank's loan operations. Given that commercial interest rates vary on a case-by-case basis, it is difficult to generalize profitability in this line of business.

One area of consumer loans that could be developed into a more profitable position is credit cards. Profit in this area relates to volume and use of the card. Since the name change, MeraBank has offered the first year of the card with no fee, but has added a $15 annual fee for each year after the first. The interest rate paid by the customer is 17.9%, which is comparable to other Arizona banks. Anyone may apply for a MeraBank credit card. The program is not tied to a deposit in the bank. Changes in the credit card program have brought MeraBank in line with the pricing policies of the major banks. However, credit card customers decreased when the changes were initiated. This is not thought to be a long-term setback.

On the liability side of the balance sheet, MeraBank offers several products that vary widely in their profit contribution. Certificates of deposits are the most profitable deposits. A bank can guarantee a certain return on the deposit, then pool them together and invest them at a higher rate. Passbook savings accounts would rank second in profitability potential. Low interest rate returns are the sacrifice for demand deposit accounts. Other less profitable deposit products would be IRAs, followed by money market accounts. The least profitable deposit account is the interest-bearing checking account, which serves as a loss leader to attract customers and to "cross-sell" other more profitable accounts. Automatic teller cards and point-of-sale cards also are only marginally profitable and serve mainly as loss leaders.

Financial planning, sales of securities, estate planning, administering trusts, and private bankers are services provided by many major banks. These services are very competitive in the Arizona market and require experienced personnel with established performance. However, MeraBank has not expanded into these areas. Though these services have been studied, MeraBank views them as marginally profitable and does not consider them as a hedge against the risk of any loan segment going soft.

Expansion

The objectives of reaching new consumers and offering convenience to all consumers drive the expansion of branch locations. Since the name change, new branches have been added in the existing service areas of Arizona and Texas. And further penetration of these states is being actively pursued.

Other expansion efforts seem to be evolving within the current eight-state southwest region that already is served by divisions of MeraBank. The southwest imagery that is projected in the corporate identity should fit well into such states as Colorado and California. Moreover, MeraBank management believes that their identity and the imagery of their logo would be acceptable to all parts of the country in any future expansion.

FUTURE CHALLENGES

MeraBank is no longer a small savings and loan. It has grown in sophistication, as its markets and competitors have. MeraBank aspires to continue its tradition of innovation and leadership. The financial services market will become more complex and turbulent. Diversification and expansion present significant opportunities, but also tough questions. MeraBank envisions establishing and sustaining a competitive advantage in terms of its customer service and service marketing strategies across its business lines and diverse geographic markets. With many different facilities, employees, and markets, setting appropriate objectives while creating the best strategies and programs to service its markets will be challenging.

MeraBank envisions using its identity as a means to powerfully exhibit who they are as a company and to provide evidence of their marketing presence. MeraBank believes that their identity can differentiate them from competitors and provide a distinct position in the market to generate sales and performance. They recognize the problems of being a service provider with many intangibilities to manage and market. Their identity must be considered all the way throughout service design, development, and delivery.

Increasingly, MeraBank has begun to consider fundamental service marketing challenges, such as: making its services more tangible for its publics; controlling its service quality; developing its service culture; enhancing the productivity of its service encounters and environments; and protecting its new identity. MeraBank's new management orientation and renewed employee enthusiasm have generated a new strategic thrust and uncovered new challenges.

Case 16

MERABANK (B)

The Resolution Trust Corporation (RTC) today was appointed receiver for MeraBank, A Federal Savings Bank, Phoenix, Arizona, by the Office of Thrift Supervision (OTS). A new federal mutual association was then created to assume all deposits and certain assets and liabilities of MeraBank. The OTS has appointed the RTC as conservator of this new institution, MeraBank Federal Savings Bank.

RTC Press Release dated January 31, 1990

On February 1, 1990, Gene Rice, CEO of MeraBank (Federal Savings Bank) of Phoenix, Arizona, pondered the events of the last 24 months that had led to the thrift's demise. The Resolution Trust Corporation, a newly formed federal agency, had just seized control of MeraBank, declaring it insolvent. Mr. Rice's vision of MeraBank, which just two years ago seemed so promising, was now a clear disaster. MeraBank's almost universally applauded strategy had not prevented failure. What was the cause—poor management or the hostile environment?

HISTORY

MeraBank, formerly First Federal Savings and Loan of Arizona, is one of the oldest financial institutions in the southwestern United States. Since its beginning in 1925, it has been a leader in the area of real estate financing. In response to deregulation in the financial services industry, First Federal Savings and Loan revised its charter in 1985 to become a federal savings bank. The new charter allowed the thrift to compete for a broader range of commercial lending activities than it could as a savings and loan. Symbolizing the new strategic direction, First Federal changed its name in January 1986 to MeraBank, Federal Savings Bank. The name change marked the beginning of a major repositioning effort. MeraBank no longer was content to be a small savings and loan; it wanted to grow into a large consumer-oriented bank. In January 1986, the future looked bright and the strategy appeared sound.

This case was prepared by Timothy B. Palmer and Rhonda K. Reger, Arizona State University.

THE ARIZONA ECONOMIC CLIMATE

While MeraBank pursued a strategy that capitalized on newfound opportunities, the banking environment continued to evolve. Leading a nationwide trend toward geographic banking deregulation, Arizona became the first state to allow full interstate banking. Beginning October 1, 1986, commercial banks headquartered anywhere in the United States could enter the Arizona market through acquisition of existing Arizona banks. *De nova,* or entry through establishing new offices, was delayed until January 1992. While savings and loan acquisitions were not affected by this state legislation, Federal regulations allowed thrifts to cross state lines if they acquired a financially troubled institution.

While many states were considering deregulation, money center banks were particularly interested in Arizona's legislation. Arizona was in a growth mode that appeared unlimited. Fueling this expansion was a building boom largely attributable to Arizona's enviable yearly population growth rate of 5%. About 66,000 new arrivals landed in the Phoenix area in 1985 alone. Population growth, however, was not the sole cause of the building boom. Other factors fueling it included easy money from lenders, abundant vacant land, few building restrictions, and generous tax incentives.

The expansion affected anyone involved in real estate developing and lending. During the height of the speculative fever, building had a wild west feeling as bankers and developers made deals over lunch. Cotton fields were transformed into strip shopping centers and Phoenix's Central Avenue became a boulevard of glass office towers.

Because of seemingly boundless opportunities for growth, large U.S. money center banks and thrifts quickly paid premiums to compete in the desert state. In fact, some banks were willing to pay "whatever it took" for the opportunity to compete. Timing, however, was not on their side. By the end of 1987, clouds rolled into the Valley of the Sun. The warning signs, however, were largely ignored. Development became reckless: planned growth gave way to wild speculation. Even by 1988 the effects of supply continually exceeding demand were discounted. Most people involved in real estate saw no downturn— only a minor correction as demand caught up with supply.

The illusion of continued expansion lasted through the spring of 1989. By the summer, however, the speculative bubble burst. Real estate prices plummeted. Undeveloped land and some commercial property lost 50% of its value in a few short months. Everyone connected to the real estate market was affected. Not only were financial institutions and large developers hurt, but home owners were as well. Home appreciation rates tumbled through 1989, falling to values below the state's inflation rate. Partly due to overdevelopment and lower in-migration rates, home sales declined 14% from 1988 levels in most communities. While this was good news for home buyers, it was bad news for sellers.

Fueling the soft Phoenix housing market were 14,000 residential foreclosures in 1989, averaging 1,482 per month. In comparison, the figure was only 687 a month in 1985. Foreclosures affected all income strata including some of

Arizona's best known citizens such as former governor Evan Mecham and former U.S. Senate candidate Keith DeGreen. Even business tycoon Gordon Hall couldn't escape the deteriorated economy. His 53,000 square foot mansion in suburban Phoenix was sold at auction for less than $4 million, about 20% of its estimated replacement cost.

Vacancy Rates

Nowhere is the effect of speculative growth in the Arizona real estate market more evident than in its vacancy rates. For example, by 1990, 10% of Tucson's apartments were empty, 13% in Phoenix. The scenario was no better in the commercial sector. Retail space was abundantly available (15% vacant in Tucson, 12% in Phoenix). Entire strip malls, built in anticipation of growth that never materialized, stood vacant, suburban reminders of the go-go years of the early 1980s. Office occupancy was no better. In Central Avenue's glistening new glass towers, empty offices are everywhere. Vacant office space in Phoenix increased 15% from 1989 to 1990: currently 24% of all Phoenix office space is unrented. In some sectors of the city, the rate climbs to 31%. Despite this fact, 3.9 million new square feet of rentable office space was added in the first half of 1990. In Phoenix alone, 35% of all industrial space was considered "available."

Employment

Construction employment continued a steep slide that began in 1986. Peaking at 117,600 jobs in June 1986, Arizona construction employment decreased by 28,200 jobs (24% decrease) by January 1989. Another 800 jobs were lost in the first half of 1990.

In addition to construction jobs lost, state politics and a slowdown in the national economy have also impacted the state's employment figures. The state of Arizona is used to more growth than it can handle. The naturally good climate, cheap labor force, and proximity to California fueled in-migration throughout the 1970s and the first half of the 1980s. Arizona, unlike many other states, had little in the way of development activities designed to attract new industry from around the country and abroad. The real estate crisis and subsequent economic downturn sent state, county, and city officials scrambling to play catch-up with other states. In addition, new businesses were increasingly skeptical about relocating in Arizona because of social and political concerns, most notably turmoil over the lack of a paid Martin Luther King day for state employees. Finally, unemployment rates increased because existing firms reduced the size of their work force in response to the sluggish national economy.

One of the state's leading employers, Salt River Project, a major Phoenix power and water supplier, has recently laid off hundreds of workers. In 1989, IBM substantially reduced its Tucson work force, and Intel decreased their head count by 200 workers in Chandler. Were these signs that the recession was spreading from real estate to other sectors, or were these unrelated coincidental events? Overall unemployment in Arizona was 5.3% in 1989, compared to 4.8% in 1986. Some observers optimistically noted that the Arizona economic crisis was primarily concentrated in real estate, banking, and thrift industries, while the rest of the economy was either continuing to do well or had felt only a minor slowdown.

The combined effects of a development bust, a decrease in in-migration, and increased unemployment left Arizona's thrift industry reeling. Unfortunately, the realization of the downturn's magnitude came too late for many. Huge new communities such as Charles Keating's Estrella were left unfinished, many abandoned. Developers defaulted on loans and lenders were left with deeds to property worth only a fraction of the loan.

The effects of the economic downturn reached beyond the state's borders to bank and thrift corporate offices. Competitors which so recently had paid premiums for the opportunity to do business in the state found ink turned quickly from black to red in nearly every Arizona financial institution. By the end of 1989, the questions on everyone's mind were: how bad will it be and how long will it last? Arizona's real estate market had experienced many downturns before, some fairly severe, but mostly of short duration.

Additionally, however, changes were occurring at a national level which would further confound the stability of MeraBank and other Arizona financial institutions. Congress was facing a national "Savings and Loan Crisis" brought on by massive bleeding of the nation's thrifts. Because depositors are protected from loss by the full faith of the U.S. treasury, Washington was compelled to enact measures to strengthen the industry. In August, President Bush signed the Financial Institutions Reform, Recover, and Enforcement Act of 1989 (FIRREA) and created the Resolution Trust Corporation (RTC) to handle disposition of defunct thrift assests. Some of the measures included in this legislation as well as other national trends that greatly affected MeraBank's competitive environment are discussed below.

New Capital Requirements

FIRREA mandated that the Office of Thrift Supervision establish minimum capital standards for thrifts that were no less stringent than those for national banks. The result was that thrifts were required to meet tighter capital standards by June 1, 1991. These standards included a provision that net worth to assets ratios be dramatically increased to about 6% from the industry average of about 4.5%. Those that would be unable to meet the standards were required to file a plan with the Federal Deposit Insurance Corporation (FDIC) by December 7, 1989.

In addition to the increased net worth ratio, the law also stipulated that tangible capital constitute at least 1.5% of total assets. For many thrifts, the definition of "capital" was at the heart of the issue. Assets, of which capital is a part, come in two types: tangible or intangible. Tangible assets include those that are physical, material, or appraisable for value such as real estate, equipment, inventory, or cash. The primary intangible asset, on the other hand, is goodwill, which represents the excess of a purchase price over the fair market value of an asset acquired. One way many thrifts accumulated goodwill in the late 1980s was through the acquisition of insolvent institutions. Because they were bought at a discount, the acquiring thrift acquired goodwill. The new capital requirements, however, no longer allowed including goodwill in the capital calculation. Congress argued that in the event an institution were liquidated to pay off depositors, the intangible value of goodwill would have no real economic worth.

At the time the 1.5% tangible capital requirement was imposed, 686 thrifts (25% of the nation's 2,949 S&Ls) flunked the test. Of the 229 largest S&Ls, each with at least a billion dollars in assets, 63 had negative tangible net worth and an additional 97 did not have the 1.5% required.

Narrow Interest Rate Spreads

During the same period, interest rates were on the rise. In April 1987, short-term interest rates paid on certificates of deposit were as low as 6.90%. By the end of 1988, however, the rate had increased to 9.65%: a rise of 240 basis points. Because a thrift's assets are generally long-term mortgage loans (typically 30 years), they roll over and reprice much more slowly than short-term certificates of deposit. The result was a compression of spreads. On the average, a spread of 2.5% is required for a financial institution to be profitable. In 1988, spreads generally ranged from a low of 1.75% to a high of 2.85%; most spreads were near 2.25%. As a result, industry-wide profits were eliminated.

America's thrifts lost over $12 billion in 1988, up from a $7.8 billion loss in 1987. The S&L industry's ROA turned negative in 1986 (-0.13%), sank even deeper in 1987 (-0.59%), and for the first six months of 1988 was a catastrophic -1.20%. In the Southwest, including Texas and Arizona, the picture was even more alarming as thrifts throughout the region continued to hemorrhage; they managed to lose a whopping $14.8 billion in 1988 for a startling 9.38% loss on assets.

Changing Tax Laws

Many analysts argue that Congress itself should shoulder some of the blame for the S&L crisis. When tax laws were relaxed in the early 1980s, incentives were created for investment funds to flow into commercial real estate. When tax reform came along in 1986, these incentives were removed. This left commercial real estate to "pencil out" on the basis of economic factors, such as income and cash flows, instead of tax breaks. Therefore, many investors who had been receiving tax advantages due to their property's losses, no longer had the incentive.

Investors of all sizes defaulted on loans because the already weak real estate market could not absorb the number of properties available. And lenders, primarily thrifts and banks, were left holding severely devalued property.

All of these factors—higher capital requirements, narrow interest rate spreads, and changing tax laws—spelled disaster for the national thrift industry. By late 1989, 600 thrifts across the nation had either been placed into federal conservatorship or were below capital requirements and required to submit plans detailing how they would bolster their capital positions. For these thrifts, regulators imposed growth and operating restrictions to prevent further decline. As a group, Arizona's thrifts fared worse. They had been dealt two blows. At the local level, they were competing against new, strong competitors in a market that had virtually dried up. Nationally, they faced regulations and trends that had crippled thrifts not faced with Arizona's woes.

While a thrift's performance is greatly affected by its environment, corporate strategists also control firm destiny. As its environment evolved, MeraBank had enacted a strong, rapid growth strategy leaving the thrift ill prepared for the new competitive arena.

MeraBank's Response to the Changing Environment

Gene Rice was well aware of Arizona's turbulent financial environment as he charted the path for MeraBank's future in 1987. Concerned over MeraBank's dependance on the Maricopa County (Phoenix) market, Rice initiated a series of tactics to reduce this exposure. With a goal of limiting assets to 20% in any one market over the next 25 years, MeraBank chose to capitalize on two opportunities: (1) high growth rates in other sunbelt states, (2) MeraBank's favorable name recognition in other Arizona markets.

First, MeraBank actively sought savings and loan acquisitions in the southwestern United States. Because of an ailing local economy, primarily due to depressed oil prices, many southwestern savings and loans found their capital positions depleted, often with a negative net worth. Of the 101 U.S. thrifts placed into federal receivership during the first eight months of 1988, the majority were located in Texas and Oklahoma. The government, however, it not in the business of running financial institutions. Through its "Southwest Plan," the Federal Home Loan Bank sought purchasers of defunct thrifts by offering attractive deals. Typically they infused enough capital into the insolvent thrift to make it solvent, hence decreasing the riskiness to the acquirer. In essence, the purchasing institution acquired a branch network, deposits, and healthy loan portfolio to begin rebuilding the savings institution.

Recognizing a relatively inexpensive opportunity to expand its market, MeraBank announced that it would become the first financial institution outside Texas to invest in that state's ailing S&L industry. In June 1988, Rice and the MeraBank team took control of two ailing savings associations, First Financial of

El Paso, and Brownfield Federal Savings in rural west Texas. With combined assets of $350 million, the transactions were smaller than had been anticipated. MeraBank therefore agreed to acquire at least $650 million more in assets from one or more Texas institutions by late September. This promise was kept through the acquisition of State Federal Savings & Loan of Lubbock in the third quarter of 1988.

Reaction to MeraBank's geographic expansion was mixed. On the one hand, the Federal Home Loan Bank was delighted with MeraBank's entrance into Texas. From their perspective, MeraBank under Gene Rice's guidance was one of the few healthy thrifts in the Southwest. Recognizing this, the board encouraged MeraBank to invest. However, MeraBank's recent financial performance had deteriorated. While the thrift's assets had grown to $6.4 billion, this growth had mainly come through acquisition. After impressive earnings of $29.1 million in 1987, MeraBank lost $12.4 million in the first quarter of 1988 in Arizona, mainly because of problems in its mortgage lending subsidiary. A few analysts were concerned that the Phoenix market was substantially overbuilt and that the only industry contributing to Phoenix's continued growth rate was growth itself. Skeptics of the MeraBank strategy felt that MeraBank's current position was too tenuous for the thrift to be expanding. But, in 1988, many were unconcerned about the long term in Arizona and felt growth would take care of any real estate problems.

Rice saw the Texas expansion as a golden opportunity that fit well with his long-run strategy of MeraBank. Responding to the riskiness of growing through Texas, Rice said, ". . . everybody thinks the savings and loan industry is gone, and Texas is gone. Both of them will come back very strong, and this is the perfect time to buy" (*Arizona Republic,* July 4, 1988). To further this strategy, MeraBank submitted a bid in October to buy the parent of Blue Valley Savings & Loan, Missouri's second largest thrift with assets of more than $900 million. Rice was also eyeing the First Financial Savings Bank of Des Moines, Iowa: MeraBank was rapidly implementing its strategy to reduce dependence on Phoenix.

MERABANK'S ARIZONA STRATEGY

Although the Phoenix metro area accounts for over two thirds of the state's economy, the rest of Arizona is tied to economic sectors quite different from Phoenix. While MeraBank maintained a statewide branch network, it was clearly a Phoenix thrift. To remedy this, the second way MeraBank sought decreased dependance on Phoenix was to consider branch expansion outside of Maricopa County, especially into Tucson where it continued to be a minor competitor.

To implement this strategy, MeraBank again capitalized on another institution's economic woes. Western Savings and Loan was taking the brunt of Arizona's deteriorating economy head-on. Unlike MeraBank, Western had no wealthy parent to turn to in the face of short-term losses. Daily, Western's stock price tumbled. Because losses were eroding stockholder's net worth, Western decided to shrink the size of the thrift (hence reducing its required net worth). To do this, Western sought a buyer for its entire branch network outside of Phoenix. MeraBank was there. On September 30, 1988, MeraBank purchased 21 non–Maricopa County branches from Western Savings. In the process, MeraBank's Arizona market share increased through 60,000 new accounts totaling $550 million in new deposits. To streamline its new operations, MeraBank successfully consolidated 18 of the 21 acquired branches into its own existing network.

Again, reaction to MeraBank's strategy was mixed. Along with MeraBank, most Arizona savings institutions were posting quarterly losses. Growth had virtually halted in most sectors of the state: Arizona's economy was plummeting. The question was—how long will it last? Responding to stockholder concerns about the thrift's recent acquisition surge in suppressed states, Rice commented that not only would the economies rebound, "but they'll come back stronger than ever. Every time we've been down in Arizona, we've come back stronger than ever." Rice added, "Arizona is one of the really great markets in the long term, and right now is a better opportunity to buy land and office buildings than any time in the past ten years/ It's the perfect opportunity if you have the money to buy and the strength to wait out the market" (*Arizona Republic,* January 1, 1989). Rice, and the MeraBank strategists, believed that ". . . as sure as the sun goes down and the sun comes up, there will be a rebirth in Texas and Arizona" (*Phoenix Business Journal,* October 10, 1988). MeraBank's executives maintained faith that the night Rice alluded to would be short. By the end of 1988, MeraBank had become Arizona's largest savings institution with 76 branches throughout Arizona and Texas and approximately 1,350 employees.

Success of the MeraBank strategy would first require weathering the deteriorating Arizona economy. For the year ending 1988, MeraBank reported a loss of $208.6 million including $205.9 million in provisions for loan and real estate losses. Of this amount, $180 million alone had occurred in the fourth quarter after MeraBank's expansion. The thrift's loan originations (granting of new loans) hit a five year low. While Rice was concerned about recent losses, his attitude remained positive. "You have to expect, if you're the biggest car insurer, that you'll have the most wrecks." Despite the losses, MeraBank's regulatory capital stood at $369 million, significantly above the federal requirement of $202 million. In addition, assets had soared 26% over the 1987 level topping $8.5 billion.

Despite Rice's faith in the Arizona and Texas economies, MeraBank's losses began to affect its relationship with its parent, the Pinnacle West Corporation. MeraBank's losses were affecting Pinnacle West's bottom line. For example, a $29.2 million MeraBank loss in the first quarter of 1989 led to a decline in Pinnacle West's earnings of over $10 million from 1988. For the twelve months ending March 31, Pinnacle West was forced to report a net loss of $5.2 million. While this would be cause for concern by any parent, Pinnacle West's other main subsidiary is Arizona Public Service, the state's largest utility.

When Pinnacle West acquired MeraBank in 1986, the Arizona Corporation

Commission, the state body regulating utilities, expressed concern over the potential that MeraBank losses could affect Arizona ratepayers. The threat was increased because Pinnacle West had agreed to a "keep well" stipulation in order to acquire MeraBank. In the event MeraBank's capital position deteriorated, Pinnacle West had agreed to keep MeraBank's capital at required levels. Members of the Corporation Commission worried that electricity consumers would be forced to bail out MeraBank.

By May 1989, corporate management began to realize the danger MeraBank could pose to Pinnacle West's future. While the thrift's regulatory capital exceeded 5% of assets, many analysts considered MeraBank insolvent by generally accepted accounting standards. A capital infusion from Pinnacle West looked inevitable. Speculation flourished over the possibility that Pinnacle West would sell MeraBank. The market for Arizona thrifts, however, was nonexistent. With few alternatives, Pinnacle West expressed renewed commitment to the MeraBank strategy. Management was fully aware that under current economic forecasts, it could take three years to turn MeraBank around.

THE MERABANK TURNAROUND STRATEGY

By the end of the first half of 1989, MeraBank had lost an additional $76 million, bringing year-to-date losses to $105.2 million. According to a MeraBank spokesperson, the losses were attributable to a deepening deterioration of the Southwest's real estate market, a drop in real estate values, and a continued increase in interest rates. With this news in hand, it became increasingly evident that MeraBank strategists would have to be more proactive than merely "weathering the storm." It was at the end of the second quarter, therefore, that the MeraBank turnaround strategy was unveiled. As reported in their second quarter financial summary, the new strategy included four elements:

1. By streamlining operations and returning to the basic business of a federally insured depository of savings accounts, we will reduce our annual overhead from $148 million to $87 million by 1992.
2. And, in order to prepare for President Bush's new bill, we expect to reduce our assets from $8 billion to approximately $4.5 billion over the next three years. Under the new law, the more assets we have, the more tangible capital is needed. We will reduce assets by not making any new loans, or replacing paid-off loans.
3. When the time comes to replenish our $5.6 billion existing loan portfolio, we will purchase, rather than originate, low-risk, geographically diversified single family home loans guaranteed by the government.
4. We also intend to sell three non-banking subsidiaries and focus our efforts on either selling our repossessed real estate at fair prices or improving the return on our underperforming assets.

> With our new plan in place our customers can be even more confident that their satisfaction and financial security are among MeraBank's highest priorities.

While it was evident that MeraBank had determined strategists at the helm, its losses continued to strain relations with Pinnacle West. Moody's Investor's Service was considering the possible downgrade of $70 million in MeraBank long-term debt. Analysts believed that a spinoff of MeraBank would substantially enhance the value of Pinnacle West's remaining assets. Said one analyst, "Arizona Public Service is a pretty attractive piece of property and is probably worth $20 a share by itself; MeraBank, on the other hand, is a bottomless pit" (*Wall Street Journal,* May 19, 1989).

CAPITAL CONCERNS FOR MERABANK

MeraBank, along with all thrifts, had been operating under the general industry-wide regulatory capital requirement imposed by the Office of Thrift Supervision. As of June 30, 1989, the savings bank had regulatory capital of $265 million, $65 million above the required level.

By July, however, legislation passed through Congress imposing more stringent capital requirements on thrifts. The bill required MeraBank to come up with an additional half a billion dollars in capital by 1991: money MeraBank did not have. At issue was $380 million of capital in the form of goodwill which MeraBank had acquired through its purchase of Western Savings' non–Maricopa County branches and from the Pinnacle West purchase of MeraBank itself.

While the news was bad for all thrifts, it soon became worse for MeraBank. In addition to raising capital levels by 1991 along with all other thrifts, regulators had notified MeraBank executives that the thrift must boost reserves immediately. Regulators argued that because of Arizona's continuing real estate decline and its detrimental effect on MeraBank's earnings, they had imposed an Individual Minimum Capital Requirement (IMCR) on MeraBank. The IMCR, which was more stringent than industry-wide capital standards, called for MeraBank's tangible capital to be increased on a phased-in schedule through 1991, with an immediate increase in capital of $192 million. Pinnacle West disputed the IMCR on legal grounds and began negotiations with the Federal Home Loan Bank Board. Pinnacle West argued that the IMCR was not only unfair, but would lead to certain receivership for the only Arizona thrift that had any chance of survival. The government, it appeared to some, was causing, not preventing, another costly S&L bailout.

To ensure that Arizona ratepayers would not have to bear the brunt of MeraBank's decline, the Arizona Corporation Commission issued an order to Pinnacle West blocking Arizona Public Service from making any unusual cash transfers to its parent. Between a rock and a hard place, MeraBank missed the deadline for its IMCR capital infusion.

DECLINE AT MERABANK

The negative spiral of 1989 continued into the third quarter. By September 30, MeraBank lost an additional $86 million bringing year-to-date losses to $191 million. While its published financial summary attempted optimism, the thrift warned of continued losses. By now, Pinnacle West had conceded that it would cost up to $600 million to restore MeraBank, approximately the entire net worth of the Pinnacle West. The more MeraBank bled, the lower Pinnacle West's stock price dropped, and the more pressure Pinnacle West felt from all quarters. Utility and thrift regulators, ratepayers, and now stockholders, all demanded that Pinnacle West do something about MeraBank.

In the midst of bad news, there were glimmers of hope. On one hand, the turnaround plan appeared to be working. Through reducing its work force, MeraBank had shaved compensation by $23.5 million. In addition, $30 million in repossessed real estate had been sold, and assets were reduced by $376 million since January. In a statement to their customers, "The new MeraBank will be leaner, more conservative and more efficient. We will specialize in savings products and be a strong competitor in our markets. We are optimistic about the future. Arizona continues to experience growth, and the real estate market will turn around. Financial institutions in Arizona will survive and prosper. And our company will be there to continue its 64-year tradition of strength and leadership."

THE FINAL QUARTER

Despite rhetoric, losses at MeraBank continued to affect the viability of Pinnacle West and Arizona Public Service. Moody's downgraded all of APS's securities ratings. Pinnacle West's stock price dropped daily. The most recent news, that Pinnacle West would be required to pump an additional $510 million of capital into MeraBank, sent the stock price into a tailspin. If no agreement could be worked out with the thrift regulators, Pinnacle West would be forced to file for Chapter 11 protection.

Facing bankruptcy, on December 6, 1989, Pinnacle West finally reached an agreement with the Office of Thrift Supervision, the Resolution Trust Corp., and the FDIC to infuse $450 million of capital into MeraBank. Upon completing that infusion, consisting of $300 million in cash and a $150 million note, Pinnacle West was released from any further financial obligations to MeraBank under the keep-well agreement signed when the bank was purchased in 1986. At that time, MeraBank was classified as a discontinued operation by Pinnacle West. Pinnacle West's 1989 annual report summed it up, "For all practical purposes, MeraBank is behind us." In its wake was a $551 million year-end loss.

Despite the capital infusion, MeraBank still faced a deficiency. Federal regulators insisted the institution needed $510 million to bring it into compliance,

$450 million was only a short-term compromise. According to Rice, "We need more, . . . somebody will have to buy the bank." A takeover of MeraBank appeared imminent as MeraBank announced more negative news. One billion dollars (16%) of MeraBank's assets were declared bad.

At 2:00 P.M. on February 1, 1990, MeraBank, Federal Savings Bank, became the thirty-second savings and loan to fail in the new decade and was seized by regulators. Reflecting the industry-wide faith in MeraBank management, both Chairman Gene Rice and President Ernest Modzelewski were asked to stay on as part of the transition team.

The transition lasted nine days. February 9 was Mr. Rice's last day with the savings and loan he had been chairman of since 1982. Prior to that, he had been president for nine years. He had charted the course for MeraBank and had taken the thrift to the top. By many, he had been viewed as the industry's premier strategist as he had successfully repositioned MeraBank as a consumer bank. Now, with his thrift in receivership, he couldn't help but wonder if a different, more cautious strategy would have saved MeraBank. Had be been too optimistic? Had MeraBank grown too quickly? Should he have downsized sooner? Was MeraBank's decline a function of poor strategy, or an overly hostile environment?

Mr. Rice wonders, "What did we miss? Could we have saved MeraBank, and how?"

S E C T I O N

C

CORPORATE-LEVEL CASES

NUCOR IN 1991

INTRODUCTION

Nuclear Corporation of America had been near bankruptcy in 1965, when a fourth reorganization put a 39-year-old division manager, Ken Iverson, into the president's role. Iverson began a process which resulted in Nucor, a steel mini-mill and joist manufacturer which rated national attention and reaped high praise.

In a 1981 article subtitled "Lean living and mini-mill technology have led a one-time loser to steel's promised land," *Fortune* stated:

> Although Nucor didn't build its first mill until 1969, it turned out 1.1 million tons of steel last year, enough to rank among the top 20 U.S. producers. Not only has Nucor been making a lot of steel, it's been making money making steel—and a lot of that as well. Since 1969, earnings have grown 31% a year, compounded, reaching $45 million in 1980 on sales of $482 million. Return on average equity in recent years has consistently exceeded 28%, excellent even by Silicon Valley's standards and almost unheard of in steel. The nine-fold increase in the value of Nucor's stock over the last five years—it was selling recently at about $70 a share—has given shareholders plenty of cause for thanksgiving.[1]

The Wall Street Journal commented, "The ways in which management style combines with technology to benefit the mini-mill industry is obvious at Nucor Corp., one of the most successful of the 40 or more mini-mill operators."[2] Ken Iverson was featured in an NBC special, "If Japan Can, Why Can't We?" for his management approach. As *The Wall Street Journal* commented, "You thought steel companies are only a bunch of losers, with stodgy management, outmoded plants and poor profits?" Well, Nucor and Iverson were different.

However, the challenges hadn't stopped. The economy made the 1980's a horrible time for the steel industry. All companies reported sales declines, most

This case was prepared by Frank C. Barnes, University of North Carolina, Charlotte. Note: Many quotes by Ken Iverson are from prepared comments and speeches and are not footnoted.

[1]Richard I. Kirkland, Jr., "Pilgrims' Profits at Nucor," *Fortune,* April 6, 1981, pp. 43–46.
[2]Douglas R. Sease, "Mini-Mill Steelmakers, No Longer Very Small, Outperform Big Ones," *The Wall Street Journal,* January 12, 1981, pp. 1, 19.

lost profitability and some, in both major and mini-mill operations, closed or restructured. Nucor's 30% plus return on equity hit 9%. Iverson, however, was one of 52 recipients of the bronze medal from *Financial World* in 1983 for holding onto profitability; they kept costs down but not at the expense of laying off their people—a near-religious commitment at Nucor.

By 1990 Nucor was the ninth largest steel producer in the U.S. and number 323 on the Fortune 500 list. But the easy gains scored by the new mini-mill operations over the integrated mills were over. The historical steel companies were arousing from their twenty-year slumber, adding modern technology, re-negotiating with their equally aged unions, and closing some mills. They were determined to fight back. Mini-mill was fighting mini-mill, as well as imports, and a number had closed. Thus the industry faced a picture of excess capacity which would be the backdrop in the battle for survival and success over the next years.

Iverson and Nucor knew how to fight the battle. They invested $325 million in new processes in 1988. They went from $185 million in idle cash in 1986 to $180 million in debt by 1988. They had opened the first new fastener plant in the U.S. in decades, completed a joint venture with the Japanese to build a plant to make structural steel products, and built the first mini-mill in the world to make flat-rolled steel, the largest market and major business of the integrated produc-ers. They had broken away from the other mini-mills and had at least a three-year headstart in taking a share of this market from the integrated mills. Iverson believed with their new products they should double sales, and probably earn-ings, by 1991. Analysts predicted a jump to 7th largest among mills and doubling or tripling share price in the immediate future.

BACKGROUND

Nucor was the descendant of a company that manufactured the first Oldsmobile in 1897. After seven years of success, R. E. Olds sold his first company and founded a new one to manufacture the Reo. Reo ran into difficulties and filed for voluntary reorganization in 1938. Sales grew 50 times over the next ten years, based on defense business, but declined steadily after World War II. The motor division was sold and then resold in 1957 to the White Motor Corporation, where it operates as the Diamond Reo Division. Reo Motors' management planned to liquidate the firm, but before it could do so, a new company gained control through a proxy fight. A merger was arranged with Nuclear Consultants, Inc., and the stock of Nuclear Corporation of America was first traded in 1955. Nu-clear acquired a number of companies in high-tech fields but continued to lose money until 1960, when an investment banker in New York acquired control. New management proceeded with a series of acquisitions and dispositions: they purchased U.S. Semi-Conductor Products, Inc.; Valley Sheet Metal Company, an air conditioner contractor in Arizona; and Vulcraft Corporation, a Florence,

South Carolina, steel joist manufacturer. Over the next four years, sales increased five times, but losses increased seven times. In 1965 a New York investor purchased a controlling interest and installed the fourth management team. The new president was Ken Iverson, who had been in charge of the Vulcraft division.

Ken Iverson had joined the Navy upon graduation from a Chicago-area high school in 1943. The Navy first sent him to Northwestern University for an officer training program but then decided it needed aeronautical engineers and transferred him to Cornell. This had been "fine" with Iverson, because he enjoyed engineering. Upon receiving his bachelor's degree in 1945 at age 20, he served in the Navy for six months, completing his four-year tour.

He wasn't too excited about an A.E. career because of the eight years of drafting required for success. Metals and their problems in aircraft design had intrigued him, so he considered a Masters degree in metallurgy. An uncle had attended Purdue, so he chose that school. He married during this time, gave up teaching geometry so he could finish the program in one year, and turned down an offer of assistance toward a Ph.D. to "get to work."

At Purdue he had worked with the new electron microscope. International Harvester's research physics department had just acquired one and hired Iverson as Assistant to the Chief Research Physicist. Iverson stayed there five years and felt he was "set for life." He had great respect for his boss, who would discuss with him the directions businesses took and their opportunities. One day the Chief Physicist asked if that job was what he really wanted to do all his life. There was only one job ahead for Iverson at International Harvester and he felt more ambition than to end his career in that position. At his boss's urging, he considered smaller companies.

Iverson joined Illium Corporation, 120 miles from Chicago, as chief engineer (metallurgist). Illium was a 60-person division of a major company but functioned like an independent company. Iverson was close to the young president and was impressed by his good business skill; this man knew how to manage and had the discipline to run a tight ship, to go in the right direction with no excess manpower. The two of them proposed an expansion, which the parent company insisted they delay three to four years until they could handle it without going into debt.

After two years at Illium, Iverson joined Indiana Steel products as assistant to the vice-president of manufacturing, for the sole purpose of setting up a spectrographic lab. After completing this job within one year, he could see no other opportunity for himself in the company, because it was small and he could get no real responsibility. A year and a half later, Iverson left to join Cannon Muskegon as chief metallurgist.

The next seven years were "fascinating." This small ($5–6 million in sales and 60–70 people) family company made castings from special metals that were used in every aircraft made in the United States. The company was one of the first to get into "vacuum melting," and Iverson, because of his technical ability, was put in charge of this activity. Iverson then asked for and got responsibility for all company sales. He wasn't dissatisfied but realized that if he was to be really successful he needed broader managerial experience.

Cannon Muskegon sold materials to Coast Metals, a small, private company in New Jersey which cast and machined special alloys for the aircraft industry. The president of Coast got to know Iverson and realized his technical expertise would be an asset. In 1960 he joined Coast as executive vice-president, with responsibility for running the whole company.

Nuclear Corporation of America wished to buy Coast; however, Coast wasn't interested. Nuclear's president then asked Iverson to act as a consultant to find metal businesses Nuclear could buy. Over the next year, mostly on weekends, he looked at potential acquisitions. He recommended buying a joist business in North Carolina. Nuclear said it would, if he would run it. Coast was having disputes among its owners and Iverson's future there was clouded. He ended his two years there and joined Nuclear in 1962 as a vice-president, Nuclear's usual title, in charge of a 200-person joist division.

By late 1963 he had built a second plant in Nebraska and was running the only division making a profit. The president asked him to become a group vice-president, adding the research chemicals (metals) and contracting businesses, and to move to the home office in Phoenix. In mid-1965 the company defaulted on two loans and the president resigned. During that summer Nuclear sought some direction out of its difficulty. Iverson knew what could be done, put together a pro-forma statement, and pushed for these actions. It was not a unanimous decision when he was made president in September 1965.

The new management immediately abolished some divisions and went to work building Nucor. According to Iverson, the vice-presidents of the divisions designed Nucor in hard-working, almost T-group-type meetings. Iverson was only another participant and took charge only when the group couldn't settle an issue. This process identified Nucor's strengths and set the path for Nucor.

By 1966 Nucor consisted of the two joist plants, the Research Chemicals division, and the Nuclear division. During 1967 a building in Fort Payne, Alabama, was purchased for conversion into another joist plant. "We got into the steel business because we wanted to be able to build a mill that could make steel as cheaply as we were buying it from foreign importers or from offshore mills." In 1968 Nucor opened a steel mill in Darlington, South Carolina, and a joist plant in Texas. Another joist plant was added in Indiana in 1972. Steel plant openings followed in Nebraska in 1977 and in Texas in 1975. The Nuclear division was divested in 1976. A fourth steel plant was opened in Utah in 1981 and a joist plant was opened in Utah in 1982. By 1984 Nucor consisted of six joist plants, four steel mills, and a Research Chemicals division.

In 1983, in testimony before the Congress, Iverson warned of the hazards of trade barriers, that they would cause steel to cost more and that manufacturers would move overseas to use the cheaper steel shipped back into this country. He commented, "We have seen serious problems in the wire industry and the fastener industry." *Link* magazine reported that in the last four years, 40 domestic fastener plants had closed and that imports had over 90 percent of the market.

In 1986 Nucor began construction of a $25 million plant in Indiana to manufacture steel fasteners. Iverson told *The Atlanta Journal,* "We are going to bring that business back."[3] He told *Inc.* magazine, "We've studied for a year now, and we decided that we can make bolts as cheaply as foreign producers and make a profit at it."[4] He explained that in the old operation two people, one simply required by the union, made one hundred bolts a minute. "But at Nucor, we'll have an automated machine which will manufacture 400 bolts a minute. The automation will allow an operator to manage four machines." Hans Mueller, a steel industry consultant at East Tennessee State University, told the *Journal,* "I must confess that I was surprised that Iverson would be willing to dive into that snake pit. But he must believe that he can do it because he is not reckless."[5]

Before making the decision, a Nucor task force of four people traveled the world to examine the latest technology. The management group was headed by a plant manager who joined Nucor after several years experience as general manager of a bolt company in Toronto. The manager of manufacturing was previously plant manager of a 40,000-ton melt-shop for Ervin Industries. The sales manager was a veteran of sales, distribution, and manufacturing in the fastener industry. The plant's engineering manager transferred from Nucor R & D in Nebraska. The Touche-Ross accountant who worked on the Nucor account joined the company as controller. The first crew of production employees received three months of in-depth training on the bolt-making machines, with extensive cross-training in tool making, maintenance, and other operations. By 1988, the new plant was operating close to its capacity of 45,000 tons.

In what *The New York Times* called their "most ambitious project yet," Nucor signed an agreement in January 1987 to form a joint venture with Yamato Kogyo, Ltd., a small Japanese steelmaker, to build a steel mill on the Mississippi River with a 600,000 ton per year capacity.[6] The two hundred million dollar plant would make very large structural products, up to 24 inches. Structural steel products are those used in large buildings and bridges. Iverson noted, "These are now only made by the Big Three integrated steel companies." The Japanese company, which would own 49% of the stock, had expertise in continuous-casting in which Nucor was interested. Their 1985 sales totaled $400 million, with approximately 900 workers. They would provide the continuous casting technology while Nucor would provide the melting technology and management style. The mill was completed in 1988 at a cost of $220 million for 650,000 tons of capacity. By the end of 1988, the plant was operating at 50% of capacity.

In August 1986, Iverson told Cable News Network, "We are talking about within the next two years perhaps building a steel mill to make flat roll products; that would be the first time a mini-mill has been in this area."[7] It was expected that approximately $10 million would be needed to develop this process. The thin-slab would also produce feed stock for Vulcraft's 250,000 tons per year steel

[3]Chris Burritt, "Foreign Steel Doesn't Scare Nucor's CEO," *The Atlanta Journal,* August 24, 1986, pp. IM, 5M.
[4]"Steel Man Ken Iverson," *Inc.,* April 1986, pp. 41–48.
[5]Burritt, "Foreign Steel Doesn't Scare Nucor's CEO," pp. 1M, 5M.
[6]"Nucor's Ambitious Expansion," *The New York Times,* June 30, 1986, pp. D1, D3.
[7]"Inside Business," Interview with Ken Iverson, Cable News Network, August 17, 1986.

deck operation. Although the project was considered pure research at the time and projected for "late 1988," the Division Manager stated, "The more we look into it, the more we feel we'll be able to successfully cast those slabs." This process would be the most significant development in the steel industry in decades and would open up the auto and appliance businesses to the mini-mills. Then in January 1987 plans were announced to build the $200 million, 800,000-ton mill for the production of high-grade flat rolled steel by the first half of 1989. They stated, "We've tested numerous approaches . . . this one is commercially feasible. It's been tested and it can do the job."[8]

The flat rolled steel was the largest market for steel products at 40 million tons in 1988 and 52% of the U.S. market. This is the thin sheet steel used in car bodies, refrigerators and countless products. Making flat rolled steel required casting a slab rather than a billit and had not been achieved in the mini-mill. Nucor had invested several million in research on a process but in 1986 chose to go with a technology developed by SMS, a West German company. SMS had a small pilot plant using the new technology and Nucor would be the first mini-mill in the world to manufacture flat rolled steel commercially.

The 800,000 ton, $265 million, plant would be built in Crawfordsville, Indiana, with an April 1988 start-up. It was expected that labor hours per ton would be half the integrated manufacturer's 3.0, yielding a savings of $50 to $75 on a $400 a ton selling price. If the project were completed successfully, Nucor planned to have three plants in operation before others could build. Investment advisors anticipated Nucor's stock could increase to double or triple by the mid 1990s. In July 1989, when Nucor announced a 14% drop in 2nd quarter earnings due to start-up costs, its stock went up $1.62 to $63. Iverson stated, "We hope this will map out the future of the company for the next decade."

However, it would not be as easy as earlier ventures. In April 1989, *Forbes* commented "if any mini-mill can meet the challenge, it's Nucor. But expect the going to be tougher this time around."[9] The flat-rolled market was the last bastion of the integrated manufacturers and they had been seriously modernizing their plants throughout the '80s.

In December 1986 Nucor announced its first major acquisition, Genbearco, a steel bearings manufacturer. At a cost of more than $10 million, it would add $25 million in sales and 250 employees. Iverson called it "a good fit with our business, our policies and our people." It was without a union and tied pay to performance.

In October 1988, Nucor agreed to sell its Chemicals Division to a New York company for a $38 million gain.

Nucor's innovation was not limited to manufacturing. In the steel industry, it was normal to price an order based on the quantity ordered. In 1984, Nucor broke that pattern. As Iverson stated, "Sometime ago we began to realize that with computer order entry and billing, the extra charge for smaller orders was

[8]Jo Isenberg-O'Loughlin and Joseph J. Innace, "Full Steam Ahead on the Nucor Unlimited," *33 Metal Producing*, January 1986, pp. 35–50.
[9]R. Simon, "Nucor's Boldest Gamble," *Forbes*, April 3, 1989, p. 122.

not cost justified. We found the cost of servicing a 20 ton order compared with a 60 ton order was about 35 cents a ton and most of that was related to credit and collection. We did agonize over the decision, but over the long run we are confident that the best competitive position is one that has a strong price to cost relationship." He noted that this policy would give Nucor another advantage over foreign suppliers in that users could maintain lower inventories and order more often. "If we are going to successfully compete against foreign suppliers, we must use the most economical methods for both manufacturing and distribution."

THE STEEL INDUSTRY

The early 1980s had been the worst years in decades for the steel industry. Data from the American Iron and Steel Institute showed shipments falling from 100.2 million tons in 1979 to the mid-80 levels in 1980 and 1981. Slackening in the economy, particularly in auto sales, led the decline. In 1986, when industry capacity was at 130-million tons, the outlook was for a continued decline in per-capita consumption and movement toward capacity in the 90–100 million ton range. The Chairman of Armco saw "millions of tons chasing a market that's not there; excess capacity that must be eliminated."

The large, integrated steel firms, such as U.S. Steel and Armco, which made up the major part of the industry, were the hardest hit. *The Wall Street Journal* stated, "The decline has resulted from such problems as high labor and energy costs in mining and processing iron ore, a lack of profits and capital to modernize plants, and conservative management that has hesitated to take risks."[10]

These companies produced a wide range of steels, primarily from ore processed in blast furnaces. They had found it difficult to compete with imports, usually from Japan, and had given up market share to imports. They sought the protection of import quotas. Imported steel accounted for 20% of the U.S. steel consumption, up from 12% in the early 1970s. The U.S. share of world production of raw steel declined from 19% to 14% over the period. Imports of light bar products accounted for less than 9% of U.S. consumption of those products in 1981, according to the U.S. Commerce Department, while imports of wire rod totaled 23% of U.S. consumption. "Wire rod is a very competitive product in the world market because it's very easy to make," Ralph Thompson, the Commerce Department's steel analyst, told the *Charlotte Observer*.[11]

Iron Age stated that exports, as a percent of shipments in 1985, were 34% for Nippon, 26% for British Steel, 30% for Krupp, 49% for USINOR of France, and less than 1% for every American producer on the list. The consensus of steel experts was that imports would average 23% of the market in the last half of the 1980's.[12]

[10]Sease, "Mini-Mill Steelmakers," pp. 1, 19.
[11]*The Charlotte Observer,* various issues.
[12]"1985 Top 50 World Steel Producers," *Iron Age,* May 2, 1986, p. 48B1.

Iverson was one of very few in the steel industry to oppose import restrictions. He saw an <u>outdated</u> U.S. steel industry which had to change.

> About 12% of the steel in the U.S. is still produced by the old open hearth furnace. The Japanese shut down their last open hearth furnace about five years ago. . . . The U.S. produces about 16% of its steel by the continuous casting process. In Japan over 50% of the steel is continuously cast. . . . We Americans have been conditioned to believe in our technical superiority. For many generations a continuing stream of new inventions and manufacturing techniques allowed us to far outpace the rest of the world in both volume and efficiency of production. In many areas this is no longer true and particularly in the steel industry. In the last three decades, almost all the major developments in steel making were made outside the U.S. There were 18 continuous casting units in the world before there was one in this country. I would be negligent if I did not recognize the significant contribution that the government has made toward the technological deterioration of the steel industry. Unrealistic depreciation schedules, high corporate taxes, excessive regulation and jaw-boning for lower steel prices have made it difficult for the steel industry to borrow or generate the huge quantities of capital required for modernization.

By the mid 1980's the integrated mills were moving fast to get back into the game; they were restructuring, cutting capacity, dropping unprofitable lines, focusing products, and trying to become responsive to the market. The President of USX explained: "Steel executives, in trying to act as prudent businessmen, are seeking the lowest-cost solutions to provide what the market wants." Karlis Kirsis, Director of World Steel Dynamics at Paine-Webber, told *Purchasing Magazine,* "The industry as we knew it five years ago is no more; the industry as we knew it a year ago is gone."[13]

Purchasing believed that buyers would be seeing a pronounced industry segmentation. There would be integrated producers making mostly flat-rolled and structural grades, reorganized steel companies making a limited range of products, mini-mills dominating the bar and light structural product areas, specialty steel firms seeking niches, and foreign producers. There would be accelerated shutdowns of older plants, elimination of products by some firms, and the installation of new product lines with new technologies by others. There would also be corporate facelifts as executives diversified from steel to generate profits and entice investment dollars. They saw the high-tonnage mills restructuring to handle sheets, plates, structurals, high quality bars, and large pipe and tubular products which would allow for a resurgence of specialized mills: cold-finished bar manufacturers, independent strip mills and mini-mills.[14]

Wheeling-Pittsburgh illustrated the change underway in the industry. Through Chapter 11 reorganization it had cut costs by more than $85/ton. They

[13]"Metals Report: Steel 1986," *Purchasing,* September 25, 1986, pp. 52–65.
[14]Ibid.

divided into profit centers, negotiated the lowest hourly wage rate ($18/hour) among unionized integrated steel plants, renegotiated supply contracts, closed pipe and tube mills, and shut 1.6 million tons of blast furnace capacity in favor of an electric furnace with continuous casting.

Paine Webber pointed out the importance of "reconstituted mills," which they called the "People Express" of the industry. These were companies which had reorganized and refocused their resources, usually under Chapter 11. These include Kaiser Steel, the Weirton Works, Jones and Laughlin, Republic, Youngstown, Wheeling, LTV, and others.

Joint ventures had arisen to produce steel for a specific market or region. The Chairman of USX called them "an important new wrinkle in steel's fight for survival" and stated, "If there had been more joint ventures like these two decades ago, the U.S. steel industry might have built only half of the dozen or so hot-strip mills it put up in that time and avoided today's overcapacity." *Purchasing* observed, "The fact is that these combined operations are the result of a laissez faire attitude within the Justice Department under the Reagan administration following the furor when government restrictions killed the planned USS takeover of National Steel (which later sold 50% interest to a Japanese steelmaker)."[15]

However, the road ahead for the integrated mills would not be easy. While it was estimated they would need $10 billion to improve their facilities, the industry had lost over $7 billion since 1982. *Purchasing* pointed out that tax laws and accounting rules are slowing the closing of inefficient plants. Shutting down a 10,000-person plant could require a firm to hold a cash reserve of $100 million to fund health, pension and insurance liabilities. The Chairman of Armco commented: "Liabilities associated with a plant shutdown are so large that they can quickly devastate a company's balance sheet."[16]

The American Iron and Steel Institute (AISI) reported steel production in 1988 of 99.3 million tons, up from 89.2 in '87, and the highest in seven years. As a result of modernization programs, 60.9 percent of production was from continuous casters. Exports of steel were increasing, 2 million tons in 1988 and forecast to 3 in 1989, and imports were falling, expected to be less than 20% in 1989. Some steel experts believed the U.S. was now cost competitive with Japan. Several countries did not fill their quotas allowed under the 5-year-old voluntary restraint agreements, which would expire in September 1989. The role of service centers in the distribution of steel continued with its fifth consecutive record year in 1988 of 23.4 million tons.

"If 1988 is remembered as the year of steel prosperity despite economic uncertainties, then 1989 is just as likely to go down as the year of 'waiting for the other shoe to drop,'" according to *Metal Center News* in January 1989.[17] The fears and the expectation of a somewhat weaker year arose from concerns of a recession, expirations of the voluntary import restraints, and labor negotiations

[15]Ibid.
[16]Ibid
[17]*Metal Center News*, January, 1989.

schedules in several companies. Declines in car production and consumer goods were expected to hit flat-rolled hard. Service centers were also expected to be cutting back on inventories. AUJ Consultants told *MCN,* "The U.S. steel market has peaked. Steel consumption is tending down. By 1990, we expect total domestic demand to dip under 90 million tons."[18] Iverson expected 1989 to be mediocre compared to 1988.

THE MINI-MILL

A new type of mill, the "mini-mill," emerged in the U.S. during the 1970's to compete with the integrated mill. The mini-mill used electric arc furnaces to manufacture a narrow product line from scrap steel. In 1981 *The New York Times* reported:

> The truncated steel mill is to the integrated steel mill what the Volkswagen was to the American auto industry in the 1960's: smaller, cheaper, less complex and more efficient. Although mini-mills cannot produce such products as sheet steel [flat rolled] and heavy construction items, some industry analysts say it is only a matter of time before technological breakthroughs make this possible.[19]

Since mini-mills came into being in the 1970's, the integrated mills' market share has fallen from about 90% to about 60%, with the loss equally divided between mini-mills and foreign imports. While the integrated steel companies averaged a 7% return on equity, the mini-mills averaged 14%, and some, such as Nucor, achieved about 25%.

The leading mini-mills were Nucor, Florida Steel, Georgetown Steel (Korf Industries), North Star Steel, and Chaparral. Nucor produced "light bar" products: bars, angles, channels, flats, smooth round, and forging billets. It was beginning to make more alloy steels. Florida Steel made mostly reinforcing bar for construction (rebar) and dominated the Florida market. Korf Industries had two mini-mill subsidiaries which used modern equipment to manufacture wire-rod.

The mini-mills were not immune to the economic slump in the early eighties. Korf Industries, which owned Georgetown Steel, found its interest charges too large a burden and sought reorganization in 1983. In March of 1983, Georgetown followed the historic wage cutting contract between the United Steel Workers of America and the major steel companies and asked its union to accept reductions and to defer automatic wage increases. In 1982 Nucor froze wages and executives took a 5% pay cut. Plants went to a four-day schedule in which workers would receive only base rate if they chose to work a fifth day doing clean-up.

[18]Ibid.
[19]"The Rise of Mini-Steel Mills," *The New York Times,* September 23, 1981, pp. D1, D6.

Florida Steel, with two-thirds of its sales in Florida, also felt the impact. At its headquarters in Tampa, a staff of over 100 handled accounting, payroll, sales entry, and almost all other services for all its facilities. Their division managers did not have sales responsibilities. Florida Steel experienced a sales decline for 1982 of 22% and an earnings drop from $3.37 per share to a loss of $1.40. The next year was also a year of losses.

Florida steel employees had faced periodic layoffs during the recession. The firm was non-union (although the Charlotte plant lost an election in 1973) and pay was based on productivity. A small facility at Indian Town, near West Palm Beach, never became productive, even with personnel changes, and had to be closed. A new mini-mill in Tennessee was completed in late 1983.

Mini-mills had tripled their output in the last decade to capture 17% of domestic shipments. Paine Webber predicted the big integrated mills' share of the market would fall to 40%, the mini-mills' share would rise to 23%, "reconstituted" mills would increase from 11% to 28%, and specialized mills would increase their share from 1% to 7%. Iverson stated mini-mills could not go beyond a 35% to 40% share due to technical limitations; mini-mills could not produce the flat rolled sheet steel used in cars and appliances.

Iverson told *Metal Center News* in 1983: "We are very interested in the development of a thin slab, which would then allow mini-mills to produce plate and other flat rolled products . . . actually, the thinnest slab that can now be produced is about 6 inches thick. . . . (That results in a plant that is too large.) There are a number of people working to develop the process. . . . We have done some work, but our primary efforts at the moment are in connection with other people who are working on it. . . . The likelihood is it would be developed by a foreign company. There are more efforts by foreign steel companies in that direction than in the United States. . . . I'd say probably a minimum of three to five years, or it could take as much as 10 to achieve this."[20]

In 1983 Iverson described the new generation of mini-mills he foresaw: "If you go way back, mini-mills got started by rolling reinforcing bar. With the advent of continuous casting and improvements in rolling mills, mini-mills gradually got into shapes. Now they have moved in two other directions: one being to larger sizes, and the other being a growing metallurgical expertise for improved product quality and production of special bar quality in alloys. Both of these represent expansion of markets for mini-mills."

By 1986 the new competitive environment was apparent. Four mini-mills had closed their doors within the year and Iverson saw that more shutdowns were ahead. The overcapacity of steel bar products and the stagnant market had made it difficult for some companies to generate the cash needed to modernize and expand their product lines. "The mini-mills are going through the same kind of restructuring and rethinking as the integrated mill. They know the problem of overcapacity isn't going to go away quickly. And, for some of the remaining firms to survive, they will have to move into more sophisticated products like special quality and clean-steel bars and heavier structurals and, once the

[20]"Iverson Alloys Usher in New Era," *Metal Center News,* August 1987, p. 29.

technology is perfected, flat-rolled products. You won't see the market growth by the mini-mills the way it was in the past until the overcapacity issue is resolved and the mills begin entering new product areas."

ORGANIZATION

Nucor, with its 18-person corporate office located in Charlotte, North Carolina, had divisions spread across the United States. The 15 divisions, one for every plant, each had a general manager, who was also a vice-president of the corporation, directly responsible to Iverson and Aycock. (See Exhibit 1.) The divisions were of two basic types, joist plants and steel mills. The corporate staff consisted of single specialists in personnel and planning and a four-person financial function under Mr. Sam Siegel. Iverson, in the beginning, had chosen Charlotte "as the new home base for what he had envisioned as a small cadre of executives who would guide a decentralized operation with liberal authority delegated to managers in the field," according to *South Magazine*.[21]

Iverson gave his views on organization:

> You can tell a lot about a company by looking at its organization chart. . . . If you see a lot of staff, you can bet it is not a very efficient organization. . . . Secondly, don't have assistants. We do not have that title and prohibit it in our company. . . . In this organization nobody reports to the corporate office; the division managers report directly to me. . . . And one of the most important things is to resist as much as possible the number of management layers. . . . I've often thought that when a company builds a fancy corporate office, it's on its way down.
>
> Each division is a profit center and the division manager has control over the day-to-day decisions that make that particular division profitable or not profitable. We expect the division to provide contribution, which is earnings before corporate expenses. We do not allocate our corporate expenses, because we do not think there is any way to do this reasonably and fairly. We do focus on earnings. And we expect a division to earn 25 percent return on total assets employed, before corporate expenses, taxes, interest or profit sharing. And we have a saying in the company—if a manager doesn't provide that for a number of years, we are either going to get rid of the division or get rid of the general manager, and it's generally the division manager.

A joist division manager commented:

> I've been a division manager four years now and at times I'm still awed by it: the opportunity I was given to be a Fortune 500 vice-president. . . . I think

21Don Bedwell, "Nucor's Lean, Mean Management Team," *South Magazine*, August 1980, p. 50.

EXHIBIT 1   **Nucor organization chart**

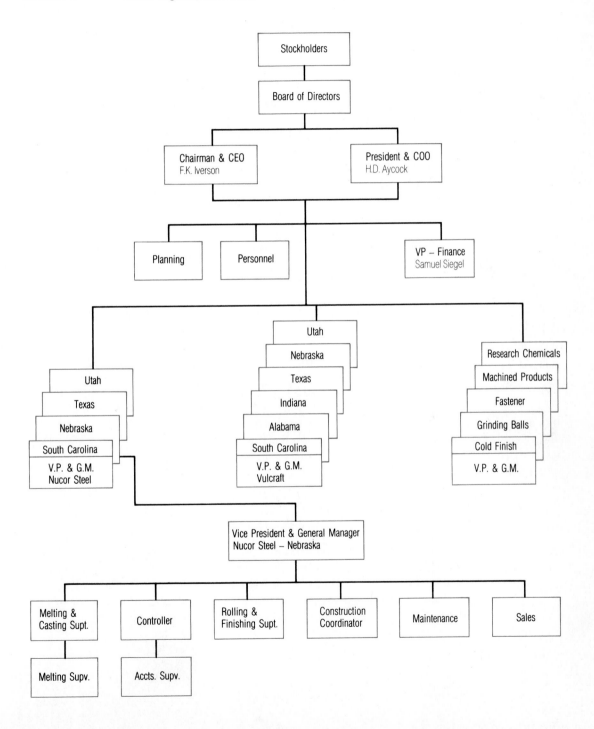

we are successful because it is our style to pay more attention to our business than our competitors. . . . We are kind of a "no nonsense" company. That is not to say we don't have time for play, but we work hard when we work and the company is first and foremost in our minds. . . . I think another one of the successes of our company has been the fact that we have a very minimum number of management levels. We've been careful to avoid getting topheavy and so consequently we put a great deal of responsibility on each individual at each level. It has often been said, jokingly, that if you are the janitor at Vulcraft and you get the right promotions, about four promotions would take you to the top of the company.

Mr. Iverson's style of management is to allow the division manager all the latitude in the world. His involvement with the managers is quite limited. As we've grown, he no longer has the time to visit with the managers more than once or twice a year. . . . Whereas in many large companies the corporate office makes the major decisions and the people at the operating level sit back to wait for their marching orders, that's not the case at Nucor. . . . In a way I feel like I run my own company because I really don't get any marching orders from Mr. Iverson. He lets you run the division the way you see fit and the only way he will step in is if he sees something he doesn't like, particularly bad profits, high costs or whatever. But in the years I've worked with him I don't believe he has ever issued one single instruction to me to do something differently. I can't recall a single instance.

The divisions did their own manufacturing, selling, accounting, engineering, and personnel management. A steel division manager, when questioned about Florida Steel, which had a large plant 90 miles away, commented, "I really don't know anything about Florida Steel. . . . I expect they do have more of the hierarchy. I think they have central purchasing, centralized sales, centralized credit collections, centralized engineering, and most of the major functions." He didn't feel greater centralization would be good for Nucor. "The purchasing activity, for example, removed from the field tends to become rather insensitive to the needs of the field and does not feel the pressures of responsibility. And the division they are buying for has no control over what they pay. . . . Likewise centralized sales would not be sensitive to the needs of their divisions."[22]

South Magazine observed that Iverson had established a characteristic organizational style described as "stripped down" and "no nonsense." "Jack Benny would like this company," observed Roland Underhill, an analyst with Crowell, Weedon and Co. of Los Angeles; "so would Peter Drucker." Underhill pointed out that Nucor's thriftiness doesn't end with its "spartan" office staff or modest offices. "There are no corporate perquisites," he recited. "No company planes. No country club memberships. No company cars."[23]

[22]Interviews conducted by Frank C. Barnes.
[23]Bedwell, "Nucor's Lean, Mean Management Team," p. 55.

Fortune reported, "Iverson takes the subway when he is in New York, a Wall Street analyst reports in a voice that suggests both admiration and amazement."[24] The general managers reflected this style in the operation of their individual divisions. Their offices were more like plant offices or the offices of private companies built around manufacturing rather than for public appeal. They were simple, routine, and businesslike.

In 1983, one of Iverson's concerns had been that as Nucor continued to grow they would have to add another layer of management to their lean structure. In June 1984 he named Dave Aycock President and Chief Operating Officer, while he became Chairman and Chief Executive Officer—they would share one management level. Aycock had most recently been Division Manager of the steel mill at Darlington. But he had been with the company longer than Iverson, having joined Vulcraft in 1955, and had long been recognized as a particularly valued and close advisor to Iverson.

Iverson explained: "The company got to the size that I just wasn't doing the job that I thought should be done by this office. I couldn't talk to the analysts and everyone else I have to talk to, put the efforts into research and development I wanted to, and get to all the units as frequently as I should. That's why I brought Dave in. And, of course, he has been with the company forever." In a February 1985 letter he told stockholders: "These changes are to provide additional emphasis on the expansion of the company's businesses."

"Dave is a very analytical person and very thorough in his thought process," another Division Manager told *33 Metal Producing,* a McGraw-Hill publication. "And Ken, to use an overworked word, is an entrepreneurial type. So, they complement each other. They're both very aggressive men, and make one hell of a good team."[25] Aycock stated: "I am responsible for the operations of all our divisions. To decide where we are going, with what technologies; what are our purposes. And what is our thrust. I help Ken shape where we are going and with what technologies. . . . I've been quite aggressive my whole career at updating, adapting, and developing new technology and new ideas in production and marketing." "Dave's the fellow who now handles most of the day-to-day operations," Iverson commented. "And he handles most of the employees who write to us"—about 10 to 15% of his time.[26]

DIVISION MANAGERS

The general managers met three times a year. In late October they presented preliminary budgets and capital requests. In late February they met to finalize budgets and treat miscellaneous matters. Then, at a meeting in May, they handled

---

[24]"Pilgrims' Profits at Nucor," *Fortune,* April 6, 1981.
[25]Isenberg-O'Loughlin and Innace, "Full Steam Ahead on the Nucor Unlimited," pp. 35–50.
[26]"Ken Iverson," *33 Metal Producing,* p. 4.

personnel matters, such as wage increases and changes of policies or benefits. The general managers as a group considered the raises for the department heads, the next lower level of management. As one of the managers described it:[27]

> In May of each year, all the general managers get together and review all the department heads throughout the company. We have kind of an informal evaluation process. It's an intangible thing, a judgment as to how dedicated an individual is and how well he performs compared to the same position at another plant. Sometimes the numbers don't come out the way a general manager wants to see them, but it's a fair evaluation. The final number is picked by Mr. Iverson. Occasionally there are some additional discussions with Mr. Iverson. He always has an open mind and might be willing to consider a little more for one individual. We consider the group of, say, joist production managers at one time. The six managers are rated for performance. We assign a number, such as +3 to a real crackerjack performer or a −2 to someone who needs improvement. These ratings become a part of the final pay increase granted.

The corporate personnel manager described management relations as informal, trusting, and not "bureaucratic." He felt there was a minimum of paperwork, that a phone call was more common and that no confirming memo was thought to be necessary. Iverson himself stated:

> Management is not a popularity contest. If everybody agrees with the organization, something is wrong with the organization. You don't expect people in the company to put their arms around each other, and you don't interfere with every conflict. Out of conflict often comes the best answer to a particular problem. So don't worry about it. You are always going to have some conflict in an organization. You will always have differences of opinion, and that's healthy. Don't create problems where there are none.

A Vulcraft manager commented: "We have what I would call a very friendly spirit of competition from one plant to the next. And of course all of the vice-presidents and general managers share the same bonus systems so we are in this together as a team even though we operate our divisions individually." The general managers are paid a bonus based on a total corporate profit rather than their own divisions' profits. A steel mill manager explained:

> I think it's very important for the general managers to be concerned with contributing to the overall accomplishment of the company. There is a lot of interplay between the divisions with a flow of services, products, and ideas between divisions. Even though we are reasonably autonomous, we are not isolated. . . . We don't like the division managers to make decisions that

[27]All quotes are either from Ken Iverson or from interviews with Nucor managers conducted by Frank C. Barnes.

would take that division away from where we want the whole company to go. But we certainly want the divisions to try new things. We are good copiers; if one division finds something that works, then we will all try it. I think that's one of our strengths. We have a lot of diverse people looking at ways to do things better.

Iverson revealed his view of management in his disdain for consultants:

They must have a specific job to do because they can't make your decisions. . . . The fellow on the line has to make decisions. . . . First he has to communicate and then he has to have the intestinal fortitude and the personal strength to make the decisions, sometimes under very difficult conditions. . . . A good manager is adaptable and he is sensitive to cultural, geographical, environmental, and business climates. Most important of all, he communicates. . . . You never know if someone is a good manager until he manages. And that's why we take people as young as we possibly can, throw responsibility at them, and they either work or they don't. In a sense it's survival of the fittest. But don't kid yourself; that's what industry is all about.

A steel division manager commented in comparing the Nucor manager to the typical manager of a large corporation:

We would probably tend to have managers who have confidence in their abilities and, very importantly, have confidence in other people in their division. And people who are very sensitive to the employees of their division. . . . But I think if you saw four or five different division managers, you'd have four or five different decision-making styles.

A Vulcraft general manager in his early 40's who had been promoted to the division manager level nine years earlier said:

The step from department manager to division manager is a big one. I can't think of an instance when a general manager job has been offered to an individual that it has been passed up. Often it means moving from one part of the country to another. There are five department heads in six joist plants, which means there are 30 people who are considered for division manager slots at a joist plant. Mr. Iverson selects the division managers.

His own experience was enlightening:

When I came to this plant four years ago, we had too many people, too much overhead. We had 410 people at the plant and I could see, because I knew how many people we had in the Nebraska plant, we had many more than we needed. That was my yardstick and we set about to reduce those numbers by attrition. . . . We have made a few equipment changes that made it easier for the men, giving them an opportunity to make better bonuses. Of course the changes were very subtle in any given case but overall in four years we have probably helped the men tremendously. With 55 fewer men, perhaps 40 to 45 fewer in the production area, we are still capable of producing the same number of tons as four years ago.

The divisions managed their activities with a minimum of contact with the corporate staff. Each day disbursements were reported to Siegel's office. Payments flowed into regional lock-boxes. On a weekly basis, joist divisions reported total quotes, sales cancellations, backlog, and production. Steel mills reported tons-rolled, outside shipments, orders, cancellations, and backlog. Mr. Iverson graphed the data. He might talk to the division about every two weeks. On the other hand Iverson was known to bounce ideas off the steel division manager in Darlington with whom he had worked since joining the company.

The Vulcraft manager commented on the communications with the corporate office: "It's kind of a steady pipeline. I might talk to the corporate office once a day or it might be once a week. But it generally involves, I would not say trivial information, just mundane things. Occasionally I hear from Sam or Ken about serious matters."

Each month the divisions completed a two-page (11" × 17") "Operations Analysis" which was sent to all the managers. Its three main purposes were (1) financial consolidation, (2) sharing information among the divisions, and (3) Iverson's examination. The summarized information and the performance statistics for all the divisions were then returned to the managers.

VULCRAFT—THE JOIST DIVISIONS

Half of Nucor's business was the manufacture and sale of open web steel joists and joist girders at six Vulcraft divisions located in Florence, South Carolina; Norfolk, Nebraska; Ft. Payne, Alabama; Grapeland, Texas; St. Joe, Indiana; and Brigham City, Utah. Open web joists, in contrast to solid joists, were made of steel angle iron separated by round bars or smaller angle iron (see Exhibit 2). These joists were costless and of lower greater strength for many applications and were used primarily as the roof support systems in larger buildings, such as warehouses and stores.

The joist industry was characterized by high competition among many manufacturers for many small customers. The Vulcraft divisions had over 3,000 customers, none of whom dominated the business. With an estimated 25% of the market, Nucor was the largest supplier in the U.S. It utilized national advertising campaigns and prepared competitive bids on 80% to 90% of buildings using joists. Competition was based on price and delivery performance. Nucor had developed computer programs to prepare designs for customers and to compute bids based on current prices and labor standards. In addition, each Vulcraft plant maintained its own Engineering Department to help customers with design prob-

EXHIBIT 2   **Illustration of joists**

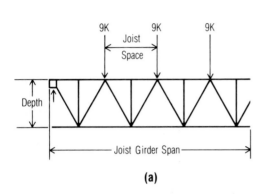

(a)

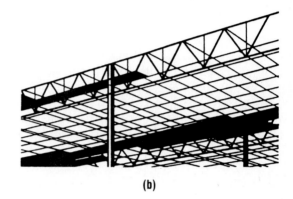

(b)

lems or specifications. The Florence manager commented, "Here on the East Coast we have six or seven major competitors; of course none of them are as large as we are. The competition for any order will be heavy, and we will see six or seven different prices."[28] He added, "I think we have a strong selling force in the marketplace. It has been said to us by some of our competitors that in this particular industry we have the finest selling organization in the country."

Nucor aggressively sought to be the lowest-cost producer in the industry. Materials and freight were two important elements of cost. Nucor maintained its own fleet of almost 100 trucks to ensure on-time delivery to all of the states, although most business was regional because of transportation costs. Plants were located in rural areas near the markets they served.

The Florence manager stated:

> I don't feel there's a joist producer in the country that can match our cost. . . . We are sticklers about cutting out unnecessary overhead. Because we put so much responsibility on our people and because we have what I think is an excellent incentive program, our people are willing to work harder to accomplish these profitable goals.

Production

On the basic assembly line used at Nucor, three or four of which might make up any one plant, about six tons per hour would be assembled. In the first stage eight people cut the angles to the right lengths or bent the round bars to the desired form. These were moved on a roller conveyer to six-man assembly stations, where the component parts would be tacked together for the next stage, welding. Drilling and miscellaneous work were done by three people between

---

[28]Interviews conducted by Frank C. Barnes.

the lines. The nine-man welding station completed the welds before passing the joists on roller conveyers to two-man inspection teams. The last step before shipment was the painting.

The workers had control over and responsibility for quality. There was an independent quality control inspector who had the authority to reject the run of joists and cause them to be reworked. The quality control people were not under the incentive system and reported to the Engineering Department.

Daily production might vary widely, since each joist was made for a specific job. The wide range of joists made control of the workload at each station difficult; bottlenecks might arise anywhere along the line. Each work station was responsible for identifying such bottlenecks so that the foreman could reassign people promptly to maintain productivity. Since workers knew most of the jobs on the line, including the more skilled welding job, they could be shifted as needed. Work on the line was described by one general manager as "not machine type but mostly physical labor." He said the important thing was to avoid bottlenecks.

There were four lines of about 28 people each on two shifts at the Florence division. The jobs on the line were rated on responsibility and assigned a base wage, from $6 to $8 per hour. In addition, a weekly bonus was paid on the total output of each line. Each worker received the same percent bonus on his base wage.

The amount of time required to make a joist had been established as a result of experience; the general manager had seen no time studies in his fifteen years with the company. As a job was bid, the cost of each joist was determined through the computer program. The time required depended on the length, number of panels, and depth of the joist.

At the time of production, the labor value of production, the standard, was determined in a similar manner. The general manager stated, "In the last nine or ten years we have not changed a standard." The standards list in use was over 10 years old. Previously, they adjusted the standard if the bonus was too high. He said the technological improvements over the last few years had been small. The general manager reported that the bonus had increased from about 60% nine years earlier to about 100% in 1982 and had stabilized at that point. Exhibits 3 and 4 show data typically computed on performance and used by the manager. He said the difference in performance on the line resulted from the different abilities of the crews.

"We don't have an industrial engineering staff. Our Engineering Department's work is limited to the design and the preparation of the paperwork prior to the actual fabrication process. Now, that is not to say that we don't have any involvement in fabrication. But the efficiency of the plant is entirely up to the manufacturing department. . . . When we had our first group in a joist plant, we produced 3½ tons an hour. We thought that if we ever got to 4 tons, that would be the Millennium. Well, today we don't have anybody who produces less than 6½ tons an hour. This is largely due to improvements that the groups have suggested."

EXHIBIT 3   **Tons per manhour, 52-week moving average**

1977	.163
1978	.179
1979	.192
1980	.195
1981	.194
1982	.208
1983	.215
1984	.214
1985	.228
1986	.225
1987	.218

EXHIBIT 4   **A sample of percentage performance, July 1982**

		Line			
		1	**2**	**3**	**4**
Shift	1st	117	97	82	89
	2nd	98	102	94	107

Management

In discussing his philosophy for dealing with the workforce, the Florence manager stated:[29]

> I believe very strongly in the incentive system we have. We are a non-union shop and we all feel that the way to stay so is to take care of our people and show them we care. I think that's easily done because of our fewer layers of management. . . . I spend a good part of my time in the plant, maybe an hour or so a day. If a man wants to know anything, for example, an insurance question, I'm there and they walk right up to me and ask me questions which I'll answer the best I know how. . . . You can always tell when people are basically happy. If they haven't called for a meeting themselves or they are not hostile in any way, you can take it they understand the company's situation and accept it. . . . We do listen to our people. . . . For instance last fall I got a call from a couple of workers saying that the people in our Shipping and Receiving area felt they were not being paid properly in relation to production people. So we met with them, discussed the situation and committed ourselves to reviewing the rates of other plants. We assured them

[29]Interviews conducted by Frank C. Barnes.

that we would get back to them with an answer by the first of the year.
Which we did. And there were a few minor changes.

The manager reported none of the plants had any particular labor problems, although there had been some in the past.

In 1976, two years before I came here, there was a union election at this plant which arose out of racial problems. The company actually lost the election to the U.S. Steelworkers. When it came time to begin negotiating the contract, the workers felt, or came to see, that they had little to gain from being in the union. The union was not going to be able to do anything more for them than they were already getting. So slowly the union activity died out and the union quietly withdrew.

He discussed formal systems for consulting with the workers before changes were made:

Of course we're cautioned by our labor counsel to maintain an open pipe-line to our employees. We post all changes, company earnings, changes in the medical plan, anything that might affect an employee's job. Mr. Iverson has another philosophy, which is, "Either tell your people everything or tell them nothing." We choose to tell them everything. We don't have any regu-larly scheduled meetings. We meet whenever there's a need. The most re-cent examples were a meeting last month to discuss the results of an em-ployee survey and three months before was held our annual dinner meetings off site.
We don't lay our people off and we make a point of telling our people this.

"In the economic slump of 1982, we scheduled our line for four days, but the men were allowed to come in the fifth day for maintenance work at base pay. The men in the plant on an average running bonus might make $13 an hour. If their base pay is half that, on Friday they would only get $6–$7 an hour. Sur-prisingly, many of the men did not want to come in on Friday. They felt com-fortable with just working four days a week. They are happy to have that extra day off." Recently the economic trouble in Texas had hurt business considerably. Both plants had been on decreased schedules for several months. About 20% of the people took the 5th day at base rate, but still no one had been laid off.

In April 1982 the executive committee decided, in view of economic con-ditions, that a pay freeze was necessary. The employees normally received an increase in their base pay the first of June. The decision was made at that time to freeze wages. The officers of the company, as a show of good faith, accepted a 5% pay cut. In addition to announcing this to the workers with a stuffer in their pay envelopes, meetings were held. Each production line, or incentive group of workers, met in the plant conference room with all supervision—foreman, plant production manager, and division manager. The economic crisis was explained to the employees by the production manager and all questions were answered.

STEEL DIVISIONS

Nucor had steel mills in five locations: Indiana, Nebraska, South Carolina, Texas, and Utah. The mills were modern "mini-mills," all built within the last 20 years to convert scrap steel into standard angles, flats, rounds, and channels using the latest technology. Sales in 1988 were 1.44 tons, a 10% increase over that of 1987. This figure represented about 70% of the mills' output, the remainder being used by other Nucor divisions. In recent years, Nucor has broadened its product line to include a wider range of steel chemistries, sizes, and special shapes. The total capacity of the mills reached 2.8 tons in 1988.

A casewriter from Harvard recounted the development of the steel divisions:

> By 1967 about 60% of each Vulcraft sales dollar was spent on materials, primarily steel. Thus, the goal of keeping costs low made it imperative to obtain steel economically. In addition, in 1967 Vulcraft bought about 60% of its steel from foreign sources. As the Vulcraft Division grew, Nucor became concerned about its ability to obtain an adequate economical supply of steel and in 1968 began construction of its first steel mill in Darlington, South Carolina. By 1972 the Florence, South Carolina, joist plant was purchasing over 90% of its steel from this mill. The Fort Payne plant bought about 50% of its steel from Florence. The other joist plants in Nebraska, Indiana and Texas found transportation costs prohibitive and continued to buy their steel from other steel companies, both foreign and domestic. Since the mill had excess capacity, Nucor began to market its steel products to outside customers. In 1972, 75% of the shipments of Nucor steel was to Vulcraft and 25% was to other customers.[30]

Iverson explained in 1984:

> In constructing these mills we have experimented with new processes and new manufacturing techniques. We serve as our own general contractor and design and build much of our own equipment. In one or more of our mills we have built our own continuous casting unit, reheat furnaces, cooling beds and in Utah even our own mill stands. All of these to date have cost under $125 per ton of annual capacity—compared with projected costs for large integrated mills of $1,200–1,500 per ton of annual capacity, ten times our cost. Our mills have high productivity. We currently use less than four manhours to produce a ton of steel. This includes everyone in the

[30]Harvard Intercollegiate Case Clearing House, Harvard Business School.

operation: maintenance, clerical, accounting, and sales and management. On the basis of our production workers alone, it is less than three manhours per ton. Our total employment costs are less than $60 per ton compared with the average employment costs of the seven largest U.S. steel companies of close to $130 per ton. Our total labor costs are less than 20% of our sales price.

In contrast to Nucor's less than four manhours, similar Japanese mills were said to require more than five hours and comparable U.S. mills over six hours. Nucor's average yield from molten metal to finished products was over 90%, compared with an average U.S. steel industry yield of about 74%, giving energy costs of about $39 per ton compared with their $75 a ton. Nucor ranked 46th on *Iron Age*'s annual survey of world steel producers. They were second on the list of top ten producers of steel worldwide based on tons per employee, at 981 tons. The head of the list was Tokyo Steel at 1,485. U.S. Steel was 7th at 479. Some other results were: Nippon Steel, 453; British Steel, 213; Bethlehem Steel, 329; Kruppstahl, 195; Weirton Steel, 317; and Northstar Steel, 936. Nucor also ranked 7th on the list ranking growth of raw steel production. U.S. Steel was 5th on the same list. U.S. Steel topped the list based on improvement in tons-per-employee, at 56%; Nucor was 7th with a 12% improvement.[31]

THE STEEL MAKING PROCESS

A steel mill's work is divided into two phases, preparation of steel of the proper "chemistry" and the forming of the steel into the desired products. The typical mini-mill utilized scrap steel, such as junk auto parts, instead of the iron ore which would be used in larger, integrated steel mills. The typical mini-mill had an annual capacity of 200–600 thousand tons, compared with the 7 million tons of Bethlehem Steel's Sparrow's Point, Maryland, integrated plant.

A charging bucket fed loads of scrap steel into electric arc furnaces. The melted load, called a heat, was poured into a ladle to be carried by an overhead crane to the casting machine. In the casting machine the liquid steel was extruded as a continuous red-hot solid bar of steel and cut into lengths weighing some 900 pounds called "billets." In the typical plant the billet, about four inches in cross section and about 20 feet long, was held temporarily in a pit where it cooled to normal temperatures. Periodically billets were carried to the rolling mill and placed in a reheat oven to bring them up to 2000°F at which temperature they would be malleable. In the rolling mill, presses and dies progressively converted the billet into the desired round bars, angles, channels, flats, and other products. After cutting to standard lengths, they were moved to the warehouse.

Nucor's first steel mill, employing more than 500 people, was located in Darlington, South Carolina. The mill, with its three electric arc furnaces, operated 24 hours per day, 5½ days per week. Nucor had made a number of improvements in the melting and casting operations. The former general manager of the Darlington plant had developed a system which involved preheating the ladles, allowing for the faster flow of steel into the caster and resulting in better control of the steel characteristics. Less time and lower capital investment were required. The casting machines were "continuous casters," as opposed to the old batch method. The objective in the "front" of the mill was to keep the casters working. At the time of the Harvard study at Nucor each strand was in operation 90% of the time, while a competitor had announced a "record rate" of 75% which it had been able to sustain for a week.

Nucor was also perhaps the only mill in the country which regularly avoided the reheating of billets. This saved $10–12 per ton in fuel usage and losses due to oxidation of the steel. The cost of developing this process had been $12 million. All research projects had not been successful. The company spent approximately $2,000,000 in an unsuccessful effort to utilize resistance-heating. They lost even more on an effort at induction melting. As Iverson told *33 Metal Producing,* "That cost us a lot of money. Timewise it was very expensive. But you have got to make mistakes and we've had lots of failures."[32] In the rolling mill, the first machine was a roughing mill by Morgarshammar, the first of its kind in the Western Hemisphere. This Swedish machine had been chosen because of its lower cost, higher productivity, and the flexibility. Passing through another five to nine finishing mills converted the billet into the desired finished product. The yield from the billet to finished product was about 93%.

The Darlington design became the basis for plants in Nebraska, Texas, and Utah. The Texas plant had cost under $80 per ton of annual capacity. Whereas the typical mini-mill cost approximately $250 per ton, the average cost of all four of Nucor's mills was under $135. An integrated mill was expected to cost between $1,200 and $1,500 per ton.

The Darlington plant was organized into 12 natural groups for the purpose of incentive pay: two mills, each had two shifts with three groups—melting and casting, rolling mill, and finishing. In melting and casting there were three or four different standards, depending on the material, established by the department manager years ago based on historical performance. The general manager stated, "We don't change the standards." The caster, the key to the operation, was used at a 92% level—one greater than the claims of the manufacturer. For every good ton of billet above the standard hourly rate for the week, workers in the group received a 4% bonus. For example, with a common standard of 10 tons per run hour and an actual rate for the week of 28 tons per hour, the workers would receive a bonus of 72% of their base rate in the week's pay check.

In the rolling mill there were more than 100 products, each with a different historical standard. Workers received a 4% to 6% bonus for every good ton sheared per hour for the week over the computed standard. The Darlington general manager said the standard would be changed only if there was a major machinery change and that a standard had not been changed since the initial

[32]Isenberg-O'Loughlin and Innace, "Full Steam Ahead on the Nucor Unlimited," pp. 35–50.

development period for the plant. He commented that, in exceeding the standard the worker wouldn't work harder but would cooperate to avoid problems and moved more quickly if a problem developed: "If there is a way to improve output, they will tell us." Another manager added: "Meltshop employees don't ask me how much it costs Chaparral or LTV to make a billet. They want to know what it costs Darlington, Norfolk, Jewitt to put a billet on the ground—scrap costs, alloy costs, electrical costs, refactory, gas, etc. Everybody from Charlotte to Plymouth watches the nickels and dimes."[33]

The Darlington manager, who became COO in 1984, stated:

> "The key to making a profit when selling a product with no aesthetic value, or a product that you really can't differentiate from your competitors, is cost. I don't look at us as a fantastic marketing organization, even though I think we are pretty good; but we don't try to overcome unreasonable costs by mass marketing. We maintain low costs by keeping the employee force at the level it should be, not doing things that aren't necessary to achieve our goals, and allowing people to function on their own and by judging them on their results.
>
> To keep a cooperative and productive workforce you need, number one, to be completely honest about everything; number two, to allow each employee as much as possible to make decisions about that employee's work, to find easier and more productive ways to perform duties; and number three, to be as fair as possible to all employees. Most of the changes we make in work procedures and in equipment come from the employees. They really know the problems of their jobs better than anyone else. We don't have any industrial engineers, nor do we ever intend to, because that's a type of specialist who tends to take responsibility off the top division management and give them a crutch.
>
> To communicate with my employees, I try to spend time in the plant and at intervals have meetings with the employees. Usually if they have a question they just visit me. Recently a small group visited me in my office to discuss our vacation policy. They had some suggestions and, after listening to them, I had to agree that the ideas were good."[34]

THE INCENTIVE SYSTEM

The foremost characteristic of Nucor's personnel system was its incentive plan. Another major personnel policy was providing job security. Also all employees at Nucor received the same fringe benefits. There was only one group insurance plan. Holidays and vacations did not differ by job. The company had no execu-

---

[33]Interview conducted by Frank C. Barnes.
[34]Ibid.

tive dining rooms or restrooms, no fishing lodges, company cars, or reserved parking places.

Absenteeism and tardiness were not problems at Nucor. Each employee had four days of absence before pay was reduced. In addition to these, missing work was allowed for jury duty, military leave, or the death of close relatives. After this, a day's absence cost them bonus pay for that week and lateness of more than a half hour meant the loss of bonus for that day.

Employees were kept informed about the company. Charts showing the division's results in return-on-assets and bonus payoff were posted in prominent places in the plant. The personnel manager commented that as he traveled around to all the plants, he found everyone in the company could tell him the level of profits in their division. The general managers held dinners at least twice a year with their employees. The dinners were held with 50 or 60 employees at a time. After introductory remarks the floor was open for discussion of any work-related problems. The company also had a formal grievance procedure. The Darlington manager couldn't recall the last grievance he had processed.

There was a new employee orientation program and an employee handbook which contained personnel policies and rules. The corporate office sent all news releases to each division where they were posted on bulletin boards. Each employee in the company also received a copy of the Annual Report. For the last several years the cover of the Annual Report had contained the names of all Nucor employees. Every child of every Nucor employee received up to $1,200 a year for four years if they chose to go on to higher education, including technical schools.

The average hourly worker's pay was $31,000, compared with the average earnings in manufacturing in that state of slightly more than $13,000. The personnel manager believed that pay was not the only thing the workers liked about Nucor. He said that an NBC interviewer, working on the documentary "If Japan Can, Why Can't We," often heard, "I enjoy working for Nucor because Nucor is the best, the most productive, and the most profitable company that I know of."[35]

"I honestly feel that if someone performs well, they should share in the company and if they are going to share in the success, they should also share in the failures," Iverson stated.[36] There were four incentive programs at Nucor, one each for production workers, department heads, staff people such as accountants, secretaries, or engineers, and senior management, which included the division managers. All of these programs were on a group basis.

Within the production program, groups ranged in size from 25 to 30 people and had definable and measurable operations. The company believed that a program should be simple and that bonuses should be paid promptly. "We don't have any discretionary bonuses—zero. It is all based on performance. Now we don't want anyone to sit in judgment, because it never is fair . . . ," said Iverson. The

[35]Ibid.
[36]"Nucor's Ken Iverson on Productivity and Pay," *Personnel Administrator*, October 1986, pp. 46–108.

personnel manager stated: "Their bonus is based on roughly 90% of historical time it takes to make a particular joist. If during a week they make joists at 60% less than the standard time, they received a 60% bonus." This was paid with the regular pay the following week. The complete pay check amount, including overtime, was multiplied by the bonus factor. Bonus was not paid when equipment was not operating: "We have the philosophy that when equipment is not operating everybody suffers and the bonus for downtime is zero."[37] The foremen are also part of the group and received the same bonus as the employees they supervised.

The second incentive program was for department heads in the various divisions. The incentive pay here was based on division contribution, defined as the division earnings before corporate expenses and profit sharing are determined. Bonuses were reported to run as high as 51% of a person's base salary in the divisions and 30% for corporate positions.

Officers of the company were under a single profit sharing plan. Their base salaries were approximately 75% of comparable positions in industry. Once return-on-equity reached 9%, slightly below the average for manufacturing firms, 5% of net earnings before taxes went into a pool that was divided among the officers based on their salaries. "Now if return-on-equity for the company reaches, say 20%, which it has, then we can wind up with as much as 190% of our base salaries and 115% on top of that in stock. We get both."[38] In 1982 the return was 9% and the executives received no bonus. Iverson's pay in 1981 was approximately $300,000 but dropped the next year to $110,000. "I think that ranked by total compensation I was the lowest paid CEO in the Fortune 500. I was kind of proud of that, too."[39] In 1986, Iverson's stock was worth over $10 million. The young Vulcraft manager was likewise a millionaire.

There was a third plan for people who were neither production workers nor department managers. Their bonus was based on either the division return-on-assets or the corporate return-on-assets.

The fourth program was for the senior officers. The senior officers had no employment contracts, pension or retirement plans, or other normal perquisites. Their base salaries were set at about 70% of what an individual doing similar work in other companies would receive. More than half of the officer's compensation was reported to be based directly on the company's earnings. Ten percent of pretax earnings over a pre-established level, based on a 12% return on stockholders' equity, was set aside and allocated to the senior officers according to their base salary. Half the bonus was paid in cash and half was deferred.

In lieu of a retirement plan, the company had a profit-sharing plan with a deferred trust. Each year 10% of pretax earnings was put into profit sharing. Fifteen percent of this was set aside to be paid to employees in the following March as a cash bonus and the remainder was put into trust for each employee

[37]Ibid.
[38]Ibid.
[39]Ibid.

on the basis of percent of their earnings as a percent of total wages paid within the corporation. The employee was vested 20% after the first year and gained an additional 10% vesting each year thereafter. Employees received a quarterly statement of their balance in profit sharing.

The company had an Employer Monthly Stock Investment Plan to which Nucor added 10% to the amount the employee contributed and paid the commission on the purchase of any Nucor stock. After each five years of service with the company, the employee received a service award consisting of five shares of Nucor stock. Additionally, if profits were good, extraordinary bonus payments would be made to the employees. In December 1988, each employee received a $500 payment.

According to Iverson: *market control*

> I think the first obligation of the company is to the stockholder and to its employees. I find in this country too many cases where employees are underpaid and corporate management is making huge social donations for self-fulfillment. We regularly give donations, but we have a very interesting corporate policy. First, we give donations where our employees are. Second, we give donations which will benefit our employees, such as to the YMCA. It is a difficult area and it requires a lot of thought. There is certainly a strong social responsibility for a company, but it cannot be at the expense of the employees or the stockholders.[40]

Nucor had no trouble finding people to staff its plants. When the mill in Jewett, Texas, was built in 1975, there were over 5,000 applications for the 400 jobs—many coming from people in Houston and Dallas. Yet everyone did not find work at Nucor what they wanted. In 1975, a Harvard team found high ? turnover among new production workers after start-up. The cause appeared to be pressure from fellow workers in the group incentive situation. A survival-of-the-fittest situation was found in which those who didn't like to work seldom stuck around. "Productivity increased and turnover declined dramatically once these people left," the Harvard team concluded. Iverson commented: "A lot of people aren't goal-oriented. A lot of them don't want to work that hard, so initially we have a lot of turnover in a plant but then it's so low we don't even measure after that."[41]

The Wall Street Journal reported in 1981:

> Harry Pigg, a sub-district director for the USW in South Carolina, sees a darker side in Nucor's incentive plan. He contends that Nucor unfairly penalizes workers by taking away big bonus payments for absence or tardiness, regardless of the reason. Workers who are ill, he says, try to work

[40]Ibid.
[41]"A Calm Hand in an Industry Under the Gun," *The Business Journal*, September 15, 1986, p. 9.

because they can't afford to give up the bonus payment. "Nucor whips them into line," he adds. He acknowledges, though, that high salaries are the major barrier to unionizing the company.[42]

.   Having welcomed a parade of visitors over the years, Iverson had become concerned with the pattern: "They only do one or two of the things we do. It's not just incentives or the scholarship program; it's all those things put together that results in a unified philosophy for the company."

AS 1990 BEGAN

Looking ahead in 1984, Iverson had said: "The next decade will be an exciting one for steel producers. It will tax our abilities to keep pace with technological changes we can see now on the horizon." Imports didn't have to dominate the U.S. economy. He believed the steel industry would continue to play a pivotal role in the growth of American industry. He pointed out comparative advantages of the U.S. steel industry: an abundance of resources, relatively low energy costs, lower transportation costs, and the change in the government's attitude toward business.

The excitement he had predicted had occurred. Imports were a challenge for steel, just as for textiles, shoes, machine tools, and computers. The old steel companies were flexing their muscle and getting back into the game. Overcapacity hadn't left the mini-mill immune; there was no safe haven for anyone. Nucor was no longer a small company, David, with free shots at Goliath.

The honeymoon appeared over. Wall Street worried about what Nucor should do. Cable News Network posed the position of some on Wall Street: "They say basically you guys are selling to the construction companies; you are selling to some fairly depressed industries. They also say, Nucor, they were a specialized little niche company. They did what they did very well; but now all of a sudden, they are going out, building these big mills to make huge pieces of steel and they are talking casted cold, all that stuff. They're worried that you may be getting into deals that are a little too complicated from what they perceive you as being able to do well."[43]

The New York Times pointed out that expansion would certainly hurt earnings for the next several years. They quoted a steel consultant. "It is hard to do all that they are trying to do and keep profits up. With the industry in the shape it's in, this is not the time to expand beyond the niche they've established."[44]

When they were sitting with $185 million in cash, Iverson told *Inc:* "It (going private) has been mentioned to us by a number of brokerage firms and invest-

[42]Sease, "Mini-Mill Steelmakers," pp. 1, 19.
[43]"Inside Business," Interview with Ken Iverson, Cable News Network, August 17, 1986.
[44]"Nucor's Ambitious Expansion," *The New York Times,* June 30, 1986.

ment houses, but we wouldn't even consider it. It wouldn't be fair to employees, and I don't know whether it would be fair to the stockholders. . . . You're going to restrict the growth opportunities. . . . You either grow or die. . . . Opportunities wouldn't be created for people within the company."[45]

Iverson told CNN: "We've decided that really we want to stay in that niche (steel). We don't want to buy any banks. . . . All of the growth of the company has been internally generated. We think there are opportunities in the steel industry today. . . . There are ample opportunities, although they are somewhat harder to find than they used to be."[46]

"Another of my strengths is the ability to stick to my knitting. The reason executives make a lot of mistakes is that sometimes they get bored—they think the grass is greener on the other side so they go out and buy a bank or an oil company or they go into businesses where they have no expertise. . . . I have never gotten bored with this company. I've done this job so long that I think I have some insight into the needs and the capabilities of the company. I'm not misled into thinking we can do something that we can't."[47]

An economics professor and steel consultant at Middle Tennessee State University told the *Times,* "You're not going to see any growth in the steel market, so the only way to make money is to reduce costs and have new technology to penetrate other companies' business."[48]

The New York Times stated: "Critics question whether it is wise to continue expanding production capabilities, as Nucor is doing, when there is already overcapacity in the steel industry and intense competition already exists between the mini-mills." Iverson insisted the strategy would pay off in the long-term. He told the *Times,* "The company's strategy makes sense for us. To gain a larger share in an ever-shrinking market, you've got to take something from someone else."[49]

They had sold the Chemicals Division, gotten into the structural steel components business, into the fastener industry, and should soon be ready to go head-to-head with the major integrated producers for the lucrative flat-rolled market. Sales and earnings were projected to double in the next two years, as the stock price doubled or tripled.

Iverson's position was clear: "We're going to stay in steel and steel products. The way we look at it, this company does only two things well, builds plants economically and runs them efficiently. That is the whole company. We don't have any financial expertise, we're not entrepreneurs, we're not into acquisitions. Steel may not be the best business in the world, but it's what we know how to do and we do it well."

[45]"Steel Man Ken Iverson," *Inc.,* April 1986, p. 48.
[46]"Inside Business," Interview.
[47]"A Calm Hand," p. 9.
[48]"Nucor's Ambitious Expansion," June 30, 1986.
[49]Ibid.

	1979	1980	1981	1982	1983	1984
For the year						
Sales, costs and earnings:						
Net sales	428,681,778	482,420,363	544,820,621	486,018,162	542,531,431	660,259,922
Costs and expenses:						
Cost of products sold	315,688,291	369,415,571	456,210,289	408,606,641	461,727,688	539,731,252
Marketing and administrative expenses	36,724,159	38,164,559	33,524,820	31,720,377	33,988,054	45,939,311
Interest expense (income)	1,504,791	(1,219,965)	10,256,546	7,899,110	(748,619)	(3,959,092)
	353,917,241	406,360,165	499,991,655	448,226,128	494,967,123	581,711,471
Earnings from operations before federal income taxes	74,764,537	76,060,198	44,828,966	37,792,034	47,564,308	78,548,451
Federal income taxes	32,500,000	31,000,000	10,100,000	15,600,000	19,700,000	34,000,000
Earnings from operations	42,264,537	45,060,198	34,728,966	22,192,034	27,864,308	44,548,451
Gain on sale of research chemicals	—	—	—	—	—	—
Net earnings	42,264,537	45,060,198	34,728,966	22,192,034	27,864,308	44,548,451
Earnings per share						
Earnings per share from operations	2.10	2.21	1.67	1.06	1.32	2.10
Gain per share on sale of research chemicals	—	—	—	—	—	—
Net earnings per share	2.10	2.21	1.67	1.06	1.32	2.10
Dividends declared per share	.11	.15	.16	.17	.20	.24
Percentage of earnings from operations to sales	9.9%	9.3%	6.4%	4.6%	5.1%	6.7%
Percentage of earnings from operations to average equity	37.5%	29.0%	17.8%	10.0%	11.4%	16.0%
Average shares outstanding	20,152,914	20,414,109	20,756,583	20,912,577	21,066,448	21,169,492
Sales per employee	145,316	150,756	155,663	133,156	148,639	176,069
At year end						
Working capital	53,826,193	48,872,282	58,349,979	66,439,942	105,402,367	152,919,689
Current ratio	1.8	1.7	1.8	2.0	2.2	2.5
Stockholders' equity per share	6.58	8.64	10.17	11.07	12.21	14.10
Shares outstanding	20,261,631	20,549,991	20,890,521	20,987,823	21,135,272	21,241,618
Stockholders	23,000	22,00	22,000	22,000	21,000	22,000
Employees	3,100	3,300	3,700	3,600	3,700	3,800

	1985	1986	1987	1988	1989
For the year					
Sales, costs and earnings:					
Net sales	758,495,374	755,228,939	851,022,039	1,061,364,009	1,269,007,472
Costs and expenses:					
Cost of products sold	600,797,865	610,378,369	713,346,451	889,140,323	1,105,248,906
Marketing and administrative expenses	59,079,802	65,900,653	55,405,961	62,083,752	66,990,065
Interest expense (income)	(7,560,645)	(5,288,971)	(964,823)	2,558,914	11,132,657
	652,317,022	670,990,051	767,787,589	953,782,989	1,183,371,628
Earnings from operations before federal income taxes	106,178,352	84,238,888	83,234,450	107,581,020	85,635,844
Federal income taxes	47,700,000	37,800,000	32,700,000	36,700,000	27,800,000
Earnings from operations	58,478,352	46,438,888	50,534,450	70,881,020	57,835,844
Gain on sale of research chemicals	—	—	—	38,558,822	—
Net earnings	58,478,352	46,438,888	50,534,450	109,439,842	57,835,844
Earnings per share					
Earnings per share from operations	2.74	2.17	2.39	3.34	2.71
Gain per share on sale of research chemicals	—	—	—	1.82	—
Net earnings per share	2.74	2.17	2.39	5.16	2.71
Dividends declared per share	.27	.31	.36	.40	.44
Percentage of earnings from operations to sales	7.7%	6.1%	5.9%	6.7%	4.6%
Percentage of earnings from operations to average equity	17.8%	12.5%	12.5%	15.4%	10.4%
Average shares outstanding	21,345,852	21,405,440	21,153,584	21,224,217	21,399,620
Sales per employee	197,011	181,983	189,116	218,838	241,716
At year end					
Working capital	213,513,319	177,297,282	87,243,967	31,651,314	86,473,389
Current ratio	2.8	2.5	1.6	1.1	1.4
Stockholders' equity per share	16.65	18.16	20.19	25.00	27.31
Shares outstanding	21,472,508	21,131,298	21,196,088	21,287,691	21,399,620
Stockholders	22,000	22,000	27,000	28,000	25,000
Employees	3,900	4,400	4,600	5,100	5,400

The consolidated financial and statistical data appearing in Exhibits 5, 6, and 7 has been compiled and extracted from annual reports and SEC filings for and during 1979 through 1989, to which reference should be made for complete details.

EXHIBIT 6   Nucor Corporation balance sheet data, 1979 through 1989

	1979	1980	1981	1982	1983	1984
Assets						
Current assets:						
Cash	8,716,950	5,753,068	8,704,859	10,668,165	6,384,795	2,863,680
Short-term investments	27,932,854	16,000,000	—	34,224,381	72,669,615	109,846,810
Accounts receivable	35,203,909	35,537,959	42,983,058	34,685,498	51,110,372	58,408,244
Contracts in process	5,004,091	7,985,985	5,719,121	3,656,643	7,058,803	8,462,815
Inventories	40,007,532	49,599,265	72,996,664	48,831,434	56,555,102	73,797,302
Other current assets	496,854	489,450	978,590	476,527	110,475	74,522
	117,362,190	115,365,727	131,382,292	132,542,648	193,889,162	253,453,373
Property, plant and equipment:						
Land and improvements	4,915,078	5,806,711	12,142,613	12,215,375	12,577,104	12,918,519
Buildings and improvements	29,875,783	34,853,546	53,037,722	53,668,523	55,971,208	58,909,921
Plant machinery and equipment	91,865,271	139,182,579	245,037,510	244,143,769	258,305,715	277,553,868
Office and transportation equipment	5,478,870	5,711,199	6,868,069	9,565,667	9,736,448	8,643,752
Construction in process and equipment deposits	29,493,880	36,323,686	2,559,867	3,279,232	2,444,220	2,576,972
	161,628,882	221,877,721	319,645,781	322,872,566	339,034,695	360,603,032
Less accumulated depreciation	35,879,558	46,021,581	66,245,946	83,782,273	107,356,805	131,867,940
	125,749,324	175,856,140	253,399,835	239,090,293	231,677,890	228,735,092
Total assets	243,111,514	291,221,867	384,782,127	371,632,941	425,567,052	482,188,465
Liabilities and stockholders' equity						
Current liabilities:						
Long-term debt due within one year	1,245,764	1,696,815	1,654,784	1,603,462	2,402,462	2,402,462
Accounts payable	26,414,666	36,640,991	32,237,889	22,948,867	37,135,084	32,691,249
Federal income taxes	15,913,361	4,362,619	10,733,627	12,535,096	14,813,909	23,705,195
Accured expenses and other current liabilities	19,962,206	23,793,020	28,406,013	29,015,281	34,135,340	41,734,778
Total liabilities	63,535,997	66,493,445	73,032,313	66,102,706	88,486,795	100,533,684
Long-term debt due after one year	41,398,138	39,605,169	83,754,231	48,229,615	45,731,000	43,232,384
Deferred federal income taxes	4,919,563	7,519,563	15,619,563	25,019,563	33,219,563	38,819,563
Minority interest	—	—	—	—	—	—
Stockholders' equity:						
Common stock	2,721,040	2,758,713	2,797,948	2,802,796	5,642,727	5,669,757
Additional paid-in capital	11,125,185	13,353,856	16,531,759	17,696,568	17,022,043	18,991,334
Retained earnings	119,891,199	161,952,033	193,355,403	211,921,654	235,569,108	275,035,788
Treasury stock	(479,608)	(460,912)	(309,090)	(139,961)	(104,184)	(94,045)
	133,257,816	177,603,690	212,376,020	232,281,057	258,129,694	299,602,834
Total liabilities and stockholders' equity	243,111,514	291,221,867	384,782,127	371,632,941	425,567,052	482,188,465

	1985	1986	1987	1988	1989
Assets					
Current assets:					
Cash	8,028,519	11,008,879	28,286,214	15,095,743	
Short-term investments	177,115,954	117,727,705	44,493,370	11,284,372	32,553,520
Accounts receivable	60,390,448	61,268,892	80,080,553	97,427,217	106,950,620
Contracts in process	10,478,296	9,120,533	8,200,366	9,356,633	—
Inventories	78,641,805	96,474,278	73,297,103	113,858,389	139,449,786
Other current assets	114,125	137,968	359,631	736,262	1,080,008
	334,769,147	295,738,255	234,717,237	247,758,616	280,033,934
Property, plant and equipment:					
Land and improvements	12,818,723	15,041,782	23,143,374	30,309,295	29,829,310
Buildings and improvements	61,709,286	75,217,588	87,690,196	113,985,857	118,362,171
Plant machinery and equipment	279,579,407	331,945,921	375,446,242	604,990,695	866,721,302
Office and transportation equipment	14,883,272	16,358,988	15,080,397	14,416,129	13,318,378
Construction in process and equipment deposits	7,505,692	18,736,585	117,174,597	178,569,987	19,781,432
	376,496,380	457,300,864	618,534,806	942,271,963	1,048,012,593
Less accumulated depreciation	150,954,339	181,431,475	199,161,904	240,368,869	294,215,015
	225,542,041	275,869,389	419,372,902	701,903,094	753,797,578
Total assets	560,311,188	571,607,644	654,090,139	949,661,710	1,033,831,512
Liabilities and stockholders' equity					
Current liabilities:					
Long-term debt due within one year	2,402,462	3,052,462	2,210,154	2,214,000	2,267,000
Accounts payable	35,473,011	53,165,551	68,459,917	93,171,767	89,746,212
Federal income taxes	27,597,464	14,309,565	24,343,944	35,803,552	13,203,371
Accrued expenses and other current liabilities	55,782,891	47,913,395	52,459,255	84,917,983	88,343,962
Total liabilities	121,255,828	118,440,973	147,473,270	216,107,302	193,560,545
Long-term debt due after one year	40,233,769	42,147,654	35,462,500	113,248,500	155,981,500
Deferred federal income taxes	41,319,563	27,319,563	19,319,563	15,319,563	18,819,563
Minority interest	—	—	23,825,439	72,704,896	81,024,425
Stockholders' equity:					
Common stock	5,732,382	8,665,397	8,701,944	8,737,064	8,781,534
Additional paid-in capital	24,299,195	25,191,988	27,379,060	30,542,937	34,226,463
Retained earnings	327,816,850	367,575,659	410,510,347	511,456,991	559,895,248
Treasury stock	(346,399)	(17,733,590)	(18,581,984)	(18,455,543)	(18,457,766)
	357,502,028	383,699,454	428,009,367	532,281,449	584,445,479
Total liabilities and stockholders' equity	560,311,188	571,607,644	654,090,139	949,661,710	1,033,831,512

EXHIBIT 7   Nucor Corporation cash flow data, 1979 through 1989

	1979	1980	1981	1982	1983	1984
Operating activities						
Earnings:						
Earnings from operations	42,264,537	45,060,198	34,728,966	22,192,034	27,864,308	44,548,451
Gain on sale of research chemicals	—	—	—	—	—	—
Net earnings	42,264,537	45,060,198	34,728,966	22,192,034	27,864,308	44,548,451
Adjustments:						
Depreciation of plant and equipment	9,712,625	13,296,218	21,599,951	26,286,671	27,109,582	28,899,421
Gain on sale of research chemicals	—	—	—	—	—	—
Changes in						
Minority interest	—	—	—	—	—	—
Deferred federal income taxes	900,000	2,600,000	8,100,000	9,400,000	8,200,000	5,600,000
Accounts receivable	(8,622,966)	(334,050)	(7,445,099)	8,297,560	(16,424,874)	(7,297,872)
Inventories	1,541,388	(9,591,733)	(23,397,399)	24,165,230	(7,723,668)	(17,242,200)
Accounts payable	2,264,519	10,226,325	(4,403,102)	(9,289,022)	14,186,217	(4,443,835)
Federal income taxes	272,537	(11,550,742)	6,371,008	1,801,469	2,278,813	8,891,286
Other	3,655,083	1,464,674	6,492,047	3,726,028	2,242,377	6,507,638
	51,987,723	51,170,890	42,046,372	86,579,970	57,732,755	65,462,889
Investing activities						
Capital expenditures	(43,343,161)	(64,054,896)	(99,521,176)	(14,023,849)	(19,971,317)	(26,333,882)
Disposition of plant and equipment	1,015,484	43,512	276,200	1,494,501	115,712	101,000
Proceeds from sale of research chemicals	—	—	—	—	—	—
	(42,327,677)	(64,011,384)	(99,244,976)	(12,529,348)	(19,855,605)	(26,232,882)
Financing activities						
New long-term debt	1,134,676	—	46,400,000	7,500,000	—	—
Reduction in long-term debt	(427,313)	(1,341,918)	(2,292,969)	(43,075,938)	(1,699,615)	(2,498,616)
Issuance of common stock	1,328,548	2,285,040	3,368,960	1,459,008	2,201,183	2,006,460
Acquisition of treasury stock	(156,100)	—	—	(120,222)	—	—
Cash dividends	(2,308,288)	(2,999,364)	(3,325,596)	(3,625,783)	(4,216,854)	(5,081,771)
	(428,477)	(2,056,242)	(44,150,395)	(37,862,935)	(3,715,286)	(5,573,927)
Increase (decrease) in cash and short-term investments	9,231,569	(14,896,736)	(13,048,209)	36,187,687	34,161,864	33,656,080
Cash and short-term investments—beginning of year	27,418,235	36,649,804	21,753,068	8,704,859	44,892,546	79,054,410
Cash and short-term investments—end of year	36,649,804	21,753,068	8,704,859	44,892,546	79,054,410	112,710,490

EXHIBIT 7   Nucor Corporation cash flow data, 1979 through 1989 (cont.)

	1985	1986	1987	1988	1989
Operating activities					
Earnings:					
Earnings from operations	58,478,352	46,438,888	50,534,450	70,881,020	57,835,844
Gain on sale of research chemicals	—	—	—	38,558,822	—
Net earnings	58,478,352	46,438,888	50,534,450	109,439,842	57,835,844
Adjustments:					
Depreciation of plant and equipment	31,105,788	34,931,520	41,793,009	56,264,631	76,571,240
Gain on sale of research chemicals	—	—	—	(38,558,822)	—
Changes in					
Minority interest	—	—	23,825,439	48,879,457	8,319,529
Deferred federal income taxes	2,500,000	(14,000,000)	(8,000,000)	(4,000,000)	3,500,000
Accounts receivable	(1,982,204)	(878,444)	(18,811,661)	(18,928,357)	(9,523,403)
Inventories	(4,844,503)	(17,832,473)	23,177,175	(44,651,570)	(16,234,764)
Accounts payable	2,781,762	17,692,540	15,294,366	25,357,059	(3,425,555)
Federal income taxes	3,892,269	(13,287,899)	10,034,379	(8,540,392)	(22,600,181)
Other	12,732,190	(6,160,986)	6,990,792	22,448,963	3,561,781
	104,663,654	46,903,146	144,837,949	147,710,811	98,004,491
Investing activities					
Capital expenditures	(28,701,463)	(86,201,391)	(188,990,476)	(345,632,411)	(130,200,982)
Disposition of plant and equipment	49,565	567,933	1,947,526	399,137	1,255,711
Proceeds from sale of research chemicals	—	—	—	78,500,908	—
	(28,651,898)	(85,633,458)	(187,042,950)	(266,732,366)	(128,945,271)
Financing activities					
New long-term debt	—	6,234,450	—	80,000,000	45,000,000
Reduction in long-term debt	(2,998,615)	(3,670,565)	(7,527,462)	(2,210,154)	(2,214,000)
Issuance of common stock	5,387,182	3,954,559	2,337,525	3,325,438	3,861,092
Acquisition of treasury stock	(269,050)	(17,515,942)	(962,300)	—	(135,320)
Cash dividends	(5,697,290)	(6,680,079)	(7,599,762)	(8,493,198)	(9,397,587)
	(3,577,773)	(17,677,577)	(13,751,999)	72,622,086	37,114,185
Increase (decrease) in cash and short-term investments	72,433,983	(56,407,889)	(55,957,000)	(46,399,469)	6,173,405
Cash and short-term investments—beginning of year	112,710,490	185,144,473	128,736,584	72,779,584	26,380,115
Cash and short-term investments—end of year	185,144,473	128,736,584	72,779,584	26,380,115	32,553,520

HANSON PLC

INTRODUCTION

Hanson PLC is one of the ten biggest companies in Britain, and its U.S. arm, Hanson Industries, is one of America's sixty largest industrial concerns. A conglomerate with over 150 different businesses in its portfolio, Hanson PLC has grown primarily by making acquisitions. By the end of 1989 the company had recorded twenty-six years of uninterrupted profit growth, cumulating in 1989 operating income of $1.61 billion on revenues of $11.3 billion and assets of $12.03 billion. The company's shareholders have been major beneficiaries of this growth. Between 1974 and 1989 the price of the company's shares on the London Stock Exchange increased eighty-fold, compared with an average increase of fifteen-fold for all companies quoted on the London Stock Exchange during this period.[1] Along the way, Hanson has gained a reputation for being one of the most successful takeover machines in the world. Its acquisitions during the 1980s included three American conglomerates (U.S. Industries, SCM Corporation, and Kidde) and three major British companies (London Brick, the Imperial Group, and Consolidated Gold Fields). So high is Hanson's profile that Oliver Stone, in his film *Wall Street,* reportedly used Sir Gordon White, head of Hanson Industries, as the model for the British corporate raider—the one who outmaneuvered the evil Gordon Gekko.

Despite this impressive track record, as Hanson enters the 1990s analysts increasingly wonder about the strategy of the company. There is speculation that the company may be on the verge of breaking itself up and returning the gains to shareholders. The age of the company's founders is fueling this speculation. The two men who built and still run the conglomerate, Lord Hanson and Sir Gordon White, are in their late sixties and both have promised to consider retiring when they are seventy. As one insider put it, "the guys that started it off will

This case was prepared by Charles W. L. Hill, University of Washington. The case was made possible by the generous assistance of Hanson Industries. It is intended as a basis for classroom discussion, rather than to illustrate either effective or ineffective handling of an administrative situation.

[1]"The Conglomerate as Antique Dealer," *The Economist,* March 11, 1989, pp. 71–73.

finish it off."[2] Another factor is that Hanson is now so big that it would take some spectacular deals to continue its historic growth rate. According to many, including Harvard Business School strategy guru Michael Porter, there simply are not that many obvious companies for Hanson to buy, thus "Even Hanson will be faced with poorer and poorer odds of maintaining its record."[3] On the other hand, at the end of 1989 Hanson had $8.5 billion in cash on its balance sheet. That, along with the billions it could borrow if need be (the company reportedly has a borrowing capacity of $20 billion), suggests that if Hanson and White should so wish, they could undertake an acquisition that would rival the RJR–Nabisco deal in size.

Other commentators question the long-term viability of the company. Some claim that Hanson PLC is little more than an asset stripper that in the long run will drive the companies it manages into the ground. According to one investment banker, "I'm not convinced that Hanson runs companies any better than anyone else. But I certainly know it squeezes them for cash, sucking the life from them."[4] Similarly, one former executive noted that "Some of the incentive programs that they write for managers actually keep the company from growing. . . . They become so concerned with profit today that they don't re-invest for tomorrow."[5] The company disagrees. Sir Gordon White clearly sees Hanson PLC as reducing inefficiencies in the companies it acquires, not stripping assets. If anything is stripped away from acquisitions, according to White, it is unnecessary corporate bureaucracy, overstaffed head offices, and top-management perks, not assets; and he steadfastly maintains that the company treats all acquired businesses as if it were going to keep them.[6]

With these issues in mind, in this case we consider the growth and development of Hanson PLC. We review the administrative systems that the company uses to manage its ongoing businesses, and we look at two acquisitions and their aftermath in depth: the 1987 acquisitions of SCM Corporation and the Imperial Group.

HISTORY

The origins of Hanson PLC go back to the port city of Hull in Yorkshire, England, in the 1950s.[7] At that time, James Hanson was learning his family's transportation business (the family operated a fleet of passenger coaches) and Gordon

[2]Quoted ibid.
[3]Quoted in John Byrne and Mark Maremont, "Hanson: The Dangers of Living by Takeover Alone," *Business Week,* August 15, 1988, pp. 62–64.
[4]Quoted in Andrew Marton, "The Buccaneer from Britain," *Mergers and Acquisitions* (February 1987), 141–146.
[5]Quoted in Byrne and Maremont, "Hanson: The Dangers," pp. 62–64.
[6]Gordon White, "How I Turned $3,000 into $10 Billion," *Fortune,* November 7, 1988, pp. 80–89.
[7]The material in this section is based on the following sources: White, "How I Turned," pp. 80–89; Marton, "The Buccaneer from Britain," pp. 141–146; and Hope Lampert, "Britons on the Prowl," *The New York Times Magazine,* November 29, 1987, pp. 22–24, 36, 38, 42.

White was selling advertising for Welbecson Limited, a magazine printing company owned by his father. James Hanson's brother, Bill, was White's closest friend, and when Bill died of cancer at twenty-nine, James and Gordon became close friends. In the late 1950s Hanson and White decided to team up in business. They formed Hanson White Ltd., a greeting card company. Although the company did well, the two soon became bored with the limited challenges and potential that the greeting card business offered, and in 1963 they sold out and began to look for acquisition opportunities.

Their first buy was Oswald Tillotson Ltd., a vehicle distribution company. This company was subsequently acquired by Wiles Group Ltd., a Yorkshire-based manufacturer of agricultural sacks and fertilizers. As part of the takeover deal Hanson and White were given a substantial ownership position in the Wiles Group. Hanson and White soon gained management control of the Wiles Group, and in 1969, after deciding that James Hanson's name had a nicer ring to it than Gordon White's, they changed the name to Hanson Trust. Because of a series of small acquisitions, by the end of 1973 Hanson Trust owned twenty-four companies with combined sales of $120 million.

By 1973, however, the British economy was in deep trouble. The stock market had collapsed; the country was paralyzed by labor disputes; inflation was increasing rapidly, as was unemployment; and Prime Minister Edward Heath of the supposedly probusiness Conservative party had blasted conglomerate companies like Hanson Trust as representing "the unacceptable face of capitalism." All of this prompted Gordon White to rethink his future. As White put it, "I was disgusted with England at the time. Disgusted with socialism and unions and excessive, antibusiness government, disgusted with the way initiative was being taxed out of existence. . . . I'd done a lot of thinking. I told James (Hanson) that maybe we should just call it a day. I thought I'd try America."[8] Hanson replied that there was no need to split up, and they agreed that Hanson would run the British operations while White tried to build operations in America.

White arrived in New York in the fall of 1973 in possession of a round-trip ticket, a one-year work visa, and $3,000 in travelers checks, which was the most that British currency controls permitted a U.K. citizen to take abroad at that time. Moreover, because of British exchange controls White could not gain access to Hanson's ample treasury without substantial penalties, and he had to struggle to convince banks that he was creditworthy. Despite this, in 1974 White managed to borrow $32 million from Chemical Bank to finance his first major U.S. acquisition, a friendly takeover of J. Howard Smith Company, a New Jersey–based processor of edible oils and animal feed that was later renamed Seacoast Products. The CEO of J. Howard Smith was David Clarke, whose family business it was. Clarke subsequently became White's right-hand man. He is now

---

[8]White, "How I Turned," p. 81.

president of Hanson Industries and the most senior executive in the United States after White.

Over the next ten years White made another six major U.S. acquisitions, all of them friendly (these are listed in Exhibit 1). Then in 1984 White was ready for his first hostile takeover, the $532-million purchase of U.S. Industries (USI). USI was a conglomerate that had grown by acquisitions during the 1960s and 1970s. White became interested in the company when he read in a newspaper that management was putting together a leveraged buyout at $20 a share for a total purchase price of $445 million. He suspected that the company was worth more than that and quickly worked out how big a loan Hanson Industries could handle, using USI's projected cash flow to cover interest charges. To USI's pre-tax earnings of $67 million he added $40 million generated by depreciation and $24 million in savings that he thought Hanson could effect by removing USI's corporate headquarters. That yielded a total cash flow of $131 million, or more than $70 million after taxes. With interest rates running at 13 percent, White figured that Hanson Industries could afford a $544-million loan. In what was to become standard White thinking, he also reckoned that even with a worst-case scenario, he could recoup his investment by selling off the disparate pieces of the company.

Hanson Industries began to buy USI shares and by April 1984 held 5 percent of the company. Hanson then made a $19 per share bid for the company, which was quickly rebuffed by USI management. Three days later White increased Hanson's bid to $22 per share. USI's management, which had yet to raise the

EXHIBIT 1   **U.S. acquisitions, 1974–1987**

Acquisition		Cost (millions)	Businesses
1974	Seacoast	$32	Fish processing, pet food
1975	Carisbrook	$36	Textile manufacturing
1976	Hygrade	$32	Castings and casing units
1977	Old Salt Seafood	$2	Prepared foods
1978	Interstate United	$30	Food service management
1978	Templon	$7	Textile manufacturing
1981	McDonough	$185	Cement, concrete
1984	U.S. Industries	$532	33-company conglomerate
1986	SCM	$930	22-company conglomerate
1987	Kaiser Cement	$250	Cement plants
1988	Kidde	$1,700	108-company conglomerate
1990	Peabody	$1,230	Coal mining

Source: Adapted from Gordon White, "How I Turned $3,000 into $10 Billion," *Fortune*, November 7, 1988, pp. 80–89; and "Hanson PLC," *Value Line*, July 20, 1990, p. 832.

financing for its own proposed leveraged buyout, responded by increasing the purchase price to $24 per share. Hanson responded by initiating a tender offer of $23 per share in cash. For stockholders cash in hand at $23 per share was far more attractive than management's promise of $24 per share if financing could be arranged, and Hanson's bid quickly won the day.

After the acquisition was completed, Hanson Industries president David Clarke spent six months at USI's corporate headquarters reviewing operations. At the end of this period USI's corporate headquarters was closed down, the staff was laid off, and financial control was centralized at Hanson Industries' small headquarters. However, most of the operating managers in charge of USI's constituent companies stayed on, lured by Hanson's incentive pay scheme and the promise that they could run their own shows. In what was also typical Hanson fashion, nine of USI's operating companies were subsequently sold off to outside investors for a price of $225 million.

The acquisition of USI was followed by three other hostile takeover bids in the United States: for SCM Corporation, Kaiser Cement, and Kidde. Of these, the SCM bid was by far the most acrimonious. SCM took a poison pill and tried to protect its position through the law courts before Hanson finally won control over the company (the SCM takeover is discussed in detail later in the case).

While White was making these U.S. acquisitions, Hanson was not sitting idle in Britain. During the 1980s the company made a series of acquisitions in the United Kingdom. These are summarized in Exhibit 2. The most notable were the 1983 acquisition of London Brick, Britain's largest brick manufacturer, against vigorous opposition from London Brick's incumbent management; the £2.36-billion acquisition of Imperial, the largest tobacco company in Britain and the third largest in the world; and the £3.61-billion acquisition of Consolidated Gold Fields, the second largest gold-mining business in the world. The acquisitions of Imperial and Consolidated Gold Fields were the two largest takeovers ever undertaken in Britain (the Imperial takeover is discussed in detail below).

EXHIBIT 2   **U.K. acquisitions during the 1980s**

	Acquisition	Cost (millions)	Businesses
1981	Ever Ready	£95	Dry cell batteries
1983	UDS	£250	Retail operations
1984	London Brick	£247	Brick manufacturer
1984	Powell Duffryn	£150	Engineering, shipping, fuel
1986	Imperial Group	£2,500	Tobacco, brewing, food
1989	Consolidate Gold Fields	£3,610	Gold mining, building aggregates

Source: Various press reports.

ACQUISITIONS PHILOSOPHY

Hanson PLC's acquisitions on both sides of the Atlantic are primarily overseen by Sir Gordon White. Lord Hanson is primarily responsible for the ongoing administration of the company. As Lord Hanson says of White, "He's the one with the gift for takeovers."[9] In turn, White says of Hanson, "James is a brilliant administrator and really knows how to run a company."[10] White claims that many of his acquisition ideas, including the USI deal, come from the newspapers. Others are suggested to him by contacts in the investment banking community, particularly Bob Pirie, president of the Rothschild investment bank, with whom White has lunch once a week.

Whenever possible, White avoids working at the office, opting instead to work from one of his four houses. Unlike corporate raiders such as Saul Steinberg and Carl Icahn, White rarely reads annual reports or detailed stock reports on a target company, claiming that he can get all of the financial information that he needs from Standard & Poor's two page summaries. In addition, his three-man takeover staff distills reams of financial data on a target and provides him with a short memo on the target company. Says White, "I'm like Churchill, tell me everything you can tell me. On one page."[11]

Under White's leadership, one of the things that has distinguished Hanson PLC from many other acquisitive conglomerates is its distinctive acquisitions philosophy (which is in essence White's philosophy). This philosophy appears to be based on a number of consistent factors that are found to underlie most of Hanson's acquisitions.[12]

1. *Target characteristics* Hanson looks for companies based in mature, low-technology industries that have a less-than-inspiring record but show potential for improving performance. Normally the objective has been to identify a poorly performing target where the incumbent management team has gone some way toward improving the underlying performance but those efforts have not yet been reflected in either the profit-and-loss account or, more importantly, the target's stock price.

2. *Research* Although White claims that he does little reading on takeover targets, his takeover staff does undertake detailed research into the potential of target companies before any bid is made. The staff routinely investigates companies undertaking leveraged buyouts.

3. *Risk assessment* One of White's most often quoted edicts is "watch the downside." What this means is that instead of considering the potential benefits of

[9]Quoted in Lampert, "Britons on the Prowl," p. 36.
[10]Quoted in White, "How I Turned," p. 81.
[11]Quoted in Lampert, "Britons on the Prowl," p. 24.
[12]The material in this section is based on the following sources: White, "How I Turned," pp. 80–89; Lampert, "Britons on the Prowl," pp. 22–24, 36, 38, 42; and Mark Cusack, *Hanson Trust: A Review of the Company and Its Prospects* (London: Hoare Govett Limited, 1987).

a deal, give consideration to what can go wrong and the likely consequences of a worst-case scenario. White will purchase a company only if he thinks that in a worst-case scenario he will be able to recover the purchase price by breaking the target up and selling off its constituent parts.

4. *Funding* White was one of the early pioneers of the highly leveraged takeover deal. All of the U.S. acquisitions have been financed by nonrecourse debt, secured on the assets of the target. This enabled White to engineer substantial acquisitions when Hanson Industries itself had a very small capital base. The British acquisitions have been funded by a mix of cash, equity, convertible securities, and loan stock.

5. *Disposals to reduce debt* After an acquisition has been completed, Hanson sends some of its own managers along with a group of external accountants to go through and audit the acquired businesses. After a thorough review, Hanson typically sells off the parts of the acquired company that cannot reach Hanson's stringent profitability targets. In the process, Hanson is able to reduce the debt taken on to fund the acquisition. The most outstanding example followed the purchase of SCM for $930 million. After the takeover Hanson sold off SCM's real estate, pulp and paper, and food holdings for a price of $964 million while holding on to SCM's typewriter and chemicals business, which in effect had been acquired for nothing. Thus, within six months of the takeover's being completed, Hanson was able to eliminate the debt taken on to finance the SCM acquisition. Similar, although less spectacular, disposals have characterized almost all of Hanson's major acquisitions on both sides of the Atlantic.

6. *Elimination of excess overhead* Another objective of Hanson's "housecleaning" of acquired companies is to eliminate any excess overhead. This typically involves closing down the corporate headquarters of the acquired company, eliminating some of the staff while sending other staff down to the operating level. Before Hanson took over, SCM had 230 people in its corporate office, USI had 180, Kidde had 200, and Hanson itself had 30. Today the total headquarters staff for all four is 120.

    Hanson also disposes of any management perks found either at the corporate or the operating level of an acquired company. For example, one of Kidde's operating companies had a collection of art and antiques, a hunting lodge, and three corporate jets. Hanson kept one jet and disposed of the rest, including the man at the top who had spent the money.

7. *The creation of incentives* Hanson tries to create strong incentives for the management of acquired operating companies to improve performance. This is achieved by (1) decentralization designed to give operating managers full autonomy for the running of their businesses, (2) motivating operating managers by setting profit targets that, if achieved, will result in significant profit enhancements, and (3) motivating managers by giving them large pay bonuses if they hit or exceed Hanson's profit targets.

ORGANIZATION AND MANAGEMENT PHILOSOPHY

In addition to its acquisitions philosophy, Hanson is also renowned for its on-going management of operating companies—of which there are over 150 in the corporate portfolio. Although Hanson does have some interests elsewhere, the strategic development of the group has centered on the United States and Britain, where a broad balance has tended to exist in recent years. Hanson PLC looks after the British operations, and Hanson Industries, the U.S. subsidiary, manages the U.S. operations. Each of these two units is operated on an entirely autonomous basis. Only one director sits on the board of both companies. Hanson PLC is headed by Lord Hanson; Hanson Industries is headed by Sir Gordon White.[13]

There are two corporate headquarters, one in the United States and one in Britain. At both locations there is a small central staff responsible for monitoring the performance of operating companies, selecting and motivating operating management, the treasury function (including acting as a central bank for the operating units), acquisitions and disposals, and professional services such as legal and taxation.

Below each headquarters are a number of divisions (see Exhibit 3). These

EXHIBIT 3   **Hanson PLC organization chart**

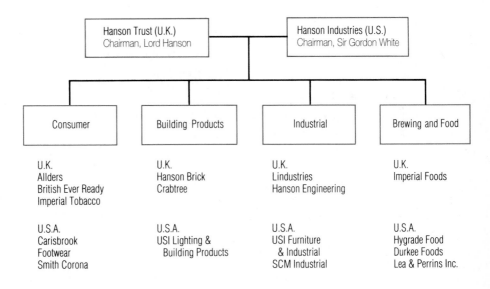

Source: Hanson Industries, *Annual Report,* 1986.

[13]The material in this section is based on the following sources: Cusack, *Hanson Trust;* "The conglomerate as Antique Dealer," pp. 71–73; Byrne and Maremont, "Hanson: The Dangers," pp. 62–64; and Gordon White, "Nothing Hurts More Than a Bogus Bonus," *The Wall Street Journal,* July 20, 1987, p. 18.

are not operating companies. Rather, they are groupings of operating companies. In 1988 there were four U.S. divisions (consumer, building products, industrial, and food) and four British divisions (again, consumer, building products, industrial, and food). There are no personnel at the divisional level with the exception of a divisional CEO. Below the divisions are the operating companies. Each operating company has its own CEO who reports to the divisional CEO. The divisional CEOs in Britain are responsible to Lord Hanson; those in the United States are responsible to David Clarke, White's right-hand man. White himself is primarily concerned with acquisitions and leaves most issues of control to David Clarke. Indeed, White claims that he has never visited Hanson Industries' U.S. corporate headquarters and as a matter of policy never visits operating companies.[14]

The following principles seem to characterize Hanson's management philosophy.

1. *Decentralization* All day-to-day operating decisions are decentralized to operating company managers. The corporate center does not offer suggestions about how to manufacture or market a product. Thus, within the limits set by centrally approved operating budgets and capital expenditures, operating management has unlimited autonomy. As a consequence, operating managers are responsible for the return on capital that they employ.

2. *Tight financial control* Financial control is achieved through two devices: (1) operating budgets and (2) capital expenditure policies. In a bottom-up process, operating budgets are submitted annually to the corporate center by operating company managers. The budgets include detailed performance targets, particularly with regard to return on capital employed (ROK). Corporate staff reviews the budgets and, after consultation with operating management, approves a budget for the coming year. Once agreed upon, the operating budget becomes "gospel." The performance of an operating company is compared against budget on a monthly basis, and any variance is investigated by the corporate center. If an operating company betters its projected ROK, the figure used as the base for the next year's budget is the actual ROK, not the budgeted figure.

   Any cash generated by an operating company is viewed as belonging to the corporate center, not to the operating company. Capital expenditures are extremely closely monitored. All cash expenditures in excess of $3,000 (£1,000 in Britain) have to be agreed upon by corporate headquarters. Capital expenditure requests are frequently challenged by headquarters staff. For example, a manager who contends that an investment in more efficient machinery will cut labor costs must even provide the names of the employees that he or she expects to lay off to achieve the savings. According to company insiders, when justifying a request for capital expenditure, a manager must

---

[14]White, "How I Turned," p. 81.

explain every possibility. In general, Hanson looks for a pre-tax payback on expenditures of three years. The quicker the payback, the more likely it is that an expenditure will be approved.

3. *Incentive systems* A major element of the pay of operating managers is linked directly to operating company performance. A manager can earn up to 60 percent of his or her base salary if the operating company exceeds the ROK target detailed in its annual budget. Bonuses are based strictly on bottom-line performance. As White puts it, "there are no bonuses for being a nice chap."[15] In addition, there is a share option scheme for the most senior operating company and corporate managers. Over 600 managers are members of the option scheme. The options are not exercisable for at least three years after they have been granted.

4. *Board structure* No operating company managers are ever appointed to the board of either Hanson PLC or Hanson Industries. The idea is to eliminate any conflicts of interest that might arise over budgets and capital expenditures.

5. *De-emphasizing operating synergy* In contrast to many diversified companies, Hanson has no interest in trying to realize operating synergy. For example, two of Hanson PLC's subsidiaries, Imperial Tobacco and Elizabeth Shaw (a chocolate firm), are based in Bristol, England, and both deliver goods to news agents and corner shops around Britain. However, Hanson prohibits them from sharing distribution because it reckons that any economies of scale that result would be outweighed by the inefficiencies that would arise if each operating company could blame the other for distribution problems.

THE SCM ACQUISITION

SCM was a diversified manufacturer of consumer and industrial products. SCM had twenty-two operating companies based in five industries: chemicals, coatings and resins, paper and pulp, foods, and typewriters.[16] Among other things, SCM was the world's leading manufacturer of portable typewriters (Smith-Corona typewriters), the world's third largest producer of titanium dioxide (a white inorganic pigment widely used in the manufacture of paint, paper, plastic, and rubber products), the sixth largest paint manufacturer in the world through its Glidden Paints subsidiary, and a major force in the U.S. food industry through its Durkee Famous Foods group (see Exhibit 4).

---

[15]White, "Nothing Hurts More," p. 18.
[16]Most of the detail in this section is drawn from two sources: Cusack, *Hanson Trust;* and Lampert, "Britons on the Prowl," pp. 22–24, 36, 38, 42.

EXHIBIT 4   **SCM divisional results for year to June 1985**

Division	Revenues		Profits	
	$m	% change from 1984	$m	% change from 1984
Chemicals	539	+49%	73.7	−100%
Coatings and resins	687	+5%	49.9	−3%
Paper and pulp	362	+3%	23.1	+10%
Foods	422	+7%	23.0	+35%
Typewriters	176	−11%	(47.4)[a]	−200%

[a]Loss after a $35m charge for restructuring.

Source: Data from Hanson Industries, *Annual Report,* 1986.

Attractions to Hanson

The SCM group was first brought to Gordon White's attention by Bob Pirie, president of Rothschild Inc. in New York. Pirie thought, and Hanson's research team soon confirmed, that SCM had a number of characteristics that made it a perfect Hanson buy.

1. *Poor financial performance* Summary financial data for SCM are given in Exhibit 5. Pre-tax profit had declined from a peak of $83.2 million in 1980 to $54.1 million in 1985. The 1985 return on equity of 7.7 percent was very poor by Hanson's standards, and earnings per share had declined by 19 percent since 1980.

2. *Beginnings of a turnaround* There were signs that incumbent management was coming to grips with SCM's problems—particularly in the troubled typewriter operation, where the 1985 loss was due to a one-time charge of $39 million for restructuring. Financial performance had improved since the low point in 1983, but the benefits of this improvement were not yet reflected in the company's stock price.

3. *Mature businesses* SCM's presence in mature proven markets that were technologically stable fit White's preferences.

4. *Low risk* Some 50 percent of SCM's turnover covered products well known to the U.S. consumer (for example, Smith-Corona typewriters, Glidden paint, Durkee foods). White felt that there would be a ready market for such highly branded businesses if Hanson decided to dispose of any companies that did not meet its stringent ROK requirements.

EXHIBIT 5   **Financial data for SCM**

	1980	1981	1982	1983	1984	1985
Net sales ($m)	1,745	1,761	1,703	1,663	1,963	2,175
Pre-tax profits ($m)	83.2	72.6	35.3	37.8	64.8	54.1
Earnings per share						
($)—fully diluted	4.76	5.01	3.20	2.63	4.05	3.85
Return on equity (%)	12.4	12.0	5.80	4.90	8.0	7.70

Source: Data from Hanson Industries, *Annual Report,* 1986.

5. *Titanium dioxide* Titanium dioxide was dominated by a global oligopoly. Hanson was aware of two favorable trends in the industry that made high returns likely: (1) worldwide demand was forecasted to exceed supply for the next few years, and (2) input costs were declining because of the currency weakness of the major raw-material source, Australia.

6. *Corporate overhead* A corporate staff of 230 indicated to White that SCM was "a lumbering old top-heavy conglomerate with a huge corporate overhead that was draining earnings."[17] He envisaged substantial savings from the elimination of this overhead.

The Takeover Battle

After reviewing the situation, in early August White decided to acquire SCM. He began to buy stock, and on August 21 Hanson Industries formally made a $60 per share tender offer for SCM, valuing the company at $740 million. SCM's top-management team responded on August 30 with its own offer to shareholders in the form of a proposed leveraged buyout of SCM. SCM's management had arranged financing from its investment banker Merrill Lynch and offered shareholders $70 per share. On September 4 White responded by raising Hanson's offer to $72 per share.

SCM's management responded to White's second offer by increasing its own offer to $74 per share. To discourage White from making another bid, SCM's management gave Merrill Lynch a "lock-up" option to buy Durkee Famous Foods and SCM Chemicals (the titanium dioxide division) at a substantial discount should Hanson or another outsider gain control. In effect, SCM's management had agreed to give its "crown jewels" to Merrill Lynch for less than their market value if Hanson won the bidding war.

[17]White, "How I Turned," p. 84.

White's next move was to apparently throw in the towel by announcing withdrawal of Hanson's tender offer. However, in contrast to normal practice on Wall Street, White went into the market and quickly purchased some 25 percent of SCM's stock at a fixed price of $73.5 per share, taking Hanson's stake to 27 percent. Furious at this break with convention, SCM's lawyers drafted a lawsuit against Hanson charging that White's tactics violated tender-offer regulations and demanding a restraining order prohibiting Hanson from making any further market purchases. Hanson quickly filed a counter suit, claiming that Merrill Lynch's "lock-up" option to buy the two SCM divisions illegally prevented the shareholders from getting the best price.

Hanson lost both suits in federal court in New York. White immediately appealed and on September 30 a U.S. court of appeals ruled in Hanson's favor. This, however, was not to be the end of the matter. On October 7 Hanson spent another $40 million to increase its stake in SCM to 33 percent, thereby effectively stalling the leveraged buyout plan, which needed approval by two-thirds of the shareholders. The following day Hanson revised its tender offer to an all-cash $75 per share offer, subject to SCM dropping the "lock-up" provision. Merrill Lynch responded by indicating that it intended to exercise the "lock-up" option because the option had been triggered by Hanson's acquiring 33 percent of SCM.

Hanson's next move, on October 10, was to file a suit to prevent Merrill Lynch from exercising the right to buy SCM's crown jewels. On October 15 it followed this with a second suit against Merrill Lynch for conspiracy. A U.S. district court ruled on November 26 that the "lock-up" was legal and that Hanson had triggered its exercise by the size of its stake. Once again Hanson appealed to a higher court. On January 6, 1986, a U.S. court of appeals overturned the lower court ruling, granting to Hanson an injunction that prevented SCM from exercising the "lock-up" option. The following day Hanson Industries won control over SCM after further market purchases. The final purchase price was $930 million, which represented a price/earnings multiple of 11.5.

After the Acquisition

Having gained control of SCM, Hanson immediately set about trying to realize SCM's potential. Within three months, 250 employees were laid off, mostly headquarters staff, and the former SCM headquarters in New York was sold for $36 million in cash. At the same time, White and his team were using their new position as owners to thoroughly audit the affairs of SCM's operating companies. Their objective was to identify those businesses whose returns were adequate or could be improved upon and those businesses for which the outlook was such that they were unlikely to achieve Hanson's stringent ROK requirements.

At the end of this process, four businesses were sold off in as many months for a total amount that recouped for Hanson the original purchase price and left Hanson with the two best businesses in SCM's portfolio: Smith-Corona typewriters and the titanium dioxide business. In May 1986 SCM's paper and pulp operations were sold to Boise Cascade for $160 million in cash, a price that represented a price/earnings multiple of 29 and was 3 times book value. Hanson felt that the outlook for those operations was not good because of a depression in paper and pulp prices. Boise Cascade obviously thought otherwise. Shortly afterward, Sylvachem, part of SCM's chemicals division, was sold for $30 million, representing a price/earnings multiple of 18.5.

In August 1986 Glidden Paints was sold to the British chemical giant and Europe's largest paint manufacturer, Imperial Chemical Industries PLC (ICI) for $580 million. This represented a price/earnings multiple of 17.5 and was 2.5 times book value. The purchase of this operation enabled ICI to become the world's largest paint manufacturer. A few days later Durkee Famous Foods was sold to another British firm, Reckitt & Colman PLC, for $120 million in cash and the assumption of $20 million in debt. This represented a price/earnings multiple of 17 and was 3 times book value. This disposal served to withdraw Hanson from an area that was subject to uncontrollable and volatile commodity price movements. For Reckitt & Colman, however, which was already one of the largest manufacturers of branded food products outside the United States, it represented an important strategic addition.

The four disposals amounted to $926 million and were accomplished at an average price/earnings multiple of 19.5. Having recovered 100 percent of the purchase price paid for SCM within eight months, Hanson had effectively acquired for nothing a number of businesses that were projected to contribute around $140 million to net pre-tax profit for their first full year under Hanson control.

Hanson held on to the titanium dioxide business for two main reasons. First, with the industry operating at close to 100 percent capacity and with projections indicating an increase in demand through to 1989, prices and margins were expected to increase substantially. Although several companies had plans to expand global capacity, given the 3-to-4-year time lag in bringing new capacity on stream, this sellers' market was likely to persist for a while. Nor did it look as if the additional capacity would outstrip the projected rise in demand. Second, two-thirds of world production of titanium dioxide is in the hands of global producers. SCM's business is ranked third with 12 percent of world capacity, behind Du Pont and Tioxide PLC. Given this oligopoly, orderly pricing in world markets seemed likely to continue.

Hanson also decided to hold on to SCM's typewriter business, despite the fact that in recent years it had been the worst-performing unit in SCM's portfolio. Hanson quickly realized that SCM management had in effect just completed a drastic overhaul of the typewriter businesses and that a dramatic turnaround was likely. In the two years prior to Hanson's acquisition, SCM's management had undertaken the following steps:

1.   A new line of electronic typewriters had been introduced to match the increasingly sophisticated Japanese models.

2. Capacity had been reduced by 50 percent, and six U.S. production facilities had been consolidated into a single assembly plant and distribution center in New York to manufacture all electronic models.
3. As a result of automation, scale economies, and labor agreements, productivity at the New York plant had increased fourfold since 1984, and unit labor costs had declined by 60 percent.
4. The manufacture of electric models had been moved offshore to a low-cost facility in Singapore.
5. Smith-Corona had just introduced the first personal word processor for use with a portable electronic typewriter, and it retailed at just under $500.

As a result of these improvements, the Smith-Corona business seemed ready to become a major profit producer. Hanson forecasted profits of $30 million for this business during 1986–1987, compared with an operating loss of $47.4 million in financial year 1985.

THE IMPERIAL ACQUISITION

On December 6, 1985, while still engaged in the SCM acquisition, Hanson opened another takeover battle in Britain by announcing a £1.5-billion offer for Imperial Group PLC.[18] Imperial Group was one of the ten largest firms in Britain. Imperial was Britain's leading tobacco manufacturer and the third largest tobacco company in the world. Its Courage Brewing subsidiary was one of the "big six" beer companies in Britain. Its "leisure" operations included 1,371 public houses (taverns), 120-plus restaurants, and over 750 specialized retail shops. Imperial manufactured over 1,000 branded food products (see Exhibit 6 for a breakdown of Imperial's divisional results). In September 1985 Imperial had sold its fourth business, the U.S. motel chain Howard Johnson, to Marriott. Howard Johnson had been purchased in 1980 and was widely regarded as one of the worst acquisitions ever made by a major British company.

Attractions to Hanson

Hanson's interest in Imperial was prompted by the news on December 2, 1985, of a planned merger between Imperial and United Biscuits PLC, a major manufacturer of branded food products. The financial press perceived this measure as a defensive move by Imperial. However, despite its well-documented problems with Howard Johnson, Imperial's financial performance was reasonably strong (see Exhibit 7). What factors made Imperial an attractive takeover target to Hanson? The following seem to have been important.

---

[18]The material in this section is based on the following sources: Cusack, *Hanson Trust;* and Lampert, "Britons on the Prowl," pp. 22–24, 36, 38, 42.

EXHIBIT 6   **Imperial divisional results for year to October 1985**

	Revenues		Profits	
Division	£m	% change from 1984	£m	% change from 1984
Tobacco	2,641	+7%	123.1	+11%
Brewing and leisure	974	+8%	97.0	+20%
Foods	719	+4%	33.0	+5%
Howard Johnson	617	+11%	11.1	−40%

Source: Data from Hanson Industries, *Annual Report,* 1986.

EXHIBIT 7   **Financial data for Imperial**

	1981	**1982**	**1983**	**1984**	**1985**
Revenues (£m)	4,526	4,614	4,381	4,593	4,918
Pre-tax profits (£m)	106	154	195	221	236
Earnings per share (pence)	12.8	16.4	18.0	20.3	22.4
Return on capital (%)	12.7	17.9	20.4	21.1	18.1

Source: Data from Hanson Industries, *Annual Report,* 1986.

1. *Mature business* Like SCM's businesses, most of Imperial's businesses were based in mature, low-technology industries. There is little prospect of radically changing fashions or technological change in the tobacco, brewing, and food industries.

2. *Low risk* Most of Imperial's products had a high brand recognition within Britain. Thus Hanson could easily dispose of those that did not stand up to Hanson's demanding ROK targets.

3. *Tobacco cash flow* Imperial's tobacco business was a classic cash cow. The company had 45 percent of the tobacco market and seven of the ten best-selling brands in 1985. Although tobacco sales are declining in Britain because of a combination of health concerns and punitive taxation, the decline has been gradual, amounting to 29 percent since the peak year of 1973. Given Hanson's emphasis on ROK and cash flow, this made Imperial particularly attractive to Hanson. Imperial had arguably squandered much of this cash flow by using it to underwrite unprofitable growth opportunities, particularly Howard Johnson.

4. *Failure of Imperial's diversification strategy* Imperial's recent track record with respect to diversification was poor. In 1978 it bought a construction company, J. B. Eastward, for £40 million. After four years of trading losses, Eastward was sold in 1982 for total loss of £54 million. In 1979 Imperial paid $640 million for Howard Johnson, the U.S. motel and restaurant chain. In 1985, after six years of declining profits, this business was sold for $341 million. These losses suggested a fundamental weakness in Imperial's top management in an area in which Hanson was strong: diversification strategy. Moreover, the failure of Imperial's diversification strategy probably resulted in Imperial's shares being discounted by the stock market.

5. *Inadequate returns in brewing and leisure* Imperial's brewing and leisure operations earned a ROK of 9 percent in 1985. This return was considered very low for the brewing industry, which was characterized by strong demand and was dominated by a mature oligopoly that had engineered high prices and margins. Hanson thought that this return could be significantly improved.

The Takeover Battle

The planned merger between Imperial and United Biscuits PLC (UB), announced on December 2, 1985, gave rise to considerable concern among Imperial's already disgruntled shareholders. Under the terms of the proposed merger, UB, although contributing just 21 percent of net assets, would end up with a 42 percent interest in the enlarged group. The implication was that Imperial's shareholders would experience significant earnings dilution. In addition, it was proposed that the corporate management of the enlarged group would primarily come from UB personnel. These factors prompted a reverse takeover by UB of the much larger Imperial group.

Hanson's interest was sparked by this controversy. Hanson's corporate staff had been tracking Imperial for some time, so when the "for sale" sign was raised over Imperial, Hanson was able to move quickly. On December 6, 1985, Hanson made a 250-pence per share offer for Imperial, valuing the group at £1.9 billion. This offer was rejected out of hand by Imperial's management.

The next major development came on February 12, 1986, when the British secretary of state of trade and industry referred the proposed Imperial/UB merger to the Monopolies and Mergers Commission for consideration. Britain's Monopolies and Mergers Commission has the authority to prohibit any merger that might create a monopoly. The referral was due to the recognition that an Imperial/UB group would command over 40 percent of the British snack-food market.

On February 17, Hanson took advantage of the uncertainty created by the referral to unveil a revised offer 24 percent higher than its original offer, valuing Imperial at £2.35 billion. On the same day, UB announced a £2.5-billion bid for Imperial and indicated that, if the offer was successful, Imperial's snack-food businesses would be sold, thus eliminating the need for a Monopolies and Mergers Commission investigation. Imperial's board duly recommended the UB offer to shareholders for acceptance.

Many of Imperial's shareholders, however, were in no mood to accept Imperial's recommendation. Under British stock market regulations, once the Imperial board accepted UB's offer, Imperial's shareholders had two months in which to indicate their acceptance or rejection of it. If the offer was rejected, then the shareholders were free to consider the hostile bid from Hanson. What followed was an increasingly acrimonious war of words between Hanson and Imperial. Hanson charged Imperial with mismanagement. Imperial responded by trying to depict Hanson as an asset stripper with no real interest in generating internal growth from the companies it owned. In the words of one Imperial executive during this period, Lord Hanson "buys and sells companies well, but he manages them jolly badly. He buys, squeezes and goes on to the next one. The only way to grow is by bigger and bigger acquisitions. Like all great conglomerate builders of the past, he's over the hill."[19]

Imperial's management failed to win the war of words. By April 17, UB had secured acceptances for only 34 percent of Imperial's shares, including 14.9 percent held by UB associates. The UB offer lapsed, leaving the way clear for Hanson. On April 18, Hanson secured acceptances for over 50 percent of Imperial's shares, and its offer went unconditional. At £2.5 billion, the takeover was the largest in British history; it implied a price/earnings multiple of 12.3 on Imperial's prospective earnings.

After the Acquisition

After the acquisition Hanson moved quickly to realize potential from Imperial. Of the 300 staff at Imperial's headquarters, 260 were laid off, and most of the remainder were sent back to the operating level. In July Imperial's hotels and restaurants were sold to Trusthouse Forte for £190 million in cash, representing a price/earnings multiple of 24 on prospective earnings and amounting to 1.7 times book value. That sale was followed in September 1986 by the sale of the Courage Brewing operations, along with a wine and spirits wholesaler and an "off-license" chain (liqueur stores) to Elders IXL, an Australian brewing company, for £1.4 billion in cash. The price/earnings multiple for that deal amounted to 17.5 times prospective earnings and represented a premium of £150 million over book value. It was quickly followed by the sale of Imperial's Golden Wonder snack-food business to Dalgety PLC, a British food concern, for £87 million in cash, representing a price/earnings multiple of 13.5 over prospective earnings.

As a result of these moves, by the autumn of 1986 Hanson had raised £1.7 billion from the sale of Imperial's businesses. Effectively, Hanson recouped 66 percent of the total cost of its acquisition by selling companies that contributed

[19]Quoted in Philip Revzin, "U.K.'s Hanson Trust Aims for Big Leagues in Takeovers," *The Wall Street Journal*, February 25, 1986, p. 30.

to just over 45 percent of Imperial's net profit forecasted for the year to October 1986. The net cost of Imperial on this basis had fallen to £850 million, with a consequent decline in the price/earnings multiple on prospective earnings from 12.3 to 7.6.

This was followed in 1988 by the sale of Imperial's food businesses for £534 million, along with the sale of various other smaller interests for £56 million. By the end of 1988, therefore, Hanson had raised £2.26 billion from the sale of Imperial's assets. It still held on to Imperial Tobacco, by far the largest business in Imperial's portfolio, which it had in effect gained for a net cost of £240 million—this for a business that in 1988 generated £150 million in operating profit.

RECENT DEVELOPMENTS

Following the SCM and Imperial acquisitions, in 1987 Hanson acquired Kidde, a 108-company U.S. conglomerate, for $1.7 billion. Kidde seemed set for the "Hanson treatment." Its headquarters was closed within three months of the take-over, and a series of disposals were arranged. These were followed in 1988 by continuing disposals of operations acquired in the Imperial and Kidde acquisitions. In total, they amounted to $1.5 billion.

In mid 1989 Hanson embarked on its biggest takeover ever, the £3.61-billion ($4.8-billion) acquisition of Consolidated Gold Fields PLC (CGF). In addition to being the second largest gold-mining operation in the world, CGF also owns a large stone and gravel operation, ARC Ltd., with major holdings in Britain. CGF came to Hanson's attention following an abortive takeover bid for the company from South African–controlled Minorco.

Hanson bought Minorco's 29.9 percent minority stake in CGF and launched its own takeover bid in July 1989. After raising its bid, Hanson won control of CGF in August. CGF also seemed set to be broken up. About half of CGF's value consists of minority stakes in publicly quoted mining companies in the United States, South Africa, and Australia. These stakes range from 38 to 49 percent, enough to hold the key to control in many of the companies. Thus Hanson should be able to extract a premium price for them. Initial estimates suggest that Hanson should be able to raise $2.5 billion from the sale of CGF's minority holdings.[20] Indeed, by February 1990 Hanson had reportedly recouped about one-third of the purchase price for CGF through disposals and was looking to sell additional operations while gold prices remained high.[21]

The CGF deal led directly to the June 1990 acquisition of Peabody Holdings Co., the largest U.S. coal producer, for a total cost of $1.23 billion in cash. CGF had a 49 percent stake in Newmont Mining Corp., the biggest U.S. gold-mining concern. In turn, Newmont owned 55 percent of Peabody. In April 1990 Hanson

[20]Mark Maremont and Chuck Hawkins, "Is Consgold Just an Appetizer for Hanson?" *Business Week*, July 10, 1989, pp. 41–42.
[21]Joann Lubin, "Hanson to Buy Peabody Stake for $504 Million," *The Wall Street Journal*, February 16, 1990, p. A4.

EXHIBIT 8   **Hanson PLC—financial record**

Income Data (million $)

Year ended Sep. 30	Revs.	Oper. inc.	% oper. inc. of revs.	Cap. exp.	Depr.	Int. exp.	Net bef. taxes	Eff. tax rate	[2]Net Inc.	% Net Inc. of revs.
[3]1989	11,302	1,609	14.2	2,141	200	533	[1]1,718	23.6%	1,313	11.6
[3]1988	12,507	1,561	12.5	724	215	485	[1]1,488	23.2%	1,143	9.1
[4]1987	10,975	1,230	11.2	522	172	493	[1]1,217	22.8%	939	8.6
[4]1986	6,196	713	11.5	848	105	359	[1]667	22.5%	517	8.3
1985	3,771	477	12.7	84	74	172	356	23.5%	272	7.2
1984	2,930	303	10.3	61	55	119	208	25.7%	154	5.3
1983	2,226	207	9.3	59	47	81	137	30.2%	94	4.2
1982	1.952	NA	NA	NA	NA	NA	NA	NA	72	3.7
1981	1,549	NA	NA	NA	NA	NA	NA	NA	62	4.0

Balance sheet data (million $)

Sep. 30	Cash	Assets	Curr. liab.	Ratio	Total assets	Ret. on assets	Long-term debt	Common equity	Total inv. capital	% LT debt of cap.	Ret. on equity
1989	8,574	12,038	5,278	2.3	17,482	8.5%	8,028	1,689	10,683	75.1	47.6%
1988	6,527	10,413	4,165	2.5	13,210	9.4%	3,592	3,707	7,878	45.6	33.5%
1987	5,025	8,236	3,422	2.4	10,471	9.3%	2,837	2,841	6,151	46.1	37.5%
1986	2,509	7,977	3,572	2.2	9,577	7.6%	2,834	2,068	5,252	54.0	29.1%
1985	1,659	2,908	1,277	2.3	4,021	7.7%	903	1,376	2,563	35.2	27.7%
1984	641	1,775	925	1.9	2,638	9.0%	981	505	1,540	63.7	36.7%

Data as orig. reptd. prior to 1986 data as reptd. in 1985 Annual Report (prior to 1984 from Listing Application of Nov. 3, 1986), Conv. to US$ at year-end exch. rates. **1.** Incl. equity in earns of nonconsol. subs. **2.** Bef. spec. item(s) in 1989, 1988, 1986. **3.** Excl. disc. opers. and reflects merger or acquisition. **4.** Reflects merger or acquisition. NA-Not Available.

Source: Standard & Poor, *Standard NYSE Stock Reports*, Vol. 57, No. 54, Sec. 12, p. 1096.

purchased the 45 percent of Peabody not owned by Newmont from three minority owners. Then in June it outbid AMAX Corporation for Newmont's stake in Peabody.

The attraction of Peabody to Hanson lies in two factors: (1) the company owns large deposits of low-sulfur coal, which is increasingly in demand because of environmental concerns; (2) the company has recently invested heavily to upgrade its plant. As a result, in the past four years labor productivity has increased 50 percent.[22] In addition, analysts speculate that the deals, by improving Newmont's financial position (Newmont has used the cash to reduce its debt), may make it possible for Hanson to sell off its 49 percent stake in Newmont for a reasonable premium.

[22]"Hanson PLC," *Value Line*, July 20, 1990, p. 832.

MICHAEL EISNER'S DISNEY COMPANY

In early 1991, Michael Eisner, chairman and CEO of the Walt Disney Company, Frank Wells, president and chief operating officer, and Gary Wilson, executive vice president and chief financial officer, were still basking in the glow generated by another year of record-breaking revenue and profit for Disney. Disney businesses were performing at an unprecedented level and confidence was high. Exhibit 1 charts the net income of the Walt Disney Company from 1985 to 1989. The problem facing the trio who had engineered Disney's turnaround was how to maintain Disney's explosive growth rate and its return-on-investment goal of increasing earnings per share by 20 percent over any five-year period, to achieve a 20 percent annual return on equity. Paradoxically, the very success of their strategy, which had originated to protect an underperforming Disney company from the rampages of corporate raiders and the threat of takeover, was causing the opposite problem: how to maintain the company's explosive growth in a business environment where attractive opportunities for expansion were becoming increasingly scarce. Eisner, Wells, and Wilson were reflecting on how to develop a five-year plan that would cement the strategy that had led to their present enviable situation and make the 1990s the "Disney Decade."

THE DISNEY COMPANY BEFORE EISNER

When Walt Disney died in 1966, he left a company that was experiencing record revenues and profits. The Disney company was at its creative peak and forging ahead at full steam on the many ideas generated by Walt Disney's creative genius. Yet by the early 1980s, all the drive in the Disney company had evaporated. Although revenues were increasing somewhat, net income and profit were dropping drastically. Although top executives believed that they were doing what "Walt would have wanted," the vision that was uniquely Walt Disney's was gone. How had this situation come about?

This case was prepared by Gareth R. Jones, Texas A&M University. Copyright, Gareth R. Jones, 1991.

EXHIBIT 1   Selected financial data (in millions, except per share and other data)

	1989	1988	1987	1986	1985
Statement of income data					
Revenues	$4,594.3	$3,438.2	$2,876.8	$2,165.8	$1,700.1
Operating income	1,229.0	884.8	776.8	527.7	345.7
Interest expense	23.9	5.8	29.1	44.1	54.6
Income from continuing operations	703.3	522.0	392.3	213.2	132.3
Net income	703.3	522.0	444.7	247.3	173.5
Balance sheet data					
Total assets	$6,657.2	$5,108.9	$3,806.3	$3,121.0	$2,897.3
Borrowings	860.6	435.5	584.5	547.2	823.1
Stockholders' equity	3,044.0	2,359.3	1,845.4	1,418.7	1,184.9
Statement of cash flows data					
Cash flow	$1,275.6	$1,075.4*	$830.6	$668.4	$518.8
Investments					
Theme parks, resorts, and other property, net	749.6	595.7	280.1	174.1	179.8
Film costs	426.7	225.7	178.3	203.7	149.9
Acquisitions	237.3	221.7			
Per share data					
Net income					
Continuing operations	$5.10	$3.80	$2.85	$1.57	$ .98
Total	5.10	3.80	3.23	1.82	1.29
Cash dividends	.46	.38	.32	.315	.30
Other data					
Stockholders at close of year	143,000	124,000	101,000	77,000	58,000
Employees at close of year	47,000	39,000	31,000	30,000	30,000

*Excludes $722.6 million unearned royalty advances.

Source: The Walt Disney Company, *Annual Report*, 1989.

Walt Disney Forms a Company

Walt Elias Disney was born in 1901. Raised on a farm, he early developed an interest in art and drawing, and his ambition was to be a cartoonist. His interest in static cartoons soon waned, however, with the appearance of animated cartoons in movies. The first cartoons were extremely crude. The figures bounced rather than moved gracefully; they were silent; and they were in black and white. Walt immediately saw the potential for developing high-quality moving cartoons and set about marshaling resources to produce his product.

After a series of setbacks, Walt had success with a character called "Oswald the Rabbit," perhaps the forerunner of Roger Rabbit. The carefully drawn cartoons were very popular with movie audiences and provided Disney with the money he needed to expand his operations and to hire additional artists and animators. However, after battles about money and profits, Disney lost control of the Oswald character to Charles Mintz, the cartoon's distributor. From that loss he learned an important lesson. From then on, he would retain all the rights to his characters, to the films produced using these characters, and to the distribution end of the film business. This was the start of Disney's fortune.

With the experience gained from Oswald, Disney set about finding a new character to pin his hopes on. In 1928 he created Mickey Mouse. Walt provided the voice, and the drawings were made by Ubbe (Ub) Iwerks, an artist and animator who had worked closely with Walt from the beginning. The Mickey Mouse cartoons were immensely popular, and their success provided Walt Disney with the resources to expand his repertoire of characters and improve his animation techniques. He and his company were always at the forefront of technological developments. The next decade saw the emergence of Disney's now-familiar cast of characters: Donald Duck, Goofy, and the Three Little Pigs, a cartoon for which Disney won an Oscar. Disney began to make cartoons in color, using Technicolor's new three-color process. He won his first Oscar for color in 1932.[1] The source of Disney's distinctive strength was this ability to meld technical developments with his emerging cast of cartoon characters. None of his competitors was able to erode this advantage. Although other studios established animation departments, none had the same success as Disney.

Full-Length Cartoon Movies

By the late 1930s, Disney's experience in short cartoons had developed his studio's skills in the three techniques needed for quality animation and cartoon making: art and drawing, perspective and sound, and color. Walt had learned the value of using a large number of drawings per second to provide his characters with realistic movements, even though doing so dramatically increased costs. He had seen the value of color as a way of making his characters more true to life. Lastly, he had developed a technique that gave depth to the previously "flat" cartoons. This was the famous Multiplane technique, which involved the use of a camera that could focus in and out of three planes of celluloid drawings: the foreground, the characters themselves, and the background. When these planes were photographed at an angle, the result was an impression of depth that gave the cartoon characters life (this technique netted an Oscar for Disney).

Utilizing these techniques, Walt Disney set about to realize his long-term dream: a full-length cartoon motion picture. He was careful in his selection of a subject. From the beginning, he believed that his subjects should be characters that were widely accepted by the public so that little learning by the public was needed. With his characteristic genius, he chose Snow White and the Seven

[1]L. Gartley and E. Leebron, *Walt Disney: A Guide to References and Resources* (Boston, G. K. Hall, 1979).

Dwarfs as his subject in 1937. *Snow White* cost a fortune to make, but it went on to make animation history and it grossed a fortune at the box office. It provided the capital that precipitated Disney into the ranks of the big studios. The money from *Snow White* allowed Disney to build his studio at Burbank, and it financed the animated films *Pinocchio* and *Bambi,* which were also very successful.

Then, in 1940, departing from his own maxim of choosing only "brand-name characters," Walt made *Fantasia*. Despite being an artistic success, the film was a commercial disaster, which, coinciding with the unpopularity of cartoons during the Second World War, plunged the Disney corporation into debt. When banks restricted the amount they were willing to lend the company, Walt Disney offered stock to the public for the first time. In 1940, Walt Disney Productions issued 155,000 shares at $25 a share and raised $3.5 million in working capital.

More Walt Disney Magic

With the end of the war, the public was once again receptive to fun and fantasy. The postwar boom years produced an audience of men and women with money in their pockets who were in search of excitement, and Walt Disney was determined to provide them with it. He began to search for new projects to exercise the talents of the Disney studios. By 1950, he had come up with new directions.

Live-action motion pictures   Disney realized that animation was not the only way to bring the public's favorite fantasy characters to the screen. Robin Hood and many other popular heroes could be depicted in live-action movies. So Disney took popular fictional characters and turned them into movies. A string of hits resulted as Disney studios came out with *Treasure Island, The Swiss Family Robinson, The Story of Robin Hood and His Merry Men, Kidnapped,* and *20,000 Leagues Under the Sea.* He also decided to create new characters, and he developed scripts for such projects as *The Shaggy Dog, The Absent-Minded Professor, Son of Flubber,* and *The Parent Trap.* Side by side with these developments Disney embarked on a series of nature or wild life projects. Between 1950 and 1960, films such as *Water Birds, The Alaskan Eskimo, Bear Country,* and *White Wilderness* were produced for enthusiastic audiences. These films are still popular.

At the same time, his interest in animation did not lapse, and animated films were a major moneymaker for the studio in the 1950s. *Cinderella* was a smash hit as was *101 Dalmatians, Peter Pan, Lady and the Tramp,* and *The Jungle Book.* By 1960 Walt was experimenting with combining animation and live action. One result was *Mary Poppins.* An all-time revenue producer for Disney and one of the greatest hits in the history of motion pictures, it won five Academy Awards.

Television   Another move that helped Walt Disney Productions at this time was Walt's decision to take his products to the television screen. While other movie studios were worrying that television would cut into their profits and reduce their audiences, Walt perceived the prospective synergies between the television and movie businesses. Disney was already producing a wide range of family-oriented entertainment: cartoons, full-length animation, live action, and wild life. What could be more logical than taking Disney characters and developing Disney products to fit a television format? Not only would this be a source of additional revenues and allow the studio to exploit its resources and people to the full, it would also provide advertising for the Walt Disney name and future product offerings. The result was that in 1954 Disney brought *The Wonderful World of Disney* to television. In 1955, *Mickey Mouse Club* was introduced, and the Disney name became part of popular American culture. For the next twenty years, Walt Disney television productions became a weekly event for the viewing public.

Theme parks   Walt Disney had another reason for entering the television market. By itself, television was not a great moneymaker for Disney. It would provide some free advertising and permit a more efficient utilization of the Disney resources, but animation was expensive compared with live action. What Walt principally saw in television was a way to promote an idea that had been on his mind for years: a permanent amusement park that could exploit the Disney characters' popularity and would offer a family a fun-filled day of Disney fantasy. Rather than passively watching a movie, amusement-park goers would become participants in the action—they would become actors in a live Disney entertainment. Television would show viewers how to take part in this experience; it would also show them what they could expect. Walt realized that theme park, television, and movies would feed on each other: each would promote the other.

After deliberation, Disney chose Anaheim, California, for his first theme park, and Disneyland opened in July 1955. Anaheim was chosen because of the huge population base of southern California and because of the weather. Less than 5 inches of rain a year meant that Disneyland could be operated all year round with little threat from the weather.

The theme-park idea was wildly successful, and since its opening Disneyland became the backbone of the Disney empire. Immense planning went into (and still goes into) the creation of the Disney experience. Every ride and attraction is crafted to highlight the Disney theme. Movies and characters are represented by different kinds of amusements and by the personal appearances of the characters. Since 1955, the number of attractions at Disneyland has grown from 17 to 62. Exhibits are constantly improved and updated to take advantage of the latest technological developments. Attractions often have a corporate sponsor that buys into a Disney theme and leases an exhibit. AT&T, Sony, and Kodak are some of the many sponsors of Disney exhibits. Disneyland is divided into seven major areas: Adventureland, Tomorrowland, Fantasyland, Frontierland, Mainstreet, Bearcountry, and New Orleans Square.

In 1965 Walt announced another part of his grand plan: the development of Disney World, including the EPCOT (Experimental Prototype Community of Tomorrow) Center in Orlando, Florida. As originally imagined by Walt, part of Disney World would include a Magic Kingdom similar to the one already established in Anaheim. However, the EPCOT center he envisaged was a "living laboratory" where from 20,000 to 30,000 people would live permanently, experimenting with advanced technology and literally providing the world with examples of future life on earth. He did not live to see either dream realized. In December 1966, Walt Disney died.

The Disney Company After Walt

Walt Disney left his company at the pinnacle of its success up to that date. The company had new films ready to distribute, plans for Disney World, steadily rising attendance at Disneyland, and a secure television audience. Yet from 1966 to 1984, when Michael Eisner took over, nothing seemed to go as well as before in the Disney organization. The company seemed to be spinning its wheels. Nobody emerged to wear Walt's crown. Nobody could provide the creative vision to lead a company whose mission was to provide fun and fantasy. There was a void in the organization, and the company accomplished little that did not already bear Walt's stamp of approval.

Walt's brother Roy took over management of the company and supervised the building of Disney World. Most of the advance planning for Disney World had been done by Walt. The first step in the plan had been to purchase a huge tract of land outside Orlando, Florida. Disney had not liked the situation that had developed outside Anaheim after the opening of Disneyland. The Disney company owns only the area on which the theme park and its parking lot are built. As a result, development around the park has proceeded unchecked, and the surrounding area has become chock-a-block with motels and hotels that Walt felt detracted from the Disney image. Moreover, the profits earned by businesses in the vicinity of the park were vastly greater than the revenues that the Disney company received from park attendance. Determined that this should not happen in Orlando, Walt arranged, through subsidiary companies, the purchase of 28,000 acres of undeveloped land, an area of 34 square miles, large enough to hold any number of hotels and amusement parks. When Disney made the announcement of the park in 1965, the value of the land increased dramatically overnight.

The Magic Kingdom was the first part of Disney World to be built. It opened in 1971 with 35 attractions; now there are over 50. Corporate sponsorship was important in financing the development of the Magic Kingdom. It was also important in financing EPCOT Center: large corporations paid $25 million for the right to sponsor an attraction there. Nevertheless, the plans for EPCOT changed dramatically after Walt's death. The Disney company realized that development costs would be enormous and that the venture as devised by Walt was not commercially feasible. Thus the company changed EPCOT's mission to provide a showcase of modern technology and of international culture. In essence, EPCOT became a kind of permanent World's Fair when it opened in 1982. It is composed of two main areas: World Showcase and Future World.

World Showcase consists of pavilions sponsored by different countries demonstrating their national culture and products. The number of countries represented is growing rapidly. Recently the Soviet Union opened a pavilion. Future World, in the spirit of Walt's original plan, showcases future developments that can be expected in all areas of human endeavor. Attractions include The Living Seas, sponsored by United Technologies; a futuristic farming exhibit sponsored by Kraft; and a journey through the human body, an exhibit highlighting advances in medical knowledge. EPCOT was the first Walt Disney "park" specifically designed to appeal to adults, although Walt always said that everything the Disney company did was designed for the child in everybody.

The development of EPCOT and Disney World was the Walt Disney Company's principal priority after Walt's death, and the opening of EPCOT attracted record crowds. However, despite high attendance, the profit margin of Disney World was lower than that of Disneyland, and both revenues and profits were disappointing given the huge investment of $1.5 billion. Moreover, by 1984, attendance at Disney World and Disneyland had dropped off from its record high, further reducing revenues. Clearly, the company had problems with its theme parks, but management did not know what to do.

Another problem was that although the company, to exploit the hotel market missed at Anaheim, had at the Magic Kingdom and at EPCOT Center three large hotels with over 2,000 rooms, chains such as Hyatt and Hilton were opening luxury hotels at the borders of Disney World. Potential Disney revenues were being lost to these chains, and the situation that had developed at Disneyland was in danger of recurring in Orlando.

Other areas of Disney's business were also not doing well. Planning for The Disney Channel had begun in the late 1970s, and it came on line in 1983 with 532,000 subscribers. The channel was a natural complement to Disney's other activities because it was an additional vehicle through which the company could exploit its skills and characters. However, the start-up costs were enormous, and even though the channel had over 1 million subscribers by 1984, it was still losing over $10 million a year. This was another drain on the company's resources and a threat to its profit margins.

Home video and consumer products   One bright spot for the Walt Disney Company was its entry into the home video market. In 1983 it began selling videocassettes of some of its movie hits. Some were contemporary films, such as *Splash,* from its new Touchstone label. The company also began marketing its classics, first selecting those that, though popular, were not its greatest hits, to see customer reaction and to protect its rerun movie revenues. *Dumbo* and *Alice in Wonderland* were released in 1983 to enthusiastic demand. Disney realized that the revenue potential from video sales was enormous and soon orchestrated the gradual release of all its classics.[2]

The sale of consumer products bearing the Disney logo had long been one of the Disney company's major lines of business. However, many analysts felt that Disney was not exploiting the potential of this market. The strategy of fran-

[2]Walt Disney Productions, *Annual Report,* 1983.

chising rights to the use of the Disney name and characters was bringing Disney some money but was making far more money for the producers and distributors of Disney products than for the Walt Disney Company itself. Analysts felt that the potential market for Disney books, comics, records, clothing, and all kinds of Disney souvenirs had yet to be exploited.

Movie making   After Walt's death, Disney's movie operations suffered because of the failure to find good scripts and projects. The performance of Disney's film business had been lackluster throughout the 1970s. Although the film division accounted for over 20 percent of Disney's profits in 1979, by 1982 it was losing money. The situation became so bad that Disney CEO E. Cardon (Card) Walker (he had taken over after Roy Disney's death in 1971) was talking about closing the film division. The division that had been Disney's core business and the source of its success was in danger. How had this come about?

The Walt Disney Company was relying on reruns of its classic movies and living on its past glory rather than on the proceeds of its present activities. Reruns were contributing over 50 percent of the revenues of the film division because Disney was having little commercial success with its new ventures. Although receiving good reviews, animated movies such as *The Secret of Nimh, Watershipdown,* and *The Black Hole* were not big moneymakers, and the live-action films that Disney had been producing, like *Something Wicked This Way Comes* and *Condorman,* lost money (those two, for example, lost over $20 million each).

Moreover, analysts were claiming that Disney was not making the best use of its film library, which contained over 700 titles. They felt that Disney could be making a much more creative use of this resource. It was in part as a response to pressure to exploit the film library that the company drew up plans for The Disney Channel. Meanwhile, top management at Disney did not like Card Walker's attitude toward the film division. They felt a turnaround in this division rather than liquidation was the answer, and in 1983 Ronald Miller became chief executive to implement a turnaround strategy.

Miller created a new film division, Touchstone Films, to produce movies that were not suitable for the family-oriented Disney label. He believed that Disney's conservative family image had prevented film makers from exploiting the opportunities in the market for new kinds of movies. Touchstone brought out *Splash* in 1983. It was a huge hit and the beginning of the desired turnaround. Yet Disney's top managers were worried that Walt would not have liked the output of Touchstone Films, and they actively sought to isolate the Touchstone division from the rest of the Disney organization. This conflict was the start of a series of fights between Disney managers and Disney stockholders over the best way to manage the company.

Roy Disney II, Walt's nephew, in particular, lost confidence in the management team. He felt that those managers lacked the Disney vision and the skills to exploit the Disney resources and, in essence, that they were destroying Walt's legacy. These open conflicts brought the Walt Disney Company to the attention of corporate raiders, and by 1984 an unfriendly takeover was an increasing possibility. To prevent such a takeover, the Disney family sided with new investors, the Bass family, to oust the old, conservative Disney management team. They then set out to recruit somebody who could restore the Disney luster in the entertainment industry. The person they fixed on was Michael Eisner, previously vice chairman of Paramount and widely regarded as the originator of a massive turnaround in the fortunes of that corporation because of his ability to identify and act on new trends in the marketplace. In September 1984, Michael Eisner took control of the Disney corporation, and a new era for Disney began. Finally, someone had emerged who could wear Walt's crown.

THE DISNEY COMPANY UNDER MICHAEL EISNER

In December 1984, Michael Eisner was sitting down with Frank Wells, whom he had recruited to help him turn the Disney corporation around, and Roy Disney, Walt's nephew, who had been instrumental in Eisner's appointment to plan Disney's future. They were looking over Disney's resources and the activities of the company's divisions and subsidiaries. Eisner and Wells were amazed at the extent and diversity of Disney's resources. Eisner decided that Disney's strengths were in its three principal business segments:

1. **Theme parks and resorts.** This division includes all the Disney theme parks and hotel businesses, together with shopping centers, conference centers, and golf courses.
2. **Filmed entertainment.** This division includes the Disney studios; Buena Vista International, which has the Touchstone label; and Buena Vista Distribution, which distributes Disney films at home and abroad.
3. **Consumer products.** This is the licensing arm of Disney. It licenses Disney characters, literary properties, songs, and music to various manufacturers, retailers, printers, and publishers.

Why were these businesses underperforming, and what could be done to turn them around? It did not take Eisner and Wells long to realize that the problem was the failure to exploit the potential of these businesses. Management in each business segment was not following any clearly defined strategy to exploit the Disney resources and had no vision of how to utilize these resources. Each division was drifting aimlessly. For example, despite Disney's raw film-making talent, the movie business was losing money. Similarly, inaction had cost Disney its television presence outside its own movie channel. Moreover, it was apparent that while Disney was not taking advantage of its opportunities, other people were.

For every dollar of revenue that Disney was collecting from its characters and theme parks, the manufacturers that were licensing Disney products and the hotel chains that were housing and feeding Disney customers at the theme parks were getting five dollars. Disney was stagnating, and new ways had to be found to exploit its revenue-generating potential and regain "Disney dollars." First, however, some exceptional executives needed to be recruited to provide leadership in the financial planning areas of the company, to back up the creative end, which Eisner and Wells would lead.

Eisner had to find the money to finance his expansion plans and to develop new business ventures. In 1985, he hired Gary L. Wilson as executive vice president and chief financial officer and made him a director. Wilson, a project finance specialist, had previously performed the same role for the Marriott, the hotel chain, and had participated in the enormous growth of that corporation. According to Eisner, Wilson's responsibility would be to "plan and implement the company's expansion programs, including internal development and acquisitions."[3] With the team set, Eisner began to change Disney.

THEME PARKS AND RESORTS

Eisner began to take a long hard look at the theme-park business. It was Disney's biggest moneymaker, but revenue growth had been slow. How could he revitalize this division's strategy? He looked at the customer groups and segments that Disney was serving. Was Disney targeting the right segment, and, moreover, what kind of product was Disney really offering?

Eisner soon discovered that 70 percent of theme-park attendance was repeat business and that more than anything else what brought people back time after time were new attractions and new novelties, not the price of the attractions. However, developing new attractions was expensive. Developing a new ride cost millions—thus the importance of corporate sponsorship. Could the price of attendance be increased to provide the revenue to finance new attractions and business ventures, or would a higher price drive customers away?

Going against the conventional wisdom that higher prices would reduce attendance, Eisner raised admission prices substantially. The result was a small falloff in attendance and a huge increase in revenues. Essentially, he had discovered that the Disney theme parks have a captive audience. When he raised the entry price again (prices rose 45 percent in two years), revenues again dramatically increased with little falloff in attendance. In fact, the increase in theme-park prices caused a 59 percent growth in company revenues and accounted for fully 94 percent of earnings growth in 1986. Pre-tax profits of Disneyland and Disney World rose by 38 percent by September 1985—to $266.4 million from $192.7 million a year earlier. This revenue provided much-needed cash for the expansion of Disney attractions and for hotel development. It is still the source of the turnaround in Disney profits.

Eisner set about revamping the theme-park concept to find ways of increasing Disney's revenues and to regain "Disney dollars" from other firms. On the

---

[3]*The Wall Street Journal,* August 9, 1985, p. 14.

theme-park side, Eisner realized that what was needed was (1) more kinds of attractions and more rides inside existing theme parks and (2) additional theme parks, or "gates," which are new collections of attractions. Competition was developing at Orlando as other entertainment companies opened attractions to capitalize on the presence of tourists. For example, Wet 'N Wild, offered a wide variety of water rides, and Sea World had opened a theme park at Orlando. The popularity of active, physically oriented attractions was accelerating. Recognizing the possibilities of such an attraction and hoping to recapture revenue, Disney planned Typhoon Lagoon. It opened in 1989 to major success and provided a reason to stay an extra day in a Disney hotel.

Disney looked for new "gate" ideas to capture tourists' imagination. In this effort, it was helped by a rival, MCA, which announced that it would build, near Orlando, Universal Studios Florida, a theme park similar to the Universal Studios park in southern California. Eisner, never slow to recognize an opportunity, rushed to come out with an alternative. Disney and MGM jointly announced that they would build on the Orlando site the Disney-MGM Studios Theme Park, which would open in 1989. The Disney-MGM park opened to enthusiastic crowds on time, ahead of Universal's park, which was not planned to open until 1990. So popular was the Disney-MGM park that Disney announced that it would double in size by 1992.

Disney is actively searching for a fifth "gate" at Disney World. There is speculation that it might take the form of a zoological park, but as of 1991 the project was being kept secret.

In the effort to wrest tourist dollars from the Orlando competition, Disney did not ignore shopping and night-time entertainment at Disney World. At night, many Disney guests were leaving Disney World to eat and play in the entertainment district of Church Street Station in Orlando. The keep patrons on the site, Disney built Pleasure Island on its land. This complex of shops, bars, restaurants, discos, and nightclubs has been very successful and provided a new dimension to the Disney experience.

Finally, the company looked at the food concession business. At Disney World and Disneyland food concessions had previously been licensed to other companies, which provided the food and paid Disney a percentage of the proceeds. Eisner realized that this practice was another source of revenue loss; and as leases and agreements expired, the Disney company began to take over all the food operations at the theme parks. Not wanting to get into the soft-drink business or the photography business, however, Eisner was content to make lucrative deals allowing Coca-Cola and Kodak to be the sole suppliers of soft drinks and film products at Disney theme parks.

Meanwhile, Eisner was ignoring neither the Magic Kingdom nor EPCOT Center at Orlando. New attractions were constantly being announced. *Captain EO,* a $17-million 3-D music video starring Michael Jackson, was developed for EPCOT Center. Also The Living Seas exhibit sponsored by United Technologies and The Wonders of Life sponsored by Metropolitan Life Insurance Company had been opened. A $32-million attraction, Star Tours, a spaceship ride, was developed with George Lucas, of *Star Wars* fame, for the Disney-MGM Studios Theme Park. Production of a ride based on the exploits of Indiana Jones was also planned.

At Anaheim, too, attractions were coming thick and fast. In 1985, Eisner announced a collaboration with George Lucas for a Star Wars attraction at Disneyland, and many additional Lucas attractions followed. In 1988, the company announced plans for Splash Mountain at Disneyland—passengers ride replicas of hollowed-out logs down huge slides populated with Disney characters. Moreover, in 1989, the company bought Henson Associates Inc., the originators of the Muppet characters, and new attractions based on Kermit the Frog and Miss Piggy are planned. Under Eisner, the cast of Disney characters constantly increases at the Disney theme parks.

The Imagineering Unit

The source of new attractions and theme-park development is Disney's Imagineering Unit. Started by Walt to actualize his ideas, the unit became responsible for all technical advances involving the design and building of Disney's new rides. In the early 1980s, when the company was experiencing problems, consideration had been given to closing this unit to save money. Under Eisner, however, the budget of the unit has been increased dramatically, and it is the source of new adventures and attractions. The Imagineering Unit cooperated with George Lucas to develop the Star Wars attractions. It also planned EPCOT Center and the Disney-MGM attraction, and it was involved in the planning for the Tokyo Disneyland and the new $2-billion EuroDisneyland. The Walt Disney Company sells the skills of this division to other interested parties. For example, Disney agreed to build a $40-million exhibit on the history of space flight for the Johnson Space Center in Houston, Texas.

Hotel and Theme-Park Developments

In developing new attractions, Eisner and his team had other moneymaking ventures in mind. Disney guests (as Disney visitors are called) needed somewhere to stay; moreover, if there were many attractions to see, they would need to stay for several days. Here was an opportunity: Disney would get into the hotel business in a big way and build luxury hotels to meet guests' needs. At Anaheim, but principally in Orlando, the new strategy went into operation. At Disney World, Eisner got his team together to discuss plans for exploiting the vast untapped land and resources on the Orlando site. Eisner realized that Disney was offering far more than eight hours of live entertainment. It could also offer a total package of Disney fun: guests could live inside a Disney world, eating, sleeping, and breathing Disney. In the years since Disney World had been built, several luxury hotels and convention facilities had been built on the boundaries—for example, the Hyatt Regency Grand Cypress and the Hilton at Walt Disney World Village. Eisner and Wilson planned to win back the hotel and food dollars for the Disney company.

They embarked on an ambitious campaign. Disney would build not one but many luxury hotels on the Orlando site, and each hotel would offer a different kind of experience to Disney guests. Then, each time guests returned, they could stay at a new Disney location and never leave Disney World. In quick succession hotels like the Grand Floridian Beach Resort and the Caribbean Beach Resort were opened. Both of them, like the other Disney hotels, enjoyed occupancy rates of over 90 percent, well above the industry average of 65 percent. Moreover, Disney built major new convention centers and hotels to reclaim the convention trade that it had let the Hyatt and Hilton corporations seize. Near EPCOT Center Disney opened four new luxury hotels, including the Walt Disney World Dolphin and the Walt Disney World Swan, which together have over 2,350 rooms and 200,000 square feet of convention space.

Using Wilson's skills, Disney management has found the ideal formula for building hotels without putting a financial debt burden on the company. As it does with Disney films, management arranges limited partnerships to finance, in this case, the Disney hotel-building program. The large hotel chains are often brought in to actually run the hotels. For example, a partnership formed by Tischman Realty and Construction, Metropolitan Life Insurance Company, and Aoki Corporation financed the Dolphin and the Swan. The Dolphin is run by the Sheraton Corporation, and the Swan is run by Westin Hotels. Providing land and the Disney name and continuing this investment strategy, Disney expects to develop 10,000 more hotel rooms by 1992. The proximity of Disney hotels and convention centers to the Magic Kingdom, EPCOT Center, and the Disney-MGM Studios Theme Park gives Disney a major advantage over the competition.

At Disneyland, Eisner's hotel and attraction development strategy was hampered by the fact that Disney did not own much of the land surrounding the park. At Disneyland, the Disney company owned a small undeveloped tract just barely big enough to contain a new "gate" or a hotel complex. But if there was no room to build hotels, maybe Disney could acquire some hotels. The previous management team had licensed the rights to use the Disney name for a hotel. The result was the Disneyland Hotel owned by the Wrather Corporation. Disney acquired a large stake in Wrather and then took over the whole operation in 1989. Disney revamped the Disneyland Hotel to upgrade it to the luxury class, carrying on the Orlando strategy.

As a part of this deal, Disney also gained control of Wrather's Long Beach entertainment complex, which consisted of the liner the *Queen Mary,* run as a hotel; Howard Hughes's *Spruce Goose* plane, the largest ever built; and an entertainment village. Disney revamped the liner as a luxury hotel complex. Eisner then realized that this complex could become Disney's second California "gate": tourists could stop at this attraction on their way to or from Disneyland. Moreover, there was all the revenue going to Sea World and Knotts Berry Farm to compete for. In 1990, Disney announced a proposal to develop the Long Beach site as the center for a Disney Sea theme park, a water-based attraction. Disney Sea will contain the largest aquarium in the world, a glass cage where tourists can go down among the sharks, and many other water-oriented rides and attractions such as Captain Nemo's submarine from *20,000 Leagues Under the Sea* (another Imagineering Unit project). Will there soon be another Disney-MGM Studios tour on the same site or in Disneyland?

Eisner also began to consider ideas for new theme parks abroad. Disney already had participated in the planning of a Disneyland outside Tokyo, Japan. It opened in April 1983 and was wildly successful. However, in that venture Disney had taken no financial stake and, pursuing its old strategy, had licensed the Disney name to a group of Japanese investors in return for 10 percent of the gate receipts and 5 percent of other proceeds. This arrangement had cost Disney much loss in profit. Now Eisner was actively considering an idea for a Disney theme park somewhere in Europe to capture the vast European market.

After much planning and up-front negotiations with several European countries, in December 1985 Eisner announced the decision to build what became a $2.1-billion EuroDisney theme park and resort complex, modeled on the Disney World concept, about twenty miles east of Paris in a suburb called Marne-la-Vallée. It opened in 1991. Disney owns 49 percent of the park; the other 51 percent is held by a company consisting of French and European investors. Disney will receive fees for operating the park and royalties on admissions, rides, food, and other operations; but the French company will control the entire project. Plans are being made for a Disney World kind of complex where, along with the Magic Kingdom, there will be Disney hotels, shopping centers, golf courses, and convention facilities to ensure that Disney is capturing all the dollars in related entertainment activities—in short, the whole successful Eisner formula.

The result of these developments on Disney theme-park revenues can be seen in Exhibit 2.

Competition in the Theme-Park Industry

Disney is by far the biggest of the theme-park companies and the most profitable. While expanding "gates" and attractions, Disney has challenged the competition. Disney Sea is a new rival for Sea World. In both California and Florida, Sea World will be competing against an expanding Disney presence into water-related entertainment. The opening of Typhoon Lagoon hurt Sea World's Orlando operation, for example.

In addition, Disney has been having a running battle with MCA, the owner of the Universal Studios tour. Sidney Sheinberg, the president of MCA, claims that his company was the originator of the idea for the Universal Studios tour in Orlando but Disney took the idea and ran with it. Competition between the

EXHIBIT 2   Consolidated statement of income (in millions, except per share data)

Year ended September 30	1989	1988	1987
Revenues			
Theme parks and resorts	$2,595.4	$2,042.0	$1,834.2
Filmed entertainment	1,587.6	1,149.2	875.6
Consumer products	411.3	247.0	167.0
	4,594.3	3,438.2	2,876.8
Costs and expenses			
Theme parks and resorts	1,810.0	1,477.2	1,285.3
Filmed entertainment	1,331.1	962.9	745.0
Consumer products	224.2	113.3	69.7
	3,365.3	2,553.4	2,100.0
Operating income			
Theme parks and resorts	785.4	564.8	548.9
Filmed entertainment	256.5	186.3	130.6
Consumer products	187.1	133.7	97.3
	1,229.0	884.8	776.8
Corporate expenses (income)			
General and administrative	119.6	96.0	70.3
Interest expense	23.9	5.8	29.1
Investment and interest income	(67.4)	(58.9)	(49.0)
	76.1	42.9	50.4
Income from continuing operations before income taxes	1,152.9	841.9	726.4
Income taxes	449.6	319.9	334.1
Income from continuing operations	703.3	522.0	392.3
Discontinued operations, net			52.4
Net income	$ 703.3	$ 522.0	$ 444.7
Earnings per share			
Continuing operations	$ 5.10	$ 3.80	$ 2.85
Discontinued operations			.38
	$ 5.10	$ 3.80	$ 3.23
Average number of common and common equivalent shares outstanding	138.0	137.4	137.8

Source: The Walt Disney Company, *Annual Report*, 1989.

Disney-MGM Studios Theme Park and Universal Studios Florida will heat up in the coming years. Moreover, after Disney announced that it would build a studio tour on its EuroDisneyland site, MCA announced that Universal would open one in Paris or London. Other competitors include Six Flags and Busch Gardens. The newest Orlando "gate" might bring Disney into direct competition with them.

Disney's expansion into hotels has also brought the company up against the major hotel chains. Competition is likely to be fierce if there is a falloff in demand for hotel rooms.

FILMED ENTERTAINMENT

While Eisner and his team were revamping the theme-park strategy, Eisner was also working on plans for a turnaround of the motion picture and television business.

When Eisner took over Disney in 1984, Disney executives were apologizing for the success of their movie *Splash* because it was not traditional Disney family entertainment. Eisner, however, as head of children's entertainment at ABC, had recognized changing trends in viewing habits and realized that new definitions of family entertainment were possible in the 1980s. Times had changed, and the family of 1985 was not the family of 1965. At Paramount, Eisner had been involved in many of the studio's huge successes. It was he who had seen the potential of *Raiders of the Lost Ark, Airplane,* and *Terms of Endearment,* all of which became blockbuster movies.[4]

At Disney, Eisner capitalized on this experience and, with Jeff Katzenberg (head of Disney's movie division), began to fashion Disney's new strategy. Katzenberg, also a Paramount veteran, was known as the "golden retriever" because of his ability to sniff out the right scripts.[5] He also is a workaholic who makes hundreds of two-minute phone calls a week to producers, directors, and others. At Paramount he was reputed to have said, "If you don't come in on Saturday, don't bother to come in on Sunday."[6]

By 1984, Disney had only a 4 percent share of box office revenues for its movies. Its movie division was losing money and had become a drain on company resources. The problem facing Eisner and Katzenberg was how to turn around the division. On the financing side, to lessen the burden on Disney and to reduce the fear of failure, Eisner negotiated an agreement with Silver Screens Management Inc. to raise money to finance Touchstone movies. Silver Screens agreed to sell limited partnerships to outside investors who would put up the money to finance Disney movies. In return, the investors would receive a percentage of a movie's subsequent revenues. By 1985, $193 million had been raised to finance fourteen new Disney movies.

With the financing in place, Eisner and Katzenberg moved to change Disney's film selection strategy. Luring talented people away from Paramount, Eisner quickly approved *Down and Out in Beverly Hills,* which grossed $62 million. To keep costs low, he focused on signing stars, such as Bette Midler and Richard Dreyfus, who at that time were not box office draws, and he added to the

[4]"Michael Eisner's Hit Parade," *Business Week,* February 1, 1988.
[5]"Disney's Magic," *Business Week,* March 9, 1987.
[6]*Time,* April 25, 1988.

production schedule films that were vehicles for their talents. Disney boasts that while other studios spend $16 million per movie, it spends about $11 million. Low cost is the hallmark of Eisner's strategy. Such films as *Stakeout* and *Outrageous Fortune* have been the result.

By 1987, Disney had captured 14 percent of the $4.2-billion movie market. The turnaround had been achieved. Film operations had become the fastest growing part of Disney operations. By 1987, Disney had turned the $10-million loss of 1984 into a huge profit.

The next part of Eisner's movie strategy involved deals for the distribution of movies to television and for videocassette sales. Disney had always distributed its own movies to theater chains through its Buena Vista Distribution subsidiary and had captured the profit rather than giving it to outside distributors. Eisner planned to use the same strategy for film distribution to television.

In 1985, the Walt Disney Company formed a new television division and hired yet another Paramount executive to head the division, orchestrate the sale of movies to television networks, and handle videocassette sales.[7] In 1986, Showtime/The Movie Channel signed an exclusive agreement to buy cable television rights for movies produced by Touchstone Films through 1990.[8] The deal started with *Down and Out in Beverly Hills* and involves over fifty movies. Disney reportedly receives from $3 to $5 million per film. Although very expensive for The Movie Channel, this deal has benefited both parties.

Eisner also went ahead with videocassette sales. He decided to release one classic a year. In 1986, for example, 1 million copies of *Sleeping Beauty* were sold. Small wonder that Disney's stock price increased by five times between 1983 and 1986. Disney is also vigorously expanding foreign sales of videocassettes.

On the television front, Disney also went through a major turnaround. Eisner moved quickly to exploit Disney's resources. First, he arranged for syndication of twenty-nine years' worth of *Wonderful World of Disney* material, cartoons, and feature films on the new networks emerging with the advent of cable television. Three packages of material put up for sale in 1987 helped to double film revenues. This market had previously been ignored.

Then, Eisner moved to make more product for the small screen. For the adult audience, *The Golden Girls* was developed. A new format was devised for *Siskel and Ebert at the Movies*. Eisner brought back *The Disney Sunday Movie* and introduces it every week, and he arranged for the development of *Duck Tales* and *Gummie Bears,* animation series to take advantage of Disney's animation skills. These cartoons, shown on afternoon television, have proved immensely popular. There were failures, however. Two series introduced in 1986, *The Ellen Burstyn Show* and *Sidekicks,* were quickly abandoned. Meanwhile, under new management The Disney Channel was doing somewhat better. Competition for subscribers is fierce in the pay TV industry, but Disney had made some headway.

[7]*The Wall Street Journal,* March 16, 1985.
[8]*The Wall Street Journal,* April 25, 1986.

By 1986 its subscriber base had grown 27 percent, to almost 3.2 million; by 1988, to 4 million.

In 1989 came another move in the television market. Disney acquired KHU–TV, a Los Angeles television station, and renamed it KCAL–TV. This takeover gives Disney a wholly owned distribution outlet for the products of its studios, so it will capture some of the value currently earned by its end users. Earlier, Disney tried but failed to acquire the 360-screen Mann theater chain (bought by Gulf and Western) and a New York television station (bought by MCA). Disney also approached CBS to buy CBS Records but was spurned by the CBS board, which eventually sold the record division to Sony. Despite these setbacks, expansion into the television station market and movie theater market is a Disney goal. As Eisner said, "We are going to be awfully conservative in what we go after, but if there was something out there that could add value to this company, we're going to go for it."[9] The search for new assets is part of Eisner's strategy to reduce Disney's heavy dependence on theme parks and movies for operating revenues.

By 1987, Walt Disney was number two (after Paramount) in share of box office revenues with 14 percent. Twenty-two of the twenty-three films produced by Disney have made a profit, a ratio far higher than the industry ratio of about 3 in 10. Then came such hits as *Three Men and a Baby,* which grossed over $160 million, *Good Morning Vietnam* ($110 million), and *Cocktail* with Tom Cruise. Disney also introduced two more animation movies—*Who Framed Roger Rabbit,* which, departing from the Disney formula of keeping costs low, cost $38 million, and *Oliver and Company.* As a result of these films, Disney took the box office lead from Paramount in 1988 with 22 percent of revenues through Labor Day, the end of the summer film season.

At the beginning of 1989, Disney established a third motion picture company, called Hollywood Pictures. It gave charge of this company to Ricardo Mestres, former president of production at Touchstone and a mega-performer in his own right. To finance between twenty-four and twenty-eight movies a year, another Silver Screens partnership was established and $600 million was raised.

By the end of 1989, Disney was the market leader with almost 20 percent of box office revenues as a result of successes like *The Little Mermaid* and *Oliver and Company.* The change in the revenues and profits of the filmed-entertainment division is given in Exhibit 2. Exhibit 3 shows Disney's balance sheet.

CONSUMER PRODUCTS

The final area that Eisner turned his attention to was improving revenues from the licensing of the Disney name to firms that wished to manufacture and sell products based on the Disney characters. Eisner would have been happy to see a

---

[9]*Business Week,* March 9, 1987.

EXHIBIT 3   Consolidated balance sheet (in millions)

September 30	1989	1988
Assets		
Cash	$ 380.8	$ 428.0
Marketable securities	662.3	668.6
Receivables	908.5	561.5
Merchandise inventories	224.3	159.9
Film costs	443.3	211.0
Theme parks, resorts and other property, at cost		
Attractions, buildings and equipment	4,143.3	3,322.5
Accumulated depreciation	(1,217.3)	(1,065.2)
	2,926.0	2,257.3
Projects in progress	407.4	511.1
Land	63.9	53.3
	3,397.3	2,821.7
Other assets	640.7	258.2
	$6,657.2	$5,108.9
Liabilities and stockholders' equity		
Accounts payable and other accrued liabilities	$1,011.4	$ 698.7
Income taxes payable	250.9	204.3
Borrowings	860.6	435.5
Unearned royalty and other advances	912.7	823.3
Deferred income taxes	577.6	587.8
Stockholders' equity		
Common stock, $.10 par value		
Authorized—300.00 million shares		
Outstanding—135.3 million shares and 133.2 million		349.6
shares	392.8	
Retained earnings	2,651.2	2,009.7
	3,044.0	2,359.3
	$6,657.2	$5,108.9

Source: The Walt Disney Company, *Annual Report*, 1989.

mouse or duck on every T-shirt, every wrist watch, and every toy or piece of baby equipment in every home in every country in the world. He started off by developing deals with major manufacturers and retailers. Disney signed an agreement with Mattel, a large toy manufacturer, to sell Disney-brand infant and preschool toys worldwide. In 1987, Disney signed a ten-year agreement with Sears to develop clothing and toys using certain Disney characters. By 1988, Disney had negotiated over 3,000 agreements with companies to manufacture over 14,000 Disney-licensed products.

Meanwhile, in 1987, the company announced plans for a large-scale expansion into retailing stores that sell nothing but Disney products produced by Disney's manufacturers. The stores sell videotapes of Disney films, children's clothing, toys, and other Disney paraphernalia. Disney hopes to have 100 stores in operation by 1992.[10] Each store is proving very profitable, and malls are fighting to attract a store.

In 1988, Disney bought Childcraft Education Corporation for $52 million. Childcraft sells educational toys and play equipment by direct mail. This purchase complements Disney's mail-order catalog sales operation, which sends out over 6 million catalogs a year, and has expanded product offerings by over 50 percent.

Given the move into mail-order and retail operations, it seems as though Disney is looking to become the Sears of the entertainment business. An important benefit to Disney from the store and catalog sales is the intangible brand-name loyalty they create for other Disney ventures. The stores are a marketing vehicle for Disney; they open up the Disney company to the public, and invite attendance at Disney theme parks and hotels.[11]

International sales of Disney products are extremely important to the company. For example, every year Japanese consumers buy over $1 billion of Disney-brand products. In Italy, the Mickey Mouse comic book, *Topolino,* sells 700,000 copies a month, and when Disney took over publishing the comic itself, it made an extra $15 million a year in profits. Videocassette sales and records are major revenue earners for Disney worldwide. In 1989, Eisner pointed to the internationalization of all Disney franchises as the source of the massive gains in the revenues of the consumer products and home video operations.[12]

Another expanding dimension of Disney's business is publishing. Disney licenses *Mickey Mouse Tales,* and *Duck Tales* to Welch Publishing. It planned the publication of *Disney Adventure Digest,* to be the official magazine of "Disney Afternoon," two hours of syndicated programming that began appearing in the fall of 1990 each weekday afternoon. The *Digest* has a planned circulation of 100,000. Many more magazine opportunities are being explored, as are books to accompany Disney movies. For example, many books were planned around Disney's successful *Dick Tracy* movie in 1990. Publishing provides new opportunities for Disney to exploit the linkages between its products. The consumer products division will mastermind international publication and sales of Disney books and magazines, a market that is likely to increase with the opening of Euro-Disneyland. In 1990, Disney sold more than 500 million books and comics worldwide.[13]

Another venture for Disney involves selling its organizational culture, which is centered on providing high-quality customer service. Disney University at Orlando puts all new recruits through a three-day program designed to make them familiar with the Disney way of doing things. Recruits learn the history of the Walt Disney Company, its mission, and its emphasis on courtesy to maximize

[10]*The Wall Street Journal,* December 23, 1987.
[11]*Advertising Age,* November 28, 1988, p. 46.
[12]The Walt Disney Company, *Annual Report,* 1989.
[13]*Folio,* April 1990, p. 57.

guests' satisfaction. This emphasis is very important given that over 70 percent of visitors are repeat customers. New employees learn the Disney language: employees are known as "cast members"; visitors are known as "guests"; and employees are said to be "on stage" when they are working and "off stage" when they are not. Disney sells its public relations expertise and its techniques to major companies. So far, over 3,000 executives from over 1,200 companies have attended a two-day Disney seminar called "Traditions" in order to learn Disney techniques so that they can improve the quality of customer service in their own companies. One of the central aims of the Disney approach is to "empower" employees so that they try to solve problems themselves as and when they occur rather than turn for help.[14] The secret to Disney's success is "pixie dust," which is a combination of training and communication and care.

DISNEY'S FUTURE

As a result of these developments, from 1984 to 1989 sales jumped from $1.46 billion to $4.59 billion, net profit rose from $97.8 million to $703.3 million, and earnings per share increased more than 10 times. The annual increase in profit was 46 percent in the 1980s. Nevertheless, Eisner and Wells have vowed to increase profits by an average of 20 percent in the 1990s. To do so, they are constantly expanding the range and scope of Disney activities as well as building on the base they have established. A new Disneyland theme park somewhere in Asia is in preparation, a new studio tours park next to EuroDisneyland is planned, as is a new theme park in southern California. New attractions based on recent successes are planned, including one designed around Dick Tracy. And Eisner has announced that Disney will have thirty hotels with over 26,000 rooms by 1995.

Observers are wondering whether Eisner and his team can maintain this growth rate and whether the company may be headed for a fall. Most of Disney's revenue comes from (1) theme parks and (2) film operations. Observers point out that increases in the price of gasoline and airplane fuel could adversely affect theme-park attendance. They also point out that historically no movie studio has been able to maintain an unbroken string of successes.

Observers also question the wisdom of Disney's current projects and the way in which the culture of the Walt Disney Company under Michael Eisner is evolving. Critics claim that there is an overabundance of conceit among Eisner and his team, who act as though they believe they can do no wrong. Eisner has been called an egomaniac—albeit by arch-critic Sidney Sheinberg, president of rival MCA—and is said to be in search of ever-greater opportunities to expand the Disney empire.

Already the largest entertainment company in the world, the Walt Disney Company is now exercising its muscle as its seeks to enlarge its share of the

[14]*Marketing News*, January 8, 1990.

television station market. But, critics ask, is such expansion wise? Disney can already sell its existing film products to the networks. Does it need the added burden of owning television stations? Eisner is looking around for new acquisitions, and CBS has been mentioned as a possible takeover target. Would the takeover of CBS add value to Disney? Critics speculate that it would add value to CBS, but perhaps not to Disney. They also wonder about some of Eisner's other projects.

In 1990, Disney announced the opening of a new record division, Hollywood Records, to produce records for the general public, not just the Disney audience. This move brought it into direct competition with huge record companies like CBS Records, which Disney bid for but did not acquire.

Disney's huge expansion into the hotel business is justified if occupancy rates stay above 90 percent. But is the resort market becoming saturated; are too many luxury hotels and conference centers being built? Any downturn in the vacation market for whatever reason might put severe pressure on hotel operations.

Against opposition from his own team, Eisner has embarked on the concept of a Disney fast-food restaurant simultaneously offering a wide array of food and exploiting the Disney cartoon characters. This is a relatively new business area for Disney, although the company operates restaurants in its own theme parks. Does Disney have the core skills to compete in the highly competitive $65-billion fast-food industry currently dominated by big chains like McDonald's and Burger King?

Moreover, although guests may like to eat, sleep, and breathe Disney on their vacations, do they want to do so 365 days a year? Is there a danger of overexposure as children wear Disney clothes, read Disney books, watch Disney television programs, sleep in Disney beds, play with Disney toys, and eat Disney food? Will there be a reaction; will people turn from Disney to new forms of excitement and fantasy? However, where would they go? Disney has co-opted George Lucas and his characters and has bought the Muppets and in films like *Dick Tracy* has captured more characters. It seems that right now Michael Eisner can force the golden goose to keep on laying golden eggs. But if the environment changes, if the film division falls on hard times, or if his new projects fail to meet expectations, the supply of eggs might stop.

FIRST GREYHOUND, THEN GREYHOUND DIAL, NOW THE DIAL CORPORATION

On June 4, 1990, John Teets, the chairman, president, and chief executive officer of Greyhound Dial Corporation, learned that Greyhound Bus Lines, the bus transportation company that he had sold in 1987, had declared bankruptcy. Although the final cost of this bankruptcy would not be known until the business and its assets had been sold, Teets was forced to take a one-time $100-million loss to establish a reserve for losses related to the bankruptcy, and the value of the 22.5 percent stake in Greyhound Bus Lines that Teets held was rather questionable. This disaster came about as the last in a series of problems that had plagued Teets while he attempted to improve the fortunes of the Greyhound Dial Corporation.

When the company had changed its name to Greyhound Dial in February 1990, to distance itself from the ill-fated Greyhound Bus Lines, he had been pleased to report an improvement in Greyhound Dial's fortunes—an increase in 1990 revenue and net income. Now Greyhound Dial was reporting a loss, and its share price was plunging as analysts wondered whether Teets would ever be able to improve the company's profitability. The price of Greyhound Dial stock had been more or less unchanged for the last six years, as Teets had consistently failed to reach his goal of 15 percent return on equity. If Teets could not solve these problems and increase Greyhound Dial's profitability, several analysts believed that the company might again be the target of a corporate raider because

This case was prepared by Gareth R. Jones, Texas A&M University. Copyright, Gareth R. Jones, 1991.

it was valued at more than twice its stock price. As a step toward this goal, Teets once again changed his company's name, in March 1991, to the "Dial Corporation" to reflect its new mission.

GREYHOUND BEFORE TEETS

In 1981 John Teets succeeded Gerry Trautman as the chief executive officer of the Greyhound Corporation. Although this was an appointment that Teets had worked hard for over the years, he succeeded a man who had changed Greyhound from a single-business bus transportation company in 1966 to a diversified conglomerate with extensive transportation, manufacturing, food, consumer products, financial, and service interests. The challenge facing Teets was to manage Greyhound's diverse businesses so that he would be able to achieve at least a 15 percent return on equity. However, many problems on the horizon might hinder the achievement of this goal. Some were the direct consequence of Trautman's ambitious expansion and diversification efforts. Others resulted from changes in environmental factors and consumer preferences. Still others stemmed from internal inefficiencies that Teets hoped he would be able to remedy. To understand the problems that Teets faced, it is necessary to look at Trautman's strategy for Greyhound Dial.

Greyhound's Early History and Growth

At the end of 1981, when Trautman turned over the driver's seat to Teets, Greyhound had the second most-recognized trademark and logo in the world, behind only those of Coca-Cola. However, Greyhound had not always been so well known. The company was founded in Hibbing, Minnesota, in 1914. Its first business was providing bus transportation to carry miners to work at the Mesabi Iron Range. Because Greyhound was the sole provider of bus service for these workers, it was immediately successful: in its very first year the new corporation started expanding its routes and acquiring interests in bus companies operating near Chicago. For the next sixteen years the young company continued purchasing interests in bus companies, extending its route structure from New York to Kansas City. In 1930 the name Greyhound Corporation was adopted, and the now-familiar running-dog logo was painted on the buses.[1]

For the next twenty-seven years Greyhound continued to acquire bus interests in order to consolidate its routes and link its various bus operations. Growth proceeded sometimes by purchase, sometimes by stock swaps, and sometimes by merger; but the result was always the same to the traveling public: it saw

[1]*Moody's Transportation Manual*, 1987.

more and more of the familiar running dog. By 1960 Greyhound had substantially achieved its objective of operating a bus system that could carry passengers to most destinations in the continental United States and Canada.

By 1962 Greyhound was facing the prospect of increasingly limited opportunities to expand its route system, which now spanned the continental United States and Canada. The bus operations, however, were generating large sums of excess cash, which could fund expansion into new businesses. Thus Greyhound's board of directors decided to diversify into operations outside of the bus transportation industry.

In 1962, Greyhound began the program of acquisition that still forms the basis of its present operations. It solidified its bus-manufacturing operations into Motor Coach industries, which became the foundation of Greyhound Dial's Transportation Manufacturing operating division. Also, in 1962, the corporation acquired Boothe Leasing Company, an enterprise that specialized in equipment leasing. Boothe Leasing was renamed Greyhound Leasing and Financial Corporation (GLFC) and became the core around which Greyhound's Financial Services operating division was to be built. Thus, by the end of 1963, Greyhound Corporation was operating in three major businesses: bus transportation, bus manufacturing, and financial services. The bus-manufacturing unit supplied buses to the bus transportation unit, as well as to other bus companies.

Trautman's Acquisitions Between 1966 and 1970

Gerry Trautman was appointed CEO in 1966, and he wasted no time in accelerating Greyhound's new strategy for expansion and growth.[2] From Trautman's installation as CEO until 1970, Greyhound acquired more than thirty widely different companies and formed a new operating division, Services, which specialized in managing transportation-related businesses, such as Border Brokerage Company, which operated two duty-free shops at the Canadian border, and Florida Export Group, which also handled duty-free commerce. In addition, Services included Manncraft Exhibitors, a company that specialized in building displays for major exhibitions; Nassau Air Dispatch, a Caribbean shipping company; and Freeport Flight Services, a Bahamian aircraft-servicing business. Trautman also brought in a line of cruise ships in the Caribbean, the Bahama Cruise Line Company.[3] Then he added Ford Van Lines of Lincoln, Nebraska, a company specializing in furniture moving; Red Top Sedan Service, a Florida limousine service; Texas, New Mexico, Oklahoma Coaches, Inc., and Carey Transportation, two regional intercity bus lines; Trade Winds Transportation Co. of Hawaii, another intercity bus carrier; Washington Airport Transport, a commuter carrier from the Washington, D.C. suburbs to Dulles Airport; and Gray Line New York

[2]A. Stuart, "Greyhound Gets Ready for a New Driver," *Fortune*, March 3, 1986, pp. 34–38.
[3]Greyhound Corporation, *Annual Reports*, 1966–1970.

Tours Corporation, a sightseeing bus line. Furthermore, he added Hausman Bus Parts to the bus-manufacturing unit.[4]

Not all the companies that Trautman acquired proved to be as profitable or as manageable as he had hoped. What he was looking for was value as well as some synergy with Greyhound's existing transportation activities. However, as the acquisition process continued, synergy became a secondary objective. When Trautman became dissatisfied with an acquisition, he would divest it as quickly as he had acquired it, and many companies were spun off. Near the end of his tenure as CEO, Trautman would boast that Greyhound had achieved "diversification within diversification."[5] What he meant was that in his view the operating groups had become diversified, so that each individually was recession-proof and all were enhancing the financial strength of the holding company.

Trautman's boldest maneuver and biggest acquisition came in 1970. He acquired Armour & Co., a large conglomerate that had many diverse business interests in food and consumer products. Trautman paid $400 million in cash, notes, and stock to take over Armour, which was primarily a large meat-packing company with more than $2 billion of sales in marginally profitable businesses. However, Armour also had interests in pharmaceuticals, cosmetics, and consumer products, such as soap, through its very profitable Dial Division.

Trautman knew that it appeared as though he had overpaid for Armour-Dial. However, he soon reduced the price of the acquisition by selling off, for some $225 million, a number of Armour divisions that he considered to be peripheral to Armour's core food and consumer businesses. In 1977 he sold off Armour's pharmaceutical division for $87 million, reducing Greyhound's net investment to $88 million.[6] What remained after the divestitures were Armour's food operations and Armour's Dial Division, from which would emerge Greyhound Dial's Consumer Products operating division.

Trautman hoped that his new acquisition would be more recession-proof than the bus business, if not countercyclical to it. However, the Armour acquisition brought to Greyhound new businesses that had management problems of their own—in areas where Greyhound had no experience, such as the price of pork bellies, cycles for meat packers' contracts, and foreign competition.

Trautman's Acquisitions and Divestitures Between 1970 and 1978

For the next eight years, Greyhound under Trautman continued buying businesses and increasing the size of the operating divisions in its corporate portfolio. By 1978 Greyhound's holding company consisted of five operating divisions: Transportation, Bus Manufacturing, Food and Consumer Products, Financial,

---

[4]Greyhound Corporation, *Annual Reports,* 1966–1970.
[5]Greyhound Corporation, *Annual Report,* 1980.
[6]"Greyhound: A Big Sell-off Leaves It Built for Better Speed," *Business Week,* July 25, 1983, pp. 88–90.

and Services/Food Service. Each of these operating divisions acquired many new businesses, so Greyhound was undergoing "diversification within diversification." Many of the new acquisitions, however, were failures. Businesses as diverse as a chicken hatchery; a European acquisition to expand Financial; the Caribbean Gray Cruise Line, Ltd.; VAVO Greyhound N.V. of Schoonhoven, Netherlands; Shannon-Greyhound Coaches; and Hausman Bus Parts proved unprofitable.[7]

Greyhound's portfolio of businesses kept changing during this period, and Trautman continued to feel that he was shaping a diversified company that would have a powerful base in many lines of business. He was willing to take the risk of acquiring some companies that would be failures as long as the overall health of the company was strengthened. However, Greyhound became more and more distant from its core business, bus transportation.

In April 1978 Trautman engineered another major acquisition by acquiring 97 percent of the stock of Verex Corporation, the largest private insurer of residential mortgages in the United States. The Verex acquisition was intended to strengthen the operations of Greyhound's Financial operating division. Verex insured first mortgages on residential real estate generally having loan-to-value ratios in excess of 80 percent. Verex was headquartered in Minneapolis but wrote insurance business in all fifty states and the District of Columbia.

By 1978 Greyhound had grown nearly as large as it would grow under Trautman's leadership. The collection of businesses that he had assembled—some by acquisition, some by internal growth, and some by selling off pieces of larger businesses—was designed to make Greyhound more resistant to economic downturns. The activities of Greyhound's five major operating divisions are summarized below.

Transportation   This operating division comprised the Intercity Services Division and the Travel Services Division. Transportation operated regularly scheduled passenger bus service between most metropolitan areas in North America and engaged in related operations, such as package shipping, sightseeing services, airport ground transportation, and deluxe tour and charter bus services. The Intercity Services Division primarily consisted of Greyhound Lines, Inc., and its Canadian subsidiary. It provided the largest intercity bus transportation system for passengers, baggage, express parcels, and mail in the United States and Canada. The Travel Services Division provided sightseeing operations in the Canadian Rockies. Other interests of this division were ground transportation services to and from airports at Detroit, Honolulu, Miami, Orlando, and Phoenix.

Bus manufacturing   The largest maker of intercity buses in North America, Bus Manufacturing had operations that were vertically integrated to fabricate bus shells of intercity design, assemble buses, and manufacture bus parts for final assembly. In addition, this operating division warehoused and distributed replacement parts to meet its own requirements and the larger requirements of the bus

[7]Greyhound Corporation, *Annual Reports,* 1970–1978.

industry. Greyhound Bus Manufacturing was the principal U.S. supplier of buses to charter operators and sightseeing companies.

Food and consumer products   The companies in this operating group manufactured and marketed products to independent retailers under private-label arrangements and distributed several products under their own trademarks. These trademarks included Dial, Tone, and Pure & Natural soaps, Armour Star and Armour Tree canned meat and meat food products, Dial antiperspirants and shampoos, Appian Way pizza mixes, Parsons' ammonia, Bruce floor care products, Magic sizing and prewash, and Malina handknitting yarns and needle products.

Services/Food Service   Companies in this operating division provided a broad range of services directed primarily to business markets, although duty-free shops located at airports and on cruise ships were targeted toward the consumer market. Greyhound Convention Services (GCS) specialized in designing, fabricating, warehousing, shipping, and setting up exhibits for trade shows, conventions, and exhibitions. GCS also served as a decorating contractor at conventions and trade show sites. The food service division, generally known as Greyhound Food Management (GFM), served approximately 400 locations in industrial plants, bus terminals, airports, office buildings, schools, colleges, and other facilities. It operated cafeterias in the United States and Belgium and provided fast-food restaurants, catering, and machine-vended services. Furthermore, GFM operated gift shops, retail shops, drugstores, newsstands, and auto-truck plazas. Another company in this operating division, Greyhound Support Services, provided housekeeping, food service, and other support services for large construction projects to industry and government agencies throughout the world.

Financial   This operating division consisted of Greyhound Computer Corporation, a company specializing in computer leasing and sales in the United States, Canada, Mexico, and Europe; Greyhound Leasing and Financial Corporation, a company specializing in worldwide industrial equipment leasing; Pine Top Insurance, an entity that reinsured commercial property and provided excess casualty insurance for large policyholders; and Verex Corporation, the leading private insurer of highly leveraged residential mortgages for primary lenders. Travelers Express Company, Inc., another company in Financial, specialized in providing traveler's checks and check-cashing services in 32,000 retail establishments and financial institutions in the United States and Puerto Rico. This company also provided draft-clearing services for more than 2,300 credit unions and savings and loan associations, making it the largest private-sector provider of such services.

Together, those five operating divisions were generating combined revenues of nearly $4.5 billion. Trautman had accomplished his objective of using profits from the bus operations to move Greyhound into other businesses.

TRAUTMAN SELECTS TEETS TO TAKE OVER GREYHOUND

Serious problems became apparent at Armour when the Food and Consumer Products operating division went from a profit of $22 million in 1979 to a loss of $1.7 million in 1980. Armour's problems came at a very inconvenient time for Trautman because he had planned to retire in 1980. Trautman wanted to solve Armour's problems while he kept business rolling at Greyhound's other groups and prepared a successor to take over the collection of companies that he had assembled. That successor was to be John Teets.

Teets was very different from Trautman. His background did not include Harvard Business School or law practice. Instead Teets had learned to be an effective hands-on manager by staying as close to the action as possible. He had worked for his father's construction company but decided that he wanted to operate a restaurant. He borrowed money, started his own restaurant, and quickly made it successful. However, soon after he had paid back his loan money and his restaurant was earning a profit, it burned to the ground. In search of a new business opportunity, Teets answered a newspaper advertisement about a position managing a Greyhound food service concession stand at the New York World's Fair in 1964.

After joining the Services/Food Service operating group, Teets quickly distinguished himself as a tight-fisted cost cutter who could make money on a miserly budget. He seemed to have a talent for squeezing every last penny out of everything he managed. Teets moved up quickly, gaining a reputation as an extremely effective manager. By 1975 he was put in charge of the Food Service group, which primarily operated a conglomeration of marginally profitable, obscure, franchised restaurants. His aggressive management style produced quick results, and in 1980 he was named the outstanding executive in the food industry. Also in 1980, in addition to his responsibilities as CEO of the Food Service group, Teets was named head of Armour in place of Trautman.

In 1981 Armour's major problem, as Teets saw it, was its paying from 30 to 50 percent more in wages and fringe benefits than its competitors. Teets asked Armour's unions for immediate wage concessions. He told the unions that if he failed to get these concessions he would have to start closing plants. After a bitter strike, wage concessions in excess of 15 percent were obtained, and with cost cutting from plant closings and more efficient operating procedures, it looked as though Armour had bought itself some time.

With Armour running more efficiently, the bus business cruising along on excess profits because of the recession and energy crunch in 1979–1980, and Financial operating division profits being generated by high interest rates in the early 1980s, it looked as though the stage was set for Trautman's retirement. In fact, all that remained to be done was to formally select a successor. It was not difficult for Trautman to make up his mind about who should be his successor. He was impressed with Teets's successes in managing the Services/Food Service group and also with the way in which Teets had dominated Armour's labor unions.

TEETS SEEKS SOLUTIONS

Although 1981 was Greyhound's most profitable year, Teets was concerned about whether Greyhound could remain as profitable in what appeared to be a more competitive and uncertain marketplace. Even though Greyhound's return on equity had hit 14.6 percent (after dropping from 15.2 percent the previous year), it had averaged only 12.2 percent since 1978. This was less of a return than investors could earn by simply putting their funds in a certificate of deposit or in an aggressive money fund. Teets knew that to be safe from a takeover bid, Greyhound would have to earn at least a 15 percent return on shareholders' equity. Achieving this objective might mean divesting businesses that seemed least likely to attain this return on equity in the next few years and that could be run better by other companies. Teets intended to achieve a 15 percent return on equity. He proceeded to position the holding company to divest itself of businesses that could not achieve a corporate-wide standard of a 15 percent return on equity.[8]

On taking over as CEO of Greyhound Corporation, Teets confronted two major problems that caused him to feel uneasy about the corporation's overall profit picture. The first problem was Armour's high production cost, which made it a weak competitor. The second was the challenge faced by Greyhound Bus Lines: the need to compete in a newly deregulated bus transportation market. He knew that if he did not find solutions for these two problems they would seriously diminish Greyhound Corporation earnings. The contribution of each operating division to Greyhound's total sales revenues in 1981 is presented in Exhibit 1.

Dealing with Armour's High Production Costs

Having been president of Armour, Teets was very familiar with the division's problems: its high production costs, the reluctance of union leadership and rank-and-file workers to agree with Greyhound's assessment of Armour's problems, and its utter inability to successfully change its marketing orientation in order to compete effectively. In addition, Teets was concerned about Armour's inefficient plants and the volatility of hog and pork belly prices, which cyclically depressed Armour's slim earnings. Although it had turned around its 1980 losses, Armour was still able to earn only $9 million. Furthermore, this profit came not from continuing operations but rather from the sale of assets after the closing of four of Armour's seventeen plants. The 1981 profit of $9 million represented a profit margin of less than 0.39 percent on sales of more than $2.3 billion.[9] Teets sensed that it was not going to be easy to make Armour a low-cost leader. Armour was

[8]"Greyhound's New Strategy: Slimmed Down and Decentralized, It's After More Market Share, 15% on Equity," *Dun's Business Month* (February 1984), 66–68.
[9]"Greyhound: A Big Sell-off," pp. 88–90.

EXHIBIT 1   **Greyhound in 1981**

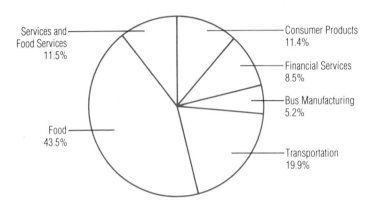

Total Revenues $5.16 Billion

Services and Food Services 11.5%

Consumer Products 11.4%

Financial Services 8.5%

Bus Manufacturing 5.2%

Food 43.5%

Transportation 19.9%

Source: Data from Greyhound Dial Corporation, *Annual Report,* 1990.

saddled with a middle management that was less than entrepreneurial, many outmoded plants, and a recalcitrant meat packers' union that intended to protect its
high-cost labor pact.

Confronting a Deregulated Bus Business

Teets was also concerned about the 1981 passage of House bill H.R. 3663, which
deregulated the intercity bus business. Greyhound Bus Lines had based its route
system on the competitive conditions that had existed in the earlier business environment. Teets, however, sensed that future success in the bus business would
be based not on the extensiveness of Greyhound's route system or on its fifty
years of experience in operating in a reguIted industry but on its ability to make
money by charging competitive fares.

With the beginning of deregulated competition in the intercity bus business
and declining passenger revenues resulting from the end of the energy crunch,
Greyhound found itself paying wages and benefits that were from 30 to 50 percent higher than those paid by its competitors. Furthermore, its chief competitor,
Trailways, having negotiated significant wage concessions from the Amalgam-
ated Transit Union, had immediately passed the savings on to customers in the
form of lower fares. Trailway's action was a frontal assault on Greyhound's most
lucrative routes in an attempt to gain market share. Greyhound's response had

been to match every one of Trailway's price cuts. Although Greyhound preserved its market share, it lost millions of dollars.

As Teets saw it, the bus operation's noncompetitive position was a problem that he could not put on hold. Since essentially all other operating costs besides wages—fuel, taxes, commissions, depreciation—were similar to those of all other carriers, the need to reduce wage costs was imperative. So Teets embarked on bitter wage negotiations. The result was a 47-day strike in 1983 and, subsequently, an agreement that included a 7.8 percent wage cut, a freeze on cost-of-living adjustments until May 1986, new employee-paid contributions into pension plans of 4 percent of annual gross wages, and larger employee contributions to health plans. In total, the agreement resulted in an 8 percent cost savings over the next three years. Teets summed up the agreement by saying, "This contract gives us the parity we were seeking and still makes the employees the best paid in the industry."[10]

Armour Foods Sold

Despite a wage freeze negotiated with the United Food and Commercial Workers Union two years before, in 1981 Armour Food Company still could not overcome the wage discrepancy with its competitors in the meat-packing industry. Teets was concerned that stodgy Armour, with its more than $2.3 billion in sales and only $13 million in net income, would always be dragging down Greyhound's prospects for improved profitability. Thus he decided to divest Armour. In preparation for the sale, he separated the Armour Food Company from Armour-Dial. On December 18, 1983, the food company was sold to ConAgra, Inc., for $166 million. With the Armour sale, Teets was chopping off nearly half of Greyhound's business. Nevertheless, even with Greyhound's revenues dropping from $5 billion in 1982 to less than $3 billion in 1984 without Armour, the sale gave Teets the opportunity to put Greyhound in better shape than it had been in years.

The Bus Line Divestiture

For Greyhound Bus Lines, the legacy of deregulation was a total inability to be a low-cost provider of bus transportation. Deregulation had brought about the emergence of lower-cost competitors in regional markets—competitors that were able to be responsive and flexible in pricing and in reacting to Greyhound's actions. As a result, Greyhound lost its competitive edge.[11] In 1986, in an effort to save the bus lines, Teets converted 120 company-owned terminals to commission

[10]"If Anyone Won the Strike, Greyhound Did," *Business Week*, December 19, 1983, pp. 39–40.
[11]"Greyhound's New Strategy," pp. 66–68.

agencies, trimming a huge overhead burden. He also created four stand-alone regional bus companies and a new travel and charter company. Finally, he franchised several of Greyhound's least profitable routes to independent operators, licensing them to use the Greyhound logo and trademark.

However, the one factor that Teets could not control was winning a new labor contract. In February 1986 an offer to freeze wages was rejected by the union. In October, in a deteriorating market, a second offer involving concessions was presented with the understanding that its rejection would prompt the sale of the company. The offer was subsequently rejected, and fifteen days later Teets announced the sale of Greyhound Bus Lines for approximately $350 million to an investor group headquartered in Dallas. Teets claimed that the actions taken by management in an effort to salvage the bus business were exactly the ones that made it an attractive acquisition for the Currey Group in Dallas.

The sale of Greyhound Bus Lines brought in $290 million in cash and equivalents, including a 22.5 percent interest in a new holding company established by the Dallas investor group. Not included in the sale were twenty-three major downtown parcels of land; Greyhound Lines of Canada; Brewster Transport Company Limited; Texas, New Mexico, Oklahoma Coaches; and the Vermont Transit Co., Inc.[12]

Divestitures in the Financial Operating Division

Besides selling Greyhound Bus Lines in 1987, Teets also sold Greyhound Capital Corporation (GCC). The decision to sell GCC reportedly reflected Teets's conviction that "some businesses just fit better into Greyhound's plans than others."[13] What this statement really meant was that GCC had become an underperformer in the face of lowered interest rates and changes in the tax laws that disallowed investment tax credits. GCC was sold for $140 million, realizing a one-time gain of $79.7 million for Greyhound.

In early 1987 Greyhound announced its intention to sell Verex. The timing of the acquisition had been a disaster given the recession in the real estate market caused by the oil bust in the early 1980s. Verex suffered huge losses generated by insurance claims from business generated before 1985. These claims were originating in states where severe downturns in farming, auto production, and oil drilling had led to a widespread inability to keep up with mortgage payments.

Not surprisingly, Teets could not find a buyer for Verex. In January 1988, Greyhound announced that it had stopped taking applications for new mortgage insurance and that it was discontinuing its mortgage insurance business. It also announced that 1987 results would reflect a one-time after-tax charge of $45 million as a result of reclassifying Verex as a discontinued operation; then Greyhound

---

[12]Greyhound Corporation, *Annual Report*, 1986.
[13]Ibid.

would manage Verex's existing portfolio to minimize continuing losses from the company's operations. Management hoped that the remnants of Verex would not be a drain on corporate resources.

With the sale of Greyhound Bus Lines, Greyhound Capital Corporation, and Armour, and the discontinuation of Verex, Teets announced that he was near the end of his mammoth task of restructuring Greyhound and shedding businesses that seemed to lack sufficient growth potential. By late 1987, Greyhound Corporation was primarily a consumer products and services company. Exhibit 2 summarizes the contribution of the different operating groups to total revenues in 1988. Compare the Greyhound Corporation that Teets structured (Exhibit 2) with the corporation that he inherited in 1982 (Exhibit 1).

TEETS'S NEW MOVES

With the restructuring in place, Wall Street looked for an improvement in Greyhound's performance. However, it soon became obvious that the stack of businesses created by Teets was not proving much more profitable than the ones he had divested. There was only an 8.8 percent return on equity in 1987, and net income after nonrecurring losses was $25.1 million, the lowest for many years. Revenue was $2.5 billion. Teets maintained that the problems with Greyhound's various divisions could not have been foreseen as the restructuring was taking place but that Greyhound was set for "substantial profits in the future." Teets

EXHIBIT 2   **Greyhound in 1988**

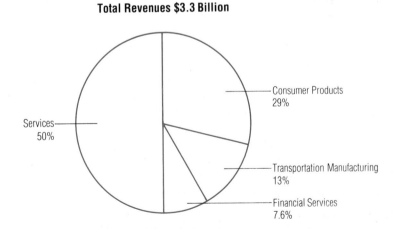

Total Revenues $3.3 Billion

- Consumer Products 29%
- Services 50%
- Transportation Manufacturing 13%
- Financial Services 7.6%

Source: Data from Greyhound Dial Corporation, *Annual Report,* 1990.

began a program of acquisitions and new product developments to strengthen Greyhound's presence in the four business areas identified in Exhibit 2 and begin the turnaround process.

Consumer Products

In the midst of the divestiture of Armour and Greyhound Bus Lines, Teets had made one major acquisition. On February 21, 1985, Teets announced the purchase of Purex Industries and its thirty household cleaning products for $264 million. Teets's aim with this acquisition was to boost profits in Greyhound's Consumer Products operating division (principally composed of the old Dial Division) by using the Dial sales force and marketing expertise to sell Purex products—Purex bleach, Brillo soap pads, Old Dutch cleanser, and Sweetheart and Fels-Naptha soap, among others.

The Purex acquisition drew mixed reviews from Wall Street. It did not meet Teets's goal of a 15 percent return, but Teets believed that it would by 1988. Analysts were also unimpressed with the purchase because Greyhound had not been successful in managing Armour. Teets responded that Dial was capable of marketing consumer products, although it had not been successful at developing its own lines. He cited as evidence the fact that Dial was marketing the number-one deodorant soap in its Dial brand. Analysts did concede that Teets should be able to realize increased profitability by using the same sales force to sell Purex and Dial products. Along with Purex's household cleaners, Greyhound also got Elio's pizza as part of the Purex acquisition. Teets was enthusiastic about expanding this frozen pizza business nationwide from its East Coast base. This was to be done by means of the Dial sales force.[14]

With the divestiture of Armour, the Dial Corporation, as it was now known, became the center of Teets's attention and the flagship of the Greyhound Corporation. In the past Dial had not had much success in launching new products, but Teets was determined to change that situation, recognizing that growth in revenue had to come from the manufacture and marketing of new products. The first product introduced by the Dial Corporation was Lunch Buckets, a range of microwaveable meals with a stable shelf life of two years. This was a new market segment. Previously all microwaveable meals had been frozen. Lunch Bucket meals were very successful and surpassed early expectations by a wide margin. By 1988 they had national distribution. By 1990 they had seized a 30 percent market share, becoming the market leader. In 1990, Dial announced new low-calorie Lunch Buckets.

Another new product introduced in 1987 was Liquid Dial antibacterial soap. This product too was very successful, and by 1990 it had achieved a 20 percent market share and was the second-best-selling liquid soap in the market, after

[14]S. Toy and J. H. Dobrzynski, "Will More Soap Help Greyhound Shine?" *Business Week*, March 11, 1985, pp. 73–78.

Procter and Gamble's Ivory Liquid. Another successful new product was Mountain Fresh Dial, a highly scented version of Dial deodorant soap. Additional developments were liquid Purex washing powder and other cleaning products.

In 1988, Teets acquired the household products and industrial specialties businesses of the 20 Mule Team division of United States Borax and Chemical Corporation. Teets announced a new advertising campaign to re-establish the market presence of Borax bleaches and cleaning powders.

Teets's formula for increasing Dial Corporation market share called for "further extensions of the Dial brand, further extensions of the Purex brand name, Parsons' ammonia working in those various regional markets. Finding new products that fit in those product niches that will augment the major shares that we have already, that will have a high enough dollar price on them to add to our income."[15] Teets's marketing plan called for close attention to the Dial Corporation's sales pattern by region and by market. This involved tailoring marketing programs and sales programs to the regions. The success of this targeted marketing strategy was shown in 1990 when Greyhound Dial scored first in a survey measuring the impact that advertising had on raising consumers' awareness of consumer products companies. The profit margins on consumer products were worrying Teets, however, because competition made it very difficult to raise prices. Instead, "The question is can we become more productive in the way we make the product? That's where it's going to have to come from—either through new equipment, new computerization, that area."[16]

In September 1990 another Consumer Products acquisition was announced: Breck hair care products. Breck had 1989 revenues of $60 million. Teets announced that integrating Breck into Dial would result in annual sales of over $1 billion for the Dial Corporation. Teets said that "Breck has been a household name for 60 years. It's a perfect fit with our other Dial products, and under Dial management the power of the Breck name will flourish."[17] Under its previous owners, Breck had languished. Teets hoped to turn the product around by applying Dial's marketing skills.

From the changes he had orchestrated Teets was hoping for sizable revenue growth and profit in the Dial Corporation. In June 1990, he announced that in the second quarter Dial had achieved a 22 percent increase in operating income (see Exhibit 3).

Services

By 1987, Greyhound's Restaura dining service was contributing the most to total revenues. It was natural, therefore, that Teets should seek to strengthen food operations. In 1987, Greyhound purchased the nation's second biggest airline

[15]"The Greyhound Corporation," *Wall Street Journal Transcript,* February 5, 1990, pp. 96, 204.
[16]Ibid.
[17]Greyhound Dial News Release, September 10, 1990.

EXHIBIT 3   **Financial statement**

(000 omitted)	Quarter ended June 30,		Six months ended June 30,	
	1990	**1989**	**1990**	**1989**
Greyhound Dial Corporation and subsidiaries	**Summary of consolidated income (unaudited)**			
Revenues	$912,318	$925,460	$1,777,822	$1,767,249
Greyhound Dial and non-financial group subsidiaries:				
Income before income taxes	$ 49,583	$ 46,090	$ 70,829	$ 67,435
Income taxes	19,520	18,487	28,987	28,936
	30,063	27,603	41,842	38,499
Net income of financial group	9,097	8,045	14,208	11,985
Income from continuing operations	39,160	35,648	56,050	50,484
Discontinued operations (Note 1)— Loss provision (net of $51,500 tax benefit) resulting from bankruptcy of Greyhound Bus Lines	(100,000)		(100,000)	
Net income (loss)	$(60,840)	$ 35,648	$ (43,950)	$ 50,484
Net income (loss) per common and equivalent share (dollars):				
Income from continuing operations	$ 0.97	$ 0.92	$ 1.39	$ 1.30
Discontinued operations	(2.51)		(2.51)	
Net income (loss)	$ (1.54)	$ 0.92	$ (1.12)	$ 1.30
Average outstanding common and equivalent shares (000 omitted)			39,809	38,440

catering and airline retailing business. The new operation had three units: Dobbs International Services, the nation's second largest provider of in-flight meals for airlines; Dobbs Houses, the operator of restaurants at many airports; and Carson International, which operated the food and beverage concession at Chicago's O'Hare Airport. In 1990, Teets announced that Dobbs had had a record year— the company had served 60 scheduled airlines in 40 cities; in addition, it had added five new accounts, including Houston International Airport.

Of Greyhound's food service businesses, Teets commented, "I see major changes in the food service business. We are exiting the service businesses that require a great deal of marketing, i.e., pizza and hamburger businesses. And, Greyhound is now primarily in the contract feeding business, be it Dobbs Houses or Restaura, our in-house catering business. Our operations in airports are primarily captive audiences. We also perform contract feeding for General Motors, IBM, office buildings and banks."[18]

[18]"The Greyhound Corporation," pp. 96, 204.

(000 omitted)	Quarter ended June 30,		Six months ended June 30,	
	1990	1989	1990	1989
Supplementary information—revenues and operating income of principal business segments				
Revenues: Consumer products	$246,867	$243,425	$ 490,807	$ 468,262
Services	444,612	418,846	852,405	795,844
Transportation manufacturing and parts	153,489	185,820	303,239	363,914
Financial	67,350	77,369	131,371	139,229
	$912,318	$925,460	$1,777,822	$1,767,249
Operating income: Consumer products	$ 30,651	$ 25,124	$ 49,403	$ 41,467
Services	41,608	35,128	63,144	58,044
Transportation manufacturing and parts	8,498	21,647	20,552	38,161
Financial	12,503	12,180	19,442	17,557
	$ 93,260	$ 94,079	$ 152,541	$ 155,229

Reclassifications have been made in revenues and operating income of principal business segments in all periods presented to combine the company's intercity coach and transit bus replacement parts sales and distribution activity (previously classified in the Services segment) with the transportation manufacturing activity (previously a separate segment) to form the Transportation Manufacturing and Parts segment.

Notes to Summary of Consolidated Income:
(1) On March 18, 1987, Greyhound Dial sold substantially all its domestic intercity bus transportation business to GLI Holding Company (GLI Holding), a new company headed by a Dallas investor group, resulting in Greyhound Dial's classification thereof as a discontinued operation. GLI Holding's principal subsidiary, Greyhound Bus Lines, filed for bankruptcy protection on June 4, 1990, as the result of a work stoppage which began March 1, 1990, and strike-related violence.
Greyhound Dial retained 22.5 percent of the common stock of GLI Holding, the parent of Greyhound Bus Lines, and also holds Greyhound Bus Lines preferred stock, a junior subordinated note and other notes and accounts receivable, and has substantial assets leased to the bus lines, as well as other contractual relationships.
On June 4, 1990, Greyhound Dial reported that it was providing a one-time charge, attributable to discontinued operations, of $100 million (after-tax), or $2.51 per share, to establish a reserve for losses related to the Greyhound Bus Lines bankruptcy. Greyhound Dial's actual loss will ultimately be determined by future developments including the bankruptcy proceedings and results of the bus line's ongoing business operations.

Source: Greyhound Dial Corporation, *Annual Report,* 1990.

Teets strengthened Greyhound Dial's Travelers Express money-order business with the purchase of Republic Money Orders, Inc., of Dallas. This acquisition made Greyhound Dial the leader in the money-order business, ahead of the U.S. Postal Service. Teets had returned to the cruise-ship industry in 1984 with the takeover of Premier Cruise Lines. In 1986, he negotiated an agreement with the Walt Disney Company making Premier Disney's exclusive cruise-ship line, with three- and four-day sailings to the Bahamas from Cape Canaveral in Florida. The cruise-lines business enjoyed record sales, and in 1989 another line was added. In June 1990, Teets announced that Greyhound Dial's other businesses in the Services operating division, such as Greyhound airport services, were enjoying steady growth and that operating income in this division had increased by 18 percent. Exhibit 3 shows the increase in revenues of the Services operating division.

Transportation Manufacturing

To strengthen the Transportation Manufacturing operating division, Greyhound purchased General Motors' unprofitable transit bus-manufacturing and bus-replacement business in 1987 and planned to produce a new model bus, the RTS, in its New Mexico coach plant. Record orders for the new bus were received in 1988 and 1989; however, the strike at Greyhound Bus Lines and its subsequent bankruptcy in 1990 severely damped down earnings. For the six months ending in June 1990, compared to the six months ending in June 1989, operating income dropped from $38 million to $21 million. Clearly, Greyhound Dial's dependency on bus operations had not ended with the sale of Greyhound Bus Lines.

Financial Services

After the disastrous Verex acquisition, the focus of Greyhound Financial Corporation (GFC) changed. Through its two major lending divisions, Commercial Finance and Real Estate Finance, GFC extends secured financing to middle-market commercial clients, like radio and television stations whose needs may be too small to attract the attention of large financial institutions.[19] It supplies services related to refinancing, recapitalization, and acquisitions funding. In 1989, the Financial Services operating division wrote $580 million of new business. Its combined net finance portfolio was approaching $2 billion by 1990.

THE NEW LOOK OF GREYHOUND DIAL

The new look of Greyhound Dial's businesses after the divestitures and acquisitions is shown in Exhibits 4, 5, and 6. Teets acknowledged the wide diversity of businesses in the company's portfolio. However, he contended that the businesses do fit together. In his words, "We are a multiservice business. We operate in niches and were number one or two in most of those niches. From a recession standpoint, I think we're going to feel it less than most major companies."[20] Teets argued that Greyhound Dial was making acquisitions to strengthen its presence in existing niches. By concentrating on a niche, the corporation avoided going head to head with major competitors. Moreover, the niches were recession-proof—small-ticket items like Lunch Buckets and soap, not refrigerators and cars. Teets argued that Greyhound Dial was positioned for growth and that man-

[19]Greyhound Dial, *Annual Report,* 1989, p. 16.
[20]"The Greyhound Corporation," pp. 96, 204.

EXHIBIT 4   **Greyhound's businesses**

Consumer Products	Services	Transportation Manufacturing	Financial Services
The Dial Corporation	Brewster Transport Company, Ltd.	Motor Coach Industries (MCI)	Greyhound Financial Corporation
Food	Consultants and Designers, Inc.	Transportation Manufacturing Corporation (TMC)	Greyhound Financial and Leasing
Personal Care	Carson International, Inc.	• Custom Coach	Greyhound Financial Services, Ltd.
Laundry and Household	Dobbs Houses, Inc.		Greyhound Bank PLC
	Dobbs International Services, Inc.		

Greyhound Airport Services Companies

Greyhound Exhibitgroup, Inc.

Greyhound Exposition Services, Inc.

Greyhound Food Management, Inc.
- Faber Enterprises, Inc.
- Glacier Park, Inc.
- GFM Engineering and Design Group
- GFM Fast Food Division
- GFM Public Service Division
- GFM Truckstop Systems
- Restaura
- Restaura, S.A.

Greyhound International Travel, Inc. (GITI)

Greyhound Leisure Services, Inc. (GLSI)
- Florida Export Warehouse
- International Cruise Shops
- Greyhound Leisure Services Duty-Free Shops
- Premier Cruise Lines, Ltd.

Greyhound Lines of Canada, Ltd.

Travelers Express Company, Inc.
- Republic Money Orders, Inc.

Universal Coach Parts, Inc.

Source: Greyhound Dial Corporation, *Annual Report,* 1990.

agement expected revenues to increase steadily over the next few years. Some analysts, however, felt that the organization was still a hodgepodge of different businesses and was still in need of rationalization. They pointed to the lack of fit between a cruise-ship line and hotel operations in Glacier National Park and contract catering, saying that Greyhound Dial was still a collection of companies with no real connection. They also argued that Greyhound Dial's breakup value was over $60 a share while its stock price had been in the range of $25 to $35 for years. Teets agreed that some minor divestitures were necessary, but he believed that the best way to proceed was to stay in the niches and manage the existing businesses more efficiently.

EXHIBIT 5 Selected financial and other data

	1989	1988	1987	1986	1985
(000 omitted)	**Operations**				
Consolidated revenues	$3,536,851	$3,304,860	$2,501,360	$2,280,736	$2,186,488
Income from continuing operations	$ 108,711	$ 93,308	$ 82,804	$ 15,661	$ 64,836
Income (loss) from discontinued operations			(51,491)	173,144	49,378
Income before extraordinary charge and cumulative effect of change in accounting principle	108,711	93,308	31,313	188,805	114,214
Extraordinary charge			(6,211)		
Cumulative effect to January 1, 1988 of initial application of SFAS No. 96—"Accounting for Income Taxes"		10,750			
Net income	$ 108,711	$ 104,058	$ 25,102	$ 188,805	$ 114,214
(Dollars)	**Income per common share**				
Continuing operations	$ 2.75	$ 2.42	$ 2.10	$ 0.32	$ 1.34
Discontinued operations			(1.32)	3.86	1.02
Extraordinary charge			(0.16)		
Cumulative effect to January 1, 1988 of initial application of SFAS No. 96		0.28			
Net income	$ 2.75	$ 2.70	$ 0.62	$ 4.18	$ 2.36
Dividends declared per common share	$ 1.32	$ 1.32	$ 1.32	$ 1.32	$ 1.26
Average outstanding common and equivalent shares (000 omitted)	39,128	38,065	38,827	44,884	47,933
(000 omitted)	**Financial position at year end**				
Total assets	$5,204,771	$5,033,879	$5,052,958	$4,585,590	$4,826,450
Long-term debt:					
Greyhound and non-financial group subsidiaries	557,095	635,675	889,986	615,198	618,965
Financial group subsidiaries	1,375,861	1,332,767	1,281,222	1,353,938	1,459,638
Total long-term debt	1,932,956	1,968,442	2,171,208	1,969,136	2,078,603
Common stock and other equity	1,074,969	1,002,088	937,051	1,027,488	1,130,692
Book value per common share (dollars)	$ 27.00	$ 26.32	$ 24.80	$ 26.04	$ 24.36
People:					
Stockholders of record	63,440	67,175	70,930	74,194	84,737
Employees (average)	36,835	37,244	29,694	35,922	36,942

(1) Includes net gains (after-tax) on sale of real estate classified as retained assets upon discontinuance of U.S. bus operations of $3,156,000 or $0.08 per share in 1989, $4,644,000 or $0.12 per share in 1988, $4,890,000 or $0.12 per share in 1987, $24,305,000 or $0.54 per share in 1986 and $19,094,000 or $0.40 per share in 1985. Also includes special loss provision of $43,810,000 (after-tax) or $0.98 per share in 1986 and an unusual loss of $19,440,000 (after-tax) or $0.40 per share in 1985.

Source: Greyhound Dial Corporation, *Annual Report*, 1990.

EXHIBIT 6 Principal business segment and geographic information

(000 omitted)	1989	1988	1987	1986	1985
Revenues					
Consumer products	$ 941,537	$ 961,825	$ 866,465	$ 848,867	$ 843,283
Services	1,762,295	1,652,592	1,135,361	975,092	860,071
Transportation manufacturing	564,509	439,551	271,979	193,857	220,891
Financial	268,510	250,892	227,555	262,920	262,243
Consolidated	$3,536,851	$3,304,860	$2,501,360	$2,280,736	$2,186,488
Operating income					
Consumer products	$ 80,522	$ 73,637	$ 69,750	$ 65,350	$ 77,329
Services	140,801	130,821	90,517	79,577	72,491
Transportation manufacturing	50,003	44,189	34,368	17,407	32,909
Financial:					
Before nonrecurring charges	33,128	24,882	17,668	8,483	10,812
Nonrecurring charges				(56,500)	(36,000)
Total financial	33,128	24,882	17,668	(48,017)	(25,188)
Consolidated	$ 304,454	$ 273,529	$ 212,303	$ 114,317	$ 157,541

(000 omitted)	1989	1988	1987	1989	1988	1987	1989	1988	1987
	Assets at year-end			Capital expenditures			Depreciation and amortization		
Consumer products	$ 615,922	$ 636,929	$ 693,322	$ 16,162	$ 29,684	$ 47,790	$ 25,945	$ 25,686	$ 24,397
Services(1)	1,830,160	1,591,218	1,652,414	71,760	71,564	46,191	61,239	59,430	39,602
Transportation manufacturing	300,776	249,514	199,967	16,811	15,379	14,611	8,381	5,834	2,772
Financial	2,050,322	2,104,654	1,986,254	1,642	1,303	1,317	1,288	1,510	1,289
Total principal business segments	4,797,180	4,582,315	4,531,957	106,375	117,930	109,909	96,853	92,460	68,060
Investment in GLI Holding Company and subsidiaries	90,598	87,372	82,588						
Investments in discontinued insurance subsidiaries	196,510	196,868	187,651						
Corporate and other assets	120,483	167,324	250,762	936	3,515	6,168	5,926	8,541	11,769
Consolidated	$5,204,771	$5,033,879	$5,052,958	$107,311	$121,445	$116,077	$ 102,779	$ 101,001	$ 79,829

	1989	1988	1987	1989	1988	1987	1989	1988	1987
	Revenues			Operating income			Assets at year-end		
United States	$3,067,559	$2,864,500	$2,190,186	$251,490	$213,649	$181,808	$4,563,857	$4,252,631	$4,285,483
Foreign	469,292	440,360	311,174	52,964	59,880	30,495	640,914	781,248	767,475
Consolidated	$3,536,851	$3,304,860	$2,501,360	$304,454	$273,529	$212,303	$5,204,771	$5,033,879	$5,052,958

(1) Assets of the Services segment include $830,855,000 (1989), $634,400,000 (1988) and $647,831,000 (1987) of funds and agents' receivables restricted for payment service obligations. Most of the increase in the assets of the Services segment during 1989 relates to the acquisition of Republic Money Orders, Inc.

Source: Greyhound Dial Corporation, *Annual Report*, 1990.

Greyhound Dial has recently gone through substantial downsizing, or what Teets calls "rightsizing." Corporate staff was reduced from 400 to 300 people. Employment at the Dial Corporation has also been reduced, and all Greyhound Dial businesses have been subjected to close scrutiny to try to reduce costs. Teets has also tried to reduce corporate debt, which after reaching a high of $850 million in 1988 was reduced to $557 million in 1989.

However, coming on the heels of improvement in revenues and earnings in 1988 and 1989 was the bankruptcy of Greyhound Bus Lines in 1990 and the poor performance of Transportation Manufacturing. It seems that just when Greyhound Dial is making strides in one operating business, problems in another wipe out the effects of the improvement. With its stock trading at $25 in October 1990—the lowest price in years—investors are wondering about Teets's claims for his recession-proof "niching strategy." Is it working, but is its success being disguised by a series of extraordinary problems like the bankruptcy of Greyhound Bus Lines? Or is the strategy a failure, and would the interest of investors be best served by the breakup of the company?

THE UPJOHN
COMPANY

The Upjohn Company is one of the consistently most profitable pharmaceutical companies in the United States. Its sales and earnings have increased steadily over the last ten years, and the company has become a major player in the global pharmaceutical marketplace. This growth, however, has been achieved only in the face of significant environmental pressures, pressures that are becoming stronger. First, there has been increasing price competition in the health care industry from the rapid growth of generic drug companies. Second, there has been an increase in legislative pressures on new drug development both at home and abroad. Third, there has been an increase in global competition as drug companies vie with each other on a worldwide basis. The problem facing Upjohn's management is how to maintain its growth in the domestic and international markets in the face of this increasing competition and regulatory pressure.

OVERVIEW

The Upjohn Company is a global, research-based manufacturer and marketer of pharmaceuticals, agricultural seeds and specialties, and health services. In 1987 it had research, manufacturing, sales, and distribution facilities in more than 200 locations worldwide. The company generated almost $2.3 billion in sales in 1986, its centennial year. This represented a 13.5-percent increase in sales and a growth in earnings per share of 24 percent over 1985. The five-year, compounded growth rate in earnings per share was 11.93 percent at the close of 1986.

The company is divided into two broad industrial segments: first, Worldwide Human Health Care Businesses, which concentrates on the development, manufacture, and marketing of drug products globally and accounted for almost 82 percent of total sales in 1986; and second, the Agricultural Division, which

This case was prepared by Douglas D. Moesel, Robert F. Elliott, and Gareth R. Jones, Department of Management, Texas A & M University. Information from Robert D. B. Carlisle, *A Century of Caring: The Upjohn Story*, used by permission of Benjamin Company, Inc.

develops and supplies seeds and drugs for use in agriculture and animal production and which accounted for just over 18 percent of company sales in 1986. Globally, that year 67 percent of Upjohn's sales revenues were generated in the United States, 15 percent in Europe, and 18 percent were scattered elsewhere across the world. By 1986 Upjohn's share of the worldwide pharmaceutical market was 1.5 percent, and top management's ambition was to achieve a minimum of 2 percent of the market by 1990. The realization of this goal would move Upjohn from the top fifteen to the top ten drug companies globally.[1]

HISTORY

For the first seventy-three years of its existence, the Upjohn Company was a family-owned and operated, domestic pharmaceutical company. In 1885, W. E. Upjohn was granted a patent on a manufacturing process that produced a "friable" pill. The new pill disintegrated rapidly in the body to speed the release of medication. This friability contrasted with the hardness of many of the mass-produced pills of the day, which often passed through the body without releasing their contents. This manufacturing process and the secrecy that surrounded it fueled the early growth of the company Upjohn founded in 1885 and made it difficult for other companies to imitate the popular product. The founder speeded the company's growth with a policy of selling his pills at about half the price of the old-style, mass-produced pill, generating considerable hostility from competitors in doing so. The company expanded its product line quickly, offering 500 products by 1892 and 2,000 by 1900.

By 1900 the new technology of compressed tablets had begun to gain favor with physicians, and Upjohn had to learn how to imitate the innovations of other companies. Tablets also disintegrated rapidly in the body but were much easier to mass-produce. The company began featuring tablets and created a tablet department to speed product development.

Upjohn was strongly aware of the need to develop marketing strengths to complement the company's research and manufacturing skills in manufacturing process innovations. Realizing early that the profit potential from mass produced tablets would be low, he emphasized the need to develop and market quality-based, high-price drug products that would give higher profit margins. Perceiving the company as operating in a luxury market, he had the insight to switch its focus from pills to tablets and to emphasize product characteristics. For example, he pioneered the development of pleasantly flavored drugs to suit consumers' tastes. One result was an important innovation called phenolax, a sweetly flavored laxative. It proved to be a big seller for more than forty years.

---

[1]Robert D. B. Carlisle, *A Century of Caring: The Upjohn Story* (Elmsford, N.Y.: Benjamin Company, 1987), p. 226.

In the next two decades Upjohn added a number of promising research areas. In 1912 bacterial vaccines became part of the company's product line. Activity was begun in endocrinology and digitalis extracts for heart failure in 1914. A pleasant-tasting alkalizer called Citrocarbonate was introduced in 1921 and reached $1 million in annual sales by 1926, the first Upjohn product to do so. This product and the intensive sales effort that accompanied it marked the emergence of the company as a first-class pharmaceutical house. A succession of other introductions followed, including new flavored versions of cough syrup and cod liver oil. Each of these research efforts was stimulated by a perceived need to respond to the demands of the medical community for improved drug products.

Upjohn was always sensitive to the needs of its main "distributors," the doctors who prescribed its products. An aggressive sales push directed toward pharmacists and doctors helped the company to grow through the tough 1930s and into the years of World War II. The Medical Department was created in 1937 by a member of the founding family, Gifford Upjohn, to upgrade company contacts with physicians. This focus became a hallmark of sales efforts at Upjohn. Through the decades that followed, the company continued to differentiate its products and match its sales strategy to the changing composition of the medical profession.

Much of the company's growth through the 1930s and 1940s was tied to vitamins. Upjohn was the first to produce a standardized combination of vitamins A and D in the United States, in 1929. Vitamins accounted for half of the $40 million in sales in 1945 and marked the company as a leader in nutritional supplements. Other products critical to Upjohn's growth included Kaopectate, estrogenic hormone products introduced in the 1930s, and antibiotics and an antidiabetic drug brought out in the 1940s and 1950s.[2]

By 1952 the Research Department had 421 employees, who viewed their research output as second in quality only to that of Merck & Co. among domestic pharmaceutical companies. The department began to establish broad research areas, which were still important in the 1980s: antibiotics, steroids, antidiabetes agents, nonsteroidal inflammatory drugs, and central nervous system agents.

The progress of the company's research efforts led to increasing demand for customized chemicals to manufacture new drug introductions. The company had purchased standardized chemicals in the past, but the growing need for unique materials led to the establishment of Fine Chemicals Manufacturing in 1949 to supply the company with its own products. The chemical division also expanded into external sales, and by 1984, 40 percent of its production was for other companies.

After World War II, the Upjohn Company continued a modest export program, sending most of its foreign sales representatives to Central and South America. The creation of the Export Division in 1952 was the first strong corporate signal that management was committed to competing globally. The

[2]Carlisle, *A Century of Caring*, pp. 13–99.

division was formed in reaction to the globalization strategies of the leading domestic drug companies, which recognized the potential in developing a worldwide market for their products.

In 1958 the twenty-member board of directors, eleven of whom were related directly or by marriage to the founder, voted to recommend public ownership. The following year, the Upjohn Company was formally accepted for listing and trading on the New York Stock Exchange. The decision to go public did not end the involvement of the extended family of the founder, W. E. Upjohn, but it did give the company the additional financial resources it needed to become a stronger force in the global pharmaceutical market.

The company continued to expand its international scope quickly to include sales subsidiaries in Canada, London, and Australia. Through the 1960s and 1970s, it added more subsidiaries and sales offices and built two major production facilities outside the continental United States: one in Belgium in 1963 and the other in Puerto Rico in 1974. By the mid-1980s these plants, in combination with the principal facility in Kalamazoo, Michigan, produced pharmaceuticals for sale in more than 150 countries.

Upjohn's first large venture out of pharmaceuticals came via its entry into animal health products in the late 1940s, when it repackaged several human products, such as antibiotics, for animal use. New products specifically for animals began flowing in 1952, and a sales force to veterinarians was established, growing from one person in 1956 to twenty in 1957. The sales force gradually increased to 130 by the mid-1980s.

Other agricultural products were added over time. After deciding against entry into fertilizers, the company acquired its core seed company, Asgrow Seed Company, in 1968 to develop new, improved strains of seeds. It added another top-ten domestic seed company, O's Gold, in 1983. The latter was chosen because its sales force and products complemented Asgrow's. In 1974 Upjohn acquired Cobb Breeding Corporation, a producer of chicken broiler breeders, to continue its expansion into animal drugs. In 1986 the company formed a joint venture with Tyson Foods, Inc., to further expand its broiler operations.

Nonagricultural diversification began in the 1960s. The company started manufacturing polymer chemical products in 1962, with the purchase of the Carwin Company, which was combined with the Fine Chemicals Manufacturing operations. The company entered cosmetics in 1964, when several other pharmaceutical companies were doing likewise. In 1969 it entered home nursing services when it purchased Homemakers, Inc.

The chemicals business was profitable for many years. After profits peaked in 1979, however, rapid decline set in because of a down cycle in the principal markets for chemicals. The polymer chemicals operation was sold in 1985, but Fine Chemicals Manufacturing was retained. The cosmetics business never proved very profitable and was liquidated in 1974. The home nursing service business was renamed Upjohn Healthcare Services. It quickly added new locations and became the market leader in 1974, a position it has held ever since.

UPJOHN'S ENVIRONMENT

By the late 1970s and early 1980s important changes were reshaping competition in the domestic and global pharmaceutical markets. First, more countries were imposing greater regulation on the drug approval process. In the United States the Kefauver-Harris amendments of 1962 placed major new constraints on pharmaceutical manufacturers. They required that companies set forth substantial proof that a drug was safe and effective before the FDA could allow it on the market. The new drug introduction process became considerably longer and more expensive as a result of this legislation, which was viewed by many as the single most important nonscientific event to affect the industry since World War II.

The Kefauver-Harris amendments marked the beginning of substantially increased regulation of the domestic pharmaceutical industry. As drug approval time was lengthened, valuable years of patent protection were being eroded. The Waxman-Hatch Act of 1984 reflected the tremendous growth in domestic political influence of the Generic Pharmaceutical Industry Association (GPIA).

Another major thrust of the bill was to speed the introduction of generic drugs after patent expiration in order to reduce their price. This put increasing pressure on the profits of the company that developed a new drug. Development costs were estimated to approach $100 million for each new drug introduced in 1986.[3] To placate the large drug companies, the bill guaranteed several drug companies, including Upjohn, the exclusive rights for five years beyond normal patent length to market four major drugs each.[4] These patent extensions were to compensate for FDA's slow handling of drug registrations over the previous few years. However, by the end of 1987 approvals for generic copies of patent-expired drugs were being issued at a very rapid pace, and the large drug companies were experiencing increased price competition on many fronts.

Similar legislative pressures were mounting in many other countries. Between 1981 and 1984 the Japanese government ordered price reductions on drugs averaging 40.1 percent.[5] Such legislation marked an industry trend toward—as Upjohn's President and Chief Operating Officer Lawrence C. Hoff put it—a "two-tier industry with innovators in one group and a large number of generic manufacturers in the other segment, competing fiercely on the sole basis of price."[6]

Many countries had begun protectionist campaigns, restricting drug marketing to products manufactured by the domestic industry. Many foreign companies also benefited from development support from their respective governments, allowing them to avoid the full cost of their research efforts. Furthermore,

---

[3]Carlisle, *A Century of Caring*, p. 24.
[4]"The Last Word," *Drug and Cosmetic Industry*, 135 (October 1984), p. 126.
[5]Carlisle, *A Century of Caring*, p. 233.
[6]Carlisle, *A Century of Caring*, p. 210.

since regulatory procedures, processes, and time orientations differ considerably from one country to another, domestic companies often experienced difficulty in obtaining information on how drugs move through foreign regulatory agencies. Although an attempt to achieve standardization of clinical procedures and disseminate intelligence on postmarketing response of users through an international information network was underway in the mid-1980s, it appeared to be years from fruition.

With increasing competition in research, and increasing difficulty and costs in achieving regulatory approval, drug companies began concentrating their research in specific fields of medicine in order to reduce the cost of developing new drugs. To maintain their profitability, companies began specializing in the world's three most lucrative markets for new drugs: heart disease, anti-inflammatory agents and analgesics, and antibiotics. This concentration of resources by major companies in a few specific areas was suggested by an Upjohn spokesperson to be the cause of the scarcity of new drugs classified as breakthrough developments by the FDA in recent years.[7]

However, the slowdown in drug innovation seems to be on the verge of reversal. The advent of biotechnology is expected to fuel a huge surge in the global pharmaceutical products as cures and medications for major diseases begin to appear. The world market for pharmaceutical drugs is projected to reach approximately $300 billion by the end of the century, in contrast to $80 billion in 1986.[8] The seven largest markets were projected to be the United States, Japan, West Germany, France, the United Kingdom, Italy, and Canada. These markets were expected to demand and have the ability to pay for new drugs treating the five major afflictions of developed nations—cancer, heart disease, chronic pain, infectious diseases, and emotional disturbances.

Although the potential for revenues from developing new drugs to suit the specific disease needs of developing nations is huge, such development carries great risks. These countries lack the funds to provide comprehensive health care, although, compared with the cost of hospitalization, pharmaceuticals are expected to be one of the most cost-effective approaches to health care services for such nations. However, the World Health Organization (WHO) is offering research opportunities for major companies through its funding of research to discover cures for six tropical diseases. Upjohn, with the support of these grants, has chosen to concentrate on the five diseases that are parasitic in nature. Although these diseases are endemic to humans, studying them may have application to Upjohn's agricultural and veterinary medicine research.

Other factors also affect the profitability of the pharmaceutical industry. International currency fluctuations influence overseas expansion. For domestic companies, strong overseas earnings are masked by a strong dollar. With downturns in the dollar in 1987, overseas efforts were expected to reflect more favor-

[7]The Upjohn Company, *Annual Report* (1986), 9.
[8]Carlisle, *A Century of Caring*, p. 226.

ably on earnings for domestic companies. The industry also seems to be subject to increasing levels of litigation as companies try to delay entry of competitors' new products or to protect essential patent rights.

Upjohn faced such a struggle in 1987 with its breakthrough hair-growth product Regaine, based on the ingredient Minoxidil. It filed a claim with the International Trade Commission (ITC) alleging that seven companies in Europe, two in Canada, one in Mexico, and ten in the United States were importing or distributing minoxidil powder, salts, and concentrates in violation of Upjohn patents.[9] The ITC had one year to complete its probe. In addition, a flood of "baldness cures," by being labeled natural products, had avoided classification as drugs and did not undergo the tests of efficacy required of drugs, but the producers of these cures were trading on the hope generated by reports about minoxidil. The effect that these seemingly useless products would have on the market facing Upjohn's Regaine was uncertain. Regaine was still awaiting final FDA approval in late 1987.

CORPORATE STRATEGY

The company's stated pharmaceutical business strategy to the year 2000 is to ensure that it delivers the greatest volume of quality pharmaceuticals to the greatest number of people while maintaining an appropriate return on investment to assure its continued growth. Three goals seem to be particularly stressed: (1) sales growth (with concurrent market share growth); (2) a continuing growth in return on investment; and (3) competition based on high quality rather than low price. Upjohn plans to achieve these goals by directing the company's resources into areas promising the greatest returns. The aggressive nature of this approach is indicated by Upjohn's quest to become one of the top ten drug companies by the 1990s. The company estimates that it will need to better the general market growth by at least 3.5 percent per year in order to attain this position.[10]

Vertical integration has been a part of Upjohn's strategy since its inception. The early process innovations which built the company reflected a desire to improve on the technologies available from external equipment suppliers. Upjohn also pursued backward integration into fine chemicals to support its drug manufacturing activities. To guarantee supplies and quality of inputs, Upjohn Production purchased most of its bulk chemicals from Upjohn Chemicals. By producing its own chemicals, the company could maintain quality control from initial chemical manufacture to the final packaging of its products.

Furthermore, rather than remain simply a drug manufacturer, the company

[9]"Upjohn Patent Complaint to be Investigated by ITC," *The Wall Street Journal,* May 14, 1987, p. 37.
[10]Carlisle, *A Century of Caring,* p. 226.

developed its own research program in the early 1900s and continually increased its research capabilities after that time to support its marketing efforts. The strong integration of research and manufacturing is the primary characteristic that distinguishes the major-brand drug segment from the generic drug segment.

While most major drug companies were acquiring biotechnical businesses in the mid-1980s as a mixed strategy of backward integration and related diversification, Upjohn decided to develop its own. In 1983 Dr. Ralph E. Christofferson, a long-time consultant, was hired by the company, assigned a budget, given a custom-constructed facility, and instructed to hire the best people in the field. The 150-person staff began working with research professionals in Upjohn's other businesses to show them how the new technology could help applied research efforts in both human health services and agriculture. The group also assisted the Chemicals division in gearing up for manipulation and cloning of genes using biotechnical methods.[11]

However, Upjohn has used acquisitions to achieve its strategic objectives of diversification and expansion in health and agriculture. It built the Agricultural Division and the Worldwide Human Health Care Businesses by related acquisitions. The key to Upjohn's success in diversification has been the degree of research synergy achievable among the individual businesses. Furthermore, potential synergies between its health and agricultural interests are becoming increasingly important. For example, although seeds were not closely related to health services at the time of acquisition, top management may have foreseen the biotechnical revolution of the late 1970s and 1980s, which served to greatly increase the research synergies between development of new plant products and new animal or human products.

The most unrelated business in the company in late 1987 was Upjohn HealthCare Services, Inc. The subsidiary has been kept relatively separate from the rest of the company since its acquisition in 1969 and has continued to lead its market. Given the high growth predicted in the home health care market, it is likely to remain successful.

Consistent with its strategy to serve the global pharmaceutical market, Upjohn has developed a manufacturing operations structure based on three tiers of ownership of manufacturing facilities. This has allowed its management flexibility in responding to changes in worldwide demand and governmental regulations. These tiers are the primary tier, where Upjohn owns and operates the facility; the secondary tier, where joint venture facilities are operated; and the third tier, where Upjohn licenses the use of its technologies or chemical formulas to an independent third-party facility, sometimes retaining marketing rights within the respective market.

The first tier concentrates capital investment and advanced technologies in three primary manufacturing facilities located in Kalamazoo, Belgium, and

---

[11]Upjohn, *Annual Report*, p. 6.

Puerto Rico. These plants combine state-of-the-art robotics and manufacturing processes to yield manufacturing economies of scale while allowing strict control over standards of quality. The Belgian location allows reductions in distribution costs for the growing European market, whereas the Puerto Rican site was selected to expand North American production capacity and at the same time receive attractive tax exemptions.

The second tier uses joint venture arrangements, typically stemming from governmental restrictions that require pharmaceuticals sold within a country's borders to be manufactured there. Joint ventures can also arise when a foreign pharmaceutical company develops a successful new drug and seeks a joint marketing arrangement with Upjohn. Joint venturing of the project allows the foreign company to use Upjohn's developmental, production, and marketing expertise, whereas Upjohn typically receives marketing rights for the new product outside of the developing company's native market.

The third-tier production facilities are not owned by Upjohn but are owned and operated by independent third parties utilizing processes and formulas licensed by Upjohn. The same governmental restrictions that explain the use of joint ventures explain the use of third-tier facilities. Besides, it is financially prudent to license rather than own facilities in certain areas of the world because of the risks involved.

Since biomedical research is increasing throughout the world, corporate officers have emphasized the need for a global orientation to research. To facilitate the acquisition of worldwide knowledge, Upjohn is developing research facilities overseas, establishing research centers in Japan and the United Kingdom. Additionally, "Discovery Centers" are being developed, in which Upjohn provides funds and research facilities to university-based scientists near the major centers of learning throughout Europe. This strategy allows Upjohn to achieve a better understanding of worldwide markets, secure access to research funded by foreign governments, gain influence and credibility within foreign markets, and acquire a differing perspective of scientific research through the monitoring of worldwide developments.

Upjohn has used joint ventures not only for manufacturing, but for research purposes as well. Realizing that its major hair-growth product Regaine could use additional developmental expertise for the consumer market, Upjohn announced a joint development project with Procter & Gamble in October 1987.[12] The agreement was to jointly develop ways to make Regaine easier to use and to develop new hair-growth products. Procter & Gamble's experience in formulating creams, gels, and lotions and its knowledge of the hair care market appeared to be the major attractions for Upjohn, even though Procter & Gamble was also sponsoring hair-growth research in England. The companies agreed to share rights to any new hair-growth products they developed.

---

[12]"Upjohn and P&G to Work on Drug Against Baldness," The Wall Street Journal, October 26, 1987, p. 30.

CORPORATE STRUCTURE

Upjohn's corporate structure in 1987 grouped its major business activities into three strategic business units (SBUs) and a central research and development functional unit, known as Scientific Administration. These are shown in Exhibit 1. The SBUs included the Worldwide Human Health Care Businesses, the Agricultural Division, and Chemicals. The Scientific Administration function is the development unit that serves the SBUs' research and development needs. These and other centrally located support functions report to the Office of the Chairman.

The Chemicals SBU, consisting of 900 employees, primarily serves as a source of fine chemicals for the other two SBUs, predominantly for Worldwide Human Health Care Businesses. It has plants in Kalamazoo and in North Haven, Connecticut. The division also has its own R&D unit, which operates separately from the central R&D group and services the other SBU's process innovation needs when necessary.

The Agricultural Division SBU is organized by its major subsidiaries, including Asgrow Seeds and animal health products. Asgrow is further broken down into a domestic unit and a number of international subsidiaries. Animal Health's international business was grouped both in the Agricultural Division and under the Worldwide Human Health Care Businesses SBU's Upjohn International, Inc., unit.

The Worldwide Human Health Businesses SBU structure in 1987 is shown in Exhibit 2. The five principal units included the Upjohn HealthCare Services subsidiary, the Consumer Products Division, Worldwide Pharmaceutical Manufacturing and Engineering, the Domestic Pharmaceutical Marketing Division, and the Upjohn International subsidiary.

Upjohn HealthCare Services, Inc., is the largest private health care provider in the nation, with 300 North American locations in 1986. The head office is located in Kalamazoo, and two regional financial centers serve as other primary hubs. Each location operates fairly autonomously, with 27 field managers and 1,500 staffers supporting the 60,000 care givers and their 200,000 patients.

The Consumer Products Division was established in July 1986 to sell and promote nonprescription drugs, primarily less concentrated versions of prescription drugs approved for consumer sales. It was moved to this higher level in the company to give it greater representation and stronger support throughout the company. The unit was created mainly because of industry predictions that the market for consumer products developed from prescription drugs would reach $50 billion by the year 2000.

Worldwide Pharmaceutical Manufacturing and Engineering is responsible for all production and facility planning for pharmaceuticals. It is divided into six subunits. These include a special projects group to plan and oversee major construction projects around the world and a licensing group to arrange

EXHIBIT 1   Corporate officers of the Upjohn Company

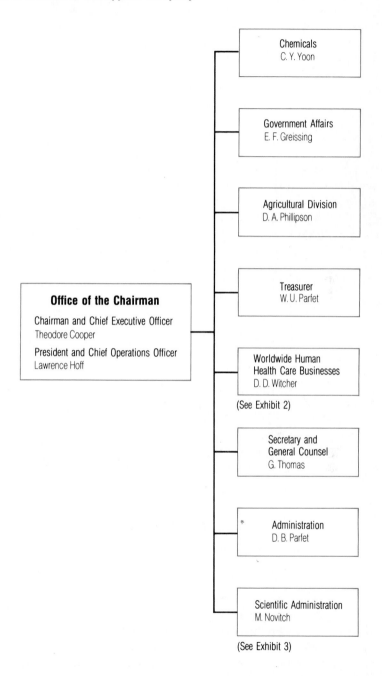

EXHIBIT 2   **Worldwide Human Health Care Businesses**

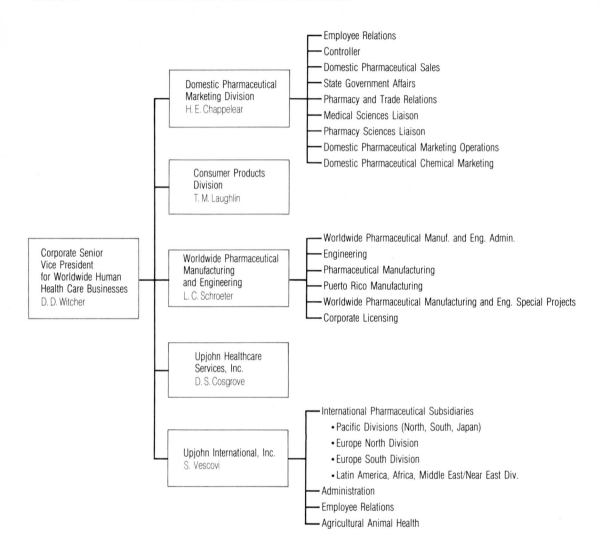

authorization and interact with other companies licensed to produce and market one of Upjohn's patented products.

The Domestic Pharmaceutical Marketing Division is responsible for sales and marketing of chemicals and prescription drugs in North America. Special offices were formed to oversee relations and promotions with medical researchers, pharmaceutical researchers, and the medical and pharmaceutical trade.

Upjohn International, Inc., is responsible for sales and marketing of pharmaceuticals and animal health products internationally. It is structured into four geographic regional subsidiary groupings: Pacific, Europe North, Europe South, and Latin America, Africa, and Middle East/Near East divisions. Agricultural Animal Health is also a subunit because its international sales force is administered separately from Asgrow's international subsidiaries and is of insufficient size to warrant a separate infrastructure.

Scientific Administration is the lone functional grouping at the corporate level. This research and development group, as shown in Exhibit 3, is structured into subgroups representing agricultural research and development, human health, or "discovery," research, pharmaceutical and consumer drug product development, clinical testing, and a Japanese R&D subunit with its own lab and development groups. A biotechnology and basic research unit works closely with all the other subgroups in providing basic research support and in overseeing academic and government research efforts funded by the company.

Upjohn employed a number of horizontal integration mechanisms to promote synergistic relations between units throughout the corporation. One such effort was the client engineering program formally established in 1980. Engineering assigned its professionals to other units on a semipermanent basis according to the changing needs of each unit. The goal was to achieve better planning and customizing of new facilities to provide maximum use for the occupying units.

The Chemicals R&D group also provided expert services to both the Agricultural Division and Worldwide Human Health Care Businesses through an extensive system of task forces and teams. It was assigned to develop synthetic chemical process and biotechnical and fermentation process innovations and analytical chemical process enhancements upon request from units within each SBU.

New product development efforts are integrated through the use of product development teams. During the development stage, experts from R&D, chemicals, engineering, and manufacturing work together under the leadership of a product manager selected from domestic or international marketing to develop the product, test it clinically, bring it into production, and introduce it to the market.

Another integrative mechanism involves Medical Sciences Liaison domestic directors. Each is assigned to a specific disease group corresponding to a Discovery Research unit, with the responsibility to transfer information from this research unit to other medical researchers and vice versa.

Several key boundary-spanning roles had been created across the company. Examples include government affairs specialists, Medical Sciences Liaison representatives, Medical Specialty representatives, Surgical Specialty representatives, and Pharmacy Sciences Liaison representatives. The regulatory, research, and professional medical groups that they target represent critical constituencies for the corporation.

EXHIBIT 3   Pharmaceutical research and development

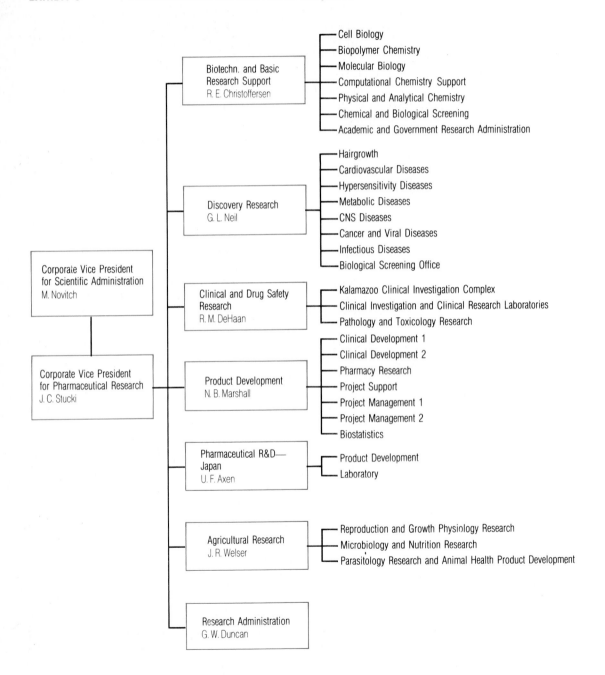

CORPORATE CONTROL

Corporate control at Upjohn centers on the corporate productivity program[13]—a major control effort formalized by Upjohn in 1984. The program established a structured approach to productivity improvement based on a model of each subunit as a production process with inputs, production activities, and outputs for "willing" customers. By early 1987 more than 1,000 organizational subunits had implemented the program. The approach was designed around a series of six steps toward unit productivity improvement.

In the first step, the subunit mission was defined by the subunit manager through a combination of five elements: (1) a statement emphasizing the nature of the subunit's activities and its expected contribution to the next higher organizational unit to which it reported; (2) a summary of products or services produced by the subunit; (3) a description of the customers for the subunit; (4) a description of the geographic scope of the subunit's responsibilities; and (5) a description of how the unit's mission related to company profit. Managers were expected to condense these five elements into a single mission statement. The manager at the next higher level then used the statements to check for gaps, overlaps, and duplication of effort within his or her span of control. In addition, cost data were available for each subunit so that the same manager could compare the cost of operating the production subunit with the operating costs of other subunits.

The second step required a process of establishing customer expectation levels for three or four primary outputs (products) and three or four primary customers. The manager of the subunit was responsible for discovering what primary customers expected of the subunit's product or service. This was usually accomplished through meetings, questionnaires, visits, or phone calls. Customer needs and expectations were then set down in written preliminary delivery agreements, which specified terms included the level or amount, timeliness, accuracy, conformity to specifications, and cost effectiveness.

In the third step, subunit managers identified required resources and inputs. Costs of capital, labor, materials, energy, equipment, technology, and service outputs from other subunits were to be determined for each product. Then direct transfer prices for products and services among units were determined through a joint bargaining process, with the option provided, "when practical," to obtain goods and services from outside vendors to encourage internal efficiency.

The fourth step required the subunit manager to select a set of three or four simple measures of subunit productivity. These measures were to include at least one quality measure, one timeliness measure, and one cost measure and were to be applied to three or four major products. Each subunit was thus allowed to select the performance measures that its manager and employees jointly felt best tracked its own performance. The measures had to focus on group rather than

[13]Cyrus C. Highlander, "Six Steps to Unit Productivity Improvement: A Corporatewide Effort at Upjohn," *National Productivity Review* (Winter 1986–1987), 20–27.

EXHIBIT 4   **Eleven-year summary: continuing operations**

The Upjohn Company and subsidiaries (dollar amounts in millions, except per share data)

Years ended December 31	1987	1986	1985	1984	1983	1982
Selected financial data						
Operating revenue	$2,529.6	$2,291.4	$2,017.2	$1,901.2	$1,738.8	$1,602.4
Earnings from continuing operations	305.0	252.6	203.2	189.5	180.1	155.0
Earnings per share from continuing operations	1.63	1.35	1.10	1.03	.99	.86
Dividends declared per share	.63	.507	.447	.427	.392	.38
Total assets	3,043.1	2,665.0	2,376.9	2,204.3	2,151.3	1,968.7
Long-term debt	436.3	423.5	377.3	382.1	548.5	461.2
Operating results						
Domestic sales	$1,556.4	$1,459.7	$1,322.8	$1,248.3	$1,111.2	$ 988.0
Foreign sales	964.6	820.6	685.7	643.3	618.9	607.4
Other revenue	8.6	11.1	8.7	9.6	8.7	7.0
Operating revenue	2,529.6	2,291.4	2,017.2	1,901.2	1,738.8	1,602.4
Cost of products and services sold	820.8	795.6	731.6	703.6	642.5	619.6
Research and development	355.5	314.1	284.1	246.7	218.0	184.8
Marketing and administrative	914.7	808.3	700.9	655.2	601.3	567.1
Operating costs and expenses	2,091.0	1,918.0	1,716.6	1,605.5	1,461.8	1,371.5
Operating income	438.6	373.4	300.6	295.7	277.0	230.9
Interest income	57.3	53.9	61.9	61.5	52.3	48.4
Interest expense	(59.0)	(58.8)	(70.2)	(76.5)	(62.3)	(55.5)
Other income (deductions)	(4.7)	(12.1)	5.5	(7.3)	(15.6)	(20.2)
Provision for income taxes	(127.2)	(103.8)	(94.6)	(83.9)	(71.3)	(48.6)
Earnings from continuing operations	305.0	252.6	203.2	189.5	180.1	155.0
(Losses) earnings from discontinued operations			(.2)	(16.2)	(19.9)	(29.0)
Net earnings	$ 305.0	$ 252.6	$ 203.0	$ 173.3	$ 160.2	$ 126.0

Years ended December 31	1981	1980	1979	1978	1977
Selected financial data					
Operating revenue	$1,610.4	$1,478.1	$1,247.6	$1,107.5	$ 945.8
Earnings from continuing operations	190.1	155.0	128.1	114.8	77.1
Earnings per share from continuing operations	1.05	.87	.72	.64	.43
Dividends declared per share	.345	.322	.27	.228	.195
Total assets	1,912.6	1,631.2	1,367.6	1,176.0	1,020.5
Long-term debt	458.1	305.7	221.5	214.9	226.2
Operating results					
Domestic sales	$ 995.3	$ 888.9	$ 741.6	$ 675.8	$ 596.7
Foreign sales	610.3	582.8	501.3	427.6	345.6
Other revenue	4.8	6.4	4.7	4.1	3.5
Operating revenue	1,610.4	1,478.1	1,247.6	1,107.5	945.8
Cost of products and services sold	634.2	594.7	497.2	423.6	383.6
Research and development	161.7	139.0	122.1	109.0	95.8
Marketing and administrative	575.1	526.1	443.8	389.4	325.5
Operating costs and expenses	1,371.0	1,259.8	1,063.1	922.0	804.9
Operating income	239.4	218.3	184.5	185.5	140.9
Interest income	39.6	22.8	17.5	9.4	5.3
Interest expense	(54.4)	(31.9)	(23.7)	(21.2)	(23.4)
Other income (deductions)	5.4	(7.2)	(9.1)	(4.5)	(4.7)
Provision for income taxes	(39.9)	(47.0)	(41.1)	(54.4)	(41.0)
Earnings from continuing operations	190.1	155.0	128.1	114.8	77.1
(Losses) earnings from discontinued operations	(8.3)	15.4	21.4	14.6	14.4
Net earnings	$ 181.8	$ 170.4	$ 149.5	$ 129.4	$ 91.5

EXHIBIT 4   Eleven-year summary: continuing operations (*cont.*)

The Upjohn Company and subsidiaries (dollar amounts in millions, except per share data)

Years ended December 31	1987	1986	1985	1984	1983	1982
Capital resources						
Accounts receivable	$ 590.5	$ 513.9	$ 409.7	$ 356.1	$ 363.5	$ 340.7
Inventories	401.4	364.7	379.3	344.5	321.0	321.8
Other current assets less (liabilities)	(251.8)	(240.8)	(229.5)	(367.5)	(238.3)	(270.0)
Working capital	740.1	637.8	559.5	333.1	446.2	392.5
Net assets of discontinued operations				110.3	105.8	103.6
Property, plant and equipment, net	1,114.4	981.5	852.1	760.3	704.8	622.6
Other assets	513.8	481.6	437.5	467.8	487.4	435.8
Total	$2,368.3	$2,100.9	$1,849.1	$1,671.5	$1,744.2	$1,554.5
Long-term financing of capital resources						
Shareholders' equity	$1,673.5	$1,470.2	$1,295.1	$1,134.2	$1,057.3	$ 973.0
Long-term debt	436.3	423.5	377.3	382.1	548.5	461.2
All other	258.5	207.2	176.7	155.2	138.4	120.3
Total	$2,368.3	$2,100.9	$1,849.1	$1,671.5	$1,744.2	$1,554.5
Major cash flows— cash provided (required) by						
Continuing operations	$ 444.4	$ 307.0	$ 253.9	$ 253.0	$ 141.3	$ 242.6
Property, plant and equipment additions	(212.0)	(201.9)	(152.6)	(129.2)	(149.6)	(131.5)
(Increase) decrease in investments	(.7)	16.3	34.1	9.8	8.7	7.1
Long-term borrowings, net	12.8	46.2	(4.8)	(166.5)	87.4	3.1
Dividends paid	(108.2)	(92.6)	(80.8)	(78.2)	(69.1)	(69.0)
All other, net	(43.4)	.5	(89.8)	117.9	(13.7)	(5.3)
Discontinued operations	(12.0)	(9.2)	145.0	(20.7)	(22.0)	(2.0)
Increase (decrease) in cash	$ 80.9	$ 66.3	$ 105.0	$ (13.9)	$ (17.0)	$ 45.0
Other data						
Common shares outstanding (thousands)	187,061	187,307	186,081	183,917	182,637	181,362
Employees	20,500	20,700	20,600	20,210	19,480	19,400
Payroll	$ 654.2	$ 596.9	$ 539.5	$ 501.1	$ 473.7	$ 457.1

Years ended December 31	1981	1980	1979	1978	1977
Capital resources					
Accounts receivable	$ 327.2	$ 322.3	$ 262.1	$ 235.3	$ 201.7
Inventories	349.8	303.4	252.0	224.5	198.0
Other current assets less (liabilities)	(270.3)	(279.0)	(140.0)	(124.0)	(82.0)
Working capital	406.7	346.7	374.1	335.8	317.7
Net assets of discontinued operations	130.6	139.3	118.8	97.5	96.8
Property, plant and equipment, net	556.7	487.7	423.5	386.6	376.8
Other assets	443.7	295.5	132.3	108.2	41.5
Total	$1,537.7	$1,269.2	$1,048.7	$ 928.1	$ 832.8
Long-term financing of capital resources					
Shareholders' equity	$ 965.3	$ 865.8	$ 743.7	$ 639.8	$ 549.0
Long-term debt	458.1	305.7	221.5	214.9	226.2
All other	114.3	97.7	83.5	73.4	57.6
Total	$1,537.7	$1,269.2	$1,048.7	$ 928.1	$ 832.8
Major cash flows— cash provided (required) by					
Continuing operations	$ 207.3	$ 140.6	$ 131.3	$ 145.1	$ 120.9
Property, plant and equipment additions	(130.9)	(99.6)	(68.0)	(30.4)	(36.1)
(Increase) decrease in investments	(148.0)	(48.9)	(66.5)	(96.6)	(41.7)
Long-term borrowings, net	152.3	84.2	6.6	(11.2)	1.2
Dividends paid	(61.6)	(57.8)	(48.7)	(39.9)	(35.4)
All other, net	(15.0)	(8.3)	45.4	17.9	(4.1)
Discontinued operations	.4	(5.1)	.1	13.9	(5.5)
Increase (decrease) in cash	$ 4.5	$ 5.1	$ .2	$ (1.2)	$ (.7)
Other data					
Common shares outstanding (thousands)	180,822	179,803	178,639	178,270	177,971
Employees	19,300	20,050	19,130	18,110	16,590
Payroll	$ 460.1	$ 418.4	$ 353.5	$ 303.7	$ 264.3

Per share data and shares outstanding reflect a three-for-one stock split effective April 6, 1987, and a two-for-one stock split effective April 7, 1986.

Source: Reprinted by permission of Upjohn Company.

EXHIBIT 5   Consolidated statements of earnings

The Upjohn Company and subsidiaries (dollar amounts in thousands, except per share data)

For the years ended December 31	1987	1986	1985
Operating revenue			
Net sales	$2,521,024	$2,280,325	$2,008,486
Other revenue	8,555	11,123	8,719
Total	2,529,579	2,291,448	2,017,205
Operating costs and expenses			
Cost of products and services sold	820,844	795,614	731,550
Research and development	355,503	314,114	284,126
Marketing and administrative	914,671	808,305	700,966
Total	2,091,018	1,918,033	1,716,642
Operating income	438,561	373,415	300,563
Interest income	57,328	53,863	61,926
Interest expense	(58,973)	(58,779)	(70,229)
Foreign exchange gains (losses)	3,331	(5,799)	3,970
All other, net	(1,526)	(4,679)	(566)
Earnings from continuing operations before income taxes and minority equity	438,721	358,021	295,664
Provision for income taxes	127,200	103,800	94,600
Minority equity in earnings (losses)	6,482	1,575	(2,129)
Earnings from continuing operations	305,039	252,646	203,193
Discontinued operations:			
Loss from operations, net of income taxes			(1,549)
Gain on sale, net of income taxes			1,311
Net earnings	$ 305,039	$ 252,646	$ 202,955
Net earnings per common share	$ 1.63	$ 1.35	$ 1.10

Per share data reflect a three-for-one stock split effective April 6, 1987, and a two-for-one stock split effective April 7, 1986.

Source: Reprinted by permission of Upjohn Company.

individual efforts and to correlate with business success but could not require excessive data gathering. The higher-level manager was directed to concentrate on how these measures improved over time. Tracking subunit performance on productivity measures allowed corrective action to be taken whenever necessary.

The fifth step was for the subunit manager to set productivity improvement goals for six-to-twelve-month intervals. The goals based on the productivity measures selected were set to be attainable but challenging. The goals were to take into account the goals and objectives of other subunits of the company, especially those of the next-higher level, to avoid conflicts.

The sixth and final step was for the subunit manager to devise and implement

EXHIBIT 6   Consolidated balance sheets

The Upjohn Company and subsidiaries (dollar amounts in thousands)

For the years ended December 31	1987	1986
Current assets:		
Cash and cash items	$ 293,027	$ 212,154
Trade accounts receivable, less allowances of $21,261 (1986: $10,928)	542,100	472,043
Other accounts receivable	48,362	41,809
Inventories	401,403	364,741
Deferred income taxes	54,167	42,825
Other	75,880	68,268
Total current assets	1,414,939	1,201,840
Investments at cost	350,914	350,200
Property, plant and equipment at cost:		
Land	45,314	39,547
Buildings and utilities	662,364	618,844
Equipment	852,215	753,698
Leasehold improvements	7,608	6,958
Construction in process	154,776	93,528
	1,722,277	1,512,575
Less allowance for depreciation	607,886	531,026
Net property, plant and equipment	1,114,391	981,549
Other noncurrent assets	152,887	131,367
Total assets	$3,043,131	$2,664,956
Current liabilities:		
Bank loans, including current maturities of long-term debt	$ 37,890	$ 44,033
Commercial paper		27,754
Accounts payable	147,175	133,244
Compensation and vacation	66,203	54,662
Taxes other than income taxes	24,532	24,351
Income taxes payable	169,113	91,588
Other	229,899	188,408
Total current liabilities	674,812	564,040
Long-term debt	436,292	423,508
Other liabilities	54,659	56,780
Commitments and contingent liabilities		

EXHIBIT 6   **Consolidated balance sheets (*cont.*)**

The Upjohn Company and subsidiaries (dollar amounts in thousands)

For the years ended December 31	1987	1986
Deferred income taxes	171,256	132,531
Minority equity in subsidiaries	32,600	17,881
Shareholders' equity:		
Preferred stock, one dollar par value; authorized 12,000,000 shares, non-issued		
Common stock, one dollar par value; authorized 600,00,000 shares, issued 188,012,658 shares (1986: 187,306,524 shares)	188,013	187,307
Capital in excess of par value	8,233	
Retained earnings	1,578,746	1,388,377
Currency translation adjustments	(72,715)	(105,468)
Less treasury stock at cost, 951,379 shares	(28,765)	
Total shareholders' equity	1,673,512	1,470,216
Total liabilities and shareholders' equity	$3,043,131	$2,664,956

Source: Reprinted by permission of Upjohn Company.

improvement plans. This was a list of actions for reaching the productivity-improvement goals. The company insisted that a clear connection be made between productivity improvement in the subunit and increased business profit.

This management-by-objectives approach to productivity was selected because it permitted economies of scale in training, integrated the company's subunits, promoted the efficient transfer of resources and R&D knowledge among subunits and SBUs, and allowed the use of common systems for planning, measuring, and tracking progress. This standardization of control processes also allowed the use of wider spans of control at many managerial levels. ⁓ Flatter ⁓

THE FUTURE

As 1989 approaches, Upjohn seems poised for the future, with several new products nearing the end of development or registration approval with the FDA. Its product strategy of high quality and high price is being threatened by a lengthening drug approval process and faster generic drug introductions after patent expiration. Should Upjohn retain the strategy and structure that have helped it reach its present position or should it be contemplating movement into new businesses or a change in strategic orientation to safeguard its position?

EXHIBIT 7   Consolidated statements of changes in financial position

The Upjohn Company and subsidiaries (dollar amounts in thousands)

For the years ended December 31	1987	1986	1985
Cash provided by continuing operations	$444,438	$307,023	$253,937
Capital investment activities provided (required)			
Property, plant and equipment additions	(211,976)	(201,920)	(152,637)
Property, plant and equipment retired	16,462	6,861	3,974
Currency translation adjustments, net	(32,547)	(15,506)	(11,918)
Other noncurrent assets acquired	(18,156)	(20,367)	
Construction funds held by trustee		7,171	15,378
	(246,217)	(223,761)	(145,203)
Financing activities provided (required)			
(Increase) decrease in investments	(714)	16,295	34,099
(Decrease) increase in short-term debt	(33,897)	2,301	(121,533)
Long-term borrowing	14,247	200,865	4,405
Reduction of long-term debt	(1,463)	(154,657)	(9,160)
Purchase of treasury stock	(34,750)		
Other financing activities	21,695	15,301	22,124
	(34,882)	80,105	(70,065)
Dividends paid to shareholders	(108,211)	(92,639)	(80,765)
Cash (required) provided by discontinued operations	(11,974)	(9,218)	144,973
Currency translation adjustments	37,719	4,829	2,119
Increase in cash and cash items	80,873	66,339	104,996
Cash and cash items, beginning of year	212,154	145,815	40,819
Cash and cash items, end of year	$293,027	$212,154	$145,815
Cash provided (required) by continuing operations			
Earnings from continuing operations	$305,039	$252,646	$203,193
Items not requiring cash			
Depreciation and amortization	96,040	81,828	69,566
Deferred income taxes	27,383	41,697	22,334
Other	2,477	(2,430)	(6,134)
Changes in			
Accounts receivable	(76,610)	(104,120)	(53,632)
Inventories	(36,662)	14,542	(34,806)
Other current assets	(7,612)	31,452	(28,090)
Other assets	(14,185)	(47,886)	(19,910)
Payables and accruals	68,047	49,681	61,146
Income taxes payable	77,525	(14,597)	40,314
Other	2,996	4,210	(44)
Cash provided by continuing operations	$444,438	$307,023	$253,937

Source: Reprinted by permission of Upjohn Company.

Case 22

BCI HOLDINGS CORPORATION (FORMERLY BEATRICE COMPANIES INC.)

In June, 1984 Beatrice Companies Inc. acquired Esmark, Inc., a food and consumer products conglomerate. Beatrice, the Chicago-based food industry giant was going through a business reorganization, and the acquisition of Esmark was seen as part of the process. Beatrice's performance had declined during the late 1970s, and its suboptimal performance record continued into the 1980s. The business reorganization plan was intended to reverse the trend. The chief executive officer, James Dutt, was optimistic about the synergies that could be reaped from the acquisition of Esmark's new businesses. However, Beatrice's future seemed uncertain, for the rationale behind the new acquisitions was unclear to many observers. Would Dutt's dream of Beatrice as "the world's premier marketer of food and consumer products" materialize?[1] Or would the company turn out to be just another "acquisition junkie" as some analysts believed?

BEATRICE FOODS: ORIGINS

Beatrice Foods Company, was founded as a partnership between George E. Haskell and William W. Bosworth in 1894 in Beatrice, Nebraska, when both men found themselves jobless after their employer, the Fremont Butter and Egg Company, went bankrupt. Haskell and Bosworth purchased the Beatrice branch of

This case was prepared by Gareth R. Jones and Rao Kowtha, Department of Management, Texas A & M University.
[1]Jo Ellen Daily, "Beatrice: An Acquisition Junkie Gets the Shakes," *Business Week,* June 3, 1985, p. 91.

the defunct company and also leased the plant of the Beatrice Creamery Company. They then began buying farm butter, eggs, and poultry and grading and shipping them to local food stores. Business prospered, and soon the company found itself shipping carloads of dairy produce to such distant markets as Boston, New York, and San Francisco. In 1898 the Beatrice Creamery Company was officially incorporated in Nebraska, with a capital of $100,000. Later Bosworth resigned from the company and opened his own business in Beatrice.

Haskell soon recognized the potential economies of scale in developing a regional dairy products business. Under his leadership, Beatrice pioneered the operation and financing of large-scale cream separators in the Prairie States. Its program of cream collection from farmers and a centrally located quality-controlled churning operation soon formed the backbone of the butter industry in the West. Beatrice grew steadily over the years, widening its collection and distribution networks, and to keep pace with the growth of business in the East, the company's general offices were moved to Chicago. In 1924 the company was reincorporated and licensed as a Delaware corporation, with headquarters in Chicago. Clinton E. Haskell, a nephew of the founder, who was elected president in 1928, was the driving force behind the diversified growth of Beatrice Foods in the years to come.

Dairy products were the core business of Beatrice throughout the early years, and the brand name Meadow Gold was used to market all the company's products. To help maintain its industry leadership, Beatrice in 1936 opened a research and new product department and a central quality control laboratory. In 1945 a sanitation program, to ensure plant cleanliness, was instituted throughout Beatrice. When its distribution networks increased, the company also developed extensive cold storage operations to preserve the quality of its products. This ensured its continuing good reputation.

GROWTH IN BEATRICE: 1945–1979

Beatrice's strengths in dairy food production, distribution, and storage provided the company with the skills and expertise to expand its business into new kinds of food products. As a result, Beatrice engaged in a diversification and expansion program, adding to its family new companies producing speciality foods. It placed particular emphasis on food products with a high sales growth potential, such as candy, pickles, and convenience and snack foods. La Choy Food Products, a pioneer in the production of American-Chinese foods, was one of the first companies Beatrice acquired. It was followed by D. L. Clark Co., Leaf, Inc. (maker of Milk Duds), Fisher Nuts Company, and a host of other convenience food companies. These companies were separated from the diary products operations and organized into the Grocery Division in 1957, to specialize in the production and marketing of convenience foods.

In 1968 the company began developing its Institutional Foods Division with the acquisition of John Sexton & Co., a leading food processor and distributor primarily engaged in selling food and other supplies to hospitals and restaurants. Other acquisitions followed. Peter Eckrich & Sons, Inc., a specialty meat producer, was acquired in 1972, and the Specialty Meats Division was thus formed. The division also included Lowrey's Meat Specialties, Inc., Rudolph Foods Company, and County Line Cheese Co., Inc. Meanwhile, the Dairy Products Division continued to expand into such products as yogurt and low-fat dairy foods with the acquisition of Dannon Yogurt (in 1959) and into soft drinks with the acquisition of the Royal Crown Cola Co. bottling operations. The latter acquisition formed the basis of Beatrice's Soft Drinks Division. The central idea that drove Beatrice through these years was growth by the acquisition of food and beverage companies.

When Beatrice realized the potential for applying its strengths in foreign markets, the next major step for the company was overseas expansion. Overseas operations, which started with Beatrice Foods (Malaysia) Ltd. in 1961, were expanded to 28 countries. By 1977 the company owned or had substantial interests in 185 overseas plants and branches. Beatrice's international operations produced dairy foods or candy in every continent except Africa; in Africa the company distributed dairy products. The growth in international operations was realized through a variety of strategies. Beatrice both acquired overseas companies and established its own foreign operations, depending on conditions in the local market and the potential for growth. For example, its entry and subsequent growth in Europe came from acquisitions as well as from start-ups. Beatrice's management strove to keep up with changing tastes at home and abroad. Generous capital expenditures were common in international operations to build, expand, or modernize new or acquired facilities. The International Division became one of the most profitable for the company, with total sales exceeding $1.1 billion by 1977.

In 1964 a new era started for Beatrice. The company began to diversify into products and businesses outside the food industry, selecting acquisitions according to their sales and earnings growth potential. One of the first such ventures was in the agricultural products business. Sensing the growing demand for protein and leather, Beatrice bought various agricultural product operations and steadily expanded to a total of fifty plants. These plants handled hides, tanned leather, processed animal oils and inedible tallow, operated wool pulleries, and produced animal protein, feed, and feed supplements.

The company soon entered the consumer goods, chemicals, and financial businesses. For example, in 1973 it acquired Samsonite Corporation, the luggage company, as well as the Southwestern Investment company (SIC), which specialized in consumer and commercial finance. In the chemicals industry, Beatrice bought specialty chemical companies, whose products included high-quality finishes for leathers (Stahl brand); vinyls and textiles (Permuthane); and paper coating and inks, high-performance metal lubricants, and paint and powder coatings (Fiberite). Many other acquisitions followed, such as Stiffel lamps, furniture, and mobile home companies.

By 1973 Beatrice had assumed a divisional form to manage its food and nonfood operations. Besides the five food divisions, Beatrice's new acquisitions were separated into five new divisions: Consumer Products, Institutional and Industrial Products, Luggage and Home Environment Products, Consumer Arts, and Leisure Products.

Beatrice, which had entered the cold storage warehouse business at the turn of the century, expanded those operations. By 1973 the company operated twenty-five cold storage facilities across the country and completed a computerized food distribution center in the Chicago warehouse. Most of these warehouses stored the company's perishable products.

By 1979 net corporate sales reached $7.5 billion, and net earnings stood at $261 million. However, even though Beatrice had steady growth in earnings, the stock market's interest in conglomerates was waning. Beatrice needed to plan its future strategy in order to consolidate its future growth.

DUTT'S REIGN AT BEATRICE

When James Dutt became chief executive officer of Beatrice in 1979, he took over a conglomerate that needed trimming. His mission was to turn Beatrice into a leader in the consumer product and food industries and to improve corporate profitability. His goal was to achieve an 18 percent return on equity. He made his first move by selling off the finance and insurance businesses of SIC for $73 million, arguing that these businesses did not fit in with Beatrice's growth plans.

Next, Dutt aggressively sought to improve Beatrice's market image. During the annual stockholders' meeting in June 1982, he announced his five-year objectives for the company. The *Annual Report* read: "A key step toward fulfilling the 18 percent return on equity objective is to achieve an annual growth rate of 5 percent, and to increase net earnings by 16 percent per year. To do so, management has identified [key business] segments of the company and will allocate the necessary funds . . . to achieve their full growth potential. A commitment to real growth also means an emphasis on brand marketing. That means among other things, stepping up advertising efforts . . . to continue emphasizing product improvement and innovation."[2] Dutt particularly emphasized diversification, market leadership, and community responsibility. He also stressed export activity and was going to expand overseas operations. A joint venture trading company was opened in Dubai to serve as a conduit for Beatrice products throughout the Persian Gulf area. In addition, joint ventures in Nigeria and the People's Republic of China were being negotiated.

To achieve these goals, Dutt instituted a vigorous asset redeployment program, which resulted in the sale of fifty-six companies, representing about $1 billion in annual sales. Prominent among these divestitures were Dannon Yogurt and the Royal Crown Cola bottling operations. The initial divestment was followed by the acquisition of a number of small companies. The rationale behind the redeployment effort was to seek acquisitions that would generate returns

[2]Beatrice Foods Company *Annual Report,* (1981), 6–7.

higher than the corporate average and to divest those businesses that were not producing a return on net assets equal to or in excess of 20 percent. The Dannon divestiture was an example of this policy. Dannon, acquired by Beatrice in 1959, had been a consistent performer until the late 1970s. It enjoyed a 30 percent market share and had net sales of $130 million in 1981. However, management believed that yogurt was a mature product and that even though yogurt appeared related to dairy products, synergies had never been realized.[3] Besides, Dannon's net earnings stood at a mere $3.5 million for 1981, a figure below the desired level of 20 percent ROA. The unit was sold to BSN-Gervais-Dannon for $384 million in 1982.

Some chronic poor performers were left untouched by the divestiture and consolidation campaign. John Sexton & Co., for example, could not have reached the return on assets goal even if its current return doubled. The business was retained because the management felt that it was a business "we should be in."[4] This lack of a coherent strategy for managing the corporate portfolio led to a lack of confidence on the part of the stock market. Consequently, when the company paid Northwest Industries, Inc., $580 million for the Coca-Cola Bottling Co. of Los Angeles in January 1982, the investment community did not react too favorably. Despite stout assertions by company officials that these actions were aimed at the long run and that the acquisition fitted well with Beatrice's strategy, many wondered what that strategy was and felt that the price paid, at twenty-two times earnings, was outrageous. Commented an analyst with a leading securities dealer: "Money put into Beatrice stock now is simply going to be dead in the water."[5] To aggravate the situation, earnings for the first quarter, ending on May 31 of that year, fell by 7.5 percent—the first such decline in thirty years.

The stock market's skepticism notwithstanding, Beatrice maintained its operating ROE at 14.6 percent for fiscal 1982, and earnings rose by 9 percent. However, the Dairy Products Division—the original business—was experiencing a steady decrease in sales and earnings because consumer consumption of nondairy beverages and products had overtaken the consumption of milk and cheese. Although sales from this division had contributed 34 percent to total corporate sales in 1969, the division contributed only 24 percent by 1982. This downward trend was expected to continue. On the other hand, ethnic and convenience food businesses and the International Food Division were posting significant gains in sales and earnings.

Two other units experiencing problems were Samsonite and Tropicana. Samsonite had been hit by the overall decline in travel due to the oil crisis and by an increase in competition from cheaper foreign products. Tropicana, an orange juice producer acquired in 1979 for $490 million, was affected by a freeze in Florida during the previous winter that limited the supply of oranges. The inept efforts of the company to cope with the shortage of fresh juice exposed a major

[3]Darry G. Kinker, "The Dannon Decision," Case Clearing Association, 1982.
[4]"The Bigness Cult's Grip on Beatrice Foods," *Fortune*, September 20, 1982, p. 124.
[5]"The Bigness Cult's Grip on Beatrice Foods," pp. 122–129.

chink in the Beatrice armor. Juice from concentrate was substituted for fresh juice without any discernible phrasing on the carton to inform buyers of the change. The action cost Tropicana substantially in sales and reputation. The matter was of no small concern because fruit juice sales contributed 4.8 percent of Beatrice's total sales volume. Beatrice, it seemed, simply did not have the marketing savvy of its major competitors such as General Foods.

Some of the best-known Beatrice brands are Samsonite luggage, Clark candy bars and Eckrich meats. However, most businesses concentrated on regional marketing, and few brands enjoyed national recognition. The name Beatrice itself did not elicit consumer awareness, even though individual brands were well known in their regions and markets. The principal reason for this obscurity was that, unlike most other conglomerates, Beatrice did not have a corporate marketing department. Beatrice was never too well known for its marketing prowess, and Dutt recognized this weakness. He began aggressive marketing programs to stress brand leadership and geographic coverage throughout Beatrice's businesses. As a first step, individual businesses were directed to expand their market coverage. For example, during 1982 Eckrich Meats expanded to Southwestern markets; the Arizona-based Rosarita Foods, which produced Mexican foods, moved into the Eastern markets; and Tropicana increased its distribution to the West Coast. These tactics paid dividends. For example, Eckrich generated 42 percent of its sales for 1982 from areas outside its original Midwest base.

During 1983 Beatrice charted a new plan for its marketing endeavors: to transform itself into a unified, directed marketing company with the ability to penetrate new markets. Advertising to create a unified corporate identity was also on Dutt's agenda. Beatrice traditionally had spent much less than its smaller competitors on advertising. For example, in 1981 advertising expenditures totaled $201 million, which was less than half of what General Foods, a slightly smaller company, spent.

Despite these efforts by Dutt to provide a new marketing identity for Beatrice in order to generate increased sales and revenues across Beatrice's individual food companies, profits continued to show a downward trend. Fiscal 1983 earnings hit an all-time low of $43 million, or 27 cents per share. It seemed that increasing marketing was not enough to improve corporate profitability—that the real problem lay with the company's portfolio of investments. Dutt began to examine the diverse collection of businesses that Beatrice had assembled and to evaluate the way corporate headquarters managed its businesses. What he found led him to realize that the time for a major overhaul at Beatrice had arrived.

IMPLEMENTING AND MANAGING CHANGE AT BEATRICE

Traditionally, Beatrice had practiced the philosophy of decentralized management, treating each individual business as an autonomous profit center. Only two levels of management stood between a profit center and corporate headquarters, the divisional level and the business-group level, and they similarly took a hands-off approach to interfering in the affairs of each business. Both business-group and corporate-level management performed mainly a portfolio-planning role. As a result, corporate headquarters was staffed with only 300 employees, while more than 100,000 people worked for the company worldwide.

Business-level and operating-strategy decisions were made at the profit center management level. Marketing, purchasing, and production decisions were largely left to the discretion of managers in the individual businesses. These decisions typically included choices concerning personnel, product mix, pricing of products, and markets.

A significant portion of executive compensation at all levels was predicated upon the profit contributions of the various businesses. Incentives included stock option plans for all salaried employees of the corporation and performance plans for executives. Executives who met their predetermined performance goals were awarded control over a profit center. The performance of a profit center was tied to overall corporate performance over a three-year period and the corporation's stock price at the end of that period.

Top management firmly believed that this decentralized management style provided the company with a sound and continuing executive development system. Beatrice made little effort to integrate individual business units and build a corporate culture. The company was built from one acquisition to the next, and new businesses that were not accustomed to operating autonomously were quickly indoctrinated into the Beatrice way. The decentralized management style allowed Beatrice to acquire companies quickly, but it did not provide any means by which business units could trade information or knowledge in order to improve corporate profitability.

Dutt realized that the diversified growth of the corporation rendered its highly autonomous operating philosophy increasingly unviable. The corporate center was unable to shape any corporate strategy when its businesses were so loosely organized. As a first step in solving this problem, Dutt changed the organization structure used to manage Beatrice's diverse operations. Beatrice's 435 individual profit centers (operating companies) were consolidated into 27 larger, freestanding divisions according to the product markets served by the businesses. Then 6 business groups were created from the 27 individual divisions according to the type of business or industry they were in (Exhibit 1).[6] Divisional managers were made directly responsible to business group managers, who were in turn responsible to corporate managers.

As a result of these changes, businesses inside a division, and divisions inside a group could now share common marketing and distribution channels. The overall thrust for marketing was provided by the Office of the Chairman, headed by Dutt. Group-level managers—each was a senior vice president of the company—were charged with the planning and execution of groupwide business strategies in task forces and teams and were directly responsible to the Office of the Chairman.

The aim behind the reorganization was to allow divisions inside each business group to share resources and trade on each other's marketing knowledge. It also gave group and corporate management more control over the performance

---

[6]Beatrice Foods Company, Form 10-K Annual Report (1984), p. 74.

EXHIBIT 1   **Beatrice Company's organization—1984**

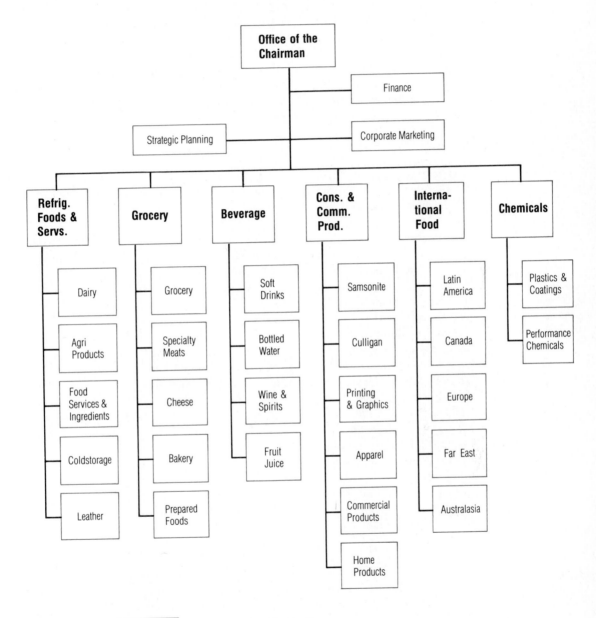

Source: Reprinted by permission of Beatrice Company.

of the division. Operating decisions were still within the local manager's realm, but corporate direction and guidance as to product development and marketing strategies increased. Moreover, control was centralized at corporate headquarters to improve integration among groups and to reduce costs. In particular, central- ization was intended to streamline functions such as purchasing, production, and marketing. For example, the number of advertising agencies used by Beatrice was cut from more than 100 to fewer than 10 worldwide firms. The consolidation was undertaken to ensure greater economies in advertising.

Group Structures and Strategies

Beatrice's six operating groups and the divisions inside the groups are discussed below, together with problems confronting the divisions. Summaries of the sales and earnings of each group are presented in Exhibits 2 and 3.

Refrigerated foods and services   The Refrigerated Foods and Services Group followed the strategy of acquiring strong regional food companies and then giv- ing their products national distribution after acquisition. One of the main prob- lems for the group centered on the price of milk, the basic ingredient used in Beatrice's dairy products. The price paid for raw milk is controlled by Federal Milk Market Orders or state regulatory agencies. These orders and agencies es- tablish the minimum price to be paid for milk. During the 1980s milk lost much of its popularity owing to the increasingly health-conscious consumer market. This decline in demand was to some extent mitigated by the introduction of low- fat milk products (Beatrice introduced low-fat yogurt and other milk products under the name brand Viva after selling Dannon). Although milk made a come- back in 1983 and 1984 with a 2 percent jump in consumption, sales projections for dairy products were not encouraging. Dairy sales continued to decline through 1984 as the whole industry struggled to recover from the losses inflicted by declining demand and surplus raw milk due to the government milk distri- bution program. Beatrice announced that the Dairy Division would be concen- trating on improving productivity and efficiency in the future. The aim was to become a low-cost producer for selected segments of the market. At the same time premium brands such as Louis Sherry ice cream and Swiss Miss chocolate milk were continued.

Beverage group   With Tropicana spearheading its competitive efforts, the Fruit Juice Division had been marketing an extensive line of citrus and other fruit prod- ucts. The Soft Drinks Division, through wholly owned subsidiaries, bottled and distributed brands such as Coca-Cola, Diet Coke, Dr Pepper, and Sprite. The Bottled Water Division consisted of Arrowhead Puritas Waters Inc. and the Great Bear Spring Company. The Wine and Spirits Division marketed and distributed imported liquor brands such as Cutty Sark scotch and Marquisat wines.

Lifestyle changes in the 1980s brought about a decline in caffeine consump- tion and an increase in the consumption of fruit juices. Some industry analysts

EXHIBIT 2   Five-year sales and earnings summary (in millions of dollars)

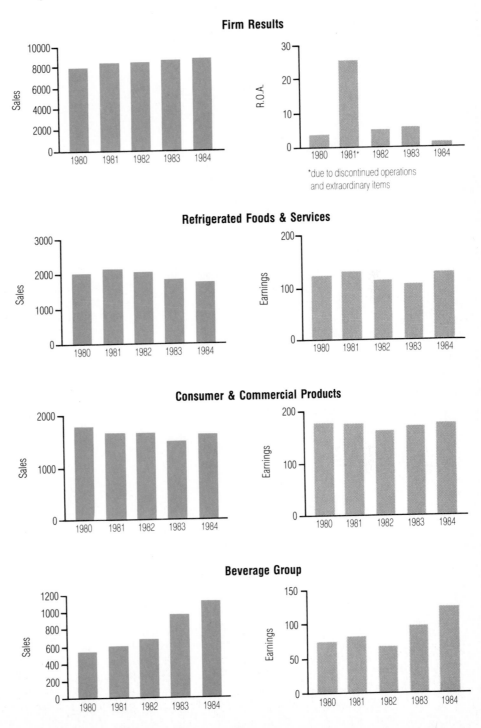

EXHIBIT 2   Five-year sales and earnings summary (*cont.*)

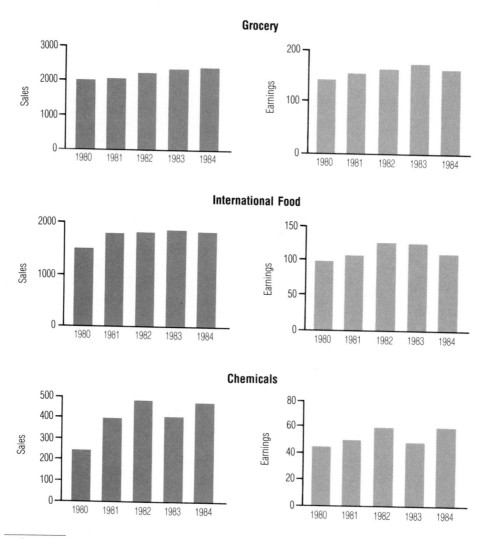

Source: Reprinted by permission of Beatrice Company.

predicted that fruit juice was ready to replace soft drinks and become the trend of the day. However, competition was stiff. A number of companies were introducing new fruit juice products, such as Procter & Gamble's Citrus Hill brand and Coca-Cola's Minute Maid brand.

The soft-drinks industry was also hit by changing demographics as the baby boomers grew older. The industry depended on the under-thirty-five age group for its sales. During the 1980s, however, the number of those between the ages

EXHIBIT 3   Sales and earnings contributions of segments—1984

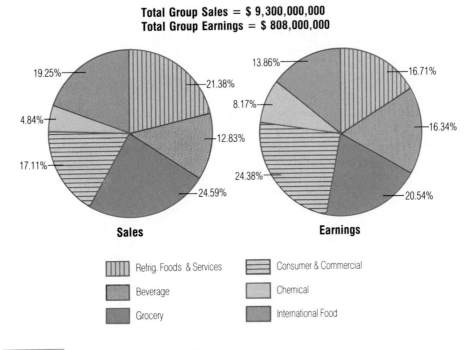

Total Group Sales = $ 9,300,000,000
Total Group Earnings = $ 808,000,000

Sales

Earnings

Refrig. Foods & Services

Beverage

Grocery

Consumer & Commercial

Chemical

International Food

Source: Reprinted by permission of Beatrice Company.

of thirty-five and thirty-nine was expected to increase by 41 percent; the number of those aged forty to forty-four, by 50 percent. Caffeine-free and low-sodium versions of soft drinks proliferated to cater to consumers' changing tastes. Diet soft drinks made up about 21.6 percent of soft-drink industry sales in 1983, estimated at $14.8 billion.[7]

Tropicana, sensing the impending changes and anticipating intense competition in the juice market, redesigned its entire product line in 1983. The packaging was changed to make the name Tropicana easily identifiable. Tropicana enjoyed strong popularity with consumers as the only major ready-to-serve orange juice. It had a higher juice content and was positioned in the market as a premium brand. These factors, combined with a renewed focus on marketing, allowed Tropicana to maintain its industry leader status in 1984.

Grocery   The Grocery Group consisted of five divisions: Grocery, Prepared Foods, Specialty Meats, Cheese, and Bakery. Grocery was the most visible part of Beatrice, offering more than 2,000 products commonly found on the supermarket shelves. The division marketed canned vegetables and sauces, pet foods, frozen foods, and

[7]"Beverages Jump 1.3% to All-Time High," *Beverage Industry* (September 1985), 4.

snacks. In addition, it had undertaken a cooperative program with the Dairy Division to market Swiss Miss chocolate milk. The division concentrated on expanding market share and improving distribution. The pet foods business was doing well with Bonkers, a cat food, holding a 30 percent market share.

Prepared Foods had traditionally been involved in the ethnic and packaged foods industry. During the 1980s, its presence in the ethnic food segment expanded. To leverage the division's strengths, all Mexican food lines were consolidated under the brand name Rosarita, and the product line was expanded to include a variety of sauces. La Choy, the leader in oriental foods, continued to market aggressively and expand its volume.

The stress on ethnic foods could not have come at a more opportune moment. As American consumers began demanding less red meat and more variety in their meals, the popularity of ethnic food surged. However, competition kept increasing as new brands arrived on the scene. Oriental foods, stagnant for a decade or so, were growing once again in popularity. Innovations such as rice crackers, rice chips, and dinners helped sales significantly. Rosarita, for its part, introduced a line of entrées and dinners in the Mexican food market. Even in the canned meat and specialty foods segment, Italian, Mexican, and oriental dishes posted strong gains, with a total of $675 million in supermarket sales in 1984.

Eckrich, the flagship brand of the Specialty Meats Division, revitalized its marketing and distribution networks. The intent was to expand a strong Midwestern presence to a nationally distributed brand. However, this business has been experiencing a flat sales volume as the consumption of beef has declined.

The Cheese Division, whose three companies had been brought under a more unified management during the reorganization, has been struggling to maintain its market share. It faced strong competition from brands such as Treasure Cave and Kraft. New product lines, including shredded natural cheese and flavored cream cheese, were introduced under the County Line brand in 1984. Government surplus distribution programs for cheese products led to a decline in sales. The Bakery Division, which produces cookies, bread, and snack foods, also had intense competition—from industry giants like Frito-Lay. The Grocery group, as a whole, emphasized increased market share and sales volume.

Consumer and commercial products   Beatrice put out a broad range of products for consumer and commercial use, including Samsonite luggage (the leader in the $1.4-billion luggage industry), Samsonite furniture, Stiffel lamps, Taylor slush and milk shake machines, and Culligan water treatment services. Exhibit 4 presents the group's structure.

Samsonite found smooth sailing in international waters after its first overseas expansion in the early 1970s. By 1984, 50 percent of the company's sales came from its international operations. Sales volume of luggage was heavily dependent on the travel conditions and airline baggage restrictions. For example, a new FAA restriction on the allowable volume of carry-on luggage, as well as growth in the business travel segment, spurred the company to develop soft-side and wrinkle-free pieces with greater capacity. It has continued to introduce new products, and it markets luggage products ranging from tote bags to trunks.

EXHIBIT 4　　　**Consumer and Commercial Products Group**

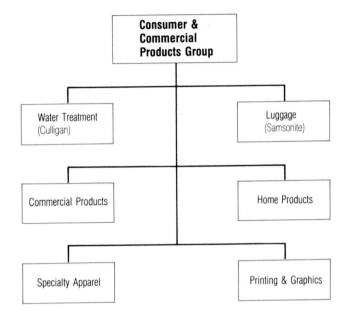

Source: Reprinted by permission of Beatrice Company.

Culligan has been doing well by catering to the industrial and residential water treatment markets. Substantial expenditures on product development and marketing slowed the growth of earnings but provided the unit with a strong identity. The Home Products Division includes furniture, Del Mar window coverings, Aristokraft cabinets and Stiffel lamps, companies that have capitalized on the growing home improvement products market. The Commercial Products and Printing & Graphics divisions are in relatively stable industries and enjoy a steady flow of earnings. The group's focus for the 1980s was defined as market penetration and geographic expansion.

International food　The International Food Group has been a profitable performer for the corporation ever since its first foray into the field in 1961. The group is organized into five world regions. These regions, with their increasing affluence and huge populations, provide fertile growth opportunities. Inside each region, businesses are grouped into distinct business areas. For example, the subsidiaries of the European division (the largest) have been grouped as snacks and confectionery, processed meats, soft drinks and fruit juices, and ice cream and dairy products. The structure has enabled the company to monitor its far-flung operations effectively and to identify market trends on a geographical and product basis. International units are usually managed by resident nationals, who are given great autonomy because competition varies from continent to continent and country to country. For example, Beatrice faced substantial competition in Australia, whereas in Latin American countries, its brands were the market leaders and experienced continuous growth and product development.

Beatrice's international operations account for nearly 20 percent of its total sales. New opportunities are opening up in Far Eastern countries such as China. However, the group's earnings are subject to currency fluctuations, which can hurt performance. For example, the troubled economies of Brazil and Venezuela hurt the dollar earnings of the division in 1984, and any decline in the value of the dollar hurts the group's operating profits.

Chemicals   Fiberite, the market leader in composite materials, continued to experience increased demand from the aerospace industry as the national defense budget swelled. Growth in electronic, business machine, and appliance markets also fueled the demand for Fiberite, and demand is likely to remain stable over the next few years. Performance Chemicals, which included Stahl leather and Permuthane Polymers, also experienced strong demand. The Performance Chemicals Division expanded its distribution to Europe during 1983–1984 and started a joint venture with Mitsubishi Chemical Industries Ltd. in Japan. The group cultivates a well-established set of customers and focuses on research and development activities to continue its strong sales and earnings trend.

Beatrice's New Face

According to Dutt, the restructuring of Beatrice in 1984 enabled the company to identify the units that did not fit in with the long-range plans. The company continued to manage the Dairy Division for cash flows and proceeded with the business realignment program through 1984. Reorganization centered on concentrating on the food and consumer products businesses while retaining profitable unrelated businesses. John Sexton & Co. was finally sold off that year. For the first time in the company's history, management decided to get rid of businesses that were poor fits with the traditional food and consumer product businesses. Increased focus on food businesses was evident as Beatrice sought to realign its portfolio for the future. However, corporate performance continued to decline, and return-on-investment goals were not being met. In an effort to improve performance, Beatrice once again turned to the acquisition path.

THE ESMARK ACQUISITION

Esmark, Inc., was another company that had grown by diversification outside its core food business during the 1970s. It had net earnings of $107 million in 1982 against total revenues of over $3 billion.[8] Among its well-known products

---

[8]Esmark, Inc., Form 10-K Annual Report (1983), 17.

are Swift processed meats and foods, Playtex apparel, Danskin knitwear, and Jhirmack shampoo.

The Swift group consisted of the company's original food-processing and marketing businesses. The processed meats and poultry division was the largest business in the group. It supplied its products to both the consumer market and the food service industry. Swift Cheese/Frozen Desserts Division sold a wide variety of cheeses and ice creams. The Dry Grocery Division marketed Peter Pan peanut butter, pet foods, and assorted commodities.

However, Playtex Inc., headquartered in Stamford, Connecticut, was the most consistently profitable unit of the corporation. With an expansive product line of intimate apparel, hosiery, and family products, Playtex operated in seventeen countries and exported to an additional twenty-six countries. In 1982 its earnings exceeded $100 million against revenues of $784 million. The dynamic head of Playtex, Joel Smilow, had been described by *Fortune* magazine as one of the ten toughest bosses in America. Smilow came to Playtex in 1965 from Procter & Gamble, where he had earned a reputation as a marketing genius.

In 1983 Esmark acquired Norton Simon Inc., another conglomerate. With Norton Simon (NSI) came new businesses such as Avis, Inc., Halston Enterprises, Inc., Max Factor & Company, Somerset Group, Inc., and Hunt-Wesson Foods, Inc. Avis is one of the leading companies in the passenger car rental business. Max Factor was a leading manufacturer of beauty products; Halston was engaged in the fashion clothing business. After the acquisition, the Hunt-Wesson grocery line was combined with the Swift group to achieve marketing synergies. Hunt-Wesson marketed nationally recognized brands of tomato products and cooking oil. Somerset Importers was a nationwide distributor of imported distilled spirits. The company also distilled and distributed bourbon whiskies.

Esmark was one of the most profitable companies in the food industry, and its return on equity had averaged above 25 percent for over a decade. Its operating philosophy was somewhat similar to Beatrice's. Decentralized divisions made business-level operating decisions while corporate managers looked after the broader policy matters and long-range business planning. However, Esmark was different from Beatrice in that close and constant attention was paid to the performance of each operating division. Donald Kelly, the highly respected chief executive of Esmark, managed the company like an investment portfolio. The units that were not performing up to expectations within planning horizons were quickly divested. For example, the entire energy segment of Esmark (Vickers Petroleum Corp.) was divested in 1980, and a substantial portion of the food business (Canadian operations and Swift Independent Packing Co.) was disposed of in 1981 when its performance declined. This approach contrasted with that at Beatrice, where often years passed before an unprofitable division or business was divested.

With the acquisition of Norton Simon, the size of Esmark assets doubled to $2 billion and long-term debt increased by more than $1.5 billion. In early 1984 the market was rife with rumors that Esmark would be bidding for Beatrice. However, as it turned out, Beatrice acquired Esmark in June of that year.

Beatrice bought Esmark for $2.8 billion. In justifying the purchase, Beatrice pointed to the synergies that could be reaped from this related acquisition. For example, Esmark had a large nationwide marketing network that would serve as a channel for Beatrice products. It would also bolster Beatrice's marketing efforts at the corporate level and provide synergies across businesses. Additionally, since Esmark was involved in many closely related products and markets, the acquisition would save the high costs and risks associated with developing new products internally. Esmark's national brands would provide Beatrice with many advantages.

Beatrice executives hailed the acquisition of Esmark as critical to the company's efforts to develop strong national brands and distribution capabilities. They felt that Esmark could be easily integrated into an already streamlined Beatrice organization that had been busy selling off assets. The "New Beatrice" would have vast marketing clout with the addition of Esmark's marketing force. For example, Beatrice's largely regional domestic food business stood to gain from Hunt-Wesson's topnotch 500-member sales organization, with its state-of-the-art inventory system. In addition, Hunt-Wesson's 16 distribution centers were to complement the network of Beatrice food brokers.

The Swift and Hunt-Wesson divisions of Esmark did fit in with the food business of Beatrice. Dutt justified the presence of Playtex and Avis on the grounds of their contribution to Beatrice's overall portfolio and their fit with Beatrice's other businesses. For example, the Consumer and Commercial Products Group would benefit from the addition of another strong performer in Playtex. Avis, Dutt said, gave the company the opportunity to participate in special ventures that represent either good growth potential or synergies with other units.[9] Meanwhile, the international business of Avis and Playtex would benefit and strengthen the International Division. However, Beatrice was buying businesses in which it had no previous management experience and in which marketing, one of Beatrice's traditional weaknesses, was of paramount importance.

The euphoria surrounding the Esmark acquisition served to hide the debt problems of Beatrice for some time. The debt-to-equity ratio of Beatrice was already one of the highest in the industry, at 49 percent in 1984. The acquisition of Esmark in June 1984, when the company had to absorb Esmark's debt load of $900 million, more than quadrupled the ratio, to 199 percent by the end of fiscal 1985. Total debt exceeded $4 billion, which Beatrice hoped to reduce by future divestitures. Bankers who financed the merger were convinced at one point that Beatrice could service its debt even though the annual interest payments of $480 million exceeded the company's 1984 earnings.

Combining the Operations

The acquisition of Esmark prompted another restructuring move. Beatrice was now the largest food marketer in the United States, with expected annual sales of over $13 billion. The task of integrating three major food and consumer goods

[9]Beatrice Companies Inc., Form 10-K Annual Report (1985), p. 22.

companies brought about a new need for reorganization. It led to conflict, as managers in both companies sought to control important operating divisions to preserve their position in the new company. The company was reorganized into four major business segments: U.S. Food, Consumer Products, International Food, and Avis/Other Operations (Exhibit 5).

U.S. Food consisted of the Beverage, Soft Drinks, Grocery, and Refrigerated Food groups. The new Beverage group, headed by John Attwood (president of the Beatrice Soft Drinks Division), combined bottled water, dairy, soft-drink, agricultural products, and warehouse businesses. Dry Grocery combined Hunt's tomato products, Orville Reddenbacher's popcorn, Peter Pan peanut butter, and Wesson Oil (all ex-Esmark) with Fisher Nuts, La Choy, Rosarita, and Martha White (Beatrice). The Refrigerated Food Group was composed of Esmark's Swift poultry, processed meats, and cheese divisions, as well as Beatrice's cheese products, Eckrich meats, and Tropicana juices. The Consumer Products group, with

EXHIBIT 5   **Beatrice Company's organization—November 1985**

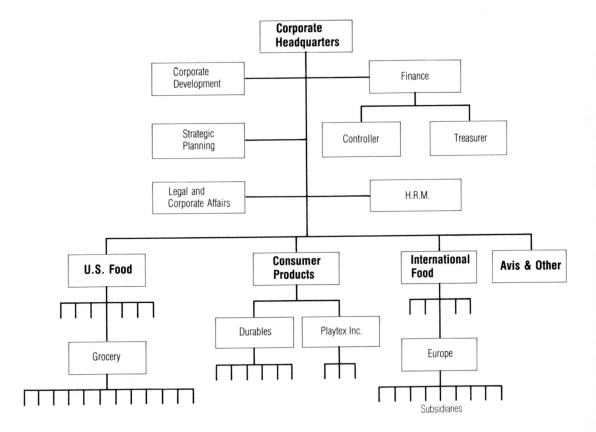

Source: Reprinted by permission of Beatrice Company.

Smilow as its president, was further divided into Personal Products and Consumer Durables. Personal Products included the Playtex line and other Esmark brands; the Consumer Durables group kept Beatrice lines such as Samsonite, Culligan, and Stiffel. This is shown in Exhibit 6. Avis, the second largest car rental company in the United States and leader abroad, formed one separate group. The International Food group was largely left untouched.

The Chemicals Group (see Exhibit 1) was entirely divested during fiscal 1985. Other nonfood interests soon followed Chemicals. Wine and spirits, food equipment, foundry, agriproducts, graphic arts, specialty apparel, and cryogenic businesses were all sold off along with the Chemicals Group for a total of $1.4 billion. Corporate debt was reduced by approximately $1.3 billion. The proceeds from the sale were used to bring down the debt-to-equity ratio to 161 percent in March 1985.[10] The company announced that more debt would be retired over the next two years through income from divestitures.

Meanwhile, the stock market reacted sharply to the merger. After the Esmark acquisition, Beatrice shares fell to $25 and were trading at nine times the earnings versus eleven times the earnings for industry stars such as Nabisco Brands, Inc., and Kellogg. Beatrice securities were downgraded to "A" from "AA" by the Standard & Poor's Index. Industry analysts commented that Beatrice turned out to be a new company every five years, and they felt that the market had lost faith in the company's ability to reorganize itself. Many thought that it was not Dutt's strategic vision that prompted the acquisition of Esmark but ego. Earlier in 1984 Esmark was found to have bought 1.5 percent of Beatrice shares. This led to the perception that Dutt was getting back at Esmark CEO Kelly for his attempt to take over Beatrice while at the same time because of Beatrice's huge debt burden, the Esmark takeover neutralized future takeover threats.

Management Changes at Beatrice

The company witnessed attrition in the ranks as Dutt grew increasingly impatient and intolerant of dissent over the next few years, when Beatrice's performance failed to improve. In three years La Choy Foods and Tropicana had three presidents each. Of the fifty-eight top corporate officers at the end of fiscal 1980, thirty-seven left the company by 1985. When Esmark's executives started to resign from Beatrice, the situation worsened, for they were experts in how to run Beatrice's new businesses. The first casualty was Frederick B. Rentschler, the head of Swift/Hunt-Wesson Foods, which accounted for $1.6 billion of Esmark's $4-billion annual sales. Smilow of Playtex stayed on as the CEO of the Consumer Products group for four months before quitting in November 1984. Walter Bregman, who succeeded Smilow at Playtex, was forced out in March 1985.

Dutt was still supported and admired by many of Beatrice's directors. However, the Esmark acquisition spelled the end of Dutt's reign. The price of Beatrice

---

[10]Beatrice Companies Inc., Prospectus, Special Meeting of Stockholders, March 11, 1986, p. F-46.

EXHIBIT 6   **Consumer products group**

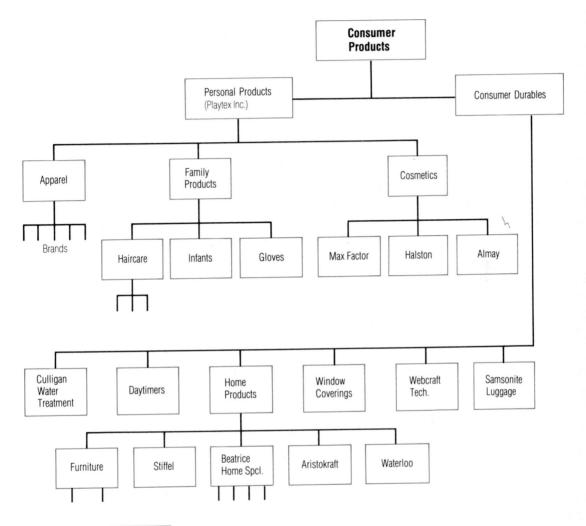

Source: Reprinted by permission of Beatrice Company.

stock plummeted when the promised synergies proved to be elusive. Matters came to a head when Senior Vice President Nolan Archibald, a Beatrice veteran and a respected manager, left the company in July 1985 in a dispute with Dutt.[11] Dutt resigned in early August and was succeeded by William Granger, the former vice chairman brought out of retirement.

[11]Kenneth Dreyfack, "Why Beatrice Had to Dump Dutt," *Business Week*, August 19, 1985, p. 34.

THE LEVERAGED BUYOUT

Granger's tenure as the chairman and chief executive of Beatrice was short. Net earnings were low because of lingering merger expenses and the strong performance of the dollar abroad. The debt-to-equity ratio still stood at a staggering 108 percent. To reduce debts further, Granger slated a number of companies from Consumer Products, as well as other companies, for sale. Among them were Danskin, Halston, Orlane, Inc., International Jensen Inc., and Avis. Granger's strategy was that Beatrice would work toward a 70 to 30 percent ratio of food to nonfood businesses in the future, the reason being that the nonfood market is cyclical but the food business is not significantly affected by the economy. He also reorganized the company into three divisions—U.S. Food, Consumer Products, and International Food—to streamline its operations. The reorganization is shown in Exhibit 7.

Meanwhile, however, Donald Kelly, former chairman of Esmark, was packaging a tender offer for Beatrice with the aid of Kohlberg, Kravis, Roberts & Company (KKR), an investment banking firm. They formed a holding company, BCI Holdings, to bid for Beatrice. Granger, with a weakened management team in the face of a hostile stock market, offered little resistance to the offer and Beatrice accepted a $40-per-share offer from KKR and Kelly in March 1986. The $6-billion leveraged buyout was the biggest in history. Beatrice was merged with BCI and was renamed BCI Holdings. Kelly commented that he wanted BCI to be private in order to take greater risks and reap greater rewards. However, Kelly's strength was in portfolio management, not in production operations. Industry analysts and executives associated with Esmark operations commented that "Mr. Kelly is not an operating manager. [He] is known for keeping that which works and finding buyers for things that don't."[12]

Thus not surprisingly, soon after the merger, the new management started to sell off companies in order to lower the debt level. The first to go was the Coca-Cola bottling business for $1 billion. Smilow, backed by a group of investors, purchased Playtex Inc. for $1,250 million. The bottled water operations were sold off to France's Perrier Group for $400 million. Rentschler took over as head of BCI's domestic food operations and carried out a trimming operation at the headquarters by reducing the number of employees from 180 to 60. In June 1987 he succeeded Kelly as the chief executive of BCI Holdings Corp.

Kelly formed another company, E-II Holdings Inc. He remained the chairman of BCI but was not actively involved in running it. Instead he shifted his focus to altering BCI's portfolio. His plan was to purchase the remaining Beatrice consumer goods companies and manage them. In other words, E-II Holdings would absorb selected businesses of Beatrice. Many specialty food businesses, including Orville Reddenbacher, Hunt's tomato sauce and Tropicana, were to be sold off to E-II. Businesses such as Samsonite and Culligan water conditioning were being considered for a spin-off to E-II.

[12]Julie Franz, "Beatrice Sell-off Due," *Advertising Age,* October 21, 1985, pp. 7, 108.

EXHIBIT 7   Beatrice Company's organization—1986

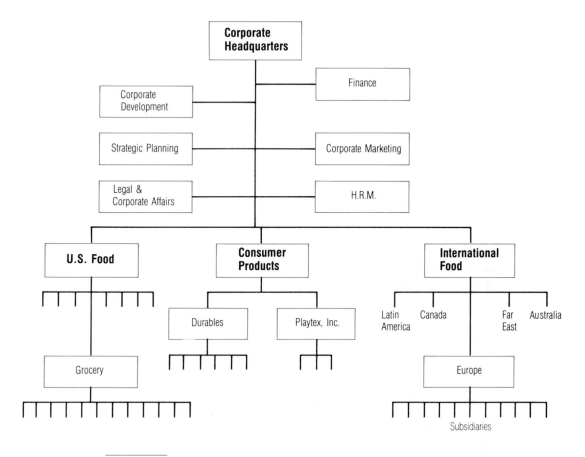

Source: Reprinted by permission of Beatrice Company.

However, not all businesses were to be brought under E-II. Many were divested. Major units sold off in the fifteen months after the merger in March 1986 were Max Factor, the Dairy Products Division (Beatrice's original business), Americold Refrigeration, and Avis. The entire International Food group was also being considered for sale.

Outsiders started to wonder what Beatrice had left. Kelly's intentions became clearer when in May 1987 E-II filed with the Securities and Exchange Commission for an initial public offering of 36 million shares. Industry observers felt that Kelly wanted to liquidate the Beatrice he had purchased and build E-II out of its remains. The old Beatrice was gone, as was the old Esmark company. A diversified conglomerate had been sold off to private investors and broken down into smaller companies. Will the new smaller companies operate more efficiently than the old Beatrice conglomerate?

EXHIBIT 8   **BCI Holdings Corporation—consolidated balance sheet (in millions)**

	As of February 28	
	1987	1986
	(Successor)	(Predecessor)
Assets		
Current assets:		
Cash	$ 16	$ 6
Short-term investments, at cost which approximates market	30	141
Receivables, less allowance for doubtful accounts of $14 and $16, respectively	384	346
Inventories	617	631
Net current assets of E-II and discontinued operations	409	656
Other current assets	129	238
Total current assets	1,585	2,018
Net property, plant and equipment	863	774
Intangible assets, principally unallocated purchase cost and goodwill, respectively	2,636	1,171
Net noncurrent assets of E-II and discontinued operations	1,492	2,810
Other noncurrent assets	348	121
	$6,924	$6,894
Liabilities and stockholders' equity		
Current liabilities:		
Short-term debt	$ 4	$ 541
Accounts payable	450	502
Accrued expenses	651	636
Current maturities of long-term debt	125	38
Total current liabilities	1,230	1,717
Long-term debt	4,244	1,147
Noncurrent and deferred income taxes	459	501
Other noncurrent liabilities	683	388
Stockholders' equity:		
Preferred stock	—	—
Preference stock	—	100
Common stock	1	212
Additional capital	418	536
Retained earnings (deficit)	(121)	2,308
Common stock in treasury, at cost	—	(12)
Cumulative foreign currency translation adjustment	10	(3)
Total stockholders' equity	308	3,141
	$6,924	$6,894

Source: Reprinted by permission of Beatrice Company.

EXHIBIT 9   **BCI Holdings Corporation—statement of consolidated earnings (in millions, except per share data)**

	Year ended February 28			
	1987			
	From April 17	To April 16	1986	1985
	(Successor)	(Predecessor)	(Predecessor)	(Predecessor)
Net sales	$4,063	$525	$4,752	$6,015
Cost of sales	2,875	381	3,436	4,455
Gross earnings	1,188	144	1,316	1,560
Selling and administrative expenses	856	112	1,050	1,233
Amortization of intangible assets	55	5	40	31
Integation and restructuring	—	—	—	264
Operating earnings	277	27	226	32
Interest expense	(317)	(14)	(117)	(145)
Change in control expenses	—	(84)	(17)	—
Divestiture gains	—	—	—	700
Miscellaneous income (expense), net	11	—	(17)	28
Earnings (loss) before income taxes and other items	(29)	(71)	75	615
Income tax expense (benefit)	36	(31)	50	258
Earnings (loss) before other items	(65)	(40)	25	357
Earnings from E-II and discontinued operations, net of income tax expense of $64, $15, $174, and $94, respectively	32	14	207	122
Extraordinary items, net of income tax benefit of $32 and $8, respectively	(36)	(10)	—	—
Net earnings (loss)	(69)	$ (36)	$ 232	$ 479
Preferred dividend requirements	(52)			
Net loss applicable to common stockholders	$ (121)			
Weighted-average common shares outstanding	82			
Earnings (loss) per share:				
Before other items	$ (1.43)			
E-II and discontinued operations	.39			
Extraordinary item	(.44)			
Net loss	$ (1.48)			

Source: Reprinted by permission of Beatrice Company.

EXHIBIT 10   BCI Holdings Corporation—statement of consolidated changes in financial position (in millions)

	Year ended February 28			
	1987		1986	1985
	From April 17	To April 16		
	(Successor)	(Predecessor)	(Predecessor)	(Predecessor)
Cash provided (used) by operations:				
Earnings (loss) before other items	$ (65)	$ (40)	$ 25	$ 357
Items not involving cash:				
Depreciation and amortization of intangibles	141	16	129	139
Net charges due to integration and restructuring	—	—	—	274
Interest expense payable in Exchange Debentures	64	—	—	—
Deferred taxes	—	2	121	258
Other items, net	29	2	24	(6)
Changes in working capital, excluding current debt:				
Divestiture proceeds received in March 1985	—	—	855	(855)
Receivables	(72)	35	2	14
Inventories	(26)	14	42	(95)
Other current assets	52	(22)	6	(98)
Accounts payable and other current liabilities	(64)	(37)	(152)	90
Cash provided (used) by operations before other items	59	(30)	1,052	78
Net cash provided (used) by E-II and discontinued operations	(52)	(27)	11	(75)
Net cash used by extraordinary items	(36)	(10)	—	—
Cash provided (used) by operations	(29)	(67)	1,063	3
Cash provided (used) by investment activities:				
Net expenditures for property, plant and equipment	(94)	(9)	(127)	(61)
Noncurrent assets of purchased businesses	—	—	(7)	(58)
Net proceeds from divested operations and other asset sales	3,385	—	360	592
Other items, net	(11)	(4)	1	(6)
Cash provided (used) by investment activities	3,280	(13)	227	467
Cash provided (used) by financing activities, excluding the merger:				
Change in debt	(3,770)	134	(1,778)	(455)
Exchange debentures issued upon exchange of redeemable preferred stock	1,230	—	—	—

EXHIBIT 10   **BCI Holdings Corporation—statement of consolidated changes in financial position (in millions) (*cont.*)**

	Year ended February 28			
	1987		**1986**	**1985**
	From April 17	**To April 16**		
	(Successor)	(Predecessor)	(Predecessor)	(Predecessor)
Redeemable preferred stock retired upon exchange of exchange debentures	(1,230)	—	—	—
Proceeds from sale of Beatrice common stock	—	—	434	—
Refund of income taxes	—	—	176	—
Common stock issued upon conversion of preference stock and debentures	—	41	157	34
Preference stock and debentures retired upon conversion into common stock	—	(41)	(157)	(34)
Common stock issued for exercises of stock options and stock warrants	—	20	85	4
Redeemable preferred stock issued as dividends and upon conversion of convertible securities	74	—	—	—
Dividends paid in redeemable preferred stock	(52)	—	—	—
Other items, net	106	(23)	(23)	42
Cash provided (used) by financing activities	(3,642)	131	(1,106)	(409)
Effect of Beatrice and Esmark acquisitions in fiscal 1987 and 1985, respectively:				
Funding	7,373	—	—	2,708
Purchase of equity securities	(6,183)	—	—	(2,708)
Debt repaid	(898)	—	—	—
Cash and short-term investments of acquired company	145	—	—	237
Increase in cash and short-term investments resulting from acquisitions	437	—	—	237
Cash provided before cash dividend payments	46	51	184	298
Cash dividends	—	(53)	(195)	(170)
Increase (decrease) in cash and short-term investments	46	(2)	(11)	128
Cash and short-term investments at beginning of period	—	147	158	30
Cash and short-term investments at end of period	$ 46	$145	$ 147	$ 158

Source: Reprinted by permission of Beatrice Company.

EXHIBIT 11   BCI Holdings Corporation—condensed consolidating financial statements
(in millions)

	NSI	Swift-Eckrich	Beatrice U.S. Food	BCI Products
Condensed consolidating income statement (Fiscal 1987):				
Net sales	$1,712	$1,318	$1,811	$1,243
Operating expenses	1,498	1,204	1,659	1,125
Operating earnings	214	114	152	118
Intercompany interest income (expense), net	(46)	(31)	(33)	(23)
Interest expense, net	(20)	(1)	(66)	(45)
Other income (expense)	—	—	9	3
Earnings (loss) before income taxes and other items	148	82	62	53
Income tax expense (benefit)	83	43	31	29
Earnings (loss) before discontinued operations and extraordinary items	65	39	31	24
Discontinued operations	4	—	41	23
Extraordinary items	—	—	—	—
Net earnings (loss)	$ 69	$ 39	$ 72	$ 47
Condensed consolidating balance sheet (As of February 28, 1987):				
Assets:				
Cash and short-term investments	$ 7	$ 1	$ 19	$ 17
Receivables, net	167	59	123	210
Inventories	353	101	187	188
Other current assets	13	1	13	16
Total current assets	540	162	342	431
Property, plant and equipment, net	434	208	204	247
Intangible assets, principally unallocated purchase cost	—	—	—	—
Other noncurrent assets	18	1	514	95
Total assets	$ 992	$ 371	$1,060	$ 773
Liabilities and stockholders' equity:				
Short-term debt and current maturities of long-term debt	$ 15	$ —	$ 5	$ 20
Accounts payable and accrued expenses	313	163	323	180
Total current liabilities	328	163	328	200
Long-term debt	228	5	40	28
Noncurrent and deferred income taxes	39	—	(1)	4
Other noncurrent liabilities	38	4	13	109
Net intercompany investments and advances	359	199	680	432
Stockholders' equity:				
Common stock	—	—	—	—
Additional capital	—	—	—	—
Retained earnings (deficit)	—	—	—	—
Cumulative foreign currency translation adjustment	—	—	—	—
Total stockholders' equity	—	—	—	—
Total liabilities and stockholders' equity	$ 992	$ 371	$1,060	$ 773

EXHIBIT 11   BCI Holdings Corporation—condensed consolidating financial statements (in millions)

	BCI International	Parent company (holdings)	Eliminations	Holdings consolidated
Condensed consolidating income statement (Fiscal 1987):				
Net sales	$2,866	$ —	$ (24)	$8,926
Operating expenses	2,719	174	(24)	8,355
Operating earnings	147	(174)	—	571
Intercompany interest income (expense), net	(11)	258	(114)	—
Interest expense, net	(19)	(538)	222	(467)
Other income (expense)	(10)	150	(273)	(121)
Earnings (loss) before income taxes and other items	107	(304)	(165)	(17)
Income tax expense (benefit)	61	(238)	53	62
Earnings (loss) before discontinued operations and extraordinary items	46	(66)	(218)	(79)
Discontinued operations	—	7	(55)	20
Extraordinary items	—	(46)	—	(46)
Net earnings (loss)	$ 46	$(105)	$(273)	$(105)
Condensed consolidating balance sheet (As of February 28, 1987):				
Assets:				
Cash and short-term investments	$ 113	$ 16	$ —	$ 173
Receivables, net	267	34	—	860
Inventories	271	—	—	1,100
Other current assets	24	102	—	169
Total current assets	675	152	—	2,302
Property, plant and equipment, net	440	74	—	1,607
Intangible assets, principally unallocated purchase cost	—	3,130	—	3,130
Other noncurrent assets	33	203	—	864
Total assets	$1,148	$3,559	$ —	$7,903
Liabilities and stockholders' equity:				
Short-term debt and current maturities of long-term debt	$ 128	$ 107	$ —	$ 275
Accounts payable and accrued expenses	387	306	—	1,672
Total current liabilities	515	413	—	1,947
Long-term debt	43	3,982	—	4,326
Noncurrent and deferred income taxes	21	420	—	483
Other noncurrent liabilities	130	545	—	839
Net intercompany investments and advances	439	(2,109)	—	—
Stockholders' equity:				
Common stock	—	1	—	1
Additional capital	—	418	—	418
Retained earnings (deficit)	—	(121)	—	(121)
Cumulative foreign currency translation adjustment	—	10	—	10
Total stockholders' equity	—	308	—	308
Total liabilities and stockholders' equity	$1,148	$3,559	$ —	$7,903

Source: Reprinted by permission of Beatrice Company.

D

INTERNATIONAL CASES

Case 23

THE GLOBAL AUTO
INDUSTRY IN
THE 1990S

INTRODUCTION

The global auto industry in 1990 looked very different from the auto industry in 1960. In 1960 the industry was fragmented into a series of self-contained national markets having relatively little trade or contact with each other. Even though companies such as Ford and General Motors had long had international subsidiaries, those subsidiaries operated on a fully autonomous basis with regard to design, production, and marketing. Typically, the structure of most national markets was consolidated, and a handful of companies dominated the local industry. For example, in the world's biggest market, the United States, the trio of General Motors (GM), Ford, and Chrysler accounted for over 90 percent of the market. The result in most nations was an absence of strong competition.

By 1990 the picture was changing rapidly. The industry was becoming more global. In particular, the volume of trade in automobiles and automobile components among the three main global markets—North America, Western Europe, and Japan—had increased rapidly. In addition, more and more companies were seeking to establish production facilities overseas as a protection against trade barriers and currency fluctuations. One consequence of these trends was the fragmentation of previously consolidated national markets and a commensurate increase in the intensity of competition around the globe. Nowhere was this result more apparent than in the United States, where by the first seven months of 1990 the market share in cars held by the big three U.S.-owned auto companies had slipped to just over 66 percent. During the same period, for the first time ever, a non-U.S. company took third place in the market for cars. Honda of America, with 9.12 percent of the market, outsold Chrysler, which held only 8.88 percent of the U.S. car market.[1]

This case was prepared by Charles W. L. Hill, University of Washington.
[1] *Automotive News*, August 13, 1990.

THE JAPANESE CHALLENGE

The driving force behind the trend toward a more competitive global auto industry has been the explosive growth of Japanese auto production since the 1960s. In 1960 Japanese companies accounted for approximately 4 percent of global auto production. By 1970 their share had risen to 16 percent, and by 1990 30 percent of the 50 million or so vehicles manufactured worldwide were made by Japanese producers.[2] Along the way Japanese companies have increased their share of the U.S. auto market from nothing to 31 percent and their share of the Western European market from nothing to 11 percent. Had it not been for a variety of import controls, "voluntary" and otherwise, in both the United States and Europe, the Japanese share would undoubtedly have been higher.[3]

Mass Versus Lean Production

Japanese production has grown because of the ability of Japanese companies to deliver a broad range of high-quality, well-designed automobiles at a reasonable cost to consumers. This ability is based on a series of process innovations pioneered primarily by Toyota and Nissan in the years following World War II.[4] Most U.S. and European automakers still utilize the mass-production technology originally pioneered by Henry Ford in the 1920s. In contrast, most Japanese producers utilize a technology that has been termed "lean production."[5] The differences between the two technologies are striking.

Mass-production technology aims to mass-produce each car model in order to spread the fixed costs of production over as many units as possible. To achieve this goal, the typical mass producer utilizes unskilled or semiskilled workers to mind expensive single-purpose machines that churn out large volumes of the same product. The mass producer also adds many buffers—extra supplies, extra workers, and extra space—in order to ensure smooth production and by-pass any bottlenecks that occur in the system (such as when a machine breaks down). In theory, this system gives the consumer lower-cost automobiles—but at the expense of some loss of variety. In practice, the extra workers, supplies, and space raise costs above the costs of the typical Japanese lean producer, and the boring and dispiriting method of work leads to an alienated work force that is likely to make mistakes. Consequently, relative to the output of lean producers, mass producers tend to turn out high-cost, poor-quality cars.

[2]Womack, J. P., Jones, D. T., Roos, D. 1990. *The Machine That Changed the World.* New York: Rawson Associates.

[3]*The Economist,* "Are America's Carmakers Headed for the Junkyard?" April 14, 1990, pp. 79–82. Tully, S. "Now Japan's Autos Push into Europe," *Fortune,* January 29, 1990, pp. 96–106.

[4]For a full description of these processes, see Cusumano, M. A. 1989. *The Japanese Automobile Industry.* Cambridge, Mass.: Harvard University Press, Table 48, p. 197. Case 27.

[5]See Womack, J. P., Jones, D. T., Roos, D. 1990. *The Machine That Changed the World.* New York: Rawson Associates.

In contrast, lean producers utilize flexible manufacturing technologies to produce limited amounts of a car at a cost that at one time could be achieved only through mass production. They utilize just-in-time inventory systems to eliminate buffer stocks of inventory. They utilize cross-functional teams composed of engineering, manufacturing, and marketing personnel in an attempt to shorten new product development times. And they form the work force into multiskilled teams, eliminating the need for many of the "specialists" and "supervisors" found in mass-production plants and thereby reducing the total work force. The team organization seems to result in a more satisfying work environment, reducing both worker alienation and the mistakes born of boredom or frustration that seem to plague mass producers.

As a result of these features, relative to the output of a mass producer, the typical lean producer can manufacture a wider range of higher-quality automobiles at a lower cost. Lean producers are also able to introduce new models more rapidly, thereby adapting themselves more quickly to trends in the marketplace. Given these advantages, it is hardly surprising that the Japanese companies who pioneered lean-production techniques—and particularly Toyota, Nissan, and Honda—are now among the strongest automobile companies in the world. Proof of this can be found in Exhibit 1, which summarizes assembly plant characteristics for a number of volume producers of different nationalities in 1989. As can be seen, relative to American and European producers, the typical Japanese producer needed fewer worker hours to assemble a vehicle, achieved superior quality, held less inventory, and had a higher percentage of the work force in teams. Clearly the challenge facing many American and European companies is to replicate this performance.

What has to be remembered, however, is that the data given in Exhibit 1 are averages. There is considerable variation in the efficiency of plants within the different national groupings. For example, the Japanese plants of Toyota, Nissan,

EXHIBIT 1   **Assembly plant characteristics for volume producers (averages for plants in each region)**

	Producers		
	Japanese in Japan	Americans in America	Europeans
Productivity (worker hours to build a vehicle)	16.8	25.1	36.2
Quality (defects per 100 vehicles)	60.0	82.3	97.0
Inventories (days' supply for 8 sample parts)	0.2	2.9	2.0
% of work force in teams	69.3	17.3	0.6

Source: Adapted from Womack, J. P., Jones, D. T., Roos, D. 1990. *The Machine That Changed the World*. New York: Rawson Associates, Figure 4.7, p. 92.

and Honda are notably more efficient than are those of some of the smaller Japanese companies (for example, Isuzu, Suzuki, and Daihatsu). Moreover, some of the best-managed plants owned by North American companies are now achieving productivity and quality levels close to those achieved at well-run Japanese plants. This seems to be particularly true of several of Ford's plants.

Diffusion of Lean Production

In the future, the productivity gap between Japanese and non-Japanese plants may close somewhat as American and European producers adopt Japanese lean-production techniques. Indeed, there are already signs that this narrowing is beginning to occur. All three U.S. auto majors have entered into joint-venture arrangements with Japanese partners in an attempt to learn more about Japanese production techniques, as have a number of European auto companies. In the early 1980s, for example, GM entered into a joint venture with Toyota to build cars in Fremont, California. This joint venture has proved to be very successful. The Fremont plant has attained productivity and quality levels comparable to those of Toyota's Japanese plants.[6] However, so far there are only limited signs that GM has been able to apply the lessons learned in the Fremont joint venture to its other U.S. plants, primarily because of the problems involved in making a huge bureaucracy like GM change direction. In recognition of the enormous inertia problems it faces in trying to change its own organization, GM set up a separate company, Saturn, to build cars utilizing "Japanese" lean-production techniques. However, it is still too early to say whether Saturn will be successful. The plant came on stream in mid 1990, but as of early 1991 it was reportedly plagued by production problems.

THE GLOBAL INDUSTRY

Roughly 50 million automobiles are produced each year worldwide. The vast bulk of this production takes place in three main regions: Japan, North America, and Western Europe. Each region accounts for approximately 30 percent of global production. The biggest single national car market is the United States, which in 1989 accounted for the sale of 9.9 million cars, plus 5 million trucks, over half of which were the light pickup trucks that many Americans use as cars. However, if Western Europe is viewed as a single car market, which it may become after the removal of trade barriers between members of the European Economic Community in 1992, then it becomes the world's largest car market with a record 13.4

[6]Womack, J. P., Jones, D. T., Roos, D. 1990. *The Machine That Changed the World.* New York: Rawson Associates.

million cars sold in 1989, a jump of 26 percent over the previous year. Japan is the third largest car market with a record 7.1 million new vehicle registrations in 1989.[7]

Viewed on a global basis, the industry looks increasingly fragmented. The [7] global market share for the world's 25 largest automakers is given in Exhibit 2. As can be seen, GM still leads the pack with 17.7 percent of the global market, followed by Ford (14.6%), Toyota (9.4%), Volkswagen (6.6%), and Nissan (6.4%). In recent years, however, GM's share has declined, particularly in the United States, while the shares of Toyota, Nissan, and Honda have increased and Volkswagen's share has held steady.

EXHIBIT 2   **Global market share for 1989**

Company	Country	Market share (%)
General Motors	U.S.	17.7
Ford	U.S.	14.6
Toyota	Japan	9.4
Volkswagen	Germany	6.6
Nissan	Japan	6.4
Chrysler	U.S.	5.4
Fiat	Italy	5.4
Peugeot	France	4.6
Renault	France	4.2
Honda	Japan	4.0
Mazda	Japan	2.8
Mitsubishi Motors	Japan	2.7
Hyundai	South Korea	1.9
Suzuki	Japan	1.7
Daimler	Germany	1.7
Daihatsu	Japan	1.4
Fuji (Subaru)	Japan	1.2
BMW	Germany	1.2
Rover	Britain	1.1
Volvo	Sweden	1.0
Isuzu	Japan	0.8
Kia Motors	South Korea	0.7
Daewood Motors	South Korea	0.4
Lada	Soviet Union	0.3
Saab-Scania	Sweden	0.3

Source: Adapted from *Business Week,* "The Business Week Global Auto Scoreboard," May 7, 1990, pp. 54–55.

[7]Figures compiled from (a) Ingrassia, P., and Graven, K. "Japan's Auto Industry May Soon Consolidate as Competition Grows," *The Wall Street Journal,* April 24, 1990, pp. 1, 10; (b) Tully, S. "Now Japan's Autos Push into Europe," *Fortune,* January 29, 1990, pp. 96–106; (c) Treece, J. B., and Melcher, R. A. "Will Japan Do to Europe What It Did to Detroit?" *Business Week,* May 7, 1990, pp. 52–53.

The United States Market

The story of the U.S. auto market in the first year of the 1990s was one of slumping sales, excess capacity, declining profits for the big three U.S. producers, and further gains made by the Japanese competition. In the first eight months of 1990 9.67 million cars and light trucks were sold in the United States. This compares with sales of 10.2 million in the first eight months of 1989. Final U.S. production for 1990 was expected to run out at no more than 12 million cars and light trucks; yet 79 plants, with a combined capacity to produce 14.4 million vehicles per year, or 16.8 million with overtime, are producing cars and trucks in North America.[8] The implication is that substantial excess capacity exists in the U.S. industry. The consequences so far have included intense price competition and slumping profits for the big U.S. producers. Compared with the first six months of 1989, during the first half of 1990 net profits slumped 63 percent at Chrysler, 58 percent at Ford, and 38 percent at General Motors. In the fourth quarter of 1990, analysts guessed, GM lost as much as $1.2 billion from its auto operations, Ford $250 million, and Chrysler up to $40 million.[9]

If anything, the situation will get worse before it gets better. Demand is likely to slip further as the U.S. economy enters a recession. Initial forecasts predict a further 41 percent fall in U.S. sales of cars and trucks during 1991. Moreover, the University of Michigan's October 1990 survey of consumer confidence showed only that 50 percent of households were inclined to buy a new car in 1991, the lowest share since the recession year of 1982.

To make matters worse still, total productive capacity will increase further during the early 1990s as major Japanese companies continue to build additional production facilities in the United States, exacerbating the excess capacity problem. The trend among Japanese companies to build production facilities in the United States began in 1985 as a hedge against import controls and currency fluctuations. Now it has developed into a major worry for the U.S. auto companies. As of 1989, Japanese automakers had opened ten auto plants in the United States. Referred to as "transplants," these facilities include some of the most efficient, most automated, and least unionized auto plants in North America. In the first half of 1989, Japanese-owned plants were already building 15 percent of the passenger cars produced in North America. Taking into account planned expansion in U.S.-based capacity, current estimates suggest that this figure could double by 1995.[10]

Despite the tough competitive environment, additional expansion of Japanese capacity in the United States is likely. The major Japanese companies have

[8]*The Economist,* "Are America's Carmakers Headed for the Junkyard?" April 14, 1990, pp. 79–80.
[9]*Automotive News,* September 10, 1990. *The Economist,* "Showdown in Motown," January 5, 1991, p. 52.
[10]*The Economist,* "Are America's Carmakers Headed for the Junkyard?" April 14, 1990. Treece, J. B., and Hoerr, J. "Shaking Up Detroit," *Business Week,* August 14, 1989, pp. 73–80.

continued to make inroads into the U.S. market in recent years, giving them an incentive to further expand U.S. capacity. This can be seen from the market-share figures given in Exhibit 3. Exhibit 3 compares the market share for cars and light trucks for the first eight months of 1989 against that for the first eight months of 1990. Both Ford and Chrysler lost share; GM managed to hold steady; and both Honda and Toyota posted substantial gains over the previous period. The Japanese gains are even more impressive if light trucks are excluded from these figures. The figures for passenger cars only show that Honda (9.22% share) outsold Chrysler (8.83% share) and Toyota was close behind (8.47% share).

Continued Japanese penetration of the U.S. market seems likely. According to a 1989 survey by J. D. Power & Associates, an automotive research firm, almost two-thirds of U.S. customers under 45 prefer Japanese cars to GM cars. They also prefer Japanese cars to Ford and Chrysler models. Winning back these younger customers, who purchase some 55 percent of all new cars, will not be easy for U.S. companies.[11] One of the principal reasons that U.S. producers have difficulty holding on to their market share appears to be the relatively poor quality of the cars and trucks that they manufacture. A survey of quality by *Consumer Reports* found that 28 of the 31 best-rated 1989 models were Japanese. Of the 33 worst-rated models, all but 1 were produced by Ford, GM, or Chrysler.[12] The same survey also found that Japanese automakers widened their quality advantage over U.S. producers in the 1989 model year when compared with the 1988 model year. This occurred despite that fact that the average quality of U.S. cars improved. Apparently, the Japanese producers improved their quality even faster.

Two other factors seem likely to increase Japanese penetration: (1) the entry of Japanese producers into the booming minivan sector and (2) the Japanese move

EXHIBIT 3   **U.S. market share in cars and light trucks in 1989 and 1990 (first eight months)**

Company	1989 (%)	1990 (%)
General Motors	35.25	35.71
Ford	23.98	25.02
Chrysler	13.74	12.06
Toyota	6.16	7.60
Honda	5.21	6.14
Nissan	4.63	4.41
All European	3.35	3.34

Source: Adapted from *Automotive News*, September 10, 1990.

[11]*The Economist*, "Are America's Carmakers Headed for the Junkyard?" April 14, 1990, pp. 79–80.
[12]Reported in *The Wall Street Journal*, "Big Three Boost Car Quality but Still Lag," March 27, 1990, pp. B1, B5.

up-market into the luxury car market. The minivan sector is currently dominated by U.S. producers, particularly Chrysler, which pioneered the minivan concept. However, after stumbling with its first attempt, Toyota came up with the 1990 Previa minivan, which looked to be one of the hits of the year. Toyota seemed sure to sell its planned output of 50,000 Previas in the United States during 1990. Indeed, Toyota dealers say they could sell 100,000 Previas if they could get them.[13]

In the luxury car market Honda's Acura and Toyota's Lexus division seem to be carving a niche for themselves. As Exhibit 4 illustrates, while traditional luxury car makers such as BMW, Cadillac (GM), Volvo, and Saab saw significant sales declines in 1990 over 1989, Lexus boosted its sales from 4,554 to 57,162 and Acura matched its 1989 sales of 140,000-plus vehicles despite a shrinking market. As elsewhere, the Japanese entry into this segment has been helped by low prices, high quality, and good customer service. For example, a fully loaded Lexus cost $40,000 in 1990. Although expensive, this compares favorably with a top-of-the-line Mercedes ($83,500) or BMW ($73,600). Indeed, the German luxury car makers seem likely to be particularly hard hit by Japanese entry into this segment. So far four out of every ten U.S. buyers of Lexus cars have traded in a German-built auto.[14]

The European Market

In the Western European car market, 1989 was a boom year. In all, 13.5 million passenger cars were sold, making Western Europe the world's largest car market.

EXHIBIT 4   **Luxury car sales in the United States in the 1989 and 1990 model years**

Make	Origin	1990	1989
Alfa Romeo	Italy	3,036	3,306
Audi	Germany	22,421	20,478
BMW	Germany	61,578	69,690
Jaguar	Britain	19,176	19,696
Mercedes	Germany	75,112	76,152
Porsche	Germany	9,244	10,609
Saab	Sweden	25,970	34,901
Stirling	Britain	4,501	5,951
Volvo	Sweden	95,419	102,625
Cadillac (GM)	U.S.	256,763	275,600
Lincoln (Ford)	U.S.	223,596	203,890
Acura (Honda)	Japan	140,305	140,713
Infiniti (Nissan)	Japan	17,115	—
Lexus (Toyota)	Japan	57,162	4,554

Source: Adapted from *The Economist,* "Elegant Nippon," December 8, 1990, p. 73.

[13]Flint, J. "The New Number Three?" *Fortune,* June 11, 1990, pp. 136–140.
[14]Templeman, J. "Infiniti and Lexus: Characters in a German Nightmare," *Business Week,* October 9, 1990, p. 64.

EXHIBIT 5   **Western European new car registrations by country, 1989**

Country	% share
Austria	2.1
Belgium	3.3
Denmark	0.6
Ireland	0.6
Finland	1.3
France	16.9
Germany	21.0
Greece	0.6
Italy	17.5
Luxembourg	0.2
Netherlands	3.7
Norway	0.4
Portugal	1.4
Sweden	2.3
Switzerland	2.5
Spain	8.5
United Kingdom	17.1

Source: Adapted from *Automotive News,* May 30, 1990.

Of these, some 73 percent were sold in four countries: France, Germany, Italy, and Britain (see Exhibit 5). Market-share figures for Western Europe for the first ten months of 1990 are given in Exhibit 6. Four big national producers (Volkswagen, Fiat, Peugeot Citroen, and Renault) plus the European subsidiaries of Ford and GM currently dominate the market.

In contrast to 1989, 1990 started slow, and industry analysts expected new car sales to slip back by 3 percent or so. As in the United States, the consequences included excess capacity, price cutting, and slumping profits. For example, compared to 1989, in 1990 profits slumped 12 percent for Fiat, 41 percent for Ford of Europe, 23 percent for General Motors of Europe, 11 percent for Peugeot, and 26 percent for Renault. Only Volkswagen among the big six European automakers saw its 1990 profits increase, by 7 percent.[15]

Despite a similar slump, long-term growth prospects in Europe are more promising than in the United States. Car ownership in Western Europe runs at about 380 per 1,000 persons, versus 580 per 1,000 persons in the United States.[16] In addition, there is the potentially large untapped demand in Eastern Europe. Ford has estimated that given growth in the East, the combined European car market could amount to 24 million cars per year by 2008, compared with a demand of only 13 million per year in the United States.[17]

[15]Melcher, R. A. "The Nasty Pileup in Europe's Auto Industry," *Business Week,* September 17, 1990, pp. 48–49.
[16]Tully, S. "Now Japan's Autos Push into Europe," *Fortune,* January 29, 1990, pp. 96–106.
[17]Treece, J. B., and Melcher, R. A. "Will Japan Do to Europe What It Did to Detroit?" *Business Week,* May 7, 1990, pp. 52–53.

EXHIBIT 6   **Western Europe's car market—January to October 1990**

Company	% market share	% change on 1989
Volkswagen	15.2	+ 1.9
Fiat	14.2	− 4.9
Peugeot Citroen	13.0	+ 1.0
General Motors	11.7	+ 2.7
Ford	11.6	− 3.7
Renault	9.8	− 5.0
Mercedes-Benz	3.3	+ 2.8
Rover	3.0	− 5.8
BMW	2.7	− 5.4
Volvo	1.8	− 10.3
Japanese	11.7	+ 6.1
Others	2.0	− 5.0

Source: Adapted from *The Economist*, "The People's Car Heads East," December 15, 1990, p. 74.

Unlike the U.S. presence in Europe, the Japanese presence in Europe is currently limited (see Exhibit 6), primarily because of stringent import controls. France restricts Japanese imports to 3 percent of sales. Italy and Spain have held the Japanese share to less than 1 percent, and even free-market Britain has set a ceiling of 11 percent on Japanese imports.[18] As a result, in the first ten months of 1990 the Japanese held only 11.7 percent of the Western European car market. However, the winds of change are now blowing through Europe. The liberalization of trade barriers between members of the European Economic Community, which is due to start in 1992, will eventually (by the end of the decade perhaps) result in the removal of most import restrictions. In the meantime, a period of transition is envisaged during which European nations will gradually lower their barriers to imported cars.

Equally significant, as in the United States, producers in Japan have begun constructing automaking capacity in Europe. Nissan, Toyota, and Honda have recently announced spending plans amounting to $2.6 billion over the next five years to build new plants in Britain, from which they can serve the Western Europe market. (Britain is favored because of low labor costs, substantial government assistance, and a productive work force.) The pioneer is Nissan, which has been building cars in Sunderland, northern England since 1986. In 1993 annual production is planned to triple to 200,000 cars. In addition, a Honda plant planned for Swindon, which lies west of London, will turn out 100,000 cars per year by 1994. Toyota will also soon break ground in the rural Midlands for a plant that will make 200,000 cars per year. Mazda and Mitsubishi are expected to

[18]Tully, S. "Now Japan's Autos Push into Europe," *Fortune*, January 29, 1990, pp. 96–106.

follow shortly. All this activity has led to predictions that Japanese production in Europe could reach over 1 million cars per year by 1998.[19]

To support their attempt to gain European sales, Toyota, Honda, Nissan, and Mazda have all set up design facilities in Europe to modify Japanese vehicles for European tastes. In addition, the companies are planning to follow the lead of GM and Ford's European operations in designing products exclusively for European use.[20] The Japanese producers are also enlarging their dealer networks. Currently, their estimated 14,400 dealerships in Western Europe barely surpass the nearly 12,000 dealerships owned by GM and Ford alone. However, Honda already has plans to swell its dealership ranks by one-third, to 2,000 by 1995.[21]

The European automakers best positioned to fight the Japanese are probably GM's European subsidiaries, Ford's European subsidiaries, and Volkswagen. In 1989 GM was the most profitable company in Europe (a fact that helped boost GM's slumping U.S. auto profits). Its subcompact Opel Corsas and Vauxhall Novas are made at a state-of-the-art low-cost factory in Saragossa, Spain. GM subsidiaries have the largest market share in the Netherlands and Denmark, and the company ranks second in Britain, Germany, and Switzerland.

Ford's dealer network of 8,000 is the strongest in Western Europe. It is number one in the large British market and ranks among the top three in Germany, Sweden, and Ireland. The company's strength is in small cars.

Volkswagen is number one in the unprotected German market and in Belgium, Austria, and Switzerland. In 1986 it acquired low-cost manufacturing facilities with the takeover of SEAT, a Spanish automaker. The company has an attractive product line ranging from the Golf (Europe's best-selling subcompact) to the sleek, high-priced Audi 100. Volkswagen's weakness has been low profitability brought on by high German labor costs. The company's response has been to move production of its smallest car, the Polo, to SEAT in Spain, freeing up high-paid and highly skilled German labor to build the company's more expensive cars.

The prospects for Fiat and Peugeot Citroen are not as bright. Both companies are heavily dependent on protected home markets for too many of their sales. Fiat sells 68 percent of its cars in Italy, and Peugeot Citroen sells 43 percent of its cars in France. Once trade barriers start to fall in Europe after 1992, Fiat and Peugeot will find their domestic market share under heavy attack from other European producers and from the Japanese.

Perhaps the most vulnerable of Europe's volume automakers, however, is Renault. This state-owned company sells about 90 percent of its cars in France and in other highly protected markets. Financially, it is by far the weakest of the big European automakers. Heavily subsidized by the French government,

[19]Tully, S. "Now Japan's Autos Push into Europe, *Fortune*, January 29, 1990, pp. 96–106.
[20]Lublin, J. S. "Japanese Auto Makers Speed into Europe," *The Wall Street Journal*, June 6, 1990, p. A13.
[21]Lublin, J. S. "Japanese Auto Makers Speed into Europe," *The Wall Street Journal*, June 6, 1990, p. A13.

Renault still has a debt-to-equity ratio of 2 to 1, which is six times the level at Volkswagen.[22]

The wild card in Europe is the newly democratic East. There is no doubt that a huge pent-up demand for cars exists in one-time communist countries like Czechoslovakia, Poland, and the former East Germany. However, that does not necessarily mean that there is cash available to buy new cars. The dismal state of most East European economies means that any boom in new car sales is likely to remain a dream for a number of years. Indeed, of the estimated 1 million Western-built cars sold in the former East Germany during 1990, some 800,000 were reportedly second-hand models.[23]

Despite this, Volkswagen, Fiat, and General Motors are investing heavily in East European car plants. On December 11, 1990, GM's Opel subsidiary announced that it was investing $680 million in a new car plant in the former East Germany. Similarly, on December 9, 1990, Volkswagen's bid to buy Skoda, a Czechoslovak automaker, was approved by the Czech government. Volkswagen aims to more than double Skoda's present production to 400,000 cars per year by 1997 and to help Skoda develop a new range of models. VW also plans to invest up to $6.4 billion in Skoda over the next ten years to update the company's antiquated manufacturing facilities.[24]

The Japanese Market

The latter half of 1990 brought an end to the boom in new car sales in Japan that had pushed demand to record levels in each of the last three years. In 1989 a record 7.1 million new cars were registered in Japan. In November 1990, however, industry sales slipped for the first time in twenty-one months, down 2.7 percent from a year ago.[25] However, Japan's auto companies believe that this slowdown is only temporary and that the domestic market is entering a period of long-term growth. They point to a number of favorable trends to back up this argument. Rural families are starting to own two cars. Women are driving more; the number of women with licenses has grown by 82 percent since 1980 compared with a 23 percent increase for men. Government plans to increase Japan's 2,700 miles of freeway to 8,700 miles by 2010 may also help things along. In addition, car ownership in Japan is still relatively low. Japan has 243 cars per 1,000 people, compared with 370 in Britain, 454 in the old West Germany, and 588 in the United States.[26]

Despite this generally favorable environment, not all is well among Japan's automakers. As the market-share figures given in Exhibit 7 demonstrate, al-

[22]Tully, S. "Now Japan's Auto Makers Push into Europe," *Fortune,* January 29, 1990, pp. 96–106.
[23]*The Economist,* "The People's Car Heads East," December 15, 1990, p. 74.
[24]*The Economist,* "The People's Car Heads East," December 15, 1990, p. 74.
[25]Miller, K. L., and Treece, J. B. "Honda's Nightmare: Maybe You Can't Go Home Again," *Business Week,* December 24, 1990, p. 36.
[26]*The Economist,* "The Car as a Fashion Statement," October 21, 1990, pp. 80–81.

EXHIBIT 7   Japan's car market

Company	1989 sales	% market share	% change in sales from 1988
Toyota	2,308,779	32.5	+8.2
Nissan	1,319,049	18.6	+12.0
Mitsubishi	665,191	9.4	+6.4
Honda	663,126	9.3	+7.5
Suzuki	510,834	7.2	−2.1
Daihatsu	509,524	7.2	−2.3
Mazda	483,759	6.8	+16.3
Subaru (Fuji)	313,245	4.4	−4.1
Isuzu	203,383	2.9	−1.1

Source: Adapted from Ingrassia, P., and Graven, K. "Japan's Auto Industry May Soon Consolidate as Competition Grows," *Wall Street Journal*, April 24, 1990, pp. 1, 10.

though the total market grew in 1989, several of Japan's small automakers experienced a sales slump! Worst hit was Subaru, which is owned by Fuji Heavy Industries. Fuji saw its sales of Subaru cars fall 4.5 percent in the middle of a sales boom, and the company registered a $146-million operating loss for the fiscal year that ended in March 1990. Suzuki, Daihatsu, and Isuzu also saw their sales fall in 1989.

In the first half of 1990 the situation got worse for these companies. Compared with the same period in the previous year, for cars of over 660cc, trucks, and buses, sales slumped by 7.8 percent at Subaru, 8.6 percent at Daihatsu, and 5.6 percent at Isuzu. Suzuki, on the other hand, staged a recovery and saw its sales surge by 27.9 percent. Over the same period, sales at Toyota increased by 14.4 percent, at Nissan by 11.8 percent, at Mazda by 21.6 percent, and at Honda by 13.7 percent. Imports also surged by 39.7 percent to take a small but significant 3.7 percent share of the Japanese market.[27]

The main factor behind the sales slumps at Subaru, Daihatsu, and Isuzu has been revisions in Japanese tax codes. For years these companies benefited from preferential tax treatment for their mini-vehicles (subcompacts and light trucks powered by engines up to 550cc). In April 1989, however, the Japanese government cut the preferential tax treatment for mini-vehicles. (At the same time the government removed a tax bias against "luxury" models with engines over 2000cc. This resulted in a surge in demand for large cars in Japan—hence the growth in imports, particularly West German imports.)

Another factor that has hurt Japan's smaller companies has been the rising yen. The value of the yen against the U.S. dollar doubled between 1985 and 1989, making it harder for Japanese producers to export. The likes of Honda, Nissan,

[27]Figures taken from *Automotive News*, July 16, 1990.

and Toyota responded to the rising yen by building plants in the United States. The smaller Japanese companies lack the capital to make similar investments and instead have seen their exports shrink.

These factors have led to predictions of consolidation in Japan's auto industry. There is already speculation that Nissan, which is the largest stockholder in Fuji (with a 4.3 percent stake), will step in to ensure Fuji's survival. In April 1990 Fuji's president announced that he would be succeeded by a former high executive at Nissan, and it seems likely that Nissan will increase its stake in Fuji over the next few years. It is also possible that other major producers may step in and take control of Daihatsu and Isuzu during the 1990s.[28] It is worth bearing in mind here that General Motors owns 38 percent of Isuzu.

Another Japanese company for which all is not smooth sailing is Honda. Honda has excelled in the United States, but it has not been able to replicate its performance in Japan. In a curious turn of events, Honda now sells twice as many cars in the United States as it does in Japan. Honda's problems in Japan stem from weak sales and distribution. Toyota has 45,000 salespeople and 4,500 dealer outlets, and Nissan has 28,000 salespeople and 3,200 outlets, but Honda has a sales force of 10,500 and 2,684 outlets. This disparity is viewed as a serious handicap in a country where customers expect top-flight service, including regular home visits by auto salespeople.[29]

STRATEGIC TRENDS IN THE GLOBAL INDUSTRY

Two strategic trends in the global auto industry began to emerge during the 1980s. One was the drive by a number of producers, particularly the major Japanese companies, to become multiregional producers. The second was a dramatic increase in the number of strategic alliances between auto companies. Both trends seem likely to continue into the 1990s.

Becoming a Multiregional Producer

With the exception of General Motors, Ford, and to a lesser extent Volkswagen, historically most auto companies have based their manufacturing in a single region and exported production to other regions. For example, until the mid 1980s Japanese producers such as Toyota, Nissan, and Honda produced all of their automobiles in Japan and exported to the rest of the world. Similarly, companies like BMW, Fiat, Renault, Rover, and Volvo continue to base most of their manufacturing in their domestic market and export to other regions. In contrast, the

[28]Ingrassia, P., and Graven, K. "Japan's Auto Industry May Soon Consolidate as Competition Grows," *The Wall Street Journal*, April 24, 1990, pp. 1, 10.
[29]Miller, K. L., and Treece, J. B. "Honda's Nightmare: Maybe You Can't Go Home Again," *Business Week*, December 24, 1990, p. 36.

ideal multiregional producers has a top-to-bottom manufacturing system in each of the world's major markets. There are a number of advantages claimed for this strategy over that of manufacturing in a single region and exporting.[30]

First, multiregional production provides protection from trade barriers and currency fluctuations. Second, despite all the talk of emerging global markets for standardized products, the simple fact is that in the auto industry consumers in the big three regional markets (North America, Europe, and Japan) continue to demand different types of vehicles. For example, the demand for four-wheel-drive vehicles, pickup trucks, and minivans is much greater in the United States than elsewhere. Consider also the example of low-end BMWs and Mercedes-Benz cars. They are sold as taxis in Germany to create a volume base for their manufacturers, but they are sold in North America and Japan at much lower volumes and much higher prices as luxury goods. These differences in approach require radically different marketing strategies and some product customization to regional requirements. Honda seems to have gone further than almost any other producer in attaching importance to these differences. During the 1990s Honda plans to develop a set of products that will be unique to each region.

A third advantage enjoyed by a multiregional producer is the ability to transfer managerial, marketing, manufacturing, and design knowhow from region to region. Experience gained in one region can often be used to solve problems and improve operations in another region. And synergies can be gained by having design teams from different regions work together on new products. With this in mind, Ford in particular has a policy of transferring managers between regional operations, and of collaboration between regional design centers, in an attempt to facilitate worldwide learning. It is important to recognize, however, that implementing such policies does require some centralization to achieve coordination. Companies like GM, which runs its overseas subsidiaries as autonomous standalone businesses, have yet to come to grips with this fact.

A fourth advantage claimed for the multiregional producer is some protection against regional cycles in the global industry. In 1989, for example, GM and Ford were able to offset slumping profits in the United States, where demand was falling, with strong profits from their European operations, where demand reached record levels. Looking back farther still, massive loans from Ford of Europe helped Ford survive the 1980–1982 auto depression.

According to a recent book by scholars at MIT, to gain all these advantages a multiregional auto company needs to have the following features:

1. Full design, manufacturing, and marketing facilities in each major region
2. An integrated, global personnel system that promotes personnel from any country in the company as if nationality did not exist
3. A set of mechanisms for continuous, horizontal information flow among manufacturing, supply systems, product development, technology acquisition, and development

[30]These arguments are set down in Womack, J. P., Jones, D. T., Roos, D. 1990. *The Machine That Changed the World.* New York: Rawson Associates.

4. A mechanism for coordinating the development of new products in each region and facilitating their sale as niche products in other regions[31]

Assessed against these features, currently Ford and Honda are the two companies that have traveled farthest down the road toward becoming full multiregional producers.

Ford has design and production facilities in each of the three major regional markets (in Japan, Ford owns 25 percent of Mazda), and Ford's corporate center is pro-active in building links between operations in each region and in encouraging joint design. Although lagging behind Ford, Honda has established design and production centers in each of the three major regions (although its European operations are nowhere nearly as well developed as those in the United States). For example, the Accord and Acura were completely designed and manufactured in the United States but are now sold in Japan. After some hesitation, the other Japanese companies, most notably Toyota and Nissan, now seem committed to traveling down this road, although they have a long way to go.

However, there are pitfalls that have to be avoided in the effort to become a multiregional company. In 1974 Volkswagen took steps toward becoming a multiregional producer with the establishment of a U.S. manufacturing plant in Pennsylvania. The idea was to provide a low-cost U.S. manufacturing base because the strong German mark had made exports to the United States increasingly uncompetitive. However, Volkswagen made two mistakes: (1) it staffed its operations with old-line manufacturing managers lured away from GM, and (2) it ran the operation as a standalone subsidiary with little input from the German operations. The results were an American rather than a German assembly plant. Costs remained high while quality tumbled, and buyers that had previously been attracted to German products were alienated. In 1989 Volkswagen finally gave up on its U.S. operations and closed them.

Global Strategic Alliances

During the 1980s the number of strategic alliances among auto companies around the globe mushroomed. For example, by 1989 Ford had entered into alliances with Volkswagen, Fiat, and Nissan, in addition to owning major stakes in Aston Martin (Britain), Mazda, and Kia (South Korea). Volkswagen also had links with Nissan, Toyota, and Porsche, and Fiat also had an alliance with Peugeot.[32]

In the early 1980s many alliances started as simple licensing arrangements under which one company would manufacture the car of another (for example, Britain's Rover group used to build Hondas under license). Now it is more typical for alliances to have one of three main thrusts:

1. The cooperating firms may jointly develop cars that both then build (e.g., the Honda Concerto and the Rover 2000 are virtually the same car).

[31]Womack, J. P., Jones, D. T., Roos, D. 1990. *The Machine That Changed the World*. New York: Rawson Associates.
[32]*The Economist*, "Spot the Difference," February 24, 1990, p. 74.

2. One company may build a car that the other then sells under its own name plate (e.g., GM's Pontiac LeMans is actually built by Daewoo Motor Co. of Korea).
3. The cooperating firms may jointly manage a manufacturing plant (e.g., under a joint-venture agreement, GM and Toyota manufacture cars in Fremont, California).

The desire to learn from competitors often appears to underlie many alliances. For example, Toyota executives argue that Toyota's joint venture with GM has allowed them to learn about U.S. supply and transportation conditions and about managing U.S. workers. This information gave Toyota the confidence to open its own production plants in the United States. Similarly, GM argues that it learned much about Japanese lean-production techniques from Toyota.[33]

However, alliances are no cure for all ills and do hold several dangers. For example, many argue that GM, by making it easier for Toyota to set up U.S. manufacturing operations, has simply created a more capable competitor. Moreover, GM seems not to have learned enough to make the alliance worthwhile. Some managers assigned to the joint venture claim that their knowledge was never put to good use inside GM. They say that they should have been kept together as a team to educate GM workers about the Japanese system. Instead, they were dispersed, to Canada, to Europe, to GM's truck division, and to GM's Electronic Data Systems subsidiary.[34]

CONCLUSION

In the 1980s the auto industry became noticeably more global in scope, with a number of producers taking steps down the road to become multiregional producers. At the same time, the leading Japanese companies underlined their position as the most productive auto companies in the world. As the world enters the 1990s a number of questions remain about the future shape of the global auto industry. Will the Japanese maintain their lead, or will the lean-production techniques on which it is based finally become diffused among international competitors? Will the industry become more consolidated, particularly in the fragmented Japanese and European markets? What will happen in the U.S. market? Will GM be able to reverse two decades of decline? Will Chrysler be able to survive the tough environment of the early 1990s? What will happen in Europe once trade barriers start to drop in 1992? Will the Japanese replicate their success in the U.S. market, or will the European producers be able to respond? And what about the newly democratic East? Will Eastern Europe eventually provide the hoped-for sales boom? And if so, which companies will benefit most?

[33]Wysocki, B. "Cross-Border Alliances Become Favorite Way to Crack New Markets," *The Wall Street Journal*, March 26, 1990, pp. A1, A6.
[34]Wysocki, B. "Cross-Border Alliances Become Favorite Way to Crack New Markets," *The Wall Street Journal*, March 26, 1990, pp. A1, A6.

TOYOTA: THE EVOLUTION OF TOYOTA'S PRODUCTION SYSTEM

INTRODUCTION

Toyota is Japan's largest car maker, largest exporter, and the third largest manufacturer of automobiles in the world. In 1989 Toyota held 33 percent of the Japanese auto market, well ahead of second-place Nissan, which held approximately 19 percent. It also held 9.4 percent of the global auto market. Only General Motors with 17.7 percent of the world market, and Ford with 14.6 percent of the world market, held a larger share.[1] Toyota's rise to these heights has been dramatic and swift. In 1990 the company sold 4.12 million vehicles worldwide. This represented an increase from 3.3 million vehicles in 1980, 1.6 million vehicles in 1970, 149,694 vehicles in 1960, and only 11,706 vehicles in 1950.[2]

This case details the rise of Toyota from an obscure Japanese auto manufacturer into the giant of today. The central focus of the case is on explaining how the revolutionary production system developed at Toyota in the 1950s and 1960s came into being. More than anything else, it is this production system that explains the rise of Toyota to global dominance.

This case was prepared by Charles W. L. Hill, University of Washington.
[1]Sources for these figures are (a) Ingrassia, P., and Graven, K. "Japan's Auto Industry May Soon Consolidate as Competition Grows," *The Wall Street Journal,* April 24, 1990, pp. 1, 10; and (b) Borrus, A. "Will Japan Do to Europe What It Did to Detroit?" *Business Week,* May 7, 1990, pp. 52–54.
[2]Figures from (a) Borrus, A. "Will Japan Do to Europe What It Did to Detroit?" *Business Week,* May 7, 1990, pp. 52–54; and (b) Cusumano, M. A. *The Japanese Automobile Industry.* Cambridge, Mass.: Harvard University Press, 1989, Appendix F.

THE ORIGINS OF TOYOTA

The original idea behind the founding of the Toyota Motor Company came from the fertile mind of Toyoda Sakichi.[3] The son of a carpenter, Sakichi was an entrepreneur and inventor whose primary interest was in the textile industry but who had been intrigued by automobiles since a visit to the United States in 1910. Sakichi's principal achievement was the invention of an automatic loom that held out the promise of being able to lower the costs of weaving high-quality cloth. In 1926 Sakichi set up Toyoda Automatic Loom to manufacture this product. He then sold the patent rights to a British textile concern, Platt Brothers, in 1930 for about 1 million yen, a considerable sum in those days. Sakichi urged his son, Toyoda Kiichiro, to use this money to study the possibility of manufacturing automobiles in Japan. A mechanical engineer with a degree from the University of Tokyo, Kiichiro in 1930 was managing director of loom production at Toyoda Automatic Loom.

At first Kiichiro was reluctant to invest in automobile production. The Japanese market at that time was dominated by Ford and General Motors, both of which imported knock-down car kits from the United States and assembled them in Japan. Given this, the board of Toyoda Automatic Loom, including Kodama Risaburo, Kiichiro's brother-in-law and the company's president, opposed the investment on the grounds that it was too risky. Kiichiro probably would not have pursued the issue, but his father made a deathbed request in 1930 that Kiichiro explore the possibilities for automobile production. In 1933 Kiichiro was able to get permission to set up an automobile department within Toyoda Automatic Loom.

Kiichiro believed that he would be able to figure out how to manufacture automobiles by taking apart U.S.-made vehicles and examining them piece by piece. He also believed that it should be possible to adapt U.S. mass-production technology to manufacture cost efficiently at lower volumes. His confidence was based in large part on the already considerable engineering skills and capabilities at his disposal through Toyoda Automatic Loom. Many of the precision engineering and manufacturing skills needed in automobile production were similar to the skills required to manufacture looms.

Kiichiro produced his first 20 vehicles in 1935. In 1936 the automobile department produced 1,142 vehicles: 910 trucks, 100 cars, and 132 buses. However, the production system was essentially craft based rather than a modern assembly line system. The struggle to manufacture might have remained uphill had not fate intervened in the form of the Japanese military. Japan had invaded Manchuria in 1931 and quickly found American-made trucks useful for moving men and equipment. As a result, the military believed that it was strategically important for Japan to have its own automobile industry. The result was passage of an

[3]This section is based primarily on the account given in Cusumano, M. A. *The Japanese Automobile Industry*. Cambridge, Mass.: Harvard University Press, 1989.

automobile manufacturing law in 1936 that required companies producing more than 3,000 vehicles per year in Japan to get a license from the government. For a company to get a license, over 50 percent of its stock had to be owned by Japanese investors. The law also placed a duty on imported cars, including the knockdown kits that Ford and GM were bringing into Japan. As a direct result of this legislation, both GM and Ford exited from the Japanese market in 1939.

Once the Japanese government passed this law, Kodama Risaburo decided that the automobile venture could be profitable and switched from opposing to actively supporting Kiichiro (Risaburo's wife, who was Kiichiro's elder sister, had been urging her husband to take this step for some time). The first priority was to attract the funds necessary to build a mass-production facility. In 1937 Risaburo and Kiichiro decided to incorporate the automobile department as a separate company in order to attract outside investors. Kiichiro Toyoda was appointed president of the new company, which was named the Toyota Motor Company. (The founding family's name, "Toyoda," means "abundant rice field" in Japanese. The new name had no meaning in Japanese.)

Risaburo and Kiichiro's vision was that Toyota should expand its passenger car production as quickly as possible. However, once again fate intervened in the form of the Japanese military. Toyota had barely begun passenger car production when war broke out, and in 1939 the Japanese government, on advice from the military, prohibited passenger car production and demanded that Toyota specialize in the production of military trucks.

THE EVOLUTION OF THE TOYOTA PRODUCTION SYSTEM

After the end of the Second World War Kiichiro was determined that Toyota should re-establish itself as a manufacturer of automobiles.[4] Toyota, however, faced a number of problems in doing this:

1. The Japanese domestic market was too small to support efficient-scale mass-production facilities such as those common in America by that time.
2. The Japanese economy was starved of capital, which made it difficult to raise funds to finance new investments.
3. New labor laws introduced by the American occupiers increased the bargaining power of labor and made it difficult for companies to lay off workers.
4. North America and Western Europe were full of large auto manufacturers that were eager to establish operations in Japan.

[4]The material in this section is drawn from three main sources: (a) Cusumano, M. A. *The Japanese Automobile Industry.* Cambridge, Mass.: Harvard University Press, 1989; (b) Taiichi Ohno, *Toyota Production System.* Cambridge, Mass.: Productivity Press, 1990 (Japanese edition, 1978); and (c) Womack, J. P., Jones, D. T., and Roos, D. *The Machine That Changed the World.* New York: Rawson Associates, 1990.

In response to the last point, in 1950 the new Japanese government prohibited direct foreign investment in the automobile industry and imposed high import tariffs on the importation of foreign cars. This protection, however, did little to solve the other problems facing Toyota at the time.

From Mass Production to Flexible Production

At this juncture a remarkable mechanical engineer entered the scene: Ohno Tai-ichi. More than anyone else, it was Ohno who was to work out a response to the problems listed above. Ohno had joined Toyoda Spinning and Weaving in 1932 as a production engineer in cotton-thread manufacture and entered Toyota when the former company was absorbed into the latter in 1943. Ohno worked in auto production for two years, was promoted and managed auto assembly and machine shops between 1945 and 1953, and in 1954 was appointed a company director.

When Ohno Taiichi joined Toyota, the mass-production methods pioneered by Ford had become the accepted method for manufacturing automobiles. The basic philosophy behind mass production was to produce a limited product line in massive quantities to gain maximum economies of scale. The economies came from spreading over as large a production run as possible the fixed costs involved in setting up the specialized equipment required to stamp body parts and manufacture components. Since setting up much of the equipment could take a full day or more, the economies involved in long production runs were reckoned to be considerable. Thus, for example, Ford would stamp 500,000 right-hand door panels in a single production run and then store the parts in warehouses until they were needed in the assembly plant, rather than stamp just the door panels that were needed immediately and then change the settings and stamp out left-hand door panels or other body parts.

A second feature of mass production was that each assembly worker should perform only a single task rather than a variety of tasks. The idea here was that a worker who became completely familiar with a single task could perform that task quickly, thereby increasing labor productivity. Assembly line workers were overseen by a foreman who performed no assembly tasks, but instead ensured that the workers followed orders. In addition, a number of specialists were employed to perform nonassembly operations such as tool repair, die changes, quality inspection, and general "housecleaning."

After working in Toyota for five years and visiting Ford's U.S. plants, Ohno became convinced that the basic mass-production philosophy was flawed. He saw five problems with the mass-production system:

1. Long production runs created massive inventories that had to be stored in large warehouses. This was expensive both because of the cost of warehousing and because the inventories tied up capital in unproductive uses.

2. If the initial machine settings were wrong, long production runs resulted in the production of a large number of defective units.
3. The sheer monotony that resulted from assembly line workers' being assigned to a single task generated defects, for workers became lax about quality. And because assembly line workers were not responsible for quality control, they had little incentive to minimize defects.
4. The extreme division of labor resulted in the employment of specialists such as foremen, quality inspectors, and tooling specialists, whose jobs could logically be performed by assembly line workers.
5. The mass-production system was unable to accommodate consumer preferences for product diversity.

In addition to those flaws, Ohno knew that the small domestic market in Japan and the lack of capital for investing in mass-production facilities made the American model unsuitable for Toyota. He decided to take a fresh look at the techniques used for automobile production. His first goal was to try to make it economical to manufacture auto body parts in small batches. To do this, he needed to reduce the time it took to set up the machines for stamping out body parts.

Reducing set-up times   Ohno and his engineers began to experiment with a number of techniques to speed up the time it took to change the dies in stamping equipment. The new techniques included using rollers to move dies in and out of position along with a number of simple mechanized adjustments to fine-tune the settings. Because these techniques were relatively simple to master, Ohno directed production workers to perform the die changes themselves. This reduced the need for specialists and eliminated the idle time that workers had previously enjoyed while waiting for the dies to be changed.

Through trial and error, Ohno succeeded in reducing the time required to change dies on stamping equipment from a full day to 15 minutes by 1962 and to as little as 3 minutes by 1971! By comparison, even in the early 1980s many American and European plants required anywhere from 2 to 6 hours to change dies on stamping equipment. As a consequence, American and European plants found it economical to manufacture in lots equivalent to 10 to 30 days' supply and to reset equipment only every other day. In contrast, because Toyota could change the dies on stamping equipment in a matter of minutes, it manufactured in lots equivalent to just one day's supply and reset equipment three times per day.

Not only did Ohno's innovations make small production runs economical, they also had the added benefit of reducing inventories and improving product quality. Making small batches eliminated the need to hold large inventories, thereby reducing warehousing costs and freeing up scarce capital for investment elsewhere. Small production runs and the lack of inventory also meant that defective parts were produced in small numbers and entered the assembly process almost immediately. As a result, workers in the stamping shops were far more concerned about quality than were their American colleagues. In addition, once it became economical to manufacture small batches of components, much greater variety could be included into the final product at little or no extra cost.

Organization of the workplace   Another of Ohno's early innovations was to group the work force into teams. Each team was given a set of assembly tasks to perform, and team members were trained to perform every task that the team was responsible for. Each team had a leader who was an assembly line worker. In addition to coordinating the team, the team leader was expected to perform basic assembly line tasks and to fill in for any absent worker. The teams were given the job of housecleaning, minor tool repair, and quality inspection (along with the training required to perform these tasks). Time was also set aside for team members to discuss ways to improve the production process (the practice now referred to as "quality circles").

The immediate effect of this approach was to reduce the need for specialists in the work place and to create a flexible work force in which individual assembly line workers were not treated simply as human machines. Workers' productivity increased.

None of this would have been possible, however, had it not been for an agreement reached between management and labor after a 1950 strike. The strike was brought on by management's attempt to cut the work force by 25 percent (in response to a recession in Japan). After lengthy negotiations, Toyota and the union worked out a compromise. The work force was cut by 25 percent as originally proposed, but the remaining employees were given two guarantees: one for lifetime employment and the other for pay graded by seniority and tied to company profitability through bonus payments. In exchange for these guarantees, the employees agreed to be flexible in work assignments. This flexibility allowed for the introduction of the team concept.

Improving quality   One of the standard practices in mass-production automobile assembly plants was to fix any errors that occurred during assembly in a rework area at the end of the assembly line. Errors routinely occurred in most assembly plants either because defective parts were installed or because good parts were installed incorrectly. The belief was that stopping an assembly line to fix such errors would cause enormous bottlenecks; thus it was thought to be most efficient to correct errors at the end of the line.

Ohno viewed this system as wasteful for three reasons. First, workers who understood that any errors would be fixed at the end of the line had little incentive to correct errors themselves. Second, once a defective part was embedded in a complex vehicle, an enormous amount of rework might be required to fix it. Third, because defective parts were often not discovered until the finished cars were tested, a large number of cars containing the same defect might be built before the problem was found.

Ohno decided to look for ways to reduce the amount of rework at the end of the line. His approach involved two elements. First, he placed a cord above every work station and instructed workers to stop the whole assembly line if a problem emerged that could not be fixed on the line. It then became the responsibility of the whole team to come over and work on the problem. Second, team members were taught to trace every defect back to its ultimate cause and then to ensure that the problem was fixed so that it would not recur.

Initially this system produced enormous disruption. The production line was stopping all the time, and workers became discouraged. However, as team members began to gain experience in identifying problems and tracing them back to their root cause, the number of errors began to drop dramatically and stops in the line became much rarer. Today in most Toyota plants the line virtually never stops.

Developing the *Kanban* System

Once reduced set-up times had made small production runs economical, Ohno began to look for ways to coordinate the flow of product within the Toyota manufacturing system so that the amount of inventory in the system could be held to a minimum. Toyota produced about 25 percent of its major components in-house (the rest were contracted out to independent suppliers). Ohno's initial goal was to arrange for components and subassemblies manufactured in-house to be delivered to the assembly floor only when they were needed, and not before (this goal was later extended to include independent suppliers).

In 1953 Ohno began experimenting with what came to be known as the *kanban* system. Under the *kanban* system, component parts are delivered to the assembly line in containers. As each container is emptied, it is sent back to the previous step in the manufacturing process. The return of the container becomes the signal to make more parts. The system minimizes work-in-progress by increasing inventory turnover. The elimination of buffer inventories means that defective components show up immediately in the next stage. The visibility of defects speeds up the tracing of defects back to the source and facilitates correction of a problem before many defective units are made. Moreover, the elimination of buffer stocks, by removing all safety nets, makes it imperative that problems be solved before they became serious enough to jam up the production process and thus creates a strong incentive for workers to ensure that errors are corrected quickly. In addition, by decentralizing responsibility for coordinating the manufacturing process to lower-level employees, the *kanban* system does away with the need for extensive centralized management to coordinate the flow of parts between the various stages of production.

After perfecting the *kanban* system in one of Toyota's machine shops, Ohno had a chance to apply the system broadly in 1960 when he was made general manager of the Motomachi assembly plant. Ohno had already converted the machining, body-stamping, and body assembly shops to the *kanban* system, but since many parts came from shops that had yet to adopt the system, or from outside suppliers, the impact of the system on inventories was initially minimal.

However, by 1962 he had extended the *kanban* to forging and casting, and between 1962 and 1965 he began to bring independent suppliers into the system.

Organizing Suppliers

The assembly of components into a final vehicle accounts for only about 15 percent of total manufacturing in automobile manufacture. The remaining 85 percent of the process involves manufacturing more than 10,000 individual parts and assembling them into about 100 major components such as engines, suspension systems, and transaxels. Coordination so that everything comes together at the right time has always been a problem for automakers.

The response at Ford and GM to this problem was massive vertical integration, in the belief that control over the supply chain would allow management to coordinate the flow of component parts into the final assembly plant. In addition, American firms believed that vertical integration made them more efficient by reducing their dependence on other firms for materials and components and by limiting their vulnerability to opportunistic overcharging. As a consequence of this philosophy, even today General Motors makes 70 percent of its own components in-house, and Ford makes 50 percent. When U.S. auto companies have not vertically integrated, they have historically tried to reduce procurement costs through competitive bidding, asking a number of companies to submit contracts and giving orders to suppliers offering the lowest price.

Under the leadership of Kiichiro Toyoda, during the 1930s and 1940s Toyota essentially followed the American model and pursued extensive vertical integration in the manufacture of component parts. Toyota had little choice, for only a handful of Japanese companies were able to make the necessary components. The low volume of production during this period meant that the scale of integration was relatively small. In the 1950s, however, the volume of auto production began to increase dramatically. This increase presented Toyota with a dilemma. Should the company increase its capacity to manufacture components in-house in line with the growth in production of autos, or should the company contract out?

In contrast to American practice, Toyota decided that although it should increase in-house capacity for essential subassemblies and bodies, it would do better to contract out for most components. Four reasons seem to have lain behind this decision:

1. The company wanted to avoid the capital expenditures required to expand capacity in order to manufacture a wide variety of components.
2. The company wanted to reduce risk by maintaining a low factory capacity in case factory sales slumped.
3. Toyota wanted to take advantage of the lower wage scales in smaller firms.
4. Toyota managers realized that in-house manufacturing offered few benefits if they could find stable, high-quality, and low-cost external sources of components.

At the same time, Toyota managers felt that the American practice of inviting competitive bids from suppliers was self-defeating. Competitive bidding might achieve the lowest short-run costs, but the practice of playing suppliers off against each other did not guarantee stable supplies, high quality, or cooperation beyond existing contracts to solve design or engineering problems. Ohno and other Toyota managers believed that real efficiencies could be achieved if the company entered into long-term relationships with major suppliers. Doing so would allow them to introduce the *kanban* system, thereby further reducing inventory-holding costs and realizing the same kind of quality benefits that Toyota was already beginning to encounter with its in-house supply operations. In addition, Ohno wanted to bring suppliers into the design process because he believed that suppliers might be able to suggest ways of improving the design of component parts based on their own manufacturing experience.

As it evolved during the 1950s and 1960s, Toyota's strategy toward its suppliers had several elements. First, the company spun off some of its own in-house supply operations into quasi-independent entities in which it took a minority stake, typically holding between 20 and 40 percent of the stock. It then recruited a number of independent companies with a view to establishing a long-term relationship with them for the supply of critical components. Sometimes, but not always, Toyota took a minority stake in these companies as well. All of these companies were designated "first-tier suppliers." First-tier suppliers were responsible for working with Toyota as an integral part of the new product development team. Each first-tier supplier was responsible for the formation of a second tier of suppliers under its direction. Companies in the second tier were given the job of fabricating individual parts.

Both first- and second-tier suppliers were formed into supplier associations. Thus, by 1986 Toyota had three regional supply organizations in Japan with 62, 135, and 25 first-tier suppliers respectively. A major function of the supplier associations was to share information about new manufacturing, design, or materials-management techniques among themselves. Concepts such as statistical process control, total quality control, and computer-aided design were rapidly diffused among suppliers by this means.

Toyota also worked closely with its suppliers, providing them with management expertise, engineering expertise, and sometimes capital to finance new investments. A critical feature of this relationship was the incentives that Toyota established to encourage its suppliers to focus on realizing continuous process improvements. The basic contract for a component would be for four to five years, with the price being agreed to in advance. If by joint efforts a supplier and Toyota succeeded in reducing the costs of manufacturing the components, then the additional profit would be shared by both. If a supplier by its own efforts came up with an innovation that reduced costs, the supplier would keep for the life of the contract the additional profit that the innovation generated.

As a consequence of this strategy, today Toyota out-sources more than almost any other major auto manufacturer. By the late 1980s Toyota was responsible for only about 27 percent of the value going into a finished automobile; the remainder came from outside suppliers. In contrast, General Motors is responsible for about 70 percent of the value going into a finished automobile. Other consequences include long-term improvements in productivity and quality among Toyota's suppliers that are comparable to the improvements achieved by Toyota itself. In particular, the extension of the *kanban* system to include suppliers, by eliminating buffer inventory stocks, in essence forced suppliers to focus more explicitly on the quality of their product.

Consequences

The consequences of Toyota's production system included a surge in labor productivity and a decline in the number of defects per car. Exhibit 1 compares the number of vehicles produced per worker at General Motors, Ford, Nissan, and Toyota between 1965 and 1983. These figures are adjusted for the degree of vertical integration pursued by each company. As can be seen, in 1965 productivity at Toyota already outstripped that at Ford, General Motors, and Toyota's main Japanese competitor, Nissan. As Toyota refined its production system over the next eighteen years, its productivity nearly doubled. In comparison, productivity essentially stood still at General Motors and Ford during the same period.

Exhibit 2 provides another way in which to assess the superiority of Toyota's production system. Here the performance of Toyota's Takaoka plant is compared with that of General Motors' Framingham plant in 1987. As can be seen, the Toyota plant was more productive, produced far fewer defects per 100 cars, and kept far less inventory on hand.

Another aspect of Toyota's production system is that the short set-up times made it economical to manufacture a much wider range of models than is feasible at a traditional mass-production assembly plant. In essence, Toyota soon found that it could supply much greater product variety than its competitors with little in the way of a cost penalty. This continues today; thus in 1990 Toyota was

EXHIBIT 1   Vehicles per worker (adjusted for vertical integration), 1965–1983

Year	General Motors	Ford	Nissan	Toyota
1965	5.0	4.4	4.3	8.0
1970	3.7	4.3	8.8	13.4
1975	4.4	4.0	9.0	15.1
1979	4.5	4.2	11.1	18.4
1980	4.1	3.7	12.2	17.8
1983	4.8	4.7	11.0	15.0

Source: Cusumano, M. A. 1989. *The Japanese Automobile Industry.* Cambridge, Mass.: Harvard University Press, Table 48, p. 197.

EXHIBIT 2   General Motors Framingham versus Toyota's Takaoka plant, 1987

	GM Framingham	Toyota Takaoka
Assembly hours per car	31	16
Assembly defects per 100 cars	135	45
Inventories of parts (average)	2 weeks	2 hours

Source: Womack, J. P., Jones, D. T., and Roos, D. 1990, *The Machine That Changed the World*, New York: Rawson Associates, Figure 4.2, p. 83.

offering consumers around the world roughly as many products as General Motors (about 150)—even though Toyota was still only half the size of GM. Moreover, it could do this at a lower cost than GM.

DISTRIBUTION AND CUSTOMER RELATIONS

Toyota's approach to its distributors and customers as it evolved during the 1950s and 1960s was in many ways just as radical as its approach to its suppliers. In 1950 Toyota formed a subsidiary, Toyota Motor Sales, to handle distribution and sales. The subsidiary was headed by Kaymiya Shotaro from its inception until 1975. Kaymiya's philosophy was that dealers should be treated as "equal partners" in the Toyota family. Thus Toyota Motor Sales provides a wide range of sales training and service training for dealership personnel.

Kaymiya used the dealers to build long-term ties with Toyota customers. The ultimate aim was to bring customers into the Toyota design and production process. To this end, through its dealers, Toyota Motor Sales assembled a huge data base on customer preferences. Much of the data came from monthly or semiannual surveys conducted by dealers asking Toyota customers their preferences in styling, model type, color, price, and other features. Toyota also used these surveys to estimate the potential demand for new models. This information was then fed directly into the design process.

Kaymiya began this system in 1952, when the company was redesigning its Toyopet model, to be used primarily by urban taxi drivers. Toyota Motor Sales surveyed taxi drivers to find out what type of vehicle they preferred. Their response indicated that they wanted something reliable, inexpensive, and with good city fuel mileage. The Toyota engineers then set about designing such a vehicle. In 1956 Kaymiya formalized this system when he created a unified department for planning and market research. The function of the department was to coordinate the marketing strategies developed by researchers at Toyota Motor Sales with product planning by Toyota's design engineers. From this time on, marketing information played a critical role in the design of Toyota's cars, and indeed in the company's strategy. In particular, it was the research department at Toyota Motor Sales that provided the initial stimulus for Toyota to start exporting during the late 1960s after predicting, correctly, that growth in domestic sales would slow considerably during the 1970s.

OVERSEAS EXPANSION

Large-scale overseas expansion did not become feasible at Toyota until the late 1960s for one principal reason: despite the rapid improvement in productivity, Japanese cars were still not competitive.[5] In 1957, for example, the Toyota Corona sold in Japan for the equivalent of $1,694. At the same time, the Volkswagen Beetle sold for $1,111 in West Germany, and Britain's Austin Company was selling its basic model for the equivalent of $1,389 in Britain. Foreign companies were effectively kept out of the Japanese market, however, by a 40 percent value-added tax and shipping costs.

Despite these disadvantages, Toyota tried to enter the U.S. market in the late 1950s. The company set up a U.S. subsidiary in California in October 1957 and began to sell cars in early 1958, hoping to capture the American small-car market (which at that time was poorly served by the U.S. automobile companies). The result was a disaster. Toyota's cars performed poorly in road tests on U.S. highways. The engines of Toyota's cars were too small for prolonged high-speed driving and tended to overheat and burn oil, and poorly designed chassis resulted in excessive vibration. As a result, sales were slow and in 1964 Toyota closed its U.S. subsidiary and withdrew from the market.

Determined to learn from its U.S. experience, the company quickly redesigned several models, using feedback from American consumer surveys and U.S. road tests. As a result, by 1967 the quality of Toyota's cars was sufficient to make an impact in the U.S. market, and production costs and retail prices had continued to fall and were comparable with those of international competitors in the small-car market.

In the late 1960s Toyota re-entered the U.S. market. Sales were initially slow, but they increased steadily. Then the OPEC-engineered fourfold increase in oil prices that followed the 1973 Israel-Arab conflict gave Toyota an unexpected boost. U.S. consumers in droves began to turn to small, fuel-efficient cars, and Toyota was one of the main beneficiaries. Driven primarily by a surge in U.S. demand, worldwide exports of Toyota cars increased from 157,882 units in 1967 to 856,352 units by 1974 and 1,800,923 units by 1984. In 1967, exports accounted for 19 percent of Toyota's total output. By 1984, they accounted for 52.5 percent.

Success, however, brought its own problems. By the early 1980s political pressures and talk of local content regulations in the United States and Europe

[5]The material in this section is based on Cusumano, M. A. *The Japanese Automobile Industry.* Cambridge, Mass.: Harvard University Press, 1989.

were forcing an initially reluctant Toyota to rethink its exporting strategy. Toyota had already agreed to "voluntary" import quotas with the United States in 1981. The consequence for Toyota was stagnant export growth between 1981 to 1984. Against this background, in the early 1980s Toyota began to think seriously about setting up manufacturing operations overseas.

TRANSPLANT OPERATIONS

Toyota's first overseas operation was a fifty-fifty joint venture with General Motors established in February 1983 under the name New United Motor Manufacturing Inc. (NUMMI). NUMMI, which is based in Fremont, California, began producing Chevrolet Nova cars for GM in December 1984.[6] The maximum capacity of the Fremont plant is about 250,000 cars per year.

For Toyota, the joint venture provided a chance to find out whether it could build quality cars in the United States using American workers and American suppliers. It also provided Toyota with experience dealing with an American union (the United Auto Workers) and with a means of circumventing "voluntary" import restrictions. For General Motors, the venture provided an opportunity to observe in full detail the Japanese approach to manufacturing. General Motors' role is marketing and distributing the plant's output. Toyota designs the product and designs, equips, and operates the plant. At the venture's start, thirty-four executives were loaned to NUMMI by Toyota, sixteen by General Motors. The chief executive and chief operating officer are both Toyota personnel.

By the fall of 1986 the NUMMI plant was running at full capacity, and the early indications were that the plant was achieving productivity and quality levels close to those achieved at Toyota's major Takaoka plant in Japan. For example, in 1987 it took the NUMMI plant 19 assembly hours to build a car, compared to 16 hours at Takaoka, and the number of defects per 100 cars was the same at NUMMI as at Takaoka—45.[7]

Encouraged by its success at NUMMI, in December 1985 Toyota announced that it would build an automobile manufacturing plant in Georgetown, Kentucky. The plant, which came on-stream in May 1988, officially had the capacity to produce 200,000 Toyota Camrys a year. Such was the success of this plant, however, that by early 1990 it was producing the equivalent of 220,000 cars per year. In December 1990 Toyota announced that it would build a second plant in Georgetown with a capacity to produce another 200,000 vehicles per year.[8] All told, when this plant comes on-stream in 1995, Toyota will have the capacity to

[6]Powell, Niland. "U.S.-Japanese Joint Venture: New United Motor Manufacturing Inc.," *Planning Review*, January–February 1989, pp. 40–45.
[7]From Womack, J. P., Jones, D. T., and Roos, D. *The Machine That Changed the World.* New York: Macmillan, 1990.
[8]Treece, J. B. "Just What Detroit Needs: 200,000 More Toyotas a Year," *Business Week,* December 10, 1990, p. 29.

build 660,000 vehicles per year in North America. If the company were to purchase GM's share of the NUMMI joint venture when the NUMMI pact expires in 1996 (which is rumored to be a strong possibility), its North American production could increase to 750,000 vehicles per year.

In addition to its North American transplant operations, Toyota has moved to set up production in Europe in anticipation of the 1992 lowering of trade barriers among the twelve members of the European Economic Community. In 1989 the company announced that it would build a plant in England with the capacity to manufacture 200,000 cars per year by 1997.

Despite Toyota's apparent commitment to expand U.S.- and European-based assembly operations, all has not been smooth sailing. A major problem has been building an overseas supplier network that is comparable to Toyota's network in Japan. In a 1990 meeting of Toyota's North American suppliers' association, Toyota executives informed their North American suppliers that the defect ratio for parts produced by 75 North American and European suppliers was 100 times greater than the defect ratio for parts supplied by 147 Japanese suppliers—1,000 defects per million parts versus 10 defects per million parts. Toyota executives also pointed out that parts manufactured by North American and European suppliers tended to be significantly more expensive than comparable parts manufactured in Japan.[9]

Because of these problems, Toyota has had to import many parts from Japan for its U.S. assembly operations. However, for political reasons Toyota is being pushed to increase the local content of cars assembled in North America. The company's plan was for 50 percent of the value of Toyota cars assembled in the United States to be locally produced by January 1991. To achieve this, Toyota embarked on an aggressive supplier education drive in the United States aimed at familiarizing its American suppliers with Japanese production methods.

PRODUCT STRATEGY

Toyota's initial production was aimed at the small car/basic transportation end of the automobile market. This was true in Japan and true of export sales to North America and Europe. During the 1980s, however, Toyota progressively moved up-market and abandoned much of the low end of the market to new entrants such as the South Koreans. Thus the company's Camry and Corolla models, which were initially positioned toward the bottom of the market, have been constantly upgraded and now are aimed at the middle-income segments of the market. This upgrading reflects two factors: (1) rising income levels in Japan and the commensurate increase in the ability of Japanese consumers to purchase mid-range and luxury cars and (2) a desire to hold on to its U.S. consumers, many of

[9]Maskery, M. A. "Toyota Talks Tough to U.S. Suppliers," *Automotive News*, November 5, 1990, p. 2.

whom initially purchased inexpensive Toyotas in their early twenties and have since traded up to more expensive models.

The constant upgrading of Toyota's models reached its logical conclusion in September 1989 when the company's Lexus division began marketing luxury cars to compete with Jaguars, BMWs, and the like. The Lexus range of cars includes the ES 250, which was initially priced at $22,000, and the LS 400, which comes fully loaded with a $43,000-price tag (a Jaguar XJ6 costs about $40,000). The initial goal of the Lexus division was to go after America's luxury car market, which amounted to sales of about 850,000 units in 1989. However, Lexus is also being sold in Japan and Europe.

Encouraged by car testers who rated the Lexus LS 400 the best in its class, Toyota initially projected worldwide sales of around 75,000 units for the Lexus models in 1990. However, the early results for Lexus fell short of expectations. Although the fully loaded LS 400 appeared to be selling well, the ES 250 model was not, primarily because it is not enough of a luxury car to appeal to luxury buyers. Moreover, a slowdown in the U.S. auto market and the specter of recession during 1990 cut into Lexus's potential sales. As a result, Toyota scaled back its projections for first-year sales from 75,000 to 60,000.[10] In the event, Toyota sold 57,162 Lexus models in North America during the 1990 model year and has expectations for selling 100,000 of the cars a year by the mid 1990s.[11]

Another addition to Toyota's product range in recent years has been a minivan. Like the Lexus, this vehicle was aimed at the North American market, where the minivan segment has grown most rapidly. Toyota first introduced a minivan in 1986, but it flopped. In typical Toyota fashion, the company dispatched product planners and design engineers to showrooms to find out why. Among the problems they identified were that the minivans lacked an aisle down the center; the short wheelbase gave them a pitchy ride; and the engine was not easy to service. Using this feedback, Toyota designers completely redesigned the vehicle and reintroduced it in April 1990 as the Previa minivan. The early results exceeded expectations. Toyota looked set to sell 50,000 Previas in its first year and believed that it could easily sell 100,000 per year in the future.[12]

TOYOTA IN 1991

As of early 1991 Toyota's position looked strong in at least two of the three major car markets of the world. In the United States, overall vehicle sales softened in response to a weak economy. For the first nine months of 1990 domestic and import vehicle sales were down 5.68 percent compared with the same period in 1989, and total car sales for 1990 looked set to fall below the 9.85 million achieved

[10]The Economist, "The Next Samurai," December 23, 1989, pp. 69–72. Landler, M., and Zellner, W. "No Joyride for Japan," Business Week, January 15, 1990, pp. 20–21.
[11]The Economist, "Elegant Nippon," December 8, 1990, p. 73.
[12]Flint, J. "The New Number Three?" Forbes, June 11, 1990, pp. 136–140.

in 1989. However, Toyota succeeded in bucking this trend with a dramatic increase in sales. For the 1990 model year, Toyota (including Lexus) sold 911,736 cars in the United States, compared with 732,807 units in the 1989 model year—an increase of 24.4 percent. In comparison, during the same period GM saw its car sales decline by 8.8 percent, Ford by 11.2 percent, and Chrysler by 16.1 percent. Indeed, if light trucks are excluded from the figures, then in 1990 Toyota surpassed Chrysler to grab third place and an 8.4 percent share in the U.S. car market behind GM and Ford.[13]

In Japan, the first half of 1990 saw a 13.4 percent surge in domestic sales compared with the same period in 1989. Most of this upward movement was concentrated at the high end of the market. Sales of cars with engines larger than 2.0 liters jumped 93.9 percent in the first half of 1990. This trend is particularly significant for Toyota, since the company is the number-one producer in the Japanese large-car luxury segment, with 37.7 percent of the market. Overall, Toyota sold 1,285,511 vehicles in Japan in the first six months of 1990, giving it a 42 percent share. Second-place Nissan sold 732,407 vehicles for a 24 percent market share.[14]

Currently Western Europe is the weak spot in Toyota's global picture. In recent years Western Europe has surpassed North America to become the world's largest car market with a record 13.46 million new passenger car sales in 1989. Moreover, there remains more room for growth in Western Europe than in the United States. Car ownership in Western Europe runs at 380 cars per 1,000 people, compared with 580 per 1,000 in the United States (Japan has only 243 cars per 1,000 people).[15] Against this favorable background, Toyota sold only 343,076 cars in Western Europe during 1989 for a 2.5 percent share of the total market. Moreover, this represented a 2.7 percent decline in sales from 1988.[16] However, to a considerable degree Toyota, along with other Japanese producers, has been held back by national quotas. For example, France restricts Japanese cars to 3 percent of sales; Italy and Spain hold the Japanese share to less than 1 percent; and even free-market Britain has limited Japanese imports to 11 percent. On the other hand, the European Economic Community is committed to abolishing national auto quotas during the 1990s. Currently, the EC is working on a proposal that would give European manufacturers temporary protection from Japanese competition (both imports and cars assembled in Europe) from 1993 to about 1997. During this period the Japanese would agree to "voluntarily" limit their European market share, and all restrictions would disappear (in theory) after 1997.[17]

---

[13]Jackson, K. "Toyota No. 3 in Car Sales, Tops Chrysler in Model Year," *Automotive News,* October 8, 1990, p. 1.

[14]Maskery, M. A. "Large Cars Are Top Gainers in Japan in the First Half of Year," *Automotive News,* 1990, p. 20.

[15]Tully, S. "Now Japan's Autos Push into Europe," *Fortune,* January 28, 1990, pp. 96–106.

[16]*Automotive News,* "Market Data Guide," May 30, 1990, p. 25.

[17]Tully, S. "Now Japan's Autos Push into Europe," *Fortune,* January 28, 1990, pp. 96–106.

Case 25

DEUTSCHE
BUNDESBAHN (A)

On the 13th of May 1982, Dr. Ing. Reiner Gohlke took over as chairman of the Deutsche Bundesbahn (DB) in a flurry of excitement and anticipation. Dr. Gohlke had been nominated to the Vorstand by the Federal Minister of Transport in January. In selecting an outsider, the Minister dramatized the need for change. During the thirty years since 1950, the DB's share of goods transport had dropped by half and it only retained one-fifth of its postwar share of personal transport. Moreover, the year prior to Dr. Gohlke's appointment, the DB reported a 1981 loss of DM 4.04 billion, with total debt outstanding of DM 34.4 billion.

OWNERSHIP AND ORGANIZATION

The German Railway had an eventful history. Founded in 1835 as a private railroad, it was nationalized during the Franco-Prussian War of 1871. The railroad was profitable until the outbreak of the First World War, after which it was reprivatized as the Deutsche Reichsbahn. An international board monitored the railroad's obligation to pay out half its profits as reparations to the Allies. This the Reichsbahn was able to do, by virtue of its monopoly on goods traffic.

After the Second World War, the Deutsche Reichsbahn was reconstituted as a public enterprise with the name Deutsche Bundesbahn, and placed under the jurisdiction of the Federal Minister of Transport. The Bundesbahn was part of the German government. Its statutes were enshrined in the German constitution of 1949. Although the 1961 revision of the Railroad Law stated that the DB was to be run like a business concern, the vast majority of upper management remained subject to the usual conditions of public service with relatively low pay, substantial long-term benefits and absolute job security. Managerial oversight was provided by a heterogeneous Board of 20 members, comprising federal and state politicians, union leaders, as well as representatives of industry (see Exhibit 1). Until 1982, the DB operations were managed by an executive committee of four members with overall responsibility for revenue and production.

Reporting directly to the executive committee were a general manager and three section managers, as well as the presidents, often Bundesbahn Dictorates, the four central staffs and the two central technical offices.

An important milestone was reached with the renewal of the Federal Railroad Law at the end of 1981. The new law allowed for restructuring of the central DB management, based on practice in the private sector. The members of the executive committee, presidents, and functional area chiefs were removed from civil servant status, by making provision for competitive employment contracts.

Dr. Gohlke's appointment seemed to signal the intention of the government to move the German economy toward a free market and away from government control and intervention (see Exhibit 2). The way was thus open to attract managers to the DB from private industry. Of the five new executive committee members taking office with Gohlke, two came from industry: Wilhelm Pällmann

EXHIBIT 1   **Simplified organizational relationships of the Deutsche Bundesbahn**

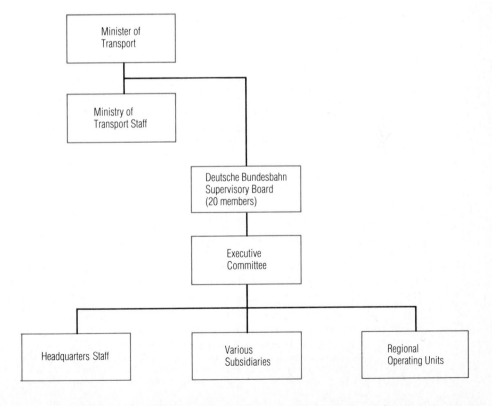

EXHIBIT 2   Comments from *Business Europe*

German privatization: sale of the century?

The German government is preparing plans for privatization of large parts of its extensive industrial holdings. The most likely method will be issues of stock, aimed mainly at small investors. But sales to companies of government-owned firms, or parts of them, are not excluded at this stage of official thinking. Make your informal soundings now for what could be the sale of the century.

Bonn is expected to announce its first privatization plans within a few weeks. The government's stockholdings, shares in which could be sold, include 74.5% of Lufthansa, the national airline; 20% of Volkswagen; 43.8% of Veba, Germany's largest industrial concern; 100% of the loss-making Salzgitter steel and shipbuilding group; and a variety of lesser interests in many fields. Stockholdings in these companies could be divested without legislation. The Finance Ministry can set the wheels in motion as an administrative measure.

Selling shares in the nationalized utilities, such as the federal railroad (Bundesbahn) and the PTT (Bundespost), would be much more complicated. But Transport Minister Werner Dollinger says he does not rule out conversion of the railroad's passenger and freight-hauling divisions into stock companies. It is, however, a massive loss-maker, which could reduce the attractions of this option.

Finance Minister Gerhard Stoltenberg has assured fellow government leaders that he will announce "very concrete steps" toward privatization before year-end, according to the chairman of the Bundestag (lower house) audit committee.

A ghost from the past

There has been speculation that the government may use the asset formation law (Vermögensbildung-BE '83 p. 259) to assist workers to acquire some of the stock to be sold. If so, they would receive tax relief for the purchases, up to certain limits. This would be a cumbersome way to distribute the stock, but would be consistent with the "shareholding democracy" ethos of the present government.

There is, however, a ghost from Germany's past history of privatization that may make ministers willing to go for the option of selling large blocks to corporate purchasers. When Ludwig Erhard's government placed Veba stock in the hands of 750,000 small investors in 1965, the value of the stock immediately fell sharply. A public outcry ensued, the stockholders not having realized that the stock was subject to the usual market risks, despite the fact that the government was involved in the issue. There has never been a subsequent issue of this kind.

Source: *Business Europe*, October, 1983.

---

(51), who previously managed the Hannoverschen Verkehrsbetriebe (Hannover Transport Company), and Henjo Klein (44), previously a Lufthansa manager and member of the board of Neckermann Marketing.

Despite the new opportunities, the 1981 law still required that substantial organizational changes be accepted first by the Board and then approved by the Federal Minister of Transport. In addition, the affected Federal States had to be consulted. A similar process applied to personnel and tariff decisions. Price changes of plus or minus 10%, or special discounts up to 30% could be decided freely, but had to be shown to the Federal Accounting Office to check whether they improved the bottom line. Moreover, the budget had to be approved by the

Minister of Finance, and wage agreements by both the Departments of Finance and the Interior. Political and other interest groups could not only influence the DB management, they were in fact required to do so by law.

The personnel of the DB, workers, employees, and civil servants were to a great extent organized in the German Railroad Union. The union represented the concerns of the personnel in the public arena, and at the Transport Ministry. Their interests were the traditional ones of the unions: working conditions and compensation, especially for the workers and employees for whom the unions negotiated wage and salary rates. After a two to three year trial period, civil servants were given employment contracts for life. Workers and employees could not be dismissed after they had spent 15 years with the DB, or were 40 years old.

The three groups, workers, employees, and civil servants, were represented internally by the Workers Council, which played an important participative role in management. In most decision areas, this role was largely consultative: management had to solicit the council's advice, but retained ultimate decision making power. However, in matters affecting the displacement, working time, or workplace of workers or employees, the Workers Council could veto management's decisions.

In terms of their attitude toward change, the civil servants fell into two groups. A small minority, perhaps 5%, could be labelled as "Young Turks" who were enthusiastic about the possibility of some movement within the organization. The vast majority, however, were much more interested in preserving their position within the status quo. Many had built long careers with the DB. They were known as "Eisenbahners" (Railroaders), especially when their association with the railroad went back one or more generations.

THE RAILROAD AS TRANSPORT SYSTEM

During the late nineteenth and early twentieth century, the German railroad developed primarily along the east-west axis of communication between Prussia and the rest of the country. But after the Second World War, the Iron Curtain cut the east-west axis. Within West Germany, the most important routes emerged in a north-south direction. As a result, the newly constituted DB found itself with a rail network that was inconsistent with the main patterns of internal trade.

In 1982, the rail network comprised 28,338 km of track of which 21,945 km were used for both goods and personnel traffic, while 11,180 km were electrified. The track density was greatest in the region of the Ruhr and the Rhine valley. The most common speed was the 60–70 km/hr possible on 40% of the track. For all connections between 100 key centers, it was observed that most commonly 1.3 to 1.5 switches between trains were required on each trip.

Notwithstanding the widespread discussion and consultation required before track could be closed down, 3,000 km of rail were shut down completely and 7,200 km were taken out of passenger service over the thirty years from 1950 to 1982. Very little new track was added: only 120 km of new subway lines and 12 km of new railroad. As can be seen from Exhibit 3, the total annual investment in the rail network, infrastructure, and vehicles remained more or less constant at about DM 4 billion between 1950 and 1982.

Over the same period, the transportation links between north and south were strengthened by the rapid expansion of the autobahn network. 136,000 km of new roads were built. The number of motor vehicles increased from 0.6 million in 1950 to 24 million in the early 1980's. In the process, the DB share of goods traffic dropped by half and its share of personal transport by more than two thirds. The recent development of kilometer tons and passenger kilometers for the main forms of transport in the Federal Republic is depicted in Exhibits 4a and 4b. Between 1968 and 1982, not only the market share, but the physical volume of goods transported by the DB declined to 57,922 billion kilometer tons. The road transport of goods more than doubled to 80,392 billion kilometer tons.

In terms of individual transport, there was a rise from 39 billion passenger kilometers to 50 billion in 1974, after which the number flattened out at 47 billion in 1982. Over the same period, air transport increased from 4 billion passenger kilometers to 11 billion in 1982.

EXHIBIT 3   **Gross investment in infrastructure and vehicles**

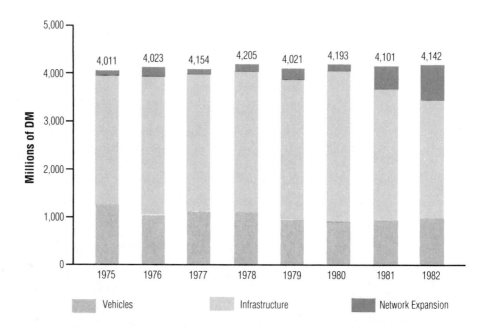

FINANCIAL RESULTS

It is ironic that the railway in Germany played an important initial role in the financing of alternative forms of transport. For example, the railroad financed the construction of the first autobahns before the Second World War. However, the DB has never received any financing in return.

The inconsistency in the financing of transportation infrastructure was keenly felt at the DB headquarters in Frankfurt. Management believed that the performance of the DB was obscured, not only by differences in the treatment of infrastructure, but also by the consolidation of public transport with the regular commercial business of the DB. The public service domain, designed to support urban and metropolitan areas, comprised primarily the short distance transport of students, senior citizens, commuters, and others travelling at a discount.

To permit a reasonable comparison between the viability of the DB and other forms of transport, its management had been experimenting with the idea of "separate accounting," known as a "Trennungsrechnung." The purpose was to provide disaggregated profit and loss statements for the commercial business, public service business, and the railroad infrastructure.

An example of the application of separate accounting to the DB income statement is shown in Exhibit 5. The third column shows the audited, consolidated 1982 Income Statement. The eliminations in column four reflect expenses, such as social security payments by the DB and the corresponding transfer payments by the Federal Government, that had nothing to do with the operations of the Bundesbahn per se. Column six shows the income statement for the DB's commercial business, estimated to have generated a net profit of DM 2.0 billion, compared to a loss of DM 0.7 billion on the public service business, and DM 5.4 billion required to support the railroad's infrastructure.

The structure of the consolidated income statements and balance sheets for the years 1981 and 1982 is shown in Exhibits 6a and 6b. Close to 90% of total assets were tied up in plant and equipment; debt made up almost 60% of total liabilities. In the income statement, personnel accounted for two thirds of all expenses.

The number of personnel dropped 38% from 512,159 in 1957 to 317,475 in 1982. However, the average salary increased almost sixfold, from DM 5,985 to DM 35,846, resulting in a more than threefold increase in total wages and salaries. In the period from 1970 to 1982, productivity measured in terms of revenues per employee climbed substantially but remained well below the productivity improvements achieved by other forms of transport (see Exhibit 7a). Productivity per unit of capacity rose more unevenly and more slowly, by less than 20% over the same 12 years (Exhibit 7b).

An overview since 1962, of the progression in personnel and total expenses relative to the main revenue categories, is provided in Exhibit 8. The shaded area reflects the annual deficit over time, given by the difference between total

EXHIBIT 4a   Freight performance: Deutsche Bundesbahn and other forms of transport

Year (1)	Deutsche Bundesbahn[1] (2)	Domestic water transport (3)	Trucking companies[2] (4)	Other trucking (5)	Foreign trucks (6)	Total (col. 4 to col. 6) (7)	Oil pipelines (over 50 km) (8)	Total (col. 2 to col. 8) (9)
			Kilometer tons in billions Change relative to previous year (%)					
1968	60,074 +6.4%	47,932 +4.7%	25,329 +11.7%	7,800 +15.5%	4,636 +10.5%	37,755 +11.4%	13,692 +37.3%	159,453 +9.1%
1969	68,445 +13.9	47,650 −0.6	27,503 +8.6	7,286 −6.6	5,087 +10.0	39,876 +5.6	14,773 +7.9	170,744 +7.1
1970	72,566 +6.0	48,813 +2.4	28,669 +4.2	7,403 +1.6	5,809 +14.2	41,881 +5.0	15,122 +2.4	178,382 +4.5
1971	66,238 −8.7	44,991 −7.8	29,478 +2.8	8,180 +10.5	6,870 +18.3	44,528 +6.3	16,265 +7.5	172,022 −3.6
1972	65,732 −0.8	43,969 −2.3	30,849 +4.7	9,540 +16.6	8,769 +27.6	49,158 +10.4	16,738 +2.9	175,597 +2.1
1973	68,361 +4.0	48,480 +10.3	33,714 +9.3	11,145 +16.8	11,003 +25.5	55,862 +13.6	16,834 +0.6	189,537 +7.9
1974	70,366 +2.9	50,972 +5.1	33,066 −1.9	12,200 +9.5	13,263 +20.5	58,529 +4.8	15,157 −10.0	195,024 +2.9
1975	56,330 −19.9	47,565 −6.7	31,772 −3.9	13,719 +12.5	13,833 +4.3	59,324 +1.4	13,086 −13.7	176,305 −9.6
1976	60,477 +7.4	45,804 −3.7	35,846 +12.8	15,924 +16.1	16,833 +21.7	68,603 +15.6	14,494 +10.8	189,378 +7.4
1977	56,899 −5.9	49,254 +7.5	36,617 +2.2	16,939 +6.4	17,926 +6.5	71,482 +4.2	13,983 −3.5	191,618 +1.2
1978	58,551 +2.9	51,489 +4.5	38,082 +4.0	15,812 −6.7	19,297 +7.6	73,191 +2.4	13,863 −0.9	197,094 +2.9
1979	67,081 +14.6	50,987 −0.1	41,020 +7.7	16,804 +6.3	20,896 +8.3	78,720 +7.6	15,960 +15.1	212,748 +7.9
1980	65,746 −2.0	51,435 +0.9	41,112 +0.2	17,467 +3.9	21,437 +2.6	80,016 +1.6	13,096 −17.9	210,293 −1.2
1981	62,538 −4.9	49,988 −2.8	40,809 −0.7	17,691 +1.3	21,695 +1.2	80,195 +0.2	11,241 −14.2	203,962 −3.0
1982	57,922 −7.4	49,401 −1.2	40,430 −0.9	17,743 +0.3	22,219 +2.4	80,392 +0.2	9,134 −18.7	196,849 −3.5

1. Total traffic excluding trucking.
2. Includes DB-related trucking.

EXHIBIT 4b   Passenger performance: Deutsche Bundesbahn and other forms of transport

Year	Deutsche Bundesbahn	Authority local public transport	Other (non-DB railroads)	Post DB bus transport	Private bus companies	Domestic air traffic	Total (col. 2 to col. 7)
(1)	(2)	(3)	(4)	(5)	(6)	(7)	(8)
	Passenger kilometers in billions Change relative to previous years (%)						
1967	3.90 −5.4%	23.1 −4.5%	1.9 +0.0%	3.9 +11.0%	18.0 +3.9%	4.0 +11.5%	89.9 −1.9%
1968	40.5 +3.7	22.6 −2.2	1.9 +0.0	4.0 +3.2	18.7 +4.3	4.5 +15.1	92.2 +2.6
1969	44.0 +8.7	23.1 +2.3	2.1 +10.5	4.5 +10.3	20.3 +8.4	5.4 +19.1	99.4 +7.8
1970	45.9 +4.3	23.8 +2.8	2.2 +7.7	4.8 +7.4	21.4 +5.6	6.6 +20.9	104.7 +5.3
1971	47.4 +3.4	24.1 +1.2	2.3 +3.1	5.1 +7.1	22.1 +3.2	7.5 +15.1	108.5 +3.6
1972	48.8 +2.9	24.1 +0.2	2.4 +3.1	5.3 +3.8	23.4 +5.7	8.1 +7.5	112.1 +3.3
1973	49.7 +1.8	24.4 +1.3	2.5 +3.4	5.6 +4.6	24.7 +5.6	7.8 −4.1	114.7 +2.3
1974	50.3 +1.3	24.4 +0.2	2.6 +4.5	5.5 −0.4	26.1 +5.6	8.1 +3.9	117.0 +2.0
1975	46.6 −7.4	24.7 +1.1	2.5 −1.8	5.6 +1.6	27.7 +6.1	8.4 +4.2	115.5 −1.3
1976	44.7 −3.9	24.4 −1.2	2.0 −20.0	4.9* −12.5	28.9 +4.3	8.9 +5.4	113.8 −1.4
1977	44.4 −0.6	24.3 −0.4	2.0 +0.0	4.6* −6.1	31.4 +8.7	9.3 +3.8	116.0 +1.9
1978	44.5 +0.3	24.5 +0.8	2.1 +5.0	4.4* −4.3	32.6 +3.8	9.9 +6.5	118.0 +1.7
1979	46.5 +4.5	25.7 +4.9	2.2 +4.8	4.2* −4.5	33.4 +2.5	10.9 +10.1	122.9 +4.2
1980	47.7 +2.5	26.5 +3.1	2.2 +0.0	4.2* +0.0	34.3 +2.7	11.0 +0.6	125.9 +2.4
1981	49.0 +2.7	27.0 +1.3	2.2 +2.4	4.1* −0.3	35.5 +3.1	10.9 −0.3	128.7 +2.2
1982	47.2 −3.7	26.3 −2.6	2.2 −1.5	3.5* −14.4	35.7 +0.5	10.7 −2.2	125.6 −2.5

*From 1 June 1976, Omnibus transport no longer included.

EXHIBIT 5   1982 Trennungsrechnung (disaggregated income statement)

	Profit & loss statement (3)	Consolidations (4)	DB total (5)	Commercial business (6)	Public service business (7)	Railroad infrastructure (8)
Revenues						
Passenger, luggage, and express packages	6.0	—	6.0	3.5	2.5	—
Freight traffic	8.9	—	8.9	8.9	—	—
Other revenues	2.6	—	2.6	2.5	0.1	—
Federal transfer payments						
Revenue enhancing	3.6	—	3.6	—	1.8	1.8
Expense reducing	5.6	5.1	0.5	—	—	0.5
Total revenues	26.7	5.1	21.6	14.9	4.4	2.3
Expenses						
Personnel	20.3	3.7	16.6	7.7	3.5	5.3
Equipment	4.3	—	4.3	3.1	0.9	0.3
Depreciation	2.8	—	2.8	1.2	0.4	1.2
Interest	2.9	1.0	1.9	0.8	0.2	0.9
Provisions	0.4	0.4	—	—	—	—
Other expenses	0.1	—	0.1	0.1	—	—
Total expenses	30.8	5.1	25.7	12.9	5.1	7.7
Profit/loss	−4.1	—	−4.1	+2.0	−0.7	−5.4

expenses and total revenues including the transfer payments for operations from the Federal Government. The accumulation of deficits caused the DB's debt to rise dramatically.

DR. GOHLKES' VIEWS

According to Dr. Gohlke, "further development (of the DB) under the conditions of the status quo, would have meant an increase in the total debt to over DM 90 billion by the year 1990, with an additional yearly net credit requirement of approximately DM 12 billion, or a total yearly funding gap, including the Federal subsidy, of approximately DM 25 billion. In the longer run, this railroad would no longer be financially supportable, despite recognition of its total economic benefits, including low land usage, small burden on the environment, energy savings, independence from oil supplies, high travel safety, and irreplaceability for commuter traffic and the transport of heavy goods."

Prior to assuming his new position, Dr. Gohlke had spent 16 years with

EXHIBIT 6a   Profit and loss statement, millions of deutsche marks

	Revenues					Expenses			
	1981		1982			1981		1982	
Deficit	$4,044	(13%)	$4,149	(13%)	Other expenses	$674	(2%)	$508	(2%)
Federal transfer payments	9,062	(34%)	9,234	(35%)	Interest	2,713	(9%)	2,926	(9%)
Other revenues	1,756	(6%)	1,840	(7%)	Equipment	7,094	(23%)	7,170	(23%)
Other transportation	795	(3%)	726	(3%)	Personnel	20,198	(66%)	20,280	(66%)
						$30,679		$30,884	
Passenger, luggage, and express package traffic	5,805	(22%)	6,007	(22%)					
Freight traffic	9,217	(35%)	8,928	(33%)					
	$30,679		$30,884						

EXHIBIT 6b   Balance sheet, millions of deutsche marks

	Assets					Liabilities			
	1981		1982			1981		1982	
Other assets	$4,257	(7%)	$4,869	(8%)	Other liabilities	$4,037	(7%)	$4,101	(7%)
Financial					Loans	33,973	(57%)	35,542	(58%)
investments	2,469	(4%)	2,431	(4%)	Cumulative surplus				
Plant and equipment	52,888	(89%)	52,244	(88%)	(equity capital) after				
	$59,614		$61,524		deduction of loss	21,064	(36%)	21,881	(35%)
						$59,614		$61,524	

IBM, most recently as General Manager of the German Text and Data Systems Group. In articles and interviews, he expressed the following views:

"A good business is the best basis for ensuring the existence of an enterprise even in the political arena."

"Above all, business activities must be oriented toward the market. Only the market and results can justify them."

"Not least, however, is the courage to do new things to keep the enterprise competitive."

"For me success alone is decisive."

There was little doubt that Gohlke would change things at the Bundesbahn. The question was what his priorities, tactics, and pace of change would be.

EXHIBIT 7a   **Revenues per employee**

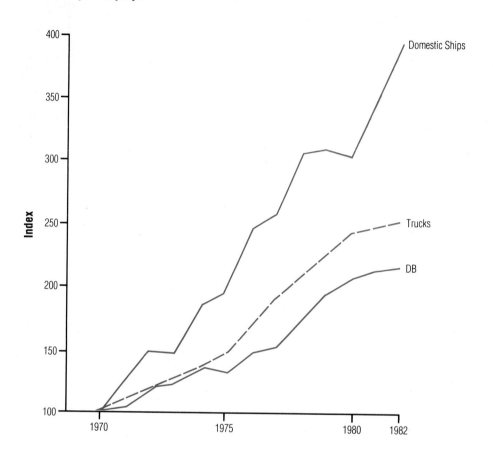

EXHIBIT 7b   Revenues per unit of load capacity

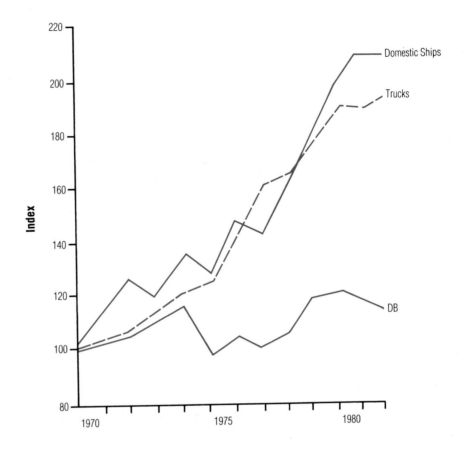

EXHIBIT 8   Financial performance summary (1962–1982)

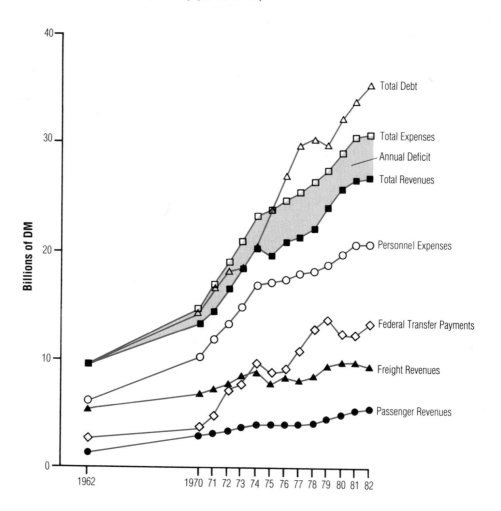

Case 26

DEUTSCHE

BUNDESBAHN (B)

Throughout 1982, German press speculated widely on the role of Dr. Gohlke, the new head of the Deutsche Bundesbahn, in reshaping the 130-year-old railroad system along commercial lines. Two aspects of the railroad's performance stood out in this thinking. First the substantial and growing subsidies were seen as an unacceptable burden on the federal budget, especially since rising unemployment had dramatically increased the budget deficit. Second, the railroad's loss of market share to road and air, both in freight and people transport, was widely believed to be at least partly caused by a lack of market orientation on the part of the DB's management.

As a first step, Dr. Gohlke established a task force of senior managers to assist him in developing a plan of action. After several months of working with the task force, Dr. Gohlke described some of the means by which he intended to achieve improved "bottom line" results at the DB. There were four main elements to his plan of change in the way the DB was to be managed.

1. *Market orientation.* The marketing effort of the DB would be strengthened by concentrating on segmenting the market along customer groups and needs. Dr. Gohlke made it clear that "improved use of existing DB facilities would not in itself lead to improved results." Rather the DB would concentrate on meeting customer needs where it had a demonstrable economic advantage over competing forms of transport. To this end, individual responsibility for product and market performance would be established.

2. *Decentralization.* The organizational changes (Exhibit 1) consolidated the headquarters staff and brought staff units directly under the responsibility of individual members of the executive board. In addition, the regional operating units were more tightly organized to eliminate a level of management. This new structure would permit an important decentralization of decision

This case was prepared by Professors Paul Strebel and George Taucher, assisted by Research Associate Robert Howard, as a basis for class discussion rather than to illustrate either effective or ineffective handling of an administrative situation. Copyright © 1987 by IMD (International Management Development Institute), Lausanne, Switzerland. Not to be used or reproduced without permission.

EXHIBIT 1   Organizational changes in the Deutsche Bundesbahn, 1982

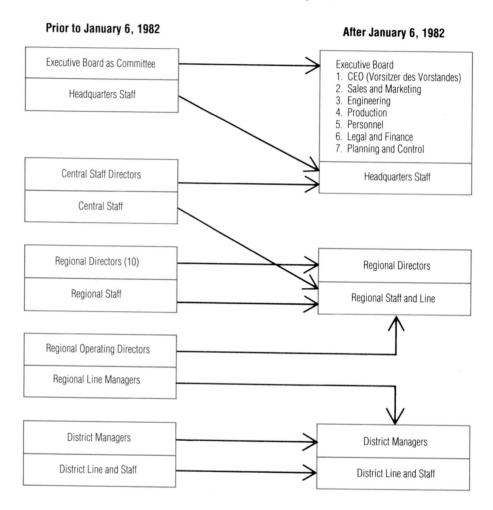

making, in Dr. Gohlke's opinion. With only three management levels, he felt that the executive board, aided by the HQ staff, would be able to delegate substantial responsibility to the regional operating units—without losing overall control.

3. *Management by objectives.* An important requirement for the decentralization of decision making would be the introduction of individual accountability with objectives controlled through improved quantitative data. While the DB had a complex and massive control system based on technical considerations and efficiency measures, there was little market-oriented information. Nor was there any real ability to measure profit contribution by product or market segments. Such information was vital if effective profit-oriented ob-

jectives were to be set, Dr. Gohlke believed. However, for an organization the size of the DB, recasting the information system would be a task of years rather than months.

4. *Open decision-making through creative conflict.* Dr. Gohlke believed that the only way to avoid "political decision-making" in the DB was to combine the decentralized decision-making process with management by objectives in as transparent a process as possible. Visibility of points of view and perspectives should be expressed as openly as possible, he believed. In this way, Dr. Gohlke hoped to improve the rationality of decisions and thereby impact the overall performance of the DB. It was a process that worked well at IBM.

IMPLEMENTATION OF CHANGE

To implement these new ideas, Dr. Gohlke began at the top. Within the first six months he announced a re-organization of the basic structure of the Vorstand (the executive board) of the DB. Essentially he introduced the system of individual responsibility for the seven members of the board. This permitted Dr. Gohlke to assign each individual executive board member direct and personal responsibility for a business function. Further re-organization took place at the same time. A five-layer organization was consolidated into three layers—essentially a single operating headquarters and a two-level field organization with 10 regional offices as before (see Exhibit 1).

To prevent the budget deficit from getting out of control, Dr. Gohlke ordered a freeze on all new hiring and investment. This measure made it possible to stabilize the deficit at DM 4 billion in 1982 and 1983.

To improve revenues, special attention was paid to marketing. The new department of marketing came up with creative ideas for improving the Bundesbahn's image and attracting new customers. These included special rail and road travel packages, differential fares designed to encourage train usage during periods of slack demand, as well as imaginative advertising. Railroad stations, for example, were converted into centers of attention by decorating them with art exhibits.

To lay a foundation for the future, Mr. Pällmann, executive board member for planning and control, was charged with the responsibility of developing a long-term plan. The plan—DB'90—had an ambitious objective of

- Increasing worker productivity by 40% in real terms
- Reducing personnel costs (on a real basis) by 30%
- Reducing overall costs by 25% (also real) between the years 1983–1990

Combining these internal efficiencies with a more effective market orientation, it was hoped that revenues would rise 1% per year faster than overall costs, thereby making a substantial improvement in the deficit.

Dr. Gohlke was fully aware, however, that his new title of "Vorsitzer des Vorstandes" did not legally correspond to the role of chief executive officer in an American company. Under German law, the role of Vorsitzer is to coordinate the decision-making role of the Vorstand. In this role he had the power to set agendas but his vote carried no more weight than other board members. In practice, the principle of collegial decision-making is well established in Germany and votes are rarely taken. Consensus is the established form of decision-making. In addition, the Vorsitzer traditionally is the "speaker" of the executive board. His task is to communicate decisions and policy to both internal and external groups. In this role, he becomes highly visible.

Dr. Gohlke realized that the changes outlined above were only a first step in moving the DB from a government organization toward a commercial enterprise. Soon after his arrival, Dr. Gohlke introduced an "open door" policy whereby he undertook to meet with as many DB personnel of all levels as possible. For example, he introduced informal breakfast meetings where he could gain better understanding of the style and culture of the DB.

SELECTED SIMULATED REMARKS OF SOME DB STAKEHOLDERS

1. Der Eisenbahner—The Railroad
Civil Servant—A Middle
Level Executive

I don't really know if Dr. Gohlke can save the railroad from the destructive forces around us. The DB has been at a significant disadvantage for many years now. The government has poured billions into building free autobahns which has resulted in declining freight and personnel transport on the railroads. Even Lufthansa has been given subsidies to increase internal traffic—surely a silly way to transport people and freight in a small country like Germany. Now we see that the EC is de-regulating truck transport, which will result in even lower freight rates and put even more pressure on us.

The railroad system is of long-term strategic importance to Germany. We must retain a basic infrastructure even if the short-term economic results are slightly negative. This fact has proved itself many times over the 130 years we have been in existence. Of course we must operate the given system as efficiently as possible—but compare us with other systems around the world. We aren't doing so badly. By European standards we are certainly one of the best. Only the French with their physical advantages have been able to do better with their new fast trains. You should really compare us to the Japanese with their densely populated coastal regions. We do a lot better than they do. You don't see any Japanese miracle there.

I see Dr. Gohlke's main task to convince the outside political authorities to accept a certain "infrastructure" cost. Within that framework we should—of course—do all we can to produce a positive result. Even now, we produce a positive result if you leave out all of the subsidized areas. Really this is a problem of accounting and public relations. The reality is that we have been making substantial progress over the years.

As far as some of the leadership measures that Mr. Gohlke has started are concerned, I think that while many are positive, we have to be careful that we don't move too far in the direction of a commercial enterprise. We still have a wider responsibility to society. For example, there is this question of individual accountability. This is OK if you have simple measures—such as in a private company. Profit counts for everything. But here, profit is only one element of our work. We have the responsibility of stewardship over the assets of the German people. If we focus only on profit, then we may end up with something like the American RR system—short-term profit orientation has resulted in the rundown and near collapse of the system. Germany can't afford that!

We hope that Dr. Gohlke will learn and respect the proven tradition of the DB.

2. The Young Turk—A High Level Headquarters Staff Executive

Dr. Gohlke's arrival at the DB has been a breath of fresh air. For the first time in my 15 years here we have a hope of change from the old ways of doing things. Too many of my colleagues around here believe that we can do very little given the political climate. After so many years and so many lost battles with the politicians to gain efficiency, too many have lost their initiative. They feel constrained within very narrow limits of possibility. Frankly there are very few of us who feel optimistic that Dr. Gohlke can really change things in a substantial way. I am strongly in favor of all of the things he is doing. His emphasis on individual accountability is sorely needed. The real test will come later when the quantitative measures have been developed and then we will know who has done well and who has not. There will be winners and losers. Will he be able to sufficiently reward the winners—given that most of us are still civil servants? What will happen to the poor performers? I know full well that in IBM, with a system of lifetime employment, the conditions are said by some to be similar—the poor performers are pushed onto a plateau where they can make some contributions but are out of the mainstream. But IBM has a positive environment of success and they are growing rapidly. None of this is true at the DB.

As far as Dr. Gohlke's management style is concerned, his "open door" policy and his real effort to communicate with people is also a terrible shock to many. This approach is totally new to nearly everyone here. We have been used to guarding our backsides—at all costs. Decisions should be defused and divided among committees to avoid risk. Frankly, much of this is seen as a threat by the bulk of executives—it is so new to them I am afraid that the changes that Dr. Gohlke wants to make will take a long time—there is just no motivation to enter the hard new world of individual responsibility for many of my colleagues.

We need some signs of success. For example, we developed a proposal, supported by outside consultants, to consolidate our railroad car workshops from eight to four locations. This would permit us to use the remaining capacity efficiently. This measure alone will save tens of millions within a few years.

Of course, there was opposition from the union and the Workers Council, but despite the fact that Dr. Gohlke was new to the job, he was successful in convincing them that this measure was necessary. Unfortunately after the proposal was formally presented to the Ministry of Transport, we were advised that government approval was unlikely. For this reason we withdrew the proposal and began to develop new ideas for a solution to the overcapacity problem in the workshops. This project is important if we are to reach our DB'90 objectives.

Dr. Gohlke's tough job will be to keep political interests out of our decision-making process as much as possible.

3. The Chairman of the Main Workers Council with the Board of Directors of the DB

Within the DB there are 3 levels to the Workers Council. The Local Councils operate in suburban areas, District Councils on a regional level and the Main Workers Council at the Board Level. In some cases the same people might work in more than one Council. All three levels work closely together and there is no formal reporting structure between the Council levels (Exhibit 2).

According to German Federal representative law, the Workers Council is elected for a period of 3 years by the staff, to participate in decisions on management of the DB.

There are three levels of participation:

1. *Information exchange.* The law obligates both partners to work together in full confidence toward the welfare of the employed. That also requires management to inform the Workers Council about all important and comprehensive procedures.

2. *Participation.* With some important issues, for example, in the organizational area, management must inform us of the development of any plans. We then give our opinion. In the event that no agreement is reached, management has the right to go ahead with its actions even without our agreement.

3. *Mutual decisions by management and the Workers Council (contribution).* On those key issues that are specifically quoted in the law, a management decision can only be passed when we have approved. In the event that no agreement is reached, the law allows an appeal to a Board of Arbitration, which, depending on the conditions of the case, delivers a recommended agreement or final decision.

This is the legal framework. We would like to work in this framework and expect the same from management. We have a responsibility to our colleagues

EXHIBIT 2   **Relationship of Workers Council to DB personnel**

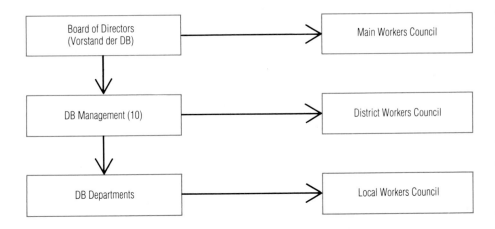

and intend to fulfill this. We meet with the Board of Directors of DB on a monthly basis and more frequently in the event that important questions are to be discussed. Dr. Gohlke has in fact brought a new leadership style to the DB. We are totally in favor of a new "transparent decision process." We also support his efforts to establish contacts with the employees of DB. Yet at the same time the danger exists that established channels of communication will be avoided. If he speaks to employees at all levels, one sometimes has the feeling that he undermines the formal organization. For example, our job is to represent the employees. He should not go around us when this could lead to misunderstanding.

We are also very worried about his objectives to reduce costs and personnel in his plan for 1990. We are all for efficiency and all for a viable railroad system, but we are concerned that some of these goals might be achieved at the expense of the employees. We think that sub-contracting might be a way of achieving these goals. This will mean that jobs now done by our people will be done by outsiders—maybe even outside of Germany. This will open the door to non-union work, lowered quality and exploitation. There is the case of the workshops, for example. We suspect that the consolidation proposal, which we opposed and was fortunately dropped after government opposition, was to be achieved by sub-contracting a lot of the work. Why not use those facilities to do other work—we could go into the metal fabrication business, for example. Management has not done enough to try to save the facilities that we have built up over the years.

4. Spokesman for the Trade Union of German Railroad Workers

The union is responsible for representing its members. I would like to stress, however, that our objective is a viable railroad system with a long-term future.

The railroad workers have never avoided the requirement of railroad rationalizations and technical modernizations. On the contrary, we have responsibly shaped
this development with the understanding that only modern and fast railroads can
maintain and strengthen their position in the traffic market. We are of the understanding that the DB has already been disadvantaged for too long in comparison
to other—sometimes less efficient—forms of transport. This was especially true
in the 1950s and the 1960s and appears to be the present attitude of the government. In the 1970s when the Social Democrats were in power, the importance of
the DB was given higher priority, but even then many of the disadvantages of
rail transport were not eliminated. This is partly a question of accounting. We
believe that the government should take responsibility for the infrastructure of
the rail system. This idea is proposed by the socialist party and we support it. It
seems that this idea may even have support in Brussels, thereby making it a
European convention. We think this would be important since Germany is not
an island. We are spending a great deal of time and effort to lay the groundwork
for these fundamental changes. If these changes were made, the public image of
the DB would rise since we would no longer require such significant subsidies.
It would at last provide an initial step to deliver DB from the red.

We work closely with the Workers Council. After all, they are mostly our
members. They actively look after the interests of the employees and appeal to
us if any problems arise. We stand by them with advice and information and also
represent their position before the court.

One of our main tasks is working together with the government and Brussels with the intention of improving the overall surroundings in which we work.
For that reason we support that European-wide, competition and distortion be
reduced in relation to all heavy freight traffic and that the financial provisions of
the European railway be improved. Only in this way can we build a good European rail network. We are also convinced that the rail network must be more
strongly promoted in the future in order to hinder a further strain on the
environment.

We hope that Dr. Gohlke will be able to improve the efficiency of the DB.
We are not in principle opposed to increases in productivity, in that the efficiency
of the DB is important for us. What we are concerned about is this craze for
"commercial results" and privatization. We are strongly opposed to "salami tactics" to privatize the DB. For example, sub-contracting seems to be increasing.
This is not only hurtful to our members but is setting a bad example for Germany. Many of these so called sub-contractors are nothing but fly-by-night operators, in many cases using "black" labor. They don't pay their share of taxes
and as a result the rest of us have to pay more. The DB is too important to
Germany to permit this jungle of illegality and exploitation. The DB must keep
its present structure as special federal property, only so it can justify its public
duty. The employees of DB must remain civil servants. This will preserve the
long tradition of the DB and create a stability that Germany needs.

We also believe that the management of DB has not done enough in the past
to compete with other transportation—especially with cars and trucks. We will

certainly support the efforts of Dr. Gohlke, to sell the DB products more effectively—but this is a job for management. We object, however, to the market orientation of DB, only to let workers go. There cannot be a continuous workforce reduction without bottlenecks occurring in different areas.

Finally, we think that management should consider the rights of the existing workforce in making decisions. We strongly believe that not enough is being done to bring work to the workers rather than workers to the work. There are areas of high regional unemployment in Germany. The DB as a major employer should concentrate its activities in those areas. The proposal to close workshops goes wholly against the needs of Germany. Several of them would have been shut down in areas of high unemployment. There are simply no employment alternatives in those regions. We think that the management of the DB should take more into account its social responsibilities—not just this craze for profits.

5. Senior Civil Servant—Ministry of Transport

The Bundesbahn is undergoing a radical but step-by-step change from a government department toward a commercial enterprise. In the good German tradition, this revolution is being conducted in an evolutionary way with careful economic and political controls to ensure that the process goes neither too fast nor too far. For the foreseeable future, government involvement will be heavy, if only because substantial parts of the railroad system will continue to be subsidized—especially, for example, suburban/city networks.

The transportation minister carries the political responsibility for the affairs of the DB. For example, the budget of the DB must be approved by the minister. The role of my department is to give the minister advisory support—an independent examination of the planning proposals. Ultimately, the minister will not make all decisions alone. Every minister of the cabinet can pose questions within his area of competence—for example, the employment minister can pose questions over unemployed personnel, and, most important, the finance minister must confirm the budget and the magnitude of state subsidization. Consequently, the fundamental plans of the DB are approved by the finance minister and sometimes at the cabinet level.

The Board of Directors has expanded its powers in executive management. Some interesting tests are going on. For example, in the relatively short distance between Cologne and Gummersbach a single manager was made responsible for operations. This manager could work with combinations of train and bus and could also establish prices independently. Unfortunately, the existing cost accounting system with average cost accounting made it difficult to compare his results with other systems. It is very important that the full-cost system of the past be replaced with a contribution system; however, to change the old well-established system is much harder than anyone believed.

Despite these good intentions and gradual steps in the direction of a market-oriented company, a strong political influence could not be avoided. The rationalization of workshops, for example (with the accompanied closings), brought on serious political debate. An approval in the Board of Directors of the DB was not expected thereafter. The Board of Directors and Dr. Gohlke should have recognized this and not made such a contested proposal in a way that aroused political emotions. This plan was so visible that it provoked public opinion sensation since over 4,000 jobs in structurally weak regions would have been eliminated. Had Gohlke used the "salami" tactic, then perhaps the plan would have had a better chance.

Case 27

DEUTSCHE
BUNDESBAHN (C)

Between 1982 and 1985 the Bundesbahn recorded an impressive improvement in its position but faced even more daunting problems ahead. Wilhelm Pällmann, a member of the executive committee who joined the Bundesbahn in 1982, made the following comments in a professional journal in early 1986:

> The impact of the new strategy on the financial return is currently stronger than had been expected. On the other hand, the risks for the period remaining up to 1990 have, if anything, become greater and the railway's basic problem of finance remains unsolved. The railways must achieve market competence in a clearly defined, limited range of services. An important starting point for this is investment in the network and in the high-speed services of the 1990s. (However) the state will not be willing to give the railways more money, or blanket terms, without constraints. (*Internationales Verkehrswesen* 2/86).

In 1985, the government announced that the projected extra state contribution of DM 2 billion per year to help finance the expansion of the rail network was not necessary and would not be forthcoming.

PROGRESS BETWEEN 1982 AND 1985

The improvement in the performance of the Bundesbahn is summarized by the financial statistics in Exhibit 1 and the graph of originally projected performance and actual losses in Exhibit 2. Whereas the loss had been projected to rise in 1983, it in fact dropped from DM 4.1 billion in 1982 to DM 3.7 billion. This was achieved by rigorous control of expenditure.

EXHIBIT 1   Summary of financial statistics

	1982	1983	1984	1985	Original projection DB90	Revised projection DB90
Loss (including federal subsidy)	4.1	3.7	3.1	2.9	1.9	4.0
Financing gap (excluding federal subsidy)	15.2	13.8	13.4	14.2	15.0	16.1
Federal subsidy	13.6	13.7	13.5	13.6	15.3	13.3
Annual borrowing	1.6	0.1	−.08	0.6	−.3	2.8
Total debt	35.5	35.6	35.5	36.1	39.5	54.9
Interest expense	2.9	2.9	2.9	3.0	3.4	4.5

Productivity increased by 10 percentage points in real terms between 1982 and 1985. Despite a slight increase in revenues, the number of personnel dropped sharply. This was the main factor behind the 9.1 percentage point drop in total expenses over the same period. Total revenues increased by 3% even though the state's subsidy hardly changed. The biggest increase came from goods traffic (5%) and individual transport (9%), primarily the postbus system.

The smaller overall loss resulted in lower borrowing. In 1984, DM 80 million of debt was actually refunded. As a result, the total debt increased by only DM 0.7 billion over the period. Nevertheless, annual gross investment increased from DM 4.1 billion to DM 5.1 billion, of which a total of DM 5 billion was used to expand the rail network.

OUTLOOK FOR 1990

The original projection for 1990 forecast a decline in the loss to about DM 1.9 billion in 1985, remaining more or less constant at that level until 1990. This assumed that the state would help finance the expansion of the rail network with an extra annual contribution of DM 2 billion starting in 1985. From the Bundesbahn's point of view, expansion and maintenance of the rail network should have been the state's responsibility, in the same way that it takes care of the road and air infrastructure.

However, the extra state contribution was not forthcoming in 1985 (see Exhibit 1). This, despite Chancellor Kohl's earlier comment that: "The railroad is indispensable." The sentiment in the Bundestag (Parliament) on the government Christian Democrat side seemed to be that things were improving at the Bundesbahn, as shown by its declining losses. Hence, an increase in the federal subsidiary was not necessary. The opposition Social Democrats argued that a change in the composition and role of the Bundesbahn board would be more useful than an increase in state financing.

EXHIBIT 2   **Annual deficit (DM billions)**

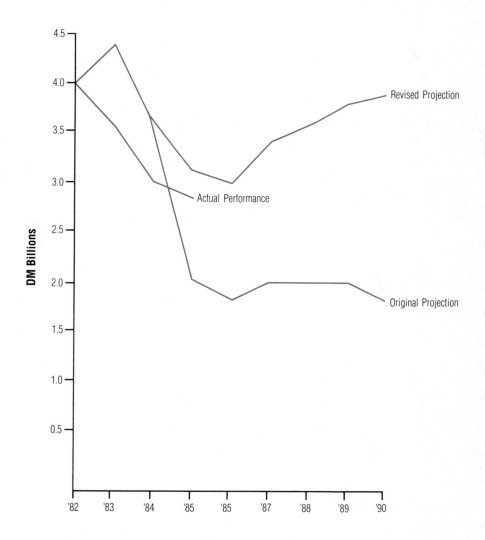

The lack of state support for the expansion of the rail network showed up immediately in higher interest expenses and a greater loss in 1985 than anticipated. As a result, the projection for 1990 had to be revised (see Exhibit 2). If the investment plan were implemented with the federal subsidy remaining at its 1982/85 level, the Bundesbahn's total debt would increase from the original projection of DM 39.5 billion to DM 54.9 billion in 1990. This would result in DM 0.5 to DM 1.5 billion of additional interest expense per year.

Another problem, which was becoming apparent in 1986, was the gradual decline in school and professional commuter traffic. The probable impact on revenues and total loss was on the order of DM 0.5 billion.

In addition, the Bundesbahn workforce was proving more resistant to change than had been hoped. "It is extraordinarily difficult to convince colleagues of the need to distance themselves from outdated notions (such as the 'State Railway') so that critical changes in performance are perceived as more than merely the railway's fate in a new age." The reason for this resistance had a lot to do with the aging of the workforce. Four out of five were staying on until retirement. In direct financial terms the result was DM 0.6 billion of extra social costs, not offset by the federal subsidy, that therefore had to be born directly by the Bundesbahn.

Adding together the additional interest expense, lower commuter revenues, and extra social costs, the revised projection for 1990 anticipated a loss of DM 4.0 billion (see Exhibits 1 and 2). The revised forecast of annual borrowing was correspondingly greater, reflecting also the loss of the anticipated increase in state financing.

The new projection did not include the impact of increasing de-regulation of trucking (road transport of goods) throughout the European Common Market. This would affect both the pricing and quantity of the demand for freight transport by rail. The railroads were at a particular disadvantage with respect to cross-border international transport. Whereas the most competitive trucker could build his business throughout Europe, the railroads were subject to a more fragmented market with many incompatible national restrictions.

Since trucking deregulation would affect the Bundesbahn's freight business, which accounted for two-thirds of its controllable revenues, the final impact might have been dramatic. Nevertheless, the Bundesbahn was hopeful that it could compete, at least within Germany, by cutting costs and introducing fast, reliable freight services between production centers, incorporating collection and distribution by road. Moreover, if revenues declined, costs could be reduced proportionately, thereby minimizing the impact on the bottom line.

Case 28

COSA BELLA, INC.

It was early evening, June 1988, and Susan Maxwell, president of Cosa Bella, Inc. (CBI), was working late on a group of fanciful ceramic table accessories featuring handpainted fish and octopus designs. The Al Mare group of dinnerware and oversized platters had done well for CBI since its introduction last season, and Maxwell wanted to follow up quickly with a collection of serving bowls, candlesticks, and pitchers in related patterns. "What a long way we've come in five years," Maxwell thought, glancing at the display of Italian dinnerware which filled shelves lining one wall of her office. From the single dinnerware line, Campagna, discovered when she was on holiday in Italy with her mother and sister in May 1983, CBI had grown to be one of the largest importers and distributors of handcrafted Italian tableware and gifts in the U.S. In 1988, CBI carried 22 lines from 20 manufacturers. Each special line, handcrafted by Italian artisans, reflected the sophisticated, tasteful image Maxwell felt was the key to her company's success.

Remembering that first trip to Italy, Maxwell smiled at how improbable the company's present success was. At thirty, with a BA degree in education, an MS in recreational therapy, and five years' experience managing a small specialty retail shop in Charlottesville, Virginia, Maxwell had moved to New York to take interior design classes at the New York School of Interior Design. When her mother offered to take Susan and her sister Frances to Italy for three weeks, Susan jumped at the chance. As luck would have it, that holiday took Susan's career in a new direction.

The Maxwell women had been so taken with the colorful dinnerware used in the dining room of the tiny San Pietro Hotel that they hired a chauffeur and went in search of the factory where it was produced. The factory—Solimene—was located in San Felice Circeo, a small fishing village. There, with the assistance of their driver's rough translations, the Maxwells met Don Vincenza, patriarch of the family business. Solimene employed some 30 artisans to make the colorful ceramic articles the Maxwells had admired. The women spent two of their vacation days negotiating prices for container-loads of the dinnerware, still

This case was prepared by Sidney Taylor Smith under the direction of Professor Richard I. Levin, UNC Business School at Chapel Hill, as a basis for class discussion rather than to illustrate either effective or ineffective handling of an administrative situation. Names and company data have been disguised.

uncertain as to how they would sell it or, indeed, what was involved in importing goods from Italy to the U.S. Filled with enthusiasm for their new project, however, the three forged ahead—and Cosa Bella (Italian for "thing of beauty") was founded.

In the course of their travels, the Maxwells met Fabio Puccinelli, a Florentine businessman with extensive import-export experience. Fabio would later become CBI's sole agent in Italy, acting as an invaluable link in coordinating the flow of merchandise from factories through the local freight carriers to customs officials. It was Fabio who first warned them, when they broached the idea of importing Solimene dinnerware to the U.S., that although "Solimene makes extremely fine ceramics . . . they are notorious . . . indeed, they are the most difficult factory to work with in all of Italy." Undeterred by Fabio's warnings, the Maxwells returned to the States, determined to investigate the intricacies of customs brokers, freight forwarders, attorneys, bankers, and to learn something about the market for high-end specialty dinnerware.

BACKGROUND

In 1987 the U.S. imported $572.5 million worth of dinnerware and tabletop items, with the bulk of imports coming from suppliers in the Far East. The dinnerware/tabletop category has grown approximately 5% annually since 1980, with most growth attributable to increased prices due to the weakened buying power of the dollar. Imports represented 70% of the total U.S. dinnerware market in 1987, a 2.3% increase over 1986 levels. Exhibit 1 shows quantity and C.I.F. value of imported dinnerware/tabletop items in 1986 and 1987.[1] Ceramic tableware from Italy represented about 3.5% of U.S. tableware imports in 1987.

Retail sales of tableware and table accessory products approached $5.6 billion in 1987. The market for high-end tabletop items, giftware, and crystal was considered an important growth segment of this market by major retailers, who attributed its importance to the booming bridal market. Bloomingdale's alone generated $20 million in tabletop business in 1987 and credited its success in this category to a policy of selecting merchandise from suppliers with limited distribution, consistent delivery schedules, and extensive customer service.

Ceramics from European artisans are noted for their design quality, and Italian design is considered the best. Despite their high cost (as much as 20–25% more expensive than handcrafted ceramics from other Southern European countries), the U.S. market was receptive to high-quality Italian products. There are six importer/distributors of ceramic tableware in the U.S., with three (including CBI) importing only Italian products. In addition to the handful of importer/distributors, most major department stores purchase directly from factories all over the world.

---

[1]C.I.F. values reflect the cost of goods plus insurance and freight to some U.S. port.

EXHIBIT 1(a)   **Imports to U.S. of tabletop items**

	Quantity (000)	
	1987	1986
Earthenware Coarse-grain & fine-grain; household ware	48,973	39,666
China Bone and non-bone tableware	20,958	20,493
Total earthenware & china	69,931	60,159

EXHIBIT 1(b)   **Imports to U.S. of tabletop items**

	C.I.F. value ($000)	
	1987	1986
Earthenware Coarse-grain & fine-grain; household ware	$344,868	$308,531
China Bone and non-bone tableware	$227,668	$234,058
Total earthenware & china	$572,536	$542,589

Source: U.S. Bureau of the Census, *U.S. Imports for Consumption*, FT246, Annual 1986, 1987.

COSA BELLA

From the moment she signed the first contract with Solimene to produce the Campagna dinnerware line, Susan Maxwell was committed to keeping her new company bound to a focused strategy. That strategy included an emphasis on handcrafted articles targeted to a sophisticated, upscale customer and dedication to customer service. Cosa Bella's first sale, in 1984, was to Neiman-Marcus. Better department stores with large tabletop and giftware departments (such as Neiman-Marcus, Gump, Bullock's, and Bloomingdale's) remained important accounts as CBI grew. Located in or close to major metropolitan areas, these retailers offered wide merchandise selections and such services as bridal registries. Most of these major retailers import some merchandise directly through their buying office in order to cut out the importer's costs, but CBI was successful in selling to these accounts on the basis of a distinctive product line and timely delivery of orders.

In order to ensure proper service to CBI accounts, Maxwell insisted that sales be handled internally rather than by independent giftware reps. CBI's three salespeople were responsible for developing accounts in three types of accounts: (1) specialty and gift stores, (2) department stores, and (3) catalog accounts. By 1988, specialty/gift shops accounted for 90% of sales, department stores accounted for 6% of CBI's sales, and catalog accounts represented 4% of sales. Sales to all three types of accounts were conducted out of permanent showrooms in Dallas, New York, and Atlanta and temporary booths at trade shows.

Maxwell carefully controlled the development of new product lines, making sure each addition to the CBI line was as special as the original Campagna line. To protect the uniqueness of the CBI product line, Maxwell negotiated verbal contracts with all suppliers to retain exclusive rights to all CBI patterns. In her five years of operation, Maxwell had added additional dinnerware lines, collections of terra-cotta cachepots and planters, heavy handblown crystal, and whimsical accessory lines. In 1988, CBI's 22 product lines reflected Maxwell's tireless search (three times a year) throughout Italy for the finest Italian crafts.

Maxwell had also carefully managed CBI's growth over the years. Conscious of her own limited experience in import-export and wholesale sales, Maxwell operated along conservative lines, relying on her policy of internally controlled sales to maintain CBI's reputation for customer service, and taking on very little debt to minimize CBI's financial risk. Maxwell credited much of CBI's success to her lean and loyal staff, which numbered twenty-five in 1988. Exhibit 2 provides a list of key players on CBI's management team and a brief description of their responsibilities. Exhibits 3 and 4 show CBI's financial statements for 1984 through 1987.

SOLIMENE

Solimene had proved to be as difficult to work with as Fabio had predicted. Don Vincenza had passed much of the managerial responsibility for the factory to his 28-year-old son, who was blatantly unscrupulous in negotiating prices and in attempting to create a bidding war for Solimene's limited output. The Vincenzas raised their prices 10% each year. Shipments were erratic and often incomplete. Maxwell was troubled by the deterioration of her relationship with Solimene and was afraid that the Vincenzas were interested in replacing her business with sales to department stores (who could afford to pay more).

Maxwell tried many tactics to improve the service she received from Solimene, including paying for goods four months in advance of receipt. But she refused to negotiate any further with the Vincenzas once prices were agreed upon and orders booked, as that would place her in the difficult position of having to bid against retail buyers who might also be her customers. Furthermore, Maxwell was concerned by the prospect of shrinking gross margins on the Campagna product line. She felt that accepting the price increases would establish a dangerous precedent.

An additional concern was that the incidence of flawed merchandise from

EXHIBIT 2   **Cosa Bella management team**

Name	Title	Responsibilities
Susan Maxwell	President	General management, sales, product sourcing and design, supplier contract negotiations.
Penny Kearns	Financial Controller	Responsible for preparation of financial statements, profitability analysis of product lines. Supervised letter of credit procedures. Responsible for Accounts Payable & Receivable.
Rick Kelly	Purchasing Manager	Responsible for ordering merchandise, quality control, lead testing, and manufacturer relationships.
Robert Miles	Director of Sales	Oversees sales and marketing. Sales responsibility for department stores.
Ellyn Brooks	Sales Manager	Supervises all showrooms and showroom personnel. Sales responsibility for catalog accounts. Sales administration for trade shows and all CBI accounts.
Mark Hunter	Design Coordinator	Showroom and office design. Trade show sales.
Frances Maxwell Robertson	Marketing/Advertising Director	Product brochure design. Art Director for all CBI advertising.
Lynn Kendrick	Office Operations Manager	Supervises office and warehouse employees. Order administration supervisor. Customer service coordinator.
Will Thompson	Warehouse Manager	Supervises order filling and shipping process. Supervises quality control.

Solimene was steadily increasing. In 1988, nearly 15% of the goods received from Solimene were second-quality goods for which Maxwell paid full price. Solimene steadfastly refused to allow CBI's deductions for flawed merchandise, and Maxwell had not been successful in achieving a compromise on this issue.

DESUIR

In an effort to limit CBI's dependence on a single supplier, Maxwell developed relationships with many other factories in Italy, and found one factory—Desuir—which was managed by a young, enthusiastic, and accommodating couple.

EXHIBIT 3   Cosa Bella, Inc., income statement ($000)

	1984	1985	1986	1987
Sales	175.69	591.43	1265.56	2271.20
Cost of sales	35.51	205.03	530.68	924.36
Other cost of sales	6.36	29.96	96.54	198.80
Gross profit	133.82	356.44	638.35	1148.04
Operating expenses				
Office	14.34	21.69	33.70	52.64
Warehouse	11.53	60.75	108.87	210.19
Wages/employee benefits	53.48	120.97	265.23	456.43
Administration	12.80	54.38	74.14	81.24
Sales administration		18.12	31.41	41.96
Total operating expenses	92.15	275.91	513.35	842.45
Marketing & sales	15.72	71.21	104.09	261.64
Buying	13.97	21.91	26.19	46.33
Total expenses	121.84	369.03	643.63	1150.43
Other income	0.62	32.15	94.04	144.71
Net profit (loss) before tax	12.60	19.57	88.75	142.33

Desuir's annual output was expected to be just over $700,000 in value (factory cost) in 1988, of which CBI would buy about $250,000. Desuir's rapid growth was hampered by space limitations, but plans for expansion were being formulated. (In contrast, Solimene's annual production was valued at just over $400,000, and the Solimene facility was approximately 50% larger than Desuir's.) Maxwell planned to add a new line of dinnerware from Desuir, and expected to place orders for $750,000 from Desuir in 1989. She estimated that Desuir's total output would reach $1.3 million in value in 1989.

In early 1988, the owners of Desuir approached Maxwell about investing in Desuir so that they could more rapidly expand their production capacity. Maxwell understood that the Desuir management wanted confirmation of CBI's long-term commitment to their business relationship, and felt that such an investment would give CBI a measure of security as well, guaranteeing a steady supply of merchandise. No specific level of investment was discussed, and Maxwell was not certain how much CBI would have to invest to establish a strong position with Desuir. She estimated, however, that an investment of around $200,000 would cover the costs of Desuir's expansion and give CBI significant clout with Desuir.

Desuir had proved to be a reliable and efficient supplier of ceramic dinnerware and terra-cotta pots in the two years Maxwell had worked with them. Desuir's product quality was good and their shipment record was consistent. In an effort to ensure adequate inventories on key Campagna accessory pieces, Maxwell asked Desuir to copy the Campagna patterns (which Maxwell had developed

EXHIBIT 4   Cosa Bella, Inc., balance sheet

Assets	1984	1985	1986	1987
Current assets				
Cash	8,052	17,287	65,483	149,694
Accounts receivable	19,335	106,707	212,037	286,099
Inventory	60,350	107,084	264,258	512,288
Prepaid expenses	0	1,786	3,033	4,453
Total current assets	87,737	232,864	544,811	952,534
Fixed assets				
Furniture & fixtures	1,710	11,262	15,017	16,804
Warehouse/office equip	128	19,542	37,391	74,049
Automobile	6,222	24,886	45,772	45,772
Leasehold improvements	231	231	500	1,140
Less accum depreciation	−908	−12,991	−37,690	−45,833
Net book value	7,383	42,930	60,990	91,932
Other assets	63	63	11,946	9,885
Total assets	95,183	275,857	617,747	1,054,351
Liabilities & stockholders' equity				
Current liabilities				
Accounts payable	5,095	65,833	327,911	500,314
Taxes payable	1,951	24,337	38,345	14,337
Total current liabilities	7,046	90,170	366,256	514,651
Long-term debts				
Notes payable	81,000	141,664	162,777	378,155
Less current maturity	0	0	0	−58,500
Total long-term debt	81,000	141,664	162,777	319,655
Total liabilities	88,046	231,834	529,033	834,306
Stockholder's equity				
Capital stock	20,000	20,000	20,000	20,000
Undistributed tax income	−25,456	0	0	0
Retained earnings	0	4,451	4,450	68,715
Net profit or (loss)	12,593	19,572	64,264	131,330
Total stockholder's equity	7,137	44,023	88,714	220,045
Total liabilities & stockholders' equity	95,183	275,857	617,747	1,054,351

at Solimene) on mugs, pitchers, casseroles, and serving pieces. While this had intensified the strained relations with Solimene, Maxwell felt that the ability to fill her customers' orders and the higher gross margins offered by Desuir made her actions justifiable. Exhibit 5 reflects 1987 product costs from Solimene and Desuir for key accessory pieces. Exhibit 6 indicates gross profit by pattern for representative product lines.

Despite Desuir's strengths, Maxwell had two reservations about making Desuir her primary supplier of ceramic dinnerware. The first had to do with her concern about incidences of lead contamination in Desuir ceramics.[2] FDA standards specified acceptable levels of extractable lead in ceramic ware used in the preparation, serving, or storage of food. "Action levels" (levels of lead contamination which required legal action and detainment of the entire shipment) varied according to category of ceramic ware. Exhibit 7 describes FDA standards for the flatware, small hollowware, and large hollowware categories.

CBI regularly tested shipments from all vendors at an independent lab in Richmond. CBI's tests had never found a contaminated piece in shipments sampled from Solimene. Unfortunately, in the past six months, one vividly colored platter made by Desuir had been tested by CBI's lab and identified as containing 7.1 parts per million of lead, slightly above legally accepted levels. Since only one piece out of the six tested was found to be contaminated, CBI management did not believe the problem was widespread. However, subsequent FDA tests of a shipment containing these pieces found that one out of three had excessive levels of extractable lead, indicating the problem was far more serious than CBI tests indicated. While Maxwell challenged the FDA test results, CBI promptly recalled the piece, which had been sold to accounts all over the U.S.

Maxwell knew that certain glaze colors contained more lead than others, and thus postulated that the problem with Desuir could be the result of the requirements of certain brightly colored designs rather than simply bad firing by Desuir. Maxwell frequently reminded all of her suppliers of the stringent FDA requirements. Nevertheless, she was concerned that dependence on Desuir could prove risky if the FDA stepped up its inspections of imported ceramics. In 1987, the FDA prohibited importation of over 1,000 shipments of ceramic articles due to lead violations, a 20-fold increase since 1983.

Maxwell's second concern was that if she decided to give up her relationship with Solimene in order to establish a stronger bond with Desuir, the Vincenzas would attempt to sell the Campagna patterns directly to major U.S. retailers. While Maxwell had a verbal understanding with the Vincenzas that the Campagna designs belonged exclusively to CBI, she was uncertain about which country's laws would protect her claim if the Vincenzas decided not to honor that agreement. On the other hand, Maxwell felt that given Solimene's erratic ship-

[2]Potters have long used pulverized lead to enhance the sheen of ceramic articles. When these articles are not fired at high enough temperatures, the glazes can break down, exposing users of the article to potentially fatal lead poisoning. In 1971, the FDA established standards regarding acceptable levels of lead releases. Imported ceramics account for the majority of violations, often due to the use of traditional methods of formulating and firing glazes.

EXHIBIT 5   **Cosa Bella, Inc., representative FOB prices, Solimene vs. Desuir**

Style #	Description	Solimene FOB price	Desuir FOB price	CBI wholesale price
1010	Mug	$ 2.60	$ 1.60	$ 6.50
1011	Pitcher	$ 8.40	$ 5.76	$22.00
1012	Casserole	$17.60	$11.12	$39.00

1. Factory prices based on average 1987 exchange rate of 1250 lire = $1.00.
2. FOB—"free on board," meaning the buyer bears the cost of shipping from the FOB point specified by the seller to the receiving point of the buyer.
3. Landed cost per piece (including freight, duty, insurance, and agents' fees) averages 28% above FOB price on these articles.

EXHIBIT 6   **Cosa Bella, Inc., schedule of gross profit by pattern**

Product line	Description	1984	1985	1986	1987
Campagna	Ceramic dinnerware & accessories				
Pattern #1		80.5%	74.6%	64.9%	67.4%
Pattern #2		79.7%	73.0%	66.7%	67.3%
Pattern #3		79.4%	75.3%	64.1%	67.6%
Pattern #4		79.5%	74.3%	66.8%	66.6%
Pattern #5		79.8%	76.1%	67.1%	66.2%
Pattern #6			73.1%	73.5%	67.9%
Insalata	Ceramic plates & serving pieces		53.3%	49.5%	46.5%
Ontano	Wooden accessories		54.0%	40.7%	46.7%
Puccinelli glass	Hand-blown stemware & accessories		49.1%	36.9%	45.9%
Buon Giorno	Ceramic dinnerware & accessories			72.0%	67.3%
De Simone	Decorative ceramic accessories			44.3%	50.8%
Fish	Whimsical fish platters			62.5%	65.8%
Veranda	Terra-cotta planters			62.5%	65.8%
Angeli	Planters				50.2%
Donatello	Handpressed bas reliefs				58.1%
Animale	Ceramic animal tureens				52.8%
Colore	Ceramic dinnerware & accessories				58.7%
Al Mare	Ceramic platters				67.3%

Note: 1987 margins on Campagna reflect weighted average of Solimene/Desuir FOB prices.

EXHIBIT 7   **Food and drug administration Compliance Policy Guide No. 7117.87**

Subject: Pottery (ceramics): imported and domestic—lead contamination

Background: Imported and domestic ceramic ware has been found to have significant quantities of extractable lead. The metal is extractable by acid foods and could cause chronic lead poisoning under continued food use.

Regulatory action guidance: The following represents the criteria for recommending legal action to the Division of Regulatory Guidance or for detaining imports.

The article   1. Is suitable to be used for liquid foods, and
2. Contains in 6 units examined, a level of lead per ml of leaching solution exceeding the action level for the category specified.

Category	Action basis	Action level parts per million
Flatware	Average of 6 units	7.0
Small hollowware	Any one of 6 units	5.0
Large hollowware	Any one of 6 units	2.5

Note:
The categories of ceramic articles, flatware, and hollowware used in the preparation, serving, or storage of food are defined as follows:

Flatware: Ceramic articles which have an internal depth as measured from the lowest point to the horizontal plane passing through the upper rim, that does not exceed 25mm.

Hollowware: Ceramic articles having an internal depth as measured from the lowest point to the horizontal plane passing through the upper rim, greater than 25mm.

Small hollowware: A capacity less than 1.1 liter
Large hollowware: A capacity of 1.1 liter or more

ping record in 1987 and 1988, it was unlikely that the Vincenzas would suddenly flood the U.S. market if they lost or abandoned CBI's business. Maxwell did feel an emotional tie to the line around which CBI was founded. She was also keenly aware that demand for the Campagna line remained strong. Campagna remained CBI's number-one product line, representing 25% of sales in 1987 (see Exhibit 8). Maxwell estimated that she could sell three to five times as much Campagna dinnerware if it were possible to get product.

Maxwell was confident that Desuir could produce dinnerware similar in quality to the Solimene product line. However, she was reluctant to risk losing her exclusive rights to the Campagna patterns. On the other hand, she was concerned by the prospect of passing on Solimene's steeply climbing prices to her customers and frustrated by Solimene's poor shipping record and high levels of flawed merchandise, all of which diminished her ability to serve her customers effectively. Maxwell felt that she must take some sort of action.

EXHIBIT 8   Cosa Bella, Inc., $ sales of Campagna line

	1984	1985	1986	1987
Pattern #1	$ 35,117	$ 66,606	$ 71,136	$ 72,319
Pattern #2	$ 45,205	$103,792	$161,282	$186,662
Pattern #3	$ 36,035	$ 57,436	$ 78,813	$106,081
Pattern #4	$ 27,026	$ 58,953	$ 69,713	$ 95,185
Pattern #5	$ 32,300	$ 56,320	$ 63,601	$ 85,392
Pattern #6		$ 14,608	$ 20,837	$ 22,118
	$175,683	$357,715	$465,382	$567,757

THE DECISION

In a May 30 meeting with CBI Controller Penny Kearns, Maxwell outlined three options (which she noted were not mutually exclusive) for dealing with the So-limene problem.

Her first option was to take no action per se, but to continue to search for ways to work with Solimene. Given the continuing popularity of the Campagna line, and the fact that she had greatly minimized the company's dependence on a single supplier, this could be the safest course of action. While the relationship with Solimene appeared to be deteriorating, Maxwell knew that she was an important customer to Solimene, and they were not likely to drop her as a customer—at this point. Kearns also pointed out that the rustic Campagna look would not remain popular indefinitely, and when demand fell off, Solimene would undoubtedly be more accommodating.

Maxwell felt that her second option was to invest in Desuir. Italian policy toward foreign investment was quite liberal, as such investment was believed to contribute to economic growth, employment, and the level of technology. Maxwell felt that she could rely on her Italian agent to assist her in negotiating with the owners of Desuir. Maxwell's consultations with lawyers in the U.S. and Italy confirmed that Italian law "guarantees repatriation of foreign capital originally invested in new 'productive' enterprises in Italy and unlimited remittance of profits therefrom."[3] Furthermore, "Italy does not limit ownership in an Italian corporation or other business entity." Maxwell was excited by the idea of investment in Desuir, as she felt that being able to better control factory deliveries would strengthen CBI's customer service image. On the other hand, Kearns pointed out that CBI's growth would soon require moving to a larger warehouse/office. Kearns felt that building a larger, more modern warehouse would also improve CBI's service capabilities, and might prove to be a more secure investment.

[3]Productive investments are those defined as adding to Italy's stock of foreign capital.

Maxwell felt that investment in Desuir was a strategic option which should be given careful thought. She knew that it might negatively impact her relations with other suppliers if they felt she was going to shift the bulk of her business to Desuir. It would almost certainly destroy her relationship with Solimene.

Maxwell's third option was to maintain the relationship with Solimene, but to investigate sourcing new lines from lower-cost producers in Spain and Portugal. The quality of ceramic imports from other countries had been improving, and Maxwell felt that she now had sufficient expertise in judging ceramics quality to select the best handcrafts available in those countries. Such a strategy could help improve CBI's gross margins, assuming she could sell the lower-cost Spanish and Portuguese articles for prices comparable to the Italian lines. Maxwell calculated that much of the initial advantage of purchasing lower-cost goods would be offset by increased travel and salary expenses. Sourcing goods from Spain/Portugal would require her to make two to three additional trips to Europe each year. Such a travel schedule would make it very difficult for her to maintain her central role in managing the home office, so Maxwell felt this plan would have to include hiring a dinner- and gift-ware merchandiser to help in sourcing, new design development, seeking local agents, and negotiating supplier contracts. Maxwell estimated that an experienced merchandiser would require an annual salary in the neighborhood of $40,000.

Maxwell felt that there must be other options for either improving relations with Solimene or minimizing CBI's risk if she were forced to drop Solimene as a supplier. Yet nothing new had come out of her meetings with Kearns and other key advisers. With her meeting with the CBI board of directors less than a week away, Maxwell removed the stack of Al Mare platters from her desk and began to outline her proposal for dealing with the Solimene problem.

ROHM AND HAAS COMPANY (A)

Rohm and Haas Company's Management Committee in 1974 knew it had to restructure the company. At a meeting late in the year, a senior vice president summed up the problem this way: "Our markets no longer fit neatly into our two domestic product divisions and our foreign operations aren't organized by product line at all. Our new corporate strategy calls for sharp increases in our marketing efforts worldwide with a broadening of the product line. No matter what else we do, we'll have to have some further subdivision of the U.S. management structure by product groups if we're to have any hope of making the new strategy work.

"Furthermore, we're trying to schedule production on a worldwide basis, but with the transfer prices the way they are, the divisions are fighting us. U.S. Chemicals is reluctant to sell to International except at prices International won't pay, and several of the subsidiaries in International disagree from time to time about who gets to produce what. We've got to do something, and do it now."

THE COMPANY

Rohm and Haas Company, a specialty chemicals manufacturer, had net income of $74 million in 1974 on net sales of $1.0 billion. With its head office in Philadelphia, it operated in most of the major markets of the world. Some of its products, such as agricultural pesticides, were used directly without further processing; most were sold to other manufacturers for use in products such as motor oils, paints, adhesives, packaging materials, and transparent plastic paneling.

Prior to 1975, Rohm and Haas was organized for managerial purposes in five operating divisions: U.S. Chemicals, U.S. Plastics, Health Products, Fibers, and International. In addition, Rohm and Haas had a Research and Development Division and various staff departments whose managers reported directly to the

This case was written by Gordon Shillinglaw. Copyright 1989 by the Graduate School of Business, Columbia University.

Chief Executive Officer. A skeleton pre-1975 organization chart is shown in Exhibit 1.

Each of the company's five operating divisions had its own marketing and manufacturing facilities and each had profit responsibility for divisional operations. Health Products and Fibers were stand-alone businesses concentrated very much in North America. The International Division had a small central staff, but otherwise operated through a set of national subsidiaries, most with their own manufacturing facilities. Regional coordination centers reporting to the management of the International Division in Philadelphia were located with supporting staff in Europe, Latin America, and the Pacific Basin.

Each subsidiary operated as a profit center. The R&D Division, like other headquarters staff groups, operated as a cost center. R&D costs were not charged to the operating divisions and subsidiaries, nor were they subdivided by product line. Subsidiaries paid varying levels of royalties to headquarters, however, the amount depending largely on local tax and exchange control regulations.

After glancing at Exhibit 1 some years later, one executive who was still with the company shook his head. "With that many senior executives reporting to the CEO," he said, "not to mention a few other staff executives you've left out, decision making was very slow."

Product transfers between the two domestic divisions and from International

EXHIBIT 1   **Rohm and Haas Company pre-1975 organization structure**

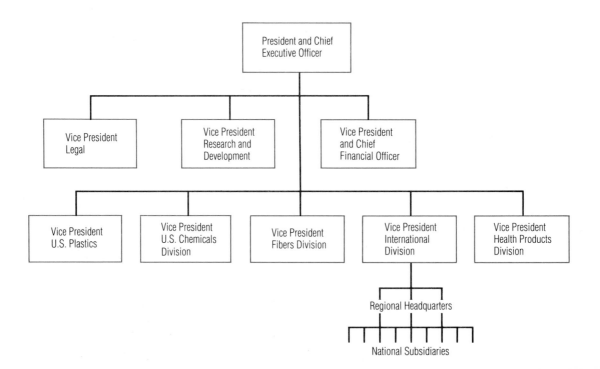

to the domestic divisions were extremely rare in 1974, except for raw material transfers from U.S. Chemicals to U.S. Plastics. U.S. Chemicals also transferred about 10 percent of its output to various International Division companies, and transfers between International Division companies were fairly frequent.

Each of the operating divisions and each foreign subsidiary was allowed to make its own sourcing decisions within guidelines set by the head office—that is, they had some freedom to choose among possible internal and external suppliers of products and feedstocks. Pricing and sourcing disputes found their way first to the regional coordination centers and then to the head office for final decisions if the regions couldn't resolve them.

One reason for the disputes was that the company had no official transfer pricing policy. The same transfer prices were used for fiscal and managerial purposes. They were set by the Treasurer, through a staff department known as the Capital Budgeting Department, to meet the company's objective of minimizing taxes and import duties within the limits set by national fiscal regulators. This led occasionally to prices that one party or another regarded as noncompetitive or noncompensatory.

THE SITUATION IN 1974

Rohm and Haas's top management had formulated a long-term strategy in 1974 that envisaged substantial growth in sales and earnings in the next decade. V. L. Gregory, Jr., Rohm and Haas's President and Chief Executive Officer, wasn't sure the company's organization structure (Exhibit 1) was the right one to carry out this strategy. As a result, he decided to establish a task force, known as the Organizational Study Group (OSG), to "undertake a thorough study of whether our existing organization—now serving us so well at the $1-billion sales level—is the optimum structure for a much bigger company, and to develop a long-term organizational strategy to match our growth objectives."

The OSG met frequently during the next six months, interviewing and collecting data from more than 150 key managers throughout the company. The Group's report, submitted in May 1975, included the following conclusions:

1. There is too much involvement of the top management in day-to-day or short-range operations.   Chandler

2. Our long- and short-range business planning systems are inadequate. Mechanisms for allocating corporate resources among businesses to achieve corporate objectives need to be developed.

3. We are not planning or running our businesses as businesses. The functional elements of the businesses are not effectively integrated.

4. Communication of technical, marketing, operating, and strategic information among overseas and domestic units of the company is inadequate.

5. Informal mechanisms that presently exist for establishing interlocking objectives and for resolving conflicts among different functions and regions are not completely satisfactory today and will not be adequate for Rohm and Haas in the 1980s.

One executive recalled recently that the second and third of these were particularly troublesome. "For one thing," he said, "top management lacked good information on the profitability of investments in individual product groups and locations. Without this information, decisions on investments in research and production facilities were quite difficult. In addition, research, manufacturing, and marketing efforts were poorly coordinated. Research found itself developing products marketing couldn't sell."

PROPOSAL: PRODUCT ORGANIZATION

As 1975 progressed, top management in Philadelphia was considering a bold new reorganization plan that it hoped would solve most of its organization-based problems. The first component of this plan was to restructure the company's product line into four broad groups:

1. Polymers, resins, and monomers (PRM)
2. Plastics
3. Industrial chemicals
4. Agricultural chemicals

Fibers and Health Products were left out of the reorganization since they were in the process of being divested.

With this structure, the company would establish a Corporate Business Department "to integrate the business plans and to coordinate the operation of the businesses on a global basis." This department would be headed by a Vice President and would include four corporate-level business group directors, one for each product group. The corporate vice presidents for research and development, finance, and legal would continue to report to the Chief Executive Officer. This portion of the organization structure is diagrammed in the right-hand portion of Exhibit 2.

THE PROPOSAL: REGIONAL STRUCTURE

The second component of the plan was to establish a regional management structure, based on customer location:

EXHIBIT 2   **Rohm and Haas Company proposed top-level organization structure**

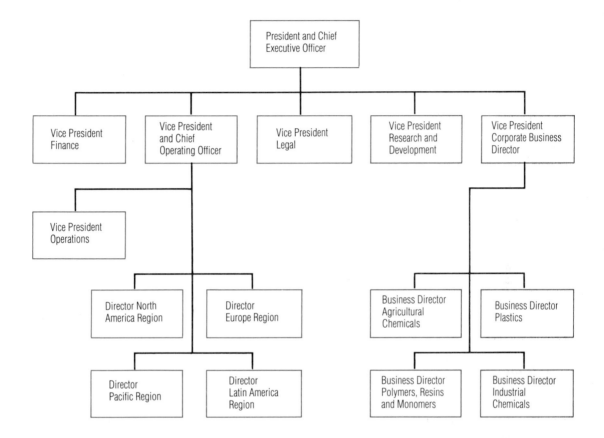

1. North America (United States and Canada)
2. Europe
3. Latin America
4. Pacific Basin

The four regional directors and a Vice President—Corporate Operations would report to the Vice President/Chief Operating Officer. The left side of Exhibit 2 diagrams this portion of the proposed organization structure.

The role of each regional organization would be to plan and run all the businesses within the region. The product structure would be built into the regional structure by the establishment of four business groups in each region, one for each product line, each headed by a regional business director. This portion of the structure is shown as the top tier in Exhibit 3, which presents a condensed version of the proposed organization structure for the North American region. The line connecting the corporate business director to the PRM group shows that

EXHIBIT 3   **Rohm and Haas Company proposed organization structure—North American region**

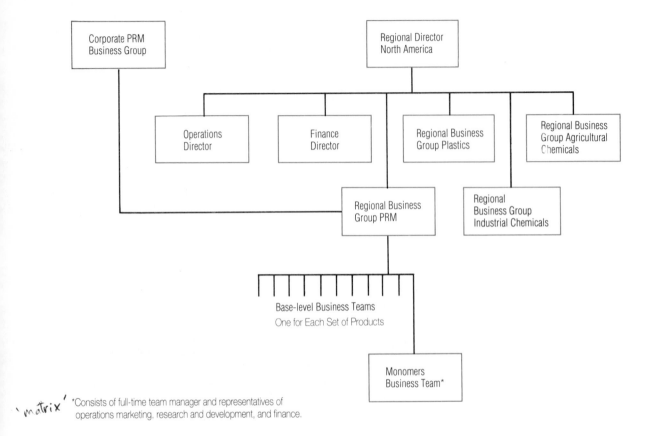

*Consists of full-time team manager and representatives of
operations marketing, research and development, and finance.

'matrix'

this regional manager would have this as a second formal reporting relationship. Similar lines of relationship for the other three regional business group directors have been omitted from the diagram to avoid clutter.

Each of the four business directors in each region would devote his or her full time to managing and coordinating the work of a business group. Each group would cover the functions of marketing, manufacturing, R&D, and finance. Each business group in the large regions would typically have separate managers for each of these functions. In the smaller regions, some functional managers would be assigned to more than one business group. The group members other than the business group director would spend about 20 percent of their time on group management activities; they would spend the rest of their time in their own functional areas. Most of the group directors would come from marketing, although some undoubtedly would come from operations, finance, or R&D.

The four regional directors for each business group, along with the research director for the business group as a whole and the worldwide business-group director, would constitute the corporate business team for that group. (R&D would be centralized, but the R&D organization would include a corporate research director for each business group.)

The proposed plan also contemplated subdividing some of the regional business groups into base-level business teams, each responsible for a subset of the group's products. Like the regional team for the product group, each base-level business team would include managers with responsibilities in marketing, manufacturing, R&D, and finance. Most of the team managers, like most of the group directors, would come from the regional marketing staffs, however. About 20 business teams would be established, all told, mainly in the North American region.

The bottom tier in the chart in Exhibit 3 shows the proposed position of the team for one base-level business in the North American region. The structure of the regional business groups and base-level business teams for the other three business groups would vary slightly, but the basic orientation would be the same.

Major product decisions, such as whether to introduce a new product or drop an old one, would be made by the corporate business groups; the regional business groups and business teams would decide such questions as when to introduce new products in their markets and how to market their products most effectively.

THE PROPOSAL: PROFIT RESPONSIBILITY

The business groups at the corporate and regional levels would be the primary profit-centered units in the new organization structure—i.e., the business would be run by region by business group. As one of the designers of the proposal put it, "The company would run its strategy by business group, but once the plans were made they would be implemented by region. The role of the regional manager would be to coordinate the business groups in his region and to control manufacturing and costs. In most regions, the regional operations manager would be the production planner and coordinator for the region, responsible for meeting delivery schedules, maintaining quality, and controlling the costs of manufacturing and administration."

Sales and marketing would remain separate functions as in the past. The company's sales people would continue to serve primarily as providers of information and advice to the company's customers. Almost all orders would continue to be received directly from customers by telephone; Rohm and Haas's sales people seldom took a sales order from a customer, and that practice would continue. The sales force would report primarily to regional or country sales managers, but would have secondary reporting lines to the base-level business teams. Individual plant managers would report both to the operations manager and to the regional business team director for the products produced in the plant.

"The lines of profit responsibility may not be as clear in your diagram as they really would be," a corporate finance manager remarked. "The base-level business team is the basic unit, next comes the regional business group, followed by the corporate business group and the corporate business director at the top. The two lowest rungs on this ladder are in the regional organization; the two highest rungs are in the Corporate Business Departments.

"Primary profit responsibility would move from the domestic divisions and foreign legal entities to business units and business teams. That way we could direct production to the facilities best equipped to meet the demand and avoid arguments about transfer prices. Our basic job at headquarters would be to decide how to allocate the product worldwide. The corporate capital budgeting staff would be responsible for analyzing relative costs and capacities and, for products supplied from another region, recommending to the business teams where they should obtain their products. We'll work out a profit reporting system to make sure their profits aren't affected by the source of the product."

THE ARGUMENTS

"I know the advantage of profit centers," a corporate finance manager said, "but they're costing us too much. We have foreign subsidiaries buying from each other when we can make the products at lower cost here. And with these distorted production and sale patterns, it's hard to figure out which products and which markets are profitable and which are not. I think the new structure will fix all that."

"That may be," one executive said, "but I'm not sure I like this plan. It seems to me the best idea is to keep responsibility for manufacturing, marketing, and profit generation in the same hands. The way your proposal reads, the people responsible for profits would have no responsibility to control manufacturing costs. I don't see anything in the proposal that would stimulate anyone to work hard on cost reduction, and that's becoming more and more important. Besides, when you take away the profit incentive at each of our subsidiaries abroad, you're weakening the linkage between effort and results."

"I disagree," another executive remembers saying. "Our markets are product-oriented, not country-oriented. We're all agreed that we should have four worldwide product groups, and we'd still have to keep the foreign corporate structure for legal reasons, but we can't have our different markets running off in different directions. To keep the product flowing smoothly, we need to make all the important production decisions here in Philadelphia anyway, so we ought to lodge responsibility where the authority is. The proposed plan does just that.

"Putting an R&D representative on the product group team should take care of the liaison problems we've been having there. The only transfer pricing problems would be on transactions between product groups, and those are few and far between. Of course, we'd still have to have official transfer prices to the foreign subsidiaries for fiscal purposes, but those would wash out in the worldwide structure because almost all transfers would be between units within the product group."

"You're wrong," a third member of the management committee remarked. "You're right about having sourcing decisions made at headquarters but when you do that you make it impossible for the foreign managers to control the amount of profit their companies can report. We have to calculate legal-entity profits for fiscal reasons, but the transfer prices that satisfy the fiscal authorities aren't likely to correspond to the prices that represent the real sacrifice to the company of providing products from the sources Philadelphia has chosen. The foreign subsidiary managers are responsible for marketing, sales, and manufacturing, but not for profits. I don't know whether that would work."

"I'm not worried about motivation for cost reduction," said the operations vice president. "Our manufacturing people are judged on quality, yield, and cost, and I don't see anything in this proposal to change that. I'm not sure about the motivation of the marketing and sales people, though."

"Well, I agree that we need to have some way to let the subsidiary managers know how they're contributing to company profits," the first executive replied, "but that's just the point. They can't see that now with the profit center structure we have, and this proposal won't make it any worse. What I'm worried about is whether we'd have to increase the size of the managerial force. Where are all these business group directors and business team managers going to come from? Won't other people have to be appointed to take over their jobs?"

"Not at all," said a member of the task force. "The same work will still have to be done as we're doing now. We're just moving responsibility from place to place and we'll be moving people to correspond to those shifts."

"Okay, but will it make decision making more efficient? We'll still have three managerial levels in the business team–regional business group–corporate business group chain. I worry that we'll have the same problems of slow responses to problems we have now."

"I don't think so," replied another member of the task force. "That's why we have those dashed-line relationships between the business teams and the business groups. The key to this thing is communication, and if we can get this new structure in place, there'll be a lot more understanding at the top of what's going on in the field, and vice versa."

ROHM AND HAAS

COMPANY (B)

"I think we could really make this product move in our market," Dave Jones remarked. "The customers are there and we're way ahead of the competition technologically."

"But is the profit margin good enough?" Rico Buonaventura asked. "We'd get only 12 cents a kilo on every sale and that's not even enough to cover our marketing costs."

"You've got a point, but let's get SAPIS to give us the usage factors. Maybe they'll make a difference."

THE COMPANY

Dave and Rico were members of the business team for vineyard fungicides in Rohm and Haas Company's European region. Rohm and Haas is a specialty chemicals manufacturer with its head office in Philadelphia. It operates in most of the major markets of the world. Some of its products, such as agricultural pesticides, are used directly without further processing; most are sold to other manufacturers for use in products such as motor oils, paints, adhesives, packaging materials, and transparent plastic paneling. It had net income of $230 million in 1988 on net sales of $2.5 billion.

The main elements of Rohm and Haas's organization structure are shown in Exhibit 1. The company's product line is structured in four broad groups:

1. Polymers, resins, and monomers (PRM)
2. Plastics
3. Industrial chemicals
4. Agricultural chemicals

EXHIBIT 1   **Rohm and Haas Company top-level organization structure**

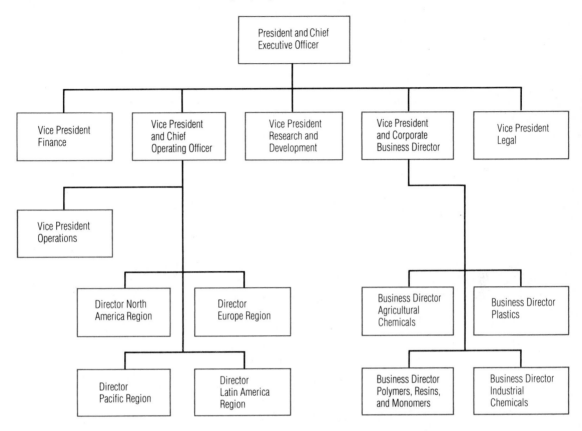

The Corporate Business Department is the main planning unit for these four product lines. Its purpose is "to integrate the business plans and to coordinate the operation of the businesses on a global basis." This department is headed by a Vice President and includes four corporate-level business group directors, one for each product group. The corporate vice presidents for research and development, finance, and legal report to the Chief Executive Officer. This portion of the organization structure is diagrammed in the right-hand portion of Exhibit 1.

The second dimension of Rohm and Haas's organization structure is the regional management structure, based on customer location, shown in the left-hand side of Exhibit 1. The four regions are:

1. North America (United States and Canada)
2. Europe
3. Latin America
4. Pacific Basin

Each region is divided into sales areas and most sales areas include two or more countries. For example, the European region includes nine sales areas, comprising 107 countries in Europe, Africa, and the Middle East. One sales area, code-named España, includes three countries (Spain, Portugal, and the Canary Islands). Another, code-named Italia, covers 48 countries. The area managers are responsible for sales activities in their respective areas.

The four regional directors and a Vice President—Corporate Operations report to the President/Chief Operating Officer. The role of each regional organization is to plan and run all the businesses within the region within the framework established by the Corporate Business Department. The product structure is built into the regional structure by the establishment of four business groups in each region, one for each product line, each headed by a regional business director.

The regional business group portion of the structure is shown as the top tier in Exhibit 2, which presents a condensed version of the organization structure for the North American region. The line connecting the corporate business director to the PRM group shows that this regional manager has this as a second formal reporting relationship. Similar lines of relationship for the other three regional business group directors have been omitted from the diagram to avoid clutter.

Some of the regional business groups are subdivided into base-level business teams, each responsible for a subset of the group's products. Like the regional business group, each base-level business team includes managers with responsibilities in marketing, manufacturing, R&D, and finance. Most of the team managers, like most of the group directors, come from the regional marketing staffs, however. About 20 business teams are established, all told, mainly in the North American region.

Major product decisions, such as whether to introduce a new product or drop an old one, are made by the corporate business groups; the regional business groups and business teams decide such questions as when to introduce new products in their markets and how to market their products most effectively.

PROFIT RESPONSIBILITY

The business groups at the corporate and regional levels are the primary profit-centered units in the organization structure—i.e., the business is run by region by business group. As one of the designers of the structure put it, "The company runs its strategy by business group, but once the plans are made they are implemented by region. The role of the regional manager is to coordinate the business groups in his region and to control manufacturing and costs. In most regions, the regional operations manager is the production planner and coordinator for the region, responsible for meeting delivery schedules, maintaining quality, and controlling the costs of manufacturing and administration."

EXHIBIT 2   **Rohm and Haas Company organization structure—North American region**

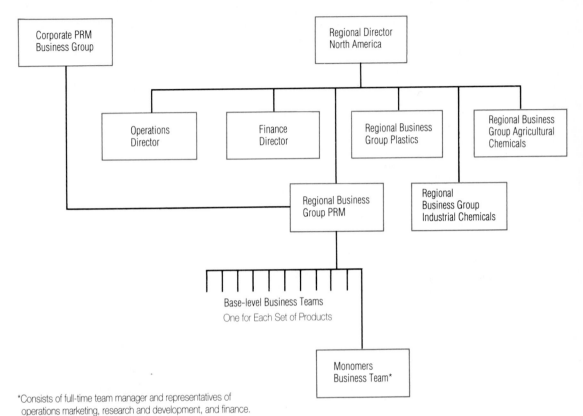

*Consists of full-time team manager and representatives of operations marketing, research and development, and finance.

"The lines of profit responsibility may not be as clear in your diagram as they really are," Mr. Smith remarked. "The base-level business team is the basic unit, next comes the regional business group, followed by the corporate business group and the corporate business director at the top. The two lowest rungs on this ladder are in the regional organization; the two highest rungs are in the Corporate Business Departments.

"The business teams may allocate some profit responsibility to the sales areas within their regions, but more usually they delegate sales and marketing responsibility to the sales personnel working for the legal entities within each sales area. These sales personnel are aware of the SAPIS profit relationships to the sales they make, and are expected to work within the base pricing parameters set by the business teams, but they don't have bottom-line, stand-alone profit responsibilities. The regional business team remains the basic building block in the profit/commercial responsibility pyramid.

"By centralizing profit responsibility in the business groups and business teams, we can direct production to the facilities best equipped to meet the demand and avoid arguments about transfer prices. Our basic job at headquarters is to decide how to allocate the product worldwide. The corporate capital budgeting staff is responsible for analyzing relative costs and capacities and, for products supplied from another region, recommending to the business teams where they should obtain their products."

SAPIS

"When we adopted the matrix organization structure in 1976," Angus Smith, Treasurer of Rohm and Haas Company, said recently, "we knew we had to do something to make sure the local managers could see the profit each product generated for the company as a whole. That's why we developed SAPIS. SAPIS is our acronym for 'Sales Area Profitability Information System.' It has two main managerial uses: (1) to give regional, area, and business team managers information on the total company profit arising from sales to outside customers, and (2) to provide both top and local management with profit reports on a geographic area and business team basis. It also provides data for external reporting by segments."[1]

The primary inputs to SAPIS are data from transactions recorded on a legal-entity (parent or subsidiary) basis. Transfers between legal entities are recorded at the prices approved by the fiscal authorities for taxation and tariff purposes. SAPIS uses a set of sales and usage conversion factors to adjust legal-entity unit profit margins based on these prices to corporate-basis margins for each geographic area and each business team and business group.

An internal Rohm and Haas document, prepared to help the company's managers understand SAPIS, uses a simple example to show how the system works. In that example, a sales area (e.g., France) markets two products, Product A, purchased for resale from a Rohm and Haas entity in the U.S., and Product B, manufactured locally from third-party materials. The legal entity records in the sales area show the following revenue and cost data:

	Product A	Product B
Unit selling price	$1.00	$1.00
Unit cost	.85	.75
Unit gross profit	$ .15	$ .25

---

[1] SAPIS doesn't report legal-entity profits. These have to come from the local books and records each subsidiary has to maintain to meet local legal requirements and for cash planning and other Treasury purposes.

Without SAPIS, the natural tendency of area management would be to emphasize product B with its 25 percent gross profit, instead of product A's 15 percent. SAPIS changes that perception by adding the inter-company mark-up to the area profit margin. In the example, product A is transferred to the sales area legal entity at a unit price of $.80; transportation costs and import duties in the sales area add $.05, to produce the entity-basis cost of $.85 presented in the table above.

The U.S. entity supplying product A to the sales area has a $.20 gross profit, however:

Unit selling price	$ .80
SAPIS unit cost	.60
Unit gross profit	$ .20

SAPIS adds this $.20 to the sales area profit by subtracting it from the entity-basis cost of goods sold, producing the following:

	Product A	Product B
Unit selling price	$1.00	$1.00
Unit cost	.65	.75
Unit gross profit	$ .35	$ .25

"The aim of this adjustment," Mr. Smith pointed out, "is to motivate area management to emphasize products that will generate the greatest corporate return, even though they may not offer the greatest return to the legal entity. Put differently, the procedure is designed to pierce the transfer pricing veil.

"SAPIS is flexible enough to handle multiple transfers within the Rohm and Haas group. For example, the U.S. sells a product known as Kerb Wet Cake to Italy where it is used to make Kerb Tech. Italy sells the Kerb Tech to Australia, where it is used to make Kerb 50W, which Australia sells to outside customers. In SAPIS, the cost reported by Australia on a sale to an outsider is adjusted both for Italy's profits on the sale of Kerb Tech and for U.S. profits on the sale of Kerb Wet Cake."

To accomplish these adjustments, SAPIS includes a file of unit-margin factors, known as the *usage file*. The file includes a separate unit-margin factor, called a "usage factor," for each source for each "usage product." The factors are updated every time manufacturing cost standards are changed, usually quarterly.

For example, the usage file for R&H Italia, Rohm and Haas's Italian legal entity, shows the following information for one end-product known as Amberlite XE-320A, made with two "usage products," Triton CF-32 and Monomer X-980:

End product		Usage product			
Code	Name	Code	Name	Usage factor	Usual supplier
79499	Amberlite XE-320A	61513	Triton CF-32	$ .37	620
79499	Amberlite XE-320A	66424	Monomer X-980	.99	001

If R&H Italia received Triton CF-32 from an internal source other than "supplier 620" (the code number for a Rohm and Haas legal entity), the transfer price and usage factor would be different.

The usage factor gives the manufacturing entity, the business team financial analysts, and the regional manager a mechanism through which the intercompany profit on an intermediate such as Triton CF-32 is credited to the end product that uses Triton CF-32, in this case Amberlite XE-320A. The allocation is a two-step process, first charging the end product with the invoiced price of the usage product and then crediting it with the usage product's internal profit, in this case, $.37 a unit.

No gross profit is reported by any unit of the company until the end-product is sold to an outside customer. SAPIS accomplishes this by crediting the gross profit on an inter-company sale to a "Profit in Inventory" (PII) file. When an end-product sale is made to an outside customer, SAPIS searches the PII file, which it relieves of any gross profit on the usage products used in the end-product. In preparing profit reports, SAPIS subtracts the amounts in the PII file from legal-entity, third-party invoiced profits.

"BELOW-THE-LINE" DATA

After SAPIS finishes processing the gross profit and profit-in-inventory data, it has two additional tasks. The first of these is to distribute legal-entity "below-the-line" data—selling and administrative expenses, research, royalties, and so forth—to the sales areas and business teams.

The below-the-line totals are relatively small, because the legal entities distribute most of their marketing, research, royalty, and administrative expenses to the strategic business units that cause costs to arise. For the remainder, SAPIS uses bases that are already generated within the system, mainly:

- Total invoiced sales
- Total region sales
- Total region sales by business team
- Total region sales by business group
- Total area sales
- Total area sales by business team
- Total area sales by business group

All "below-the-line" items are fully distributed each quarterly reporting period.
Exhibit 3 shows an abbreviated income statement for one area/legal entity set. It illustrates the magnitude of the adjustments SAPIS makes to convert entity-basis statements to SAPIS-basis statements and shows the elements that enter into the calculation of operating profit after taxes for an area entity.

EXHIBIT 3   **Rohm and Haas Company area versus legal-entity (invoiced) results for Area X for the full year 1989 (in thousands of dollars)**

	Area (SAPIS)	Invoiced	Difference
Sales to customers	$108,500	$98,600	$ 9,900
Inter-company sales	0	500	(500)
Total sales	108,500	99,100	(9,400)
Cost of goods sold	63,100	82,300	(19,200)
Materials variances	(300)	(400)	100
Discards/writedowns	100	(100)	200
Operating variances	500	0	500
Inventory adjustments	(700)	0	(700)
Other	1,200	300	900
Total oper. cost of sales	63,900	82,100	(18,200)
Operating gross profit	44,600	17,000	27,600
LIFO adjustment	(200)	(200)	0
Translation adjustment	1,100	400	700
Other adjustments	(600)	0	(600)
Total adjustments	300	200	100
Total gross profit	44,300	16,800	27,500
Selling expense—direct	5,700	4,200	1,500
Selling expense—allocated	3,600	2,000	1,600
Commissions	0	(300)	300
Administrative expense:			
Direct	4,600	2,100	2,500
Management services	1,400	0	1,400
Allocated	1,600	0	1,600
Research expense	6,200	0	6,200
Other income/expense	(2,900)	(1,200)	(1,700)
Total other income/expense	20,200	6,800	13,400
Operating profit before tax	24,100	10,000	14,100
Taxes	9,500	5,700	3,800
Operating profit after tax	$ 14,600	$ 4,300	$10,300

RONA REPORTS

SAPIS's final chore for management is to prepare and print reports of gross profit, operating profit after taxes (OPT), and return on net assets (RONA). Gross profit is calculated for each product within each business group and within each area, with suitable summary tabulations. OPT and RONA are calculated by area, region, business team, business group, and total company.

For this purpose, inventory and net fixed assets are distributed using sales and usage factors. For example, intermediates and raw materials are allocated on standard usage relationships to finished products and net fixed assets follow the depreciation distribution. Inventories are reported at FIFO cost, after deducting the gross profit in inventory amounts extracted from the PII file.

DISCUSSION

Case writer: I noticed that SAPIS charges materials variances and operating variances to sales areas and to business teams. How is that done?

Mr. Smith: Both of them are allocated in proportion to sales. We take the materials variances all the way down to the product level and the operating variances to the business team level.

Case writer: What do those variances include?

Mr. Smith: Both materials price and materials usage variances go first to a Variances in Inventory account and are released to income as sales take place. The operating variances cover most other variances from standard manufacturing cost, including labor and manufacturing overhead. They also go through a Variances in Inventory account and are released as sales take place.

Case writer: Doesn't that conflict with the idea of controllability? The area managers and business team managers can't control those variances, can they?

Mr Smith: No, the manufacturing variances, particularly yields, are controlled by the Operations Director and the Plant Manager. Anyway, the SAPIS reports aren't designed to pinpoint control responsibility. They are used to help decision makers decide what to produce and sell. Since these decisions are affected by the variances, we need to allocate them.

Case writer: Are all the operating variances product-specific?

Mr. Smith: No, most of them aren't. It seems reasonable to assume, however, that they are likely to be roughly proportional to dollar volume.

Case writer: What about the allocations of assets and below-the-line items? Aren't they pretty arbitrary?

Mr. Smith: No allocations are perfect, but we think we do a good job of picking the right allocation base. Of course, any legal-entity expenses that are fully traceable to a sales area or a business team are assigned directly there; it's only the nontraceable items we have to allocate. That cuts the problem down a lot.

Case writer: I noticed in the table we've labeled Exhibit 3 that SAPIS changes the number on every line but one. I'm having trouble understanding that. I thought that SAPIS was designed mainly to reduce the cost of goods sold number to the companywide base. Why does it produce a different number for sales to customers, for example, and different numbers for direct selling expense and direct administrative expense?

Mr Smith: I'm glad you asked that question. The answer is a little complicated, so let me concentrate on the big picture. The main difference, other than the cost of goods sold adjustment you just mentioned, is that areas sales and expenses include amounts relating to shipments that go directly to customers in the area from legal entities outside the area, without going through the accounts of the legal entities in the area. Exhibit 3 shows that $9.9 million of sales were made this way in Area X in 1989. The SAPIS-adjusted cost of goods sold on these items is included in the $63.1 million area cost of goods sold. Selling and administrative expenses that are direct to those sales also show up in the area column, as do some related minor items.

Most of the other differences arise from allocations we either don't make to the legal entities—research expense, for example—or make on a basis that differs from the basis used for legal-entity allocations.

THE DECISION SITUATION

The end-product Dave and Rico were discussing in the conversation quoted at the beginning of this case was Hittite 07, a chemical designed to keep grapes free of fungus without leaving toxic residues in the fruit. It had been introduced successfully in the U.S. in 1988 and Dave and Rico were discussing the possibility of introducing it in the European region at a price equivalent to $3.47 a kilo. The invoiced cost, including average variances, would be $3.35 a kilogram. The average variance to be assigned to Hittite 07 would be $.16.

If introduced in the European region, Hittite 07 would be manufactured in France. It would incorporate two usage products from sources outside France, as follows:

Usage product	Usage factor
Chaldee T-46	$.24
Baalbeck TF-13	.79

Rohm and Haas's regional director for Europe, after consulting with the area marketing directors, estimated that initial marketing expenses totaling $500,000 would have to be incurred the first year, with continuing product-related expenditures of about $200,000 a year thereafter to achieve a 400,000-kilogram annual sales target for Hittite 07 by 1992. Sales were expected to reach 200,000 kilograms in 1990 and 300,000 kilograms in 1991.

Index